1001 PLANTS
YOU MUST GROW BEFORE YOU DIE

1001 PLANTS
YOU MUST GROW BEFORE YOU DIE

GENERAL EDITOR LIZ DOBBS

FOREWORD BY GRAHAM RICE

◔ *Drosera capensis*, also known as the sundew, is a carnivorous
plant that can be found on every continent.

A Quintessence Book

First published in Great Britain in 2016 by Cassell Illustrated
A division of Octopus Publishing Group Limited
Carmelite House
50 Victoria Embankment
London EC4Y 0DZ
www.octopusbooks.co.uk

An Hachette UK Company
www.hachette.co.uk

ISBN: 978-1-84403-792-6
QSS.PLTS

A CIP catalogue record for this book is available from the British Library.

This book was designed and produced by
Quintessence Editions Ltd.
6 Blundell Street
London N7 9BH
www.1001beforeyoudie.com

Project Editor	Sophie Blackman
Editors	Rebecca Gee, Fiona Plowman
Proofreader	Jane Simmonds
Designer	Damian Jaques
Picture Researchers	Sophie Blackman, Liz Dobbs, Ouassila Mebarek, Hannah Phillips
Production Manager	Anna Pauletti
Editorial Director	Ruth Patrick
Publisher	Philip Cooper

Colour reproduction by Bright Arts in Hong Kong
Printed in China by Midas Printing International Ltd.

Contents

Foreword Graham Rice

My mother, trying to encourage an interest in gardening, gave me some radish seeds to sow when I was five. They mature so quickly that she thought they'd be ready before I lost interest. She was right – but the taste! I spat out the first mouthful and it was more than a decade before I again paid attention to plants. During those years my interest in the garden was confined to digging for night crawlers for fishing bait, squirting the bees with water and hiding behind shrubs to avoid sowing any more seeds. My mother had the right idea but chose the wrong plant. My grandson developed his interest in plants from tasting the tiny wild strawberries growing outside his back door and learning the patience to wait until they were bright red before picking them. Next, he learned to identify plants from the smell of their leaves: rosemary, mint, basil. . . Now he's a little older – and a little more bloodthirsty – insectivorous plants have grabbed his attention.

We come to our enjoyment of plants and gardens in different ways – even digging for night crawlers I began to notice that there were more crawling in the rich flower borders than in empty stone corners. I loved home-grown pole beans and could even be persuaded to help carry the poles, although sowing the seeds was still a step too far. I don't think I became interested in flowers until I realised girls liked them. The point is that there's a vast variety of different ways in which we enter and explore the world of plants and the 1001 plants in this book represent all the ways in which plants appeal: fresh picked peas, so sweet and juicy that the pods are split and the peas tasted before they ever reach our kitchen; perfumed petunias decorating the deck, helping it transform into our home's favourite summer room; perennials bringing colourful pleasure to the coldest, and hottest, climates; the aromas of herbs adding life to home cooking; shrubs bringing us a variety of colourful features at different seasons through the year; cut flowers bringing stylish, ever-changing new décor to our homes; and, yes, the radishes, strawberries and insectivorous plants as well.

There are plants tough enough to grow in the coldest climes or the driest beds, in tropical zones or cool and damp areas, and for everywhere else. There are wild flowers from wild places – the Himalayas, for example, and the Rockies – from rainforests and river banks, from mountains and meadows, from deserts and from sweeping forests. Many were discovered during pioneering explorations by the great plant collectors of the 1800s; some were found much more recently. With plants, you can bring the wild places of the world to your own back garden. Alongside this vast variety of intriguing wild flowers are plants discovered or developed in gardens and nurseries and by plant breeders around the world who are dedicated to developing exciting new varieties and cultivars.

But it's not just the beauty or flavour of the plants themselves. The transatlantic team of experts who bring their insight and expertise to this book reveal why every one of these trees, shrubs, perennials, annuals, vegetables, fruits and herbs deserve a place in your garden. They intrigue us with the stories behind the plants, including the native perennial developed in the Netherlands that now grows on New York's High Line, the herb grown by Thomas Jefferson, the dye plant mentioned by Shakespeare and the new form of a Chinese evergreen shrub first introduced by a British plant hunter that was discovered in the United States. Plants, as you can see, are now an international enthusiasm.

The names are fascinating, too. Look out for the plants named after comedians (*Camellia japonica* 'Bob Hope'), plants named for botanists and horticulturalists around the world (*Omphalodes* 'Cherry Ingram'), and those named for a cellist (*Rosa* 'Jacqueline du Pré'), a classical guitarist (*Narcissus* 'Segovia') and for a rock band (*Phlox drummondii* 'Moody Blues'). There are plants named for American towns (*Fragaria* x *ananassa* 'Fort Laramie'), a film (*Phygelius* 'African Queen'), a character in a film (*Picea pungens* 'Fat Albert'), members of the British Royal family (*Clematis texensis* 'Princess Diana'), food (*Heuchera* 'Tiramisu'), a bird (*Penstemon* 'Raven'), an animal (*Ricinus* 'Impala'), a dance (*Salpiglossis* 'Bolero'), well known and lesser known gardens (*Heliotropium arborescens* 'Chatsworth') – even an Irish folk song (*Rosa* Wild Rover) . . . anything to mark their unique qualities and tempt us into growing them. And believe me, all the plants in this book are well worth growing.

We have an intimate, fundamental tie with plants of all kinds. We use their wood to build shelter; we eat their fruits, roots and leaves; we depend on the oxygen they produce with every breath; they provide drugs to keep us healthy; and we use their aromas to smell sweet and lift our spirits. They create atmosphere, they furnish our outdoor rooms and bring us beauty and fragrance everywhere.

Every plant chosen for this book is inspiring: for its colour, its fragrance, the elegant style of the way it grows, its taste or simply its big bold impact. Perhaps you can't grow every one – but grow some.

Graham Rice

Introduction Liz Dobbs

'I have never been one for collecting varieties; I have preferred to collect species and to select varieties.'

Graham Stuart Thomas, *Perennial Garden Plants*

Growing plants is good for the mind, body and soul, not to mention the local environment. For some people, the seed is sown early: raising sunflowers at school or helping grandparents to harvest potatoes. Many people take an interest when they reach adulthood, tackling the 'outdoor room', whereas for others, gardening brings joy in later years. Often, the active retired have the best gardens, but it is a pity to leave it so late in life to start gardening. Be proactive and begin your learning curve with forty growing seasons in front of you rather than ten. And remember that the lack of a garden is no barrier to raising plants: think about container or window-sill plants, get an allotment or volunteer in a community garden.

Despite the title of this book, I don't know any gardeners who aim to grow a specific number of plants. However, I do meet plenty of people who are confused about which plants to buy, who don't know what to grow where, or who have a 'black hole' garden where plants go into the ground each spring but disappear thereafter. There are also many excellent plants out there, both old and new, that many gardeners never hear about: if these plants aren't grown in our gardens they may disappear altogether. Fortunately, this is the perfect book to inspire and inform our selections.

Our time and capacity to grow plants is limited – let us use both wisely.

Aim to grow a diverse collection of plants for intellectual stimulation, simple satisfaction and sensory pleasure, but within that, do be discerning. Life is too short to be a martyr to the garden and there is no shortage of 'recommended' plants that suit all needs. Growing trials, record keeping, competitions and generous information sharing are invaluable resources to the majority of horticulturists and plant societies the world over. However, if you would prefer personal advice, there is a fine tradition of garden writing to explore, and now, of course, social media. Plant suppliers, such as nurseries and garden centres, are also a useful source of local information. By whichever means you make your selection, be mindful that plants need space: we are not stamp collecting, but nurturing and caring for living things.

Gardening is a great leveller but plant snobbery does exist. In one corner are those who eschew anything popular, are sniffy about 'trade' and take a pride in saying that they can't remember the last time they visited a garden centre. Instead, they seek out rare but subdued species (ideally nothing a fellow human has had a hand in); these can be 'blink and you miss them' plants. At the other extreme, some gardeners are so fixated on their annual splashes of colour that thirty years on their gardens haven't developed because they start from scratch each year and follow the same routine. The type of gardener you are or become is up to you – and it might change over the years – but my aim in this book has been to present you with garden-worthy but exciting plant choices that have earned their recommendations. Some will be beautiful, others curious; there are fragrant flowers, aromatic foliage and tasty treats; a mix of old and new. Naturally, a garden-worthy plant offers more than a beautiful flower. Expert judges and experienced gardeners will look at the whole package: foliage, plant shape and constitution, as well as how the plant holds itself, and how robust and reliable it is. I have also noticed a new criteria creeping in: the need for plants to be easy and foolproof to grow, but there is a danger that many great plants will fall by the wayside because of this extra hurdle.

The Royal Horticultural Society (RHS) has been trialling a wide range of plants for more than a century. These trials form the basis of its Award of Garden Merit (AGM), overseen by judging panels organised by plant committees. AGM plants are an excellent starting point because their criteria bears the gardener in mind rather than commercial companies, but this still leaves a bewildering amount of choice. If you have the time and inclination to delve a little deeper, extension services at universities in the United States offer impartial, research-based information on a range of subjects, including horticulture and gardening – as do some botanical gardens, such as the Missouri Botanical Garden. There are also numerous organisations ready to point you in the direction of new varieties. For example, in the United Kingdom, Gold Standard Rose Trials are run by professional rose breeders through the British Association of Rose Breeders. All-America Selections (AAS) is a non-profit organisation that tests new varieties in impartial trials in North America, highlighting and promoting the best garden performers as AAS winners. But who blows the trumpet for the heritage plants? Often it is the keen amateur, handing down passalong plants from one generation to another, or small nurseries, seed libraries and keen collectors propagating and swapping plants. In the United Kingdom, the charity Plant Heritage encourages the conservation of cultivated plants via its National Plant Collections housing more than 600 varieties.

Although award-winning plants will always warrant inclusion in any list of recommended plants, the rationale behind the selection here focuses on gardening as a pursuit of personal pleasure within one's own space. It is not focused on agriculture, or even commercial horticulture, so plants such as wheat, rice and the most commercially important varieties of fruits, vegetables and cut flowers do not feature here. I decided to exclude trees, not because they are unimportant or do not contribute to a garden, but because, while it is fine to experiment with smaller plants, there is much more to consider when planting a tree in your garden. For those who have room for a tree in their garden, please, plant one or more. The right tree in the right place will mark the spot for generations, and will provide shelter and food for all manner of wildlife. Research your purchase carefully, and buy from the tree nurseries available in your locality. For most of us, though, our outdoor space for private growing shrinks with each decade. Not only do we have less physical space in which to plant, but open, sunny spots are at a premium where neighbouring buildings cast shadows. Consequently, in this book, the focus is on plants that offer a lot in a small package: several seasons of interest, forms that are suitable for container growing and varieties that are amenable to pruning and training. The approach has been pragmatic rather than academic, because the aim is to guide readers to plants that will bring them pleasure.

We start with the simplest, cheapest, minimal commitment plants and move through to those that require more investment and long-term care. Annuals will reach their peak in a single growing season and cost little to get started, so if you make a mistake, it won't be permanent and you can start again with something else in the next growing season. Bulbs are great because half of the work has been done for you: the flower has already formed within the bulb, but you still get the satisfaction of plant raising and the grand reveal. Perennials give your garden movement and pace, changing with the seasons, and they shoot up, do their stuff and die down. Then there are the woody structural plants: shrubs offering spring blossom, autumn tints and evergreen structure. Climbers require commitment to tame their wandering vine-like nature, but they allow you to dress garden features such as arches, walls and pergolas. Although roses are summer-flowering shrubs, quite a few are also climbers, therefore it seemed sensible to give the world's favourite flower its own chapter. Indoor and patio plants are brought together to show what can be grown in various light or undercover spaces. Finally, given the welcome rise in interest in home-grown food, the book concludes with chapters on edibles. Here you will find delicious herbs, vegetables and fruits. Again, these are starter suggestions for what I hope will be a 'grow your own' experience that will last a lifetime.

This is not a botanist's book – the aim is to point gardeners in the direction of plants that are worth growing – but we have used botanical names for ordering the plants within each chapter because common names, although often charming, are not standardised. Each plant entry starts with a fact box that gives practical pointers for growing the plants – to enable you to select the right variety for a given place in the garden. This box includes the plant's main features of interest and the maximum size it should grow to in five years, as well as whether it requires or prefers sun, copes with partial shade or tolerates a shady position. For the more permanent plants, which one hopes will survive the winter, a hardiness rating is supplied. In the United Kingdom, the revised RHS hardiness ratings, introduced in 2013, are based on the absolute minimum winter temperatures. All these measurements come with the caveat that plants are variable!

In addition to the facts, there is nothing like a personal recommendation to help you select and grow plants. And this is where our contributors come in, each writing about the plants that they particularly value and why they are worth growing. Among their number are nursery owners, garden designers, plant writers, garden historians, industry insiders, horticulturists and passionate plantaholics – each of whom offers their own perspective – and I would like to thank them all. Once you have selected your plants, it may not always be possible to buy all of them, because the availability of a plant in an area depends on the seed company listing it, the nursery propagating it and the garden centre stocking it. Consequently, the contributors have been precise with the plant headings where it matters to source the plant, but if you cannot obtain the one you want, try one of the listed alternatives. Sometimes the same plant is sold under an alternative name or it may be easier to source a closely related cultivar or species. Furthermore, your local region may be limited by a list of 'invasive' or 'banned' plants drawn up to protect local habitats or farming. These change from region to region and over time. Buying plants from recognised stockists, nurseries or garden centres in your area, or from reputable online retailers, is the best protection against introducing banned plants to your region.

This book focuses more on the personal 'why grow' rather than the 'how to grow', but there is no shortage of advice on the basics of gardening. One of the common stumbling blocks for beginners is getting into the seasonal rhythm of the growing season. For example, the time to plant bulbs for spring flowers is the autumn before, but that is only half of the story if you want to take your bulb growing to the next level. The optimum way to acquire specific varieties of tulip is to order them from mail-order bulb specialists in the summer, and the way to decide which tulips you would like is to see them blooming in the spring. This is not to say that you can't have tulips instantly in spring, by visiting a garden centre and buying potted plants in flower, but these will be the more common varieties. Gardening teaches patience, and planning a garden is a slow but rewarding experience. Today, not enough people experience the joy and satisfaction of growing and raising plants. So, dip into this book and discover the plants that appeal to you, check if they might work in your plot, and set about obtaining and growing them.

Index by plant name

A

Abelia × grandiflora
'Kaleidoscope' **436**
Abies lasiocarpa var. arizonica
'Compacta' **437**
Abutilon 'Kentish Belle' **676**
Abutilon megapotamicum
'Orange Hot Lava' **677**
Acer palmatum 'Bloodgood' **439**
Acer palmatum 'Katsura' **439**
Achillea 'Moonshine' **235**
Aconitum carmichaelii 'Arendsii' **235**
Actaea simplex Atropurpurea Group
'James Compton' **236**
Actinidia kolomikta **584**
Actinidia deliciosa 'Jenny' **926**
Adiantum venustum **237**
Adlumia fungosa **585**
Aeonium 'Zwartkop' **678**
Aesculus parviflora **440**
Agapanthus Headbourne hybrids **239**
Agastache 'Blue Fortune' **812**
Agave americana **678**
Ageratina altissima 'Chocolate' **239**
Ageratum houstonianum
'Blue Horizon' **22**
Akebia quinata **586**
Alcea rosea Halo Series **23**
Allium cowanii **130**
Allium hollandicum
'Purple Sensation' **133**
Allium sativum var. ophioscorodon
'Lautrec Wight' **858**
Allium schubertii **131**
Allium tuberosum **814**
Allium ampeloprasum var. porrum
'Lincoln' **854**
Allium cepa 'Jermor' **855**
Allium sativum 'Solent Wight' **857**
Allium fistulosum 'White Lisbon' **857**
Allium schoenoprasum **813**
Aloe vera **681**
Aloysia citrodora **815**
Amaranthus cruentus × powellii
'Hopi Red Dye' **24**
Amaryllis belladonna **133**
Amberboa moschata **25**
Amelanchier alnifolia 'Saskatoon' **927**
Ammi majus 'Graceland' **27**
Ampelaster carolinanus **587**
Anchusa azurea 'Loddon Royalist' **27**

Anemone hupehensis
'Hadspen Adundance' **240**
Anemone coronaria
De Caen Group **134**
Anemone blanda **134**
Anethum graveolens 'Fernleaf' **816**
Angelica archangelica **817**
Angelonia angustifolia
'Serenita Pink' **28**
Anthriscus cerefolium **818**
Antirrhinum majus 'Night and Day' **28**
Antirrhinum majus 'Twinny Peach' **29**
Apium graveolens var. secalinum
'Par-cel' **819**
Aquilegia canadensis **242**
Arctosis × hybrida **681**
Argyranthemum
'Jamaica Primrose' **682**
Arisaema candidissimum **136**
Arisarum proboscideum **137**
Aristolochia macrophylla **588**
Artemisia ludoviciana
'Valerie Finnis' **242**
Artemisia dracunculus **820**
Arum italicum subsp. italicum
'Marmoratum' **138**
Asarum europaeum **243**
Asparagus officinalis **859**
Aspidistra elatior **683**
Asplenium scolopendrium
Crispum Group **243**
Astelia chathamica
'Silver Spear' **684**
Aster amellus 'Veilchenkönigin' **244**
Aster × frikartii 'Mönch' **245**
Aster 'Little Carlow' **247**
Aster novae-angliae
'Harrington's Pink' **248**
Astilbe chinensis 'Visions' **249**
Astilbe × arendsii 'Fanal' **250**
Astrantia 'Roma' **251**
Athyrium niponicum var. pictum **252**

B

Baptisia australis **253**
Begonia Dragon Wing Red **29**
Begonia Fragrant Falls Series **31**
Begonia Big Series **31**
Begonia Million Kisses Series **32**
Berberis valdiviana **440**
Bergenia 'Bressingham White' **254**

Beta vulgaris 'Alto' **860**
Beta vulgaris 'Burpee's Golden' **860**
Beta vulgaris 'Bright Lights' **861**
Bignonia capreolata **589**
Billardiera longiflora **590**
Bomarea edulis **591**
Borago officinalis **820**
Bougainvillea × buttiana **593**
Brassica oleracea 'Glamour Red' **33**
Brassica oleracea 'Savoy King' **861**
Brassica rapa var. chinensis
'Joi Choi' **862**
Brassica oleracea 'Cavolo Nero' **863**
Brassica oleracea 'Petit Posy' **864**
Brassica oleracea 'Dynamo' **865**
Brassica oleracea 'Artwork' **866**
Brassica oleracea 'Redhead' **866**
Browallia speciosa **34**
Brugmansia suaveolens **685**
Brunfelsia pauciflora **686**
Brunnera macrophylla 'Jack Frost' **255**
Buddleja davidii Buzz Series **441**
Buddleja 'Lochinch' **441**
Buddleja globosa **442**
Buddleja sempervirens **442**

C

Caesalpinia pulcherrima **686**
Calamagrostis brachytricha **256**
Calathea zebrina **687**
Calendula officinalis 'Indian Prince' **35**
Calendula officinalis **823**
Calibrachoa Can-Can Series **36**
Calliandra haematocephala **687**
Callicarpa bodinieri var. giraldii
'Profusion' **444**
Callistemon citrinus 'Splendens' **688**
Callistephus chinensis
'Milady Mixed' **37**
Calluna vulgaris 'Silver Queen' **445**
Camassia quamash **139**
Camellia × williamsii 'Donation' **446**
Camellia japonica 'Bob Hope' **448**
Camellia 'Quintessence' **689**
Campanula 'Sarastro' **257**
Campanula garganica **258**
Campsis × tagliabuana
Indian Summer **593**
Canna 'Phasion' **141**
Canna 'Erebus' **141**
Capsicum annuum 'Basket of Fire' **868**

Annuals are plants that complete their life cycle in a single growing season: sow a seed in spring; watch it grow and flower in summer; the end. The annuals featured in this chapter are ornamentals, but always remember there are many other varieties: most vegetables are annuals and so too are many of the climbers.

Biennials complete their life cycle in two years, but they have been included here because they are plants that strictly speaking are perennial but are treated by gardeners as annuals.

Many gardeners get their annuals from seed suppliers, but even quicker results can be obtained from young plants.

ANNUALS AND BIENNIALS

❂ *Papaver commutatum* 'Ladybird' is a sow and forget annual for summer colour.

Ageratum
A. houstonianum 'Blue Horizon'

Main features Flowers in summer; attracts butterflies; cut as fresh flowers or dry as winter decoration
Height 45 cm (18 in.) **Spread** 30 cm (12 in.)
Position ○ ◑ **Hardiness** Annual

Many varieties of *Ageratum* are popular summer-flowering bedding plants. So why choose *A. houstonianum* 'Blue Horizon'? Most modern varieties are bred to be dwarf plants for bedding schemes, but 'Blue Horizon' – apart from having attractive, fluffy, mid-blue flowers and simple ovate leaves – has the added bonus of having a taller growing height, up to 45 centimetres (18 in.), which means it can be used in the middle of a flower bed or at the back of a border. It also makes excellent cut flowers that will remain in good condition for at least two weeks in water. Whole stems can be cut as the flowers open for drying.

Apart from its use in garden borders, 'Blue Horizon' (also commonly known as Mexican paintbrush or mistflower) is often planted in large containers, where its vigorous, branching plants and clusters of cushion-like flowers on long stems combine well with other species such as red *Salvia splendens* and the yellows and oranges of American Marigolds. 'Blue Horizon' was originally bred by the Sakata Seed Corporation in Japan. It has since been followed by a similar tall variety called 'Blue Planet', bred by Syngenta in the Netherlands.

Ageratum are popular summer-flowering annuals, which, because of their soft, pastel flower shades of blue and pink together with white, make great foil plants for stronger colours in the garden, in addition to attracting butterflies. Most varieties are low growing and can be used as border edgings or in colour drifts. Grow *Ageratum* in full sun or partial shade, remove fading flowering heads, and keep well fed and watered to prolong flowering until the arrival of frosts. Although not invasive, plants may be toxic if ingested in large quantities due to a defensive chemical produced to deter pests. **TS**

Alternatives

Ageratum houstonianum 'Blue Mink', *Ageratum houstonianum* 'Blue Planet'

Alcea
A. rosea Halo Series

Main features Bicoloured summer flowers; exceptional range of colour combinations
Height 2 m (6 ft) **Spread** 45 cm (18 in.)
Position ○ ◑ **Hardiness** Annual

Hollyhocks – *A. rosea* – are classic cottage garden plants. Their tall stateliness is captured in nineteenth-century paintings of Victorian English gardens and from there they were taken around the world. Their wild origin is unclear, having been grown in gardens for so many centuries, but it is thought to be western Asia.

The Halo Series, of twelve colours, was developed at Thompson & Morgan in Suffolk by Charles Valin, one of the leading contemporary plant breeders. These dramatic cultivars feature bicoloured flowers in which the centre of each single bloom contrasts boldly in colour with the rest of the flower. Most often seen as a mixture of all the colours, individual colours are also available and these include 'Halo Appleblossom' (white with a crimson centre), 'Halo Apricot' (apricot pink with a crimson centre), 'Halo Blush' (pale pink with a red centre and a yellow throat), 'Halo Candy' (blushed white with a wine-red throat), 'Halo Cream' (creamy white with a magenta centre) and 'Halo White' (white with a yellow centre, pictured).

These are perennial plants but are usually grown as biennials and raised afresh from seed each year, because after their first year of flowering, they tend to decline or suffer from disease. They are grown for their tall, upright, spikes (1.5–2.4 m/5–8 ft) of single and double, flared, trumpet-shaped flowers (5–10 cm/2–4 in.), which line the upper half of the stems and open in a wide variety of colours in summer. These are held tight to the stems to create impressive spires of colour. At the base the bold rounded leaves, which are rough in texture, tend to become ragged by flowering time. Rust disease can be a problem, as with all hollyhocks. Growing them as biennials helps and the foliage can also be sprayed with an appropriate fungicide. **GR**

Alternatives

Alcea rosea Chater's Double Group, *Alcea rosea* 'Nigra', *Alcea rosea* Spotlight Series

Amaranthus
A. cruentus × powellii 'Hopi Red Dye'

Main features Flowers in summer; good for cutting and drying; edible leaves and seed; attracts wildlife

Height 1.2 m (4 ft) **Spread** 60 cm (24 in)

Position ○ **Hardiness** Annual

The upright flower spikes of *A. cruentus × powellii* 'Hopi Red Dye' bear little resemblance to the more familiar weeping tassels of the species *A. caudatus,* known as love-lies-bleeding. However, the decorative and productive 'Hopi Red Dye' is sometimes listed as a cultivar of *A. caudatus*. What is not in doubt is that with its brilliant burgundy flowers and purple-red foliage, it makes an impressive statement in borders or roomy containers in your summer garden. 'Hopi Red Dye' grows best in full sun but can tolerate a variety of conditions, from humid to arid. Given a sheltered spot, you can expect a height of 1.2 to 1.5 metres (4–5 ft) and a spread of around half of that. Add fuel to the fire and create some glorious bonfire tints by planting tall annual *Rudbeckia* in front. Both look spectacular when backlit by the sun. Use twiggy sticks for support, pushed in when the plants are around knee high.

Like other members of the genus, 'Hopi Red Dye' is a real multipurpose plant. The young shoots can be harvested either as microgreens to add a dash of colour to salads, or when more mature, when the leaves are better stirfried or added to soups. In addition, the plentiful seed can be ground down into gluten-free flour or used to make a snack similar to popcorn.

Of course, as the name suggests, this amaranth was originally famed as a dye plant, being rich in betacyanins. It was used by the Hopi Native American tribe (from the western United States) to make a ceremonial deep red dye used to colour corn bread. In addition, the flowers are attractive to bees and butterflies and can be cut fresh for the vase or hung up to dry for winter display. Left in situ, the seed is greedily devoured by birds. Many will fall and regrow the following year. Amaranths can be prolific self-seeders, but you can cut off flower spikes as they fade if you would rather prevent this. **GS**

Alternatives

Amaranthus caudatus 'Fat Spike', *Amaranthus tricolor* 'Joseph's Coat'

Amberboa
A. moschata

Main features Flowers in summer; sweetly scented; fluffy thistle-like flowers in mainly soft pastel shades
Height 60 cm (24 in.) **Spread** 25 cm (10 in.)
Position ○ **Hardiness** Annual

This appealing fragrant annual for borders and for cutting is related to the more familiar cornflower, *Centaurea*, and was once classified with it. However, *Amberboa* is now placed in a small genus of six species, owing to significant differences in the seed. One species in particular is grown more widely than others although, sadly, it is now seen less often, but it is a lovely plant. The summer-flowering *A. moschata* – commonly known as sweet sultan – grows naturally in south-west Asia and is appreciated in gardens for its soft colouring and its attractive fragrance. It is more dependent than most annuals on fertile soil that is never parched.

Reaching about 60 centimetres (24 in.) in height, its leaves are deeply divided and the soft, thistle-like heads (4 cm/1.5 in.) are filled with petals that are noticeably dissected at their tips. Wild plants have purple flowers, whereas garden forms come in an appealing range of delicate shades of purple, lilac, rose pink and yellow, together with a creamy white. The colours are never strident, and in many forms the centre of each flower is also a soft cream colour. 'Imperialis' is the mixture most commonly seen and includes a vivid canary yellow along with softer shades. The flowers of 'The Bride' are pure white with a rich cream-coloured centre.

Sweet sultan is now primarily regarded as a cut flower. It is usually sown in spring; however, sowing in autumn will give larger plants that flower earlier. Plants should produce up to eight stems per plant for cutting, although this may be significantly reduced if plants are short of nutrients. The sweet honey-scented flowers are long lasting in water (up to ten days) and are best cut when the flowers are about one-third open; if cutting sprays, the first flower should be three-quarters open when cut. **GR**

Alternatives

Amberboa moschata 'The Bride,' *Cyanopsis muricata*, *Centaurea cyanus*

Ammi
A. majus
'Graceland'

Main features Flowers from early to midsummer;
excellent for cutting; attracts pollinators
Height 1.4 m (4.5 ft) **Spread** 45 cm (18 in.)
Position ○ ◑ **Hardiness** Annual

Every garden needs a touch of cool sophistication to
counterbalance attention-seeking plants, and *A. majus*
'Graceland' – with its cloud of ferny foliage topped by a
froth of small, flat, white flower heads – is a stylish way to
get that contrast. Its height and billowing shape make it a
perfect border filler, and in recent years the simple white
umbels have been incorporated increasingly into garden
designs. They have a look that suits the trend towards
using informal tapestries of plants grown closely together.
This graceful annual plant is easy to grow from seed, not
too fussy about what soil it grows in and flowers as well
in light shade as in full sun, so it is very versatile. It seldom
needs any support and is good for wildlife, attracting a
host of insects to its nectar-rich flowers, including lesser-
known pollinators such as hoverflies and small, solitary
wasps. It flowers for months from early to midsummer,
and is long lasting as a cut flower too. It looks good with
other annuals such as pot marigolds and cornflower. **JS**

Alternatives

Syn. *Ammi glaucifolium. Ammi visnaga, Orlaya grandiflora*

Anchusa
A. azurea
'Loddon Royalist'

Main features Unusual vivid blue flowers in late spring
to early summer; attracts bees; edible flowers
Height 90 cm (3 ft) **Spread** 60 cm (2 ft)
Position ○ ◑ **Hardiness** RHS H7

'Loddon Royalist' was discovered about fifty years ago
in the United Kingdom, although *A. azurea* belongs to
the borage family and has been grown for centuries.
The hairy stems and coarse leaves might have made
it a plant only its mother could love, but the vivid blue
flowers transform it into a real crowd-pleaser. The blooms
are small but plentiful, held in clusters over rosettes of
foliage on long, stiff stems. They are a beautiful blue that
looks good in sunlight and appears luminous in low light,
so it seems to stand out in dull, wet weather or as the
light fades at the end of the day. Flowering through late
spring and early summer, it can help to fill the awkward
gap as the early flush of spring bulbs and flowers fades
before summer bloomers get into their stride. It combines
equally beautifully in the middle of a border with an
orange geum such as 'Totally Tangerine', as with the more
upright spires of yellow verbascums. It can grow quite
tall, in which case stems will need support. **JS**

Alternatives

Syn. *Anchusa italica. Anchusa azurea* 'Dropmore'

 Ammi majus 'Graceland' produces copious cut flower material even in poor soils.

Angelonia
A. angustifolia
'Serenita Pink'

Main features Summer-long blooms; suitable for mass planting or containers; attracts bees and butterflies
Height 30 cm (12 in.) **Spread** 15 cm (6 in.)
Position ○ **Hardiness** RHS H1c

If you are keen for variety in your summer display, the characterful annual or tender perennial *A. angustifolia* is ideal. Unlike many of the top-selling bedding plants, such as French marigolds and begonias that are round in shape, 'Serenita Pink' has pink, dark-throated flowers arranged in elegant spikes that contrast well with carpeting trailers in containers, beds or baskets. Individually, the flowers are as intricate and exotic as an orchid. *Angelonia* performs outstandingly well in wet, humid or dry weather. In fact, in warm, frost-free climates, the plants will thrive year-round and exceed their usual height and spread. This is not surprising, considering they are native to Brazil. Pruning and deadheading is not normally required, but a straggly plant can be rejuvenated with a hard prune. Sow seed in a greenhouse, porch or on a warm windowsill in early spring. Plant out at 20 to 30 centimetres (8–12 in.) after the last frost. **GS**

Alternatives

Angelonia angustifolia 'Serenita Raspberry', *Angelonia angustifolia* 'Purple', *Angelonia* Serena Series

Antirrhinum
A. majus
'Night and Day'

Main features Showy flowers in boldly contrasting crimson and white; prolific bushy plants
Height 45 cm (18 in.) **Spread** 30 cm (12 in.)
Position ○ **Hardiness** RHS H6

These slightly woody perennial plants – almost always grown as annuals to be raised from seed each year – are among our most attractive summer flowers. Their spikes of two-lipped flowers, set against dark semiglossy foliage, come in an exceptional range of colours and bicolours. *A. majus* 'Night and Day' is the modern version of an old Victorian type. The upright plants feature foliage that has sultry bronze-purple tints, while the lips of the flowers are deep blood-red, which contrasts sharply with the pure-white throat. The result is flowers that show a striking and rare contrast between the two colours. 'Night and Day' is short enough to grow in a sunny border without staking, yet tall enough to be cut for the house, where it makes an appealing companion to old roses. Sow seeds of 'Night and Day' in spring for flowering through the summer; pinch out the seedlings when 7 to 10 centimetres (3–4 in.) high and deadhead regularly. **GR**

Alternatives

Antirrhinum majus 'Black Prince', *Antirrhinum majus* 'Madame Butterfly', *Antirrhinum majus* Liberty Classic Series

Antirrhinum
A. majus
'Twinny Peach'

Main features Unique, scented, double-ruffled flowers; bedding or container plants; good cut flower
Height 30 cm (12 in.) **Spread** 30 cm (12 in.)
Position ○ **Hardiness** RHS H6

There are hundreds of *Antirrhinum* varieties, but Twinny is the first dwarf bedding hybrid to exhibit fragrant, double-flowered plants. These in themselves are very attractive, but the added bonus is that the tightly curled, ruffled flowers do not permit entry to bees; no pollination means plants do not go to seed and will continue to flower through summer into the autumn. Strictly speaking, the alternate name, snapdragon, is not appropriate for Twinny, as it refers to the traditional two-lipped single 'butterfly' flower type. There are a number of flower colours in the family, such as violet, bronze, yellow and white, but 'Twinny Peach' is considered the best and holds the distinction of being an All-America Selections winner. Plants reaching a height of 30 centimetres (12 in.) are compact, bushy and multi-stemmed with good flowering potential. Plants have good vigour and are heat tolerant; they grow best in a sunny site with well-drained soil. **TS**

Alternatives

Antirrhinum majus 'Floral Showers', *Antirrhinum majus* 'Kim', *Antirrhinum majus* 'Magic Carpet'

Begonia
Dragon Wing Red

Main features Virtually year-round blooms; handsome, glossy leaves
Height 36 cm (14 in.) **Spread** 60 cm (24 in.)
Position ○ ◐ ● **Hardiness** RHS H1c

Many enthusiasts believe Dragon Wing Red is the best begonia. A super-sized version of the wax begonia, it is tough, growing in sun or shade, and forms a pleasing umbrella shape without any pinching or pruning. Best of all, being incapable of setting fertile seed, it puts all its efforts into nonstop flowering. The exact parentage of Dragon Wing Red is open to debate. It has a fibrous root system, like its parent plants, wax begonia (*Begonia* × *semperflorens*) and possibly an angelwing begonia (*B. coccinea*). However, its hybrid qualities surpass both parents with bigger, wing-shaped leaves, bolder flowers and a denser, more robust growth habit. Available in red, pink and white, the loose clusters of flowers are cleanly shed, thus avoiding rot. With their thick, succulent stems, plants can miss the odd watering, but in hot climates they are best in semi-shade. Mature plants can be trimmed back and overwintered indoors. **GS**

Alternatives

='Bepared'. *Begonia* 'Million Kisses Amour', *Begonia* 'Santa Cruz Sunset', *Begonia* 'Perfectly Pink'

Begonia
Big Series

Main features Flowers throughout summer; large vividly coloured blooms against green or bronze foliage
Height 60 cm (24 in.) **Spread** 38 cm (15 in.)
Position ○ ◑ ● **Hardiness** RHS H1c

Begonia
Fragrant Falls Series

Main features Fully double flowers summer to autumn; trailing plants suitable for baskets; distinctive fragrance
Height 30 cm (12 in.) **Spread** 30 cm (12 in.)
Position ○ ◑ **Hardiness** RHS H1c

In the plant world, bigger blooms are not necessarily better. You only have to look at some highly bred pansies nodding over to see the problems it can bring. However, recent developments to get more mileage from fibrous-rooted or wax begonias have given them a new lease of life. Bred by seed company Benary and introduced in 2008, there are now five variations: rose flowers with a bronze or green leaf, red flowers with a bronze or green leaf and the latest offering, pink flowers with a green leaf. The Big Series is a great choice for landscaping or containers, though to succeed in suspended containers, their vigour demands a generous-sized basket or bowl. They have an upright, arching habit and dense growth. Blooms are more than twice the size (5–8 cm/2–3 in. across) of *Begonia* × *semperflorens*. Plants can be grown from seed or bought as plugs or garden-ready specimens. They thrive in sun or shade, but in full sun you may need to water every other day in hot spells. Try them with banana plants and cannas for a touch of the tropics. **GS**

Tuberous begonias with the extra attraction of fragrance are derived from a primrose-scented species found growing wild in the Andes in 1886. It was introduced by the French nursery Lemoine et Fils, who also developed some scented hybrids. Then the inventor of the 'Stargazer' lily, Leslie Woodriff, also introduced fragrant cultivars, and it is thought that Belgian breeder Arnold van Peteghem developed his 'Aromatics' from these. However, the scent was still not strong. So Thompson & Morgan in Suffolk developed tuberous begonias that combined double flowers with a stronger fragrance. In 2011 the Fragrant Falls Series debuted at the Chelsea Flower Show, then in 2014 they introduced the Fragrant Falls Improved Series. Plants have a trailing habit suitable for hanging baskets and fully double flowers. Unusually, different colorus in the series have different scents: 'Apricot Delight' comes with a rose fragrance, 'Lemon Fizz' has a sharp citrus scent while the rose-scented 'Rose Syllabub' is pale pink with a dark pink picotee edge. **GR**

Alternatives

Begonia 'Glowing Embers', *Begonia* 'Whopper Mixed'

Alternatives

Begonia 'Aromatics', *Begonia* 'Red Glory'

 Begonia **Big Series** is a great statement plant for shady corners.

Begonia
Million Kisses Series

Main features Semi-trailing habit with attractive pendulous flowers; exceptionally long flowering season
Height 40–50 cm (16–20 in.) **Spread** 80 cm (32 in.)
Position ○ ◑ **Hardiness** RHS H3

There are about 900 wild species of begonia growing mainly in tropical and subtropical South America, but, until relatively recently, *B. boliviensis* had rarely been grown in gardens. Although introduced from Bolivia and Argentina in 1864, and used as part of the development of the colourful tuberous begonias grown in summer gardens today, its most striking feature had been lost along the way. Its pendulous, four-petalled, fiery-red flowers appear all summer, but these original plants were too spindly and sparse in flowers to be widely popular. However, seeds were again collected in the wild in 1990, and cultivars have been developed that build on its attractive flower form but improve the growing habit.

The result is the Million Kisses Series, developed by Fred Yates in the United Kingdom, of which nine cultivars have been introduced. All feature a relatively compact, semi-trailing habit of growth; neat, pointed leaves; and a long, prolific flowering season with the flowers held conveniently just outside the mass of foliage and so showing themselves off well. Flowering continues until frost, and in autumn, plants can be moved into a conservatory to continue the display. The most popular cultivars in the series, with pendulous flowers, are Amour ('Yamour'), with red flowers and bronze-tinted foliage; Devotion ('Yadev'), with red flowers and green leaves; and Elegance ('Yagance'), with especially lovely pink and white bicoloured flowers (pictured). **GR**

Alternatives

Begonia Bonfire Series, *Begonia* Bossa Nova Series, *Begonia* 'Santa Cruz Scarlet', *Begonia* Sparkler Series

Brassica
B. oleracea 'Glamour Red'

Main features Three-season foliage effect; spectacular as cut foliage material
Height 30–45 cm (12–18 in.) **Spread** 30 cm (12 in.)
Position ○ **Hardiness** RHS H4

If you have never considered the impact ornamental brassicas can have on your winter to spring display, then you have been missing out on a treat. Imagine a tight rosette of vivid magenta pink, frilly leaves that can grow to dinner plate proportions, and then consider what else would be capable of creating the same drama in the dead of winter. In 2011, *B. oleracea* 'Glamour Red' was the first ever kale to win an All-America Selections award in seventy-eight years of trialing. Lacking the characteristic waxy coating associated with kales, the gloss rather than matt finish results in a more intense colour. Typically grown as annuals, ornamental kales derive from the wild *B. oleracea* that grow under exposed conditions on coastal cliffs in western and southern Europe. In their second year, in common with other brassicas, they produce a tall flower spike studded with yellow blooms.

Leaves begin to assume their rich colours when night temperatures fall below 13°C (55°F) for more than two weeks and get more intense after the first frost. These kales are generally hardier than ornamental cabbage, and the red selections tend to be tougher than the whites in both groups, though all may perish in severe cold spells. It takes around ninety days from seed to the first sign of leaf colour, which makes early summer the ideal time to sow seeds. Alternatively, buy young plants in the autumn. They look a treat planted in hollow pumpkins or in pots or beds with bulbs and violas in the spring. **GS**

Alternatives

Brassica oleracea 'Peacock Red', *Brassica oleracea* 'Peacock White', *Brassica oleracea* 'Chidori Red'

Browallia
B. speciosa

Main features Smothered in tubular, star-shaped flowers from early summer to early autumn; frost tender
Height 45 cm (18 in.) **Spread** 45 cm (18 in.)
Position ○ ◑ **Hardiness** RHS H1b

Also known as the bush violet, *B. speciosa* has star-shaped, tubular violet-blue flowers (4 cm/1.5 in. across) with white throats. It is a neat, rounded plant with a long display of flowers, and fresh green leaves that feel slightly sticky to the touch. Native to Colombia, it is actually a perennial, but is grown as a summer bedding plant or indoor plant in temperate climates. Plants or seeds may be sold as species or by a variety name but plants are similar being either shades of blue or white.

 B. speciosa thrives when grown as an annual bedding plant outdoors, discarded after flowering. It can be grown in the ground, in fertile, well-drained soil, but it is particularly suited to containers and hanging baskets.

The plant needs a minimum temperature of 13°C (55°F) year-round to thrive and can therefore also be grown as a houseplant. Grow it in a greenhouse or conservatory and protect it from direct sunlight. Keep the compost moist and give it a balanced liquid feed every month. Pinch out the growing tips to ensure bushy plants and pick off the flowers as they fade. In winter, water sparingly. *B. speciosa* is usually bought at a nursery when it is in flower, but it can be easily grown from seed. Sow in early spring in a heated greenhouse for outdoor plants; for indoor plants, sow in late winter for late spring and summer flowers or in summer for winter flowers. Aphids and whitefly may be a problem under glass. **VP**

Alternatives

Browallia speciosa 'Blue Bells', *Browallia speciosa* 'Silver Bells', *Browallia speciosa* 'Blue Troll'

Calendula
C. officinalis 'Indian Prince'

Main features Summer-long blooms that are edible;
medicinal qualities; good as cut flowers
Height 60 cm (24 in.) **Spread** 45 cm (18 in.)
Position ○ **Hardiness** Annual

C. officinalis 'Indian Prince' is indeed a prince among calendulas, for it displays the brilliant Day-Glo colours so typical of this lovely annual marigold, but unlike the others, the dark orange ray petals are backed with rich mahogany red. It also provides long stems for cutting that can last up to a week in the vase. Cut or deadhead regularly to keep the flowers coming.

For the sturdiest plants, in milder climates sow pot marigolds in late summer and autumn. These will overwinter and be quicker to flower than those from a more traditional early-spring sowing under glass. They can also be sown directly into the garden soil by mid to late spring. Some will scatter their seeds and pop up the following year. For containers, look for more compact varieties like 'Fiesta Gitana'.

Like many of the plants that form the mainstay of the classic cottage garden, *C. officinalis* earned its place not for purely decorative reasons. Its petals were also edible, and it had medicinal properties. Over the centuries, the flowers have been considered beneficial in reducing inflammation and promoting healing.

All pot marigolds look a treat in among dark-leafed kale, red cabbage and ruby chard and their bright flower heads will also lure in beneficial insects, such as aphid-eating hoverflies. Strip off the spicy flavoured individual petals and scatter them over salads as a feast for both the eyes and the taste buds. **GS**

Alternatives

Calendula officinalis 'Orange Porcupine', *Calendula officinalis* 'Geisha Girl', *Calendula officinalis* 'Princess Orange Black'

Calibrachoa

Can-Can Series

Main features Semi-trailing plants; prolific trumpet-shaped blooms; unusual colours and colour combinations
Height 30 cm (12 in.) **Spread** 60 cm (24 in.)
Position ○ **Hardiness** RHS H3

About two dozen species of *Calibrachoa* grow in scrub and grassland from the southern United States and south into Brazil. Wild plants are twiggy, sprawling evergreens with neat leaves and prolific, small, reddish or purplish petunia-like flowers. Closely related to petunias, they are distinct in several botanical details, and gardeners will appreciate that calibrachoas are neater, more dainty and less blowsy.

Calibrachoas had been overlooked as garden plants until the 1990s, when a number of species were brought together and hybrids between them created. The first was the Million Bells Series, and million bells is now sometimes used as a common name for all calibrachoas. The Can-Can Series and its sister series, the Double Can-Can Series, are more vigorous than many calibrachoas and develop into well-branched, semi-trailing plants that become woody at the base as the plants mature.

From early summer until late autumn, the neat, five-lobed, trumpet-shaped flowers open in an increasing range of distinctive colours, including some striking bicolours. Unlike earlier introductions they perform well in rainy and cloudy conditions; the flowers remain open on the dullest of days and they do not become bare at the base. Note that flowering may tail off if plants are not fed regularly.

Can-Can calibrachoas are perfect used in hanging baskets, and two or three carefully chosen cultivars can be grown together in one basket for a sparkling all-season effect. Among the many, unusually distinctive cultivars available are: Can-Can Dark Purple ('Balcanark') in deep crimson, Can-Can Coral Reef ('Balcanoree') in peachy pink and Can-Can Hot Pink Star ('Balcanosar') in pink and white. Can-Can Apple Blossom (pictured) is soft pink with deep-magenta veins. **GR**

Alternatives

Calibrachoa Cabaret Series, *Calibrachoa* Double Can-Can Series, *Calibrachoa* Superbells Series

Callistephus
C. *chinensis* 'Milady Mixed'

Main features Spectacular late-summer flowers; good for cutting; single blooms attract bees
Height 25 cm (10 in.) **Spread** 25 cm (10 in.)
Position ○ **Hardiness** Annual

The common name 'aster' comes from the ancient Greek word *astron*, meaning 'star'. This refers to the shape of the flowers. However, asters are gaining momentum only in late summer, when many of the most popular bedding plants are beginning to look tired, so they are stars twice over. Whether you are looking for compact ones to fill narrow beds, containers, window boxes and baskets, or taller ones that will impress as cut flowers, there are plenty to choose from. Flower shapes vary from needle pointed to single eyed, ostrich plumed and pompom.

C. chinensis 'Milady Mixed' is a sturdy, long-established, dwarf cultivar with 8-centimetre-wide (3 in.) blooms in blue, pink, rose, rose red and white that last well into the autumn. It has been awarded a Royal Horticultural Society Award of Garden Merit, having proved over time to be outstanding as a bedding plant. This is partly due to the fact that it shows good resistance to the disease aster wilt. Once present, this damaging disease can persist in the ground, preventing plants from drawing moisture from the soil. However, you can still enjoy them in containers.

'Milady Mixed' looks superb interplanted with dwarf annual *Rudbeckia,* such as 'Toto'. Both can be purchased as plug plants and potted up individually to grow on before planting out in early summer after all danger of hard frost has passed. Alternatively, you can sow aster seeds under cover in trays of potting compost in early spring in gentle heat, just covering with more compost or vermiculite. For the best quality plants, pot seedlings into individual pots or cell trays. You will also avoid the transplant shock that seed tray-grown plants can suffer when split and set out in show containers or the open garden. They will not be harmed by light spring frost if properly hardened off. **GS**

Alternatives

Aster chinensis 'Duchess Mixed', *Aster chinensis* 'Teisa Stars', *Aster chinensis* 'Ostrich Plume Mixed'

Celosia
C. argentea
Plumosa Group

Main feature Long-lasting, upright summer plumes in vibrant fiery colours on bushy plants
Height 35 cm (14 in.) **Spread** 30 cm (12 in.)
Position ○ **Hardiness** Annual

The development of *C. argentea* – an annual, originally from the Asian tropics and related to *Amaranthus* – has run along two different paths. All celosias are colourful annuals, with huge numbers of tiny flowers in distinctive heads. Those in the Cristata Group (known as cockscomb) develop tightly congested, rippled flower heads, whereas in the more elegant Plumosa Group, the flower heads develop into pointed plumes and are known as Prince of Wales feathers, feather celosia or feathered amaranth. In the Plumosa Group, taller series have been developed for cut-flower use while shorter series, such as Fresh Look Series (pictured), are intended for borders and containers; the latter are noticeably bushy plants. Each plume is made up of a huge number of tiny flowers that open over a long period to create an extended display. Colours are in the red, orange and gold ranges, while some cultivars also feature reddish leaves. **GR**

Alternatives

Celosia argentea First Flame Series, *Celosia argentea* Kimono Series, *Celosia argentea* New Look Series

Centaurea
C. cyanus
'Black Ball'

Main feature Sultry, deep-reddish, purple flowers for borders or cutting
Height 60–90 cm (2–3 ft) **Spread** 30 cm (12 in.)
Position ○ **Hardiness** Annual

Blue cornflowers were once a feature of the British countryside, and in 1640, they were said to be 'furnishing, or rather pestering, the cornfields'. Modern agricultural techniques have largely eliminated this delightful annual, with its slightly downy stems and vivid thistle-like flowers, from the fields, and it is in the garden that we now find cornflowers more than anywhere else. For both colourful summer borders and in vases inside, 'Black Ball' is a variety that always excites interest. The flowers are not black but come in a rich, deep-crimson purple, with a shimmer that catches the light on bright days. Although the stems look wiry, they often need some discreet support both to show off the flowers and to ensure straight stems for cutting. Seed can be sown in spring or autumn. Autumn sowing is preferred as this ensures more flowers over a longer season with an earlier start. Deadhead, or cut, regularly, otherwise the flowering season may be brief. **GR**

Alternatives

Centaurea cyanus 'Blue Diadem', *Centaurea cyanus* 'Blue Ball', *Centaurea cyanus* 'Midget Blue'

● *Celosia argentea* var. *cristata* Plumosa Group in the cutting garden of Château de Chenonceau in early autumn.

Cerinthe
C. major 'Purpurascens'

Main features Flowers in summer; handsome foliage;
good for cutting; attracts bees
Height 60 cm (24 in.) **Spread** 45 cm (18 in.)
Position ○ **Hardiness** RHS H3

C. major somehow looks like an exotic plant that should
be difficult to grow, although the truth is, it could not be
easier. With fleshy, grey-green leaves and arching stems,
from which hang large sea-green bracts and tubular
purple flowers, it could be mistaken for some kind of
euphorbia, but is, in fact, a member of the borage family.

Everything about 'Purpurascens' is elegant, from the
way the leaves are arranged around the slender stems, to
the drooping tips with their clusters of nodding bracts
and flowers in subtle, steely hues of blue and purple.
This is a classy-looking plant that would fit into a modern
garden, a container or a cottage-garden–style border
with white larkspur and orange marigolds.

Although it might be tough enough to overwinter
in a sheltered spot in mild regions where it might even
prove evergreen, the plant is not very hardy and in most
gardens should be treated as an annual. It will self-seed
freely, though, so can often be relied on to reappear even
if the original plants have died over winter. Collect seed
in autumn and start it off in spring to replenish your stocks.

The plant originated in the Mediterranean and is
very popular with bees, which led to the common name
honeywort. It is trouble-free and will flower for months
from late spring to late summer, as long as it is positioned
in the sun and growing in well-drained soil. The only
work you will need to do to keep the plants tidy is to cut
the stems back when flowering has finished. **JS**

Alternatives

Cerinthe major 'Blue Kiwi', *Cerinthe major* 'Yellow Gem',
Cerinthe major 'Zingaro'

Clarkia
C. unguiculata 'Apple Blossom'

Main features Easy seed-raised hardy plant; flowers in
summer; good cut flowers; attracts bees
Height 90 cm (3 ft) **Spread** 30 cm (12 in.)
Position ○ ◑ **Hardiness** Annual

The frilly blooms of this lovely garland flower are a
delicate shade of apricot with hints of white, which
is very distinctive, although might not be what you'd
expect from the name 'Apple Blossom'. Plants throw
up masses of racemes, with dark-green leaves that
become festooned with flowers and have all the charm
of miniature hollyhocks. They have plenty of vigour, too,
flowering for many weeks in summer. They also make
terrific cut flowers. Cut them as the top bud opens, and
all the others on the stem will open in the vase.

They are great to use among perennials, where a bit
of extra colour is needed. When plants are small, it is
a good idea to put in some pea sticks to support the
growing stems, which can be floppy in full flower, and
regular deadheading as soon as the petals start to wilt
helps to keep fresh blooms forming.

A wildflower from California, *Clarkia* is often included
in packs of wildflowers and is also sold in seed packs of
mixed colours that can be a very inexpensive way of
filling gaps in your border. Look for packs with names
like 'Double Mix' and see what comes up. It is a very easy
plant to raise from seeds and will start to flower within
as little as eight weeks of sowing. It is best to start seeds
off directly in the ground, sowing a couple of times at
intervals to keep the display going as long as possible.
It will often self-seed, giving you another display the
following year. **JS**

Alternatives

Syn. *Clarkia elegans. Clarkia unguiculata* 'Double Mix',
Clarkia unguiculata 'Pretty Polly Mix'

Cleome

Senorita Rosalita

Main features Adaptable plants; exceptionally long season of colour; plentiful flower heads
Height 60 cm (24 in.) **Spread** 45 cm (18 in.)
Position ○ **Hardiness** Annual

This tall summer annual is especially popular in areas with hot, humid summer weather. Growing wild mainly in South America, there are more than 150 species but only *Cleome hassleriana* has made an impact in gardens up to now. However, in spite of its bold heads of large and colourful spidery flowers, its sticky leaves, unpleasant-smelling foliage and spiny stems have limited its appeal. In recent years a number of hybrid cultivars have been developed that, although less flamboyant, come without these off-putting features.

The best of these new hybrid cultivars so far is Senorita Rosalita; it is more compact and branches more effectively than other cultivars to produce a tight and bushy plant. Plants have no spines, the foliage is not sticky and it has no unpleasant odour. While *C. hassleriana* cultivars tend to develop a few tall stems topped with large heads of flowers – a long succession of flowers open in each flower head – plants in the Senorita Series develop far more flower heads. These are smaller but come in a continuing succession, with the new flower heads overtopping the old.

The overall effect is a colourful plant flowering well into the autumn and better suited to today's gardens and the tastes of today's gardeners. The Senorita Series was developed in Germany and at present includes two colours. The flowers of Senorita Blanca are white with a pink tint and held on pale-pink stalks, while the flowers of Senorita Rosalita are pink and held on dark-pink stalks. Plants in the Senorita Series thrive in cooler summers as well as in heat and humidity; they are compact enough to make impressive plants for large containers, and their exceptionally long flowering season makes them ideal in small spaces. These plants are sterile, though, so do not expect to find self-sown seedlings. **GR**

Alternatives

='Inncleosr.' *Cleome* Senorita Blanca, *Cleome* Sparkler Series

Cleome
C. serrulata 'Solo'

Main features Flowers summer to autumn; drought tolerant; attracts bees and butterflies
Height 60 cm (24 in.) **Spread** 30 cm (12 in.)
Position ○ **Hardiness** Annual

Smaller and more subtle than the well-known spider flower *Cleome hassleriana* and its cultivars, *C. serrulata* 'Solo' produces stunning heads of light pink to white flowers with protruding, fuzzy, crimson stamen on sturdy thornless stems. It is a quick-growing plant that blooms within ten weeks of sowing, and it continues to flower over a long period. Easily grown by sowing directly into open ground, these compact annuals have buff-green foliage and prefer full sun, handling drought with ease. They also are tolerant of pests, are remarkably disease free, and perform best with little or no feeding.

Actually a cultivar of a North American wildflower native to the intermountain west and prairies, 'Solo' blooms from early summer through to the first frost. It will reseed at random, creating the impression of a perennial planting, and is a perfect addition to any border, looking particularly good planted en masse in a cottage-garden–style planting. The nectar-filled blossoms are clustered in elongated racemes near the top portion of the stems. They produce copious amounts of nectar, thereby attracting bees and other pollinators to the garden. The plant continues flowering as the stalks elongate, while the distinctive pod-like fruits, up to 10 centimetres (4 in.) long, droop downward in a spidery fashion. The seed are important food for doves and other small birds.

C. serrulata was one of many new plants collected in 1804 during the Lewis and Clark expedition. Although widely cultivated today as a bee forage plant, *Cleome* was grown by Native Americans who consumed young leaves as a potherb in spring and boiled the plant down to a syrup as a remedy for stomachaches and other ailments. It was also used as a basis for paints and dyes used to decorate pottery and textiles. **KK**

Alternatives

Cleome Senorita Rosalita, *Cleome serrulata*

Consolida
C. regalis

Main feature Clouds of purple, blue or white flowers over many summer weeks
Height 60 cm (24 in.) **Spread** 30 cm (12 in.)
Position ○ ◑ **Hardiness** Annual

Larkspur is a classic cottage garden annual closely related to the perennial delphinium. Botanists separate the two by details of their flower structure while gardeners notice that larkspur, or *Consolida*, is an annual, and delphiniums are mainly perennials. Larkspurs fall into two groups, both of which are delightful annuals, with the main focus on their brilliant blue flowers. The rocket larkspur, *C. ajacis*, is more formal in appearance, relatively unbranched, with crowded upright spikes of semi-double flowers.

Branched larkspurs are derived from *C. regalis*, a species from the Caucasus that became an agricultural weed in Europe but is now dying out. Plants are well branched and more airy, the dark-green, wiry stems reaching 60 centimetres (24 in.), or a little more, and are more delicate in their appearance although not in their constitution. Their single flowers are spaced out along the stems, and the effect is of a cloud of small butterflies dancing over the foliage. Wild plants tend to come in purple-blue shades, while in garden selections, the 2.5-centimetre-long (1 in.) flowers come in pale and dark blues and in white. 'Blue Cloud' is a deep and vivid blue, a very striking colour, which is lovely interplanted among more robust annuals and with perennials.

Flowering is in summer, but when seeds are sown in the autumn, and rosettes develop before the winter, flowering begins in late spring or early summer and continues for many weeks. Spring-sown plants begin to flower later and are less prolific. Growing conditions have a significant impact on the performance of *C. regalis* and, in rich, fertile soil and a sunny site, perhaps with an occasional liquid feed, results can be very impressive compared with neglected plants in less suitable situations. Plants may suffer from mildew in late summer, especially in hot, dry seasons. **GR**

Alternatives

Consolida regalis 'Snow Cloud', *Consolida regalis* 'Cloudy Skies', *Consolida regalis* 'Blue Cloud'

Coreopsis
C. tinctoria

Main features Flowers summer to autumn; attracts a
wide range of pollinating insects
Height 90 cm (3 ft) **Spread** 45 cm (18 in.)
Position ○ **Hardiness** Annual

This sunny little annual is popular for its distinctive
bright-yellow flowers with maroon or brown centres.
Being a member of the daisy family, it has a central disk
in the same dark red hue. Commonly known as tickseed
or golden tickseed, C. tinctoria seem to burst with vitality,
bearing an explosion of thin, branching stems and
smooth, narrow leaves. They form balls of colour when
in full flower, and carry on blooming through most of
summer and autumn. Tickseed is often still sold as a
wildflower but it has become increasingly popular as a
garden plant, and can be used as a hardworking border
filler, in pots or planted in drifts. It is also effective as a
cut flower.

A native of the plains regions of the United States and
the state wildflower of Florida, C. tinctoria is now found
in many regions across the country. Plants prefer full
sun but can grow in partial shade. They are easy to raise
from seeds, which can be sown directly into the ground
in autumn where winters are mild, or in spring in colder
regions. They grow quickly and usually self-seed and
therefore reappear in subsequent years and can become
a weed. They are popular plants with pollinating insects,
including bees and butterflies.

There are perennial species of tickseed too, and both
kinds have become a favourite of breeders, not least
the innovative Terra Nova nurseries in the US state of
Oregon. There are a huge number of different varieties
in a rainbow of colours such as the Lemonade Series and
C. tinctoria 'Roulette' from Thompson & Morgan in
the United Kingdom, which has striking maroon and
yellow tiger-striped flowers. Some of them are barely
recognisable as tickseed, but they do generally share
the same easy charm and low-maintenance needs of
the original species. **JS**

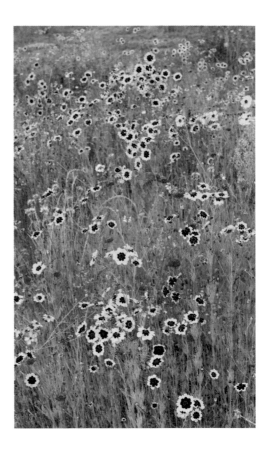

Alternatives

Coreopsis tinctoria 'Mahogany Midget', *Coreopsis* 'Ruby
Frost', *Coreopsis* 'Jethro Tull', *Coreopsis* 'Cosmic Eye'

Cosmos

C. sulphureus
'Polidor'

Main features Bright, breezy summer to autumn blooms;
good for beds, containers and cutting; attracts wildlife
Height 30–60 cm (12–24 in.) **Spread** 30 cm (12 in.)
Position ○ **Hardiness** Annual

In the sort of hot, baking conditions that would see some
annuals quickly seed and die, this dazzling star of the
plant world keeps on blooming. As you would expect,
C. sulphureus (or yellow cosmos) is native to arid countries
like Mexico, where it was much admired by Spanish
explorers who brought seeds back to Europe. The native
plant can grow up to head height, but modern strains,
such as 'Polidor', are more compact with a greater range
of hot, Day-Glo colours in the orange, red and yellow
spectrums, set against finely divided foliage that makes
them well suited to contemporary gardens and colour
schemes. Besides performing a floral marathon from early
summer to late autumn, the incurved, 5- to 7-centimetre
(2–3 in.) wide blooms are attractive to bees and butterflies.
Like its cousin, *Cosmos bipinnatus*, it is not prone to pests
and diseases and comes freely from seed. Harvest flowers
in the cool, early morning and pick regularly. **GS**

Alternatives

Cosmos sulphureus, Cosmos sulphureus 'Ladybird Dwarf
Red', *Cosmos sulphureus* 'Klondyke Mixed'

Cosmos

C. bipinnatus
Sonata Series

Main features Compact; prolific and long flowering
summer to autumn; four distinct colours
Height 60 cm (24 in.) **Spread** 38 cm (15 in.)
Position ○ **Hardiness** Annual

Introduced from Mexico in 1799, *C. bipinnatus* makes a tall
plant with fresh bright leaves and lovely daisy-like flowers
in red, pink and white shades with bright yellow centres.
The problem is that as these large plants mature, they
are easily damaged by wind. Flowers can be sparsely
scattered across the plant, and the result is large green
plants without enough flowers. Shorter and bushier
cultivars have been developed, the best of which is the
Sonata Series. The plants are less than half the height
of earlier cultivars, so they can be grown in almost any
sunny situation. They also feature more flowers and less
foliage; they start to flower earlier in the summer and
flower well into the autumn if deadheaded. There are four
colours: 'Sonata Carmine' is deep carmine red, 'Sonata
Pink' (pictured right) is pale rose pink, 'Sonata Pink Blush' is
rich rose pink with a fuchsia-pink ring round the eye and
'Sonata White' (pictured above and right) is pure white. **GR**

Alternatives

Cosmos bipinnatus Cosimo Series, *Cosmos bipinnatus*
Gazebo Series

Cosmos bipinnatus Sonata Series is the right size to make a pretty gap filler in summer beds. ➲

Cucurbita
C. pepo

Main features Fascinating summer fruits that will keep indefinitely when dried; long growing season
Height 6 m (20 ft) **Spread** 1.2–1.5 m (4–5 ft)
Position ○ **Hardiness** Annual

Ornamental gourds are a great way to get the young gardening. Harvested and laid out to ripen, the diverse range of shapes (star, club, turban), colours and patterns (plain, speckled, striped) and textures (smooth, warty, ridged) cannot fail to amaze. Some of the larger fruited types can be carved to make water scoops and birdhouses. Ornamental gourds will be happy trailing over open, sunny ground, but they are space invaders, and fruits that form will be more prone to uneven ripening than those that are trained upwards. They are great at disguising eyesores or decorating a wood, bamboo or metal-framed tunnel or arch, where mature fruits hang down seductively at eye level. Although related to squashes, the hard-skinned fruits are not edible. Sow under cover in spring in individual pots and then plant out after frost. Fruits are ready to harvest when the skins are firm and the colours are at their most intense. Store in a warm room or greenhouse for two weeks to finish ripening. **GS**

Alternatives

Cucurbita pepo 'Crown of Thorns', *Cucurbita pepo* 'Harrowsmith Select', *Cucurbita pepo* 'Small Fruited Mix'

Cuphea
C. ignea

Main features Frost tender evergreen shrub; distinctive tubular flowers over a long season
Height 60 cm (24 in.) **Spread** 60 cm (24 in.)
Position ○ **Hardiness** RHS H1c

Flowering from seeds in its first year, this evergreen shrub can be treated as an annual for summer containers. It is native to Mexico and Jamaica and has been grown in gardens since 1845. Of the 260 *Cuphea* species, *C. ignea* is the one most often seen. The cigar flower makes an attractive specimen, with bright-red stems and pointed, glossy, green leaves, each with a central white stripe running along the midrib and less distinct veins branching from it. The distinctive flowers are made up of a bright-red tube about 2.5 centimetres (1 in.) long, which, at the tip, is rolled back to reveal the purple interior of the tube. The upper lip of this flare is bright white, and the result is a flower that, perhaps rather fancifully, resembles a cigar with ash at its tip. In warm areas the cigar flower is hardy outside; in cooler areas it is sometimes grown as a conservatory or greenhouse plant. Where plants are not hardy, it is more often grown as a summer container plant. It can be raised from seeds or from cuttings. **GR**

Alternatives

Cuphea ignea 'Dynamite', *Cuphea ignea* 'Matchmaker Pink', *Cuphea hyssopifolia*, *Cuphea viscosissima*

⊖ *Curcubita pepo* includes mixed ornamental gourds, such as these, raised from seeds.

Cynoglossum

C. amabile

Dahlia

'Harlequin'

Main feature Sky blue summer flowers
Height 38–60 cm (15–24 in.) **Spread** 20 cm (12 in.)
Position ○ ◑
Hardiness RHS H5

Main features Flowers from summer to autumn; good
cut flower posies; attracts bees and butterflies
Height 30–45 cm (12–18 in.) **Spread** 40 cm (16 in.)
Position ○ **Hardiness** RHS H2

There are relatively few plants with flowers a genuine clear, pure blue, with no purple or reddish tints, and many of these are found in the borage family. Unlike borage, the flowers of *C. amabile,* or Chinese forget-me-not, are a lovely sky blue that associates well with plants in a range of other colours: they even look good with scarlet and orange. Growing wild in Sichuan, Yunnan and other provinces of southern China, Chinese forget-me-not is found in meadows and forests and along roadsides and riverbanks; in its natural habitat it behaves as a herbaceous perennial, although a relatively short-lived one. Plants are generally upright in growth with lance-shaped, slightly greyish, velvety foliage that feels soft to the touch. The individual flowers are small (12 mm/ 0.5 in. across), but as the branches of the flower heads unfurl, they build into a delightful display. Easy to grow, and happy in any well-drained soil in sun or partial shade, *C. amabile* makes a lovely, long-lasting cut flower. **GR**

There are thousands of *Dahlia* cultivars, but 'Harlequin' has an extremely attractive flower form, with its central, secondary row of flower petals in a contrasting colour to that of the main flower. This feature led to it being known as a 'collarette' type. The bushy, yet compact plants with mid-green foliage flower in a wide range of double-flower colours. Bred in Holland, 'Harlequin', like other dahlias, is most correctly classified as a perennial but is usually grown as an annual, flowering through summer and into the autumn, where it will stand a few degrees of frost. Collarette types need a lot of attention to keep the flower type pure with a high degree of 'rogueing' to remove 'off' types in the seed crops. In addition to its use as a bedding plant, 'Harlequin' performs equally well planted in large containers and looks effective planted with an edging of trailing blue *Lobelia.* Dahlias need good light intensity and duration to maximise their flowering potential. They are adaptable to different soil types. **TS**

Alternatives

Borago officinalis, *Echium vulgare* 'Blue Bedder'

Alternatives

Dahlia 'Yankee Doodle Dandy', *Dahlia* 'Figaro White'

Dianthus

D. barbatus
Green Trick

Main features Flowers from summer to autumn;
long-lasting cut flowers
Height 45 cm (18 in.) **Spread** 30 cm (12 in.)
Position ○ ◑ **Hardiness** RHS H4

D. barbatus Green Trick really does have a trick up its
sleeve. In fact, this plant, with its extraordinary-looking
fluffy pom-pom shape, is not a flower at all but a fuzzy
globe of very fine petals on top of tall, straight stems
with long, narrow foliage. The plants grow vigorously,
producing plenty of these strange blooms over the
summer and well into autumn. The vibrant green colour
makes it a useful addition to borders where it would
contrast well with the gentle orange of *Achillea* 'Terracotta'
or the dark purple *Dahlia* 'Summer Night' but it can also
be grown in a container, where the same colour contrasts
could be worked with *Begonia* 'Non-stop Orange' or
purple petunias. Green Trick is often referred to as a
carnation, but it is in fact a sweet william that was originally
bred for the cut-flower market. Cut blooms last for several
weeks. Deadheading will keep it producing, and it should
be watered regularly if growing in a container, but it is
generally easy to grow. Propagate in late summer. **JS**

Alternatives

= 'Temarisou'. *Zinnia elegans* 'Envy', *Nicotiana* 'Lime Green'

Dianthus

D. × barbatus
'Diabunda Purple Picotee'

Main features Flowers spring, summer, autumn; fragrant
blooms; good cut flowers; attracts bees and butterflies
Height 22–30 cm (9–12 in.) **Spread** 22–30 cm (9–12 in.)
Position ○ ◑ **Hardiness** RHS H5

The much-loved sweet william, valued both as a cottage-
garden–style plant and a cut flower, has been given
a face-lift. By crossing it with *Dianthus chinensis,* the
plant breeders at Syngenta have produced a stunning,
award-winning plant. *D. × barbatus* 'Diabunda Purple
Picotee' can be grown for spring, summer or autumn
flowering on compact plants that require little attention.
Picotee-edged white flowers have another frilly-edged
purple centre blending the two colours to perfection. The
individual flowers are larger than the traditional sweet
william, but plants are more compact. Each successive
new flower stem grows slightly taller than previous ones,
thus obscuring the spent flowers and avoiding the need
for deadheading. It makes an excellent cottage garden
border plant but can also be used in containers. A mass
planting as a bedding plant is striking. The name is derived
from the name *Dianthus* combined with the plant's ability
to flower abundantly, hence 'Di-abunda'. **MP**

Alternatives

Dianthus 'Doris', *Dianthus* 'Gran's Favorite'

Dichondra
D. *argentea* 'Silver Falls'

Main feature Long trails of shimmering silver leaves and stems
Height 5–7.5 cm (2–3 in.) **Spread** 90–180 cm (3–6 ft)
Position ○ ◑ **Hardiness** RHS H1c

Any gardener who likes to create living pictures and to blend their annuals together for the most pleasing effects will appreciate the value of grey foliage. It acts as a soothing go-between when two colours such as orange and pink collide, and it also adds new tones and textures to cool and fashionable all-white arrangements. In appearance, the small, kidney-shaped leaves of *D. argentea* 'Silver Falls' are more silver than grey. A downy coating of hairs makes the leaves reflect light, a feature that is almost unique in the plant world. Unlike the foliage, the tiny greenish-yellow to white spring flowers are not showy.

The growth habit of 'Silver Falls' is distinctive: the long trails of foliage fall vertically like a waterfall from baskets and tall pots, unlike the much stiffer *Helichrysum petiolare*, which makes good ground cover. If allowed to reach the ground, 'Silver Falls' will quickly form roots and create a tight silver carpet. Alternatively, the rooted pieces can be snipped off and given away to fellow enthusiasts. Pot-grown plants may be purchased in the spring from nurseries or, if a larger quantity is required, 'Silver Falls' can be grown from seeds sown under cover in early spring.

As would be expected from a plant that is native to desert regions of the south-western United States, 'Silver Falls' is very drought tolerant, and its surface hairs help to prevent water loss from the leaf. It will recover well from the odd missed watering, but the best plants will be grown if watering occurs before the foliage wilts. Try 'Silver Falls' as a stand-alone plant in a hanging basket or as an understory and foil to the arching stems and hot blooms of *Begonia* Dragon Wing Red. Alternatively, keep it cool with blue *Scaevola aemula*, also known as the fairy fan-flower. **GS**

Alternatives

Dichondra sericea 'Emerald Falls', *Helichrysum petiolare* 'Silver Mist'

Digitalis
D. purpurea f. albiflora

Main feature Stately spires of bell-shaped flowers
in midsummer
Height 90–150 cm (3–5 ft) **Spread** 60 cm (24 in.)
Position ◑ ● **Hardiness** RHS H7

This beautiful foxglove often graces the show gardens
at the Chelsea Flower Show in London, but it is
rarely seen in 'real' gardens. This is a shame, because
the plant deserves to be more widely grown. It
produces elegant spires of white, bell-shaped flowers
in midsummer, held above rosettes of large, hairy, dark-
green leaves. As with most foxgloves, the flowers of
D. purpurea f. *albiflora* are produced on only one side
of the stem.

Foxgloves are found naturally in open woodland and
in hedgerows, so they will grow in a shady spot in the
garden, and they are particularly good for bringing light
to a shady border. They are equally at home in a cottage-
style garden or in a more contemporary setting, and look
especially attractive planted between evergreen shrubs,
such as box balls, for a classy, fresh aesthetic. They would
be an essential component of a wildlife garden and also
of a white garden, planted among other white-flowered
plants, such as *Allium* 'Mount Everest'.

D. purpurea f. *albiflora* is a biennial or short-lived
perennial. It should self-seed freely if it is happy, but in
order to ensure plants every year, sow seeds annually in
a cold frame in late spring. It will flower the next year.
Foxgloves enjoy moist, humus-rich soil and prefer a little
shade. The flowers are loved by bees and make good cut
flowers. After the plants have flowered, cut down the
spikes to encourage more side shoots to grow. A second
flush of flowers may grow later in the season. Beware that
the plant is poisonous. Other foxgloves include
D. purpurea Excelsior Group, which has pastel flowers in
colours that range from creamy white to purple and pink
and can reach a height of 2 metres (6.5 ft). *D. purpurea*
Foxy Group has deep-red, pink, pale yellow or white
flowers, copiously spotted with maroon. **VP**

Alternatives

Digitalis purpurea Excelsior Group, *Digitalis purpurea*
Foxy Group

Digitalis

D. purpurea
'Sutton's Apricot'

Main features Summer flowering; unusual colour flower; cut flowers; attracts bees and butterflies
Height 90–120 cm (3–4 ft) **Spread** 45 cm (18 in.)
Position ○ ◑ **Hardiness** RHS H7

'Sutton's Apricot' has two standout features: its unique apricot pink colour, which had not been seen before its introduction in the 1960s, and its dwarf, sturdy growth habit, which makes it very suitable for open and exposed gardens. This foxglove is often thought of as a quintessential British cottage garden plant, and it has been popular for many generations. Foxgloves are usually biennials or short-lived perennials, flowering the year after sowing, but recent breeding work in the United States has resulted in annual flowering types. Flowering can last up to two months, and if the main stem is removed after flowering, the side shoots will come into bloom to prolong flowering. New plants will easily propagate from seeds falling from seeding flower heads. 'Sutton's Apricot' was bred by the UK company Suttons Seeds, which was formed in 1806. The cultivar is a winner of the prestigious RHS Award of Garden Merit. **TS**

Alternatives

Digitalis purpurea Excelsior Group, *Digitalis purpurea* Foxy Group, *Digitalis purpurea* Dalmation Series

Echium

E. vulgare
'Blue Bedder'

Main features Summer-long blooms; attracts butterflies, moths and bees
Height 30 cm (12 in.) **Spread** 45 cm (18 in.)
Position ○ **Hardiness** RHS H7

'Blue Bedder' is a short, bushy and free-flowering form of *E. vulgare*, a handsome biennial native to most of Europe and western and central Asia. The species is also common in North America. It is happiest out in the open, exposed to wind and sun, spilling onto paths or popping up through gravel or among rocks. The flowers emerge from the base of bristly coiled bracts and move up in succession, finishing with the last blooms at the very top. As the flowers fade they turn to shades of pink. 'Blue Bedder' makes a lovely colour contrast with orange pot marigolds, and both will oblige by producing self-sown seedlings that will give a repeat viewing the following year. Try it with other sun-worshipping annuals, such as *Zinnia* and California poppies. As with several other hardy annuals – cornflowers and scabious – 'Blue Bedder' can be sown in the autumn to give bigger and earlier flowering plants in the spring. **GS**

Alternatives

Echium vulgare 'Pink Bedder', *Echium vulgare* 'White Bedder'

Echium vulgare **'Blue Bedder'** thrives in hot, well-drained sites. ➔

Eryngium
E. giganteum

Main feature Dramatic silver colouring on bold
but manageable plants
Height 75–120 cm (30–48 in.) **Spread** 75 cm (30 in.)
Position ○ ◑   **Hardiness** RHS H7

There are more than 200 species of *Eryngium,* and they
grow all over the world, in a variety of climates. They
all have character, but *E. giganteum* is one of the most
distinctive. Found wild in the Caucasus region of Europe
between the Black Sea and the Caspian Sea, this biennial
has been grown in gardens since 1820 and came to
prominence when British horticulturist Ellen Willmott
created a notable garden at Warley Place, Essex. In its
first season *E. giganteum* develops a rosette of green,
paddle-shaped leaves, neatly toothed along the edge,
and the following year the flower heads erupt. These are
punchy and dramatic: the ruff of jaggedly sharp bracts
beneath each flower head stiffens and matures from fresh
green to silver. It cradles a cylindrical head with packed
florets that creates an overall blue-green effect. Willmott
had an unusual way of popularising the plant. When she
visited other gardens, she surreptitiously scattered seeds
in the borders. The following year, the flowering of the
ghostly silvered plants reminded her host of her visit. **GR**

Alternatives

This is the only biennial species of *Eryngium.*

⊙ *Eryngium giganteum* casts a silver, ghost-like presence
at Piet Oudolf's nursery, Hummelo, in the Netherlands.

Erysimum
'Apricot Twist'

Main features Flowers from early spring to summer;
sweet, slightly spicy fragrance; attracts bees
Height 45 cm (18 in.) **Spread** 60 cm (24 in.)
Position ○   **Hardiness** RHS H4

A wallflower that grows fast into a low mound of woody
stems, *Erysimum* 'Apricot Twist' has slender, jagged leaves
in grey-green. These leaves, which remain all winter, make
a lovely backdrop to the profuse clusters of soft apricot-
coloured flowers. The blooms open from dark-red buds
from early spring, and the combination of red and orange
is highly attractive. These clusters of flowers combine
beautifully with tulips, such as 'Brown Sugar', 'Apricot Foxx'
and 'National Velvet' and they should carry on flowering
long after the tulips have finished. Trim them back by
about a third in midsummer, when the only flowers left
are at the tips of the stems, and they will regrow and often
flower again later. Another delightful feature of 'Apricot
Twist' is that the flowers change colour slightly as they
mature, so plants will display various shades of orange at
the same time. This is common with wallflowers. There
are some, such as 'Plant World Lemon', that will carry
flowers of completely different colours on each cluster,
which makes for an eye-catching display. **JS**

Alternatives

Erysimum 'Plant World Lemon'

Erysimum

Sugar Rush Series

Main features Compact and prolific plants; flowers
in autumn and spring
Height 30–35 cm (12–14 in.) **Spread** 30–35 cm (12–14 in.)
Position ○ **Hardiness** RHS H4

Although the colours of traditional wallflower cultivars,
many grown for more than a century, are lovely and the
fragrance almost intoxicating, *Erysimum* is a large plant
that demands a long growing period before its late-spring
blooming season. This season also extends into the time
when summer flowers are usually planted out, which
many gardeners find inconvenient. Moreover, all traditional
wallflowers require a period of cooling temperatures and
cold weather to initiate flower buds; in other words, they
flower after the winter.

Erysimum Sugar Rush Series does not have this
requirement, so the first flowers appear in the autumn,
they open sporadically through mild spells in winter and

are at their peak earlier in spring than the older types.
The 'Sugar Rush' cultivar is relatively dwarf, but not short
and squat. It branches exceptionally well, and the result
is a mass of flowers on short plants. The flowers also carry
a lovely fragrance, and with bursts of blooms in both
autumn and spring, they give exceptional value. Seeds
(or plants) are usually available as a mixture of six colours:
'Sugar Rush Bronze', 'Sugar Rush Orange', 'Sugar Rush
Primrose', 'Sugar Rush Purple Bicolor', 'Sugar Rush Red'
and 'Sugar Rush Yellow' although other colours are
sometimes seen. Plant them with violas and pansies and
with dwarf bulbs, such as crocus, dwarf tulips and dwarf
daffodils. Wallflowers are still sometimes listed under
their old name, *Cheiranthus cheiri*. **GR**

Alternatives

Erysimum Bounty Series, *Erysimum* Treasure Series,
Erysimum Sunset Series, *Erysimum* Bedder Series

Eschscholzia
E. californica Thai Silk Series

Main features Flowers in summer; finely cut blue-green foliage; excellent for colour drifts
Height 20 cm (8 in.) **Spread** 15 cm (6 in.)
Position ○ **Hardiness** Annual

Native to the United States and Mexico, this poppy is a common wildflower, and it is the state flower of California. However, recent breeding work, with the addition of other colours and flower forms, has rendered this flower almost unrecognisable compared with the original. *E. californica* Thai Silk Series is somewhat of a quantum leap, with its large semi-double frilled flowers in many colours. These flowers, opening with the sun, are often up to 5 centimetres (2 in.) in diameter and come in a wide range of bright and pastel colours, including red, rose, pink, orange, yellow and cream. They are well held above attractive, finely cut, blue-green foliage. The beautiful texture of the petals and the unique wavy nature of the flowers were the inspiration for the Dutch breeder – Sahin Seeds (now part of Takii) – to name this variety of *E. californica* 'Thai Silk'. The first colour was introduced in 1994, and others were added and improvements made through to 2010. It is an RHS Award of Garden Merit winner.

Eschscholzia produces a long taproot. Because of possible damage to this root, it is best sown directly in the spot where it is to flower. However, this long root has the benefit of sustaining the plants during drought conditions. *Eschscholzia* is normally grown as an annual, sown in spring after the danger of frost is past, and it flowers during the summer months. In warm areas it can be sown late summer or autumn and overwintered for early-summer flowering. **TS**

Alternatives

Eschscholzia californica 'Mission Bells', *Eschscholzia californica* 'Jelly Beans'

Euphorbia

E. *hypericifolia* Diamond Frost

Main features Prolific small white flowers; small green
leaves; container, hanging basket or border plant
Height 30–45 cm (12–18 in.) **Spread** 25–30 cm
(10–12 in.) **Position** ○ ◑ **Hardiness** RHS H2

Most gardeners like to try something a bit different, and
this diminutive and unlikely relative of the poinsettia is
not to be missed. A billowing cloud of tiny white flowers
hovers above wiry stems bearing small green leaves, like
the first flakes of snow on a lawn. The flowers might be
tiny, but collectively they make an impact. Usually treated
as an annual, although in mild climates it is perennial, this
award-winning, dome-shaped plant will bloom from
spring throughout summer and up to the first frost.

The original species is native to both tropical and
subtropical America, but *E. hypericifolia* Diamond Frost
is a huge improvement, making it an interesting addition
to the garden. Thriving in any well-drained soil, it

enjoys full sun or partial shade. Deer and rabbits find it
unpalatable, which is a huge bonus for those plagued
by these garden pests. Care must be taken, as with all
Euphorbia, because the milky sap can be an irritant.

A shapely container filled with Diamond Frost alone
makes an eye-catching sight. In mixed containers it
provides great contrast with bold flowers or foliage, or
perhaps a spiky foliage plant. A pink-leaved *Cordyline*,
such as 'Pink Passion', surrounded by Diamond Frost
would be striking. Use it at the base of a spring-flowering
container shrub, such as a camellia, to add summer
interest, or for mass planting at the front of a border –
spacing the plants 25 to 30 centimetres (10-12 in.) apart.
It will look after itself and not need deadheading. **MP**

Alternatives

= 'Inneuphe'. *Euphorbia griffithii* 'Dixter', *Euphorbia rigida*,
Gypsophila elegans

Evolvulus
E. glomeratus

Main features Trailing plant with bright-blue, saucer-shaped flowers over long summer season
Height 30–45 cm (12–18 in.) **Spread** 60–90 cm (24–36 in.)
Position ○ **Hardiness** RHS H3

The bindweed family, *Convolvulaceae*, is dominated by twining climbers, some of which are all too familiar as garden weeds. *Evolvulus*, however, is a sprawler and does not twine. There are about one hundred species, and these are native from the northern United States as far as southern Argentina, although only one or two are ever grown in gardens. There is some uncertainty about whether *E. glomeratus* and *E. pilosus* are the same species, as they appear to be very similar.

This sprawling, well-branched evergreen plant has slightly silvery leaves and saucer-shaped 2.5-centimetre-long (1 in.) flowers that have purplish tints and look a little ruffled. It also has neat wide 2.5-centimetre (1 in.) leaves that tend to be broadest towards the tips and livened by silvery hairs. Clusters of flowers are carried at the shoot tips and in the leaf joints over a long season; each blue, rounded, almost flat-faced bloom has a white centre. Unlike the wild species, which may go through phases when flowering is sparse, the flowers of named forms such as 'Hawaiian Blue Eyes' open consistently throughout the season. The flowers tend to close at night and on dull days.

The sprawling habit of this plant, combined with its branching growth and its blue flowers, makes it ideal for hanging baskets and large containers. There are so many flowers produced that there is no need to deadhead. **GR**

Alternative

Syn. *Evolvulus pilosus, Evolvulus glomeratus* 'Hawaiian Blue Eyes,' *Evolvulus* 'Blue My Mind'

Gaura
G. lindheimeri

Main features Flowers late spring to autumn; drought tolerant
Height 1 m (3.5 ft) **Spread** 45 cm (18 in.)
Position ○   **Hardiness** RHS H4

One of the big success stories of the plant world since it was first introduced, G. lindheimeri is a subtle rather than showy plant that has become a staple of numerous garden designs. Pinky-white flowers shaped like butterflies adorn the willowy stems, massed above bushy growth with slender leaves. They grow quickly into clumps and flower continuously for months from late spring.

G. lindheimeri can be grown easily from seeds and will reach flowering size in one year. It looks good in informal groups, such as in cottage gardens, and it can be grown successfully in a pot. The upright, wispy shape of the flower stems also works really well with ornamental grasses, adding light colour and echoing the way that grasses sway in the breeze. This is not surprising because Gaura was originally a prairie plant from the southern states of North America.

A popular plant with breeders, G. lindheimeri is reasonably hardy, but it does not like being in waterlogged conditions, especially in winter, or being grown on heavy soil, where it will often disappear after one season. If these conditions are avoided, it is very easy to grow and has few problems with pests or diseases. There are now many different cultivars on the market. The flowers of all of them are various shades of white and pink, and most will grow to a similar size and shape. However, a few have begun to establish themselves as good alternatives to the species. 'Siskiyou Pink' is a lovely variety with bright-pink flowers, whereas 'Crimson Butterflies' and 'Passionate Pink' are both more compact. 'Rosyjane' has gorgeous pink picotee blooms, while 'Corrie's Gold' has yellow variegated leaves. Both 'The Bride' and 'Whirling Butterflies' have almost entirely white flowers. **JS**

Alternatives

Gaura lindheimeri 'Whirling Butterflies', Gaura lindheimeri 'The Bride', Gaura lindheimeri 'Siskiyou Pink'

Gazania
'Gazoo Red with Ring'

Main features Flowers early summer to autumn;
loved by butterflies
Height 30 cm (12 in.) **Spread** 30 cm (12 in.)
Position ○ **Hardiness** RHS H2

Breeders have taken great strides forwards in recent years with regard to these dazzling South African daisies. Cultivars are now more compact, with larger blooms and an ability to open them under lower light levels. *Gazania* 'Gazoo Red with Ring' typifies these qualities. However, gardeners who wish to conjure up images of carpets of exotic blooms that stop viewers in their tracks should grow their *Gazania* where the plants can soak up every ray of sunshine, because this is still the safest way to achieve the best results.

Gazania petals may be striped or single coloured in various shades of red, purple, orange, bronze, white, pink and yellow. Some, such as 'Gazoo Red with Ring', have a distinctive dark ring around the central disk, which adds to the dramatic effect. Although grown mainly as an annual, *Gazania* can be overwintered, either as a mature plant lifted from the garden or brought indoors in its summer display pot. If space is at a premium, rooted cuttings can be taken in late summer. In frost-free areas, 'Gazoo Red with Ring' will become a permanent feature, flowering throughout the year, although it does not relish heat when it is accompanied by high humidity. It can be raised from seeds sown in the spring or bought as a young, pot-grown plant in early summer.

The plants thrive in dry, parched soil, in rock walls, and among gravel, pebbles and boulders. Terra-cotta pots will suit them better than plastic ones because they let in air and will be less likely to get too wet. Snip off dead heads to keep the plants tidy and to encourage more blooms. 'Gazoo Red with Ring' looks superb with other dry regime plants, such as *Portulaca* and succulent-leaved *Echeveria*. Avoid any tall partners that may cast shade. **GS**

Alternatives

Gazania Kiss Series, *Gazania* Daybreak Series, *Gazania* Talent Series, *Gazania* Dynastar Series

Gomphrena
G. globosa

Hamelia
H. patens

Main features Exceptionally heat and humidity tolerant; long-lasting summer flower heads
Height 20–60 cm (8–24 in.) **Spread** 15–25 cm (6–10 in.)
Position ○ **Hardiness** Annual

Main features Vivid orange tubular flowers; attracts hummingbirds and butterflies
Height 90 cm (3 ft) **Spread** 80 cm (2.5 ft)
Position ○ **Hardiness** RHS H3

Of the ninety *Gomphrena* species, only two or three are grown in gardens, and *G. globosa* – also known as the globe amaranth – is the only one seen frequently. Growing wild in Panama and Guatemala, *G. globosa* is also naturalised in parts of Texas and Louisiana. It is a rather upright but well-branched annual, with intriguing globular flower heads that are made up of tiny individual flowers that open sequentially over a long period. Flowering usually begins on young plants, the heads held above pale, rather rough, foliage. The wild species has flowers in a rather uncompromising magenta pink, but those grown in gardens cover a range of colours, along with bicolours and white. There have been two approaches to the plant's development. Breeders have created dwarf, bushy types, such as the Buddy Series, for use as pot plants and summer plants for containers. At the same time, attention has focused on cut flowers: the QIS Series, in carmine, orange, red, pale pink and white, can last up to two weeks in water without flower food. **GR**

There are around forty species of *Hamelia*, a member of the coffee family, but *H. patens* is the one commonly grown. Found wild in subtropical regions from Florida south to Argentina, it is a large, bushy evergreen shrub, but can be treated as an annual container plant. The red stems carry tiers of slightly hairy, bright-green leaves with pale veins. There are two phases to the appeal of the flowers, which are gathered in clusters at the shoot tips. The tubular buds are about 2.5 centimetres (1 in.) long, and bright orange-red in colour. They remain closed for an unexpectedly long period, and it is these buds that contribute most to the colourful display. As they approach opening, they become slightly more orange in colour. When the flowers finally open they are bright orange, and the yellow-orange inside of the tube is revealed as a spark of light. The flowers are followed by small, juicy, many-seeded edible berries. The seeds can be sown fresh or cuttings or young plants can be purchased at the start of the growing season. **GR**

Alternative

Gomphrena haageana

Alternative

Hamelia ventricosa

Helianthus
H. annuus 'Italian White'

Helianthus
H. annuus 'Solar Flash'

Main features Distinctive flower colour; heritage type; easy-to-grow border plant; good cut-flower variety
Height 1.2–1.5 m (4–5 ft) **Spread** 25–30 cm (10–12 in.)
Position ○ **Hardiness** Annual

Main features Distinctive flower colour; compact, bushy habit; border or patio use; pollen-free cut flowers
Height 60–75 cm (24–30 in.) **Spread** 40 cm (16 in.)
Position ○ **Hardiness** Annual

A heritage variety, *H. annuus* 'Italian White' is known and loved for its distinctive, creamy-white flowers. They often have a yellow base to the petals, giving the impression of a yellow ring surrounding the middle of the chocolate-coloured flower centre. The flowers, some 8 to 10 centimetres (3–4 in.) in diameter, are plentiful, and they are borne on branching, sturdy stems. 'Italian White' may be grown towards the back of a border for garden decoration, where its bright, clear flowers will enliven the dullest day. Alternatively, the blooms make very good, long-lasting cut flowers and are a great foil for delphiniums, for example. For flowering throughout the summer, it is best to sow at fortnightly intervals from spring through the summer. Plants will flower some sixty days after sowing, and a degree of self-seeding should ensure further generations. In the United States, 'Italian White' is used in wildlife areas, providing pollen for butterflies and bees, and the seed heads are a useful source of food for seed-eating birds. **TS**

One of a new generation of sunflowers, bred to possess a dwarf, bushy growth habit and to flower over a long period, *H. annuus* 'Solar Flash' is ideal for large containers and bedding schemes. The other main feature of 'Solar Flash' is the very distinctive flowers: they are bronze maroon with yellow petal tips and a chocolate centre to the bloom. This striking sunflower is one of the new generation of multi-stemmed varieties in which the large central head, approximately 18 centimetres (7 in.) in diameter, is followed by a series of side shoots bearing slightly smaller flowers, to continue the display for several weeks. In order to achieve this, it is important to remove the main central flower as it fades, to encourage further flowering of the side shoots. The blooms of 'Solar Flash' may also be used as cut flowers, and they are pollen-free, which means no sticky mess underneath the vase. A late-spring sowing, followed by another two to three weeks later, should see flowering through late summer, until the autumn frost. **TS**

Alternatives

Helianthus annuus 'Vanilla Ice', *Helianthus annuus* 'Fantasia'

Alternative

Helianthus annuus 'Suntastic Yellow'

Helianthus
H. annuus 'Suntastic Yellow'

Main features Flowers in summer; easy to grow; ideal for pots or borders; attracts bees and insects
Height 25–60 cm (10–24 in.) **Spread** 38 cm (15 in.)
Position ○ **Hardiness** Annual

Sunflowers produce stunning annual plants with bright, cheerful flowers. There are hundreds of sunflower varieties to choose from: tall types, intermediate ones for cut flowers, and dwarf types for pot growing. The problem with most dwarf varieties is that they do not flower for very long, which is rather a waste if they have been planted in a container. However, one recently bred dwarf variety is causing quite a stir. The Suntastic Series has been bred to flower for at least eight to nine weeks, by developing a multi-stemmed growth habit. In other words, the central flower is followed by blooms from the numerous side shoots to prolong flowering. There are a number of flower colours in the Suntastic Series, but yellow with a black centre is the most popular. Bred by Clause in France, it was an All-America Selections Award winner in 2014.

The height of the plant can vary somewhat according to growing conditions, and the flower can grow up to 13 to 15 centimetres (5–6 in.) in diameter. 'Suntastic Yellow' is single rather than double flowered, and it is a versatile variety in that it can be used in pots and containers, as a border edging, or as colour drifts in a border. The plants produce up to twenty blooms each during the season. There are, of course, many other good dwarf sunflower varieties – single, anemone or double flowered – but there is no doubt that the Suntastic Series is a real breeding breakthrough.

Sunflowers need full sun to produce the best flowering results, but they are fairly tolerant of soil conditions. Dwarf types may be sown indoors and planted out for early flowering or sown direct in late spring for mid- to late-summer blooming. Remove the flowers once they begin to fade in order to encourage new growth. **TS**

Alternatives

Helianthus annuus 'Ms. Mars', *Helianthus annuus* 'Teddy Bear', *Helianthus annuus* 'Waooh', *Helianthus annuus* 'Sunspot', *Helianthus annuus* 'Solar Flash'

Helianthus
H. annuus 'Valentine'

Main features Lovely pale-lemon flowers with a black
disk; medium-tall branching plants; long summer season
Height 1.5 m (5 ft) **Spread** 40 cm (16 in.)
Position ○ **Hardiness** Annual

Of the seventy or eighty wild species of sunflowers, there
are only a few annuals, and one of them, *H. annuus*, is by
far the most widely grown and has the most cultivars.
Growing wild in North and Central Americas, *H. annuus*
carries large daisy-like flower heads, singly or in small
numbers, on stout upright stems. The bold, rough
leaves are more or less heart-shaped, and the flowers
are made up of yellow ray florets (petals), which surround
a brownish central disk that matures to produce the
large, familiar seed.

Many hundreds of cultivars have been developed over
the years, and the range is now impressively varied, from
record-breaking tall types to small cultivars for containers.
Some are well branched whereas others have huge
individual flower heads. A number of cultivars are
intended as cut flowers and produce no pollen, to avoid
staining the furniture and provoking allergic reactions. At
the same time, an unexpected array of new colours and
bicolours – rich and sultry to pale and pastel – has been
introduced, and *H. annuus* 'Valentine' is one example.
Reaching about 1.5 metres (5 ft) in height, the plant
branches well from the base and carries 15-centimetre-
wide (6 in.) heads of pale lemon-yellow flowers, which
shade to a richer yellow around the black disk. Ideal at the
back of a sunny border, 'Valentine' has a delightful, subtle
colouring, and with regular deadheading, it makes a
valuable long-season backdrop to other summer flowers.

'Valentine' is also good for cutting (although it is not
one of the pollen-free cultivars). Cut the stems when
the first one or two petals start to unfurl, strip almost all
the leaves off straight away, and plunge in water with
added flower food. If sowing seed in pots, do not allow
the plants to dry out or become pot bound because this
will significantly restrict growth. **GR**

Alternatives

Helianthus annuus 'Full Sun', *Helianthus annuus* 'Italian
White', *Helianthus annuus* 'Pacino', *Helianthus annuus*
'Teddy Bear', *Helianthus annuus* 'Velvet Queen'

Helianthus
H. annuus 'American Giant'

Main features One of the tallest sunflowers; large flower heads; attracts wildlife to the garden
Height 4.2–4.8 m (14–16 ft) **Spread** 60–90 cm (24–36 in.)
Position ○ **Hardiness** Annual

One thing that appeals to gardeners young and old is to have a go at growing a giant sunflower. There are a number of varieties to choose from, but one of the best for this purpose is the well-known *H. annuus* 'American Giant', which can grow up to 4.8 metres (16 ft) and beyond. It produces thick, sturdy, branching stems with large leaves and big yellow flowers with dark-brown centres. These blooms can reach up to 28 centimetres (11 in.) in diameter. Although the stems are sturdy, some plant support may be necessary, particularly in windy areas. For this reason 'American Giant' is often grown against a sunny wall or fence. The plants are very fast growing and, despite their size, they can come into flower in only sixty-five to seventy-five days from sowing. 'American Giant' is a very wildlife-friendly variety, producing pollen and nectar for the butterflies and bees, as well as seed after flowering for seed-eating birds. It is often seen growing in wildlife areas where it self-seeds naturally. **TS**

Alternatives

Helianthus annuus 'Kong', *Helianthus annuus* 'Russian Giant'

Hesperis
H. matronalis

Main features Perfumed summer flowers; attracts wildlife to the garden
Height 90 cm (3 ft) **Spread** 45 cm (18 in.)
Position ○ ◑ **Hardiness** RHS H7

This popular biennial or short-lived perennial, also known as sweet rocket, is an essential element of the classic cottage garden, grown for both its rich perfume and generous show of blooms. Like the wallflower, it is a member of the mustard family, and the two plants work well together as *H. matronalis* takes over the late-spring display of scent and colour from the wallflower and carries it forwards into midsummer. The name *Hesperis* is Greek for 'evening', and it alludes to the clove-like scent that becomes more intense as the light fades. Interestingly, the white-flowered form is the most strongly perfumed. Sweet rocket self-seeds freely to form dense colonies in shades of lavender, purple, pink and white, which, like foxgloves, look wonderful in the wilder parts of the garden. It was introduced into the United States in the seventeenth century and has since become naturalised. However, it has reached pest proportions in some states, and there are restrictions on its cultivation. **GS**

Alternatives

Hesperis matronalis 'Alba', *Hesperis matronalis* 'Alba Plena'

Hesperis matronalis has long been valued for its evening clove-like fragrance. ➲

Hunnemannia

H. fumariifolia 'Sunlite'

Main features Bright-yellow tulip-shaped flowers; prettily cut blue-green leaves
Height 38–45 cm (15–18 in.) **Spread** 38–45 cm (15–18 in.)
Position ○ **Hardiness** RHS H3

There are about 200 species in the poppy family, and although each one is easily recognisable as a poppy, they are sometimes less easy to distinguish from one another. However, there is only one species of *Hunnemannia*, which is a perennial in the wild and most closely related to the annual California poppy, *Eschscholzia*, and the shrubby tree poppy, *Dendromecon*. Originating high in the dry Mexican mountains, *H. fumariifolia* is a sparkling and sunny plant. In its natural habit, it is a short-lived perennial with a fat but brittle rootstock, but in gardens it is usually grown as an annual. Through its striking blue-green, narrowly divided foliage, tall stems emerge, each carrying only one noticeably tulip-shaped, four-petalled flower –

hence the common name tulip poppy. Sometimes the petals are a little pleated at the edges, but they come in the most wonderful, clean, pure sunshine yellow.

Unfortunately, this is not an easy plant to grow as a perennial in gardens. It demands exceptionally good drainage, all-day sunshine and a relatively infertile garden soil; even damp and muggy weather can instigate rot. As a result *H. fumariifolia* is most often grown as a spring-sown annual, so it does not have to deal with difficult winter conditions. It is a fast grower and may be in flower in as little as six weeks after a late-spring sowing. *H. fumariifolia* 'Sunlite' is an exceptionally beautiful form, and it differs from the wild type by having an extra row of four petals; but beware plants without the extra petals are sometimes sold as 'Sunlite'. **GR**

Alternatives

Eschscholzia californica, Dendromecon rigida

Impatiens

Sunpatiens Series

Main features Bright, showy flowers; shiny foliage
Height 38–122 cm (15–48 in.)
Spread 40–91 cm (16–36 in.)
Position ○ ◑ **Hardiness** RHS H1c

Occasionally, something comes along in the world of flower breeding that really takes a gardener's breath away, and *Impatiens* Sunpatiens is one such plant. Originally conceived from a hybrid of a New Guinea type and a wild species, the series has really come to the fore over the past few years. It has large weather-resistant flowers in bright, showy colours and glossy, green foliage, which is variegated on some varieties, all on neat, bushy plants. Unlike its well-known cousin, the *Impatiens walleriana,* also known as the busy Lizzie, which in parts of the world has been decimated in recent years by the fungal disease downy mildew, Sunpatiens does not suffer from this affliction and so has become increasingly

popular. The plants are happy to grow in sun or in partial shade and they have a good resistance to rain and wind damage, largely due to the thick leaves and flower petals that characterise the species. Strictly speaking, Sunpatiens is a half-hardy perennial, but it is normally grown as an annual and will flower continuously from midsummer through to the first frost with no deadheading of the flowers required.

There are three different groups in Sunpatiens: compact types are suitable for pots and containers; spreading types are ideal for hanging baskets and compact ground cover; and vigorous types are popular for landscape use and for filling large borders. These latter plants can grow surprisingly tall and wide in hot, sunny conditions, so plant and plan with caution. **TS**

Alternatives

Impatiens Divine Series, *Impatiens* Florific Series

Impatiens
I. hawkeri 'Florific Sweet Orange'

Main features Seed-raised flower; flowers from summer to first frost; baskets, containers or bedding plant
Height 25–35 cm (10–14 in.) **Spread** 30–38 cm (12–15 in.)
Position ◑ ● **Hardiness** Annual

A seed-raised strain of the New Guinea busy Lizzie that is not susceptible to downy mildew is a winner, and *I. hawkeri* 'Florific Sweet Orange' is an unusual bicoloured addition to the Florific Series. Flowering from summer through to the first frost, the two-tone peachy-orange blooms have darker orange markings on large flower heads – 5 centimetres (2 in.) in diameter – which are held well above the dark foliage, thereby making a striking combination. If orange is not the colour for you, then the Florific Series also offers red, white, lavender and pink flower shades over green or bronze foliage. The name *Impatiens* is derived from the Latin word meaning 'impatient', and this has led to the common name 'touch-me-not' for the whole genus. When touched, the ripe seeds pods explode and are a constant source of amusement to children.

Grown as an annual plant for summer display, the plants are naturally well branched and can be spaced generously, about 25 to 30 centimetres (10–12 in.) apart, to give excellent ground cover as bedding plants. They can also be used in containers and hanging baskets. Although the Florific Series is perfect for difficult shady sites, it can also be grown in sunny parts of the garden, but prefers light shade in the heat of the day. It is best to delay planting until the night temperatures remain above 7°C (45°F), because lower temperatures may prevent plant establishment. Keep the plants moist at all times during the growing season.

I. hawkeri 'Florific Sweet Orange' looks stunning en masse as a bedding plant, but it can be enhanced by a backing of the silver-leaved, shade-tolerant *Plectranthus argentatus*, or by the fibre-optic effects of the annual grey-green grass *Panicum elegans* 'Frosted Explosion' used as a dot plant. **MP**

Alternatives

Impatiens omeiana, Impatiens niamniamensis

Isotoma
I. axillaris

Main feature Fine, mounded foliage covered with a
profusion of star-shaped flowers
Height 30 cm (12 in.) **Spread** 30 cm (12 in.)
Position ○ **Hardiness** RHS H3

A heat-loving Australian perennial, *I. axillaris* is usually
grown as an annual in cooler climates. It is frost tender,
so plant it out only after all danger of frost has passed
in spring. *I. axillaris* is also sold as *Laurentia*, as it was
previously classified as *Laurentia axillaris*. It is sometimes
sold as *Solenopsis axillaris*, or as Australian harebell.

The plants bear a profusion of small, fragrant, star-
shaped, pale to deep blue (and occasionally white)
flowers – 4 centimetres (1.5 in.) in diameter – from
summer to autumn. They form an attractive mounded
shape, with delicate, narrow foliage. In its native Australia,
I. axillaris is found on rocky outcrops, so not surprisingly,
the plant likes a well-drained soil (any type) in full sun
and copes well in dry conditions. As a low-growing,
bushy plant, it is useful for edging beds or pathways,
and looks good spilling over a low wall or in a rockery.
Alternatively, grow it in a container to show off its
distinctive, mounded shape. Buy established plants at
the garden centre in spring, or for a better choice of
varieties, grow from seeds (start them off early in late
winter in a heated propagator for flowers in the summer).
Pinch out the young growth to make the plant even
bushier but take care when handling because the sap
may irritate the skin. Plants shed spent flowers on their
own, but deadheading will ensure even more blooms.

I. axillaris 'Blue Star' (pictured), or blue star creeper,
is a charming cultivar, with a mound of sky-blue, star-
like flowers. The flowers of 'Stargazer Mixed' are white,
pink and purple and are scented in the evening whereas
the Avant Garde Series includes uniform, vigorous F1
hybrids in shades of blue, pink and violet. Other popular
cultivars include 'Indigo Stars', a compact variety with
bright-violet flowers, and 'White Star', a vigorous variety
with white flowers. **VP**

Alternatives

Isotoma axillaris 'Blue Star', *Isotoma axillaris* 'Stargazer Mixed'

Lantana
L. camara
Landmark Series

Main features Flowers summer and autumn; attracts
hummingbirds, bees, and butterflies; aromatic
Height 90 cm (3 ft) **Spread** 90 cm (3 ft)
Position ○ **Hardiness** RHS H3

Plants in the Landmark Series of *Lantana* grow fast,
producing mounds of large, jagged-edged leaves with
deep veins. The flower heads appear above and in among
these leaves, starting out as a halo of tiny blooms around
buds that soon open to form the small balls of bright
colour for which *Lantana* is known. Often, these colours
are mixed on a single head, so there might be a group of
yellow flowers at the top of a head surrounded by pink or
orange, all in vibrant shades. They are great plants if you
live in a hot or humid climate as they thrive in heat and
strong sunlight, but they also grow and flower surprisingly
well in more temperate regions, as long as they are in
free-draining soil. With their long stems and upright
shape, plants in the Landmark Series will become quite
large so would be great to fill out a border, especially
accompanied by other bright plants such as *Echinacea*
'Marmalade'. They can also be grown in a pot as long as
they are not mixed with anything too delicate. **JS**

Alternatives

Lantana camara 'Miss Huff', *Lantana camara* Lucky Series

Lavatera
L. trimestris
Beauty Series

Main features Summer flowering; may be used as cut or
dried flowers; attracts butterflies and bees
Height 60–90 cm (2–3 ft) **Spread** 45 cm (18 in.)
Position ○ **Hardiness** RHS H1c

Before the introduction of varieties such as the award-
winning Beauty Series, *Lavatera*, although always very
showy, tended to be tall and rather weak growing, which
made the plants susceptible to wind and general weather
damage. That changed when plant breeders produced
the Beauty Series: dwarf plants with a bushy growing
habit, and larger flowers too. A great way to fill large
borders with vibrant colour, the plants can be grown as
biennials if overwintered indoors, but more commonly
they are grown as annuals as they will flower in as little as
twelve weeks from sowing. The large single flowers are
stunning – reaching 10 centimetres (4 in.) in diameter –
and the petals glisten with a natural sheen. They can be
used as specimen plants or in colour drifts. Unlike some
species, *Lavatera* is happy to be transplanted, so may
be started indoors in spring for early flowering outside;
alternatively, it may be sown outside, where it will flower
in late spring/early summer. **TS**

Alternatives

Lavatera trimestris 'Mont Blanc', *Lavatera trimestris* 'Parade'

Leonotis
L. leonurus

Limnanthes
L. douglasii

Main features Flowers in summer and autumn; attracts bees, butterflies and birds
Height 2 m (6 ft) **Spread** 60 cm (24 in.)
Position ○ **Hardiness** Annual

Main features Nectar rich; yellow-centred, white-tipped flowers; attracts insects
Height 15 cm (6 in.) **Spread** 20 cm (8 in.)
Position ○ **Hardiness** Annual

If gardeners want to create a hot, exotic-looking border or to add something dramatic to their planting, then *L. leonurus* would be an ideal plant to grow. Whorls of elegantly curving, tubular orange flowers are spaced along strong stems, which keep producing more blooms throughout the summer and into autumn, only being stopped by the first frost. Typical of the mint family to which it belongs, *L. leonurus* has square stems that are surprisingly strong given how slender they are. Its leaves are long, narrow, veined and hairy, which gives the plant some character. The vibrant flower colour can easily match the brightness of other South African natives such as red hot pokers (*Kniphofia*), but this is a surprisingly versatile plant and it would look as good grown with *Agapanthus* as well as in a bed of dahlias. It could be surrounded by the huge, palm-shaped leaves of *Ricinus communis* or planted with humble annuals such as cornflower and cosmos. Best of all, it is easy to grow from seeds. **JS**

Seven species of *Limnanthes* grow in the western United States, mostly in California and mostly along or near the coast. They are usually found in sunny but damp conditions, in marshes or by pools; some species are now classified as endangered. Named for the plant collector David Douglas, *L. douglasii* is a sprawling or sometimes more upright annual with bright, slightly fleshy, divided foliage that makes an appealing background to the broadly cup-shaped 2.5-centimetre-wide (1 in.) flowers. Each flower is egg-yolk yellow in the centre with a striking white rim, hence the common name poached egg plant. The flowers are sweetly scented and rich in nectar; they are popular with bees and hoverflies. *L. douglasii* is worth planting for that reason alone, because hoverfly larvae are voracious predators of aphids. The subspecies with all-yellow or all-white flowers are very occasionally seen, and there is also a very pretty variety with pink veins, whose flowers fade to pale rose pink. **GR**

Alternative

Leonotis leonurus var. *alba*

Alternatives

Limnanthes douglasii subsp. *nivea*

Lobelia

L. *erinus* Super Star

Main features Large, distinctive, bicoloured flowers; spreading, trailing growth habit
Height 10 cm (4 in.) **Spread** 38 cm (15 in.)
Position ○ ◑ **Hardiness** Annual

Aptly named, this relative newcomer is a real eye turner. The flowers of *L. erinus* Super Star are deep indigo-blue in colour with a large white eye, which is larger and more clearly defined than in previous varieties of *Lobelia*. Originally a native of South Africa, the plant has seen much developmental work over the years in order to produce the trailing and upright forms that we know and love today. Super Star was bred in Germany, and currently, it is only available as cutting-raised plants from tissue culture. This helps to maintain the distinctive flower markings. It also tends to mean that the plants have more vigour than seed-raised ones and therefore will flower from midsummer to the autumn frost. Extensive trials have shown cutting-raised plants to be more tolerant of hot weather than normal seed-raised types.

The growth habit of Super Star is semi-trailing, which keeps the plants looking bushy in containers, yet the flowering shoots still trail to some 38 centimetres (15 in.) in length. Again, this is an advantage over seed-raised types, which can appear rather thin and spindly later in the growing season. In addition to their suitability for growing in containers and hanging baskets, *Lobelia* can be used for ground cover in the flower border. Super Star looks really effective when planted with *Impatiens* 'Sunpatiens' or other New Guinea *Impatiens*. It is fairly easy to grow as long as it is kept moist and fed with a liquid fertiliser later in the season. **TS**

Alternatives

= 'Weslosu'. *Lobelia erinus* 'Richardii', *Lobelia erinus* 'Fountain Mix', *Lobelia erinus* 'Sapphire'

Lobularia
L. maritima Snow Princess

Main features Multi-use variety; distinctive fragrance; flowers in as little as six weeks; easy to grow
Height 10–20 cm (4–8 in.) **Spread** 60 cm (24 in.)
Position ○ ◑ **Hardiness** RHS H7

A free-flowering, heat-tolerant cultivar, *L. maritima* Snow Princess does not set seeds; it is raised from cuttings or bought as young plants. Other cultivars include 'Snow Carpet' and 'Snow Crystals'. *L. maritima*, also known as sweet alyssum, is compact, branching and ground hugging, which makes it ideal for ground cover.

Sweet alyssum is much loved for its honey-like scent and its versatility in both formal and informal planting schemes. You can use plants as neat border edgings, as part of a red, white and blue scheme or in loose drifts within cottage-garden–style plantings. White is still by far the most popular colour, and there are many white cultivars that will do the same job for the home gardener. Even in contemporary or town gardens, white alyssum looks stylish as an underplanting for a piece of topiary or a specimen standard. These plants are neat enough even for hanging baskets, small pots or for growing on rockeries. Plants can be started indoors and planted out, or sown direct in any weed-free soil to flower in as little as six weeks. They grow well in full sun or partial shade and attract butterflies, bees and other pollinators to your garden. Plants will flower throughout the summer if watered well, but will run out of steam if allowed to dry out. Strictly speaking, *L. maritima* is a tender perennial but is more commonly grown as an annual each year to get the precise, neat shape and flowering impact. **TS**

Alternatives

= 'Inlbusnopr'. *Lobularia maritima* 'Wonderland White', *Lobularia maritima* 'Aphrodite White'

Lunaria
L. annua

Main features Attractive seedpods; fragrant flowers; attracts bees, butterflies, moths and other wildlife
Height 75–90 cm (2.5–3 ft) **Spread** 30–45 cm (12–18 in.)
Position ○ ◑ **Hardiness** RHS H7

Any plant that offers two seasons of interest has to be a winner, and *L. annua*, or honesty, does just that. Overwintered plants start to flower in early spring, producing branching heads of fragrant, lilac-coloured, four-petalled flowers that bloom for several weeks. These are followed, in late summer, by roundish, flat seedpods. Both sides of the flat seedpod flake off, and the seeds disperse to reveal moon-shaped, silvery disks that are most attractive and give the plant one of its other names: silver dollars. The name *Lunaria* refers to these moon-like pods, which remain on the plant all winter alongside rather coarse, pale-green basal leaves. Honesty is excellent for use in light woodland areas, where it can be encouraged to naturalise. It is a stalwart of the cottage-style border, but also makes an impressive statement in a winter garden. Allow the plant to self-seed among the coloured stems of dogwoods, so the silver dollars shine in the winter sun. The scented flowers can be cut and enjoyed indoors with other spring blooms. **MP**

Alternative

Lunaria rediviva

Mimulus
Maximus Series

Main features Flowers in many colours; often brightly marked; very quick to bloom
Height 30 cm (12 in.) **Spread** 40 cm (16 in.)
Position ○ ◑ **Hardiness** RHS H3

The *Mimulus,* or monkey flowers, have long been known as bright and colourful plants. Once thought to be botanically linked to the superficially similar penstemons and snapdragons, research now suggests that this may not be the case. Plants in the Maximus Series reach about 30 centimetres (12 in.) in height and have succulent stems and glossy foliage. The lobed, trumpet-shaped flowers open at the leaf joints, and at 5 centimetres (2 in.) in diameter, they are twice the size of the flowers of other *Mimulus*. The flowers come in an extensive range of colours and are very quick to bloom. Even small plants will flower as soon as there is twelve and a half hours of daylight, as long as they are not allowed to dry out. Although plants in the Maximus Series are perennials, they are usually grown as annuals because they mature and flower so quickly after sowing. Work in England and Japan has led to the development of shorter, well-branched plants also with flowers in a very wide range of colours, both plain and with bold spots. **GR**

Alternatives

Mimulus Magic Series, *Mimulus* Mystic Series

◉ *Lunaria annua* showing spring flowers and forming seedpods.

Moluccella
M. laevis

Main features Imposing summer spikes of green bracts; much loved by flower arrangers
Height 90 cm (3 ft) **Spread** 30 cm (12 in.)
Position ○ **Hardiness** Annual

Known as Bells of Ireland, this erect annual is not native to Ireland; it originates from western Asia, including Turkey and Syria. There are records of *M. laevis* being grown by the royal botanist to James I in 1570, when it was considered a symbol of good luck. Today, it is cultivated primarily as a home-grown cut flower. From a packet of seeds you get plenty of impressive flower spikes that can be used in both fresh and dried arrangements; in the latter it dries to an appealing straw colour, adding structure and interest to displays.

Plants flower in late summer. From a distance what appear to be green, shell-like flowers are actually the bracts; the true, two-lipped flowers are white or pale pink and neatly contained in the pale-green, bell-shaped shells (or calyxes). Although a member of the mint family, the plants do not smell particularly of mint but more of vanilla. For garden display use it as part of a green-themed bed or border and include the green, weeping tassels of *Amaranthus* and *Zinnia* 'Envy'.

Growing from seeds can be tricky if you sow direct into cold ground, so give them a flying start by putting the seeds in the refrigerator for a week, then sowing in the optimum temperature under cover in the spring. Sowing in modular trays or small pots will avoid damaging the taproot when planting out. Line them in a row after the last frost if you are planning to harvest them for cut flowers. Grow in a sunny sheltered place and give them plenty of water in dry spells; they will need staking in open or windy sites.

The flowering stems are hollow, so flower arrangers often insert wire stakes to secure them in arrangements. For dried flowering stems, harvest them in dry weather at the end of the summer or early autumn and hang the stems upside down in a well-ventilated area. **GS**

Alternatives

Helichrysum bracteatum, Limonium platyphyllum

Moluccella laevis paired with tall ageratums. ➲

Myosotis
M. sylvatica 'Royal Blue'

Main features Tiny, deep-blue flowers in spring and early summer; an excellent foil for spring bedding
Height 30 cm (12 in.) **Spread** 15 cm (6 in.)
Position ○ ◑ **Hardiness** RHS H7

Planted en masse, *M. sylvatica*, or forget-me-not, erupts into a carpet of pretty, tiny flowers in spring and early summer. In shades of blue, white or pink, the plants are the perfect complement to tulips, wallflowers and spring-flowering shrubs. Although many forget-me-nots are sky blue, *M. sylvatica* 'Royal Blue' has deep-blue flowers, held above a rosette of grey-green, softly hairy leaves. It flowers early and blooms freely, and its height of around 30 centimetres (12 in.) makes it taller than other cultivars. Blue is a handy colour in the garden: use 'Royal Blue' to underplant taller tulips that are white, yellow, orange, pink or red. It looks great in beds, borders and rockeries, as well as in gaps in paving. Although biennial forget-me-nots self-seed readily in borders, for a reliable bedding display, discard the plants after flowering and replant in autumn. Alternatively, sow seeds outdoors in summer for flowers the following year. Naturally found in woodland, 'Royal Blue' will grow well in sun or light shade. **VP**

Alternatives
Myosotis sylvatica 'Blue Ball', *Myosotis sylvatica* 'Ultramarine', *Myosotis sylvatica* 'Sylva Blue'

Nemesia
'Sweet Lady'

Main features Sweet-scented flowers from summer to autumn; ideal for containers
Height 30 cm (12 in.) **Spread** 20 cm (8 in.)
Position ○ **Hardiness** Annual

Finding scented flowering plants for the smallest of spaces is a real challenge, especially for the window box or patio, but this particular cultivar really delivers. *Nemesia* is a small unassuming 'basket filler', rather like *Diascia*; the Lady Series brings together three scented varieties, and of these 'Sweet Lady' is the one that flowers for the longest, from two months or more. Wild forms of *Nemesia* are found in the mountains of South Africa. They lack the habit and flowering impact to make good garden plants but the Lady Series has been bred to be highly scented with improved flowering. Use 'Sweet Lady' as a single subject for hanging baskets or pots; three young plants will fill the diameter of a 30 centimetre (12 in.) wide container. Alternatively, use as container fillers in mixed planting or in a free-draining soil as a border edging or rockery plant. It is best treated as an annual by buying young starter plants each year, although technically, it is a half-hardy perennial. **LD**

Alternatives
Nemesia 'Vanilla Lady', *Nemesia* 'Scented Lady', *Nemesia* 'Sweet Scented'

⊕ *Myosotis sylvatica* 'Royal Blue' works well under these tall tulips.

Nemophila
N. menziesii

Main features Sky-blue, upwards-facing flowers with white centres; low, often spreading plants
Height 20 cm (8 in.) **Spread** 30 cm (12 in.)
Position ○ ◑ **Hardiness** Annual

The eleven species of *Nemophila* grow naturally in the western and southern United States, especially in California. They are delightful small annuals, often blooming in spring in the wild but flowering in summer in gardens. *N. menziesii* is by far the most widely grown. Plants may be upright or spreading, and the fleshy, rather brittle stems carry neat, pale, slightly hairy, broadly divided leaves. The flowers are saucer shaped – 4 centimetres (1.5 in.) in diameter – and they are held individually above the leaves on relatively long stems. Each flower is a gorgeous sky-blue colour, with a white centre, and the five anthers stand out in royal blue. The related *N. maculata* has white flowers with five bold, deep-blue spots around the edge.

Nemophila comes from the Greek word meaning 'woodland loving', and although plants will grow well in sunny sites, they will often tolerate some shade. They are also more tolerant of damp conditions than most annuals but will not thrive in dry soil. Sow seeds in spring to flower in summer or, in mild areas, sow in late summer and autumn to flower the following spring. It pays to sow where the plants are to flower, because they do not transplant well. If happy, plants usually self-seed and find their favourite places in the garden: the cracks in partially shaded paving are popular. *N. menziesii* also makes a fine plant to grow in a pot in a cool conservatory. Sow a few seeds thinly in late summer in the pot in which the plants are to flower. **GR**

Alternatives

Nemophila maculata, Nemophila aphylla, Nemophila parviflora, Nemophila pulchella

Nicotiana
N. mutabilis

Main features Multi-coloured flowers; cottage-garden–style border plant; attracts hummingbirds and moths
Height 90–150 cm (3–5 ft) **Spread** 45–60 cm (18–24 in.)
Position ○ ◑ **Hardiness** RHS H2

This unusual relative of the scented ornamental tobacco plant (*N. alata*) is full of surprises. From the slightly hairy and sticky basal foliage arises an abundance of wiry stems that branch to create a bush effect. Each branch bears a profusion of 2.5-centimetre-wide (1 in.) trumpet-shaped flowers with petals spreading at the tips. The surprise comes from each flower, as it is pure white when it opens but gradually ages through pale pink to deep pink and finally magenta, thus showing three different colours at once. Its species name, *mutabilis*, means 'changing', in reference to this attractive feature.

Introduced from South Brazil, where it is a favourite with hummingbirds and moths, *N. mutabilis* sadly lacks the strong evening scent that is so often a feature of its close relatives. Some authorities claim that the faint scent is stronger on the darker pink flowers. *N. mutabilis* would look most attractive planted in front of a purple-leaved smoke bush (*Cotinus coggygria* 'Royal Purple'), or any other purple-leaved plants, to show off the three different colour blooms to best effect. The plant flowers all summer, continuing until the first frost, and it would enhance any cottage-garden–style border. However, allow each plant ample space for its prolific number of flowers to develop. *N. mutabilis* performs best in full sun or a lightly shaded position in any well-drained soil. The individual flowers fade gracefully, so there is no need for repeated deadheading to keep it looking good. **MP**

Alternatives

Nicotiana sylvestris, Nicotiana langsdorfii, Nicotiana obtusifolia, Nicotiana alata

Nicotiana
N. sylvestris

Main features Bold plant with prolific white summer flowers; strong perfume
Height 1.5–2 m (5–6 ft) **Spread** 60–90 cm (2–3 ft)
Position ○ ◑ **Hardiness** RHS H3

There are two distinct types of *Nicotiana*. The species grown for tobacco, *N. tabacum*, is found nowhere in the wild and is thought to be an ancient garden hybrid, whereas the more ornamental species grow wild in warmer parts of Australia, North America and South America. It is from this latter group that the many garden plants are derived.

The short- and medium-sized cultivars, in a wide range of colours, are derived mainly from *N. alata*, but the most impressive, in terms of its stature, display and fragrance is *N. sylvestris*. Growing naturally in Argentina, often in partially shaded areas, the stout upright stems reach between 1.5 and 2 metres (5–6 ft) in height and carry large, sticky, dark-green, oval leaves up to 35 centimetres (14 in.) long. The stems are topped with dense clusters of long, white pendulous flowers, which have a long tube and a flared, five-lobed face. The flowers are not only striking and attractive but powerfully fragrant, especially in the evening and at night, when they attract pollinating moths. Unlike the flowers of some species, those of *N. sylvestris* often remain open during the day.

Grow this tall, bold plant at the back of a border or on the corner of a patio, where its fragrance can be enjoyed on warm evenings. Normally raised from seeds sown in heat in spring and planted out, in mild areas seeds can be sown in autumn and the plants overwintered for a more impressive late-spring and summer display. The cultivar 'Only the Lonely' is no different from the species. **GR**

Alternatives

Nicotiana 'Fragrant Cloud', *Nicotiana* Perfume Series

Nierembergia
N. scoparia 'Mont Blanc'

Main features Long season of white flowers; compact, dark-leaved plants
Height 15 cm (6 in.) **Spread** 30 cm (12 in.)
Position ○ **Hardiness** Annual

The *Nierembergia*, also known as the cup flower, is an unlikely member of the potato family. It includes about twenty species, some of them a little woody, and although *N. scoparia* is naturally a perennial, it is usually grown as an annual. In its natural habitat in Brazil, Uruguay and Argentina, *N. scoparia* makes a sprawling plant with short, dark, slender leaves that resemble those of broom (*Cytisus*), hence its alternative common name.

N. scoparia branches well towards the tips of the shoots, and at the end of each side branch a single cup- or trumpet-shaped flower opens. Each 2.5-centimetre-long (1 in.) flower is white and shades to a slightly greyish purple toward the centre with a few dark veins radiating

out into the flower; at the heart of each bloom is a bright yellow star.

Cultivated forms vary in two ways; they may be shorter and bushier, even tightly compact, and the flowers can come in different colours. Developed in Japan, 'Mont Blanc' matures into a surprisingly neat plant reaching only about 15 centimetres (6 in.) in height, although spreading to 30 centimetres (12 in.). Its mound of small, dark-green leaves makes an ideal background to its flowers, which are pure white with gold hearts and sit tightly just above the leaves. This appealing habit of growth makes 'Mont Blanc' an ideal edging plant for a sunny place, and it will spill prettily over the edge of a low raised bed. It is also attractive planted at the edge of a sunny container. **GR**

Alternative

Nierembergia scoparia 'Purple Robe'

Nigella
N. hispanica 'Midnight'

Main features Flowers from early spring to midsummer; attracts bees; flowers and seedpods are good for cutting
Height 75 cm (2.5 ft) **Spread** 30 cm (12 in.)
Position ○ ◑ **Hardiness** Annual

There is something almost extraterrestrial about the blooms of this flower. The colours are eye-catching, thanks to the deep, velvety-purple sepals, and the spidery shapes of the seedpod and stamen are worth a close look too. When blooms finish, the quirky dark-purple seedpods carry on the display.

The common name 'fennel flower' refers to the very delicate ferny foliage of *N. hispanica* 'Midnight', which could be mistaken for the fennel herb (*Foeniculum vulgare*) before the pretty flowers appear. Although *N. hispanica* is very much shorter than fennel, it also develops into bushy plants and shares the ability to self-seed freely around the garden. It is such a beauty that it will normally be welcomed when it reappears year after year and pops up in different places.

N. hispanica 'Midnight' will flower from early spring, especially if sown the previous autumn, providing early food for the bees. Traditionally, it is grown in cottage-garden–style schemes with other annuals, such as cornflowers and corn marigolds, but the plant can also be grown in the front of mixed borders, with perennials and grasses, where its informal style and handsome flowers can easily be appreciated. If you cannot find 'Midnight', or if you would like a lighter or brighter colour, there are quite a few cultivars to choose from, such as *N. hispanica* 'African Bride', which has dramatic pure-white flowers with black centres. *N. damascena* 'Miss Jekyll' has a double layer of paler blue sepals, while seed mixes such as *N. damascena* 'Persian Jewels' contain a range of colours, and *N. papillosa* 'Delft Blue' has beautifully patterned, light-blue flowers said to resemble Dutch Delft pottery. All these *Nigella* plants are easy to grow. They can simply be sown in the ground where you want them to appear, and they are unfussy about their soil. **JS**

Alternatives

Nigella damascena 'Miss Jekyll', *Nigella damascena* 'Persian Jewels', *Nigella sativa*

Ocimum

O. × *africanum* Pesto Perpetuo

Main features Compact, tender plant; handsome
variegated foliage; edible leaves
Height 60 cm (24 in.) **Spread** 30 cm (12 in.)
Position ○ **Hardiness** RHS H1c

This is a particularly ornamental basil, with attractive
cream-variegated leaves that grow upwards in almost a
pyramid shape. You get plenty of foliage on small plants
that take up very little ground space; they are the perfect
shape for planting at the ends of window boxes or as a
single subject in a tall pot. Plants keep their shape through
the summer and add an elegant touch in a contemporary
garden. In fact, until you give it a squeeze, you might not
even recognise it as a basil, but the leaves are edible,
and the yield per plant is good. Another attraction of
'Perpetuo' is that it does not flower or set seeds. While
not unattractive in themselves, letting basil flowers form
results in a falling off of leaf size and quality. This selection
puts all its energies into producing a nonstop supply of
leaves on upright plants that have that classic sweet basil
flavour – spicy with a hint of lemon.

'Perpetuo' was discovered as a sport (a freak shoot)
on the variety O. × *africanum* 'Lesbos' by Pierre
Bennerup of Sunny Border Nurseries, Connecticut, in
the United States. From this single shoot, the plant has
been patented, propagated, widely distributed and
has become a favourite herb, both fresh and dried, to
flavour many meat and vegetable dishes, soups, salads
and desserts, as well as to make a classic pesto sauce.
Fresh leaves can be washed and frozen for winter
recipes by using a food processor to purée the leaves
with olive oil, then freezing the mixture in an ice-cube
tray. Alternatively, plants can be overwintered indoors
in a well-lit, warm spot.

Young plants of 'Perpetuo' are best purchased in late
spring and early summer. However, wait for a week or
two longer than you normally would when setting out
tender plants in the garden, for basil is very likely to suffer
in cold weather. **GS**

Alternatives

= 'Perpetuo'. *Ocimum × Africanum* 'Siam Queen', *Ocimum*
'African Blue', *Ocimum basilicum* 'Dark Opal'

Origanum
'Kent Beauty'

Main features Pink overlapping bracts;
low, bushy plants
Height 60 cm (24 in.) **Spread** 30 cm (12 in.)
Position ○ **Hardiness** RHS H4

Members of the mint family are especially known for their aromatic foliage, and oregano is amongst the most widely grown. All *Origanum* are low perennials or small twiggy shrubs, and they originate in the mountains of the Mediterranean region, North Africa and eastern Asia. They have been grown for culinary use as oregano or marjoram, or as a medicinal herb since ancient Egyptian times, and they are unexpectedly varied.

The familiar oregano and marjoram are herbaceous perennial plants with small green leaves and tiny purplish or pinkish flowers in slender flowering spikes. *Origanum* 'Kent Beauty' is different. It makes a neat, twiggy, bushy, trailing shrublet, and the wiry stems are lined with pairs of small, stiff, oval, bluish leaves with silvery veins. However, it is the flower heads that are so impressive: not the individual flowers themselves, which are small and pale lilac-pink, but behind each individual flower is a large leafy structure, a broad bract about 2 centimetres (0.75 in.) in length and width. Through summer and autumn, these overlapping bracts are gathered into pendulous heads, rather like the seed heads of hops. They open pale green, then turn white and finally mature to pink as the heads stretch to 5 centimetres (2 in.) in length. It is these flower heads that give the plants their appeal.

'Kent Beauty' is a hybrid between the *O. scabrum* from Greece and the Turkish *O. rotundifolium*. It was spotted by Elizabeth Strangman, perhaps best known as a pioneer breeder of hellebores, as a chance seedling at her nursery in Kent. A surprisingly hardy and adaptable plant, although usually grown as a perennial in screes, raised beds and troughs, 'Kent Beauty' is also grown as an annual raised from cuttings each year, and it does well planted in window boxes and hanging baskets. **GR**

Alternatives

Origanum rotundifolium 'Barbara Tingey',
Origanum 'Buckland'

Orlaya
O. grandiflora

Main features Flowers summer and autumn; attracts a
wide range of pollinating insects; lasting cut flowers
Height 60 cm (24 in.) **Spread** 30 cm (12 in.)
Position ○ **Hardiness** Annual

The *O. grandiflora* is a subtle and understated plant, but
its charms have nonetheless made it very popular with
gardeners, designers and florists. The foliage is lovely
in itself – finely dissected and a fresh shade of green –
giving a billowing, ferny and very airy look to the plants.
When the white blooms appear, they add to the appeal,
with a beautifully poised arrangement of small individual
umbellifer flowers that combine to create distinctive
flat flower heads with a lace-like appearance, hence the
common name white lace flower. The natural grace of
the plants makes them suitable for growing in informal
areas, such as traditional cottage or gravel gardens, or
at the edge of a border, where the foliage can disguise
the hard edges of a path.

Attractive to pollinators, like other members of the
Apiaceae family, *O. grandiflora* has its own insect fans,
such as hoverflies, small solitary wasps and various
flies. It is sometimes forgotten that all these insects are
important pollinators, and you may well find the odd
small spider climbing aboard the flower heads to catch
a meal too.

O. grandiflora can be grown from seeds, but it is not
the easiest to raise. Although it will self-seed freely in the
correct circumstances, it can be temperamental when it
is sown indoors. Rarely will all the seeds germinate, and
it can be erratic in the time that it takes, so gardeners
need to be patient. It is probably easier to sow the seeds
directly into the soil, which can be done in autumn, in
areas that are not too cold for a half-hardy plant over
winter, or in spring in colder regions. Grow *O. grandiflora*
with a scabious, such as *Scabiosa atropurpurea* 'Black Cat',
a deep-red *Dianthus cruentus* or a dark-purple cornflower,
Centaurea cyanus 'Black Ball'. These combinations will
also work well for cut flowers. **JS**

Alternatives

Ammi majus, Ammi visnaga 'Casablanca', *Anthriscus
sylvestris* 'Ravenswing'

Osteospermum
Serenity Series

Main features Free-flowering plants with exotic shades for summer-into-autumn blooms
Height 35 cm (14 in.) **Spread** 50 cm (20 in.)
Position ○ **Hardiness** RHS H2

These glorious South African daisies, formerly known as *Dimorphotheca*, are among the most obliging of all plants because even in dry, neglected conditions they will display a summer-through-to-autumn torrent of vibrant blooms. They are traditionally grown from seeds, and plant breeders have made great strides in recent years to produce more compact plants and to extend the colour range from pinks, purples and white. However, it is the plants raised from cuttings, such as the *Osteospermum* Serenity Series, that really deliver the most subtle and distinct colours. Some cultivars, such as 'Serenity Bronze' (pictured), have bronze petals that become suffused with purplish pink towards the centre and turn to rich pink as they age. One of the most recent and most desirable selections is 'Blue Eyed Beauty', a bicolour with shimmering yellow petals that contrast with the purple-eyed centre spot. Cultivars with 'Magic' in the name, such as 'Serenity Sunset Magic', change colour as the flowers open; in this case, from pale yellow to peachy tones, then pink.

Although commercial growers apply growth regulants to restrict plant height, 'Serenity Bronze' branches naturally to make compact, mounded plants. You can expect the flowers to conceal the foliage, and one plant will fill a 30-centimetre-wide (12 in.) pot. Each flower lasts about a week, and snipping off spent blooms, although not essential, will keep the plant looking neat. Narrow-bladed florists' snips are more efficient at getting in among the dense shoots than bulky secateurs. Plants raised from cuttings can be purchased as young plugs in the early spring and grown on before planting out, or bought as more mature specimens in the summer. To keep them from one year to the next, move them into a cool, well-lit room before the first frost. **GS**

Alternatives

Osteospermum 'Akila', *Osteospermum* 'Falling Stars', *Osteospermum* 'Passion Mixed'

Panicum
P. elegans 'Frosted Explosion'

Main features Fascinating form of North American
native; long-lasting flower heads
Height 60–75 cm (24–30 in.) **Spread** 45 cm (18 in.)
Position ○ **Hardiness** Annual

'Frosted Explosion' is a dainty and decorative ornamental
grass, whether used at the stage when the green seed
tassels are just emerging from the tops of the stems or
after 'detonation', when the long panicles hover in a cloud.
A fairly new cultivar related to the North American native
switch grass, it has become established as a favourite
with both gardeners and flower arrangers.

In the garden, as an annual grass, it soon produces
the flower heads that add movement and texture to
beds and borders. The haze of purple-tinted seed heads
surround larger blooms, such as *Rudbeckia*, so that they
appear to float in the border. Each plant produces over
twenty stems, so not many are required to make an
impact. It is not a tall ornamental grass, and the stems are
rather lax, so plant in broad drifts. Even a single plant of
'Frosted Explosion' looks effective in container schemes.
The changing form of the seed heads adds interest both
through the seasons and at different times of day, when
covered in early-morning dew or backlit by the sun.

The cut stems make an excellent foil for other
cut flowers, such as sweet peas, whether used in a
bouquet or in a vase. The fine green haze offers a more
contemporary effect than the traditional sprays of baby's
breath (*Gypsophila*). The seed heads are also good for
dried arrangements; in 2010, 'Frosted Explosion' was
voted the best dried flower of the year by the Association
of Specialty Cut Flower Growers.

Seed is best sown under cover in early spring before
being planted out late spring to early summer, because
when planted directly in the soil, it is hard to tell the
emerging seedlings from weeds. Young plants can be
slow to establish in individual pots or cell trays, but when
planted out, they soon make up for lost time and by
midsummer, the fireworks will begin. **GS**

Alternatives

Briza maxima, Lagurus ovatus, Panicum virgatum 'Heavy
Metal', *Panicum virgatum* 'Rehbraun'

Papaver

P. commutatum
'Ladybird'

Main features Cheap and cheerful summer flowers;
suitable for beds, containers and cutting
Height 45 cm (18 in.) **Spread** 15 cm (6 in.)
Position ○ **Hardiness** Annual

Few plants are as aptly named as this annual poppy. The four brilliant crimson petals are marked with a large black spot near the base, and they gleam in the sunlight as though coated in varnish. At 8 centimetres (3 in.) in diameter, the flowers are not as large as the perennial *P. orientale*, but *P. commutatum* 'Ladybird' is such an extrovert that size is not an issue. It is a relative of the cornfield poppy and it was developed using a species introduced from Russia in 1876 by Mr William Thompson, the founder of Thompson & Morgan Seed Company. 'Ladybird' is sturdy and upright, with each plant producing a succession of two dozen or more short-lived blooms. Try it on the edge of the border for classic cottage garden appeal, or planted into the wildflower meadow. 'Ladybird' falls into the category of 'sow and forget', which makes it an ideal choice of plant to get children experiencing the pleasure and satisfaction of seed raising. **GS**

Alternatives

Papaver rhoeas, *Papaver nudicaule*, *Papaver orientale* 'Cedric Morris'

⊖ *Papaver commutatum* 'Ladybird' adds a splash of colour at Painswick Rococo Garden, Gloucestershire, UK.

Pentas

P. lanceolata
New Look Series

Main features Clusters of colourful starry flowers;
attracts butterflies and hummingbirds
Height 25 cm (10 in.) **Spread** 30 cm (12 in.)
Position ○ **Hardiness** RHS H2

This species, a member of the coffee family, stands out for its impressive flowers and its appeal to butterflies. The Egyptian star cluster *P. lanceolata* is native to parts of east Africa and Yemen, and it has become naturalised in Florida. The glossy, deeply veined, pointed leaves provide a fine background to the large, crowded, flower clusters. Each five-pointed flower is only 12 millimetres (0.5 in.) in diameter, but the combined effect is very colourful. Breeders have developed plants in various flower colours on neater and bushier forms that can be used as summer bedding or as pot plants. The *P. lanceolata* New Look Series comes in red, violet, pink and white, sometimes with white centres to the flowers. In completely frost-free areas, New Look Series will flower almost year-round, as one tiny flower follows the next and as one cluster follows another. **GR**

Alternatives

Pentas lanceolata Butterfly Series, *Pentas lanceolata* Graffiti Series, *Pentas lanceolata* Kaleidoscope Series

Petchoa
SuperCal Series

Main features Trailing or upright plants; trumpet-shaped flowers; wide range of colours and patterns
Height 30 cm (12 in.)   **Spread** 35 cm (14 in.)
Position ○   **Hardiness** RHS H3

The *Calibrachoa* and *Petunia* are two closely related genera, perhaps surprisingly found in the potato family. Although *Petunia* has been popular with gardeners since the 1800s, it was not until the 1990s that the smaller-flowered *Calibrachoa* also became widely grown. The next step was for Japanese plant breeders to create a hybrid between the two. The *Petchoa* SuperCal Series combines the best features of both parent types. The plants are colourful and prolific and come in a wide range of colours and bicolours. They are early flowering, develop well in cool conditions and are tolerant of a range of pH levels. The plants are unusually good in rainy conditions – the flowers stand up to rain and recover well after a downpour – and they also tolerate both light frost and hot summer sun. Upright selections, such as SuperCal 'Artist Rose', are more suited to filling out tubs, whereas trailing types, such as SuperCal 'Pink Ice', are better choices for planting at the edges of tubs and in hanging baskets. **GR**

Alternatives

Calibrachoa Million Bells Terracotta = 'Sunbelkist',
Petunia 'African Sunset'

Petunia
P. exserta

Main features Flowers summer to autumn; attracts hummingbirds
Height 30–60 cm (12–24 in.)   **Spread** 30 cm (12 in.)
Position ○   **Hardiness** RHS H3

This rare petunia was not discovered and named until 1987, and it is nearly extinct in its native Brazil. Fortunately, seeds were collected, so *P. exserta* – the only truly red petunia – will remain preserved in gardens. It is a profuse bloomer, with 6-centimetre-long (2.5 in.) tubular flowers whose yellow stamens extend from the throat. The species grows as an upright mound and its stems weave charmingly into its neighbours. It is also an example of a plant that has evolved a specialised pollinator relationship. While other petunias are nocturnally fragrant, thus attracting moths, this non-scented petunia targets hummingbirds, which have no sense of smell and show a marked preference for red flowers. It is surprising that *P. exserta* has come to the brink of extinction, for it is not particularly threatened by human encroachment. The problem is that it is interbreeding with other petunias to the point of its own disappearance as a distinct species. It is most susceptible to its cousin *P. axillaris*. **KK**

Alternatives

None, as this is the only naturally occurring, true red petunia.

Petunia

'Crazytunia Pulse'

Main features Summer-long blooms; exciting colours and combinations
Height 25 cm (10 in.) **Spread** 30 cm (12 in.)
Position ○ **Hardiness** RHS H3

With such a distinctive name, you'd expect something out of the ordinary, and this new generation of petunias does not disappoint. Produced by the German breeders Westhoff, there are over a dozen selections to date that represent the most desirable colours and shapes available. Bred for resistance to sun and rain, they are vigorous, though their growth is compact, with no bare stems in the centre. 'Crazytunia Pulse' (pictured) is a striking mix of dark purple with gold, star-shaped patterns. 'Crazytunia Green with Envy' is a delightful confection of green and pink; the flowers start off with pink splashes on a lime-green background, then as they age, the pink dominates. 'Crazytunia Black Mamba' shows none of the instability of earlier types, when the black would fade or irregular stripes would appear. Fiery colours radiate out from the centre of 'Crazytunia Mandeville', whereas 'Crazytunia Wedgwood Blue' is more formal with smart blue splashes on each petal, leaving a white star in the centre. **GS**

Alternatives

Petunia Shock Wave Series, *Petunia* Priscilla = 'Kerpril',
Petunia 'Phantom'

Petunia

Priscilla

Main features Neat, semi-trailing plant; dark-veined, lavender-mauve, fragrant double flowers
Height 30 cm (12 in.) **Spread** 90 cm (3 ft)
Position ○ **Hardiness** RHS H3

The native petunias of South America – with their purple, red or white flowers – are wild and straggly, and while they can be well-scented, they produce too few flowers on too much leggy growth to satisfy today's demanding gardeners. Consequently, plant breeders set out to improve them. Part of the Tumbelina Series, Priscilla was developed in Cambridgeshire, England, and introduced in 1997. It has many special features. The individual flowers are fully double, so plants last longer than those with the more familiar single flowers. Each flower is pale lavender-mauve with plum-purple veins and a strong fragrance. The flowering season is long, often from early summer and well into the autumn, with a consistent spread of flowers across the display. Other well-scented plants in the series include 'Angela', with larger dusky-pink flowers and 'Belinda' in rich blue. 'Joanna' is very pale lilac-mauve with a darker centre, and 'Melissa' is white with lemony overtones. **GR**

Alternatives

= 'Kerpril'. *Petunia hybrida* Angela, *Petunia hybrida* Belinda,
Petunia hybrida Damson Ripple, *Petunia hybrida* Eliza

Phlox
P. *drummondii* 'Moody Blues'

Main features Distinctive blue flowers; fragrant blooms; good cut-flower posies; attracts pollinators
Height 25 cm (10 in.) **Spread** 30 cm (12 in.)
Position ○ **Hardiness** Annual

Known as creeping phlox, the species *P. drummondii* is a native of central and eastern Texas that has become naturalised in many southeastern states of America. The species is named after Thomas Drummond, a Scottish naturalist who spent nearly two years surveying the botany of Texas from 1833 until his death. He sent more than 700 plant species from his Texas collections around the world; phlox was sent to England in 1835, where it was considered exotic.

Phlox is one of the few plants that has flowers in every colour of the rainbow, which probably explains its continuing popularity. Among the annual phlox available, there is no shortage of single colours and mixes, but as there is only a limited number of any blue-flowered annual, it is worth seeking out 'Moody Blues' for its colour and slight fragrance. The flowers come in varying shades of blue, and an occasional white flower. There is nothing plant breeders can do about the white flowers – it is just a characteristic of the plant's genetics, but it does not detract from its use as informal bedding plant, gap filler in borders or as a container plant.

The medium-sized flowers (up to 2.5 cm/1 inch in diameter) form as clumps on compact, branching plants that flower from midsummer through to the autumn. Plants are well suited to cottage-garden–style plantings and attract both butterflies and pollinating insects. For colour contrast 'Moody Blues' looks superb grown alongside golden marigolds. The cut flowers also have a reasonable vase life, although as its common name creeping phlox implies, the stems are short and are therefore better suited to posy arrangements. *P. drummondii* can be grown from seeds started indoors and planted out, or seeds can also be sown directly into the ground where they are to flower. **TS**

Alternatives

Phlox Promise Series, *Phlox* Summer Majesty Hybrid Mixed, *Phlox* Dwarf Beauty Mixed, *Phlox* Tapestry Mixed

Plectranthus
Mona Lavender

Main features Flowers in the autumn;
spring to autumn foliage
Height 60 cm (24 in.) **Spread** 60 cm (24 in.)
Position ◐ ● **Hardiness** RHS H1c

The *Plectranthus* is a tropical plant, related to mint, and it is best known as the houseplant *P. verticillatus*, the culinary herb *P. amboinicus* and the summer container plant *P. argentatus*. Most species of the plant are grown for their foliage, so *Plectranthus* Mona Lavender is quite a departure, because its chief appeal is its showy flowers. Although it has attractive bicolour foliage (dark-green leaves with vivid purple undersides), it becomes a true showstopper when it erupts into bloom in autumn as the days shorten. Its dramatic lavender spikes are vaguely similar to *Coleus* flowers, but they are much more substantial and stout, reminiscent of lilac or buddleja.

Mona Lavender is also quite easy to grow. Like all *Plectranthus*, it prefers shade, and it can thrive with less moisture than other common shade lovers, such as *Impatiens* or *Coleus*. In frost-free regions, it is quite drought tolerant when grown as an inground perennial, but elsewhere treat as an annual and use as a bedding plant. Mona Lavender is even amenable to that most dreaded of garden aspects: dry shade. In a container it makes an upright, vigorous, dense bush that is 60 centimetres (24 in.) tall and wide. Flowers appear over a long period – up until the first frost – and if brought indoors to pass the winter as a houseplant it will flower continually with deadheading until spring. As with most of its tribe, Mona Lavender is easily propagated by cuttings, which root readily in water and offer a secondary route to overwintering a cherished specimen.

Rarely afflicted by pests or disease, this wonderful plant is a hybrid of *P. saccatus* and *P. hilliardiae*, and it was bred by horticulturist Roger Jaques at Cape Town's renowned Kirstenbosch National Botanical Garden. First released in 2002, Mona Lavender is gradually becoming more widely available. **KK**

Alternatives

= 'Plepalila'. Plectranthus 'Velvet Elvis', Plectranthus *zuluensis*, Plectranthus *ecklonii*

Plectranthus

P. argentatus 'Silver Shield'

Main features Summer foliage and flowers; architectural plant; attracts bees and butterflies
Height 90 cm (3 ft) **Spread** 90 cm (3 ft)
Position ○ ◑ ● **Hardiness** RHS H1c

The *P. argentatus* 'Silver Shield' is primarily grown as an annual or tender perennial foliage plant. Its silver leaves – 5 to 10 centimetres (2–4 in.) long – sit in opposite pairs on the square stems and have scalloped edges. Both the leaves and the stems are covered in a myriad of flattened hairs that trap air and give the effect of a velvety sheen. Later in the summer, elegant, upright terminal spires of small, tubular, bluish-white flowers appear clustered around the stems, and these blooms are loved by bees. Unlike many of its relatives in the large mint family, 'Silver Shield' has only slightly aromatic foliage.

This vigorous plant, native to Australia, makes a dramatic contrast to subtropical plants. Its silver leaves offset brighter gem-like colours to perfection. Try planting it adjacent to the multi-coloured foliage of *Canna* 'Durban' or among purple-leaved, vibrant dahlias, such as 'Bishop of Canterbury' (deep purple) or 'Bishop of Llandaff' (bright red) for a calming influence. Reasonably tolerant of drought, but intolerant of wet conditions, the silver spur flower can be used in large containers too. It is easily propagated by cuttings or seeds, and regular pinching of the new growth will encourage a more compact plant, which associates well with white or blue agapanthus. In a shady location, try 'Silver Shield' among white or blue hydrangeas, or for summer simply add its silver foliage to bright, golden variegated evergreens such as *Choisya ternata* 'Sundance'. **MP**

Alternatives

Plectranthus ciliatus 'Sasha', *Plectranthus oertendahlii* 'Lime Light', *Plectranthus madagascariensis* 'Variegated Mintleaf'

Portulaca
P. oleracea Rio Series

Main features Large, bright, exotic flowers; low
maintenance; some drought resistance
Height 10–20 cm (4–8 in.) **Spread** 30–38 cm (12–15 in.)
Position ○ **Hardiness** Annual

The Rio Series of *P. oleracea* provides exotic, tropical-looking blooms in many different colours. With its ability to tolerate a certain amount of drought, it offers a low-maintenance solution to brightening up hot, dry, sunny sites such as banks or hot patios.

The series is the result of a breeding program that started in Costa Rica in 2002 with the aim of producing plants with larger flowers in more colours and with an improved growth habit compared to other *Portulaca*. One of the parents was purslane (*P. oleracea*), a native of India whose semi-succulent foliage is known around the world as an edible; another is the rose moss (*P. grandiflora*). There are six colours in the series: Rio Rose

(pictured), Rio Orange, Rio Scarlet, Rio Apricot, Rio White and Rio Yellow.

The five-petalled flowers (4 cm/1.5 in. in diameter) open with the sun, and each bloom lasts only a single day before being replaced throughout the summer months, so there is no need for tedious deadheading to ensure a good display. The plant's growth habit is low growing, which makes it ideal for ground cover use in sunny borders or trailing from baskets and containers. Pinching out the growing tips early on produces better plants. Water is stored in the semi-succulent foliage, hence the drought resistance, but in wet soils or in container mixes with poor drainage, or if overwatered, it can suffer from rot. **TS**

Alternatives

Portulaca oleracea Lazy Days Mix, *Portulaca oleracea*
Sundaze Mix, *Portulaca oleracea* Sundial Mix

Ricinus
R. communis 'Impala'

Main features Exotic specimen plants; suitable for containers and beds
Height 1.2–1.5 m (4–5 ft) **Spread** 1.2 m (4 ft)
Position ○ ◑ **Hardiness** Annual

When gardeners invest time in growing plants from seeds, it is always worth the extra effort to seek out the best varieties. *R. communis* 'Impala' is a showstopper, and its huge leaves are the most intense shade of purple-red when compared to its green- or bronze-leaved cousins. In addition, the spiny seedpods that follow creamy-yellow flowers are even more conspicuous, in a rich shade of maroon red. The plant is compact and well branched, rarely exceeding shoulder height in a season unless grown in warm, frost-free climates. 'Impala' is indigenous to areas of the Mediterranean, eastern Africa and India, but is widespread throughout tropical regions and widely grown elsewhere as an ornamental. It looks superb amongst other plants grown for their striking architectural foliage. Aim for contrasts of leaf shape and texture by planting with narrow-leaved *Cordyline* and *Phormium*, *Canna* 'Tropicanna Gold', and *Coleus* and *Iresine* around the base. Beware that the seedcoats are poisonous. **GS**

Alternatives

Ricinus communis 'Carmencita', *Ricinus communis* 'Zanzibarensis'

Rudbeckia
R. hirta 'Prairie Sun'

Main features Flowers in summer and autumn; long flower stems for cutting; plant roots have medicinal uses
Height 60–75 cm (24–30 in.) **Spread** 40 cm (16 in.)
Position ○ ◑ **Hardiness** RHS H3

An All-America Selections Gold Medal winner, *R. hirta* 'Prairie Sun' was bred in Germany by the old established seed company Benary. Its breeding objective was to create a *Rudbeckia* cultivar that would flower over a long period and be suitable for the middle or back of a border. At this time there were some very good varieties available, but most were late maturing, flowering in the autumn. Benary produced a variety that flowered much earlier (as few as twelve weeks after sowing) and also carried on flowering into the autumn. 'Prairie Sun' plants become smothered in large flowers up to 13 centimetres (5 in.) in diameter. The blooms are golden yellow with a light-yellow tip to the petals and a green centre to the flowers. They make great plants for a border or for a large container and complement blue *Ageratum* and *Lobelia*. *Rudbeckia* is easy to grow, and the flowers attract butterflies and pollinating insects. The flowers are long lasting as cut blooms and may also be used for drying. **TS**

Alternatives

Rudbeckia hirta 'Cappuccino', *Rudbeckia hirta* 'Rustic Dwarfs', *Rudbeckia hirta* 'Moreno', *Rudbeckia hirta* 'Toto'

Rudbeckia hirta 'Prairie Sun' starts flowering in summer and continues into autumn. ➡

Rudbeckia
R. hirta 'Indian Summer'

Main features Long-lasting showy blooms; good cut flower; attracts bees and butterflies
Height 60 cm (24 in.) **Spread** 30 cm (12 in.)
Position ○ **Hardiness** RHS H3

With flower heads that can be larger than the span of your hand, and an ability to flower from early summer until the frost, it is not surprising that this variety of *R. hirta* is a standout plant. Combining a robust constitution that makes it tolerant of heat and drought with ease of growth, this selection of a native to the eastern and central United States has received gongs on both sides of the Atlantic, including an All-America Selections Award and the Royal Horticultural Society Award of Garden Merit in the United Kingdom.

The species is named for Olof Rudbeck, a Swedish botanist; 'hirta' refers to the fine hairs on the plant stems. Cultivars offer larger flower heads, and flower for longer; some alternatives have red or bronze flowers, but it is the rich yellow of *R. hirta* 'Indian Summer' that associates so well with ornamental grasses and the Michaelmas daisies in the autumn.

Each bloom is long lasting and rain resistant, thanks in part to the prominent central cone and reflexed yellow petals that shed moisture so efficiently. The plant is a favourite nectar source for butterflies and equally popular with flower arrangers. At around 60 centimetres (24 in.) tall, it is possible to cut good length stems for the vase without removing too many unopened buds. 'Indian Summer' is grown mainly as a half-hardy annual although it is, in fact, a short-lived perennial. Sow seeds in early spring under cover or order young starter plants to arrive by post. These may be more expensive, but will save heating bills if you do not have a heated propagator or heated greenhouse in which to grow them on. Starter plants will develop more quickly and not suffer when planted out if potted into individual 8-centimetre-wide (3 in.) pots or cell trays. Alternatively, buy young plants in bud after the last frost date. **GS**

Alternatives

Rudbeckia hirta 'Cherry Brandy', *Rudbeckia hirta* 'Cherokee Sunset', *Rudbeckia hirta* 'Chim Chiminee'

Salpiglossis
S. *sinuata* 'Bolero'

Main features Flowers in summer; large, exotic,
trumpet-like flowers; fragrant blooms
Height 30–45 cm (12–18 in.) **Spread** 22–30 cm (9–12 in.)
Position ○ **Hardiness** RHS H1c

This species originally comes from Chile, and its flowers
have always held a fascination, hence the common
names painted tongue and velvet trumpet flower. Seed
companies offer packets of mixed-flower colours that can
include a medley of blue, mauve, pink, red, orange or
yellow. If you want the single colours, raise them in pots,
then pick out the flower colours you want, or look out for
specialist suppliers who sometimes offer blue separately.

'Bolero', an F2 hybrid, is known for its large,
impressive, tubular trumpet-like blooms, which come
in many colours, including blue (pictured). The blooms
are attractively marked with contrasting coloured veins
and marbled patterns, and the flowering stems are
often used for cut flowers during the summer months.
'Bolero' produces flowers remarkably quickly, in as little
as ten weeks, and will continue to flower throughout
the summer until the first frost. The flowers are lightly
fragrant, and it is often grown in containers on the patio
to appreciate the scent. 'Bolero' was bred in the United
States by Bodger Seeds in California's Lompoc Valley.
As very little breeding had been done on *Salpiglossis*
previously, the interest was immediate and 'Bolero' was
soon being grown around the world.

Although the plants are grown as annuals, botanically
they are short-lived perennials. *Salpiglossis* grows best in
full sun, although too high a temperature can inhibit
growth. Plants are equally at home in a border as well as
on the patio; you can also grow them in a conservatory
or as a pot plant on a well-lit kitchen windowsill. Outdoor
plants usually need staking, as the stems are lax, but if
you pinch out the main growing tip when the plants
are 15 centimetres (6 in.) tall, this will encourage bushier
plants. Thereafter, apply a balanced fertiliser and water
as necessary. **TS**

Alternatives

Salpiglossis sinuata F1 'Royale Mix', *Salpiglossis sinuata*
'Burlesque', *Salpiglossis sinuata* 'Superbissima'

Salvia

S. coccinea
'Summer Jewel Pink'

Main features Unique, soft-pink colour; flowers
continually over a long period; aromatic foliage
Height 45 cm (18 in.) **Spread** 30–38 cm (12–15 in.)
Position ○ ◑ **Hardiness** Annual

The virtually maintenance-free *Salvia splendens* is a well-
known sight in many gardens around the world, bringing
as it does vibrant colour. *S. coccinea* 'Summer Jewel Pink'
is a relative newcomer and an All-America Selections
award winner that many people believe is even better.
It has attractive shell-pink flowers and a more compact
growth habit, which gives improved weather resistance,
as well as the added benefit of aromatic foliage. 'Summer
Jewel Pink' flowers quickly and continuously on multi-
bloomed stems, and the flowers are long lasting. In beds,
borders or large containers, it goes well with the soft
blue of *Ageratum* in a pastel-coloured scheme. Plants are
also ideal for an informal wildlife garden, as the continuous
blooming and subsequent nectar in the flowers
encourage bees, butterflies and even hummingbirds.
Sow seeds early in the season and pinch the plant to
encourage sturdy branching prior to planting. **TS**

Alternatives

Salvia coccinea 'Summer Jewel White', *Salvia coccinea*
'Summer Jewel Red', *Salvia coccinea* 'Hummingbird Mixed'

Salvia

S. farinacea
'Victoria Blue'

Main features Flowers from summer to first frost;
attracts bees and butterflies; good cut or dried flowers
Height 40–60 cm (16–24 in.) **Spread** 30–38 cm (12–15 in.)
Position ○ ◑ **Hardiness** RHS H2

This striking, purple-flowered variety of the sage offers
an upright habit ideal for mixing amongst lower growing
plants. Spikes of small blue flowers are clustered around
the stems and appear from a mealy calyx to give a slightly
two-tone effect. The linear, dark-green leaves are covered
in white hairs beneath. Consequently, *S. farinacea* 'Victoria
Blue' makes an ideal dot plant in a bedding scheme,
where it will flower all summer until the frost. It is equally
at home in a cottage-garden–style border, planted singly
or in groups, or even grown as a cut flower because the
heads can be dried for winter decoration. The upright
habit makes it ideal as the centrepiece in a container.
Blue is a versatile colour that not only complements the
hot shades – reds, oranges and yellows – but also looks
good with the cooler pinks and whites. A more compact
variety of *S. farinacea* is the award-winning 'Fairy Queen',
with blue-and-white effect flower spikes. **MP**

Alternatives

Salvia elegans, *Salvia microphylla* 'Cerro Potosi', *Salvia
officinalis* 'Purpurascens'

Salvia
S. *viridis* var. *comata* 'Claryssa Mixed'

Main features Vivid spikes of bracts for display, cutting and drying; attracts beneficial insects
Height 45 cm (18 in.) **Spread** 30 cm (12 in.)
Position ○ **Hardiness** Annual

A significant breakthrough when it first appeared in the 1980s, *S. viridis* var. *comata* 'Claryssa Mixed' was shorter, well branched and had richer colours than earlier strains of clary. Amongst its many virtues are what appear to the casual observer to be terminal clusters of blooms, in delicious shades of blue, pink and white – marked with darker veins – but are, in fact, coloured bracts. It can be sown along pathways in cottage-style gardens to make a multi-coloured 'hedge' or more informally in great drifts in borders where it will act as a magnet to lure bees and butterflies. 'Claryssa Mixed' is also superb for cutting and drying, and plants can be raised in cell trays under cover and lined out in the cutting garden for extra early flower spikes or sown straight into the ground in spring. The foliage of clary has a pleasing fragrance and the plant was added to liquors in the past to increase potency. It also has antiseptic qualities. **GS**

Alternatives

Syn. *Salvia horminum*. *Salvia horminum* 'Bouquet Mixed', *Salvia horminum* 'Blue Denim'

Salvia
S. *guaranitica* 'Black and Blue'

Main features Fast growing; lightly aromatic leaves; attracts bees, butterflies and hummingbirds
Height 1.2 m (4 ft) **Spread** 90 cm (3 ft)
Position ○ **Hardiness** RHS H2

One of the most stately and striking of all the many and varied sages is *S. guaranitica* 'Black and Blue'. A bushy plant with lightly aromatic leaves, it will grace the latter part of summer and autumn with tall spires of hooded blue flowers, backed by the black calyxes that give it its name. 'Black and Blue' will form into big, upright clumps, its strong, branching stems producing a steady supply of blooms until the first frost. Like all *Salvia*, it is very popular with bees, but the length of the flowers makes it difficult for some bees to gain access. Bumblebees especially will resort to 'nectar robbing' by chewing a hole in the base of the flower from the outside, through which they can access the nectaries. *Salvia* comes in many different shapes and sizes and from numerous parts of the world, but *S. guaranitica* and its cultivars, as natives of South America, are not as hardy as some and would need protection to survive any but the mildest winters. **JS**

Alternatives

Salvia 'Amistad', *Salvia* 'Purple Majesty', *Salvia guaranitica* 'Blue Enigma', *Salvia* 'Wendy's Wish'

Scabiosa
S. atropurpurea 'Chile Black'

Main features Prodigious, scented summer blooms for display and cutting; attracts wildlife
Height 90 cm (3 ft) **Spread** 45 cm (18 in.)
Position ○ **Hardiness** RHS H2

This native to the Mediterranean region was first introduced into cultivation in the late sixteenth century, but it is surprising how few gardeners are still not familiar with the unique qualities of *Scabiosa*. Famed for the torrent of blooms that pour forth throughout the summer months (and even into winter in the absence of heavy frost), *S. atropurpurea* can be gathered in armfuls, and its flowers used to fill every vase in the house. Flower colours range from pure white through blues and violets to pinks, ruby reds, mauve and a very deep purple-plum shade that appears black in dull light, such as *S. atropurpurea* 'Chile Black'. As the flowers age, tiny violet stamen peep out. The blooms have the most delicious honey fragrance, which bees, butterflies and other wildlife find irresistible.

Each flower lasts approximately one week in water, and as with sweet peas (*Lathyrus odoratus*), the more blooms you pick, the more will reappear. However, it is a good idea to allow a number of heads to produce seeds every now and again. These can be saved as an insurance policy, because 'Chile Black' will only overwinter successfully in mild climates on well-drained soil. There is also a subtle beauty in the seed heads, which can be picked for indoor display or left in the garden for hungry birds to feast on.

Seeds can be sown indoors in spring and transplanted into beds a month or so later. Alternatively, it can be sown directly in the garden where the plants will flower in mid- to late spring. Sow in straight drills, and it will be easy to distinguish 'Chile Black' from annual weed seedlings. It takes around ten to twelve weeks from sowing for the first eagerly anticipated flower to appear. Although this plant is a short-lived perennial, it is more often grown as an annual. **GS**

Alternatives

Scabiosa atropurpurea 'Oxford Blue', *Scabiosa atropurpurea* 'Ace of Spades', *Scabiosa atropurpurea* 'Imperial Mix'

Scaevola
S. aemula 'Blue Wonder'

Main features Fan-shaped flower heads on trailing
stems; flowers summer to first frost; attracts bees
Height 22–45 cm (9–18 in.) **Spread** 30–60 cm (12–24 in.)
Position ○ ◐ **Hardiness** RHS H1c

The uniquely shaped blooms of *S. aemula* 'Blue Wonder'
make its common name – fan flower – most appropriate.
The five petals of each flower are arranged solely on
one side of the flower, in the shape of a fan. These
petals are blue, with a hint of purple, a whitish eye, and
a yellow throat. The individual flowers are clustered into
terminal heads that keep extending, thereby producing
a succession of blooms throughout the summer until
the first frost. 'Blue Wonder' has attractive green foliage
stems and flower heads that have an arching habit, trailing
outwards from the plant. This makes it an excellent choice
for hanging baskets and containers, but also as a useful
bedding plant. The flower clusters on the trailing stems
always face up to the light, so present themselves well in
any situation. There is no need to deadhead this variety
because it does not set seeds and must be propagated
by cuttings.

Although this plant would make an impressive basket
planted on its own, try using 'Blue Wonder' trailing over
the edge of containers topped with the vibrant red,
pink, orange or white colours of the Nonstop Series
of begonias for a summer-long display that requires
little attention. As a bedding plant, a carpet of the blue
flowers could be interplanted using the dwarfer-growing
varieties, earlier-flowering forms of *Canna indica* as dot
plants or an obelisk covered in the climbing black-eyed
Susan vine, *Thunbergia alata*.

The species is native to Australia, occurring in
southeast Queensland and throughout New South
Wales, and it has been much improved. It grows in any
reasonable soil but dislikes waterlogged conditions. A
sunny or lightly shaded position will suit it well. This plant
is typically bought afresh each spring as a young plant
raised commercially from cuttings. **MP**

Alternatives

Scaevola aemula 'Brilliant', *Scaevola aemula* 'White Wonder',
Scaevola aemula 'Topaz Pink', *Scaevola aemula* 'Zig Zag'

Schizanthus

S. *pinnatus* 'Hit Parade'

Main feature Neat plants covered in multi-coloured flowers like small, prettily patterned butterflies
Height 30 cm (12 in.) **Spread** 30 cm (12 in.)
Position ○ ◑ **Hardiness** RHS H1b

The potato family includes some unexpected gems amongst its 2,600 species, and *S. pinnatus* is one of the most colourful. All the dozen annual species are appealing, but *S. pinnatus* is the one from which garden forms have been developed. It is a native of Chile, but plant populations are declining in the wild. The rather brittle plants carry fresh green leaves that are twice divided into pairs of short slender segments. The summer flowers are purple, pink or white and, like the leaves, are split into slender lobes, sometimes with purple streaks and/or a yellow splash.

Schizanthus has been cultivated since the early 1800s, and over the centuries plants have been selected that were smaller, bushier, less brittle and easier to manage. The flowers developed broader lobes to the petals to create more impact, the purple veins became blotches, and the yellow eyes intensified. The range of colours has also been extended impressively, and the colours fixed.

Plants of *S. pinnatus* 'Hit Parade' are neat, bushy and very well branched, so their clusters of flowers are held in tight heads above the foliage. The flowers come in red, pink and lavender, plus white, all with a yellow eye with a purple or pink zone around it. 'Hit Parade' is usually grown as a cool season annual – it hates summer heat but is also frost tender. Sow seeds in the late summer or autumn and overwinter the plants in a greenhouse if necessary. In warmer areas, *S. pinnatus* can be planted outside. **GR**

Alternatives

Schizanthus Atlantis Series, *Schizanthus* 'Royal Pierrot', *Schizanthus pinnatus* 'Star Parade'

Tagetes
T. tenuifolia 'Lemon Gem'

Main features Flowers in summer; fragrant, dark-green foliage; good spreading plant; attracts butterflies
Height 22 cm (9 in.) **Spread** 30 cm (12 in.)
Position ○ **Hardiness** Annual

Smaller flowered than their illustrious cousins, the French and African marigolds, these lovely little plants have a charm all their own. *T. tenuifolia* 'Lemon Gem' produces masses of blooms of only 2 centimetre (0.75 in.) in diameter, but what they lack in size, they make up for in numbers. The plants become literally covered in blooms by midsummer. In some respects this is a shame, because the lacy, finely cut foliage is very attractive. In addition, brushing against the plants will release a lovely citrus-like aroma, and the flowers can even be eaten in salads and desserts. Is there anything this little plant does not do?

'Lemon Gem' is ideal as border edging or in colour blocks. It has a wonderful, spreading, mounded growth habit, so is good at filling space and looks superb grown with red *Salvia* or blue *Petunia*. There is even a place for it in large containers.

If lemon yellow is not an appropriate colour in your scheme, then there are golden, tangerine and red bicolour types to choose from. Alternatively, *T. tenuifolia* looks good grown as a mixture. The plants are fast growing and will flower in as little as ten weeks from sowing. They are easy to grow, starting in trays and planting out when they are some 15 centimetres (6 in.) tall. *T. tenuifolia* is practically maintenance-free, and it produces so many flowers that no deadheading is required. In good conditions the plants will continue to flower through to the first frost. **TS**

Alternatives

Tagetes tenuifolia 'Golden Gem', *Tagetes tenuifolia* 'Tangerine Gem', *Tagetes tenuifolia* 'Paprika Gem'

Tagetes
T. erecta

Main features Flowers in summer; good for bedding, borders, or cutting; tall, architectural plant
Height 60–90 cm (2–3 ft) **Spread** 30 cm (12 in.)
Position ○ **Hardiness** RHS H1c

There are numerous African marigolds with superb uniformity in flower size, colour and growth habit. Consequently, it is difficult for the many species of *Tagetes* to find a niche in this popular market. However, there are a couple of African marigold cultivars that offer something a bit different. *T. erecta* 'Simba' (pictured) has orange flowers and ruffled petals rather like a lion's mane. It is quite a tall cultivar that can reach nearly 90 centimetres (3 ft). Strong, orange colours come into their own when summers are overcast and weather is dull, also where there is planting with plenty of bold foliage and you want some powerful colour highlights. *T. erecta* 'Key Lime' has unusual green lime-yellow flowers. There is something quite special about this particular colour: it almost has an iridescent glow, particularly towards evening on a hot day. It also makes an excellent, long-lasting, cut flower with a life in water of up to three weeks. In addition, it is a scentless variety for gardeners who do not appreciate the distinctive marigold fragrance. 'Key Lime' was bred by Burpee in the Netherlands. *T. erecta* 'Vanilla Ice' is a white-flowered cultivar, which is useful for subtle gap filling in cooler-colour schemes, such as those with blue or mauve flowers.

African marigolds are excellent plants for growing at the back of beds, borders or in large containers; they can reach 60 to 90 centimetres (2–3 ft), dependent on location and fertiliser levels. Plants are easy to grow and can be started indoors for early-summer flowering or sown directly outside for mid- to late-summer blooms. Seed germination is usually quick, and plants grow away strongly. The use of a general fertiliser is recommended, and watering is important until the plants are established. Fading flower heads should be removed to prolong flowering into the autumn. **TS/LD**

Alternatives

Tagetes erecta 'Marvel Gold', *Tagetes erecta* Jubilee Series, *Tagetes erecta* Climax Series, *Tagetes erecta* 'Inca Orange'

Tagetes
T. patula 'Cinnabar'

Main features Flowers summer to autumn; drought
tolerant; fiery colour departure from typical marigolds
Height 90–120 cm (3–4 ft) **Spread** 90 cm (3 ft)
Position ○ ◑ **Hardiness** Annual

Marigolds get little respect. Derided as common and
despised as garish, perhaps they are simply too easy
to grow. Nevertheless, British horticulturalist Gertrude
Jekyll was a fan as long ago as 1916: '...a valuable annual
should not be neglected because it is so common and
easy to grow and because it was so much overdone
... if the plant was misused it was not the fault of the
plant but that of the general acceptance of a poor sort
of gardening.'

T. patula 'Cinnabar' is different. Even marigold haters
lust after this elegant variety of French marigold. It is
a princess among commoners, bred at Great Dixter
in the south of England, where gardener Christopher
Lloyd painstakingly selected taller, redder plants year
after year. 'Cinnabar' has rich, terra-cotta red flowers
with the faintest mustard-yellow edging on single,
fluted, bee-friendly flowers featuring a central button
of frothy-yellow stamen. It is poised and statuesque, well
branching, and willowy, weaving in among other plants
if permitted. Useful as a summer filler for empty spots
that open up in beds and borders as spring wanes, it
obligingly and reliably blooms from summer until the
first frost. Even the feathery, ferny foliage is attractive
and refreshingly scented of pine and camphor. It is an
excellent flower for cutting.

In some respects the long flowering 'Cinnabar' is
every inch a marigold. It is easily sown outdoors in spring,
shakes off early-season deluges, scoffs at late-summer
drought, and withstands light frost in early autumn. It
flowers exuberantly without fertilising, deadheading
or much else from the gardener. It will come true from
collected seeds, providing the mother plant has been
kept away from other marigolds. It suffers from almost no
pests or diseases and also attracts pollinating insects. **KK**

Alternatives

Tagetes patula 'Striped Marvel', *Tagetes patula*
'Tall Scotch Prize'

Tagetes
T. patula 'Tiger Eyes'

Main features Neat marigold for containers and raised beds; attracts insects; good for companion planting
Height 20 cm (8 in.) **Spread** 20 cm (8 in.)
Position ○ **Hardiness** Annual

French marigolds come in a variety of forms, but *T. patula* 'Tiger Eyes' is one of the most distinctive. A long-established favourite, it has showy double blooms with crested orange-yellow centres and drooping outer rings of mahogany-red petals that curl in to reveal a yellow reverse. With its large, easy to handle, bristly seeds (which germinate like mustard and cress), rapid growth and nonstop blooms, 'Tiger Eyes' is the perfect introduction to growing bedding plants for junior gardeners. It also makes a delightful edging to a bed or window box and looks great growing amongst red- and green-leaved, nonhearting lettuce, such as 'Salad Bowl' (*Lactuca sativa*). It is strongly aromatic, and the scent from these marigolds is thought to act as a deterrent to whitefly when grown alongside tomatoes, making 'Tiger Eyes' an ideal companion plant in a traditional cottage-style garden.

Sow seeds indoors in the spring in trays of seed compost. Maintain gentle warmth and keep the compost moist. Transplant (prick out) into individual pots or trays when the plants are large enough to handle and plant out after the last frost. 'Tiger Eyes' can also be sown directly into the garden soil in late spring, but as the plants are very prone to damage by slugs and snails, they may struggle compared to larger pot-grown plants that will get off to a flying start. Beer traps can be employed to drown the offenders, and night-time forays with a flashlight will reveal the culprits who can be picked off and despatched. Regular deadheading will keep the plants tidy and prolong the display. Fading heads can be snapped off easily between thumb and forefinger. This is a lot quicker (and more satisfying) than using snips or secateurs, but care is needed because the foliage may aggravate skin allergies. **GS**

Alternatives

Tagetes patula 'Sparky Mix', *Tagetes patula* 'Dainty Marietta', *Tagetes patula* 'Bolero'

Tagetes
T. patula 'Harlequin'

Main features Flowers summer to autumn; drought
tolerant; good for companion planting with edibles
Height 90 cm (3 ft) **Spread** 90 cm (3 ft)
Position ○ ◑ **Hardiness** Annual

This heritage nineteenth-century marigold has recently
been rediscovered. Technically a French marigold (*Tagetes
patula*), it, in fact, hails from Mexico, as do all marigolds.
It was the Aztecs who domesticated this pretty tough yet
useful plant, and even today an unimaginable number of
local heritage varieties are grown in its native land. There
they are used medicinally, in dyes and most importantly,
as the *flor de muertos* (flower of the dead) in Day of the
Dead celebrations. Curiously, the marigold occupies
an equally central place in religious observance on the
Indian subcontinent, although it was only introduced
there some 350 years ago.

As for *T. patula* 'Harlequin', it was rediscovered as
a result of the renewed interest in edible gardening.
Marigolds are useful in integrated pest management
in the organic kitchen garden, and although out of
fashion and out of commerce, 'Harlequin' was saved as a
'passalong' plant by generations of home gardeners who
were charmed by its simple beauty and its usefulness. Its
roots repel harmful soil organisms, its pleasantly pine-
scented leaves repel aphids and the charming single
flowers attract beneficial insects, including pollinators, to
the kitchen garden. Old-fashioned, heritage 'Harlequin'
is in many ways the modernist ideal: the perfect fusion
of good form and function.

It is not necessary to have a kitchen garden to desire
'Harlequin'. It is well branching and full of single flowers,
striped gold and mahogany red, like little pinwheels or
court jesters. Taller than modern marigold hybrids, it
blooms exuberantly from summer to the first frost. The
striping is more pronounced in cooler weather, so its
flowers are more yellow during summer extremes. It is
as pretty in a border as in a kitchen garden, for it weaves
and blends well with other border denizens. **KK**

Alternatives

Tagetes 'Mr Majestic', *Tagetes* 'Striped Marvel', *Tagetes*
'Tall Scotch Prize', *Tagetes* 'Villandry'

Thymophylla
T. tenuiloba

Main features Prolific display of bright-yellow daisies; prettily divided aromatic foliage
Height 30 cm (12 in.) **Spread** 45 cm (18 in.)
Position ○ **Hardiness** RHS H1c

It can be confusing when botanists feel the need to change the name of a plant, and then change it again, when research creates new insight and reveals the need for a rethink. It often results in the plant becoming less widely grown because it is listed under different names in different places, and gardeners become understandably irritated. Over the years *T. tenuiloba* has been known as *Chrysanthemum tenuilobum*, *Dyssodia tenuiloba* and *Hymenatherum tenuilobum*, all names that refer to the narrow-lobed foliage that is finely divided into pairs of slender leaflets. Although sometimes described as pungent, the leaves are appealingly aromatic and bright in colour; they make an ideal backdrop for the flowers that emerge through the foliage to open.

The close relationship between *Thymophylla* and *Tagetes* (marigolds) is clear from the 12 millimetre (0.5 in.) daisy-like flowers, with their bright-yellow ray petals set around a slightly orange-yellow centre. From early summer the blooms begin to open, but flowering may fade in late summer; clipping over with shears followed by a drench with water will usually promote a late flush. *T. tenuiloba* is quick to flower and often self-seeds freely. These self-sown seedlings will usually flower late the same year, thereby extending the season. Ideal at the front of a sunny border, the species also makes a good plant for growing in hanging baskets or at the edges of large containers. The flowers last well in small posies.

Native to southern Texas and northern Mexico, *T. tenuiloba* is actually a short-lived perennial plant in the wild and in gardens in the southern United States, but it is more often grown as a spring-sown annual. Untroubled by pests, it enjoys hot sunshine and good drainage but will flower for longer in less heat and with more moisture. **GR**

Alternatives

Thymophylla tenuiloba 'Golden Dawn', *Thymophylla pentachaeta*, *Thymophylla pentachaeta* var. *belenidium*

Tithonia
T. rotundifolia 'Torch'

Main features Flowers from late summer to autumn; attracts bees and butterflies; good cut flower; drought tolerant **Height** 1.8 m (6 ft) **Spread** 60 cm (24 in.) **Position** ○ **Hardiness** Annual

Plants that can be grown easily from seeds are always a great find, especially if they grow as quickly and become as spectacular as does the Mexican sunflower in one growing season. *T. rotundifolia* 'Torch' grows very tall very fast, producing successive large, bright-orange flowers for months from midsummer to the first frost. The blaze of late-summer colour that it provides can be hard to achieve at that time of the year. Height does vary depending on where it is grown and the weather, usually at least 90 centimetres (3 ft) and often up to 1.8 metres (6 ft).

Dark-green, lobed leaves cover branching stems, which, along with the velvety orange petals and fetching bright-yellow flower centre that is a typical feature of the daisy family, help to give the plant its universal appeal. A native of Mexico, it needs plenty of sun to flower well, so give it a prime spot in your border, where it can bask all day long. Plant it with dark-red dahlias or purple *Cleome* for dramatic contrast, or team it with *Ricinus communis* and *Rudbeckia hirta* 'Cherokee Sunset' for a truly hot combination.

In very warm climates, Mexican sunflowers can be sown directly into the soil, but because it needs heat, in colder regions, a better option would be to start the seed off in spring indoors, then plant out when all danger of frost has passed. Both bees and butterflies love the blooms, and it makes a striking cut flower, although it needs some care when being picked, as the stems are hollow and easily damaged. It can be sown in succession if you are growing it as a cut flower; the orange flowers are particularly welcome in the autumn. *Tithonia* 'Fiesta del Sol' packs all the punch of 'Torch' but is much shorter (75 cm/2.5 ft) so would be a better option in a smaller space or in a patio pot. The species is considered invasive in Australia and parts of Africa. **JS**

Alternatives

Tithonia rotundifolia 'Yellow Torch', *Tithonia rotundifolia* 'Fiesta del Sol', *Tithonia rotundifolia* 'Goldfinger'

Torenia
T. fournieri

Main features Flowers summer to autumn;
tolerant of shade
Height 15–30 cm (6–12 in.) **Spread** 25–30 cm (10–12 in.)
Position ◑ ● **Hardiness** RHS H2

A bushy annual that is noted for its ability to bloom well in shady conditions, *Torenia* features two-lipped, tubular, trumpet-shaped flowers that are usually bicolour. As a member of the figwort family, its bright and quirky upturned flowers resemble snapdragons, with wide-open mouths showing off delicate throats marked with anthers that join at the tips in the shape of a chicken's wishbone (hence the common name, wishbone flower). Visiting bees delight in these cheerful flowers and break the wishbone while pollinating.

T. fournieri is native to Vietnam, but most of the hybrids in commerce are the result of crosses with other species native to subtropical regions of Asia and Africa. Tolerant of shade, heat and humidity, they brighten summer landscapes, flowering copiously just as many other flowering plants take a pause. Since *T. fournieri* is a perennial in frost-free climates, it can be taken in and overwintered as a houseplant. The species is typically light blue, but hybridisers have been busy, and cultivars are available in a wide range of colours, including blue, lavender, pink, white and burgundy. The white cultivar is perhaps the most elegant, because it is a pure white marked with a single golden splotch just inside the mouth, acting as a sort of landing pad for bees.

Grown easily from seeds but frequently offered as young plants, *Torenia* is self-cleaning, it blooms nonstop until the first frost, and is rarely bothered by pests or disease. Lovely as a patio edger, it excels in hanging baskets and window boxes because the plants form mounds that eventually trail over and down the sides. It is also useful as a seasonal ground cover in shady gardens, because stems will root where they touch moist soil, which means that *Torenia* will propagate easily from cuttings too. **KK**

Alternatives

Torenia fournieri 'Summer Wave Blue', *Torenia fournieri* 'Clown Blue', *Torenia fournieri* 'Moon Indigo'

Trachelium
T. caeruleum Devotion Series

Main features Broad domes of tiny flowers; long-lasting
cut flowers; good container plants
Height 45–90 cm (18–36 in.) **Spread** 30 cm (12 in.)
Position ○ **Hardiness** RHS H3

This delightful relation of *Campanula* has been popular
since Victorian times. *T. caeruleum* grows wild on the
northern and southern sides of the Mediterranean (in
Portugal, Spain and Sicily, as well as in Algeria and Morocco)
in damp or shady places, usually on limey soil. The
resemblance to *Campanula* is clear: the broad, domed
heads – up to 15 centimetres (6 in.) in diameter – are made
up of a large number of very small flowers, like upturned
bells, with five points around the edge. These flowers tend
to be mauve or violet blue rather than a clear, pure blue.
The flower clusters are held on strong upright stems that
are clothed in alternately arranged, dark-green, pointed
leaves, which contribute especially well to the plant's value
as a cut flower. In the wild *T. caeruleum* is a perennial, but
in gardens it is usually grown as a spring-sown annual.

Two types of *T. caeruleum* have been developed. In
the 1800s tall types were grown, often in greenhouses,
either to be used as cut flowers or as large and impressive
pot plants, reaching up to 90 centimetres (3 ft) in height.
Nowadays, shorter, bushier types, including *T. caeruleum*
Devotion Series – with flowers in blue, burgundy,
purple and white – have been developed as pot plants,
reaching about 45 centimetres (18 in.) in height. These
varieties can also be planted in sunny, well-drained
situations outside, and they are well suited to large
containers. However, they will flower poorly in high heat
and high humidity.

T. caeruleum 'Lake Michigan' – in blue, purple, deep
violet and white – is a series of cultivars that is specifically
used as cut flowers, reaching 90 centimetres (3 ft) in
height. In *T. caeruleum* 'Hamer Pandora', the deep violet-
blue flowers are combined with purple-tinted foliage.
Cut the whole stem when about a quarter of the flowers
are open, and they should last about two weeks. **GR**

Alternatives

Trachelium caeruleum 'Lake Michigan', *Trachelium
caeruleum* 'Hamer Pandora'

Trachymene
T. coerulea 'Blue Lace'

Main features Dome-shaped heads of almost blue
blooms; good cut flower; attracts pollinators
Height 60 cm (24 in.) **Spread** 20 cm (8 in.)
Position ○ **Hardiness** Annual

Although it would be fair to assume that the flowers of
this wild Australian native would be blue, in fact, they are
never true blue and even the flowers of garden cultivars
have a touch of mauve. Sometimes listed under its old
name, *Didiscus caeruleus*, *T. coerulea* 'Blue Lace' includes
pink and white forms, but it is as close to a pure blue as
can be found, with the faintest lavender tints and a purple
eye to each floret. It is a member of the vast carrot family
and, like many of its relations, lasts unusually well in water
as a cut flower. Reaching about 60 centimetres (24 in.) in
height, its olive-tinted leaves are finely divided in the same
way as carrot leaves. Plants are usually well branched,
without the need for pinching, and the tiny florets bloom
through the summer, opening first around the edge of the
domed heads and then opening progressively towards
the centre. The clusters of unopened florets are a darker
shade. 'Blue Lace' also makes an attractive container
plant, especially as the flowers have a sweet scent and
are much appreciated by hoverflies. **GR**

Alternative

Trachymene coerulea 'White Lace'

Tropaeolum
T. majus Alaska Series

Main features Bright-green leaves marbled in white;
trumpet-shaped flowers in a range of fiery colours
Height 30 cm (12 in.) **Spread** 50 cm (20 in.)
Position ○ **Hardiness** Annual

The origins of the nasturtium, *T. majus*, are slightly unclear.
This vigorous annual sprawler and climber is found
apparently growing wild in the South American Andes,
from Columbia south to Bolivia. However, it seems likely
that it is, in fact, an ancient hybrid derived from three or
four genuinely native *Tropaeolum* species. Introduced into
northern gardens in 1684, its succulent stems carry large,
rounded, peppery-tasting, bright-green leaves, which are
rich in vitamin C. Trumpet-shaped orange flowers open
on long stems all summer and are followed by large seed.
The flowers are often hidden by the leaves. *T. majus* Alaska
Series is a bushy form, with the additional special feature
of its foliage being marbled and mottled in white. The
series includes a wide range of flower colours, including
scarlet, salmon, rose, gold, orange and yellow, as well as a
peachy shade. Grow Alaska Series in a sunny place at the
front of the border, trailing over a low wall or billowing
over the edge of a raised bed. It also works well in large
tubs and even in hanging baskets. **GR**

Alternative

Tropaeolum majus 'Jewel of Africa'

Tropaeolum majus Alaska Series brings quick colour to raised beds. ➲

Verbena
V. bonariensis

Main features Contemporary, summer-long blooms; good for garden display, wildlife and cutting
Height 2.4 m (8 ft) **Spread** 1.2 m (4 ft)
Position ○ **Hardiness** RHS H3

Like many things, gardening has been subject to the whims of fashion for centuries, and plants can plummet from being the latest must-have choice to being an also-ran in a matter of a few years. However, the demand for the distinctive qualities of this easy-to-raise *Verbena* shows no sign of tailing off. Perhaps this is because the plant lends itself so well to associations with ornamental grasses and other prolific self-seeders, such as purple fennel, as well as with broad drifts of perennials, such as *Achillea* and *Helenium*. The sparse branching habit of *V. bonariensis* means that it can be sited close to border edges in traditional or gravel gardens to give valuable height without shading out other plants. It has one of the longest flowering periods of any plant – from late spring to early autumn – although young plants grown from spring-sown seeds may only really get up steam by late summer. The small purple flowers are rated highly as a nectar source for bees and butterflies. **GS**

Alternatives

Verbena bonariensis 'Lollipop', *Verbena bonariensis* 'Little One', *Verbena rigida*

Verbena
V. tenuisecta 'Imagination'

Main features Clusters of deep, violet-blue flowers; good spreading plant
Height 22 cm (9 in.) **Spread** 60 cm (2 ft)
Position ○ **Hardiness** RHS H4

The *Verbena* is a varied group of around 250 species, including annuals, perennials and shrubby types, as well as upright and spreading, extremely frost hardy and rather tender types. *V. tenuisecta* is a desert species from South America, but it is naturalised all across the southern United States, from Florida through Texas to California. Although it grows wild in hot sun and dry, well-drained soil, in gardens, the plant is more adaptable. *V. tenuisecta* 'Imagination' was developed in Germany and introduced in 1993. Originally thought to be a hybrid, it was selected for its rich violet flower colour, its prolific flowering and its low, spreading but more restrained habit. The clusters of purple flowers arise on stalks from the leaf joints, and each cluster is made up of up to fifteen small florets, each with five lobes divided at the tip and with a tiny white eye. 'Imagination' is ideal growing in hanging baskets and trailing from other containers. It also makes an effective summer ground cover when planted in sunny borders. **GR**

Alternatives

Verbena tenuisecta 'Decked Out', *Verbena tenuisecta* 'Desert Jewels', *Verbena* Aztec Magic Series

❧ *Verbena bonariensis* has small flowers that are very rich in nectar.

Verbena

Lanai Twister Pink

Viola

Sorbet Series

Main features Flowers summer to first frost; attracts
bees, butterflies and moths; good bedding plant
Height 25 cm (10 in.) **Spread** 30–45 cm (12–18 in.)
Position ○ **Hardiness** RHS H2

Main feature Flowers in a huge range of charming
colours and patterns on neat plants
Height 15 cm (6 in.) **Spread** 20 cm (8 in.)
Position ○ ◑ **Hardiness** Annual

Two-tone flowers such as *Verbena* Lanai Twister Pink
always add a bit of glamour to a planting. A multitude
of individual, five-petalled flowers are arranged in a circle
at the end of the shoots. The three outer petals are white,
with a hint of pink, while the two inward-facing petals
are sugar pink, and the new buds peek enticingly through
the centre of the flower head. The award-winning Lanai
Twister Series has been bred to flower right through
summer until the first frost. It loves the heat, so should
preferably be grown in full sun. Grown as a cutting-raised
annual, Lanai Twister Pink looks stunning trailing down
the edge of a tall container topped with a puff of blue
Ageratum houstonianum, or a cherry pie-scented heliotrope.
When used for mass planting, try interspersing it with
the occasional rich ruby-coloured leaves of *Iresine herbstii*
'Brilliantissima'. Other colours in the series include Twister
Red and Twister Blue, both with two-tone flowers. **MP**

The *Viola* is among the most charming of small perennials
and annuals, and there are about 500 wild species and
thousands of cultivars; there are even a few small shrubs.
Although common in the cooler regions of the northern
hemisphere, a few species can be found in South America
and Australasia. In gardens, the types most frequently
seen are pansies and violas, and here the names are a
little confusing. *Viola* is the botanical name for the genus,
and 'viola' is used as the popular name for the colourful,
small-flowered annuals and biennials often grown from
seeds in gardens. Seed-raised violas for autumn, spring
and summer displays are mainly neat plants with dark-
green stems topped with distinctive five-petalled flowers,
in pure colours, bicolours and pretty patterns, often with
charming dark whiskers. *V.* Sorbet Series was developed
in Japan and includes more than two dozen cultivars in
an exceptional range of cheerful colours. **GR**

Alternatives

Verbena rigida, *Verbena rigida* f. *lilacina* 'Polaris',
Verbena 'Seabrooks Lavender'

Alternatives

Viola cornuta Floral Power Series, *Viola cornuta* Penny
Series, *Viola cornuta* Velour Series

Viola Sorbet Series are neat plants that can bring colour to the smallest container. ➔

Viola
V. cornuta
Endurio Series

Main features Flowers in autumn, winter and spring;
scented; spreading, slightly trailing shape
Height 15 cm (6 in.) **Spread** 25 cm (10 in.)
Position ○ ◐ **Hardiness** RHS H5

The *Viola* is sold as winter-flowering bedding, but the
majority of types will only really bloom well when
the temperature starts to rise in spring. Plants in the
V. cornuta Endurio Series are unusual in that they will
start to flower in autumn and can carry on blooming
when temperatures drop in winter in northern temperate
regions, even when they are under a light covering of
snow. The series includes a wide range of colours, and
it is often sold as a mixture, either of similar colours or a
more random mix that can look very bright and lively.
Typically, *V. cornuta* has a delicious, sweet scent, and at its
best will be covered in a mass of small blooms. Endurio is
often described as a trailing plant, but it is mostly quite
upright and spreading, only trailing slightly when plants
start to grow faster in spring. Plant it with ornamental
kale or cabbage, or with a shrub such as the handsome
Skimmia japonica 'Rubella', and some trailing ivy. **JS**

Alternatives

Viola cornuta Teardrops Series, *Viola cornuta* Avalanche
Series, *Viola wittrockiana* × *cornuta* 'Cool Wave'

Viola
V. cornuta
'Deltini Honey Bee'

Main feature Flowers autumn, winter, spring and early
summer
Height 15 cm (6 in.) **Spread** 20 cm (8 in.)
Position ○ ◐ **Hardiness** RHS H5

The blooms of *V. cornuta* 'Deltini Honey Bee' are an unusual
shade of warm mustard green, with markings that look like
cute little faces, and a delightful, sweet scent. It can flower
through surprisingly cool winter weather and is capable
of flowering from autumn into late spring if temperatures
do not drop too low. During cold weather the striking
mustard colour will change to a combination of yellow
and purple, but it soon reverts to its original colour when
temperatures start to rise. 'Deltini Honey Bee' is a stocky
little plant that is uniform in shape and flowering time,
which keeps the display neat and floriferous. Its upright
shape makes it best suited to pot growing, but it does
well in the ground too. Make the most of winter flowers
by combining them with foliage plants, such as *Hebe
ochracea* 'James Stirling', which has a similar mustard-
green hue; the evergreen sedge *Carex oshimensis* 'Evergold';
or the bronze-leaved *Primula vulgaris* 'Claddagh'. **JS**

Alternatives

Viola cornuta 'Sorbet Peach Melba', *Viola cornuta* 'Sorbet
Morpho XP', *Viola* × *wittrockiana* 'Envy'

Zinnia

Z. hybrida
Profusion Series

Main features Bright and colourful, single or double
summer flowers; short spreading plants
Height 38 cm (15 in.) **Spread** 50 cm (20 in.)
Position ○ **Hardiness** RHS H1b

The *Zinnia* is a colourful flower in the daisy family, native
to grassland and open scrub. The largest concentration
of species is in Mexico, but its distribution stretches north
into the south-western United States. Almost all *Zinnia*
are annuals, although there are also some slightly shrubby
species. The *Z. hybrida* Profusion Series, developed in
Japan, makes neat plants that are wider than they are
high. All the colours in the series are well-matched for
size and flowering time. They are also unusually heat and
drought tolerant, and their dependable disease resistance
allows gardeners to grow them without fear of their
display being ruined by disease. The Profusion Series is
divided into two parts. Plants in the original series have
single flowers in purple, pink, orange, yellow and white
shades. The more recent Profusion Double Series has
double flowers in similar shades, and it matches the
single-flowered cultivars for size and development. **GR**

Alternatives

Zinnia elegans Dreamland Series, *Zinnia marylandica*
Zahara Series

Zinnia

Z. marylandica
'Zahara Double Fire'

Main features Flowers summer to first frost; suitable as a
bedding, border or container plant; good cut flower
Height 45 cm (18 in.) **Spread** 50 cm (20 in.)
Position ○ **Hardiness** RHS H1b

An award-winning *Zinnia* that is really worth growing,
the vibrant orange-red *Z. marylandica* 'Zahara Double
Fire' adds real zing to the garden. The fully double
flowers are held above the mid-green foliage, and the
compact nature of the plant, growing into a flower-filled
mound, makes it ideal as a plant for borders, bedding and
containers. Grown as a summer annual, *Zinnia* – originally
from Mexico – is drought tolerant once established,
shows good disease resistance and is best grown in full
sun. If vibrant colour is not for you, *Z. marylandica* 'Zahara
Double Strawberry' is an excellent alternative with the
same fully double flowers, but in deep pink. For a tall
container, fill the top with 'Zahara Double Fire' and set
off this gem of a plant with the trailing silver foliage of
Dichondra argentea 'Silver Falls', or perhaps surround the
bold orange-red blooms with the dainty white flowers
of *Euphorbia hypericifolia* 'Diamond Frost'. **MP**

Alternatives

Zinnia marylandica 'Zahara Sunburst', *Zinnia marylandica*
'Zahara Starlight Rose', *Zinnia elegans* Benary's Series

BULBS, CORMS AND TUBERS

Here are plants that last from one year to the next, thanks to an underground storage phase in their life cycle. The benefit for the gardener is that this dormant stage is the ideal time to buy and plant them without too much concern about planting times and watering. Within this chapter are bulbous plants best considered as annuals – amaryllis and forced hyacinths, for example – alongside plants that just get better and better each year: naturalised snowdrops or species cyclamen.

The most familiar bulbs are those such as the daffodils and tulips that flower in springtime. Planting their dry bulbs the previous autumn is a measure of a gardener thinking ahead to the next season. But there are bulbs for all seasons: for summer scent, colour and cut flowers, for the last hurrah of autumn and for the earliest flowers of winter.

◉ *Tulipa* 'Flaming Parrot' creates excitement in spring thanks to autumn planting of dry bulbs.

Allium
A. cowanii

Main features Flowers in spring; excellent as cut flowers; scented blooms
Height 40 cm (16 in.) **Spread** 7 cm (3 in.)
Position ○ ◑ **Hardiness** RHS H3

Grown for their showy flower heads, alliums belong to the group of small-flowered ornamental onions. Closely related to *Allium neapolitanum* and *Allium subhirsutum*, *A. cowanii* distinguishes itself from the latter two varieties by its noticeably larger flower, which keeps well for quite some time. The stalk is three-sided and grows up to 40 centimetres (16 in.) in height. In the beginning of the growing period, the stalk looks like a corkscrew, but it straightens out shortly before the flowers start to open. The delicate snow-white flower umbel comprises fifteen to twenty short-stemmed flowers with contrasting green pistils. Originally from southern Europe and North Africa, *A. cowanii* flowers in early spring and is a good cut flower with a pleasant scent; it regularly features in bridal bouquets. The flowers can also be eaten in salads. Best grown in full sun or dappled shade and in fertile, well-drained soil, it is striking planted in combination with *Brunnera* (Caucasian forget-me-not). This bulb is also good for perennialising.

There is a story that onions became universally known after the Fall from Grace, when the devil deserted Paradise. On the places where the devil's right foot defiled the earth, onions grew; where his left foot troubled the earth, garlic sprouted; and where his tail fouled the soil, leeks grew. The sulphurous odour he gave forth created the smaller species of allium. In spite of its origins, alliums were also regarded as holy. Ancient Egyptian priests treated the form of an onion bulb as a symbol of the universe. In the round globe they saw heaven, hell and Earth. As an allium bulb has seven 'skirts' (layers), it is thought to protect against seven evil spirits and also against witches and devils. Fresh allium contains antibiotic properties and is used medicinally to treat various conditions. **FR/MS**

Alternatives

Syn. *Allium neapolitanum* Cowanii Group. *Allium zebdanense, Allium triquetrum, Allium unifolium*

Allium
A. schubertii

Main feature Eye-catching, starburst flower heads in summer
Height 50 cm (20 in.) **Spread** 20 cm (8 in.)
Position ○ **Hardiness** RHS H4

If you want to introduce a touch of drama to your garden, look no further than the large-headed *A. schubertii*. It is one of the most distinctive of all the alliums, with gigantic dark-pink/purple flower heads that look like exploding fireworks in summer. Each flower head is made up of around fifty tiny flowers that radiate outwards on stalks of varying lengths, which add to the spectacular starburst effect.

Allium bulbs are best planted in September, at least 15 centimetres (6 in.) deep; you may also come across them in pots at the garden centre at flowering time. As the flower heads are so large (around 30 cm/12 in. across), plant them at least 38 centimetres (15 in.) apart for maximum impact. These ornamental onion bulbs should come back and flower for many years. They prefer a well-drained soil (if you do not have this, add plenty of grit when planting and ensure it does not become too waterlogged) and enjoy a good baking in summer. Divide large clumps in spring or autumn. Their stems are shorter than some alliums (around 50 cm/20 in.), and as with many varieties, the strappy leaves begin to die back before flowering, which can look unsightly. Best planted en masse or at a minimum of three plants. Grow them through lower-growing perennials, such as hardy geraniums or *Alchemilla mollis*, to conceal any unsightliness.

In its native Eastern Mediterranean, the giant seed head separates from the plant and rolls in the wind – like a tumbleweed dispersing seed. It will self-seed in your garden too. The flower heads are attractive to butterflies, bees and other pollinating insects and are also much loved by flower arrangers, who use the heads either fresh or dried. You could spray the dried heads gold, silver or red for a dramatic Christmas decoration – they make a perfect star for the top of the tree. **VP**

Alternatives

Allium cristophii, Allium amethystinum 'Red Mohican', *Allium atropurpureum × schubertii*

Allium

A. hollandicum 'Purple Sensation'

Main features Late-spring to early-summer flowers; attracts bees and butterflies; good cut flower
Height 90 cm (3 ft) **Spread** 15 cm (6 in.)
Position ○ ◑ **Hardiness** RHS H7

Sturdy stems topped with long-lasting, richly coloured pompom flowers make 'Purple Sensation' a favourite with garden designers. The deep-purple blooms open in early summer as the grey-green leaves are dying back, and their lollipop heads create dramatic displays when planted en masse alongside grasses, cream-coloured camassias and hardy geraniums. After flowering, the performance continues as plants form impressive seed heads resembling green-tipped exploding stars. These plants are ideal for gravel or wildlife gardens; they can also lend colour and architectural interest to smaller gardens or balconies planted in raised beds or patio containers. This reliable allium was bred from *A. hollandicum* and has deeper coloured, more compact flower heads than its parent. Plant in groups in the autumn, ideally behind later flowering perennial plants that will form a screen to disguise the dying foliage. **ZA**

Alternatives

Allium 'Beau Regard', *Allium* 'Rosenbachianum', *Allium* 'Globemaster', *Allium* 'Mount Everest', *Allium nigrum*

 Allium hollandicum '**Purple Sensation**' is a simple way to bring strong colour and form to early summer beds and borders.

Amaryllis

A. belladonna

Main features Early to mid-autumn fragrant flowers; good cut flower
Height 60–75 cm (24–30 in.) **Spread** 45 cm (18 in.)
Position ○ **Hardiness** RHS H3

Not to be confused with the indoor amaryllis (*Hippeastrum*), *A. belladonna* is hardier and can be grown outside in warm, sheltered positions in direct sunlight. It produces smaller, pink, fragrant, trumpet-shaped flowers up to 10 centimetres (4 inches) long in clusters from six to twelve in autumn. These are good for garden colour and are excellent for cutting and indoor decoration. Plant in summer with the tip of the bulb level with the soil or compost surface, 30 centimetres (12 in.) apart. The long, strap-like leaves appear after the flowers and last through winter and into the following summer. They are susceptible to cold and frost, so in cold climates it is important to mulch the plants in autumn and cover in winter. Alternatively, grow them in containers and overwinter indoors. Keep the foliage of pot-grown plants growing for as long as possible and feed monthly, when in leaf, with a liquid feed to strengthen the bulb. Be aware, this plant is harmful if eaten. **GH**

Alternatives

Amaryllis belladonna 'Johannesburg', *Amaryllis belladonna* 'Kimberley', *Amaryllis belladonna* 'Cape of Good Hope'

Anemone
A. blanda

Main features Saucer-shaped flowers; blooms in spring; dormant in summer; attracts bees
Height 13 cm (5 in.) **Spread** 25 cm (10 in.)
Position ○ ◑ **Hardiness** RHS H5

An established colony of this anemone is one of the joys of the spring garden. Three-lobed and toothed leaves emerge in early spring, flushed with red on the underside, and carpet the ground. Daisy-like flowers appear, held above the foliage, usually in blue, with a boss of creamy stamen in the centre, but pink or white forms are also common. The specific name 'blanda' means 'enchanting', which suits this diminutive tuberous-rooted perennial. By early summer the show is over, and this plant, belonging to the buttercup family, vanishes underground until next spring. Before planting the wizened tubers, soak them overnight in water and they will plump up. There is not a right or wrong way to position the tubers when planting; they will sort themselves out. For best effect plant in bold drifts 5 to 8 centimetres (2–3 in.) deep in a well-drained, humus-rich soil. If they are happy, they will self-seed and become naturalised. They can be grown in containers but are happiest in the open ground. **MP**

Alternative

Anemone nemorosa 'Robinsoniana'

Anemone
A. coronaria
De Caen Group

Main features Flowers in spring and summer; blooms in red, blue and white; good cut flower
Height 30 cm (12 in.) **Spread** 15 cm (6 in.)
Position ○ **Hardiness** RHS H5

A genus from the family *Ranunculaceae*, many anemones are pretty garden varieties that are grown for their attractive flowers. *A. coronaria* De Caen loves a warm sunny spot in the garden. Besides being a good perennialiser, it is also an excellent cut flower. Instead of cutting, however, twist the flower stem and pull. This makes them last longer in a vase. Tuberous anemones (corms) are well known as summer flowers, but they also bloom in the spring. In southern areas, anemones are the first plants to bloom, but, as a rule, tuberous anemones bloom at any desired time. For spring flowering, the corms must be planted in autumn, but they must not be planted too deep because the leaves need to be allowed to form quickly. In autumn, plant a handful of anemones between tulip bulbs and you will have a dazzling combination in spring. If they are planted in spring, they flower in midsummer. Before planting corms, soak them in warm water for a few hours and they will root better. **FR/MS**

Alternative

Anemone coronaria Harmony Series

Anemone coronaria **De Caen Group** grown in rows in a cutting garden by planting corms in the autumn or spring. ●

Arisaema
A. candidissimum

Main features Flowers in summer; fragrant flowers; architectural plant
Height 30–40 cm (12–16 in.) **Spread** 15 cm (6 in.)
Position ○ ◑ **Hardiness** RHS H4

This must surely be the beauty queen of this interesting and curious group, whose relatives probably rank among the weirdest and most otherworldly looking of all plants. It is well into summer before the typical arum-style flower of *A. candidissimum* emerges, so mark the spot carefully. The flower consists of a white spathe, striped with green outside and pink inside. Another surprise is that the flowers are sweetly scented, and are closely followed by a single leaf consisting of three large leaflets. These persist until the autumn, when they turn buff yellow before vanishing to survive the winter as an underground tuber. A clump of the foliage is in itself attractive.

This is one of the easier to please of this group of plants. Growing to 30 to 40 centimetres (12–16 in.), these gems prefer a sunny or lightly shaded, moisture-retentive, but well-drained soil rich in leaf mould. The tubers are very vulnerable to drying out if lifted, so it is preferable to buy pot-grown plants. The plant originates from western China and was introduced by George Forrest in 1914. A good alternative is *Anemone griffithii*, from the Himalayas. The spathe is netted in maroon and white and arches over, giving it a sinister, hooded appearance.

A. candidissimum associates well with earlier-flowering woodland plants – such as *Anemone blanda*, *Anemone nemorosa* or even *Cardamone quinquifolia* – all of which have completed their life cycle and died down before the *Arisaema* emerges, thus making good use of the same piece of ground. Alternatively, plant a group adjacent to the Japanese painted fern (*Athyrium nipponicum* var. *pictum*), where the colour and texture of the leaves will complement each other. Although hardy for many regions, plants could be grown in a cool greenhouse in very cold areas. Note that plants are harmful if eaten and can irritate the skin and eyes. **MP**

Alternative

Arisaema sikokianum

Arisarum
A. proboscideum

Main features Spring foliage and flowers; summer dormant; popular with children
Height 15–20 cm (6–8 in.) **Spread** 30 cm (12 in.)
Position ◐ ● **Hardiness** RHS H5

There are not too many plants that 'hide their light under a bushel', but this endearing plant – also known as the mouse plant or mouse-tailed arum – does just that. In early spring a carpet of shiny, green, broadly arrow-shaped leaves emerges, growing to a height of 15 to 20 centimetres (6–8 in.). Later in spring the 'mice' appear, hidden among the leaves. The flowers are typical of the *Araceae* family and have a tubular spathe, white at the base, that gradually becomes striped with deep maroon. The spathe continues to elongate – creating the tail of the mouse – and can be up to 15 centimetres (6 in.) long. The spadix is concealed inside the 'mouse's body' and gives off a mushroom-like smell to attract fungus gnats that act as pollinators. It is the perfect plant for children to explore and find the 'mice'.

A native of Mediterranean regions, *A. proboscideum* enjoys a lightly shaded position in any damp soil. Plant the rhizomes in the autumn, 10 centimetres (4 in.) deep and 30 centimetres (12 in.) apart. By midsummer the leaves and 'mice' will have vanished, leaving behind hardy underground tubers to survive the drier summer conditions. The initial clump will spread slowly. It can also be grown in a container and would make an interesting and easily viewed subject for an alpine house. Make sure to protect the plants from slugs and snails, which eat and spoil the emerging growth.

As this plant goes dormant in summer, leaving the ground bare, it offers the ideal opportunity for layer planting of later-flowering species. *Roscoea purpurea* does not emerge until the *A. proboscideum* foliage is dying away, so can be planted in the same space. The variegated form of Solomon's seal (*Polygonatum × hybridum* 'Striatum') may also be used in the same way, as can the tall stately stems of a close relative, *Arisaema tortuosum*. **MP**

Alternative

Arisarum vulgare

Arum

A. *italicum* subsp. *Italicum* 'Marmoratum'

Main features Marbled winter to late-spring foliage;
greenish-yellow spring flowers; orange-red autumn berries
Height 30 cm (12 in.) **Spread** 20 cm (8 in.)
Position ◑ ● **Hardiness** RHS H6

Ideal for woodland gardens, the eye-catching marbled foliage of this arum covers the ground from autumn through to early summer, making a decorative blanket of glossy cream and green leaves beneath trees and shrubs. Although the large arrow-shaped foliage is its star quality, in autumn, 'Marmoratum' produces elegant poker-like flower heads wrapped in greenish-yellow petal-like spathes. The blooms are followed by spikes of bright orange-red berries, which form after the foliage has died back. In very cold areas the foliage may die back in winter, reappearing as soon as temperatures climb.

Team 'Marmoratum' with spring bulbs, including snowdrops, daffodils and woodland anemones, (*Anemone nemorosa*), together with autumn crocuses (*Colchicum autumnale*), which make a good match for the arum's bright berries. Also try it with hostas, which enjoy the same shady position and fill the gap when the arum's leaves die down in summer. Another arum to consider is *Arum maculatum,* which shares many of the same characteristics as the Italian form, but its purple-spotted foliage is not as showy. The slightly tender *A. creticum* has large, scented pale-yellow flowers and plain green leaves, and makes a decorative late-spring container plant, where it can be protected from frost. One word of caution: all parts of this plant are toxic if eaten, and are skin and eye irritants, so it is not a good choice for family gardens.

Plants grow from tubers, but 'Marmoratum' is most commonly sold as a perennial in a pot. In autumn, plant it in a shady spot in moisture-retentive soil – dig in well-rotted compost or manure a few weeks beforehand to help it establish. Within a few years it will form large clumps; remove unwanted seedlings to prevent it from becoming invasive. **ZA**

Alternatives

Arum maculatum, Arum creticum, Arum italicum subsp. *italicum* 'Tiny'

Camassia
C. quamash

Main features Spikes of early-summer purple-blue starry flowers; strap-shaped foliage; good cut flower
Height 50 cm (20 in.) **Spread** 20 cm (8 in.)
Position ○ ◑ ● **Hardiness** RHS H7

The shortest of the camassias, reaching just below knee height, this diminutive bulb produces a splash of early-summer colour, plugging the gap between spring bulbs and the raft of perennial summer flowers. A North American meadow plant – *C. quamash* was traditionally used as a food crop by Native American peoples – this dainty camassia features spikes of dark purple-blue starry flowers with bright golden stamen above a mound of sword-shaped foliage. Its relaxed habit makes it ideal for naturalising in rough grass and open meadow, or use it at the front of an informal planting scheme. Happy in boggy soils, it can also be planted along the margins of a pond or stream.

Partner up your camassias with primulas, low-growing hardy geraniums, such as the white *Geranium maculatum* f. *albiflorum* or *Geranium sylvaticum* 'Album' backed by leafy hostas, epimediums and ferns. For the best results, in autumn choose a sunny or partially shaded spot and plant groups of bulbs about 7 centimetres (3 in.) deep in moisture-retentive soil. Although camassias enjoy damp conditions, they will tolerate soils that dry out in summer. Bear in mind that camassias become dormant in summer and you will need later-flowering plants in front to hide the gaps. Also, if planting in grass, do not mow until the flowers and foliage have died down.

Other camassias worth trying include the cultivar 'Blue Melody', which has the same deep-blue flowers but with an underskirt of cream-edged foliage. Alternatively, if you are looking for a taller plant, *Camassia leichtlinii* subsp. *suksdorfii* grows up to 1.2 metres (4 ft) in height and sports blue or white flowers, depending on the variety. For earlier-flowering examples, opt for *Camassia cusickii*, a tall, blue form that blooms in late spring. **ZA**

Alternatives

Camassia leichtlinii subsp. *suksdorfii* Caerulea Group,
Camassia leichtlinii subsp. *suksdorfii* 'Alba'

Canna
'Erebus'

Main features Flowers in late summer; attractive foliage;
suitable for water gardens
Height 1.8 m (6 ft) **Spread** 80 cm (2.5 ft)
Position ○ **Hardiness** RHS H3

Originally from tropical and subtropical America,
C. 'Erebus' is a curiosity among cannas because it needs
to grow in water. It is a herbaceous perennial with long,
sturdy, unbranched flower stems bearing spires of delicate
pink flowers with a blush of salmon. Each plant produces
stunning soft, grey-green, lance-shaped leaves edged
with a cream-coloured pinstripe. This foliage in particular
provides a tropical touch to the garden. In cooler climates
the plants are not hardy and should be brought into a
frost-free greenhouse in autumn. There, the pots should
be kept moist but not saturated. These cannas are useful
in the garden and water garden, as they are fast growers.
They require full sun and medium-wet to wet soil. They
grow rapidly to 1.8 metres (6 ft) in height, and flower in
late summer. In spring, water cannas can be placed in
containers with fertile soil in ponds with no more than
15 centimetres (6 in.) of water over the roots. They can
also be integrated in well-watered borders; potted plants
can be stood in deep saucers of water. **FR/MS**

Alternatives

Canna 'Endeavour', *Canna* 'Ra', *Canna glauca*

Canna
'Phasion'

Main features Flowers and striking foliage in summer
and autumn; architectural plant
Height 1.8 m (6 ft) **Spread** 60 cm (2 ft)
Position ○ ◑ **Hardiness** RHS H3

This is not a plant for the fainthearted, but for those who
love drama C. 'Phasion' is a must. The large paddle-shaped
leaves are held upright and offer a psychedelic mix of
purple, yellow and orange perpendicular stripes, topped
on stiff, tall stems by orange flowers. It is spectacular if
positioned so that the foliage is backlit by the sun. Given
a warm growing season and plenty of water, this plant
can reach 1.8 metres (6 ft) when in bloom and is the
perfect addition to any subtropical-themed border. In
summer the large flowers are held well above the leaves.
In mild climates the underground rhizomes may survive
outdoors, especially if given a generous layer of mulch,
but for those in colder climes, it is preferable to lift the
roots and store them in frost-free conditions in winter.
It makes a striking dot plant emerging from lower, hot
colour-themed, summer bedding schemes. It can also
be used to make a centrepiece for a large container,
perhaps with *Plectranthus argentatus*, whose silver leaves
add a calming effect to the vibrant canna foliage. **MP**

Alternatives

Canna 'Stuttgart', *Canna* 'Striped Beauty', *Canna* 'Striata'

◑ *Canna* 'Erebus' is a water canna that thrives in wet ground.

Chionodoxa
C. luciliae

Main features Small, blue, star-shaped spring flowers;
strappy, mid-green leaves; good for naturalising
Height 15 cm (6 in.) **Spread** 5 cm (2 in.)
Position ○ ◑ **Hardiness** RHS H7

No rock or gravel garden is complete without this dainty
spring bulb. Forming carpets of star-shaped blue flowers
with white centres surrounded by tiny strap-shaped
leaves, its diminutive size belies a hardy nature; an alpine
from Turkey, *Chionodoxa* will survive cold winters, and
flowers at the beginning of spring, when temperatures are
still low, justifying its common name, glory of the snow.
Although a sunny site encourages the flowers to open, it
is also happy at the edge of deciduous woodland, where
light levels remain high before the tree leaves emerge.
Or plant bulbs in shallow pots filled with gritty compost
to brighten up a patio, balcony or roof garden. Perfect
planting partners include dwarf narcissi, crocuses and
Iris reticulata, which all bloom at about the same time
and enjoy similar conditions. In early autumn, plant bold
drifts of bulbs 5 centimetres (2 in.) deep in free-draining
soil. The bulbs are relatively inexpensive, so plant them
generously for the most rewarding display. **ZA**

Alternatives

Chionodoxa sardensis, Chionodoxa forbesii 'Blue Giant',
Chionodoxa 'Valentine Day'

Colchicum
'Waterlily'

Main features Flowers in autumn; blooms without
planting in soil
Height 13 cm (5 in.) **Spread** 8 cm (3 in.)
Position ○ ◑ **Hardiness** RHS H5

Originally from a species found in Colchis, Asia Minor,
east of the Black Sea, C. 'Waterlily' has been bred from
two *Colchicum* species with white flowers, although it
in fact has mauve-coloured, double flowers. Each flower
consists of more than twenty florets, which bloom in early
autumn when the garden is on its way into hibernation.
Colchicum has the remarkable ability of being able to
flower without having been planted in soil, for example,
in a warm spot on a windowsill. After, it should be planted
in a well-drained sunny position. Some species like
Colchicum autumnale will also grow in semi-shade. When
planted in the right spot, 'Waterlily' will come back, year
after year, and provide the autumn garden with a splash
of colour. Great companions are low-growing plants, like
Artemisia schmidtiana and *A. stelleriana* (both wormwood
species), *Geranium* Dusky Crûg, *G. renardii* and creeping
phlox. Note that all parts of this bulbous plant contain
colchicine, which is toxic if eaten. **FR/MS**

Alternatives

Colchicum autumnale 'Album', *Colchicum* 'Giant',
Colchicum 'Lilac Wonder'

● *Chionodoxa luciliae* has small flowers so plant in generous bands or drifts.

Colchicum
C. speciosum 'Album'

Main features Autumn-flowering bulb; enormous pure-white goblet-shaped flowers
Height 25 cm (10 in.) **Spread** 15 cm (6 in.)
Position ○ **Hardiness** RHS H7

The perennial *C. speciosum* 'Album' produces a dozen or more large white goblets of flower in the second half of autumn, the pristine flowers coming up when much of the garden is in decline. *C. speciosum* 'Album' is one of the last to flower and one of the finest, but many *Colchicum* need careful placing because their large leaves appear very early in the year and then take ages to wither and die. For this reason they jar against spring bulbs, so the temptation is to sink them into deep shade where they fail to perform. They need good light and exposure to summer rain in order to flourish. Sunny edges of autumn-flowering borders work well because their foliage has died down before these borders get going. When the border comes to life in late summer and early autumn they add extra pizzazz. Or use them around mature trees or on a grassy west-facing slope. Their common name naked ladies suits them well, for the flowers appear as if by magic through bare earth. **VB**

Alternatives

Colchicum autumnale 'Nancy Lindsay', *Colchicum agrippinum*, *Colchicum tenorei*

Convallaria
C. majalis

Main features Fragrant, white, bell-shaped late-spring flowers; wide, spear-shaped green leaves; good cut flower
Height 25 cm (10 in.) **Spread** 30 cm (12 in.)
Position ◑ ● **Hardiness** RHS H7

The inspiration for many perfumes, the flowers of this elegant bulb are highly fragrant and guaranteed to lift the spirits when they bloom in late spring. The tantalising scent is emitted from clear white flowers, which hang like scallop-edged bells from arching stems, against a backdrop of broad, dark-green leaves. No wonder this exquisite plant is a favourite for spring wedding bouquets. Shy of full sun, lily-of-the-valley makes a decorative carpet of flowers and foliage beneath trees and shrubs, or plant it in pots to add fragrance to a patio or balcony. Match it with plants that like similar conditions, such as the blue-flowered *Corydalis flexuosa* and pink bleeding heart, *Dicentra formosa*. Wood anemones (*Anemone nemorosa*) and dwarf narcissi form a prelude, flowering earlier in spring, while ferns make a more permanent partner, creating a leafy layer when the *Convallaria* flowers fade. In autumn the leaves of lily-of-the-valley turn a golden yellow and red berries may appear. This is toxic if eaten. **ZA**

Alternatives

Convallaria majalis 'Albostriata', *Convallaria majalis* 'Variegata', *Convallaria majalis* 'Flore Pleno'

Convallaria majalis is better known as the highly fragrant lily-of-the-valley. ➡

Crinum
C. × *herbertii*

Crocus
C. *flavus* subsp. *flavus*

Main features Flowers from summer to autumn; fragrant flowers; drought tolerant; low maintenance
Height 30 cm (12 in.) **Spread** 30 cm (12 in.)
Position ○ **Hardiness** RHS H5

Main features Brilliant orange-yellow flowers in spring; attracts bees
Height 5 cm (2 in.) **Spread** 5 cm (2 in.)
Position ○ **Hardiness** RHS H5

These heritage bulbs (actually amaryllids not lilies) are so long-lived and carefree that they are often found marking abandoned homesteads or plantations in the southern United States. Several species of *Crinum* have been found growing along the routes of the slave trade, signalling their origin in Africa, but *C.* × *herbertii* is the classic milk-and-wine lily hybridized in 1819 by English botanist Dean William Herbert by crossing *C. scabrum* and *C. bulbispermum*. The milk-and-wine lily is the most cold hardy, and has been rediscovered in recent years as a handsome, fragrant low-maintenance heritage. The bulb alone looks exotic, and an old one can easily exceed 30 centimetres (12 in.) in length. Even young bulbs are large, and a bulb that has been growing and multiplying undisturbed for a long time can be a challenge to unearth. Plants have clumps of strappy, glaucous foliage above which the flowers appear. The clusters of red-and-white-striped blooms fill the air with fragrance. They demand only full sun and patience to reach their potential. **KK**

This small crocus is one of the first yellow flowers to appear as a messenger of spring. *C. flavus* subsp. *flavus* has fragrant bright yellow-orange flowers, which are slightly darker in the throat, and linear leaves usually with a silvery central stripe. It is much smaller than the 'Dutch Yellow' or 'Yellow Mammoth', which are often sold as the yellow crocus. The big flowers are probably grown from crosses with *C. flavus*, but are unscented. A very hardy plant, it will grow well outdoors in a well-drained sunny spot, in the rock garden, or in thin grass. It flowers in spring and shows its full beauty when the sun is out. However, be aware, it is very short – grass left long in autumn will hardly show the beauty in late winter and early spring. It has the characteristic of self-sowing, with moderate freedom, and a colony will develop in two to five years after the first few corms have been planted. Make sure that the planting spot is not too dry and warm in summer. In the garden it looks good with *Crocus tommasinianus* or with smaller snowdrops and other early bulbs. **FR/MS**

Alternatives

Crinum 'Ellen Bosanquet', *Crinum* 'Mrs James Hendry'

Alternatives

Crocus 'Dutch Yellow', *Crocus* 'Yellow Mammoth'

Crocus
C. sativus

Main features Flowers in autumn; prominent orange filaments; produces saffron
Height 13–15 cm (5–6 in.) **Spread** 8 cm (3 in.)
Position ○ **Hardiness** RHS H5

There is a real thrill growing *C. sativus*, the plant that provides the world with saffron – the most expensive spice. You can see close-up how the orange strands of saffron start life as part of the crocus's female stigma; its three branches are so long, they hang down between the mauve-purple petals. In Europe, saffron is used in rice dishes, such as paella, but it is also added to buns and cakes. Commercial production of saffron is very labour-intensive: picking the delicate strands from each flower, drying and toasting them. For those serious about harvesting saffron, plant at least twenty-five dry bulbs as soon as they are available in late summer in a well-drained soil in a sunny spot. Plant 10 centimetres (4 in.) deep, and they will flower within six to eight weeks, often as it starts to rain. Heavy rain can spoil the flower display, but in dry weather they are pretty and smell sweet. After a while the grassy leaves go dormant, so mark the position if growing among other plants. In colder areas, lift bulbs to overwinter. **LD**

Alternative

Crocus cartwrightianus 'Albus Tubergen'

Crocus
C. speciosus 'Albus'

Main features Showy pure-white flowers in autumn; attracts bees
Height 10 cm (4 in.) **Spread** 10 cm (4 in.)
Position ○ **Hardiness** RHS H4

A showy fall-flowering crocus, *C. speciosus* 'Albus' is one of two varieties of *C. speciosus* that were cultivated in the Netherlands. *C. speciosus* 'Albus' has large pure-white flowers with an orange throat and is an excellent grower, superb for naturalising in grassy areas. This variety is also known as white Bieberstein's crocus. It flowers from early autumn onwards, without leaves as these appear only in the spring. The autumn-flowering species are too little known. They are easy to grow and require a sunny spot with poor, well-drained soil. Great for a rock garden in between other low-growing plants that can support them, they tend to fall over when they are standing on their own. They can be used for naturalising in grassy areas, grow well in lawns and borders, and can propagate well from their own seed. The flowers of other varieties of *C. speciosus* are large, cup-shaped, and come in colours from dark blue to metallic blue-violet. They are a great companion to *Geranium macrorrhizum*, which also grows well in poor conditions. **FR/MS**

Alternatives

Crocus speciosus 'Aitchinsonii', *Crocus speciosus* 'Artabir'

Crocus
'Pickwick'

Main features Plant in autumn, flowers in spring; white-and-violet-striped petals; attracts bees
Height 13 cm (5 in.) **Spread** 5–10 cm (2–4 in.)
Position ○ ◑ **Hardiness** RHS H3

This crocus is a round, large-blooming hybrid of *C. vernus* with a beautiful blue-violet colour and a grey-white background; the colour becomes more intense at the base of the flower. 'Pickwick' is excellent for naturalising in grass. It is also good used in pots, in combination with later-flowering spring bulbs, such as grape hyacinths, botanical tulips and short-stemmed botanical narcissi. Try mixing them with early-flowering purple pansies, such as *Viola tricolor*. The late Christopher Lloyd of Great Dixter, Sussex, recommended planting *C. vernus* hybrids under rose beds to provide interest during the spring ('vernus' means 'spring'). 'Pickwick' is the best multi-coloured *C. vernus* hybrid and was developed by W. Eldering in 1950, in the Netherlands.

'Pickwick' normally flowers in midspring. Plant the corms in full sun or light shade, spacing them 5 to 10 centimetres (2–4 in.) apart and covering them with 5 to 10 centimetres (2–4 in.) of soil. *C. vernus* hybrids can tolerate poor to moderate soil as long as it is well drained. For the earliest spring bloom, plant them in a sunny protected spot; for later enjoyment plant them in clusters on the north side of a wall, hedge or building in dappled shade.

The spring-blooming *C. vernus* grows wild in the Alps and the mountains of southern Germany and southern Europe, from the Pyrenees to Slovakia. The colour varies from white to purple and the plant can be striped. This colour pattern is the same for all the hybrids that have been bred from this species and variety. The hybrids created from *C. vernus* are all available as large-flowering Dutch crocuses and appear in both blue and white. The corm and the flower are larger than those of the wild ones and they bloom a little later. There are dozens of varieties; by 1774 twenty had been registered. **FR/MS**

Alternatives

Crocus 'Jeanne d'Arc', *Crocus* 'Remembrance', *Crocus* 'Flower Record', *Crocus* 'Vanguard'

Crocus
C. × *sieberi* subsp. *sublimis* 'Tricolor'

Main features Plant in autumn, flowers in spring; striking purple, yellow and white petals; attracts bees
Height 7 cm (3 in.) **Spread** 5 cm (2 in.)
Position ○ **Hardiness** RHS H4

An elegant dwarf crocus flowering from early to midspring, C. × *sieberi* subsp. *sublimis* 'Tricolor' has beautiful flowers in a unique combination of colours, and excellent growing quality. It has a yellow throat, very attractive deep lilac-blue flowers with a white zone, and a brilliant orange stamen. It grows wild in the Balkans, Greece and Crete. In England it is known as the snow crocus because it flowers when the last snow is still around and while the frost is still in the soil. This happens particularly when the crocuses have naturalised over many years. They will then always flower earlier than the ones that were planted more recently.

C. *sieberi* is marked by brilliant orange, which is mostly confined to the stamen and style, fading through the bottom third of the petal. It distinguishes itself from subspecies *atticus* and *nivalis* by the clear presence of hairs in the throat of the flower. Corms should be planted 5 centimetres (2 in.) deep and 5 centimetres (2 in.) apart. Bulbs are tolerant of summer moisture in well-drained soil.

Other C. *sieberi* varieties that are widely available include C. *sieberi* 'Bowles's White', which is clear white with an orange throat and goblet-shaped flowers. It is a superb garden plant. C. *sieberi* subsp. *atticus* 'Firefly' is violet pink with an extraordinary orange stamen. Last but not least, C. *sieberi* 'Hubert Edelsten' is lilac purple with a white-and-yellow centre.

Crocuses grow in rather diverse biotopes. Some species are found only in rocky terrain, others in grassy areas, whereas others thrive on barren rocky slopes. They exist rarely if ever on elevations higher than 3,000 metres (10,000 ft). Other species grow in evergreen oak thickets and coniferous forests. Crocuses are also found at low elevations and even at sea level. C. *sieberi* is found on lower altitudes. **FR/MS**

Alternatives

Crocus sieberi 'Violet Queen', *Crocus sieberi* subsp. *atticus* 'Firefly', *Crocus sieberi* 'George', *Crocus sieberi* 'Ronald Ginns'

Crocus
C. tommasinianus

Main features Plant in autumn, flowers in spring; linear leaves with central silver stripe; attracts bees
Height 7 cm (3 in.) **Spread** 5 cm (2 in.)
Position ○ **Hardiness** RHS H5

This very showy crocus originates in the Balkans and was imported to the Netherlands in 1847. *C. tommasinianus* was named by Dean William Herbert after his friend, Signor Tomasino. This charming species propagates itself well by seed. The background colour is dark violet-blue and is distinguished from *Crocus vernus* by its glossy throat. An interesting characteristic is that it is more darkly coloured on the inside than the outside, the colours ranging from light lilac to deep red-purple. The other surfaces of the petals are often silver or cream coloured.

It is ideal for naturalising and has gained the Royal Horticultural Society's Award of Garden Merit. The long-tubed flowers appear from early spring, depending on the weather. Plant in clusters or just scatter them in sunny areas and grow them where they have fallen.

There are several varieties of *C. tommasinianus*, ranging from white with tints of rose, violet and blue to purple. The cultivar 'Barr's Purple' has large, amethyst-purple flowers. 'Ruby Giant' (1956) from Roozen-Kramer in the Netherlands has festive, deep-violet flowers with a lighter flower base and a light border on the petals. It has the largest flowers within the group. *C. tommasinianus* is one of the earliest flowering crocuses, sometimes as early as January. Bees can be seen busily collecting their first food of the year from this crocus's flowers, which provides them with much-needed protein and vitamins after winter. **FR/MS**

Alternatives

Crocus tommasinianus 'Whitewell Purple', *Crocus tommasinianus* 'Roseus'

Cyclamen
C. hederifolium

Main features Small, pink flowers in autumn; patterned, ivy-shaped, green-and-silver foliage; good for naturalising
Height 10 cm (4 in.) **Spread** 15 cm (6 in.)
Position ◑ ● **Hardiness** RHS H5

While most bulbs sparkle in spring or summer, this little beauty puts on a show when others have faded, its flowers appearing a little before autumn or as the patterned leaves emerge. The dry soil and shade beneath trees provide a perfect home for this cyclamen, and just when you have forgotten all about it, small pink blooms start to unfurl, reminding you that winter is on its way. Their delicate petals look like butterflies fluttering in the breeze, while the sculptural ivy-shaped foliage, often intricately patterned, sustains interest after the flowers are over.

A natural woodlander, plant ivy-leaved cyclamen in partial shade at the front of a border, or use it as ground cover beneath trees and shrubs. Combine it with other cold-season blooms – such as winter aconites, snowdrops, and early primroses – which all enjoy similar conditions. Ferns, including *Asplenium scolopendrium* and *Polystichum*, make good partners, too, adding colour and texture to schemes during the cyclamen's summer dormancy. The leaves also make a decorative addition to winter containers and work well with other shade-lovers, such as violas and dead nettle (*Lamium*).

Plant the tubers in groups and mulch the ground with leaf mould as the leaves die down in spring. The tubers prefer dry soil in summer; plant them in raised beds or pots of gritty soil-based compost if prone to waterlogging. In areas that experience hard frost, add a layer of protective bark chips. **ZA**

Alternatives

Cyclamen hederifolium 'Amaze Me Series', *Cyclamen hederifolium* 'Ruby Strain', *Cyclamen hederifolium albiflorum*

Cyclamen
C. coum Pewter Group

Main features Flowers in winter and spring; attractive
winter foliage
Height 5–8 cm (2–3 in.) **Spread** 15 cm (6 in.)
Position ○ ◑ ● **Hardiness** RHS H5

A plant that braves the winter elements in order to flower
deserves a place in any garden. The rounded leaves of
C. coum Pewter Group have a dull pewter-coloured sheen,
edged with green, as well as green veins, although the
foliage can vary. This distinguishes the Pewter Group from
the plain green leaves of the *C. coum* species. The leaves
appear in the autumn and sprawl close to the ground,
concealing the flower buds. The chubby, snub-nosed
flowers, in shades of pink, have a darker blotch at the
base, but still have the typical swept-back petals of the
species and are held above the foliage, therefore giving
an interesting combination of flower and leaf colours.
The flowers may be small, but this is a tough and hardy
plant that grows from a small underground tuber, which
is best planted 2.5 centimetres (1 in.) deep in a humus-rich,
but well-drained soil. This makes it reasonably drought
tolerant and suitable for growing under deciduous trees.
It can be grown in sun or shade, and makes an interesting
addition to a rock garden, in a lightly shaded position. **MP**

Alternatives

Cyclamen coum Silver Group, *Cyclamen repandum*

Cyrtanthus
C. elatus

Main features Large scarlet-red, trumpet-like flowers
from late summer to midautumn; usually grown indoors
Height 50 cm (20 in.) **Spread** 30 cm (12 in.)
Position ○ ◑ **Hardiness** RHS H2–3

The Scarborough lily, or *C. elatus,* is an elegant and
colourful pot plant for indoor flowering. Its large, slightly
fragrant flowers will brighten up a well lit windowsill or
conservatory. Flowers (10 cm/4 in. wide) are produced in
clusters at the top of stout stems from late summer to
midautumn. These are surrounded by strappy, evergreen
basal leaves. Although hardy down to -5°C (23°F), it is
rarely grown outside, except in warm climates, where it
needs to be grown at the base of a sunny wall. Another
option is to grow it in a pot and move the pot into the
garden during flowering, bringing it back under cover
before the first severe frost. Plant with the tip of the bulb
above compost level, one bulb to a 13 to 15 centimetre
(5–6 in.) pot. Keep the compost moist and feed weekly
with a liquid fertiliser when in growth. After flowering,
water sparingly, especially in winter. The plants flower
best when potbound. Be aware of various names
including *C. purpureus, C. speciosus, Vallota speciosa*, and
V. purpurea. Note also that the bulb is poisonous **GHo**

Alternatives

Cyrtanthus elatus 'Cream Beauty', *Cyrtanthus elatus* 'Delicatus'

◀ *Cyclamen coum* **Pewter Group** is a winter-flowering *Cyclamen* with interesting foliage.

Dahlia
'Bishop of Llandaff'

Main features Bright-red flowers from midsummer to
autumn; insect friendly; superb cut flower
Height 90 cm (3 ft) **Spread** 45 cm (18 in.)
Position ○ **Hardiness** RHS H3

This heritage dahlia, a veteran of over seventy years, is
still a star performer in the garden today, and it even
flowers profusely in cooler conditions. 'Bishop of Llandaff'
is bushy in habit, with almost-black ferny foliage framing
bright-red flowers. It is rarely out of flower and does not
need staking. Given a space at the front of the border, this
dahlia will shine and create a focal point, flattering fall-
flowering blue or mauve asters, such as 'Little Carlow'. Its
warm-red flowers suit fiery schemes with tropical plants
using warm yellows and oranges too. It was personally
selected from thousands of seedlings by Joshua Pritchard
Hughes, then Bishop of Llandaff, in 1928 from Treseder's
Nursery in Cardiff. It has spawned other bishops since,
although none are quite as splendid as the original, which
combines the best dahlia foliage with bright-red regalia.
It stands supreme, combining beauty with a rugged
constitution. Protect from slugs in the early stages and
deadhead regularly to encourage more buds. Lift the
tubers in late autumn, unless your garden is frost-free. **VB**

Alternatives

Dahlia 'Tally Ho', *Dahlia* 'Grenadier'

Dahlia
'David Howard'

Main features Khaki foliage topped by butterscotch-
orange miniature decorative flowers; a superb cut flower
Height 90 cm (3 ft) **Spread** 45 cm (18 in.)
Position ○ **Hardiness** RHS H3

This first-rate garden dahlia was raised from a seed
capsule collected from 'Bishop of Llandaff' by Norfolk
nurseryman David Howard in the late 1950s. Dahlias
were an early obsession, and Howard raised thousands
of seedlings on his village allotments, but realised that
this was the finest of all. When National Service (drafting)
took him away from home for eighteen months, his last
words to his parents were 'look after my dahlia'. They
passed it to a local nurseryman, who propagated it and
christened it 'David Howard'. It has inherited a rugged
constitution from 'Bishop of Llandaff', along with elegant
lines and an ability to perform whatever the weather.
A succession of fully double flowers in soft butterscotch
orange, held on strong dark stems, rise above rather
ordinary olive-green foliage. However, that warm-orange
flower colour is a perfect foil for blues and purples, or it
can be swirled through tropical cannas, fiery crocosmias
and red-hot pokers. Lift the tubers in late autumn, unless
your garden is frost-free, and stake as you plant. **VB**

Alternatives

Dahlia 'Thomas A. Edison', *Dahlia* 'Sam Hopkins'

Dahlia
'Mystic Illusion'

Main features Chocolate-brown foliage; bright-yellow, single flowers; insect friendly; superb cut flower
Height 1.2 m (4 ft) **Spread** 45 cm (18 in.)
Position ○ **Hardiness** RHS H3

The original name for this dahlia, raised by New Zealander Keith Hammett, was 'Knockout', and it lives up to its name brilliantly. The red-tinted, dark-mahogany foliage highlights the sunshine yellow of the pristine flowers. Each displays eight perfectly formed petals of great regularity. However, it is the orange-rimmed chocolate eye in the middle of each bloom that makes this dahlia a dazzler, because it marries flower and filigree foliage together. Use it as an architectural feature or mix it with vibrant, warm reds, yellows or purples. It performs brilliantly in cool conditions and, being bred in New Zealand, as one of the Mystic Series, it is tough. Hammett has also bred the velvet-red 'Dovegrove' and the deep-pink 'Magenta Star'. However, both have to be cutting-raised, because they fail to produce tubers in any quantity. Despite this, Hammett's single dahlias are in the top rank, flowering prolifically, although the foliage would be enough for some on its own. Lift the tubers in late autumn, unless your garden is frost-free. **VB**

Alternatives

Dahlia 'Twyning's After Eight', *Dahlia* 'Happy Single Wink'

Dahlia
'Pooh Swan Island'

Main features Red-and-yellow collarette dahlia; strong constitution; flowers prolifically; superb cut flower
Height 1 m (3.5 ft) **Spread** 45 cm (18 in.)
Position ○ **Hardiness** RHS H3

Collarette dahlias have single flowers and a distinct middle, surrounded by an inner ruff of shorter petals that are often quilled. Many have been named in recent years, but often the flowers are malformed and messy, so neatly formed collarettes, such as 'Pooh', are rare. 'Pooh Swan Island', released in 1998, produces neat orange-and-yellow flowers, with orange outer petals evenly tipped in yellow. The clear, yellow central ruff matches the petal tips exactly and it is one of the few collarettes to satisfy the show bench exhibitor, the gardener and the florist. This green-leaved dahlia produces massive tubers and stiff upright stems, indicating its vigour, and it copes with mixed planting well – pushing up through herbaceous plants. Used with late-summer performers, its sunny presence adds extra sparkle from midsummer until late autumn. The orange-and-yellow flowers are best placed closer to blues and the late-flowering deep-blue *Aconitum carmichaelii* 'Arendsii' makes a great jewel-box combination. Protect from slugs and stake as you plant. **VB**

Alternatives

Dahlia 'Trelyn Crimson', *Dahlia* 'Hootenanny'

Dierama
D. pulcherrimum

Main features Flowers in summer; evergreen foliage; architectural plant
Height 1.5 m (5 ft) **Spread** 60 cm (24 in.)
Position ○   **Hardiness** RHS H5

The common name – angel's fishing rod – is very apt for this worthwhile member of the iris family. The tough, green, grasslike foliage is evergreen and grows to about 90 centimetres (3 ft), thus making a strong clump. In summer thin, wirelike flower stems, up to 1.5 metres (5 ft) or more in height, arch over and above the foliage with the weight of the flowers. It is as if a small fish is taking a bite at the bait with every passing breeze. The clusters of pendulous flowers are variable in colour and can be white, pale pink to dark pink and even magenta, with silvery bracts that add to the charm. The flowers open over a long period from mid- to late summer.

Native to South Africa, *D. pulcherrimum* loves a perfectly drained, yet moisture-retentive, soil in a sunny location. Give each clump plenty of space to enjoy its graceful habit. It grows from an underground corm, which should be planted 5 centimetres (2 in.) deep in spring, but it can be raised from seed too, if your patience allows. Grow *D. pulcherrimum* in a gravel garden or border, where it will not be overcrowded; on a patio it may self-seed prolifically into the cracks between the paving slabs. However, this plant is deep rooted and does not take kindly to being disturbed or grown in a pot.

A pure-white selection, *D. pulcherrimum* var. *album* is available, and the variety 'Merlin' has extremely dark-purple flowers. 'Blackbird' is a good form too, with darkish, but slightly variable coloured blooms. Try growing a clump so that it rises out of a ground covering of the blue-flowered hardy perennial *Geranium* 'Rozanne'. Alternative species to sample include *D. dracomontanum*, which is shorter in stature, with coral-pink to red flowers; *D. pauciflorum*, with narrow leaves and more upright purple-pink flowers; and *D. igneum*, a free-flowering species with coral flowers. **MP**

Alternatives

Dierama dracomontanum, Dierama pauciflorum, Dierama igneum

Dierama pulcherrimum given space to sway in the breeze at the Dillon Garden, Dublin, Ireland. ➔

Eranthis
E. hyemalis

Main feature Colourful flowers from midwinter
to early spring
Height 10 cm (4 in.) **Spread** 10–15 cm (4–6 in.)
Position ○ ◑ **Hardiness** RHS H5

The *E. hyemalis* flowers at the same time as snowdrops and is a perfect companion to these plants. The lemon-yellow flowers brighten up dull winter days, especially when they are planted in bold groups. Only 2.5 centimetres (1 in.) wide, the dainty, cup-shaped flowers are produced above finely cut, bright-green leaves and surrounded by an attractive ruff of leaf-like bracts. As a woodland plant, *E. hyemalis* generally prefers cool conditions. Consequently, it can be grown in partially shaded beds and borders and makes superb ground cover under deciduous trees and shrubs, or alongside early-flowering perennials, such as hellebores. It can also be grown naturalised in light grass cover or in pots in a cold greenhouse, or indoors for flowering from midwinter onwards. *E. hyemalis* Cilicica Group and *E. hyemalis* (Tubergenii Group) 'Guinea Gold' tolerate more sun than other cultivars in the species and are suitable for humus-rich soil in rock gardens and at the front of sunny borders. **GHo**

Alternatives

Eranthis hyemalis Cilicica Group, *Eranthis hyemalis* (Tubergenii Group) 'Guinea Gold'

Erythronium
'Pagoda'

Main features Yellow flowers in mid- to late spring;
mottled, shiny, green foliage
Height 30 cm (12 in.) **Spread** 15 cm (6 in.)
Position ◑ **Hardiness** RHS H5

The 'Pagoda' is an extremely popular cultivar thanks to its large, attractive flowers produced from mid- to late spring. With prominent stamen and reflexed petals, the blooms are lemon-yellow and elegantly swept back. Three to five gracefully nodding flowers are produced on each 30 centimetre (12 in.) stem, which rises above the shiny, green foliage, mottled with bronze or maroon. 'Pagoda' loves cool shade, making it a star performer that is well worth growing in any lightly or partially shaded position in the garden. It is perfect for rock gardens and mixed borders, where it is shaded by other plants, but it is at its best in the dappled shade under trees or in woodland gardens. It can also be grown in pots to adorn patios and other areas of the garden that are cool and shady. Growing 'Pagoda' around other plants that shade the soil will prevent the bulbs becoming baked in summer. Once established, it forms good-sized clumps that provide a spectacle of colour. **GHo**

Alternatives

Erythronium tuolumnense, Erythronium dens-canis 'Snowflake', *Erythronium dens-canis* 'Charmer'

◑ *Eranthis hyemalis* offers a cheerful midwinter carpet under deciduous shrubs.

Erythronium

E. *californicum* 'White Beauty'

Main features Flowers as spring arrives; elegant ivory-white flowers; handsome mottled foliage
Height 20 cm (8 in.) **Spread** 20 cm (8 in.)
Position ◑ **Hardiness** RHS H5

'White Beauty' produces ivory-white Tiffany lamp–style flowers with six upturned petals that fly outwards, somehow catching the exuberant spirit of spring. Viewed from above, there is a cool hint of green as the flower meets the stem, and this echoes the glint of green found in the anthers suspended beneath each flower. Gaze inside the bloom, and there is a brown necklace of dots that tones with the handsome mottled foliage below. These features make 'White Beauty' a stunning plant, and it is a wonderful starting point for beginner gardeners, because it is easy to grow and floriferous. However, *Erythronium* bulbs are very fragile, so handle them carefully.

In the wild, *Erythronium* emerges as the snow melts, following a cold winter. It appreciates cool temperatures and moist soil when flowering, so the plants need to be positioned away from the midday sun. Each 20-centimetre-long (8 in.) stem will bear three flowers, and they soon bulk up, making 'White Beauty' very showy. Furthermore, the brown-and-green scale pattern on the foliage, which gives the plant the common names trout lily and fawn lily, makes much more of an impact than plain green leaves. Divide the clumps with care as they die down and water each one well before lifting. Place it onto newspaper and gently tease apart the white, waxy bulbs. Carefully replant them into friable soil that has been dug over well. **VB**

Alternatives

Erythronium 'Pagoda', *Erythronium* 'Hidcote Beauty', *Erythronium dens-canis* 'Snowflake'

Erythronium
E. revolutum

Main features Autumn planting; flowers in spring; attractively marked foliage
Height 15 cm (6 in.) **Spread** 20 cm (8 in.)
Position ◑ **Hardiness** RHS H7

An excellent woodland plant that enjoys partially shaded conditions, E. revolutum is decorative and graceful, but quite difficult to grow. It resembles a miniature lily and usually has beautifully marked or flecked leaves, which give it a pleasing appearance, even when not in bloom. Commonly, these leaves are two per bulb and they grow near to the ground. Each bulb sends up a long, naked stalk bearing one or two showy flowers. The stalk bows at the end, so that the face of the flower points to the ground. There are six tepals in shades of pink or light purple, which may have yellow or white spotting towards the centre of the flower. The tepals tend to curve more strongly as the flower ages.

The bulbs have no protective shell and are easily harmed by a dry environment. Planting them early and immediately after obtaining them is essential. The tube-formed little bulbs should be planted in groups in damp soil. Choose an area in dappled shade and plant them 10 centimetres (4 in.) apart and 7.5 centimetres (3 in.) deep. If they are left undisturbed, they will gradually produce more of their pretty spring flowers. E. revolutum originates from Canada and northern areas of the United States, while in Europe, the equivalent species is the dog's tooth violet, E. dens-canis. This only has one flower per stem in white or purple-pink, but also has mottled foliage. It is less fussy about soil than most species so it is worth trying to grow it in chalky or sandy soils. **FR/MS**

Alternatives

Erythronium japonicum, Erythronium dens-canis 'Lilac Wonder', *Erythronium* 'Kondo', *Erythronium* 'Pagoda'

Eucharis
E. amazonica

Main features Houseplant or greenhouse pot plant; fragrant flowers
Height 60 cm (24 in.) **Spread** 20 cm (8 in.)
Position ◑ **Hardiness** RHS H1b

The name *Eucharis* originates from the Greek language, and it is a combination of *eu*, meaning 'good', and *charis*, meaning 'attractive', in reference to the beauty of the plant's flowers. Each stem of *E. amazonica* carries between three to six white, narcissus-like pendant flowers. These flowers open one after another, and the flowering period is fairly long. The flowers often bloom later in the winter and in the spring, but, in fact, they can bloom at any time of the year. They sometimes come into flower two or three times a year. With a delightful fragrance, they are often used in bridal bouquets. The six broad petals of the perianth are flat and wide open when fully mature, and the short calyx has a corolla that forms a light-green bowl in the middle of the flower. A member of the Amaryllidaceae family, *E. amazonica* is an attractive plant found growing in the understorey of rainforest.

To induce flowering, grow in pots (under cover in most regions) with a watering and temperature regime. The procedure for year-round production is to keep the plants dry and cool for a few weeks, until the leaves droop but not wither (otherwise, the bulbs would weaken). When the wilted flower stalk has been removed, a new set of leaves will appear. The temperature in the greenhouse has to be kept at 27°C (80°F) during the flowering period and at 20°C (68°F) during the dormant period, with a relatively high humidity, imitating the plant's natural growing conditions. **FR/MS**

Alternatives

Syn. *Eucharis × grandiflora*, other species *Eucharis candida*, *Eucharis astrophiala*

Eucomis
E. comosa 'Sparkling Burgundy'

Main features Dark reddish-purple leaves; pineapple-shaped, purple-pink flower heads; purple seedpods
Height 60 cm (24 in.) **Spread** 30 cm (12 in.)
Position ○ ◑ **Hardiness** RHS H5

Pineapple plants are exotic-looking perennial bulbs with flower heads topped with leafy bracts that resemble the fruits after which they are named. The species is beautiful, but *E. comosa* 'Sparkling Burgundy' makes a dramatic focal point in the garden. With long, strappy, dark reddish-purple leaves with wavy margins and stems packed with star-shaped, purple-pink blooms, it is hard to beat for a tropical-themed garden in a cool climate.

After flowering throughout the summer, 'Sparkling Burgundy' produces deep-purple seedpods that continue the performance up to the first frost, when it will die back. Combine it with *Dahlia*, *Crocosmia*, *Kniphofia* and *Aster* for a blaze of colour in a border, or plant it in a large

decorative pot partnered with summer bedding. For an exotic look, try it alongside *Phormium*, *Canna* lilies, and *Fatsia japonica* to create a jungle-like effect. 'Sparkling Burgundy' also combines well with the green-leaved species, *E. comosa*, which grows a little taller and has small greenish-white flowers and green seedpods.

Despite appearances, 'Sparkling Burgundy' is quite hardy and will survive freezing conditions as long as the bulbs are planted deep enough and the ground is quite dry over winter. In spring, plant the bulbs in a sunny spot in free-draining soil or pots of soil-based compost. Keep the plants well watered in summer. If planted in a container, tip it on its side and place in a sheltered area in winter, which helps prevent the bulbs from rotting. **ZA**

Alternatives

Eucomis comosa, *Eucomis bicolor*, *Eucomis autumnalis*, *Eucomis montana*

Fritillaria

F. imperialis
'Maxima Lutea'

Main features Flowers in spring; architectural plant for mixed borders
Height 90 cm (3 ft) **Spread** 25–30 cm (10–12 in.)
Position ○ ◑ **Hardiness** RHS H6

The *F. imperialis* is native to the Middle East, where it is usually red or orange in the wild. *F. imperialis* 'Maxima Lutea' is a vigorous variety with extra large yellow flowers. From a huge bulb arise strong stems clad with an abundance of glossy foliage. The leafy stem gives way to a clear section topped with a tuft of leaves, from under which develops a cluster of pendulous yellow bells. Peer into the individual flowers, and the base has six prominent, shining, white nectaries, with the stigma and anthers in the centre. The dramatic flowers will make a bold statement in the spring garden, rising above the emerging foliage of herbaceous perennials. *F. imperialis* 'William Rex' has dark bronze-red flowers, while *F. imperialis* 'Aurora' has blooms that are more orange. As the shoots emerge in spring, they give off a strange smell, often described as 'foxy.' This appears to deter deer, rabbits, moles and mice. **MP**

Alternatives

Fritillaria persica 'Adiyaman', *Fritillaria pallidiflora*, *Fritillaria pyrenaica*, *Fritillaria imperialis* 'Aureomarginata'

Fritillaria

F. meleagris

Main features Purple-and-pink checkered, bell-shaped, spring flowers; grass-like foliage; good for naturalising
Height 30 cm (12 in.) **Spread** 15 cm (6 in.)
Position ○ ◑ **Hardiness** RHS H6

The nodding bells of this diminutive *Fritillaria*, with its intricate pink-and-purple chequerboard patterning, mark it out from the bright, brash bulbs that appear alongside it in midspring. Its subtle, yet sophisticated good looks have been admired for centuries, and it was a favourite in Elizabethan gardens. Today, this dainty bulb is back in fashion and can be used to decorate damp meadow schemes, lawns and gravel gardens. A sunny or partially shaded site will promote the best display. Take care not to upstage *F. meleagris* with dazzling colours or blowsy blooms: grass makes the perfect foil for its delicate hues, or choose buff-coloured gravel to show off the patterned bells. Twinning the graceful white form with the purple variety also makes an eye-catching display. If planting in a border, team it with small-cupped, white or pale-yellow daffodils, such as 'Ice Wings' and 'Minnow', and the blue *Scilla siberica*, with leafy ferns providing a backdrop. **ZA**

Alternatives

Fritillaria meleagris var. *unicolor* subvar. *alba*, *Fritillaria elwesii*, *Fritillaria pontica*, *Fritillaria acmopetala*

Fritillaria meleagris is known as the snake's head fritillary and its petal markings have been admired since Elizabethan times. ➔

Fritillaria
F. persica

The *F. persica* originally comes from the Middle East, specifically from the eastern Mediterranean to Iran. It is one of several bulbous plants that were brought from Constantinople to Vienna by Flemish diplomat and herbalist Ogier Ghiselin de Busbecq. The bulbs arrived in Vienna in April 1576 and bloomed there for the first time in 1583. These spike-shaped flowers occur on Cyprus, and they can be found on grave sites, where they have apparently been used in funeral services because of the flower's almost black colour. *F. persica* 'Adiyaman' is a good form with darker bells; there is also *F. persica* 'Ivory Bells' with greenish-white flowers.

A stately plant and member of the *Liliaceae* family, *F. persica* has leaves and a stem frosted with blue. The purple (almost black) bell-shaped flowers number from ten to forty or more on the terminal of the stalk, and they produce a soft scent. The outer side of the flower is sometimes covered with dusty purple lines but is never flecked. In fact, this plant has such a special and almost overpowering appearance that it is hard to find it good companions in the garden. Neighbouring plants should be modest in order to bring out the best in *F. persica*. Lavender and *Santolina* are ideal; their grey leaves match perfectly with the dark-purple flowers and grey-green leaves of this *Fritillaria*. In addition, the evergreen leaves of *Sesleria nitida* make it a great supporting plant. All these plants like the same situations: sunny and warm.

F. persica blooms in the middle of spring. Any fertile garden soil will do, but do not plant the bulbs in an area where the plant is at risk of becoming waterlogged, because if it is too wet, you may lose the bulb to fungal rots. Although *F. persica* is robust, in colder areas it is advisable to provide a winter cover with mulch. **FR/MS**

Alternatives

Fritillaria persica 'Ivory Bells', *Fritillaria persica* 'Adiyaman', *Fritillaria persica* 'Midnight Bells'

Fritillaria
F. pontica

Main features Autumn planting; flowers in spring
Height 30 cm (12 in.) **Spread** 12 cm (4.5 in.)
Position ◐
Hardiness RHS H3

The *F. pontica* was introduced in 1826 from Albania, the north of Greece, Bulgaria and Turkey. It likes a semi-shaded position in the garden and moist, peaty soil, but can be cultivated without any problems. Each stem will produce between one and three hanging flowers. Their colour is unusual and is best described as light green and purplish-brown at the edge. In the heart of the flower are six dark ambrosia spots like large eyes. When the plant is in full bloom, place your hand under the flower, agitate the stem a little, and you can taste the sweet drops of nectar.

In autumn, tubers should be planted directly upon arrival. The bulbs are naked, which means 'without a shell', and they are therefore susceptible to drying out. Once established, *F. pontica* will happily seed. Although it is an easy bulb to grow, the planting spot should not be too hot or dry and preferably in dappled shade, where the colour of the flowers will stand out. In a semi-shaded woodland area or in a raised bed with morning sun, it will grow happily and return each spring. Together with other spring bulbs, such as *Scilla siberica* 'Alba' and graceful ivory-white *Narcissus* 'Ice Wings' or 'Jenny', it will make an attractive display. Good perennial companions are *Alchemilla mollis*, *Tiarella cordifolia* and *Milium effusum* 'Aureum', an ornamental grass with lime-green leaves in spring.

The genus *Fritillaria* belongs to the family *Liliaceae*, and the name *fritillaria* derives from the Latin word *fritillus*, meaning 'chessboard'. Perhaps the most recognisable feature of the genus is that it usually has hanging flowers, but often the flowers are chequered too. There are more than one hundred spring-flowering species, many of which are very interesting, and *F. pontica* has been honoured by the Royal Horticultural Society's Award of Garden Merit. **FR/MS**

Alternatives

Fritillaria acmopetala, *Fritillaria michailovskyi*, *Fritillaria meleagris*, *Fritillaria pallidiflora*, *Fritillaria uva-vulpis*

Galanthus

'Lady Beatrix Stanley'

Main features Dainty, low-growing double snowdrop;
forms large clumps that really make a show
Height 10–13 cm (4–5 in.) **Spread** 10 cm (4 in.)
Position ◑ ● **Hardiness** RHS H5

Lady Beatrix Stanley was a great friend of Edward
Augustus Bowles, the gentleman who coined the
word 'galanthophile', meaning 'a person who collects
snowdrops'. They shared a love of bulbous plants,
particularly snowdrops, iris and crocuses, and went
plant hunting together from the 1920s onwards. This
snowdrop – a dainty double, short in stature – was almost
certainly collected on one of their trips. 'Lady B' planted it
in her garden at Sibbertoft Manor in Northamptonshire,
and after her death, bulbs were lifted by her daughter,
Barbara Buchanan. The cultivar was named by the British
galanthophile Richard Nutt in 1981, and every snowdrop
lover should plant it.

This amenable snowdrop, the favourite double of
very many gardeners, has dainty little pips on the outers
and neatish middles. As the flowers age, the narrow
outers wither slightly, and many have likened their shape
to large molar teeth. Few snowdrops push out as many
flowers as this one, and its ability to grow and flower in
dank shade is highly useful.

Many snowdrops like to be lifted every three to four
years, but 'Lady Beatrix Stanley' is best left undivided so
that it makes wide show-stopping clumps. If you want
to divide it, do so as the foliage dies down, making sure
that the bulbs are not flaccid. Replant in small clumps,
not single bulbs in this case, and 'Lady Beatrix Stanley'
will romp away again. **VB**

Alternatives

Galanthus 'Ophelia', *Galanthus* 'Rodmarton', *Galanthus*
nivalis 'Flore Pleno', *Galanthus* 'Farringdon Double'

Galanthus
'S. Arnott'

Main feature Large, single snowdrop of great substance
Height 30 cm (12 in.) **Spread** 10 cm (4 in.)
Position ◐ ●
Hardiness RHS H5

The *Galanthus* 'S. Arnott' is an elegant single snowdrop with thickly textured, pearl-drop flowers that open slightly on warmer days, releasing their strong honey scent. The Audrey Hepburn of the snowdrop world, it is all about clean lines and elegant poise, and when happy this cultivar will rise to a surprising 30 centimetres (12 in.) in height. The neat foliage sits close to the ground, so the flowers stand proud. Gaze inside, and the vertical green lines on the inners add to this pristine snowdrop with the bold-green sinus mark.

Known as the giant snowdrop, this vigorous hybrid was distributed by Samuel Arnott, a well-connected Scottish galanthophile, as 'Arnott's Seedling'. Edward Augustus Bowles, the snowdrop authority of the day, rechristened it 'S. Arnott' in 1956. When displayed at a Royal Horticultural Show in London, it sparked off a new wave of galanthophilia, which confirmed its reputation. The bulbs were rediscovered after the severe winter of 1947 at Hyde Lodge, a sloping Gloucestershire garden that had been planted up by the previous owner Walter Butt in the 1920s. They had multiplied over the decades, and as the snow melted, thousands of flowers appeared, much to the amazement of the new owners, Brigadier Leonard and Mrs Winifrede Mathias. Their chauffeur, Herbert Ransom, helped them restore the garden and the Giant Snowdrop Company, trading between 1951 and 1968, rekindled this snowdrop's popularity. **VB**

Alternatives

Galanthus 'Brenda Troyle', *Galanthus plicatus* 'Colossus', *Galanthus* 'Byfield Special', *Galanthus elwesii* 'Fred's Giant'

Galanthus
G. elwesii

Main features Single snowdrop with wide, grey-green leaves; white flowers boldly marked in dark green
Height 20 cm (8 in.) **Spread** 10 cm (4 in.)
Position ○ ◑ **Hardiness** RHS H5

This species snowdrop, collected by plantsman Henry John Elwes near Smyrna in Turkey in 1874, makes a bold, upright statement with its blunt-tipped, grey-green foliage and clean-white flowers held aloft on strong stems. Markings vary greatly, generally from a single green mark to double barring, but many aberrants have been named, and they include the green-tipped 'Comet' and the six-petalled 'Godfrey Owen'. *G. elwesii*, although very hardy, does best in well-drained soil that gets a good summer bake. Give it good light on the edge of woodland shade or use it at the front of a mixed border among hybrid hellebores, miniature daffodils and other spring woodlanders. Like all snowdrops, it loves a slope because this provides better drainage. Elwes's garden, Colesbourne Park in Gloucestershire, is still one of the world's great snowdrop gardens, and some of its finest seedlings have been named after family members, including 'Lord Lieutenant' and 'George Elwes'. **VB**

Alternatives

Galanthus plicatus, *Galanthus* 'Atkinsii', *Galanthus reginae-olgae*, *Galanthus woronowii*

Galtonia
G. candicans

Main feature Flowers from summer to autumn; colourful, lightly scented blooms
Height 90 cm (3 ft) **Spread** 20 cm (8 in.)
Position ○ **Hardiness** RHS H4

The summer hyacinth is a stately summer flower, which looks regally elegant and deserves to be planted in any herbaceous or mixed border. Its tall spires of up to thirty nodding, bell-shaped, white flowers rise above the glossy, strap-like leaves in late summer and early autumn. They are up to 5 centimetres (2 in.) long, lightly scented, and open in succession, providing an attractive display over quite a long period of time. In order to extend flowering even further, you can plant in early spring for flowers from mid- to late summer or delay planting until late spring to have flowers from late summer into autumn. *G. candicans* is particularly useful for flowering above the faded foliage of earlier-flowering perennials. However, it does not look as impressive when dotted about and grown as individual plants, so instead plant bold groups of seven to ten bulbs. Alternatively, try planting the bulbs individually in small pots, or three or five bulbs together, in early autumn for flowers in late spring or early summer. **GH**

Alternatives

Galtonia candicans 'Moonbeam', *Galtonia viridiflora*, *Galtonia regalis*

◉ *Galanthus elwesii* looks after itself in a well-drained soil.

Gladiolus
G. communis subsp. *byzantinus*

Main features Magenta, trumpet-shaped flowers; sword-shaped foliage; good cut flower; attracts bees
Height 70 cm (28 in.) **Spread** 40 cm (16 in.)
Position ○ **Hardiness** RHS H5

One of the hardiest gladioli and one of the earliest to flower, *G. communis* subsp. *byzantinus* has spires of vivid magenta, trumpet-shaped blooms that set gardens ablaze from late spring to early summer. A wild flower of the Mediterranean region, this colourful corm can be seen growing among olive groves in Spain and southern France, and while the blooms are not as big as many later-flowering cultivars, it sits more easily in relaxed wildlife and informal planting schemes. The green, sword-shaped foliage also offers architectural structure and continues to provide colour after the flowers have faded.

Given free-draining soil, a mild climate, and a sunny site, this gladiolus makes a bold statement when planted in naturalistic groups in rough grass or meadows. It also integrates well into more formal border schemes, providing focal points among lower-growing hardy geraniums, such as *Geranium himalayense*, and ground cover roses, which bloom at roughly the same time. In autumn, plant corms 15 centimetres (6 in.) deep in sandy soil, or if you have clay, plant them in raised beds. Alternatively, buy young plants in late spring if you live in a frost-prone area, and add them to large pots or a sunny border. In autumn in mild areas, cover plants with a thick insulating mulch of mushroom compost or similar dry material. When growing in frost-prone areas, lift the corms and store them in a garage or cool room indoors over winter.

Another small-flowered, relatively hardy gladioli is the *Gladiolus nanus* species, which includes the pink-and-cream-flowered 'Carine', white 'Nymph' and orange 'Amanda Mahy'. Alternatively, opt for a *Gladiolus primulinus*, such as 'Mirella', or the *Gladiolus tubergenii* species, which includes the lavender-pink 'Charming Lady'. These forms are all planted in spring and flower later in summer. **ZA**

Alternatives

Gladiolus nanus 'Carine', *Gladiolus nanus* 'Nymph', *Gladiolus nanus* 'Amanda Mahy', *Gladiolus primulinus* 'Atom'

Gladiolus
G. murielae

Main features Flowers in summer; suitable for borders and containers; swordlike foliage
Height 60 cm (24 in.) **Spread** 25 cm (10 in.)
Position ○ **Hardiness** RHS H3

The first *G. murielae* arrived in Europe in 1930 from Somalia and Eritrea, when it became known as the Abyssinian gladiolus. It is also called *Acidanthera murielae*, and this name originates from *akis*, meaning 'point' and *anthera*, meaning 'helmet peaks', in reference to the plant's horned anthers. The flowers have the shape of an equilateral triangle; the outer petals are larger than the inner ones, and the flower is wide open. Pure white with a burgundy blotch at the centre of the petals, the flowers grow in spikes. Each spike bears between four and eleven flowers; flowering from the bottom to the top, only one or two flowers come into bloom at the same time. The flowers have a diameter of 10 centimetres (4 in.) and produce a heavenly scent, the purpose of which is to attract the hummingbird hawk moth that pollinates the flowers in its native habitat. The foliage is narrow and sword-like and up to 60 centimetres (24 in.) high, which makes quite a statement border shape even before the flowers appear.

These corms require full sun and well-drained soil. In the right climate and planting conditions, they are a great addition to the summer-flowering border, scattered and planted in between existing perennials. Mulch well overwinter. In colder regions or on wetter soil, grow them in containers from the start. Put five or six corms in a container with Mexican daisies (*Erigeron karvinskianus*) or with *Bidens ferulifolia* 'Bellamy White' and enjoy a great scented combination all summer. Alternatively, plant corms in their own pots to use as seasonal late-summer gap fillers. If you plant some in midspring and more in late spring, you will have a spread of flowering plants to fill beds or enjoy in the house. *G.* 'Nymph' is similar, but about half the height with bright-pink markings on white flowers. **FR/MS**

Alternatives

Hesperantha coccinea, Watsonia borbonica, Watsonia pillansii, Gladiolus carneus, Gladiolus carneus 'Georgina'

Gladiolus
G. tristis

Main features Flowers in early summer; good cut flower; suitable for borders and containers
Height 80 cm (2.5 ft) **Spread** 15 cm (6 in.)
Position ○ **Hardiness** RHS H3

A lesser-known species of *Gladiolus*, *G. tristis* is native to the marshy areas and riverbanks of South Africa and is also known in parts of Australia and coastal California as an introduced species. It grows from a corm and produces three narrow leaves. The inflorescence is a spike of between two to eight large, fragrant blooms. Each individual flower has six sulphur-yellow petals with a darker-yellow, green, or purplish line in the middle. These flowers are fragrant in the evening, and the scent resembles that of carnations. Consequently, *G. tristis* makes a good conservatory or veranda pot plant. Use tall pots because the plants grow up to 80 centimetres (2.5 ft) high, and the corms will need planting about 10 to 15 centimetres (4–6 in.) deep.

In some regions *G. tristis* can grow in the ground. Thanks to its native habitat, it is tolerant of water but planting corms on a layer of sand is recommended. In colder areas it will need some winter protection, such as an insulating mulch of bark chips. If planted in the right position and in ideal conditions, it spreads easily by seed; however, for growing in pots it is easier to start with fresh corms each spring.

This plant offers something different for the early-summer flowers in a mixed border; it can also be planted in rows in a cutting garden. In order to enjoy early-summer flowers, plant no later than midspring, as the corms develop best in cool soil. Because of its elegance and subtle colouring, *G. tristis* is at its best in perennial borders where the striking flowers will give the extra touch that is needed. It is also a good addition to borders among ornamental grasses, such as *Sesleria* and *Miscanthus*. Try *G. tristis* in a large container, such as a half-barrel size, with *Carex comans* 'Mint Curls' and *Gaura lindheimeri* 'Whirling Butterflies'. **FR/MS**

Alternatives

Gladiolus primulinus, *Gladiolus tubergenii* 'Charming Henry', *Gladiolus communis* subsp. *byzantinus*

Habranthus
H. robustus

Main features Flowers in summer; suitable for rockeries and pots
Height 25 cm (10 in.) **Spread** 15 cm (6 in.)
Position ○ **Hardiness** RHS H2

The *Habranthus* is one of the several related genera known as rain lilies. *H. robustus* is a herbaceous flowering bulb, and in its native habitat the flowers appear after rain, typically from late summer to early autumn. They are followed by narrow, linear or strap-shaped leaves. The pale-pink flowers resemble small amaryllis flowers: starry, funnel-shaped, and either solitary or in umbels of up to four flowers. In fact, *Habranthus* is a member of the family *Amaryllidaceae*. The genus name comes from *habros*, meaning 'elegant' and *anthos*, which means 'flower' in the Greek language. The *H. robustus* species is native in southern Brazil and Argentina, as well as in Bolivia, Mexico, Paraguay, Arizona, New Mexico and Texas. It was formerly classified under the genus *Zephyranthes*, as *Z. robusta*, but the two are now considered separate. With *Habranthus*, the flowers point upwards at an angle and have unequal stamen in four different sizes, whereas the flowers of *Zephyranthes* point straight up, and the stamen are more equal.

In cooler climates, *H. robustus* can be raised in pots or planted in sheltered rockeries, where the stones will reflect warmth on the areas where the corms have been planted. In late spring plant five or six corms in a 15-centimetre (6 in.) pot to a depth of 5 to 8 centimetres (2–3 in.). Normally, plants start to flower late in summer, and if the weather cooperates, they may flower more than once. When planted in containers, the pots should be taken inside in late autumn and stored in a frost-free place during winter. Other species to try include the yellow-flowering *H. tubispathus* or *H. tubispathus* var. *texensis*, which is found in Texas and Louisiana and has yellow flowers with bronze tints. It blooms after a good rain in summer, or in areas where summer is dry, the blooms appear after the first rain in the autumn. **FR/MS**

Alternatives

Habranthus tubispathus (syn. *Habranthus andersonii*, *Habranthus texanus*)

Hippeastrum
H. cybister 'Chico'

Hippeastrum
H. papilio

Main features Thin delicate petals; unique
spider-like form; flowers in winter
Height 55 cm (21 in.) **Spread** 35 cm (14 in.)
Position ○ ◑ **Hardiness** RHS H2

Main features Orchid-like variety; ideal as a houseplant
or in the garden depending on region
Height 50 cm (20 in.) **Spread** 35 cm (14 in.)
Position ◑ **Hardiness** RHS H2

A member of the Amaryllidaceae family, *Hippeastrum* is a
genus with seventy to seventy-five species and more than
600 hybrids and cultivars. *H. cybister* is native to Bolivia
and Argentina, and 'Chico' is one of the new varieties that
have been introduced to the market relatively recently.
The bulbs are very well known because they are popular
gifts at Christmas, and they are mostly grown as indoor
plants. The flower petals of 'Chico' are thin, oxblood red,
and accented with a green throat, which makes the plant
look very much like an orchid. However, the unique shape
of the delicate flowers has led to the plant being referred
to as a spider amaryllis. Each stem will produce four to
five flowers, but compared to the regular *Hippeastrum*,
this variety produces fewer leaves. At room temperature
'Chico' can flower for at least seven to nine weeks. After
that the plant will need special treatment to get it to
flower again. **FR/MS**

Native to Brazil, *H. papilio* was named in 1970 by Argentine
botanist Pedro Félix Ravenna with reference to the
similarity of the flower's tepals to a swallowtail butterfly's
tail wings. It produces two to three blooms per stem, and
the greenish-white petals are tinged with contrasting
maroon-red-striped markings. Sometimes the plant will
not bloom in its first season, but it becomes more reliable
as the bulb gets older. However, *H. papilio* is an evergreen,
so it can be grown as a houseplant year-round in a sunny
window. When not in bloom, its strap-like, arching and
glossy green leaves add an interesting element to a
collection of potted plants. Outdoors, *H. papilio* requires
some protection from the hot afternoon sun. A shaded
area in an open position is ideal, for example, under trees
with a transparent canopy and in the company of graceful
ornamental grasses, such as the grey-green *Bouteloua
gracilis* and the feathery *Nassella tenuissima*. **FR/MS**

Alternatives

Hippeastrum cybister 'Merengue', *Hippeastrum cybister*
'La Paz'

Alternatives

Hippeastrum 'Sumatra', *Hippeastrum* 'Star of Holland',
Hippeastrum 'Belinda'

Hippeastrum papilio is more sophisticated than run-of-the-mill types sold as gift sets. ➲

Hyacinthoides
H. italica

Main features Blue, purple or white flowers in spring; great woodland plant
Height 40 cm (16 in.) **Spread** 15 cm (6 in.)
Position ◑ **Hardiness** RHS H4

This spring-flowering bulbous perennial is native to northern Italy, southern France and north-eastern Spain, where it naturalises very well in neglected woodland. It is part of the genus *Hyacinthoides*, to which the common or English bluebell *H. non-scripta* and the Spanish bluebell *H. hispanica* also belong, but *H. italica* is a little bit smaller than these more common bluebells, with a stem up to 40 centimetres (16 in.) long. The flowers are blue, purple or white outfacing in pyramidal racemes, and the leaves are linear-lanceolate. This species likes soil that is nutritious and humid, and therefore it is at its best in woodland areas. Here, in dappled shade, the pale-blue colour of the flowers stands out, whereas it would fade and grow dull in full sun.

Plant *H. italica* early in autumn, preferably in large quantities that will turn into beautiful drifts of blue flowers in spring. There are numerous spring-flowering bulbs and perennials that will combine well with this pretty blue flower. Spring bulbs that like the same circumstances and have a similar, rather natural appearance include *Ornithogalum nutans* and *Leucojum aestivum* 'Gravetye Giant', which both flower midspring. A little bit earlier are the 'Sailboat' and 'Jenny' cultivars of *Narcissus jonquilla*. Perennials – such as *Pulmonaria* 'Sissinghurst White', *Omphalodes verna* and *Cardamine heptaphylla* – also complement *H. italica*, and all of them like a woodland habitat. A characteristic of the *H. non-scripta* is that the flowering stems hang down and the flowers are sweetly scented. *H. hispanica* is more vigorous and also hybridises with the English bluebell, so to protect native populations, the planting of *H. hispanica* is discouraged near wild populations. If purchasing English bluebells, buy from a quality supplier to make sure bulbs have not been taken illegally from the wild. **FR/MS**

Alternatives

Hyacinthoides hispanica 'Rose Queen', *Hyacinthoides hispanica* 'Azalea', *Hyacinthoides non-scripta*

Hyacinthus
H. orientalis 'Royal Navy'

Main features Flowers in spring; densely packed double blooms; sweet fragrance; winter-flowering indoors
Height 30 cm (12 in.) **Spread** 8 cm (3 in.)
Position ○ ◐ **Hardiness** RHS H4

If the rich, sweet scent of this sought-after hyacinth is not enough to turn a gardener's head, the stout stems packed with dark-blue, double blooms certainly will. The deep colour of *H. orientalis* 'Royal Navy' contrasts beautifully with golden daffodils and fiery-red tulips in formal bedding schemes or use the plant in a patio container on a garden table, where its intricate petal formation can be viewed at closer quarters.

Plant 'Royal Navy' in bold groups in sun or part shade against a background of bright gravel or set alongside hyacinths in complementary colours. Flowering in mid spring, it also combines well with white or yellow primulas and violas, and dwarf narcissi such as the small-cupped 'Hawera' and 'Yellow Cheerfulness'. Species tulips, including 'Little Beauty' and 'Clusiana', which flower at the same time, also make pretty partners.

In autumn, plant groups of bulbs 10 centimetres (4 in.) deep and 7.5 centimetres (3 in.) apart, either in free-draining soil in the ground or in pots of gritty soil-based compost, but remember to place the pots on 'feet' to allow good drainage. The stems may bend under the weight of the large flower heads, so be prepared to add small stakes to prop them up. As the blooms fade, remove the flower stems but leave the foliage to die down naturally. The bulbs are hardy and can be left in situ, although plants will form looser flower heads in subsequent years, so add new bulbs each fall to maintain the display.

Plants can be forced to flower in winter. To do this, buy prepared bulbs as soon as available in early autumn. Plant in pots and keep cool (7–10°C /45–50°F) to encourage rooting. When the shoots are 5 centimetres (2 in.) high, bring the pots into a light room, no warmer than 21°C (70°F). These plants are toxic and are a skin irritant. **ZA**

Alternatives

Hyacinthus orientalis 'Delft Blue', *Hyacinthus orientalis* 'Festival Blue', *Hyacinthus orientalis* 'Blue Star'

Hyacinthus
H. orientalis 'Woodstock'

Hymenocallis
H. × festalis

Main features Flowers in spring; fragrant; good cut flower; attracts bees
Height 30 cm (12 in.) **Spread** 8 cm (3 in.)
Position ○ **Hardiness** RHS H4

Main feature Fragrant flowers in summer
Height 45 cm (18 in.) **Spread** 30 cm (12 in.)
Position ○
Hardiness RHS H1c

Perhaps best known for its intoxicating perfume, the original wild hyacinth is blue, and although blue, pink and white forms prevail, there are some striking alternatives. *H. orientalis* 'Woodstock', a sport of the vivid carmine 'Jan Bos', is not the darkest hyacinth, but it is a sumptuous magenta purple. The beetroot shading is intense because the individual, thick-textured blooms are so densely packed into the dome-topped cylindrical heads. For a new take on cottage-garden–style, mix 'Woodstock' with early-blooming plum- and berry-coloured tulips, with violas, hybrid primroses or polyanthus. In a contemporary setting, try it as a single subject or with splashes of lime in sleek metallic planters. Historic, or 'heirloom', hyacinths had their heyday in the 1800s and included single- and double-flowered forms. Hyacinths are harmful if eaten and their sap and bulbs can be a skin irritant, so always wear gloves when handling these bulbs. **JH**

Few bulbs burst into bloom more quickly than this *H. × festalis*, which produces big, fragrant flowers some 10 centimetres (4 in.) wide. These white, scented flowers have the shape of a church bell and appear only a few weeks after planting. *H. × festalis* makes a great border plant where the large, double row of strap-like leaves will provide an excellent fresh, green touch. Its height serves it well as a solitaire plant dotted in between lower-growing plants – such as *Anaphalis triplinervis*, *Lavandula angustifolia*, *Artemisia cana* and *Diascia integerrima* – which complement one another and grow well under the same circumstances. This tropical bulbous plant originally comes from the Pacific (Polynesia), where it is a common plant in the wild. Plant it in full sun in rich garden soil or compost, covering the bulbs with 13 centimetres (5 in.) of soil. Space bulbs about 30 centimetres (12 in.) apart in borders, or half that distance in containers. **FR/MS**

Alternatives

Hyacinthus orientalis 'Jan Bos', *Hyacinthus orientalis* 'City of Haarlem', *Hyacinthus orientalis* 'Gipsy Queen'

Alternatives

Hymenocallis 'Sulphur Queen', *Hymenocallis longipetala*, *Hymenocallis harrisiana*

◑ *Hyacinthus orientalis* '**Woodstock**' is a rich magenta-purple and offers plenty of scope for colour combinations, both indoors and out.

Ipheion
'Rolf Fiedler'

Main features Scented, sky-blue, starry spring flowers;
strappy pale-green leaves; good cut flower
Height 15 cm (6 in.) **Spread** 8 cm (3 in.)
Position ○ **Hardiness** RHS H5

Hailing from South America, this small but eye-catching
bulb sports a profusion of sky-blue flowers that form
carpets of starry upturned faces when they appear over
many weeks from early spring. Although the underskirt of
short, strappy leaves smells of onions when bruised, the
flowers themselves emit a sweet honey-like scent and are
prized as cut flowers, adding to this tiny plant's charms.

Use 'Rolf Fiedler' en masse to cover sunny banks or
grow it in a sheltered gravel or rock garden alongside
dwarf narcissi, crocuses and white squills (*Puschkinia
scilloides* var. *libanotica* 'Alba'), which have matching
needs and flower at the same time. The bulbs can
also be planted in pots, either on their own or with
other early-flowering bulbs. *Ipheion* naturalises freely,
given the right conditions, but becomes dormant in
summer; mask the gaps with later-flowering plants,
such as *Armeria maritima*, *Helianthemum* and *Campanula
carpatica*. The bulbs are quite hardy, as long as the
soil is free-draining, so if you have heavy clay in the
garden, plant 'Rolf Fiedler' in raised beds or containers.
Other *Ipheion* to look out for include 'Jessie', which
is similar to 'Rolf Fiedler' but has darker blue flowers;
'Alberto Costello', a taller cultivar with large white
blooms; and 'Charlotte Bishop', with its white-centred,
deep-pink flowers. An attractive violet-blue option is
I. uniflorum 'Wisley Blue', which blooms for a long period
from late winter. **ZA**

Alternatives

Syn. *Ipheion uniflorum* 'Rolf Fiedler'. *Ipheion* 'Jessie', *Ipheion
uniflorum* 'Wisley Blue', *Ipheion uniflorum* 'Charlotte Bishop'

Iris
I. *reticulata* 'Joyce'

Main features Flowers in spring; suitable for borders and containers; fragrant
Height 15 cm (6 in.) **Spread** 5 cm (2 in.)
Position ○ **Hardiness** RHS H7

There are numerous types of *Iris*, but the best known are *Iris germanica* and *Iris sibirica*, which are both rhizomatous, herbaceous perennials that are vigorous and prominent in the garden. The early-flowering bulbous plant *I. reticulata* has a totally different appearance and comes in various varieties, including 'Joyce' (sky blue with an orange blotch), 'Natascha' (white), 'Pauline' (deep purple) and 'Cantab' (pale blue). The Greek word *iris* means 'rainbow' and refers to the plant's endless number of colours and to the beauty of the flowers. The name may also refer to the way the outer petals are bowed like a rainbow.

I. reticulata 'Joyce' reaches a height of approximately 15 centimetres (6 in.) and has fragrant flowers. It prefers a sunny spot and well-drained, limy soil. Like the snowdrop (*Galanthus*), it is one of the first to flower in spring, or even very late winter, so should be planted in groups of various sizes to get the best effect. After flowering, the grey-green grassy leaves begin to appear, and these offer a graceful addition to the display too.

The best area in the garden for 'Joyce' is a raised bed or a warm edge along a wall. However, *I. reticulata* can also perform very well in containers. Plant it as a first layer in a lasagne pot, with *Crocus* in the second layer and a tiny low-growing *Narcissus* such as 'Jack Snipe' or 'Tête-à-Tête' in the third layer. In the wild, they grow in north and south Turkey, Iraq, Iran and the southern part of the Caucasus. **FR/MS**

Alternatives

Iris danfordiae, Iris histrioides 'George', *Iris reticulata* 'Katharine Hodgkin'

Iris
I. xiphium

Lachenalia
L. aloides

Main features Flowers in early summer; good cut flower; suitable for beds and borders
Height 75 cm (2.5 ft) **Spread** 30 cm (12 in.)
Position ○   **Hardiness** RHS H5

Main features Flowers in summer; pot plant or rockery; plant with summer flowers
Height 25 cm (10 in.) **Spread** 20 cm (8 in.)
Position ○ ◑   **Hardiness** RHS H2

The *I. xiphium* is common in Portugal, Spain, Sicily and northern Africa, and it is one of the small bulb irises. It bears blue, violet, white or yellow flowers, and each flower consists of six perianth segments, joined together by a short tube above the ovary. The outer three are called 'falls' and grow out horizontally or half vertically, then turn downwards towards the tips. The three inner standards are somewhat smaller and vertical. The falls have a different colour from the standards and are often delightfully blotched with a third colour. The flowers stand on graceful, sturdy stems, and the foliage is narrow and linear. These greyish-green leaves emerge in autumn. *I. xiphium* is great for rock gardens, in raised beds and along a sun-facing wall. It requires a sunny position and well-drained soil. Blue is the most popular colour, such as *I.* 'Professor Blaauw' followed by the bronze *I.* 'Bronze Beauty'. **FR/MS**

The *L. aloides* is a bulbous perennial, belonging to the *Hyacinthaceae* family, and it is native to the Western Cape and Namaqualand in South Africa. In Europe, *Lachenalia* was seen for the first time at Schönbrunn Palace in Vienna, where Baron Nikolaus von Jacquin studied the plant and named it *L. aloides*, after Werner de Lachenal, a well-known professor in Basel, Switzerland. *L. aloides* has fleshy stems, bearing tubular, pendant flowers that are 2.5 centimetres (1 in.) long. These flowers come in various colours: yellow, reddish and pink are popular as well as bicoloured. *L. aloides* also has green flowers banded with red and yellow, whereas the flowers of *Lachenalia bulbifera* combine coral red, yellow and purple. In general *L. aloides* is cultivated as a houseplant, but it is sometimes seen in rock gardens, in regions where it is warm enough for it to grow outside. It grows best in at least four hours of direct sunlight a day, but should be kept cool at night. **FR/MS**

Alternatives

Iris hollandica 'Autumn Princess', *Iris hollandica* 'Eye of the Tiger', *Iris xiphium* 'Casablanca', *Iris hollandica* 'Blue Magic'

Alternatives

Lachenalia liliiflora, Lachenalia longituba, Lachenalia longibracteata

Leucocoryne
'Andes'

Main features Flowers in early summer; suitable for beds and borders
Height 45 cm (18 in.) **Spread** 5 cm (2 in.)
Position ○ ◑ **Hardiness** RHS H3

Native to South America and seen in large numbers in the dry rocky mountain areas of Chile, *Leucocoryne* grows at altitudes of 2,000 metres (6,500 ft). The colours of the flowers can range from blue to lilac, but there are also several pinks. *Leucocoryne* 'Andes' has pale, purplish-blue flowers with cranberry-coloured centres and tiny green eyes. It grows on graceful stems with grass-like leaves, and there are a number of fragrant blossoms on each stem. The foliage, like that of all other *Leucocoryne*, is wispy and disappears about the time the blossoms appear. This happens in midsummer, when it will flower for a couple of weeks. A great addition to the midsummer border, 'Andes' is superb amid early-flowering rockery plants, such as *Arabis*, *Cerastium* and *Phlox subulata*. It will also do well in containers, alongside annual plants, such as *Erigeron karvinskianus* and makes a great cut flower that will last for a long time. **FR/MS**

Alternatives

Leucocoryne ixioides 'Blue Ocean', *Leucocoryne* 'Dione', *Leucocoryne* 'Sunny Stripe', *Leucocoryne* 'White Dream'

Leucojum
L. aestivum
'Gravetye Giant'

Main features Flowers in late spring; snowdrop-like, green-tipped flowers; strappy foliage; slightly fragrant
Height 60 cm (24 in.) **Spread** 30 cm (12 in.)
Position ○ ◑ **Hardiness** RHS H7

The slightly fragrant blooms of *L. aestivum* 'Gravetye Giant' are like giant green-tipped snowdrops, and the bells hang in small clusters from tall, arching stems that shoot up between strappy, dark-green leaves. Robust yet dainty in appearance, 'Gravetye Giant' thrives in full sun or the dappled shade of a woodland edge. This European native reaches just above the knees, or slightly taller. It makes the perfect match for bluebells and red campion (*Silene dioica*) in woodland situations, or the nodding white flowers combine with candelabra primulas in bog gardens next to streams and water features. 'Gravetye Giant' can also be grown successfully in a large container, as long as the soil is kept moist throughout spring. The earlier-flowering spring snowflake, *L. vernum*, makes a good companion for its cousin; it is shorter in stature but produces larger nodding white flowers with green spots. Both plants are good subjects for wildflower gardens. **ZA**

Alternatives

Leucojum aestivum, *Leucojum vernum* 'Podpolozje', *Leucojum vernum* var. *carpathicum*

Lilium
L. canadense

Main feature Summer flowers for beds and borders
Height 45–150 cm (18–60 in.) Spread 30 cm (12 in.)
Position ○ ◑
Hardiness RHS H4

Known as the Canada lily, wild yellow lily or meadow lily, *L. canadense* is a native of eastern North America. It grows in Quebec and Nova Scotia, and from there southward, in moist meadows, along watersides and in semi-shaded wood margins. The species is variable: it can cross-pollinate and set seed, as well as be propagated by bulbs (stolon). Consequently, the height of the plant varies greatly from 45 to 150 centimetres (18–60 in.). The flowers come in orange, yellow or red, and they are spotted on the insides of the petals to a greater or lesser extent. The blooms emerge in summer, nodding like clusters of small bells, and they attract a great many bees.

This bulb prefers a sunny or partially shaded site, but it requires a moist position in slightly acidic soil. It is important that the soil does not dry out during the growing season, and leaf mould can be used to help improve the soil if necessary. Plant the bulbs in autumn and ensure that they are planted at least 15 centimetres (6 in.) deep and fairly wide apart. Roots will also appear along the stalks, hence the advantage of deep planting. In spring make sure that the plants are well protected against slugs and snails. Plants that go well with these elegant lilies are those that prefer the same moist soil, such as *Rodgersia*, *Iris sibirica*, *Filipendula* and *Carex*. Alternatively, *L. canadense* can be planted in amongst ferns or rhododendrons to provide summer highlights.

The flower buds and roots of *L. canadense* were once gathered and eaten by North American native tribes. The plant was introduced to Europe by the French in the 1620s, and it was the first American lily to be known there. By the middle of the seventeenth century, it was being grown in English gardens. The species was named *Lilium canadense* by the Swedish botanist Carl Linnaeus in 1753. **FR/MS**

Alternatives

Lilium regale, Lilium lancifolium, Lilium martagon, Lilium henryi

Lilium
L. mackliniae

Main features Flowers early summer; good for rock
gardens and woodland areas
Height 30–90 cm (12–36 in.) **Spread** 15 cm (6 in.)
Position ◑ **Hardiness** RHS H5

Also known as the Shirui or Siroi lily, *L. macklinae* is native
to India where it grows more than 1,700 metres (5,700 ft)
above sea level, in the Manipur region, close to Myanmar
(formerly Burma). It was discovered on the windswept
ridges of the mountains in 1946 by English botanist and
plant explorer Frank Kingdon-Ward, who named the plant
after his second wife, Jean Macklin. According to local
folklore the flower helps keep evil spirits away and brings
wealth and happiness. *L. mackliniae* is a distinctive plant,
which, being the state flower of Manipur, has become a
tourist attraction in north-eastern India. Unfortunately, it
has also become an endangered species.

This rare and outstandingly beautiful lily is not
very tall, between 30 and 90 centimetres (12–36 in.) in
height. Each stem bears up to seven flowers, which hang
down like bells and are a pale, bluish pink colour, which
is flushed reddish purple at the base. The bell-shaped
flowers will nod gently in the breeze. The long, narrow,
mid- to dark-green leaves are typical of most lilies. It is
a shade-loving plant that blooms during the monsoon
months of June and July. There are several forms in
cultivation, including the descendants of Myanmar's
original seed introduction; most of these are less than
40 centimetres (16 in.) tall. More recent introductions
show much taller plants, carrying pale to darker pink
flowers. Most bulbs that are found on the market today
are all raised from seeds.

The bulb of *L. mackliniae* is diminutive in size; it likes
soil rich in humus that does not dry out. It feels at home
between small ericaceous shrubs and even grows well
in compost that is comprised almost entirely of organic
matter. Plants prefer a spot sheltered from direct sun
and where there is a high percentage of humidity. Water
plants when they are in flower. **FR/MS**

Alternatives

*Lilium leucanthemum, Lilium sargentiae,
Nomocharis aperta*

Lilium
L. lancifolium 'Splendens'

Lilium
Pink Perfection Group

Main features Flowers in summer; good cut flower; highly scented
Height 90 cm (3 ft) **Spread** 30 cm (12 in.)
Position ○ ◑ **Hardiness** RHS H7

Main features Flowers late summer; good cut flower; plant in perennial borders and ornamental thickets
Height 2 m (6.5 ft) **Spread** 30 cm (12 in.)
Position ○ ◑ **Hardiness** RHS H6

The *L. lancifolium* (also called *Lilium tigrinum*, the tiger lily) is one of the prettiest lilies. The tiger lily was originally described in 1712 by German naturalist Kaempfer but became established in Europe in 1804 by Thurnberg, a student of Swedish botanist Linnaeus. The sturdy, long stem of the cultivar 'Splendens' holds many crimson-spotted orange flowers with recurved petals, like a turk's cap. It grows in well-drained, moist soil. It has contractile roots but it also forms roots on its stems, so plant at least 15 centimetres (6 in.) deep. It flowers from midsummer and can be used in combination with shrubs, especially those with a strong leaf colour, like *Physocarpus opulifolius* 'Luteus' (yellow leaves), 'Diabolo' (red leaves) or specimen ferns (bright-green leaves). Alternatively, plant against ornamental grasses, which form a powerful yet subtle background, such as *Calamagrostis × acutiflora* 'Overdam' or varieties of *Miscanthus*. **FR/MS**

Pink Perfection belongs to the division of trumpet lilies: tall lilies in gorgeous shades, such as white, cream, yellow, apricot, copper and pink. Most of them have contrasting tones on the reverse of the petals. Pink Perfection also comes in shades of pale- or deep-purplish pink, and the large, trumpet-shaped flowers are very fragrant. They flower in midsummer in short racemes, or umbels on top of thick, rigid stems with plenty of narrow, dark-green leaves. The showy flowers provide colour, contrast and impact in the perennial border between tall ornamental grasses, but they can also be good companions to not too tall, flowering shrubs like *Hydrangea macrophylla* 'Lanarth White' or 'Bouquet Rose'. Plant in groups of three to five bulbs in well-drained, neutral, moist soil. Like most lilies, Pink Perfection should be planted deep, at 15 to 20 centimetres (6–8 in.), and spaced 30 to 45 centimetres (12–18 in.) apart for a good display. **FR/MS**

Alternatives

Lilium martagon, Lilium martagon var. 'Album', *Lilium candidum, Lilium canadense*

Alternatives

Lilium regale, Lilium nepalense, Lilium 'Casa Blanca', *Lilium* 'African Queen'

 Lilium lancifolium 'Splendens' brings summer flowers to partially shaded corners.

Lilium
L. regale

Lilium
L. martagon

Main features Flowers in summer; good cut flower; highly scented
Height 90 cm (3 ft)   **Spread** 20 cm (8 in.)
Position ○ ◑   **Hardiness** RHS H6

Main features Purple-pink summer flowers with purple-spotted swept-back petals; whorls of dark-green leaves
Height 1.2 m (4 ft)   **Spread** 30 cm (12 in.)
Position ○ ◑   **Hardiness** RHS H7

The regal lily – *L. regale* – was discovered in 1903 in western China, near the Tibetan border, by English plant collector Ernest Wilson. The only place where these lilies were found was in a narrowly enclosed valley, the Min River Valley, in the high mountains. There, it is very hot in summer and can be extremely cold in winter. In 1910, Wilson collected a large number of bulbs from this area. The 6,000 bulbs that he brought back were the source of the many millions that we now have today. *L. regale* belongs to a group of trumpet hybrids. It has a large bulb, which should be planted in autumn or spring in a sunny, well-drained area. All lilies need 'cold feet', so plant them between plants that provide shade, such as hostas. Each stem has three to eight trumpet-shaped, white flowers, which produce a heady summer scent. They face outwards from the stem and hang slightly downwards. The heart of the flower is bright yellow, and the outside is covered with a red-pink to purple-brown

This striking lily is no shy bystander. Its towering stems of purple-pink flowers pack a punch in summer, upstaging more demure woodlanders in the twinkling light beneath the deciduous trees. Sporting up to fifty blooms per stem and above whorls of dark-green leaves, the nodding flowers, with their signature swept-back spotted petals, dance like pirouetting ballerinas when touched by the breeze. Although blooms are normally purple pink, some may appear in other colours, and while they are strongly scented, the perfume is not pleasant, so plant away from seating areas. Turk's cap lilies are too tall and brightly coloured for mixing with dainty woodland flowers, and look best rising up among shrubs – such as Christmas box, *Sarcococca confusa* and viburnums – or the male fern, *Dryopteris filix-mas*. Alternatively, plant bulbs in a sunnier spot together with cottage garden favourites, such as delphiniums, lupins and geraniums. The lily's common name refers to the turbans worn by Turkish sultans. **ZA**

Alternatives

Lilium martagon, Lilium martagon var. 'Album', *Lilium candidum, Lilium henryi*

Alternatives

Lilium martagon var. 'Alba', *Lilium martagon* × 'Terrace City', *Lilium martagon* × 'Claude Shride'

Lilium martagon lilies left to naturalise at the back of a border in dappled shade. ➤

Muscari
M. azureum

Main features Powder-blue conical, scented flower heads; grass-like grey-green foliage; attracts insects
Height 10–15 cm (4–6 in.) **Spread** 10–15 cm (4–6 in.)
Position ○ ◑ **Hardiness** RHS H7

The distinctive powder-blue flowers of this grape hyacinth, *M. azureum*, form a bright carpet of colour beneath deciduous trees in spring gardens. The conical flower heads are comprised of up to forty tiny scented bells, and they appear on clear stems above four or five grass-like, grey-green leaves, which wither and die when the plant becomes dormant in summer. Distinct from the more common species, *M. armeniacum*, which has darker blue flowers, the azure grape hyacinth rarely becomes invasive. Blooming best in woodland settings, its flowers appear before the tree leaves unfurl, and make good partners for crocuses, dwarf narcissi and the woodland anemone, *Anemone nemorosa*, as well as larger spring flowers, including *Epimedium* and the dog's tooth violet, *Erythronium*. Azure grape hyacinths are also perfect for hanging baskets, or combine them with white narcissi and ferns to complement contemporary patio displays of box topiary and evergreen shrubs. **ZA**

Alternatives

Muscari armeniacum, Muscari latifolium, Muscari aucheri 'White Magic', *Muscari armeniacum* 'Album'

Muscari
M. latifolium

Main features Two-tone dark-blue spring flower heads topped with bright-blue blooms; attracts pollinators
Height 15–22 cm (6–9 in.) **Spread** 10 cm (4 in.)
Position ○ ◑ **Hardiness** RHS H7

Prized for its unusual two-tone blooms, *M. latifolium* is the queen of the grape hyacinths. It stands slightly proud of its cousins, reaching up to 23 centimetres (9 in.) in height, and in spring sports bunched grape-like heads of tiny, inky-blue flowers topped with bright-blue tufted hats. Each baby bloom is wrapped in one or two wide grey-green leaves, forming little posies that produce a mesmerising display when planted en masse in a border or large container. Plant them in broad naturalistic drifts under deciduous trees and shrubs, either on their own, or with seams of other diminutive spring bulbs, such as narcissi, wood anemones, white *Ipheion* and lily of the valley (*Convallaria majalis*). They also make superb rock garden plants and work well in containers. Try partnering them with violas, ferns, heucheras, dwarf hebes and other small bulbs in pots, baskets and window boxes, but take care when matching them with other blue-coloured flowers – they may clash. **ZA**

Alternatives

Muscari aucheri 'Mount Hood', *Muscari macrocarpum* 'Golden Fragrance', *Muscari paradoxum*

◔ *Muscari azureum* at close quarters to show the structure of the flower head.

Narcissus
'Crackington'

Main features Strong growing, double-flowered daffodil; good cut flower; weather resistant; fragrant
Height 30 cm (12 in.) **Spread** 15 cm (6 in.)
Position ○ ◐ **Hardiness** RHS H6

'Crackington' belongs to the division of double-flowered narcissi and has been described since 1620. It flowers with a double, mixed orange-yellow bloom that resembles a rose. The flowers are fragrant and appear on 30-centimetre (12 in.) stems with strap-shaped leaves, making it an excellent cut flower. It is easy to grow and, once planted, it behaves like a perennial, coming back each spring without any special treatment. These double narcissi are lovely for beds and borders; they prefer a sheltered location in full to part sun. They will tolerate most soils but prefer a fertile, well-drained soil that remains moist during the growing season. Their flowering period starts in early spring and, depending on the location, can last until late in the season. This narcissus received a Royal Horticultural Society Award of Garden Merit because it is a robust daffodil that copes with the often unsettled weather in early spring.

'Crackington' can be planted in various situations, for example, in perennial borders together with *Primula elatior* (oxlip), *Aquilegia* (columbine) and the ornamental grass *Milium effusum* 'Aureum' (golden grass). It also works in formal beds, with white or blue forget-me-not (*Myosotis*). Last but not least, it is lovely planted in meadows, with other spring-flowering bulbs, like *Narcissus poeticus* var. *recurvus*, *Leucojum aestivum* 'Gravetye Giant' and *Camassia cusickii*.

Other well-known narcissi of the double-flowered group are 'Van Sion', 'Rip van Winkle' and 'Sir Winston Churchill'. 'Van Sion' is visually the most extravagant of these. It is an early-spring-flowering species that has golden-yellow flowers, but these can sometimes be golden yellow all over with perfect double trumpets, sometimes resembling shaggy powder puffs, marked with green. **FR/MS**

Alternatives

Narcissus 'Van Sion', *Narcissus* 'Rip van Winkle', *Narcissus* 'Sir Winston Churchill', *Narcissus* 'Cheerfulness'

Narcissus
'Hawera'

Main features Buttery-yellow, swept-back petals;
creamy-yellow cups; strappy foliage; good cut flower
Height 25 cm (10 in.) **Spread** 15 cm (6 in.)
Position ○ ◑ **Hardiness** RHS H6

One of the best of the late-spring-flowering daffodils, this
dainty bulb has myriad charms. The nodding blooms with
their swept-back petals resemble fluttering birds about to
land, and each bulb produces several flower stems, rising
above slim, strappy foliage. Up to five slightly fragrant
blooms form on each stem, their pale-yellow petals
teamed with creamy cups, creating a two-tone effect.

Raised in New Zealand, this dwarf daffodil has the
Maori name 'Hawera', referring to a town on the North
Island. Like all daffodils, 'Hawera' creates the most
dramatic display when grown in groups or swaths. It
thrives in the dappled shade beneath deciduous trees
and shrubs and is an ideal match for those that come
into leaf with or just after the daffodil's blooms, such as
Cotinus and *Ribes*. Its late appearance also makes 'Hawera'
an ideal partner for tulips, *Leucojum*, and wallflowers in
a border, the pastel flowers combining well with most
colours. Alternatively, use the bulbs in containers and
deep window boxes alongside other late-spring flowers
and small leafy shrubs, such as hebes.

'Hawera' is one of the triandrus group of daffodils,
which all produce two to six small blooms on each
flowering stem. In autumn, plant the bulbs 10 to 15
centimetres (4–6 in.) deep and 8 centimetres (3 in.) apart
in free-draining soil or pots of loam-based compost.
Choose a spot that is sunny in spring – the bulbs tolerate
some shade in summer when dormant. Nip off the faded
blooms, apply a liquid feed, and leave the foliage to die
down naturally after flowering. Other triandrus group
daffodils include 'Silver Chimes', which has white petals
and yellow cups; 'Stint', with its lemon-yellow blooms; and
'Puppet', which has yellow petals contrasting with orange
cups. For white blooms try 'Thalia' or 'Ice Wings'. **ZA**

Alternatives

Narcissus 'Silver Chimes', *Narcissus* 'Stint', *Narcissus* 'Puppet',
Narcissus 'Thalia', *Narcissus* 'Ice Wings'

Narcissus
'Jack Snipe'

Narcissus
'Kokopelli'

Main features Early-spring flowers; white swept-back petals and yellow trumpets; green strappy leaves
Height 22–30 cm (9–12 in.) **Spread** 15 cm (6 in.)
Position ○ ◑ **Hardiness** RHS H7

Main features Elegant narcissus; flowers late spring; good for beds and borders
Height 25–30 cm (10–12 in.) **Spread** 13 cm (5 in.)
Position ○ **Hardiness** RHS H6

Amongst the first daffodils to open, elegant 'Jack Snipe' is justifiably popular, its nodding flowers with white swept-back petals and contrasting buttercup-yellow trumpets making a splash from early to mid spring. This dwarf daffodil produces only one flower per stem, but each bulb can give rise to six or more blooms, which appear above grass-like foliage. Group these beauties close to deciduous trees and shrubs in moist soil, where the flowers will produce spectacular displays in the early spring. In small gardens or on a patio, allow their blooms to shine on their own in plain terra-cotta pots or partner them in large pots with leafy evergreens that enjoy similar conditions, such as *Ajuga*, shield ferns (*Polystichum*) and Japanese spurge, *Pachysandra terminalis*. 'Jack Snipe', with its cyclamen-like petals, is a cyclamineus daffodil. It enjoys moist, slightly acidic soil and is more successful on heavy soils than many other spring bulbs. **ZA**

'Kokopelli' belongs to the group of jonquil daffodils, which come from the Iberian Peninsula, southern France, northern Africa, Italy and the Balkans. The name 'jonquil' originates from the Latin word for 'reed'. Reeds are slender, elegant plants, and the same holds true for the this narcissus. 'Kokopelli' grows up to 30 centimetres (12 in.) tall; one bulb produces a number of stems, each one bearing two fragrant yellow flowers. At the start of the flowering period, the darker centre, or cup, shows a green colour at the base; the six petals are slightly paler yellow than the cup and form a flat, round flower from which the shallow cup protrudes. Plant at the start of autumn before the soil gets too cold. They prefer a sunny location, where they will thrive and naturalise. They make a beautiful show planted with late-flowering orange tulip 'Ballerina' and creamish-white tulip 'Spring Green'. Or sprinkle them as solitaires in a group of *Aquilegia* 'Silver Queen'. **FR/MS**

Alternatives

Narcissus cyclamineus, *Narcissus* 'February Gold', *Narcissus* 'Jetfire', *Narcissus* 'Rapture', *Narcissus* 'Little Witch'

Alternatives

Narcissus 'Baby Moon', *Narcissus* 'Bell Song', *Narcissus* 'Pipit', *Narcissus* 'Quail'

● *Narcissus* 'Jack Snipe' planted in rough grass.

Narcissus
N. papyraceus

Main features Great for forcing; strongly scented; multi-flowered; good cut flower; popular Christmas bulb
Height 40 cm (16 in.) **Spread** 15 cm (6 in.)
Position ○ ◑ **Hardiness** RHS H4

One of a few species known as paperwhites, *N. papyraceus* belongs to the division of tazetta daffodils. The tazetta was one of the narcissi that attracted attention in ancient times due to its scent, which was thought to be healing. It is a perennial, bulbous plant, native to the western Mediterranean region. Usually white with a yellow cup, it is the earliest flowering narcissus: it blooms from Christmas until midspring. In its native habitat *N. papyraceus* requires average, well-drained soil in full sun or partial shade. Paperwhite narcissi can be used in the garden, but they are best known as pot plants. The bulbs are excellent for forcing and, in contrast to other narcissi, can come into flower in a cool room in full light, so that they produce roots and leaves at the same time. They flower three weeks after potting. Other scented paperwhites include *Narcissus tazetta* 'Grand Soleil d'Or' (showy golden-yellow flowers with orange cups) and *N. tazetta* 'Ziva' (masses of pure-white flowers). **FR/MS**

Alternatives

Narcissus 'Geranium', *Narcissus* 'Golden Dawn', *Narcissus* Minnow', *Narcissus* 'Martinette', *Narcissus* 'Falconet'

Narcissus
N. poeticus var. recurvus

Main features Flowers late spring; fragrant blooms; good cut flower; naturalises well
Height 30–45 cm (12–18 in.) **Spread** 10 cm (4 in.)
Position ○ ◑ **Hardiness** RHS H6

Practically the last daffodil to bloom, *N. poeticus* var. *recurvus* produces its pure-white, sweetly fragrant heads in late spring. The petals are elegantly swept back, and the shallow yellow cup is highlighted by a crinkled flame rim, the overall look reminiscent of a pheasant's ringed eye (hence, its common name old pheasant's eye). This rather dainty daffodil has upright tufts of narrow, ribbed leaves. It revels in rough grass, blooming alongside cowslips, cuckoo flower (*Cardamine pratensis*) and snakeshead fritillary. It can be found blooming in vast numbers in damp meadows, alpine pastures and light woodlands across central Europe. Though noted for its ability to naturalise in grass, it makes a fine addition to the late-spring border, provided the ground remains reasonably moist. This wild daffodil is grown commercially in France and the Netherlands where its potent essential oil is extracted for perfumery. Cut for the house, two or three stems are enough to scent a room. **JH**

Alternatives

Narcissus 'Actaea', *Narcissus* 'Salome', *Narcissus* 'February Gold', *Narcissus* 'Sweetness', *Narcissus* 'Yellow Cheerfulness'

Narcissus
'Segovia'

Main feature Flowers spring; good cut flower; suits borders and semi-shaded woodland areas
Height 18 cm (7 in.) **Spread** 8 cm (3 in.)
Position ○ ◑ **Hardiness** RHS H6

The narcissus of early times was not considered worth collecting. Later, when bulbous plants became more popular, the Netherlands was the centre of narcissi production. Around 1880, activity shifted to England and Ireland, where wild gardening, for which the narcissus was highly suitable, took hold. Today, the narcissus is the United Kingdom's most popular cut flower. *N.* 'Segovia' is a typical small-cupped narcissus. Distinguishing characteristics are one flower to a stem, with the cup, or corona, no more than one-third the length of the outer perianth segments. 'Segovia' has a white perianth with a greenish-yellow cup, and it flowers in late spring. It naturalises well and belongs to a group of narcissi that bloom profusely. It is also an excellent cut flower, lovely in bouquets with forget-me-nots and *Allium cowanii*. It prefers a not-too-shady spot in the garden and is at its best planted in small drifts in between perennials, such as *Heuchera* or *Dicentra formosa* (bleeding heart). **FR/MS**

Alternatives

Narcissus 'Barrett Browning', *Narcissus* 'Mite', *Narcissus* 'Snipe', *Narcissus* 'Polar Ice', *Narcissus* 'Sea Princess'

Nerine
N. bowdenii

Main features Spring planting; flowers in the autumn; good cut flower
Height 50 cm (20 in.) **Spread** 20 cm (8 in.)
Position ○ **Hardiness** RHS H5

The South African lily *N. bowdenii* grows wild on the Cape of Good Hope and on Table Mountain. It blooms as a cluster of flowers on a leafless stem; the leaves appear as a rosette at the bottom of the stem. Each flower is trumpet-shaped, and the petals curl backwards. With its tall scapes, terminated by a loose umbel of five to ten trumpet-shaped, shocking-pink flowers, it is perhaps the most exotic autumn-flowering bulb and lifts the spirits on a dull fall day. *N. bowdenii* flowers at the end of the growing period (early autumn) when the foliage has almost withered and flowers till late autumn. It is good planted against a sunny wall with plants such as *Erysmium* 'Bowles Mauve', *Asphodeline* and *Iris unguicularis*. Another attractive combination is with the blue-flowering *Ceratostigma*, which flowers in late summer. It should be planted shallowly in a very sunny, sheltered spot in the garden. It can also be planted in containers that can be brought inside during the cold season. **FR/MS**

Alternatives

Nerine bowdenii 'Albivetta', *Nerine sarniensis*, *Nerine undulate*

Nerine
N. sarniensis

Main feature Flowers from autumn to winter; exotic blooms from shocking pink to pure white; sparkling petals
Height 13–15 cm (5–6 in.) **Spread** 13–15 cm (5–6 in.)
Position ○ **Hardiness** RHS H2

To have fresh flowers appear in late autumn is a wonderful treat, and those of *N. sarniensis* have a particular glistening sheen to the petals – hence the common name diamond lily – that is best appreciated at close quarters. Another desirable feature is the flower's wavy petals. Nerines are, in fact, related to the amaryllis rather than lilies.

The light-reflecting petals have marked this species out as a plant for the serious collector or breeder, and *N. sarniensis* has been known in Europe since 1635, with records of selections and breeding from 1820 onwards. The Victorians admired the metallic 'dusting' of the petals. In the 1930s nerines were bred by the Rothschild family at Exbury Gardens in the United Kingdom.

Cultivars (or hybrids with other nerines) are more reliable plants than the species, although plants often hybridise too readily. Named nerines are only available from a few specialists who propagate them by offsets so the best advice is to buy plants in flower. Choose one with a colour and flower you like – there are pinks, reds, oranges, purples and whites. The plants are frost tender, so are grown in a cool greenhouse or conservatory and put on display for their moment of glory, then moved out of the limelight. The leaves follow on later, then die down again in spring. While growing, plants need good light and a feed. Over summer the plant appears to be dormant, but that is when the flower buds are forming; a temperature between 24 and 27°C (75–80°F) at this time is the secret to good flowering in the autumn. **LD**

Alternatives

Nerine filifolia, Nerine flexuosa, Nerine undulata

Nerine
'Zeal Giant'

Main features Flowers in early autumn; pink trumpet-shaped flowers; good for wall-side borders, pots and tubs
Height 80 cm (2.5 ft) **Spread** 20 cm (8 in.)
Position ○ **Hardiness** RHS H3

All nerines are summer dormant, perennial bulbs with erect leafless stems, each bearing a terminal umbel of funnel-shaped flowers with strap-shaped or linear leaves that appear after the flowers. All nerines are native to South Africa and they belong to the family of Amaryllidaceae.

N. 'Zeal Giant' is relatively new and was raised by the late Terry Jones, a specialist nerine breeder from Devon. It is a rather hardy cross from *N. bowdenii* and *N. sarniensis*. 'Zeal Giant' is a vigorous, bulbous perennial that lives up to its name with large clusters of at least twelve deep-pink, trumpet-shaped flowers, each 10 centimetres (4 in.) in diameter with swept-back petals.

This nerine should be planted in spring in a moderately fertile, sun-warmed and well-drained soil, preferably in a sheltered location. Wall-side borders and areas under an overhang are perfect. However, they also grow well in gravel gardens and on patios in pots and tubs. The bulbs should not be planted too deep: 5 centimetres (2 in.) of soil on top will do. In colder areas the plants should be protected with a deep, dry mulch over winter. All 'Zeal' varieties carry a virus; not enough to stunt their growth or affect flowering, but most gardeners keep 'Zeal' apart from other nerine species and varieties.

'Zeal Giant' does not need flowering partners to put on a good show, however, it is good in combination with earlier flowering *Cistus* (rock rose), which requires the same conditions. **FR/MS**

Alternatives

Nerine 'Zeal Salmon', *Nerine* 'Zeal Purple Stripe'

Ornithogalum
O. dubium

Main features Plant in spring, flowers in summer; showy, tightly-packed, vibrant flowers; good cut flower
Height 30–50 cm (12–20 in.) **Spread** 8 cm (3 in.)
Position ○ **Hardiness** RHS H2

The tropical-looking bulbous perennial *O. dubium* is also known as 'chincherinchee' – a term used to describe the sound made by the dry stalks rubbing together in the wind as it blows through flowers in the hedgerows of South Africa's Cape Province. Other common names include star of Bethlehem, orange star flower and snake flower. It grows up to 50 centimetres (20 in.) in height, and the flower at the end of the stem is a pyramid-shaped cluster that produces around twenty small flowers. The colour of the flowers is yellow to deep orange; the leaves are dark green, lance-shaped and short. The Royal Horticultural Society gave this striking bulbous plant the Award of Garden Merit.

Unfortunately, it is only very seldom that this bulb can be bought through catalogs, as it is mainly grown by professional growers who focus on cut flowers. *O. dubium* makes a great cut flower that lasts in bouquets for at least three weeks. However, the circumstances in which it grows well are so particular (temperature, degree of moisture, soil) that it can deter most gardeners. Frost tender, the plants are best overwintered in a frost-free greenhouse, then repotted in spring. Soil must be well-drained; plants need plenty of watering during the early growth cycle but none when dormant. In the same group, there are other *Ornithogalum*, including *O. saundersiae, O. arabicum* and *O. thyrsoides,* which make wonderful summer-flowering bulbs. **FR/MS**

Alternatives

Ornithogalum thyrsoides, Ornithogalum arabicum, Ornithogalum saundersiae

Ornithogalum
O. thyrsoides

Main features Dense clusters of white star-shaped
flowers in summer; long-lasting cut flower
Height 38–50 cm (15–20 in.) **Spread** 10 cm (4 in.)
Position ○ **Hardiness** RHS H2

Known since 1605, *O. thyrsoides* is a tender species
commonly found in the Cape Province of South Africa,
where it is also known as 'chincherinchee'. It is a wonderful
architectural plant and a definite bonus for the garden
in late summer. Gardeners will find it easy to cultivate.
Each round white bulb produces at least two to three
sturdy stems, each bearing a dense raceme of thirty
to fifty star-shaped flowers. The lovely white flowers
have brown centres and prominent yellow stamen.
The flowering period is from late summer to midautumn.
Plant the bulbs in warm and sunny positions in light,
well-drained, humus-rich soil in spring, planting only
5 centimetres (2 in.) deep and 10 centimetres (4 in.) apart.

The broad leaves do not develop fully when grown
outdoors, consequently the bulbs should be dug up
after flowering and then discarded.

It makes a fabulous companion to ornamental grasses
such as *Pennisetum* (fountain grass) and *Hakonechloa*,
but it also partners well with late-flowering perennials,
such as *Aster*. Additionally, it grows well in containers;
O. thyrsoides works beautifully together with *Carex
testacea* or with *Bidens* 'Bellamy White'.

This *Ornithogalum* is cultivated on a commercial scale
as a cut flower since it lives longer in water than any
other flower. If cut in bud and placed in water that is
topped up regularly, every bud will blossom and a bunch
can last up to four weeks. **FR/MS**

Alternatives

*Ornithogalum arabicum, Ornithogalum saundersiae,
Ornithogalum magnum, Ornithogalum nutans*

Polianthes
P. tuberosa

Main features Highly fragrant; flowers in late summer and early autumn; usually grown as a pot plant
Height 60 cm (24 in.) **Spread** 15 cm (6 in.)
Position ○ **Hardiness** RHS H1a

The *P. tuberosa* is highly sought after for its sweetly scented flowers, but it can be tricky to source and to grow. Three species occur in Mexico and Central America, but only *P. tuberosa* was domesticated by the indigenous civilisations of Mexico, as noted when Spanish conquistador Hernán Cortés arrived in 1521. The Inca sweetened their chocolate with parts of the plant and the Aztec used it in traditional medicine. The Spanish took *P. tuberosa* back home, where it was grown in gardens; it also found its way to France and India and now grows in Africa and China too. In Victorian times *P. tuberosa* was a very popular plant, grown in greenhouses and market gardens.

With pure-white flowers, *P. tuberosa* 'The Pearl' is the best-known tuberose. It is also known as mistress of the night and scent of the night, when the plant releases its fragrance. This scent has been described as being floral: deep and rich like a honeysuckle or a gardenia. In the garden it should be planted in mid- to late spring in a warm location. It will then flower in the early autumn. Unfortunately, the flowers are not very rain resistant and will soon spoil. Consequently, it is advisable to plant 'The Pearl' in pots in midspring and to place them in a cold frame. Plant one bulb per 15 centimetre (6 in.) container, with the top of the bulb just visible on the compost surface. Once the plant has rooted sufficiently, it can be moved inside, and if the pots are brought in at intervals of a few weeks, you can have flowering plants on the terrace or in the house in late summer and again in the early autumn. During the growing period, 'The Pearl' needs a lot of water. After flowering leave the foliage to grow on and feed if you want to keep the bulbs. However, although the plant is perennial in tropical climes, it is usual to buy fresh bulbs each year. **FR/MS**

Alternatives

Ornithogalum arabicum, Ornithogalum saundersiae, Ornithogalum dubium 'Namib Gold'

Puschkinia
P. scilloides var. libanotica

Main features Flowers in spring; pale-blue to near-white
flowers with blue stripes; strappy upright foliage
Height 10–13 cm (4–5 in.) **Spread** 5 cm (2 in.)
Position ○ ◑ **Hardiness** RHS H5

Originally from Asia Minor, *P. scilloides* var. *libanotica*
was named for the Russian botanist and collector who
discovered this bulbous plant in 1805. As the name
suggests, this plant has much in common with *Scilla*,
and they flower in the same period, in midspring. *Scilla*
is the dark-blue, earlier-flowering one, while *Puschkinia*
flowers a little later. The species is seldom cultivated, but
the variety *P. scilloides* var. *libanotica* is widely grown. This
plant has larger flowers that are light blue to near white,
with a blue stripe on every petal. Each spike carries up to
ten near-white flowers. The broad leaves arise, sheath-like
and upright, around the stem. The plant has gained the
Royal Horticultural Society's Award of Garden Merit. There
is also a white variety, *P. scilloides* var. *libanotica* 'Alba'.

Both varieties are normally used for naturalising under
trees and shrubs, as well as in grass, where undisturbed
they will form good-sized clumps. They grow well
in dappled shade, but if the soil is moist enough,
they will also grow in full sun. They naturalise well, and
once you have planted them they will come back, year
after year. They should be planted 5 centimetres (2 in.)
deep and a similar distance apart in well-drained soil in
early autumn.

P. scilloides var. *libanotica* is one of those bulbous
plants that suits anywhere – in woodland areas, under
trees and shrubs, in borders, but also in containers. It is
pretty intermingled with other (early) spring-flowering
bulbs, such as *Crocus, Scilla, Chionodoxa* and *Narcissus*
'Jack Snipe' and *N. cyclamineus* 'Tête-à-Tête'. However, be
careful not to overcrowd them. It is also a great addition
to (perennial) ground-covering *Ajuga* (carpet bugle) and
Campanula portenschlagiana (bellflower). Try planting
P. scilloides var. *libanotica* in containers with *Bellis* (English
daisy) and *Myosotis* (forget-me-not). **FR/MS**

Alternatives

Puschkinia scilloides var. *libanotica* 'Alba', *Scilla
mischtschenkoana, Scilla siberica, Scilla siberica* 'Alba'

Roscoea
R. cautleyoides

Main features Flowers in summer; orchid-like flowers; good for rockeries and containers
Height 30–45 cm (12–18 in.) **Spread** 30 cm (12 in.)
Position ◗ **Hardiness** RHS H5–6

Chinese hardy ginger is a perennial, herbaceous plant, occurring in the Chinese provinces of Sichuan and Yunnan. Members of the ginger family usually grow only in tropical areas, but *R. cautleyoides* also grows in colder, mountainous regions. The plant usually has four or five linear leaves. Flowers sometimes appear before the leaves start to develop. Flowers come in various colours, including purple, white and pale pink (rare) but yellow is most common. The flower looks like a cross between an iris and an orchid. It prefers dappled shade and needs humus-rich soil with good drainage; keep moist during summer when flowering. It is a great rockery plant, but because of its unusual appearance, it is hard to combine with other plants, as it wants to stand out on its own. The best companions are those that either are at their best earlier or later in the season, like *Cyclamen coum* and *C. hederifolium,* or foliage plants such as *Ophiopogon planiscapes* 'Nigrescens'. **FR/MS**

Alternatives

Roscoea × beesiana, Roscoea alpina, Roscoea purpurea 'Red Ghurka'

Scadoxus
S. puniceus

Main features Flowers in summer; attractive, globe-shaped umbels of orange-red flowers; good pot plant
Height 60 cm (24 in.) **Spread** 20 cm (8 in.)
Position ◗ **Hardiness** RHS H2

Commonly known as paintbrush lily, *Scadoxus* is a native plant of southern and eastern Africa. Other common names include snake lily, royal paintbrush and African blood lily. A well-known synonym is *Haemanthus natalensis*. It has been cultivated as an ornamental in the Netherlands since the beginning of the eighteenth century. *S. puniceus* can be found in cool, shady habitats, such as forests, where it grows in moist, leafy litter. The large, decorative, ball-shaped umbel of 200 orange-red flowers makes *Scadoxus* an unusual but very attractive plant. The thick, rigid stems can grow to 60 centimetres (24 in.) and carry mid-green, oblong-lanceolate leaves. In cooler climates, *Scadoxus* is best as a pot plant. If potted in early spring, it will flower in the middle of summer. Plant with the tip of the bulb just above the potting compost; the pot should be twice the circumference of the bulb. Like many tender summer bulbs, it prefers bottom heat. A start temperature of 13°C (55°F) is perfect. **FR/MS**

Alternatives

Scadoxus multiflorus subsp. *multiflorus, Sprekelia formosissima, Sandersonia aurantiaca*

Scilla
S. litardierei

Scilla
S. siberica

Main features Flowers in late spring; grape-hyacinth-like flowers in lilac-lavender blue
Height 10 cm (4 in.) **Spread** 6 cm (2.5 in.)
Position ○ **Hardiness** RHS H5

Main features Nodding, bell-shaped, bright-blue early-spring flowers; two to four strappy mid-green leaves
Height 20 cm (8 in.) **Spread** 5 cm (2 in.)
Position ○ ◑ **Hardiness** RHS H7

Part of the *Scilla* genus, this hardy, bulbous, clump-forming perennial was introduced to western Europe in 1827 from the Balkans. The stems of *S. litardierei* (pictured above, left) carry numerous starry, soft-lilac and lavender-blue flowers that grow closely together. They look like a mixture of *S. bifolia* and *Muscari*. After flowering in late spring – much later than the various *Muscari* that it resembles – the flower's leaves fold themselves over the stamen. These bulbs need moist but well-drained soil and are very easy to grow. In a warm and sunny spot, the plant naturalises well, especially on banks, and is good for border edges or in raised beds. Together with other sun-loving plants – like *Cerastium*, *Dianthus*, *Diascia* and *Helianthemum* – it will make a great show. In containers, it can be part of a 'lasagne' planting to give a sequence of flowering, starting with *Chionodoxa* planted on top, then *Narcissus* 'Segovia' in the second layer, and *S. litardierei* in the third layer, at the bottom. **FR/MS**

The tiny blue lanterns that decorate this diminutive bulb paint the ground with colour when they emerge in early spring. Formed of single stems bearing a handful of nodding, bowl-shaped flowers above glossy grass-like leaves, the Siberian squill (*S. siberica*) is less than impressive when grown in small numbers, but once established, it sets seed and spreads rapidly, often popping up in unexpected nooks and crannies to create breathtaking displays throughout the spring. Easy to naturalise in a lawn or beneath deciduous trees and shrubs, it also makes a good subject for rock and gravel gardens. Combine it in turf with other small early-flowering spring bulbs, such as narcissi and crocuses, or with pasqueflowers (*Pulsatilla vulgaris*), *Puschkinia scilloides*, *Iris reticulata* and aubretia. You can also add the dainty bulbs to baskets and pots, but ensure they are not overwhelmed by bright or brash blooms. Ideal partners for containers are compact spring-bedding plants, such as violas and dwarf daffodils. **ZA**

Alternatives

Scilla mischtschenkoana, Scilla siberica, Scilla bifolia, Chionodoxa forbesii 'Blue Giant'

Alternatives

Scilla siberica 'Spring Beauty', *Scilla siberica alba, Scilla siberica* 'Boreas'

Scilla
S. peruviana

Main features Flowers late spring; showy violet flowers; low growing; good for borders and containers
Height 38 cm (15 in.) **Spread** 25 cm (10 in.)
Position ○ ◐ **Hardiness** RHS H4

The Peruvian lily, *S. peruviana*, was introduced in 1607. Contrary to its name it does not originate from Peru. Its original habitat is a region of the western Mediterranean, including Italy, Iberia, North Africa and the island of Madeira. The plant was misnamed by Clusius when he was told that the bulbs came from a ship called *Peru*. *Scilla* is a large genus of the lily family that takes its name from 'squilla'; not surprisingly these plants are therefore commonly called 'squills.' This species is known as the Portuguese squill. *Scilla* comes from the word *'scullo'* meaning 'damaging' because the bulbs were thought to be poisonous.

In mid- to late spring, sturdy stems appear with bulb-shaped flowers on top; these consist of large, dense racemes of up to one hundred starry, deep-violet flowers with decorative yellow anthers. The foliage – five to ten shiny green leaves – grows at the bottom of the plant, in a star formation. The bulbs are large but should not be planted too deep: with only 1.5 centimetres (0.5 in.) of soil on top of the nose. Proper planting depth is critical for best plant growth, vigour and performance of the bulb. The plants prefer full sun to light shade and a well-drained soil. Bulbs planted in a border will need winter protection by adding protective mulch. Breathtaking as it is, *S. peruviana* needs modest neighbours in the border. Good choices include *Milium effusum* 'Aureum' (golden grass), *Sesleria nitida* (moor grass) and *Euphorbia cyparissias* 'Fen's Ruby' (cypress spurge).

Also worth planting is *S. peruviana* 'White Moon', a beautiful variety of the species. The starry, white flowers have green stripes in the middle of their petals. Both *S. peruviana* and the white variety make great pot plants, which can be stored in a frost-free greenhouse during wintertime. **FR/MS**

Alternatives

Scilla peruviana 'White Moon', *Scilla peruviana* 'Alba', *Scilla peruviana* var. *elegans*

Sparaxis
'Moonlight'

Main features Flowers in summer; good in raised beds, borders and pots
Height 20 cm (8 in.) **Spread** 8 cm (3 in.)
Position ○ **Hardiness** RHS H3

Known as the harlequin flower, *Sparaxis* is a genus with about thirteen species endemic to the Cape Province in South Africa, and it has been in cultivation for more than 200 years. As a member of the *Iris* family, it is closely related to *Freesia* and *Ixia* and has flowers with six equal segments forming a widespread perianth with a very short floral tube. In its native habitat *Sparaxis* is a perennial that grows during the wet winter season, flowers in spring, and survives underground as a dormant corm over summer. In cooler climates it is not hardy and should be treated as you would an annual summer-flowering bulb.

The most common species in cultivation is *S. bulbifera*, with flowers in several colours, from cream to yellow or purple. Another species, *S. tricolor*, has bright-red blooms with yellow-and-black centres. *S.* 'Moonlight' is one of several hybrids that have been bred from crossing *S. bulbifera* with *S. tricolor*. 'Moonlight' has white flowers with a yellow centre. There are pinkish-red flames towards the tips of the petals; more on the outsides of the flowers than on the insides. They grow on 20-centimetre-high (8 in.) stems, accompanied by narrow, pointed leaves, arranged in two ranks. Despite the short stems, they make good cut flowers.

'Moonlight' should be planted in a sheltered, sunny spot where the soil is light and well drained. A rockery, raised bed or the base of a sunny wall would be ideal. Plant the corms 5 centimetres (2 in.) deep, from midspring onwards, covering them with a little coarse sand before replacing the soil. They must be lifted for frost-free winter storage after the foliage has died back, usually in early autumn. The corms can also be grown in containers, to sit on the patio in summer, as long as they go back under glass once the first frost has blackened the foliage. **FR/MS**

Alternatives

Sparaxis 'Red Reflex', *Sparaxis elegans*, *Sparaxis grandiflora* subsp. *acutiloba*

Tigridia
T. pavonia

Trillium
T. grandiflorum

Main features Bright pink, red, yellow, orange and white summer flowers; green strappy foliage
Height 45 cm (18 in.) **Spread** 10 cm (4 in.)
Position ○ **Hardiness** RHS H4

Main features Spring-flowering woodlander; three-petalled white flowers held above green bracts
Height 30 cm (12 in.) **Spread** 30 cm (12 in.)
Position ● **Hardiness** RHS H5

The sizzling colours of the tiger flower (*T. pavonia*) lend an exotic note to garden displays, their spotted petals making 'leopard flower' a more appropriate name for this Mexican native. Slim flower stems rise up above narrow, sword-shaped foliage, each topped with an unusual three-petalled bloom balanced like a spinning saucer on a pole. Individual flowers last only a day or two, but they open in succession, keeping the show going for weeks. Tiger flowers will sparkle in a sun-drenched gravel garden or flower border, where they combine well with other summer bulbs – try dahlias and the white Abyssinian *Gladiolus murielae* – together with contrasting blooms in cool shades, such as spiky blue salvias, and leafy plants like *Melianthus* and *Artemisia*. A backdrop of blue passion flowers (*Passiflora caerula*) will add to the exotic ambience. Tigridia is not ideal for containers, since the blooms are fleeting and plants can look a little scruffy after they have faded. **ZA**

This neat North American woodland species has white flowers that nestle above green bracts resembling leaves. Often called wake-robin, in the wild it appears as the snow melts, staying in leaf for many months before dying down. As it emerges through the ground in the garden setting, it is very vulnerable to slug attack. The secret of success is to endeavour to keep your plant in leaf for as long as possible after flowering, so that the rhizomes build up food for next year's flowers. Water and feed if needed. *Trillium* is not the easiest of garden plants. It needs good drainage and cool, moist conditions in spring when it flowers. It resents exposed positions, because it is prone to wind damage, and needs deep, friable soil. However, it is well worth the effort. Find it the right position, and when it becomes established, it will flower for many weeks, bridging spring and early summer. If possible, buy a ready-grown plant rather than a dry rhizome. **VB**

Alternatives

Tigridia pavonia 'Alba Grandiflora', *Tigridia pavonia* 'Speciosa'

Alternatives

Trillium kurabayashii, *Trillium choloropetalum*

◑ *Tigridia pavonia* 'Aurea' adds a neat but exotic note at the front of a sunny border.

Trillium
T. luteum

Main feature Flowers spring; lemon-scented flowers; variegated foliage; good for woodland areas
Height 40 cm (16 in.) **Spread** 30 cm (12 in.)
Position ◑ **Hardiness** RHS H7

Also known as yellow wake-robin or yellow trillium, *T. luteum* gets its name from the Greek word *'tri'* meaning 'three'. The flower, bract and the leaf of this plant each consists of three parts. The species is native to the Great Smoky Mountains and surrounding areas of the United States. It occurs in parts of North Carolina, Georgia, Tennessee and Kentucky, usually in the shade of mature, deciduous trees. It is especially abundant around Gatlinburg. Groups of *Trillium* make an elegant understorey planting in woodland or shady, naturalised areas. They grow in clumps and flower in late spring. *T. luteum* is often sold under its earlier name of *T. sessile* var. *luteum*. The plant has a Royal Horticultural Society Award of Garden Merit.

Trillium belongs to the Liliaceae (lily) family and is a rhizomatous herb with unbranched stems. *T. luteum* has pale yellow-green flowers atop a trio of leaves, which are often mottled with a paler shade of silvery-green. The flowers are faintly fragrant of lemon oil, and they grow up to 40 centimetres (16 in.) tall. The leaves are broad and end in a point. These plants like rich, moist, well-drained soil with a neutral to acidic pH; they also like to grow in dappled shade, hence, they are ideal for woodland areas. They will definitely benefit from annual mulching with organic matter.

After the flowering period they go dormant in summer and are therefore best planted with other shade-loving perennials to share their space until they reappear the following spring. Try combining with varieties of ferns, such as *Polystichum setiferum* (soft shield fern), *Smilacina racemosa* (false Solomon's seal) and *Cornus canadensis* (bunchberry). *Trillium* propagates readily by division when plants are dormant in late summer or early autumn. **FR/MS**

Alternatives

Trillium erectum, *Trillium erectum* var. 'Album', *Trillium recurvatum*, *Trillium grandiflorum*

Trillium
T. sulcatum

Main features Flowers in spring; rich dark-red to maroon flowers; good for shady, woodland areas
Height 60 cm (24 in.) **Spread** 30 cm (12 in.)
Position ◑ **Hardiness** RHS H5

Endemic to the southern Appalachian Mountains of the United States, *T. sulcatum* is also commonly known as southern red trillium or furrowed wake-robin. It is a perennial wildflower that blooms in late spring. It has dark-red to maroon flowers with recurved petals, which turn into red berries later in the season. The anthers are usually yellow or purple. The three-petalled flower sits atop a flower stem above three large, bright-green leaves. The tips of the sepals are 'sulcate', meaning that they are upturned and rolled in, like the prow of a canoe; hence the name *'sulcatum'*, which was only given in 1984. Prior to that time, *T. sulcatum* was categorised with *T. erectum*, to which it is similar, except that *T. sulcatum* is more robust.

This is a multi-stemmed, herbaceous perennial that makes a bold and attractive statement in the shady woodland garden. It is one of the most beautiful and easy to cultivate of the species, growing up to 60 centimetres (24 in.) in height. It prefers a well-drained, neutral to slightly acidic soil in partial sun to light shade. It makes a compatible companion with other woodland plants, such as *Stylophorum distichum* (celandine poppy), *Polystichum acrostichoides* (Christmas fern), *Phlox divaricata* (woodland phlox) and *Mertensia virginica* (Virginian bluebells).

These plants do not actually produce any true leaves or stems above ground. The 'stem' is simply an extension of the horizontal rhizome; the above-ground plant is technically a flowering scape and the leaf-like structures are actually bracts subtending the flower. Despite their morphological origins, the bracts have an external and an internal structure, similar to that of a leaf. They function in photosynthesis, and most garden writers refer to them as 'leaves'. **FR/MS**

Alternatives

Trillium grandiflorum 'Flore Pleno', *Trillium viridescens*, *Trillium catesbaei*

Tritonia

T. *crocata* 'Pink Sensation'

Main features Early-summer flower; great in rock gardens and containers
Height 35 cm (14 in.) **Spread** 15 cm (6 in.)
Position ○ **Hardiness** RHS H2

Consisting of thirty species, *Tritonia* is a genus that originates, like so many others, from South Africa, Natal Province and Cape Province. The name *Tritonia* comes from Triton, the son of Poseidon, god of the sea. Images of the mythological character were used on weather vanes; he is shown as a figure whose lower body has been turned into the tail of a fish, and he is blowing on a conch shell. As Triton came to be connected with weather vanes, the *Tritonia* plant was named after him, because the stamen of its flowers point in various directions.

T. *crocata* was discovered by English botanist John Ker-Gawler. It belongs to the *Iris* family and was first described in 1802. It has orange, brown, yellow and pinkish flowers, which are dusted with a deeper shadow and are fragrant. There are seven to nine flowers per stem. Flowering time is early to midsummer. The leaves are linear and fan-shaped, like the gladiolus, and at some point another popular name for *Tritonia* was *Gladiolus crocata*. These plants also look a lot like *Ixia* and *Crocosmia*. The species has orange flowers, but several named varieties, such as *T. crocata* 'Pink Sensation', now offer a dusky pink. There is also a white variety (*T. crocata* 'Baby Doll'), plus several different shades of orange, from salmon to tangerine hues.

'Pink Sensation' needs a sunny, well-ventilated spot in the garden, in well-drained soil. It also requires heavy drenching every once in a while during the growing season. In the right place, and if treated well, it will multiply rapidly in warm climates. In colder climates it is a good (seasonal) plant for rock gardens and for containers. A great combination, for example, is 'Pink Sensation' amid silver-leaved *Helichrysum* or ground-covering *Artemisia*. It is very attractive to bees and grows up to 35 centimetres (14 in.) in height. **FR/MS**

Alternatives

Tritonia laxifolia, Tritonia lineata var. *parviflora, Tritonia disticha* subsp. *rubrolucens*

Tulbaghia
T. violacea 'Silver Lace'

Main features Flowers in summer; variegated, aromatic
foliage; fragrant flowers; good cut flower; edible flowers
Height 45 cm (18 in.) **Spread** 30–38 cm (12–15 in.)
Position ○ ◑ **Hardiness** RHS H7

This plant is a South African native belonging to the
onion family. The variety 'Silver Lace' is reminiscent of
a delicate agapanthus. The narrow grey-green, grassy
leaves edged with white are attractive on their own and
emit a typical onion-garlic scent, but only if crushed.
From summer through to autumn, 45-centimetre-tall
(18 in.) flower spikes appear topped by a generous cluster
of lilac-coloured, six-petalled, star-shaped flowers that
open in succession. This gives a long season of interest,
in much the same style as an agapanthus or an allium,
with the flower stalks erupting from one point.

Regular deadheading of the faded flower spikes
encourages more to develop. Remove flowered stems
at the base as they finish to keep the display going. Grow
them in a sunny position in well-drained soil, in very
mild climates. Not reliably frost hardy, it needs its foliage
cut back in late autumn, and cover the root zone with a
generous mulch for insulation. In colder areas grow it in
a container, which can be moved into a cool greenhouse
for the winter. Allow the pot to remain dry for its resting
period. Plants benefit from division of the rhizomes in
the spring every couple of years or so, as this improves
flowering. The flowers are pleasantly scented, especially
in early morning and evening, and should you wish, the
flowers are also edible. They have a mild onion flavour
and are perfect on a salad with a summer barbecue.

Excellent in a sunny, yet sheltered border, it is also a
good coastal garden plant. Planted in containers, 'Silver
Lace' will look good grouped together with other pot
plants that have contrasting foliage. Try it planted with
the bold dark purple foliage of *Heuchera* 'Plum Pudding'
or *H.* 'Frosted Violet' together with a pot of the blue-grey
leaved *Echeveria* to complement the attractive 'Silver
Lace' foliage. **MP**

Alternatives

Tulbaghia cernua, Tulbaghia leucantha,Tulbaghia
'Purple Eye'

Tulipa
'Apricot Beauty'

Main features Flowers in spring; slightly scented; good for containers, borders and also as a cut flower
Height 38 cm (15 in.) **Spread** 8 cm (3 in.)
Position ○ **Hardiness** RHS H6

Belonging to the division of early-blooming single tulips, this is an outstanding *Tulipa* variety that grows up to 45 centimetres (15 in.). The flowering period is early to midspring, and as long as the weather is not unusually hot, the flowers will last for at least three weeks. The blooms have a soft, salmon-pink colour with a touch of orange. They are also fragrant and make very good cut flowers. *Tulipa* 'Apricot Beauty' was bred in 1953 and has proved to be a strong, long-lasting variety, which is suitable for perennialising in borders.

Most varieties of *Tulipa* require a sunny, well-drained spot in the garden. Originally, the plants grew in similar circumstances in the high mountains of Central Asia and therefore, their preference for this kind of area is in their genes. 'Apricot Beauty' should be planted when the soil has started to cool down, normally in mid- to late autumn. After planting it must be watered, so that roots can start to grow as soon as possible. Once it has rooted, the plant cannot be damaged by frost.

'Apricot Beauty' can be easily mixed with other early-flowering tulips in the same range of colours, such as 'Couleur Cardinal' (scarlet red with a plum blush) and 'Prinses Irene' (vibrant orange with a purple stripe). Or grow a longer-lasting combination of *Tulipa* and include later-flowering varieties, such as 'Abba' (double-flowered red), 'Orange Emperor' (large orange petals with a pale-yellow base) and 'Negrita' (deep-purple with beetroot veins), which provide a sequence of flowers for a couple of weeks. Alongside early perennials – such as *Geranium*, *Brunnera*, *Aquilegia* and *Euphorbia* – these *Tulipa* will make an attractive early-spring border. However, they should be left in the soil and undisturbed after their flowering period to guarantee another abundance of flowers the following spring. **JK**

Alternatives

Tulipa 'Christmas Dream', *Tulipa* 'Couleur Cardinal', *Tulipa* 'Prinses Irene'

Tulipa
'Ballerina'

Main features Flowers in mid- to late spring;
lightly scented
Height 50 cm (20 in.) **Spread** 8 cm (3 in.)
Position ○ **Hardiness** RHS H6

'Ballerina' is a late-season orange tulip for the discerning gardener. The overall shape of the plant – from the long, thin stems to the profile of its lily-shaped flower – is elegant, and it brings not only colour but also a graceful touch to mixed borders with emerging hummocks of foliage and to gravel gardens of ornamental grasses. Furthermore, tulips that flower a bit later in spring have many more potential foliage companions; not only herbaceous plants, but deciduous shrubs too, in particular the Japanese *Acer*.

The flower colour of 'Ballerina' is a very warm, rich orange, with shades of red and subtle touches of yellow, so there is plenty of scope for planting schemes. It goes particularly well with the bronze-leaved forms of ornamental grasses, such as *Carex comans,* or the pale-green *Stipa tenuissima*. A few well-placed clusters of 'Ballerina' punctuating a long border will make the garden glow with energy. Among spring-bedding displays that include combinations of tulips, this variety really lifts the dark-coloured tulips, such as the purple-black 'Queen of Night' or the rich purple 'Negrita', and the contrasting flower shapes complement one another, too. 'Ballerina' is often grown in containers, although sometimes the tall stems look out of proportion. Place them at the back of a group of other containers, so that the tulips with shorter stems are at the front.

'Ballerina' is one of the few tulips to have a light scent, similar to that of the much older, single early tulip 'Generaal De Wet' (1904). The latter is known to be an orange sport of 'Prince of Austria', a scented orange-scarlet tulip dating back to 1860. Registered in 1980 by J. A. Borst and classed as a lily-flowered tulip, 'Ballerina' is much more than a shapely flower; it has echoes of tulips of old and therefore is in a class of its own. **LD**

Alternatives

Tulipa 'Queen of Sheba', *Tulipa* 'Elegant Lady', *Tulipa* 'Fly Away', *Tulipa* 'Mariette'

Tulipa
'Ballade'

Main features Flowers in spring; elegant blooms; good for beds and borders
Height 45–55 cm (18–22 in.) **Spread** 8 cm (3 in.)
Position ○ **Hardiness** RHS H6

The *Tulipa* 'Ballade' is a late-flowering variety that belongs to the division of lily-flowered tulips. These plants all have elegant flowers with gracefully pointed, reflexed petals. The leaves, with a greyish colour, are not as wide as those of other divisions of tulips, and this adds to the airiness of the whole plant. 'Ballade' has reddish-magenta flowers, edged white with a yellow base. It thrives in full sun, where the colours are striking, even from a distance. When open, the flowers form six-pointed stars, which will return to their goblet shape at the end of the day. 'Ballade' is a strong variety and makes a good cut flower, but it can be used in many different ways, for example, in formal beds, with a base of pink or blue forget-me-nots, or as the last one in a sequence of tulips to brighten up a pink perennial spring border. In the latter case, plant 'Ballade' amongst 'Flaming Purissima' (creamy-white base with rosy-pink tips), 'Don Quichotte' (rich pink), 'Ronaldo' (deep purplish red) and 'Mistress' (soft dusky pink). **JK**

Alternatives

Tulipa 'Aladdin', *Tulipa* 'Elegant Lady', *Tulipa* 'Flashback', *Tulipa* 'Mariette'

Tulipa
'Black Hero'

Main features Dark maroon-black double flowers; grey-green leaves; excellent cut flower
Height 65 cm (26 in.) **Spread** 6 in. (15 cm)
Position ○ **Hardiness** RHS H6

Bursting into bloom in late spring, the flowers of this highly prized tulip look like scoops of dark-chocolate ice cream balancing on tall, sturdy stems. The maroon-black double blooms have a satin sheen, and contrast beautifully with the wide blue-green leaves. Ideal for beds, borders and containers, the blooms are also fêted by florists, their brooding colour and frilly petals perfect for contemporary indoor displays. *Tulipa* 'Black Hero' produces the greatest impact when planted in groups and makes a good companion for other tulips of almost any colour. Try a stylish black-and-white combination with the white 'Mount Tacoma' or opt for a rich colour theme with 'Angélique', its strawberry ice cream flowers offering the perfect match. 'Black Hero' also looks the part in terracotta or glazed pots, edged with a frill of white violas or *Lobularia maritima*. Although you can lift and store the bulbs after the blooms have faded, flowering tends to be more successful if you plant new bulbs each year. **ZA**

Alternatives

Tulipa 'Queen of the Night', *Tulipa* 'Paul Scherer', *Tulipa* 'Black Parrot', *Tulipa* 'Blackjack', *Tulipa* 'Café Noir'

○ *Tulipa* 'Ballade' makes a great impact in a border.

Tulipa
T. clusiana

Main features Flowers in spring; good for containers and for warm and dry areas in the garden
Height 22 cm (9 in.) **Spread** 4 cm (1.5 in.)
Position ○ **Hardiness** RHS H4–5

The *T. clusiana* is a species tulip, which means that it belongs to the division of tulips that are 'wild'. It originates from countries around the east of the Mediterranean and Central Asia and was described for the first time in 1803. However, long before that, in 1607, it flowered in the garden of Carolus Clusius, a well-known French botanist after whom this tulip is named.

T. clusiana needs a warm, sheltered area and the best drainage. It will very much feel at home in gravel gardens or rock gardens, where it will spread abundantly. It has only four leaves, which are greyish green, narrow and undulated. The tapered flowers are red on the outside and white on the inside, with a basal blotch of deep purple that becomes visible as soon as the flowers open. They will only open in sunny weather, but when they do, they look like little stars, and their unbelievable colour combination can be seen at its best.

The original *T. clusiana* has various descendants, including *T. clusiana* var. *chrysantha* (inner petals deep yellow, outer petals crimson with a yellow edge), *T. clusiana* var. *chrysantha* 'Tubergen's Gem' (outer petals red, inner petals sulphur yellow), *T. clusiana* 'Cynthia' (outer petals red with a chartreuse-green edge, inner petals red) and *T. clusiana* 'Lady Jane' (tall with white petals tinged with pink-red on the outside). This last variety is elegant and a good choice for small containers, together with the ornamental grass *Stipa tenuissima*. **JK**

Alternatives

Tulipa clusiana 'Cynthia', *Tulipa clusiana* var. *chrysantha* 'Tubergen's Gem', *Tulipa clusiana* 'Lady Jane'

Tulipa
'Fancy Frills'

Main features Flowers in spring; good for beds and
borders with seasonal plants; good cut flower
Height 38 cm (15 in.) **Spread** 8 cm (3 in.)
Position ○ **Hardiness** RHS H6

A tulip with a very showy appearance, this plant belongs
to the division of fringed tulips, also known as crispa tulips.
They have been bred from single late tulips and for that
reason, they flower late in spring. *Tulipa* 'Fancy Frills' dates
from 1972 and grows up to 38 centimetres (15 in.) high.
The outer petals have an ivory-white base, which blends
into pink, mixed with ivory-white flames and ends at the
top in a crystalline whitish-rose fringe. A great cut flower,
'Fancy Frills' is outstanding as an addition to bouquets
that include different leaf shapes, or ornamental grasses.

Like many other tulips, this one requires a warm and
sunny position. Because of the extravagant shape of the
flowers, it can be difficult to find an appropriate spot in

the garden, but as long as the surrounding plants are
quite simple and ancillary, 'Fancy Frills' will stand out
and play a leading role, as intended.

It looks particularly attractive in beds with biennials;
for example, a red flowering *Bellis perennis* or a pink
flowering *Myosotis sylvatica*. However, 'Fancy Frills' can
also be mixed into the perennial border, together with
evergreen/evergrey plants, such as *Lavandula* and
Santolina, or with perennials that start their leaves early,
such as *Geranium*. If earlier-flowering tulips are added to
the scheme, it is possible to create a pink-to-red mixture
that will colour the garden from early spring onwards.
In this case, 'Rosalie' (soft pink), 'Christmas Dream' (deep
pink) and 'Renown' (pinkish red) are the best choices. **JK**

Alternatives

Tulipa 'Swan Wings', *Tulipa* 'Red Hat', *Tulipa* 'Blue Heron',
Tulipa 'Maja'

Tulipa
T. sprengeri

Tulipa
T. sylvestris

Main features Flowers in late spring/early summer; good for naturalising
Height 38 cm (15 in.) **Spread** 5 cm (2 in.)
Position ○ ◐ ● **Hardiness** RHS H6

Main features Flowers in spring; slightly scented; good for borders and wild conditions
Height 25 cm (10 in.) **Spread** 5 cm (2 in.)
Position ○ ◐ **Hardiness** RHS H5

A native to Turkey, this tulip has two unique attributes. Firstly, it is the latest to flower, appearing in late spring/early summer. Secondly, it seems perfectly happy growing in light shade and also in sun. The urn-shaped flowers are held above green leaves and open from a pointed bud. The inner three pointed petals are bright scarlet, while the outer three often have a buff marking, which gives a two-tone effect when viewed from the side. *T. sprengeri* likes to become established and will then seed freely, popping up wherever it feels the inclination. It associates perfectly with the attractive foliage of herbaceous perennials, such as the acid yellow flowers of *Euphorbia epithymoides* or the silver-green leaves and blue flowers of *Pulmonaria* 'Diana Clare'. It even appears to be happy growing under deciduous trees, taking advantage of the light before the tree leaves emerge. A white-flowered cherry tree with scarlet tulips scattered at random beneath is an arresting sight. **MP**

This tulip originates from southern Europe, the Balkans and Asia Minor, and it was described for the first time in 1753. It is a slender plant and has a graceful appearance with drooping flower buds. The petals are golden yellow, with a green hue and a touch of maroon at each tip. Each petal is pointed and quite long and narrow; the inside is pale yellow. Slightly scented, the flowers of *T. sylvestris* appear in midspring. The name 'sylvestris' suggests that this is a woodland plant, but in this case, *sylvestris* should be interpreted to mean 'wild' as opposed to 'cultivated'. *T. sylvestris* prefers full sun, but it will also grow in light shade. It needs a rather rich soil, and bulbs should be dug up every three to four years in summer and replanted immediately. This has to be done because they tend to pull themselves deeper into the soil, after which they stop producing flowers. As an alternative, wire netting can be put into the soil before planting, and this will prevent the bulbs from growing deeper. **JK**

Alternatives

Tulipa linifolia Batalinii Group 'Bright Gem', *Tulipa turkestanica*

Alternatives

Tulipa tarda, *Tulipa turkestanica*, *Tulipa saxatilis* Bakeri Group 'Lilac Wonder'

Tulipa sylvestris grows wild in a cornfield in Italy, yet is unusual to see in a garden. ➔

Tulipa
'White Triumphator'

Main features Flowers in spring; great for borders;
good cut flower
Height 60 cm (24 in.) **Spread** 5 cm (2 in.)
Position ○ ◑ **Hardiness** RHS H6

A late-flowering tulip introduced in 1942, *Tulipa* 'White
Triumphator' has pure-white flowers with pointed,
reflexed petals. It is tall stemmed, and its leaves are rather
narrow, which adds to the gracefulness of each plant.
Although it is a superb garden plant, 'White Triumphator'
is also a great cut flower. Plant it in a potager garden, with
other lily-flowered varieties – such as 'Marilyn' (creamy
white with red flame), 'Purple Dream' (deep purple with
an ivory heart), 'Jacqueline' (rose pink) and 'Red Shine'
(deep ruby-red) – and you will have a bouquet both
in the garden and in the vase. 'White Triumphator' is
also one of the best varieties for perennialising: leave it
undisturbed in the soil after the flowering period, allow
it to die back, and deadhead it as soon as the petals do
not close at night anymore. Thus treated, it can come
back for many years. The best spot in the garden is full
sun, but this variety also thrives in dappled shade, where
it looks like a little lantern in between ornamental grasses
such as *Geranium* and *Brunnera*. **JK**

Alternatives

Tulipa 'Ballerina', *Tulipa* 'Merlot', *Tulipa* 'Yonina'

Tulipa
'Spring Green'

Main feature Flowers in mid- to late spring
with a green stripe
Height 50 cm (20 in.) **Spread** 8 cm (3 in.)
Position ○ ◑ **Hardiness** RHS H6

Viridiflora is a group of tulips that have a green stripe
or flame on the back of the petals, and the best-known
variety is *Tulipa* 'Spring Green', which combines the green
with a cream-white edge. It is one of the taller Viridiflora
and more natural looking than some, working well in
mixed border plantings with bold foliage plants, such as
hostas and ferns. It flowers in mid- to late spring, often
when *Euphorbia* is in flower, and these two plants look
good together too. 'Spring Green' was registered in 1969 by
P. Liefting and it has been a popular tulip ever since. There
have been some interesting variations recently, including
'Flaming Spring Green', which is identical to the original
but with the addition of red markings on the petals. These
small splashes of colour add a little extra zing. Other new
Viridiflora cultivars include 'Yellow Spring Green' and
'Red Spring Green', in which the white is replaced either
by a strong yellow or red. However, there is something
refreshing about the 'Spring Green' combination of white
and green that gives it the edge. **LD**

Alternatives

Tulipa 'Flaming Spring Green', *Tulipa* 'China Town'

◉ *Tulipa* 'White Triumphator' is a classic choice for pairing with *Myosotis*.

Tulipa
'Flaming Parrot'

Main features Flowers in spring; great for beds with
seasonal plants and for borders; excellent cut flower
Height 50 cm (20 in.)   **Spread** 8 cm (3 in.)
Position ○   **Hardiness** RHS H6

The *Tulipa* 'Flaming Parrot' was introduced in 1968 and
has been popular ever since, because of its big, bowl-
shaped flowers and stunning appearance. The petals,
which are deeply fringed and ruffled, have a base colour
of pale yellow, decorated with fire-engine-red flames.
However, because of the long stems and the relatively
heavy flowers, 'Flaming Parrot' needs a sheltered position,
so that it will not be damaged by strong winds and heavy
rain. Whereas many tulip varieties can be planted in
groups, 'Flaming Parrot' is at its best in small numbers.
The flower is so striking and so magnificent that in a
perennial border only a few are needed to make a good
show. Five to seven bulbs per 1 square metre (3 sq ft) are
perfect, preferably amid humbler companions, such as
ornamental grasses, *Lavandula*, and *Alchemilla mollis*.
Alternatively, in a base of yellow or red bedding plants,
such as pansies or *Bellis perennis*, 'Flaming Parrot' will
finish the spring-flowering bulbs in a splendid way. **JK**

Alternatives

Tulipa 'Black Parrot', *Tulipa* 'Rococo',
Tulipa 'Green Wave'

Tulipa
'Menton'

Main feature Large, cream-pink flowers in late spring
Height 65 cm (26 in.)   **Spread** 10 cm (4 in.)
Position ○
Hardiness RHS H6

Tulip cultivars fall in and out of favour but *Tulipa* 'Menton'
remains distinctive for its huge egg-shaped flowers and
unusual colour. The flowers are pink, and close-up, there is
an apricot-orange flush; in fact, the blooms almost glisten
when you see them in the flesh. Named after Menton
on the French Riviera – renowned for its gardens and
flower displays of citrus trees, palms and mimosas in the
sunny, subtropical climate – this plant was introduced
by W. Dekker & Sons in 1971, and it arose as a sport of
Tulipa 'Renown', a well-regarded tulip introduced in 1949.
Both cultivars have the characteristic shape of the yellow
historic *Tulipa* 'Mrs John T. Scheepers'. 'Menton' flowers
late in the season, which can be a challenge if you want
to grow it alongside other tulips, but the large white-
flowered 'Maureen' will make a good companion. It is
best to view the former in person in spring, at a reputable
supplier exhibit, then order dry bulbs for autumn delivery,
because not all tulips sold as 'Menton' are true to type. **LD**

Alternatives

Tulipa 'Avignon', *Tulipa* 'Maureen',
Tulipa 'Pink Diamond'

◐ *Tulipa* 'Flaming Parrot', with its fringed and ruffled petals, creates a touch of the exotic.

Tulipa
'Orange Princess'

Main features Flowers in spring; scented; good
for containers and borders
Height 30 cm (12 in.) **Spread** 8 cm (3 in.)
Position ○ **Hardiness** RHS H6

Introduced in 1983, *Tulipa* 'Orange Princess' is a descendent
of *Tulipa* 'Prinses Irene', which was named after a sister
of Princess Beatrix, the former queen of Holland. It is in
the division of double late-flowering tulips, and as the
cultivar name indicates, it has orange-coloured flowers
with a bronze flame on each petal. Other attractive
features are its fragrance and dark stem. Because of the
relatively short stem, 'Orange Princess' is a great tulip
to be used in containers. A 25-centimetre-wide (10 in.)
container can easily host seven of these tulips, with
seasonal flowers, such as deep-red pansies or grey-leafed
Calocephalus brownii, planted underneath. However,
when planting tulips in a container, do not plant them
too close to the edge, because of possible frost damage.
In a perennial border there are several choices for good
companion plants, including red-leafed *Heuchera,*
Euphorbia polychroma and *Santolina rosmarinifolia.* Or
try a mixture of late-flowering tulips – 'Orange Princess',
'Pieter de Leur', 'Ballerina' – and ornamental grasses. **JK**

Alternatives

Tulipa 'Angélique', *Tulipa* 'Black Hero', *Tulipa* 'Red Princess'

Uvularia
U. grandiflora

Main features Flowers in spring; woodland plant;
attracts bees
Height 45–60 cm (18–24 in.) **Spread** 30 cm (12 in.)
Position ◐ ● **Hardiness** RHS H5

This delightful, herbaceous perennial relative of *Colchicum*
is native to the woods of eastern North America, but it
makes a fine addition to the woodland garden. In early
spring, shoots emerge from the rhizomatous rootstock.
The stems lengthen, clasped alternately by mid-green,
oval-shaped, downy leaves. The flowers at the tips of
these stems are clusters of yellow flowers that hang
down demurely. Peeking out from the leafy stems are six
slender petals that are slightly twisted and splayed at the
tips. In a woodland setting *U. grandiflora* could be planted
in the same patch as the earlier-flowering *Anemone
blanda,* the leaves of which will vanish in summer. A carpet
of the delightful, but somewhat rampant, white star-
like flowers of *Galium odoratum* would make a pleasing
background too. A desirable, paler flowered form,
U. grandiflora var. *pallida* is much sought after and has a
slightly glaucous hue to its leaves. *U. grandiflora* 'Lynda
Windsor' is a butter-yellow–leafed variety, but the flowers
do not show up too well against the foliage. **MP**

Alternatives

Uvularia sessiliflora, Uvularia perfoliata

Veltheimia
V. bracteata

Main feature Flowers in summer; grows well in pots and tubs
Height 60 cm (24 in.) **Spread** 30 cm (12 in.)
Position ◑ ● **Hardiness** RHS H2–3

In cooler climates, *V. bracteata* is at its best when grown as a pot plant. It starts as a 30-centimetre-wide (12 in.) rosette of glossy, green, fleshy leaves that are broadly strap-shaped with crisp or wavy margins. From there the flower's stem starts to grow: a long stalk, reaching a height of up to 60 centimetres (24 in.). The inflorescence is a dense raceme of tubular flowers in various colours. They range from pale pink to dusty pink, orange pink, and deep rose-pink to occasionally greenish yellow. The flowers are held upright when in tight bud and are pendant when open. *V. bracteata* looks good as part of an arrangement of pot plants that could include *Carex elata* 'Aurea', *Nicotiana sylvestris* 'Only the Lonely' and *Solenostemon scutellarioides*. Whether grown in pots or beds, this plant requires well-drained soil that is rich in humus. However, it thrives in shaded or semi-shaded gardens, which is a great advantage because there are not many summer-flowering, showy plants that do well in dappled shade. **FR/MS**

Alternatives

Veltheimia capensis, *Veltheimia viridiflora*

Zantedeschia
Captain Series

Main feature Flowers in summer
Height 60 cm (24 in.) **Spread** 35 cm (14 in.)
Position ○
Hardiness RHS H4

The *Zantedeschia* Captain Series is a collection of plants of various sizes with both spotted and solid leaves that are broadly spade-shaped and medium green. Flowering freely in late spring and summer, these Dutch hybrid cultivars are particularly suited for container culture. The blossoms are solidly coloured or bicoloured, in a wide range of colours (pictured is Captain Safari). It is difficult to believe that these elegant, sculptural flowers grow from such odd-looking, knobbly tubers. In fact, a good *Zantedeschia* tuber has a short growing period and a high flower production. Plant it in a well-drained soil, but be aware it will need water to flower and a sunny site. No flowers usually means there was not enough water or sun, or perhaps too much nitrogen in the soil. Too much nitrogen makes the plant grow a lot of foliage but fewer flowers. The best companion plants for *Zantedeschia* depend on the type of planting or arrangement, but all companion plants should have shallow, noninvasive root systems and a high tolerance of sun and moist soil. **FR/MS**

Alternatives

Zantedeschia 'Captain Maori', *Zantedeschia* 'Captain Amigo'

Zantedeschia

Z. aethiopica 'Crowborough'

Main features Flowers in summer; grows near ponds or on banks; good container plant; cut flower
Height 90 cm (3 ft)   **Spread** 50 cm (20 in.)
Position ○   **Hardiness** RHS H4

This is a cultivar of the common calla lily, *Z. aethiopica*. The species originates in South Africa and is evergreen, where rainfall and temperatures are adequate, but deciduous where there is a dry season. Its preferred habitat is in streams and ponds or on banks. Officially, the calla lily is hardy only in mild, subtropical areas, but *Z. aethiopica* 'Crowborough' is more cold tolerant and will last in cooler areas, provided that there is a heavy winter mulch. It was found in Sussex, growing in a herbaceous border. Until this discovery, calla lilies were thought to need planting in water or in a bog garden.

It is a tuberous perennial, and each tuber forms a sturdy clump of leathery, lance-shaped, or arrow-shaped green leaves, bearing tall stems of white flowers with a showy, hood-like spathe (15 cm/6 in. in length) and a prominent yellow spadix. The plant has a great texture, and the flowers are excellent for cutting. It can grow up to 90 centimetres (3 ft) in height with a spread of 50 centimetres (20 in.), but this will take five to ten years.

Z. aethiopica 'Crowborough' requires full sun and clay or loam soil, which must be moist. It can be grown in planting baskets (in heavy loam soil) in water up to 30 centimetres (12 in.) deep. The tubers must be planted shallowly, so that the top of the tubers is slightly exposed. Instead of mulching them for wintertime, the baskets can be removed from the water in late autumn and placed in a frost-free environment. **FR/MS**

Alternatives

Zantedeschia 'Edge of Night', *Zantedeschia* 'Kiwi Blush', *Zantedeschia* 'Green Goddess'

Zephyranthes
Z. minuta

Main feature Bright-pink flowers in summer; good in rockeries and containers
Height 25 cm (10 in.) **Spread** 15 cm (6 in.)
Position ○ **Hardiness** RHS H2

The *Z. minuta* is a perennial flowering plant, native to Mexico, Colombia and Central America. It is also widely cultivated as an ornamental and naturalised in the West Indies, Peru, Argentina, and Brazil and in the United States from Texas to Florida. The plant bears solitary, upwards-facing flowers that resemble little stars. They are bright pink, fragrant, around 10 centimetres (4 in.) wide, and surrounded by green, strap-like leaves. They are known as rain lilies, which refers to their habit of flowering soon after a heavy rainfall.

These plants are great for rockeries or along a sun-facing wall, where they need well-drained, not too heavy, soil and full sun. They will stand out in the company of other plants that like similar circumstances, including *Leontopodium alpinum* (edelweiss), *Houstonia caerulea* (mountain bluets) and *Campanula carpatica* (Carpathian bellflower), to name a few. When planted in pots or planters, *Z. minuta* can easily hibernate: in the autumn, cover the pot in a plastic bin bag and store it in an area that avoids severe frost, for example, a garage. In late spring remove the bag, trim any winter growth, and leave it as it is in the planter or separate bulbs and transplant them. Most of the time, however, *Z. minuta* is used as an annual or as a container plant. Another South American species is *Z. candida*, which is hardy as it is found in marshes. It has the same rush-like leaves, but has pure-white flowers that look like a crocus. **FR/MS**

Alternatives

Zephyranthes candida, Habranthus robustus,
Zephyranthes citrina

When you are ready for plants that return time and again, it is time to fall in love with perennials. They remain in the garden from year to year, thus reducing the need for annual planting. Perennials bring pace and excitement to plantings, they shoot up above ground and put on a show. Then the top growth dies down, although the roots live on.

Within this chapter are not only much-loved flowering border plants, from day lily and iris to peonies, but also plants with evergreen foliage, such as ferns and ornamental grasses with their architectural grace. Grow perennials for seasonal interest and movement: they add permanence, yet most are amenable to being moved around and are great for sharing. Buy them either as bare roots or as pot plants, but for named forms seek out reputable suppliers, because the truest plants are often propagated by cuttings or division, rather than raised from seed.

◑ *Yucca gloriosa* 'Variegata' provides architectural shape and colourful foliage year after year.

Achillea
'Moonshine'

Main features Flowers in summer and autumn; attracts beneficial insects; good cut and dried flower
Height 60 cm (24 in.) **Spread** 45 cm (18 in.)
Position ○ **Hardiness** RHS H7

The classic yellow achillea for the middle of sunny borders has to be *Achillea* 'Moonshine'. Always one of the first to bloom, its wide flat heads of sulphur-yellow flowers add sparkle to borders all summer and attract beneficial insects. If the weather stays dry and not too humid, the display can last well into autumn. The flower heads are good for cutting and retain their colour well if dried as soon as the blooms have fully opened. The evergreen, feathery, grey-green foliage of this bushy variety is another bonus as it sets off the flowers so well. 'Moonshine' thrives in full sun in any well-drained soil, but good winter drainage is essential. 'Moonshine' looks at home in cottage garden and prairie-style schemes. Good partners include blue- and purple-flowered sun lovers – *Agapanthus*, *Salvia*, *Echinacea purpurea* (coneflower) and lavender – as well as soft grasses like *Stipa tenuissima*. Many people dislike the scent of achillea leaves, so avoid planting them where you will brush past them regularly. **GP**

Alternatives

Achillea decolorans 'W. B. Child', *Achillea filipendulina* 'Cloth of Gold', *Achillea filipendulina* 'Gold Plate'

Aconitum
A. carmichaelii 'Arendsii'

Main features Autumn flowers; attracts bees; good cut flower; spring to autumn foliage
Height 1.2 m (4 ft) **Spread** 45 cm (18 in.)
Position ○ ◐ **Hardiness** RHS H7

This monkshood, *A. carmichaelii* 'Arendsii', is taller and later flowering than most, and a choice variety for adding height and colour to the back of a border in fall. From a distance it resembles a delphinium – one that is oddly resistant to slugs, snails and mildew! The handsome spires of rich, blue-violet, helmet-shaped flowers are held erect on tall stems that rarely need staking in sheltered sites unless the soil is very rich. 'Arendsii' is an outstanding cut flower and popular with bees too. It has a long season of interest because its glossy, dark-green, deeply divided foliage appears very early in the year. This makes an ideal backdrop for variegated foliage and for pale-yellow and white flowers. The blooms contrast well with typical autumn colours; try weaving them between autumn-colouring shrubs and acers or partnering with yellow perennial sunflowers, rudbeckias and bronze chrysanthemums. Wear gloves, as it contains aconitine, one of the most toxic plant compounds. **GP**

Alternatives

Aconitum carmichaelii Wilsonii Group, *Aconitum* 'Spark's Variety', *Aconitum* 'Bressingham Spire'

---

❸ *Achillea* 'Moonshine' is a garden classic for a sunny, well-drained border.

Actaea
A. simplex Atropurpurea Group 'James Compton'

Main features Flowers in late summer; purple foliage; fragrant flowers; architectural plant; attracts bees
Height 1.5–2.2 m (5–7 ft) **Spread** 60 cm (24 in.)
Position ◑ **Hardiness** RHS H7

Late-summer-flowering plants are an asset to any garden. Growing from a rhizomatous rootstock, *A. simplex* 'James Compton' dies down for the winter. In spring, dark-purple ferny foliage emerges, which contrasts well with the greens and yellows of other emerging leaves. In late summer, tall deep-purple flower stems give a strong vertical and architectural structure. The pink buds open to darker pink flowers clustered, like an elongated bottle brush, around the top 30 to 38 centimetres (12–15 in.) of the stems and contrast against the purple stems. The added bonus is that they are delightfully scented.

Grow these striking hardy perennials in a moisture-retentive soil in partial shade. They are even happy in a clay soil. In northern Europe the purple-leaved forms perform equally well in sun provided the soil stays moist. In areas with hotter summers, keep them in partial shade. The clumps are quite slow to establish, but your patience will be rewarded. This variety was selected by Piet Oudolf, the Dutch plantsman, a great proponent of naturalistic-style planting.

These plants suit all styles, from cottage gardens to herbaceous borders, and even light woodland, but it is their association with ornamental grasses that is so appealing. Try a combination including *Miscanthus sinensis* 'Morning Light', *Echinops* 'Veitch's Blue', and sedums, leaving the seed heads to add structure to the garden in winter. Note that this plant is poisonous and a skin irritant. **MP**

Alternatives

Actaea pachypoda 'Misty Blue', *Actaea rubra*

Adiantum

A. venustum

Main features Attractive, delicate-looking fronds; excellent evergreen ground cover over a long season
Height 15–20 cm (6–8 in.) **Spread** 60 cm (24 in.)
Position ○ ◑ **Hardiness** RHS H7

We tend to think of maidenhair ferns as plants for warm gardens, shady windowsills or for the shady corners of the conservatory, and for most of the two hundred species from around the world, this is true. However, a small number are hardier, and the Himalayan maidenhair, *A. venustum,* is one of the hardiest of all perennials.

The lance-shaped, pale-green fronds are made up of similar delicate-looking individual leaflets as those of its less hardy relations, each leaflet is wedge-shaped at the base, rounded at the tip and divided into several lobes. As they mature the fronds tend to be held horizontally on strong, wiry, glossy, black stems and overlap to create a lacy look. The appeal begins as the new fronds unfurl

in spring, with their distinctive reddish-bronze colouring, and extends well into winter as the foliage is amongst the last of the perennials to succumb to frost. However, those pretty new spring fronds are surprisingly delicate and are easily damaged when weeding or mulching.

Another useful feature of this plant is that once established, it will thrive in a few hours of sunshine, again belying our expectation that it needs shade all day. *A. venustum* needs better drainage than we might assume – in the wild it tends to grow on shady rocks where the rhizomes are exposed to the air and not covered by soil. Once happy, however, the Himalayan maidenhair spreads steadily and makes lovely ground cover in shade alongside small hostas and epimediums, for example. **GR**

Alternatives

Adiantum aleuticum, Adiantum pedatum

Agapanthus
Headbourne hybrids

Main features Flowers in midsummer; attracts bees
and butterflies; architectural seed head; good cut flower
Height 75 cm (2.5 ft)   **Spread** 75 cm (2.5 ft)
Position ○   **Hardiness** RHS H6

Headbourne hybrids are one of the best-known strains of
this stately South African perennial. Raised in England in
the late 1940s, they are one of the hardiest, most vigorous
and free-flowering agapanthus available. They add drama
and a touch of the exotic to late-summer displays, when
their glorious orbs of blue (or occasionally white) trumpet
blooms soar above their fountains of narrow, strap-like
leaves. The blooms are attractive to bees and butterflies
and excellent for cutting. By midautumn they evolve into
handsome seed heads. Leave these on for winter interest
or cut them for dried flowers. Headbourne hybrids are
usually raised from seeds, so they vary in height, flower
colour and flower size. Full sun is essential for agapanthus
to flower well, and they do best in fertile, moist but well-
drained soil. Headbourne hybrids are excellent container
plants. In borders they combine well with grasses, such
as *Miscanthus* and *Stipa*, or late-flowering cottage garden
perennials, such as *Crocosmia* and *Nepeta*. Golden- or
bronze-leaved shrubs make an effective backdrop. **GP**

Alternatives

Agapanthus 'Loch Hope', *Agapanthus* 'Northern Star'

Ageratina
A. altissima 'Chocolate'

Main feature Burgundy-purple foliage from spring to
summer, especially on new growth
Height 90 cm (3 ft)   **Spread** 90 cm (3 ft)
Position ○ ◑   **Hardiness** RHS H7

White snakeroot (*A. altissima*) is a hardy perennial related
to joe pye weed, and until recently, grouped with it under
the name *Eupatorium*. These plants all have in common
flower heads that are similar in style to those of the
familiar bedding *Ageratum*: they are a little like daises, but
without the petals, and coloured in purple, pink or white.
Clump-forming white snakeroot is native to eastern and
central North America. 'Chocolate' is a shorter form, with
red stems and deep-burgundy tints to its foliage (centre),
especially in the shoot tips, although the leaves becomes
greener towards the end of the season. The upright,
red-tinted stems carry pairs of leaves similar to those of
stinging nettles, but without the stings. In summer and
autumn these are topped with branched, flat-topped
clusters of white fluffy flowers. White snakeroot grows
wild in meadows, woods and along roadsides. Leaf colour
is best in full sun but plants will wilt in dry conditions. It
makes a fine foliage foil for grasses and a bold contrast
to scarlet crocosmias and blue cranesbills. **GR**

Alternatives

Ageratina 'Braunlaub', *Ageratina ligustrina*

 Agapanthus **Headbourne hybrids** and *Stipa gigantea* at Trentham Gardens, UK.

Anemone

A. *hupehensis* 'Hadspen Abundance'

Main features Flowers in late summer/autumn; rich pink-purple saucer-shaped flowers; good cut flower
Height 75 cm (2.5 ft) **Spread** 60–90 cm (2–3 ft)
Position ○ ◑ **Hardiness** RHS H7

Japanese anemones (*A. hupehensis*) actually originate from the Hubei province of China and are an essential ingredient of the late-summer garden. *A. hupehensis* 'Hadspen Abundance' has leaves consisting of three large, ovate, mid-green leaflets that emerge in spring from a gently suckering rootstock. The flowers appear in late summer and continue to bloom well into the autumn. Five roundish petals, in slightly varying shapes and a rich deep purplish-pink, have a boss of yellow stamen in the centre, surrounding a green spherical central blob. This all adds to the charm of this variety that grows to a height of about 75 centimetres (2.5 ft). When the petals fall, small, round, bobbly seed heads remain, which eventually open to reveal seed covered in white fluff.

All anemones in this group are easy to grow, but they tend to be a bit slow to establish. They are tolerant of most soil types, even moderately wet soils, but prefer a rich, moist site, and can be grown in sun or part shade. In hot climates, partial shade is preferable. In cooler climates, established clumps can be tolerant of dry shade. Their versatility makes them ideal for perennial borders, cottage-garden–style plantings or for use on the edge of woodland schemes. *Aster* × *frikartii* varieties make excellent companions with them for the late-summer border. They associate particularly well with grasses, such as diamond grass (*Calamagrostis brachytricha*) or *Miscanthus sinensis* 'Yakushima Dwarf'.

Other Japanese anemones include *A. hupehensis* var. *japonica* 'Pamina', which has a multitude of pink petals, whereas *A. hupehensis* var. *alba* has five simple, rounded, white petals, the reverse of which are flushed with purple. *Anemone* 'Bowles' Pink' is a very similar variety, but the petals have a characteristic twist. Note that contact with the sap may cause skin irritation. **MP**

Alternatives

Anemone × *hybrida* 'Honorine Jobert', *Anemone* Wild Swan = 'Macane001'

Anemone hupehensis 'Hadspen Abundance' will bring impact to a late-summer border. ➔

Aquilegia
A. canadensis

Main features Charming red-and-yellow bicoloured
spring flowers; attracts hummingbirds and bees
Height 30–70 cm (12–28 in.) **Spread** 30 cm (12 in.)
Position ○ ◐ **Hardiness** RHS H7

There are about seventy species of these delightful,
distinctive, appealing perennials spread around the
cooler parts of the northern hemisphere, with about
twenty growing in North America and one in the United
Kingdom. Only one, however – *A. canadensis* – has a close
relationship with a migratory hummingbird. Columbines
provide the nectar that is so valuable to hummingbirds.
The only species to grow naturally in eastern North
America, columbine is found on sunny and partly shaded
banks, rocky slopes and woodland margins. The long-
stalked leaves at the base are divided into three, and then
divided into three again, and from among them arises
upright, rather wiry, red-tinted stems. Individual flowers
are turned to face downwards, the outer parts red with
striking upwards-pointing projections (spurs) and the
inner parts yellow. *A. canadensis* is a lovely spring flower
for informal plantings. **GR**

Alternatives

Aquilegia buergeriana 'Calimero', *Aquilegia* 'Red Hobbit',
Aquilegia canadensis 'Little Lanterns'

Artemisia
A. ludoviciana
'Valerie Finnis'

Main features Spring to autumn aromatic foliage;
good cut and dried flower
Height 60 cm (24 in.) **Spread** 60 cm (24 in.)
Position ○ **Hardiness** RHS H7

One of the most spectacular of all the silver foliage plants,
this bushy variety is prized for the startling whiteness of its
young growth. It is a wonderful foil for other perennials –
particularly those with purple or bronze leaves – and an
invaluable buffer between colour-clashing neighbours.
The broad lance-shaped leaves of *A. ludoviciana* 'Valerie
Finnis' are more vibrant than those of other white sages.
This variety is also better behaved, as it spreads more
slowly and is usually self-supporting when grown in full
sun. Many prefer to grow this variety purely as a foliage
plant. The tiny insignificant flowers can add textural
interest, but they tend to detract from the plant's allure
and make it look untidy. To avoid this, cut the whole plant
down when it starts to flower in midsummer. You will be
rewarded with a second display of sparkling new growth
that will look luminous throughout the autumn. This plant
is good for the front of borders and in containers. **GP**

Alternatives

Artemisia absinthium 'Lambrook Silver', *Artemisia lactiflora*,
Artemisia schmidtiana 'Nana'

Asarum
A. europaeum

Main features Attractive glossy evergreen foliage; good low ground cover; broken roots emit ginger scent
Height 15 cm (6 in.) **Spread** 50 cm (20 in.)
Position ● ◑ **Hardiness** RHS H7

There are about a hundred species of these shade-loving ground covers growing wild in Europe, North America and Asia. For decades hardy gingers were looked on with more fascination than enthusiasm, but as US collectors found attractive forms in the wild, and plant hunters visiting Asia found new species, interest has grown. The European ginger, *A. europaeum*, is one of the few that has been both popular and widely available, partly because it was grown as a medicinal herb. The glossy, dark-green leaves are about 5 centimetres (2 in.) across and spread into low, dense mats, making valuable low ground cover. It is easy to miss the bell-shaped reddish-purple or brown flowers that are formed at ground level. In North America, *A. canadense* and *A. hartwegii* are most often seen and are suited to hot summers. *A. canadense* is deciduous but vigorous whereas *A. hartwegii* has variants with silvery patterns in the foliage and reddish flowers. Unlike other species, *A. hartwegii* prefers open, sunny sites. **GR**

Alternatives

Asarum caudatum, Asarum splendens

Asplenium
A. scolopendrium
Crispum Group

Main features Bold, broad, wavy evergreen foliage; handsome specimen in shady borders
Height 30–60 cm (12–24 in.) **Spread** 30–60 cm (12–24 in.)
Position ● **Hardiness** RHS H7

The most striking thing about this tough and resilient fern is that at first sight, it does not look like a fern at all. There are about 700 species of *Asplenium* growing in temperate and tropical regions around the world. What they all have in common are rather leathery fronds, compact crowns, and elongated spore-bearing areas (in most ferns, the spore-bearing areas are roundish). *A. scolopendrium* has a tight rhizome from which arise bold, upright or slightly arching, broad undivided fronds that look like straps. They can be up to 60 centimetres (24 in.) long and 5 centimetres (2 in.) wide, and a mature plant with many of these fronds is very impressive. Plants in the Crispum Group have wavy fronds, an effect caused by the fact that the edges of each frond are longer than the midrib. Many plants in this group have their own names and are difficult to distinguish, but what they all share is a distinctive stature that is invaluable in shady borders and an ability to tolerate dry conditions. **GR**

Alternative

Asplenium scolopendrium Cristatum Group

Aster

A. *amellus* 'Veilchenkönigin'

Main features Violet, yellow-eyed daisy flowers in late summer; attracts bees and butterflies; good cut flower
Height 45 cm (18 in.) **Spread** 45 cm (18 in.)
Position ○ **Hardiness** RHS H7

This beautiful European aster (*A. amellus*) is a great choice for injecting a burst of late colour and vibrancy into sunny borders (pictured left, bottom). Masses of intense violet, yellow-eyed daisies, about 2.5 centimetres (1 in.) wide, draw the eye for weeks from late summer until the first frosts arrive. Bees and butterflies love them. The 45-centimetre-high (18 in.) sprays of bloom are excellent for cutting, too, lasting up to a fortnight in a vase.

Like other *A. amellus* varieties, this compact, bushy perennial is immune to mildew, the scourge of the more widely grown *A. novi-belgii* New York asters. It also thrives in drier soils than the New York asters – in fact, good drainage in winter is essential, so dig some sharp grit into your soil if necessary. It is also better to plant 'Veilchenkönigin' in spring rather than autumn so that the roots can become fully established before being subjected to winter wet. Most *amellus* asters have stems that tend to flop but 'Veilchenkönigin' is sturdy and will not need staking.

A mid-border position among other late summer-flowering perennials such as pink-flowered penstemons, *Solidago* (golden rod), *Aconitum* and Japanese anemones suit this aster as does a backdrop of leaves that turn yellow or orange in the autumn. It is also useful for hiding the untidy remains of perennials that flowered earlier in the year such as oriental poppies and delphiniums. The plants are slow to bulk up so plant in groups of at least three to give a bold splash of colour.

The variety name, 'Veilchenkönigin', is German for 'violet queen' and the plant was bred by German nurseryman Karl Foerster. In fact it is sometimes sold as *A. amellus* 'Violet Queen', however, other varieties may also be sold under this name so it is probably best to seek out plants sold as 'Veilchenkönigin'. **GP**

Alternatives

Aster amellus 'Jacqueline Genebrier', *Aster amellus* 'King George'

Aster
A. × *frikartii* 'Mönch'

Main feature Intense lavender-blue daisy flowers from summer to autumn
Height 50–90 cm (20–36 in.) **Spread** 10–50 cm (4–20 in.)
Position ○ **Hardiness** RHS H7

Most plant experts and gardeners agree that A. × *frikartii* 'Mönch' is simply a must-have plant – worthy of the best spot in any garden (far right). It puts on the finest show of flowers all season long. An original hybrid from a cross between the short, long flowering A. *thomsonii* and the taller, brief-flowering A. *amellus*, it was one of three seedlings, all named after famous mountains, raised in Switzerland by Frikart in the 1920s, but A. × *frikartii* 'Mönch' stood out. It blooms for much longer than A. *amellus*, producing an abundance of clear lavender-blue flowers from midsummer to autumn, and does so without regular deadheading. These are the crowning glory to its other positive attributes: elegant, strong growing, upright, freely branching and resistant to mildew.

Although bloom colour is an outstanding feature, 'Mönch' is gentle, not strident, and blends well with many other flowers. For pink-and-blue combinations, plant it beside *Geranium* 'Mavis Simpson' with *Lavatera* × *clementii* 'Rosea' behind them. In complementary colour schemes, pair it with *Helianthus* 'Lemon Queen' or the buttery-yellow, red-hot poker *Kniphofia* 'Wrexham Buttercup'. Easy to grow, it reaches 90 centimetres (3 ft) in height, and is generally a bushy plant; in some locations top growth can be lanky. Cutting back by one-half in late spring or early summer will improve this, but it may delay flowering. In cooler climates the top growth is best left on for winter and not cut until spring. In spring mature, established clumps can be lifted out of the border and split into sections, then the healthiest ones replanted.

A. 'Wunder von Stäfa' is another popular aster with flowers of a similar colour; it is a taller plant and usually needs staking or pruning for habit and height control. Other hybrids include A. *x frikartii* 'Flora's Delight', with rose-lilac flowers on compact plants. **RC**

Alternatives

Aster × frikartii 'Eiger', *Aster × frikartii* 'Flora's Delight', *Aster × frikartii* 'Wunder von Stäfa'

Aster
'Little Carlow'

Main features Flowers late summer to late autumn;
attracts bees and butterflies; good cut flower
Height 90 cm (3 ft) **Spread** 60 cm (24 in.)
Position ○ ◐ **Hardiness** RHS H7

Perennial aster 'Little Carlow' has the most electrifying lilac-blue blooms of the healthy, mildew-free types of aster and in the autumn, these bushy plants are smothered with them. The dainty 2.5-centimetre-wide (1 in.) daisy-like blooms have contrasting bright yellow centres, which are irresistible to nectar-seeking butterflies and bees. The graceful sprays are good for cutting too, lasting up to a fortnight in a vase.

Despite its name, 'Little Carlow' typically grows up to 90 centimetres (3 ft) tall. The plants are usually self-supporting but the dense clumps of leafy stems often eventually arch to give a mound-like effect so you may want to stake them for a more formal, upright look.

Hugely popular in the United Kingdom (where it was bred in the 1930s), 'Little Carlow' is a hybrid between the small-flowered North American *A. cordifolius* and the popular New York aster, *A. novi-belgii*. Happily, this robust variety has not inherited the latter's susceptibility to unsightly mildew and can thrive in any soil that does not become waterlogged or bone dry. It is often more floriferous when grown in full sun, but can look more beguiling in light shade where its pale blooms almost appear to glow.

Good companions include ornamental grasses and other late-flowering perennials including *Solidago* (goldenrod), taller sedums, *Anthemis tinctoria*, rudbeckia and echinacea (coneflowers). It suits both cottage-garden–style and prairie-style schemes and because it is an attractive plant even before it flowers, it can be put in a prominent position and even used as an edging plant along a wide path or drive. This lovely aster is also useful for hiding the untidy remains of perennials that have finished flowering such as oriental poppies and delphiniums. **GP**

Alternatives

Aster × *frikartii* 'Mönch', *Aster* × *frikartii* 'Wunder von Stäfa'

⊖ *Aster* 'Little Carlow' has soft lilac blooms that set it apart from the darker asters.

Aster

A. *novae-angliae* 'Harrington's Pink'

Main features Flowers late summer to mid-autumn;
attracts bees and butterflies; good cut flower
Height 1.2 m (4 ft) **Spread** 60 cm (24 in.)
Position ○ ◑ **Hardiness** RHS H7

A wonderful cut flower, this vigorous North American aster produces large clusters of long-rayed soft pink daisies from late summer – much to the delight of nectar-seeking butterflies and bees. The sprays of bloom top 1.2-metre-tall (4 ft) sturdy stems making 'Harrington's Pink' a great back of the border plant. Unless the soil is particularly fertile, it rarely needs staking if grown in full sun. It looks particularly effective when planted in bold swaths and makes a compatible partner for ornamental grasses such as *Miscanthus* and other late-flowering prairie-style/cottage-garden–style perennials such as *Agastache*, *Echinacea purpurea* (coneflowers) and *Sanguisorba officinalis* (great burnet).

As you would hope, 'Harrington's Pink' is reasonably resistant to mildew, the scourge of several other *A. novae-angliae* varieties and of the more widely grown *A. novi-belgii* New York asters. This variety also has excellent resistance to rust disease. The plants will thrive and flower well in most spots receiving at least six hours of sun a day as long as the soil is reasonably moist and fertile. They will tolerate dry soil once established but the lower leaves will then tend to die off and look tatty, so it is best to anticipate this by growing smaller, more drought-tolerant perennials in front of the plants.

Flowering typically peaks in early autumn but it is easy to extend the display by pinching out the growing tip of some of the stems when they are about 15 centimetres (6 in.) tall in late spring/early summer. This will make these stems bloom later. They will be shorter and bushier than unpinched stems, too. After flowering, cut back the plants to ground level for neatness and to prevent self-seeding – any offspring are sadly unlikely to be as attractive as the original. Dividing the plants every third spring will help to keep them vigorous. **GP**

Alternative

Symphyotrichum novae-angliae 'Rosa Sieger'

Astilbe

A. chinensis 'Visions'

Main features Upright purple plumes; robust dark
green leaves
Height 50 cm (20 in.) **Spread** 50 cm (20 in.)
Position ○ ◑ **Hardiness** RHS H7

The elegance and dependability of astilbes is appreciated
by many gardeners as is their enjoyment of conditions
that are wetter than many perennials can stand. Their
divided, often dark or bronze-tinted, foliage is particularly
attractive and their plumes of summer flowers in red,
purple and pink shades, as well as white, are much valued
in borders. Most, however, are insistent on damp soil
and are unhappy in hot summers. All astilbes dislike
hot, dry conditions.

A. chinensis is valuable to gardeners because it is more
tolerant of dry conditions than other species and also,
instead of making tight clumps as others do, it tends to
spread steadily. In fact, when happy, *A. chinensis* makes
a very effective weed-smothering ground cover. The
foliage is dark green, divided in three and then twice
divided in three again, and wiry green stems covered in
brown hairs strike vertically through the foliage. Towards
the tips, the stems branch into distinctive, tightly upright
sprays of small pink or white flowers.

'Visions' represents a further step towards the goal
of creating astilbes that better meet the needs of
gardeners. A more compact, more manageable plant,
the robust and noticeably glossy foliage makes a good
background for the fat, sturdy, upright purple plumes.
'Visions' was the first in two series of astilbes developed
in the Netherlands by astilbe specialist Wim van Veen.
'Vision in Red' (pictured) has purplish-red plumes held
on red stems above slightly bronzed foliage whereas
'Vision in White' has more open, white plumes over dark
green leaves. Both varieties match the original 'Visions'
in height, although the pink-flowered 'Vision in Pink' is
a little taller at 65 centimetres (26 in.). Plants in the Little
Visions Series, with pink and purple flowers, are shorter
at about 40 centimetres (16 in.). **GR**

Alternative

Astilbe chinensis var. *pumila*

Astilbe
A. × arendsii 'Fanal'

Main features Narrow, deep red plumes in summer and early autumn; red-tinted divided foliage; cut flower
Height 60 cm (24 in.) **Spread** 60 cm (24 in.)
Position ○ ◐ **Hardiness** RHS H7

Astilbes are tough perennial members of the saxifrage family from Asia and North America that grow naturally in wet meadows and damp woodland clearings. About five of the twenty wild species are grown in gardens and all have been used in the development of those that come under the heading of *A. × arendsii*. These hybrids were developed in Germany by nurseryman Georg Arends. One of these is 'Fanal', which is German for 'signal'.

These are winter hardy, moisture-loving herbaceous perennials, some with tight, compact, rather woody rootstocks. The foliage is lobed and divided, often tinted in bronze when it first opens. The distinctive feathery heads open in summer and early autumn, the tiny five-petalled flowers packed into plumes or sprays, which are sometimes bold and erect and sometimes more spreading and airier in appearance. They range in colour from purples, reds and pinks to cream and white. In autumn the old plumes turn biscuit brown or rust coloured and persist into the winter giving an additional seasonal appeal. Astilbes are invaluable perennials for damp but sunny situations and are increasingly used as cut flowers.

The upright crimson stems hold narrow, deep red plumes, which open above glossy leaves in midsummer. The foliage, whose reddish tint is most pronounced when the leaves first open, remains reddish through the summer. These astilbes are ideal partners for hostas, providing the colourful flowers that hostas lack. **GR**

Alternatives

Astilbe x *arendsii* 'Burgundy Red' ('Burgunderrot'), *Astilbe japonica* 'Montgomery', *Astilbe japonica* 'Red Sentinel'

Astrantia
'Roma'

Main features Flowers early to late summer; good cut and dried flower; attracts bees and butterflies
Height 60 cm (24 in.) **Spread** 60 cm (24 in.)
Position ○ ◑ **Hardiness** RHS H7

This plant deserves a place in every garden, if only to give the owner the chance to repeat the common name (masterwort) of *A*. 'Roma' to visitors. Deeply lobed, mid-green leaves appear from a clump in spring. In summer, wiry stems topped with clusters of pink, pincushion-style flowers appear, each one consisting of a host of tiny individual flowers packed together, and surrounded by a ruff of pink bracts. Growing to 60 centimetres (24 in.), the flowers are held well above the foliage. This vigorous selection flowers over a longer period than other varieties, and was bred in the Netherlands by Piet Oudolf.

Easy to grow in any rich, moisture-retentive soil, it tolerates sun or partial shade, but prefers climates with cooler summers, so should be grown in light shade in hotter locations. Clumps may be divided in early spring, but resent root disturbance. The do not take kindly to container culture. It is a sterile hybrid, so does not have the annoying habit of self-seeding into other plants.

The flowers are excellent for cutting fresh, or for use when dried. Pick the stems when in full bloom and hang upside down in a cool airy place to dry. It is worthy of a place in cool colour-themed borders, perhaps teamed with blues of *Salvia × sylvestris* 'Mainacht' or *Geranium* Rozanne. It is equally at home in cottage-garden–style or contemporary plantings, associating well with some of the shorter-growing ornamental grasses, such as the blue-leaved oat grass (*Helictotrichon sempervirens*). **MP**

Alternatives

Astrantia major 'Sunningdale Variegated', *Astrantia major* var. *involucrata* 'Shaggy', *Astrantia maxima*

Athyrium
A. niponicum var. *pictum*

Main feature Lacy foliage patterned in silver and purple
Height 30 cm (12 in.) **Spread** 60 cm (24 in.)
Position ◑ ●
Hardiness RHS H7

The painted lady ferns, *Athyrium*, are a group of easy to grow ferns that have grace, delicacy and increasingly lovely combinations of colours in their fronds. There are around 200 creeping or clump-forming species growing in damp woodland and forests around the world, including the United Kingdom and North America, but mainly in Asia.

Japanese painted fern (*A. niponicum* var. *pictum*) is a low, steadily creeping plant from the forests of northeast Asia. It rarely reaches more than 30 centimetres (12 in.) in height. The rather narrow fronds, which tend to arch over appealingly, are divided into alternate divisions and each division is again split into small segments. As they unfurl, the new fronds may be greyish or completely silvery grey. They soon mature to greyish green with a grey stripe along the centre of the main divisions and purple colouring along the main midrib. Plants are a little variable, but all are worthy of a place in the garden. The Japanese painted fern is easy to grow in fertile soil with at least some shade and in soil that does not dry out. Note that plants can die in dry or hot and sunny conditions. This is a beautiful plant for a shady perennial tapestry that includes smaller hostas, hellebores, corydalis, pulmonarias and epimediums.

Treasured and admired for many decades, in recent years the Japanese painted fern has been used to develop a range of newer types. These are generally larger, with broader fronds and with more dramatic colouring. The result is a range of plants that retain the delicate appearance but are even more striking. 'Ghost' is almost completely grey, 'Silver Falls' is especially vigorous with an almost reflective silver colouring, whereas 'Ursula's Red' has grey fronds, with pink veins and a heavy deep stripe along the centre. **GR**

Alternatives

Athyrium 'Ghost', *Athyrium niponicum* var. *pictum* 'Silver Falls', *Athyrium niponicum* var. *pictum* 'Ursula's Red'

Baptisia
B. australis

Main features Early summer blooms; good foliage throughout season; interesting seedpods
Height 90–120 cm (3–4 ft) **Spread** 60 cm (24 in.)
Position ○ **Hardiness** RHS H7

Hailing from a genus of about thirty-five species of North American perennials, *B. australis* (commonly known as blue false indigo) became popular as part of the movement towards low-maintenance gardening and as a result of the rediscovery of native North American plants. It is revered as one of modern perennial gardening's great backbone plants and is often recommended as a replacement for classic garden lupins, which do not thrive in the summer heat and humidity of most of North America, and because it has similar typically leguminous flowers.

Although slow to establish, blue false indigo forms a neat, shrub-like plant. In early summer, 30-centimetre-long (12 in.) upright stalks of intense blue flowers rise above handsome, grey-green leaves that remain an attractive feature all summer. It has a rugged character and blooms are followed by prominent dark seedpods that complement the foliage and make an interesting rattling sound in the breeze. Plants are extremely long lived and have a long taproot making them highly drought tolerant – they can barely be pried out of the garden once established.

As a legume, *Baptisia* can fix nitrogen in the soil, rarely needs fertilising and is perfect for a lean site in full sun. The botanical name is derived from the Greek word for 'dip' or 'dye', and indeed early English colonists in North America cultivated it as a dye similar to (but weaker than) the true indigo of the tropics.

Other species of *Baptisia* have flowers that bloom white, yellow or varying shades of blue/purple. There has recently been much hybridising between the different species to produce plants with better or more interesting colours, but the same fortitude and drought tolerance characteristic of the unimproved species, which is extending the usefulness of this genus. **KK**

Alternatives

Baptisia 'Carolina Moonlight', *Baptisia* Decadence 'Dutch Chocolate', *Baptisia sphaerocarpa* 'Screamin' Yellow'

Bergenia
'Bressingham White'

Main features White bell-shaped flowers open from coral pink buds in spring; evergreen leaves flecked with pink in winter **Height** 45 cm (18 in.) **Spread** 60 cm (24 in.) **Position** ○ ◑ ● **Hardiness** RHS H6

Dramatic evergreen leaves and long-lasting spring flowers combine to make bergenias a great asset to any planting scheme, and while most have pink or red blooms, 'Bressingham White' stands out from the crowd with clusters of clear white bells, opening from coral pink buds. An underskirt of sculptural oval dark-green foliage provides a striking foil for the flowers and weed-suppressing ground cover year-round. The leaves also feature pink tints during the winter months.

This bergenia is ideal for edging a woodland garden or shady border, where it will form a decorative fringe of leathery leaves. Combine it with other woodlanders, such as daffodils, Jacob's ladder (*Polemonium caeruleum*) and bluebells, as well as textured foliage plants, including ferns, hostas, the foam flower (*Tiarella cordifolia*) and heucheras. This easy-going plant is equally happy in sun, where it makes a good partner for summer snowflakes (*Leucojum*), tulips, alliums and other spring- and early summer-flowering blooms.

Almost anyone can grow bergenias, and they thrive in most situations and soils, including free-draining sand and heavy clays. Plant them in early autumn or spring for the best results and remove the flower heads after they have bloomed. Cut off damaged or scruffy leaves as new growth emerges in spring, and lift and divide large or congested clumps at the same time.

Other bergenias include 'Silberlicht', which produces white flowers that fade to pale pink; 'Harzkristall', with white blooms that feature a hint of pink on the petals; and the slightly smaller species *B. ciliata*, which also has white flowers with a pink tinge. *Bergenia* 'Bach' has sugar-pink flowers that mature to white, whereas 'Ice Queen' has red-edged leaves and greenish-white flowers that appear slightly earlier than 'Bressingham White'. **ZA**

Alternatives

Bergenia ciliata, *Bergenia* 'Silberlicht', *Bergenia* 'Harzkristall', *Bergenia* 'Bach', *Bergenia* 'Ice Queen'

Brunnera
B. macrophylla 'Jack Frost'

Main features Sprays of tiny, forget-me-not-like blue flowers in late spring; white and green, heart-shaped foliage **Height** 40 cm (16 in.) **Spread** 60 cm (24 in.) **Position** ◑ **Hardiness** RHS H7

Shimmering in the shade, the heart-shaped leaves of this deciduous perennial, with their dramatic frosted design, make a bold statement from spring to autumn. The ice-white and green-veined foliage of *B. macrophylla* 'Jack Frost' is joined in late spring by delicate sprays of tiny blue flowers that resemble forget-me-nots, creating a winning combination of colour and texture in borders and woodlands gardens. 'Jack Frost' remains dormant in winter, but new leaves are quick to emerge in early spring.

Use 'Jack Frost' to edge a woodland path, or to brighten up a bed beneath trees and shrubs where the soil remains moist. Try mixing it with spring bulbs, such as daffodils, snakeshead fritillaries (*Fritillaria meleagris*) and bluebells, together with other shade plants that feature decorative leaves, including ferns, hostas and *Dicentra formosa*. In a flower border, the silvery leaves provide a foil for foxgloves, hardy geraniums, *Anemone hupehensis*, *Corydalis* and pink and red *Astrantia*.

To thrive, *Brunnera* requires moist but free-draining soil and some shade – it will lose its patterning in deep shade or full sun. Improve the soil with well-rotted manure or compost a few weeks before planting in spring or early autumn. Add some all-purpose slow-release fertiliser to the soil when planting, and water regularly until the roots have established. Cut out any plain green leaves as soon as you see them, and remove spent flower heads in early summer.

Other varieties of Siberian bugloss worth considering include *Brunnera macrophylla* 'Dawson's White', which has cream-edged leaves; 'Betty Bowring', with its plain green leaves and pure white flowers; and 'Hadspen Cream', which has a thin cream margin around the green leaves. Another variety, 'Looking Glass', has solid silver leaves. **ZA**

Alternatives

Brunnera macrophylla 'Alba' (syn. *Brunnera* 'Betty Bowring'), *Brunnera macrophylla* 'Langtrees'

Calamagrostis
C. brachytricha

Main features Upright, architectural habit with feathery plumes of flower heads; flowers summer/autumn/winter
Height 90–150 cm (3–5 ft) **Spread** 45–90 cm (18–36 in.)
Position ○ ◐ **Hardiness** RHS H7

A group of *C. brachytricha* makes a stunning sight. A single specimen is irresistibly attractive. It is a grass that demands attention – garden visitors want to know its name. This robust grass is a reliable performer. A central clump of erect linear leaves gives it a bushy habit, with upright stems bearing feathery plume-like sprays of flowers high above. Like elegant millet, its purple-tinged flowers put on a show from late summer and early autumn. As a bonus they persist into winter, turning silver grey. Fresh or dried, they are wonderful for flower arrangements.

   C. brachytricha looks good in monoculture drifts, it also mixes well with a range of different planting styles. Excellent on slopes where breezes add more movement to leaves and flower heads, it is equally at home in mixed cottage-garden–style planting or as a single specimen in a container. It is particularly good in airy meadow-style schemes with other such as *Agapanthus* Headbourne hybrids, *Sanguisorba officinalis* 'Red Thunder' and *Verbena bonariensis*. Easy to grow, it is happy in full sun or partial shade, and not fussy about soil type as long as it is well drained.

   C. × *acutiflora* 'Karl Foerster' is another feather reed grass of the same size and upright habit, but its bronze flower heads are not as airy. The same is true for *C.* × *acutiflora* 'Overdam', but this attractive variegated form has green and white striped leaves that make a good foil for its pinkish flower plumes. **RC**

Alternatives

Calamagrostis × *acutiflora* 'Overdam', *Calamagrostis* × *acutiflora* 'Karl Foerster'

Campanula
'Sarastro'

Main features Flowers summer; attracts bees, butterflies and hummingbirds; good cut flower
Height 60 cm (24 in.) **Spread** 60 cm (24 in.)
Position ○ ◑ **Hardiness** RHS H7

This superb, relatively new bellflower hybrid is fast becoming a mid-border classic. Unlike many *Campanula*, 'Sarastro' flowers all summer long. Masses of intense violet-blue tubular bells each 6 centimetres long (2.5 in.), open from slender buds of the deepest purple. They dangle from slender arching 60-centimetre-tall (2 ft) leafy stems, which are often so laden with blooms they need some support – a small price to pay. The blooms are outstanding for cutting. There is no need to worry about this *Campanula* taking over your border either. Unlike one of its thuggish parents (*C. punctata*), 'Sarastro' has a neat, dense, clumping habit and is guaranteed to not self-seed as it is a sterile hybrid.

While it is often described as being a shorter more compact version of *C.* 'Kent Belle' (which shares the same parents), 'Sarastro' is more floriferous and has a longer flowering period and more upright habit. Like most bellflowers, this variety does well in full sun or part shade in any soil that does not become waterlogged or bone dry. Boggy conditions will rot the roots – especially in winter – so dig some sharp grit into your soil to improve drainage if necessary.

'Sarastro' works well alongside alliums (ornamental onions) and grasses such as the golden *Hakonechloa macra* 'Aureola'. It is also effective combined with other cottage garden plants such as roses, hardy geraniums, penstemon, lupins, hosta and phlox. **GP**

Alternatives

Campanula lactiflora 'Prichard's Variety', *Campanula poscharskyana* 'E. H. Frost', *Campanula alliariifolia* 'Ivory Bells'

Campanula
C. garganica

Main features Compact growth; neat foliage; long summer succession of starry flowers
Height 5–10 cm (2–4 in.) **Spread** 30 cm (12 in.)
Position ○ ◑ **Hardiness** RHS H7

The Adriatic bellflower, *C. garganica,* is a European species growing wild in Greece and Italy with a particular liking for rocky outcrops and crevices, but usually in the shade. It makes a neat, clump- or cushion-forming plant with small, heart-shaped, bright-green, finely toothed leaves about 2.5 centimetres (1 in.) across. It is usually evergreen, though may lose its leaves in hard winters. From midsummer slender 15-centimetre (6 in.) stems emerge from the tight crown to carry five-pointed starry flowers, each flower usually blue with a white centre; the flowers tend to turn to face the brightest light. Although in the wild this is generally a plant of shade, in gardens it thrives in sun. It can be grown in rock crevices and the cracks in the walls of raised beds or at the front of well-drained borders, and when happy will often produce self-sown seedlings, which may flower in the cracks in paving. 'Dickson's Gold' is the best-known cultivar, and one of the few bellflowers with golden foliage. Colouring best in full sun, the bright foliage sets off the blue flowers perfectly. **GR**

Alternatives

Campanula portenschlagiana, Campanula poscharskyana

Cautleya
C. spicata 'Robusta'

Main features Exotic-looking perennial with spikes of yellow blooms; flowers late summer and autumn
Height 1 m (3.5 ft) **Spread** 60–90 cm (24–36 in.)
Position ◑ **Hardiness** RHS H5

The hardier members of the ginger family, *Zingiberaceae*, are becoming increasingly popular. The hardiest are in the genus *Cautleya*, which grow in the Himalayas in moist and shady conditions. *C. spicata*, the Himalayan ginger, is the most widely grown in gardens. This is a stout herbaceous perennial, the fat, reddish vertical stems carrying large lance-shaped, fresh, green leaves up to 30 centimetres (12 in.) long. Growth starts unusually late in spring but is rapid. The bright-yellow hooded flowers open from red bracts, starting at the base of the long spikes and opening in succession over some weeks. 'Robusta', sometimes labelled as 'Autumn Beauty', has darker yellow flowers with a little orange tinting, opening from rich dark-red bracts in spikes that are longer than those of the wild species. Use it in a planting scheme that also features the hardier palms (*Chamaerops humilis* and *Trachycarpus fortunei*), the larger phormiums, tree ferns, bamboos, pawlonias and *Hedychiums*, which are also members of the ginger family. **GR**

Alternatives

Cautleya gracilis, Cautleya gracilis 'Edinburgh Lemon'

Cautleya spicata **'Robusta'** has yellow flowers
that emerge from red bracts over several weeks. ➡

Chelone
C. obliqua

Main features Flowers late summer to early autumn; striking blooms on vertical stems; attracts bees
Height 30–90 cm (12–36 in.) **Spread** 30–90 cm (12–36 in.)
Position ◑ ● **Hardiness** RHS H7

This is a late-summer showstopper, so gardeners who only shop for plants in spring will miss the opportunity to be seduced by the easy-care North American native. *C. obliqua*, also known as turtleheads, are cousins of penstemons and have fascinating flowers similar to snapdragons where the upper lip arches over the lower lip, giving the flower a resemblance to the heads of open-mouthed turtles. It is an excellent, sturdy, vertical perennial with rounded stems, medium texture and deep-green, boldly veined leaves on short stalks. Weather-resistant flowers are dark pink or purplish red, borne in short, dense, terminal spikes. The flowers are tubular two-lipped blooms, with a sparse yellow beard inside each lower lip. Turtlehead is an ideal plant for the middle of the border as it will provide a good contrast for other perennials and small shrubs. It is best grown in partial shade with moist soil, but it will tolerate dense shade. The botanical name comes from the Greek for tortoise, referring to the turtlehead-shaped blooms. **KK**

Alternatives

Chelone lyonii 'Hot Lips', *Chelone glabra*

Chionochloa
C. rubra

Main features All-year foliage interest; flowers summer; architectural plant
Height 1.2 m (4 ft) **Spread** 1.2 m (4 ft)
Position ○ **Hardiness** RHS H4

An established clump of this evergreen tussock grass, native to New Zealand, is an impressive sight when shimmering in the sun or being gently buffeted by the wind. It forms graceful open mounds of slender, almost wire-like leaves in shades of orange-brown and olive green, that arch out from a compact rootstock. Each plant should be allowed sufficient space to show off its architectural structure. Although grown primarily for its foliage, willowy stems appear in late summer bearing lax panicles of flowers (the same colour as the leaves), which move in the slightest breeze. Plant this impressive grass in full sun in any well-drained soil. Cut out the old flower spikes in winter and comb out dead leaves in spring. Take care as the leaves have sharp edges. The arching, elegant shape makes it an ideal plant for a large container. It offers year-round interest, and can be used effectively in gravel gardens and prairie-style plantings. It associates well with the orange flowers of *Kniphofia* 'Mango Popsicle' or the spires of the foxtail lily, *Eremurus* 'Cleopatra'. **KK**

Alternatives

Chionochloa conspicua, Chionochloa flavescens

Chrysanthemum
'Mrs Jessie Cooper'

Main feature Prolific display of vibrant cerise-pink
flowers in late summer and autumn
Height 90 cm (3 ft) **Spread** 45 cm (18 in.)
Position ○ **Hardiness** RHS H4

Chrysanthemums have been developed for centuries
and probably come in more different types, sizes, forms
and colours than any other plant. They are classified into
thirty groups, some of which have up to seven subgroups.
Rubellum chrysanthemums are hardy garden specimens
carrying sprays of usually single, but sometimes semi-
double or double flowers, often nicely scented. They also
often have a tendency to run at the root when almost
all other types are more clump forming. The 1930s saw
an influx of new introductions of easy to grow, outdoor
chrysanthemums with good floral shape and strong
colours, among them 'Mrs Jessie Cooper'. Originally
introduced simply as 'Jessie Cooper' by Amos Perry in the
United Kingdom, the 5-centimetre (2 in.) single flowers
are a vibrant cerise pink with a narrow white ring around
the large yellow disks. Relatively late to flower, sometimes
extending its display into early winter, the combination of
colour, prolific flowering late in the season, and hardiness
has ensured that it remains popular with gardeners. **GR**

Alternatives

Chrysanthemum 'Clara Curtis', *Chrysanthemum* 'Mary Stoker'

Chrysanthemum
'Mei–Kyo'

Main feature Small, pink, pompon flowers on neat,
twiggy plants
Height 60 cm (24 in.) **Spread** 45 cm (18 in.)
Position ○ **Hardiness** RHS H4

Perennial chrysanthemums come in a huge variety of
forms and colours to enhance autumn borders. Some of
the most distinctive are those with small, almost button-
like (pompon) flowers. Not only are the flowers little more
than 2.5 centimetres (1 in.) across, but the leaves are also
unusually small and neat. This type is ideal in spaces
where many hardy chrysanthemum plants are too big.
Small flowers do not mean a small display – the stiff,
upright stems branch repeatedly at the top to provide
a mass of colour. Pink-flowered 'Mei-Kyo' was the first of
these delightful pompon types. Its name means 'treasure
of Kyoto' and it arrived in the United Kingdom in an
unusual way. Cuttings came from Japan in a matchbox,
were rooted, and the plant was introduced in 1961. Ten
years later, a customer noticed a sport on a plant of
'Mei-Kyo' that had bronze flowers. It was sent back to
the nursery who introduced it and it is still available as
'Bronze Elegance'. A white, 'Purleigh White', and a yellow,
'Nantyderry Sunshine', followed in the same way. **GR**

Alternatives

Chrysanthemum 'Anastasia', *Chrysanthemum* 'Ruby Mound'

Clematis
'Alionushka'

Main feature Rich, pink, bell-shaped flowers
midsummer to early autumn
Height 1–1.5 m (3.5–5 ft) **Spread** 30 cm (12 in.)
Position ○ ◑ **Hardiness** RHS H6

This herbaceous clematis deserves to be more widely grown for there are not many specimens offering rich pink flowers from midsummer to early autumn. 'Alionushka' keeps the interest going in a mixed border of shrubs and perennials, and in the hands of someone who enjoys putting together plant combinations, it will be a rewarding plant.

The plentiful bell-shaped flowers, borne on stiff stems, nod attractively. Examine the flower close-up and you will notice a darker pink stripe and the petals – strictly speaking these are tepals – twist slightly. The flower colour combines well with other pinks, purples, blues or whites but it also blends well with silver- or purple-leaved shrubs. This clematis does not cling – you can allow it to weave around the middle of a sunny border between the shrubs and front perennials. Alternatively, in a small garden you might want to tie it into a small or medium support bearing in mind its modest height. The heights and spread given here assume the plant grows with support. Despite looking very special this plant is hardy and not fussy about its site or soil. Cutting back the stems to ground level in late winter to early spring makes it a feasible choice even in a narrow border or small garden. Mature clumps will need lifting and dividing after four years, replanting a healthy section into enriched soil.

'Alionushka' is a hybrid of the Integrifolia Group; it was raised in the Nikitsky Botanical Garden in Crimea, Ukraine, in the early 1960s. It was awarded a British Clematis Society Certificate of Merit in 1998 and a Royal Horticultural Society Award of Garden Merit in 2002. *C. integrifolia* is a European species that has been grown since the sixteenth century but many of its hybrids currently recommended were bred in the 1990s. **LD**

Alternatives

Clematis 'Arabella', *Clematis* 'Pangbourne Pink', *Clematis* Petit Faucon = 'Evisix'

◐ *Clematis* 'Alionushka' does not cling but can be tied to short supports.

Clematis
C. × *durandii*

Main features Flowers in early to late summer; scrambling habit
Height 2 m (7 ft) **Spread** 90 cm (3 ft)
Position ○ ◐ **Hardiness** RHS H6

Expect the unexpected with this clematis, for it does not have the ability to climb in the true sense of the word. The leaf stalks are unable to twine around any support, as happens with the majority of clematis. However, it is still a worthy addition to any garden once its habit has been mastered. It is best described as a deciduous scrambler, with a remarkably long flowering season. From early to late summer, 10-centimetre-wide (4 in.), deep indigo-blue flowers, each with four to six petals (technically tepals), and a cluster of creamy-coloured stamen in the centre are produced from lax stems. In full sun the colour may fade a bit.

Growing best in most moisture-retentive soils in full sun, C. × *durandii* is also quite tolerant of partial shade. In common with most clematis, it prefers a cool root run in a neutral to alkaline soil. The flowers are produced on the new season's growth, and it can grow up to 2 metres (7 ft) or more in a season. Pruning is simplicity itself, as it can be cut to the ground in early spring before the new growth starts. It needs something to scramble through and makes the perfect companion to an early-flowering shrub, such as the red-flowered *Chaenomeles* 'Rowallane', or pink-flowered *Clematis* 'Pink Lady'. If given a start in the right direction, it will happily scramble through a shrub rose or over a tree stump, or can even be left to sprawl along the ground over a bark or gravel mulch to keep the flowers clean.

Durand's clematis is thought to be a hybrid between the truly climbing 'Jackmanii' and the truly nonclimbing, but much smaller-flowered, *C. integrifolia*. It has been in cultivation since 1874. The purplish-blue flowers partner well with golden-leaved or silver-leaved foliage shrubs. Surplus blooms can be cut and used indoors as cut flowers. **MP**

Alternatives

Clematis 'Arabella', *Clematis* 'Alionoushka', *Clematis* × *jouiniana*, *Clematis* Petit Faucon = 'Evisix'

Cortaderia
C. selloana Silver Feather

Main feature A specimen grass with ornamental
flower stems in the autumn
Height 1.5–2.4 m (5–8 ft) **Spread** 1.5–2.4 m (5–8 ft)
Position ○ **Hardiness** RHS H5

With over 650 genera and more than 10,000 wild species
growing just about everywhere across the globe, the
grasses have the fifth-highest number of species of all
plant families. Amongst those grasses the pampas grasses
are some of the largest and most imposing.

There are twenty-four fibrous-rooted, evergreen,
herbaceous perennial pampas grass species. Most of
them grow in South America, but there are a few in New
Zealand. Pampas grasses are invasive in California and
other suitable climates. The vast majority of those seen
in gardens are forms of the species *C. selloana*.

Native to Argentina, Brazil and Chile, *C. selloana*
is nothing if not dramatic. Reaching up to 3.6 metres
(12 ft) in height, with none shorter than about 1.2 metres
(4 ft), the plant has a crown that becomes increasingly
tough as the years pass. From this woody crown arise
long, slender, sharp-toothed leaves, which in the largest
forms can be 2.4 metres (8 ft) long. The mass of leaves
arches in a graceful fountain of foliage and makes an
impressive clump even before the flower spikes emerge.

From early autumn, stout, vertical stems appear
carrying large, fluffy plumes of flowers, usually in
white or cream shades, which vary in length from 30 to
90 centimetres (1– 3 ft), depending on the cultivar. There
are also a number of selections with variegated foliage,
the pale slender stripes running along the length of the
individual leaves. This feature ensures that the plants are
valuable additions to the garden in the months before
the flowers emerge, and as they mature they become
truly impressive. Some have golden stripes; some are
more are striped in silver. *C. selloana* Silver Feather is
a sport of the relatively small *C. selloana* 'Pumila', and
features bright-silver stripes and is especially valuable
for its neat habit. **GR**

Alternatives

= 'Notcort'. *Cortaderia selloana* 'Aureolineata', *Cortaderia
selloana* 'Silver Fountain', *Cortaderia selloana* 'Splendid Star'

Corydalis
C. flexuosa

Main features Spring-blooming blue flowers;
fragrant flowers
Height 15–30 cm (6–12 in.) **Spread** 15–30 cm (6–12 in.)
Position ◑ ● **Hardiness** RHS H5

This gorgeous perennial has delightful, ferny foliage that covers itself in spikes of dangling, tubular, sky-blue flowers, which emit a sweet coconut-like scent for a couple of weeks in late spring. Few gardeners can resist its charms, and few gardeners can grow it as anything other than an annual. Heavily promoted in fashionable garden circles in the last decade, a number of named but similar-looking cultivars were released in rapid succession. *C. flexuosa* resents drought and is challenging to grow as a perennial in areas other than the Pacific Northwest, parts of the United Kingdom, and other locales where summer evenings are cool and the soil remains constantly moist. It needs not only exquisite drainage but also consistent moisture, and under the best of conditions, it routinely goes dormant when the heat of summer arrives, sometimes coming up again in autumn only to be felled by frost.

C. flexuosa was discovered by English plant explorers on an expedition to western China in 1989. It was found near China's main panda preserve. Some gardeners report more success with *C. flexuosa* in containers as the tubers, positioned shallowly below the soil surface, are more easily kept moist. As an alternative, some nurseries tout *C. elata*, also discovered in the last twenty years in China. Similar in appearance to *C. flexuosa* with true-blue flowers (scent of gardenia), it tends to greater longevity because it sprouts from a crown rather than tubers. **KK**

Alternatives

Corydalis flexuosa 'Blue Panda', *Corydalis flexuosa* 'China Blue', *Corydalis flexuosa* 'Père David', *Corydalis elata*

Crocosmia
'Lucifer'

Main features Spring to autumn foliage; late-summer flowers; attracts hummingbirds; flowers and seed heads good for cutting **Height** 1.2 m (4 ft) **Spread** 60 cm (24 in.) **Position** ○ ◑ **Hardiness** RHS H5

Justifiably one of the most popular crocosmia of all, fiery-red 'Lucifer' adds drama and a touch of the exotic to late-summer borders. Once established, you can expect a dazzling display of upwards-facing blooms on a profusion of tall, arching stems. They are a hummingbird favourite and good for cutting too. This imposing variety has fans of handsomely ridged, sword-shaped leaves that provide added interest – these are just the right shade of green to flatter the sprays of scarlet blooms. Even the seed heads are attractive and useful in floral arrangements.

'Lucifer' combines well with cannas, dark-red dahlias and castor oil plants (*Ricinus communis*) to give a tropical effect. It also looks at home in cottage-garden–style schemes, alongside deep blue nepetas (cat mint), yellow and orange heleniums, yellow coreopsis and red-hot pokers (*Kniphofia*). Crocosmias flower best in full sun but also thrive in light shade. Strictly speaking, crocosmias should be classed as bulbs but their corms soon multiply, forming dense perennial-like clumps, and this is how they are normally sold (either in pots or as bare-rooted plants). In fact, it is better to avoid buying them as dry corms as these often fail to sprout.

'Lucifer' is one of the hardiest crocosmias, but in cold areas it is worth planting it about 5 centimetres (2 in.) deeper than it was originally, to give added insulation from freezing temperatures. Also apply a 10-centimetre-deep (4 in.) layer of bark over the plants each autumn. **GP**

Alternatives

Crocosmia 'Emberglow', *Crocosmia* 'Hellfire', *Crocosmia* 'Severn Sunrise', *Crocosmia* 'Spitfire'

Cynara
C. cardunculus

Main features Architectural plant; midsummer to autumn flowers; attracts bees and butterflies; good cut flower
Height 1.8 m (6 ft) **Spread** 1.2 m (4 ft)
Position ○ **Hardiness** RHS H6

A living sculpture, *C. cardunculus* is one of the most architectural of all herbaceous perennials. Soaring to 1.8 metres (6 ft) plus, it is a fine choice for adding year-round drama and interest to the back of sunny borders. In spring it resembles a giant silver fern with its upright rosettes of deeply dissected grey leaves that grow up to 90 centimetres (3 ft) long. From midsummer the towering candelabra of luminous violet-blue, thistle-like flowers become the main attraction. By autumn the flowers will have evolved into a skeleton of attractive seed heads, which is well worth keeping until spring. The foliage and flowers are both useful in floral arrangements, and the flowers dry well.

Originating in Mediterranean regions, *C. cardunculus* needs full sun and well-drained soil to thrive. It is less likely to need staking if sheltered from strong winds. Established clumps are pretty hardy, but young plants are vulnerable to winter cold and wet, so plant them in spring to give them time to get their roots down and then cover the crown (centre) with a 15-centimetre-deep (6 in.) layer of straw or bark for the first winter, at least. Watch out for blackfly in early summer and squash or spray off before they look unsightly.

This is a plant that it is best to see before buying as many are seed-raised, and some have more ornamental leaves than others. In particular, try to ensure that you are not sold plants of the edible globe artichoke instead (*C. cardunculus* Scolymus Group), as this has greener, sparser leaves and fewer flowers. Edible artichoke plants also tend to be less hardy and do not grow to such a magnificent size. This species is considered to be an invasive weed in some parts of California and Australia, where it has formed large colonies in the wild. It has been banned from sale in many parts of Australia. **GP**

Alternative

Cynara cardunculus 'Cardy'

Dactylorhiza
D. foliosa

Main features Bold spikes of purple or pink flowers on strong-growing plants; easy to cultivate
Height 40–60 cm (16–24 in.) **Spread** 30 cm (12 in.)
Position ○ **Hardiness** RHS H5

Orchids from temperate climates, which can be grown outside in areas that are too cold for the more familiar tropical orchids, always excite gardeners – especially when they discover that they are not difficult to grow. The marsh orchids, *Dactylorhiza*, combine a slightly exotic look with colourful spikes of flowers and a perhaps unexpected ease of cultivation that is always appealing.

The best species of all for gardens is the Madeiran marsh orchid, *D. foliosa*. Growing wild only on the island of Madeira, it makes tall spikes of flowers above a rosette of slightly succulent leaves. Up to ten dark, glossy, sword-shaped leaves make a low rosette, and from it emerges the upright flower spike. Sometimes opening in spring, but more often in summer, the purple or pink flowers are packed into a crowded, pointed 18-centimetre (7 in.) spike; each flower (2.5 cm/1 in. across) is hooded and has its lip split into three parts. Growing in moist woods and grassland in the wild, the Madeiran marsh orchid thrives best in gardens in rich, moist conditions in full sun, where it will sometimes increase rapidly to make extremely impressive clumps. Self-sown seedlings may also occasionally appear. On poor soils, liquid feeding will ensure that it grows well. Young plants are sometimes eaten by mice or deer, which appreciate the slightly tuberous roots.

The classification of these orchids is complicated, since hybrids between species are common, so the experts vary in their assessment of how many species there are: some say about thirty-five, whereas others suggest about seventy-five species. They are native in a wide area, with many growing wild in Europe, two in North America, and others in the Middle East and Asia. Unlike many tropical orchids, which are epiphytic (growing on trees), the marsh orchids are herbaceous perennials. **GR**

Alternatives

Dactylorhiza fuchsii, Dactylorhiza maculata

Darmera
D. peltata

Main features Fragrant flowers in late spring;
architectural plant; attracts bees and butterflies
Height 90 cm (3 ft) **Spread** 50–100 cm (20–36 in.)
Position ○ ◑   **Hardiness** RHS H6

If you have a damp site and yet have not got room for
the giant-leaved *Gunnera*, then *Darmera* is an excellent
alternative. This deciduous, herbaceous perennial grows
from thick rhizomes that lie partly on the surface of the
ground. In late spring strong 60-centimetre-long (24
in.) stems arise, well before the leaves emerge, topped
with a head consisting of a rounded cluster of pale-pink,
five-petalled flowers. As the flowers fade the foliage
emerges. Large, mid-green, rounded leaves are attached
with the stalk in the centre of the back. The veins radiate
out like the spokes of an umbrella. Each leaf can be
45 centimetres (18 in.) across by 1.5 metres (5 ft) high,
with a lobed edge. In autumn, before the foliage dies
down, the leaves adopt shades of yellow, orange and
red, especially if grown in a sunny position.

This plant needs a moist site, so it is ideal to grow
at the edge of large ponds or in bog gardens. It prefers
a sunny – or in very hot climates, a partially shaded –
position in any soil type. The chunky rhizomes spread
slowly to form a colony 50 to 90 centimetres (20–36 in.)
across, which makes a bold statement in the garden.
It would associate well with other moisture-loving
plants, such the tall, fluffy, pink flower of *Filipendula
rubra* 'Venusta', *Iris sibirica* 'Silver Edge' and *Ligularia* 'The
Rocket', giving interest throughout the growing season.

Native to the western United States, and belonging to
the saxifrage family, this easy, hardy perennial deserves
a space in any garden large enough to accommodate
it. *D. peltata* 'Nana' grows to 60 by 60 centimetres
(24 x 24 in.), so can be used where space is limited. This
herbaceous perennial is grown primarily for its clumps of
large parasol-like leaves. The flower stems are impressive
when they appear in spring before the foliage, but they
can be damaged by late frost. **MP**

Alternative

Darmera peltata 'Nana'

Delphinium

D. elatum New Millennium Series 'Sweethearts'

Main feature Rich, pink flowers with white centres on bold spikes
Height 1.8–2.4 m (6–8 ft) **Spread** 90 cm (36 in.)
Position ○ **Hardiness** RHS H7

Delphiniums are famous for the most intense blue colouring of any hardy perennials and for their statuesque presence at the back of sunny borders in temperate climates around the world. If you need a tall, blue-flowered perennial, there is only one answer. However, over the long period of their development, which began in the 1850s, and as other colours were developed, delphiniums have become genetically complicated. Firstly, all modern varieties have double the number of chromosomes compared with the wild delphiniums from which they originally arose. This gives the plants extra vigour and the leaves and flowers extra substance.

Also, each individually named variety has a unique genetic blend that brings it not only its special flower colour, but also its petal shape and flower form, the length of its flower spike, how the flowers are arranged on the spike, the robustness of its stems and more. To preserve that unique blend of characteristics, most delphiniums are propagated by dividing plants or taking spring cuttings. However, each plant yields very few cuttings, so plants are always in short supply. Seeds collected from these varieties produce unpredictable results, so plant breeders have worked to develop delphiniums that are intended to be grown from seeds.

Terry Dowdeswell in New Zealand has been at the forefront of this work, and his New Millennium Series combines the widest range of colours with the best habit of growth and the most reliable consistency of colour. 'Sweethearts' is one of the most popular around the world. Each flower is rich, rose pink at the edge, paler pink towards the base, and with a white centre. The precise shade of pink varies slightly from plant to plant, but all the colours are all lovely. Take care to protect the seedlings from slugs. **GR**

Alternative

Delphinium Dusky Maidens Group

Delphinium
'Faust'

Main feature Bold spikes of dark-blue flowers in summer
Height 1.8–2.4 m (6–8 ft) **Spread** 75 cm (30 in.)
Position ○ **Hardiness** RHS H7

'Faust' is one of the best *Delphinium* varieties produced by the British nursery Blackmore & Langdon. Introduced in 1960, it has long, slender spikes of dark-blue, semi-double flowers with a pale streak through the centre of each petal and a slightly purplish tinge towards the centre. The classic English delphinium arose in the nursery of nineteenth-century French breeder Victor Lemoine. He grew wild *D. elatum*, a species from eastern Europe and western Asia with pale-blue flowers, alongside other species including *D. grandiflorum* with larger, dark-blue flowers. Lemoine sold seed from his *D. elatum* that had clearly cross-pollinated with the neighbouring species. He noticed how good these plants were and began to name and distribute selections. Over the years hundreds were introduced, and it is from these that the fine summer pillars of blue – and purple, pink, white and yellow – have been developed. This is a dramatic and colourful back-of-the-border perennial but, it is important to propagate only by division or from cuttings taken in early spring. **GR**

Alternatives

Delphinium 'Clifford Sky', *Delphinium* 'Fenella'

Dennstaedtia
D. punctilobula

Main feature Bright-green, hay-scented, low-maintenance ground cover
Height 30–60 cm (12–24 in.) **Spread** Indefinite
Position ◑ ● **Hardiness** RHS H7

The *D. punctilobula* is a fast-spreading ground cover of soft, bright-green, bipinnate fronds, which has the distinct aroma of newly mown hay. Native to eastern North America, its tenacity can be a virtue in the right location. Hay-scented fern has triangular- to oval-shaped fronds that are heavily divided into lacy leaflets. It thrives in moist soil, but is also tolerant of drought and poor, rocky soil. It is a perfect ground cover for locations where one needs to cover a large expanse quickly and inexpensively, as it spreads by underground rhizomes as well as by seeding about its spores. It is also ideal for difficult situations, like slopes and inclines. It is best planted with other vigorous partners, as it can overwhelm small plants. It is lovely paired with spring bulbs – such as daffodils, hyacinths and tulips – as it nicely covers over their dying foliage as the season progresses. Later in the summer, it pairs well with asiatic lilies and columbines. In autumn the fronds turn a coppery-orange, providing a vibrant and stunning carpet beneath the changing leaves of the trees. **KK**

Alternatives

Dryopteris marginalis, *Onoclea sensibilis*

● *Delphinium* 'Faust' with its dark-blue flowers alongside white *Delphinium* 'Butterball'.

Dianthus
D. gratianopolitanus

Main features Prolific display of single, pink or purplish flowers; grey foliage; sweetly scented flowers
Height 10–15 cm (4–6 in.) **Spread** 30 cm (12 in.)
Position ○ **Hardiness** RHS H7

There are about 300 species of pinks growing wild, mainly in Europe and Asia, and mostly in mountainous areas. Relatively few of the wild species are grown in gardens; but Cheddar pink, *D. gratianopolitanus*, is a species that is often seen – and deservedly so. Native to Central and Western Europe, its common name arises from the fact that its best-known British location is on the limestone rocks and cliffs of Cheddar Gorge, a dramatic landscape feature in western England. Cheddar pink is a low-growing evergreen, rooting in cracks and crevices, and forming low mats of slender grey foliage. In summer, plants are covered with 2.5-centimetre-wide (1 in.) flowers held singly on short stems up to 8 centimetres (3 in.) tall; the flowers are strongly scented and vary in colour from pale-pink to pink-purple. It is a fine plant for well-drained, alpine-raised beds and for the cracks in retaining walls. Give a neat trim after flowering to reveal the bright-grey, sometimes steely, foliage that is such a feature when the plants are not flowering. **GR**

Alternatives

Dianthus 'Bath's Pink', *Dianthus* 'Feuerhexe'

Dianthus
Sugar Plum

Main features A very long season of colourful, double flowers; spicily fragrant blooms; attractive grey foliage
Height 25 cm (10 in.) **Spread** 30 cm (12 in.)
Position ○ **Hardiness** RHS H7

Britain has always been the centre for development of new cultivars of garden pinks, and in recent years those developed by H. R. Whetman have found favour in North America and elsewhere; testing plants in new areas has informed decisions on which cultivars are best suited to different climates. The range now includes garden pinks for well-drained borders, patios, pots and cutting. The Scent First series not only focuses on garden performance, but also on fragrance. It comes in two groups, for larger and smaller containers and patio beds; Sugar Plum is one of the most striking of the taller types. With dense compact mounds of silvery, evergreen foliage, it has an exceptionally long flowering season, from midspring until autumn. The flowers have up to fifteen wavy petals, opening from distinctive chocolate-brown buds, and each petal is reddish-maroon with a pale-pink edge, giving a highly distinctive look. There is a strong, spicy fragrance. Sugar Plum is ideal as a specimen in an attractive pot or in a raised patio border. **GR**

Alternatives

='Wp08 Ian04'. *Dianthus* 'Candy Floss'

Dianthus
'Cranmere Pool'

Main features Large, faintly blushed, white, double
flowers in summer; scented blooms; good cut flower
Height 25 cm (10 in.) **Spread** 25 cm (10 in.)
Position ○ **Hardiness** RHS H6

Modern garden pinks originated in the early 1900s when
Montagu Allwood, a grower from the United Kingdom,
crossed perpetually-flowering carnations with an old-
fashioned pink called 'Old Fringed White'. This and other
old pinks flowered in June, but one of the special features
of what became known as *D.* × *allwoodii* was that it
flowered over a very long season. Development has
continued over the years, and one of the cultivars still
grown is 'Cranmere Pool'. The flowers are faintly blushed
white in colour, darkening towards the bright-red zone
in the very centre, and sometimes with red spots on the
pink-tinted, white areas. The petals are slightly toothed,
the flowers are scented, though not strongly, and are held
on 25-centimetre-long (10 in.) stems. The long succession
of flowers is set against long, slender, grey-blue evergreen
foliage. This is a prolific and reliable plant, although for
some the effect is spoiled by the tendency of the petals to
burst out of their calyx (the leafy organs clasping the base
of the flower), which can create a slightly untidy look. **GR**

Alternatives

Dianthus 'Alice', *Dianthus* 'Doris', *Dianthus* 'Haytor White'

Diascia
D. barberae 'Ruby Field'

Main features Dark coral-red flowers; unusually long
summer to autumn flowering season
Height 20 cm (8 in.) **Spread** 40 cm (16 in.)
Position ○ **Hardiness** RHS H4

Many valuable perennials originate in South Africa,
but in the 1970s and 1980s a series of promising new
genera were introduced. The twinspurs, *Diascia*, has
made the most impact. There are about fifty species
and all are low-growing plants with a spreading habit
and a tendency to run at the root. The shoots carry pairs
of small, toothed leaves that vary in shape from long
and narrow to broad and heart-shaped and are topped
by clusters of open-mouthed flowers. In the wild the
flowers are almost always pink, although other colours
have been developed in gardens. The five-lobed, flared
blooms feature a pair of yellow zones at the base of the
two upper lobes. *D. barbarae* was the first species to
become popular, the stems tending to lie on the soil and
turn up at the tips to carry prolific clusters of dark salmon-
pink flowers. *D. barbarae* 'Ruby Field' is distinguished by
its more upright growth and its deep coral-red flowers.
Like other diascias, it tends to be short-lived, but can
easily be propagated by division or cuttings. **GR**

Alternatives

Diascia barberae 'Belmore Beauty', *Diascia* Breezee Series

Dodecatheon
D. meadia

Main features Delightful lavender to vivid-pink flowers with reflexed petals; summer dormant
Height 30–40 cm (12–16 in.) **Spread** 25 cm (10 in.)
Position ○ ◑ **Hardiness** RHS H7

Take a look at the herbaceous *D. meadia*, also known as shooting star, and its place in the plant kingdom is clear: the flowers look as if they belong to a cyclamen, whereas the leafy plant itself is more reminiscent of a primula. Shooting star, in fact, belongs to the primula family as does the familiar cyclamen species seen on windowsills and rock gardens.

Native to every American state except Hawaii, as well as Russia, *D. meadia* has a definite preference for moist conditions; it grows naturally by the sides of streams and in wet patches in woods and meadows. Moisture is more important than sun, although plants dislike deep shade. From the centre of a rosette of oval leaves up to 20 centimetres (8 in.) long, vertically erect or arching stems arise that reach 35 to 40 centimetres (14–16 in.) in height. In spring, these are topped with clusters of remarkably beautiful flowers in lavender to magenta-pink shades with strongly reflexed petals, which look very similar to those of cyclamen. Plants with white flowers are occasionally found in the wild. Well over one hundred flowers have been counted on a single head, but from fifteen to twenty-five is more common. After flowering, seedpods develop and at the same time the rosette of foliage dies away, so that by midsummer the plant appears to be dead. Do not be deceived: this is a reaction to the drier summer conditions; the plant will remain dormant until early the following spring, when it once again enters into growth.

A number of garden forms of shooting star have been named, including two with lilac-pink flowers. In 'Goliath', the flowers are carried on stout stems up to 70 centimetres (28 in.) tall, which are excellent for cutting, and at the opposite end of the spectrum is the 30-centimetre-tall (12 in.) cultivar 'Queen Victoria'. **GR**

Alternatives

Dodecatheon pulchellum, Dodecatheon dentatum

Dryopteris
D. filix-mas 'Crispa Cristata'

Main features Robust and tolerant fern with bold
crested fronds; impressive specimen for shady borders
Height 60 cm (24 in.) **Spread** 40 cm (16 in.)
Position ● **Hardiness** RHS H7

These tough and resilient, mostly deciduous, ferns grow in
woods and other shady places, as well as in swamps and
alongside lakes and streams across temperate regions of
the northern hemisphere. This is a large group, around 300
species, although only about a dozen account for most
of those grown in gardens. Compact crowns carry bold
oval- or lance-shaped fronds in a more or less shuttlecock
formation; the fronds are sometimes held noticeably
upright and sometimes more arching in growth. Each
frond is divided at least once into toothed segments, and
as plants mature they can make impressive specimens
for shady borders. In the wild the fronds may grow from
45 centimetres (18 in.) to 1.8 metres (6 ft) long, depending
on the situation. They die away very late in the season.
Unexpected offspring may appear in the cracks of walls
and other shady places.

The most popular is the male fern, *D. filix-mas*,
so-called in comparison to the lady fern, *Athyrium filix-
femina*, which is more delicate looking. It grows wild in
a few places in North America, more widely in Asia, and
is common in Europe. Its lance-shaped fronds are split
into staggered rows of leaflets, each of these split into
staggered lobes on the undersides of which four to six
round, rusty-coloured, spore-bearing bodies develop.

'Crispa Cristata' is one of the most visually fetching
forms of *D. filix-mas*. The tips of each rather pale-green
frond, along with the tips of each of the main segments,
are crested crisply, creating a very appealing waved and
ruffled effect. While the simplicity of the wild species is
effective, the additional interest provided by this crested
form is valuable in moist, shady borders. *D. filix-mas*
'Crispa Cristata' looks attractive combined with hostas,
hellebores, lilies, brunneras and other shade-loving and
shade-tolerant plants. **GR**

Alternatives

Dryopteris filix-mas 'Barnesii', *Dryopteris filix-mas* 'Cristata'

Echinacea
E. purpurea 'Ruby Giant'

Main features Flowers in midsummer to midautumn; attracts bees, butterflies and hummingbirds; attractive seed heads **Height** 90 cm (3 ft) **Spread** 60 cm (24 in.) **Position** ○ **Hardiness** RHS H7

Huge, boldly coloured flowers coupled with a strong constitution make *E. purpurea* 'Ruby Giant' a choice coneflower. Deep-pink, honey-scented daisies up to 18 centimetres (7 in.) across are borne on sturdy, tall stems from midsummer into the autumn. Its double row of petals are held almost horizontally for maximum impact, and the orange-brown central cone can grow up to 5 centimetres (2 in.) tall. The cones evolve into attractive seed heads that can be used as dried flowers. It is worth leaving some for winter interest – they look striking when covered in frost and may attract seed-eating birds. *Echinacea* flower best in full sun. They enjoy reasonably moist soil, but it must drain well in winter. They are best planted in spring rather than autumn, so the roots can become established before being subjected to winter wet. 'Ruby Giant' suits cottage-garden–style and prairie-style schemes. It looks wonderful planted in drifts with grasses, sea hollies, red-hot pokers and persicaria. **GP**

Alternatives

Echinacea purpurea 'Kim's Mop Head', *Echinacea* 'Twilight'

Echinacea
E. purpurea 'Coconut Lime'

Main features Impressive, white, double-flower heads; blooms summer to autumn; excellent cut flower **Height** 60–75 cm (24–30 in.) **Spread** 30 cm (12 in.) **Position** ○ **Hardiness** RHS H7

The *E. purpurea* 'Coconut Lime' is a vigorous cultivar that is considered the world's first white, double coneflower. Each flower head sports a ring of petals surrounding a large pompom of creamy-white to pale-green florets. When the flower first opens, it appears like a normal single coneflower with a typical centre cone surrounded by petals. However, as days pass, the centre cone swells into the characteristic pompom while the large horizontal petals appear to shrink backwards and downwards. As the flower matures, the cone takes on the creamy white with green overtones and is then surrounded by a fringed skirt of fully reflexed, pure-white petals. At the topmost centre of the cone there often remains a small button of pale orange – this is what is left of the actual cone while the rest of the pompom is composed of tiny petals. Plants bloom continuously through summer, and each bloom lasts a few weeks. 'Coconut Lime' is a good addition to a cottage garden or a formal border. **KK**

Alternatives

Echinacea purpurea 'Meringue', *Echinacea purpurea* 'Magnus'

● *Echinacea purpurea* 'Ruby Giant' is a coneflower with particularly sturdy stems.

Echinacea
E. purpurea 'Kim's Mop Head'

Main features Eye-catching white blooms; flowers in summer to autumn; lightly scented
Height 30–45 cm (12–18 in.) **Spread** 30 cm (12 in.)
Position ○ **Hardiness** RHS H7

Purple coneflower (*E. purpurea*) is a member of the *Aster* family and is related to sunflowers, *Rudbeckia* and other daisies. Long used as a medicinal plant by Native American tribes for numerous ailments, it was widely cultivated in the United States by early settlers in herb and kitchen gardens and has been rediscovered in recent years as a supplement for stimulating the immune system and fighting infection.

Although the botanical name implies a purple colour, the unimproved species is a pink to magenta shade. Recent breeding efforts have resulted in a wide range of flower colours, as well as double-flowered forms. Easy to grow and requiring little care other than deadheading, coneflowers reward the gardener with blooms all summer to early autumn in a full-sun position in moist, well-drained soil. They suffer few pest or disease problems, are tolerant of urban pollution, and adaptable to both dry and moist locations, thus making them an ideal choice for a low-water garden.

E. purpurea 'Kim's Mop Head' is a sport of the pink-flowered cultivar 'Kim's Knee High' and features beautiful, 8-centimetre-wide (3 in.), lightly scented, white daisy flowers with a compact habit. Ideal for the front of the border, it could be used in both formal and cottage-garden–style designs. It is a wonderful addition to a naturalised wildflower garden, the cut-flower border and even the herb or vegetable garden. It is also valuable for attracting bees, butterflies and birds to the garden. Coneflowers are especially useful in attracting overwintering goldfinches for whom the seed is the perfect forage. If the last flush of blooms is not deadheaded in the autumn, the little birds will perch just below the blackened seed head to peck, thereby bringing life and activity to the garden in winter. **KK**

Alternatives

Echinacea purpurea 'Kim's Knee High', *Echinacea purpurea* 'Fragrant Angel', *Echinacea purpurea* 'White Swan'

Epimedium
E. × youngianum 'Niveum'

Main features Pure-white bell-shaped flowers; attractive bronzed foliage; good weed-suppressing ground cover
Height 30 cm (12 in.) **Spread** 30 cm (12 in.)
Position ◑ ● **Hardiness** RHS H7

These deciduous and evergreen perennials, with their dainty flowers and attractive, resilient foliage, have become increasingly popular in recent years, and more new species and cultivars have appeared. The popularity of epimediums is now well established among gardeners needing plants for shady situations. Evergreen species and hybrids make the best weed-suppressing ground cover: the dense all-year carpets of low, leathery leaves smother many weeds very effectively. However, deciduous species and hybrids often bring together the prettiest flowers and the most attractive foliage.

For many years the same few species and hybrids were usually grown. Then, as gardeners realised that shade was not a situation to be tolerated and filled with dull, evergreen shrubs but instead, an opportunity to grow a huge range of attractive and intriguing plants, attention focused on epimediums. More and more selections of wild species were made in a widening range of flower colours, and new species were introduced from Asia and selections made from these.

Hybrids occur naturally in the wild, and more frequently when species that do not grow in natural proximity to each other are grown together in gardens. *E. × youngianum* is an early hybrid between *E. diphyllum* and *E. grandiflorum* that occurs naturally in Japan and has also been found in gardens. It makes a small, compact plant with purple-tinted young foliage and up to a dozen small bell-shaped flowers. 'Niveum' provides the perfect combination of white flowers and coppery-bronze new foliage that look lovely together. *E. grandiflorum* is a species that hybridises more readily than most and, taking inspiration from long-established hybrids such as this one, specialists have now crossed it with a number of other species. **GR**

Alternatives

Epimedium × youngianum 'Merlin', *Epimedium × youngianum* 'Roseum', *Epimedium × youngianum* 'Tamabotan'

Epimedium
E. grandiflorum 'Rose Queen'

Main features Pretty pinkish-purple, spider-shaped flowers; purple-tinted new foliage
Height 45 cm (18 in.) **Spread** 30 cm (12 in.)
Position ◑ ● **Hardiness** RHS H7

The *Epimedium* is a plant that is a great deal tougher than it looks. The delicate flowers and fragile-looking young foliage may tempt you into thinking that it needs careful pampering and incessant care, but once you know that it is related to barberries, *Berberis*, your ideas will head in a more appropriate direction.

Valuable herbaceous perennials for shade, these unexpected relatives of the tough deciduous and evergreen shrubs have slender, branched roots, which in some species stay tight and compact while in others spread more widely. (Note, however, that vine weevil can seriously damage the roots.) Unlike some barberries, *E. grandiflorum* is never invasive. Wiry stems hold evergreen or deciduous leaves, which are split into three, six or nine segments that vary from lance-shaped to heart-shaped and have tiny teeth along the edges. Many emerge in spring in coppery or bronze shades. Each flower has two pairs of four petals in what is usually referred to as a spidery shape, and they are spread along wiry flowering stems in spring, usually hanging pendulously. They may be red, pink, white or yellow, or combinations of two shades.

In all there are about sixty evergreen or deciduous species, mainly found in Asia, with a few in Europe. New species are still being found in Asian habitats that have not previously been explored. *E. grandiflorum* is deciduous and one of the most widely grown species. It is found in deciduous woods in Japan and Korea. It features nine oval leaflets that are copper-tinted as they emerge. Up to eighteen flowers hang from each stem, each about 2.5 centimetres (1 in.) in diameter, and these may be white, pale yellow or various shades of pink. 'Rose Queen' is an old favourite, with purplish-bronze new foliage and large pinkish-purple flowers. **GR**

Alternatives

Epimedium grandiflorum 'Lilafee', *Epimedium grandiflorum* 'White Queen', *Epimedium grandiflorum* 'Yellow Princess'

Eremurus
E. robustus

Main features Dramatic, tall spikes of pink flowers; early-summer blooms
Height 3 m (10 ft) **Spread** 90 cm (3 ft)
Position ○ **Hardiness** RHS H7

At times gardens need a big, tall perennial, and *Eremurus*, known as foxtail lilies, deliver exactly that. These majestic plants reach 3 metres (10 ft) or more in height. There are over forty species, although only a few are ever seen in gardens. Foxtail lilies grow naturally in dry, stony and rocky places in the mountains of Asia, however, some also grow very well in gardens.

All the species produce a mass of fleshy roots coming together at the base of a fat bud from which grow the leaves and flowers. The foliage is long, narrow and pointed and makes a slightly untidy mass. Then, in late spring and summer, vertical stems arise, topped with long spikes of starry flowers in yellow, pink or white. After flowering, the leaves and flower stems dry up and die as the plant goes dormant until the following spring, leaving an empty space by mid- and late summer; large bushy plants, such as asters, can be planted nearby and will fill the space with late-season flowers.

E. robustus is probably the tallest of all the foxtail lilies, with long leaves reaching 1 metre (3.3 ft) in length and 10 centimetres (4 in.) in width, usually tinted in blue. The flowering stems can reach more than 3 metres (10 ft) in height and the flowering area can be 1 metre (3.3 ft) long and packed with hundreds of flowers; each flower (4 cm/1.5 in. across) is a pale peachy-pink with yellow stamen. *E. robustus* is also sometimes known as giant desert candle.

This is a dramatic back-of-the-border plant, but it poses some problems for the gardener. Reaching such a great height, the flowering stems usually need staking, however, with such a mass of roots, the stake needs careful placing. Also, because the roots can spread to 60 centimetres (24 in.) around the stem, it is unwise to plant other plants too close to *E. robustus*. **GR**

Alternatives

Eremurus himalaicus, Eremurus stenophyllus, Eremurus × isabellianus 'Cleopatra'

Eryngium
E. bourgatii 'Oxford Blue'

Main features Architectural summer plant offering
flower and foliage interest; attracts bees
Height 40 cm (16 in.) **Spread** 40 cm (16 in.)
Position ○ **Hardiness** RHS H5

It is well worth seeking out a good form of this sea
holly, and *E. bourgatii* 'Oxford Blue' is one of the best
available. The deeply divided basal leaves, marked with
silver veins, are attractive on their own. From midsummer
40-centimetre-tall (16 in.) stems arise bearing round
thistle-like heads in deep metallic-blue, surrounded by
very, very spiny silvery-blue bracts. At first sight it appears
an unlikely member of the cow parsley family (*Apiaceae*),
as it lacks the typical, strong, umbel-shaped flower heads.

Well-drained soil, in full sun, is the essential requirement
for this distinctive-looking, clump-forming plant. It is
drought tolerant, once established, and the clumps can
be divided in the spring with care or can be propagated
by root cuttings taken in the dormant season. The old
seed heads can be left on the plant, and when touched
by a hoar frost look even more spiny. Under favourable
conditions self-sown plants can appear, but they may
be variable in colour.

E. bourgatii 'Oxford Blue' is the ideal plant for a
sunny gravel garden, planted singly or in clumps. It
associates well with ornamental grasses, such as the
feathery *Stipa tenuissima*, and the bold, flat, yellow heads
of *Achillea* 'Moonshine'. Allow the easy-to-grow, burnt-
orange flowers of Californian poppies (*Eschscholzia
californica* 'Mikado') to self-seed among 'Oxford Blue'
for a striking combination. Other good varieties of
E. bourgatii include 'Picos Blue' (lavender blue), and Graham
Stuart Thomas Selection (strong blue). This plant would
be equally at home in the front of a herbaceous border,
where the long-lasting colour of the bracts is so valuable.
E. bourgatii and *E. planum* are European species; there
are lots of other species from North America that make
interesting specimens, including *E. yuccifolium*, but they
are not blue. **MP**

Alternatives

Eryngium alpinum 'Amethyst', *Eryngium alpinum*
'Jade Frost'

Erysimum
'Constant Cheer'

Main feature Orange flowers mature to purple over
many spring weeks
Height 45 cm (18 in.) **Spread** 45 cm (18 in.)
Position ○ **Hardiness** RHS H4

The cabbage family is one of the most varied of those
grown in gardens. From cabbages, Brussels sprouts and
Chinese mustard to honesty, perennial candytuft and
stocks, the distinctive spikes of four-petalled flowers
are borne by an unexpected range of both edible and
ornamental species – including wallflowers, *Erysimum*.

There are two types of wallflower. Biennial
wallflowers, grown from seeds, have always been more
popular in the United Kingdom than anywhere else.
They are traditionally grown for late-spring flowering in
seasonal schemes with tulips, and their rich colours and
distinctive scent are much appreciated. There is also a
group of wallflowers grown as short-lived shrubs. Usually
in softer shades, and sometimes with flowers changing
colour as they mature, these are grown from cuttings
and often have unusually long flowering seasons.

Erysimum 'Constant Cheer' is one of the latter,
shrubby types. Developing into stiff, twiggy, rounded
evergreen bushes clothed in slender, dark-green leaves,
the spikes of flowers in the tip of each shoot begin to
open in late spring, and flowers keep coming until
midsummer. Purple buds open to spikes of orange-red
flowers with dark-purple veins, which change to pale
purple with dark veins as they mature.

This is a fine plant for a Mediterranean garden, a
sunny raised bed, or it can also be grown as a specimen
plant in containers; it tolerates drought once established.
Note that strong winds may loosen the plants and lead to
early death. Snipping off the faded flower spikes as they
go over helps retain the vigour of the plant and most
definitely improves its appearance. No other pruning is
needed. After three to five years, plants are best replaced;
the next generation can be grown from short cuttings
taken from shoots without flowers in summer. **GR**

Alternatives

Erysium 'Bowles' Mauve', *Erysium* Walberton's Fragrant
Sunshine = 'Walfrasun'

Eupatorium
E. maculatum Atropurpureum Group

Main features Architectural plant; flowers in late summer to early autumn; attracts bees, butterflies; good cut flower
Height 1.8 m (6 ft) **Spread** 1.2 m (4 ft)
Position ○ ◑ **Hardiness** RHS H7

Atropurpureum Group plants are an imposing sight, even before they flower. Their robust, burgundy stems, clothed with whorls of dark-green leaves, soar to 1.8 metres (6 ft) yet rarely need staking. From midsummer into autumn, these stems are topped with a profusion of frothy maroon-pink flowers in large, flat clusters up to 25 centimetres (10 in.) across. Nectar-seeking butterflies, bees, and hoverflies find them irresistible. They are good for cutting too. You need not worry about this plant being too much of a border giant for you, either. It is clump forming, but not a rapid spreader, and you can easily reduce its ultimate height by cutting the stems back to about 60 centimetres (24 in.) in late spring or early summer. The fluffy seed heads also look attractive well into winter.

An improvement on the North American native *E. maculatum*, Atropurpureum Group plants are more winter hardy and have greater visual impact, as they are more floriferous and the stems and blooms are a darker, more intense colour. Like all spotted Joe-pye weeds, these plants need moist or boggy soil to thrive. If the soil does become dry, powdery mildew disease is likely to become a problem, so water if need be. Before buying, check the plants are mildew-free.

Atropurpureum Group plants provide a handsome, architectural backdrop for other perennials, particularly if you have space to plant them in a large group. They suit informal schemes, including bog gardens and naturalised areas alongside ponds and streams. Good waterside companions include hostas, *Gunnera tinctoria*, *Aruncus dioicus* and *Rodgersia pinnata*. In drier – but still moist – soils, try combining them with tall grasses, such as *Miscanthus* or pampas grasses, and other late-summer flowering perennials, such as *Artemisia lactiflora*, *Rudbeckia*, *Helenium* and *Hemerocallis*. **GP**

Alternatives

Syn. *Eutrochium maculatum*. *Eupatorium maculatum* 'Riesenschirm' (*Eutrochium maculatum* 'Riesenschirm')

Euphorbia
E. characias subsp. *wulfenii* 'Lambrook Gold'

Main features Bold, yellow flower heads; imposing plants covered in attractive bluish foliage
Height 2 m (7 ft) **Spread** 1.5 m (5 ft)
Position ○ **Hardiness** RHS H4

Many of the cactus-like plants found in the deserts of the Americas are euphorbias, as is the wild ancestor of this rather woody perennial plant from the Mediterranean region. *Euphorbia* is an extraordinarily diverse genus covering around 2,000 species. The Mediterranean spurge, *E. characias*, grows wild in sunny, dry and rocky places throughout the Mediterranean and is often split into two types. Both feature large clusters of small, saucer-shaped flowers in heads that are quite variable in shape but which, at their most dramatic, are tall and cylindrical. In spring, stout woody stems emerge from the base of the plant and develop through summer and into autumn; on these shoots the flower heads develop in late winter. They then tend to shrivel and die as the seed heads mature, to be replaced by new growth from the base of the plant. Euphorbias are popular with gardeners for their distinctive overall form.

Towards the western end of the Mediterranean, from Portugal to Crete, grows subsp. *characias,* which is distinguished by black nectaries in its yellow flowers; this distinctive feature gave rise to the common name of frog spawn bush. To the east, from southern France to Anatolia, the taller subsp. *wulfenii* is found, and this has uniformly yellow flowers. The evergreen foliage is also striking; long, slender leaves line the stems and vary in colour from dark-green to bluish to being covered in silvery hairs. *E. characias* subsp. *wulfenii* 'Lambrook Gold' is a substantial and dramatic selection with blue-green leaves and golden-green cylindrical flower heads. It was selected at East Lambrook Manor in Somerset, England, by plantswoman Margery Fish, and is thought to have been introduced in the 1960s. It should be propagated from cuttings, not from seeds. The milky sap can burn the skin, so wear gloves when handling this plant. **GR**

Alternatives

Euphorbia characias subsp. *wulfenii* 'John Tomlinson',
Euphorbia characias subsp. *wulfenii* 'Lambrook Yellow'

Euphorbia
E. sikkimensis

Main features Yellow summer flowers; attractive red stems add interest
Height 1.2–1.5 m (4–5 ft) **Spread** 45 cm (18 in.)
Position ○ ◑ **Hardiness** RHS H5

One of the joys of the spring border is to see the pink-tinged new shoots of the *E. sikkimensis* spurge pushing through the ground. Spurges show some of the greatest variations in plant form on the planet. This is a clump-forming herbaceous perennial. As the shoots grow, the stems retain some of the pinkish-red colouring, which extends into the central vein of each of the leaves that spiral up the stems. By midsummer the leaf's veins have faded to white, but the stalks remain reddish. The tall, willowy stems are topped in summer by flattish heads of acid-yellow bracts, which look good through until late summer. In autumn, the reddish stems remain and look attractive well into winter. Plant in full sun to slight shade. It may flop if there is insufficient light. Use in the middle to back of borders, where the new shoots add spring interest as well as late flower colour. Team it with red-hot pokers for vibrant effect, or calm the acid yellow with blue-flowered *Campanula lactiflora*. **MP**

Alternatives

Euphorbia schillingii, Euphorbia griffithii 'Dixter'

Farfugium
F. japonicum
'Aureomaculatum'

Main features Architectural perennial with year-round foliage; autumn and winter flowers
Height 30–60 cm (12–24 in.) **Spread** 45–60 cm (18–24 in.)
Position ◑ **Hardiness** RHS H3

For lovers of architectural foliage, this yellow-spotted *Farfugium* (also known as the gold-spotted leopard plant) will be a sought-after specimen. In sheltered gardens not overly troubled by frost – a shady city courtyard or coastal plot sheltered from wind and sun scorch – this broad-leaved perennial remains evergreen. The glossy, deep-green, kidney-shaped plates have a rather jagged margin and grow up to 30 centimetres (12 in.) across. With its golden splashes giving the effect of dappled light shining through a forest canopy, this variegated form of *F. japonicum* adds a tropical flavour. Try teaming it with clump-forming bamboos or tree ferns for jungle drama. Plants may bloom at the very end of the year, throwing up loose, branched heads of golden-yellow daisies. In a fertile, moisture-retentive but drained border, it works well as a foliage foil for daylilies and flame-coloured crocosmias or dahlias. It is useful for colonising narrow, lightly shaded strips between house walls and paving. **JH**

Alternative

Farfugium japonicum 'Argenteum'

Farfugium japonicum 'Aureomaculatum' is an eye-catching foliage plant for shady spots. ➲

Festuca
F. glauca 'Elijah Blue'

Filipendula
F. rubra 'Venusta'

Main features Year-round foliage; attracts wildlife
Height 30 cm (12 in.) **Spread** 25 cm (10 in.)
Position ○
Hardiness RHS H4

Main features Architectural plant; fragrant, candy
floss–like flowers in summer; attracts wildlife
Height 1.5 m (5 ft) **Spread** 50–100 cm (20–40 in.)
Position ○ ◑ **Hardiness** RHS H5

Tactile tussocks of dusty blue make 'Elijah Blue' a standout plant. The original species, *F. glauca,* comes from southern France, but this handsome, semi-evergreen form was found growing in the East Coast region of the United States. The neatly symmetrical domes of needle-like leaves colour best in full sun, but in hot regions, they may benefit from a partially shaded site to avoid scorching. In midsummer greenish flower stems push through, opening to feathery heads that later turn a pale-biscuit shade. Good drainage is critical to health and winter survival. 'Elijah Blue' associates well with sun-loving alpines, herbs and drought-tolerant succulents, like sedums. Plant in Mediterranean-style gravel gardens and raised beds. Though silver- and grey-leaved plants blend easily, brown- and maroon-toned foliage, as well as orange and red blooms, make the fluffy, blue domes come to life. Planted in dense blocks or strips, they add a contemporary note to urban courtyards of glass, chrome and concrete. JH

Big, bold and beautiful, the aptly named queen of the prairie (also known as meadowsweet) has much to recommend it, especially to lovers of easy-care gardening. The candy floss–like flower heads, appearing from early to midsummer, are sweetly fragrant and attract pollinating insects. As the weeks go by they turn from a clear rose to pale pink and finally to a not unattractive brown. Despite reaching 1.5 to 2.4 metres (5–8 ft) when in bloom, these statuesque, herbaceous perennials do not require staking. All they need is fertile, moisture-retentive soil. Try them at the back of a deep, mixed border with roses. The vertical deep-red stems carry jaggedly cut, aromatic, green leaves and make the perfect foil for this giant's frothy blooms, especially when topped with upright-pointing, palm-shaped leaves. Though not as exotic or dramatic, purple meadowsweet (*F. purpurea*) from Japan enjoys similar conditions. It has deeper-pink blooms and only reaches 80 centimetres (32 in.) in height. JH

Alternatives

Festuca glauca, Festuca glauca 'Blaufuchs', *Festuca glauca* 'Golden Toupee'

Alternatives

Filipendula purpurea, Filipendula ulmaria 'Aurea', *Filipendula ulmaria* 'Variegata'

◉ *Festuca glauca* 'Elijah Blue' adds form, texture and colour to a range of planting styles.

Gaillardia
G. × *grandiflora* 'Arizona Apricot'

Main feature Large, single flowers whose golden petals shade to apricot at the base
Height 30 cm (12 in.) **Spread** 30 cm (12 in.)
Position ○ **Hardiness** RHS H7

There are around 23,000 species in the daisy family, and about thirty species of sun-loving, annual and perennial blanket flowers come under the *Gaillardia* genus. They grow wild in meadows and prairies throughout the Americas and provide attractive garden plants as the blanket flower is so dependably colourful. *G.* × *grandiflora* is a hybrid between the perennial *G. aristata* and the annual *G. pulchella*. *G. aristata* has yellow or yellow-and-purple, daisy-like flowers, whereas *G. pulchella* has yellow, purple or brown flowers, sometimes bicoloured. The hybrid *G.* × *grandiflora* is a short-lived perennial, sometimes grown as an annual, and is produced in a range of bright colours, including bicolours.

Developing a basal rosette of hairy, lobed or toothed, lance-shaped leaves, from summer to autumn, *G.* × *grandiflora* carries individual single or double, daisy-like flowers in a variety of red, purplish, orange and yellow shades, including some highly striking two-colour forms. Usually grown as annuals – from cuttings or seeds depending on the cultivar – plants can be persuaded to last more than one season by deadheading spent flowers regularly and by cutting the whole plant back hard, to about 15 centimetres (6 in.), in late autumn. Flowering may tail off or plants die during winter if not deadheaded regularly.

Many seed-raised forms of *G.* × *grandiflora* have been developed. The Arizona Series is particularly renowned for its early flowering, compact habit, bright-green foliage, and for its tolerance of a greater variety of growing conditions. It includes three colours: red, yellow and 'Arizona Apricot' (pictured), which has multi-petalled single flowers in golden-yellow shading to apricot around the green-centred, honey-coloured eye. It is perfect for containers or for filling gaps in borders. **GR**

Alternatives

Gaillardia 'Arizona Sun', *Gaillardia* × *grandiflora* 'Goldkobold'

Gentiana
G. septemfida

Main feature Vivid-blue summer flowers on low
spreading plants
Height 20 cm (8 in.) **Spread** 40 cm (16 in.)
Position ◑ ● **Hardiness** RHS H7

The idea of growing gentians always seems to set
gardeners' hearts racing. That uniquely vivid-blue colour
of the showy trumpet-shaped flowers, combined with
the completely mistaken idea that gentians are difficult
to grow, inspires admiration; awe, almost; coupled with
unfounded regret. It is true that many of the 400 gentian
species, all from temperate climates, are particular about
how they are grown, and some are annoyingly choosy
about where they grow. However, for many, as with
other perennials and alpines, it is usually simply a matter
of giving them what they need – and some are not
fussy at all.

Amongst all these gentians there are evergreen
and deciduous perennials, as well as some annuals and
biennials. They grow either in free-draining, rocky or
stony, mountainous habitats or in richer conditions in
shady woods. They may flower in spring, in summer,
or in autumn. The crested gentian, _G. septemfida_, is one
of the easiest of all to grow. This is a plant that spreads
steadily, its trailing stems carrying pairs of 4-centimetre-
long (1.5 in.), strongly veined oval leaves. At the tips of the
shoots, in summer, clusters of 4-centimetre-long (1.5 in.)
flowers open; each flower is a rich bright blue in colour,
sometimes slightly purplish, with a white throat.

In some species the glossy, green leaves are spread
out in pairs along the flowering stems, which may be
upright or arching or lay flat on the ground; in others
the leaves are gathered in a rosette from which upright
flower stems emerge. The large, usually trumpet-shaped
flowers most frequently come in that captivating classic
rich blue and sometimes seem disproportionately large
for the size of plant. Less frequently, flowers also come
in paler blue shades as well as purple, red, pink, white
and yellow. **GR**

Alternatives

Gentiana asclepiadea, Gentiana makinoi

Geranium
G. clarkei 'Kashmir White'

Main features White flowers with pink-purple veins;
deeply cut green foliage; attracts butterflies and bees
Height 45 cm (18 in.) **Spread** 60 cm (24 in.)
Position ○ ◑ **Hardiness** RHS H7

Dainty yet tough, this carpeting geranium is a cottage garden favourite. Long-lasting sprays of white saucer-shaped flowers appear from summer to early autumn, but even when not in bloom, the deeply cut foliage provides much to admire. Use *G. clarkei* 'Kashmir White' to create a frilly edge for sunny or partly shaded borders, or as an addition to wild gardens, where it will provide a cool contrast to hot-hued flowers, such as roses, lupins and penstemons. Alternatively, include it in a rock garden or plant it in dappled sunlight at the edge of a woodland. An easygoing geranium, it will soon spread and may self-seed, given the right conditions, to form a textured, weed-suppressing ground cover. Native to alpine meadows in the mountains of Kashmir, it prefers a moist but free-draining soil, and full sun or partial shade. However, it will tolerate drier conditions once established. Tired-looking plants can be rejuvenated by removing old flowering stems and faded leaves. **ZA**

Alternatives

Geranium phaeum 'Album', *Geranium macrorrhizum* 'White-Ness', *Geranium pratense* 'Laura'

Geranium
G. renardii

Main features Prettily veined white flowers;
rounded, sage-like foliage
Height 38 cm (15 in.)
Position ○ **Hardiness** RHS H7

There are about 300 species, mostly perennial, of *Geranium,* but around 1,700 different forms have been grown in gardens over the years. From an often woody rootstock, which may be tight and clump forming or more extensive in its travels, the leafy growth develops in one of two ways. In some species, stems trail across the soil and produce flowers in their leaf joints. In most, a mass of basal foliage is produced from the crown, and then through it, the flower stems grow, the blooms opening above the leaves. *G. renardii* belongs to the latter group, but is not typical in the style of its foliage. In this species the leaves are gently lobed and covered in greyish hairs; they have the colour of culinary sage. The flowers, too, are distinctive. Clusters of more or less outwards-facing flowers, each petal notched at the tip, are white, but with a fan of short, purple veins towards the base and often with greyish tints. They open in late spring and early summer, but the soft foliage is attractive for many months. **GR**

Alternatives

Geranium renardii 'Zetterlund', *Geranium renardii* 'Tcschelda', *Geranium* 'Philippe Vapelle'

 *Geranium clarkei* 'Kashmir White' forms part of a pretty carpet of summer flowers.

Geranium
G. maderense

Main features Evergreen, architectural leaves; flowers in spring to midsummer; attracts bees
Height 1.5 m (5 ft) **Spread** 1.5 m (5 ft)
Position ○ ◑ **Hardiness** RHS H3

The *G. maderense* is the largest and one of the most impressive species of *Geranium*. With a height and spread of up to 1.5 metres (5 ft), this evergreen giant is a spectacular focal point when in flower but is worth growing for its foliage alone. It has huge rosettes of intricately dissected fern-like leaves that can grow up to 60 centimetres (24 in.) long. The leaves are bright green, but they have contrasting red stems that have the curious habit of bending down to the soil surface as they age. By the time the plant flowers, the lower leaves will have died off, but the leaf stalks remain intact, acting as props for the now top-heavy plant. Another unusual habit of *G. maderense* is that it does not flower until it is at least two years old. When it does, it produces a magnificent bouquet of magenta flowers with dark centres. These blooms are borne on wiry stems that are covered with purple hairs that glow when they catch the light. Removing faded flower stems helps to prolong the display. **GP**

Alternatives

Geranium 'Dilys', *Geranium* Cinereum Group, *Geranium renardii*, *Geranium* x *riversleanianum* 'Mavis Simpson'

Geranium
Rozanne

Main features Flowers summer into the autumn; good habit for growing in mixed plantings
Height 30–45 cm (12–18 in.) **Spread** 30–60 cm (12–24 in.)
Position ○ ◑ **Hardiness** RHS H7

This is a gardener's plant, so perhaps it is not surprising that it was found as a natural hybrid in a retired couple's garden in Somerset. Being keen gardeners, they noticed the plant's large flowers and long flowering period and then contacted Adrian Bloom at Bressingham Gardens to trial and introduce it. Although the registered name is 'Gerwat', the selling name Rozanne pays tribute to one of the garden owners who found it. For a hardy geranium the five-petalled flowers of Rozanne are large (5 cm/2 in. in diameter) and well displayed above the mid-green foliage, but it is the length of the flowering time – late spring to the first frost – that marks it out as a noteworthy variety. In addition it has a growth habit that gently weaves in and out of its neighbours without taking over or being invasive. With its gorgeous violet-blue flowers, Rozanne makes a welcome companion in a mixed herbaceous border or as an underplanting for any rose bed. **LD**

Alternatives

= 'Gerwat'. *Geranium* 'Jolly Bee', *Geranium* 'Brookside', *Geranium* 'Orion'

Geranium Rozanne will add extra flowering interest at the base of shrubs. ➲

Geranium

G. *cinereum* Cinereum Group 'Ballerina'

Main features Flowers in summer; attracts bees and butterflies; year-round foliage
Height 15 cm (6 in.) **Spread** 30 cm (12 in.)
Position ○ ◑ **Hardiness** RHS H5

With blooms for several weeks between late spring and midsummer or beyond, this neat little *Geranium* has bags of garden potential. The first thing that strikes you is the beautifully marked, pale lilac-pink flowers that float above the daintily cut, soft-textured, grey-green leaves. A dark 'eye' highlights each flower, and the nectar guides are clear, radiating out from the centre, like lines hand drawn in maroon ink. With such bold advertising it is not surprising that this diminutive form attracts bees and butterflies.

'Ballerina' was raised by British plantsman Alan Bloom, from the internationally known Norfolk nursery Blooms of Bressingham. Other Cinereum Group cultivars include 'Laurence Flatman', which is darker than 'Ballerina' and has two-tone petal shading; 'Alice', a pale lilac-pink flower with silvery green foliage; and 'Purple Pillow', with ruffled, plum-red petals and foliage red tinged in winter. Although you can run this noninvasive ground cover plant along the front of a well-drained border, or use it to edge a path, planting it above ground level allows for easier inspection of the delicate markings. An alpine scree, raised bed or trough would be perfect. 'Ballerina' also makes a good patio container specimen, planted among dwarf lavenders, and works well in Mediterranean-style gravel gardens, alongside grasses, such as *Stipa tenuissima* and *Festuca glauca* 'Elijah Blue'.

The fragile appearance of 'Ballerina' is deceptive. Plants are long-lived and easy to grow on most well-drained soils. They are wind tolerant and will still bloom in partial shade. The flowers are produced on trailing stems, and if plants appear to run out of steam midseason, you can cut them back to their basal foliage clump, and a fresh crop of flowers typically follows in the autumn. **JH**

Alternatives

Geranium cinereum 'Laurence Flatman', *Geranium sanguineum* 'Album', *Geranium sanguineum* 'Max Frei'

Geranium

'Mavis Simpson'

Main features Rose-pink flowers from summer to autumn; evergreen in temperate regions; attracts bees
Height 45 cm (18 in.) **Spread** 90 cm (3 ft)
Position ○ ◑ **Hardiness** RHS H4

Describing a plant as 'useful' might suggest that it is not attractive, but 'Mavis Simpson' is very pretty. The usefulness of this cranesbill geranium stems from its ability to cope with almost any type of soil as long as it is well drained; it will also flourish in sun or light shade and cover bare ground, yet it needs very little maintenance. Its prettiness comes, as you might expect, from the small but plentiful rose-pink flowers with delicate purple veins, though also from the cloud of soft and shapely grey-green leaves that cover its rambling stems.

Capable of spreading to quite a size, 'Mavis Simpson' can still be grown close to other perennials in a border, where it will weave its way through surrounding plants. The flowers open nonstop from early summer to autumn without any need to deadhead, and they are a magnet for bees. It may be less vigorous on heavy soil than on light soil, but it will still grow and flower well. If it does encroach, or if its trailing stems start to look a little tired or get a touch of mildew, simply trim with shears to tidy it up and it will keep going until the first frost slows it down. In mild areas it often keeps enough of its leaves in winter to make it a good addition all year round.

All cranesbill geraniums make good cottage-garden–style plants, but 'Mavis Simpson' also grows well in a gravel garden and fits into any informal mixed planting, including contemporary schemes. It fits well with salvias, such as the slim columns of *Salvia* 'Caradonna', or with the lime-green flowers of *Alchemilla mollis* (also known as lady's mantle). Plants with a short season of interest, such as many spring-flowering shrubs or peonies, benefit from it growing alongside. The shade of the pink flowers of 'Mavis Simpson' goes well with many rose-coloured flowers, and an underplanting or edging is an easy way to achieve a summer colour combination. **JS**

Alternatives

Geranium × *oxonianum* 'Wargrave Pink', *Geranium* 'Dilys', *Geranium* 'Orkney Cherry', *Geranium* Rozanne = 'Gerwat'

Gerbera
Garvinea Series

Geum
'Fire Opal'

Main features Vivid daisy flowers in a wide range of colours; unusually hardy plants
Height 38 cm (15 in.)   **Spread** 30 cm (12 in.)
Position ○   **Hardiness** RHS H3

Main features Flowers in late spring and summer; attracts bees
Height 60 cm (24 in.)   **Spread** 50 cm (20 in.)
Position ○ ◑   **Hardiness** RHS H7

Plants in the daisy family are popular with gardeners around the world. There is something about the basic daisy shape – the resemblance to an eye, perhaps – that people, across all cultures, find appealing. Among the 23,000 plus species in the family are many popular garden plants and flowers, including gerberas. These are widely grown as cut flowers, as seasonal summer flowers, and, in some climates, as hardy perennials. Usually making a bold rosette of lobed or more sharply divided leaves, which are dark green above and woolly underneath, stout upright stems carry large, bright daisy flowers from late spring to late summer. Their flowers are noted for their long life and vivid colours. Cold tolerance has been the focus of much recent development, and the Garvinea Series is the most impressive example. The flowers open from spring to autumn, up to a hundred blooms on each plant, and come in a huge range of single colours, bicolours, and doubles in the complete rainbow of shades. **GR**

Herbaceous perennials with hot-coloured flowers tend to feature in late summer, so it is refreshing to discover _Geum_, which packs a punch early in the season. In late spring the clump-forming _G._ 'Fire Opal' sends up airy, deep maroon-red branching stems that carry semi-double blooms of vibrant orange suffused with scarlet. At the centre is a boss of stamen – a tempting treat for early insects – for which the handsomely scalloped, fresh-green, hairy leaves provide a cool foil. 'Fire Opal' will put fizz into a cottage garden border, working well with the new lime-green sprigs and shoots of plants such as _Valeriana phu_ 'Aurea', as well clear-blue forget-me-nots and purple aquilegia or _Tulipa_ 'Queen of Night'. A few twiggy sticks pushed in around the plants in spring will ensure that the stems are well supported as they lengthen. The striking orange also works for contemporary schemes, and bold, block plantings of 'Fire Opal' contrast nicely with the linear leaves of coppery grasses and sedges, as well as purple-black _Heuchera_. **JH**

Alternative

Gerbera Sweet Series

Alternatives

Geum 'Prinses Juliana', _Geum borisii_, _Geum_ 'Lady Stratheden'

Gillenia
G. trifoliata

Main feature Starry white flowers in late spring/early summer followed by a rich leaf colour in autumn
Height 1.2 m (4 ft) **Spread** 60 cm (24 in.)
Position ○ ◑ **Hardiness** RHS H7

Indian physic, *G. trifoliata*, is an unlikely looking member of the rose family, one of only two species in the genus, both of which are North American natives. The more familiar *Spiraea* is its best-known close relative. The root was used by Native Americans and early settlers as a herbal treatment. Sometimes known as *Porteranthus stipulatus*, *G. trifoliata* grows wild in eastern North America and is found in various habitats, including woods where the shade cover is not too dense, open rocky hillsides and also roadsides. Rather woody at the base, with unusually fat questing roots, reddish upright stems carry veined foliage divided into three distinct leaflets. In the tips of the branches, clusters of flowers open. Each flower has five slender, usually twisted petals. The petals are often white, though they also come in pink, and are spaced to create a star-like effect. 'Pink Profusion' has rose-pink flowers and red-tinted foliage held on deep-red stems. The species, *G. stipulata*, is similar but shorter in growth, more delicate in appearance, and less prolific in flower. **GR**

Alternatives

Gillenia trifoliata 'Pink Profusion', *Gillenia stipulata*

Gunnera
G. tinctoria

Main feature Spring to autumn architectural foliage (all year in frost-free areas)
Height 1.8 m (6 ft) **Spread** 1.8 m (6 ft)
Position ○ ◑ **Hardiness** RHS H5

This prehistoric-looking plant is one of the biggest, most dramatic, and architectural perennials available. From a distance it resembles a large rhubarb plant – the two species are not related – and it is grown for its huge, leathery, umbrella-shaped leaves. In addition to its handsome foliage, *G. tinctoria* produces curious, primeval-looking spikes of tiny, greenish-brown flowers in early summer. These evolve into knobbly, corn-cob–like structures packed with reddish berries, thereby adding to the exotic appeal of this majestic plant. *G. tinctoria* looks best in a semi-natural setting near water, but ensure that the crown of the plant remains above the surface of the water and soil, otherwise it will rot. For the biggest leaves, plant it out of full sun, but take care, because in some parts of the world, the plant is considered to be an invasive weed. Good companions include other strong-growing moisture lovers, such as *Eupatorium*, *Eutrochium*, and *Iris pseudacorus*. For a more exotic pairing, try *Phyllostachys* bamboos. **GP**

Alternatives

Gunnera chilensis, *Gunnera scabra*, *Gunnera manicata*

Gymnocarpium
G. *dryopteris* 'Plumosum'

Main feature Attractive, luxuriant but lacy fern that spreads well
Height 10–30 cm (4–12 in.) **Spread** 45 cm (18 in.)
Position ◐ ● **Hardiness** RHS H7

Ferns are the obvious first choices for shady situations. Gardeners appreciate their tendency to creep steadily through borders, providing foliage ground cover and filling the spaces between deciduous and evergreen shrubs and around bolder, more imposing perennials, such as hostas. Ferns ensure that no bare soil invites weeds to become established, they create attractive plant associations with their neighbours, and some are also handsome in their own right. One of the most useful of this type is the oak fern, *G. dryopteris*. The 20-centimetre (8 in.) fronds emerge from roots that spread just below the surface and take hold wherever there is enough light to support the fronds they generate. These triangular fronds are held on vertical stems and are divided two or three times into opposite pairs of leaflets, creating a lacy look. The fronds are pale green, but in deep shade, they develop bluish tints. *G. dryopteris* 'Plumosum' has more impact than the original wild species, as the fronds have broader segments and develop a more leafy look. **GR**

Alternative

Gymnocarpium oyamense

Gypsophila
'Rosenschleier'

Main features Clouds of tiny, double, pale-pink flowers; grey-green, semi-evergreen leaves; good cut flower
Height 30 cm (12 in.) **Spread** 30 cm (12 in.)
Position ○ **Hardiness** RHS H6

Like a shimmering pink cloud billowing over beds and borders, 'Rosenschleier' forms a hazy ball of tiny blooms for many weeks in summer. A semi-evergreen perennial, its airy clusters of silvery-pink double flowers are held on wiry stems over a low mound of narrow, grey-green leaves, which add structure during the winter months. The perfect addition to a bridal bouquet, the delicate blooms of 'Rosenschleier' combine beautifully with roses and cottage-garden–style perennials, such as penstemons, lupins and delphiniums, forming soft pillows that help to cover the bare legs of the taller plants. You can also use baby's breath to blur the hard edges of patios or pathways, or allow the stems and flowers to flow over the sides of a raised bed. In a gravel garden it happily rubs shoulders with other drought-tolerant plants, such as *Sedum spectabile*, *Nepeta*, *Cistus* and *Salvia*, flowing between its partners like morning mist. Given a sunny site, it grows in most soils, although it especially enjoys drained, slightly alkaline conditions. **ZA**

Alternatives

Syn. *Gypsophila* 'Rosy Veil.' *Gypsophila paniculata* 'Bristol Fairy'

Haberlea

H. rhodopensis

Main features Bold, evergreen rosettes; lilac
or purplish flowers
Height 15 cm (6 in.) **Spread** 40 cm (16 in.)
Position ◑ ● **Hardiness** RHS H7

Most of the 3,200 species in the African violet family are herbaceous, and many grow from bold basal rosettes of foliage. *Haberlea* falls into this group and is one of the hardiest of all the plants in the family. An evergreen perennial from the Balkan region, *H. rhodopensis* grows wild on rocky and stony hillsides. It has dark-green, egg-shaped, heavily textured leaves – boldly notched along the edges – which are wider towards the tip and gathered into flat rosettes. In spring and early summer the flowers open. Carried on short stalks arising from the centre of the rosette, the rather open heads have about six flared flowers, split to create five lobes. In *H. rhodopensis* the rosettes may reach 30 centimetres (12 in.) across on mature plants, and the leaves are covered in soft hairs. The flowers are pale bluish lilac to bluish purple – the upper lip often darker than the lower lip – with a pale speckled throat. *H. rhodopensis* prefers shady conditions and good drainage, and it is ideal to grow in the vertical cracks between the stones of shady retaining walls. **GR**

Alternative

Haberlea ferdinandi-coburgii

Hacquetia

H. epipactis 'Thor'

Main feature Bright, white-splashed foliage and clusters
of tiny yellow flowers
Height 15 cm (6 in.) **Spread** 25 cm (10 in.)
Position ◑ **Hardiness** RHS H7

With circular flat heads of tiny, usually white flowers, supported a little like the spokes of an umbrella, plants in the carrot family are very distinctive. They are found wild mostly in the temperate parts of the northern hemisphere and less often across the rest of the world. *H. epipactis* is a tightly clump-forming perennial that grows naturally in woodlands in the Alps and Carpathian Mountains of Europe. Short stems carry a ring of about six leafy, yellow-green bracts, each 1 to 2 centimetres (0.3–0.7 in.) long and resembling petals. In the centre is a mass of tiny yellow flowers, and the overall effect is like a rather greenish buttercup. The flowers open close to the soil in late winter, but the stems steadily stretch, so that eventually the flowers are held 10 to 13 centimetres (4–5 in.) above ground. Then the glossy, green leaves develop, each split into three to five lobes, which are again lobed or toothed. *H. epipactis* 'Thor' is a dramatic variegated form, with the leaves, and especially the bracts, brightly splashed in white towards the edges. **GR**

Alternative

Hacquetia epipactis

Hakonechloa
H. macra 'Alboaurea'

Main feature Waterfall of slender variegated foliage
Height 38 cm (15 in.) **Spread** 75 cm (2.5 ft)
Position ○ ◑
Hardiness RHS H7

Ornamental grasses have become very fashionable. Their soft informality and attractive and sometimes colourful foliage, as well as their robustness and dependability, mark them out as some of the most valuable garden perennials. Many also feature attractive flowers. The flowers of all *H. macra* types, however, are unexceptional. Fortunately, the elegance of these relatively short plants and their foliage colouring will ensure that even gardeners who have little enthusiasm for most ornamental grasses will grow one of these.

Making tight and slowly expanding clumps, the slender stems and long, narrow, pointed leaves develop into plants that are about 38 centimetres (15 in.) high. The bright-green leaves arch over appealingly from the tops of the stems, producing a lovely waterfall effect, and in late summer, airy heads of small flowers create an additional softness. In autumn, and extending into winter, the foliage turns pale brown and is lovely with other fall colours and when frosted on early-winter mornings.

Striped in various ways along the length of the leaves, the variegated forms of *H. macra* are the most popular, and 'Alboaurea' is one of the two most often seen. Its leaves feature long stripes in both white and deep yellow as well as green stripes that are narrower than both. It is less vigorous than similar forms, and so is ideal in small spaces and in containers. The similar *H. macra* 'Aureola' has bright-yellow stripes and even thinner green stripes.

'Alboaurea' is a lovely plant to grow in rich soil at the front of a sunny or partially shaded border and partners especially well with blue-leaved and variegated hostas. However, white parts of the leaves may scorch in very sunny, dry conditions. In a terra-cotta container it makes a very elegant specimen plant, but should be fed regularly and never allowed to dry out. **GR**

Alternatives

Hakonechloa macra 'All Gold', *Hakonechloa macra* 'Aureola', *Hakonechloa macra* 'Nicolas'

Hedychium
H. coccineum 'Tara'

Main features Orange flower spikes that bloom summer
to autumn; architectural foliage; fragrant flowers
Height 1.8 m (6 ft) **Spread** 1.2 m (4 ft)
Position ○ ◑ **Hardiness** RHS H4

Known as ginger lily, this genus includes the edible ginger,
but 'Tara' is an ornamental cultivar valued for its hardiness.
In some regions this is sufficient to make it a perennial
border plant, albeit with deep planting and a generous
mulch. So the leap from ornamental gingers as a Victorian
conservatory plant into the perennial border makes them
a candidate for impressive specimens in tropical-style or
jungle planting in temperate regions.

'Tara' originated from seeds collected by Tony
Schilling of Kew Gardens in Nepal. The resulting seedlings
were uniform and named after his daughter in 1972. At
the time it was thought to be a selection of *H. coccineum*,
although current thinking is that it is a natural hybrid of
this species, possibly with *H. gardnerianum*. Why this
could matter is that not all forms of 'Tara' have scented
flowers or the desirable blue-green tinge to the foliage,
so buy in person or from a reputable specialist if those
characteristics are important to you. The main feature for
most is the showy orange-red flower spike, impressive
from afar and fascinating close-up.

The plants grow from rhizomes similar to root ginger,
so soil condition is important. In the growing season they
need it fertile, with plenty of moisture, but over winter,
it needs to be well-drained. The rhizomes can be lifted
over winter, but plants do not flower well if disturbed.
A warm, sheltered spot will help the flower spike form
and keep the foliage from damage, but they can take
partial shade. There are a couple of other species that are
hardy, such as *H. densiflorum*, plus, there are lots grown
as patio plants. If they grow for you, they can become
addictive. Plant hunters and breeders are continuing their
search for other hardy ginger lilies, and a few specialist
nurseries are now listing new selections of *H. coccineum*
from seeds collected at high altitudes in India. **LD**

Alternatives

Hedychium densiflorum 'Assam Orange', *Hedychium
densiflorum* 'Stephen'

Helenium
'Sahin's Early Flowerer'

Main features Flowers in summer and autumn; autumn
seed heads; good cut flower; attracts bees and butterflies
Height 1 m (3.5 ft) **Spread** 40 cm (16 in.)
Position ○ **Hardiness** RHS H7

Gardeners love an easy, dependable, hardy perennial
that flowers for a long time, and this one fits the bill
perfectly. Many *Helenium* varieties grow too tall and
require staking, but this one is much better behaved.
The typical daisy-shaped flowers consist of yellow
petals, streaked with orange and red, surrounding a
chocolate-brown spherical central 'cone', from which
yellow pinhead stamen appear. The colouring makes
it an obvious choice for a hot colour–themed border.

Helenium 'Sahin's Early Flowerer' grows up to 1 metre
(3.5 ft) high, with mid-green leaves spaced up the stem,
and flowers from midsummer onwards. Grow this tough,
vigorous, clump-forming plant in full sun, in any fertile

soil that stays moist but is well drained. Occasional
deadheading of the earliest flowers will keep it looking
pristine, and encourage more flowers. Later in the
season, leave it well alone as the spherical cone makes
an interesting feature for the autumn when the petals
have dropped. Lifting and dividing in early spring every
two or three years will ensure the plants remain vigorous.

This versatile plant makes an excellent addition to a
herbaceous or cottage-garden–style border, but it looks
equally at home in a mixture of grasses and other warm-
coloured perennials, such as *Rudbeckia* and *Crocosmia*.
For a more adventurous display, team it with the purples
and blues of *Agastache* and *Salvia*. 'Sahin's Early Flowerer'
also makes a useful cut flower. **MP**

Alternatives

Helenium 'Moerheim Beauty', *Helenium* 'Dunkle Pracht',
Helenium 'Gelbe Waltraut'

Helianthus

'Lemon Queen'

Main features Lemon-yellow daisy-like flowers; tall stems; veined, dark-green leaves; good for cutting
Height 1.8 m (6 ft) **Spread** 45 cm (18 in.)
Position ○ **Hardiness** RHS H7

The towering stems of this sought-after sunflower create walls of colour in sunny gardens from late summer to autumn, the graceful wands of lemon-yellow blooms offering much-needed interest when many perennials are dying back. Veined, green leaves stud the stems and provide a cool contrast to the bright blooms. *Helianthus* 'Lemon Queen' is perfect for the back of a border or wildlife garden, where bees and other beneficial insects will head straight for the nectar-rich flowers. Be bold and plant it in groups for the greatest impact and to ensure you have some stems for cutting. It makes a beautiful backdrop to shorter blooms that flower at the same time, such as *Aster* × *frikartii* 'Mönch', white *Leucanthemum* ×

superbum, *Helenium*, *Sedum spectabile* and spires of blue *Agastache*. Add in some tall grasses, such as *Calamagrostis* × *acutiflora* 'Karl Foerster' and *Miscanthus* for a late-season display of seed heads and daisy blooms.

Perennial sunflowers are deciduous and remain dormant overwinter, reemerging the following spring. They like a fertile, moist but well-drained, preferably neutral to alkaline soil. Improve the soil a few weeks before planting by incorporating some well-rotted manure or compost, and continue to water plants regularly until they are established. Despite their towering size, these sturdy plants do not require staking and quickly form good-sized clumps, which you can divide every three or four years to maintain their vigour. **ZA**

Alternatives

Helianthus 'Carine', *Helianthus* 'Capenoch Star', *Helianthus* 'Happy Days', *Helianthus angustifolius*, *Helianthus salicifolius*

Helictotrichon
H. sempervirens

Main features Architectural evergreen grass; flowers in summer; attracts wildlife
Height 1–1.5 m (3.5–5 ft) **Spread** 50–100 cm (20–40 in.)
Position ○ **Hardiness** RHS H7

Some plants are evocative of particular locations, and *H. sempervirens* immediately conjures visions of hot, sunny places where the earth is rocky and parched. Its evergreen leaves, like slender porcupine quills, are a powdery blue and arranged in stiff, upright tussocks. The grass deserves space for its architectural qualities to be admired, and a gravel garden, or a position adjacent to a flat expanse of stone paving, shows off these vertical sculptures admirably. In midsummer biscuit-coloured flower spikes open above the foliage, rather like heads of oats. With its steely-blue leaves, *H. sempervirens* is safe to blend with a range of grasses and drought-tolerant sedges like *Carex*, perhaps as part of a collection of potted specimens. It also teams effectively with the broader leaves of variegated and purple-leaved *Phormium* and *Cordyline*. For more vibrancy consider running *H. sempervirens* in broad ribbons through swaths of orange and terra-cotta yarrows, such as *Achillea* 'Walther Funcke'. **JH**

Alternative

Helictotrichon sempervirens 'Saphirsprudel'

Heliopsis
H. helianthoides
var. *scabra* 'Benzinggold'

Main feature Tough plant with a long season of bright, golden-yellow daisies
Height 1.5 m (5 ft) **Spread** 90 cm (3 ft)
Position ○ **Hardiness** RHS H7

Native to North and South America, these robust, prolific, and colourful perennials carry bright daisy flowers with yellow petals in summer. However, although they are dramatically colourful, some *Heliopsis* can be rather coarse. Those that combine colour with a more refined look are mainly *H. helianthoides*. This species is widespread across eastern and mid-North America, Canada and Mexico, where it is found in open woods, tallgrass prairie and along roadsides. The vertical stems are clothed with lance- or egg-shaped leaves, and in *H. helianthoides* var. *scabra*, the stems and leaves are rough to the touch. Most of the cultivars grown in gardens are grouped under var. *scabra*, and 'Benzinggold' is one of the best. Its large flowers feature two or three rows of golden-yellow petals around a slightly darker eye. It is ideal at the back of the border, and the stems are long enough for it to make an effective cut flower. Plants can be cut back by half in late spring to reduce their eventual flowering height. **GR**

Alternative

Heliopsis helianthoides var. *scabra* 'Sommersonne'

Heliopsis helianthoides var. *scabra* 'Benzinggold' is the tallest flowering plant in this late-summer planting. ➲

Helleborus
H. niger

Main features Gold-centred white flowers;
blooms in midwinter
Height 30 cm (12 in.) **Spread** 45 cm (18 in.)
Position ◑ **Hardiness** RHS H7

A popular winter flower, *H. niger* is the best known of this group of tough, evergreen perennials. Growing wild in the mountains of central Europe, its five-petalled pure-white flowers with golden-yellow centres are carried singly on upright green stems. Wild plants are sometimes found with pink buds, pinkish flowers or red stems, but it is the purity of the white flowers that is the main appeal. They range from 5 to 13 centimetres (2–5 in.) in diameter, and blooms are produced generously from the centre of the plant. Unfortunately, they are often overtopped by dark, leathery, evergreen foliage and this can spoil the effect. The remedy is simple: in late autumn, cut the old leaves away, so that the flowers can reveal themselves. Many modern varieties are significant improvements on older types. They flower more reliably at Christmas and are less fussy about growing conditions. Look for plants with the initials HGC (Hellebore Gold Collection) in their names. These German selections are especially reliable. **GR**

Alternatives

Helleborus niger 'HGC Jacob', *Helleborus niger* 'HGC Josef Lemper', *Helleborus niger* 'HGC Joshua'

Helleborus
H. foetidus

Main features Architectural foliage; late-winter to
midspring flowers; attracts bees; good cut flower
Height 60 cm (24 in.) **Spread** 90 cm (3 ft)
Position ◑ **Hardiness** RHS H7

The *H. foetidus* is hard to beat amongst robust perennials that look good all year round. It is a handsome evergreen foliage plant with distinctive, deep-green leaves that are divided into long, narrow fingers. It is also an uplifting harbinger of spring, because it starts blooming in the depth of winter. The leafy flower stems bear nodding clusters of pale-green, thimble-sized bells that become edged with maroon as they age. These are a welcome early source of nectar for bees and are excellent for cutting, as is the foliage. Native to Western and Central Europe, *H. foetidus* is often found growing in woodlands, so it would suit being planted in a shady border or woodland garden. Try growing it in broad drifts as a ground cover par excellence. For added interest combine it with evergreen ferns, spring-flowering bulbs and hardy cyclamen. *H. foetidus* is also a good choice for planting at the base of deciduous shrubs, because its architectural form will show up strongly in winter against such a backdrop. **GP**

Alternatives

Helleborus foetidus Wester Flisk Group, *Helleborus × sternii* Blackthorn Group, *Helleborus argutifolius* 'Silver Lace'

 Helleborus niger cultivars flower reliably in midwinter so are known as Christmas roses.

Helleborus
H. argutifolius

Main features Flowers in winter and early spring; striking, evergreen foliage
Height 90 cm (3 ft) **Spread** 90 cm (3 ft)
Position ○ ◑ **Hardiness** RHS H5

Tough and handsome, this *Helleborus* is deservedly popular. Stiff stems clothed in long, curved fingers of dark-green, leathery leaves grow into an impressive clump with a striking, architectural shape. In the dead of winter loose clusters of large, lime-green flowers spill over the foliage, every bit as stylish as the spiny-edged leaves.

Flowers in winter are a relatively rare sight, and large flowers even more unusual, so these muted, creamy cups are very welcome. They are a good source of nectar for winter flying insects, and the large, stiff sepals keep their shape for a long time, the colour slowly fading as the central flower parts drop away. Grow *H. argutifolius* in the company of other winter stars, such as *Cornus*

alba 'Sibirica' or *Hamamelis*, and low evergreens, such as *Carex oshimensis* 'Evergold'. It is impressive enough to grow as a feature plant and, like other *Helleborus*, does surprisingly well in a pot.

A native of Corsica and Sardinia, *H. argutifolius* will be happy in full sun and will also grow well in part-shade. As long as the soil is not acidic or prone to extremes of drought or waterlogging, it is an unfussy plant and will look all the better for not having too many nutrients, which can make stems long and floppy. The only maintenance it needs is to have its stems removed when flowers have faded, which is usually in spring. Old foliage can also be cut back in late winter, just before new growth gets going. **JS**

Alternatives

Helleborus argutifolius 'Silver Lace', *Helleborus foetidus*, *Helleborus* 'Anna's Red', *Helleborus* 'Penny's Pink'

Helleborus
H. × hybridus

Main features Single or double flowers; huge variety of colours and colour combinations in winter and spring
Height 45 cm (18 in.) **Spread** 45 cm (18 in.)
Position ○ ◑ **Hardiness** RHS H7

This is a supreme winter perennial, and it comes in a vast variety of colours and colour patterns, single-flowered and double-flowered. Big, bold, dark evergreen foliage grows from a tight, woody, compact crown, from the centre of which the winter and early-spring flowers emerge. These flowers – 5 to 8 centimetres (2–3 in.) in diameter – are held in clusters at the top of stout, upright stems and at their simplest they are made up of five broad petals around a ring of small, tubular organs in the centre. These produce nectar to attract early bees.

The flowers of *H.* × *hybridus* may be white, pink, dusky red, purple, yellow or black – in fact, almost any colour except scarlet and true blue. Often they are patterned with red blotches or speckles. There are double forms, with a mass of extra petals, and anemone-centred types with a dense cluster of short, fat petals in the middle. The blooms are followed by plump seedpods. In late spring and early summer, these pods split to reveal black seed, which are carried off by ants to germinate around the garden. A few years later they will produce new plants, but with flowers in unpredictable colours.

Best left to grow into individual specimen plants, *H.* × *hybridus* is happy in full sun (if the soil never becomes parched) or in partial, dappled shade. Rich, fertile conditions will ensure the development of prolific plants. Good partners include snowdrops, crocuses and other early bulbs. **GR**

Alternatives

Helleborus × *hybridus* Early Purple Group, *Helleborus odorus*, *Helleborus* × *hybridus* 'Walberton's Rosemary'

Hemerocallis
'Stafford'

Main feature Deep-red flowers with a splash of yellow
Height 1.1 m (3.75 ft) **Spread** 75 cm (2.5 ft)
Position ○
Hardiness RHS H7

It is undeniable that of the more than 60,000 different *Hemerocallis*, or day lily, cultivars that have been introduced over the decades, the vast majority have been developed in North America. After all, it is the United States' favourite perennial, partly because it thrives in a variety of climates across the country. In the United Kingdom development began in earnest in the 1950s when two iris breeders turned to developing *Hemerocallis*. Leonard Brummitt's introductions can often be noted from their 'Banbury' prefix, while those of Harry Randall were often named for towns near his home in Buckinghamshire. Randall began by importing plants from North America, especially those developed by top US breeders of the time, Herbert Fischer and Orville Fay. He used these US plants as breeding parents from which he went on to create plants that were more suited to the British climate. Randall's other claim to fame was that, as chairman of the London Electricity Board, he commissioned the construction of the Bankside Power Station, now known as London's Tate Modern. He was also a pioneer breeder of irises and wrote a book on irises.

Hemerocallis 'Stafford', introduced in 1959 and named for a town that was not local to Randall's home, is a tall plant, reaching about 1 metre (3.5 ft) and carrying 13-centimetre-wide (5 in.) flowers in a deep but vibrant red. Each petal shows a bright contrast: the petals often feature dark, crimson-red tones, while a sharp, yellow streak runs along the centre of each petal. The overall shape of the flower is rather starry, as is the case with so many introductions from that era, but it continues to bloom throughout an unusually long season, from midsummer until early autumn. Other *Hemerocallis* introductions by Randall that are still popular today include 'Amersham' and 'Missenden'. **GR**

Alternatives

Hemerocallis 'Seductor', *Hemerocallis* 'Tom Wise', *Hemerocallis* 'Summer Wine'

Hemerocallis 'Stafford' is a 1950s day lily still valued for its long flowering period. ➲

Hemerocallis
'Burning Daylight'

Main feature Vivid, orange, fragrant flowers
Height 60 cm (24 in.) **Spread** 60 cm (24 in.)
Position ○
Hardiness RHS H7

In some ways 'Burning Daylight' is a typical *Hemerocallis*, or day lily, but in other ways it is rather special and makes a notable impact in informal cottage gardens. It is also an example of a long-established cultivar that is still appreciated, even though many thousands have been introduced since its first arrival. There are numerous orange varieties, and some of the wild species from which garden day lilies are descended, including *H. dumortierii* and *H. fulva*, have flowers in this colour range. However, although the 10-centimetre-long (4 in.) flowers of 'Burning Daylight' are smaller than those of many modern cultivars, they come in an unusually fluorescent colour: a bright and brilliant shade that outshines many others. In the garden the flowers require a close look, because the colouring has a subtlety to it: the inner three petals are a shade or two darker than the outer petals, while darker and lighter tones alternate across the petal surface. In addition, the inner petals feature slightly waved edges. Finally, all the petals are unusually heavy in texture and therefore stand up well to sun and bad weather.

Of the many tens of thousands of day lilies that have been introduced over the years, relatively few are fragrant. 'Burning Daylight', however, has an unusually heavy and intense scent. Its flowers are carried low on the plant and mingle with the tips of the leaves, a feature that some enjoy and others do not appreciate. Its relatively late flowering season means that it usually misses infection by the destructive gall midge.

Introduced by Herbert Fischer in 1957, 'Burning Daylight' is noticeably tolerant of dry conditions. Its relatively narrow petals mark it out from the majority of more recent introductions, but the more starry shape blends in with other perennials more effectively. The foliage dies away in winter. **GR**

Alternatives

Hemerocallis 'Primal Scream', *Hemerocallis* 'Sparkling Orange', *Hemerocallis* 'Tuscawilla Tigress'

Hemerocallis
'Bela Lugosi'

Main feature Large, rich-purple, sunproof flowers with green throats
Height 85 cm (2.75 ft) **Spread** 85 cm (2.75 ft)
Position ○ **Hardiness** RHS H7

There is a long tradition of plants being named for actors, who then participate in publicising the plant, and this tactic usually guarantees that a new plant will be featured heavily in the media. Plants are also named to mark the anniversary of an actor's birth or death, and that is the case here. However, attaching the name of an actor to a plant is not a guarantee of the plant's quality, and many cultivars that are named in this way disappear after a few years. The quality of the plant, not the fame of the actor, determines the value of the plant in the long run. *Hemerocallis* 'Bela Lugosi' is an example of a fine plant that was named for an actor's anniversary, forty years after his death. Lugosi is best known for playing Count Dracula in the original 1931 film directed by Tod Browning, a classic of its genre.

Considered to be a premium day lily, 'Bela Lugosi' is a low-maintenance, adaptable plant, performing well in a range of different climates. The 15-centimetre-long (6 in.) flowers are a very striking, rich and sultry purple colour and feature a contrasting vivid, green throat. They have overlapping petals, which are prettily crimped. Important in dark-coloured day lilies such as this, the colour does not fade in the sun. The stems branch well and carry a long succession of buds, so flowers open continually to create an extended summer display. The long, slender foliage is semi-evergreen; it will be cut down by frost in cold areas, but in milder zones it will remain evergreen through the winter.

Developed by Ohio day lily breeder Curt Hanson, 'Bela Lugosi' is a tetraploid. This means that it has double the usual number of chromosomes, which results in a more robust plant with a heavier texture to its flowers and foliage. It also has better resistance to fading and to pests and diseases. **GR**

Alternatives

Hemerocallis 'Darker Shade', *Hemerocallis* 'Quest for Excalibur', *Hemerocallis* 'Strutter's Ball'

Hemerocallis
'Stella de Oro'

Main features Long season of soft, golden-yellow flowers; dwarf plants
Height 30 cm (12 in.) **Spread** 75 cm (2.5 ft.)
Position ○ **Hardiness** RHS H7

Dwarf day lilies are essential in today's smaller gardens as fewer and fewer plots have space for the fat clumps of the taller types that were once so popular. Another feature of some modern *Hemerocallis* that endears them to contemporary gardeners is a long blooming period, because those that produce a long season of colour provide the best possible value from every inch of the border. Both features – dwarf habit and a long flowering season – are essential characteristics of plants that are to be used in pots and tubs. Consequently, a limited number of day lilies are also suited to containers.

An alternative planting option is to grow dwarf day lilies en masse, either in a long line to look like an edging or on a slope. The leaves look fresh for a long period, there are plenty of blooms, and the extended reflowering period can make a notable difference to a garden.

H. 'Stella de Oro' is the most popular day lily and is the bestselling variety of all time. Reaching only 30 centimetres (12 in.) in height, and only 75 centimetres (2.5 ft) wide, its golden, sweetly scented flowers are nicely rounded in shape while each flower features a tiny green throat, and petals that roll back attractively. Although the flowers are small, matching the stature of the plants and the rather narrow grassy foliage, their special quality is that they open continuously over a long season. The first blooms may open in late spring and flowers keep coming into the autumn.

This continuous production of flowers takes a great deal of energy: rich soil that does not dry out, plenty of sunshine, and prompt deadheading help ensure that the display is continuous. It is also advisable to lift plants, divide them, and replant them in fresh soil every two or three years. **GR**

Alternatives

Hemerocallis 'Happy Returns', *Hemerocallis* 'Mini Stella', *Hemerocallis* 'Yellow Lollipop'

Hepatica
H. nobilis

Main feature Flowers in early spring; bright, starry flowers in blues, pinks, or white
Height 10 cm (4 in.) **Spread** 15 cm (6 in.)
Position ◑ **Hardiness** RHS H5

Species of *Hepatica* are amongst the smallest plants in the buttercup family, but their six-petalled flowers shine like jewels in the woods. Most closely related to *Anemone*, the ten species grow in northern temperate regions of North America, Asia and Europe. All are tight, clump-forming, usually evergreen, herbaceous perennial plants that grow best in shady parts of flood plains, on valley bottoms, and on woodland slopes. Held on short stems, the five-lobed, smooth or hairy foliage may have silvery markings on the upper surface with purple on the underside. The starry flowers open in early spring in purple-blue, blue, pink or white.

Most of the plants that are easily available and grown in gardens on both sides of the Atlantic are forms of the European *H. nobilis*. However, there are also two North American natives: *H. acutiloba* and *H. americana*. The kidney-shaped or rounded leaves, up to 6 centimetres (2.5 in.) long, are purple underneath and sometimes lightly patterned in paler shades. The 2.5-centimetre-wide (1 in.) flowers open in early spring, and mature plants can produce them in large numbers. Plants are most often sold simply by flower colour and then planted in pots or troughs to be viewed at close quarters.

In nursery catalogues Japanese varieties of *Hepatica* are often listed separately. They can be very expensive, because in Japan, the development and cultivation of *Hepatica* has reached a high art. *H. japonica* and *H. pubescens* are the two species grown, and they were first seen in gardens in Japan in the early seventeenth century. However, since the 1970s, many hundreds of named forms have been developed. These include double-flowered and bicoloured varieties, forms with yellow flowers and plants with flowers that have stamen in a contrasting colour. **GR**

Alternatives

Hepatica acutiloba, Hepatica × media, Hepatica transsilvanica

Hesperantha
H. coccinea 'Major'

Main features Small, bright-red blooms; sword-shaped mid-green foliage; good cut flower
Height 60 cm (24 in.) **Spread** 30 cm (12 in.)
Position ○ **Hardiness** RHS H3–H4

Prized for its late-season, bright-red starry blooms, this exotic-looking plant is the prima donna of the autumn garden. The small flowers are held aloft on sturdy stems above narrow sword-shaped foliage, and if it is given sun and plenty of moisture, this striking beauty will continue to bloom until the first frost or beyond. The tough flowers will withstand rain and cold weather, opening up to greet the day at dawn, then closing like demure Cinderellas as night falls. Combine *H. coccinea* 'Major' with other late blooms that enjoy similar conditions, such as dahlias and Michaelmas daisies (*Aster novi-belgii*), positioning clumps just behind the front line in a sunny border. An edge of small leafy plants, such as *Carex* or *Euonymus*, will hide the gaps earlier in the year before 'Major' gets going. This plant also adds splashes of colour to the banks of streams and looks beautiful against a backdrop of textured ferns.

Hailing from the wet areas of the South African Cape, *Hesperantha* has exacting standards, requiring a very specific site and particular soil conditions to succeed. You can buy ready-potted plants or dry bulbs. Plant the bulbs at a depth of 5 centimetres (2 in.) in spring in a sunny, sheltered position and in soil that is consistently moist during the summer, but drier in winter. Dig in plenty of organic matter before planting, and water plants regularly when they are in growth. In colder areas protect the bulbs from frost with horticultural fleece or a thick mulch of straw or compost. *Hesperantha* tends to flower poorly if left in one spot for too long, so lift and divide clumps every two or three years.

The red 'Major' cultivar is the most widely available form, but gardeners can also choose white varieties, which include *H. coccinea* f. *alba* and *H. coccinea* 'Snow Maiden'; pink forms, such as *H. coccinea* 'Mrs. Hegarty'; and the larger-flowered, shell-pink *H. coccinea* 'Jennifer'. **ZA**

Alternatives

Hesperantha coccinea 'Snow Maiden', *Hesperantha coccinea* 'Jennifer', *Hesperantha coccinea* 'Mrs. Hegarty', *Hesperantha coccinea* 'Rosea', *Hesperantha coccinea* f. *alba*

Heuchera
'Rave On'

Main features Spikes of bright coral-pink flowers; silver-marbled purple foliage; ideal for containers
Height 45 cm (18 in.) **Spread** 30 cm (12 in.)
Position ○ ◑ **Hardiness** RHS H7

Silver-marbled leaves, etched with dark-green veins and purple below, are prized features of this striking *Heuchera*, but it is the prolific number of bright coral-pink flowers that sets it apart from the rest. The tiny bell-shaped blooms appear from late spring to summer on slender spires above lobed semi-evergreen foliage, creating an unbeatable fusion of colour and long-lasting interest.

Plant this little beauty along the edge of a pathway or flower bed, or add it to a rock or gravel garden: pale stones create the perfect foil for the decorative leaves and flowers. Its semi-evergreen foliage is also a useful addition to baskets, containers and window boxes, performing throughout the year in mild areas or where sheltered from harsh winter weather on a terrace close to the house. If the leaves do fall, fresh growth will reappear in spring. Combine *Heuchera* 'Rave On' in borders or pots with spring bulbs, including tulips and daffodils, and evergreen sedges, such as *Carex morrowii* 'Ice Dance', or the blue grass *Festuca glauca* to create eye-catching textural contrasts. Other silver-leaved coral bells include 'Can-Can', which has ruffled burgundy leaves with silver marbling and cream flowers; 'Cascade Dawn', with its silver and dark-purple foliage and cream blooms; and 'Glitter', which has deep-purple and silver leaves, and pink flowers.

'Rave On' is best grown in fertile, moist but well-drained soil, and in full sun in cool climates or part shade. Add well-rotted manure, compost or leaf mould to the soil a few weeks before planting in early autumn or spring, and mulch afterwards to protect the roots. Remove faded flower stems to encourage more blooms to form, and divide clumps in spring. Also check for vine weevil damage; the grubs eat the roots, causing plants to collapse. **ZA**

Alternatives

Heuchera 'Can-Can', *Heuchera* 'Cascade Dawn', *Heuchera* 'Glitter', *Heuchera* 'Silver Scrolls', *Heuchera* 'Hollywood'

Heuchera

Rosemary Bloom

Main features Prolific show of soft coral-pink flowers; tall spikes
Height 60 cm (24 in.) **Spread** 45 cm (18 in.)
Position ○ ◑ **Hardiness** RHS H7

The *Heuchera* is an evergreen member of the saxifrage family, and in the last thirty years it has become one of the most popular perennials. During the first waves of enthusiasm for the plant in the 1930s and then the 1950s, a wide range of cultivars was developed, mainly by Alan Bloom, founder of the British nursery that still bears his name. The flowers were the plant's most important feature, and they were intended both for display in borders and also as cut flowers.

From the late 1980s, plants with standout foliage came to the fore, largely through the work of Charles Oliver and Dan Heims in the United States. However, *Heuchera* Rosemary Bloom, developed by Alan Bloom in the late 1980s, harks back to the heyday of the plant breeder's earlier work. His original introductions included such prolific plants as 'Red Spangles', 'Scintillation' and 'Snowflake' and he returned to the theme of prized flowers with Rosemary Bloom, crossing two unnamed seedlings and selecting Rosemary Bloom from among the offspring. From a mound of glossy, green, lobed, evergreen foliage, wiry, honey-coloured stems reach about 60 centimetres (24 in.) high and carry upright, slender sprays of small, pale, coral-pink bells that are pale yellow deep in the throat. Flowering usually runs through early and midsummer.

Named for the wife of Alan Bloom's son, Rosemary, this is a fine summer-flowering perennial, suitable for woodland gardens, rock gardens, sunny borders and as a cut flower, its soft colouring a pastel shade that is always popular. For use as a cut flower, cut the stems when about half the individual flowers on the spike are open. The use of flower food will make a significant difference to the life of the stems in water and will encourage all the buds to open. **GR**

Alternatives

= 'Heuros'. *Heuchera* Bressingham hybrids, *Heuchera* 'Florist's Choice', *Heuchera* 'Scintillation'

Heuchera
'Tiramisu'

Main feature Chartreuse foliage with an ever-changing red and silver overlay
Height 30 cm (12 in.) **Spread** 30 cm (12 in.)
Position ○ ◑ **Hardiness** RHS H7

When *Heuchera* was first popular many decades ago, it was its flowers that appealed to gardeners, but in recent years it has been those plants grown for their foliage that have become more desirable. The shapes, colours and patterns in the foliage have reached an extraordinary variety, and with its neat growth and tolerance of cold winters, as well as the ease with which *Heuchera* can be propagated by nurseries, it is now amongst the most sought-after perennials.

All varieties develop compact mounds of evergreen foliage, which may be lobed or toothed, or sometimes tightly ruffled. The colours are amazingly varied; they range from almost black, mahogany and charcoal tones through crimsons and purples, oranges, golds and yellows to ginger and increasingly fiery shades. There are also shades of green, of course, although greens are much less in evidence. Many feature silvery overlays, veins in dark, contrasting colours, and other variations. It is the mingling of all these colours, and the way that they change over the year, that makes modern *Heuchera* cultivars so astonishing. In spring, the chartreuse foliage of *Heuchera* 'Tiramisu' is veined and tinted in brick red. Then, in summer, the colouring becomes paler and the leaves develop a noticeable silver cast; in autumn, the colour intensifies again, and a brick shade dominates each leaf, leaving only a narrow greenish-yellow rim. The spikes of white summer flowers are unremarkable and best snipped off.

'Tiramisu' was developed in France by Europe's top breeder, Thierry Delabroye, who also developed 'Caramel' and 'Citronelle'. Unusually tolerant of both cold winters and hot and humid summers, it makes a fine specimen in a small container, is a good companion at the front of large containers, and thrives in partial shade. **GR**

Alternatives

Heuchera 'Electra', *Heuchera* 'Miracle', *Heuchera* 'Caramel', *Heuchera* 'Citronelle'

× *Heucherella*
'Kimono'

Hosta
'Blue Mouse Ears'

Main features Low-spreading plant; boldly marked, silver-and-green evergreen foliage
Height 30 cm (12 in.) **Spread** 30 cm (12 in.)
Position ◑ ● **Hardiness** RHS H7

Main features Attractive leaves from spring to autumn; scented flowers in summer
Height 15 cm (6 in.) **Spread** 30 cm (12 in.)
Position ◑ ● **Hardiness** RHS H7

The increasing range of × *Heucherella* cultivars unites the extraordinary range of foliage colours of modern *Heuchera* and the vigour and impressive flowering of modern *Tiarella*. These hybrids tend to inherit the cut foliage and flower spikes of *Tiarella*, but the basic colouring of the foliage comes from *Heuchera*. × *Heucherella* 'Kimono' is the variety that made gardeners realise the value and potential of these tough plants. The individual evergreen leaves are dramatically lobed and up to 22 centimetres (9 in.) long. Each pointed leaf is green overlaid with silver and with bold maroon markings; the foliage develops metallic-pink tones in winter. In spring the plants are topped with small, tawny-white flowers opening from pink buds. However, many gardeners prefer to nip them off so that the colourful patterned foliage stands out more effectively. 'Kimono' makes an effective ground cover at the front of shaded and partially shaded borders. **GR**

The small but perfectly formed foliage of *Hosta* 'Blue Mouse Ears' may not be as showy as the large-leaved beauty of some *Hosta*, and it might never carpet the amount of ground that the larger varieties cover, but it has a charm of its own. It grows into a neatly shaped, dense mound of symmetrically arranged, rounded leaves, which have a slight curl to them that resembles a mouse's ear. In summer, it produces a mass of perfectly proportioned scapes of lilac lily-like flowers. As *Hosta* is primarily grown for its foliage, it has been suggested that the flower scapes should be removed, but the flowers are very much a part of the appeal of this diminutive plant. The blue-green leaves keep their colour well throughout the season, as long as they are not planted in hot afternoon sun. The size of 'Blue Mouse Ears' makes it ideal for the front of a damp area around a pond, woodland gardens, damp rock gardens or shady borders. **JS**

Alternatives

× *Heucherella* 'Alabama Sunrise', × *Heucherella* 'Tapestry', × *Heucherella* 'Quicksilver'

Alternatives

Hosta 'Blue Cadet', *Hosta* 'Frosted Mouse Ears', *Hosta* 'Snow Mouse', *Hosta* 'Dancing Mouse'

Hosta 'Blue Mouse Ears' is very small but perfectly formed, right down to its flowers. ➔

Hosta
'Krossa Regal'

Main features Bold blue-green foliage; large, dramatic plant
Height 90–150 cm (3–5 ft) **Spread** 1.8 m (6 ft)
Position ◑ **Hardiness** RHS H7

The *Hosta* comes in a vast array of shapes and sizes, from tiny miniature varieties – for pots or for a prominent and highly visible situation at the front of a rich border – to majestic plants that create fine focal points and bold backgrounds that are best admired from a distance. *Hosta* 'Krossa Regal' is most definitely one of the latter varieties, and perhaps the finest of its kind.

A seedling of *H. nigrescens*, which grows wild on Honshu island, Japan, 'Krossa Regal' is a low-maintenance plant that develops into a large, vase-shaped plant with a striking mass of elegant foliage about 90 centimetres (3 ft) high. It will occupy a large space in a shady garden and may spread as widely as 1.8 metres (6 ft) as it matures. Its distinctive shape is created by the combination of the leaf stems, which strike upright from the crown, and the broad leaf blades that are held almost at right angles to their stems and, which as they expand, tend to force the stems outwards. The effect is almost unique and allows smaller *Hosta*, other perennials and annuals to be planted beneath.

Each oval leaf, with its gently lobed base, matures to about 30 centimetres (12 in.) long and is very gently waved along its edge. In colour, the leaves are a lovely greyish green at first, the hue created by a thick, white bloom that is repeated even more deeply on the undersides. By midsummer the foliage has turned green, but in the autumn it often becomes a remarkable buttery-gold colour. In midsummer 1.5-metre-tall (5 ft) stems surge through the foliage and up to forty flared lavender flowers open, crowded into the top 30 centimetres (12 in.) of the stem. When the flowers fade, the stems soon turn brown and are best removed. Although slugs and snails are attracted to *Hosta*, the solidity of the foliage of 'Krossa Regal' means that these pests are rarely a problem. **GR**

Alternatives

Hosta 'Regal Splendor', *Hosta* 'Tom Schmid', *Hosta nigrescens*

◉ *Hosta* 'Krossa Regal' has an elegant vase-shaped profile and makes a dramatic focal point.

Hosta

'Paul's Glory'

Main features Vivid, gold-centred, blue-green leaves;
vigorous plant
Height 1 m (3.5 ft) **Spread** 1.8 m (6 ft)
Position ◑ **Hardiness** RHS H7

Variegated varieties of *Hosta* were amongst the very first
types to be grown in gardens. Their willingness to sport
(to produce shoots that are different from the rest of the
parent plant) has ensured that there is a constant stream
of new variegated cultivars. These come in a range of
different styles. Some have a pale colouring around the
edge of the leaf, whereas others have a pale colouring
in the centre. The colour of the variegation can be deep
gold through yellow and cream to pure white, set against
a basic leaf colour from the greens and blues of the *Hosta*
foliage spectrum. The margin between the variegation
and the main leaf colour can be clean, or less precise, and
the variegation may change or fade through the season.

Hosta 'Paul's Glory' is special, because not only does
it make a dramatic specimen plant, but it also does
so quickly – in three or four years. The leaf colour is
unusually intense, and the leaves are relatively thick so
slugs find them less appealing. 'Paul's Glory' makes a
large mound of foliage, more than twice as wide as it is
high, with each heart-shaped leaf slightly puckered and
gently waved along the edges. The leaves may be blue
as they emerge, but soon develop a broad central zone
that begins chartreuse, matures to bright gold, and is
feathered at the edges where it meets the darker margin.
Around the vivid centre is a narrow, blue-green zone
that matures to rich, dark-green by midsummer. As the
margins turn green, the funnel-shaped, pale-lavender
flowers are held well above the leaves. **GR**

Alternatives

Hosta 'Gold Standard', *Hosta* 'Janet', *Hosta* 'September Sun'

Hosta
H. plantaginea var. japonica

Main features Heavily scented evening and night-time white flowers; mounds of glossy, green leaves
Height 75 cm (2.5 ft) **Spread** 1.5 m (5 ft)
Position ◐ **Hardiness** RHS H7

The *Hosta* is the finest foliage perennial that we grow, and it is for the vast variety of its foliage that the various plants are appreciated around the world. However, there are a few cultivars for which the flowers are the main appeal, and this is the case with *H. plantaginea*, the first hosta to be introduced from Asia and grown in the West.

Seeds of *H. plantaginea*, the fragrant plantain lily, were sent to Europe from China in 1789, and plants were soon being grown by Joséphine Bonaparte in her garden at Malmaison in France. At first, the plant was grown in glasshouses, but it soon became so popular as an outdoor plant that it was known as the 'Parisian Funkia'. (*Funkia* was the botanical name used before *Hosta*.)

The glossy, bright-green leaves are oval in shape, boldly lobed at the base, and with a neat pointed tip. As plants mature, they form a mound of foliage. *H. plantaginea* var. *japonica* is very similar to *H. plantaginea,* but differs in its longer and narrower leaves, the more upright shape of the plant as it matures, and the narrower lobes on the flowers. The fragrance is equally impressive. Up to fifteen large, pure-white, trumpet-shaped flowers open in crowded clusters midsummer and early autumn and are held just above the leaves on 75-centimetre-long (2.5 ft) stems. Individual flowers begin to open in early evening and remain open until the following afternoon. The cooler the day temperature, the longer they remain open; on hot days, they may close early in the afternoon. Their heavy scent is at its most powerful in the evening. **GR**

Alternatives

Hosta 'Aphrodite', *Hosta* 'Invincible', *Hosta* 'Royal Standard'

Iris
'Sunny Dawn'

Main feature Intermediate bearded (IB) iris with bright-yellow flowers sparked by an orange beard
Height 55 cm (21 in.) **Spread** 50 cm (20 in.)
Position ○ **Hardiness** RHS H7

There are very many thousands of bearded irises, and their sparkling and varied colouring has won fans all around the world for centuries. In order to help differentiate between the various plants, irises are classified according to their height and flower size. In ascending order, the classifications are miniature dwarf bearded (MDB), standard dwarf bearded (SDB), intermediate bearded (IB), miniature tall bearded (MTB), border bearded (BB) and tall bearded (TB). Often it is only the abbreviations that are used. The IB iris covers plants that reach 40 to 70 centimetres (16–28 in.) in height when in bloom, and with flowers that are up to 12 centimetres (4.5 in.) across. 'Sunny Dawn' is a fine example of this class.

Towards the top of the height range for an IB iris, 'Sunny Dawn' has slightly scented, ruffled flowers with bright-yellow standards (the three upright petals) that become paler towards the base. The falls (the three drooping petals) are also bright yellow but with a pale-bronze overlay and a darker bronze veining toward the base. In addition, each flower has a bright tangerine-orange beard (the beard serves to attract pollinators) at the base of the falls, which adds a vital fiery spark to its colouring. The blooms appear on strong stems (up to four per stem) through grey-green, sword-shaped leaves. Flowering is in late spring, a little before the main flowering of the most popular group: the tall bearded irises.

'Sunny Dawn' was developed by US iris breeder Bennett Jones, who introduced a large number of fine irises and was given the Hybridizer Award by the American Iris Society in 1974. Twelve of his irises received medals from the American Iris Society, and his irises have also won awards from iris societies in Germany, Austria, Italy and England. **GR**

Alternatives

Iris 'Harmonium', *Iris* 'Hot Glow', *Iris* 'Ming', *Iris* 'Season Ticket'

Iris

'Bumblebee Deelite'

Main feature Miniature tall bearded (MTB) iris with
cheerful yellow and maroon flowers
Height 50 cm (20 in.) **Spread** 30–45 cm (12–18 in.)
Position ○ **Hardiness** RHS H7

More and more new bearded irises, called flag irises in the
United Kingdom, are introduced every year, and in order
to help gardeners understand them they are organised
into groups according to their main features. One way
of classifying irises is by their heights and the sizes of
their flowers (see opposite). Another complementary
approach is to group them according to the pattern of
colouring in the flowers.

There are eight groups. Selfs have standards (the
upper three petals) and falls (the lower three petals) that
are more or less the same colour, while others come in
various colour combinations. Amoenas have standards
in a paler version of the colour of the falls; bicolours have
the standards and falls in different colours; and in bitones
the falls are the same colour as the standards but darker.
Blends have two or more colours intermixed; luminatas
have a white or yellow base washed over with colour;
plicatas have pale standards and falls with a boldly
contrasting colour around the edges; and variegatas
have yellow standards and dark, usually maroon, falls.

Variegatas are so called because their colouring is
similar to that of the wild species *I. variegata*, one of the
species that was used to develop modern bearded irises.
'Bumblebee Deelite' is a dramatically coloured variegata
type, and it is also classified as a miniature tall bearded
iris. Its flowers are small, but boldly coloured. The bright-
yellow standards curve inwards at the top and are slightly
stained in maroon at the base. The falls are held more
or less horizontally and are maroon with a bright-yellow
edge and with a yellow beard.

'Bumblebee Deelite' is a popular, eye-catching
variety with a striking pattern that more than makes up
for its small flowers. However, do not allow the plants to
become crowded, or flowering will diminish. **GR**

Alternatives

Iris 'Ancient Echoes', *Iris* 'Supreme Sultan', *Iris* 'Plum Quirky',
Iris 'Jack's Pick'

Iris

'Jane Phillips'

Main feature Tall bearded iris, pale sky-blue flowers on robust and vigorous plants
Height 90 cm (3 ft) **Spread** 50 cm (20 in.)
Position ○ **Hardiness** RHS H7

Colourful – flamboyant, even – and in a multitude of colours and colour combinations, tall bearded irises are the classic irises of the early-summer garden. There was a time when large country estates created beds and borders, sometimes enclosed within neatly trimmed yew hedges, planted entirely with tall bearded irises, to give a stunning early-summer display. The display would last for only two or three weeks, but during that time it would be unforgettable. Nowadays, gardeners integrate irises into the mixed plantings of more modest spaces, and 'Jane Phillips', first introduced in 1946, has the vigour and strength to hold its own alongside other perennials. Its pleasingly fragrant flowers have clear, pale-sky blue, gently ruffled standards and falls (the upper and lower petals) with a golden-yellow beard at the base of the falls to indicate where the bees should aim. It associates well with Oriental poppies in pastel shades and with white sweet rocket (*Hesperis matronalis* var. *albiflora*). **GR**

Alternatives

Iris 'Az Ap', *Iris* 'Cannington Bluebird', *Iris* 'Time Zone'

Iris

I. unguicularis
'Mary Barnard'

Main features Fragrant flowers from midwinter to early spring; attracts bees
Height 30 cm (12 in.) **Spread** 60 cm (24 in.)
Position ○ **Hardiness** RHS H5

The *I. unguicularis* 'Mary Barnard' bears its exquisite butterfly blooms in mild spells from the depth of winter to early spring. These are rich purple, with yellow markings, and measure 5 to 8 centimetres (2–3 in.) across. They are beautifully scented too, but in order to appreciate this, they need to be picked in bud and brought indoors to unfurl. Each flower lasts only a few days, but they are produced in succession for weeks. 'Mary Barnard' is the connoisseur's choice when it comes to winter-flowering irises because it has the darkest blooms, and its strap-like leaves are narrower, shorter and a darker green. It is one of the first varieties to flower too. However, full sun is essential for it to flower well, and the soil needs to be very well drained. A spot at the foot of a sunny wall is ideal, preferably where the plant will not be too prominent during summer as the foliage can look rather untidy. Good companions include drought-tolerant evergreens, such as *Lavandula*, *Cistus*, and *Santolina*. **GP**

Alternatives

Iris unguicularis 'Abington Purple', *Iris unguicularis* 'Walter Butt'

 *Iris* **'Jane Phillips'** is an elegant tall bearded iris that is robust enough for mixed planting.

Iris

'Broadleigh Carolyn'

Main feature California hybrid with pale lilac-blue
flowers that look up from short stems
Height 45 cm (18 in.) **Spread** 25 cm (10 in.)
Position ○ ◑ **Hardiness** RHS H5

The Pacific Coast irises are an interesting group of about
fifteen relatively dwarf species that grow wild in California,
Oregon and Washington states. In gardens they have
been developed into a wide variety of prettily patterned
forms, with flowers in an appealing range of colours
and bicolours. In the wild, all the species are relatively
short, with tough, sinewy rhizomes producing wiry roots,
narrow leaves and unbranched flowering stems. Some
are evergreen and some deciduous.

Most wild species produce only one or two flowers
on each stem, and these may be purple, blue, mauve,
lavender, cream, yellow or orange, depending on the
species. *I. douglasiana*, with lavender or mauve flowers

veined in purple, and *I. innominata*, in a variety of darkly
veined colours, are the species most often seen in the
wild. However, these are not widely seen in gardens,
where the hybrids between them, known collectively as
the California Hybrids (CH), are grown instead. They are
well known for their exquisite colouring, and the long,
narrow leaves make a mass of foliage through which
the flowering stems emerge in late spring and early
summer. These prettily veined flowers are carried two
or three per stem, resulting in a very colourful display.
'Broadleigh Carolyn' is an impressive hybrid developed
by Christine Skelmersdale at Broadleigh Gardens in
Somerset. Its flowers are pale lilac blue, with a deeper-
purple flash at the base and a yellow throat. **GR**

Alternatives

Iris 'Broadleigh Angela', *Iris* 'Broadleigh Amiguita', *Iris*
'Broadleigh Mitre'

Iris

I. × *fulvala* 'Violacea'

Main feature Rich purple flowers on leafy plants
Height 70 cm (28 in.) **Spread** 50 cm (20 in.)
Position ○
Hardiness RHS H7

The Louisiana irises make up a group of colourful, large-flowered plants native to the southern United States. Although their flowers are large and very attractive, they demand wet, even swampy, conditions to thrive, so ideal positions include along streams and in water gardens. *I.* × *fulvala* is a hybrid between two Louisiana irises – *I. fulva* and *I. brevicaulis* – both of which grow wild in the Mississippi river basin. *I. fulva* is a robust species, but its flowers are relatively small; about 6 centimetres (2.5 in.) across. They are carried just one or two per stem, but are especially valuable for their colouring: in red, orange and coppery shades. Unusually, both standards (the upper petals) and falls (the lower petals) tend to flop.

The other parent of the richly colourful *I.* × *fulvala* is the shorter *I. brevicaulis*. This is a very leafy plant, with 2.5-centimetre-wide (1 in.) leaves that tend to hide the flowers, but it does produce several blooms on each stem. Each one is up to 10 centimetres (4 in.) in diameter, comes in a bright bluish-violet, and has large, broad falls and small spreading standards.

The hybrid between these two species occurs naturally and was raised by the British iris pioneer W. R. Dykes in 1910. In colour, it is intermediate between the two parents; the flowers are reddish purple, and it can reach 70 centimetres (28 in.) in height. Like *I. brevicaulis*, the leaves overtop the flowers, but to a lesser extent. *I* × *fulvala* 'Violacea' is a form with rich, purple flowers. **GR**

Alternatives

Iris brevicaulis, Iris fulva, Iris hexagona, Iris fulva 'Marvel Gold', *Iris* 'Black Gamecock'

Iris
I. ensata 'Caprician Butterfly'

Main feature Large, white, wavy flowers with boldly contrasting purple veins
Height 90 cm (3 ft) **Spread** 60 cm (24 in.)
Position ○ **Hardiness** RHS H7

The water irises from Japan, *I. ensata*, are some of the most exotic looking of all irises, with flowers in forms and patterns not seen elsewhere. Related to the British native yellow flag iris, *I. pseudacorus*, which has become invasive in some parts of North America, this very variable species is always well behaved.

Having been cultivated and collected in Japan since the seventeenth century, *I. ensata* already had hundreds of named forms by the end of the eighteenth century. Individual pot-grown plants were taken into the house, so that the unfurling of the flowers could be appreciated at close quarters. The wild species – native to China, Japan, Korea and Russia – has long, very slender foliage and purple flowers, about 10 centimetres (4 in.) across, which are carried in pairs at the top of erect stems. Each flower has yellow flashes on the falls (the lower petals) and rather small standards (the upper petals).

In cultivated forms the summer flowers may be as large as 30 centimetres (12 in.) or more in diameter, and they come in a variety of unexpected forms, including flowers with no standards, flowers with double the usual number (three) of falls, and even flowers with nine or more petals. In colour, purple and blue predominate, but white and pink forms are also seen, and yellow-flowered hybrids are now appearing. The slightly ruffled flowers also feature a wide variety of patterns, including contrasting colours. The veining, stippling, splashing and picotee edging create some very attractive and desirable forms.

I. ensata 'Caprician Butterfly' stems carry up to six double flowers, each with six broad, waved, pristine-white falls, boldly veined in purple and with a picric yellow flash at the base. In the centre is a short contrasting cluster of dark-purple styles. **GR**

Alternatives

Iris ensata 'Cascade Crest', *Iris ensata* 'Light at Dawn', *Iris ensata* 'Katy Mendez', *Iris ensata* 'Flying Tiger'

Iris
I. *ensata* 'Variegata'

Main feature White-striped foliage and purple flowers
Height 70 cm (28 in.) **Spread** 45 cm (18 in.)
Position ○
Hardiness RHS H7

Considering the huge number of different irises grown in gardens around the world, it is surprising that there are so few variegated forms. Fewer than twenty have been named, and only a small number of these are currently available from nurseries. However, although most irises have quite a limited flowering season, forms with variegated foliage – which is attractive for many months – offer much greater appeal and a more structural shape in the garden. The slender, often dark-green foliage – with white, yellow or cream stripes – not only makes a striking feature but also combines well with plants that have broad leaves or more feathery foliage. Choosing companion plants that enjoy the same growing conditions is, of course, essential.

I. ensata 'Variegata' is one of three variegated Japanese water irises, but it is the only one that is widely available from nurseries. Its slender, upright, slightly greyish-green leaves have vertical white stripes; about one-half to one-third of each leaf is variegated. This provides a very long season of colour, from when the shoots first emerge in spring until they die back in autumn. The summer flowers are small by the standards of this species, but they are an attractive, sultry purple colour and have a bright-yellow flash at the base of the falls (the lower petals). Although *I. ensata* 'Variegata' enjoys plenty of moisture, it is important that the plant is not left standing in water over the winter.

I. laevigata 'Variegata' is a very similar plant, but it can be distinguished by its smooth leaves and its bluish flowers. The leaves of *I. laevigata* 'Variegata' have a ridged midrib and its purple flowers feature a bright-white flash on each of the falls. Both species are distinguished from the widely grown *I. foetidissima* 'Variegata', which has dull-lilac flowers and evergreen foliage. **GR**

Alternatives

Iris laevigata 'Variegata', *Iris foetidissima* 'Variegata', *Iris pallida* 'Variegata', *Iris pallida* 'Argentea Variegata'

Iris
I. sibirica 'Strawberry Fair'

Main feature Large, ruffled, magenta-pink flowers on upright stems
Height 75 cm (2.5 ft) **Spread** 60 cm (24 in.)
Position ○ **Hardiness** RHS H7

In the group of Siberian irises are eleven very hardy species that grow naturally in Central Europe and eastern Asia, usually in damp conditions. The Siberian irises grown in gardens are mainly hybrids, between *I. sibirica*, from Europe and northern Asia, and *I. sanguinea*, from Russia and Japan. Combining tolerance and robustness with elegant upright stems of attractive flowers in a wide range of colours, these irises bring together garden appeal and ease of cultivation. Available in purple, blue, pink, white and yellow, older cultivars tend to have drooping falls (the lower three petals), while some more recent introductions have horizontal falls. The flowers of *I. sibirica* 'Strawberry Fair' are sometimes described as strawberry pink. They can more accurately be said to have broad, ruffled, magenta-pink falls held horizontally with paler lavender-pink standards. There is a blue zone and then a white zone around the yellow throat. 'Strawberry Fair' will flower well for many years with little care, but responds even better to more generous treatment. **GR**

Alternatives

Iris sibirica 'Eric the Red', *Iris sibirica* 'Ruffles and Flourishes'

Iris
I. chrysographes

Main feature Almost-black flowers with yellow flashes on the falls
Height 50 cm (20 in.) **Spread** 25 cm (10 in.)
Position ○ **Hardiness** RHS H7

There are around 300 species of *Iris* spread across the northern hemisphere. All are perennials, a few are evergreens, and many are very winter hardy. They are divided into bearded irises – mainly the flamboyant early-summer irises in a rainbow of colours – and the beardless irises, which include a wide range from very varied habitats. *I. chrysographes* is a beardless iris, and it is striking, almost unique, for one main reason: the colour of its flowers. At its best, both the standards and the falls are almost black. In fact, the flowers, carried in pairs at the top of unbranched stems, vary in colour from rich burgundy red through deep purple, and the black colour often proves to be elusive. Seed taken from the darkest plants may produce seedlings that are dark red or dark purple, so it is only by lifting and dividing the clumps of plants with the very best colours that true plants can be produced. Plants labelled 'black-flowered' are usually seedlings and should be chosen in flower to be sure of a good form. **GR**

Alternatives

Iris sibirica 'Reddy Maid', *Iris sibirica* 'Ruffles Plus'

Iris chrysographes varies in colour so buy plants when they are in flower. ➜

Kirengeshoma
K. *palmata* Koreana Group

Main features Late-summer and autumn woodland perennial; architectural plant
Height 50–120 cm (20–24 in.) **Spread** 50–100 cm (20–24 in.) **Position** ◑ **Hardiness** RHS H7

In spring woodland gardeners have a wealth of plants to choose from, but as the seasons progress, relatively few flowering herbaceous plants, shrubs and bulbs are available. Bucking the trend, *K. palmata* Koreana Group is just getting started towards the end of summer, with scores of developing buds ready to continue its exotic flower display into autumn. *Kirengeshoma* is elegance personified, from the light-green mounds of maple-shaped leaves to the graceful, branching stems coloured red-purple that hold the flowers clear of the foliage. The rounded buds carry the same dark tints until they pop, revealing the waxy-textured, pale-yellow petals. The large, pixie cap–shaped blooms hang down, arcing the branches over as their weight increases. Overall height varies according to the age of the plant and how good the growing conditions are. Koreana Group individuals grow taller than the species and can reach up to 1.5 metres (5 ft) in optimum conditions. They also have slightly larger flowers.

One perennial to try with *Kirengeshoma* that enjoys similar conditions and shares the same flowering time is *Gentiana asclepiadea*, which offers tubular, deep-blue flower contrast. Another blue companion, provided the soil is acidic, could be selected from one of the mophead or lacecap hydrangeas. Japanese maples with tinted foliage would layer in more texture and colour.

Typical drained woodland-type soils, rich in leaf mould and with good moisture-retaining qualities, work best for *Kirengeshoma*. If all other conditions are met, the plants will tolerate some lime in the soil. Provide a position that is sheltered from wind with some shade, especially in regions that have relatively low rainfall. Cut back after flowering, and if necessary, divide the rhizomatous clumps in spring. **JH**

Alternative

Kirengeshoma palmata

Kniphofia
'Timothy'

Main features An elegant, summer-flowering poker; unique shade of coral red with pink overtones
Height 1.2 m (4 ft) **Spread** 50 cm (20 in.)
Position ○ **Hardiness** RHS H5

'Timothy' produces pink-toned, orange pokers that appear in late summer, without any hint of yellow. It is warm but never brash, with loosely arranged florets on shapely pokers supported on slightly curved, dark stems, and is therefore more airy, elegant and ethereal than many red-hot pokers. It suits gravel gardens, or it could be mass planted with delicate grasses, which could include the much taller *Stipa gigantea* or the delicate golden *Deschampsia cespitosa* 'Bronzeschleier' ('Bronze Veil'). 'Timothy' also suits modern prairie planting.

Bred by Carlile's Nursery in the United Kingdom in 1976, it has endured the test of time and is made more special by having red-flushed stems. Its garden-worthy brother 'Jonathan', also bred by Carlile's in 1992, is a deeper, brighter red, although the flowers do have yellow at the base. Both won Awards of Garden Merit at the RHS Wisley trial held between 2007 and 2009, and both survived a severe winter in their first year.

Try to plant all pokers in spring and, once they grow, frisk the leaves and remove snails early in the year or they will do considerable damage to emerging lower buds. Remove the faded flowers from the base as they go over, low down, because many will send out more flowers after rain. This will also prevent unwanted seedlings from popping up. Leave the foliage intact over winter to protect the crown. Tidy the clump in late spring using pruning shears. If you wish to propagate more plants lift and divide them in spring, never in the autumn.

Kniphofias are a diverse bunch, flowering randomly between midsummer and autumn, and they come in many shades of cream, lime green, yellow, orange, coral and warm red, offering both warm and cool tones. They have attracted the attention of plant breeders since the 1930s and new kniphofias continue to appear. **VB**

Alternatives

Kniphofia 'Safranvogel', *Kniphofia* 'Bees' Sunset'

Kniphofia
'Wrexham Buttercup'

Main features Yellow poker with great presence; flowers mostly in midsummer but also in autumn
Height 1.3 m (4.25 ft) **Spread** 50 cm (20 in.)
Position ○ **Hardiness** RHS H5

A well-known yellow poker, bred by Bakers of Codsall in the United Kingdom in 1946, this is still one of the finest *Kniphofia* today, despite its age. It produces lots of substantial warm-yellow pokers from midsummer onwards, often giving a late and very welcome flourish in autumn. It is strong, reliable, and lovely to look at, with green buds that develop into glowing yellow flowers packed with hundreds of neat florets. 'Wrexham Buttercup' is the easiest yellow of all – widely available and widely grown – and it avoids being brash, thanks to a hint of green in the young flower heads. Expect forty to fifty flowers from a happy, well-established clump on fertile soil, and remember to deadhead because more flowers may come if there is enough moisture in the ground. The flowers are held on slender stems well above the foliage, and because 'Wrexham Buttercup' is such a lucid yellow, it can used with most colours. It will brighten red and orange *Helenium*, clash with purple *Dahlia* and contrast with a true blue *Agapanthus* such as 'Northern Star'. **VB**

Alternatives

Kniphofia 'Sunningdale Yellow', *Kniphofia* 'Innocence'

Kniphofia
'Tawny King'

Main features Cream, apricot and tawny-brown poker; lots of nectar; attracts bees, wasps and butterflies
Height 1.2 m (4 ft) **Spread** 50 cm (20 in.)
Position ○ **Hardiness** RHS H5

This floriferous poker produces masses of flowers from early summer to midautumn, for a far longer period than most *Kniphofia*. The narrow foliage is tidier than other *Kniphofia* too, with dusky stems supporting apricot flowers that fade to warm brown. The neatly arranged spike, always with a ruff of cream florets at the base, offers tempting glances of the stem through the flower head. As a result 'Tawny King', which can produce thirty flowers at once, smolders warmly in a border like butterscotch in a sweet shop. Use it with toning oranges, such as *Dahlia* 'David Howard' and *Helenium* 'Sahin's Early Flowerer' or mix it with late-season *Miscanthus sinensis*. It will create a great contrast with rich-blue *Agapanthus* or *Aconitum* 'Spark's Variety'. When given space to shine, this architectural plant will add drama in summer- and autumn-flowering borders. 'Tawny King' prefers good growing conditions, with plenty of summer rain, but remember to frisk the leaves and remove snails early, or they will do considerable damage to emerging lower buds. **VB**

Alternatives

Kniphofia 'Toffee Nosed', *Kniphofia* 'Percy's Pride'

Kniphofia 'Tawny King' produces plenty of poker flowers from summer to autumn. ➲

Lamprocapnos
L. spectabilis 'Alba'

Main features Arching stems with white, heart-shaped, pendent flowers; fern-like, green deciduous foliage
Height 90 cm (3 ft) **Spread** 45 cm (18 in.)
Position ◑ ● **Hardiness** RHS H7

Like strings of heart-shaped pearls, the exquisite flowers of this bleeding heart hang from arching stems in late spring above deeply cut fern-like foliage. Few plants surpass *Lamprocapnos* for sheer elegance, and its graceful habit and dainty flowers suit both contemporary and traditional settings. The only drawback is that it is dormant from summer to winter, so plant later-flowering perennials or bulbs in front to mask its fading foliage and the gaps it leaves behind. Try *L. spectabilis* 'Alba' in groups alongside rich burgundy or pink tulips in a formal bed edged with a clipped box, or mix it up with other cottage garden staples, such as *Polemonium*, *Aquilegia*, *Astrantia*, and *Geranium*, which also enjoy light shade. Alternatively, try a tallish *Geranium*, such as 'Orion' or 'Patricia', in front of 'Alba' to fill the gaps when it disappears below ground for the summer. 'Alba' also shines out from woodland gardens, its rows of bead-like flowers creating a focal point above low-growing partners, such as *Erythronium*, *Epimedium* and *Corydalis flexuosa*. **ZA**

Alternatives

Dicentra formosa f. *alba*, *Dicentra* 'Langtrees'

Leucanthemella
L. serotina

Main feature Late display of large white daisies on tall plants
Height 1.8 m (6 ft) **Spread** 60 cm (24 in.)
Position ○ **Hardiness** RHS H7

Two *Leucanthemella* species grow wild from southeastern Europe through to eastern Asia, but only one of them, *L. serotina*, is seen in gardens. A tall perennial, it has hairy stems and leaves at the base that are dark green and more or less lance-shaped. Gently lobed, and with forwards-pointing teeth along the edges, these leaves are arranged alternately. The stems are topped with branched heads of long-stemmed flowers. Each bloom has white petals – sometimes with reddish tints – that circle a bold, greenish-yellow central eye. The flowers open late in the season, at the end of summer and well into the autumn, so they are ideal at the back of borders featuring *Chrysanthemum*, *Aster*, and late grasses. Think carefully about where to plant *L. serotina* because the flowers follow the sun from morning till dusk. Consider the time of day you will be looking at the site and from which direction. This slow spreader will need thoughtful staking; alternatively, the shoots can be nipped back in late spring to reduce the eventual height of the plant. **GR**

Alternative

Lecanthemella serotina 'Herbsstern'

◐ *Lamprocapnos spectabilis* 'Alba' brings light and grace to a shady bed in late spring.

Leucanthemum
L. × superbum 'Wirral Supreme'

Main features White double flowers; serrated dark-green leaves; good cut flower
Height 90 cm (3 ft) **Spread** 75 cm (2.5 ft)
Position ○ ◑ **Hardiness** RHS H7

The sturdy stems of this popular Shasta daisy are topped with large, white, double, daisy-like flowers, which bloom for a long period from midsummer to early autumn. Comprising reflexed petals and a central disk of pale yellow, shorter petals, and a green eye, the flowers stand tall above simple dark-green leaves and create a striking focal point in beds and borders. Team the white blooms of *L. × superbum* 'Wirral Supreme' with flowers of any colour, except perhaps cream, which may look dirty against these sparkling daisies. The blooms work well with traditional cottage garden plants – such as roses, lupins, delphiniums, phlox, salvias and asters – or used in a contemporary scheme matched with clipped box cubes and ornamental grasses. The plants may need staking. These daisies originate from Mount Shasta in California, where botanist Luther Burbank first developed the parent plant, *L. × superbum,* in the 1890s. **ZA**

Alternatives

Leucanthemum × superbum 'Aglaia', *Leucanthemum × superbum* 'Highland White Dream'

Lewisia
L. cotyledon Ashwood Strain

Main feature Slightly bluish, succulent rosettes carry neat clusters of vivid flowers in five colours
Height 23 cm (9 in.) **Spread** 23 cm (9 in.)
Position ◑ **Hardiness** RHS H7

The *Lewisia* was named for Captain Meriwether Lewis, who collected a specimen during the Lewis and Clark expedition across the eastern states to the Pacific in the early 1800s. It is a small perennial that develops a rosette of foliage, from the centre of which the flowering stems emerge. Some species produce rather small leaves, which die away in the summer after flowering, but *L. cotyledon* produces larger evergreen foliage. Plants are frost hardy but their crown is vulnerable to wet so they are often planted on their sides. Their site should be open but shaded from the midday sun. The stems carry loose clusters of pink-purple or white flowers. Each flower has up to nine petals and is often streaked in darker or paler shades. The Ashwood strain, developed by John Massey at Britain's Ashwood Nurseries (pictured) has colourful, vivid flowers, while his Ashwood Carousel hybrids are smaller but more weather-resistant, so easier to grow. **GR**

Alternatives

Lewisia cotyledon 'Elise', *Lewisia cotyledon* Sunset Group, *Lewisia cotyledon* 'Regenbogen'

Libertia
L. grandiflora

Ligularia
'Britt Marie Crawford'

Main features White summer flowers; evergreen foliage; good cut flower; architectural plant
Height 90 cm (3 ft) **Spread** 60 cm (24 in.)
Position ○ ◑ **Hardiness** RHS H4

Main features Mid- to late-summer flowers; dramatic summer foliage; good cut flower; architectural plant
Height 1 m (3.5 ft) **Spread** 1 m (3.5 ft)
Position ○ ◑ **Hardiness** RHS H6

This evergreen member of the *Iris* family makes a useful addition to many gardens. It is a clump-forming perennial with sword-shaped, leathery, dark-green foliage all year around. In early summer rigid stems bear dense clusters of rounded, pure-white, six-petalled flowers. These are followed by dark, decorative seedpods, giving added autumn/winter interest. The stiff foliage of *L. grandiflora* provides a strong vertical accent and looks at its best if not overcrowded. This reliable and long-lived plant works well in gravel gardens where it would associate with the prostrate sea-green foliage of *Euphorbia myrsinites*. It can even be encouraged to colonise light deciduous woodland, where the winter interest is valuable. In sunny borders, try associating it with the satin-pink spires of *Sidalcea* 'Elsie Heugh', or the fluffy, purple flower heads of *Thalictrum aquilegifolium*. Or let it emerge from a carpet of pink-flowered *Silene* × *lempergii* 'Max Frei'. **MP**

Named after a lady in whose nursery in Scotland it was found, 'Britt Marie Crawford' is a clump-forming, deciduous, herbaceous perennial worth growing for its foliage alone. Large, shiny, roundish, maroon-black leaves emerge in spring, held on the same coloured stalks. The undersides of the leaves are a rich burgundy and show up when blown by the wind. In mid- to late summer, the flower stems appear, topped with loose heads of vivid orange-yellow daisy flowers, 5 to 8 centimetres (2–3 in.) in diameter. The flowers look striking set against the dark foliage, and they are loved by butterflies. Grow 'Britt Marie Crawford' as a single specimen in smaller gardens, or as a massed group in a large area, along with partners such as the blue foliage of *Hosta sieboldiana* var. *elegans* and a white-flowered Japanese or Siberian iris. A position beside water or in a moist border, where its architectural features can be appreciated, is ideal. **MP**

Alternatives

Libertia ixioides, Libertia ixioides 'Goldfinger', *Libertia caerulescens, Libertia pereginans*

Alternatives

Ligularia dentata 'Desdemona', *Ligularia dentata* 'Othello', *Ligularia* 'The Rocket', *Ligularia przewalskii*

Liriope
L. muscari

Main features Flowers in late summer and autumn;
evergreen foliage
Height 30–40 cm (12–16 in.) **Spread** 45 cm (18 in.)
Position ○ ◑ ● **Hardiness** RHS H5

This architectural evergreen perennial from East Asia
pretends to be a grass, but it certainly is not. Amazingly
tolerant of a wide range of soils and locations, the strap-
shaped, leathery, deep-green leaves form a tufted clump
that spreads very slowly to 45 centimetres (18 in.). In very
late summer or early autumn, spikes of tiny purple flowers
cluster around purple, flushed, upright stems that reach
30 to 40 centimetres (12–16 in.) in height. They are vaguely
reminiscent of a grape hyacinth (*Muscari*), hence its
specific name, but *L. muscari* has longer flower spikes.
The flowers are sometimes followed by shiny black berries.

Although this perennial is happy in full sun, it is even
more content, and therefore useful, in partial or even
densely shaded areas, where the flower spikes and
foliage tend to be a bit taller. The plant's only vice is that
the clumps of foliage can start to look a bit tatty, but this
can be resolved by occasionally trimming off the leaves
in spring before the new shoots emerge. Alternatively,
when grown as massed ground cover, a lawn mower,
with the blades set high, could be used.

L. muscari's tolerance of shade makes it an ideal
member of a woodland garden, where it will add
valuable flower interest in the autumn. The choicer
varieties make good container plants for shade. Although
the variety *L. muscari* 'Big Blue' is often sold for its large
blue flowers, it may be no different from the species.
L. muscari 'Monroe White' bears large white spikes of
flowers held above the foliage and seems to prefer a
shady spot. Colourful foliage includes: *L. muscari*
'Variegata' (pictured), *L. muscari* 'Gold Banded', as its
name suggests, has yellow- and green-striped foliage,
whereas *L. muscari* 'Okina' is unusual in that the foliage
emerges in spring, almost white, and gradually turns
green as the season progresses. **MP**

Alternatives

Liriope muscari 'Big Blue', *Liriope muscari* 'Monroe White',
Liriope muscari 'Okina', *Liriope spicata*

Lobelia
L. cardinalis 'Queen Victoria'

Main features Spikes, bright-scarlet flowers; rich, beetroot, bronze foliage
Height 1.2 m (4 ft) **Spread** 25 cm (10 in.)
Position ○ ◑ **Hardiness** RHS H7

The cardinal flower, *L. cardinalis*, is a red-flowered, hardy perennial relation of the trailing blue species of *Lobelia* that is so popular each year in summer hanging baskets. It grows wild in most of the United States, with the exception of parts of the northwest, as well as in eastern Canada and south into Central America as far as Columbia. In its natural habitat *L. cardinalis* grows well in sunny and partially shaded positions, as long as the soil is damp. It grows on pond and lake margins, in swamps and seeps, along riverbanks, and even in the water of shallow creeks.

The plant overwinters as small rosettes, often made up of only a few rudimentary leaves and gathered into groups as the crowns steadily expand. This is an exceptionally frost-hardy plant, often overwintering in water and soil that is frozen solid for months. In spring the narrow 10-centimetre-long (4 in.) leaves develop, often bronze-tinted at first, and reduce in size as they extend up the stem.

In summer the boldly vertical stems, which may be unbranched or with a few branches just below the flowers, are topped with a 20 to 40 centimetre (8–16 in.) length of vivid scarlet flowers. Each flower is 2.5 to 4 centimetres (1–1.5 in.) long and split into three large lower lobes and two narrow, flared upper lobes. The overall effect is of a rather starry, five-pointed flower. Vivid scarlet is the most common colour, but deeper red is sometimes seen, as is an occasional white. The flowers are popular with hummingbirds.

In *L. cardinalis* 'Queen Victoria', the tendency towards bronze-tinted leaves is enormously enhanced so that the stems are purple and the foliage is beetroot bronze. This colouring is perfect in partnership with the plant's scarlet flowers. **GR**

Alternatives

Lobelia cardinalis 'Bees' Flame', *Lobelia cardinalis* 'Chocolate Truffle'

Lobelia
L. siphilitica

Main features Attractive blue flowers; tall slender spikes
Height 90 cm (3 ft) **Spread** 15 cm (6 in.)
Position ◑
Hardiness RHS H7

This great blue *Lobelia* – other blue-flowered species have smaller flowers – is one of many herbaceous perennial species native to North America and Canada. However, most *Lobelia* species are from warmer, more southerly climates. *L. siphilitica* grows over central and eastern United States and Canada. It prefers damp conditions, growing in swamps, seeps, and lake- and streamsides, as well as in damp, less-shaded, woodland sites. It is particularly intolerant of sun combined with drought. Its name is derived from the fact that the plant was once used as a cure for syphilis.

The striking, usually unbranched, vertical green stems arise from an overwintering rosette of slightly hairy, elliptical or lance-shaped leaves that can be as much as 15 centimetres (6 in.) long. In summer they are topped by spikes that reach 60 centimetres (24 in.) in length and are packed with flowers that open in clusters in the leaf joints from the bottom of the spike upwards. Each 2.5-centimetre-long (1 in.) flower is divided into two lobes – the upper lobe split in two and the lower into three segments. These lobes may be pointed or rounded and come in a range of blue shades, sometimes a deep violet blue, held on a darker-coloured tube. White-flowered forms are occasionally seen too.

This summer- and early-autumn blooming perennial has a tight, compact root system, and it is relatively short lived – four or five years is its expected lifespan. While still appreciating moisture, the great blue *L. siphilitica* is a little more tolerant of dry conditions than the more often seen cardinal flower, *L. cardinalis*. These two species – *L. cardinalis* and *L. siphilitica* – are the parents of several lovely hybrids with purple, cranberry-red, and almost ruby-coloured flowers. Those in the Kompliment Series and Fan Series are especially impressive. **GR**

Alternatives

Lobelia × speciosa 'Fan Blau', *Lobelia × speciosa* 'Kompliment Blau'

Lunaria
L. rediviva

Main features Fragrant flowers; attracts butterflies
and bees; flowers and seed heads good for cutting
Height 90 cm (3 ft) **Spread** 45 cm (18 in.)
Position ○ ◑ ● **Hardiness** RHS H7

There are few more amenable cottage-garden–style
plants than perennial honesty – it will even cope with
dry shade. *L. rediviva* has a longer season of interest than
most, too, commencing in late spring with 90-centimetre-
tall (3 ft) branching sprays of small but superbly scented
lilac-white, cross-shaped flowers. These attract bees and
butterflies and are lovely for cutting. The flowers of the
more widely grown *L. annua* are not scented at all, but
both species produce very decorative seed heads, so do
not be tempted to deadhead them.

L. rediviva has flat, pointed, oval seedpods that are up
to 8 centimetres (3 in.) long. These eventually shed their
outer coverings – you can help with this – to reveal the
translucent silvery remains that are beloved of dried-
flower arrangers. The common name 'honesty' was first
used in the sixteenth century and is thought to be a
reference to the transparency of these seedpods. If left
on the plant, they can be an attractive feature all winter
if the weather is kind. The plant itself is a neat, clump-
forming perennial with branching stems clothed in fresh,
green, heart-shaped leaves that are up to 8 centimetres
(3 in.) long. It is unlikely to need staking.

Traditionally, honesty is said to grow best when the
landowner is honest, but this is not to be relied upon.
L. rediviva is a European native found in damp shady
places including woodlands. It prefers some shade and
fertile, moist, well-drained soil, but the plant is drought-
tolerant once established and can do well in full sun too.
It suits informal planting schemes – including woodland
gardens, cottage-garden–style borders and wildflower
meadows – and is best planted in swathes of at least
five. Try some near a seating area so you can enjoy the
fragrance on a warm summer evening. It will self-seed
if happy. **GP**

Alternatives

Lunaria annua var. *albiflora*, *Lunaria annua* var. *albiflora*
'Alba Variegata', *Lunaria annua* 'Munstead Purple'

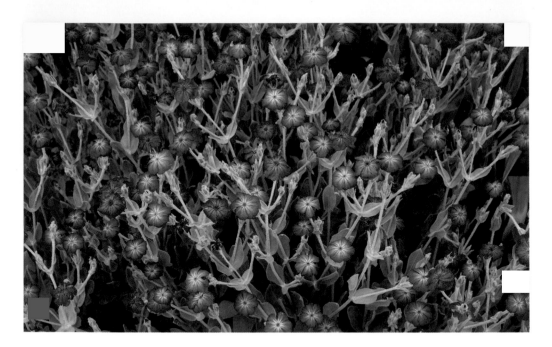

Lychnis

L. coronaria

Main features Late-summer perennial; vivid magenta flowers; attracts butterflies
Height 50–100 cm (20–40 in.) **Spread** 10–50 cm (4–20 in.)
Position ○ ◑ **Hardiness** RHS H7

Borders often start to flag beyond midsummer, especially after a hot spell, but when *L. coronaria* (also known as rose campion) comes into bloom, it adds renewed sparkle. The flat, circular blooms are a vivid, almost glowing magenta, carried at the top of finely branched silver stems. These rise from a clump of downy, grey-green leaves. Being light and airy in stature, rose campion is a great border-gap filler. It looks striking weaving its way between late-flowering shrubs, such as yellow forms of *Potentilla fruticosa*, *Buddleja davidii* 'Buzz Magenta', and the blue-flowered *Caryopteris* × c*landonensis* 'Heavenly Blue'. It also works as a foil for larger-flowered perennials, such as the pale-yellow *Leucanthemum* × *superbum* 'Broadway

Lights', and architectural verbascums, echinops and agapanthus. On a smaller scale its vertical flower stems contrast handsomely with low ground-cover plants, like catmint (*Nepeta* × *faassenii*) and purple sedum.

Rose campion is a short-lived perennial or biennial, but it seeds generously, making it easy to keep plants in the border year after year. The grey-white, felted seedlings are easy to spot and transplant as soon as large enough to handle, either in autumn or spring. Self-sown seedlings rarely end up in the wrong spot, though, and the colour blends with any late-summer shade, even a potentially clashing orange. There are several forms of *L. coronaria*, including the pure-white 'Alba' and the Atrosanguinea Group, which has darker blooms than the species. **JH**

Alternatives

Lychnis coronaria 'Alba', *Lychnis coronaria* Atrosanguinea Group, *Lychnis coronaria* Gardeners' World = 'Blych'

Macleaya
M. cordata

Main features Summer flowers and foliage that persist through autumn; architectural plant
Height 1.5–2.4 m (5–8 ft) **Spread** 90–150 cm (3–5 ft)
Position ○ ◐ **Hardiness** RHS H6

Tall, architectural and handsome, *M. cordata* does not look like the other members of the poppy family that give it its common name (plume poppy). It is easy to grow and is that rare thing: a tall, graceful herbaceous plant that does not need staking.

Plume poppy is a slow starter, taking a few seasons to get into full growing stride. However, it develops into a very robust plant that spreads quite rapidly through its growth habit of strong shoots spreading out below ground. Above ground, upright clumps of tall stems bear palmate lobed leaves in an attractive shade of grey green. Each stem is topped in summer with airy panicles of buff-white flowers opening from delicate coral-pink

buds. Its strong stems flex naturally in the breeze, making the flowers shimmer as they move.

Give it plenty of space to reach its full architectural potential. In smaller gardens a single plant brings real presence to the back of a border; in larger gardens group planting makes a bold statement. *M. cordata* has a similar presence to *Miscanthus sinensis*, *Stipa gigantea* and *Cortaderia selloana* and is hardier than the equally fine-foliaged *Melianthus major*. In small spaces it can be grown in a container sunk into the ground to control its spread. Alternatively, planted in large containers it makes a statuesque accent in any garden. Avoid planting taller plants in front of *M. cordata*, because its foliage reaches all the way down to the ground. **RC**

Alternatives

Macleaya microcarpa 'Kelway's Coral Plume', *Macleaya × kewensis* 'Flamingo', *Macleaya microcarpa* 'Spetchley Ruby'

Maianthemum
M. racemosum

Main feature Bold foliage topped with creamy-white plumes, followed by red berries
Height 90 cm (3 ft) **Spread** 60 cm (24 in.)
Position ◐ ● **Hardiness** RHS H7

The *M. racemosum* is a bold, herbaceous, hardy perennial with a stout, slowly spreading rhizome from which individual arching shoots emerge. Here, finely pointed, narrowly elliptical leaves stand out alternately in a more or less flat plane and in a gentle zigzag pattern. They turn yellow or brown in autumn. With its ranks of leaves standing out alternately from the arching stems, it very much resembles *Polygonatum*, but *Convallaria* is also closely related genetically. The uncertainty of the botanical relationships of *M. racemosum* is indicated by the fact that *Polygonatum* was previously known as *Smilacina racemosa* and is still often listed under this name by nurseries.

In late spring and early summer the shoots of *M. racemosum* are tipped with dense, fluffy, 15-centimetre-wide (6 in.) heads of creamy-white flowers, which give way to green berries, spotted in red at first and then maturing fully to bright red. The berries tend to be eaten promptly by birds, but may last long enough to coincide with the autumn foliage colouring. Both the rhizomes and berries were once eaten by humans.

Distributed over the whole of the United States, except Hawaii, and throughout most of Canada *M. racemosum* grows in moist woods, by damp roadsides, and in other partially shaded sites that are not dry. In gardens it makes a fine specimen plant for the shade and woodland garden, especially as it looks so handsome even before the flowers open. **GR**

Alternatives

Maianthemum bifolium, Maianthemum oleraceum

Matteuccia
M. struthiopteris

Main feature Spring and summer foliage; winter interest from fertile fronds; architectural plant
Height 1.2 m (4 ft) **Spread** 60 cm (24 in.)
Position ◐ ● **Hardiness** RHS H7

The unfurling croziers of ferns in the spring garden are a sight to please most gardeners, and this fern fits the bill well. *M. struthiopteris* spreads gently via underground stolons to create impressive colonies, if space permits. The new sterile fronds emerge in spring – curled inwards, in a vase-like cluster from a knobbly rootstock – and gradually splay out to form the characteristic shuttlecock shape of light-green, finely divided, pinnate foliage. Later in summer brown fertile fronds emerge from the centre of the shuttlecock.

Ideally, this easy, reasonably hardy, architectural fern likes a moisture-retentive soil in shade or partial shade. It prefers a neutral to slightly acidic soil and is even tolerant of clay. Although the foliage is deciduous and can be cut back in the autumn, the fertile fronds can be left for winter effect, especially if touched by a hoar frost. Surplus plants can be lifted and replanted in spring.

M. struthiopteris, together with *Polygonatum*, is perfect for growing in moist or dappled shade on the edge of a deciduous woodland garden or pushing through a carpet of *Geranium macrorrhizum*. In a bog garden it associates well with other moisture-loving perennials, such as *Primula* and *Astilbe*. The feathery fronds contrast beautifully with the bold blue foliage of *Hosta sieboldiana* var. *elegans* or the large, dark purple-black leaves of *Ligularia* 'Britt Marie Crawford'. *M. struthiopteris* 'The King' is larger in all its parts and is renowned for its better heat tolerance when grown in warm climates. **MP**

Alternative

Matteuccia orientalis

Mertensia
M. virginica

Main features Flowers in spring; attracts bees, butterflies and wildlife
Height 30–60 cm (12–24 in.) **Spread** 30–45 cm (12–18 in.)
Position ◐ **Hardiness** RHS H7

The *M. virginica* is a plant full of charm. It is a native of eastern North America – the region east of the Mississippi – from Canada in the north, down to Georgia. It brings intense blue carpets of colour to a garden in spring, offering the perfect combination of colour and freshness that comes with the new season.

Ideally suited to planting beneath taller trees and shrubs, *M. virginica* prefers moist woodland conditions. A true carpeting herbaceous perennial, it has smooth, oval, greyish-green leaves that cushion arching, branched stems. In spring these bear 2.5-centimetre-long (1 in.) tubular-shaped flowers that start off pink and turn a striking violet blue. These are slightly pendulous, which gives them a nodding appearance. In early spring they are a magnet for bees, but only the largest bumblebees can push their way up the funnel-shaped flowers. Butterflies and moths also make perfect pollinators.

This perennial is dormant in summer, when a little dryness is tolerated, so it is best to plant *M. virginica* among ferns and hostas that will take over as it begins to diminish in high season. Plants that naturally make good partners include *Athyrium filix-femina* and any variety of hostas, because these have suitably lush top growth that will fill in the gaps from midsummer onwards. *M. virginica* will spread easily by self-seeding to make a delightful colony.

Other notable species include *M. ciliata*, from the Rocky Mountains, which has slightly longer leaves and smaller, light-blue tubular flowers. *M. maritima* is a native of the cooler regions of northern Europe. Its beautiful glaucous leaves are liberally sprinkled with pale-blue, narrow, bell-shaped flowers. As a coastal plant, *M. maritima* needs well-drained soil in full sun to thrive, so sandy soils and areas of gravel are ideal. **RC**

Alternatives

Syn. *Mertensia pulmonarioides, Mertensia ciliata, Mertensia maritima, Mertensia sibirica*

Miscanthus
M. sinensis 'Morning Light'

Main feature Summer and autumn flowers that linger into winter
Height 90–150 cm (3–5 ft) **Spread** 50–90 cm (20–36 in.)
Position ○ **Hardiness** RHS H6

The *Miscanthus* genus contains some of the most beautiful of all the ornamental grasses. *M. sinensis* is a tall, rangy plant reaching up to 1.8 metres (6 ft), and Japanese artists often portrayed its wispy flower heads in their work. Out of the many free-flowering cultivars available today, *M. sinensis* 'Morning Light' is a great choice for any garden.

A compact form reaching a maximum of 1.5 metres (5 ft), 'Morning Light' is a perfectly named plant. A single specimen makes a focal point that lights up a border all season long with its arching, narrow, linear leaves edged with white. In the autumn a haze of pink-tinged flower plumes further enhances the effect: they appear to float above stems and leaves. In short it is a plant of great beauty and refinement, superb as a single specimen, dramatic planted in a large drift and excellent in a container.

M. sinensis cultivars bring graceful animation to gardens of all sizes; they range in height from 90 centimetres (3 feet) to an impressive 3 metres (10 ft). Some are deciduous, like 'Morning Light', whereas others are evergreen. They are easy to grow in any aspect, but full sun brings out the best in them. 'Morning Light' can be slow to increase in size, but it is well worth the wait.

M. sinensis 'Kleine Fontäne' is another similar-sized variety that produces graceful mounds of green foliage and masses of soft-pink flowers from late summer. As autumn progresses, these turn an attractive silver grey. *Miscanthus* is genuinely low maintenance and requires only one cut back per year, in early spring. As with other ornamental grasses, it is more a case of grooming the plants to remove dead foliage and old flowered stems in early spring to prepare them for the new season. It does not like excessive winter wet, and cultivars produce flowers more freely in cooler locations. **RC**

Alternatives

Miscanthus sinensis 'Ferner Osten', *Miscanthus sinensis* 'Kleine Silberspinne', *Miscanthus sinensis* 'Septemberrot'

Miscanthus
M. sinensis 'Zebrinus'

Main feature Summer and autumn flowers that linger into winter
Height 90–150 cm (3–5 ft) **Spread** 50–90 cm (20–36 in.)
Position ○ **Hardiness** RHS H6

The *M. sinensis* 'Zebrinus', commonly known as zebra grass, stands out from the herd of other cultivars in the same way that its namesake is a distinctive presence in the wild animal kingdom. Its singular qualities make 'Zebrinus' very desirable: it is not only perfect as a stand-alone focal feature, but it also harmonises well with a range of planting schemes. Growing to 1.5 metres (5 ft) in height, it forms a dense clump of tall, bright-green stems with slim arching leaves that become distinctively marked with bands of creamy yellow as summer progresses. Although the flowers are not prolific, they have an attractive copper tint.

'Zebrinus' is particularly effective when grown near water or in a position where its leaves are backlit by the sun, which maximises their appearance. This ornamental grass can be planted either in spring or autumn, in a high-quality, well-drained soil. Sometimes a little slow to establish at first – the eye-catching foliage markings only appear after midsummer – it develops into a low-maintenance plant with impressive looks that last beyond the summer.

'Zebrinus' makes a striking backdrop for taller plants with bold-coloured flowers, such as *Crocosmia* 'Lucifer'. Another similar banded-leaved cultivar is *M. sinensis* 'Strictus'. More erect and spiky leaved than zebra grass, it is sometimes shorter growing and topped with pink-red flowers in late summer. For different variegated foliage effects, *M. sinensis* 'Variegatus' has narrow, arching, green leaves that are striped with white. It grows to around 2 metres (7 ft) and sometimes produces sparse reddish flowers in early autumn. *Miscanthus* grows in any aspect and full sun brings out the best in it. The various species can be either deciduous or evergreen; they are easy to grow but do not like excessive winter wet. More compact forms make great container plants. **RC**

Alternatives

Miscanthus sinensis 'Kleine Fontäne', *Miscanthus sinensis* 'Kleine Silberspinne', *Miscanthus sinensis* 'Morning Light'

Molinia
M. *caerulea* subsp. *caerulea* 'Variegata'

Main features Late-spring to early-winter foliage; late-summer flowers; autumn to early winter seed heads
Height 24 in. (60 cm) **Spread** 24 in. (60 cm)
Position ○ **Hardiness** RHS H7

One of the best variegated grasses on the market, *M. caerulea* subsp. *caerulea* 'Variegata' is one of the most cumbersomely named, too. This elegant variety has arching, slender foliage that emerges yellow and matures to green with bold, cream stripes. It grows as a neat, dense hummock about 45 centimetres (18 in.) high. From mid- or late summer, there is an explosion of tall, airy stems topped with a haze of purple-tinged flowers, and by the autumn the whole plant turns a luminous pale gold. Even in regions where summers are short, this ornamental grass will produce its flowers.

The see-through qualities of 'Variegata' make it ideal as a focal point for the front of a border. Good companions include flowers with a defined shape, such as *Echinops ritro* and *Eryngium* species, or autumn daisies, such as *Aster* and *Rudbeckia*. Plants with contrasting foliage – such as *Hosta*, *Bergenia*, *Heuchera* and *Alchemilla mollis* – make an effective partnership too. This variety is also well worth considering for planting beside a pond or along a path, but bear in mind that it is deciduous and does not hold on to its old leaves and flower stems through the winter like some grasses. Because it does disappear underground, it is wise to mark its position, so you do not forget that it is there and dig it up by mistake.

Like all moor grasses, 'Variegata' prefers a sunny spot in neutral to acidic soil that does not dry out. If your soil is alkaline, you could grow it in a container filled with an ericaceous (lime-free) compost. When buying 'Variegata', opt for a plant that is big enough to give instant impact, as young small plants take a while to become decent-sized clumps. Where space permits, aim to have a group of three or five, with a planting distance of 60 centimeres (24 in.) or so between each one. Alternatively, plant two or three young plants together in the same hole. **GP**

Alternatives

Molinia caerulea subsp. *caerulea* 'Moorhexe', *Molinia caerulea* subsp. *arundinacea* 'Transparent'

Monarda
M. fistulosa

Main features Attracts insects; lavender flowers; aromatic foliage
Height 90–120 cm (3–4 ft) **Spread** 60–90 cm (2–3 ft)
Position ○ ◑ **Hardiness** RHS H7

The *Monarda* is one of the most popular native North American perennials. A hardy, easy-to-grow member of the large and varied mint family, *M. fistulosa* makes an upright plant, its square stems springing from steadily, sometimes vigorously, spreading roots. The slightly purplish stems are clothed in a series of oppositely arranged, oval leaves edged in fine teeth, which have an aromatic fragrance. In summer the stems are topped with branched heads of lavender flowers, which are sometimes formed in two or three tiers. The individual florets are tightly clustered into a slightly domed disk, the first opening in the centre and then falling away as the outer florets open. Each head of flowers is surrounded by leafy bracts. The flower colour varies slightly, and in a large population such as is often seen in open meadows, plants with a range of pale- and dark-lavender flowers may be seen. Plants with white flowers also occur occasionally. **GR**

Alternatives

Monarda 'Aquarius', *Monarda* 'Elsie's Lavender', *Monarda* 'Fire Marshall', *Monarda* 'Fishes'

Monarda
'Marshall's Delight'

Main features Vivid, purple-pink flowers; easy-to-grow, disease-resistant plant; attracts bees and butterflies
Height 90 cm (3 ft) **Spread** 90 cm (3 ft)
Position ○ ◑ **Hardiness** RHS H7

Plants that combine bright and colourful flowers over a long season, a robust habit, good winter hardiness, aromatic foliage and ease of propagation are hard to beat. Fortunately, 'Marshall's Delight' fits all these requirements. It is derived from two favourite North American species: scarlet-flowered *M. didyma* has rich, green foliage and heads of vivid, scarlet flowers; lavender-flowered *M. fistulosa* has paler foliage, to go with flowers in a much softer shade, and is hardier and less troubled by mildew. The result, developed in Canada, is a plant with stout, upright stems clothed in shiny, pale-green foliage. From midsummer to autumn, the tight heads of attractive, arching, two-lipped flowers open consecutively over up to eight weeks, each one a lovely bright pink with purplish overtones. Deadheading will extend the display. The stems last well in a vase, but wait until the flowers are almost all open before cutting. **GR**

Alternatives

Monarda 'Balance', *Monarda* 'Twins', *Monarda* 'Petite Delight'

Monarda 'Marshall's Delight' provides large blooms over a long flowering period. ➲

Monarda
M. citriodora 'Lambada'

Main features Attracts bees, butterflies and hummingbirds; highly aromatic, citrus-scented foliage
Height 30–75 cm (12–30 in.) **Spread** 22–30 cm (9–12 in.)
Position ○ **Hardiness** RHS H2

A hybrid of the lemon bee balm *M. citriodora* (also known as lemon mint or purple horsemint), *M. citriodora* 'Lambada' is a distinctive, elegant form with beautiful, summer-long, tall spires of flowers arranged in circular whorls. The flower heads are a mixture of white and pale mauve, with lovely purple-dotted markings, while the showy bracts are pink. These colour combinations make 'Lambada' especially desirable as a garden plant and as a cutting flower.

As a mixed border or bed plant, it performs well with flowers right up to the first frost. Unlike many *Monarda*, it can tolerate dry conditions and is considered to be less likely to suffer from powdery mildew. This is thanks to the parent *M. citriodora,* a native plant found in dry, sandy, or rocky sites from South Carolina and Florida, westward to Missouri, Texas and Mexico. 'Lambada' is becoming increasingly popular as a cutting flower, and the long flower spikes also dry well with the lemon aroma retained in the foliage. The flowers are loved by bees, butterflies and hummingbirds.

Although 'Lambada' can be considered, along with many other *Monarda*, for wildflower or naturalised planting, its short stature and neatness makes it particularly useful in small gardens for filling in gaps in a herb bed or gravel garden, or as part of a cottage-garden–style bed. It is a first-year flowering perennial and easy to raise from seed, so is often treated as an annual. There are other lovely dwarf *Monarda* that are becoming very popular worldwide for use as container plants, as flowering impact and mildew resistance improves. At only 30 centimetres (12 in.) high, *M. didyma* 'Cranberry Lace' (rose pink), *Monarda* 'Pardon My Pink' (rich pink or purple) and 'Petite Pink Supreme' (cerise pink) are all worth a try. **FRe**

Alternatives

Monarda citriodora, Monarda hybrida 'Bergamo', *Monarda citriodora* subsp. *Austromontana* 'Bees' Favourite'

Monarda
M. punctata

Main features Attracts bees and butterflies; deer
resistant; aromatic foliage
Height 60 cm (24 in.) **Spread** 30 cm (12 in.)
Position ○ ◑ **Hardiness** RHS H7

This *Monarda* differs from most in that it is the noticeable
bracts (leaf-like structures below the true flowers) rather
than the petals that provide the pink, white or purple
colour. Look closely, and you will see the true flowers;
these are generally yellow but can sometimes be white
to green for much of the summer. They have dotted
markings on the petals, which has led to the plant also
being referred to as spotted bee balm, dotted horsemint
or dotted bee balm.

The species is a North American native, found in the
eastern United States, northeastern Mexico and eastern
Canada, and there are ten subspecies. *M. punctata* has a
strong thyme scent due to its high level of the essential
oil thymol. It was commonly used medicinally by Native
American tribes as a treatment for colds, headaches and
fevers. An infusion was also used to treat skin problems,
and it was dried and hung up for its aroma.

Today, we value the distinctive appearance of
M. punctata and the nectar-rich flowers that are enjoyed
by bees and butterflies. If you have enough space, a
mass planting as part of a meadow or as part of a wild
or naturalised garden is very economical because it can
be raised from seeds. Even a couple of plants in a herb
garden or a herbaceous border are worthwhile if you
take appropriate steps to limit their spread. Heights vary
greatly, and plants can reach 1.8 metres (6 ft) in their
natural habitat. In cultivation it is generally much less;
more like 60 centimetres (24 in.) or so. In its native habitat
M. punctata thrives in dry, sandy soil, but it will tolerate
most soil types provided that they are well drained.
However, it may suffer from powdery mildew in high
humidity. *Monarda* spreads by runners to form large
clumps, and it may self-seed prodigiously. Remove the
flowers once they are over in order to limit the latter. **FRe**

Alternatives

*Monarda fistulosa, Monarda didyma, Monarda
bradburiana, Monarda citriodora, Monarda menthifolia*

Myosotidium
M. hortensia

Main features Bold evergreen foliage; clusters of large, blue forget-me-not flowers
Height 45–60 cm (18–24 in.) **Spread** 60 cm (24 in.)
Position ◑ **Hardiness** RHS H4

This plant is a member of the *Boraginaceae* family, which includes heliotrope, comfrey and forget-me-nots. It grows mainly in dunes around the coasts of the Chatham Islands, which are in the Pacific Ocean, a little more than 650 kilometres (400 miles) southeast of New Zealand. It grows nowhere else. Oddly, genetic studies have revealed that its closest relatives in the family are in the genus *Omphalodes*, and the species to which it is most closely allied grows in the Mediterranean. *M. hortensia* is a bold and impressive evergreen perennial for milder areas. From the stout roots emerge broad, rounded, rather succulent leaves with a noticeable pattern of parallel veins. They are slightly reminiscent of the leaves of *Hosta* or *Bergenia*. In early summer, the flowers open, closely resembling those of forget-me-nots, except for their larger size. The individual, five-lobed flowers are usually dark blue in the centre and pale blue at the edges, with a small yellow eye. A white-flowered form is occasionally seen. **GR**

Alternatives

Syn. *Myosotidium nobile*, *Myosotidium hortensia* 'True Blue', *Myosotidium hortensia* white-flowered

Nelumbo
N. nucifera

Main features Ancient sacred plant of all-round beauty; a challenge to grow
Height 60–90 cm (24–36 in.) **Spread** 60–90 cm (24–36 in.)
Position ○ **Hardiness** RHS H7

A symbol of beauty, purity or fertility, as well as being an edible plant with medicinal properties, the sacred lotus has been in cultivation for more than 3,000 years. Above all, *N. nucifera* is a breathtakingly beautiful aquatic plant, and the flowers rise up on long stalks held well above the water's surface. Each flower is fragrant and opens in the morning, but by afternoon the petals start to fall. If fertilised, the subsequent seedpods are works of natural art in themselves: when mature, they bend towards the water's surface and release their seed to give the next generation a chance to grow. The foliage comprises of rounded, dark-green leaves, some of which float on the surface; others are submerged. If you enjoy a plant-growing challenge, you will want to have a go at *N. nucifera*. The most important thing is to give the plant a long, warm growing season to build up its roots. The experience of seeing your first homegrown flower open in the warming sun cannot be beaten. **PM**

Alternatives

Nelumbo nucifera 'Alba Striata', *Nelumbo lutea*, *Nelumbo* 'Emerald Daybreak', *Nelumbo* 'Momo Botan'

Nelumbo nucifera, the sacred lotus, is beautiful, symbolic and a challenge to grow. ➜

Nepeta
N. *grandiflora* 'Bramdean'

Main features Deciduous fragrant foliage; summer-long flowers; attracts bees and other pollinators; deer resistant
Height 75–100 cm (2.5–3.5 ft) **Spread** 60–90 cm (24–36 in.)
Position ○ **Hardiness** RHS H6

An elegant and popular cultivar of *Nepeta*, this plant was deservedly recognised with the Royal Horticultural Society Award of Garden Merit in 2012. Grown for many years in the double, mirror-image herbaceous borders of the renowned garden of Bramdean House in Hampshire, England, it was reintroduced for sale in the mid-1980s under the name *N. grandiflora* 'Bramdean'. It is favoured for its particularly long spikes of delightful deep-blue tubular flowers. Furthermore, its shape is striking because it offers stronger, upright stems and an open, less dense shape than some other *Nepeta* varieties, making it less likely to fall onto paths when used as a border or edging plant.

The billowing forms of *Nepeta* are great garden stalwarts because they are easy to grow and maintain, as well as being long-lasting. They work well as edging plants, where they are renowned for their architectural shape, aromatic grey-green foliage and summer-long flower spikes. Excellent companions in planting schemes, they are often used as ground cover for rose beds and can be interspersed in traditional herbaceous borders with complementary or contrasting planting. If you find cats a problem, *Nepeta* has a euphoric effect on the feline species, so consider growing some of their favourite *N. cataria* elsewhere to act as a decoy. 'Bramdean' flowers over a long period during the summer, but by cutting it back after its first bloom, this variety will flower again in the same season.

This plant does particularly well in a position where the border is deep, the soil is well drained and the aspect is sunny. 'Bramdean' also fits in well when planted in drifts within Mediterranean-style plantings, gravel gardens or in limey garden soil, such as that at Bramdean House. **FRe**

Alternatives

Nepeta racemosa 'Walker's Low', *Nepeta* × *faassenii*, *Nepeta* 'Six Hills Giant'

Nepeta
N. subsessilis

Main features Deciduous fragrant foliage; summer-long flowers; good cut flower; attracts butterflies
Height 50–100 cm (20–40 in.) **Spread** 45–60 cm (18–24 in.)
Position ◑ **Hardiness** RHS H6

The *N. subsessilis* is an easy-to-grow and striking, strong, bushy, upright variety. The large, deep, violet-blue, tubular flowers at the end of erect stems last all summer. By cutting back after first flowering, both a more compact shape and repeat flowers will be achieved. A native of the moist mountain slopes of Japan, *N. subsessilis* is more cold, moisture and shade tolerant than many of the other varieties of *Nepeta*, but unlike these forms *N. subsessilis* is not a drought-tolerant choice. Its allure is enhanced by its extremely large, slightly glossy, fragrant leaves, which are a richer green than the grey-green shades of other cultivars. In addition, it is hard to ignore the plant's appeal as a sturdy mid- or edge-of-border choice that combines particularly well with paler-toned neighbours, such as those with pink and grey hues. Similarly, the strong shape and summer-long colour of *N. subsessilis* make it a great option for container growing or rock gardens. Although, like all *Nepeta*, it can be attractive to cats, it is a less popular choice. When mature it spreads underground but is not invasive.

N. subsessilis has also been cultivated to produce a number of delightful forms, including some compact varieties. 'Laufen' is a very striking smaller version in which the leaves and the flowers are very large in proportion to the plant size, whereas 'Nimbus' is only 25 centimetres (10 in.) in height and spread, with distinctive lip markings on purple-blue flowers. There are also some pink-flowering compact forms, such as 'Pink Dreams' and 'Sweet Dreams'. Alternatively, try some other species of *Nepeta*, such as *N. manchuriensis* 'Manchu Blue', which has beautiful, large, lavender-colour flowers and is thought to be more damp tolerant than most varieties, or *N. sibirica*, which is hardier than most and has large blue flowers. **FRe**

Alternatives

Nepeta sibirica, Nepeta yunnanensis, Nepeta troodii, Nepeta manchuriensis

Nymphaea
'James Brydon'

Main features Peony-like flowers; green foliage
blotched with purple
Height 10 cm (4 in.) **Spread** 1.5 m (5 ft)
Position ○ **Hardiness** RHS H7

The 'James Brydon' is a true beauty of a water lily. It produces peony-like, carmine-red flowers and a delicious scent of ripe apples. Like most water lilies, it prefers to grow in still water, and for this variety a minimum water depth of 50 centimetres (20 in.) is required. It needs a sunny position, and once happy, the flowers – with orange stamen to add to the colour burst – are produced in summer and can reach 13 centimetres (5 in.) in diameter. 'James Brydon' is also an adaptable variety that can survive in less than perfect conditions, hence it has a Royal Horticultural Society Award of Garden Merit. In order to keep the plant looking good, it is best to remove the flowers as they fade. This encourages new growth, but also stops the risk of nutrient imbalance in the pond due to the dead blooms rotting down. Remember that blooms will close in the early evening and night, reopening in the midday sun, so wait until they start to turn brown before removing them. **PM**

Alternatives

Nymphaea 'Pink Sensation', *Nymphaea* 'Marliacea Flammea'

Nymphaea
'Marliacea Chromatella'

Main feature Aquatic plant grown for its summer
flowers and speckled foliage
Height 10 cm (4 in.) **Spread** 90–150 cm (3–5 ft)
Position ○ **Hardiness** RHS H7

This water lily is a superb choice for any still-water pond. It produces numerous flowers for a long period, and although it is a very old variety, it is highly recommended and has a Royal Horticultural Society Award of Garden Merit. 'Marliacea Chromatella' prefers a sunny position but is tolerant of shade as long as it receives four hours of sun a day. The blooms are large, reaching 15 centimetres (6 in.) in diameter, and appear from midsummer through to the start of autumn. The olive-green leaves have purple splashes, which are useful to mark out this variety when growing it alongside plain, green-leaved varieties, as if the plants grow into one another, you can separate them. 'Marliacea Chromatella' will grow in quite shallow water for a water lily and will adapt to a medium-sized or large pond: a depth of 25 centimetres (10 in.) of water is sufficient. It benefits from a feed once growth is underway in late spring and will flower consistently after it has been established for a couple of years. **PM**

Alternatives

Nymphaea 'Moorei', *Nymphaea* 'Odorata Sulphurea Grandiflora'

⬅ *Nymphaea* 'James Brydon' is a reliable, hardy water lily for garden ponds of all sizes.

Omphalodes
O. cappadocica 'Cherry Ingram'

Main features Sprays of small, blue, forget-me-not-like flowers; oval-shaped, mid-green, evergreen foliage
Height 20–30 cm (8–12 in.) **Spread** 40 cm (16 in.)
Position ◐ ● **Hardiness** RHS H7

Carpeting the ground with oval evergreen leaves, this unassuming but useful woodlander sparkles in spring when it produces airy sprays of small blue flowers that fade to violet. The tiny blooms have the same charm as those of its relative the forget-me-not, but *Omphalodes* is a perennial and will form a permanent feature in the garden, creating a weed-suppressing layer of lush green foliage. For the best results grow *O. cappadocica* 'Cherry Ingram' in partial shade at the front of a border with a backdrop of ferns, *Hosta* and *Dicentra formosa*. Ideal for a woodland setting beneath deciduous trees and shrubs, it also combines well with dwarf daffodils that flower at the same time, presenting an eye-catching colour combination. Or add it to a shady rock garden with *Viola*, *Primula* and *Erythronium* for a colourful spring display. Native to Turkey, *Omphalodes* prefers moist, well-drained soil and is best planted in autumn or early spring. **ZA**

Alternatives

Omphalodes cappadocica 'Starry Eyes,' *Omphalodes verna*, *Omphalodes verna* 'Alba'

Onoclea
O. sensibilis

Main features Attractive divided foliage; vigorous spreading plants
Height 30–60 cm (12–24 in.) **Spread** 60 cm (24 in.)
Position ◐ ● **Hardiness** RHS H7

Ferns are often rather lacy in their looks, with delicate, repeatedly divided foliage. However, although *O. sensibilis* has a slightly ferny look, you would be forgiven for mistaking it for a flowering perennial – at first. From a slender creeping root, which can spread quickly when plants are growing well, leaves are held on individual stems; each green frond is egg-shaped in outline but is actually divided into a pair of lobed leaflets. The stems of the fronds are coppery in colour, and the whole frond may be tinged pink in spring as its fiddleheads unfurl. Ferns reproduce not from flowers but from spores. In most ferns these develop as rusty patches on the undersides of the fronds, but in *O. sensibilis* it works differently. In late summer, amongst the mature leafy fronds, growth carrying only spores develops. This resembles a vertically branched twig lined with black beads, and these beads are what produce the spores from which new plants develop. **GR**

Alternatives

Osmunda cinnamomea, Osmunda claytoniana, Osmunda japonica, Osmunda regalis

Ophiopogon
O. planiscapus
'Nigrescens'

Main features Inky-black, evergreen leaves; spikes of small, bell-shaped, pale-mauve or white summer flowers
Height 25–30 cm (10–12 in.) **Spread** 30 cm (12 in.)
Position ○ ◑ **Hardiness** RHS H6

Masquerading as a grass, this compact evergreen perennial has jet-black, arching leaves that appeal to many garden designers. The tufted foliage is joined in summer by short spikes of tiny, white or pale-mauve, bell-shaped flowers, followed by shiny, black berries, which add to the plant's glamorous good looks. *O. planiscapus* 'Nigrescens' needs a pale backdrop to shine, because its impact will be lost in a bed surrounded by soil. Plant it in gravel or against contrasting gold, silver or bright-green-leaved plants, such as *Heuchera*, *Asplenium scolopendrium*, and the sedge *Carex siderosticha* 'Variegata'. 'Nigrescens' is also a beautiful container plant, ideal for terra-cotta and stone pots. Or use it in blocks in a contemporary scheme alongside other textured, low-growing plants, such as *Echeveria* or *Stachys*. 'Nigrescens' is easy to grow, when given moist but free-draining soil and a position in sun or partial shade. Plant it in early autumn or spring. **ZA**

Alternatives

Ophiopogon planiscapus 'Little Tabby', *Pennisetum setaceum* 'Rubrum', *Uncinia rubra*

Origanum
'Rosenkuppel'

Main feature Purple flowers and bracts on neat dome-shaped plants
Height 35 cm (14 in.) **Spread** 30 cm (12 in.)
Position ○ **Hardiness** RHS H7

It is convenient to split marjorams and oreganos, all of which are classified under *Origanum*, into two groups: those that are aromatic and useful in the kitchen, and those that are less aromatic but valued as ornamentals. Among the latter species, with a less-pungent aroma than others that are grown as ornamentals, *O. laevigatum* is one of the most popular. It is the parent of the cultivar 'Rosenkuppel', which is a neat and prolific form with a mass of purple summer flowers opening amongst purple bracts, which provide colour after the flowers have faded. 'Rosenkuppel' has a valuable role in naturalistic- or prairie-style planting schemes, where it weaves around amongst ornamental grasses or more solid shapes, such as the larger sedums. Garden designer Piet Oudolf has used the long-lasting colour it provides as part of his large-scale plantings at Scampston Hall in North Yorkshire. It will also add interest to a gravel garden or as path edging. **GR**

Alternatives

Origanum 'Barbara Tingey', *Origanum* 'Kent Beauty', *Origanum* 'Rotkugel'

Osmunda
O. regalis

Main features Architectural plant; fine foliage
Height 1.5–2.4 m (5–8 ft) **Spread** 45–90 cm (18–36 in.)
Position ◐ ●
Hardiness RHS H7

There is nothing quite like *O. regalis*; its height gives it a truly regal stature. Lush tropical looks hint at the exotic, but in reality disguise its hardiness, and it is one of the tallest ferns that can be grown in cooler temperate regions. Spring's arrival sees its fronds begin to unfurl. As they unfold, colour changes from coppery brown, through green in summer, to red brown, yellow tan and darker shades in autumn. Fine-textured summer foliage contrasts well with larger-leaved plants that thrive in similar conditions, such as *Gunnera*, *Ligularia* and *Rodgersia*. *O. regalis* cultivars of interest include 'Cristata' – with fronds, pinnae and pinnules that are forked or crested at the tips, giving them a frilled appearance – and 'Purpurascens', with new spring growth that is purplish in colour. *O. regalis* is easy to grow. It thrives in the moist, peaty soil of poorly drained bogs or at the edges of streams and ponds, where roots are kept cool. Prune old leaves in late winter to allow new fronds to emerge. **RC**

Alternatives

Osmunda regalis 'Cristata', *Osmunda regalis* 'Purpurascens', *Osmunda cinnamomea*, *Osmunda claytoniana*

◷ *Osmunda regalis*, the regal fern, showing its autumn colours at Cambridge Botanic Garden.

Osteospermum
'Weetwood'

Main feature Long season of bright-eyed white daisies
Height 20 cm (8 in.) **Spread** 40 cm (16 in.)
Position ○
Hardiness RHS H4

The 'Weetwood' is one of the hardier varieties in the genus. Its spreading stems are clothed with greyish, evergreen leaves, and from early summer into the autumn, the flowers stand up on single stems. Each sparkling flower has bright-white ray petals, with a narrow purple ring around the eye. The unopened anthers in the centre of the eye are blue; they open to yellow and mature to bronze, thereby creating a series of concentric rings. The other osteospermums are a mixed bunch and include annuals, perennials and dwarf evergreen shrubs. There are about seventy species, most of them growing wild in South Africa, but with a few from the mountains of Yemen and Saudi Arabia. All have linear or reverse egg-shaped leaves, the edges of which may be smooth, toothed or lobed, and their daisy flowers are either held singly or in branched sprays. The flowers come in shades of pink, yellow or white, although other colours have been developed in gardens. **GR**

Alternatives

Osteospermum 'Cannington Roy', *Osteospermum* 'Lady Leitrim', *Osteospermum* 'Nairobi Purple'

Pachysandra
P. terminalis

Main features Neat carpet of year-round foliage; fragrant flowers in spring
Height 20–25 cm (8–10 in.) **Spread** 40 cm (16 in.)
Position ○ ◑ ● **Hardiness** RHS H5

This plant is a member of the small boxwood family, *Buxaceae*, and is native to Japan, Korea and China. It tends to be a 'love it' or 'hate it' sort of plant, but when growing well, it is extremely useful. *P. terminalis* makes an evergreen carpet of stems, growing from spreading rhizomes and topped by a cluster of dark-green, leathery leaves with random serrated edges. In spring erect spikes of greenish-white flowers appear, which consist of a cluster of prominent stamen. They are not the most strikingly beautiful flowers, but they are sweetly scented.

This versatile, hardy perennial, or subshrub, is perfect for growing in sunny or shady locations. It is slow to spread, so should be planted fairly close together if reasonably rapid ground cover is to be achieved. It prefers a neutral to acidic soil that is well drained, but it is capable of tolerating reasonable drought periods.

Although not perhaps the most attractive of plants, when grown as a raft of ground cover, *P. terminalis* is a useful workhorse and looks best with deciduous shrubs emerging from it. Its tolerance of shade makes it extremely valuable. Try using it to underplant a specimen of the wedding cake tree, *Cornus controversa* 'Variegata', where the dark-green *Pachysandra* foliage would contrast with the white-variegated *Cornus* leaves, or plant a group of three white clematis up stylish obelisks in a large circle of *Pachysandra* in a sunny position. Both the white variegated form, *P. terminalis* 'Variegata' (pictured), and the plain green form make useful woodland floor plants.

Known as Japanese spurge, *P. terminalis* looks effective in Japanese garden-style plantings, whether used on a large scale as a horizontal surface or as small tufts in amongst moss. One of the few plants that can grow under yellow-stemmed bamboo, it makes an excellent foil to the vertical yellow canes. **MP**

Alternatives

Pachysandra terminalis 'Green Carpet', *Pachysandra terminalis* 'Green Sheen'

Paeonia
'Bartzella'

Main feature Abundance of long-lasting, lemon-yellow, frilly flowers, each with a touch of egg yolk in the middle
Height 60–90 cm (2–3 ft) **Spread** 75–90 cm (2.5–3 ft)
Position ○ **Hardiness** RHS H5

This short, showstopping, hybrid peony can, once it is happy and established, produce fifty to sixty 20-centimetre-wide (8 in.), fragrant, lemon-yellow, semi-double blooms. It resembles a tree peony in form, with woody stems, but it only reaches between 60 and 90 centimetres (2–3 ft) in height. It is also sterile, meaning that it does not produce seeds, and this accounts for its flower power and its ability to hang onto its flowers for weeks.

'Bartzella' was raised in the United States in 1976 by Roger Anderson, a peony breeder. He had been inspired by an earlier Japanese breeder called Toichi Itoh, who made 1200 crosses in the mid-1960s before finally persuading the yellow tree peony *P. × lemoinei* 'Alice Harding' and the double-white *P. lactiflora* 'Kakoden' to set seeds. Sadly, Itoh died before any of the plants flowered, but his son-in-law carried on his work. Luckily, US peony enthusiast Louis Smirnow recognised the plant's potential and introduced the Itoh hybrids into the United States, thus encouraging a new wave of breeding. 'Bartzella' took the United States by storm, so much so that customers were paying a thousand dollars for one root. Thankfully, it is now much more affordable, and just as glorious.

Alternative Itoh hybrids with different colour blooms include 'Cora Louise' (large, semi-double, white flowers with purple at the centre) and 'First Arrival' (very large, semi-double, pink flowers with a centre of yellow stamen). *Paeonia* should be left alone undisturbed in a border because if the roots are lifted and divided, flowering may be disrupted. In autumn gather up any dead leaves and dispose of them. Although 'Bartzella' is a tree peony hybrid, this cultivar will die down in winter, so mark its presence well for the next season, so it is not disturbed accidentally. **VB**

Alternatives

Paeonia 'Cora Louise', *Paeonia* 'First Arrival', *Paeonia* 'Going Bananas'

Paeonia

'Coral Sunset'

Main feature Shallow, saucer-shaped, orange-tinted petals surrounding a boss of insect-friendly stamen
Height 90 cm (3 ft) **Spread** 60–90 cm (2–3 ft)
Position ○ **Hardiness** RHS H7

This US-bred hybrid peony, jointly released by Samuel Wissing and Carl Klehm in 1981, is the best of the coral, orange-toned, and coral-pink peonies. When mature, one clump of 'Coral Sunset' will produce twenty saucer-shaped flowers, and these will gradually change colour from apricot to coral pink before fading to shades of pale yellow and clotted cream. If you want a peachier flower opt, for 'Coral Charm', or if shocking pink is preferred, plant 'Pink Hawaiian Coral'.

'Coral Sunset' was a late arrival, because earlier breeding had concentrated on producing pinks, whites and reds, which sold well as cut flowers. This peony is superb when picked at the 'marshmallow' stage – the size of an average marshmallow – and the blooms can be left to open naturally or coldstored until needed. Long-lived and hardy, peonies make excellent flowers for a picking garden. In the vase 'Coral Sunset' changes colour from day to day; in the garden it will also change, but more slowly. With handsome foliage, it mixes well with shorter roses, such as floribundas, or can be used in an early-summer herbaceous border. Peonies often flower best if left undisturbed, so choose the initial planting site with care, making sure it is sunny. Winter cold promotes more flower buds with peonies, so place the tuberous roots just 5 centimetres (2 in.) below the ground, because planting too deeply or too shallowly can adversely affect future flowering. **VB**

Alternatives

Paeonia 'Coral Charm', *Paeonia* 'Pink Hawaiian Coral', *Paeonia* 'Claire de Lune', *Paeonia* 'Buckeye Belle'

Paeonia
P. *lactiflora* 'Duchesse de Nemours'

Main feature Fully double, cream-white peony with a heavenly citrus scent
Height 90 cm (3 ft) **Spread** 60 90 cm (2–3 ft)
Position ○ **Hardiness** RHS H7

This French peony, bred by Jacques Calot in 1856, dazzles on every front, with its glossy, green foliage and fully double, cream-white flowers that demand to be sniffed. They do not disappoint, either: there is a hint of lemon from the moment the flowers open. It is a distinctive fragrance that makes them good in a vase or a border. The pale 'Duchesse de Nemours' is best used with bright roses, such as the deep-pink 'You're Beautiful' and deep-mauve 'Rhapsody in Blue' because they will flatter each other. Although there is only one flush of flower, the handsome foliage endures until autumn.

'Duchesse de Nemours' is one of many peonies bred for the cut-flower trade. Breeder Félix Crousse bought

Calot's nursery stock after his death and went on to produce the bombe-shaped, double-pink 'Monsieur Jules Elie' and the magenta-carmine P. *lactiflora* 'Félix Crousse'. Victor Lemoine then acquired Crousse's collection in this game of 'pass the peony' and came up with the pretty, pink 'Sarah Bernhardt' and the 'Solange'. The latter has cream-white blooms with a hint of salmon-pink. P. *lactiflora* hybrids come in many flower forms, from single to stamen-packed Japanese. However, fully double flowers last longer in the garden and can shrug off summer rain, having evolved in Japan and China, where there is a six-week rainy season just as the plants flower. Support the plants with semicircular metal hoops to prevent them from drooping during downpours. **VB**

Alternatives

Paeonia lactiflora 'Monsieur Jules Elie', *Paeonia lactiflora* 'Solange'

Papaver
P. orientale 'Karine'

Main features Attractive leaves; flowers in early summer; attracts bees
Height 60 cm (24 in.)   **Spread** 60 cm (24 in.)
Position ○   **Hardiness** RHS H7

Oriental poppies have extravagant, blowsy flowers that demand attention in the garden, and with a host of tempting colours to chose from, it can be hard to make a decision on which varieties to grow. *P. orientale* 'Karine' is a bit different in that it is daintier than most. The simple, saucer-shaped flowers have delicate colouring that is much less glaring than many poppies, the subtle shade of pink providing a gentle contrast to splashes of beetroot-purple at the base of the petals, and the froth of dark-purple stamen. These flowers, although typically short-lived, are large, plentiful and held face-up, waiting to be admired. The stems of 'Karine' are slender, so the flowers dance around in the lightest breeze. They are surprisingly strong, though, so there is rarely any need for elaborate support. The delicate look of the flowers is deceptive, as the waxy petals hold their shape well, even after heavy rain, and their open shape makes life easy for the many bees that are attracted to them. **JS**

Alternatives

Papaver orientale 'Lady Frederick Moore', *Papaver orientale* 'Patty's Plum', *Papaver* 'Bright Star' Super Poppy Series

Pennisetum
P. setaceum 'Rubrum'

Main features Accent plant with attractive foliage; seed heads in winter; flowers in summer
Height 1.2 m (4 ft)   **Spread** 90 cm (3 ft)
Position ○   **Hardiness** RHS H2

The strong combination of colour and shape makes this plant one of the most dramatic-looking grasses to grow. Glossy, burgundy foliage grows in narrow-based clumps that arch outwards, the tips of the leaves almost reaching the ground when fully grown. The look is completed in summer by a throng of eye-catching purple flower spikes that can almost cover the leaves. They are long, fluffy and irresistibly tactile. A fast-growing grass, *P. setaceum* 'Rubrum' can reach a substantial size in one season. It is best grown in full sun in well-drained soil, and once established, it will romp away even in dry conditions. The mass of flower stems start to open in midsummer, and flower heads gradually fade to beige in late summer. Seed heads have burgundy tints and can be left on the plant until no longer attractive. The plant often keeps its shape over winter. If there is space, 'Rubrum' looks stylish planted in groups with *Veronicastrum virginicum* 'Album' and works well as an accent plant in a mixed border. **JS**

Alternatives

Pennisetum setaceum 'Vertigo', *Pennisetum glaucum* 'Purple Majesty', *Pennisetum alopecuroides* 'Hameln'

Pennisetum setaceum **'Rubrum'** dotted around a summer bed adds texture and movement, thanks to its flower spikes. ●

Penstemon

'Andenken an Friedrich Hahn'

Main features Summer flowers of good colour; attracts bees; long flowering
Height 60 cm (24 in.) **Spread** 30 cm (12 in.)
Position ○ **Hardiness** RHS H5

This Swiss-bred *Penstemon*, raised by Hermann Wartmann in about 1918, was introduced in the 1930s by Alan Bloom. He gave it the name 'Garnet', and it is still sold under this name. 'Andenken an Friedrich Hahn' is arguably the finest of the garden varieties because the rich, red-burgundy flowers appear to glow. The narrow foliage makes the plant long-lived and hardier than many other types, and the tubular flowers are slender and graceful rather than fat and flared. In addition, 'Andenken an Friedrich Hahn' produces numerous bee-friendly spikes starting in midsummer.

The various species of *Penstemon* vary in hardiness. Do not be tempted to cut back the plants in the autumn, because it will kill them off. This may mean that you are stuck with ragged plants during bad winters. However, few plants flower for as long or as late in the year as 'Andenken an Friedrich Hahn', so it is worth putting up with any winter shabbiness and cutting them back in late spring. Deadheading will encourage more flowers.

Take cuttings in summer, preferably fairly early. Select pieces of semiripe growth – with a little strength in the stem – and pick off the flower buds if necessary. The cuttings root easily in a mixture of sand and compost, or grit and compost, as well as in one hundred per cent coarse horticultural sand. Overwinter the cuttings and pot up in spring so that you can plant out a rooted young plant in early summer. **VB**

Alternatives

Syn. *Penstemon* 'Garnet', *Penstemon heterophyllus*, *Penstemon* 'Alice Hindley'

Penstemon
P. *digitalis* 'Husker Red'

Main features Semi-evergreen with attractive leaves; flowers early to midsummer; attracts bees and butterflies
Height 90 cm (3 ft) **Spread** 45 cm (18 in.)
Position ○ ◐ **Hardiness** RHS H7

In any garden it makes sense to have some plants like *P. digitalis* 'Husker Red' that are unfussy but look good over a long period. As the plants start to grow in spring, the new leaves are deep purple, matching the upright stems. Later, the leaves become dark green, with purple tints and veins, but the stems remain dark purple and make a good contrast to long racemes of white tubular flowers, which often have a fetching pink blush.

Once the flowers are fully out, the stems may start to lean, especially if plants are being grown on fertile soil and have become tall. However, they rarely need staking and are easily supported by surrounding plants. It is best to deadhead whole stems when flowering finishes, as the dead flowers tend to hang on and can spoil the look of the plants. Flowering begins in early summer, as is expected with *Penstemon*, but once it finishes, which usually occurs in midsummer, 'Husker Red' rarely reflowers. The foliage effect will still be good, though, and can last into the early days of winter if frost is light, only becoming damaged when harder frost sets in. Whatever happens to the stems during winter, it is best to leave them on until spring, when any damaged parts can be trimmed.

This versatile plant looks good in a variety of situations. Try it with grasses in prairie-type plantings, with other perennials in a mixed border or in a wildflower garden where it will attract pollinating insects. **JS**

Alternatives

Penstemon 'Dark Towers', *Penstemon* 'Blackbird', *Penstemon* 'Raven'

Penstemon
'Raven'

Main feature Sultry plant with beautifully marked sooty flowers
Height 90 cm (3 ft) Spread 30 cm (12 in.)
Position ○ Hardiness RHS H3

This almost-black penstemon is the best of Ron Sidwell's Bird Series, which was bred on Bredon Hill in Worcestershirein the 1970s. Other notable 'birds' include 'Osprey' and 'Blackbird'. He plotted the Worcestershire hills for frost-free positions in order to site plum orchards, and built a house on one of the most benign spots. Once there, he collected southern-hemisphere plants with less-than-hardy dispositions – including penstemons from Mexico.

'Raven' is beautifully marked, with flared flowers barred in smoky lilac and purple, but no white. The backs of the flowers look almost sooty, so it is excellent with all silvers, such as *Lavandula*, *Artemisia* and *Salvia*. Care must be taken to give it some space, because this glamorous penstemon is not the strongest grower. As long as the plant has enough room, placing 'Raven' is easy because its low spires of flower mingle well in a traditional border. However, flower size varies among cultivars, and those with slender trumpets are easier to position. Once planted, it is reliable and will often flower until late autumn.

Penstemon is native to North and Central Americas. It has been cultivated extensively in Europe, and breeding continues to be centred near Pershore, in Worcestershire. The genus belongs to *Scrophulariaceae*, a free-flowering family that includes snapdragons and foxgloves. Of the 250 species of *Penstemon*, most prefer well-drained soil and sun. However, it is possible to add grit or build up raised beds to improve drainage, and some garden varieties are tolerant of light shade. These repeat-flowering plants benefit from deadheading, which will keep them in flower until late in the year. Hardiness can be a problem, so success will depend on where you live, and how well your soil drains over winter. **VB**

Alternatives

Penstemon 'Stapleford Gem', *Penstemon* 'Hidcote Pink', *Penstemon* 'Osprey', *Penstemon* 'Blackbird'

Perovskia
P. atriplicifolia 'Little Spire'

Main features Spires of tiny violet-blue flowers; silver-grey, aromatic leaves; attracts bees and butterflies
Height 60 cm (24 in.) **Spread** 60 cm (24 in.)
Position ○ **Hardiness** RHS H7

Compact and aromatic, the small, silver-grey leaves of this woody-based perennial have a sage-like scent when crushed, and from late summer to autumn, the slender grey-white stems terminate in cloud-like clusters of tiny, tubular, violet-blue flowers. This Russian sage cultivar is a valuable addition to the garden, introducing plenty of late colour and structure and masking the fading flowers of early-season blooms.

Weave ribbons of *P. atriplicifolia* 'Little Spire' through the front of a border or gravel garden alongside other late-season performers, such as *Echinacea*, *Aster amellus*, *Sedum*, and ornamental grasses. You can use this compact plant for edging paths too, where the intense scent from the leaves will be released as visitors brush past. It is also ideal for coastal gardens, since it shrugs off the effects of salt-laden winds, and for wildlife schemes, where the numerous spires of flowers will lure butterflies and bees.

Although the foliage smells of sage or lavender, *Perovskia* is actually a member of the mint family. However, unlike mint, it prefers free-draining soil and a sunny position – if the soil is too fertile, it will produce leaves at the expense of the flowers. Plant it in a raised bed or large container if the garden has heavy clay. Although 'Little Spire' is less likely to flop than its taller cousins, it is still advisable to prune the stems in late spring to encourage bushy growth. Cut them back to about 15 centimetres (6 in.) from the ground when the leaf buds start to open; do not be tempted to do this earlier as the plant may die. Other good Russian sages to try include *P. atriplicifolia* 'Blue Spire', the taller parent of 'Little Spire', which boasts the same flowers and foliage. 'Filigran' is also tall and has more finely cut leaves and an upright habit. **ZA**

Alternatives

Perovskia atriplicifolia, *Perovskia atriplicifolia* 'Blue Spire', *Perovskia* 'Filigran'

Persicaria
P. amplexicaulis Taurus

Phlomis
P. russeliana

Main features Flowers in summer and autumn; good cut flower; attracts butterflies
Height 90–120 cm (3–4 ft) **Spread** 60 cm (24 in.)
Position ○ ◐ **Hardiness** RHS H7

Main features Flowers in summer; architectural plant; attracts bees and butterflies
Height 90 cm (3 ft) **Spread** 60–90 cm (2–3 ft)
Position ○ ◐ **Hardiness** RHS H7

Originating in the Himalayas, this useful, robust, herbaceous perennial belongs to the knotweed family (*Polygonaceae*). Handsome, bold, pointed, heart-shaped leaves that clasp the stems emerge in spring and make a good weed-repelling clump. In midsummer, slender, upright, flowering stems appear, topped with clusters of small but showy, vibrant, red flower spikes. *P. amplexicaulis* Taurus is renowned for its long flowering season. The striking foliage is effective from early summer, whereas the flowers will keep the plant looking good well into autumn. Taurus associates particularly well with ornamental grasses – such as the shorter *Miscanthus*, *Pennisetum* or *Calamagrostis* – in a prairie-style planting, along with the blue flowers of *Scutellaria incana* and the fluffy heads of *Aruncus* 'Horatio'. Its long flowering season makes it a valuable member in a herbaceous border or mixed with other cottage-garden–style plants. MP

This easy member of the deadnettle family (*Lamiaceae*) has heart-shaped, coarse-textured, virtually evergreen leaves. In summer the flower stems have tightly clustered whorls of mid-yellow, hooded flowers at intervals up the stems. The flowers open in succession to give a long-lasting display all summer. In autumn, the flower-stem leaves drop, leaving brown stems studded at intervals with the brown flower bracts. These winter seed heads are enjoyed by birds. The summer show is good, but when *P. russeliana* is planted in association with the buff winter foliage of ornamental grasses such as *Calamagrostis* × *acutiflora* 'Karl Foerster' or *Miscanthus sinensis* 'Yakushima Dwarf' – along with the orange-red stems of *Cornus sanguinea* 'Midwinter Fire' or *Cornus sericea* 'Cardinal' – the winter effect is stunning. *P. russeliana* is also a handsome spreading plant that makes an excellent weed-suppressant ground cover. MP

Alternatives

= 'Blotau'. *Persicaria amplexicaulis* 'Orange Field', *Persicaria amplexicaulis* 'Alba', *Persicaria amplexicaulis* 'Rosea'

Alternatives

Phlomis italica, *Phlomis tuberosa* 'Amazone', *Phlomis fruticosa*

Phlomis

P. tuberosa 'Amazone'

Phlox

P. paniculata 'Uspekh'

Main features Prolific purple stems; clusters of lavender-purple flowers
Height 1.5 m (5 ft) **Spread** 90 cm (3 ft)
Position ○ **Hardiness** RHS H7

Main features Short, eye-catching, purple-and-white flowers; attracts insects; excellent cut flower
Height 60–75 cm (24–30 in.) **Spread** 60–75 cm (24–30 in.) **Position** ○ **Hardiness** RHS H7

This is an upright plant with tuberous roots that are said to be edible, and it grows on well-drained slopes and meadows in Europe and Asia. The soft, arrow-shaped, deeply veined green leaves are up to 25 centimetres (10 in.) long, and in summer there are clusters of 2.5-centimetre-long (1 in.) lavender-purple flowers. 'Amazone' develops a mass of distinctive, upright, purple flowering stems, which are surprisingly good for cutting. When the flowers have faded, the seed heads are attractive, so refrain from deadheading until they look ragged. This is a drought-tolerant plant, once established, and although the roots spread widely, the top growth develops from a tight crown. There are a hundred *Phlomis* species, and they include herbaceous perennials, along with evergreen, woody-based perennials and shrubs. Many combine fine ornamental qualities with fragrant foliage, but some are grown solely as ornamentals. **GR**

The hardiness of this North American *Phlox* has made it a popular plant in Europe and Russia, where winters are particularly savage. *P. paniculata* 'Uspekh' is a short purple variety, smartened up by a bright-white eye piped onto each flower. What it lacks in stature is made up by sheer flower power, because 'Uspekh' produces lots of stems topped with well-spaced, large flowers. It will also repeat flower when deadheaded, giving a long show of fragrant flowers in an unusual cool-purple hue. Add some garden flair by placing it in front of an orange *Crocosmia*, or plant it at the front of an autumn border to add some sultry touches. The mophead shape of the flower, arriving from the second half of summer onwards, breaks up the monopoly of the rayed daisy, so it is superb in a mixed border. The stiff stems and foliage are also a feature, and some varieties, such as 'Starfire', have almost black foliage. **VB**

Alternatives

Phlomis russeliana, Phlomis samia, Phlomis tuberosa 'Bronze Flamingo'

Alternatives

Phlox paniculata 'Franz Schubert', *Phlox paniculata* 'Miss Ellie'

Phlox

P. *divaricata* subsp. *laphamii* 'Chattahoochee'

Main features Pale lavender-blue flowers with crimson eyes; purple winter foliage
Height 30 cm (12 in.) **Spread** 60 cm (24 in.)
Position ○ ◑   **Hardiness** RHS H7

The *Phlox* was among the first American native plants to be sent back to the Old World after the Americas were settled. The various species are some of the most colourful plants in the landscape, and early settlers would have come across them almost everywhere in what was to become the United States and Canada.

With the exception of one variety grown widely as an annual, most species are evergreen or deciduous perennials, but they vary from tall, upright, summer-flowering plants to low, spring-flowering creepers. They grow in a range of habitats, from woodland to dry Mexican country. One of those most often seen in the eastern forests, and of most value to gardeners, is *P. divaricata*.

This species is a neat plant of rich woodland soils, and it sometimes occurs in impressive, widely spreading colonies. From among glossy, lance-shaped leaves arise vertical stems topped by loose heads of up to thirty flowers. The flowers, each about 2 centimetres (0.75 in.) across, are described as light blue, but they are often more of a lavender or lavender-blue shade. Found in the wild in Florida, *P. divaricata* subsp. *laphamii* 'Chattahoochee' was introduced in the mid-1940s. It is noted for its pale lavender-blue flowers, each with a crimson centre, and foliage that turns deep purple in winter. Since then, a number of similar plants have been grown under the 'Chattahoochee' name, and all retain these basic features. Plants flower most prolifically in just a little shade. **GR**

Alternatives

Phlox divaricata 'Chattahoochee Variegated', *Phlox divaricata* 'Clouds of Perfume'

Phlox
P. paniculata 'Monica Lynden-Bell'

Main features Fragrant silver-pink flowers with dark stems; handsome green foliage
Height 90 cm (3 ft) **Spread** 90 cm (3 ft)
Position ○ **Hardiness** RHS H7

The *P. paniculata* 'Monica Lynden-Bell' was named in the 1970s after the Hampshire gardener who discovered this seedling in her garden. It is now widely grown and admired for its silver-pink flowers that emerge from dark buds above good, green foliage. It is one of three species of *Phlox* that tolerate poor soil; the other two are the variegated *P. paniculata* 'Norah Leigh' and the white and airy *P. paniculata* 'Alba Grandiflora'. All three thrive in dry conditions and on light or chalky soil.

Phlox was an Edwardian favourite that was planted in every garden, but the plants fell from favour largely due to timing. These late-summer performers look ragged in garden centres because pot culture does not suit them.

Try to get 'Monica Lynden-Bell' early in the year. Most plants will need deep, fertile soil, and summer rain to avoid mildew, but they are capable of thriving on light soil and in drier conditions.

Luckily, *Phlox* is having a revival and deservedly so, because these plants are both stiff-stemmed and fragrant. In recent years taller varieties have been raised by the Dutch breeder Coen Jansen, specifically for prairie planting. These include *P. × arendsii* 'Luc's Lilac', *P. × arendsii* 'Hesperis' and *P. × arendsii* 'Utopia'. Deadheading will produce more flowers, and you can shake off spent flowers to improve the look of the plant. Cut the stems back to ground level in the autumn and remove any stems that have distorted leaves. **VB**

Alternatives

Phlox paniculata 'Bright Eyes', *Phlox paniculata* 'Eva Cullum'

P. paniculata 'Shortwood'

Main features Vivid, rosy-pink flowers;
mildew-resistant plants
Height 1.2 m (4 ft) **Spread** 90 cm (3 ft)
Position ○ ◑ **Hardiness** RHS H7

One of the most striking, easy-to-grow, colourful, fragrant
and popular hardy perennials is *P. paniculata*. Native to
eastern and central United States, introduced to Europe
in 1732, and named by Carl Linnaeus in 1753, this plant
has long been an essential ingredient in cottage garden
borders, as well as in more contemporary herbaceous
perennial and mixed plantings. It has also long been
valued as a cut flower.

Growing wild in rich soil, especially in flood plains,
along river- and streamsides, and in clearings in damp
woods, it usually grows in partial or dappled shade.
This is in contrast to its use in gardens, where it is most
often planted in full sun. *P. paniculata* has been grown
in gardens for so long that in some wild situations, it is
difficult to determine if populations are native or if they
are the result of plants escaping from gardens. From a
steadily creeping root, a mass of relatively stout, upright
stems arise, which are lined with opposite pairs of more
or less elliptical, dull-green leaves up to 15 centimetres
(6 in.) long. In mid- and late summer, the stems are
topped with large domed heads of scented flowers,
sometimes in the hundreds, and each five-lobed flower
is about 2.5 centimetres (1 in.) in diameter. In the wild the
flowers are usually purple or magenta. However, they are
sometimes pink, and occasionally white.

P. paniculata 'Shortwood' is one of many cultivars,
and it is more similar to the wild type than many recent
dwarf introductions. It is admired for its mass of rosy-pink
flowers and for its resistance to powdery mildew, which
disfigures so many other cultivars in gardens. However,
'Shortwood' will suffer from mildew if grown in hot
and dry conditions. It was developed in Pennsylvania
by crossing two well-known and highly rated cultivars:
P. paniculata 'David' and *P. paniculata* 'Eva Cullum'. **GR**

Alternatives

Phlox paniculata 'Eva Cullum', *Phlox paniculata* 'Flamingo',
Phlox paniculata 'Miss Pepper'

Physostegia
P. *virginiana* 'Vivid'

Main features Flowers late summer and autumn;
attracts hummingbirds and butterflies; good cut flower
Height 60 cm (24 in.) **Spread** 60 cm (24 in.)
Position ○ ◑ **Hardiness** RHS H7

The *P. virginiana* 'Vivid' is one of the oldest varieties of
this North American native, but it is still one of the most
prized because it is at its luminous best in autumn rather
than in summer. Like other *Physostegia*, it is easy to please
but is less likely than most species to take over garden
borders or to need staking. 'Vivid' is a compact variety,
growing up to 60 centimetres (24 in.) tall, with beautiful
spikes of numerous light-purple, snapdragon-like blooms
from midsummer. Long-lasting as cut flowers, it also
attracts butterflies and hummingbirds. Attractive seed
heads often follow. These can be cut for dried-flower
arrangements or left on the plant to extend the season of
interest even further. The upright stems become reddish
in the autumn and can look decorative until midwinter.

The common name, obedient plant, is derived from
the fact that the flowers, if pushed to one side, often
remain in their new position temporarily, as if they
were hinged. Many gardeners worry that the plants
themselves are less obedient. The species is notorious
for spreading aggressively by underground rhizomes,
but this variety is more restrained. 'Vivid' is shallow-
rooting, too, so it is easy to pull up the plants if need be.
However, if space is a concern, why not grow it in a pot?
It thrives in fertile, moist, but well-drained soil, although
it is drought-tolerant once established. Consequently,
only water and feed the plants if you want to encourage
them to spread.

A recipient of the Royal Horticultural Society's
Award of Garden Merit, this colourful variety is ideal
for naturalising in a wildflower garden or meadow, as
well as for planting in borders. It combines well with
autumn-flowering perennials with a more airy habit,
such as Japanese anemones and Russian sage. The spiky
flowers are also a nice contrast with *Aster* and *Sedum*. **GP**

Alternatives

Physostegia virginiana 'Summer Snow', *Physostegia
virginiana* var. *speciosa* 'Bouquet Rose'

Polyanthus
Gold Laced Group

Main feature Clusters of dark flowers with golden edges
Height 15–25 cm (6–10 in.) **Spread** 30 cm (12 in.)
Position ◐
Hardiness RHS H7

For gardeners in the industrial towns of nineteenth-century Britain, competitive horticulture was an enjoyable distraction from a tough life. Gooseberries, rhubarb and the so-called 'florists' flowers' – tulips and carnations, for example – were very popular. Small plants, the superiority of whose intricate detail was judged in competitions, were widely grown, including auriculas and gold-laced polyanthus, related perennials in the genus *Primula*.

Gold Laced polyanthus (*Primula* Gold Laced Group) is distantly derived from two British native perennials: the primrose *Primula vulgaris*, and the cowslip *Primula veris*. Through centuries of cross-fertilisation and selection – coupled with the rigorous standards imposed in competitions – the colours and forms have been refined. From a neat rosette of wrinkled, often evergreen leaves, short stems arise, each carrying a cluster of flowers. The flat face of each flower is made up of five two-lobed petals, so that the flower appears to have ten petals encircling the golden centre. Each lobe is chocolate brown, deep crimson, or even black and finely edged in gold. In the best forms the face of the flower is completely flat, the lobes are evenly sized, the dark petals are uniform in shape and colour, and the narrow, edging is also completely uniform. Although these details are important for serious exhibitors, everyone else can enjoy the plants grown in terra-cotta pots, window boxes and containers, where they can be viewed close-up. **GR**

Alternatives

Primula Gold Laced Beeches Strain, *Primula* Gold Laced Jack in the Green, *Primula* Silver Laced Group

Polygonatum

P. × hybridum

Main features Late-spring flowers; architectural plant
Height 90–150 m (3–5 ft) **Spread** 60 cm (24 in.)
Position ○ ◐ ●
Hardiness RHS H7

An essential ingredient in any garden for its spring display, this hardy perennial has a rhizomatous rootstock and spreads slowly to form impressive colonies. The new shoots emerge in spring, with all the leaves tightly wrapped in a beautiful overlapping sequence. Gradually, these elongate, and the graceful stems arch over, the leaves flexing slightly upwards from the horizontal to reveal the flowers beneath. The mid-green leaves have a slightly bluer underside, and alternate up the stems. From each leaf joint, a small cluster of creamy-white, bell-shaped flowers hangs down, with each petal tipped with green. The flowers appear in late spring and are followed by black berries.

This hybrid is more vigorous than its parents and can grow up to 1.5 metres (5 ft) under ideal conditions. Plant *P. × hybridum* in any moisture-retentive soil in sun, shade, or partial shade. It is prone to attack by sawflies that skeletonise the foliage, but this does not usually happen until after flowering. The foliage can be cut to the ground in the autumn, and clumps can be easily divided in the spring before the delicate shoots emerge. *P. × hybridum* associates well in light woodland, with other shade-tolerant plants, such as *Hosta* and *Lamprocapnos spectabilis*, and makes a useful follow-on plant emerging from a carpet of *Cardamine quinquefolia*. It is a classic component of a traditional cottage-style garden, but it looks equally at home in a herbaceous border. **MP**

Alternatives

Polygonatum × hybridum 'Betberg', *Polygonatum × hybridum* 'Striatum', *Polygonatum verticillatum*

Polypodium
P. cambricum 'Cambricum'

Main feature Prettily divided, wintergreen fronds on steadily creeping plants
Height 25 cm (10 in.)   **Spread** 25 cm (10 in.)
Position ◑ ●   **Hardiness** RHS H7

Many ferns have obliged us as gardeners by producing a number of variants, both in the wild and in gardens. These include the male ferns, *Dryopteris*; the shield ferns, *Polystichum*; and the lady ferns, *Athyrium*. The polypody ferns, *Polypodium,* have also provided us with fine plants, although on a smaller scale. Found growing wild across the temperate and tropical world, there are about 150 species of creeping fern, which derive their name (meaning 'many little feet') from the way their rhizomes spread. All produce a stout, creeping, scaly, brown rhizome, which can be seen when the plants spread over rocks. The evergreen fronds are produced singly along the rhizomes. Each frond is split into opposite pairs of leaflets, the rusty-coloured spores are clustered in broad rows on the undersides of the divisions. 'Cambricum' is distinctive in that the fronds are rather thin, deeply divided, sharply pointed, and never produce spores. **GR**

Alternatives

Polypodium cambricum 'Grandiceps Fox', *Polypodium cambricum* 'Richard Kayse'

Polystichum
P. tsussimense

Main feature Neat, glossy, pale-green fronds held on black stems
Height 30 cm (12 in.)   **Spread** 30 cm (12 in.)
Position ◑ ●   **Hardiness** RHS H6

The shield ferns (*Polystichum*) are found around the world in temperate and tropical regions and they include some of the best hardy ferns for gardens. Most are evergreen; the mature fronds are rather leathery to the touch and arise in a ring from a tight crown. The emerging fronds, with their striking crozier shape, are an appealing spring feature and may be covered in gingery or silvery scales before they open to fronds. *P. tsussimense* is an Asian species, growing from Thailand to Japan along streams, around lakes, and in moist, rocky woods. This small species rarely reaches more than 30 centimetres (12 in.) tall, with pale-green, glossy, narrowly triangular or lance-shaped fronds divided twice into slender pointed leaflets and held on black stems. It is evergreen in mild areas, but may lose its leaves in winter in colder regions. Oddly, this species was once sold as a houseplant. It is, in fact, hardy in many areas and ideal in a shady trough or raised bed. **GR**

Alternatives

Polystichum rigens, *Polystichum setiferum* Divisiloblum Group, *Polystichum aculeatum*

Potentilla
'Arc-en-Ciel'

Primula
P. florindae

Main features Small double flowers in late spring to summer; attractive foliage
Height 40 cm (16 in.) **Spread** 30 cm (12 in.)
Position ○ **Hardiness** RHS H7

Main features Flowers in summer; winter seed heads; fragrant flowers; good cut flower
Height 1.2 m (4 ft) **Spread** 30–60 cm (12–24 in.)
Position ○ ◑ **Hardiness** RHS H7

The attractive leaves of this *Potentilla* are small, dark green and soft, with deep veins and serrated edges that mark it out as a relative of the strawberry. The plants are much more substantial than any strawberry, though, and the flowers are less easily recognisable and much more glamorous. In fact, relaxed glamour sums up the appeal of 'Arc-en-Ciel'. The mounds of leaves and languorous stems are adorned with deep-red, rosebud-shaped, double blooms, with showy flashes of gold on the petal's edges. Planted at the edge of a bed or next to a path, it will spill out and clothe the soil with gorgeous flowers. Surround it more closely with other plants, and the stems will thread their way through, so the flowers appear to mingle with the neighbours. In fact, the stems can produce copious amounts of flowers almost continuously from late spring to late summer and require little more work than trimming back when the flowers have finished. **JS**

This long-lived herbaceous perennial is the largest of the *Primula* species. The basal rosette of leaves is 20 centimetres (8 in.) long and mid-green in colour, with toothed-edge, ovate leaf blades held on long stalks. *P. florindae* is one of the latest primulas to flower, and in summer, mealy covered stout stems are topped by a terminal cluster of up to eighty pendulous, bright-yellow, fragrant flowers. Like the stems, the individual flower stalks and the outside of the flowers are covered in a white meal known as farina. *P. florindae* associates well with water and will grow happily beside a stream or in a bog garden accompanied by ferns, such as *Matteuccia struthiopteris* or *Osmunda regalis*. White *Astilbe* and white- or purple-flowered *Iris ensata* would make excellent companions in a cool, moist site, and mass plantings look particularly effective. *P. florindae* 'Ray's Ruby' has deep ruby-red flowers, and other orange/red flower selections are available. **MP**

Alternatives

Potentilla 'Volcan', *Potentilla thurberi* 'Monarch's Velvet', *Potentilla* × *hopwoodiana*

Alternatives

Primula japonica 'Postford White', *Primula rosea*, *Primula denticulata*, *Primula* 'Guinevere'

Primula
P. sieboldii

Main feature Attractive flowers
Height 20 cm (8 in.) **Spread** 20 cm (8 in.)
Position ◑
Hardiness RHS H5

There are many types of *Primula*, some of which are very familiar – cowslips, primroses, auriculas, candelabras and drumsticks – but there is also a spectacular Japanese woodland type, which has been quite overlooked everywhere except in Japan. There, *P. sieboldii* is regarded as one of the classic garden plants, and it is known as *sakurasou*, literally 'flower of the cherry', in reference to its similarity to another Japanese favourite: cherry blossom. Its season begins in late winter, with a pale-green rosette that looks like a lush clump of salad leaves. In spring flower spikes appear, each with up to twenty bell-shaped flowers held in loose rings. The flowering period is usefully long, from early spring to early summer.

There are a few hundred named cultivars, and this is an indication of the variety of flower colours – there is every shade of *P. sieboldii*, from white through pink and magenta to blue and purple – and of petal shapes: plain, wavy, notched, filigree-like snowflakes and bowl shaped. All of them are very pretty, so it is difficult to choose only one variety. In fact, many people become quite addicted to the plant, adding new forms to their gardens when they find them. *P. sieboldii* 'Geisha Girl' is one of the more widely available cultivars, and it has overlapping, notched, light-pink petals with a white centre. A collection of little potted plants would make an impact in the smallest of spaces.

Japanese woodland primulas prefer a position that is not too dry, in dappled shade. They will also clump slowly, even migrating small distances, so would look wonderful at the edge of an open lawn, near (but not too near) trees. A good tip is to mark their location, because they disappear completely during the dormant season, from high summer through to late winter. **ER**

Alternatives

Primula denticulata, Primula sieboldii 'Dancing Ladies',
Primula sieboldii 'Geisha Girl', *Primula sieboldii* 'Snowdrop',
Primula sieboldii 'Winter Dreams'

Primula sieboldii is a Japanese primula that grows in woodlands. ➲

Primula
P. japonica 'Miller's Crimson'

Main features Tiered clusters of small reddish-purple flowers; crinkled, pale-green, semi-evergreen foliage
Height 45 cm (18 in.) **Spread** 45 cm (18 in.)
Position ◗ **Hardiness** RHS H7

Few plants can compete with the eye-catching blooms of this elegant primrose, which offer a dazzling feast of colour in late spring when reflected in the glassy surface of a stream or pond. Clusters of small dark reddish-purple flowers are held in tiers up the sturdy stems, giving rise to the candelabra primrose's common name. The blooms appear above a skirt of textured, pale-green, semi-evergreen foliage.

Demanding constant moisture to thrive, *P. japonica* 'Miller's Crimson' is ideal for a bog garden next to a pond or the banks of a stream. It will also thrive at the edge of a woodland on clay soil, where the trees' shady canopies guarantee damp conditions. Combine 'Miller's Crimson'

with hardy ferns and *Hosta*, as well as other moisture-loving flowers – such as *Astilbe*, *Trollius*, *Ligularia* and *Iris sibirica* – but ensure that its flowering stems are given space to perform among taller partners. Other species of candelabra primrose to try include *P. pulverulenta*, which has crimson flowers with orange eyes, held on silvery stems, or the taller, yellow-flowered *P. prolifica*.

For the best results, plant 'Miller's Crimson' in the autumn or early spring in a partly shaded area with moist soil. If conditions are too dry, create a bog garden by digging a large hole and lining it with pond liner. Do not remove the flower stems after blooming if you want the plant to self-seed and naturalise, and divide large clumps after flowering in early summer. **ZA**

Alternatives

Primula japonica 'Postford White', *Primula japonica* 'Apple Blossom', *Primula japonica* 'Carminea', *Primula prolifica*

Pulmonaria
'Diana Clare'

Main features Semi-evergreen ground cover; flowers in spring; silver-speckled leaves; silver rosettes
Height 30 cm (12 in.) **Spread** 50 cm (20 in.)
Position ◗ ● **Hardiness** RHS H6

Finding flowering plants for shady positions is tricky, so ground cover plants like this handsome, semi-evergreen *Pulmonaria*, which actually prefers shade and offers both flower and foliage interest, are prized. 'Diana Clare' blooms from late winter to late spring, producing larger than usual, deep violet-blue, bell-shaped flowers held in clusters on upright stems. The small leaves that punctuate this cultivar's flowering stems are speckled silver, but when the flowers are coming to an end, a new basal rosette of lance-shaped leaves emerges, and this is heavily variegated. In fact, the only green parts showing are along the margins, where the solid silver starts to break up and then down the midrib.

'Diana Clare' is vigorous and, given the right woodland soil conditions, it spreads to form colonies. Use it beneath deciduous spring- and summer-flowering shrubs, along with hellebore hybrids, perhaps followed by hardy blue geraniums, whose cut leaves will provide a strong contrast. Alternatively, grow this plant to cover shady banks accompanied by swaths of naturalised snowdrops and dwarf daffodils. Cut back the stems and old foliage after flowering to make way for the new growth and to reduce the risk of fungal disease. Watering and feeding at the same time encourages strong regrowth. Other varieties to try include 'Majesté', with slightly paler, two-tone blooms, and 'Ocupol', with cool, pale-blue flowers and very heavily spotted leaves. **JH**

Alternatives

Pulmonaria 'Majesté', *Pulmonaria* 'Ocupol',
Pulmonaria 'Lewis Palmer', syn. *Pulmonaria* 'Highdown'

Pulmonaria
'Sissinghurst White'

Main features Ground cover for shade; white flowers in spring; silver-spotted leaves persisting until autumn
Height 30 cm (12 in.) **Spread** 30–45 cm (12–18 in.)
Position ◐ ● **Hardiness** RHS H7

White flowers are unrivalled when it comes to brightening up a shady spot, and if the leaves also have pale variegation the combination really lifts the gloom. This particular plant was discovered by author and plantswoman Vita Sackville-West at Sissinghurst in Kent, which has a white garden of international renown. From midspring until early summer, clusters of pure-white bells open from pink buds on stems peppered with silver-spotted leaves. For a refreshingly cool look, intersperse clumps of 'Sissinghurst White' with the lime-green grass *Milium effusum* 'Aureum' and the soft-blue *Anemone nemorosa*. 'Sissinghurst White' will benefit from regular lifting and dividing, perhaps every two or three years, either in the autumn or spring. Grow it on moisture-retentive ground, rich in organic matter, and cut back after flowering. 'Roy Davidson' is a good alternative to try: its two-tone blooms start pink and then fade or darken to sky blue. **JH**

Alternative

Pulmonaria 'Roy Davidson'

Pulsatilla
P. rubra

Main features Flowers in late spring; silky, hairy leaves; attractive seed heads; attracts bees
Height 30 cm (12 in.) **Spread** 30 cm (12 in.)
Position ○ **Hardiness** RHS H5

This wine-red–flowered form of the northern European native *Pulsatilla* is a plant of exceptional beauty. It is a deciduous, herbaceous, clump-forming perennial. In spring, leaves appear from the clump covered in silky hairs. They are followed in late spring by solitary bell-shaped flowers, initially hiding demurely among the leaves, but then elongating to be held, slightly nodding, above the foliage. The petals are magenta to rusty red, and inside is a boss of yellow stamen – a delightful combination. As the flowers fade, they are replaced by charming, fluffy, silky, hairy seed heads, giving an extended season of interest, especially when the light shines through them. A hardy plant, *P. rubra* requires a well-drained site on calcium-rich soil in full sun. It grows in calcareous grassland in its native habitat, but it adapts well to a garden situation at the front of a border or in a rock garden. A raised alpine bed enables the beauty of the flowers to be more easily appreciated. **MP**

Alternatives

Pulsatilla alpina subsp. *apiifolia*, *Pulsatilla halleri*

Rodgersia
'Blickfang'

Main feature Generous pink plumes over bold, richly coloured foliage
Height 90–120 cm (3–4 ft) **Spread** 90 cm (3 ft)
Position ○ ◐ **Hardiness** RHS H7

The saxifrage family is a varied one, not only in the look of the plants, but in the habitats in which they grow. There are almost 800 species found in the Himalayas, eastern Asia and western North America. Rodgersias are most closely allied to bergenias. In the wild they are found growing in China, Korea and Japan by lakes, streams and in woods. All are summer-flowering perennials for moist conditions with attractive bold foliage. There are seven species of herbaceous perennial with steadily spreading, branching roots from which long stems arise that hold bold foliage divided into large leaflets. The foliage is often tinged with bronze. In summer, large clusters of small white, cream or pink flowers are carried on separate leafy stems, which later develop good seed heads. 'Blickfang' was first thought to be a form of *R. aesculifolia,* but is now considered a hybrid. The foliage is split into five leaflets, usually with darker veins and bronze tints, and the dark-red flowering stems hold clusters of pink flowers. **GR**

Alternatives

Rodgersia aesculifolia 'Irish Bronze', *Rodgersia* 'Parasol'

Rodgersia
R. podophylla
'Rotlaub'

Main feature Deep-bronze leaf colour all season with white summer flowers
Height 1.2 m (4 ft) **Spread** 1.2 m (4 ft)
Position ◐ **Hardiness** RHS H7

There are situations when a garden benefits from a bold foliage plant to provide impact throughout the whole season. In dappled or partial shade, in soil that never becomes too dry, rodgersias are an inspired choice, and not only do they feature impressive foliage, but they also have summer flowers. *R. podophylla*, a tall perennial that grows wild in Japan by shady lakes and streamsides and in damp woods, makes a stout but elegant and spreading plant. The large leaves can be up to 90 centimetres (3 ft) across, each made up of five broad segments, each toothed and lobed, usually only towards the tips. 'Rotlaub', means 'red leaves', and the leaves open with bronze tints in spring. They lose their richness as summer approaches only to develop red tones again in autumn. During the green-leaved period in summer, large clusters of small, white flowers open. For the best foliage, make sure the soil is not allowed to dry out, and enrich it with garden compost. **GR**

Alternatives

Rodgersia podophylla, Rodgersia podophylla 'Braunlaub'

Rudbeckia

R. fulgida var. sullivantii 'Goldsturm'

Main features Flowers in summer/autumn; winter interest; good cut flower; attracts bees and butterflies
Height 45–60 cm (18–24 in.) **Spread** 60 cm (24 in.)
Position ○ ◑ **Hardiness** RHS H7

This versatile plant is a stalwart of the late-summer garden. The dark-green, slightly rough foliage emerges in spring and is followed by a generous display of stems. These bear deep-yellow, daisy-shaped flowers. The petals radiate out from a dark-brown, cone-shaped centre. As each flower fades, the cone remains, set against a ruff of green sepals that last well into winter. Tough and accommodating, *R. fulgida* var. *sullivantii* 'Goldsturm' will grow in virtually any soil, including clay. It rarely needs staking and is drought tolerant once established. Grow it in groups in herbaceous borders, cottage gardens, or as a long-lasting cut flower. The strong yellow flowers add vibrancy to a hot-colour-themed border, but are equally at home teamed with silvers or blues. 'Goldsturm' associates perfectly with ornamental grasses, both when in flower and during the winter, when the dark cones contrast against the buff shades of deciduous grasses. **MP**

Alternatives

Rudbeckia hirta, Rudbeckia hirta 'Toto', *Rudbeckia hirta* 'Cappucino', *Rudbeckia laciniata* 'Herbstsonne'

Salvia

S. nemorosa 'Caradonna'

Main features Spikes of violet-blue flowers on dark stems; aromatic grey-green foliage; attracts bees and butterflies
Height 60 cm (24 in.) **Spread** 60 cm (24 in.)
Position ○ ◑ **Hardiness** RHS H7

The *S. nemorosa* 'Caradonna' produces dense spikes of intense violet-blue flowers on dark purple-black stems, providing the perfect counterpoint to daisies and flat-topped flowers. In addition to its exceptionally long flowering season, which runs from summer to midautumn, 'Caradonna' is also fêted for its compact habit and aromatic foliage. Like all *S. nemorosa*, it retains a rosette of evergreen leaves over winter. Choose 'Caradonna' for the front of a sunny or lightly shaded border, and use the blue spires to contrast with hot hues or pastel shades. It looks particularly beautiful in swaths alongside plants with contrasting flower shapes, such as *Achillea, Astrantia, Helenium, Rudbeckia, Sedum* and *Hemerocallis*. Combine it with these plants in naturalistic and wildlife gardens, where its flowers will attract butterflies and bees. 'Caradonna' also works well in gravel gardens and raised beds, and will form a low wall along the edge of a path. **ZA**

Alternatives

Salvia nemorosa 'Ostfriesland', *Salvia nemorosa* 'Amethyst', *Salvia nemorosa* 'Sensation Blue', *Salvia* × *sylvestris* 'Mainacht'

 Rudbeckia fulgida var. *sullivantii* '**Goldsturm**', lilac *Perovskia atriplicifolia* and white *Cimicifuga* at Rifkind Garden, Long Island, New York.

Salvia
S. pratensis

Main features Spikes of intense blue, white, violet or pink flowers; aromatic foliage
Height 90 cm (3 ft) **Spread** 38 cm (15 in.)
Position ○ **Hardiness** RHS H6

With around 1,000 different species, *Salvia* includes annuals, perennials and evergreen shrubs. The many herbaceous perennial species tend to form tight clumps of square, upright stems clad in relatively small leaves. The tubular flowers break into two lips for easy bee pollination and come in a range of colours. The meadow clary, *S. pratensis*, is a rare British native species that grows across Europe. It has a preference for well-drained soils over limestone and chalk and is mostly seen in meadows and roadsides. It forms a low rosette of heart-shaped leaves up to about 15 centimetres (6 in.) long, then through the summer, clusters of four to six flowers open on vertical stems; flowers are usually blue, but they can also be violet, pink or even white. Each flower has a hooked upper lip. This plant is the parent of the hybrids grouped under *S. × sylvestris*, but the blue-flowered, true species is a fine plant for rough grass and wildflower meadows and is more adaptable than its natural habitat might indicate. **GR**

Alternatives

Salvia pratensis Haematodes Group, *Salvia pratensis* 'Indigo', *Salvia pratensis* Ballet Series

Salvia
S. × sylvestris 'Mainacht'

Main features Flowers in summer; good cut flower; aromatic foliage; attracts bees, butterflies and wildlife
Height 45–60 cm (18–24 in.) **Spread** 45 cm (18 in.)
Position ○ ◑ **Hardiness** RHS H7

This German hybrid is a valuable addition to many garden styles. It is a deciduous, herbaceous perennial that forms compact clumps. In early to midsummer, dark-purple flower stems arise, bearing dense spikes of two-lipped flowers in deep violet blue. If the first flush of flowers is deadheaded promptly, then another flush usually appears in late summer, giving a long season of interest. Typical of *Salvia*, the grey-green foliage is slightly aromatic if crushed. The numerous flower spikes, although not very tall, give a useful vertical element among other flower forms, such as creamy-yellow *Leucanthemum × superbum*, or the bold flowers of *Hemerocallis*. *S. × sylvestris* 'Mainacht' associates well with pink flowers, such as roses and peonies, and fits perfectly into a mixed cottage-garden–style planting. In more formal herbaceous borders, it looks impressive planted in groups towards the front. Single plants are equally at home dotted through a prairie-style area or even in a gravel garden. **MP**

Alternatives

Salvia officinalis 'Purpurascens', *Salvia uliginosa*, *Salvia leucantha*

Salvia × sylvestris 'Mainacht' combines well with *Achillea* 'Moonshine' in a mixed cottage-garden–style planting. ➔

Sanguinaria
S. canadensis f. multiplex 'Plena'

Main features Fully double, pure-white, spring flowers; bold foliage
Height 20–30 cm (8–12 in.) **Spread** 25 cm (10 in.)
Position ◐ ● **Hardiness** RHS H7

One of the highlights of the shade garden in spring, and of the eastern American and Canadian forests, is the appearance of the fleeting flowers of the wild bloodroot, *S. canadensis*, which confirms that winter is departing. The first spring sign of growth is the emergence of the rust-tinted new shoots as they push through the soil. These become greyer as they stretch, the developing leaves rolled protectively around the flowering stems, the veins picked out in rusty orange. The flower buds quickly stretch from within their shielding leaf, and as the buds open, the rounded foliage also unrolls and develops a blue-green colouring. Later, the leaves become green and round, with large or small lobes, and they make an attractive summer feature.

The shining white flowers, each with eight petals, open flat on sunny days, but close at night and in dull and wet weather. Soon after the flower is pollinated, the petals drop; consequently, in some seasons, there is only a show for a few days. However, the foliage continues to expand over the following weeks, becomes green as it matures, and opens out above the developing seedpods. These canoe-shaped pods are 5 centimetres (2 in.) long – or slightly more – narrow, and pointed.

The double-flowered form *S. canadensis* f. *multiplex* 'Plena' has two significant advantages for the gardener over the wild single-flowered form. Firstly, it is an unusually beautiful flower, with a mass of white petals and a slightly cream-coloured centre. Secondly, because it is incapable of producing seed, and therefore is never effectively pollinated, the flowers last for much longer than those of the single-flowered type. Sap from the roots was once used as a red dye, hence the common name (bloodroot). However, the sap can be toxic, so it is necessary to wear gloves when handling the plant. **GR**

Alternatives

Sanguinaria canadensis f. *multiplex*, *Sanguinaria canadensis*, *Sanguinaria canadensis* early-flowering

Sanguisorba
S. officinalis 'Red Thunder'

Main features Flowers in late summer; autumn colour;
attracts insects
Height 1.8–2 m (6–7 ft) **Spread** 60 cm (24 in.)
Position ○ ◑ **Hardiness** RHS H7

Follow in the footsteps of renowned Dutch garden
designer Piet Oudolf and plant *S. officinalis* 'Red Thunder'.
A beautiful and useful provider of flowers from summer
through autumn, it is one of his favourites. Like other
Asian forms, 'Red Thunder' is taller and later flowering
than European *Sanguisorba*. It was selected specifically for
its tall, stiff stems and good, red-coloured flowers heads.
Feathery grey-green clumps of foliage make attractive
ground cover in spring. Stems emerge and shoot upwards
to support minibranches bearing masses of distinctive,
tiny, catkin-style red flowers in late summer.

Sanguisorba goes well with grasses; indeed, some
varieties look very grass-like when surrounding plants
hide their basal foliage and when their bobble-shaped
flowers hover above planting. An all-round good mixer
with other plants, 'Red Thunder' has the ability to go
with the flow of breezes, making it particularly perfect
for prairie-style planting. Try *Panicum virgatum* 'Squaw'
as a neighbour for colourful autumn highlights; it turns
a similar shade to 'Red Thunder' flowers as summer
moves into autumn. Be sure to copy Oudolf's style and
leave the flower heads on through winter – they make
an attractive sight in the pale light of the late season.

Other species of note include *S. canadensis*, which is
a native to eastern North America. Its stems reach up to
1.8 metres (6 ft) in height from bold central clumps, and
from midsummer through to midautumn, these bear
clouds of white flowers that resemble tiny bottlebrushes.
Frost add showy red and copper hues to an already good-
looking plant. 'Cangshan Cranberry' was found in the
Yunnan province of China in 1996 and was introduced
by plantsman Dan Hinckley from the United States. It
produces rich burgundy flowers on tall, thin, reddish
stems, reaching more than 1.8 metres (6 ft) tall. **RC**

Alternatives

Sanguisorba officinalis 'Red Buttons', *Sanguisorba officinalis*
'Shiro-fukurin', *Sanguisorba* 'Tanna'

Saponaria
S. × *lempergii* 'Max Frei'

Main features Flowers in summer and autumn;
semi-evergreen foliage; mat forming
Height 30–40 cm (12–16 in.) **Spread** 30–40 cm (12–16 in.)
Position ○ **Hardiness** RHS H5

This less well-known but well-behaved *Saponaria* is a vigorous hybrid perennial selected in Switzerland. Small grey-green, slightly hairy leaves – in opposite pairs – on trailing stems cover the ground. These are followed by an abundance of clusters of 2.5-centimetre-wide (1 in.), soft-pink flowers, each with five petals opening over a prolonged period, giving colour from mid- to late-summer. The foliage makes a semi-evergreen mat in winter.

S. × *lempergii* 'Max Frei' grows to between 30 to 40 centimetres (12–16 in.) in height by the same width. Plant it in full sun in a well-drained, neutral to slightly alkaline soil, but avoid acidic locations. 'Max Frei' hates waterlogged soils and intense heat, so is more suited to a temperate climate. It makes excellent ground cover planted en masse, but looks equally at home in a rock garden, where its noninvasive habit is an advantage. It also makes a good edging plant for borders and can be used to trail down a wall. For the best results, trim back the old growth in spring.

This is a plant that looks most striking growing in bold groups among other low-growing, sun-loving plants on a shallow bank. Team it up with the purple-leaved sage *Salvia officinalis* 'Purpurascens' and the silver-leaved dwarf cotton lavender *Santolina chamaecyparissus* 'Nana'. Alternatively, try it alongside a low-growing sun rose, such as the white-flowered *Cistus* × *dansereaui* 'Decumbens', or a grey-leaved rock rose, such as *Helianthemum* 'Wisley Primrose'. 'Max Frei' would be equally effective grown in a sunny gravel garden, where it would flower in summer and give foliage effect in winter. S. × *lempergii* 'Fritz Lemperg' is another popular but more compact cultivar. It is earlier flowering and produces deeper-pink flowers over a longer period. **MP**

Alternatives

Saponaria ocymoides, *Saponaria* 'Bressingham',
Saponaria × *olivana*, *Saponaria officinalis*

Sarracenia
S. flava

Main features Bold, upright pitchers in yellow or red; large yellow flowers in spring
Height 60–120 cm (2–4 ft) **Spread** 45 cm (18 in.)
Position ○ **Hardiness** RHS H5

There is a diverse range of carnivorous plants that have adapted to trap insects and digest them as a way of acquiring nutrients in habitats where the levels of soil nutrients are naturally very low. Some, such as the tropical *Nepenthes*, root in the crotches of tree branches, where they may develop into plants so large that they can even digest small animals. Others, such as bladderworts, *Utricularia*, float free in ponds and trap tiny waterborne organisms. The pitcher plants in the genus *Sarracenia* are herbaceous perennials with colourful funnels growing in wet conditions.

These pitcher plants have two kinds of leaves. Many develop relatively small, flattened leaves in the autumn; these persist through the winter. In spring the much larger and more dramatic-looking pitchers develop. These pitchers are large leaves that have become modified into cylinders with the tops formed into a hood. Insects slip down inside the pitchers until they fall into a digestive liquid in the base; the hood prevents the pitcher from filling with rain. The large nodding flowers open on individual stems and can be very showy, with a sweet scent, or sometimes a more musky odour.

In the yellow pitcher plant, *S. flava*, the colour and size of the pitchers are noticeably variable: they may be yellow–green (f. *flava*), a more vivid lime green, usually with a flare of red veins under the hood or they may be much more strongly veined throughout or even completely red. They vary in height from 25 to 100 centimetres (10–40 in.). The 2.5- to 4-centimetre flowers (1–1.5 in.) are yellow and unpleasantly scented. This species grows in swamps and bogs from Virginia south to Florida, but has become much less common as its habitats have been drained. Take care never to allow plants to dry out. **GR**

Alternatives

Sarracenia leucophylla, Sarracenia purpurea, Sarracenia flava subsp. *flava* var. *rubricorpora*

Saxifraga
S. × *urbium* 'Variegata'

Main features Flowers in early summer; year-round variegated foliage
Height 30 cm (12 in.) **Spread** 30 cm (12 in.)
Position ○ ◑ **Hardiness** RHS H5

S. × urbium epitomises the traditional English cottage garden and was celebrated by Noel Coward in his song 'London Pride' in 1941: 'London Pride has been handed down to us, London Pride is a flower that's free.' It makes low, ground-hugging, compact, evergreen rosettes of spoon-shaped, tooth-edged leaves. It spreads, but not in an invasive way, to form mats, making it an ideal edging plant. In early summer, slender, upright wiry stems that grow to 30 centimetres (12 in.) hold the open heads of small, pink, five-petalled flowers, faintly dotted with red and yellow spots.

This hybrid is very similar to *S. umbrosa*, but differs by being more vigorous and with taller flower stems. In sun or partial shade and in any soil, this delightful plant could be used as a formal edging in a rose garden or as a charming informal edging in a cottage-garden–style planting. The evergreen foliage adds interest to any planting scheme in winter. It is also suitable for growing under roses. Its tolerance of partial shade means it can also be used as ground cover in light woodland. Tough and drought tolerant, this versatile little plant deserves a place in every garden. The rosettes can easily be divided in spring to make extra plants for elsewhere in the garden or to give to your gardening friends.

S. × urbium 'Variegata' offers all the above advantages but with the bonus of yellow splashes on the foliage. *S.* 'Rubrifolia' is a choice plant for a cool, moist, shaded spot, with shiny, bronze-red leaves, and in the autumn, stems of white star-shaped flowers. *S.* 'Jenkinsiae' forms a tight clump of lime-encrusted foliage topped by pale-pink flowers, ideal for a sink garden or alpine house. *S.* 'Cloth of Gold' makes a spreading cushion of golden foliage covered in white flowers from spring to summer, best in light shade to avoid foliage scorch. **MP**

Alternatives

Saxifraga 'Rubrifolia', *Saxifraga* 'Jenkinsiae', *Saxifraga* 'Cloth of Gold'

Sedum
'Herbstfreude'

Main features Flowers late summer and autumn; attracts helpful insects; architectural foliage; good cut flower
Height 60 cm (24 in.) **Spread** 60 cm (24 in.)
Position ○ **Hardiness** RHS H7

This deservedly popular perennial is hard to beat for year-round interest. 'Herbstfreude' earns its keep as soon as its succulent green leaves emerge. These grow up to 14 centimetres (5.5 in.) long and 6 centimetres (2.5 in.) wide, and they provide a wonderful foil for plants that flower in late spring and summer. By midsummer this robust variety will have grown leafy stems up to 60 centimetres (24 in.) tall. These are topped with waxy, green flower buds packed into huge calabrese-like heads, which grow up to 20 centimetres (8 in.) in diameter. The flattened domes of tiny starlike blooms open into a pale dusky-pink in late summer, deepening in colour as they age to a coppery-crimson shade by autumn. These flowers are excellent for cutting and are popular with hoverflies and bees, but sadly butterflies prefer *S. spectabile* varieties. By late autumn the flowers will have evolved into rich chestnut-brown seed heads, which remain attractive all winter.

'Herbstfreude' thrives in full sun in any neutral or slightly alkaline, well-drained soil – even quite poor ones – and is very drought tolerant once established. However, good winter drainage is essential to prevent rot, so dig some coarse grit into the soil if need be. Once established, the clump may splay open under the weight of the flowers, especially if it is grown in fertile soil or out of full sun. In order to prevent this problem, do not feed the plants and cut them back in spring by about a third of their height once they are about 15 centimetres (6 in.) tall, which will promote bushier growth. Unfortunately, the sap may irritate the skin, so it is best to wear gloves when handling the plant.

A front or midborder position suits this variety best. It combines well with all types of *Aster* and with numerous ornamental grasses. It makes an impressive edging and container plant too. **GP**

Alternatives

Sedum 'Bertram Anderson', *Sedum* 'Matrona', *Sedum* 'Red Cauli', *Sedum* 'Ruby Glow', *Sedum* 'Mr Goodbud'

Sedum
'Matrona'

Main features Flowers in late summer and autumn;
attracts beneficial insects; architectural foliage
Height 60 cm (24 in.) **Spread** 60 cm (24 in.)
Position ○ **Hardiness** RHS H7

In full bloom the clouds of starry-pink flowers of 'Matrona'
will light up a border and be buzzing with a wider range
of insects than almost any other flowers in the garden.
These blooms sit on top of sturdy, purple stems above
typically fleshy leaves, which are dark grey green suffused
with maroon and edged with jagged serrations. The
foliage looks good in its own right and makes a perfect
background to the flowers. In fact, the great shape and
proportions of 'Matrona,' combined with its foliage colour
and flowers, transform it from an unassuming garden
favourite into an outstanding plant.

It is also one of the easiest plants to have in the
garden and comes into its own in late summer, when

other plants start to look tired. All it really needs is some
sun. One of the longest-flowering sedum varieties,
'Matrona' will give up to ten weeks of glorious colour,
lasting well into autumn. Its strong stems make it less
prone to flopping open at the middle than many sedum
cultivars, and it is ideal on poor soil, since it will still flower
well, although the stems will be shorter and sturdier than
when grown in richer conditions. In cold winter regions,
flower stems left on over winter can look very attractive
covered in frost. 'Matrona' looks great combined with
Ophiopogon planiscapus 'Nigrescens' in a smart town
garden, with *Echinops ritro* or *Eryngium planum* 'Blue
Hobbit' in a gravel garden or with ornamental grasses
in a natural-looking mixed border. **JS**

Alternatives

Sedum spectabile 'Autumn Joy', *Sedum* 'Mr Goodbud',
Sedum telephium subsp. *maximum* 'Gooseberry Fool'

Sedum

'Red Cauli'

Main feature Red stems carry clusters of reddish-pink,
late-season flowers opening from red buds
Height 60 cm (24 in.) **Spread** 45 cm (18 in.)
Position ○ **Hardiness** RHS H7

'Red Cauli' is one of the best of all late-summer and
autumn perennials for sunny sites. It has uniquely deep
colouring and is a hybrid of the ice plant (*S. telephium*)
developed by British sedum specialist Graham Gough.
The 8-centimetre-long (3 in.) leaves are carried on upright
or rather spreading red stems, the lowest leaves are pale
green, and the upper leaves are dark green and strongly
tinted in purplish brown. In late summer and autumn,
clusters of 10-centimetre-wide (4 in.) flower heads packed
with tiny cherry-pink flowers open from cherry-red buds.
They mature into rich brown seed heads, which can be
left on the plant until spring. In appearance the clusters
look more like sprouting broccoli than cauliflower.

Sedum belongs in the stonecrop family: between
1200 and 1500 species of succulent plants, including
trees, woody-based perennials and some aquatics,
although many are adapted to dry conditions. Other
popular plants in this family include *Sempervivum*,
Kalanchoe, and *Echeveria*. About 600 species of *Sedum*
are found in the northern hemisphere, and they range
from shrubs to creeping plants suited to ground cover,
and from herbaceous perennials to annuals and
biennials. Botanists have long thought that the
herbaceous perennial species are sufficiently distinct to
be given a genus of their own. The only problem is that
they cannot agree where their new home should be: in
Hylotelephium or, more likely, in *Orostachys*. **GR**

Alternatives

Sedum 'Marchant's Best Red', *Sedum telephium*
Atropurpureum Group 'Purple Emperor'

Sedum

S. telephium Atropurpureum Group 'Karfunkelstein'

Main features Rich, red foliage; red buds opening
to pink flowers in late summer and autumn
Height 50 cm (20 in.) **Spread** 50 cm (20 in.)
Position ○ **Hardiness** RHS H7

Flowering perennials are always more appreciated in small
gardens if they have a second season of interest. Some –
including many ornamental grasses, perennial clematis
and *Iris foetidissima* – have attractive fruits after the flowers.
Others have colourful foliage that provides interest before
the flowers open, and these include *Aquilegia*, many
peonies and some euphorbias. A number of sedums also
fall into this second category, and as they tend to flower
towards the end of the season, this ensures that in spring
and summer, the plants still capture attention.

Sedums grown as hardy perennials tend to have
fat, fleshy foliage. In many varieties this is an attractive
greyish blue-green; in some other very striking cultivars,

the foliage is variegated and has a bright, cream-coloured
edge to the leaves, which can be quite dramatic. An
increasing number of cultivars have rich, red stems and
red leaves, and this red colouring is evident from when
shoots first appear in spring.

S. telephium 'Karfunkelstein' is a relatively compact
and self-supporting plant that has green stems boldly
stained in dark red and lined with pairs of slightly
toothed, oblong leaves up to 10 centimetres (4 in.) long.
These are green at the base of the plant and tend to clasp
the stems, but towards the top of the plant, where there
is more light, they become bright, beetroot in colour. In
late summer and autumn, after this long display of
foliage colour, the red buds open to pink flowers. **GR**

Alternatives

Sedum 'Vera Jameson', *Sedum telephium* Atropurpureum
Group 'Xenox'

Sempervivum
S. arachnoideum

Main features Diminutive rosettes of textured green foliage; starry-pink flowers; drought tolerant
Height 10 cm (4 in.) **Spread** 30 cm (12 in.)
Position ○ **Hardiness** RHS H7

Rooting between the cracks in walls or forming a textured cushion in a shallow pot, the leafy rosettes of this unusual houseleek resemble baby water lilies covered with cobwebs. The evergreen foliage is green, although red forms are also available, and in early summer, flowering stems topped with starry-pink blooms shoot up from the centres of mature rosettes. Individual plants die after flowering, but because this diminutive succulent is quick to spread, the gaps are soon filled.

Ideal for very small containers on a sunny patio, *S. arachnoideum* complements other succulents, such as *Sedum* and *Leontopodium alpinum*, in an alpine trough. It can also be squeezed between the stones of a rock

garden or dry stone wall, or allow it to creep through the gaps in patio paving. Alternatively, grow this tiny succulent on a sloping roof, where it will spread to form a layer of downy rosettes, which will help to insulate a home or garden building.

S. arachnoideum hails from the alpine regions of Europe, where its fine webbing helps to trap moisture in the dry, rocky conditions. It is hardy, but requires sun and excellent drainage to survive and will quickly rot in moist soil. Grow it in sandy soil or a gravel bed, or in pots of soil-based compost mixed with sharp horticultural grit. In areas that experience wet winters, keep the plants in pots and move them next to the house or into an unheated greenhouse from autumn to spring. **ZA**

Alternatives

Sempervivum arachnoideum subsp. *tomentosum*,
Sempervivum arachnoideum 'Boule de Neige'

Sidalcea
'Elsie Heugh'

Main feature Silky, pale-pink, summer flowers
Height 90 cm (3 ft) **Spread** 45 cm (18 in.)
Position ○
Hardiness RHS H7

Despite the huge number of new plants that have been introduced from around the world in recent years, sometimes the old favourites are still among the best, and these include classics, such as *Forsythia* × *intermedia* 'Lynwood Variety' from 1935, *Narcissus* 'Geranium' from 1930 and *Clematis* 'Perle d'Azur' from 1885. Many fine hardy perennial plants have also stood the test of time, including *Aster* × *frikartii* 'Mönch' from about 1920, *Hosta sieboldiana* var. *elegans* from 1905, and *Iris* 'Jane Phillips' from 1946. Another dependable old-timer that is still widely grown, and deservedly so, is 'Elsie Heugh', first introduced in 1936.

This prairie mallow, a member of the hollyhock family, which also includes such diverse plants as okra and cotton, is a hybrid between two of the twenty species of *Sidalcea* that grow across western North America, usually in sunny places on well-drained soil. One parent of this hybrid, *S. candida*, from the southwestern United States, has white flowers, while the other parent, *S. malviflora*, from the west, has pink or purple flowers with white veins. 'Elsie Heugh' is usually an upright plant, spreading steadily at the root, with rounded, lobed leaves up to 8 centimetres (3 in.) long at the base and reducing in size up the hairy stems; towards the top they split into five narrow segments. The five-petalled flowers, which resemble small hollyhock blooms, open through the summer, with secondary branches developing below the original spike. The 5-centimetre-long (2 in.) silky petals are pale pink, slightly frilled along the edges and drop off as they age, leaving a very clean look. Although 'Elsie Heugh' reaches only a modest height, discreet support is sometimes necessary, especially in exposed situations. Unfortunately, the plants may be attacked by the same rust disease that attacks hollyhocks. **GR**

Alternatives

Sidalcea 'Little Princess', *Sidalcea* 'Party Girl', *Sidalcea* 'William Smith'

Solidago
S. *rugosa* 'Fireworks'

Main features Flowers in late summer and autumn;
attracts butterflies
Height 1.5 m (5 ft) **Spread** 60 cm (24 in.)
Position ○ ◑ **Hardiness** RHS H7

A relatively recent introduction (1993) from the United
States, this eye-catching form of *Solidago* stands head
and shoulders above the rest, not in stature but in class.
It is a valuable, late-flowering, much more elegant variety,
without the weedy habit of some of its relations. Sturdy,
but thin, purple-flushed stems grow to 1.5 metres (5 ft)
in height, supporting lance-shaped leaves in pairs. Slender
arching flower stems spread out from the top, bearing
countless clusters of pale-yellow florets along the length
of each wand. The overall effect of a clump in bloom is
reminiscent of a shower of fireworks and makes a striking
addition to the late-summer and autumn garden, where
butterflies and other pollinating insects adore them.

Low-maintenance *S. rugosa* 'Fireworks' is a slowly
spreading, very hardy, herbaceous perennial that is
suitable for any soil type, including heavy clay. Grow it
in sun or partial shade, and in soil that stays moist but is
well drained. The plant is equally tolerant of hot summer
conditions or a more temperate climate. The slender but
robust stems support themselves without the need for
staking, but faded flower stems are best removed to
prevent unwanted self-seeding.

'Fireworks' looks at ease in many planting styles,
but it is particularly effective when combined with the
ornamental grasses, *Helenium*, *Crocosmia* and *Aster* in a
prairie-style garden. In a traditional herbaceous border,
its airy effect would add contrast to some of the bold
spikes of late-flowering *Aconitum*. Because 'Fireworks' is
late flowering, it is in bloom when the autumn tints of
many woody plants have started to turn. Try planting it
alongside deciduous *Azalea*, *Spiraea thunbergii* or *Cotinus*
'Flame'. The pale-yellow flowers would also look very
effective against a backdrop of purple-leaved *Cotinus*
or *Physocarpus*. **MP**

Alternatives

Solidago 'Gardone', *Solidago* × *luteus* 'Lemore',
Solidago canadensis

S. *cernua* var. *odorata* 'Chadd's Ford'

Main features Flowers in late summer and autumn;
spikes of strongly scented white flowers
Height 45–60 cm (18–24 in.) **Spread** 50–75 cm (20–30 in.)
Position ○ ◑ **Hardiness** RHS H7

The idea of growing orchids outside in the garden is
something that appeals to many gardeners – even if they
suspect that it may not actually be possible. However, it
can be done, and the American native *Cypripedium*, the
British native *Dactylorhiza fuchsii*, the Asian *Bletilla* and
Calanthe and more are surprisingly winter hardy in cold
climates. One of the loveliest, most fragrant and easiest
to grow of the hardy orchids is *S. odorata*. It is one of
twenty-three North American native *Spiranthes* species
growing wild all over the United States and Canada,
and it grows mainly in mid-Atlantic and southern states.
However, these wild species are not usually grown in the
garden, and gardeners are more likely to opt for *S. cernua*
var. *odorata* 'Chadd's Ford' because it is more vigorous,
taller and has longer spikes of larger and more strongly
scented flowers.

Up to six, narrow, 20-centimetre-long (8 in.), evergreen
leaves make a low rosette, and then in late summer,
spikes up to 60 centimetres (24 in.) in height, standing
upright. The top parts of the stems are packed with
flowers – up to fifty flowers are found on some plants –
displayed in an intriguing spiral arrangement. The waxy,
pure-white, bell-shaped flowers tend to lay flat against
the stem in bud, then stand out from the stem as they
open. They have a powerful vanilla–jasmine fragrance,
and in mild areas may continue opening until early spring.

'Chadd's Ford' was discovered in a ditch in Delaware,
and named for the hometown of the grower who first
gained an award for the species. In the wild it grows in
very wet sites, and the flower spikes may even emerge
from shallow water. Consequently, in the garden it is
important that the soil be kept moist, but also well
drained; standing water is not necessary, but the plants
will appreciate sun. **GR**

Alternatives

Spiranthes cernua, Spiranthes spiralis

Stachys
S. macrantha 'Superba'

Main features Dense spikes of deep, pinkish-purple
flowers; steadily spreading plants
Height 50 cm (20 in.) **Spread** 50 cm (20 in.)
Position ○ **Hardiness** RHS H7

The sage family provides gardeners with a huge number
of attractive garden plants; some are grown for their
foliage, but most are grown for their flowers. Many,
including *Salvia pratensis*, are salvias: sages that have
almost three times as many species as any other genus
in the family. *Scutellaria*, which is not often grown and
Stachys come next in the family's hierarchy.

Previously known as *S. grandiflora*, *S. macrantha*
originates in Turkey and Caucasus, where it grows in sunny
places on slopes and amongst scrub. The dark-green,
rather wrinkled, basal leaves are about 10 centimetres
(4 in.) long, and among them vertical unbranched
stems emerge from late spring to midsummer. These
carry tightly packed clusters of 4-centimetre-wide
(1.5 in.) purplish-pink flowers that are larger than those
of other species. *S. macrantha* 'Superba' has flowers in
an especially deep shade of pinkish purple.

Some species of *Stachys* are grown for foliage and
others for flowers; there is even one species, *S. affinis*, that
produces small, curly, edible tubers. With its soft, woolly,
silvery leaves, *S. byzantina* is one of the most popular
low-growing foliage plants, whereas the species grown
for their flowers are generally very colourful and are
reminiscent of a more robust *Agastache*. There are around
three hundred *Stachys* species in total, distributed across
a range of temperate and tropical habitats all around
the world. In addition to herbaceous perennials, there
are woody-based perennials, shrubs and annuals. The
perennials tend to form slowly spreading clumps with
opposite pairs of leaves carried on square stems, each
leaf noticeably veined and neatly toothed around the
edge. The two-lipped flowers are held in clusters above
the leaves on vertical stems and come in purplish or
pinkish shades. **GR**

Alternatives

Stachys macrantha 'Robusta', *Stachys macrantha* 'Violacea'

Stipa
S. gigantea

Main features Clump-forming habit; spectacular oat-like flower heads in summer, autumn and winter
Height 1.5–2.4 m (5–8 ft) **Spread** 50–90 cm (20–36 in.)
Position ○ **Hardiness** RHS H7

The *S. gigantea* is one of the top-ten ornamental grasses. It puts on a superb performance each year and is truly majestic in full flower: a plant with real presence. Give it plenty of space so that its stately habit makes maximum impact. An evergreen bunch grass, native to southern Europe, *S. gigantea* has arching linear leaves that make up the foliage base from which emerge tall blond stems bearing oat-like flowers. These large flower panicles have long-awned, purple-hued heads that ripen to gold and catch the sun. The plant flowers earlier than most grasses, and its stems will persist through autumn and winter, but they can be battered by wind and rain. Remove damaged stems by cutting them off at the base. Another cultivar of similar stature is *S. gigantea* 'Gold Fontaene', a selection made by German nurseryman Ernst Pagels that has enormous golden flower heads held upright above the foliage base. *S. gigantea* 'Pixie' is a more compact form. **RC**

Alternatives

Stipa gigantea 'Gold Fontaene', *Stipa gigantea* 'Pixie', *Stipa calamgrostis, Stipa tenuissima*

Thalictrum
T. delavayi
'Hewitt's Double'

Main features Flowers in summer; good cut flower
Height 90–150 cm (3–5 ft) **Spread** 10–50 cm (4–20 in.)
Position ◑
Hardiness RHS H7

Amongst the many species of *Thalictrum*, *T. delavayi* 'Hewitt's Double' stands out not only on account of its height but also because of the massed miniclouds of flowers it produces in summer. These look great on the plant and are also excellent for cutting for indoor displays. It has a base typical of *Thalictrum*, made up of divided, lacy, grey-green leaves similar in appearance to *Aquilegia* or *Adiantum*. Purple-tinged stems emerge upwards from this clump and are topped off with large clouds of blooms, formed by sprays of very small lilac-purple double flowers. Up close, these look like tiny pompoms. 'Hewitt's Double' excels in a woodland garden or moist sunny border. It is adaptable: it contrasts well with larger-leaved plants that thrive in the same conditions, for example *Ligularia* and *Lobelia cardinalis*, and looks equally at ease in a species-rich, cottage-garden–style planting or in more contemporary matrix planting mixes. **RC**

Alternatives

Thalictrum aquilegifolium 'Thundercloud', *Thalictrum aquilegifolium* 'Black Stockings', *Thalictrum delavayi*

Thamnochortus
T. insignis

Thermopsis
T. villosa

Main feature Tall, crowded tussocks of attractive colourful stems
Height 1.2–2.4 m (4–8 ft) **Spread** 60 cm (24 in.)
Position ○ **Hardiness** RHS H4

Main features Bright yellow, late-spring flowers; showy spikes; attractive to bees
Height 90 cm (3 ft) **Spread** 60 cm (24 in.)
Position ○ **Hardiness** RHS H7

Sometimes, after years of being ignored, a group of plants suddenly starts to capture gardeners' attention, and this is exactly what has happened with restios. These are plants in the family *Restionaceae*, a distinct group that, along with sedges and rushes, falls under the broader heading of grasses. However, restios are evergreen perennial plants, very much like small bamboos in appearance. There are almost 500 species, with the main concentrations in South Africa and Australia, and they are distinct in having almost no leaves. *T. insignis* is one of the most widely grown and it is used for thatching in South Africa. It makes tight, crowded tussocks of stems, the older growth arching over to make a broad plant. In colour the stems are alternately green, amber and rusty brown, and with their elegant habit and dense growth, they make attractive long-term foliage plants. In summer the stems are tipped with golden flower clusters. **GR**

There are about twenty species of *Thermopsis* growing across a wide area, including Asia, Siberia, India and North and South Americas. The close relationship with *Baptisia* is clear, but *Thermopsis* is distinct in its foliage, which often has a bluish tint. In addition, once the slender spikes of yellow flowers are over, the seedpods remain flat and do not swell as they do in *Baptisia*. *T. villosa* grows wild down North America's east coast, from Maine to Alabama and Georgia. From fat, fleshy roots arise upright stems carrying leaves split into three lance-shaped segments. The plant makes a clump of vertical stems carrying slightly hairy green leaves, covered in silky hairs on the undersides. In late spring tall spikes of yellow pea-like flowers open, each about 5 centimetres (2 in.) long, followed by flat, hairy seedpods. Unlike some species, *T. villosa* is well behaved and does not have invasive spreading roots. **GR**

Alternatives

Elegia capensis, Elegia tectorum, Restio tetraphyllus, Rhodocoma capensis

Alternatives

Thermopsis lanceolata, Thermopsis rhombifolia var. *montana*

Tiarella
T. cordifolia

Main features Fluffy, white flowers; attractive, lobed evergreen leaves
Height 20–30 cm (8–12 in.) **Spread** 60 cm (24 in.)
Position ◐ ● **Hardiness** RHS H7

Small, neat, and easy-to-grow plants for shade gardens are invaluable to today's gardeners, and this in part accounts for the popularity of a group of very hardy perennials in the saxifrage family. Heucheras, in their vast variety of foliage colours, are the best known; heucherellas, of which heucheras are one of the parents, are quickly gaining recognition. Tiarellas, the other parents of heucherellas, are the least well known, but are perhaps most effective at combining attractive foliage with delightful flowers in a natural way. While the flowers of heucheras are basically bell-like, those of tiarellas are lighter and fluffier. Carried above the leaves on vertical stems, large numbers of the tiny blooms often begin as pink buds at the top and open to pure and creamy-white, star-shaped flowers.

There are around five *Tiarella* species: one grows wild in China whereas the others are all North American. *T. cordifolia* is found in the wild across eastern North America, from Quebec south to Georgia. It comes in a clump-forming type, sometimes known as *T. wherryi*, and a type that runs more vigorously at the root. The soft, heart-shaped evergreen leaves (8 cm/3 in. across) are gently lobed and toothed around the edges. New growth may be purple-tinted in spring whereas mature foliage may be striped or tinted in purple or maroon. Plants with especially attractive leaves occasionally stand out in wild populations. Plants can be aggressive when growing well.

T. cordifolia is a plant for partial or dappled shade in rich woodland soil, and it appreciates similar conditions in gardens. It is the parent of many hybrids with other *Tiarella* species, as well as with heucheras. For a natural look, and if you prefer a genuinely native plant instead of a man-made garden hybrid, choose the heartleaf foam flower. **GR**

Alternatives

Tiarella 'Mystic Mist', *Tiarella* 'Pink Bouquet', *Tiarella* 'Spring Symphony', *Tierella wherryi* 'Bronze Beauty'

Tiarella
'Pink Skyrocket'

Main features Showy pink flowers in spring and
summer; attractive year-round foliage in mild locations
Height 15–30 cm (6–12 in.) **Spread** 25–30 cm (10–12 in.)
Position ◑ ● **Hardiness** RHS H7

The creators of *Tiarella* 'Pink Skyrocket', Terra Nova
Nurseries in Oregon, rate it as the best of their pink-
flowering cultivars. It is showier in every sense than
many other foam flowers. Attractive red veins enhance
its deeply cut mid-green leaves. In sunnier locations its
foliage becomes burnished with bronze tints, giving us
beautiful autumn colour. In deeper shade, autumn leaf
colour is a glamorous black. When rimed with winter
frost, the foliage becomes even more beautiful – this
plant stays evergreen in mild winter regions.

Such distinctive leaves are combined with a compact
habit: the base clump is about 15 centimetres (6 in.) in
height, with flowers rising to 30 centimetres (12 in.). Flower
heads are more pyramidal in shape, and hold masses of
prawn-pink flowers – it is one of the largest-flowered
hybrids ever introduced. 'Pink Skyrocket' is an excellent
plant that relishes woodland conditions. It makes a
stunning edging to tall shrub borders or beneath tree
groups when planted in drifts. It beautifies the ground
under high-branching, early-flowering shrubs such as
Chimonanthus praecox 'Grandiflorus', *Corylopsis pauciflora*
and *Hamamelis* × *intermedia*.

Foam flowers are easy-care plants that reward with
many weeks of display. Tidy leaves in spring before
flowers appear; remove faded flower heads as flowering
diminishes. *T. wherryi* is another popular choice of foam
flower. It is native to the woodlands of Tennessee, North
Carolina and Alabama and is a parent to a number of
new hybrids. Slightly more compact and slow growing,
in early summer it bears short sprays of wispy, white
flowers that, up close, have a sweet fragrance. *T. wherryi*
'Heronswood Mist' has elegant leaves and explodes
with masses of prawn-pink flowers held on upright, tiny,
cone-shaped heads. **RC**

Alternatives

Tiarella cordifolia, *Tiarella* 'Spring Symphony', *Tiarella
wherryi* 'Heronswood Mist'

Tricyrtis
T. formosana

Main features Flowers late summer and autumn; wide range of colours and colour combinations
Height 30–90 cm (12–35 in.) **Spread** 45 cm (18 in.)
Position ◐ ● **Hardiness** RHS H7

If you have shady areas in your garden, you will notice that many shade-loving plants tend to flower in the spring. Most grow wild in deciduous forests and woods, where increasing spring temperatures combine with high light penetration through a canopy that has not yet closed over. The soil also tends to be moist in spring, and the relatively open canopy allows most rainfall through. These factors combine to encourage growth and flowering in spring as plants take advantage of this opportunity. So shade gardens are colourful in spring but less bright later in the season.

Toad lilies (*Tricyrtis*) are a valuable yet easy-to-grow exception to this tendency, flowering as they do in late summer and autumn. About twenty species grow wild in Asian woods and forests and make steadily spreading plants with thick stems, which may be upright, spreading, or more arching in growth. The slightly succulent, more or less lance-shaped leaves are at times attractively freckled with dark spots. The flowers are said to be orchid-like, but having six petals, are more like those of lilies. They come in a wide variety of colours, including purple, pink, lavender, yellow and white; are often boldly spotted and speckled; and are held in open sprays or lining the shoot tips.

T. formosana is a vigorous plant from Taiwan, spreading strongly at the root, with 5-centimetre-long (2 in.) glossy, heart-shaped leaves with a tendency to clasp the stems. Clusters of flowers open at the shoot tips in autumn and are usually lavender with purple spots. 'Dark Beauty' has dark-green foliage and deep-purple flowers whereas 'Gilt Edge' is short with yellow edges to the leaves and white-spotted purple flowers. Plants in the Stolonifera Group are especially vigorous and earlier flowering, with purplish-pink flowers with darker spots. **GR**

Alternatives

Trycirtis hirta, Trycirtis latifolia, Trycirtis macropoda

Trollius
T. chinensis 'Golden Queen'

Main features Upwards-facing, large orange blooms;
flowers late spring to early summer
Height 75 cm (30 in.) **Spread** 45 cm (18 in.)
Position ○ ◑ **Hardiness** RHS H7

Globeflowers come in all guises. Some are smooth globes
or open goblets that add a touch of elegance to areas of
the garden. Others raise up their feathered heads, and
T. chinensis 'Golden Queen' is one of these. It provides a
dazzling explosion of pumpkin-orange in late spring to
early summer. 'Golden Queen' is an exceptionally large-
flowered form of *T. chinensis*. Also known as the Chinese
globeflower, it comes from northeast China and Siberia,
and grows in damp, cool meadows, where summer
rainfall tends to be heavy. Winters are cold, so hardiness
is not a problem. Nor is supply as most commercially
available plants are seed-raised.

Globeflowers have a reputation for being difficult,
but they are easy to grow if placed in a cool position
in soil that does not dry out in summer, or become
waterlogged in winter. If you can emulate a damp
meadow, they will perform well. Add friable, humus-
rich material – preferably garden compost – to your
planting hole to trap moisture and improve drainage. If
planting close to water, position plants 30 centimetres
(12 in.) above the highest waterline. Winter wet will
kill them, and this applies to most meadow plants.
Once planted, keep them well watered during their
first growing season. Mulch with fine bark to preserve
moisture and do not cover the crown.

Trollius will grow with other moisture-loving plants,
such as traditional willowy forms of Siberian irises. They
also mix well with various streamside plants, including
Asian candelabra primula varieties, such as 'Miller's
Crimson'. Other potential partners are tall *Thalictrum*,
Astilbe and moisture-loving *Euphorbia*, for example, the
orange-flowered *E. griffithii*. *Trollius* also enjoy the same
conditions as ornamental rhubarbs, such as *Rheum
palmatum* 'Atrosanguineum'. **VB**

Alternatives

Trollius chinensis 'Imperial Orange', *Trollius yunnanensis*

Trollius
T. × cultorum

Main feature Globe- or cup-shaped flowers related to the buttercup family
Height 60–90 cm (24–36 in.) **Spread** 60 cm (24 in.)
Position ○ ◐ **Hardiness** RHS H7

Globe flowers are distinctive in that their flowering stems are topped by one large, individual, often more or less spherical or sometimes more bowl-shaped, flower, usually in yellow or orange. These vertical stems arise from tight crowns, which carry basal leaves that are boldly lobed, each division then itself toothed or more sharply divided. Similar, though smaller, leaves are carried on the stems. *T. × cultorum* is a hybrid group derived from two main species, *T. europaeus* and *T. chinensis,* with a little help from *T. asiaticus. T. europaeus* is a British native that also grows in other parts of Europe, whereas *T. chinensis* grows in China and *T. asiaticus* grows in China and Russia. All have yellow or orange flowers and grow naturally in wet meadows, scrubs and thin woodlands.

The hybrid globe flowers retain the clump-forming habit of their parents and the handsomely divided basal leaves are attractively dark green in colour. Cup-shaped or more or less spherical flowers (5–8 cm/2–3 in. in diameter) open on individual stems in late spring and early summer. There are many cultivars of these popular perennials, including 'Dancing Flame' in vivid orange, 'Goldquelle' in bright yellow, 'Lemon Queen' in lemon yellow, 'New Moon' in cream yellow, 'Orange Princess' in deep orange, 'Superbus' in golden yellow and 'Taleggio' in pale ivory yellow. They all grow well in a sunny or partially shaded border.

Trollius is a member of the buttercup family, *Ranunculaceae.* Together with hellebores, winter aconites, marsh marigolds and, of course, buttercups themselves, it is obvious that globe flowers fit in the family. You might not immediately guess that delphiniums, aconitums, columbines and thalictrums also belong in the buttercup family, but look closely at their flower structure and it is clear that they do. **GR**

Alternatives

Trollius europaeus, Trollius chinensis

Trollius × cultorum as part of a mixed planting near to a garden pond. ➔

Veratrum
V. nigrum

Main feature Bold pleated foliage followed by tall flower and seed heads
Height 60–120 cm (24–48 in.) **Spread** 60 cm (24 in.)
Position ● **Hardiness** RHS H6–7

The unique, pleated foliage of these dramatic woodland perennials – the veratrums, or false hellebores – is enough to make them well worth growing. This is, perhaps, fortunate, for although the flowers are interesting and impressive in their way, most are far from colourful. About twenty species of false hellebores grow around the northern hemisphere and all have two features in common: the distinctive foliage and their need for shady conditions.

From thick, black roots that spread steadily, bold leaves arise. First displayed in a rosette as they emerge in spring, then extending higher up the stems as they stretch, individual, more or less egg-shaped leaves can be 35 centimetres (14 in.) long and half as wide. However, their most distinctive feature is that the foliage is dramatically pleated and veined along its length. Plants stand out boldly both in the spring woods and the spring garden. *V. nigrum* is from southern Europe, Asia and Siberia. It has the largest leaves of those usually seen so this species is the most widely grown.

In summer, defiantly upright stems carry leaves that become smaller towards the top and above which the mass of flowers appears. The vertically branched spikes carry huge numbers of small, reddish-brown, almost black, but unpleasantly scented flowers. As they mature they develop 2.5-centimetre-long (1 in.) seed capsules. All parts of the plant are toxic when eaten, and the sap from the leaves and stems may cause a skin allergy. *V. nigrum* has been used to treat a wide range of medical problems, including high blood pressure, and it has also been used to kill fleas. In spite of the common name, these plants are not in any way related to hellebores (*Helleborus*); the two things they have in common, however, are their black roots and toxicity. **GR**

Alternatives

Veratrum album, Veratrum viride

Verbascum
'Gainsborough'

Main feature Dramatically tall spikes of pale-yellow
flowers bloom from summer to autumn
Height 90–150 cm (3–5 ft) **Spread** 10–50 cm (4–20 in.)
Position ○ **Hardiness** RHS H6

All members of the mullein family (*Verbascum*) produce
tall spikes of flowers all summer long even on the poorest
soil. However, the beauty of the 'Gainsborough' cultivar
(Cotswold Group) starts at ground level, with a large basal
rosette of grey-green, hairy leaves. From the centre of
this soft, crinkled platform of foliage, a tall spire emerges,
reaching up to 1.5 metres (5 ft) in height, and this is
studded with large, saucer-shaped, pale primrose-yellow
flowers from early summer through to early autumn.

'Gainsborough' is a good-looking space filler – it adds
instant height and a sense of maturity to any garden.
Simply plant it in well-drained soil in full sun. It fits in
beautifully with informal, cottage-garden–style planting
schemes, and it also adds great presence to more sparsely
planted gravel gardens. Allow 'Gainsborough' plenty
of room for maximum impact, to ensure that its
shape and form can be fully admired. A little light trim
before flowering finishes produces the reward of fresh
growth in the form of secondary spikes. It is a semi-
evergreen, short-lived perennial but easy to grow – root
cuttings are simple to take to ensure its continued
attractive presence.

Other cultivars of interest in the Cotswold Group
of *Verbascum* include 'Pink Domino'. Slightly lower
growing at 1.2 metres (4 ft), this mullein combines dark-
green leaves with spikes of dark-centred, deep rose-pink
flowers. The giant mullein, *V. olympicum*, is even taller,
reaching over 2 metres (7 ft) in height; its woolly, white-
stemmed flower spikes resemble young tree saplings.
With a less refined quality than 'Gainsborough', an
open site is essential for such a rugged individualist. Its
downy base rosette of large grey-white leaves reaches
90 centimetres (3 ft) across. A short-lived perennial, it can
be grown as a biennial or left to self-seed. **RC**

Alternatives

Verbascum 'Golden Wings', *Verbascum* 'Tropic Sun'

Verbena
V. rigida

Main features Intense purple flowers that bloom from summer to autumn; fragrant blooms; attracts butterflies
Height 90 cm (3 ft) **Spread** 90 cm (3 ft)
Position ○ **Hardiness** RHS H3

Planting *V. rigida* adds a dash of South American pizzazz to a garden. Upright stems have oblong leaves and support delicate branches that resemble tiny candelabras. These branches bear clusters of intense purple flowers in late summer. Blooms persist into autumn, only disappearing at the first frost. Overall, the density of blooms and intensity of colour create a vivid purple haze. A flexible plant, it suits a range of garden styles: use it as an edge of border plant, in a gravel garden or as a patio and container subject in any style of garden. It is excellent planted among silver-leaved plants such as *Artemisia ludoviciana* 'Valerie Finnis', *Anaphalis triplinervis* 'Sommerschnee' and *Stachys byzantina* 'Silver Carpet'. Or combine it with *Achillea* 'Moonshine', *Pennisetum villosum* and *Dianthus carthusianorum* for a wildflower meadow–style planting. *V. rigida* is native to Brazil and Argentina, and in cooler locations it is treated as an annual, but its seeds invariably survives frost, especially on well-drained sites. **RC**

Alternatives

Verbena rigida f. *lilacena* 'Lilac Haze', *Verbena hastata*

Veronica
V. gentianoides
'Barbara Sherwood'

Main feature Spikes of pretty, pale-blue flowers with dark-blue veins from late spring to early summer
Height 40 cm (16 in.) **Spread** 40 cm (16 in.)
Position ○ **Hardiness** RHS H7

As with many large genera – there are about 500 species of *Veronica* – a number of different groups are represented. These include annuals, biennials, herbaceous and woody-based perennials, as well as trees and shrubs. *V. gentianoides* is one of the shorter species, known as broad-leaved speedwell. Growing in thin woods and damp meadows in Turkey, the Caucasus and Ukraine, it spreads to form a low mat of rosettes made up of glossy, lance-shaped leaves that knit together to make a dense cover. In early summer pointed spikes of small blue or pink flowers appear. 'Barbara Sherwood' is a little shorter and a little more vigorous than most cultivars, but with very pretty, pale-blue flowers noticeably veined in dark blue. Plant in a fertile, well-drained soil that does not dry out. Because of its rather crowded growth, this is a plant that benefits from being lifted, split into small pieces and the healthiest of those pieces replanted. Do this every two or three years to prevent flowering from tailing off. **GR**

Alternatives

Veronica gentianoides 'Pallida', *Veronica gentianoides* 'Variegata'

 Verbena rigida provides an edge of solid colour to a late summer border in a rural garden.

Veronicastrum
V. virginicum 'Adoration'

Main feature Tall, slender, branched spikes of lavender flowers opening from pink buds
Height 1.2 m (4 ft) **Spread** 60–90 cm (2–3 ft)
Position ○ ◐ **Hardiness** RHS H7

Culver's roots, or *Veronicastrum*, are impressively tall and elegant plants related to *Veronica*. Their long and slender flower spikes are superb at the back of a border and essential ingredients of modern informal meadow and prairie-style plantings. About twenty species of *Veronicastrum* grow in North America and Asia, but it is the North American *V. virginicum* that is most often seen. Found wild in much of the east of the United States and southern Canada, this is a tall plant with upright stems carrying lance-shaped leaves arranged in clusters of six to eight at points up the stem. The common name refers to an eighteenth-century physician who advocated the medicinal use of the roots of *V. virginicum*.

Above the leaves, the slender flower heads begin as a single spike of tiny cream-coloured flowers, but this is followed by pairs or trios of lower side spikes, also growing vertically, to create a candelabra of candles. In the wild, culver's root is found along woodland edges and in meadows, usually in soil that is not parched in summer. The flower heads are cream-coloured but garden forms in a range of pink, lilac and purple have been introduced in recent years; some have probably arisen through hybridisation with other species. 'Adoration' has bright-pink buds that open to tall spires of lavender flowers. It is now thought to be a hybrid, perhaps with the purple-flowered *V. sibiricum*, which comes from China, Japan, Korea and Russia. 'Adoration' may suffer from mildew in dry seasons.

These are signature plants of the Dutch garden designer and plantsman Piet Oudolf, who has utilised them so effectively with grasses and other perennials in his naturalistic style of planting seen on the High Line in New York City and the Millennium Garden at Pensthorpe Natural Park in the United Kingdom. **GR**

Alternatives

Veronicastrum 'Erica', *Veronicastrum* 'Fascination', *Veronicastrum virginicum* 'Lavendelturm'

Vinca
V. minor 'Ralph Shugert'

Main feature Violet-blue flowers in spring against neat, cream-edged, dark-green leaves
Height 30–38 cm (12–15 in.) **Spread** 45 cm (18 in.)
Position ○ ◑ ● **Hardiness** RHS H7

It is only fair to say that there are two views on these trailing perennials known as periwinkles (*Vinca*). In the United Kingdom and Europe, they are regarded as valuable, weed-suppressing ground-cover plants that will grow in any reasonable soil in sun or shade. However, in much of North America they are seen as destructive, invasive plants, and planting them is discouraged. It pays to follow local guidance and remember that this plant can take over.

There are seven species of these mainly evergreen, mat-forming, woody-based plants growing in a variety of shady places in Europe, North Africa and Asia. Stems spread across the ground, rooting from the leaf joints as they go, or are more arching in growth, rooting where the tips touch the soil. As more stems and shoot tips root, an interlocking mass of low growth develops. The glossy, oval leaves are carried in pairs along the stem. In spring the flowers open. Each 2.5 to 5 centimetre (1–2 in.) flower consists of five slightly unevenly shaped petals held in a star shape on a short tube and with a white ring round the throat. They are held singly on short stalks in the leaf joints. Wild plants have blue or white flowers, although other colours have been developed for gardens.

In the lesser periwinkle, which grows wild in much of Europe and central Asia, the 2- to 4-centimetre-long (0.75–1.5 in.) leaves are neat and usually very dark green in colour, and they are so glossy that on sunny days they sparkle in the light. The slightly purplish-blue flowers open in spring with more sometimes appearing sporadically throughout the summer. 'Ralph Shugert' is especially valued for its large, violet-blue flowers and its neat, cream edge to the relatively small leaves. It is essentially a variegated form of 'La Grave', which is also known as 'Bowles's Blue'. **GR**

Alternatives

Vinca minor 'Argenteovariegata', *Vinca minor* 'Aureovariegata', *Vinca minor* 'Silver Service'

Viola
'Jackanapes'

Main feature Flowers from spring to early autumn on slightly sprawling plants
Height 20 cm (8 in.) **Spread** 35 cm (14 in.)
Position ◑ **Hardiness** RHS H7

Although there are about 500 *Viola* species growing in temperate climates around the world, relatively few are grown in gardens. A popular choice is *V. tricolor*, also known as wild pansy. Growing wild all over Europe, this cheerful little plant is an annual or short-lived perennial. The flowers have five petals: the upper two usually blue or purple; two on each side, which are paler; and one at the bottom that may be similar to the side petals in colour, or white or yellow. Short, dark whiskers radiate from the centre, and there is usually a yellow eye. This is one of the species that is in the background of modern pansies and violas, but it is also in the background of 'Jackanapes'. A little bushier than *V. tricolor*, but equally short-lived, its flowers open over a long season from spring to early autumn, each flower having the upper two petals in brownish crimson and the lower three in bright yellow, with short crimson whiskers. 'Jackanapes' was introduced by Gertrude Jekyll, who is said to have named it for her pet monkey. 'Jackanapes' offers colourful flowers for a shady spot. **GR**

Alternatives

Viola 'Bowles's Black', *Viola* 'Green Goddess'

Viola
V. labradorica

Main feature Deep-violet flowers over purple-tinted foliage
Height 15–20 cm (6–8 in.) **Spread** 30 cm (12 in.)
Position ● **Hardiness** RHS H7

This is an interesting case of a name becoming attached to the wrong plant, and for decades, longer perhaps, gardeners thought they were growing one thing when, in fact, they were growing something else. The true Labrador violet, *V. labradorica*, is a North American native growing in Greenland, most of Canada and south as far as Florida. It has sharply pointed, gently toothed, heart-shaped leaves, and deep-violet flowers in late spring and summer. It is very rarely grown in gardens. The plant that is almost always grown under its name is *V. riviniana* Purpurea Group, a form of the British and European native, dog violet, with purple-tinted blue leaves. The two plants are very similar, the deep-violet flowers of *V. labradorica* distinguishing it from the pale-blue flowers of *V. riviniana*, but the situation is complicated by that purple leaf colouring. The richness of the colour varies with the season, temperature and the amount of moisture in the soil. So the plant grown as *V. labradorica* is, almost without exception, *V. riviniana* Purpurea Group. **GR**

Alternatives

Viola cornuta, *Viola sororia*

Woodwardia
W. radicans

Yucca
Y. gloriosa 'Variegata'

Main feature Impressive ferns with large, evergreen or partially evergreen fronds
Height 60–180 cm (2–6 ft) **Spread** 60–180 cm (2–6 ft)
Position ◑ **Hardiness** RHS H4

Main feature Striking, variegated evergreen leaves all-year-round
Height 90–150 cm (3–5 ft) **Spread** 90 cm (3 ft)
Position ○ **Hardiness** RHS H6

The chain ferns, *Woodwardia*, include up to twenty species related to the hard ferns, *Blechnum*, and are found growing in moist woods in warm, temperate and subtropical parts of the northern hemisphere. All have large fronds, some reaching 3 metres (10 ft) in length, divided twice, or even three times, into slender segments. The name chain fern comes from the arrangement of the spores on the undersides of the fronds. Some species develop bulbils – embryonic plants – along their fronds, often towards the tips, and in these species the fronds often arch over attractively. *W. radicans*, *W. fimbriata*, and *W. unigemmata* are popular with gardeners. The giant chain fern, *W. fimbriata*, is a tall evergreen with slightly spreading upright fronds: a slowly spreading plant for damp conditions. The European chain fern, *W. radicans*, produces long, oval, or lance-shaped, arching, evergreen fronds. *W. unigemmata*, the giant Chinese chain fern, is like a less evergreen version of the European chain fern, with red-tinted young growth and arching fronds. **GR**

Exotic-looking blooms and striking, architectural foliage are so often features associated with a tender disposition. Happily, this glorious yucca breaks the mould. With its explosion of sword-shaped, creamy-yellow-edged leaves, it makes a dramatic contrast to more amorphous plants, and in late summer it has huge panicles of cream, bell-shaped flowers. It is surprisingly hardy and can cope with winter temperatures well below freezing when grown in free-draining soil, as well as shrugging off the summer heat of its native southeastern United States. It will live as happily in a windy coastal location as in a town garden, and grow as well in a pot as in the border, although it deserves to be given a prominent position, and needs some room around it to be fully appreciated. Although fairly slow growing, it will produce a new set of leaves each growing season, and the older leaves at the base will die back (these should be removed). Plants need to be reasonably mature before they flower, but once they start, they will usually flower every year afterwards. **JS**

Alternatives

Blechnum chilense, *Matteuccia struthiopteris*

Alternatives

Yucca gloriosa 'Bright Star', *Yucca flaccida* 'Golden Sword'

Shrubs are perennials, but with woody stems that create a framework that remains above ground throughout the year. Shrubs bring a permanent presence to a garden: each year they will grow outwards as well as upwards, and at some stage they will need pruning. These are investment plants that grow in beauty year after year, provided that you have researched the site and are prepared to do a modicum of annual maintenance.

Shrubs are either evergreen, retaining their leaves throughout the year, or deciduous, which means that their foliage is shed annually. In addition, most shrubs flower or bear fruit, so there is scope for several seasons from a single plant.

Shrubs can be bought either as bare roots or as pot-grown plants. It is important to buy fresh stock, since shrubs are prone to becoming 'pot bound' if confined for too long, and then they fail to thrive when planted out because their roots have grown in a circle.

◑ *Hebe* 'Midsummer Beauty' is an evergreen shrub with plenty of summer flowers.

Abelia
A. × *grandiflora* 'Kaleidoscope'

Main features Vibrantly coloured, small-leaved,
semi-evergreen shrub; fragrant flowers
Height 75 cm (2.5 ft) **Spread** 1.2 m (4 ft)
Position ○ ◑ **Hardiness** RHS H3

In small gardens, plants have to work hard to earn their
place, so when multi-season introductions like
'Kaleidoscope' come along, they create an instant buzz.
This American selection from 2006 is glossy leaved, semi-
evergreen, and constantly produces new and yet more
colourful versions of itself. In spring the new leaves on
this low, rounded shrub are a radiant lime green with a
lemon-yellow edge. Through summer the foliage darkens
to gold, but plants appear colour washed with peachy
orange. The first main flush of fragrant, white-tinged pink
flowers appears in late spring, but blooming continues
through to autumn. The rosy sepals surrounding the
flower buds persist, adding to the display. With the arrival
of cooler nights in autumn, the next wave sweeps across
'Kaleidoscope', turning the shoot tips intense orange
with maroon highlights. These colours develop through
winter, making this a superb container specimen.

Situated close to the front of a sunny border,
'Kaleidoscope' could be partnered with herbs and
perennials preferring fertile, well-drained soil. Blue
grasses and silver- or purple-shaded herbs make a great
foil for the leaves of this abelia. Echo the peachy tints
with apricot patio roses, achilleas and echinacea; in
autumn, contrast with blue- and purple-flowered
Caryopteris, *Perovskia* and *Ceratostigma*.

The glossy abelia, *A.* × *grandiflora* with dark-green
foliage, is noted for its long flowering period that attracts
bees and butterflies. It is much larger than the compact
'Kaleidoscope' or the other gold-leaf or variegated forms.
These include the dainty, white-variegated 'Confetti' and
the yellow-green 'Francis Mason', which also develops
bronzy winter tints and, like 'Kaleidoscope', orange-
shaded spring growth. 'Hopleys' has cream-yellow to
white-edged leaves. **JH**

Alternatives

Abelia × *grandiflora* 'Confetti', *Abelia* × *grandiflora* 'Francis
Mason', *Abelia* × *grandiflora* 'Hopleys'

Abies
A. lasiocarpa var. *arizonica* 'Compacta'

Main features Evergreen, blue and grey foliage;
structural form; versatile plant
Height 4 m (13 ft) **Spread** 2.4 m (8 ft)
Position ○ **Hardiness** RHS H7

Since their popularity in the 1960s and 1970s, conifers have largely fallen out of favour in gardens – never was a group of plants so snubbed! Thankfully, the realisation that there is a wonderful variety of species available that do not automatically grow into giants has brought about a sea change in attitudes, which means that these versatile plants are reclaiming their place as valuable additions to any varied planting scheme.

A. lasiocarpa var. *arizonica* 'Compacta' (commonly known as Compact corkbark fir) is an outstanding example of a conifer that would add a positive dimension to any garden. It is a very luxuriant, blue-needled tree, specially cultivated to grow slowly. Bushy, low-growing and medium-sized, it fits into the dwarf conifer category, growing anywhere between 4 to 8 centimetres (1.5–3 in.) a year and reaching its ultimate height of 4 metres (13 ft) in anything from ten to twenty years. It makes a dense pyramid that is usually very symmetrical in form and for this reason is popularly grown as a Christmas tree. Large cones are held vertically on its upper branches – a good way to tell fir from spruce, whose cones are pendent.

This evergreen fir can be used in a border to anchor successional planting schemes; as a vertical focal point, to offset contrasting plants; in a group of other diverse conifers; or as an individual specimen in its own right. Successful planting schemes contain a balance of different sizes, forms and colours with layers of varying textures. This corkbark fir will form a juxtaposition with any nonconiferous plant, and therefore is a winning choice to make. Combine with the spreading form of a Japanese maple (ideally a purple cultivar) or set drifts of *Hakonechloa macra* 'Aureola' at its feet to give definition to all the elements and make a tremendously pleasing planting combination. **ER**

Alternatives

Picea pungens Glauca Group 'Globosa', *Picea pungens* Glauca Group 'Hoopsii'

Acer

A. palmatum 'Bloodgood'

Main features Wine-red summer foliage; scarlet autumn foliage
Height 3 m (10 ft) **Spread** 1.8 m (6 ft)
Position ○ ◑ **Hardiness** RHS H6

Deservedly the most popular and widely grown of the red-leaved Japanese maples, 'Bloodgood' lives up to its name with dark twigs that carry abundant purple-red, lobed leaves that turn rich scarlet in autumn. The stems are ascending and quite upright on young plants, the habit becoming broader and more spreading as the shrub grows. More mature plants carry attractive, red, winged fruits in hanging clusters in late summer and autumn. This robust variety needs an open, sunny position for best foliage colour, and it copes with more wind and exposure than many other varieties of Japanese maple. As one of the best purple-foliage subjects, 'Bloodgood' makes a striking planting partner for contrasting silver, golden or variegated shrubs. It is also ideal as a focal point in a bed or border of lower-growing shrubs and perennials. Evoking images of the Japanese landscape, it associates well with gravel, stones and water. 'Bloodgood' is the ideal choice as a foliage tree for a small garden, or for a courtyard or balcony if grown in a large container. **AMcl**

Alternatives

Acer palmatum 'Fireglow', *Acer palmatum* 'Shaina'

◐ *Acer palmatum* **'Bloodgood'** showing summer foliage brings a tree-like structure to small spaces when grown in a pot.

Acer

A. palmatum 'Katsura'

Main features Leaves pale-orange when young; rich, orange autumn foliage
Height 1.5 m (5 ft) **Spread** 1.2 m (4 ft)
Position ○ ◑ **Hardiness** RHS H6

This is a delightfully delicate Japanese maple of refined character. Pale-green leaves with long, pointed lobes and finely serrated, red-flushed edges are poised gracefully, appearing to hang along the branches, especially when young. The new leaves unfurl pale orange in early spring, a delight with early blue flowers, such as muscari and myosotis. Throughout summer the young leaves at the tips of the shoots retain an orange hue, until the foliage changes to a richer orange and deep yellow in autumn. 'Katsura' is a petite Japanese maple that will convey the maturity of a bonsai in a small garden. It is at its best in partial shade, in a sheltered position away from strong winds. It is an excellent subject for a well-chosen pot or container, particularly when grouped with caramel-leaved heucheras, ferns or *Ophiopogon*. 'Katsura' suits minimalist and contemporary planting schemes where its form and foliage can be shown off to advantage. The leaves of this drought-sensitive shrub may brown and curl at the tips or scorch in strong sunlight. **AMcl**

Alternatives

Acer palmatum 'Beni-Maiko', *Acer palmatum* 'Orange Dream'

Aesculus
A. parviflora

Main features Attractive white flower spikes;
architectural foliage and form; attracts pollinators
Height 4 m (13 ft) **Spread** 4.7 m (15.5 ft)
Position ◑ ● **Hardiness** RHS H5

Despite being native to the open woodlands of the
southeastern United States, *A. parviflora* is largely
underused on both sides of the Atlantic, a situation
that deserves rectifying. For this plant is arguably one of
the best flowering shrubs for shady areas. Also known as
bottlebrush buckeye, it is a handsome, well-built plant –
mostly wider than it is tall – that makes a good tiered
shape. Its foliage is an attractive feature in its own right:
large compound leaflets, unfurling bronze, settling into
a dark green and finally turning yellow before falling.
In midsummer, masses of white, conical, fluffy flower
heads appear, standing about 30 centimetres (12 in.) tall
above the horizontally held leaves, providing a pleasing
directional contrast. These appear cream-coloured from
a distance, but up close they are a treat: each tiny flower
is splashed with orangey red and throws out immensely
long stamen, like the most luxuriant eyelashes. This
versatile plant is an absolute winner when used as a lawn
specimen or in a mass planting for difficult places. **ER**

Alternative

Aesculus parviflora var. *serotina* 'Rogers'

Berberis
B. valdiviana

Main features Drooping clusters of saffron-yellow
flowers in spring; glossy evergreen
Height 2.4–4 m (8–13 ft) **Spread** 2.4–4 m (8–13 ft)
Position ○ ◑ **Hardiness** RHS H4

In late spring grape-like bunches of saffron-yellow flowers
festoon this evergreen native of the Valdivia Province in
Chile. Later, in the autumn, the flowers give way to black,
round fruits. *Berberis* is popular for the almost year-round
interest it provides from the flowers, fruits and foliage.
This bushy species possesses long, smooth, dark-green
leaves, polished to a shine and almost without the sharp
spines that arm many of the other 450 species. Although
slow growing at first, *B. valdiviana* is worth the wait. When
it eventually reaches full height, at any age between ten
and twenty years old, it is much admired, not only for its
wonderful, drooping racemes of flowers but also for its
rarity. It is notoriously difficult to propagate, particularly
from seed, but enthusiasts willing to persevere might have
better luck from cuttings. Once established, *B. valdiviana*
is relatively easy to grow and very adaptable. It thrives in
most kinds of soil – clay, sand, chalk and loam – as long as
it is not waterlogged, and it is a useful ornamental plant
for gardeners with more acidic soils. **RSJ**

Alternatives

Berberis darwinii, Berberis × *frikartii* 'Amstelveen'

Buddleja
B. davidii Buzz Series

Main features Flowers in summer and autumn;
attracts butterflies
Height 1.2 m (4 ft) **Spread** 1.2 m (4 ft)
Position ○ ◑ **Hardiness** RHS H5

Butterflies linger on the nectar-rich flowers of all types of
B. davidii, so what makes the Buzz Series special? These
plants are bred for small gardens and containers, so any
outside space can be transformed into a butterfly-feeding
station. Although the plants will reach only 1.2 metres (4
ft) in height, less than half that of a typical *Buddleja,* the
flower spikes are still long and packed with nectar. The
Buzz Series really comes into its own when grown in a
container, because the height is further reduced to 60 to
90 centimetres (2–3 ft). If you keep it fed and watered and
remove the faded flower spikes promptly, new flowers
will form from summer to the first frost. The series was
bred by Thompson & Morgan in Suffolk, and launched
in 2009 with Buzz Magenta (pictured). Others in the
Buzz Series have followed, but Buzz Magenta – with its
intense red-purple flowers – has the edge for a gardener.
It looks a bit classier than other varieties and, like most
dark flowers, it appears less scruffy than plants with white
or pale blooms if you neglect the deadheading. **LD**

Alternatives

Buddleja 'Blue Chip', *Buddleja davidii* 'Black Knight'

Buddleja
'Lochinch'

Main feature Deciduous shrub with scented
summer flowers
Height 2–2.4 m (6–8 ft) **Spread** 2–2.4 m (6–8 ft)
Position ○ **Hardiness** RHS H5

This is the buddleja to grow if you want a choice 'blue'
flowered shrub to set off other flowers in a mixed border
or to include in a wildlife garden. The flowers are borne
on erect, cone-shaped panicles in summer; close up,
you will find that they are scented, and in addition to
the lovely, soft, violet-blue petals, each flower has an
orange eye. The foliage, which is grey when young and
later green grey with whitish undersides to the leaves,
complements the flowers. 'Lochinch' is a medium-sized
shrub, easily kept in check by annual pruning. It has the
familiar hardy *B. davidii* as one of its parents, but the more
interesting foliage and flower features are from its other
parent, *B. fallowiana.* This species from southwest China
was introduced to the West by plant collector George
Forrest in 1921. It has white woolly young stems and leaves
and very fragrant flowers of lavender-blue but needs a
sheltered spot. 'Lochinch' arose as a chance seedling in
the grounds of Lochinch Castle in Scotland and is cold
hardy to -15°C (5°F). **LD**

Alternatives

Buddleja davidii 'Glasnevin Hybrid', *Buddleja* 'Ellen's Blue'

Buddleja
B. globosa

Main features Fragrant and attractive orange flowers; attracts wildlife; good screening foliage
Height 5 m (16 ft) **Spread** 5 m (16 ft)
Position ○ ◐ **Hardiness** RHS H5

Buddlejas do well in gardens and are generally referred to as butterfly bushes for their ability to draw multitudes of these insects to their nectar-packed flowers. Gardeners should also be as attracted to the unusual orange, honey-scented flowers of the orange ball tree *B. globosa*. Fuzzy, golf-ball–shaped buds open to reveal intense tangerine-coloured clusters of blossom. A comparatively early bloomer, it gets going before many butterfly species are about, but it still attracts bees. The leaves are mid-green and rough-textured, with pale woolly undersides. Lanceolate and growing up to around 15 centimetres (6 in.) or more, they provide useful screening. Although strictly classified as deciduous, given a sheltered site, this buddleja will drop its leaves in only the harshest winters. At the back of a border this eye-catching buddleja looks sensational set against something early flowering and blue, like *Ceanothus arboreus* 'Trewithen Blue'. Avoid pruning unless absolutely necessary as the hollow stems can become waterlogged. If needed, do so in spring. **ER**

Alternatives

Buddleja asiatica, Buddleja alternifolia

Buxus
B. sempervirens

Main features Evergreen foliage; fragrant flowers; architectural shape as topiary or hedges
Height 5 m (16 ft) **Spread** 5 m (16 ft)
Position ○ ◐ ● **Hardiness** RHS H5

There cannot be many gardens that do not have one or more box plants, often fashioned into intricate topiaries or used to create the elaborate patterns in knot gardens and parterres. Many historic houses and gardens have huge numbers of box hedges, reflecting its importance as a plant in the history of garden design. An evergreen shrub or small tree, it can reach 9 metres (29 ft) if left unpruned. The small, dark-green, leathery leaves are arranged in opposite pairs along the shoots, and in spring, inconspicuous clusters of scented flowers appear. The foliage also has a distinct smell. It is a hardy, bushy shrub, although the new spring growth is prone to frost damage. It will grow in sunny or even densely shaded sites, and the combination of its tolerance of close clipping and evergreen nature makes it a versatile shrub. It has many uses in the garden apart from traditional topiary balls, cubes and pyramids, which all add formality and structure to borders. *Buxus* can be clipped into formal or informal shapes with usually only one clipping per season. **MP**

Alternatives

Buxus sempervirens 'Suffruticosa', *Buxus microphylla* 'Faulkner'

Buxus sempervirens clipped into spiral and balls in a small topiary garden designed by Sue Milward. ➲

Callicarpa
C. bodinieri var. giraldii 'Profusion'

Main features Berries and tinted foliage in autumn; cut branches of berries for flower arrangements
Height 3 m (10 ft) **Spread** 2.4 m (8 ft)
Position ○ ◐ **Hardiness** RHS H5

This shrub, originating from central and west China, is worthy of a place in any medium to large garden, purely for the spectacular colour of its autumn fruits and foliage. Surprisingly, it is a member of the dead nettle family (*Lamiaceae*). This deciduous shrub (also known as beautyberry) grows to 3 by 2.4 metres (10 x 8 ft) with opposite pairs of pointed leaves that emerge a bronze-purple shade, later turning plain green. In summer, clusters of compact, tiny, purplish, rather inconspicuous flowers appear in the leaf axils, and these develop in autumn into amazing metallic-purple clusters of conspicuous, tiny bead-like berries. These show up better after the leaves have turned to shades of soft-rose madder and then fallen.

To ensure good pollination, it is advisable to plant more than one beautyberry. Plant in a sunny or partial shaded position, in any neutral to acidic soil that is well drained. A soil that is too alkaline will cause leaf yellowing. It requires no regular pruning, making it easy to manage in the garden. If necessary, prune back stems in spring. Bare branches of the striking berries can be cut for use in the home.

Use this plant to brighten up an autumn border or as part of a mixed shrub border next to a white-and-cream evergreen variegated shrub, such as the cream-variegated privet (*Ligustrum ovalifolium* 'Argenteum'), to show up the berries. Alternatively, try it next to the equally striking shrub with metallic-blue berries known as sapphire berry (*Symplocos sawafutagi*). It makes an excellent specimen group when three are planted together in a circular bed in a lawn and underplanted with late-flowering autumn crocuses (*Colchicum*). Wherever you decide to plant it, 'Profusion' will be the talk of your neighbourhood. **MP**

Alternative

Callicarpa japonica 'Leucocarpa'

Calluna
C. vulgaris 'Silver Queen'

Main features Year-round interest from evergreen, often coloured, foliage; late-summer and autumn flowers
Height 40 cm (16 in.) **Spread** 60 cm (24 in.)
Position ○ ◑ **Hardiness** RHS H7

This lovely heather (*C. vulgaris* 'Silver Queen') is a dense, low-growing, evergreen shrub ideal for using as ground cover. The foliage is covered with fine hairs, creating a silvery-grey effect, and the stems are tipped in late summer and early autumn with generous sprays of tiny, pale pinkish-purple flowers. These are rich in nectar with a delicious scent and are highly attractive to bees. Where heather grows wild, in Europe and Asia Minor, it can cover large tracts of ground, allowing bees to produce much-prized heather honey. The flowers are also good for cutting and, once dried, will retain their colour and last almost indefinitely.

Heathers are popular, ornamental plants that are easy to grow provided you have an acidic soil with a good moisture supply without waterlogging. They are very hardy and revel in an open, sunny position, such as an island bed or the south side of a mixed border. Plants can tolerate moderate shade. Heathers also work well in containers, providing year-round colour and interest. Just make sure they have ericaceous (lime-free) compost and are not allowed to dry out. To keep the plants neat, prune off the dead flowers and most of that year's growth in winter or spring. This is a quick, easy job using shears.

There are hundreds of different varieties of heather to choose from, with flower colours ranging from white through all shades of pink and purple. Foliage variations are even more striking and include lime green, gold, silver, white, red and orange, often with seasonal changes. 'Kinlochruel' has long sprays of ice-white, double flowers over dark foliage, whereas 'Darkness' is a deep red-purple with bright-green leaves. 'Wickwar Flame' has mauve flowers with foliage that is bright orange and yellow in summer, deepening to copper and gold in winter. **RKW**

Alternatives

Calluna vulgaris 'Annemarie', *Calluna vulgaris* 'Firefly'

Camellia
C. × *williamsii* 'Donation'

Main features Shade-tolerant evergreen; semi-double spring flowers
Height 2.4 m (8 ft) **Spread** 1.2 m (4 ft)
Position ○ ◑ ● **Hardiness** RHS H5

Described in the standard work *The Hillier Manual of Trees and Shrubs* as the most beautiful camellia raised in the twentieth century, *C.* × *williamsii* 'Donation' arose in 1938 at Borde Hill Garden in West Sussex, when head gardener Walter Fleming crossed *C. japonica* 'Masayoshi' with the pale-pink-flowered *C. saluenensis*. All three plants are still in the extensive and historic gardens at Borde Hill. The 'Donation' cultivar was soon recognised by the Royal Horticultural Society, first in 1941 with an Award of Merit, and it still holds its own with a present-day revised RHS Award of Garden Merit. The name 'Donation' was given by Stephenson Robert Clarke, the present garden owner's great grandfather, who wanted to make the plant a gift to the nation.

There are a great many other *C.* × *williamsii* crosses to choose from, and they all tend to have the foliage of the *C. japonica* cultivars combined with the beautiful flowers of *C. saluenensis*. Some are seedlings or crosses of 'Donation', such as 'Julia Hamiter' and 'Glenn's Orbit'. *Camellia* makes a beautiful, long-lasting shrub, offering smart foliage and impressive spring flowers. It can be allowed full rein to mature as a free-standing shrub in a woodland garden or shrub border, thriving where the soil is moist, acidic or neutral, but it is versatile enough to fit in smaller spaces too. For example, it is amenable to being trained on a wall or fence (any aspect except where the early morning sun can damage frozen buds). Its shade tolerance also makes it a classic choice for urban or city courtyards: a specimen will thrive in a tub of ericaceous (lime-free) compost, and in the shelter of buildings, the blooms last for ages. Just remember that over the summer, all camellias need moisture at their roots, because that is when the buds are formed for the following spring. **LD**

Alternatives

Camellia × *williamsii* 'Elsie Jury', *Camellia* × *williamsii* 'J. C. Williams', *Camellia* × *williamsii* 'Glenn's Orbit'

Camellia × *williamsii* '**Donation**' is one of the most garden-worthy camellias. ➔

Camellia
C. japonica 'Bob Hope'

Main features Blowsy flowers in spring; dark-green, glossy evergreen leaves
Height 2.4–4 m (8–13 ft) **Spread** 1.5–2.4 m (5–8 ft)
Position ○ ◑ **Hardiness** RHS H5

Bob Hope was an English-born American actor and comedian who did nothing by halves. Beloved by his adopted country and devotees worldwide, he was married for sixty-nine years, his career spanned nearly eighty years and he lived until he was one hundred years old. Just like its namesake, *C. japonica* 'Bob Hope' is a long-lived showstopper.

The deep-red, showy flowers, with yellow stamen and pretty ruffled petals, are semi-double. They are 10 to 13 centimetres (4–5 in.) in diameter and put on a spectacular performance in spring, appearing either solo or in blowsy ensembles against a backcloth of the evergreen, glossy *Camellia* leaves that are so familiar to gardeners. A stalwart of the woodland garden or semi-shaded garden areas, 'Bob Hope' must be thoughtfully planted in a sheltered position out of the way of cold dry winds and early morning sun. It should also be protected from late frost, because frost will damage the flower buds, thereby causing the gardener undue disappointment.

Cultivated in 1972 at Nuccio's Nurseries in Altadens, California, 'Bob Hope' can reach up to 4 metres (13 ft) by the time it is fully grown, which can be anytime between ten and twenty years, depending on its growing conditions. This plant is a bushy but compact cultivar, and it grows well in most soils, acidic and neutral, as long as they are well drained. However, it does not enjoy waterlogged feet. Grow this gregarious performer with *Rhododendron*, *Azalea* and *Iris* in a shady flower border to create the wow factor in spring and welcome greenery in the winter. Borders under walls will provide it with the shelter it needs. 'Bob Hope' is well suited to less exposed urban and courtyard gardens and will flourish in pots on patios, benefiting from more protected areas in the garden when temperatures drop. **RSJ**

Alternatives

Camellia japonica 'Alba Plena', *Camellia japonica* 'Elegans', *Camellia japonica* 'Gloire de Nantes'

Carpenteria
C. californica 'Elizabeth'

Main features Clusters of large, cup shaped flowers in
summer; glossy, evergreen leaves; flaky bark
Height 1.5–2.4 m (5–8 ft) **Spread** 1.5–2.4 m (5–8 ft)
Position ○ **Hardiness** RHS H5

It is no surprise that *C. californica* 'Elizabeth' hails from
the Golden State of California. This rare genus – named
after Dr William Marbury Carpenter, a botanist from
Louisiana – comprises only one species. Although it is only
found on a few scrubby, dry slopes and in pine forests in
Fresno County, California, there is nothing scrubby about
the cultivar 'Elizabeth'. A compact evergreen shrub, it is
named for another Californian, the little-known botanist
Elizabeth McClintock, who specialised in taxonomy and
flowering plants native to California. It is more common
now in gardens than in its natural habitat.

From early to midsummer, narrow, glossy, dark-
green, evergreen leaves are peppered with masses of
pure-white flowers that have a froth of egg-yolk yellow
stamen at their centres. A close relative of *Philadelphus*
(mock orange), 'Elizabeth' often goes by the common
name of tree anemone and has deliciously fragrant
flowers like its cousin. If grown in a sunny position
against a wall – to protect it from damage to its leaves
in harsh winters – this plant will eventually reach up to
2.4 metres (8 ft) in height and almost as much in width.
It suits any kind of well-drained soil, but prefers dry soils
akin to its natural habitat, because in wet areas it can be
prone to fungal leaf spot.

A perfect plant for courtyard gardens and sheltered
mixed borders, 'Elizabeth' is also a useful shrub for
the low-maintenance garden, providing evergreen
structure in the winter. Some gardeners like to lift the
crown to show off the attractive flaky bark on more
mature stems. In the wild, seedlings of 'Elizabeth' are
few and far between, but luckily, it possesses the ability
to regenerate from sprouting stumps after wildfires.
Fortunately, gardeners do not need to go to that extreme
and can propagate from semi-hardwood cuttings. **RSJ**

Alternatives

Carpenteria californica 'Bodnant', *Carpenteria californica*
'Ladhams' Variety'

Caryopteris

C. × *clandonensis* 'First Choice'

Main features Compact, aromatic shrub with deep-blue flowers; attracts butterflies from summer to autumn
Height 60–90 cm (24–36 in.) **Spread** 90–120 cm (3–4 ft)
Position ○ **Hardiness** RHS H5

Standing out from the crowd of gentle blue *Caryopteris*, 'First Choice' (also known as bluebeard) produces a long succession of ultramarine blooms from summer to early autumn. The indigo sepals covering the flower buds persist long after the petals have disappeared. Dusky hues run through the plants with stems crimson tinged and the grey-green leaves suffused purple with winter cold. Being so densely branched, the effect is intensified. Although there are other dark bluebeards, 'First Choice' has the edge because of its neat, compact habit, slightly longer flowering, and the handsome flower-foliage combination. Its blooms make a dramatic foil for smoldering autumn foliage, and if space allows, it is worth repeating this front-of-the-border plant at intervals or grouping close to shrubs with orange, red and purple leaf tints for greater impact. In most of the cultivars, the blooms are set against lavender-scented, light grey-green leaves with toothed edges. The look is distinctly Mediterranean. **JH**

Alternative

Caryopteris × clandonensis 'Heavenly Blue'

Ceanothus

'Concha'

Main features Evergreen foliage; abundant early summer flowers; attracts bees and butterflies
Height 3 m (10 ft) **Spread** 2.4 m (8 ft)
Position ○ **Hardiness** RHS H4

Evergreen 'Concha' in full bloom is an arresting sight, as the whole shrub erupts like a spectacular firework in a cloud of sapphire blue. In a sheltered position, in full sunshine, this Californian lilac steals the garden show for around three weeks, before returning to its role as a small-leaved, evergreen shrub. For the rest of the year its loose habit and arching branches are a lighter addition to the garden than many other evergreens provide. In full bloom the fluffy, deep-blue flower clusters are a magnet for bees and butterflies. It makes a wonderful planting partner for silver- and golden-foliage shrubs and associates well with roses. 'Concha' can be grown as a free-standing subject in a bed or border; its lax habit also makes it ideal as a wall shrub. 'Concha' is perhaps the most reliable and easy-to-grow evergreen ceanothus. It grows on most soils but dislikes wet conditions and shallow, dry chalk soils. Evergreen ceanothus grow quickly and flower from an early age, but they are not long-lived. **AMcI**

Alternatives

Ceanothus thyrsiflorus 'Skylark', *Ceanothus* 'Italian Skies'

Ceanothus 'Concha,' in a warm and sheltered location, will produce a wonderful flowering display in early summer. ➔

Cercis
C. canadensis
'Forest Pansy'

Main features Heart-shaped leaves; clusters of pea-like flowers
Height 12 m (40 ft) **Spread** 8 m (26 ft)
Position ○ ◑ **Hardiness** RHS H5

There are around ten species of shrubs and small trees in the genus *Cercis*. In their natural habitat they grow in woodland or on rocky hillsides, from the Mediterranean to North America and Central and eastern Asia. Distinctive for their heart-shaped leaves, pea-like flowers in shades of pink, red or white, and pods of seeds, *Cercis* species have made an easy transition from wild plant to well-loved garden plant. They make excellent specimen plants but are just as happy trained against walls or planted in borders. The leaves of *C. canadensis* start life as a deep shade of bronze, then mature to bright green; the foliage finally turns yellow in the autumn. In the meantime this species produces pale-rose flowers in late spring to early summer. 'Forest Pansy' is considered to be one of the loveliest cultivars. The great plantsman Graham Stuart Thomas described it as 'remarkable' and waxed lyrical about its outstanding, deep red-purple foliage. **RSJ**

Alternatives

Cercis canadensis 'Ruby Falls', *Cercis canadensis* Lavender Twist = 'Covey', *Cercis chinensis* 'Avondale'

Chaenomeles
C. speciosa
'Moerloosei'

Main features Tough shrub; useful in shade; attractive spring flowers; amenable to training; autumn fruits
Height 2.4 m (8 ft) **Spread** 2.4 m (8 ft)
Position ○ ◑ **Hardiness** RHS H6

Known as flowering quince, *Chaenomeles* is a hardy, deciduous genus of spiny shrubs, producing masses of flowers in colours from white, through pink, salmon and coral to cherry red. *C. speciosa* 'Moerloosei' is considered to be one of the best cultivars for its large, white and blush-pink, apple-blossom–like flowers, that smother its bare branches from early spring. Glossy, dark-green leaves take over, and in late summer yellow fruits appear. The fruit can be used for its high-pectin content to make jellies, although the plant is no relation to the edible quince tree (*Cydonia oblonga*). It is a spiny, rather unruly specimen, which works well as a hedge. If left in a border as a free-standing shrub, it might be considered dull after the glory of its flowers has passed; however, if trained, or espaliered, against a wall, it provides a great framework upon which to grow climbers, like clematis. Prune after flowering, reducing the previous year's growth by half. **ER**

Alternatives

Chaenomeles speciosa 'Geisha Girl', *Chaenomeles speciosa* 'Nivalis', *Chaenomeles × superba* 'Crimson and Gold'

 Cercis canadensis **'Forest Pansy'** is valued for its red-purple foliage, as is shown here in a garden in Spokane, Washington, USA.

Chamaerops
C. humilis

Chimonanthus
C. praecox 'Grandiflorus'

Main features Evergreen foliage; architectural plant
Height 1.5–2 m (5–7 ft) **Spread** 1.5–2 m (5–7 ft)
Position ○ ◑
Hardiness RHS H4

Main features Spicy winter scent; intriguing waxy flowers
Height 3 m (10 ft) **Spread** 3 m (10 ft)
Position ○ ◑ **Hardiness** RHS H5

The dwarf fan palm is one of only two palms native to Europe and is found wild in southwest Europe and North Africa, where it grows on the sides of mountains in coastal areas. It is a variable plant in size, colour and habit, some being more upright with a short trunk whilst others are more ground hugging and bushy in shape. The large leaves are deeply divided into stiff leaflets, creating a fan-like appearance. The entire plant is mound shaped with a mass of leaves emanating from the centre. Mature plants may produce a cluster of rather insignificant flowers, followed by fruits resembling dates. Its robust nature makes it an ideal specimen for windy and coastal areas, where it has a high salt-level tolerance. A mature plant will usually regenerate from the base if cut back by severe weather. This palm is exceedingly drought tolerant, making it ideal for a large container. It can also be planted in a gravel garden. It associates well with yuccas and *Kniphofia caulescens*. **MP**

If there is little that excites you in the winter garden, plant the large-flowered wintersweet *C. praecox* 'Grandiflorus' in a sunny spot on a wall near the house, and you will gladly await winter's arrival. The main attraction is the penetrating spicy scent of the waxy blooms, which appear from autumn to spring. Indeed, viewed from a short distance, this shrub or small tree appears rather unremarkable, but the unique flowers demand closer inspection. There are two rings of waxy petals – the outer ones a fragile cream yellow while the inner petals are splashed conspicuously with purple. Place a cut stem indoors, in a cool spot to preserve the scent. As an added bonus the mid-green leaves, which arrive towards the end of the flowering spell, also give off a perfume when crushed. Wintersweet's upright, rounded shape will complement either spire-shaped or horizontally inclined plants. Plant spring bulbs, such as hyacinths and narcissus, around its base to boost the border's impact. **ER**

Alternative

Chamaerops humilis var. *argentea*

Alternative

Chimonanthus praecox, syn. *Chimonanthus fragrans*

Chionanthus
C. virginicus

Choisya
C. × dewitteana
'Aztec Pearl'

Main features Pendulous fringes of flowers, followed by berries; deciduous shrub; glossy, green foliage
Height 2.4–3.4 m (8–11 ft) **Spread** 2.4–3.4 m (8–11 ft)
Position ○ **Hardiness** RHS H5

Main features Evergreen aromatic foliage; scented flowers in summer and autumn
Height 1.5–2.5 m (5–8.5 ft) **Spread** 1.5–2.5 m (5–8.5 ft)
Position ○ **Hardiness** RHS H4

The snowflower, or North American fringe tree, is a member of the olive family. In the right conditions this large shrub is festooned with long, pendulous fringes of cream-white, spidery blooms. Each flower has between four and five narrow strap-like petals and a slight but fresh scent. In between the floriferous mayhem is the deciduous foliage of large, glossy, dark-green leaves that can grow up to 20 centimetres (8 in.) long. Flowers are not produced on young plants; to reach its full-flowering potential, C. virginicus needs hot summers and cold winters, so flowering of this shrub is best in a continental climate. Yet, when conditions allow, the flowers of C. virginicus appear from early to midsummer, followed by dark-blue berries. C. virginicus will grace sunny borders and beds beneath walls where the shelter protects the leaves and stems from winter temperatures. The shrub's discovery is credited to John Banister, a missionary, who travelled to Virginia in 1678. **RSJ**

All types of choisya enrich a garden with their sweetly scented flowers. C. × dewitteana 'Aztec Pearl' was the first hybrid, created in 1989. It combines the repeat-flowering quality of C. ternata with the more graceful foliage shape of C. arizonica. The results are the truly lustrous 'Aztec Pearl'. It is an excellent small evergreen shrub with a rounded habit, making loose domes of aromatic, bright-green, slender, palm-shaped leaves. In late spring it is covered with large highly fragrant flowers. These are white opening from pink-tinged buds, and as a bonus, this floral show is repeated in autumn. 'Aztec Pearl' has yet more going for it: drought resistant, genuinely low maintenance – it needs no regular pruning to keep it looking good – and its good looks extend right down to ground level. It suits all styles of garden and does really well against a sunny wall in particular. Plant highly fragrant 'Aztec Pearl' in a sunny, sheltered spot to make the most of it. **RC**

Alternative

Chionanthus retusus

Alternatives

Choisya × dewitteana 'White Dazzler', Choisya ternata

Cistus
C. × lenis 'Grayswood Pink'

Main features Low-growing, evergreen, ground-cover shrub; profusion of pink summer blooms
Height 30–90 cm (12–36 in.) **Spread** 90–150 cm (3–5 ft)
Position ○ **Hardiness** RHS H4

For weeks from early to midsummer, this aromatic evergreen opens a succession of circular blooms, each lasting a day. Reminiscent of a dog rose, the single flowers are clear pink, shading to white at the centre, with a bold tuft of golden stamen. The evergreen, grey-green leaves, narrowly oval in shape, are carried on a network of densely clothed prostrate branches, often little more than 30 centimetres (12 in.) high.

C. × lensis 'Grayswood Pink' is perfect for fronting a sunny mixed border alongside purple-flowered Salvia × sylvestris 'Mainacht' or lavender, together with a backdrop of Jerusalem sage (Phlomis fruticosa) or Ceanothus. It will carpet the ground for 1.5 metres (5 ft) or more in time and could be used to tumble over a retaining wall or to fill a sizeable space in a gravel garden, with the evergreen grass, golden oats (Stipa gigantea) added for vertical accent. In small urban gardens, plant 'Grayswood Pink' in a narrow border and let the stems spill out to soften an expanse of paving. Aptly named the rock rose, all cistus thrive on poor, stony ground. Despite their Mediterranean origins, some, like 'Grayswood Pink,' are reasonably hardy given sharp drainage and a sunny, sheltered spot. The backdrop of a warm wall provides extra winter protection in colder regions. Once established, no pruning or watering is required. Limiting fertiliser keeps plant growth compact.

Another excellent compact cistus alternative, which does not spread as widely is C. × pulverulentus 'Sunset', which carries hot-pink flowers and is ideal for sunny, city courtyards. If you are looking for a country-garden feel, why not try C. × purpureus, a large-flowered rock rose with maroon spots at the centre of its tissue paper–like blooms. 'Alan Fradd' is a pure-white form with similar maroon blotches. **JH**

Alternatives

Cistus × pulverulentus 'Sunset', Cistus × purpureus, Cistus × purpureus 'Alan Fradd'

Clerodendrum
C. trichotomum var. *fargesii*

Main features Deciduous bush or small tree; fragrant
white flowers and red sepals; metallic-turquoise fruits
Height 4 m (13 ft) **Spread** 4 m (13 ft)
Position ○ ◑ **Hardiness** RHS H4

The fabulously named harlequin glorybower takes
on an exotic air from the moment its broad, heavily
veined leaves unfurl in spring. The young shoots and
leaf stems are shaded purple-red, and this colouring is
echoed at flowering time, in mid- to late summer, when
clusters of pinkish-red 'pods' pop to reveal starry, highly
fragrant white blooms with protruding stamen. The
small, round-headed trees or large shrubs are a sight to
see in full bloom, as the tresses of flowers can almost
cover the leafy canopy. Yet in autumn, it is obvious that
the harlequin glorybower has saved the best till last.
A ring of swept-back sepals, now deep crimson-red,
surrounds the developing fruits, which starts out green
as you would expect, but then morph into an incredible
metallic turquoise and finally a lustrous peacock blue.
The unexpected colour is enough to stop you in your
tracks. Underplanting with the low, shrubby *Ceratostigma
willmottianum* adds even more vibrant-blue, autumn
colour. White-flowered Japanese anemone also work
well with the glorybower's berries, or try white colchicum.

There is a striking variegated form of *C. trichotomum*
var. *fargesii* called 'Carnival,' whose young leaves have a
broad, cream-yellow, wavy margin that pales to a white
edge over time. It does not have the vigour or hardiness
of the parent and needs more shelter and protection
from full sun than the variety *fargesii*. However, it does
also flower and fruit well.

Grow *C. trichotomum* var. *fargesii* in full sun or partial
shade in any reasonably fertile and moisture-retentive
soil with added organic matter. Find a spot sheltered
from strong winds to avoid leaf damage. Minimal
pruning is needed in early spring. Seedlings may occur.
Avoid disturbing the foliage as it releases an unpleasant
odour. Note that the fruits can be toxic. **JH**

Alternative

Clerodendrum trichotomum var. *fargesii* 'Carnival',
Clerodendrum bungei

Clethra
C. alnifolia 'Ruby Spice'

Main features Showy, deciduous, shade-tolerant shrub; pink bottlebrush blooms; strongly fragrant flowers
Height 1.2–1.8 m (4–6 ft) **Spread** 90–150 cm (3–5 ft)
Position ◑ ● **Hardiness** RHS H5

While spring gardens are full of shade-loving, flowering shrubs, it is difficult to find showy specimens to take over in summer. However, C. alnifolia 'Ruby Spice', also known as the sweet pepper bush, fills that niche perfectly. From mid- to late summer it opens its candy-pink buds to reveal fluffy bottlebrushes, a pleasing contrast to the domed heads of hydrangeas. Each flower has deep-pink edges with a white centre, giving a pretty two-tone effect. Bees and butterflies are lured in by its warm, spicy clove-like fragrance: this is definitely a shrub to site within sniffing distance of a door, pathway or terrace. However, take care to plant some winter evergreens, like skimmia, in the foreground, as sweet pepper bush – or summersweet as it is also called – is relatively late into leaf.

'Ruby Spice' is a fully hardy, upright shrub – no more than 1.2 to 1.8 metres (4–6 ft) high – sufficiently compact for urban sites. A sport spotted in 1992, it arose from the blush-rose-coloured 'Pink Spires'. Like other clethra, its dark-green leaves are crisp looking, with deep veins and serrated edges. Some yellow autumn colour can be expected, and the dark seed heads persist well into winter. The species C. alnifolia is pure white. For a showier version, go for 'Paniculata'. Another white variety, 'Hummingbird', is petite and ideal for small gardens.

Preferring acidic, humus-rich soils, the sweet pepper bush enjoys moisture-retentive, but not constantly wet, ground. It thrives in light, dappled shade, but is shy to flower in deep shade. Grow in woodland glades, at the fringes of bog gardens, or in streamside swaths. It also works well in a lightly shaded shrub border. Although suckering occurs, spread is controllable. In winter remove a portion of the oldest stems. The new shoots in spring act as replacements. After pruning, apply a leaf-mould mulch around the base of the plant. **JH**

Alternatives

Clethra alnifolia 'Paniculata', *Clethra alnifolia* 'Pink Spires', *Clethra alnifolia* 'Hummingbird'

Cornus
C. florida 'Daybreak'

Main features Sculptural, with prominent flower bracts; large, brightly variegated leaves; pink autumn colour
Height 1.8–2.4 m (6–8 ft) **Spread** 3 m (10 ft)
Position ○ ◑ **Hardiness** RHS H5

This variegated, flowering dogwood is an absolute showstopper with both flowers and foliage vying for attention. Through late spring into early summer, as the leaves are expanding, C. Florida 'Daybreak' unfolds four, pure-white bracts around each green flower cluster. Its deeply veined leaves are edged with a generous, irregular, cream-yellow margin. As the broad blades enlarge they become somewhat ruffled. With the approach of autumn, the now mostly ivory variegation takes on pink tints and on patches of yellow, the effect is peachy. Finally, the whole shrub turns a deep, pinkish-red.

Sometimes sold as 'Cherokee Daybreak', this plant has an upright habit and becomes broadly conical, forming a medium to large shrub or small tree over time. Grow it as a lawn specimen or to add height and colour in a mixed border. For example, you could follow on from its early flower show with the late-summer blooms of *Hydrangea paniculata* 'Unique'. Its lacy heads take on pink tints in autumn, picking up on the dogwood's foliage. Although *C. florida* thrives along the margins of woodland or under light tree canopy, 'Daybreak' can tolerate full sun, avoiding leaf scorch, provided the site is reasonably sheltered.

Two more variegated forms include the yellow-edged, pink-bract–bearing 'Sunset' and white-bract–bearing 'Rainbow', which has a rich medley of autumn colours. A spectacular flowering tree for a small garden is the green-leaved 'Cherokee Chief', whose pink bracts smother its branches in late spring. Fruits formed by *C. florida* and cultivars in late summer are attractive to birds. Grow on well-drained but humus-rich, neutral to acidic soil. 'Daybreak' and 'Sunset' are moderately resistant to anthracnose disease. Water establishing plants in drought and apply a thick mulch. **JH**

Alternatives

Cornus florida, *Cornus florida* f. 'Cherokee Chief', *Cornus florida* 'Sunset', *Cornus florida* 'Rainbow'

Cornus
C. alba 'Sibirica'

Main features Slender, ruby-red stems in winter; flat heads of cream-white flowers in summer
Height 1.5 m (5 ft) **Spread** 1.5 m (5 ft)
Position ○ ◐ **Hardiness** RHS H7

A very easygoing shrub, C. alba 'Sibirica' is grown mainly for its ruby-red bark, which is revealed in its full brilliance in winter after the leaves have fallen and the stems are lit up by the low sun. More subtle attractions are provided by flat heads of cream-white flowers in early summer, followed by white berries. As a prelude to the winter display, the leaves become flushed with red-purple tints, turning bright red before they drop.

'Sibirica' tolerates most growing conditions, including wet or dry soils and shade, although the best colour is produced in a sunny spot. Younger stems have the brightest bark, and the shrubs can get very large if left alone, so the best way to manage them is by hard pruning. Simply cut all the stems down each year, in early spring, to within two or three buds at the base. On poor soils, and with coloured-leaved varieties, cut down only one-third to half of the stems each year.

Dogwoods look very good planted next to water, but they also work well in mixed borders, bringing welcome seasonal change to contrast with evergreens, and their see-through branch structure in spring makes them an ideal partner for snowdrops, primroses and other dainty spring flowers. Later on, the dark-green leaves make a good foil for more flamboyant summer show-offs. Several varieties of C. alba, including 'Elegantissima' and 'Spaethii' have highly attractive, variegated foliage, giving them genuine year-round appeal. **RKW**

Alternatives

Cornus alba 'Aurea', Cornus alba 'Kesselringii', Cornus alba 'Sibirica Variegata'

Cornus
C. kousa 'Miss Satomi'

Main features Showy, deep-pink flower bracts; deep-red and purple foliage in autumn
Height 1.5 m (5 ft) **Spread** 1.5 m (5 ft)
Position ○ ◑ **Hardiness** RHS H5

Few shrubs and trees have the arresting beauty of the flowering dogwoods. 'Miss Satomi' is more petite in stature than most, with wide-spreading, arching branches and a height of 1.5 metres (5 ft) in five to ten years, making her more suitable for the smaller garden. This is a lovely flowering shrub to associate with purple-leaved Japanese maples and azaleas, or to underplant with hostas, pulmonarias, and dwarf bulbs.

'Miss Satomi' is prized for her butterfly-like, salmon-pink bracts, which are amongst the showiest of all. The true flowers are insignificant and gathered into a tiny ball; each ball of flowers is surrounded by four showy bracts resembling petals. The blooms are carried on short upright stems above the leaves that are all along the branches. The bracts gradually develop from pale green through pale salmon to deep pink; the colour being richer and deeper in an open, sunny position. The flower clusters sometimes develop into pink, strawberry-like fruits. However, the main autumn feature is the colour of the foliage, which turns to shades of deep red and purple.

Most other varieties of *C. kousa*, including 'China Girl' and 'Teutonia' have cream-white bracts, which may blush pink in full sun as they age. *C.* 'Porlock' has profuse cream-white bracts that also blush pink. It is larger growing than 'Miss Satomi' and has the bonus of showy strawberry-like fruits in autumn. *C. kousa* varieties grow on most fertile soils, but need adequate moisture. **AMcI**

Alternatives

Cornus kousa var. *chinensis* 'China Girl', *Cornus kousa* 'Teutonia', *Cornus* 'Porlock'

Cornus

C. sanguinea
'Midwinter Fire'

Main features Brightly coloured winter stems; brilliant autumn foliage colour
Height 1.2 m (4 ft) **Spread** 90 cm (3 ft)
Position ○ ◑ **Hardiness** RHS H6

Perhaps the most vivid of all the dogwoods grown for their winter stems, *C. sanguinea* 'Midwinter Fire' glows in the winter garden, whatever the weather. The olive-green leaves of summer turn to shades of gold and orange in autumn, before they reveal the flame-and-gold bark of the winter stems. The colour becomes more intense as the days get colder and winter light reaches the bark, now unprotected by a mantle of foliage. The new leaves at the tips of the shoots are bronze green in spring. 'Midwinter Fire' is suitable for any garden, whether planted individually or in drifts in larger spaces. It is attractive when underplanted with *Hedera*, *Vinca*, or *Carex* for ground cover. Stunning winter effects can be achieved by planting 'Midwinter Fire' with other cornus, such as *C. alba* 'Sibirica' and *C. sericea* 'Flaviramea'. Individual plants make striking winter container subjects. The secret of strong stems of vibrant colour is hard pruning to 15 centimetres (6 in.) above ground level in early spring. **AMcI**

Alternatives

Cornus sanguinea 'Magic Flame', *Cornus* 'Winter Beauty'

Cornus

C. sericea
'Hedgerows Gold'

Main features Colourful foliage in spring and summer; white berries in autumn; red winter stems
Height 1.5 m (5 ft) **Spread** 1.5 m (5 ft)
Position ○ ◑ **Hardiness** RHS H7

From a distance this shrub has a bright, lemon-yellow appearance, but up close the leaves are actually pale green with a broad, irregular margin that starts off yellow and fades to cream white. Autumn sees a range of pink and red tints appearing, whereas in winter the plant presents a different picture with its mass of upright, leafless red stems that are striking in the snow. It is great for group planting on damp, difficult soils, or to stabilise streamsides, especially when matched with other dogwoods in different colours. It also makes a fine individual specimen, perhaps underplanted with variegated ivy for winter interest and spring bulbs. Red osier dogwood is native to much of northern and western North America, where it favours damp soil, spreading underground to produce dense thickets. In a garden it will tolerate most growing conditions except very hot and dry. All varieties produce dull, off-white flowers, but in a good year the berries that follow can be showy. **RKW**

Alternatives

Cornus sericea 'Flaviramea', *Cornus sericea* 'Kelseyi'

◐ *Cornus sanguinea* **'Midwinter Fire'** shown in winter with box balls and a white-stemmed birch tree at Sir Harold Hillier Gardens, Hampshire.

Corylopsis
C. pauciflora

Main feature Scented spring flowers
Height 1.5 m (5 ft) **Spread** 2.4 m (8 ft)
Position ◑
Hardiness RHS H5

That *C. pauciflora*, the winter hazel, is underused as a garden plant is ludicrous as it counts as one of the very finest spring-flowering shrubs. In early to midspring, constellations of deliciously scented buttercup-yellow blossoms dangle charmingly from bare branches, illuminating any gloomy space that may need a lift. *Pauciflora* means 'scarcity of flowers', which is a paradox in this instance, as its ample quantities of blooms ensure a show that will take your breath away, the effect increased by the lack of foliage during the flowering period.

There is more going for this plant than just its flowers though. It will please year-round. The leaves start to appear as the flowering dwindles, delicate slivers of bronze that unfurl, turning bright green as they mature, retaining a fringe of copper. The leaves are toothed and veined – rather like a hazel – and in autumn they provide a dying display of saffron and gold. Even in its winter nakedness, *C. pauciflora* maintains an elegant silhouette.

It is slower growing than other *Corylopsis* species, and its compact shape makes it the ideal choice where space is at a premium. Place in a sheltered position, preferably near an entrance or path to appreciate the fragrance, which is reminiscent of cowslips. *C. pauciflora* makes a dense and spreading shape, with a graceful branching habit. Its handsome structure means that pruning is rarely needed. It does not appreciate competition, so grow it as a specimen or allow it enough space amongst a selection of ground-covering woodland plants. **ER**

Alternative

Hamamelis × intermedia 'Pallida'

Cotinus
C. coggygria Golden Spirit

Main features Golden summer foliage; fluffy, late-summer flowers; pale orange foliage in autumn
Height 1.5 m (5 ft) **Spread** 1.5 m (5 ft)
Position ○ ◑ **Hardiness** RHS H6

Golden Spirit is one of the finest foliage shrubs, with its abundant rounded leaves, golden yellow in full sun; yellow green in shade. Unlike many yellow-leaved shrubs, it does not scorch in strong sunlight, retaining its foliage quality from late spring until autumn, when the colour often changes to pale orange. Wherever it is planted, Golden Spirit associates more happily with its neighbours, and is less brazen than many other yellow-leaved shrubs.

The fluffy flower plumes are not as large or profuse as they are on other smoke bushes. However, their red-brown colour stands out well against the leaves in late summer. Golden Spirit is compact in habit with upright branches, and it can be kept to 1.5 metres (5 ft) in height with some pruning. It makes an eye-catching focal point in any planting scheme and contrasts well with purple-leaved shrubs, such as other cotinus. In shade it makes a lively planting partner for *Hydrangea paniculata* or *Hydrangea arborescens* varieties. It is also effective as a backdrop for a garden feature, such as a seat or a statue.

Originally discovered as a seedling in a Dutch nursery in 1990, Golden Spirit is the only widely grown form with golden-yellow foliage. Other popular choices have copper or purple leaves. *C. coggygria* 'Royal Purple' is the best known, with deep wine-purple leaves. 'Velvet Cloak' is similar. *C.* 'Grace' is larger and more vigorous, with soft copper-red leaves and large wine-red flower plumes. Prune in winter to control shape and size; harder pruning promotes more vigorous growth. **AMcI**

Alternative

= 'Ancot'. *Cotinus coggygria* 'Royal Purple'

Cotoneaster
'Rothschildianus'

Main features Semi-evergreen foliage; flowers in
summer; berries in summer and autumn; attracts bees
Height 1.8 m (6 ft) **Spread** 1.8 m (6 ft)
Position ○ ◑ **Hardiness** RHS H6

This is an excellent shrub if you have space to fill. Its
elegant, arching stems can spread to 5 metres (16 ft) high
and wide, but it is easy to keep to 1.8 by 1.8 metres
(6 x 6 ft) with an annual prune. Alternatively, plants can
initially be trained on a single stem, then allowed to
branch to form a small tree, or trained against a wall.
'Rothschildianus' is semi-evergreen, with long, narrow,
oval leaves, pale green with deep veins. Large sprays of
cream-white flowers cover the plant in early summer;
they are followed by profuse bunches of lemon-yellow
berries. The variety 'Exburiensis' is similar but with apricot
berries, tinged pink in winter. Both were raised at Exbury
Gardens in England, owned by the de Rothschild family.
If you want to provide food for birds, then one of the
red-berried forms will be popular. 'Cornubia' is a large,
arching shrub or small tree smothered in clusters of fruits
in late summer and early autumn, when the foliage takes
on shades of bronze to add to the show. **RKW**

Alternatives

Cotoneaster 'Exburiensis', *Cotoneaster* 'Cornubia'

Cotoneaster
C. × *suecicus*
'Coral Beauty'

Main features Flowers in summer; autumn fruits;
evergreen foliage; good ground cover; attracts bees
Height 90 cm (3 ft) **Spread** 1.8 m (6 ft)
Position ○ ◑ **Hardiness** RHS H6

The *Cotoneaster* is a real workhorse in the garden, doing
a brilliant job where other plants would not succeed. An
indispensable ground cover plant, this hybrid between
C. conspicuus and *C. dammeri* is a useful plant, popular
with professional landscapers, but also invaluable in the
domestic garden. It forms a dense mound of arching
branches bearing small, ovate, shiny, evergreen leaves.
In early summer an abundance of small white flowers
are produced, which are followed by a profusion of
bright orange-red berries. Bees love this plant, and their
activity helps to ensure a bumper crop of berries every
year. This is a robust plant that is tolerant of a wide range
of conditions. Plant in sun or partial shade in any well-
drained soil, and it will ultimately create a mound of
branches that, once established, give good weed control.
It is an ideal plant for covering a bank that is too steep
to mow safely, but can also be used to underplant large
deciduous shrubs. **MP**

Alternative

Cotoneaster procumbens 'Queen of Carpets'

Cryptomeria
C. japonica
'Globosa Nana'

Main features Dwarf globe appearance; attractive green foliage; soft tactile foliage
Height 90 cm (3 ft) **Spread** 90 cm (3 ft)
Position ○ ◐ **Hardiness** RHS H6

Japanese cedar (*C. japonica*) is a conifer that has produced a wide variety of cultivars available in the West. They range from tiny miniature forms to giants that can reach 45 metres (150 ft) in their native Japanese habitat, rather like redwoods and sequoias. 'Globosa Nana' is suitable for smaller gardens. This dwarf version is considered one of the best of the mounding cryptomerias, with attractive bright-green foliage and tidy needles held in dense sprays that seem to explode outwards from the crown and then droop very slightly, forming an agreeable globe shape. The foliage is quite soft to the touch, and its inviting texture earns it the occasional pat in passing. In a formal garden it substitutes well for topiary boxwood balls, and it can even be trained into standard lollipops. Left to grow naturally, it looks wonderful in clumps of three or more, interspersed with lavender or ornamental grasses. It can be clipped to produce a tighter shape; this is best done from midspring through summer. **ER**

Alternative

Cryptomeria japonica 'Elegans Compacta'

Daboecia
D. cantabrica
'William Buchanan'

Main features Evergreen; long flowering period in spring, summer, and autumn
Height 38 cm (15 in.) **Spread** 50 cm (20 in.)
Position ○ ◐ **Hardiness** RHS H5

This pretty, long flowering evergreen makes an ideal container plant where its red-purple blooms can be enjoyed close-up from late spring to midautumn. Try it in a trough with spring bulbs and dwarf gentians, or in a hanging basket with a few trails of a small-leaved, variegated ivy. William Buchanan was an alpine-plant enthusiast, and this variety would be a welcome addition to a rock garden or gravel area. It also finds a place around the margins of acid-loving shrubs, such as camellias and rhododendrons, or spreading beneath the branches of dwarf pines and other conifers. The *Daboecia* is related to heathers and is the prima ballerina of the family, with its fine stems and delicate, hanging blooms like tiny balloons, a dozen or more per stem. It is named for St Dabeoc, a Welsh prince of the fifth or sixth century who founded a monastery in the west of Ireland, where the plant grows wild. Keep plants neat by shearing off dead blooms once flowering is over. **RKW**

Alternatives

Daboecia cantabrica 'Bicolor', *Daboecia cantabrica* 'Vanessa'

Daphne
D. × transatlantica
Eternal Fragrance

Main features Heavily scented flowers from spring to early autumn; semi-evergreen
Height 90 cm (3 ft) **Spread** 90 cm (3 ft)
Position ○ **Hardiness** RHS H5

Eternal Fragrance is a hybrid cross between *D. caucasica* and *D. sericea*. It was bred by Robin White of the now-closed Blackthorn Nursery in Hampshire. As a plant that ticks all the boxes of a garden-worthy shrub – long flowering, highly scented, tolerant of most soils, and easy to propagate – it has been a great commercial success worldwide. Eternal Fragrance has white flowers flushed with the palest shade of pink. The flowers appear from pink buds mainly in the spring, but there are clusters of flowers here and there until the autumn. However, the ability to flower over a long period is completely superseded by the powerful and sweet scent that this plant exudes, filling the garden: a joy in the spring but a wonderful bonus for the rest of the season. In the autumn the flowers are followed by red berries. *Helleborus* is an ideal companion in the spring and *Anemone* × *hybrida* 'Honorine Jobert' later in the year. **RSJ**

Alternatives

= 'Blafra'. *Daphne* × *transatlantica* 'Jim's Pride', *Daphne* × *transatlantica* Pink Fragrance = 'Blapink'

Daphne
D. bholua
'Jacqueline Postill'

Main features Highly fragrant winter and early-spring flowers; attracts early bees
Height 1.8 m (6 ft) **Spread** 90 cm (3 ft)
Position ○ ◑ **Hardiness** RHS H4

If you only grow one shrub for fragrance, choose this one. 'Jacqueline Postill' may not be the most elegant shrub: the growth habit is upright and the narrow, semi-evergreen leaves unremarkable. However, the scent of the flowers from midwinter to early spring is unsurpassable. Fat clusters of flower buds develop at the tip of every tan-stemmed shoot. The purple-pink buds open to starry lilac-white flowers, purple on the reverse of the petals. The perfume is sweet and strong, and a plant in flower will fill the whole garden with its fragrance. Plant 'Jacqueline Postill' close to the house, where you can enjoy it. Small sprigs of the flowers can be cut and brought indoors when in bloom. However, the flowers do not last well in water. This is a good shrub to plant with a variegated pittosporum, which will give foliage interest when the shrub is not in flower. Underplant with *Helleborus* × *hybridus* for more impact in winter and early spring. **AMcI**

Alternatives

Daphne bholua 'Gurkha', *Daphne* × *transatlantica* Eternal Fragrance = 'Blafra'

Daphne bholua **'Jacqueline Postill'** in late winter is a semi-evergreen with fragrant flowers. ➜

Daphne
D. odora Rebecca

Main features Heavily scented winter flowers; striking variegated foliage
Height 1.2 m (4 ft) **Spread** 1.5 m (5 ft)
Position ○ ◑ **Hardiness** RHS H4

This *Daphne* is a sport of *D. odora* 'Aureomarginata' and it was discovered in Devon in 1989. It has an excellent pedigree. The species *D. odora* from China and Japan produces one of the most evocative and delicious scents of all winter-flowering shrubs, while 'Aureomarginata' has a yellow margin to its leaves and is hardier than the species. This cultivar's clusters of pale-lavender, star-like flowers start off from purple-red buds and are fully open by late winter, releasing their sweet scent into the garden. Rebecca has evergreen, variegated foliage that is nothing short of striking. Clear green leaves with yellow margins – broader and brighter than 'Aureomarginata' – mean that it more than earns its place in the garden for year-round interest. Plant in winter-interest shrub borders or woodlands with *Skimmia* and *Sarcococca*. The continuous trickle of heady perfume will gladden gardeners' hearts in winter. **RSJ**

Alternatives

= 'Hewreb'. *Daphne odora* 'Aureomarginata', *Daphne odora* 'Mae-jima'

Deutzia
D. × hybrida 'Strawberry Fields'

Main feature Early to midsummer flowers
Height 1.8 m (6 ft) **Spread** 1.5 m (5 ft)
Position ○ ◑
Hardiness RHS H5

If *Deutzia* flowers were fragrant these shrubs would be more widely planted, and 'Strawberry Fields' would be the most popular. Strong, arching stems carry pointed mid-green leaves and clusters of beautiful, mauve-pink blooms delicately etched with white in midsummer. A shrub in full flower is a beautiful sight for about four weeks, as buds in each flower cluster open in succession. 'Strawberry Fields' is a vigorous shrub with a clump of strong stems arising from its base. Cutting out some of the flowered stems right after flowering results in those strong, arching stems that display the flower clusters so perfectly. After leaf fall, the tan-coloured, peeling bark is revealed. 'Strawberry Fields' fits well with roses and summer-flowering perennials, such as peonies, geraniums and salvias. It is the perfect shrub for a mixed border to add graceful height to a planting scheme. It is disease free and reliable if given plenty of direct sunlight. **AMcl**

Alternatives

Deutzia × *hybrida* 'Mont Rose', *Deutzia* × *hybrida* 'Magicien Lemoine', *Deutzia* × *hybrida* 'Contraste'

⊝ *Daphne odora* **Rebecca** has eye-catching foliage as well as scented winter flowers.

Dicksonia
D. antarctica

Main feature Majestic plant with architectural form
Height 4 m (13 ft) **Spread** 4 m (13 ft)
Position ◑ ●
Hardiness RHS H3

Tree ferns are exactly that – plants that combine the delicate fronds of a fern raised above ground level by a stout trunk. Native to Australia, where it populates wet, shady gullies, *D. antarctica* is one of the oldest types of plant in the world. The soft tree fern, or Australian tree fern, has a strong personality – introduce it to your garden and it will immediately transform the space into something redolent of the dinosaur age. This majestic plant looks especially good planted in numbers. Grow ferns and ornamental grasses below, or make an architectural statement by scattering different-sized boxwood (*Buxus sempervirens*) balls around the base of its trunks.

The trunk consists of a slender stem surrounded by fibrous roots that support the structure. The plant produces a terminal rosette of arching, deeply divided, dark-green fronds that grow to 3 metres (10 ft) in length. It prefers a shady spot; however, it will tolerate a sunny site if the trunk is kept moist (this is where the roots are and therefore where the water spray should be directed). A generous daily soaking is vital, especially in the first six months after planting.

Frost hardy in warmer climes, *D. antarctica* holds its fronds throughout winter, but where temperatures dip to below freezing, they are likely to die back. Cut back old fronds to 15 centimetres (6 in.) long – these stalks help form the trunk – and protect it through winter by stuffing the crown with fallen leaves, or straw, and wrapping in frost fleece. As the tree fern grows, its hardiness increases because the growing point becomes naturally better insulated. When purchased, the soft tree fern may well resemble a lifeless log. But fear not! Once it has been set only about 10 centimetres (4 in.) into the soil, it will slowly come to life in spring with new fronds unfurling from the crown. **ER**

Alternative

Dicksonia squarrosa

Dipelta
D. floribunda

Main features Fragrant, pale-pink, early-summer flowers; attractive bracts; peeling bark
Height 3–4 m (10–13 ft) **Spread** 2.7 m (9 ft)
Position ○ ◐   **Hardiness** RHS H5

Some shrubs deserve to be better known and *D. floribunda* is a good example. It has probably remained underused because it is difficult to propagate, and therefore not often found in nurseries. However, it is well worth the search. It is closely related to *Weigela* (and, in fact, the flowers are very similar to that species) and is reminiscent in appearance of a *Kolkwitzia* on steroids. It is another introduction from China by the distinguished plant collector Ernest Wilson.

This large, vase-shaped deciduous plant grows at a moderate rate, as a multi-stemmed shrub. The upright stems can reach 3 to 4 metres (10–13 ft) high, with an ultimate spread of about 2.7 metres (9 ft) wide; therefore, the plant is not really a subject for the small garden. The mid-green, simple shaped leaves are held in opposite pairs. Unfortunately, the autumn tints are not much to shout about. However, the scented flowers compensate for this. They open in late spring or early summer and are trumpet shaped, consisting of five fused petals that are cream white, tinged with pale pink. The throats of the flowers have orange markings, probably as nectary guides for pollinating insects. After flowering, greenish papery bracts develop, and these blush to pink as they enlarge and mature, adding interest for later in the summer. The two-seeded fruits that develop distinguish *Dipelta* from *Kolkwitzia*, which has single-seeded fruits.

When the leaves have fallen, the structure of the stems is visible, and the brownish bark on mature stems is shed in long strips. Grow *Dipelta* at the back of a border or as a screen. It is tough and easy to grow in any soil that is well drained, and it flowers best in full sun, but light shade can be tolerated. This shrub is reasonably hardy, but will need shelter from cold winter winds, so avoid exposed sites in cooler climates. **MP**

Alternatives

Dipelta ventricosa, Dipelta yunnanensis

Disanthus
D. cercidifolius

Main feature Heart-shaped foliage with spectacular autumn hues

Height 1.5 m (5 ft) **Spread** 2.4 m (8 ft)

Position ◑ **Hardiness** RHS H5

The *D. cercidifolius* is a shrub that resembles a witch hazel (*Hamamelis*) and hails from China and Japan. It displays a similar habit to witch hazel, but the species name, *cercidifolius*, reflects the appearance of the leaves, which could easily be mistaken for those of *Cercis siliquastrum*.

Disanthus is a monotypic genus, meaning that there is only one species in the genus. It is, however, related to the glorious genus *Liquidambar,* the beautiful trees that are well known for the wonderful autumn hues displayed by their deeply lobed leaves. In the autumn, *D. cercidifolius* puts on a similar, though arguably more spectacular, turn as the deciduous heart-shaped leaves that begin a glaucous blue green evolve into various shades of purple, crimson and orange. It is a dramatic finale to the season and outshines most shrubs. In comparison to the foliage, the flowers are less impressive unless viewed close up. Minuscule, maroon and spider-like, with five petals, they are very slightly fragrant and appear on stalks in pairs.

D. cercidifolius makes a wonderful specimen shrub with all kinds of planting possibilities: in low-maintenance gardens, as long as you do not mind raking up the leaves; in cottage-style gardens; and in flower borders. For the best results, the soils needs to be moist, well drained, humus rich and lime free. Partial shade is best but this plant can tolerate some sun. For the best foliage display, make sure it is sheltered from cold winds and frost. **RSJ**

Alternatives

Disanthus cercidifolius 'Ena-nishiki', *Hamamelis* 'Vesna', *Hamamelis* 'Jelena'

Elaeagnus
E. × ebbingei 'Gilt Edge'

Main features Evergreen; good hedge and windbreak;
drought tolerant; salt tolerant; fragrant flowers in autumn
Height 1.8 m (6 ft) **Spread** 1.8 m (6 ft)
Position ○ ◑ ● **Hardiness** RHS H5

Tough as old boots, with brilliant, year-round colour and
fragrant flowers, this shrub can be a real winner in the
most challenging situations. It is drought resistant, copes
with virtually any soil and tolerates exposed positions
and salt-laden wind or road spray. It will even grow in
shade, although it does best in a sunnier spot.

'Gilt Edge' has large, oval, leathery leaves in bright
green, with a broad, golden-yellow margin. It can reach
3.6 by 3.6 metres (12 x 12 ft) but is easily kept to half this
with regular trimming. It makes a striking specimen
plant, a colourful hedge and effective shelter belt. Small,
silvery flowers produced in autumn and would go
undetected but for their strong, sweet scent. They are
sometimes followed by orange-red berries. *E. × ebbingei*
'Coastal Gold' is another vivid variety with mostly bright
yellow leaves within an irregular, green edge. It is an
excellent plant to enliven a golden border. For a more
subtle backdrop, look for the plain green Ebbingei's
silverberry (*E. × ebbingei*). This has dark-green leaves, but
looks more lively in spring when the young foliage is
covered in silvery scales.

Another related species, *E. pungens*, is similarly easygoing and tolerant of difficult conditions. The evergreen
leaves are somewhat narrower, with wavy edges, and it
also produces scented flowers and berries. The most
popular variety is 'Maculata', where each leaf is a jazzy
mixture of dark green, light green and yellow. **RKW**

Alternatives

Elaeagnus × ebbingei, *Elaeagnus × ebbingei* 'Coastal Gold',
Elaeagnus pungens 'Maculata', *Elaeagnus pungens* 'Frederici'

Enkianthus
E. cernuus f. rubens

Main features Early summer display of small, but numerous, pendulous red blooms; rich autumn colour
Height 1.5–2.4 m (5–8 ft) **Spread** 1.5–2.4 m (5–8 ft)
Position ◑ **Hardiness** RHS H5

With its open habit and spreading branches, the nodding or drooping red *E. cernuus* f. *rubens* adds an elegant and informal touch to any shady cottage- or woodland-style garden. Its oval, subtly serrated leaves are arranged in whorls, and the arrival of autumn sees the foliage acquire opulent red and plum shades. Yet this relative of heather, rhododendron and blueberry first draws an admiring gaze in late spring, when elegant, long-lasting clusters of red bells open beneath the leaves.

Although it has sufficient presence to attract from a distance, this is a plant that rewards when up close. The pendulous, somewhat glossy ruby blooms hang at different heights within the cluster, adding to its appeal. More rounded than bell-shaped, they are reminiscent of Chinese paper lanterns, and the mouth of each is prettily toothed. From slightly further away, you would be forgiven for thinking the flowers to be luscious red berries. Persistent seed heads add to the autumn display.

For textural contrast combine drooping *Enkianthus* with large-leaved rhododendrons, camellias and deciduous azaleas, and at the other end of the textural spectrum, with filigree-fingered Japanese maples and lacy ferns. In informal areas, naturalise late-spring bulbs in swaths around the base and encourage cow parsley and other shade-loving wildflowers to colonise. In a more conventional border, try it underplanted with blue camassias or the pure-white *Geranium phaeum* 'Album'. Another lovely species of *Enkianthus,* which has given rise to several choice forms and cultivars, is *E. campanulatus*, which has white bells edged with raspberry red. *E. perulatus* is pure white, with an autumn display of flame reds and oranges. Grow *E. cernuus* f. *rubens* in humus-rich, moisture-retentive, neutral to acidic soil, with protection from wind. **JH**

Alternatives

Enkianthus campanulatus, Enkianthus perulatus, Enkianthus var. *campanulatus* f. *albiflorus, Enkianthus campanulatus* 'Pagoda'

Erica
E. × *darleyensis* 'Kramer's Rote'

Main features Evergreen; good ground cover; long
flowering period in winter and spring; good cut flower
Height 30 cm (12 in.) **Spread** 60 cm (24 in.)
Position ○ ◑ **Hardiness** RHS H6

The dense, bronzy, evergreen, weed-smothering foliage
on this dwarf shrub is reason enough to grow it, but
add to that vivid, magenta blooms from late winter to
early spring, and it genuinely is a winner. This species
is a hybrid between the tall Mediterranean heath
(*E. erigena*) and the low-growing winter heath (*E. carnea*).
It appeared at the end of the nineteenth century in Darley
Dale nurseries, Derbyshire. Since then, it has produced
many varieties, both naturally and by deliberate breeding,
including the program run by German nurseryman Karl
Kramer, who is responsible for this variety, which translates
as 'Kramer's red'.

Most varieties come in various shades of pink, but red-
purples and whites are also available. The small flowers
are bell-shaped or tubular. Some have yellow foliage,
while many varieties produce coloured tips on the new
foliage in spring, which may be red, white, cream or pink.
Most varieties grow to around 30 centimetres (12 in.) tall,
with a spread of 60 centimetres (24 in.), and can be lightly
trimmed to keep them tidy after flowering. 'Darley Dale'
is the original variety, with shell-pink flowers from late
autumn to midspring, and mid-green foliage tipped with
cream in spring. The blooms of 'Furzey' open lilac pink,
maturing to purple over a similar period, with dark-green
foliage tipped pink in spring. 'White Perfection' starts a
little later, and the bright-green foliage develops yellow
tips during the spring months.

These are some of the most adaptable heaths,
growing in any well-drained soil, in sun or semi-shade.
They will form a reliable element in a traditional, mixed
shrub border, but will also work well in providing winter
colour for more modern planting combinations with
grasses or silver-foliaged perennials. The flowers are also
good for cutting and are very long-lasting. **RKW**

Alternatives

Erica × *darleyensis* 'Darley Dale', *Erica* × *darleyensis* 'Furzey',
Erica × *darleyensis* 'Ghost Hills', *Erica* × *darleyensis* 'J. W.
Porter', *Erica* × *darleyensis* f. *albiflora* 'White Perfection'

Erica
E. carnea 'Myretoun Ruby'

Main features Long flowering period in winter and spring; evergreen
Height 15 cm (6 in.) **Spread** 45 cm (18 in.)
Position ○ ◑ **Hardiness** RHS H7

Bearing deep rose-pink flowers from midwinter to midspring, 'Myretoun Ruby' brings a welcome blast of colour to any garden at a time when few other plants are in bloom. It also provides a valuable source of nectar for early-foraging bees. This low-growing, evergreen shrub is versatile, too, thriving anywhere from a patio or balcony container to drifts planted around deciduous shrubs and trees. In sunny positions, you could create a patchwork with other dwarf shrubs flowering at different times to create year-round appeal. Good choices are dwarf hebes, lavenders, rock roses or Japanese *Spiraea*. This heather also thrives in partial shade, where it can be teamed with variegated euonymus, dwarf rhododendrons and spring-flowering bulbs, such as hardy cyclamen. These plants have leaves like tiny needles, normally dark green, although there are also varieties with yellow foliage. Flowers are in the white/pink/magenta/purple spectrum, depending on the variety. **RKW**

Alternatives

Erica carnea 'Ann Sparks', *Erica carnea* 'Rosalie'

 Erica carnea **'Myretoun Ruby'** planted in generous drifts provides plenty of nectar for early-foraging bees.

Erica
E. vagans f. *alba* 'Kevernensis Alba'

Main features Evergreen; long flowering period in summer and autumn; good in containers; attracts bees
Height 20 cm (8 in.) **Spread** 40 cm (16 in.)
Position ○ **Hardiness** RHS H6

If you fancy growing 'lucky white heather' all year round, then this variety will plug the late-summer to autumn gap between the true heathers (*Calluna*) and the winter heaths (*Erica carnea*). It is a neat, pretty plant with compact, tapering spikes of small, white flowers above fine, dark, evergreen foliage. The flowers are nectar rich and appear at a good time to help bees stock up for winter. 'Kevernensis Alba' is a good choice for containers. Planted in the centre of a large tub, it will provide a permanent backdrop for small spring bulbs and trailing summer bedding, then turn on its own display to prolong the show of blooms into autumn. Other options are window boxes, rock gardens and narrow beds along paths. Grow in any well-drained soil in a sunny position. 'Kevernensis Alba' grows wild on the Lizard Peninsula in the English county of Cornwall, as well as parts of Ireland, western France and Spain. It produces flowers in a variety of pinks, pale purples and white. **RKW**

Alternatives

Erica vagans 'Birch Glow', *Erica vagans* f. *alba* 'Cornish Cream'

Escallonia
E. bifida

Main features Clusters of white flowers;
evergreen foliage
Height 3 m (10 ft) **Spread** 2.4 m (8 ft)
Position ○ ◑ **Hardiness** RHS H4

There are around forty species of *Escallonia*, and several are popular among gardeners as evergreen hedges and for their suitability for coastal gardens. In its natural habitat *E. bifida*, the cloven gum tree, is an upright shrub found on cliffs and hillsides in Brazil and Uruguay. In the garden it is much appreciated for its late-season flowers – from late summer to early autumn – and evergreen foliage. Fully deserving of a Royal Horticultural Society Award of Garden Merit, *E. bifida* produces showy clusters of small, white, 2.5-centimetre-wide (1 in.) flowers, which provide nectar for foraging butterflies and bees. This is a substantial and bushy shrub with small pointed leaves around 7 centimetres (3 in.) long and it is a reliable wind-tolerant hedge. Gardeners in colder areas should take care to plant *E. bifida* in sheltered positions to prevent the foliage from being damaged. Clipping or pruning should be carried out only after the shrub has flowered, to be sure that it will flower the following season. **RSJ**

Alternatives

Syn. *Escallonia montevidensis*, *Escallonia* 'Donard Radiance', *Escallonia rubra* 'Crimson Spire'

Eucalyptus
E. gunnii

Main features Sculptural evergreen foliage; good for
borders or large patio pots; good for cutting
Height 1.5 m (5 ft) **Spread** 1.5 m (5 ft)
Position ○ **Hardiness** RHS H5

The *E. gunnii* is a striking metallic-blue colour, and its precision-cut leaves and stems give it a contemporary or exotic feel. Cut or coppiced annually once established, it produces abundant whiplike stems clothed in almost spherical, wax-coated leaves set in regularly spaced pairs. Popular with flower arrangers who are attracted by the texture and colour of the young growth, cut material from *E. gunnii* lasts well in arrangements. Furthermore, the foliage has a pleasant eucalyptus oil aroma when crushed. Naturally fast growing, a newly planted *E. gunnii* will rocket up to become a tall, slender tree with peeling bark if you fail to prune it. The adult foliage of the tree is different to that of the juvenile type on stooled or coppiced plants: sickle shaped and more grey than blue. In cool climates fluffy white flowers can appear in summer. Try partnering this plant with a purple or variegated *Phormium* or train a young, potted *E. gunnii* seedling into a pretty lollipop-headed standard for the patio. **JH**

Alternatives

Eucalyptus gunnii Azurea = 'Cagire', *Eucalyptus pauciflora* subsp. *niphophila*

Eucryphia
E. glutinosa

Main features Deciduous; attracts bees; white blooms in mid- to late summer; autumn foliage colour
Height 4–8 m (13–26 ft) **Spread** 2.4–4 m (8–13 ft)
Position ○ ◑ **Hardiness** RHS H4

Unusually for this group of southern-hemisphere shrubs, this species of *Eucryphia* is deciduous, developing flaming orange and red tones in autumn. In mid- to late summer the small, upright and broadly columnar shrub or tree is covered in large bowl-shaped blooms with a mass of prominent, red-tipped stamen. Set against the dark-green foliage, the overall effect is striking. And if you needed another excuse to grow *Eucryphia*, the flowers are bee magnets. This plant is ideal in light woodland, where the roots are shaded but the branches are in a reasonable amount of sunlight. However, with its architectural good looks, *Eucryphia* would work well in a modern city garden or courtyard, and given sufficient moisture, it could be set to grow up against a wall. It is an excellent free-flowering variety and one of the hardiest, with handsome single and three-lobed leaves. The foliage makes an effective backdrop for other flowers when the plants themselves are not in bloom. **JH**

Alternatives

Eucryphia × *nymansensis* 'Nymansay', *Eucryphia lucida* 'Ballerina', *Eucryphia lucida* 'Pink Cloud'

Euonymus
E. europaeus 'Red Cascade'

Main features Attractive autumn fruits and foliage tints
Height 3–6 m (10–20 ft) **Spread** 2.4 m (8 ft)
Position ○ ◑
Hardiness RHS H5

Pink and orange are colours not normally put together, but this plant marries them to perfection in its fruits. The wood of the branches is very hard and was traditionally used to make spindles for spinning wool. The species is native to Europe and can often be found growing as a small tree or in hedgerows, where it thrives on nutrient-rich, calcareous soils. The variety 'Red Cascade' makes a broadly conical, slightly weeping small tree or large shrub. In early summer inconspicuous greenish-yellow flowers appear, which, when insect pollinated, develop into four-lobed, deep-pink capsules that split to reveal the orange seed. The branches are often weighed down by the fruits, which hang on the tree until long after the leaves have turned purple, and turn to rich shades of red in the autumn. Plant as a specimen or at the back of a border. Other late-flowering plants will enhance the picture, including red-hot poker, *Kniphofia rooperi*, whose flaming torches will contrast with the spindle foliage. **MP**

Alternatives

Euonymus alatus 'Compactus', *Euonymus fortunei* 'Emerald 'n' Gold', *Euonymus planipes* 'Sancho'

Euonymus
E. fortunei
'Emerald 'n' Gold'

Main features Variegated, evergreen foliage; good ground cover; drought resistant
Height 45 cm (18 in.) **Spread** 90 cm (3 ft)
Position ○ ◑ **Hardiness** RHS H5

'Emerald 'n' Gold' provides a cheerful splash of colour year-round with its neat, green-and-yellow, evergreen leaves. Suited to all kinds of gardens, it is a low-maintenance shrub, happy in all soils except very wet ones. Left to its own devices, it forms a low-spreading shrub, ideal for ground cover, for filling in between larger shrubs or for providing welcome winter interest in a cottage-garden–style border. Plant it next to a wall, however, and this shrub starts to climb, producing longer shoots with ivy-like aerial roots to help it hold on. 'Emerald 'n' Gold' also works well in formal situations, where it can be clipped to form a low hedge, or balls and cones. There are many good varieties of *E. fortunei* with gold or silver variegation in various shapes and sizes. 'Silver Queen' is one of the largest and has broad, silvery-green, white-edged leaves. 'Blondy' is similar to 'Emerald 'n' Gold' in growth, but has bright-green leaves with a central, yellow blotch. **RKW**

Alternatives

Euonymus fortunei 'Emerald Gaiety', *Euonymus fortunei* 'Harlequin', *Euonymus fortunei* 'Wolong Ghost'

Fabiana
F. imbricata
f. violacea

Main features Evergreen that thrives in warm, sheltered spots; summer flowering
Height 1.5–2.4 m (5–8 ft) **Spread** 90–150 cm (3–5 ft)
Position ○ **Hardiness** RHS H4

As a member of the *Solanaceae* family, *F. imbricata* is related to the humble potato. It comes from Chile, where it thrives in poor soil on dry slopes and has numerous sprays of upright branches and stems coated with masses of tiny, scale-like, evergreen leaves. In early summer the branches are festooned with hundreds of small, white, tubular flowers. The foliage is used in traditional and homeopathic medicine as a digestive and diuretic. Also known as the violet pichi, *F. imbricata* f. *violacea* is similar to the species with its bushy habit, but it has pale-lilac flowers that have a sweet honey scent that attracts pollinating butterflies and bees. Although this plant will grow well in warm areas, it needs a sheltered position in full sun. It thrives in sand, chalk or loam and is happy in either acidic or neutral conditions. It is a useful addition when planting tricky sunny slopes and banks or in a large rock garden. **RSJ**

Alternatives

Fabiana imbricata 'Prostrata', *Fabiana imbricata*, *Fabiana nana*, *Fabiana foliosa*

◉ *Euonymus fortunei* 'Emerald 'n' Gold' shines all year.

Fatsia
F. japonica

Main features Architectural plant; bold, evergreen foliage; winter flowers
Height 1.8 m (6 ft) **Spread** 1.5 m (5 ft)
Position ◑ ● **Hardiness** RHS H5

The big, green, glossy, hand-shaped leaves of *F. japonica* add a touch of the tropics to any planting scheme. This versatile shrub, sometimes grown as a houseplant, lends itself to shady situations, both in the open ground and in pots and containers. The white, intricately structured flower heads in winter are a bonus, although the main reason to grow this shrub is as a striking, architectural evergreen foliage subject.

This plant is closely related to ivy (*Hedera*); both leaves and flowers are clues to this relationship. Upright stems, which become bare at the base as the plant matures, carry the large leaves on stout, horizontal leaf stalks. These stems can become leggy with age; however, hard pruning soon produces vigorous new shoots, and results in rejuvenation of the plant.

In the shadow of neighbouring buildings or under the light shade of trees, the bold leaves of *Fatsia* contrast with an underplanting of small-leaved *Hedera*, *Vinca* or *Lonicera pileata*. The dark-green leaves of *F. japonica* and the white-and-green *Euonymus fortunei* 'Emerald Gaiety' will together form the basis of a green-and-white planting combination for shade. *F. japonica* is both exotic and contemporary in appearance when grown as a stand-alone specimen in a large pot – the perfect choice for a modern balcony or courtyard. Variegated forms are seldom seen, but the best known, 'Variegata', has leaf lobes tipped with cream-white. **AMcI**

Alternatives

Fatsia japonica 'Variegata', *Fatsia japonica* 'Spider's Web', × *Fatshedera lizei*

Forsythia

F. × intermedia Week End

Main features Spring flowers; autumn foliage tints
Height 1.8 m (6 ft) **Spread** 1.8 m (6 ft)
Position ○ ◐
Hardiness RHS H5

Few early-spring flowering shrubs are as reliable as the forsythias, which were named for William Forsyth, a Scottish botanist, head gardener and founder member of the Royal Horticultural Society. Belonging to the olive family (*Oleaceae*), forsythias originate from Central Europe and Asia. This relatively new variety, selected in 1982, was found as a mutation of the old stalwart 'Lynwood Variety'.

Week End is a tough, versatile variety with the qualities of ease of cultivation, colour and floriferousness of its parent, but in a compact form. The branches are more erect, with mid-green leaves that sometimes colour well before dropping in autumn. The golden-yellow bells clothe the bare branches in late winter and early spring.

It can be grown almost anywhere, although it will flower at its best in a sunny location. Partial shade does not mar its performance. Any soil conditions will suffice, provided it is not waterlogged for prolonged periods. To keep the bush to a good shape, it is advisable to thin out some of the old wood from the base every year or so.

It can be grown as a freestanding shrub in a border, adding a traditional feel to a cottage-garden–style planting scheme, and it looks stunning surrounded by blue spring flowers, such as scillas, grape hyacinths, forget-me-nots or blue pulmonarias. Alternatively, it can be trained against a wall and used as the support for a summer-flowering annual, such as *Asarina scandens*, *Thunbergia alata* or *Ipomoea lobata*. **MP**

Alternatives

= 'Courtalyn'. *Forsythia* Maree d'Or = 'Courtaneur',
Forsythia suspensa 'Nymans'

Fothergilla
F. major

Main features Deciduous shrubs grown for their autumn foliage colour; flower spikes in spring
Height 1.5–2.4 m (5–8 ft) **Spread** 90–150 cm (3–5 ft)
Position ○ ◑ ● **Hardiness** RHS H5

The *Fothergilla* genus is named after the eighteenth-century physician and plant collector Dr John Fothergill, who assembled an important collection of US shrubs in his botanical garden near Stratford in London. Also known as the mountain witch alder, *F. major* is one of only two species in the genus. Related to the witch hazel, both species come from the woodlands of the southeastern United States.

Well deserving of a Royal Horticultural Society Award of Garden Merit, *F. major* is a slow-growing bushy shrub that produces full, bottlebrush-like spikes of lightly fragrant white flowers in spring, just before or at the same time as the leaves start to emerge. It is these deeply veined, deciduous leaves that are the plant's greatest asset. They start life dark, glossy, green, and slightly downy on their undersides, but by the time autumn is in full swing, they have turned dramatic shades of red, orange and yellow.

F. major is an ideal shrub for low-maintenance gardens because it requires little specialist care, yet it still performs to its full potential. It will grow in any position in the garden as long as it is sheltered from cold winds. Although it does best in acidic soils, it is happy in loam, clay or sand. For the best autumn colours, plant *F. major* in full sun in borders or on the edge of the woodland garden. Popular varieties to try include the sweetly scented *F. major* Monticola Group (pictured), which is lower growing than the species, or *F. × intermedia*: a hybrid between *F. gardenii* and *F. major* that seems to have captured the best of both species. Handsome, fragrant, compact and hardy – with *F. major*'s ability to tolerate poor soil – *F. × intermedia* also produces the white catkin-like flowers and autumn colouring of the leaves found in both parents. **RSJ**

Alternatives

Fothergilla major Monticola Group, *Fothergilla × intermedia*

Fuchsia
F. magellanica var. *gracilis* 'Versicolor'

Main features Deciduous shrub with pretty foliage variegation; long flowering period from summer to autumn
Height 90–150 cm (3–5 ft) **Spread** 60 cm (24 in.)
Position ○ ◑ **Hardiness** RHS H4

This elegant, hardy fuchsia is adorned with pendent blooms through summer, continuing well into autumn. The tubular and long, tapered sepals are crimson red, and the petal 'skirts' rich purple. In classic fuchsia fashion, the heads dangle from the arching stems, and their stamen protrude, adding to the delicate, drop-earring effect. Unlike in green-leaved forms, where the flowers can disappear against the dark backdrop, in 'Versicolor' – or 'Tricolor,' as it is also known – the pale foliage makes a perfect foil. Spring and early-summer growth is flushed coppery pink, the colour remaining in the shoots' tips, while the rest of the small, pointed leaves turn grey green with a variable cream edge.

All fuchsias prefer a fertile soil with good moisture retention, and 'Versicolor' is happy in full sun or light shade. It looks well mixed with herbaceous and cottage-garden–style plantings, or adding a light touch to a mixed border in a sheltered town plot or breezy coastal garden. Try contrasting its fine foliage with trumpet-flowered day lilies and blue hostas, or combine with airy ornamental grasses and bold agapanthus for a late-summer show. In autumn consider a foreground of salmon-coloured *Hesperantha*, with a backdrop of hydrangeas.

Another excellent form of *F. magellanica* var. *gracilis* is the yellow-green-leaved cultivar 'Aurea'. Shorter growing than 'Versicolor', it prefers a shaded spot to prevent leaf scorch. 'Variegata' is of similar stature and has bold, cream-white leaf margins. Happy in sun or shade, it is pretty when planted together with blue cranesbills.

Cut *F. magellanica* back hard in spring to just above where the new shoots are sprouting. In colder regions, protect it by planting the crowns about 5 centimetres (2 in.) below the surface of the ground and apply a deep mulch during the autumn. **JH**

Alternatives

Fuchsia magellanica var. *gracilis* 'Aurea', *Fuchsia magellanica* var. *gracilis* 'Variegata'

Gaultheria
G. *mucronata*

Main features Heather-like flowers; berries in winter
Height 90–150 cm (3–5 ft) **Spread** 90–150 cm (3–5 ft)
Position ◑ ●
Hardiness RHS H5

This South American native thrives in the coastal mountains and interior valleys of Chile. A member of the *Ericaceae* family, *G. mucronata* has been in cultivation for nearly 200 years and is valued for its reliable year-round garden interest. A dense bushy mass of wiry stems is shrouded in small, pointed, shiny, evergreen leaves. From late spring to early summer, there are clusters of white, bell-shaped flowers, but by midsummer the flowers have begun the slow transformation into winter berries. These fleshy fruits, which are white or shades of red and pink, are fully formed by the autumn and last until spring. *G. mucronata* is perfect for banks, slopes and flower borders in all aspects, except for the coldest and shadiest. For guaranteed success as ground cover, planting in large groups creates the best effect. Many *Gaultheria* species are dioecious, meaning that they produce male and female flowers on separate plants. However, 'Bell's Seedling' (pictured) is a hermaphrodite form with large, dark-red fruits. **RSJ**

Alternatives

Gaultheria mucronata 'Crimsonia', *Gaultheria mucronata* 'Pink Pearl', *Gaultheria mucronata* 'Wintertime'

Genista
G. *tinctoria* 'Royal Gold'

Main features Tough shrub with plenty of late-spring flowers; winter colour from the stems
Height 50–90 cm (20–36 in.) **Spread** 50–90 cm (20–36 in.)
Position ○ **Hardiness** RHS H6

In nineteenth-century Britain, *G. tinctoria* was grown for its yellow flowers, which provide a yellow dye. Wool was dipped in this dye and then into a blue dye – either woad or indigo – resulting in a shade of deep green that was known as Kendal or Lincoln green and brought about the plant's common name: dyer's greenweed. Legend has it that this green cloth was worn by Robin Hood and his merry men; these men and their attire were immortalised in Shakespeare's *Henry IV*: 'How couldst thou know these men in Kendal green'. Like the species, 'Royal Gold' possesses the typical yellow, pea-like flowers, but it flowers more freely, resulting in clusters of small, deep, golden-yellow, blooms from spring until early summer. The deciduous leaves are small, narrow and dark green, but because the bare stems are green, this shrub provides a useful element of winter colour. 'Royal Gold' is a most amenable shrub: it will thrive in any position in full sun, but take care not to overdo any pruning. **RSJ**

Alternatives

Genista tinctoria 'Flore Pleno', *Genista tinctoria* 'Golden Plate', *Genista tinctoria* 'Humifusa'

Grevillea
G. *rosmarinifolia*

Main feature Evergreen, drought-tolerant shrub with unusual flowers
Height 90–150 cm (3–5 ft) **Spread** 1.8 m (6 ft)
Position ○ **Hardiness** RHS H3

You could mistake this Australian native for a bushy, well-clothed rosemary: the narrow, dark-green leaves with needle tips are very similar, and the plant also goes by the name of rosemary grevillea. The spidery blooms of this gracefully spreading evergreen are as attractive as they are fascinating. A relative of the South African proteas, it carries dense, ruby-red clusters towards the ends of its branches, and close examination reveals no petals, just colourful, curly sepals and long, protruding stigmas. In a favourable spot it can flower from late winter well into summer. For similar but showier blooms, look out for 'Canberra Gem', whereas 'Jenkinsii' is a pink form (pictured) and *G. juniperina* f. *sulphurea* has yellow flowers. Being compact, *G. juniperina* fits most plots, and no pruning is needed. In colder regions, grow it against a warm wall for protection. It works well with Mediterranean-style plantings that include silver- and grey-leaved companions to act as a foil for its dark foliage. **JH**

Alternatives

Grevillea 'Canberra Gem', *Grevillea rosmarinifolia* 'Jenkinsii', *Grevillea juniperina* f. *sulphurea*

Halesia
H. *carolina* Vestita Group

Main features Clusters of snowdrop-like flowers on bare stems in early summer; distinctive fruits
Height 3 m (10 ft) **Spread** 3 m (10 ft)
Position ○ ◑ **Hardiness** RHS H5

If there is ever a shrub to provoke admiration from fellow gardeners, *H. carolina* Vestita Group is it. In early summer this deciduous shrub, or small tree – which also goes by the more elegant and evocative common name of snowdrop tree – is covered with clusters of white bell-shaped flowers. Lightly scented, these hang on long, slender stems from branches that have yet to come into leaf. Occasionally, the flowers of plants in the Vestita Group have a faint tinge of pink, and they are almost always larger than the flowers of the species. The flowers make way for light-green, four-winged fruits that remain on their stems until autumn. Oval leaves that start out a blue green with downy undersides allow this shrub another opportunity to perform when they turn a yellow hue in the autumn. Ideal for woodland gardens, this is a plant that could be given pride of place in any garden. Although exotic in appearance, it is easy to grow, but requires well-drained, ericaceous (lime-free) soil. **RSJ**

Alternatives

Halesia carolina 'Uconn Wedding Bells', *Halesia diptera* Magniflora Group

× Halimiocistus
× H. wintonensis 'Merrist Wood Cream'

Main feature Cream-yellow flowers with
deep-maroon centres
Height 10–50 cm (4–20 in.) **Spread** 50–90 cm (20–36 in.)
Position ○ **Hardiness** RHS H4

Mediterranean and North African sun-lovers *Halimium*
and *Cistus* are members of the *Cistaceae* family. They
are bushy, low-growing plants that thrive in sunny, dry
gravel and rock gardens. × *Halimiocistus* species have
substantial saucers of flowers made up of five petals,
either white or yellow, and with striking colouring at
the base of each petal. × *Halimiocistus wintonensis* is
thought to be the result of a union between *H. lasianthum*
subsp. *formosum* and *C. salviifolius*, which was raised
in Hampshire. 'Merrist Wood Cream' is a sport of
× *H. wintonensis*. Like the species, it has greyish leaves and
large flowers with a dramatic centre of yellow surrounded
by a rich, deep maroon. The difference is that 'Merrist
Wood Cream' has the palest cream-yellow flowers rather
than white. It thrives in full sun, preferring places that
are sheltered from winds. A lovely plant for borders in
coastal, courtyard and urban gardens, it will easily take
to being cultivated in a patio pot. **RSJ**

Alternatives

× *Halimiocistus* 'Ingwersenii,' × *Halimiocistus revolii*

Halimium
H. lasianthum

Main feature Bright-yellow flowers with deep-purple
blotches at the bases of the petals
Height 45 cm (18 in.) **Spread** 90–150 cm (3–5 ft)
Position ○ **Hardiness** RHS H3

The woolly rock rose *H. lasianthum* is one of only seven
species of the genus *Halimium*, which are close relatives of
the sun roses (*Cistus*) and the rock roses (*Helianthemum*).
Originally from North Africa, Portugal and Spain, this is a
sun-loving plant for very dry soil. In late spring and early
summer, *H. lasianthum* has deep golden-yellow, saucer-
shaped flowers, around 4 centimetres (1.5 in.) across, often
with a contrasting purple blotch at the base of each
petal and a mass of evergreen, grey-green leaves. There
are several other outstanding cultivars: 'Concolor' has
yellow petals without the blotches, whereas 'Sandling' has
significant crimson blotches. 'Hannay Silver' is altogether
more vigorous and larger than some of the other cultivars.
It has yellow petals without blotches, but is most admired
for its silky grey leaves. *H. lasianthum* needs full sun,
shelter from cold winds and protection from frost. For
a pleasing combination, plant with heron's bill (*Erodium
trifolium*), which enjoys similar growing conditions. **RSJ**

Alternative

Halimium lasianthum subsp. *alyssoides*

Halimium lasianthum in full flower with other sun-loving plants in early summer. ➲

Hamamelis

H. × *intermedia* 'Vesna'

Main features Fragrant winter flowers; rich, autumn foliage colour
Height 1.5 m (5 ft) **Spread** 1.2 m (4 ft)
Position ○ ◑ **Hardiness** RHS H5

There are three qualities to look for in a witch hazel: impressive flowers freely produced, strong fragrance and rich, autumn foliage colour. *H. × intermedia* 'Vesna' has all three in abundance. In midwinter the upright branches of this vigorous shrub carry large, ribbon-petalled orange-yellow flowers with hints of red at their hearts. The scent is powerful; sweet but spicy and lingering. In autumn the foliage turns from green to shades of orange flame and gold. Altogether this is a hardworking shrub with two stunning seasons of interest. Although 'Vesna' is a large shrub, it is slow-growing and compact in habit compared to many other witch hazels. Position it where the low winter sun can shine through the flowers, ideally against a backdrop of dark evergreens. As hamamelis prefer a neutral to acidic soil, they are ideal partners for heaths and heathers. Those with gold or orange winter foliage are ideal for underplanting. They have a naturally graceful character, so pruning should be avoided. **AMcl**

Alternatives

Hamamelis × intermedia 'Aurora', *Hamamelis × intermedia* 'Aphrodite', *Hamamelis × intermedia* 'Robert'

Hebe

'Midsummer Beauty'

Main features Evergreen; showy flower display over many months; attracts bees and butterflies
Height 2 m (7 ft) **Spread** 1.5 m (5 ft)
Position ○ ◑ **Hardiness** RHS H4

This stalwart evergreen blooms far beyond the first flush of summer, and while many shrubs and perennials run out of steam late in the season, the rounded form of this shrubby veronica remains clothed in tapering amethyst wands well into the autumn. It is quick to mature and makes a useful addition to any new shrub or mixed border, rapidly filling its allotted space. The narrow, pointed, somewhat fleshy leaves have a refined quality and are flushed purple when young. Blooms, produced in abundance, begin as slender purple cords, which, as the individual flowers open, fluff out to form showy, upright-to-arching heads. Aging from lilac to white, they create an attractive two-tone effect. The lilac-mauve colouring of 'Midsummer Beauty' makes it the perfect foil for a wide range of plants in the mixed border, including roses, hydrangeas, as well as perennials such as day lilies, dahlias and white Japanese anemones. For drama, drop in a dark-purple foliage shrub like a smoke bush (*Cotinus*). **JH**

Alternatives

Hebe 'Great Orme', *Hebe* 'Nicola's Blush', *Hebe* Autumn Glory'

Hebe 'Midsummer Beauty' produces a generous flower display all summer and into autumn. ➲

Helianthemum
'Fire Dragon'

Main features Flowers in summer; attracts bees and butterflies; drought tolerant; evergreen ground cover
Height 15 cm (6 in.) **Spread** 38 cm (15 in.)
Position ○ **Hardiness** RHS H4

A low-growing, evergreen shrub with unbeatable flower power, 'Fire Dragon' is smothered in smoldering, deep orange-red blooms from late spring to midsummer. Cut it back with shears after flowering, and it will reclothe itself in neat, grey-green foliage that will survive all but the harshest winters. Needing a well-drained soil and sunny position, it is perfect for rockeries, raised beds or containers. 'Fire Dragon' can also be used along the front of borders, beside paths or in planting pockets among paving. The simple, five-petalled flowers produce a generous supply of nectar, so are attractive to bees and butterflies. This variety could be teamed with species tulips, such as spidery, red-and-yellow *Tulipa acuminata*, or star-like, yellow-and-white *T. tarda*. These bulbs will enjoy the same growing conditions as the rock rose and provide flowers earlier in the year. To follow on in late summer, try dwarf lavender or purple sage. Rock roses come in a variety of colours, from white to deep red, with various shades of yellow, pink and orange in between. **RKW**

Alternatives

Helianthemum 'Henfield Brilliant', *Helianthemum* 'Jubilee'

Heptacodium
H. miconioides

Main features Flowers late summer to autumn; peeling bark; fragrant flowers; architectural plant; attracts bees
Height 4–5 m (13–16 ft) **Spread** 3 m (10 ft)
Position ○ ◐ **Hardiness** RHS H5

This unusual and handsome plant, known as the seven son flower, originates from China. First discovered by Ernest Wilson in 1907, it was only introduced to cultivation in 1980. It is closely related to viburnums and forsythias. The dark-green leaves hang down in pairs in a curious fashion, with deep veins running the length of the leaf, parallel with the smooth leaf edges. The groups of five-petalled, white flowers appear in terminal clusters in late summer and early autumn. As the petals fall, the remaining calyx matures to a deep red, giving the impression of more flowers. The bark is grey to tan when mature, but reddish on younger shoots. Thin, papery strips exfoliate, adding to the interest. Prune in late winter or early spring to maintain a good shape. Use it as a specimen in a lawn or wild meadow, underplanted by a generous quantity of spring bulbs. These could emerge through an early-summer flowering, evergreen ground cover of the barren strawberry (*Waldsteinia ternata*), which flowers in early summer before this shrub has taken off. **MP**

Alternative

Dipelta floribunda

⊖ *Helianthemum* 'Fire Dragon' basking in a hot, dry spot.

Hibiscus
H. syriacus 'Diana'

Main features Showy midsummer to autumn flowers; tolerates heat and air pollution
Height 1.5–2.4 m (5–8 ft) **Spread** 90–150 cm (3–5 ft)
Position ○ ◑ **Hardiness** RHS H5

A goddess of the garden, *H. syriacus* 'Diana' is a shrub that you can really look forward to once the spectacle of spring bulbs and early perennials has faded. The pure-white blooms of this particular shrub are like ruffled satin petticoats, and unusually, each flower stays open at night and lasts more than a day. Given a sheltered location in full sun, the large blooms are produced continuously from midsummer right through to the first frost. The secret? 'Diana' is sterile and therefore incapable of setting seeds and so flowers for longer. The first plants were released in 1970, the result of a cross made by Dr Donald Egolf at the United States National Arboretum.

A relatively tall but upright-growing shrub – well-clothed with dark-green, lobed leaves – 'Diana' can be used as an informal screen. It oozes charm set among other sun worshippers, with its silver or grey-green leaves and blue or purple flowers. Such plants provide an elegantly understated foil for the white, hollyhock-shaped blooms. Simply surround 'Diana' with lavender, or use a catmint, such as *Nepeta* 'Six Hills Giant', *Caryopteris* × *clandonensis* 'Heavenly Blue' or *Perovskia atriplicifolia* 'Blue Spire' to similar effect. Other hardy hibiscus include 'Oiseau Bleu' (mauve blue), 'Red Heart' (white) and 'Woodbridge' (deep pink), each with a dark maroon-red blotch.

Although exotic looking, these shrubs of Far Eastern origin are surprisingly tough. Tolerant of pollution, they are useful for city plots where they help to attract butterflies. With its upright habit, 'Diana' fits into relatively narrow beds and large containers, which makes it ideal for courtyard gardens. Grow the plant on reasonably fertile, well-drained but moisture-retentive, neutral to alkaline soil. Prune this shrub in early spring to shape the plants and to encourage more flowering sideshoots. **JH**

Alternatives

Hibiscus syriacus 'Oiseau Bleu', *Hibiscus syriacus* 'Red Heart', *Hibiscus syriacus* 'Woodbridge'

Hippophae
H. rhamnoides

Main feature Attractive long-lasting fruits
Height 2–4 m (7–13 ft) **Spread** 2–4 m (7–13 ft)
Position ○ ◑
Hardiness RHS H7

This interesting shrub is now being planted on a commercial scale for the nutritional and medicinal benefits of the berries and other parts of the plant. Used in herbal medicine for centuries, the fruits contain an impressive array of antioxidants and are very rich in vitamin C. On a domestic scale, the fruits can be used to make marmalades and jams. In addition, *H. rhamnoides* is an attractive plant for the wilder areas of the garden. It is native to sand dunes and sea cliffs in many parts of Eurasia.

Also known as sea buckthorn, it makes a bushy, very spiny, deciduous plant growing between 2 and 4 metres (7–13 ft) in height with narrow, willowlike, silvery leaves. The plants are dioecious, which means that the male and female flowers are borne on separate plants, so it is important to grow several plants to ensure cross-pollination and a good crop of berries. When raised from seeds, this process is subject to much guesswork, but named 'sexed' varieties are available. *H. rhamnoides* 'Leikora' is one such female clone, and *H. rhamnoides* 'Pollmix' is a male. Ideally, plant one male to five females.

The flowers are small, yellow and insignificant, but they are clustered on the stems in vast numbers. The fruits that develop in midsummer can sometimes stay on the shrubs until well into the New Year, because they contain a substance unpalatable to birds. They are very acidic, and although edible, should be avoided when pregnant. *H. rhamnoides* will grow in any sunny or lightly shaded site on well-drained soil. It is exceptionally drought, wind and salt tolerant, making it ideal for coastal planting. It is also tough and hardy, and the roots have the ability to remove nitrogen from the air, in association with other organisms. This shrub suckers freely and may become invasive in some situations. **MP**

Alternatives

Hippophae salicifolia 'Streetwise', *Hippophae rhamnoides* 'Leikora'

Hydrangea

H. arborescens 'Annabelle'

Main feature Summer and autumn colour from leaves and flowers
Height 1.5–2.4 m (5–8 ft) **Spread** 1.5–2.4 m (5–8 ft)
Position ○ ◑ **Hardiness** RHS H6

This plant is all about the flowers. In full bloom from summer through autumn, their elegant appearance belies the plant's hardiness and provides a graceful accent to any garden. Launched in the mid 1970s by Gulf Stream Nursery, *H. arborescens* 'Annabelle' was discovered growing wild, rather than bred, near Anna, Ohio, in the United States, and it is from here that it takes its name. Unsurprisingly, given its origins, 'Annabelle' is a natural survivor of cold, snow-filled winters and hot, dry summers. A deciduous, small, bushy shrub with oval leaves, it produces huge round heads of white flowers measuring up to 25 centimetres (10 in.) across in summer. These flowers are sterile, showier than smaller fertile ones, and persist through autumn into winter. They fade gracefully from white to lime green into buff. Winter frost makes them sparkle as it highlights their tracery. After rain, the size of the flowers on 'Annabelle' can cause branches to droop and flatten the shrub. Decorative plant supports, planting in groups, and pruning sparingly so that stems are thicker are options to counter this tendency.

Other popular cultivars of *H. arborescens* with white flowers include the slightly smaller-flowered 'Grandiflora' and the more compact 'Hayes Starburst', the latter found by Hayes Jackson in his garden in Anniston, Alabama. Its white dome-shaped flower heads are made up of masses of double florets that give a starburst effect. 'Invincibelle Spirit' is a pink-flowered cultivar. **RC**

Alternatives

Hydrangea arborescens 'Invincibelle Spirit', *Hydrangea paniculata* 'Limelight', *Hydrangea quercifolia* 'Snow Queen'

Hydrangea
H. paniculata 'Limelight'

Main features Flowers in late summer and autumn;
dry winter flower heads
Height 1.5 m (5 ft) **Spread** 1.2 m (4 ft)
Position ○ ◑ **Hardiness** RHS H5

Upright stems clothed in dark-green leaves carry large,
densely packed, lilac-like flower heads composed of
soft lime-green florets in late summer. As the season
progresses, these turn from white to pink and then
parchment as autumn turns to winter. The pink colouring
is more pronounced in a sunny position. The lime-green
flowers of *H. paniculata* 'Limelight' have an almost
luminous quality, making it a superb choice to plant with
dark evergreens or to use as part of a green-and-white
planting scheme with variegated foliage shrubs, such as
Euonymus fortunei 'Silver Queen'. Planting with evergreens
maintains the foliage interest when the hydrangeas lose
their leaves in late autumn.

The secret of success with *H. paniculata* is hard
pruning in late winter. This stimulates vigorous, upright
growth raising the flower heads towards eye level, where
they are most visible. *H. paniculata* is a versatile shrub,
which sits well in the company of other shrubs and
perennials. It is a good choice to grow behind earlier-
flowering perennials where it will add structure and
extend the flowering season. In full bloom this shrub
is a wonderful sight under the light shade of deciduous
trees, perhaps underplanted with ferns, lungworts and
other ground-cover subjects. The lime-green flower
colour of 'Limelight' is unique. Most other cultivars are
white, or display pink coloration at an earlier stage in
the season. **AMcI**

Alternatives

Hydrangea paniculata 'Kyushu', *Hydrangea paniculata*
'Unique', *Hydrangea paniculata* 'Vanille Fraise'

Hydrangea
H. macrophylla Teller Series

Main features Showy flowers over a long period; good for containers; good cut flower
Height 1 m (3.5 ft) **Spread** 1 m (3.5 ft)
Position ○ ◑ **Hardiness** RHS H5

The Teller Series of *H. macrophylla* was bred in Switzerland in the 1950s as pot plants, and it does well in large containers for balconies, patios and gardens, maintaining a neat shape and flowering over a long period from a young age. As a lacecap hydrangea, it produces flowers with clusters of small, fertile florets in the centre, surrounded by a ring of showy, sterile florets. Closely related mophead hydrangeas have flowers composed entirely of large, sterile florets. Most varieties flower between mid- to late summer and early to midautumn. Both types of flower head are good for cutting fresh and will last indefinitely when dried.

All told, there are twenty-six varieties in the Teller Series, and most of them were given German bird names, although nowadays they are often sold by colour. Teller Blue is 'Blaumeise' (blue tit) and Teller Pink is 'Taube' (pigeon), although this latter variety is a lovely shade of blue when grown in acidic soil. Teller Red is 'Rotkehlchen' (redbreast) and Teller White 'Libelle' (dragonfly). Another popular variety is 'Möwe' (gull), which has a cream centre and rose-red outer florets.

H. macrophylla needs a fertile, moist but well-drained soil, and a position in sun or semi-shade. Although it is hardy over winter, tender young leaves and flower buds can be damaged by late-spring frost and cold winds, so a sheltered position is best. In milder areas it can thrive in coastal gardens. These shrubs do best in acidic or neutral soils, but they will tolerate some lime. Blue-flowered varieties will turn pink in alkaline conditions and require regular treatment with hydrangea colourant to keep their blue colour. All varieties look good planted in small groups and underplanted with spring bulbs and winter-flowering hellebores to extend the period of interest. **RKW**

Alternatives

Hydrangea macrophylla 'Lanarth White', *Hydrangea macrophylla* 'Quadricolor', *Hydrangea macrophylla* 'Zorro'

Hydrangea
H. quercifolia Snow Queen

Main features Flowers in summer; attractive foliage; autumn colour; good cut flower
Height 1.2 m (4 ft) **Spread** 1.2 m (4 ft)
Position ○ ◐ ● **Hardiness** RHS H5

A medium-sized, deciduous shrub, *H. quercifolia* Snow Queen is a good choice for prominent positions and smaller gardens, as it provides interest year-round. The deeply lobed leaves are up to 20 centimetres (8 in.) long and unfurl from downy shoots to reveal a dark-green upper surface and a greyish-white underside. The flowers open from midsummer in long conical sprays on the ends of new shoots, starting off cream white and aging to rose pink, eventually becoming brown and papery. In autumn the leaves turn bronze red, then drop to reveal peeling bark on mature plants, which is an attractive cinnamon brown underneath. Snow Queen needs no special care, but shortening the shoots back after flowering will help to retain a compact shape.

Most species of *Hydrangea* originate in Asia, but the oak-leaved variety is native to the southeastern United States, from Tennessee to Florida, thriving in a woodland setting. In gardens it prefers a well-drained soil and will tolerate drier, shadier conditions than other hydrangeas. However, it needs a sunny position to produce good autumn colour, which can include shades of red, yellow, orange and purple. The flowers are less showy than the named varieties, but are still attractive. *H. quercifolia* 'Harmony' was found growing wild in Alabama and has large flowers, with individual florets nearly 2.5 centimetres (1 in.) across. 'Snowflake' has double flowers, and 'Pee Wee' is a more compact form. All these cultivars have white flowers, which age to pink, and good autumn colour.

In acidic soils, team *H. quercifolia* Snow Queen with dwarf azaleas and rhododendrons to bring evergreen foliage and colourful late-spring flowers to the garden. If the soil is more limey, try varieties of winter-flowering heath (*Erica carnea*), many of which also have colourful spring foliage. **RKW**

Alternatives

= 'Flemygea'. *Hydrangea quercifolia* 'Harmony', *Hydrangea quercifolia* 'Pee Wee', *Hydrangea quercifolia* 'Snowflake'

Hydrangea
H. serrata 'Bluebird'

Main features Flowers in summer and autumn; burgundy-flushed foliage
Height 90 cm (3 ft) **Spread** 75 cm (2.5 ft)
Position ○ ◑ **Hardiness** RHS H5

A delightful summer-flowering shrub, *H. serrata* 'Bluebird' is the perfect choice for any garden that does not have the space for one of the larger lacecap hydrangea varieties. 'Bluebird' is a slender shrub, with upright tan-coloured stems and pointed dark-green leaves flushed purple red. In midsummer the delicate lacecap flower heads appear; these are purple-pink on alkaline soils, but bright gentian-blue on acidic soils. Each flower head consists of a flattened cluster of tiny fertile florets surrounded by larger, showier, sterile or ray florets. 'Bluebird', along with other *H. serrata* varieties, has smaller, more refined flower heads than familiar lacecap hydrangeas. As the season progresses, the colour of the flowers changes to purple-green, and the wine-red colour of the foliage becomes more intense towards the autumn.

'Bluebird' is a lovely hydrangea to grow in sun or in light shade with perennials and roses. Its compact habit makes it suitable for narrow borders. Plant it with evergreen shrubs such as *Choisya* and *Viburnum tinus*, in order to extend the season of interest. *H. serrata* 'Tiara' is similar in habit to 'Bluebird', but it has more sterile florets in each flower head. The flower colour is more mauve, and the autumn foliage more intensely crimson in the sun. *H. serrata* 'Rosalba' has fewer, large sterile florets, which are initially white but soon change to crimson. Its autumn foliage is rich purple-red. *H. serrata* 'Miranda' has very dome-shaped flower heads, which turn a vibrant shade of blue in acidic conditions.

This species produces many slender stems from the base of the plant. Cut out some of the older stems each year in order to encourage new growth from ground level. These older stems are easily identified by their more branching habit and dull brown colouring, in contrast to the tan-coloured bark of the new stems. **AMcI**

Alternatives

Hydrangea serrata 'Tiara', *Hydrangea serrata* 'Rosalba', *Hydrangea serrata* 'Miranda'

Hypericum
H. kalmianum

Main features Bright-yellow flowers; prominent stamen; pale-brown flaky bark
Height 1 m (3.5 ft) **Spread** 1 m (3.5 ft)
Position ○ ◑ **Hardiness** RHS H7

A vast genus, *Hypericum* comprises around 370 species of trees, shrubs and herbaceous perennials. Some are from the United States, others are from eastern Asia, and yet more come from Europe. They are well known worldwide by the common name of St John's wort. *H. kalmianum* is a native of eastern North America, specifically the Great Lakes, where it grows in dry woods and at lakesides. It is named after Peter Kalm, who was a student of the great Swedish botanist Carl Linnaeus and who is thought to have discovered this species in the mid 1700s.

Species of *Hypericum* from the United States tend to be of the smaller-flowering kind. However, this is not always the case, and *H. kalmianum* bucks the trend with its clusters of up to seven relatively large, bright-yellow flowers that have an exuberant froth of stamen at their centres. After the flowers come the fruits, which are oval and brown, and can last until spring. *H. kalmianum* is a long flowering species, with blooms appearing throughout late summer. It is happy in full sun or partial shade, enjoys well-drained soil and will even put up with drought – but not for prolonged periods. The slender evergreen leaves start life a bright-green colour but turn grey-green as they mature. The bark on the main stems is pale brown, papery and flaky.

With long-lasting fruit and evergreen foliage, this bushy shrub is a show-off of a *Hypericum* that will make an excellent year-round hedge. Plant one or two at the edge of a pond, on a rocky slope or in a border, and it promises never to disappoint. Two Chinese species to try are *H. forrestii*, which forms a neat shrub with attractive foliage colours in the autumn, and *H. kouytchense*, which is also compact with plenty of flower. *H. olympicum* f. *uniflorum* 'Citrinum' is an excellent European species with pale-lemon flowers. **RSJ**

Alternatives

Hypericum forrestii, Hypericum kouytchense, Hypericum olympicum f. *uniflorum* 'Citrinum'

Ilex

I. *aquifolium* 'Handsworth New Silver'

Main features Evergreen foliage; brightly coloured berries; good for hedging; many variegated varieties
Height 90 cm (3 ft) **Spread** 60 cm (24 in.)
Position ○ ◐ **Hardiness** RHS H6

Despite the name, this variety of holly is more than 160 years old, and its longevity shows what a good garden plant it is. The evergreen leaves are somewhat longer than most hollies; they have neat spines and a broad white border. Small, white flowers, popular with bees, are followed by bright-red berries. It will grow in most soils, except very wet ones, and is happy in sun or partial shade, but needs shelter from icy winds, especially when young.

I. aquifolium 'Handsworth New Silver' will eventually grow into a small tree, but it is easily kept smaller by pruning annually in late summer. Clipped specimens can be used to create year-round focal points: they look smart paired on either side of an entrance and make good container plants. Being spiny, this variety also makes an impenetrable hedge and creates a safe haven for nesting birds, providing them with winter food.

Native to Europe and western Asia, *I. aquifolium* has many religious, magical and folkloric connections, and it has been central to Christmas decorations for centuries. Slow growing, it produces a dense, white wood that is easily turned on a lathe and absorbs staining well. Consequently, it was often used to produce chess sets. There are scores of garden varieties of *I. aquifolium*, which may have few or many prickles; yellow, cream or white variegation; and yellow, orange or red berries. Plants are either male or female, and both are needed for the females to produce berries. **RKW**

Alternatives

Ilex aquifolium 'Alaska', *Ilex aquifolium* 'Bacciflava'. *Ilex aquifolium* 'Ferox Argentea', *Ilex aquifolium* 'J. C. van Tol'

Ilex

I. *verticillata* 'Maryland Beauty'

Main features Oval, rich-green leaves; clusters of bright-red winter berries
Height 1.5–2 m (5–7 ft) **Spread** 1.5–2 m (5–7 ft)
Position ○ ◑ **Hardiness** RHS H7

This *I. verticillata* 'Maryland Beauty' belongs to the holly family, but the foliage looks not in the least bit like the evergreen hollies that we associate with winter. Instead of the typical, spiny, evergreen holly leaves, 'Maryland Beauty' has deciduous oval leaves, with slightly serrated edges and downy undersides. They begin a mid-green colour but turn bronze yellow in the autumn. After the somewhat unexciting, greenish-white flowers in spring come vivacious clusters of berries that are bright scarlet. These last for a good while throughout winter and into early spring and are a welcome source of food for birds.

'Maryland Beauty' is dioecious, which means that there are separate male and female plants. The berries appear only on female plants that have been pollinated, so planting one male, such as *I. verticillata* 'Jim Dandy', among several females should guarantee a generous display. A shrub that demands little maintenance, 'Maryland Beauty' makes an excellent hedging plant. Slow growing and suckering, it should be pruned in spring to keep it in check. Being native to swampy habitats or woodland at the edge of ponds or streams in eastern North America, the species will tolerate damp feet, but it does not like chalky soil. It is also a useful plant for urban gardens, where it will fend off air pollution with ease. The form *I. verticillata* f. *aurantiaca* has orange fruits, while *I. verticillata* 'Christmas Cheer' and 'Winter Red' are both recommended for their lovely bright-red fruits. **RSJ**

Alternatives

Ilex verticillata f. *aurantiaca, Ilex verticillata* 'Christmas Cheer', *Ilex verticillata* 'Winter Red'

Indigofera
I. heterantha

Main features Spikes of dark pink-mauve flowers; delicate fern-like leaves
Height 1.5–2.4 m (5–8 ft) **Spread** 1.5–2.4 m (5–8 ft)
Position ○ **Hardiness** RHS H5

A native of the northwestern Himalayas, *I. heterantha* belongs to a genus of around 700 species of tropical and subtropical shrubs and herbaceous plants. The pea-like flowers of deep pink-mauve are produced in luscious thick spikes in the axils of the fern-like pinnate leaves, continuously from summer until autumn. However, planting conditions will dictate how high *I. heterantha* grows in the garden situation. It can be planted in the open in a border of any aspect, where it will grow quite happily; however, if *I. heterantha* is planted against a wall in full sun, where it is better protected from harsh frost and cold winds, the plant will grow to a more impressive height. Planting *I. heterantha* with repeat-flowering, climbing roses, such as *Rosa* 'Pink Perpetue' and 'Gertrude Jekyll', or with late-flowering *Clematis viticella* will achieve a truly stunning and rather exotic effect. Another lovely species of *Indigofera* is *I. himalayensis,* and particularly the form *I. himalayensis* 'Silk Road', which was introduced in 2006 and has vivacious purple-pink flowers. **RSJ**

Alternatives

Indigofera 'Claret Cascade', *Indigofera himalayensis* 'Silk Road'

Itea
I. virginica 'Henry's Garnet'

Main features White racemes of large fragrant flowers; good autumn colour
Height 1–1.5 m (3.5–5 ft) **Spread** 1–1.5 m (3.5–5 ft)
Position ◑ **Hardiness** RHS H7

The *I. virginica* is the only one of around fifteen species of *Itea* that comes from the United States. The rest are from eastern Asia. The genus includes evergreen and deciduous small trees and shrubs, and *I. virginica* is a deciduous, rounded shrub with sweeping arches for branches. The leaves are oval and dark green, and they turn gorgeous shades of red through orange to gold in the autumn. The flowers are white and deliciously fragrant, appearing en masse in spring on heavy drooping racemes. *I. virginica* 'Henry's Garnet' is a form of the species that was discovered in 1982 by Dr Michael Dirr at Swarthmore College in Pennsylvania. It is similar to the species in all but the size of the flowers, which are larger, and the autumn colours of the leaves, which are deep, rich shades of red and purple; hence the allusion to the semiprecious stone in its name. Like the species, the leaves remain much longer on the plant than many other shrubs and trees, often until winter, when some leaves are still green. **RSJ**

Alternatives

Itea virginica 'Beppu', *Itea virginica* Little Henry = 'Sprich'

Kalmia
K. latifolia 'Olympic Fire'

Main features Flowers in summer; evergreen foliage
Height 1.5–4 m (5–13 ft) **Spread** 1.5–4 m (5–13 ft)
Position ○ ◑
Hardiness RHS H7

Native to the eastern parts of North America, *Kalmia* is considered by many to be the loveliest flowering shrub. Of all its cultivars, *K. latifolia* 'Olympic Fire' is especially highly rated for its deep-red, crimped buds that look like they have been squeezed out of the nozzle of an piping bag. These open to reveal candy-pink blooms, creating a striking colour contrast. The open flowers are cup-shaped, with their petals fused together, and each contains ten stamen that are reflexed and fused to the bowl, giving the inside of the flowers a spotted appearance where the dark pollen-loaded anthers tuck into the petals. The foliage is handsome, glossy and dark green, providing year-round interest and a foil for the rosy flowers. In the garden, 'Olympic Fire' provides a great backdrop in a border or as an informal hedge in a natural landscape, such as a woodland garden. Mix it with other ericaceous plants, such as rhododendrons and azaleas, in a relaxed shrub border or place it somewhere gloomy to bring some summer relief. **ER**

Alternative

Kalmia latifolia 'Freckles'

Kerria
K. japonica 'Pleniflora'

Main features Green winter stems; flowers in late spring; easygoing plant; good cut foliage
Height 1.2 m (4 ft) **Spread** 1.5 m (5 ft)
Position ○ ◑ ● **Hardiness** RHS H7

Pretty, egg-yolk-yellow pompoms decorate this shrub in mid- to late spring, and they often continue intermittently until autumn. The narrowly triangular leaves with toothed margins are a fresh, light-green colour, giving an attractive, airy effect. Even after leaf fall, the slender, arching stems remain vivid green and continue to make a significant contribution to the garden display in winter. *K. japonica* 'Pleniflora' is an easygoing shrub that will thrive in sun or shade; it tolerates most soils, except very wet ones, and bounces back from damage. Left alone it will eventually form a substantial thicket, but if you cut out all the flowered branches as they fade you can keep its size in check, and it will flower all the better for it. 'Pleniflora' works well with other light-foliaged plants, such as bamboo, and makes a good foil for evergreen shrubs. Mix it with red-barked, variegated dogwood and yellow-barked willow, underplant with blue-flowered ground cover – such as *Vinca*, *Brunnera* or *Pulmonaria* – and you will have a low-maintenance, year-round display. **RKW**

Alternatives

Kerria japonica 'Golden Guinea', *Kerria japonica* 'Picta'

Kolkwitzia
K. amabilis 'Pink Cloud'

Main features Flowers in summer; winter bark
Height 1.8–3 m (6–10 ft) **Spread** 1.8–3 m (6–10 ft)
Position ○ ◐
Hardiness RHS H7

This is an easy, tough shrub that can be relied upon to perform and give a display that lives up to its common name: beauty bush. Introduced from China in 1901, the original species was collected by prolific plant hunter Ernest Wilson. This improved variety, *K. amabilis* 'Pink Cloud' was selected at the Royal Horticultural Society's garden at Wisley, England, in 1946.

A medium- to large-sized suckering shrub, it has arching stems that are festooned in pink trumpet-shaped flowers with faint, yellow vein markings in the throat. On close inspection, the flowers appear from incredibly hairy calyxes and have equally hairy flower stalks. 'Pink Cloud' is beautiful sight in full bloom in summer. However, the leaves are unremarkably green, ovate shaped, and lack any significant autumn interest.

Grow this floriferous shrub at the back of a border where its summer glory can be appreciated, flanked by other shrubs to add interest in other seasons. *Buddleja* would add late-summer interest, and an evergreen *Berberis darwinii* or *Pieris japonica* would be ideal for spring. Use 'Pink Cloud' as a shapely specimen arising from a carpet of an evergreen ground-cover plants, such as *Pachysandra terminalis* 'Variegata' or *Vinca difformis*. The flowers are produced on the previous season's wood, so thinning out some of the older wood immediately after flowering will prevent overcrowding and keep a good shape. **MP**

Alternatives

Kolkwitzia amabilis, Kolkwitzia amabilis Dream Catcher = 'Maradco', *Dipelta floribunda*

Lagerstroemia

L. *indica* 'Pocomoke'

Main features Rose-pink flowers all summer; good in beds and in containers
Height 90 cm (3 ft) **Spread** 90 cm (3 ft)
Position ○ **Hardiness** RHS H5

The crepe myrtle *L. indica* has a miniature named form, 'Pocomoke', which is a bushy, deciduous shrub with rose-pink, crepe-like flowers that smother the glossy, green, leafy shoots throughout summer. In hot, sunny regions, it provides a mass of summer colour, as well as some rich bronze-red tints to the foliage in the autumn. Grow it in a mixed border, en masse on a sunny bank, or in a container, where it can be appreciated on a terrace or deck.

'Pocomoke' is one of several hybrids bred at the United States National Arboretum in Washington, DC. One parent is the larger *L. indica*, which originated from China and is grown as a large wall shrub. The other is *L. fauriei*, a species introduced to the arboretum in the 1950s from Japan. Selections made there by Dr Donald Egolf over many years resulted in garden-worthy hybrids that are smaller and neater, with a high mildew resistance and a wide range of flower colours. 'Pocomoke' has only been available for gardeners to buy since 2000.

The plant is hardier than might be expected, and shoots damaged by frost will reshoot. However, a long period of hot sun is needed for the flower display, so 'Pocomoke' is most popular in regions such as the southern US states. To propagate new plants, take softwood cuttings from nonflowering shoots in early summer, root them in ericaceous (lime-free) compost, and overwinter in a cold greenhouse or frame. Plant out the young plants for amazing displays the following summer. **PM**

Alternatives

Lagerstroemia 'Chickasaw', *Lagerstroemia* 'Firecracker', *Lagerstroemia* 'Ozark Spring'

Lavatera
L. × *clementii* 'Rosea'

Main features Rose-pink flowers all summer; attractive grey-green foliage; good plant for beds and containers
Height 2.4 m (8 ft) **Spread** 2.4 m (8 ft)
Position ○ **Hardiness** RHS H5

There is no doubt that *L.* × *clementii* 'Rosea' is an outstanding tree mallow to have in the garden. Masses of rose-pink, funnel-shaped, hollyhock-like flowers (up to 6 cm/2.5 in. across) festoon plants in midsummer through to the autumn, with grey-green leaves adding to the display. This popular lavatera produces upright plants perfect for mixed borders or as specimens. This plant can also be grown in a large container to brighten up a patio. It does need a sunny position to flower well; however, any type of well-drained, fertile soil will suffice. The grey-green leaves of plants such as *L.* × *clementii* 'Rosea' are usually an indication of drought tolerance.

However, what this vigorous shrub does need is plenty of space to spread out because it is fast growing – 90 centimetres (3 ft) of growth in a year is common. Diseases tend not to bother *L.* × *clementii* 'Rosea', and most pests are preoccupied attacking other plants around it. To keep plants looking compact and less straggly, it is a good idea to give the woody branches a good prune in spring. Cut back all shoots to around 30 centimetres (12 in.) above soil level before growth bursts into life, but after the last frost. This encourages a more squat and bushy plant to be produced. In exposed areas cut back the branches by half in the autumn to prevent them from rocking and snapping in the wind.

This long flowering variety of *Lavatera* can be a relatively short-lived shrub lasting five or six years. This life expectancy can be extended by overwintering container-grown specimens in a cold greenhouse, by ensuring all plants are grown in sharply drained soil or compost, and by growing against a warm, sheltered wall to minimise frost and wind damage in colder areas. Otherwise, simply sit back and enjoy the show. *L.* × *clementii* 'Rosea' will not disappoint. **PM**

Alternatives

Syn. *Lavatera arborea* 'Rosea'. *Lavatera olbia* 'Rosea'

Lavatera × *clementii* 'Rosea' is a quick-growing, short-lived shrub for a sunny bed. ➔

Lavandula

L. × intermedia 'Gros Bleu'

Main features Attracts bees and butterflies; fragrant foliage; scented flowers from summer to autumn
Height 75 cm (2.5 ft) **Spread** 90 cm (3 ft)
Position ○ **Hardiness** RHS H5

The cultivar 'Gros Bleu' is one of the most outstanding of the more recent French hybrid lavenders. It has many star qualities that give it the edge over other cultivars and species. First, its evergreen, grey-green foliage makes a substantial mound that is perfectly robust. Tall flower stems grow above this bushy base, each ending with a fabulous, 10-centimetre-long (4 in.), slender, tapering bloom spike. Flowers have deep-purple, woolly calyxes with intense, dark-violet corollas. They are very sweetly scented, with fewer camphor notes than other lavenders. Distinctive colour and fragrance make its flowers perfect for both fresh and dried bouquets. Finally, flowering extends from summer through to autumn.

A single specimen brings timeless fragrance to any style of garden; for maximum impact, plant it near a doorway, at the corner of a patio or to mark the end of border. A row of them makes an aromatic, low hedge, perfect for adding presence around herb borders or a formal rose garden. A wide swath of many plants conjures a vision of the lavender fields of Provence in southern France. In warmer climates other Mediterranean natives make good planting partners, for example, rock rose (*Cistus*), the common olive (*Olea europaea*), rosemary and sage. In cooler regions grow 'Gros Bleu' in containers, which can be placed outside in summer and moved indoors when shelter is required during winter. A warm spot in summer sunshine enhances its fragrance and will attract numerous bees and butterflies to the garden. Trimming stems as flowers fade will extend the flowering season.

'Grosso' is another tall, dark-flowered French lavender cultivar, but it is less compact than 'Gros Bleu.' Reaching 90 centimetres (3 ft) in height, 'Grosso' is one of the most widely grown lavenders for essential oil in the world. **RC**

Alternatives

Lavandula × intermedia 'Grosso', *Lavandula × intermedia* 'Hidcote Giant', *Lavandula dentata*

Lavandula
L. × ginginsii 'Goodwin Creek Grey'

Main features Attracts bees and butterflies; drought
tolerant; fragrant flowers in summer and autumn
Height 60–90 cm (24–36 in.) **Spread** 60–90 cm (24–36 in.)
Position ○ **Hardiness** RHS H5

Fragrance and distinctive flowers are produced by all
lavenders, so what is it that makes *Lavandula × ginginsii*
'Goodwin Creek Grey' so special? Upright and bushy,
its silver-grey, tooth-edged leaves set off intense,
deep-lavender to violet-purple flowers from late spring
through summer and autumn, even into winter in mild
climates. Lavender specialist Jim Becker discovered this
cultivar in 1991 at Goodwin Creek Gardens in southwest
Oregon. It was a hybrid seedling, parented by French
lavender (*L. dentata*) and woolly lavender (*L. lanata*,
pictured). This determines its original, ornamental
appearance. Its leaves are fuzzy with very fine leaf hairs
that give it a highly tactile quality. Its flower clusters have
longer, tiny bracts going up to the top of the conical-
shaped flower heads.

'Goodwin Creek Grey' suits all garden styles, from
traditional cottage gardens to cool contemporary
minimalist spaces. A single plant punctuates the front of
a border with fragrance; a row forms a neat, low hedge,
makes a stand-alone statement, accentuates a path, or
delineates the edge of planting behind; multiple rows
create a sweetly scented 'river' of blue, either straight or
in meandering curves. This shrub is a natural in gravel
gardens planted with fellow Mediterranean natives rock
rose (*Cistus*) and rosemary. It is also perfect for growing
in containers, which can be moved into winter shelter
as required – useful in colder locations.

There are several other lavenders that make
rewarding shrubs. One of the most noteable groups is
the English lavender (*Lavandula angustifolia*) cultivars
such as 'Hidcote' and 'Folgate.' All lavenders need sun,
lean soil and not too much water – the conditions in
their native region – because excess water makes them
leggy and shortens their life span. **RC**

Alternatives

Lavandula × intermedia 'Gros Bleu', *Lavandula angustifolia*
'Hidcote', *Lavandula dentata*, *Lavandula lanata*

Lespedeza
L. thunbergii subsp. thunbergii

Main feature Rose-purple flowers on long racemes in the autumn
Height 2 m (7 ft) **Spread** 3 m (10 ft)
Position ○ **Hardiness** RHS H5

Known as the Thunberg lespedeza, or Thunberg bush clover, this member of the pea family has long, arching stems bearing rose-purple flowers that fill the flower gap at the end of summer, and it makes a lovely plant for many gardens in milder regions. Native to northern China and Japan, *L. thunbergii* subsp. *thunbergii* has stems that grow up to 2 metres (7 ft) long, each capable of producing racemes of blooms. The whole plant dies down at the end of autumn, but it returns more strongly every spring. Unlike its edible pea relatives, the woody stems are not affected by diseases or pests. This shrub blooms in the early autumn on growth that has been produced in the same year, so pruning is best done in early spring to allow the new growth to mature and flower in the same year. A well-drained soil is all that is required to produce an impressive display in the first cool days of autumn. **PM**

Alternatives

Lespedeza thunbergii subsp. *thunbergii* 'White Fountain',
Lespedeza thunbergii subsp. *formosa*

Leucosceptrum
L. stellipilum

Main features Spikes of pinkish-mauve blooms in autumn; coarsely serrated leaves
Height 90 cm (3 ft) **Spread** 90 cm (3 ft)
Position ◑ ● **Hardiness** RHS H5

For shady spots beneath trees and shrubs there is no better plant to grow than Japanese forest mint, *L. stellipilum*. As the flowering frenzy of summer fades, it bristles into bloom with a gentility and sophistication ushered in by the first days of a cool autumn. *L. stellipilum* is a semi-woody perennial plant originating in Japan. The rounded, coarsely serrated leaves fill the space beneath overhanging trees from midspring, with elaborately constructed spikes of flowers appearing in autumn. Individual blooms are pinkish-mauve in colour, the first bloom opening at the base of the spike, with others following suit over a two-week period. Imagine the construction of a foxglove, the appearance of a bottlebrush and the colour of lavender and you have *L. stellipilum*. It is the perfect companion to many shade-loving ferns and hostas. Hydrangea leaves are not dissimilar to the foliage, and both plants also work well together. **PM**

Alternatives

Leucosceptrum japonicum, *Leucosceptrum stellipilum* var. *formosanum*, *Leucosceptrum stellipilum* var. *tosaense*

Leucothoe
Scarletta

Main features Compact evergreen; rich red and purple seasonal colouring
Height 90 cm (3 ft) **Spread** 1.8 m (6 ft)
Position ◑ ● **Hardiness** RHS H6

Whether potting up containers for the winter patio or planning a shady border for year-round interest, *L.* Scarletta has to be on the shopping list. This glossy evergreen is a chameleon. In spring the new growth emerging from the mid-green mound of narrow, tapered leaves is touched maroon and scarlet. Dark, glossy, green prevails through summer, but in autumn, the leaves once again transform, this time becoming burgundy. Cold winter spells promote additional red and bronze highlights, keeping the display vibrant. Try growing Scarletta as part of a festive-season patio feature and add some trailing ivy, red mini cyclamen and white hellebores. In a woodland-style border with spring bulbs, foxgloves and geraniums, use Scarletta along with flowering *Skimmia* to inject rich winter colour. It makes neat, weed-suppressing ground cover, and it is easy to keep the slowly spreading clumps in check by trimming in late spring. **JH**

Alternatives

= 'Zeblid'. *Leucothoe axillaris* 'Curly Red', *Leucothoe* 'Zebekot', *Leucothoe fontanesiana* 'Rainbow'

Leycesteria
L. formosa
Golden Lanterns

Main features Golden summer and autumn foliage; flowers in summer; autumn fruit clusters
Height 1.8 m (6 ft) **Spread** 1.5 m (5 ft)
Position ○ ◑ **Hardiness** RHS H6

A beautiful pheasant berry, with upright, arching, green stems and soft golden leaves, *L. formosa* Golden Lanterns is an easy shrub to grow. The perfect choice to lift a corner of the garden, it will lighten heavy, evergreen planting partners, mixes well with golden variegations and contrasts superbly with purple-foliage shrubs, which also highlight the wine-red flower clusters. In late summer and autumn, pendent clusters of purple berries and wine-red bracts hang from the branches, creating a pleasing effect. The leaves do not scorch in sun and become intensely golden yellow by midsummer. The colour is more subdued in shade, but it retains a fresh lime-yellow hue. Naturalised and regarded as 'wild' in some areas, *L. formosa* is a useful garden shrub grown for its green winter stems and hanging clusters of purple fruits surrounded by red-purple bracts. It is best tidied in autumn to remove twiggy growth, but retain the green stems for winter interest. **AMcl**

Alternatives

= 'Notbruce'. *Leycesteria formosa*, *Leycesteria formosa* 'Purple Rain', *Leycesteria formosa* 'Gold Leaf'

Ligustrum
L. ovalifolium 'Aureum'

Main feature Handsome variegated foliage
Height 1.5 m (5 ft) **Spread** 1.2 m (4 ft)
Position ○ ◐ ●
Hardiness RHS H5

Privet is not generally regarded as an exciting plant. In the United Kingdom it is associated with provincialism, because it is so often grown in suburban gardens. However, its omnipresence does not make it dull, and privet deserves to be better respected. *Ligustrum* is widely used because it is so brilliant, so uncomplaining, so smart, and so tough; moreover, it comes in gold. It is a very handsome plant and more people should include it in their gardens.

Perhaps the most magnificent variety is golden privet, *L. ovalifolium* 'Aureum', a variegated form of the familiar green hedging plant: vigorous, tough and versatile. Its leaves are glossy green, edged with rich golden yellow. It withstands clipping as well as the species does, it so makes an excellent, dense hedge, and it is also well-suited to more elaborate topiary designs. It is particularly fitting for urban areas, as it is very resistant to pollution. Grown as a hedge, it can reach up to 4 metres (13 ft), but may top 5 metres (16 ft) if left to grow freely as a shrub. Do remember to promptly pinch out any shoots that revert to green.

Privet will grow in most moist, free-draining soils and is as happy by the coast as it is in a sheltered site. In very cold winters it may lose its leaves, but on the whole it behaves as an evergreen. In late summer it produces white flowers, followed by glossy, black berries, making it very popular with butterflies and songbirds. Despite the benefits to wildlife of leaving privet unpruned to flower, in practice it is nearly always trimmed before it flowers because the blooms have an unpleasant smell. A size of 1.5 by 1.2 metres (5 x 4 ft) assumes a plant is up to five years old and is trimmed annually, typically as a hedge. Single specimens can also be bought trained as a standard lollipop (pictured) and kept trimmed. **ER**

Alternative

Syn. *Ligustrum ovalifolium* 'Aureomarginatum'.
Ligustrum ovalifolium 'Lemon and Lime'

Lonicera

L. × *purpusii* 'Winter Beauty'

Main features Deciduous to semi-evergreen shrub;
very strong winter perfume
Height 1.5 m (5 ft) **Spread** 1.5 m (5 ft)
Position ○ ◑ **Hardiness** RHS H5

Few things lift the spirits in winter better than detecting wafts of heavenly perfume drifting across the garden. When *L. × purpusii* is planted as part of a larger shrub border, you might search around a while for the source of the scent. This is not a showy plant and seems far too delicate to be winter flowering, and yet this rounded, semi-evergreen shrub, with fine, wiry stems, produces scatterings of tiny, paired, cream flowers from midwinter to early spring. During particularly mild spells, especially after a long freeze, many more blooms open together. If you cannot wait and want to enjoy a taste of spring early, cut a few stems from a mature, established plant, bring them indoors, and put them in a vase of water.

L. × purpusii is a naturally occurring cross between two hardy Chinese species, which were brought together at the Darmstadt Botanical Garden in Hessen, Germany. The parents, *L. standishii* and *L. fragrantissima*, have long been grown for their winter fragrance. The hybrid's name, *L. × purpusii*, remembers two German brothers, Carl and Joseph Purpus, who were plant collectors in the late 1800s. *L. × purpusii* 'Winter Beauty' is the most widely available selection, which, like the others, bears small, oval leaves in pairs.

Site 'Winter Beauty' at a short distance from a doorway or thoroughfare. Planted in a front garden, it will enchant passersby. However, take care next to pathways: plants can spread wider than anticipated, and branch tips may root where they touch the ground. If space is limited, train the plant against a wall, spreading out and thinning the stems to form a framework. Prune around one-third of the oldest wood immediately after flowering. Grow 'Winter Beauty' on moisture-retentive but not boggy soil and in drier conditions. Mulch with well-rotted manure in winter. **JH**

Alternatives

*Lonicera standishii, Lonicera fragrantissima,
Lonicera × purpusii*

Lupinus
L. arboreus

Main features Fragrant summer flowers; attracts bees and butterflies
Height 90–150 cm (3–5 ft) **Spread** 90–150 cm (3–5 ft)
Position ○ ◑ **Hardiness** RHS H4

Few plants rival *Lupinus* in full flower because it is an exuberant sight that lights up any garden. Perhaps this is only to be expected, given that it originates in the Golden State, specifically coastal California. A fast-growing medium shrub, *L. arboreus* loves sunny, well-drained sites. Its relaxed, sprawling habit is made elegant by its palm-shaped leaves that look like tiny fingers, especially when they are dappled with dew or the residue of rain. From spring through summer, it is covered with pea-like, buttery-yellow flowers held in dense, erect racemes up to 25 centimetres (10 in.) long. As a bonus these are deliciously fragrant.

Suitable for a wide range of garden styles, *L. arboreus* will need some space in order to show off its qualities. It is particularly good on sunny slopes with poor soil, where it may naturalise, but it can become invasive in the coastal dunes of the northwestern United States. It can also be short-lived, so consider its short-term uses; for example, grow *L. arboreus* for instant stature and for filling gaps between slower-growing, sun-loving shrubs. An upside of its vigorous growth rate is that the soil around it becomes more fertile as it grows, because it fixes nitrogen into the soil.

Other noteworthy cultivars include *L. arboreus* 'Blue Boy', which has blue-purple flowers, and the cool white-blooming 'Snow Queen'. Plant the yellow form with 'Blue Boy' for a perfect complementary colour association. *L. arboreus* also mixes well with lavender, rosemary and *Eryngium*, which all like the same conditions. However, it does not tolerate clay soil and grows best on well-drained, acidic to neutral sandy soil. Perfectly at home in coastal conditions, this shrub is low maintenance and generally no pruning is required. Cut it back hard if it takes over too much space. **RC**

Alternatives

Lupinus arboreus 'Blue Boy', *Lupinus arboreus* 'Snow Queen'

Magnolia
'Susan'

Main feature Attractive flowers
Height 2–4 m (7–13 ft) **Spread** 1.5–1.8 m (5–6 ft)
Position ○ ◑
Hardiness RHS H7

This magnolia is the opportune result of a cross between *M. stellata* 'Rosea' and *M. liliiflora* 'Nigra', which was made by William F. Kosar and Dr Francis de Vos at the United States National Arboretum in Washington, DC, in the mid-1950s. 'Susan' is one of eight selections, known collectively as 'The Girls', which were created to produce a glorious display that, crucially, would be delayed a week or two later than *M. stellata* and *M.* × *soulangiana*, thereby reducing the possibility of spring frost damage to the flower buds. In addition to 'Susan', the magnolias 'Ann', 'Betty', 'Judy', 'Randy', 'Ricki', 'Jane' and 'Pinkie' are all small trees or large shrubs that burst onto the scene in spring in shades of pink and purple.

'Susan' is the best known of the group and the only one with an Award of Garden Merit from the Royal Horticultural Society. It is also the one with the most impressively purple buds. Initially protected by a furry covering, the buds emerge standing upright on the bare stems, glossy and cerise. The goblet-shaped petals (strictly speaking, these are tepals) twist open to give glimpses of the slightly paler, rosy-pink interior, fragrant on a warm day. Mid-green leaves follow shortly afterwards.

The tree makes a fantastic addition to a small garden, grown as a large shrub or trained on a strong leading stem into a small tree. It also looks great planted in a border along with a crab apple for company, perhaps, or on its own as a specimen. 'Susan' prefers a sunny position, but will tolerate light shade if not crowded in. Although it is hardy, it will not perform at its best if sited in an exposed situation. Placed ideally in a nonchalky, well-drained soil with a high organic matter content, 'Susan' offers year-round interest and will give its all with hardly any fuss at all. **ER**

Alternatives

Magnolia stellata 'Rosea', *Magnolia stellata* 'Rosea Massey', *Magnolia* 'Ann', *Magnolia* 'Betty'

Magnolia
M. stellata 'Waterlily'

Main features Silky winter buds; flowers in spring
Height 1.5–3.6 m (5–12 ft) **Spread** 1.2–3 m (4–10 ft)
Position ○ ◑
Hardiness RHS H7

Always popular, *M. stellata* 'Waterlily' is one of the most beautiful spring-flowering shrubs. Silky winter buds – resembling large, pussy-willow catkins – burst in spring to release rosettes of pure-white, ribbon-shaped petals. The blooms are carried on elegantly divided, horizontal branches, well before the soft green leaves appear. They open into flattened stars, like exotic waterlilies, the petals often reflexing and curling with grace. Although delicate in appearance, the flowers are more frost resistant than those of the large, tulip-flowered magnolias. The slow, compact growth habit makes this shrub suitable for the smaller garden and for containers. Any gardener considering a magnolia for the average garden should consider this one first.

'Waterlily' makes a wonderful specimen shrub planted where its shape can be left to develop naturally. Underplant with dwarf spring bulbs, such as *Muscari* and *Calanthus*, or *Cyclamen hederifolium* for autumn flowers and winter foliage. A large-flowered, white or cream clematis grown through the magnolia will add later-summer flowers, thus extending the season. 'Waterlily' is one of the best magnolias for alkaline soils; most prefer neutral to acidic conditions. It grows well on heavy clay soils, providing that they are not too waterlogged. Prune with care after flowering to control shape and size, but avoid pruning if possible to preserve natural shape.

Raised in Long Island, New York, *M. stellata* 'Royal Star' is a very large-flowered cultivar. It has pink-tinged buds and pure-white flowers. 'Centennial' hails from the Arnold Arboretum in Boston, Massachusetts; it is large, vigorous, and free-flowering with slightly pink-tinged blooms. Derived from 'Rosea' and raised in Portland, Oregon, 'Jane Platt' is the best pink variety, with profuse, deep-pink blooms. **AMcl**

Alternatives

Magnolia stellata 'Royal Star', *Magnolia stellata* 'Centennial', *Magnolia stellata* 'Jane Platt'

Magnolia stellata **'Waterlily'** makes a fine specimen if allowed to grow naturally with minimal pruning. ➔

Mahonia
M. × media 'Winter Sun'

Main features Scented winter flowers; evergreen foliage; architectural form
Height 4 m (13 ft) **Spread** 2.4 m (8 ft)
Position ◑ ● **Hardiness** RHS H7

This plant is highly rated for its impressive architectural stature and fragrant winter flowers. *M. × media* 'Winter Sun' is one of the best hybrids within the family. It is smaller than its relations 'Charity' and 'Lionel Fortescue', which makes it simpler to appreciate the slender spikes of gorse-yellow flowers that flare upwards and outwards in giant sprays from the centre of rosettes of glossy, evergreen, spiky leaves. However, the impact is more than visual: the flowers, produced during the winter months, also impart a delicious scent – not unlike lily of the valley – that is a welcome addition to a garden empty of other winter interest. Birds also enjoy eating the buds and the berries that follow. The flowers give way to attractive dark-purple fruits, which sprawl between the stems elegantly in summer. These are used to produce Oregon grape jelly, a popular preserve in the United States.

M. × media combines the best qualities of its parents – *M. lomariifolia* and *M. japonica* – both for looks and for robustness, tolerating extreme cold and shade, as well as sun. In fact, it will adapt perfectly to wherever it is placed and should need little care once planted. This independence makes it valuable in a low-maintenance garden, where it can be teamed with clump-forming bamboos (*Phyllostachys*) or larger types of ornamental grass, such as *Miscanthus*, to deliver an impactful, year-round, architectural display. Add shade-tolerant perennials such as *Epimedium* to cover the ground around its feet.

'Winter Sun' needs space to stretch its limbs, but if it outgrows its allotted area, it can be pruned hard. It will break from stems cut back in spring to a few feet from ground level, flowering again within a couple of years. Alternatively, grow it in a container. **ER**

Alternatives

Mahonia × media 'Charity', *Mahonia × media* 'Lionel Fortescue', *Mahonia × media* 'Buckland'

Mahonia
M. eurybracteata subsp. *ganpinensis* 'Soft Caress'

Main features Spikes of yellow flowers from late summer to autumn; year-round, soft, ferny foliage; attracts bees
Height 1.2 m (4 ft) **Spread** 1.2 m (4 ft)
Position ○ ◑ ● **Hardiness** RHS H5

If you consider mahonias to be tough, prickly shrubs, then this new cultivar should prompt a rethink, as it has narrow leaves with no sharp, spiny edges. However, it still has the mahonia virtues of being a robust, evergreen shrub with late-season flowers and berries. The botanical name is a mouthful, but it points to its origin because *M. eurybracteata* is an upright shrub with jagged-toothed leaves of variable shape and colour. It was found in central and southern China and introduced into cultivation in 1980 (as *M. confusa*) by UK-based plant hunter Roy Lancaster.

'Soft Caress' is a recent selection from a subspecies that has narrower foliage. The year-round foliage is the main attraction, although in typical mahonia style, it produces spikes of lemon-yellow, scented flowers followed by dark-blue berries, often with a silver bloom on them, which will attract birds to the garden in the winter months. The flowers appear from late summer into the autumn, rather than in winter. A compact, medium-sized shrub, it will make a hardworking, backbone plant for a mixed border.

The shrub will be happy in either sun or semi-shade, but it will prove most useful for shady areas that are challenging for flowering shrubs. Pests and diseases leave it alone, although, of course, bees enjoy the unseasonal flowers, and birds appreciate the flower buds and berries. Its size and compact form make this useful shrub a great choice for smaller gardens, including for larger pots, where it will provide year-round interest. Even in medium and large gardens, it will be appreciated, as it copes well with shade. At present it is tricky to propagate, so costs more than run-of-the-mill mahonias, but as it becomes more widely available, it will become a staple evergreen shrub. **PM**

Alternative

Mahonia eurybracteata 'Sweet winter'

Nandina
N. *domestica* Obsession

Main features Evergreen foliage; bold autumn and winter leaf colour
Height 45 cm (18 in.) **Spread** 30 cm (12 in.)
Position ○ ◑ **Hardiness** RHS H6

This is a wonderful, more recently introduced dwarf variety of the sacred bamboo. Compact, upright stems of *N. domestica* Obsession carry fern-like, evergreen leaves with pointed leaflets in an elegantly layered habit. The foliage is olive and dark green, tinged with orange red in places through summer. In autumn the colour starts to intensify, becoming brilliant coral red by midwinter. As a result this superb dwarf shrub is the ultimate evergreen with year-round appeal for small gardens and containers. Unlike most evergreens, it presents a changing picture and is at its best in winter, when many other hardy plants are at their dullest. It combines well in the open ground or in pots with the dark foliage of *Ajuga* and *Ophiopogon*. Try it in a black- or red-glazed pot to create a Japanese effect.

Mature plants produce conical heads of small, white flowers in midsummer. These may be followed by red berries in autumn in a warm, sunny year. Obsession does not flower and fruit as freely as *N. domestica*, and the flowers are very secondary to the foliage interest. *N. domestica* 'Fire Power' is a widely planted form of dwarf sacred bamboo with abundant olive-green foliage and orange-red winter colour. The leaflets are larger, and the habit is looser but heavier than Obsession. Plum Passion is another US introduction but taller with deep red-purple new growth and strong autumn and winter colour. Native to China and Japan, 'Richmond' is a cultivar of the species that grows to form a medium-sized evergreen shrub with fine foliage, spikes of white flowers in summer and clusters of red fruits in winter.

Nandina is useful and popular as an evergreen for its lighter, finer foliage and slender upright habit. It can be planted towards the front of beds and borders to add height and texture. Although the shrub dislikes cold and waterlogged situations, it requires no pruning. **AMcI**

Alternatives

= 'Seika'. *Nandina domestica* 'Fire Power', *Nandina domestica* Plum Passion = 'Monum', *Nandina domestica* 'Richmond'

Osmanthus
O. heterophyllus 'Goshiki'

Main features Evergreen foliage; easy to grow; good for hedging and containers; drought resistant; variegated
Height 90 cm (3 ft) **Spread** 90 cm (3 ft)
Position ○ ◑ **Hardiness** RHS H5

The term 'goshiki' is Japanese for 'five coloured' and may be familiar as a description for some of the most highly coloured koi carp. It is a bit of a stretch to describe this shrub as five coloured, but the leaves are very thoroughly mottled with small areas of dark green, light green and cream yellow with the addition of pink on new spring foliage. *O. heterophyllus* 'Goshiki' is a tough, evergreen shrub that is slow growing and well-behaved. It is a member of the olive family, but has leaves that are remarkably similar to those found on holly. Amenable to clipping, it remains clothed with leaves right down to ground level, so it makes an excellent hedge or screening plant. Being slow growing, it is also an excellent choice as a container specimen.

'Goshiki' rarely flowers, but in late summer and autumn the plain-green species produces clusters of small, tubular, white flowers that are sweetly scented. 'Gulftide' is more compact and very prickly. Other colour variations include 'Variegatus', with broad, yellow leaf margins, and 'Purpureus', which has young, purple shoots. A related species, *O.* × *burkwoodii*, has small, glossy, evergreen, nonspiny leaves, and it produces strongly fragrant, small, white flowers all along the stems in spring.

O. americanus is a large, evergreen shrub or small tree native to the southeastern United States, from Virginia to North Carolina, but grown as a garden plant in somewhat colder areas too. It is commonly known as wild olive, or as devil wood because the timber is difficult to split and work. Small but highly fragrant cream flowers are produced on shoot tips in early spring, and the black berries – 1.2 centimetres (0.5 in.) in diameter – are popular with birds. *O. americanus* favours moist but well-drained, acidic to neutral soil in sun or partial shade, but self-sown seedlings can become a nuisance. **RKW**

Alternatives

Osmanthus heterophyllus 'Gulftide', *Osmanthus heterophyllus* 'Purpureus', *Osmanthus americanus*

Philadelphus
'Belle Étoile'

Main features Orange-blossom-scented blooms;
flowers in summer
Height 1.8 m (6 ft)   **Spread** 1.5 m (5 ft)
Position ○ ◑   **Hardiness** RHS H6

The spicy, orange-blossom perfume of 'Belle Étoile' –
one of the most glorious scents of summer – will fill the
garden with fragrance in late spring or early summer.
Of the varieties of mock orange, this is a good choice
for its moderate size and beautiful, large, white flowers
marked with a central, pale-purple flush. The downside
to all this beauty is that out of flower, it is a rather untidy
shrub with dull leaves, so is best positioned with other
plants that will take over the display for the rest of the
year. Butterfly bushes and shrubby mallows make good
partners, as they are cut back hard in late winter, provide
a leafy foil in spring and early summer, then bring on the
flower power in late summer and autumn. In front of all
these tall shrubs, add low-growing varieties of evergreen
shrubs, such as hebe and skimmia. Alternatively, choose
mock oranges with more interesting foliage. 'Innocence'
has striking cream-yellow marbling whereas *P. coronarius*
has smaller flowers but retains the rich perfume. **RKW**

Alternatives

Philadelphus 'Innocence', *Philadelphus coronarius* 'Variegatus'

Phyllostachys
P. aureosulcata
f. *spectabilis*

Main feature Green-grooved yellow stems
Height 6 m (20 ft)   **Spread** 4 m (13 ft)
Position ○ ◑
Hardiness RHS H5

Bamboos are not suitable for every region or site, but this
one can be an absolute gem in the right place. The green-
grooved yellow canes can reach 6 metres (20 ft) tall and
are tinged red when young. Grown in a sunny position, it
can create a colourful hedge or screen. It is also a
showstopper when grown as a specimen container plant.
The leaves of *P. aureosulcata* f. *spectabilis* are narrow and
15 centimetres (6 in.) long. The canes are impressive and
look superb when grown alongside the black stems of
P. nigra. Originating in China, showy yellow-groove
bamboo grows best in fertile soil that is moist but well
drained. When grown in poor soil, it stays as a clump but
in fertile soil it will quickly produce runners that will invade
the garden. It can be restricted by using planting
membrane to line the planting trench and by cutting roots
once they reach a particular area. Once established it will
produce a display that not only looks terrific, providing
wildlife with nesting sites, but also sounds wonderful. **PM**

Alternative

Phyllostachys nigra

Phyllostachys aureosulcata f. *spectabilis* well maintained at RHS Rosemoor, Devon, UK. ➲

Physocarpus
P. opulifolius 'Diabolo'

Main features Dark purple foliage; summer flowers;
colourful fruits; good for wildlife; autumn foliage colour
Height 1.2 m (4 ft) **Spread** 1.2 m (4 ft)
Position ○ ◑ **Hardiness** RHS H7

This plant must have some of the darkest leaves to be
found on a shrub – a deep, dark purple, creating a perfect
contrast to yellow and lime-green foliage, and a foil for
white, pink or pale-blue flowers. *P. opulifolius* 'Diabolo'
itself has fluffy, white flowers, often pink tinged, in dense,
flat clusters. These are followed by sprays of small, bright
red fruits. In winter the peeling bark on mature branches
reveals a range of shades from cinnamon to russet, hence
the common name ninebark.

In the wild ninebark has dark green leaves, white
flowers, and pink-green fruits. Native to the central and
eastern United States, it is very hardy and undemanding
in its growing conditions, tolerating virtually any soil
from wet to dry, and having a role stabilising unsettled
ground. The shrub prefers a sunny position and makes an
effective screen or hedge. The flowers are a good source
of nectar, and its dense growth is popular with nesting
birds, which can also feed on the seed.

Gardeners are showing more interest in ninebarks as
new colours come on to the market. 'Dart's Gold' is a
golden-leaved form that does not scorch in the sun.
'Amber Jubilee' opens up in shades of gold and russet-
orange, turns lime green in summer and purple in autumn.
'Donna May' (syn. Little Devil) is similar in colour to
'Diabolo' but 'Chameleon' is jazziest of all with leaves
opening green with bright-red flushing and golden edges
maturing to bronzy purple with a cream edge. **RKW**

Alternatives

Physocarpus opulifolius 'Amber Jubilee', *Physocarpus
opulifolius* 'Chameleon'

Picea
P. pungens 'Fat Albert'

Main features Year-round foliage colour; drought and pollution tolerant; resistant to rabbits and deer
Height 3–4.5 m (10–15 ft) **Spread** 2–3 m (7–10 ft)
Position ○ **Hardiness** RHS H7

Despite its weighty name, 'Fat Albert' is a perfectly formed conifer. Its growth habit naturally keeps it a trim conical shape. Also known as Colorado spruce, it is a native of the southwestern United States; the typical form has been superseded by the many glaucous-leaved forms, which make handsome garden trees. 'Fat Albert' is a selection raised at the Iseli Nursery in Boring, Oregon. It was named after a fictional character created by Bill Cosby, the US comedian.

Key to its shape is its strong, naturally straight leader branch. Closely spaced, ascending branches develop and fill out to make a full conical form that endures from the young plant to the mature tree. Bushy branches are covered in silver-blue needles; this colour remains uniform throughout the year. It is a very easy-to-grow, shapely plant requiring no staking, training or pruning. Its uniformity has established it as a standard – it resembles a conifer drawn to a precise design blueprint. This has also made it a popular choice as a Christmas tree. *P. pungens* Glauca Group 'Hoopsii' is similar in most respects but narrower at the base.

One specimen makes a beautiful focal point in a small to medium-sized garden. In larger spaces a group of them makes an outstanding copse of year-round, steely-blue foliage. For good ground cover around it, consider heathers, such as *Erica × darleyensis*. 'Fat Albert' also looks at home set among large boulders and rocks. **RC**

Alternatives

Picea pungens Glauca Group 'Hoopsii', *Picea pungens* Glauca Group 'Globosa'

Pieris

P. japonica 'Carnaval'

Main features Variegated evergreen foliage; colourful new growth; flowers early spring
Height 90 cm (3 ft) **Spread** 75 cm (2.5 ft)
Position ◐ ● **Hardiness** RHS H5

This is a delightful, compact evergreen shrub with abundant, leathery, dark-green leaves, narrowly edged with silver and flushed with copper towards the tips of the shoots in winter. In early spring the bright-red leaves of the new growth are edged with pink, turning the whole shrub into a mound of changing colour. The small sprays of white spring flowers resemble lily of the valley, hence the common name Japanese lily of the valley. These open from tiny beaded sprays of pinkish buds that grace the plant through winter.

Introduced in 1999, 'Carnaval' is one of the most colourful, small, evergreen shrubs, which presents a changing picture throughout the year and is perfect for the small garden. It is an ideal plant for a pot or container in shade or semi-shade, if planted in an ericaceous (lime-free) compost. In the open ground it enjoys a sheltered position, where the delicate new growth will be protected from severe frost. However, because of its small leaves and compact habit, it is not as vulnerable as the larger-leaved pieris. 'Carnaval' makes an attractive planting partner for a red-leaved Japanese maple or one of the leucothoes with evergreen leaves that change to red in winter.

P. japonica 'Ralto' is similar to 'Carnaval' but with pink flowers and a rather more open habit. 'Little Heath' has small, narrow, grey-green leaves, edged with silver and pink new growth. It is a pretty foliage shrub, but flowers reluctantly. 'Flaming Silver' is more open in habit and altogether larger. The new growth is red.

All pieris are ericaceous plants and do not tolerate alkaline conditions. 'Carnaval' requires no pruning and will naturally retain a compact, rounded habit. Simply snip off any frost damage growth or old flower stems in spring. **AMcI**

Alternatives

Pieris japonica 'Ralto', *Pieris japonica* 'Little Heath', *Pieris japonica* 'Flaming Silver'

Pieris
P. japonica 'Katsura'

Main features Evergreen foliage; spectacular
mahogany-red new growth; winter buds; flowers spring
Height 90 cm (3 ft) **Spread** 75 cm (2.5 ft)
Position ◑ ● **Hardiness** RHS H5

Shining, elegantly curved, deep-green leaves appear
to be carried in whorls on the straight, young, green
stems of this dome-shaped lily of the valley bush. This
wonderful foliage provides the perfect setting for the
mahogany-red new growth that makes the shrub such
an arresting sight in spring. The new shoots appear like
exotic blossoms, so spectacular they draw attention
away from the flowers, which open about the same
time. The drooping flower panicles carry rose-pink bells,
opening from red-pink buds. If a shrub flowers freely, new
growth is restricted until the flowers have faded. If there
is profuse new growth, flowers are fewer. 'Katsura' is a
compact evergreen shrub with year-round appeal and
a peak of interest in spring.

'Katsura' is reputed to have been discovered near a
Shinto shrine in Japan. Partnered with *Nandina*, Japanese
maples, or dwarf bamboos, it is an ideal subject for a
contemporary or Japanese-garden planting scheme.
It makes the perfect specimen for a well-chosen pot or
container in shade or semi-shade, close to the house,
where the new growth will be protected from frost in
colder areas. Pot in ericaceous (lime-free) compost.

There are several other attractive varieties of *P. japonica*.
'Valley Valentine' is grown for its profuse, deep, dusky-
red flowers carried in large drooping clusters; the new
foliage growth is copper. 'Mountain Fire' is a Canadian
selection with young, red leaves turning to shining
chestnut-brown and white flowers. 'Pink Delight' was
selected in New Zealand. It is grown for its abundant
pale-pink flowers that fade to white as they age.

Pieris are perfect for an acidic or neutral soil but
do not thrive in alkaline soil. Generally, no pruning is
necessary, but light pruning to control shape can be
carried out in spring after flowering. **AMcI**

Alternatives

Pieris japonica 'Valley Valentine', *Pieris japonica* 'Mountain
Fire', *Pieris japonica* 'Pink Delight'

Pinus
P. mugo 'Carsten'

Main features Conifer with year-round foliage interest; winter colours
Height 45–60 cm (18–24 in.) **Spread** 60–90 cm (24–36 in.)
Position ○ **Hardiness** RHS H7

Mountain pine takes its name from the high altitudes of central Europe from where it originates. It is a very hardy group of large shrubs or small trees that have adapted to harsh conditions. 'Carsten' stands out as a small conifer that undergoes a beautiful colour change in winter; it adds a spark of gold to the garden in dark winter months. It is a slow-growing dwarf conifer with naturally rounded habit that becomes more spreading with age. Short branches are so densely covered with needles that they resemble a handful of green bottlebrushes. Bright-green summer foliage turns a rich gold as summer moves into autumn, deepening to orange tinged in winter. This transformation is more marked when it is planted in an open, sunny position. Each spring it reverts to green. On heavy soils grow 'Carsten' in a raised bed or in a container. 'Carsten' works well with spare, contemporary plantings, and it mixes well with grasses, such as *Festuca glauca*. **RC**

Alternatives

Pinus mugo 'Ophir', *Pinus mugo* 'Winter Gold', *Pinus mugo* 'Winter Sun'

Pinus
P. parviflora
'Bonnie Bergman'

Main features Year-round colour; evergreen; drought tolerant
Height 1.5–2.4 m (5–8 ft) **Spread** 90–150 cm (3–5 ft)
Position ○ **Hardiness** RHS H7

Japanese white pine *P. parviflora* has a natural sculptural quality that makes it an outstanding conifer choice. The species is the picturesque pine so well-known globally by the 'willow tree' pattern, widely cultivated in Japan for bonsai training. The sculptural appearance of 'Bonnie Bergman' comes from the open spread of branches; this look is achieved naturally without any special pruning or training. Its upswept branches are covered with short, dense, silver-blue needles. These seem to be slightly twisted, giving the plant a tousled look. In late spring, branches bear orange-red flowers, and in summer conspicuous red male cones add a seasonal highlight. 'Bonnie Bergman' makes a good specimen, bringing the look of a bonsai to a garden, but without the painstaking labour. Grow in a container or planted in moist, well-drained soil surrounded by a swath of ornamental grass, such as *Hakonechloa macra* 'Alboaurea'. **RC**

Alternatives

Pinus parviflora 'Adcock's Dwarf', *Pinus parviflora* 'Negishi'

Pittosporum

'Garnettii'

Main features Year-round attractive variegated foliage;
deep-purple flowers; good cut foliage
Height 2.4–4 m (8–13 ft) **Spread** 2.4–4 m (8–13 ft)
Position ○ ◑ **Hardiness** RHS H4

This is an elegant, dependable shrub with beautiful
evergreen foliage that adds brightness and structure all
year. The variegated leaves of 'Garnettii' make it a standout feature plant, but it also associates well with a variety
of other plants and is perfectly suited to many planting
styles. Native to New Zealand, it is bushy and upright,
with branches covered with rounded grey-green leaves
edged with cream margins that take on a pinkish tinge
and become freckled with red in autumn and winter.
Small, deep-purple flowers are held in clusters. Good in
shrub groups to divide up the space in gardens, it can also
be used for hedging or trimmed as topiary, although its
natural shape is very pleasing. 'Garnettii' makes a pretty
foil to other flowering plants, particularly those with
blooms in the pink to burgundy colour palette, such as
Astrantia 'Roma', *Penstemon* 'Raven' or any of the day lilies
with flowers in the same range. **RC**

Alternatives

Pittosporum tenuifolium 'Irene Paterson', *Pittosporum
tenuifolium* 'Silver Queen'

Platycladus

P. orientalis
'Franky Boy'

Main features Yellow-green to bronze-coloured foliage;
slow-growing evergreen
Height 90 cm (3 ft) **Spread** 60 cm (24 in.)
Position ○ **Hardiness** RHS H6

This slow-growing, evergreen shrub is a bit of a show-off.
Chartreuse-coloured leaves develop from yellow shoots
in spring, and as the weather cools, the whole plant takes
on a bronze tint. The exquisite thread-like branches, with
flattened, scaly leaves, form a beautiful teardrop shape.
P. orientalis 'Franky Boy' looks impressive as a dot plant
in mixed borders, alongside other conifers, and is
especially eye-catching when underplanted with dark-
flowered tulips. As the tulips flower, 'Franky Boy' excels.
Many gardeners mistake this shrub for a tuft of ornamental
grass, but it is very much a conifer. Selected from an
Austrian nursery seedbed of young plants in 1990, it has
gone on to become a firm favourite with gardeners
around the world. The changing leaf colour over the year
is the main feature, but the plant's easy-to-grow character
also makes it appealing. If any branches turn brown,
simply cut them off to retain the shape of the plant. **PM**

Alternatives

Platycladus orientalis 'Aurea Nana', *Platycladus orientalis*
'Rosedalis'

Podocarpus
'County Park Fire'

Main features Buttery-yellow, salmon-pink, green and purple foliage; year-round interest
Height 60 cm (24 in.) **Spread** 90 cm (3 ft)
Position ○ **Hardiness** RHS H6

This handsome dwarf shrub was a winner the moment it was first spotted growing in an Essex garden. Young growth starts out a buttery yellow in colour, turning a subtle salmon pink, which eventually develops to a beautiful mid-green. As a bonus, if 'County Park Fire' puts on a growth spurt in late summer, all three colours can be seen on the same plant at once. Then finally, as winter approaches, the foliage transforms once more into a rich purple-bronze. This is a truly amazing foliage plant.

'County Park Fire' is a low-spreading conifer and is perfect for growing in a container where its unusual foliage will make it an excellent focal point. It can also be used as a hedging plant. Granted a Royal Horticultural Society Award of Garden Merit, it grows best in full sun, where the colour changes are more intense. Forming a low-mound shape, it needs a fertile, free-draining soil or, if growing in a container, a loam-based potting mix. Additional feeding is not required, as excessive fertilisers will stimulate soft, leggy growth that will detract from the plant's natural shape. Once the plant is established, all that is required to maintain its natural beauty is a light prune in midspring. Simply nip back any shoots that are growing in the wrong direction or have become damaged during winter. It is important to not prune excessively, as this will only create an artificial-looking plant, unless it is being pruned for bonsai purposes. Pest and diseases overlook 'County Park Fire,' resulting in a trouble-free plant.

This is a relatively hardy, slow-growing conifer and will only reach 60 centimetres (24 in.) in height, with a 90-centimetre-wide (3 ft) spread in ten years. It is the perfect size for a permanent container, but 'County Park Fire' also makes a good candidate for rockery gardens. **PM**

Alternatives

Podocarpus nivalis 'Kilworth Cream', *Podocarpus salignus*, *Podocarpus totara* 'Aureus'

Prunus

P. incisa 'Kojo-no-mai'

Main feature Attractive, winter twigs; beautiful spring blossom; autumn foliage colour; architectural plant
Height 1.5–2.4 m (5–8 ft) **Spread** 1.5–2.4 m (5–8 ft)
Position ○ ◐ **Hardiness** RHS H6

The original species of this attractive cherry heralds from the volcanic slopes of Mount Fuji, Japan. This particular variety gives several seasons of interest, making it an excellent garden plant. It is hardy and makes a compact, slow-growing, deciduous shrub, growing 1.5 to 2.4 metres (5–8 ft), although it can be kept considerably smaller by careful shaping. In fact, it is a popular choice for bonsai enthusiasts because it brings all the seasons – spring blossom, green summer foliage, autumn tints and sculptural bare twigs – into a small courtyard. The twiggy stems appear to grow in a zigzag fashion, giving the bare branches considerable winter interest. In early spring fat buds open to very pale-pink (almost white) clusters of flowers before the leaves emerge. The leaves are small, with neatly toothed edges, and they turn to vibrant shades of yellow, orange and red in the autumn. 'Kojo-no-mai' can be purchased already grafted onto a stem to make a standard shape. It will grow in any moisture-retentive, well-drained soil, ideally in a sunny position.

The compact habit of this shrub makes it an ideal choice for the smaller garden, although where more space is available, a group could be planted. It makes a useful addition to a winter garden, where its zigzag twig formation will contrast well with the coloured stems of dogwoods and evergreens. It also makes an excellent specimen shrub for a rock garden, particularly if underplanted with small, blue-flowered scillas. 'Kojo-no-mai' can also be grown in a container, which could be moved around to best view its different seasonal interests. Growing it permanently in a container will keep it at half the size and spread of a plant growing in the ground. No routine pruning is required, but any damaged, diseased or congested branches can be removed after flowering. **MP**

Alternatives

Prunus 'Accolade', *Prunus lusitanica* 'Myrtifolia', *Prunus* 'Ukon', *Prunus tenella* 'Firehill'

Pseudopanax
P. lessonii 'Gold Splash'

Main features Architectural shrub; eye-catching evergreen foliage
Height 6 m (20 ft) **Spread** 2.4 m (8 ft)
Position ○ ◑ **Hardiness** RHS H3

Throughout the winter, evergreen trees and shrubs with variegated foliage brighten up the garden and help lift the gardener's spirits, and this is no exception. This plant is, quite literally, a very good sport! It was discovered in a garden in New Zealand in 1969 – a variegated variation growing from the base of a *P. lessonii*. Botanically speaking, a sport is a naturally occurring genetic mutation, resulting in a section of the plant showing different characteristics from the parent. This section can be propagated by cuttings to produce new plants. So *P. lessonii* 'Gold Splash' may be a freak of nature, but it is a positive and attractive addition to the garden.

Some *Pseudopanax* species look like they belong on a different planet – quirky, spiky-leaved, architectural, evergreen shrubs – they have great eccentricity value. 'Gold Splash' is certainly unusual looking, but elegant rather than weird. In fact, it is a very handsome plant, with striking long, leathery, wavy-edged, palmate leaves that are randomly splashed with gold around the central vein of each leaflet. It looks a bit like the houseplant *Schefflera*, or perhaps an interesting shrubby version of a horse chestnut.

It tends to grow on a single stem for a few years, branching out when it reaches about 3 metres (10 ft) tall. The leaves extend out and away from the main stem, which gives the plant an attractive form that is perfect for an exotic-style garden. Do not be put off by measurements of it reaching 6 metres (20 ft): this is when it is left to grow naturally. In practice it can be pruned to size, which is worth doing now and again to encourage the younger foliage. Also, growing it in a container, which anyone in a colder area will need to do, will restrict its roots and therefore its height, making it a suitable plant for a conservatory. **ER**

Alternative

Pseudopanax ferox, Pseudopanax lessonii 'Goldfinger', *Pseudopanax lessonii* 'Rangitira', *Pseudopanax lessonii* 'Forest Gem', *Pseudopanax lessonii* 'Nigra'

Rhododendron
'Lem's Cameo'

Main features Dark, evergreen leaves; frilly pink flowers
Height 1.8 m (6 ft) **Spread** 1.5 m (5 ft)
Position ○ ◑
Hardiness RHS H3

This evergreen shrub is a real eye-catcher, with its large globes of frilly flowers. The pink buds open to pale-pink flowers with tones of cream and apricot, with a nice red eye in the heart of their throats. Feeding with suitable fertiliser ensures rich, green foliage; the young leaves are a lovely bronzy brown when they first develop, giving an extra show after the mid-season flowering.

In a suitable region and with regular moisture, 'Lem's Cameo' forms a dense shrub that stays compact for many years before eventually becoming quite large. If planting a rhododendron bed, it is worth spacing widely for the long-term development, and interplanting with other shorter-lived shrubs, such as *Buddleja*, *Hydrangea*, *Lavatera* and *Fuchsia*. All these can be pruned quite hard to keep their shape and will give colour for a long season through high summer, after the rhododendrons have finished flowering and become all-green mounds. In around ten years time, as the rhododendrons fill out, these shrubs will be getting past their prime and can be removed.

All rhododendrons need an acidic soil with plenty of organic material. Peat and leaf mould are ideal. Plant shallow; the roots will grow out sideways just under the surface, and feed on the decomposing leaf litter. Be sure to make good use of fallen leaves by spreading them thinly under the rhododendrons. Chopped prunings, twigs, and even dead fern fronds can be laid on top to stop the leaves from blowing everywhere again.

The name 'Lem's Cameo' comes from the breeder, Halfdan Lem of Seattle, Washington, who bred a number of fine rhododendrons in the mid-twentieth century, many of which also bear his name. They have been much used in breeding newer varieties, such as 'Nancy Evans'. **ED**

Alternatives

Rhododendron 'One Thousand Butterflies', *Rhododendron* 'Point Defiance', *Rhododendron* 'Lem's Monarch', *Rhododendron* 'Horizon Monarch'

Rhododendron

Obtusum Group 'Hinomayo'

Main features Evergreen; neat bushes covered with flowers in spring
Height 90 cm (3 ft) **Spread** 90 cm (3 ft)
Position ○ ◐ **Hardiness** RHS H5

This delightful azalea is one of the many Japanese varieties, forming a tight, rounded bush smothered every spring with dainty, soft-pink flowers. All the Japanese varieties are described as evergreen, but they do lose older leaves at the end of the season. These drop under the bush and are best left there, forming a valuable layer of dead leaves. This layer protects and feeds the plant as it rots down, adding to the peaty soil in which the shallow roots do best. Evergreen azaleas make a spectacular show along the edges of woods in dappled shade. Colours range from white through pink to rich red, and also tomato red, mauve and purple. In Japan the wild ancestors of these azaleas cover whole hillsides making a lovely show. They are widely used in gardens there, often trained into little trees and clipped into mounds and hedges. This shape is known as cloud pruning. 'Hinomayo' is an old hybrid introduced in 1910, which is earlier and smaller flowered than other Japanese azaleas. **ED**

Alternatives

Rhododendron 'Kokin-shita', *Rhododendron* 'Macrostemon'

Rhododendron

'Klondyke'

Main features Golden-yellow flowers in spring; rich autumn leaf colour
Height 1.5 m (5 ft) **Spread** 1.2 m (4 ft)
Position ○ ◐ **Hardiness** RHS H6

Few plants are as well named as this lovely azalea, which is immediately linked with the Yukon Gold Rush. The rich, golden-yellow flowers are greatly complemented by the young, dark-bronze leaves, making it one of the most striking of the deciduous azaleas and a superb spectacle in mid- to late spring. The leaves often turn to rich colours before they drop at the end of the season. Hardy and reliable, it grows into a compact, upright shrub. Planting out with other azaleas and compact rhododendrons will produce a superb display border. If there is space, lower-growing Japanese evergreen azaleas in front of it will give a longer season and hide the stems, especially in winter. Hardy geraniums are also good planted in front of and among 'Klondyke'. As with all rhododendrons, including both deciduous and evergreen azaleas, the ideal position is in semi-shade, copying the wild woodland conditions. They are also fairly tolerant of warmth and dryness. **ED**

Alternatives

Rhododendron 'Golden Eagle', *Rhododendron* 'Harvest Moon'

◉ *Rhododendron* Obtusum Group 'Hinomayo' is smothered with flowers in spring.

Rhododendron
'Razorbill'

Main feature Upright, small, pink flowers on a compact evergreen shrub
Height 90 cm (3 ft) **Spread** 90 cm (3 ft)
Position ○ ◑ **Hardiness** RHS H4

If you expect rhododendrons to be big solid bushes, this one may come as a surprise. With its slight stature, small leaves, and 2.5-centimetre-long (1 in.) tubular flowers, it can be hard to identify. 'Razorbill' is one of the dwarf and compact varieties that are so useful in smaller modern gardens, on rockeries, raised beds, and at the front of borders. It is often more spreading than tall and is very reliably free flowering. These dwarfs are also good grown in tubs, such as old wooden barrels. Tubs can be put in a prominent position when flowering, and tucked away at other times. This means that they can be grown even in a small yard or if the garden soil is unsuitably heavy or alkaline. Being raised up above ground level enables the flowers to be appreciated more. The Cox family in Perth, Scotland, bred this and many other dwarf rhododendrons, nearly all named after birds, including 'Ptarmigan' and 'Curlew', as well as good evergreen azaleas, such as the late-flowering 'Squirrel' and 'Wombat'. **ED**

Alternatives

Rhododendron 'Puncta', *Rhododendron* 'Caerhays Crossbill', *Rhododendron* Seta Group 'Seta'

Rhododendron
'White Lights'

Main features Deciduous; pink-white flowers in spring; attractive foliage colour in autumn
Height 1.5 m (5 ft) **Spread** 1.2 m (4 ft)
Position ○ ◑ **Hardiness** RHS H5

'White Lights' is one of the earlier-flowering, deciduous azaleas with pink buds that start opening on bare twigs before the leaves, which soon follow. They open to nearly pure white, making a fine show, although with little scent. Curiously, there is no need to deadhead them, as the flowers are sterile and the pods never develop seeds, but just drop. This is one of the Northern Lights Series of azaleas bred at the University of Minnesota, with the goal of developing varieties that are bud-hardy there and in other northern states. The particularly hardy native roseshell azalea (*R. prinophyllum*) grows in Quebec and New England and across a wide area of the northeastern United States. This has been crossed with various Mollis and Exbury varieties. Others in the series include 'Golden Lights', 'Orchid Lights', 'Boulters Pink Lights' and 'Spicy Lights'. All deciduous azaleas grow well in the open or in dappled shade and look attractive grown under the light shade of trees, such as Japanese cherry or dogwood. **ED**

Alternatives

Rhododendron 'Persil', *Rhododendron* 'Daviesii', *Rhododendron* 'Oxydol', *Rhododendron* 'Northern Lights'

Rhododendron
R. fortunei

Main features One of the few hardy rhododendrons with scented flowers from mid- to late spring; evergreen
Height 1.5 m (5 ft) **Spread** 1.5 m (5 ft)
Position ◐ **Hardiness** RHS H5

This is an evergreen rhododendron of real quality. It is distinguished by glossy leaves, which almost always have purple leafstalks (petioles). The flowers are pale lilac-pink or white and each has seven petal lobes and often a golden flush in the throat. Perhaps the most special feature is that *R. fortunei* is one of the few scented, hardy rhododendrons – a sweet candy scent, perhaps with a hint of chocolate. It is named after the Scottish plant collector Robert Fortune, who first took tea plants from China to India. This species is a moderate grower, staying compact and suitable for a relatively small space for at least a couple of decades. Mature plants develop into a small tree with an attractive smooth trunk and casting light shade so it can be underplanted. Like all rhododendrons, it grows best in a light, peaty, leaf-mouldy soil, with its roots growing just under the surface. However, a raised bed filled with the right soil often works well for a species this size. **ED**

Alternatives

Rhododendron fortunei subsp. *discolor* Houlstonii Group,
Rhododendron 'Sir Charles Butler'

Rhododendron
'Taurus'

Main features Dark evergreen leaves; bright, red flowers
Height 1.8 m (6 ft) **Spread** 1.5 m (5 ft)
Position ○ ◐
Hardiness RHS H5

'Taurus' is one of the best red rhododendrons available. A large variety, it flowers in midspring. The bright, red flower trusses are profusely borne over healthy dark-green foliage, which complements the flower colour so well and makes a good evergreen statement year-round. This is a surprisingly hardy, strong, and yet compact grower; as with all rhododendrons, it is a long-term project of many years before large plants outgrow their space. Light, sandy soil is best, but do remember to irrigate as this is the first soil to dry out. Rhododendrons will grow in other soils so long as it is not too heavy or alkaline. As with all rhododendrons and azaleas, plant them shallow with plenty of peaty, leaf-mould-type material. Do not worry if the leaves roll and hang down in very cold weather; they do this to conserve moisture and perk up again when the weather gets warmer. 'Taurus' was bred in Vancouver, Canada, by the pollination of a flower on 'The Honourable Jean Marie de Montague'. **ED**

Alternatives

Rhododendron 'Grace Seabrook', *Rhododendron* 'Red Jack',
Rhododendron 'Robert Croux'

Rhododendron
R. vaseyi

Main features Deciduous; pale-pink flowers in spring; attractive autumn leaf colour
Height 1.5 m (5 ft) **Spread** 1.2 m (4 ft)
Position ○ ◑ **Hardiness** RHS H5

Commonly known as pinkshell azalea, *R. vaseyi* produces distinctive pale-pink flowers on bare twigs each spring before the leaves develop. Some varieties have white or darker pink flowers. It grows wild in North Carolina and is naturalised in Massachusetts. It is named after George Vasey, who found it in 1878. It is a hardy upright shrub, which in the wild grows in quite moist conditions, such as on the edges of swamps, but not in waterlogged conditions, as the roots need air. It grows best in moist, peaty, acidic soil, with the roots a little below the surface growing outwards. In heavy, unsuitable conditions, it can be grown in a thick layer of humus-rich material. This is perhaps the most distinctive of the azalea species growing wild in the United States, many of which are scented, from *R. occidentale* in California to *R. atlanticum* and *R. viscosum* in the eastern states. These are pastel coloured; others, such as *R. calendulaceum* and *R. cumberlandense,* flower in hot, fiery colours. **ED**

Alternatives

Rhododendron schlippenbachii, Rhododendron albrechtii

Rhus
R. typhina 'Dissecta'

Main features Summer foliage; striking autumn foliage tints; winter structure; architectural plant
Height 1.8–3 m (6–10 ft) **Spread** 1.8–3 m (6–10 ft)
Position ○ ◑ **Hardiness** RHS H6

This handsome, deciduous, small ornamental tree is grown mainly for its striking foliage. Native to eastern North America, it has a flat-topped appearance. The branches are stout, and when young, are covered thickly with reddish-brown hairs. The large leaves can be up to 60 centimetres (24 in.) long and are finely divided to give a fern-like effect. In the autumn these turn to vibrant shades of yellow and orange. The flowers are fairly inconspicuous and appear in summer, but as the seed heads develop they become much more visible as fat, conical, hairy crimson 20-centimetre (8 in.) 'candles'. These persist well into the winter months, adding interest to the structure of the branches. This easy plant likes a sunny position to get the best autumn foliage tints. The architectural shape and ferny leaves lend themselves to a subtropical planting style, but it looks equally at home at the back of a traditional border. It also adds rich tints to a prairie-style planting of grasses, perennials and winter stems. **MP**

Alternatives

Rhus typhina Tiger Eyes = 'Bailtiger', *Rhus typhina* Radiance = 'Sinrus'

Rhus typhina 'Dissecta' makes a striking feature plant in the autumn, combining colourful foliage with dark-red 'candle' seed heads. ➜

Ribes
R. odoratum

Main features Fragrant, yellow blooms in midspring;
vigorous shrub
Height 2.4 m (8 ft) **Spread** 2.4 m (8 ft)
Position ○ **Hardiness** RHS H5

The clove currant, or buffalo currant, is an easy-to-grow, spring-flowering shrub for a tough spot in the garden. This shrub is native to the central United States, but is so reliable and trouble-free that it is the backbone of many spring gardens around the world. The yellow blooms are produced in little bunches in midspring and last until the start of summer. They give off a spicy fragrance that is rich and heady – visitors usually smell the plant before they see it. Leaves are bright green in spring and summer, turning red and purple with the onset of autumn. *R. odoratum* is a vigorous shrub, but it responds well to pruning; tackle after flowering, so that it has time to ripen wood for the following year's blooms. This will mean you forgo the berries, but these are not a main feature. Also cut out one in three of the older stems, cutting back to the base every winter. The best spot for this plant is in sun and planted in fertile soil that stays moist, but not waterlogged. However, *R. odoratum* will perform in most locations. Aphids can be a problem. **PM**

Alternative

Ribes speciosum

Ribes
R. × beatonii

Main features Two-tone blooms in spring; hardy,
easy-to-grow shrub
Height 1.5 m (5 ft) **Spread** 1.5 m (5 ft)
Position ○ ◑ **Hardiness** RHS H7

Gordon's currant, as its down-to-earth name suggests, is a very hardy, flowering shrub that produces masses of spring blooms in a two-tone of red and yellow. This hybrid first appeared after Donald Beaton, a renowned Victorian gardener and plant breeder, crossed the clove-scented buffalo currant, *R. odoratum*, with the more commonplace *R. sanguineum*. The resulting plant was named *R. × gordonianum* in honour of his employer, William Gordon, but has since been renamed *R. × beatonii*. It flowers for a month at the start of spring. Each flower has red outer petals and apricot-yellow inner petals. The scent comes from its mother's side of the family (*R. odoratum*) whereas the overall vigour is down to its father's side (*R. sanguineum*). Leaves are bright green in spring and summer and can turn a brilliant reddish-brown in autumn. This shrub is a candidate for mixed borders, where it adds spring interest, or as a specimen, perhaps in a front garden. Flowers are carried on the previous season's growth, so trim after flowering has finished. **PM**

Alternative

Ribes sanguineum 'Pulborough Scarlet'

◒ *Ribes odoratum*, kept in check by regular pruning, offers plenty of fragrant spring flowers.

Romneya
R. *coulteri* 'White Cloud'

Main features Fragrant flowers; attractive summer foliage; drought tolerant; attracts bees and butterflies
Height 1.5–2.4 m (5–8 ft) **Spread** 1.5–2.4 m (5–8 ft)
Position ○ **Hardiness** RHS H5

The Matilija poppy is a veritable queen of California's native wildflowers in terms of height and size of flower. 'White Cloud' is a choice cultivar; statuesque, it makes a magnificent sight in full flower. This cultivar is slightly more restrained than the species, but it is still a vigorous subshrub with strong woody stems. These shoot upwards each year, reaching over 1.8 metres (6 ft), and bear attractive blue–grey–green leaves, which are lobed and finely cut. In late spring, stems are topped with huge pure-white, cup-shaped flowers. Measuring 15 to 20 centimetres (6–8 in.) across, they resemble wide-open crêpe-paper blooms, with slightly frilled edged petals. At the centre of each flower, there is a dome of bright yellow stamen; flowers resemble large fried eggs. A distinctive fragrance, which is as sweet as apricot, is its crowning feature.

Although slow to get going, once established, this plant spreads vigorously by strong underground rhizomes that can travel some distance, so give it plenty of space. It thrives in a moist but well-drained soil; shelter is required in colder regions. In warmer climates similar to its native habitat, it declines in summer and dies back nearly to ground level by autumn. In this case, cut the plant back to 8 to 10 centimetres (3–4 in.), which improves its looks and encourages new growth. In cooler regions, top growth can be cut back in late winter or early spring. Plant alongside other shrubs, such as *Ceanothus*, *Cotoneaster* and *Viburnum* species. **RC**

Alternatives

Romneya coulteri, *Romneya coulteri* var. *trichocalyx*

Rubus
R. odoratus

Main features Masses of pinky-purple blooms from summer to autumn; scented flowers; pale-green leaves
Height 2.4 m (8 ft) **Spread** 2.4 m (8 ft)
Position ◑ **Hardiness** RHS H7

The flowering raspberry, or American bramble, is a suckering shrub that produces flowers – loved by butterflies and bees from early summer to early autumn – on both last year's and the current year's growth. A native of eastern North America, *R. odoratus* is a shrub for a large wildlife or woodland garden, or for growing on a shady slope.

It produces plentiful flowers around 5 centimetres (2 in.) in diameter, with a light rose scent. These are borne in clusters at the end of flowering shoots, and the pale-green, attractive maple leaves complement the flowers. This rampant, deciduous shrub produces suckers and quickly forms a thicket in favourable conditions. As an edge-of-woodland plant, it prefers partial shade, so the blooms are shielded from the midday sun, but they will tolerate sun or shade. Some shade results in longer-lasting blooms and more intense coloration.

The stems are strong, erect and grow up to around 2.4 metres (8 ft) in length and exhibit gorgeous peeling bark. When plants become thick and congested, they can be pulled apart and replanted. Make sure that each new plant has roots at the base of the division before replanting, which is best done every couple of years in late autumn or winter. When plants lose their simple, toothed leaves in autumn, it reveals flattened red berries. These are edible, but somewhat lacking in flavour compared to real raspberries. The bonus is that gardeners need not panic as birds flock to devour them. **PM**

Alternative

Rubus parviflorus

Rubus
R. rolfei 'Emerald Carpet'

Main features Dense, mat-forming evergreen shrub; ivy-like leaves; good ground cover; red berries in autumn
Height 30 cm (12 in.) **Spread** 1.5 m (5 ft)
Position ○ ◐ **Hardiness** RHS H5

This is a superb, ground-hugging ornamental shrub, capable of growing in dry or moist conditions and produces colourful red berries in autumn. Add to that the sensational autumn leaf colour, and it is no surprise that the Royal Horticultural Society granted it an Award of Garden Merit in 2012. *R. rolfei* 'Emerald Carpet', also known as creeping bramble, is a robust and fast-growing shrub, but not one that bullies its way over the soil. It is ideal for planting under trees or wherever ground cover is required without any effort or worry. The trailing, woody stems bear rounded, ivy-like, sage-green, crinkled leaves the texture of fine-grade sandpaper and it is these that turn a brilliant scarlet colour as temperatures drop. The plant does flower in summer, although the white, saucer-shaped blooms are insignificant and easily missed. However, the spherical, orange-red fruits that sometimes follow cannot be overlooked and that includes by a range of wildlife and birds.

    R. rolfei 'Emerald Carpet' will grow in full sun or partial shade in dry conditions, but thrives when there is a drop of moisture in the soil. As the stems grow, they root at points where they touch the soil surface. This quickly results in a mat of weed-suppressing growth. It can take a couple of years for a tangled mass of leaves to form, but as the stems are thornless, it is easy and painless to pull out any opportunistic weeds. This charming, trailing woody plant grows well with other ground covers, under shrubs and large perennials. It will grow in any soil and soil acidity does not concern this shrub, with pests and diseases giving it a wide berth. If the plant gets out of control, it is a simple job to cut back the long stems. Shred the prunings before adding to the compost heap, so that they break down sooner. Do any pruning in early spring and the plant will thrive for years. **PM**

Alternative

Syn. *Rubus calycinoides*. *Rubus rolfei* 'Green Jade'

Ruscus
R. aculeatus 'John Redmond'

Main features Evergreen foliage; colourful red berries; tolerates extreme shade and poor soil
Height 30 cm (12 in.) **Spread** 90 cm (3 ft)
Position ○ ◑ ● **Hardiness** RHS H6

If you lack a single spot in your garden that is gloomy and inhospitable, then you are fortunate. For the rest of us, however, these places are a source of frustration and misery. There is an excellent solution, butcher's broom – a prickly little evergreen shrub that will put up with dense shade in the dry soil between tree roots. Not only that, it will reward you for your neglect with a brilliant show of marble-sized red berries that appear in summer and last right through the winter months, guaranteed to perk up even the grimmest corner of your garden.

Once upon a time you would need two plants to get the wax-red berries as the male and female flowers were borne on different plants, but now there are hermaphrodite forms available, which fruit all on their own for our convenience. *R. aculeatus* 'John Redmond' is one such useful cultivar, which is also appreciated for its more compact form than the species. It is evergreen – even its stems are green – and its tough, spiky green 'leaves' are leathery and glossy.

R. aculeatus is a little odd botanically, because its 'leaves' are actually flattened stems called cladodes (also known as cladophylls). Therefore the rather insignificant flowers and the beautiful berries that follow sit nestled in the centre of these, which is a unusual set up.

In days gone by, as its common name butcher's broom suggests, bunches of stems were used to scrub the blocks of butchers. They were also used to clean chimneys and repel rats and mice. This shrub might even still be useful in the garden for this purpose, although it seems to be most popular these days for its wonderful berries, stems of which, brought into the house at Christmas and kept in water, will last for weeks. Another common name is knee holly, quite an apt description of its height and prickly leaves. **ER**

Alternative

Danae racemosa

Ruta
R. graveolens 'Jackman's Blue'

Main features Beautiful blue-grey foliage; clusters of yellow flowers in summer
Height 90 cm (3 ft) **Spread** 90 cm (3 ft)
Position ○ ◑ **Hardiness** RHS H7

Originating in southeastern Europe, this shrub is valued for its exquisitely coloured, blue-grey foliage and for its ability to thrive in dry conditions. *R. graveolens* 'Jackman's Blue' is a bushy plant that looks great in the dry border or even in a container on a hot, sunny patio. Gardeners can admire it growing in mixed borders, ideally in sun but happily in semi-shade, and in dry conditions if nothing else is on offer.

The blue-grey is outstanding, and the yellow four-petalled flowers, produced in clusters in summer, are delightful. The foliage is fascinating, as it looks dainty, almost like a maidenhair fern, but it is the intense glaucous nature of the scented, pinnately lobed leaves that makes them tough, resulting in it being an ideal plant to grow in coastal areas. Well-drained soil is essential to avoid any chance of root rot. Wherever it is grown, the metallic-blue bloom to the leaves is sensational. If the plant becomes too large, it is easy to cut down after flowering; shorten stems by a half. Take care when pruning and disposing of the cuttings. Although *R. graveolens* 'Jackman's Blue' is classed as an evergreen, in severe winters the leaves can look scruffy. This is nothing to worry about as the fresh spring growth is lush, abundant and beautiful.

R. graveolens is also known as rue, an ancient herb that medicinal texts generally quote as an effective cure for headaches. However, great care must always be taken when handling this plant, as severe skin irritation and blistering can form after contact with bare skin in the presence of sunlight; always wear gloves. Do not use it medicinally unless you are qualified to do so. With such a powerful internal system capable of causing skin irritations, it is unsurprising to find that pests steer well clear, leaving the plant to thrive. **PM**

Alternatives

Ruta graveolens, Ruta graveolens 'Variegata', *Ruta chalepensis*

Salix

'Boydii'

Main features Attractive grey, felt-like leaves on
slow-growing branches; architectural plant
Height 30 cm (12 in.) **Spread** 20 cm (8 in.)
Position ○ ◐ **Hardiness** RHS H7

This compact, very slow-growing, and gnarly hybrid
willow is steeped in history and has been honoured
with a Royal Horticultural Society Award of Garden Merit.
S. 'Boydii' is an absolute gem. It has only ever been
found once growing in the wild and that was during the
Victorian era. It is reported that Dr William Boyd, a keen
gardener, spotted it growing in the 1890s on Glen Fiagh,
near Glen Clova in Angus, Scotland, and was besotted
with its beauty. Soft, round, hairy, veiny leaves grow on
branches that eventually reach up to 90 centimetres (3
ft) high, and little greyish-yellow catkins are produced in
spring (the catkins on male plants are showier than on
female ones). In winter, when the leaves have fallen and
its catkins are a distant memory, the plant has an almost
primeval architectural allure – even when young – looking
like a craggy survivor of many a rugged Scottish winter.

'Boydii' is easy to grow, but it does best in full sun
although it will tolerate a little bit of shade. It does need
moisture in the soil, but should never be waterlogged
or allowed to become bone-dry. As plants are so slow
growing, individuals can be started in containers or
troughs and grown for years before being transferred
to the garden. They are perfect for dotting around
rockeries and screes, where they will rarely outgrow
their allotted space.

Aphids have a penchant for the soft new shoots of
this willow, but these are easily stopped by spotting
attacks before they get out of hand. If left to gorge,
unattended aphids will cause the growing points to
become damaged with resultant shoots distorted.
Clear up all dropped leaves in autumn and nip off any
damaged leaves during the growing season to ensure
that the plant is open to good air circulation. This keeps
possible disease risks low. **PM**

Alternatives

Salix helvetica, *Salix reticulata*, *Salix reticulata*
subsp. *nivalis*

Salix

S. *alba* var. *vitellina* 'Yelverton'

Main feature Vibrantly coloured winter stems
Height 1.8 m (6 ft)   **Spread** 1.2 m (4 ft)
Position ○ ◑
Hardiness RHS H6

This superior form of golden willow is selected for its dazzling, yellow-orange shoots, which gradually deepen to fiery red towards their ends. For strength of stem colour, *S. alba* var. *vitellina* 'Yelverton' is unrivalled. It excels during the winter months when there is little else to provide colour interest, and the classic way to use it is in a mass waterside grouping, planted in a situation where the low winter light can backlight the stems. The reflection of this spectacle in the water beneath creates astonishing impact, like a bonfire in an otherwise bleak landscape.

If left alone, 'Yelverton' will grow to a great size; the secret to its striking appearance is hard pruning or coppicing the plants to ground level every two to three years, which produces masses of thin, whippy shoots. Coppicing not only reduces the size of the plant, but also maximises the quantity of colourful stems produced. For those with less space, leaving a stem of a single plant to grow to around 1.8 metres (6 ft) and then cutting back all the branches to this height (pollarding) every few years will produce a blazing fireball of orange and red stems to appreciate at head height.

'Yelverton' makes a wonderful display when combined with other brightly stemmed plants, such as *Cornus sericea* 'Flaviramea', *C. alba* 'Kesselringi' and *Salix alba* 'Hutchinson's Yellow'. These plants together will provide a display of stem colours ranging from yellow and lime green, through orange, coral, scarlet, to darkest purple – enough to brighten any frosty landscape. **ER**

Alternative

Salix alba var. *vitellina* 'Britzensis'

Salix
S. hastata 'Wehrhahnii'

Main features Silvery-white catkins in spring; attractive stems in autumn; compact shrub; attracts wildlife
Height 1.5 m (5 ft) **Spread** 1.5 m (5 ft)
Position ○ ◐ **Hardiness** RHS H6

This willow is the perfect choice for a smaller space and for people wanting to attract wildlife into the garden. It is certainly not one of the large willows seen growing in public parks – *S. hastata* 'Wehrhahnii' is select, choice and controllable. Silvery-white catkins are produced in early spring, and when in full bloom, the whole plant can take on the appearance of an icicle-encrusted skeletal shrub. After the early, intrepid bees have had their rewards for venturing out, the catkins fade and the sea-green leaves emerge. Oval-shaped and bright green on the upper surfaces, with glaucous grey undersides, they create a well-rounded shape until they drop in autumn. Beautiful, dark reddish-brown stems are then revealed.

This lovely willow is a slow-growing shrub requiring either a sunny spot or partial shade. Soil must never become waterlogged nor should it dry out. It will grow happily in sandy or clay soil and at most pH values. It is best not to use fertiliser on the soil around the plant, as this encourages softer growth that is susceptible to aphid damage. If shoots and leaves become distorted, or if you see numerous ants running up the stems to the growing tips, aphids have got a hold of them. Deal with them as you would anywhere else in the garden.

Willows are beautiful plants, but they generally need space. 'Wehrhahnii' is a bushy plant, but it fits neatly into most garden settings. It has been awarded the Royal Horticultural Society Award of Garden Merit for its consistent performance in real garden situations. **PM**

Alternative

Salix helvetica

Salix
S. integra 'Hakuro-nishiki'

Main feature Spectacular white, green and pale-pink foliage; elegant shape
Height 1.5 m (5 ft) **Spread** 1.5 m (5 ft)
Position ○ ◐ **Hardiness** RHS H5

This willow has an elegant shape with long, drooping branches and flamboyant leaves in white, green, and pale pink. Usually grown and trained into a lollipop shape, *S. integra* 'Hakuro-nishiki' is pretty as a container specimen or anywhere in the garden. It thrives in a sunny spot where the dappled coloration of the leaves is strongest, but it is equally at home in a partially shaded position. All specimens are best pruned in early spring. This not only maintains the shape of the tree, but also encourages new shoots. Branches start life growing in all directions, helping to create a wild, firework effect, but soon begin to droop under their own weight as the leaves develop. In autumn the leaves are shed to reveal coral-coloured stems. Plants will not grow tall but pruning will ensure bushy growth that is packed full of colour. As the leaves age they quieten down to green and white, but even that still creates an impressive show. **PM**

Alternatives

Syn. *Salix integra* 'Albomaculata'. *Salix integra* 'Flamingo', *Salix integra* 'Pendula'

Sambucus
S. nigra porphyrophylla 'Thundercloud'

Main features Dramatic black foliage; flat umbels of tiny pink flowers; edible flowers and berries
Height 2.4 m (8 ft) **Spread** 1.8 m (6 ft)
Position ○ ◐ **Hardiness** RHS H4

The common elder (*S. nigra*) is an unexceptional plant ubiquitous in most of Europe, but popular for its flowers and berries, which have culinary and medicinal uses. The cultivar *S. nigra* f. *porhyrophylla* 'Thundercloud' is particularly dramatic, with green leaves that, given a sunny site, rapidly become a chocolate-purple colour, more maroon and less black than other varieties. In spring large, flat umbels of ruby flower buds appear, which open to a rich pink, becoming paler as they age. The contrast between the pink flowers and the dark foliage is stunning. The shrub has a bushy, erect habit and provides interest from spring through to early winter. It will also grow in almost any soil, but it needs sun to colour fully. It is vigorous, but it will stand heavy pruning in late winter. Use it in a border to provide depth behind herbaceous plants or mixed with golden-leaved plants, such as *Berberis thunbergii* 'Aurea' for great colour contrast. **ER**

Alternatives

Sambucus nigra f. *porphyrophylla* 'Eva', *Sambucus nigra* f. *porphyrophylla* 'Gerda'

 Salix integra 'Hakuro-nishiki' kept manageable and in peak condition by regular pruning.

Sarcococca
S. hookeriana var. *digyna* 'Purple Stem'

Main features Fragrant winter flowers; loves dry shade; tolerates pollution; low maintenance
Height 1.2 m (4 ft) **Spread** 1.2 m (4 ft)
Position ○ ◑ ● **Hardiness** RHS H5

All the sweet box family bring welcome fragrance to a garden in winter. The distinctive, dark purple-pink, flushed, upright stems of *S. hookeriana* var. *digyna* 'Purple Stem' grow to 60 to 90 centimetres (2–3 ft) in the first five years, and their colour extends into leafstalks and midribs. The leaves are tapering and elegant; in late winter, the plant stems carry a host of small, cream-white-coloured, highly fragrant flowers. It is a plant whose presence is smelled before it is seen and it will stop visitors to the garden in their tracks as they search for the source of the scent. Small, blue-black, glossy spherical berries follow on from its flowers as the evergreen shrub reverts back to a supporting role.

'Purple Stem' originates in western China. Like the species, it is a small, evergreen, suckering shrub that thrives even in the shaded, root-filled soil beneath larger trees, and it can also tolerate urban pollution.

A popular new hybrid is *S. hookeriana* 'Winter Gem', which has inherited the best qualities of its parents *S. hookeriana* var. *digyna* 'Purple Stem' × *S. hookeriana* var. *humilis*. Larger leaved, its strongly scented white flowers are followed by round, glossy, red berries that eventually ripen to black. *Sarcococca confusa* is a taller cultivar, which reaches to 2.4 metres (8 ft).

'Purple Stem' is hardy and relatively easy to grow in humus-rich, well-drained soil; it spreads by underground runners to cover the ground, in sunny conditions as well as in partial or full shade. It is genuinely a low maintenance shrub, because it keeps a neat shape and appearance without the need for regular pruning. There is no garden that does not have space for at least a single specimen. That is all it takes to add a welcome scent to the dreary days of winter. However, do be aware that this plant is harmful if eaten. **RC**

Alternatives

Sarcococca confusa, Sarcococca hookeriana 'Winter Gem'

Shibataea
S. kumasaca

Main features Dense and compact plant; dark-green leaves; pale-green canes
Height 1.5 m (5 ft) **Spread** 90 cm (3 ft)
Position ○ ◑ **Hardiness** RHS H5

The *S. kumasaca* is a dwarf, compact bamboo that produces leafy clumps of pale-green canes with dark-green leaves. It will not outgrow the garden and is therefore a favourite for gardeners who are ordinarily wary of bamboos. Originating in China and Japan, *S. kumasaca* is suited to sun or partial shade, provided that it has its roots in moist soil. If the soil dries out, the leaves begin to turn crispy at the edges. It is also worth testing the pH of the soil before planting, because this bamboo thrives in acidic conditions. Anything alkaline, and the leaves will turn brown. In ideal conditions, this Royal Horticultural Society Award of Garden Merit winner will thrive for years.

S. kumasaca belongs to the group of bamboos that are classified as 'runners'. This means that it has the capability to send out shoots all over the garden. Although this species does do this, the shoots do not go very far, so the plant never becomes a menace. It also grows superbly well in a container in which it is best to use ericaceous (lime-free) compost. Watering with stored rainwater will ensure a healthy plant, and an annual mulch with pine needles will maintain the correct acidity. In winter the tips of the leaves occasionally turn white, especially in extreme cold. This adds even more beauty to the leaf and is not detrimental.

Free from the usual running bamboo problems and untroubled by pests, *S. kumasaca* in a row can make a lovely, dense, and relatively short hedge. Plant small specimens about 90 centimetres (3 ft) apart to ensure that each has plenty of water and nutrients during the developmental years. Spindly stems can be removed to maintain fresh, vigorous growth. If flower shoots form, it is best to cut these out to enable the plant to concentrate its energy on producing canes and leaves. **PM**

Alternative

Syn. *Phyllostachys ruscifolia*. *Shibataea lancifolia*

Sinocalycalcanthus
S. raulstonii
'Hartlage Wine'

Main features Exotic summer flowers; golden foliage
Height 1.8 m (6 ft)   **Spread** 1.5 m (5 ft)
Position ○ ◑
Hardiness RHS H5

S. raulstonii 'Hartlage Wine' is a multi-stemmed magnolia-like shrub with upright but spreading branches carrying large, broad, mid-green leaves that turn to a rich golden-yellow in autumn. From early summer fat, red-brown flower buds appear in the leaf axils. These open to glorious lotus-like blossoms around 8 centimetres (3 in.) across. The narrow, graceful, incurved petals are burgundy maroon, tipped with cream white in the centre of each bloom. The flowers are long lasting, delicately fragrant, and are produced over a long period through midsummer on even the youngest plants. Few other hardy shrubs produce such captivating flowers. The richly coloured blooms are shown at their best when planted alongside a shrub with copper- or wine-coloured foliage, such as *Physocarpus opulifolius* 'Diable D'Or', or a red-leaved smokebush (*Cotinus*). Originally, the genus was *Sinocalycalcanthus,* but it is now recognised as *Calycanthus,* and plants are sold with either name. **AMcI**

Alternatives

Calycanthus chinensis, Calycanthus floridus

Skimmia
S. japonica
'Nymans'

Main features Berries in early summer; evergreen
Height 90 cm (3 ft)   **Spread** 1.5 m (5 ft)
Position ○ ◑
Hardiness RHS H5

Evergreen plants are indispensable in any garden, the permanence of their forms providing a consistent, year-round structural framework and foundation around which plants with seasonal highlights can be organised. *Skimmia* is a consummate representative of this evergreen community, with its dark-green, glossy leaves forming compact mounds of foliage that gives off an aromatic fragrance when crushed. The leaves are waxy, rather like those of holly but without the vicious prickles. The plants produce attractive and scented flowers that remain in bud over winter and open in spring. However, *Skimmia* is also celebrated for its berries. For a good display of clustered beads of bright-red berries, it has to be *S. japonica* 'Nymans', with lots of relatively large fruits. Berries are produced on female plants and need a male plant nearby to pollinate, such as *S. japonica* 'Rubella'; the combined display of these two cultivars together is greater than the sum of its parts. **ER**

Alternatives

Skimmia japonica 'Temptation', *Skimmia japonica* 'Veitchii'

Skimmia
S. japonica 'Rubella'

Main features Sculptural plant; shade-tolerant evergreen; colourful, long-lasting winter flower buds
Height 90 cm (3 ft) **Spread** 90 cm (3 ft)
Position  **Hardiness** RHS H5

From late autumn to early spring *S. japonica* 'Rubella' carries luscious crimson flower buds in tight, cone-shaped clusters, the colour deepening towards year's end. In spring they open to reveal fragrant, pink-tinged white blooms. 'Rubella' shines as a handsome foliage plant, tolerating even moderate shade. The glossy, deep-green leaves have a sculpted look – oval with a neat crease down the centre – and at flowering time, form whorls around the flower heads, creating a posy effect at the end of each branchlet. The tidy, dome-shaped shrubs associate well with other shade-loving woodlanders. Those with smaller or more intricately cut leaves, such as ferns, hardy fuchsia, pieris and Japanese maple, are ideal. Hydrangeas also make good partners, as their foliage is matt against the skimmia's gloss, and the summer-into-autumn blooms have a lacy quality. 'Rubella' is popular as a container specimen; in summer the foliage creates a backdrop for patio plants, such as fuchsias and begonias. **JH**

Alternatives

Skimmia × confusa 'Kew Green', *Skimmia japonica* 'Nymans'

Skimmia
S. × confusa 'Kew Green'

Main features Evergreen; winter buds; flowers in spring; fragrant flowers; attracts bees
Height 75 cm (2.5 ft) **Spread** 75 cm (2.5 ft)
Position ◐ ● **Hardiness** RHS H5

Although skimmias with red buds or berries may draw the eye, *S. × confusa* 'Kew Green' is best as a garden plant. Forming a rounded mound of bright-green leaves, carried in rosettes at the end of straight green stems, 'Kew Green' retains its foliage quality and colour, even when planted where it gets some direct sunlight. In a similar situation most other skimmias yellow and fade. Large conical clusters of green winter buds open to dense heads of cream spring flowers with dark stamen. Their fragrance is powerful, reminiscent of lily of the valley. 'Kew Green' is wonderful for cutting for floral decoration, both for its winter buds and scented spring flowers. It is an excellent choice for a shady border, either with dark evergreens, such as *Viburnum davidii*, or cream-variegated shrubs, such as *Euonymus fortunei* 'Silver Queen'. It also makes an excellent subject for a pot in a shady situation where it has year-round appeal. Skimmias are happy on most soils, and yellowing is usually caused by too much sunlight. **AMcI**

Alternatives

Skimmia japonica 'Fragrans', *Skimmia japonica* 'Magic Marlot'

Sophora
Sun King

Main features Evergreen foliage; flowers late winter and early spring; architectural plant
Height 1.8 m (6 ft) **Spread** 1.8 m (6 ft)
Position ○ **Hardiness** RHS H4

Every so often a really good new variety of plant appears by chance. Sun King was spotted as a seedling in 1982 at the Hillier Nurseries, in Hampshire, and has proved to be a real winner. Its possible parents originate from Chile, and it is a member of the *Papilionaceae* family, related to peas. If you are looking for an impressive shrub for early blooms, then look no further.

This is an evergreen, bushy shrub. The pinnate leaves consist of up to twenty small, shiny, dark-green leaflets arranged on each side of the central stalk. The long-lasting bunches of clear, bell-shaped, yellow flowers, with prominent stamen, hang in pendulous clusters. They open in late winter or early spring and stand out well against the dark-green foliage. After the plant has flowered, 15- to 20-centimetre-long (6–8 in.) slender pods will develop.

This unusual, attractive shrub has an exotic feel and can be grown in any reasonable soil, provided it is well drained. It will perform best in a sunny, sheltered position. It is reasonably hardy, but it is best to shelter this plant from strong winds. It can be grown as a freestanding shrub and would look good underplanted with blue scillas or grape hyacinths. As a wall shrub, trained onto wire or trellis, it could have an annual climber scrambling through it to flower during the summer months. The blue-flowered grass pea (*Lathyrus sativus* var. *azureus*) would be an ideal choice. **MP**

Alternatives

= 'Hilsop.' *Sophora* 'Little Baby', *Styphnolobium japonicum*, *Sophora tetraptera*

Sorbaria
S. sorbifolia 'Sem'

Main features Compact, multi-season shrub; bright and unusual colouring
Height 90–120 cm (3–4 ft) **Spread** 90–120 cm (3–4 ft)
Position ○ ◑ **Hardiness** RHS H5

Tropical sunset colours seldom feature in the spring garden, but when the buds on the upright stems of *S. sorbifolia* 'Sem' burst forth, prepare to be dazzled. The bright chartreuse of the shoot tips become suffused with bronze red, pink, and salmon. This showstopping performance eases back to leave plants a fresh green by midsummer. This is when frothy cream flower plumes open to cooling effect. The large pinnate leaves produce a second display in autumn, developing rich, red tones. Try fronting 'Sem' with a swath of the long flowering orange geum 'Totally Tangerine' or the blue *Geranium* Rozanne.

Still a fairly new plant to many gardeners, this false spiraea appeared on the scene in the early 2000s.

It was bred by a Dutch nurseryman crossing two *Sorbaria* species, collected from the Urals in Russia, to produce the seedlings from which 'Sem' was chosen. This selection is more compact and colourful than other false spiraea. Its surprising hardiness and wind tolerance comes from its lineage, and in cold gardens you can create the illusion of a warm climate by growing it alongside other large-leaved architectural specimens such as *Miscanthus sinensis* 'Zebrinus', New Zealand flax (*Phormium*) and blue-green hostas. Add some potted bronze canna and dark-leaved dahlias for extra summer drama.

If space in the border is limited, this plant makes a fine container specimen. Its unusual colour and strong form create a look that sits well in contemporary gardens. **JH**

Alternatives

Sorbaria sorbifolia, *Sorbaria sorbifolia* var. *stellipila*, *Sorbaria sorbifolia* 'Gimborn's Pygmy'

Spiraea
S. *japonica* Magic Carpet

Main features Changing foliage colour; flowers in summer; attracts bees and butterflies
Height 60 cm (24 in.) **Spread** 60 cm (24 in.)
Position ○ **Hardiness** RHS H6

This hardworking, easy-to-please little shrub will earn its keep in any garden. It forms a neat, compact mound of foliage that opens bright red in spring, fading through orange to yellow, but continuing to produce young red shoots for most of the season. Small, deep-pink flowers in fluffy, rounded clusters appear from mid- to late summer. Magic Carpet needs a sunny position, but it copes with most soils except heavy, wet ones. Trim plants over with shears in early spring to keep them neat, and encourage new shoots. Magic Carpet makes a good container plant, perhaps underplanted with a small-leaved ivy, for winter interest, and early-spring bulbs, such as snowdrops, scillas or winter aconites. It is also an ideal front-of-border plant, good as a path edging, or as ground cover between larger shrubs. Purple-leaved shrubs, such as *Cotinus cogyggria* 'Royal Purple' or *Acer palmatum* 'Bloodgood' work well with this variety all through the season. Alternatively, create a contrast in form with large-leaved perennials, such as hostas, bergenias or verbascums. **RKW**

Alternatives

= 'Walbuma'. *Spiraea japonica* 'Candlelight'

Stachyurus
S. *praecox*

Main features Red-brown stems; hanging flower clusters in early spring; attracts bees and butterflies
Height 1.8 m (6 ft) **Spread** 1.8 m (6 ft)
Position ○ ◑ **Hardiness** RHS H5

Arching, red-brown stems carry narrow, tapering leaves that fall to leave a graceful, multi-stemmed shrub. As the leaves fall, stiff, pendent clusters of dark buds are revealed, and they remain there, tightly closed, through winter. In early spring the drooping flower clusters open into icicles of pale-yellow, cup-shaped flowers. The effect of a shrub in full bloom in soft, spring sunshine is quite wonderful. *S. praecox* is at its best when seen as a specimen, rising out of low underplanting. It is lovely over a carpet of early-flowering bulbs, such as blue *Anemone blanda*. The flowers are shown off to greatest advantage against a background of evergreen leaves, or when backlit by the sun. The lovely *S. praecox* 'Isaai' is perhaps the best cultivar to grow, as it flowers reliably from an early age and has drooping flower clusters up to 30 centimetres (12 in.) in length. Most varieties have plain green foliage, but *S. chinensis* 'Joy Forever' has dark-green leaves, edged and sometimes spotted with yellow, thus continuing the colour and interest after it flowers. **AMcI**

Alternatives

Stachyurus 'Magpie', *Stachyurus chinensis* 'Celina'

● *Spiraea japonica* 'Magic Carpet' has summer flowers that are loved by bees and butterflies.

Syringa
S. × *hyacinthiflora* 'Esther Staley'

Main features Fragrant spring flowers; good cut flower
Height 2.4 m (8 ft) **Spread** 1.8 m (6 ft)
Position ○ ◑
Hardiness RHS H6

Everyone loves lilac (*Syringa*) for its sweet fragrance and soft hue. This lovely hybrid lilac is earlier to bloom than most and has the classic lilac flowers that are so familiar. With mid-green, heart-shaped leaves on upwards-sweeping stems, it forms a sturdy shrub, similar to the common lilac (*S. vulgaris*), one of its parents. The other parent, *S. oblata* from China, gives *S. × hyacinthiflora* a tolerance of hot weather, making it the best lilac for warmer climates.

Two weeks before other large-flowered lilacs, *S. × hyacinthiflora* opens its deliciously fragrant blooms. These may be single or double, depending on variety, packed in broad, conical flower heads that are wonderful for cutting. Hard pruning after flowering encourages vigorous growth to carry the following year's flowers.

The original hybrid was created by Victor Lemoine of France in 1876. Since then, from the same parents, more compact and earlier-flowering *S. × hyacinthiflora* hybrids have been raised in California and Canada. Because of its earlier flowers, this shrub has the ability to grow and set flowers in a shorter growing season, hence its popularity in Canada and parts of the United States. *S. × hyacinthiflora* 'Esther Staley' is one of the best-known varieties, with red buds opening to single pink flowers in densely packed clusters. It is exceptionally free-flowering and reliable. Other varieties to try include *S. × hyacinthiflora* 'Maiden's Blush', which has pale-pink flowers in large panicles; *S. × hyacinthiflora* 'Pocahontas', with violet, single flowers; or *S. × hyacinthiflora* 'Sweetheart', which has double pink flowers opening from dark-pink buds. Most lilacs flower only once in spring; after that they are plain-leaved deciduous shrubs. However, the season of interest can be extended to late summer by planting a late-flowering *Clematis viticella* to grow through the lilac. **AMcI**

Alternatives

Syringa × *hyacinthiflora* 'Pocahontas', *Syringa* × *hyacinthiflora* 'Maiden's Blush', *Syringa* × *hyacinthiflora* 'Sweetheart'

Syringa
S. meyeri 'Palibin'

Main features Compact, pollution-tolerant shrub; fragrant, late-spring and early-summer flowers
Height 90–150 cm (3–5 ft) **Spread** 90–150 cm (3–5 ft)
Position ○ ◐ ● **Hardiness** RHS H5

For those seeking the charm and fragrance of traditional cottage-garden lilacs but who lack the space to accommodate one, then Korean lilac is the perfect choice. Unlike the many forms of *Syringa vulgaris*, which grow into large shrubs or trees, *S. meyeri* 'Palibin' keeps its small stature and is only very slow growing.

The 'Palibin' lilac has dainty, rounded leaves and starts flowering young. The starry blooms are a deep red-purple in bud, opening to pale lilac-pink, and broad, cone-shaped clusters smother the plant from top to bottom from late spring to early summer. 'Palibin' forms a dome-shaped bush or can be trained as a short-stemmed standard, ideal for large containers. It has the right proportions for the narrow borders of small town gardens, and provided the ground is fertile and moisture-retentive with plenty of added organic matter, 'Palibin' could be grown in the raised bed of a courtyard or roof garden. In larger plots it works well at the front of a sunny shrub or mixed border, especially next to pathways where its sweet fragrance can be relished. Or use it as a 'tree' feature in a rock garden, especially on its preferred alkaline or chalky soil.

'Red Pixie' is a variety similar to Korean lilac. It is slightly later flowering, with eye-catching red buds opening into pink flowers. However, if you have more space, another lilac – ultimately taller but with similarly petite elements and colouring – is *Syringa pubescens* subsp. *microphylla* 'Superba'. Its principal flowering is mid- to late-spring, but it continues to throw out flower heads sporadically till the autumn. The flowers are rosy pink. Lightly prune and deadhead all dwarf lilacs after the main flush of flowering and follow with a thorough watering and fertiliser feed. Mulch with well-rotted manure or homemade compost in late winter. **JH**

Alternatives

Syringa 'Red Pixie', *Syringa pubescens* subsp. *microphylla* 'Superba'

Syringa
S. *vulgaris* 'Madame Lemoine'

Main feature Strongly scented flowers in late spring to early summer

Height 4 m (13 ft) **Spread** 3 m (10 ft)

Position ○ **Hardiness** RHS H6

Ask anyone to name a scented flower, and as often as not 'lilac' will be the response. Adored in the West since it was introduced, *Syringa* has become less popular in recent times. This is probably due to the mistaken belief that its short flowering period negates its other uses. However, this perception is dreadfully misguided, because *S. vulgaris* produces the most sumptuously beautiful and heavily scented blooms at a time when most spring bulbs are finished and summer colour has yet to appear, thereby gracefully filling a void in the garden programme.

S. vulgaris 'Madame Lemoine' is an heritage lilac and was selected in 1890 in Alsace, France. It bears lavish, double, white flowers in late spring to early summer. Three generations of the Lemoine family at Nancy named 214 cultivars of French lilac over seventy years, many of which are still in commercial cultivation: a rare achievement for a plant produced more than a hundred years ago. This particular plant was named for the wife of the first Monsieur Lemoine.

In order to maximise the flowering period, and make the most of the delicious scent, cut 'Madame Lemoine' stems for display in large vases around the house. Sarah Raven, doyenne of the cut flower in the United Kingdom, recommends removing all the leaves from the stems first, then searing the ends in boiling water for thirty seconds. Plunge them into a bucket of cold water and then leave overnight somewhere dark before arranging the following day. 'Madame Lemoine' lasted longer in her tests than any other cut lilac. Outdoors, use this plant as a hedge for screening or as a single specimen in a sunny spot, ideally in alkaline soil. Judicious post-flower pruning and deadheading will keep it looking good, and its open habit provides the perfect framework for a summer-flowering clematis. **ER**

Alternatives

Syringa vulgaris 'Madame Abel Châtenay', *Syringa vulgaris* 'Madame Casimir Périer', *Syringa vulgaris* 'Miss Ellen Willmott'

Syringa vulgaris '**Madame Lemoine**' in the walled garden at Henbury Hall, Cheshire, UK. ➔

T. *ramosissima* 'Pink Cascade'

Main features Light feathery plumes of rich, pink flowers; attractive foliage; versatile shrub or tree
Height 4.5 m (15 ft) **Spread** 4.5 m (15 ft)
Position ○ ◑ **Hardiness** RHS H5

This graceful shrub is indispensable for coastal dwellers, and beside the sea is where you will mostly find tamarisks. Most species are from the Mediterranean region, but this species (*T. ramosissima*) is Russian. 'Pink Cascade' is a very garden-worthy form with large plumes of rich-pink flowers. Arching glaucous fronds of ferny foliage flex in the sea breezes, then, in summer, the plant becomes shrouded in a mass of hazy, candy-floss blossoms. The salty air so destructive to most plants is excreted by glands in tamarisk leaves, and their flexible structure helps them withstand strong winds. Although their natural habitat is by the sea – where they thrive in light soils, because the salt in the air acts as a moisture regulator – if grown inland, they require more substantial soil that remains slightly moist. It is easy to imagine such a fragile-looking plant to be on the tender side, but it is robust enough to endure life on the coast, and hardy to boot. Another popular tamarisk species, *T. tetranda*, flowers in spring.

Normally grown as a shrub or small tree, as an effective wind break or in a border, *T. ramosissima* also makes a good hedge. Left to its own devices it will form a rather untidy tree about 4.5 metres (15 ft) high, although an annual late-winter prune will not only establish a cloud-like form but also encourage flowering.

Tamarisk is ideal when used as a specimen in a gravel garden setting or in a border underplanted with tulips, and later in the season with bold-coloured flowers like dahlias (those who are of faint heart may wish to avoid the yellows). The feathery foliage contrasts well with any plant with significant broadness of leaf. Unfortunately, *T. ramosissima* has become invasive in the southwestern United States and the desert region of California, where it is consuming volumes of groundwater, which is having a negative impact on native flora and fauna. **ER**

Alternatives

Tamarix tetrandra, Cotinus coggygria 'Royal Purple'

Taxus
T. baccata

Main features Hedging and topiary plant; evergreen;
architectural plant
Height 40 ft (12 m) **Spread** 26 ft (8 m)
Position ○ ◐ ● **Hardiness** RHS H6

This plant is synonymous with majestic hedges and giant topiaries in grand British country gardens and is generally acknowledged to be the classic plant for the task. So if you are desirous of clipped figures or substantial and elegant planted structures, *T. baccata,* or the English yew, is the obvious choice. There is only one drawback, and that is you will need a degree of patience, for yew grows more slowly than many other popular topiary or hedging plants; that given, once established, a well-looked after yew hedge may put on up to 30 centimetres (12 in.) a year.

In all other departments the yew prevails: it is tremendously long-lived, possibly to 600 years of age. In fact, there are ten yews in the United Kingdom thought to predate the tenth century; it is also fairly easygoing about where it goes, putting up with most soils except the most compacted or waterlogged. It can be easily maintained by trimming once in late summer or early autumn; it is mostly trouble-free, although sudden oak death (*Phytophthora ramorum*) has recently become more of a problem. Another bonus is that it will regrow from old wood, making it really useful for renovating neglected plants, and for topiary. Cut back hard, and new growth will break from the centre rather than the shortened branches, which is what gives the shrub such an excellent dense form.

If not clipped, *T. baccata* will grow into a broadly conical tree, with spreading branches. Male plants carry yellow cones whereas female plants produce fleshy, red fruits. If fruits are required, then both plants are needed. Note that all parts except the fleshy, red arils are toxic.

Yew hedging is a favourite choice for structure and screening in a formal garden and makes a superb dark-green backdrop for colourful plants. The cultivar 'Dovestonii Aurea' has golden-yellow foliage. **ER**

Alternative

Taxus baccata 'Dovestonii Aurea'

Tetrapanax
T. papyrifer 'Rex'

Main features Architectural foliage; attractive to bees
Height 4.5 m (15 ft) **Spread** 3 m (10 ft)
Position ○ ◑
Hardiness RHS H3

The clue to this plant's qualities really is in the name – shorten it to *T.* 'Rex' and you get an idea of what to expect – a monster (not a dinosaur), but please do not let that put you off! It is a wonderful plant, named such for its massive leaves, which at anything up to 1.2 metres (4 ft) in diameter will always create a talking point in your garden. The huge, lobed, mid-green leaves, which are fuzzy on the undersides, are an essential requirement for any exotic garden, but this plant will look handsome in any border, for its capacity to contrast so brilliantly with most other plants. Although its growth might be limited in cooler climates to around 3 metres (10 ft) in height (more than double that in more favourable climes) it does need space to stretch out.

T. papyrifer was introduced from Taiwan in 1850 and is commonly known as the rice paper plant, as the fibres in the stem are used to make a type of rather pithy paper. 'Rex' is hardier, with larger leaves than the species, and it produces clusters of woolly, white flowers in the autumn, which are very attractive to bees. The flowers are similar to those of *Fatsia japonica,* which is a close relative. 'Rex' is now the variety you are most likely to come across in cultivation. It was introduced to gardeners fairly recently by the Welsh nursery Crug Farm Plants, whose owners collected it in 1993 in a mountainous region of Taiwan.

For a tropical effect, try combining 'Rex' with *Musa basjoo* (banana palm) and cannas. However, use caution when handling, as the fuzzy filaments can irritate skin and be a problem for asthma sufferers. This plant is on the edge of hardiness in many regions; outdoors, cultivate in any well-drained soil in full sun with shelter from strong winds. In frost-prone areas it may behave deciduously. If it is cut back by frost, however, it may regrow from suckers. **ER**

Alternative

Fatsia japonica, Tetrapanax papyrifer 'Variegata', *Tetrapanax papyrifer* 'Empress', *Tetrapanax papyrifer* 'Steroidal Giant'

Thamnocalamus
T. crassinodus 'Kew Beauty'

Main features Attractive canes; evergreen, architectural foliage
Height 4 m (13 ft) **Spread** 1.8 m (6 ft)
Position ◑ **Hardiness** RHS H6

This shrub is a very beautiful and elegant bamboo that forms a dense clump of upright, gently arching canes of statuesque proportions. The canes are blue grey when young and become mahogany with age. The branches are attractively tinged with red, cupped in parchment-like sheaths that remain in place at the nodes of the canes. The mid-green leaves are small and narrow – around 8 centimetres (3 in.) long – creating a light, airy effect.

T. crassinodus 'Kew Beauty' is at its best when grown as a freestanding specimen, rising above stones or low ground-cover planting. The beauty of the canes is shown to greatest advantage if the lower side branches are removed, cutting right back to the canes. This also displays the characteristic zigzag base of some of the canes. The plant is more open in habit, and the new shoots are allowed space to grow if a few of the older canes are removed each year. As a clump-forming bamboo, 'Kew Beauty' is noninvasive and does not run and spread like many of its relatives. However, patience is needed when growing this bamboo; it may be very slow to start and takes time to get established.

'Kew Beauty' grows well in light shade in a sheltered position away from cold winds. Most well-drained soils are suitable, but this cultivar dislikes shallow chalk. In severe winter weather the leaves may drop, leaving the older canes quite bare. It is a lovely choice for a Japanese-style scheme and is very effective alongside still water. Other varieties to try include *T. crassinodus* 'Gosainkund', which has lovely blue-grey canes that retain their colour. It is named after a Nepalese lake, where it was originally found, and is not as hardy as the species or other cultivars. *T. crassinodus* 'Langtang' is smaller in stature, with green canes and fine branches carrying very small leaves. The overall effect is frothy and delicate. **AMcI**

Alternatives

Thamnocalamus crassinodus 'Langtang', *Thamnocalamus crassinodus* 'Merlyn', *Thamnocalamus spathiflorus*

Thuja

T. occidentalis 'Rheingold'

Main feature Brightly coloured foliage all year round
Height 1.5 m (5 ft) **Spread** 90 cm (3 ft)
Position ○
Hardiness RHS H6

Some gardens can be rather dull affairs in the middle of winter, so including evergreen shrubs that not only bolster the structural 'bones' of the space but also inject colour can make a big difference, especially in very cold places where snow is a regular event. Also known as white cedar, *T. occidentalis* is an evergreen conifer from eastern and central North America. It can grow up to 18 metres (60 ft) in height over time in the wild and is often used for hedging because it is extremely hardy and trouble-free.

It is too large for most gardens, but luckily, many small cultivars have been selected so gardeners can enjoy a greater selection of these wonderful plants that require so little attention. Top performer *T. occidentalis* 'Rheingold' is a relatively old variety, but it is still unmatched for its showstopping attribute: foliage colour. This slow-growing, large dwarf – it will reach about 1.5 metres (5 ft) after ten years in most gardens – has flat, fan-shaped sprays of feathery foliage, which is citrus-golden in colour during the summer months, when it combines really well with dark-leaved plants. In the autumn the leaves start to change colour, turning a burnished copper-gold and providing an extraordinary winter show. Because it moves through such a broad colour palette, 'Rheingold' is a source of ever-changing seasonal interest.

Like the species, this variety will make an excellent low hedge, but it is also good as an accent plant in the border or lawn. In fact, 'Rheingold' is an essential requirement for a gold-themed planting. It will also look great in a large container, and although no pruning is required, it can be tidied up with shears to present a formal shape. The colourful branches can be utilised in the winter to decorate the house, and they will impart an aromatic pineapple fragrance when crushed. **ER**

Alternatives

Thuja occidentalis 'Golden Tuffet', *Thuja occidentalis* 'Sunkist'

○ *Thuja occidentalis* 'Rheingold' provides winter colour and structure.

Trachycarpus
T. fortunei

Main feature Exotic, architectural palm that is hardier than it looks
Height 8 m (26 ft) **Spread** 2.4 m (8 ft)
Position ○ ◑ **Hardiness** RHS H5

It is not necessary to have an exotic garden to possess one of these plants, because they are a great addition to all kinds of gardens. However, if you are designing an exotic garden, then this cold-hardy palm is a crucial feature. Tolerating temperatures down to -17°C (1.4°F) makes *T. fortunei* capable of growing at a more northerly latitude than any other trunked palm, and it is therefore one of the most popular palms for temperate gardens. Commonly known as the Chusan palm, or windmill palm, it originates from the foothills of the Himalayas and was introduced into the United Kingdom by Scottish botanist Robert Fortune at the end of the nineteenth century. He sent some seed to the Royal Botanic Gardens at Kew in London, where they were raised in the Palm House until gardeners realised that the plants would do very well outside, once they were mature at a few feet tall.

The resilience of *T. fortunei* is not the only reason for its popularity. It is also a very handsome plant, with a slim trunk – normally hirsute from the remains of leaf bases – and large, fan-shaped leaves up to 90 centimetres (3 ft) in diameter. This shrub makes an attractive and structural focal point and, understandably, is a mainstay of any exotic plantings, where interesting architectural leaves are essential. *T. fortunei* likes a position in sun or partial shade; in fact, less light will encourage the leaf stems to lengthen and therefore increase its jungle appearance. It prefers a moist but well-drained soil, but make sure that it is positioned out of the wind, because the leaves will become quite bedraggled if they are buffeted constantly. If the leaf tips go brown, they can be snipped off to improve their appearance. Stripping the old leaf bases from the stem provides a more formal, smooth trunk, which some gardeners may prefer. **ER**

Alternative

Syn. *Chamaerops fortunei. Trachycarpus wagnerianus, Trachycarpus latisectus*

Tsuga
T. canadensis 'Cole's Prostrate'

Main features Fine, evergreen foliage; deeply fissured
bark; long-lived large tree
Height 30–180 cm (1–6 ft) **Spread** 90–120 cm (3–4 ft)
Position ○ ◑ ● **Hardiness** RHS H7

With sweeping sprays of fine foliage, *T. canadensis* is a
vigorous, conical, evergreen tree. Its short, green, needle-
like leaves are silver underneath and grow in flattened
sprays carried horizontally on the branches. The purple-
grey, deeply fissured bark becomes more beautiful as the
tree matures, and small brown cones are produced in
autumn. Other species of *Tsuga* hate limey soil, but
T. canadensis tolerates it. Although it dislikes very dry
conditions, the shrub grows well in a sunny or shady position.

   T. canadensis is a very beautiful specimen, but it is
a tree for very large gardens and parks. Consequently,
for most gardens, it is best to choose one of the large
number of dwarf varieties that are smaller in stature, and
it is the dwarf forms that have become very popular for
small gardens. Their attractive shape and texture make
them ideal specimens for rock and gravel gardens or
for containers, whereas the prostrate forms are best for
banks and raised beds.

   T. canadensis 'Cole's Prostrate' is totally unlike the
species. The long branches grow along the ground
to form extensive carpets of silver-green needles. It is
a striking subject for a large rock garden or as ground
cover for a bank. If trained or purchased as a standard,
it will cascade down from an upright stem (pictured),
which makes it more of a feature plant for mixed borders
or for use as a specimen. Alternatively, try *T. canadensis*
'Jeddeloh', a lovely dwarf form with a dimpled mound
of arching branches that form a green 'doughnut', or
T. canadensis 'Minuta', which is even smaller and forms
a bun of tightly packed foliage. The latter is suitable for
the smallest spaces and is a total contrast to the habit
of the species. *T. canadensis* 'Pendula' is larger, growing
into a low mound of pendulous branches, around
1.8 metres (6 feet) high, with a broader spread. **AMcI**

Alternatives

Tsuga canadensis 'Jeddeloh', *Tsuga canadensis* 'Minuta',
Tsuga canadensis 'Pendula'

Viburnum
V. × *bodnantense* 'Dawn'

Main features Deciduous shrub; highly fragrant
winter flowers
Height 1.5–2.4 m (5–8 ft) **Spread** 90–150 cm (3–5 ft)
Position ○ ◑ **Hardiness** RHS H6

There is something magical about the scent of flowers
drifting across the garden in the depths of winter. One
of the most reliable – releasing its sweet almond perfume
from a succession of blooms starting in late autumn and
continuing until early spring – is the Bodnant viburnum.
The plant is a valuable resource for early- and late-foraging
bees seen hovering around them on warmer days.

An upright, densely branched shrub, this winter
beauty was created at Bodnant Garden on the edge of
the Snowdonia mountain range in North Wales during
the 1930s. *Viburnum grandiflorum* was crossed with the
fragrant *V. farreri*. An earlier attempt had been made by
Charles Lamont at the Royal Botanic Gardens in

Edinburgh, but with disappointing results. The two-tone,
rose-pink and white 'Dawn' was an obvious award-
winner. The heavily veined leaves are burnished bronze
in spring, turning dark green through summer. After leaf
drop the tufted clusters of reddish-pink buds become
visible, opening sporadically during mild spells.
Pink pompoms sprout from the bare stems and make a
good show at the back of a mixed border with other
winter-interest plants, such as red-berried cotoneasters,
Mahonia × *media* 'Winter Sun', and the flame-stemmed
dogwood, *Cornus sanguinea* 'Midwinter Fire'.
V. × *bodnantense* 'Deben' is a paler pink than 'Dawn', and
the name 'Charles Lamont' was given to the third clone,
a pretty pure-white form, in his honour. **JH**

Alternatives

Viburnum × *bodnantense* 'Deben', *Viburnum* ×
bodnantense 'Charles Lamont', *Viburnum farreri*

Viburnum
V. × burkwoodii 'Mohawk'

Main features Attractive flowers; strong scent; autumn colour **Height** 2.4 m (8 ft) **Spread** 2.4 m (8 ft)
Position ○ ◑ ●
Hardiness RHS H6

Medium-sized, evergreen shrubs with the bonus of flowers are always of interest to the gardener seeking year-round interest, and this particular one has a great deal going for it. It is prized for its showy, spring flowers, and of more than 150 varieties of *Viburnum*, it is one of the most fragrant. *V. × burkwoodii* is the result of a cross between *V. carlesii*, with its highly fragrant flowers, and *V. utile*, for its attractive foliage and resistance to bacterial disease. Don Egolf, a plant breeder at the United States National Arboretum, further improved the hybrid by backcrossing *V. × burkwoodii* with *V. carlesii*, thereby producing the cultivar *V. × burkwoodii* 'Mohawk', launched commercially in 1966.

'Mohawk' has very desirable flowers: the glossy red buds appear in early spring and, after a few weeks, they open to clusters of exquisite, white, waxy flowers with a spicy, clove-like fragrance that perfumes the air for a considerable distance. These flowers, and the berries that follow, are a magnet for wildlife, especially butterflies and birds. The foliage is an attractive glossy green through the growing season, followed by a tour de force of dramatic autumn colour. 'Mohawk' has undemanding growing needs, with good resistance to bacterial leaf spot and powdery mildew, which tend to beset some viburnums. It will grow in any position or soil; just make sure to put it somewhere where the glorious scent can be appreciated. **ER**

Alternatives

Viburnum × burkwoodii 'Park Farm Hybrid', *Viburnum × burkwoodii* 'Anne Russell'

Viburnum
V. carlesii 'Diana'

Main feature Sweetly fragrant late-spring flowers
Height 1.2 m (4 ft) **Spread** 1.2 m (4 ft)
Position ○ ◑
Hardiness RHS H6

This is a rounded shrub of open habit, with straight twigs and soft, slightly downy, grey-green leaves, tinged with purple when young. In leaf it is unremarkable; its moment of glory comes in late spring, when clusters of red-pink buds open to pure-white flowers, salmon pink on the outside of the petals and tube. The scent is strong, sweet, powerful and to be savoured. The effect of the flower clusters, carried at the end of the twigs, over the grey-green leaves is delightful.

'Diana' is light, airy and mixes well with other shrubs and perennials. It makes a good planting partner for *Cornus alba* 'Sibirica Variegata' with its soft, green and white variegated leaves, flushed with pink. The cornus maintains interest in the planting when the flowers of the viburnum have faded. The viburnum produces some autumn foliage colour. *V. carlesii* is an easy shrub to grow and it fits nicely into almost any garden. It combines well with roses, shrubs and perennials and is valuable for its early flowers. *V. carlesii* can be pruned lightly, immediately after flowering to control shape and spread, but this is rarely necessary. It is a usually grown as a grafted plant, so it is important to look out for suckers arising from the rootstock. Left to develop these will quickly take over and weaken the shrub.

A very similar viburnum is *V. carlesii* 'Aurora'. Raised at Slieve Donard Nursery in Northern Ireland, it also has red flower buds opening to pink blooms, which are white on the inside. *V.* × *juddii* is a hybrid of *V. carlesii* with *V. bitchiuense*. It is bushier in habit, with similar flowers and was raised by William Judd, propagator at the Arnold Arboretum in Boston, Massachusetts. *V.* × *carlcephalum* is another hybrid of *V. carlesii*, this time with *V. macrocephalum*. It is compact in habit, with large flower clusters and colourful autumn foliage. **AMcI**

Alternatives

Viburnum carlesii 'Aurora', *Viburnum* × *juddii*, *Viburnum* × *carlcephalum*

Viburnum
V. opulus 'Compactum'

Main features Attractive flowers, berries, and autumn
colour; valuable as a wildlife shrub
Height 1.5 m (5 ft) **Spread** 1.5 m (5 ft)
Position ○ ◑ ● **Hardiness** RHS H6

A common sight in British ditches and hedgerows,
V. opulus is one of the most ornamental European native
plants, with lacy-white flowers, a bumper crop of berries,
and impressive autumn colour. It is also known as the
guelder rose, and across the Atlantic, it is commonly
known as the European cranberry bush, although it is
neither a cranberry nor a rose.

The species is generally too vigorous and bulky for
most gardens, so it is helpful that there is a garden-
worthy version. *V. opulus* 'Compactum' is a reduced
form, as its name suggests, reaching only 1.5 metres
(5 ft) in height – but this does not compromise its ability
to produce flowers and fruit liberally. The white flowers
are similar to those of the lacecap hydrangea, consisting
of loose corymbs (flattened clusters) that begin to open
around the edges first. Although the flowering period is
brief, it is followed by lustrous bright-red berries, which
can easily persist through winter. Technically, these are
edible as well as being ornamental, but they are not
particularly appetizing and are best left for the birds,
who are very keen on them. In the autumn the compact
guelder rose leaves turn vibrant red and orange.

From a design point of view, 'Compactum' is a
generous plant, providing interest through most of the
year. It is also very low maintenance and easily managed
by pruning if it outstretches its limits. It is best used in
an informal, mixed garden, where wildlife is welcome.
In addition 'Compactum' makes an attractive hedge,
either singly or combined with plants, such as *Prunus
spinosa* (blackthorn) and *Crataegus monogyna* (common
hawthorn). Underplant it with early-flowering bulbs to
span the seasons. The species plant, *Viburnum opulus*,
may be listed as potentially invasive in certain US states,
but there is no record of this cultivar being a problem. **ER**

Alternatives

Viburnum opulus 'Roseum', *Viburnum opulus*
'Xanthocarpum'

Vitex
V. *agnus-castus* f. *latifolia*

Weigela
'Praecox Variegata'

Main features Aromatic foliage; flowers in summer;
attracts bees and butterflies
Height 1.8 m (6 ft) **Spread** 1.8 m (6 ft)
Position ○ **Hardiness** RHS H5

Main feature Compact, variegated shrub with late-
spring blooms for sun or shade
Height 90–150 cm (3–5 ft) **Spread** 90–150 cm (3–5 ft)
Position ○ ◑ ● **Hardiness** RHS H6

The *Vitex* has long been gathered and cultivated in the Mediterranean and parts of Asia. It is an excellent, drought-tolerant shrub and is ideal at the foot of a sunny wall, alongside paving or to add structure in a gravel garden. Its straight, silver-grey, downy stems carry green, aromatic, hemp-like leaves with pointed leaflets. The growth is slender and makes a light, airy mound of graceful character that moves gently in a breeze. Hailing from warmer regions, *Vitex* is a sun lover and tolerates dry, stony soil. From mid- to late summer, the stems are tipped with slender, buddleja-like sprays of mauve-violet flowers that are produced well into autumn. Varieties to try include *Vitex agnus-castus* f. *alba* 'Silver Spire', which has pure-white flowers and is delightful against a purple *Berberis* or in a silver scheme. *Vitex agnus-castus* f. *latifolia* is more vigorous and hardy with broad leaflets. It is perhaps the most reliable variety for most situations. Prune to remove the old flowered shoots in late winter or early spring before new growth commences. **AMcl**

It is unusual to find a shrub that is grown as much for its foliage as for its flowers, but this one has the complete package. In spring, along with bulbs, it adds vibrancy to borders, its new leaves emerging from wiry stems. Narrowly oval and tapered to a fine point, the blades have broad, cream-yellow margins. At this time there is often a fine pink edging. Clusters of deep-pink flower buds develop in the leaf axils, adding to the colourful display. Especially in full sun, the variegation pales to cream-white, making a perfect foil for the rose-pink, funnel-shaped blooms in late spring and early summer. The flowers have a light honey scent and are loved by bumblebees. Its airy, upright-to-spreading form works well in informal settings, such as beneath a light tree canopy, growing with foxgloves, ferns and forget-me-nots. Like other variegated weigelas, it will not lose its colouring in shade, though it may not flower as profusely. In a sunny mixed border the dainty foliage sets off bold-flowered perennials, like peonies, delphiniums and lilies. **JH**

Alternative

Vitex agnus-castus f. *alba* 'Silver Spire'

Alternatives

Weigela florida 'Florida Variegata', *Weigela* 'Victoria'

Weigela
'Red Prince'

Main features Attractive flowers in late spring and again in late summer; deciduous
Height 1.5 m (5 ft) **Spread** 1.5 m (5 ft)
Position ○ ◑ **Hardiness** RHS H6

In Victorian times *Weigela* was very fashionable, and it is now having a long-overdue renaissance after being thought to be dull out of season. It is an easy-care shrub, and, far from dull, *Weigela* 'Red Prince' is a blooming powerhouse. In late spring it produces an abundance of deep, ruby-red trumpets on languidly graceful branches, perhaps the brightest blooms of all the *Weigela* family. Often, there is another burst of blooms in late summer for double delight. Moreover, 'Red Prince' is content in any moist, well-drained soil; has no serious pest problems; and will fit perfectly into a typical mixed border. Other options in the garden include growing it permanently in a container or training it into a lollipop standard. However, 'Red Prince' does like lots of sun and needs some protection from winter winds. It is a good choice for urban areas and will also perform well as a hedge if it is fully hardy in your region. If you are lucky enough to entertain hummingbirds in your garden, this is a plant they will visit in droves. **ER**

Alternatives

Weigela Carnaval = 'Courtalor', *Weigela* 'Eva Rathke'

Xanthoceras
X. sorbifolium

Main features Flowers in late spring; attractive foliage
Height 1.8 m (6 ft) **Spread** 90 cm (3 ft)
Position ○
Hardiness RHS H5

The *X. sorbifolium* is a very beautiful deciduous shrub with attractive foliage and flowers. As the specific name suggests, the pale-green pinnate leaves resemble those of *Sorbus aucuparia*, but they are larger. The flowers are a stand-out feature, and these appear in late spring in upright panicles, starry white with crimson centres. *X. sorbifolium* flowers from an early age, but it requires a warm, sunny position to ripen the wood for the best flowers, and with luck you will get walnut-like fruits developing later in the year. These contain large, chestnut-like seed that gardeners often pass on to family members to sow. *X. sorbifolium* is a lovely specimen for the centre of a lawn or against a wall. It is an interesting alternative to *Rhus* or *Koelreuteria*, the latter of which it resembles. Ultimately *X. sorbifolium* could grow to the size of a tree (5 m/16 feet), but in practice, much depends on how hardy it is in your region. In addition the shrub can be controlled to a typical height of 180 by 90 centimetres (6 x 3 ft) by selective pruning after flowering. **AMcI**

Alternative

Koelreuteria paniculata

These plants have evolved to reach up to sunlight by using one of several adaptations: tendrils, curling leaf stalks, twinning stems, or hooked thorns. Climbers can be annuals, herbaceous perennials, or woody-stemmed growths. Annuals, such as sweet peas, are the easiest ones to start with, because any support needs to hold only one season's top growth.

The woody-stemmed climbers need very sturdy permanent supports, but can result in impressive garden features: for example, a gorgeous wisteria up a house wall, or an ornamental vine over a pergola. Flowering climbers offer colour and often scent for an arch, arbour or trellis screen, while foliage climbers can screen out eyesores and soften hard landscaping. Climbers need attention in their early training, and often annual pruning, but the rewards are the privacy and atmosphere they bring to a garden.

CLIMBERS

● *Actinidia kolomikta* is a deciduous climber that displays pink coloration on its green foliage.

Actinidia

A. kolomikta

Main features Unusually colourful, summer leaves; tiny, fragrant, white flowers
Height 4–8 m (13–26 ft)
Position ○ **Hardiness** RHS H5

Pink leaves are not a common feature of plants, which makes the pretty, pink-and-white splashed, heart-shaped leaves of this twining, woody climber unusually attractive. The secret for the best show is to plant it against a brick wall or up a strong tree and ensure it gets a good amount of sunshine. The charm is that the colouring is varied and looks as if someone has walked along and randomly flicked a paintbrush at it. In Japan, *A. kolomikta* grows wild in woodland. The species was originally collected in 1878 in Sapporo, on the northern island of Hokkaido, and sent to Veitch Nurseries in the United Kingdom, who are famed for their interest in new and unusual species and who quickly introduced it into Western horticulture.

The deciduous *A. kolomikta*, which is also known as the Chinese gooseberry or variegated kiwi vine, is purely ornamental. It is the hardiest of the species, but is still susceptible to late frost. With this amount of foliage colour, flowers are almost superfluous. However, *A. kolomikta* is actually named from the Greek word *akis* – meaning 'ray' – after its star-shaped flowers and clusters of tiny, fragrant, white flowers, which appear fleetingly in early summer. Species plants can be male or female, with the female producing fruits, but cultivated *A. kolomitka* are all male. Vigorous growth of up to 5 metres (16 ft) can be rapid, even in the first year, so ensure it has suitable support and free-draining soil and prune if necessary in late winter. The plant is attractive to cats, which can damage the vines. **JWo**

Alternative

Actinidia kolomikta 'Arctic Beauty'

Adlumia
A. fungosa

Main features Vigorous biennial vine with a long season of flower; white to pale-pink flower bells
Height 4.5 m (15 ft)
Position ○ ◑   **Hardiness** RHS H7

The Allegheny vine is an underappreciated North American native that is becoming increasingly rare in the wild. Although it is distributed from Quebec and Manitoba south down the eastern side of the United States to North Carolina and Tennessee, and as far west as Iowa and Minnesota, it is most often seen in the Allegheny Mountains, from Pennsylvania to Virginia. It grows in moist conditions amongst rocks and in open woodland.

This biennial vine is one of two *Adlumia* species that belong in the poppy family and are most closely related to the fumitories, *Fumaria*. A stout tap root and a rosette of feathery foliage develops in its first year, then the following season, long, fleshy, rather weak, pale reddish-green stems develop carrying much divided and lobed leaves that behave as tendrils and clasp their supports. The flower clusters develop at the leaf joints from early summer into the autumn, up to thirty flowers in each cluster, and are usually white to pale pink in colour, although pink-purple forms are also seen. The first flower to bloom may well have developed seeds while flower buds further up the stems are yet to open.

This is a climber to grow through shrubs; in gardens it tolerates drier conditions than in the wild. It is ideal sprawling through *Euphorbia characias* with blue foliage, such as 'Blue Hills', and through spring-flowering shrubs, including azaleas and weigelas. While it is not suited to hot and humid conditions and regions with warm winters, it is unusually hardy and thrives in very cold climates. **GR**

Alternatives

Dactylicapnos macrocapnos, Dactylicapnos scandens

Akebia
A. quinata

Main features Semi-evergreen with fragrant, cup-shaped spring flowers; attractive foliage
Height 6 m (20 ft)
Position ○ ◑　**Hardiness** RHS H7

A semi-evergreen, this plant gets its common name chocolate vine from the colour of its flowers rather than its fragrance, although the flowers do have a delicious vanilla scent. In early spring purple, three-petalled flowers hang in bunches among the leaves. In regions with mild springs and long, hot summers, 10-centimetre-long (4 in.), sausage-shaped, violet fruits appear in the autumn. The fruits split open to reveal black seed in a white pulp, which is edible if not particularly exciting – the taste is similar to tapioca pudding. There is a late-season bonus when the attractive foliage of five, rounded leaflets becomes tinged purple in winter.

A native of Japan, China and Korea, *A. quinata* makes an excellent scrambler over old stumps, up sturdy trees and across walls or pergolas. It is very vigorous, growing to 6 metres (20 ft) or more. That vigour can lead to the plant dominating others in the garden if care is not taken to shorten it after flowering to restrict growth. Furthermore, in some regions, where it fruits and seeds, it is considered invasive and not recommended where it could out-compete native plantings or simply be too vigorous to maintain. However, in the right place it has merit. In temperate gardens *A. quinata* can be reluctant to flower or to fruit, as two plants are needed to ensure fertilisation, but it still provides attractive foliage and good screening. It is found at forest edges in Asia, so the plant can take some shade, but it does better when grown in sun, giving a greater chance of fruit.

The cultivar 'White Chocolate' has cream flowers and is available from specialist nurseries. Modern plant hunters have collected *A. longeracemosa*, a new form from northern Taiwan, with considerably longer racemes hanging below the three-petalled flowers, giving it an even more impressive look. **JWo**

Alternatives

Akebia × pentaphylla, Akebia longeracemosa

Ampelaster
A. carolinianus

Main features Vigorous climber; very late season of fragrant pink daisy-like flowers in autumn
Height 3–6 m (10–20 ft)
Position ○   **Hardiness** RHS H6

The fact that this unique species – known as the climbing Carolina aster – is native in the southeastern United States, from North Carolina to Florida, and grows naturally along streams, in swamps and in wet woodlands tells you a great deal about the requirements of this plant. This is a tall, vigorous, rather floppy, vine-like climber, which sprawls over and through neighbouring shrubs and trees. Its stems branch widely, so that it may cover a broad area and carry untoothed, greyish-green foliage up to 8 centimetres (3 in.) long, which varies noticeably in shape from oval or lance shaped to egg shaped.

In Florida, the climbing aster may flower all year round, but further north it tends to be at its peak in late autumn and winter. Up to fifteen fragrant flowers are gathered in open sprays, each flower is up to 5 centimetres (2 in.) across, with up to seventy pale rosy-purple to pale-pink petals around a yellow disk. The flowers attract bees and butterflies well into autumn. For the best flower display, plants need as much sun as possible. The climbing aster also needs support, such as a fence or trellis, for its mass of growth, and it can smother neighbouring plants if not controlled by cutting back in spring.

This perennial vine is a fine plant if it is hardy in your region. It appreciates moist conditions, although it will take some drought once established. However, it needs a long, hot summer for the flowers to develop. In cooler summer climates, such as the Pacific Northwest and in the United Kingdom, it rarely flowers at all. The plant was known for many years as *Aster carolinianus* but, then as botanists developed a deeper understanding of these plants and divided them into a number of different genera, it became classified as *Ampelaster carolinianus*. Note that catalogues and websites may still list it under its previous name. **GR**

Alternative

Syn. *Aster carolinianus*

Aristolochia
A. macrophylla

Main features Vigorous, large-leaved, deciduous vine; large, dark, beautifully patterned flowers
Height 9 m (30 ft)
Position ○ ◑   **Hardiness** RHS H7

The *Aristolochia* group of plants is more often described as interesting than colourful. There are about 300 evergreen or deciduous species, which vary greatly in their hardiness, but almost all are twining vines. The foliage is usually more or less triangular, sometimes quite large, making a mature plant an impressive spectacle. In some species the summer flowers are very large and flared, often densely patterned in purple, maroon, brown and white; in others they are smaller and more obviously the origin of the common names of some species – Dutchman's pipe.

The hardiest of those that are grown most often is *A. macrophylla*, a vigorous 7.5 to 9 metre (25–30 ft) vine with 30-centimetre-long (12 in.) heart-shaped leaves and small 2.5-centimetre-long (1 in.) green flowers hidden among the leaves; it is handy for covering tree stumps or eyesores. *A. clematitis* is a little less hardy, but it is distinct in being a 90-centimetre-tall (3 ft) hardy herbaceous perennial that spreads at the root, the upright stems carrying 8- to 15-centimetre-wide (3–6 in.) heart-shaped leaves with yellow, flared, tubular flowers. *A. gigantea*, however, is a very vigorous tropical vine, growing wild in Brazil and Panama, and valuable for frost-free zones. Its dark, evergreen triangular leaves are 8 to 10 centimetres (3–4 in.) long and it produces a succession of fascinating 15-centimetre-long (6 in.) flared purple flowers with intricate white veining held on individual stems facing outwards, where their pattern can be appreciated.

In cold areas it is recommended growing the less hardy types of *Aristolochia* in a conservatory, although their vigour can pose problems. Some have had success growing it in a large container, cutting back its mass of growth hard in the autumn and moving it to a frost-free porch. Provide stout supports and maintenance so that it does not smother neighbouring plants. **GR**

Alternatives

Aristolochia grandiflora, Aristolochia littoralis, Aristolochia gigantea (syn. *Aristolochia clypetala*)

Bignonia

B. capreolata

Main features Very vigorous vine; clusters of scented orange-red flowers
Height 6–15 m (20–50 ft)
Position ○ **Hardiness** RHS H6

This colourful and unexpectedly hardy vine is related to the familiar trumpet vine, *Campsis*, under which name it was once included. It is a very vigorous plant, clinging both by its twining stems and by the small suckers at the tips of the tendrils that develops between the two leaf segments. *B. capreolata* grows wild in shady situations from Virginia and Illinois, south to Louisiana and Florida, usually in damp, acidic soil and often along riverbanks and lakesides, where its roots are constantly wet. It grows high into the forest canopy. An evergreen in the southern part of its range and in southern gardens, it tends to lose at least some of its foliage in areas with cold winters.

The glossy, dark-green leaves are up to 15 centimetres (6 in.) long and are split into two oval or lance-shaped, wavy-edged leaflets with the tendril between; in autumn or winter they often develop attractive bronze tones. In late spring or early summer, on growth made the previous year, clusters of 5- to 10-centimetre-long (2–4 in.) tubular flowers develop, each orange red in colour with five lobes that flare to reveal a golden interior. The flowers are chocolate scented and are followed by slender, 18-centimetre-long (7 in.) seed capsules. The plant may re-bloom sporadically later in the summer.

A number of forms of *B. capreolata* have been named, including 'Atrosanguinea', which has purple flowers, and 'Jekyll', with smaller foliage and orange and yellow, unscented flowers. In the southern areas of the United States, this plant will need space to rampage through trees and on long fences; in cooler areas it prefers the shelter of a sunny wall, and its growth will be much less vigorous, so make sure the soil is fertile, moist and well-drained. Cut back after flowering in order to keep growth in check. In cold regions *B. capreolata* can be grown in a large conservatory. **GR**

Alternatives

Bignonia capreolata 'Atrosanguinea', *Bignonia capreolata* 'Dragon Lady', *Bignonia capreolata* 'Jekyll'

Billardiera
B. longiflora

Main features Lovely late-season, purple-blue fruits; modest grower so not too vigorous
Height 1.8–3 m (6–10 ft)
Position ○ ◑　**Hardiness** RHS H5

One of twenty species of Australian twining plants, *B. longiflora* is a well-behaved evergreen vine, grown mainly for its colourful fruits. It grows in damp forests and woods in New South Wales, Victoria and Tasmania. This slender twiner has alternately arranged, lance-shaped, dark-green leaves, each with a pale central vein. From late spring through summer, clusters of flowers appear at the leaf joints towards the tips of the shoots. Each 2.5-centimetre-wide (1 in.) tubular flower is pale greenish yellow – often greener at first and then becoming slightly more yellow later – and sometimes develops pinkish tints as it matures or even becomes rather purplish. In late summer and autumn the flowers are followed by cylindrical berries – about 2.5 centimetres (1 in.) long – usually in deep purplish blue but sometimes in purple, carmine, red, pink or white. The berries are edible, with a pleasing apple flavour, but they are rather too full of seed to be truly appetizing.

In cold areas *B. longiflora* can be grown outside in a container and brought into a conservatory in autumn. Alternatively, it makes a fine permanent conservatory plant. In fact, it is more manageable in this environment than many vines that enjoy warm climates outside. In the garden, where it is hardy, it is best grown in a sunny situation against a wall or somewhere sheltered from cold winds. Its roots prefer a cool site, so plant *B. longiflora* behind a low evergreen, or be sure to mulch the roots well. The ideal site is a humus-rich, neutral or acidic soil that does not dry out. In subtropical areas this plant is ideal scrambling over low shrubs, twining on a low lattice fence, or trailing over a retaining wall. Its top growth can be cut back by light frost, but it will usually regrow in spring unless the frost is prolonged. 'Cherry Berry' is an attractive red-fruited form of *B. longiflora*, whereas 'Fructo-albo' is white. **GR**

Alternatives

Billardiera longiflora 'Cherry Berry', *Billardiera longiflora* 'Fructo-albo'

Bomarea
B. edulis

Main features Colourful flowers summer to autumn; berries in autumn; twining vine for outside or conservatory
Height 1.8–3 m (6–10 ft)
Position ○ ◐ **Hardiness** RHS H2

We are all familiar with alstroemerias, either as unusually, long-lasting, cut flowers or as colourful, garden perennials. However, closely related to them is *Bomarea*, a group of about 120 species from South America grown for their flower clusters and their fruits, many of which are well-behaved climbers. Growing from spreading rhizomes, in the same way as alstroemerias, many *Bomarea* species are twining climbers, although some are more floppy and more spreading. They can be found from Mexico south to Chile; some species are coastal and some grow in the Andes mountain range, although many forms grow in humus-rich, woodland conditions, often in areas of cloud forest.

B. edulis is the species most often seen in gardens and is common in the wild from the Caribbean to Brazil. It is evergreen in climates above 5°C (40°F), but deciduous in cooler winters, and develops edible tubers. The 6- to 13-centimetre-long (2.5–5 in.), lance-shaped leaves have the unusual feature, as in all species of *Bomarea*, of their stems being twisted through 180 degrees, so that what appears to be the upper surface of each leaf is, in fact, the underside. On the outside, the 4-centimetre-long (1.5 in.), bell-shaped flowers are usually pink-salmon, rose, magenta-tinted or even red, and on the inside, yellow or green and prettily flecked with dark-red speckles. Flowers open from early summer to autumn and, in favourable climates, they will be followed by tight, round clusters of orange-red berries encased in papery coverings.

Bomarea grows well in full sun in mild coastal areas; in hotter and drier regions, give it partial shade and a humus-rich, moist soil. Where cold winters are a problem, it can be grown in a large pot in the conservatory, where it will bloom almost year round. Plants may suffer from spider mites in dry conditions. **GR**

Alternatives

Bomarea multiflora, Bomarea salsilla, Bromarea acutifolia

Bougainvillea
B. × buttiana

Main feature Vivid and vibrant flowers for
tropical climates
Height 3–12 m (10–40 ft)
Position ○   **Hardiness** RHS H2

These flamboyant trees, shrubs and vines are favourites
with gardeners in frost-free climates worldwide for their
brilliant colours, reliability and tolerance of minimal care.
There are fourteen species – some are almost deciduous
but most are evergreen – and all grow wild in South
America. *Bougainvillea* is often sold simply by colour –
reds, purples, vibrant pinks, yellows and white – and it
may be necessary to source plants from a specialist if
particular species or cultivars are needed. Generally
vigorous and sometimes thorny, the rather unruly plants
can be tamed by growing over strong pergolas or up
balconies. Clusters of flowers in fluorescent shades open
mostly in spring and autumn, and in many climates, into
winter. They flower best when days and nights are more
or less the same length and when rainfall is light. Plants
need the stout support of a wall, fence or trellis but can
also be grown in containers. They make good boundary
hedges and can even be trained as trees. **GR**

Alternatives

Bougainvillea × buttiana 'Poulton's Special'

Campsis
C. × tagliabuana
Indian Summer

Main features Impressive, exotic-looking flowers for
late-season interest; attracts hummingbirds
Height 9 m (30 ft)
Position ○   **Hardiness** RHS H4

C. × tagliabuana is a hybrid of the only two species in the
genus, both of which are attractive deciduous climbers
grown for their flowers. *C. radicans* is native to the woods
of the southeastern United States, where it climbs into
trees using aerial roots. As its name suggests, *C. grandiflora*
has large, beautiful flowers; it was introduced to the West
from China in 1800. There are two cultivars of the hybrid
C. × tagliabuana to look for: the 8-centimetre-wide (3 in.)
flowers of Indian Summer are peach-orange with a red
throat, and appear from late summer to autumn. They
attract hummingbirds, whose curved beaks reach into
the trumpets, hence its common name, the hummingbird
vine. The flowers bloom earlier and are larger than either
parent. However, it is not as vigorous as other cultivars,
such as 'Madame Galen'. Although hardy to -10°C (14°F),
Campsis needs shelter from cold winds. The key to good
flowers is strong sunshine. Control growth with annual
pruning of side shoots in late winter. **JW**

Alternative

= 'Kudian'. *Campsis × tagliabunda* 'Madame Galen'

⊖ *Bougainvillea* thriving against a stone wall in rural Spain.

Celastrus
C. scandens

Main feature A mix of colourful autumn fruits
Height 6 m (20 ft)
Position ○ ◐
Hardiness RHS H7

This attractive, North-American native, deciduous vine grows wild from Quebec to Saskatchewan in the north, to Texas in the south, and as far west as Montana; it is found in deciduous woods, scrub, rocky slopes and roadsides. *C. scandens* is one of thirty species, and the others grow mainly in tropical, subtropical and temperate zones of Asia, Australia and South America.

Clinging with its twining stems, it features shiny, oval, alternate leaves of 5 to 10 centimetres (2–4 in.) – toothed along their edges – that develop an attractive yellow colour in autumn. Small and yellow white in colour, the flowers – gathered into heads of six or more at the ends of the shoots – do not make much of an impact. Male and female flowers are carried on separate plants, and the plants need to be fairly close together for pollination to take place and for fruit to be set on the females. And it is the fruits that are the main feature. In autumn each fruit splits to reveal the yellow interior of the three ridged lobes. These lobes surround a bright, orange-red seed, thus providing a vivid contrast that catches the eye.

It is important to note that the species *C. orbiculatus*, which grows wild in China, Japan and Korea – has become an invasive weed in the northeastern United States after having been grown as an ornamental in gardens. It is easily distinguished by its clusters of up to three fruits, which develop at the leaf joints along the stems instead of at the shoot tips, as in the native *C. scandens*. Planting *C. orbiculatus* is now prohibited in many states. **GR**

Alternative

Celastrus orbiculatus Hermaphrodite Group

Clematis
C. alpina 'Stolwijk Gold'

Main feature Violet-blue spring flowers set against golden-yellow foliage
Height 1.8 m (6 ft)
Position ○ ◑ **Hardiness** RHS H7

Clematis have been popular for centuries, so it is perhaps surprising that only two forms of clematis with golden leaves have appeared over the years. The most effective of these is *C. alpina* 'Stolwijk Gold'. This golden-yellow leaved selection from spring-flowering *C. alpina* has a highly appealing combination of flower and foliage colours. The stems are slightly reddish, and the leaves are split into nine toothed, oval leaflets that are bright yellow from when they first open in spring. They retain their colour after flowering, slowly maturing to chartreuse.

The nodding, violet-blue, four-petalled flowers open in spring and early summer, while the foliage colour is still at its peak, so the richly coloured blooms stand out impressively against the bright leaves. The flowers are followed by fluffy seed heads made up of a mass of 2.5-centimetre-long (1 in.) silky tails, one for each seed.

Modest in growth, the winning combination of flowers and foliage makes 'Stolwijk Gold' a good specimen plant for a trellis on a fairly expsoed wall, preferably in fairly well-drained soil. Alternatively, it could be trained over a mature boxwood. It is very cold hardy, but it is not suited to subtropical zones or hot, dry conditions.

The other gold-leaved clematis is 'Celebration'. It is a form of the 'Jackmanii Alba', which features 15-centimetre-long (6 in.) double white flowers. Introduced in 2010, 'Celebration' has stems and yellow leaves edged in red, but the slightly bluish-white colouring of the flowers does not sit well with the yellow leaves. **GR**

Alternative

Clematis 'Celebration'

Clematis

'Betty Corning'

Main feature Lavender-blue, bell-shaped flowers in
summer and autumn
Height 1.8–2.4 m (6–8 ft)
Position ○ ◐   **Hardiness** RHS H7

Found in 1932 by Elizabeth Corning, 'Betty Corning' is
one of the finest clematis hybrids. One of its parents is
the American native *C. crispa*, which grows across much
of the southeastern United States and is known by the
common name of swamp leather flower. It has pitcher-
shaped flowers in shades of lavender and purple. The
other parent is *C. viticella* from southern Europe, where
it grows on banks and old walls. Its nodding, bell-shaped
flowers in blue or purplish shades are held on long stems
away from the foliage.

Each flower of 'Betty Corning' is like a lavender-
blue bell split into four reflexed lobes, with a paler
stripe through the middle on the inside of each lobe.
The flowers are held away from the foliage and have a
sweet, sharp fragrance (though some people cannot
detect the scent). Grow it as a specimen on a steel
pyramid or on a wall in bright light, and prune back to
15 to 30 centimetres (6–12 in.) each spring. It is sometimes
wrongly listed under *C. viticella*. **GR**

Alternatives

Clematis 'Emilia Plater', *Clematis* 'Little Bas'

Clematis

C. texensis 'Princess Diana'

Main feature Luminous, pink-flared flowers from
midsummer and well into autumn
Height 1.8 m (6 ft)
Position ○ ◐   **Hardiness** RHS H5

A very pretty American native vine, *C. texensis* grows wild in
a small area of south central Texas. The partially nodding,
pitcher-shaped flowers are especially appreciated for
their colouring, which in the most desirable forms is
a vivid scarlet. In many gardens this species behaves
as a more or less herbaceous perennial, tending to die
back to the ground in winter, but considering its native
range it is surprisingly hardy. Since its arrival in Europe
in 1880, *C. texensis* has been used by a number of plant
breeders to combine its red colouring with the larger
flowers of many hybrids. 'Princess Diana' was raised by
UK breeder Barry Fretwell, who used 'Bees Jubilee' with
mauve flowers and a pink stripe, as the other parent.
Sometimes listed as 'The Princess of Wales', it has flowers
in an elongated bell shape and is shimmering pink in
colour, with a deeper-pink central stripe. It pays to cut
the plant back hard in spring and allow it to grow into
a mature flowering climber, although in cold regions it
may die down to the ground naturally. **GR**

Alternatives

Clematis 'Duchess of Albany', *Clematis* 'Ladybird Johnson'

Clematis **'Princess Diana'** in full bloom during the summer. ➜

Clematis
C. armandii 'Apple Blossom'

Main features Spring blossom; year-round foliage; highly scented flowers; fast growing

Height 8 m (26 ft)

Position ○ ◑   **Hardiness** RHS H4

Native to China, *C. armandii* was introduced to the West by well-known plant hunter Ernest Wilson in 1900. It was named in honour of the Jesuit priest Père Armand David, who discovered the giant panda in China in the 1860s. Evergreen *C. armandii* has beautifully polished, long, dark-green leaves; wonderful, fragrant, white flowers; and a strong growing habit that lets it romp away and fill almost any available space. 'Apple Blossom' is a form with particularly choice flowers. Each bloom is 5 to 8 centimetres (2–3 in.) in diameter, and flowers are produced prolifically in large clusters. The buds emerge deep pink and turn to white, with just a hint of pink as they develop.

This climber is fast growing – up to 1.8 metres (6 ft) in a year – and is best positioned where it can be allowed to grow unfettered: over a shed roof, along a fence, or up a suitably strong tree. Plant where the spring scent can be enjoyed, but keep in mind that the old leathery leaves can linger, and when they do fall, they are slow to decompose. However, if you have the right spot for 'Apple Blossom' it is a gorgeous plant for an early spring garden, and its magnificent vanilla fragrance will not go unnoticed.

There are some caveats, however. It flowers early in the year on shoots that were produced the previous summer. Left unpruned it may ultimately achieve 8 metres (26 ft), so some maintenance will be necessary. Prune back the plant to a framework of a trellis or netting immediately after flowering. This will mean taking off the new with the old, so flowering might be disrupted for the following year. Rest assured, the plant will make a comeback. Although 'Apple Blossom' is frost hardy, it has a reputation for being a little tender. For success, it is best if its roots can be in a warm, sheltered spot. **JWo**

Alternatives

Clematis armandii 'Enham Star', *Clematis armandii* 'Little White Charm', *Clematis armandii* 'Snowdrift'

Clematis

Crystal Fountain

Main features Short clematis; bred for patio containers; flowers during the summer
Height 1.5 m (5 ft)
Position ○ ◑ **Hardiness** RHS H7

The development of clematis varieties for the patio has meant that growing this plant is now within reach of more gardeners, and clematis fans can fit even more of these neat climbers into their gardens. The breeding of patio varieties started in 1992, when Guernsey-based Raymond Evison, in association with the Danish rose-breeding company, Poulsen, set up a programme to develop a range of compact clematis that would flower up and down the stems instead of just at the ends. As a result, varieties now exist that are not only short and easy to manage at around 1.5 metres (5 ft) tall, but they can flower for several months at a time. Thus, the clematis can be placed on the patio alongside summer bedding and modern repeat-flowering roses. They are also pretty additions to flower beds and borders.

The Crystal Fountain variety has double flowers that form on new growth each year, so it is a true double, with no single flowers. Annual pruning is simple: in late winter to early spring, cut down all the stems so that they are 15 to 25 centimetres (6–10 in.) from the base. A lot of patio clematis cultivars are now available, but Crystal Fountain is eye-catching, reliable, and widely accessible; therefore, it is a good starting point for those wishing to train a clematis in a pot or up an obelisk in a bed.

Some of the new patio clematis varieties are only 60 to 90 centimetres (24–36 in.) high, so they can just about grow into mounds. A patio clematis can be left in a container permanently if it has been planted in good compost and has plenty of drainage. Simply replace the top few centimetres of compost each spring with a fresh layer. You can add low-growing summer bedding to finish the container display and then refresh it with new spring bedding in the autumn – as this is a deciduous clematis, there will not be any activity through the winter. **LD**

Alternatives

='Evipo038'. *Clematis* Josephine ='Evijohill', *Clematis* Diamantina ='Evipo039', *Clematis* Arctic Queen ='Evitwo'

Clematis
'Tie Dye'

Main feature Eye-catching bicoloured summer flowers
Height 4 m (13 ft)
Position ○ ◑
Hardiness RHS H7

'Tie Dye' is a comparatively new cultivar that has attracted attention due to the eye-catching markings on its blooms. A late, large-flowered type, it has been bred from the familiar 'Jackmanii', which has long been recognised as one of the most reliable of the large-flowered clematis varieties, and it was possibly the first – raised by father and son William and George Jackman at their nursery in the United Kingdom in 1859. 'Tie Dye' was discovered in Walworth, New York, in 2001 and has been available since 2008.

This is a vigorous cultivar that flowers prolifically from midsummer to early autumn. The four tepals, which are about 5 to 10 centimetres (2–4 in.) wide, are violet blue. Fine, white stripes that coat the tepals irregularly, from the base to the tip, give the plant its distinct 'batik' appearance. The irregularity of the stripes makes the blooms look as if they have been individually hand painted. 'Tie Dye' has the same growth habits, time of bloom and prolific bloom of its parent, 'Jackmanii'. The main difference is the white marbling, and as an additional bonus it has proved to be less susceptible to the powdery mildew that can affect 'Jackmanii'.

The strength of the plant enables it to comfortably climb along a fence or up a long pergola. In good soil it can reach 4 metres (13 ft) high, but it will need to be hard pruned. This is easily done: in spring each year, simply chop through all the stems to about 30 centimetres (12 in.) off the ground. This will produce a mass of perfect summer flowers. There are other late, large-flowered *Clematis* varieties related to 'Jackmanii', although flowers of the dark, violet-purple colour tend not to show up as well as they do in 'Tie Dye'. However, they look effective with pink repeat-flowering roses, yellow perennial flowers or foliage of the golden hop. **JWo**

Alternatives

Clematis 'Jackmanii', *Clematis* 'Jackmanii Alba', *Clematis* 'Jackmanii Rubra', *Clematis* 'Jackmanii Superba'

Clematis
'Bill MacKenzie'

Main features Bright-yellow flower; attractive
seed heads
Height 5–6 m (16–20 ft)
Position ○ ◐ **Hardiness** RHS H7

This is a late-flowering clematis with open, bell-shaped, single, yellow flowers. An added attraction – a result of the long flowering season, which lasts from late spring to late summer – is the combination of flowers and fluffy seed heads together. 'Bill MacKenzie' is a hybrid of *C. tangutica* and *C. orientalis* from China, two closely related species with yellow flowers. Plant breeders have had to look east as a starting point, because all yellow clematis originate there (as did, of course, all yellow roses). Unfortunately, seedlings of these crosses are variable, so finding a true strain is tricky. The best advice is to buy from a clematis specialist or buy plants in flower, looking for blooms that are at least 6 centimetres (2.5 in.) across, with four yellow sepals that feel thick (the common name orange-peel clematis indicates the texture) and have purple filaments.

Soon after the first wave of blossoms, seed heads begin to form, and the later crop of flowers is wonderfully set off by the shimmering seed heads, which gave rise to the other common name, old man's beard. This clematis is a vigorous grower, with almost no limit if left unchecked, but it also flowers happily if reduced. There is a compact yellow-flowered clematis with *C. tangutica* parentage called *C.* Aztek that reaches 1.5 metres (5 ft) in height. Allow it to freely grow up into a tree or cover a fence or wall at the back of border; it looks fantastic with blue, late-flowering perennials or other primary colours, such as yellow or red.

Cut back hard when the flowers have gone, in winter or early spring. 'Bill MacKenzie' needs to be pruned, and to do this, simply chop down to 30 centimetres (12 in.) above the ground. This clematis is named for William MacKenzie, a long-serving curator of the Chelsea Physic Garden in London. **JWo**

Alternatives

Syn. *Clematis orientalis* 'Bill MacKenzie'. *Clematis* Aztek = 'Daihelios'

Clematis
'Étoile Violette'

Main feature An abundance of summer flowers
Height 3–4.5 m (10–15 ft)
Position ○ ◐
Hardiness RHS H6

One of the easy-to-grow clematis, this plant suffers little from mildew or clematis wilt, and its care is straightforward: it is pruned hard once a year when to within 30 centimetres (12 in.) of the ground. This simplicity delights inexperienced clematis growers, while the abundant delicate flowers of 'Étoile Violette' please all. Its parent, the native *C. viticella* species from southern Europe and western Asia, is a vigorous, deciduous, scrambling vine that makes its way along with twining leaf stalks. This parentage makes 'Étoile Violette' perfect for growing through shrubs, and its velvety, purple flowers easily thread their way over and through vegetation. It is often grown entwined with roses, but is equally good up and over arches or pergolas. 'Étoile Violette' makes elegant ground cover, too, and is a good choice for a smaller garden. As the flowers appear along the growing stem, it has the bonus of a long flowering time, from midsummer to midautumn.

C. viticella is characterised by its bell-shaped or saucer-shaped flowers and sits in the group three category of plants that flower later in the year on new growth. It can be cut back each spring, which is ideal because the habit tends to be untidy as the plant matures. Its pedigree is long and impeccable. Bred by Francisque Morel in France in 1885, 'Étoile Violette' has stood the test of time, and in 1993 received the Award of Garden Merit from the British Royal Horticultural Society as a mark of its quality. **JWo**

Alternative

Syn. *Clematis viticella* 'Étiole Violette', *Clematis* 'Venosa Violacea'

Clianthus
C. puniceus

Main feature Flamboyant, exotic-looking flowers in bright red
Height 1.8–5 m (6–16 ft)
Position ○ ◑ **Hardiness** RHS H5

There are two flamboyant species in the genus *Clianthus*, one of which is very difficult to grow successfully and this one – *C. puniceus* – which is easy. Growing wild in the North Island of New Zealand, this species – known as lobster claw or parrot's bill – has become increasingly rare and is now known to grow wild on only one island off the northwest coast. It is a rather floppy, evergreen shrub, with widely diverging branches, that is ideally suited to training on walls. The dark-green leaves – up to 15 centimetres (6 in.) long – are divided into pairs of leaflets, like those of roses, each with up to twenty-five oblong segments.

The distinctive 8-centimetre-long (3 in.) flowers – their striking exotic shape gives the plant its common names – hang from the branches in clusters of up to fifteen; each flower is a bright, vivid red. There are also other named forms offering versions in white or pink. In mild areas flowers appear in early spring, and in cooler areas they open in early summer.

In warm areas lobster claw can be grown on a wall or as a freestanding plant, when its growth may need restricting. In cooler regions it is best grown with the protection of a sunny wall, whereas in cold areas it is best planted in a container that can be moved into shelter in winter. However, if cultivated outside and damaged by frost, it will often regrow from the base. In temperatures of 29°C (85°F) it is better in partial shade; in cooler areas full sun and a well-drained soil is preferred. **GR**

Alternative

Syn. *Clianthus puniceus* 'Red Admiral'. *Clianthus puniceus* 'White Heron', *Clianthus puniceus* 'Red Cardinal'

Cobaea
C. scandens

Main features Flowers in summer and autumn; year-round foliage; fragrant flowers
Height 6 m (20 ft)
Position ○ ◑ **Hardiness** RHS H2

The evergreen climber *C. scandens* is known by various common names, such as cup-and-saucer plant, cathedral bell, monastery bells and Mexican ivy. It has large, showy, 5-centimetre-long (2 in.) flowers that hang like bells. The scented flowers open as a cream-green colour with a musky smell and then mature to purple, developing a sweeter scent. In their native Mexico the flowers are pollinated by bats. Flowers are produced through summer into autumn, but in cooler regions, sow the seed early to guarantee flowers before the end of the growing season. Keen gardeners often collect their own seeds to sow fresh. The great plantsman Christopher Lloyd recommended picking a seed pod with a length of stalk before the first frost and ripening it in a glass of water on a windowsill.

The flowers are held on long stalks clear of the foliage, which comprises leaves that split into four leaflets and a tendril. Large egg-shaped seed pods are filled with rows of large seeds that are easy to handle and sow, and generally germinate well. Once germinated, the seedling grows rapidly, grasping at nearby plants with its tendrils as it climbs. The robust, vigorous character of this climber makes it appealing.

In temperate climates, with winter frost, *C. scandens* is treated as an annual and sown indoors for planting outside once the frost has gone. It is a perennial in frost-free climates, and when established it can grow up to 20 metres (70 ft) high. It is more commonly grown as an annual to 6 metres (20 ft). To control the size of a conservatory-grown plant, cut it back hard in late autumn after flowering. For permanent planting, grow it on a sturdy pergola, and for annual use, try growing it through a large hedge. There is a green-tinged, white variety, but it is not as effective as the stronger, more exotic-looking purple-flowered plant. **PWi**

Alternatives

Cobaea scandens f. *alba*, *Cobaea paneroi*, *Cobaea pringlei*

Codonopsis
C. grey-wilsonii

Main feature Blue, saucer-shaped flowers on
twining stems
Height 1.2–1.8 m (4–6 ft)
Position ◑ **Hardiness** RHS H5

The forty-two species of *Codonopsis* are closely related
to the bellflowers (*Campanula*) that spread across much
of Asia, and almost all *Codonopsis* grow wild in China.
They are all herbaceous perennials that grow from fat,
carrot-like roots, which are a feature of Korean cuisine.
The stems of *Codonopsis* carry alternating leaves and vary
from weak and floppy to upright; some have climbing
stems that twine around the stems of their host.

The flowers each have five pointed lobes and open
on individual stalks at the shoot tips or opposite the
leaves. They come in purple, blue, white, green, brown or
yellow and some are patterned in the throat. They can be
usefully divided into two groups: in one, the unscented,
purple, blue or white flowers are flared into a saucer
shape; in the other, the more tubular or bell-shaped,
green, yellow or brown flowers have a musty smell.

For many years there has been uncertainty and
disagreement about the classification of this plant,
although recent investigation has clarified the situation.
It turned out that the plant grown for decades as
C. convolvulacea was, in fact, a new species, which was
named *C. grey-wilsonii* after Christopher Grey-Wilson, the
expert on the Himalayan flora.

This easy-to-grow climber is more robust than its
extremely slender twining stems might indicate. Its pale,
2.5- to 5-centimetre-long (1–2 in.) leaves are oval or
lance shaped with a heart-shaped base, and the saucer-
shaped flowers come in shades of blue. They open in
summer and early autumn and each features a purple or
deep-red ring around the centre. 'Himal Snow' is a white-
flowered form. Preferring ericaceous (lime-free) soil, this
is an ideal, well-behaved twiner to allow to scramble
through azaleas and other acid-loving shrubs. Be aware
that slugs may damage the new growth. **GR**

Alternatives

Codonopsis forrestii, Codonopsis rotundifolia

Dactylicapnos
D. scandens

Main feature Long season of yellow lockets on long self-clinging, climbing stems
Height 4 m (13 ft)
Position ○ ◑   **Hardiness** RHS H7

There are relatively few hardy perennial vines, and two of the best were once classified with the North American and Asian native bleeding hearts in the genus *Dicentra*. Now, however, they have been recognised as sufficiently different to be split off into a genus of their own – *Dactylicapnos*. There are ten species in all, but only two are found in gardens, and both have fleshy, frost-tender top growth and yellow flowers. *D. scandens* produces yellow lockets that are followed by fleshy, purple seed capsules. Its large, repeatedly divided leaves are up to 35 centimetres (14 in.) long, and the leaf stalks twist to cling onto supports in the same way as clematis. From late spring until autumn, clusters of up to thirty 2.5-centimetre-long (1 in.), yellow, heart-shaped flowers appear on the opposite side of the stem to a leaf; some develop reddish tints. This plant appreciates mild winters and cool, moist summers. It is best grown through mature shrubs and on stout fences; shelter from frost will extend flowering. **GR**

Alternatives

Syn. *Dicentra scandens*. *Dactylicapnos macrocapnos*,
Dactylicapnos scandens 'Athens Yellow'

Decumaria
D. barbara

Main feature Fragrant, white, summer flowers on a self-clinging vine
Height 6–9 m (20–30 ft)
Position ○ ◑ ●   **Hardiness** RHS H5

Many gardeners are surprised that there are types of hydrangeas that climb trees, but, in fact, there are four different plants in the hydrangea family that climb. These include the North American native vine *Decumaria barbara*, also known by the name of wood-vamp.

There are two species of *Decumaria*. The evergreen *D. sinensis* from China, and *D. barbara*, which is native to Long Island, New York, and the southeastern United States, as far south as Florida. Evergreen in milder areas, deciduous in colder zones, reddish stems carry 8- to 13-centimetre-long (3–5 in.) dark-green, oval, oppositely arranged leaves that turn yellow in autumn. In late spring and summer, small, fluffy, fragrant, white flowers are carried in rounded heads 5 to 8 centimetres (2–3 in.) across. Plant in moist soil at the base of deciduous trees and guide the stems to the trunk, where they will soon secure themselves. Young plants need guidance before clinging effectively. **GR**

Alternatives

Hydrangea anomala subsp. *petiolaris*, *Schizophragma hydrangeoides*

× Fatshedera
× *F. lizei* 'Annemieke'

Main feature Bold, evergreen leaves, brightly splashed in yellow
Height 1.2–1.8 m (4–6 ft)
Position ◐ ● **Hardiness** RHS H3–H4

In 1910 a French nurseryman put pollen of *Hedera hibernica*, a common ivy of western England, onto the flower of a compact form of the evergreen shrub *Fatsia japonica* called Moseri. They are closely related botanically, and the result was a plant that became known as × *Fatshedera lizei*. This is a handsome, vigorous, evergreen shrub that is not usually self-supporting and so needs tying onto a trellis or a fence. Its stout stems carry 10- to 25-centimetre-long (4–10 in.) dark-green, leathery leaves split into five pointed divisions; the young growth has a dusting of rusty hairs. In mid- and late autumn it produces 20- to 25-centimetre-long (8–10 in.) sprays of small greenish-white flowers. 'Annemieke' is a form that has a yellow splash at the centre of each leaf. This is a fine plant for shady corners and dark fences and walls and is especially useful in urban or city gardens. It is not suitable for the coldest areas, but in an average cold winter (-10–-5°C/14–23°F), it often regrows from ground level after all the top growth has been frosted. **GR**

Alternative

× *F. lizei* 'Variegata'

Fremontodendron
'California Glory'

Main feature Prolific display of large, bright-yellow flowers
Height 2.4–6 m (8–20 ft)
Position ○ **Hardiness** RHS H4

Two species of colourful, evergreen shrubs or small trees, which have become popular in milder gardens, grow naturally on the hot, dry slopes of the California chaparral. Individual plants of these two *Fremontodendron* species, also known as flannel bush, vary in the way they grow; some are noticeably upright (*F. mexicanum*), whereas others are more spreading, with the branches laying flat on the ground in some cases (*F. californicum*). 'California Glory' is a hybrid between these two species and was created at the Rancho Santa Ana Botanic Garden in Orange County, California, in 1952. It has shallow, cup-shaped, lemon-yellow flowers up to 6 centimetres (2.5 in.) across, which become red on the backs as they mature. It is unusually vigorous and flowers prolifically over a long period. This is the flannel bush usually seen in gardens. Rancho Santa Ana Botanic Garden used 'California Glory' and a low-growing form of *F. californicum* to create 'Pacific Sunset,' which has brighter lemon-yellow flowers and more spreading growth. **GR**

Alternative

Fremontodendron 'Pacific Sunset'

Garrya
G. *elliptica* 'James Roof'

Main features Catkins in winter; year-round foliage
Height 5 m (16 ft)
Position ◐ ●
Hardiness RHS H4

The *G. elliptica* is a wall shrub or free-standing evergreen and something of an unsung hero in the garden. There is nothing sensational about it in terms of colour – the simple leaves are grey-green, tough and leathery – but in an understated way this is a star performer. The surprise element is that *G. elliptica* makes its maximum impact in winter, when everything else in the garden is at a low ebb, by producing cascades of magnificent dangling catkins. It has been described rather nicely as a 'subdued shrub in summer and autumn but luxuriously flamboyant in winter and early spring'. *Garrya* is dioecious, having separate male and female plants, and although both forms produce catkins, it is the male *G. elliptica* 'James

Roof' that is generally acknowledged as the best cultivar. It has exceptionally long tassels – 20 centimetres (8 in.) or more – of petalless flowers boasting a more silvery hue than the species. As the overall summer effect can be dark, it is often beneficial to have lighter-colour-leaved companions, such as the bushy evergreen *Euonymous fortunei* 'Silver Queen', or a variegated *Pittosporum,* such as *P. eugenioides* 'Variegatum', planted nearby.

Garrya is a woodland scrub, native to the western coast of the United States and to Central America, and it is often used as a windbreak. Useful for a shady aspect, where it can be trained up a wall, or where soil is thin and free draining, this plant is long-lived but not particularly vigorous. Wait until the tassels have started to fade before pruning it to the shape and size wanted. **JWo**

Alternatives

Garrya elliptica 'Evie', *Garrya* × *issaquahensis* 'Glasnevin Wine'

Gelsemium
G. sempervirens 'Margarita'

Main features Fragrant, twining climber; prolific yellow, funnel-shaped flowers
Height 3–6 m (10–20 ft)
Position ○ ◑   **Hardiness** RHS H5

Yellow jessamine, or *G. sempervirens*, is the state flower of South Carolina. It is an evergreen twiner that is native to Virginia, south to Florida and west to Texas. It is found mainly in clearings at a forest's edge and climbs into shrubs, spreads over walls and fences and may grow into small trees. It is a familiar plant in warmer climates and signals spring across much of the southern United States. Farther north, it is sometimes grown in a container and moved inside for the winter or grown in a conservatory.

'Margarita' has significantly larger flowers with a light fragrance. It was introduced by Don Jacobs of Eco Gardens in Georgia. It is also noticeably hardier than the species *G. sempervirens* and will often survive winters in colder areas. The stems twine anticlockwise and carry oppositely arranged, oval- or lance-shaped, glossy, green leaves between 5 and 10 centimetres (2–4 in.) long. The flowers develop in clusters of up to three along the branches; each yellow, funnel-shaped flower is flared into five lobes and is about 2.5 centimetres (1 in.) wide and 4 centimetres (1.5 in.) long.

Yellow jessamine flowers in early or late spring, depending on the climate; sometimes with additional flowers in the autumn. The flowers vary from pale yellow to deep yellow in colour, usually with orange throats. They are strongly scented and draw a wide range of pollinators to their nectar. Flower buds emerge from the leaf axils of the previous season's growth, and a happy vine can have thousands of flowers. **GR**

Alternatives

Jasminum officinale, Jasminum azoricum

Gloriosa
G. *superba* 'Rothschildiana'

Main feature Eye-catching flowers in summer and into the autumn

Height 1.8–2.4 m (6–8 ft)

Position ○ **Hardiness** RHS H1c

Also known as the glory lily, this plant lives up to its name, and its vibrant colours and exotic shape immediately indicate its tropical origins. It is the national flower of Zimbabwe, native in tropical and southern Africa and Asia, and now naturalised in Australia and the Pacific. In addition it is widely cultivated in greenhouses around the world. *G. superba* 'Rothschildiana' is named after Lionel Walter, the 2nd Baron Rothschild of the UK banking family and a keen zoologist, who brought the plant back from Africa in the early twentieth century. He was not to know at the time, but he may have saved the plant, because it is near to extinction in the wild in parts of Africa and the Indian subcontinent where it is harvested for Ayurvedic medicine. For this reason the Royal Botanic Gardens at Kew in London is monitoring *G. superba* as part of the Red List of endangered plants. Meanwhile, in Australia, it has naturalised so well that it is listed to be suppressed as a weed.

A tuberous perennial member of the *Liliaceae* family, 'Rothschildiana' needs a high rainfall for growth in spring and a dry season to die down. The white tubers are oddly finger-shaped and grow fast in spring to produce thin, glossy, bright-green leaves, which end in distinctive tendrils used by the plant to attach itself to the support: a host in the wild or a climbing frame in a conservatory. The showy flowers appear in summer through to the autumn. Opening bright red with contrasting yellow bases and margins, the petals have a gently ruffled texture and curve around a cluster of protruding stamen. In tropical-themed gardens 'Rothschildiana' is particularly effective when scrambling through surrounding plants and up trees. In conservatories it needs support for the tendrils to cling to. It is poisonous if ingested, and contact with the stem and leaf can cause skin irritation. **JWo**

Alternative

Syn. *Gloriosa rothschildiana. Gloriosa superba* 'Lutea', syn. *Gloriosa lutea*

Hardenbergia
H. violacea

Main feature Vigorous twiner with pendulous spikes of purple flowers
Height 2.4–6 m (8–20 ft)
Position ○ ◑ ●   **Hardiness** RHS H3

Some of the best known of all climbers belong to the pea family – think sweet peas, wisterias and pole beans. Many are adapted to cold climates and so do well in very cold gardens, but there are also climbing peas for tropical climates and these include the glorious jade vine, the notoriously invasive kudzu vine and the lablab bean. The purple coral pea is one of a group of three evergreen Australian species of twining climbers, although they are sometimes seen trailing and tumbling rather than climbing. The alternately arranged, oval leaves are usually divided into three, or sometimes five, parts, but the outer divisions are sometimes so small as to hardly be noticeable. Small, purple, pea-like flowers are carried in dangling spikes in spring and summer.

In the eastern half of Australia – from Queensland, south to Tasmania, where it is endangered – from the coast to mountains, the purple coral pea, *H. violacea*, scrambles through forest shrubs. From a long carrot-like root, vigorous twining stems carry dark-green, leathery, lance-shaped leaves up to 13 centimetres (5 in.) in length on which the outer divisions have been reduced to nothing. The small, 1.2-centimetre-wide (0.5 in.), purple flowers each have two green or yellow spots and hang in spikes 10 to 13 centimetres (4–5 in.) long, which develop at the leaf joints from late winter into summer. Plants are best pruned after flowering to encourage more blooms.

The purple coral pea is a very useful plant for drier tropical zones, because it is drought tolerant once established. It will cling to fences or trellis, and it can be guided into a stout host plant or be planted to trail over retaining walls. In colder areas it is grown large in conservatories or in hanging baskets. *H. violacea* 'Happy Wanderer' is a particularly vigorous form, and there are also other varieties with white and pink flowers. **GR**

Alternatives

Hardenbergia violacea f. *alba* 'Happy Wanderer',
Hardenbergia violacea f. *rosea*

Hedera
H. colchica 'Sulphur Heart'

Main features Year-round, good cut foliage; architectural plant
Height 4.5 m (15 ft)
Position ○ ◑ ● **Hardiness** RHS H5

This plant is worth seeking out for the colouring on its large leaves. The edge of the leaf is dark green, and the centre a light lime green; between them is often an area of intermediate colour. These coloured zones follow the lines of the leaf veins, giving a distinctive look. As with all *Hedera*, once the plant reaches a certain height, it produces adult foliage and starts to flower. The adult foliage is a different shape from the juvenile: less lobed and usually narrower. The leaves on some *H. colchica* varieties tend to roll in at the edges, which makes it look as if it is wilting, but 'Sulphur Heart' suffers less from this. Ivies are self-clinging, so no wires are needed on walls or fences. *H. colchica* is less inclined to 'stick' to a wall than most *Hedera* species, but after a while it will get a grip and start to climb. In addition to being a handsome wall plant, 'Sulphur Heart' makes very good ground cover. The large leaves do a good job of smothering weeds, and its colour lifts the gloom often found under trees. **PWi**

Alternative

Syn. *Hedera colchica* 'Paddy's Pride', *Hedera colchica*

Hedera
H. helix 'Buttercup'

Main features Year-round, good cut foliage; attracts wildlife
Height 1.8–3 m (6–10 ft)
Position ○ ◑ **Hardiness** RHS H5

An evergreen climber that clings tightly against a wall, fence or tree, 'Buttercup' is one of the more popular of around 300 selections of *H. helix*. The bright-yellow, bluntly lobed leaves colour best in full sun. Too much shade will cause the leaves to become green. The mature foliage at the very top of an ivy plant is a different leaf shape from that lower down. It is narrower and less lobed and will bear flowers. Several insects, including wasps, feed on these flowers, and birds will feed on the subsequent berries and then nest amongst the foliage. Most varieties of *Hedera* are robust and reliable, and 'Buttercup' is no exception. Although it is tolerant of poor soil and dry conditions, you will get better results if you properly prepare the planting site by incorporating some organic matter and fertiliser. Large untidy ivies that have grown out from a wall can be given a hard shearing, much as you might cut back a hedge. You will be rewarded with a set of fresh new shoots and foliage. **PWi**

Alternative

Hedera helix 'Goldchild'

 *Hedera colchica* 'Sulphur Heart' provides colourful, year-round interest on a sturdy arch.

Hibbertia

H. scandens

Main features Long season of bright-yellow flowers; a twining vine or ground cover
Height 3–6 m (10–20 ft)
Position ○ ◑ **Hardiness** RHS H1c

Gardeners rarely consider using vines as ground cover plants, but at times vines can be very effective. Some, such as *H. scandens* – the snake vine – make a dense cover that also efficiently suppresses weeds.

The snake vine is one of about 150 evergreen trees, shrubs, and vines that grow naturally, mainly in Australia. Almost all *Hibbertia* species have similar yellow flowers, each with five, egg-shaped petals and a cluster of between four and 200 golden stamen in the centre. The foliage is variable in shape, and in some species the leaf stalks clasp twigs and branches for support.

Also known as the Golden Guinea Vine and the Climbing Guinea Flower, *H. scandens* grows wild in eastern Australia. It is found in a wide variety of habitats, from coastal areas to mountain valleys. Its reddish-brown stems carry elliptical or egg-shaped, dark, glossy, green leaves up to 10 centimetres (4 in.) long. The leaves are paler and softly hairy underneath, sometimes with a few teeth towards the tips.

The 5- to 8-centimetre-wide (2–3 in.), bright-yellow flowers open in late spring and summer and are wavy edged and slightly notched. Each flower remains open for one or two days, but the blooms open continually over a long period. Their smell is rather unpleasant but is not usually noticeable except at close range. This is a fine self-supporting vine and a ground cover develops into a tangled mass of growth. It grows very well in coastal areas, but may it smother smaller plants. **GR**

Alternative

Hibbertia aspera

Humulus

H. lupulus 'Aureus'

Main features Flowers summer to autumn; hanging,
yellowish-green, aromatic flowers
Height 4–7.5 m (15–25 ft)
Position ○ **Hardiness** RHS H6

Golden hop is an ornamental version of the same plant
used to produce hops for brewing beer. *H. lupulus* 'Aureus'
is a vigorous, herbaceous perennial spreading by
underground shoots and sending up twining stems as
high as 6 metres (20 ft) in a single season. The leaves are
15 centimetres (6 in.) and deeply lobed into between
three and five leaflets; they show their best colour when
grown in full sun. The narrow stems are rough with
downwards-facing bristles that help the plant grip
whatever host it is scrambling through. As the whole plant
is bristly, it is best to wear gloves when cutting stems.

Hop plants are either male or female, and it is the
female plants that produce the hanging, yellow-green
aromatic flowers that become hops. Male flowers are
small and not showy. Fortunately, you can now get sexed
plants, so you can be sure to get hops if you want them.

This is a good plant for a pergola or for training into
a small tree, as well as an ideal plant for those who are
never sure about pruning. Pruning 'Aureus' is simple –
the whole plant is cut to the ground during the winter,
and new shoots will sprout from the ground in spring.
If the old stems are left standing from year to year, an
unsightly tangle will build up. Grow this plant alongside
any of the *Clematis viticella* varieties that have a strong
purple flower. Not only does this flower colour go well
with the yellow foliage, but both climbers are cut back
during the winter, thereby making it an easy combination
to manage. **PWi**

Alternative

Humulus compactus 'Golden Tassels'

Hydrangea
H. anomala subsp. *petiolaris*

Main features Large flowers; fast-growing climber; good shade tolerance
Height 9–15 m (30–50 ft)
Position ○ ◑ ● **Hardiness** RHS H5

This hydrangea is valued as one of the few climbers that is happy to grow in shade and on a cool, shady wall. Wall, not fence, because this is a vigorous climber with thick stems that attach themselves by adventitious roots, which, after a while, will cause a fence to give way. It may damage a wall too, but it takes much longer, and meanwhile, there is much enjoyment to be had from the impressive, white, lacecap flower heads that appear in midsummer. The clusters of flowers are huge – up to 25 centimetres (10 in.) across – and as flat as plates. The tiny, white, fertile flowers sit in the centre of the flower head, surrounded by a ring of cream-coloured sterile ones. Flowers last almost to the autumn, or longer if they are cut and brought into the house for arrangements. Although *H. anomala* subsp. *petiolaris* is deciduous compared to the evergreen *H. serratifolia*, the flowers make up for this. After flowering, remove the spent flower heads and trim back wayward shoots to healthy buds. **JWo**

Alternatives

Hydrangea anomala subsp. *petiolaris* var. *ovalifolia*,
Hydrangea serratifolia

Ipomea
I. purpurea 'Grandpa Otts'

Main features Deep-purple flowers with a red central star; vigorous annual vine
Height 3–6 m (10–20 ft)
Position ○ **Hardiness** RHS H1c

Morning glory, sweet potato and bindweed are all members of the genus *Ipomoea*, but among the more than 500 species, it is the flowering vines that enjoy the most affection, especially those with the trumpet-shaped flowers. Some species of this type are perennials, but they are so tender and so vigorous that they are usually grown as annuals; others are true annuals. The easiest of these true annual types is *I. purpurea*. This fast-growing plant has slender, hairy or even bristly stems that twine anticlockwise around supports. They carry slightly rough, oval leaves, sometimes split into three lobes. In summer, clusters of up to seven large flowers – up to 6 centimetres (2.5 in.) across – open at the leaf joints. 'Grandpa Otts' is one of the original varieties of the Seed Savers Exchange (SSE) in 1975. Seeds of 'Grandpa Otts' was given to SSE founder Diana Whealy by her grandfather, Baptist John Ott, who had brought it from Bavaria in 1870 and grown it every year on his farm in Iowa. **GR**

Alternatives

Ipomoea purpurea 'Crimson Rambler', *Ipomoea purpurea* 'Kniola's Purple-black', *Ipomoea purpurea* 'Star of Yelta'

Ipomea
I. lobata

Main features Long, crowded spikes of red-and-yellow flowers; vigorous vine
Height 1.8–4.5 m (6–15 ft)
Position ○ **Hardiness** RHS H1a

This vigorous perennial vine, growing wild in Mexico and Central and South America, is almost always grown from seeds as an annual. It needs a sunny spot, but any well-drained, fertile soil that does not dry out will do. In one growing season it can make a mass of heavy growth, so it needs a stout support. The stems and flower stalks of *I. lobata* are richly tinted in red and carry alternately arranged, toothed, oval leaves with three bold but narrow lobes and a heart-shaped base. One-sided flower spikes are held away from the foliage and packed with up to thirty gently curved flowers, which are scarlet in bud. They turn orange, then yellow, and as the buds open they become cream; at this stage the stamen and styles extend well outside the petals. Soon after, the tube of petals falls away. The result is a mass of extremely colourful flower spikes, although almost all the colour comes from the flowers before they open. The cultivars 'Exotic Love' and 'Jungle Queen' are very similar to the wild species. **GR**

Alternatives

Ipomoea lobata 'Exotic Love', *Ipomoea lobata* 'Jungle Queen'

Jasminum
J. humile 'Revolutum'

Main features Bushy and compact; fragrant flowers in late spring to early summer
Height 2 m (7 ft)
Position ○ ◐ **Hardiness** RHS H4

This jasmine is often described as a 'semiscandent' shrub, meaning that it has partially climbing stems so can be grown as a climber or as a free-standing shrub. The main feature is the bright-yellow flowers that appear in clusters from late spring to early summer. This plant is also semi-evergreen, meaning that the leaves can be deciduous in a hard winter, but the stems are green. 'Revolutum' is a compact variety, so it is easy to find a place for it somewhere sheltered: sunny in a mild region or undercover in cooler climates. There is some fragrance, which is brought out best in warm conditions. Any moist, well-drained soil will do but the plant can be damaged during hard winters. The earliest form of *J. humile* to arrive in Europe came in the seventeenth century, and it was known in British gardens as the 'Italian yellow jasmine'. There are several forms of *J. humile*, including *J. wallichianum*, which has more leaflets but fewer, more pendulous flowers. All are worthy of cultivation. **MB**

Alternatives

Syn. *Jasminum reevesii, Jasminium humile wallichianum, Jasminium mesnyi, Jasminium floridum*

Jasminum
J. officinale

Main features Vigorous twining climber; deliciously
fragrant flowers from midsummer to autumn
Height 7.5 m (25 ft)
Position ○ ◑ **Hardiness** RHS H5

A strong-growing, deciduous, twining climber, with
leaves formed of five to nine leaflets, *J. officinale* is arrayed
with the most beautiful white flowers – from midsummer
to midautumn – whose sweet, sophisticated perfume
is at its most intense in warm sunshine. Found in the
wild from the Caucasus, northern Iran and Afghanistan
through the Himalayas to China, it is said to have been
introduced from the British Isles in 1548 and is a highlight
in gardens worldwide. In cooler climates *J. officinale* will
need some warmth and shelter – against a sunny wall, for
example – but in milder climates it flourishes in a more
open situation, providing the soil is moisture retentive.
Its natural vigour can be put to good use climbing over
a shed, porch, arbor, outbuilding or old tree stump;
alternatively, it can be trained up a wall with the support
of wires. An ideal spot is by a door or window or where the
air is still enough to capture the fragrance. Young plants
can be shy to flower, so keep pruning to a minimum. **MB**

Alternatives

Jasminum officinale f. *affine*, *Jasminum officinale*
'Argenteovariegatum', *Jasminum officinale* 'Clotted Cream'

Jasminum
J. nudiflorum

Main feature Weather-resistant flowers in winter, carried
on naked stems
Height 8 ft (2.4 m)
Position ○ ◑ ● **Hardiness** RHS H7

Winter jasmine is one of the most widely grown jasmines.
It is robust in regards to hardiness and aspect, but most
of all its flowers provide cheer at a dull time of year. There
are masses of yellow, waxy flowers, borne in pairs or
singly along its angular, arching, naked stems. Flowering
occurs on wood produced the previous summer, so the
show is particularly good after a hot summer. The plant's
natural inclination is to trail over the ground, not climb,
so the main shoots will need tying onto a trellis or wires.
J. nudiflorum was introduced into cultivation in 1844 by
Robert Fortune, who collected plants in China for the
Horticultural Society (now the Royal Horticultural Society).
It was not the first time it had been discovered: botanist
Dr John Lindley found it had already been distributed
as a pressed plant by the Imperial Russian Chinese
Herbarium. Good variegated versions include 'Aureum',
which has yellow markings or almost all-yellow foliage,
and 'Mystique' with leaves edged in cream white. **MB**

Alternatives

Jasminum nudiflorum 'Aureum', *Jasminum
nudiflorum* 'Mystique'

Jasminum nudiflorum is a tough plant whose winter flowers are always welcome. ➜

Lapageria
L. rosea

Main feature Beautiful, waxy, bell-like flowers from summer to autumn
Height 4.5 m (15 ft)
Position ◗   **Hardiness** RHS H3

The Chilean bell flower *L. rosea* is the national flower of Chile, and it was named for Josephine La Pagerie, wife of Napoléon Boneparte, 'who rendered great services to botany by the cultivation of exotic plants in the beautiful gardens of Malmaison near Paris and by the encouragement she gave to works on botany'. The first introduction to the Royal Botanic Gardens, Kew, in 1847 was by Richard Wheelwright, 'an American gentleman who has been instrumental in establishing steam navigation in the Pacific, and thus enjoyed the superior means for the transport to England'. It arrived in commerce in a less grandiose manner when plant hunter William Lobb sent plants to Veitch Nurseries in 1848. With

it was a coloured drawing of the plant in flower in its native habitat. When *L. rosea* flowered it was compared with the painting and described as 'unusually faithful'.

This plant is a twining, evergreen climber, with wiry stems and deep-green, leathery leaves. It has beautiful hanging, bell-shaped, waxy, red to pink flowers that are up to 10 centimetres (4 in.) long, with flecks in the flower tube. *L. rosea* is a plant of cool temperate forests; it needs a damp, partly shaded spot and high humidity in acidic, humus-rich, well-drained soil. Grow it outdoors in mild districts – coastal California, for example – or as a container plant in a large tub of ericaceous (lime-free) compost in a cool conservatory in colder regions. Cultivars include 'Myrtle Wolf's Pink', which is a soft blush pink, and there are whites, bicolours and reds too. **MB**

Alternative

Lapageria rosea var. *albiflora*

Lathyrus
L. *odoratus* Solway Series

Main features Short-growing vines; wide range of colours
Height 90–120 cm (3–4 ft)
Position ○ **Hardiness** RHS H2

Sweet peas are probably the world's favourite annual vines. They make tall, self-clinging plants that are perfect in the right place, but what if you enjoy the flowers and the fragrance, but need a smaller plant? As early as 1893 a tiny dwarf sweet pea, 'Cupid', appeared. It is still available and reaches only 15 centimetres (6 in.) in height. Since then, a succession of shorter sweet peas has been introduced; most are bushy in growth, and they produce more and larger flowers over a long period. But what if you are looking for neither a tall vine nor a dwarf and bushy type?

A sweet pea breeder from the northwest of England, J. Dickson Place, provided the answer. In the 1990s he developed the Solway Series of *L. odoratus*. Plants in this series climb and cling by tendrils in the same way as traditional sweet peas, but they only reach about 90 to 120 centimetres (3–4 ft) in height. There are now about a dozen different colours in the series, all with the 'Solway' prefix. They tend to have smaller foliage and a shorter length of stem between the leaves than conventional sweet peas, but they do come with fragrant flowers in a wide variety of colours and colour combinations. These include 'Solway Ballerina' (pictured) with flowers of the palest pink; 'Solway Blue Vein', which is white with blue markings; the magenta-and-mauve 'Solway Serenade' and 'Solway Sunset', which has white flowers with red markings. They are all ideal in patio containers, scrambling on short fences, and even tumbling over sunny retaining walls. **GR**

Alternative

Lathyrus odoratus 'Teresa Maureen'

Lathyrus
L. odoratus 'Erewhon'

Main features Vigorous vine; strongly scented, reverse bicoloured flowers
Height 1.8 m (6 ft)
Position ○ **Hardiness** RHS H2

A new species of *Lathyrus* was discovered in Turkey in 1987. *L. belinensis* has small flowers with yellow-orange upper petals (standards) – boldly veined in red – and yellow side petals (wings), and botanically, it is closely related to the familiar sweet pea, *L. odoratus*. With its yellow colouring, *L. belinensis* offered the possibility of introducing the elusive yellow flower colour into sweet peas, and New Zealand plant breeder Dr Keith Hammett set about crossing the two species. Obtaining seeds after pollination proved unexpectedly difficult, but by using laboratory techniques, he succeeded and spent many years developing the offspring.

What was surprising was that the yellow colour continued to prove elusive; however, it became possible to develop two other features. Previously, bicoloured sweet peas had always had standards that were darker than the wings, but by using *L. belinensis*, it became possible to create plants in which the wings were darker than the standards, and these varieties are known as reverse bicolours. The new species also made it easier to enhance the blue colouring. *L. odoratus* 'Erewhon' is a fine example of a blue reverse bicolour, which – many generations in its background – has blood from both traditional sweet peas and the new species. The standards are pink lavender and the wings are dark mauve. The name is derived from the novel *Erewhon* (1872) by British novelist Samuel Butler, which was set in a land where everything happens in reverse. The name is also partly based on a visit to New Zealand, where this variety was developed. The scent of 'Erewhon' is exceptionally strong, and the plant makes a fine cut flower, as well as a good garden vine. As with all sweet peas, keep the soil consistently moist and deadhead plants regularly to prolong the flower display. **GR**

Alternatives

Lathyrus odoratus 'Blue Shift', *Lathyrus odoratus* 'Porlock', *Lathyrus odoratus* 'Turquoise Lagoon'

Lathyrus
L. *odoratus* 'Matucana'

Main features Powerfully scented; maroon and
purple flowers
Height 1.8 m (6 ft)
Position ○   **Hardiness** RHS H2

There are a number of sweet peas grown in gardens
around the world that are supposed to be the original
wild sweet pea. Few of them actually are. The sweet pea
L. odoratus grows wild in Sicily and on the southern tip
of the Italian mainland. It reaches anything from
50 centimetres (20 in.) to 1.8 metres (6 ft) in height in the
wild, sprawling over scrubland in open places. Its winged
stems carry pairs of narrow leaves up to a little more than
8 centimetres (3 in.) in length, with two smaller leaf-like
appendages at the base. One or two fragrant flowers,
up to 4 centimetres (1.5 in.) in length, are carried at the
leaf joints on short stems. Each flower has maroon
standards (upright petals) and violet wings (side petals).

Seed of this wild sweet pea was sent to England in
1699 by Sicilian monk Francisco Cupani, and by 1724, seed
was being offered for sale. It soon began to provide
flowers in different colours: first a pink-and-white bicolour
that became known as 'Painted Lady', and then a pure-
white variety. The powerful fragrance, richness of colour,
and charm of growing the original wild sweet pea have
all encouraged the cultivation of plants that resemble it.

At times, plants with various cultivar names, such as
'Cupani', 'Cupani's Original', 'Original', 'Quito' and
'Matucana' have all been credited with being the
original wild sweet pea, but most are, in fact, throwbacks
from cultivated varieties or garden selections of plants
that originated in the wild. The majority of them have
larger flowers and up to four flowers per stem, which
indicates their garden origin. 'Matucana' is definitely
worth growing for its rich purple-magenta colour,
superb strong scent and prolific flowering. Plant it in a
rich but well-drained soil in full sun, or in a large
container. 'Matucana' was first collected in the place of
that name in central Peru. **GR**

Alternatives

Lathyrus odoratus 'Cupani's Original', *Lathyrus odoratus*
'Original', *Lathyrus odoratus* 'Cupani'

Lonicera

L. × tellmanniana

Main features Colourful flowers from late spring to midsummer; lush foliage
Height 3.6 m (12 ft)
Position ○ ◑   **Hardiness** RHS H5

Regarded by many as the most successful of all *Lonicera* hybrids, this spectacular plant combines the finest characteristics of one of the showiest Chinese species with one of the most beautiful of the American ones (*L. tragophylla* × *L. sempervirens*). Raised in the Royal Horticultural School in Budapest, Hungary, and introduced into cultivation by Spath, a German nursery, in 1927, it has long been enjoyed in gardens.

Although fragrance free, this bold, bright, deciduous climber boasts masses of brightly coloured, eye-catching blooms. The oval, green leaves, with white undersides, form saucers around clusters of six to twelve red-flushed buds, followed by golden-orange blooms up to

5 centimetres (2 in.) long. It is uplifting and invigorating in full flourish, enlivening a garden with its energy and exotic exuberance.

Although it is happy to grow in full sun, the flower colour is more intense in light shade; it is ideal for growing on trellis or wires against a house wall or spilling over a boundary. The roots like a cool shady position. It is ideal as a backcloth for bright colours – red, yellow and bronze – transporting the viewer to the tropics, yet despite its appearance, it is hardy in most regions. This hybrid is widely available, but you might find recently introduced named cultivars, such as orange-flowered 'Joan Sayers' or large, yellow flowers of 'Pharaoh's Trumpet' available from specialists. **MB**

Alternatives

Lonicera × *tellmanniana* 'Joan Sayers', *Lonicera* × *tellmanniana* 'Pharaoh's Trumpet'

Lonicera

L. tragophylla

Main features Eye-catching flowers from early to
midsummer; attractive foliage
Height 2.4 m (8 ft)
Position ○ ◑ ● **Hardiness** RHS H5

This, the largest-flowered and most flamboyant of all
climbing honeysuckles, is extremely ornamental and will
be sought after by those seeking summer flowers for a
shady spot. One fascinating feature is that the upper
leaves, just below the flower cluster, are fused at the base,
so the flower stem appears to grow through; the pair of
leaves below it just clasp the stem, and the pair below
that become short-stalked leaves. The foliage is bronze
when young. The bright, brilliant-yellow flowers are in
clusters of ten to twenty, each bloom up to 9 centimetres
(3.5 in.) long and the two lips at the end of each flower,
around 2.5 centimetres (1 in.) wide. They are at their peak
from early to midsummer and are followed by red berries.

This glorious climber was discovered in the Chinese
province of Hupeh by Dr Augustine Henry, who then
sent plant material to the Royal Botanic Gardens, Kew. It
was later introduced into cultivation by the plant
collector Ernest Henry Wilson in 1900, who found it to
be fairly common. Known in China as the 'great gold and
silver flower', it was regarded by Wilson as the most
showy of all the Chinese species. It flowered for the first
time in July 1904 at James Veitch's nursery in Coombe
Wood, Surrey.

This fast-growing climber is ideal for growing over a
trellis or pergola or scrambling into a tree. It dislikes
competition at the roots from other plants, so improve
the soil so that it holds moisture yet drains away. **MB**

Alternatives

Lonicera tragophylla 'Maurice Foster', *Lonicera
sempervirens*

Lonicera
L. periclymenum
'Graham Thomas'

Main features Beautiful, white to yellow, fragrant
flowers; mid-green foliage; attracts bees
Height 6.5 m (21 ft)
Position ○ ◑   **Hardiness** RHS H5

This vigorous twining, scrambling climber, renowned
for its beauty and fragrance, was a chance discovery in
a hedgerow in Warwickshire, United Kingdom, in 1960. It
was discovered by Graham Stuart Thomas, a garden plant
adviser to the National Trust, Britain's major conservation
charity for historic houses and gardens. The two-lipped
white flowers, carried at the shoot tips, gradually mature
to yellow with a hint of copper, giving the flowers a
bicoloured appearance, and are followed by glistening
red berries. The sweet fragrance of the flowers, which
attracts pollinating bees and other insects, has beguiled
many. At its finest in early morning and late evening, it
is the perfect deciduous climber for arbours, trellis and
doorways, where the luxuriant fragrance is carried on the
breeze. The plant has a good habit for growing through
hedges or over tree stumps too. This climber produces
flowers on the previous year's growth, so if you need
to prune this honeysuckle, do so after flowering. **MB**

Alternative

Lonicera periclymenum 'Belgica'

Lonicera
L. × brownii
'Dropmore Scarlet'

Main features Scarlet flowers from midsummer to
autumn; attracts bees
Height 3.6 m (12 ft)
Position ○ ◑   **Hardiness** RHS H7

The scarlet-trumpet honeysuckle is a vigorous climber
that is worth growing for two notable features. Firstly, the
mass of cheerful, bright-scarlet flowers with an orange
throat, from midsummer to autumn, which look glorious
against the blue-green foliage. Secondly, the upper
leaves that are fused at the base so the stems appear
to pass through the centre of a single, rounded, saucer-
shaped leaf. This delightful hybrid between *L. hirsuita* and
L. sempervirens was first recorded in 1854. 'Dropmore
Scarlet' was raised in Canada, but it did not become
popular until much later and was awarded a Gold Medal
during trials at Boskoop in 1964. Sadly, it is not a scented
honeysuckle but it is still worth growing as an ornamental
evergreen to semi-evergreen. Grow it over trellis or against
a wall to lend a rustic cottage-garden–style. Little pruning
is required, but since it flowers on the previous year's
growth, if you need to keep it tidy and within its allotted
space, prune immediately after flowering. **MB**

Alternative

Syn. *Lonicera sempervirens* 'Dropmore Scarlet'

Lophospermum
L. erubescens

Main feature Delicate but colourful flowers from summer to autumn
Height 4.5 m (15 ft)
Position ○ **Hardiness** RHS H2

Grow this dainty, half-hardy Mexican climber for its natural elegance and foxglove-like, magenta to rose-pink flowers. It climbs using twining flower stems and is ideal for lightweight frames, wire, twiggy sticks or slender bamboo canes. Blooming from early summer to midautumn, this plant is happy to trail from hanging baskets or troughs for an understated summer display. There are several excellent selections to choose from, including *L. erubescens* 'Bridal Bouquet' (pictured), with beautiful white trumpets; 'Red Dragon' in carmine red; and 'Magic Dragon' in shades of pink and red. As *L. erubescens* is not frost hardy, choose a growing technique to suit your climate. Sow annually in spring, harden off, and plant out in a sunny position once the danger of frost has gone; seed-raised plants flower freely in the first year, although the colour may be variable. In order to maintain good colour forms, take cuttings from nonflowering shoots in mid- to late summer. **MB**

Alternative

Syn. *Asarina erubescens*

Mandevilla
M. laxa

Main features Fragrant summer flowers; lush, evergreen leaves
Height 3.6 m (12 ft)
Position ○ ◐ **Hardiness** RHS H2

This is a glorious plant for a conservatory, greenhouse, border or garden, depending on your climate. In summer the twisted buds, which look like tightly rolled-up umbrellas, unfurl to reveal five-petalled white flowers. These have a vanilla fragrance, which is at its most potent in the evening. *M. laxa* is one of several *Mandevilla* species with a Royal Horticultural Society Award of Garden Merit, but it is the only one with a vanilla scent. In garden centres, you may come across the Rio Series and the Sundaville Series, the latter of which contains many different shades of red and pink. Despite the exotic appearance of *M. laxa*, it can tolerate winter temperatures down to 5°C (40°F) for short periods, providing the compost remains on the dry side; below this temperature the plant becomes deciduous and sheds its leaves. *M. laxa* is superb grown up a trellis or over obelisks because the supple stems twine easily up wires, tripods or canes. Stems should be trained horizontally for optimum flowering. **MB**

Alternatives

Mandevilla × *amabilis* 'Alice du Pont', *Mandevilla boliviensis*

Pandorea
P. jasminoides

Main features Clusters of flowers at the shoot tips; attractive evergreen foliage
Height 9 m (30 ft)
Position ○ ◐   **Hardiness** RHS H1c

The *P. jasminoides* vine is a vigorous, evergreen climber that is found from warm, temperate to tropical areas from eastern Queensland to northern New South Wales in Australia. Clusters of large, tubular, pale-pink or white flowers with magenta throats grow in small clusters at the shoot tips, backed by leaves of four to seven oval, glossy, green, lance-shaped leaflets. It is a very beautiful plant and recommended cultivars include 'Charisma' (pictured) with variegated foliage.

P. jasminoides is fast growing and ideal for training over a pergola, up walls through a large trellis, along chain-link fencing, or over outbuildings. For the best results, improve the soil, if necessary, with well-rotted organic matter, water well, and tie young growth into its support until the plants are established. Feed with general fertiliser in spring for the first two years to build up the framework. Although *P. jasminoides* is vigorous, it can be controlled easily by pruning or growing in containers. In its native Australia it is advised not to plant it near underground pipes.

In regions where summers are cool, it is advised to choose a warm, sheltered microclimate, where the plant will flower sporadically. Alternatively, grow it in a conservatory, where it will flower prolifically. Planted in a large container of loam-based compost, *P. jasminoides* can be trained to grow over a tripod or obelisk, thereby creating an outdoor display on the terrace or patio after the last frost of spring until the arrival of autumn. Feed with a high-potash fertiliser, such as a tomato fertiliser, to encourage flowering. Propagation of *P. jasminoides* is by layering the stems or by taking stem cuttings in late summer. Alternatively, you could sow fresh seeds in spring. It is best to avoid hard pruning, but if the plant needs to be kept within bounds, prune it in spring. **MB**

Alternatives

Pandorea jasminoides 'Alba', *Pandorea jasminoides* 'Rosea Superba', *Pandorea pandorana*

Passiflora
P. citrina

Main features Spectacular lemon-yellow flowers in summer; attractive leaves
Height 3 m (10 ft)
Position ○ ◑ **Hardiness** RHS H2

One of the few yellow-flowered passionflowers, *P. citrina* was discovered in 1989 by John McDougal, an American botanist noted for his work on the classification of passionflowers, who has discovered several new species. He found it at a high altitude in the humid hills of western Honduras and in eastern Guatemala in Central America, growing inside and on the margins of moist pinewoods, scrambling over shrubs or tall grasses. It is believed to be the only yellow-flowered, hummingbird-pollinated passionflower in the world; the small fruits become yellow when ripe.

The dainty, bright, citrus-yellow flowers appear from midspring to midsummer in temperate climates or even longer when grown under glass, where it flowers constantly apart from a small break from mid- to late-winter, when light levels are reduced. In addition to the bright-yellow flowers, it has attractively veined leaves, each shaped like a duck's foot. This is an ideal climber for growing up trellis or supported by a tripod of canes when growing in a pot. Grow it in full sun or partial shade outdoors or in a cool, frost-free conservatory. It needs moist but well-drained soil. Water daily during the growing period. Alternatively, use as a houseplant. This passionflower is also suitable for containers and can be propagated by seeds or cuttings.

The amber- to peach-flowered hybrid *P. citrina* 'Adularia', which has *P. citrina* as one of the parents was introduced in 1993. It is vigorous and free flowering when grown under glass, reaching up to 4 by 10 metres (13 x 33 ft), if allowed to grow to its full extent. Like *P. citrina* it makes an attractive plant for windowsills or hanging baskets with regular trimming. Both passionflowers are excellent conservatory plants in cooler climates, but they dislike temperatures below 2°C (35°F). **MB**

Alternatives

Passiflora 'Adularia', *Passiflora* 'Amethyst', *Passiflora* × *exoniensis*

Passiflora
P. caerulea
'Constance Eliott'

Main features Beautiful flowers from midsummer to
early autumn; orange fruits in some regions
Height 6 m (20 ft)
Position ○ ◑   **Hardiness** RHS H4

P. caerulea 'Constance Eliott' is an old, much-loved cultivar
with ivory-white blooms. It is a parent of the special
'White Wedding;' the other parent is *P. eichleriana*, a hot-
house passionflower with wonderful pure-white blooms.
'White Wedding' is the result of a collaboration between
two breeders: Dr Roland Fischer in Germany and Henk
Wouters, a Dutch grower who has cultivated more than
300 types of passionflower. This new cultivar has only
been available since 2004. 'White Wedding' is a vigorous
passionflower with large, lightly fragrant, white blooms
that are up to 10 centimetres (4 in.) in diameter, followed
by rounded orange fruits. It needs a free-draining soil
that is low in nutrients, in a sheltered spot in either sun
or partial shade. Its hardiness is still being evaluated, but
a minimum temperature of 5°C (23°F) is recommended. If
growing outside, a mulch in winter to protect the roots
is a wise precaution. **MB**

Alternatives

Passiflora caerulea 'White Wedding', *Passiflora caerulea*
'White Lightning'

Passiflora
P. × violacea

Main feature Exotic-looking flowers from summer to
autumn
Height 8 m (26 ft)
Position ○   **Hardiness** RHS H2

This is the oldest of all the passionflower hybrids and was
raised in London and introduced into cultivation in 1821. It
is a beautiful, sumptuously exotic plant with bowl-shaped,
deep reddish-purple flowers and filaments that are deep
violet with white tips. Flowers appear from summer to
autumn. There are several other forms in cultivation; one
with the filaments half deep purple and half white, and
sold as *P. × tresederi* or 'Lilac Lady'. Another has filaments
that are a quarter deep purple and the remainder, white –
the form most often found in Europe. 'Celia Costen', a
hybrid between *P. × violacea* and *P. caerulea* 'Constance
Eliott', is easy to grow and has leaves with narrow lobes,
with white flowers and mauve-and-purple filaments. They
flower under glass or outdoors from midsummer to early
autumn and need a minimum temperature of 0°C (32°F).
When growing outside they need a sunny, sheltered spot
in a low-fertility, free-draining soil. **MB**

Alternatives

Passiflora × violacea 'Tresederi' (syn. *Passiflora* 'Lilac Lady'),
Passiflora × violacea 'Victoria'

Passiflora × violacea is a passionflower that has stood the test of time. ➲

Passiflora

P. incarnata

Main features Beautiful architectural flowers from summer to autumn; deciduous
Height 6 m (20 ft)
Position ○ ◑ **Hardiness** RHS H5

One of the hardiest of all passionflowers, *P. incarnata* is reported to have survived temperatures down to -19°C (-2°F) at which point it dies back to ground level but often regrows vigorously the next growing season. The sweet-scented flowers, ranging from mauve to lilac, or white, sometimes on the same plant, appear from summer to autumn and are followed by egg-like fruit, which become lime green or yellow when ripe. The ripe fruits are edible (although the species grown specifically for passion fruit is *P. edulis*). The plant's dried foliage has been utilised in medicine to make a tincture that is used as a mild sedative and calmative. More recently, it has been used to treat Parkinson's disease.

In cooler climates the plant can be grown outdoors against a warm, sunny wall. It will thrive in dry, free-draining soil, but a mulch will help protect the roots over the winter. The alternative is keeping this plant in a cool conservatory, but you will need to hand-pollinate the flowers if you want to ensure a good crop of fruits. This species is native to the southeastern United States, where it is known as maypop and is often found growing on road and rail embankments. It makes a good wildlife plant, particularly for bees and butterflies. *P. incarnata* is the parent of several hardy hybrids most notably 'Incense', which has deep-purple flowers; the filaments have white and violet bands at the base and are white and crinkled toward the apex, creating a remarkable visual effect. **MB**

Alternatives

Passiflora × colvillii, *Passiflora incarnata* 'Incense'

Podranea

P. ricasoliana

Main features Masses of beautiful blooms; attractive leaves
Height 9 m (30 ft)
Position ○ **Hardiness** RHS H3

This popular plant is often seen in Mediterranean and tropical gardens although the species originally comes from South Africa. *P. ricasoliana* climbs rapidly on thin woody stems, the new growth having a graceful arching habit, but beware because it is vigorous. The main feature is the masses of loosely clustered, delicate, bell-like flowers that reach 8 centimetres (3 in.) in length. The exterior of the flower is lilac pink, whereas the interior is exquisitely marked with dark purple-pink lines and spots as if deftly decorated by an artist with a fine pen. After flowering, new branches develop behind the spent flowers, and the leaves, made up of small leaflets, are attractive too.

A climber suitable for growing over a sturdy trellis, pergola or wall, *P. ricasoliana* becomes deciduous in cold weather. It was a popular plant in Victorian conservatories and on the French Riviera, as well as in coastal cities in Italy, such as Sorrento. It is still grown there in large clay pots and its graceful branches are trained up the terra-cotta walls of hotels and restaurants. *P. ricasoliana* also makes useful ground cover for large banks, rooting where the stem tips touch the ground. If you want to propagate the plant, this can be done by layering, by sowing seeds in spring, or by taking semiripe or hardwood cuttings. In warmer countries and the tropics, it can be in flower for most of the year; in cooler regions it flowers from late summer to autumn. **MB**

Alternatives

Syn. *Pandorea ricasoliana, Tecoma ricasoliana*

Schisandra
S. rubriflora

Main features Deciduous, twining plant; attractive buds; flowers in spring, followed by fruits
Height 6 m (20 ft)
Position ○ ◑   **Hardiness** RHS H5

This twining, woody climber – suitable for growing on fences, walls or into trees – is one of two species of this genus that has a Royal Horticultural Society Award of Garden Merit and so is considered garden worthy. The main features of interest are the flowers and fruits. In the case of *S. rubriflora*, the solitary buds, resembling ripe cherries, open to hanging, fragrant, dark- crimson, saucer-shaped flowers up to 2.5 centimetres (1 in.) across.

For fruits to be formed, male and female plants are needed, so some nurseries sex their *Schisandra*, offering both male and female plants. When both sexes are planted together, the female plant will produce 15-centimetre-long (6 in.) clusters of scarlet, fleshy fruits that ripen in the autumn. In their native habitat in parts of China, India and Myanmar, the fruits are eaten fresh or dried. The cultivar 'Bodnant Redberry', which originated in Bodnant Gardens, North Wales, is a female with clusters of hanging fruit up to 20 centimetres (8 in.) long.

The closely related *S. grandiflora* is similar to *S. rubriflora*, but the flowers are white to pink, and they are in bloom in late spring and early summer. The shiny, edible, red fruits are held in extremely ornamental clusters up to 10 centimetres (4 in.) long. *S. grandiflora* is a native of west Sichuan, China and northeast India, and it was introduced to the West from Mount Emei by plant collector Ernest Henry Wilson in 1908. Both species have aromatic bark and leathery leaves and can be grown as wall plants, trained up wires up a vertical post, or through trees or large shrubs. In order to keep the plants within their allotted spaces, prune in late winter, removing dead or badly placed growth. They prefer acidic soils but tolerate alkalinity, so dig in plenty of well-rotted organic matter, such as garden compost, before planting. Water frequently during dry periods and mulch in winter. **MB**

Alternatives

Schisandra rubriflora 'Bodnant Redberry', *Schisandra grandiflora* var. *cathayensis*

Schizophragma

S. hydrangeoides var. *concolor* 'Moonlight'

Main features Deciduous climber for shade; beautiful leaves; attractive autumn colour
Height 6 m (20 ft)
Position ○ ◑ ●   **Hardiness** RHS H7

When gardeners ask for a deciduous climber to brighten up a shady wall, the climbing hydrangea *Hydrangea anomala* subsp. *petiolaris* is often recommended. However, another excellent option is *S. hydrangeoides* var. *concolor* 'Moonlight', which, as its name suggests, is very much like the climbing hydrangea. Both species grow together in the woods, forests, and mountains of Japan, where they climb using aerial roots.

The selection 'Moonlight' is notable for its silver-grey leaves, with prominent veining, that turn shades of yellow and orange red in the autumn. Small, cream-white flowers in flat clusters from midsummer to early autumn are surrounded by heart-shaped bracts, which act as flags to draw the attention of passing insects to the tiny flowers. There is also a selection *S. hydrangeoides* var. *hydrangeoides* 'Roseum' with rose-pink bracts.

'Moonlight' is not too fussy about its position in the garden and will grow up walls, large trees, or over old stumps. In warmer climates this climber prefers a shady position, but in cooler climates it thrives in sunshine. The flowers of those grown in shade last longer than those produced in sunshine, but the leaves remain a desirable feature because the plant can be slow to flower wherever it is grown. Plant 'Moonlight' 45 to 60 centimetres (18–24 in.) from the base of the wall so it will catch the rain. It needs a moist, fertile soil, so it is best to enrich it with garden compost. Patience will be rewarded because although the plant may take a while to flower and is slow to establish, 'Moonlight' is moderately vigorous once it has done so. Attach young plants to a support, such as a bamboo cane, to guide where they climb; aerial roots attach much more readily to moist surfaces, so spraying the support with water will help establishment. **MB**

Alternatives

Schizophragma hydrangeoides var. *hydrangeoides* 'Roseum', *Schizophragma integrifolium*

Solanum
S. crispum 'Glasnevin'

Main features Clusters of bright, starry, deep-mauve
flowers; lax habit; often grown as a wall shrub
Height 3.6 m (12 ft)
Position ○ **Hardiness** RHS H4

This species is a member of the potato family, and it was
introduced into cultivation around 1830. The main feature
is the clusters of fragrant flowers backed by dark-green,
oval leaves, and these resemble the flowers on a potato
plant. The deep-mauve stars, with a prominent spike of
stamen in the centre, are eye-catching, and they emerge
continuously from midsummer to late autumn. The
selection 'Glasnevin' is hardier than the species and longer
flowering, sometimes blooming in mild winters. However,
it is always at its best in milder locations. 'Glasnevin' is
semi-evergreen but becomes deciduous if temperatures
drop. In warm climates the flowering season is longer,
from spring to autumn, and the plant can be grown as
a free-standing shrub. A warm, sheltered site with plenty
of sun is the key thing for flowering. Lax in habit, the
stems need tying in against trellis or wires attached to a
wall. It looks spectacular growing on an outbuilding or
shed where it will spread to 1.5 metres (5 ft). **MB**

Alternatives

Syn. *Solanum crispum* 'Autumnale'. *Solanum laxum*,
Solanum laxum 'Album', *Solanum laxum* 'Aureovariegatum'

Sollya
S. heterophylla

Main features Beautiful flowers followed by fruits;
plant of modest height
Height 1.8 m (6 ft)
Position ○ ◑ **Hardiness** RHS H3

The colour blue is not well represented in the plant world,
so growing this elegant, twining evergreen climber with
nodding clusters of gentian-blue flowers is a particular
pleasure. Native to southwest Australia, it is only for
planting in the ground in mild regions, but it makes a
good container plant in a conservatory. *S. heterophylla*
blooms appear from midsummer to early autumn, and
they are backed by slender, lance-shaped, evergreen
leaves, which are also the perfect backdrop for the eye-
catching, blue berries that follow. Reaching 1.8 metres
(6 ft) in height, *S. heterophylla* is perfect for growing up
an arch or trellis or on the upright support of a pergola.
In addition, it is neat enough to grow in a container
around a tripod of canes, and therefore makes a suitable
patio subject. The plant was introduced into cultivation
in the 1930s by the plant physiologist and anatomist
Richard Horsman Solly, who discovered it growing in
open woodland and forest in the 1930s. **MB**

Alternatives

Syn. *Billardiera heterophylla*, syn. *Sollya fusiformis*. *Sollya
heterophylla* 'Alba', *Sollya heterophylla* 'Pink Charmer'

 Solanum crispum 'Glasnevin' will provide summer colour if you have the right spot for it.

Tecoma
T. stans 'Orange Jubilee'

Main features Drought tolerant; long flowering season;
nectar-rich flowers for hummingbirds
Height 60–360 cm (2–12 ft)
Position ○ ◑   **Hardiness** RHS H2

The species *T. stans* is native to Florida, Mexico, the West
Indies and northern Venezuela and Argentina. In regions
with cold winters, this plant is grown in a container as
a summer patio plant and its height range is as above.
However, in frost-free areas, it can reach 6 metres
(20 ft) in height and blooms nearly year round. It is then
overwintered in a conservatory or in a brightly lit room.
The bell-shaped flowers are the plant's main feature; they
are slightly scented, and it is worth deadheading them
so that more flowers appear. The flowers are pollinated
by hummingbirds that visit the plant to sip from the
nectar-filled blooms hanging in clusters from the ends
of the branches. *T. stans* 'Orange Jubilee' is a form with
bright copper-orange trumpet flowers that appear year
round in hotter climates. A complete joy in the garden,
it is often found planted alongside the species. 'Orange
Jubilee' is amenable to pruning and can be grown as a
free-standing specimen, espaliered against a wall, over
a trellis, or even as an attractive small tree. **MB**

Alternatives

Tecoma stans, *Tecoma stans* 'Flaming Belles'

Thunbergia
T. grandiflora

Main features Long flowering; clusters of attractive
blooms; attractive to bees
Height 8 m (26 ft)
Position ○ ◑   **Hardiness** RHS H2–3

The profusion of glorious flowers makes *T. grandiflora* a
must-have plant for Mediterranean and tropical gardens.
They are displayed in clusters, each flower trumpet-
shaped, velvety and a lovely violet-blue colour with a
beautiful, soft, pale-yellow mark in the throat that is
illuminated when backlit by the sun. No surprise that this
plant is often known as the sky vine or blue-trumpet vine,
appellations that fit it perfectly. There is a pure-white form,
'Alba', which is absolutely beautiful too. In addition, this
twining evergreen has alternating, heart-shaped, coarsely
toothed leaves. The plant is very vigorous and is therefore
useful for covering buildings, growing over a pergola, or
being trained along wires. In Australia it is considered to
be a weed on agricultural land and is a threat to native
plants. In a conservatory or greenhouse, it needs a large
container or border to restrict the growth, yet the natural
vigour ensures that it still makes an impact. Even here,
T. grandiflora requires trimming in spring to keep stems
within their allotted space. **MB**

Alternative

Thunbergia grandiflora 'Alba'

Thunbergia
T. gregorii 'Lemon Star'

Main features Annual climber with summer flowers; perfect for small containers or lightweight supports
Height 2.4 m (8 ft)
Position ○ ◐ **Hardiness** RHS H2–3

Annual climbers are always useful in the garden, particularly for small spaces where a permanent climber is not practical. The genus *Thunbergia* includes several varieties, such as those sold as a mix of colours or as an orange with the characteristic black eye. *T. gregorii* 'Lemon Star' is a variation on this theme and is a lovely lemon-yellow colour. It was introduced from Germany in 1999 and stands out like a beacon among the orange tones of its peers. Plants can be raised each year from seeds for use in summer displays, and they will flower even in a cool summer providing that the compost is moist and there are no checks in growth. 'Lemon Star' is perfect as ground cover and in window boxes, but also for twining up a tripod of bamboo canes or along a trellis or fence. It is often sold ready-planted in hanging baskets as a bit of instant summer colour, although it may climb up the chains rather than trail down. Other colour selections include 'Superstar Orange' with intense orange flowers and 'Red and Orange' with almost burnt-orange flowers. **MD**

Alternatives

Thunbergia alata 'Lemon Queen', *Thunbergia gregorii*

Trachelospermum
T. jasminoides

Main features Fragrant flowers; handsome evergreen foliage
Height 9 m (30 ft)
Position ○ ◐ **Hardiness** RHS H4

This climber is the garden designer's secret weapon because it seems to work as well in partial shade (useful for a wall or fence that has morning sun) as it does in full sun in all but the coldest areas. Confederate, or star jasmine, as it is commonly known (although it is not related to Jasmine), provides a dense, evergreen curtain of oval, glossy, dark-green leaves, the perfect backdrop for the profusion of cream-white fragrant flowers that overrun the stems from midsummer. *T. jasminoides* is elegant, understated and smells glorious. It has no special soil requirements apart from a moist, free-draining site. Moreover, it deserves praise for its behaviour, because it is easily controlled and will form a tidy screen at the back of a mixed border. *T. jasminoides* is also useful as a specimen grown in a pot, in a city, or courtyard garden, as it does not become leggy and retains leaves and flowers along its entire length. Growing over a pergola or arch brings the flowers to roughly head height – all the better to appreciate the wonderful scent and splendid flowers. **ER**

Alternative

Syn. *Rhynchospermum jasminoides*

Tropaeolum
T. speciosum

Main features Herbaceous plant; colourful flowers from mid- to late summer; unusual metallic-blue berries
Height 3 m (10 ft)
Position ◑ **Hardiness** RHS H5

This slender herbaceous climber grows from a potato-like tuber to produce bright-red flowers that are up to 2.5 centimetres (1 in.) in diameter. These flowers are followed by bright-blue berries. The foliage is a rich green, and the pretty leaves have five lobes. The overall effect is not too overwhelming when grown over shrubs or up trees.

T. speciosum first appeared in an account of plants that were collected in South America by Eduard Friedrich Poeppig, a professor of zoology at Leipzig, Germany. He landed at the port of Valparaíso in Chile in 1827, collected extensively in the area and also in Peru, then canoed down the Amazon River to the Atlantic coast. The plant is found growing in *Nothofagus* forests and up through bamboos. It was introduced into cultivation in the United Kingdom by plant collector William Lobb, who was employed by Veitch Nurseries, and it flowered for the first time in June 1847 in the gardens in Exeter.

For the best results, plant *T. speciosum* in a shallow hole around 15 centimetres (6 in.) deep, then gradually fill it with loose, organic, rich soil as the shoots appear. Plenty of water and humidity in summer, along with drier conditions in winter, guarantees optimum growth. Train the plant up fences, in the shade of walls, at the base of a yew hedge, or scrambling over rhododendrons. *T. speciosum* needs shelter and cool, moist conditions but it should not be in waterlogged soil over the winter. The tubers can be lifted and stored in compost in a cool, dry, frost-free place, then replanted the following spring. Unfortunately, slugs can be a problem, so take the necessary precautions, especially with young plants. Although the establishment of *T. speciosum* takes a little care, do not be put off this climber, because when it is mature and in full flower, it is a wonderful sight to behold. **MB**

Alternative

Tropaeolum tuberosum var. *lineamaculatum* 'Ken Aslet'

Tropaeolum
T. tricolor

Main features Attractive foliage; twining stems; shoals of unusual flowers
Height 1.8 m (6 ft)
Position ○ ◑ **Hardiness** RHS H4

From early spring to early summer, the unusual flowers of *T. tricolor* appear like a shoal of small tropical fish swimming amongst the foliage, making this an outstanding plant to grow. Each individual bloom is architectural and colourful; the bright-red outer part of the flower has purple-tipped lobes, and the yellow petals are only just visible.

T. tricolor can be found in a range of habitats in Chile, from temperate forests at high altitude, to the point where the Atacama Desert meets the coast. Here, it scrambles among cacti and spiny shrubs and is watered by fog rolling in from the sea. In the garden, provide the plant with a moist but free-draining soil or compost in full sun or dappled shade. *T. tricolor* was first illustrated in 1828 in *The British Flower Garden* from plants at Chelsea Physic Garden, United Kingdom, grown from seed received from the daughter of the British Vice-Consul in Valparaíso, Chile.

The foliage dies back and regrows annually from a tuber. It is very vigorous, and when grown in a pot of free-draining, loam-based compost, such as John Innes no. 2, with added grit, it can easily cover a support 1.8 metres (6 ft) high. In a cool, frost-free greenhouse, plant *T. tricolor* in the autumn, watering slightly, and increasing the volume of water as the first growth appears. It will then flower in early spring. It is best to minimise watering once the plant has flowered, to prevent the leaves from withering. Alternatively, plant it outdoors in spring, once the risk of frost has passed. Water freely, feed when in growth, and keep the tubers dry when dormant. In regions where frost is not a problem, tubers can be left in the ground but mulched as a precaution. A faster-growing annual climber is *T. peregrinum* (syn. *T. canariense*), which has bright-yellow flowers from summer to autumn with blue-green lobed leaves. **MB**

Alternative

Tropaeolum peregrinum (syn. *Tropaeolum canariense*)

Vitis

'Brant'

Main features Ornamental vine; rich autumn foliage
colour; bunches of black grapes
Height 6 m (20 ft)
Position ○ ◐ **Hardiness** RHS H6

Any gardener who wants to grow an ornamental *Vitis*
outdoors would do well to pick the cultivar 'Brant', a
vine renowned for the brilliance of its autumn foliage.
The small dark-purple fruits, which make very pleasant
eating but are full of seed, can be left to complement
the orange, purple and pink foliage and green or yellow
veins, or it can be turned into wine. The juice of the fruit
is also excellent when fresh.

'Brant' was raised by Charles Arnold of Paris, Canada,
in the 1860s and was introduced to Britain in 1886. The
plant makes an impressive garden feature growing over a
sturdy pergola because the grapes hang down from the
roof. An alternative is to train the plant against a sunny
wall using horizontal wires. If 'Brant' is allowed to grow
unrestrained, the grape crops will be smaller and more
difficult to harvest. It is much better to adopt a pruning
style, such as the double Guyot system, recommended
in many specialist fruit books, which allows the growth
to be controlled, thus ensuring good crops of healthy
grapes. Remember to protect the grapes from birds
when they ripen in midautumn. Water well in drought
and thin out the foliage during growth.

Sited in plenty of sunshine or partial shade, 'Brant' is a
long-lived plant that will flower and fruit on the current
year's growth. When planting, it is worth remembering
that small one-year-old plants establish better than older
specimens. A mature, well-grown specimen is a delight
to behold in the autumn sunshine. **MB**

Alternative

Vitis coignetiae

Vitis
V. vinifera 'Spetchley Red'

Main feature Grapevine grown for its rich, red, autumn colour and black fruits
Height 8 m (26 ft)
Position ○ ◑ **Hardiness** RHS H6

This selection of the common grapevine was made at Spetchley Park, Worcestershire, England, for its intense, red, autumn colour by plant collectors Bleddyn and Sue Wynn-Jones. They describe the plant as 'a slender vine with peeling woody stems bearing smooth-surfaced palmate leaves which transform to one of the best intense autumnal reds available'. This outstanding vine looks effective in any garden, trained against a wall or trellis, draped over a pergola, waiting to illuminate the garden with the onset of autumn. The small, black grapes make excellent wine too. As with any grapevine, it is important to consider the site because the plants will last for many years. *V. vinifera* 'Spetchley Red' prefers somewhere that

gets sun or partial shade on a free-draining, preferably alkaline to neutral, soil. Grow it against a warm wall in cool, temperate climates and keep the plants well watered in a drought. All the previous year's stems should be cut back to a main framework of older wood when vines are dormant in midwinter; if you leave it too late, when the sap has started to flow, they will bleed. Small, one-year-old plants establish better than older specimens. It may not be the best vine for grapes, but for vivid autumn colour in the garden, 'Spetchley Red' is hard to beat.

Other grapevines grown for their ornamental foliage include *V. vinifera* 'Apiifolia', known as the parsley vine, because the leaves are deeply divided. 'Fragola', or dusty miller grape, has grey-green foliage dusted with white down and black fruits. **MB**

Alternatives

Vitis vinifera 'Apiifolia', *Vitis vinifera* 'Fragola'

Wisteria
W. brachybotrys
'Shiro-kapitan'

Main feature Beautiful and fragrant flowers in late spring
to early summer
Height 7.5 m (25 ft)
Position ○ ◑   **Hardiness** RHS H5

Despite the relatively short flowering period of this large
vine, the flowers are so breathtakingly beautiful when
they appear that *W. brachybotrys* 'Shiro-kapitan' must
be one of the most desirable climbers. It has the largest
flowers of the genus and the most fragrant. The beautiful,
pea-like, white flowers – with a central yellow stain –
appear in loose, wide clusters as the copper-green leaves
emerge in late spring or early summer. 'Shiro-kapitan'
is also known as the silky wisteria because the leaves
are soft and downy on both sides. The classic climber
for growing against walls and fences, over buildings, or
into trees, it can also be grown up a single vertical post
as a 'standard'. Correct annual pruning is essential for
wisteria growing against a house wall or on a post: cut
the side shoots back to four to six buds in late summer
and again to two to three buds in late winter. Pruning in
early summer or heavy pruning will reduce flowering. **MB**

Alternatives

Wisteria brachybotrys 'Okayama', *Wisteria brachybotrys*
'Showa-beni', *Wisteria brachybotrys* 'Burford'

Wisteria
W. floribunda
'Domino'

Main features Beautiful bicoloured flowers; stems of
character when mature
Height 7.5 m (25 ft)
Position ○ ◑   **Hardiness** RHS H5

Known as Japanese wisteria, this genus is the one usually
seen in gardens. The flowers are fragrant and the colour
depends on the cultivar: *W. floribunda* 'Domino' has
blooms that are a delightful pale lavender to deep lilac,
and this two-tone colour creates a pleasing bicolour
effect. Flowers appear in late spring and early summer
at the same time as the leaves emerge, which is a great
advantage, because if you plant a wisteria, you want it
to flower as soon as possible after planting. One way to
grow 'Domino' is as an espalier, as you would an apple or
pear against a sunny fence or wall, by training it against
horizontal support wires. When growing it over an arch,
reduce the number of trusses before the plant starts to
flower, thereby giving those that remain room to develop
to their full glory. Not as vigorous as some, 'Domino' can
be grown as a standard in a container of loam-based
compost, which makes it ideal for a small garden. **MB**

Alternatives

Syn. *Wisteria × formosa* 'Domino'. *Wisteria floribunda* 'Alba',
Wisteria floribunda 'Rosea', *Wisteria floribunda* 'Multijuga'

Wisteria floribunda 'Domino' is a less vigorous cultivar that has two-tone flowers. ➲

More than simply popular summer-flowering shrubs, roses have a special place in human civilisation and culture. Since roses can be shrubs and climbers, it makes sense to bring our featured rose varieties together here in one place. Rose plants come in all shapes and sizes, so you can find one to fill a space of any size. While the flowers and their scent are our highest priority, we must also consider the whole plant, and here are examples of roses with interesting foliage or colourful hips, which remind us that roses have value as a hedging and wildlife plant too.

As well as much-loved old rose varieties, with their historical associations and romantic names, we bring you examples of modern roses selected for their natural disease-resistance and easy-to-grow nature. In addition, we highlight a few lesser-known species valued for their robustness and charm.

◉ *Rosa* **Princess Alexandra of Kent** is a modern rose with old rose fragrance.

Rosa
Iceberg

Main features Summer flowers that last into the autumn; lightly scented; fresh-green foliage and stems
Height 1.2 m (4 ft) **Spread** 1.2 m (4 ft)
Position ○ **Hardiness** RHS H6

The pure-white blooms complemented by the fresh green of the stems and foliage make this a rose that will fit in with any style of planting. Bred by German rose breeder Reimer Kordes in 1958, *R.* Iceberg was used extensively by English landscape designer Russell Page in the 1960s and 1970s, which helped to raise its profile around the world. His signature pairing for clients' gardens was to have beds of Iceberg edged with trimmed box plants. This simple classic look has a timeless appeal for a formal garden or courtyard, but this rose is equally at home in a mixed border of shrubs and perennials, where it looks good underplanted with a froth of hardy *Geranium* or *Nepeta*. It is a robust rose that requires little attention and even a single bush in the front of a suburban garden is worthwhile.

A climbing sport arose in 1968, introduced by Cants of Colchester, England. When a rose produces a climbing sport it is not necessarily an improvement, but in the case of 'Climbing Iceberg' the longer stems give the plant an added elegance. At 3.6 metres (12 ft) tall, the climbing form is the ideal height for sizable obelisks and arches, where its full flowering potential can be displayed. When the flowers fade, the petals drop off the plant cleanly and do not remain on the plant looking brown.

The clusters of double blooms last well, and Iceberg is a repeat flowerer, so it is fine to cut a few for an indoor display. Flowering can continue into the autumn depending on the weather, and the plant has been known to flower almost all year round in hot climates. A light, fresh scent that is not too overpowering adds to the appeal. Within its ancestry are a red hybrid musk, 'Robin Hood', and a white hybrid tea, 'Virgo'. Consequently, if you inspect Iceberg close up you may see a faint red or pink streak to the blooms. **LD**

Alternatives

= 'Korbin'. *Rosa* 'Schneewittchen', *Rosa* 'Fée des Neiges'

Rosa **Iceberg** in a bed edged with *Salvia officinalis* 'Berggarten', designed by Louise van den Akker. ➡

Rosa
R. gallica var. officinalis

Main features Large, semi-double, light crimson, fragrant flowers; tough and reliable rose
Height 1.2 m (4 ft) **Spread** 1.2 m (4 ft)
Position ○ **Hardiness** RHS H5

This is a rose of great historical interest, and it was probably introduced around 1400. For many centuries it was grown in huge quantities, especially around Paris, for cosmetic, culinary and medicinal purposes. The fact that *R. gallica* var. *officinalis* is still popular proves that it is not only very beautiful, but also very tough and reliable. The individual blooms are large, semi-double, and a light crimson colour, with a bunch of golden stamen in the middle and a pure, old-rose fragrance. It is bristly rather than thorny, and so is more gardener friendly than many modern roses. *R. gallica* var. *officinalis* stays relatively compact when kept lightly pruned. When grown from a cutting, or planted deeply as a budded plant, it will sucker freely and form an attractive thicket, and so can make a very good hedge. Although it does not repeat flower, it is still an extremely worthwhile rose. A similar cultivar, *R. gallica* var. *officinalis* 'Versicolor' (pictured), appeared around the year 1600. Its flowers are crimson and striped with white. **MM**

Alternatives

Rosa 'Tuscany Superb', *Rosa* 'The Herbalist'

Rosa
'Francis Meilland'

Main features Large, fragrant, shell-pink flowers; disease-resistant plant
Height 90 cm (3 ft) **Spread** 90 cm (3 ft)
Position ○ **Hardiness** RHS H6

This is the perfect variety for anyone dipping their toes into the intoxicating world of roses. 'Francis Meilland' has everything: strong growth; gorgeous, pink hybrid tea flowers; and an old-rose, fruity fragrance that will fill the still air on a midsummer evening. In hot, sunny conditions, the blooms fade to white, and whatever the weather decides to do, diseases will not take hold. Once the blooms fade, they naturally fall off the plant, leaving a clean-looking specimen ready for new growth and more buds. Growth is fast and compact, but if late summer brings warm, humid conditions, do not be surprised to see the plants putting on a growth spurt. In fact, stems can take on the appearance of a climbing rose. 'Francis Meilland' is a great variety to grow in among perennials, where the vigorous growth, glossy, olive-green leaves, and red-thorned stems combine well with neighbouring plants. Winner of a UK Gold Standard award in 2009 and the All-America Rose Selection in 2013, 'Francis Meilland' is without doubt a rose for every garden. **PM**

Alternatives

Rosa 'Meitroni', *Rosa* 'Prince Jardinier', *Rosa* 'My Garden'

◑ *Rosa gallica* var. *officinalis* is an ancient rose that is tough and reliable with an old-rose fragrance.

Rosa

R. × *odorata* 'Mutabilis'

Main features Medium-sized, single, coppery-yellow to coppery-crimson flowers; extremely healthy
Height 1.8 m (6 ft) **Spread** 1.8 m (6 ft)
Position ○ **Hardiness** RHS H3

With its flowers of ever-changing colour, *R.* × *odorata* 'Mutabilis' is one of the most instantly recognisable of all roses, but strangely, its origins are obscure. It was introduced commercially in 1933 by a Swiss nurseryman, Henry Corrévon, who acquired it from a garden on Lake Maggiore, where it was called Tipo Ideale.

The pointed copper-flame buds open to butterfly-like, coppery-yellow single flowers on light, airy growth. Their colour gradually changes to pink, and eventually to a much darker coppery-crimson, thus creating a delightful mix. There are numerous other roses with single flowers, such as the pale-pink and extremely healthy 'Rosy Cushion', or 'The Alexandra Rose', with smaller flowers that change colour to a certain extent. In warm climates the flowers will be produced continuously all through the year, although unfortunately, there is only a light fragrance. The leaves are attractive, too, and are a dark bronze colour when young, turning to a dark, shiny green.

'Mutabilis' is not a very winter-hardy rose, and in cooler climates, unless given a warm position, it will not grow very strongly and may well be cut back in winter if not protected. However, it sits delightfully in a mixed border next to a wide range of other plants and will make a superb hedge in which the bronze-coloured leaves will create a fine show. Roses generally love a soil that is rich in organic matter and that does not dry out quickly. Feeding, mulching and watering will help the rose grow strongly and repeat flower more quickly. **MM**

Alternatives

Rosa 'Rosy Cushion', *Rosa* 'The Alexandra Rose'

Rosa
Munstead Wood

Main features Very beautiful, deep velvety-crimson
flowers; strongly fragrant
Height 1.2 m (4 ft) **Spread** 90 cm (3 ft)
Position ○ **Hardiness** RHS H5

Munstead Wood is one of the best known and most
popular of the English rose varieties, and it belongs to a
relatively new group that breeder David Austin has been
working on since the 1940s. His aim was, and indeed
continues to be, to develop a group of roses that have the
charm, fragrance and beauty of the old roses, combined
with the repeat flowering and wide colour range of the
modern roses (hybrid tea roses and floribundas).

Munstead Wood was introduced in 2007 and has
the most beautiful, deep velvety-crimson flowers, the
eighty or so petals of which are arranged in the form
of a rosette. Matching the colour is a superb fragrance,
which is old rose in character, with an additional fruity

note of blackberry, blueberry and damson. The growth
is quite bushy, forming a broad shrub that has flushes of
blooms from summer through to the frost.

This plant can be used in formal rose gardens as a
single variety in a bed or more informally in borders,
purely among other roses, or mixed in with perennials
(the addition of the latter will help to keep them healthy).
It is particularly effective alongside plants with blue
flowers, although apricot blooms create a wonderful
contrast. Similar varieties include 'Darcey Bussell' and
'L.D. Braithwaite', although both of these lack the
glorious fragrance, and the colour is not quite so rich.
Munstead Wood has won prizes for both its fragrance
and its qualities as a shrub, including the Award of
Garden Merit from the Royal Horticultural Society. **MM**

Alternatives

= 'Ausbernard'. *Rosa* 'Darcey Bussell', *Rosa* 'L.D. Braithwaite'

Rosa
R. glauca

Main features Distinctive coppery-mauve foliage;
simple pink flowers; dark-red hips in the autumn
Height 1.8 m (6 ft) **Spread** 1.5 m (5 ft)
Position ○ **Hardiness** RHS H7

With its coppery-mauve foliage, *R. glauca* is immediately recognisable. The colour of the leaves varies considerably between forms and how exposed they are to sunlight: the sunnier it is, the darker, more plum-purple the leaves are; in partial shade they are more of a slate grey. In order to ensure good leaf colour, buy this variety as a budded plant when in leaf at a garden centre or nursery, because those raised from seed can be variable. Close examination of the leaves will often reveal a very wide range of colours, the veins and petioles being more of a dark red. In the autumn the leaves will briefly turn soft yellow.

The small, five-petalled flowers are a rich pink, paling to white in the centre and have a simple charm. *R. glauca* produces only one crop of flowers each season, followed by dark-purple hips that become rounded and bright red with age and last well into the winter. Unpruned, it will become a large shrub, but the arching, almost thornless stems give it an airy grace, and it is perfect for wilder parts of the garden. At the back of a mixed border it will stand out among perennials, and with its dark-purple stems be a showy permanent structure through the winter.

Flower arrangers also like *R. glauca* for adding a distinct colour to their displays; they often prune it back hard in winter to encourage the fresh young growth, which will have larger leaves and the best colour. If this variety is grown as a wildlife shrub, like most species of roses, it is best left unpruned to encourage as many flowers as possible. It is best grown in regions with a cold spell in winter, although it will be fine when summers are hot. No other species offers this foliage colour, but for wild-looking roses of a similar size, try *R. canina*, *R. villosa*, or *R. californica*. All of these have simple pink flowers that are attractive to bees, followed by an excellent crop of hips. **MM**

Alternatives

*Rosa canina, Rosa villosa, Rosa californica, Rosa nutkana,
Rosa willmottiae, Rosa webbiana*

Rosa
'Darlow's Enigma'

Main features Flowers in summer and autumn; fragrant flowers; ornamental autumn hips; low maintenance
Height 1.5 m (5 ft) **Spread** 1.5 m (5 ft)
Position ○ ◑ **Hardiness** RHS H7

'Darlow's Enigma' is a 'found' rose, discovered in Oregon in 1993 and believed to be a hybrid musk. It has everything that gardeners might want in a rose, including vigour, constant bloom and sweet fragrance. It covers itself with large clusters (up to one hundred flowers per cluster) of single, pure-white flowers with golden-yellow stamen. These flowers are so fragrant and borne in such abundance that they can perfume the garden for quite a distance. However, the plant is lovely even before it blooms, with new red canes and small, glossy, dark-green leaves. It mounds itself into a sizable shrub but is also flexible enough to be bent horizontally and trained as a climber along a fence. It is so vigorous that it can be cut back almost to the ground each winter and will still flower as a small shrub later in the season. One possible drawback is that it has ferocious thorns, but this is negated by the fact that it needs no fungicides or pesticides, and still blossoms without needing regular fertilising.

A wonderful rose for a cottage or rustic garden, 'Darlow's Enigma', growing fast and dense, is a good candidate for hiding eyesores or creating a screen. It is a perfect starter rose for the gardener who has given up on roses, because it is relatively easy to grow. One caveat: it is best to grow this rose on its own roots, as the annual production of new basal canes is key to the shrub's long-term survival, as well as to its aesthetic appeal and functional versatility. Perhaps this is the secret to its vigour, as roses grown on their own roots seem much stronger and more drought tolerant. Anyone with an interest in plant propagation will find 'Darlow's Enigma' a rewarding test subject. Unfortunately, few garden centres carry own-root roses, but there are a number of good sources for these plants online. **KK**

Alternatives

None that have the same reputation and mysterious origin of *Rosa* 'Darlow's Enigma'.

Rosa
'Cécile Brünner'

Main features Small, pink, miniature, hybrid tea-shaped, scented flowers; perfect for small bouquets
Height 90 cm (3 ft) **Spread** 90 cm (3 ft)
Position ○ **Hardiness** RHS H6

This is a charming rose with dainty, blush-pink, thimble-sized blooms throughout most of the summer and early autumn months. The plant naturally produces short joints, resulting in a shrub rose of compact looks, ideal for midborder planting. It is also well proportioned for growing in containers, where it can be placed near walkways to delight passersby with its divine fragrance. The blooms of 'Cécile Brünner' are perfect for making into a posy. Choose buds that are just beginning to open, picking early in the morning, when they are full of water. Once arranged the buds will fully open within a day. The smooth, dark-green leaves are the perfect foil to the blooms whether in an arrangement or on the plant. 'Cécile Brünner' is an old rose, having been bred in France in 1881, and it performs consistently year after year with little or no trouble from the usual rose problems. There is an equally good climbing sport, *Rosa* 'Climbing Cécile Brünner', which grows to 6 metres (20 ft) and can be trained over garden features. **PM**

Alternatives

Rosa 'White Cécile Brünner', *Rosa* 'Climbing Cécile Brünner'

Rosa
'Firefighter'

Main features Large, fragrant, red flowers on strong stems perfect for cutting; plants are disease resistant
Height 1.8 m (6 ft) **Spread** 90 cm (3 ft)
Position ○ **Hardiness** RHS H6

The *Rosa* 'Firefighter' is a truly impressive red rose with perfume, vigour and strength. Named in honour of the firefighters who lost their lives in the 9/11 terrorist attacks in 2001, 'Firefighter' is a must-have rose for every garden. It is exactly what you immediately picture when someone says 'red rose'. Stems are long, strong and topped by large hybrid tea flowers. They are perfect as cut flowers, lasting for at least a fortnight and filling rooms with evocative perfume. Left to bloom on plants, they will add rich, velvety-red colours to any hot-colour-themed borders or perform superbly as dot plants in cool-colour-themed schemes. The dark-green foliage is disease resistant, with a subtle matt foil to any other plantings. Occasionally a little shy to flower in the first couple of years after initial planting, 'Firefighter' soon gets into its stride and blooms profusely in the summer months. When planting, dust the roots with a root dip of mycorrhiza to help quick establishment, and always keep newly planted roses well watered in the first few years of growth. **PM**

Alternatives

Rosa 'Oradal', *Rosa* 'Hacienda', *Rosa* 'Red 'n' Fragrant'

● *Rosa* '**Climbing Cécile Brünner**' trained over an arch is the perfect way to display the small blooms.

Rosa
Wild Rover

Main features Plenty of flowers from summer to
autumn; disease-resistant plants
Height 1.2 m (4 ft) **Spread** 1.2 m (4 ft)
Position ○ **Hardiness** RHS H7

Rosa
Love & Peace

Main feature Large, yellow-and-pink flowers on
tall plants
Height 1.2–1.8 m (4–6 ft) **Spread** 90 cm (3 ft)
Position ○ **Hardiness** RHS H5

The rich-purple blooms of *R*. Wild Rover make it a
gorgeous addition to any garden. It is perfect as a stand-
alone shrub in a mixed border or used en masse in a rose
bed as a bank of bloom where both colour and scent
are required. Around 8 centimetres (3 in.) in diameter,
each flower develops from a claret-coloured bud and
opens to a vibrant shade of purple, with beautiful yellow
stamen and a central ivory-coloured eye. The flowers
then age gracefully to a subtle mauve hue, maintaining
a light scent throughout their lifespan. Wild Rover also
has good resistance to rose diseases – such as blackspot,
rust and mildew – and the dense, matt-green foliage
grows best in full sun. With newly planted specimens,
light pruning is best done in early autumn, but once
established, one or two of the oldest stems can be hard
pruned to encourage vigorous new shoots to develop.
This variety tries hard for the gardener, and although it
was only introduced in 2007, Wild Rover already has a
Royal Horticultural Society Award of Garden Merit. **PM**

With the world-famous *Rosa* 'Peace' as one of its parents,
'Love & Peace' has no other option than to be a superb
hybrid tea rose, and it is. Producing mildly scented blooms
in a blend of yellow and pink on long stems that are
perfect for cutting, the plants are well-shaped and avoid
the 'legginess' exhibited by many hybrid tea roses. Stems
cut for indoor display will last for several weeks, with each
bloom opening to an impressive 15 centimetres (6 in.) in
diameter. When grown in a sunny position, 'Love & Peace'
produces its glossy, green leaves from the soil surface up
to blooming height. It is a fully clothed plant, and forms
a dense barrier; it is therefore wonderful when used in a
mixed hedge or grown as a specimen, where its stately,
almost noble, appearance will add height and grandeur
to the back of a mixed border. When planted en masse, a
bed of 'Love & Peace' is simply breathtaking. It produces
flower flushes throughout the summer, and blooms
appearing toward the autumn will be more intense in
colour as will any produced in cooler conditions. **PM**

Alternative

= 'Dichirap'. *Rosa* Rhapsody in Blue = 'Frantasia'

Alternatives

= 'Baipeace', *Rosa* 'Bright Spirit', *Rosa* 'Orient Express'

Rosa
Temptress

Main features Plentiful red blooms produced over a long period of time; great disease resistance
Height 5 m (16 ft) **Spread** 1.5 m (5 ft)
Position ○ **Hardiness** RHS H6

A modern climbing rose with shiny, almost polished-red blooms, *R*. Temptress has good resistance to many rose diseases and is a wonderful choice if you want stunning flowers over archways, up pillars and against walls. This variety is also a repeat-flowering rose, which means that the gorgeous blooms are produced over a long period of time. You can expect the first to appear in late spring, and flowering can continue well into autumn. In order to keep the blooms coming, always nip off fading flower heads. Individual flowers are only lightly fragrant, but they are displayed in large clusters; each bloom is a semi-double, so there is plenty of visual appeal. With dark-green, glossy, and disease-free foliage, Temptress is a vigorous climber: grow it up a house wall or train it over thick rope swags or a pergola, allowing for 5 metres (16 ft) of growth over its lifetime. In 2008, Temptress was awarded the Gold Standard after a three-year trial, and the Royal Horticultural Society Award of Garden Merit sealed the plant's position as a great rose for all gardeners. **PM**

Alternative

= 'Korramal'. *Rosa* 'Dortmund'

Rosa
R. nutkana 'Plena'

Main features Small, semi-double, fragrant flowers of deep rose-pink; flowers once; tough and reliable
Height 2.4 m (8 ft) **Spread** 2.4 m (8 ft)
Position ○ ◑ **Hardiness** RHS H5

This rose is closely related to the original species of rose, although there is some confusion as to its actual origin. The authorities say that it was bred, or at least introduced, by Rudolf Geschwind in 1894. Wherever it comes from, it is a first-class plant for the wilder parts of the garden or the back of a very large border. Once mature, it will form a wonderful, dense shrub that will be covered with small- to medium-sized, semi-double, very fragrant, deep rose-pink flowers. Although it does not repeat flower and only sets the occasional hip, this should not be a deterrent to planting it where space allows. In order to extend its period of interest, it could be used as a support for a climber, perhaps one of the varieties of *Clematis alpina* for spring flowers, *C. viticella* for late-summer flowers, or *Tropaeolum speciosum* for bright-red flowers. *R. nutkana* 'Plena' is an extremely tough and healthy variety that will cope with less-than-ideal conditions for both the soil and hours of sunshine. However, the better the conditions, the better the display. **MM**

Alternatives

Rosa spinosissima 'Stanwell Perpetual', *Rosa macrophylla*

Rosa
'New Dawn'

Main features Vigorous, healthy climber; masses of silvery-pink flowers
Height 2.4–4 m (8–13 ft) **Spread** 2.4 m (8 ft)
Position ○ ◑ **Hardiness** RHS H7

The *R.* 'New Dawn' is a fantastic rose, and rewards the gardener without needing any fuss and attention. It is the forerunner of the modern perpetual-flowering climbers, so it is an important variety in the history of rose breeding too. Introduced by US rose breeder Henry Dreer in 1930, 'New Dawn' was the first plant ever to be patented. It arose as a repeat-flowering sport from *R.* 'Dr W. Van Fleet' – a variety with some *R. wichurana* in its parentage – which is particularly valued for its hardiness, climbing vigour, elegant flower form and value as a cut rose.

Still widely grown today, the plant produces masses of pale, silvery-pink flowers from early summer to late autumn. Depending on when, or even if, winter strikes, blooms can continue well into the colder months, and it is hardy in most regions. 'New Dawn' is a large climber, and the attractive double blooms are sweetly scented and best produced when the stems are tied in horizontally. This encourages the plant to produce flowers at the expense of leafy growth. However, the foliage is a healthy, glossy, mid-green colour and resistant to many rose diseases. Left to climb without any training, the plant will reach 2.4 to 4 metres (8–13 ft) yet still flower profusely. Its arching habit makes it a perfect variety for climbing up walls, over arches and around pergolas.

'New Dawn' will grow in partial shade as well as in full sun and is not concerned whether it is positioned in a sheltered or exposed site. In 1993 its overall vigour, health and reliability made it an ideal candidate for the Royal Horticultural Society's prestigious Award of Garden Merit. 'New Dawn' has produced two sports: a white form with red tips to its buds ('White New Dawn') and *R.* Awakening, a strongly fragrant, fully double sport that is light pink. **PM**

Alternatives

Rosa Awakening = 'Probuzení', *Rosa* 'Weisse New Dawn'

Rosa
R. nitida

Main features Vigorous, prickly and low growing; perfect low-growing hedge
Height 90 cm (3 ft) **Spread** 90 cm (3 ft)
Position ○ ◐ **Hardiness** RHS H7

This little shrub is known as the shining rose due to its glossy, green, narrow leaves. It is one of the hardiest roses and one of the few species of *Rosa* that is suitable for a small garden. Native to the northeastern United States and Canada, it will survive the worst of the winter weather. This tough rose can be grown as a single plant, but it is often used as a dense hedge or for growing on slopes or banks. The foliage is dark green in summer, turning into hues of yellow, red and purple in the autumn. Flowering is brief, but when the 5-centimetre-wide (2 in.) blooms appear, they are vibrant pink with a prominent yellow centre of stamen; the flowers are slightly scented. Add to this a display of small rose hips in brilliant red, and *R. nitida* provides plenty of year-round interest for a small shrub.

R. nitida is ideal as a low, informal boundary hedge, with the prickles deterring unwanted animal visitors to the garden, or as a quick-growing, groundcover plant. It is not bothered about having the perfect soil. It thrives in poorer ground and can tolerate soils that become waterlogged; in the wild it is often found growing at the edges of ponds and bogs. *R. nitida* is robust and tough and copes well with hot and cold conditions. When in flower the plant attracts bees to its single blooms, and other wildlife make full use of the plant's dense thicket growth as hiding places and nesting sites. It requires little attention during the year, and once planted it can be left to simply get on with its job. If you have a tough site, there are several rose species, or varieties with wild species in their makeup, that are worth seeking out. *R. nitida* 'Stanwell Perpetual' produces soft-pink blooms and lots of prickles; 'Lavaglut' is a small rose with numerous velvety-red blooms that appear all summer long; and 'The Fairy' is a world favourite, a small but vigorous-growing rose. **PM**

Alternatives

Rosa 'Stanwell Perpetual', *Rosa* 'Lavaglut', *Rosa* 'The Fairy'

Rosa
'Ghislaine de Féligonde'

Main features Clusters of apricot and yellow blooms, fading to peach and white; almost thornless
Height 3 m (10 ft) **Spread** 1.2 m (4 ft)
Position ○ ◑ **Hardiness** RHS H6

This variety is fantastic if you need a shorter-growing rambling rose and one that attracts wildlife to the garden. 'Ghislaine de Féligonde' is less vigorous than other rambling roses and produces orange-coloured buds that open to small, apricot flowers with a yellow base. These then fade to peach, white and pink, with clusters of differently aged blooms actually looking akin to a bunch of different rose varieties on the same plant. In autumn the flowers tend to be more pink in colour.

Bred by horticulturist Eugène Turbat in France in 1916, 'Ghislaine de Féligonde' is an old rose. It is a special variety suitable for growing around doorways, pergolas and archways because the blooms appear throughout the year and produce a musky fragrance. In addition the stems are almost thornless; consequently, there is little danger from scratches as garden visitors get up close to take in the scent. Flower buds are usually produced well in winter months, even though they have little chance to open. Wildlife, and in particular bees, are attracted to the blooms, and birds devour the hips in the colder months. The stiff branches of 'Ghislaine de Féligonde' make it easy to train against a wall, and this variety flowers profusely if the branches are trained horizontally. The glossy, green leaves also provide good protection and potential nesting sites for birds.

Most roses prefer a sunny position in the garden, but 'Ghislaine de Féligonde' is happy and will flower well in any shadier spots. However, the soil needs to be moist and fertile for good, strong growth. In ideal conditions, each plant will quickly cover 3 by 1.2 metres (10 x 4 ft) and will be disease resistant. 'Ghislaine de Féligonde' is without doubt a striking rose, and it was honoured with the Royal Horticultural Society's Award of Garden Merit in 2012. **PM**

Alternative

Rosa 'Goldfinch'

Rosa 'Ghislaine de Féligonde' is a repeat-flowering rose with a flower colour that changes with the weather. ➲

Rosa
'Buff Beauty'

Main feature Fragrant flowers in summer and autumn
Height 1.5 m (5 ft) **Spread** 1.5 m (5 ft)
Position ○
Hardiness RHS H4

'Buff Beauty' was introduced in 1939 and belongs to the popular group of roses called the hybrid musks, most of which were bred in the early part of the twentieth century by the Reverend J. Pemberton. It is a lovely group that flowers very freely from summer through to the frost and is generally very fragrant too.

The warm apricot-yellow, five-petalled flowers of 'Buff Beauty' are medium sized and have a strong and delicious tea-rose scent. These semi-double blooms can be solitary or may grow in clusters. The plant has a beautiful arching habit, and so will make a good-sized, rounded shrub that will measure about 1.5 by 1.5 metres (5 x 5 ft) when pruned each winter. It is the most vigorous of the hybrid musk group and so even in the United Kingdom it will make an excellent climber at some 2.5 to 3 metres (8–10 ft) high. In warmer climates it can reach 6 metres (20 ft) or more.

As a shrub, 'Buff Beauty' looks superb at the back of a wide border mixed in with other roses or with perennials. It complements plants with purple flowers especially well, including *Salvia*, *Nepeta* and *Verbena*, although with its soft coloration, it will combine happily with most colours. As a climber it is superb on a wall, trellis, or obelisk, although it can just as easily be grown into a small- to medium-sized tree, depending on the climate. Roses love a soil that is rich in organic matter and does not dry out quickly. Feeding, mulching and watering will help the rose grow strongly and repeat flower more quickly.

Other excellent climbers of a similar colour are 'Crown Princess Margareta' and 'Teasing Georgia', both of which are significantly hardier than 'Buff Beauty', at least as healthy and have the advantage of dropping their petals more cleanly. Like 'Buff Beauty' both of these varieties can also be grown as large, arching shrubs. **MM**

Alternatives

Rosa 'Teasing Georgia', *Rosa* 'Crown Princess Margareta'

Rosa
'Veilchenblau'

Main features A rambler with small dark-magenta
flowers that fade to lilac; delicious orange scent
Height 4.5 m (15 ft) **Spread** 2 m (7 ft)
Position ○ **Hardiness** RHS H7

'Veilchenblau' is distinctive for two reasons. The first is
the colour of the flowers, which open to dark magenta
and then fade to lilac and are often streaked with white.
The second is the fact that the long, arching stems are
completely thornless, which is a rarity in the rose world.
'Veilchenblau' is the best known and most widely grown
of a small group of purple-flowered ramblers, of which
it is the palest. All of them were introduced in the early
1900s by rosarian Hermann Kiese in Germany. As with
most ramblers it does not repeat flower, but when in
bloom it is very prolific, and the semi-double, five-petalled
flowers have a rich, orange scent. Unfortunately, no hips
are produced.

Because 'Veilchenblau' has no thorns, it is not very
well suited to growing into trees without tying in. It is
best suited to growing on a pergola in full sun or perhaps
climbing up a tall pillar or obelisk, although it is quite
vigorous, so any support needs to be quite substantial.
As there is no repeat flowering, growing a later-flowering
climber through it can be most effective. The various
varieties of *Clematis viticella* and *C. texensis* are very
good companion plants because they flower later in
the season. *Ipomoea purpurea* and *I. tricolor* (morning
glory) will complement 'Veilchenblau', as they will flower
at the same time as the rose and for several weeks
afterwards. As a rambler this plant is relatively tough,
but it can be subject to some disease, and so preparing
the ground well using plenty of organic matter will be
very worthwhile. The roots will also benefit from an
occasional deep soaking.

Similar rambling roses to 'Veilchenblau' are the
other varieties in this group: 'Bleu Magenta', 'Violette'
and 'Rose-Marie Viaud', all of which have rather darker
flowers and have few or no thorns. **MM**

Alternatives

Rosa 'Bleu Magenta', *Rosa* 'Violette', *Rosa* 'Rose-Marie Viaud'

Rosa
Princess Alexandra of Kent

Main features Very large flowers of warm, glowing pink; about 130 petals; very tough, reliable and healthy
Height 1.2 m (4 ft) **Spread** 1.2 m (4 ft)
Position ○ **Hardiness** RHS H5

Princess Alexandra of Kent is a particularly impressive variety of rose. Its fully double flowers are very large, often as wide as 13 centimetres (5 in.) in diameter, with as many as 130 petals arranged in the form of a beautiful rosette. The overall colour is a warm, glowing pink, with paler outer petals that create a lovely contrast. These flowers are produced freely, either singly or in small groups, and although they are very large, they are never clumsy, being held nicely poised on an upright well-rounded shrub. The fragrance matches the colour for strength: a delicious tea, changing to lemon and eventually taking on hints of blackcurrant.

Princess Alexandra of Kent was bred by David Austin in the United Kingdom, and it was introduced in 2006. The plant flourishes in a wide range of climates, from those of its native country to much warmer ones, but it always remains between 90 and 120 centimetres (3–4 ft) both tall and wide. It is generally a very tough, reliable and healthy variety. Its relatively compact size makes it extremely effective in formal beds where the flowers will be produced more or less from the ground up. It is also very effective in a more informal border with or without other plants, be they perennials, biennials or annuals. Planting it close to the edge of a border will make the flowers easily accessible for regular sniffing and for cutting to bring into the house.

Similar to Princess Alexandra of Kent is *Rosa* 'Gertrude Jekyll', which is one of the most fragrant of all roses. *Rosa* 'Harlow Carr' has rather smaller but equally fragrant flowers and is extremely prolific if rather thorny. All roses love a soil that is rich in organic matter and does not dry out too quickly. Feeding, mulching and watering will help the plant grow strongly and repeat flower more quickly. **MM**

Alternatives

= 'Ausmerchant'. *Rosa* 'Gertrude Jekyll', *Rosa* 'Harlow Carr'

Rosa **Princess Alexandra of Kent**, shown here in the garden of the breeder David Austin. ➔

Rosa
Jacqueline du Pré

Main features Blush-white flowers with a musky scent; long blooming period
Height 90 cm (3 ft) **Spread** 90 cm (3 ft)
Position ○ ◑ **Hardiness** RHS H6

This is a superb shrub rose that starts flowering early and repeat flowers through to the autumn. It is a garden-worthy variety introduced by UK rose breeder Jack Harkness in 1988 after crossing *Rosa* 'Maigold' – the yellow-flowered cultivar well known for flowering a month before most roses – with one of his pale-pink fragrant roses, *Rosa* 'Radox Bouquet'. With its blush-white blooms, *Rosa* Jacqueline du Pré complements many other flowering plants in a mixed border. Its delicate flowers have a light, musky scent and are cup-shaped at first, opening to semi-double blooms within days. The prominent golden centres of each bloom are a particular feature. The plants themselves are tough and vigorous, with good disease resistance. Although Jacqueline du Pré performs best in a sunny spot in the garden, it will do well in partial shade too.

Plants can be left to their own devices to reach full height; alternatively, they can be gently pruned in autumn to maintain a more rounded appearance. The leaves are glossy and dark green – just the right backdrop to set off the blooms and neighbouring perennials. Wherever you grow Jacqueline du Pré, feed the plants generously in spring and water them in dry weather in order to keep more flowers coming. Mulching around the base of the plant with garden compost in spring is a great way to encourage strong growth too. It is always a good idea with any rose variety to cut back hard one or two of the older canes every year. This encourages the plant to produce fresh, vigorous shoots leading to even more blooms in subsequent years.

This variety was named in honour of Jacqueline du Pré, a noted British concert cellist who died in 1987 of multiple sclerosis. It received the prestigious Royal Horticultural Society's Award of Garden Merit in 1994. **PM**

Alternatives

= 'Harwanna'. *Rosa* Keros = 'Har pacific', *Rosa* Simple Peach = 'Harwarmth'

Rosa
'Felicia'

Main features Large, silvery-pink, fragrant flowers from early summer to the frost; extremely healthy
Height 1.5 m (5 ft) **Spread** 1.5 m (5 ft)
Position ○ **Hardiness** RHS H4

Rosa 'Felicia' is one of the best of Reverend J. Pemberton's group of roses called the hybrid musks, which he bred in the early part of the twentieth century. It was introduced in 1928, the result of a cross between the early hybrid tea 'Ophelia' and the short rambler 'Trier', both of which are highly fragrant. Most hybrid musks are substantial shrub roses with lovely flowers and a strong aromatic fragrance, and 'Felicia' is no exception. The flowers are loosely double, and the colour is silvery pink with hints of apricot. The plant is often seen in gardens covered in flowers, looking very healthy when many other roses around it have lost their leaves.

'Felicia' will develop into a large shrub and will sometimes reach more than 1.5 metres (5 ft) in height, and nearly the same across, if lightly pruned. In warmer climates, as a climber, it can grow up to 3.6 metres (12 ft) tall. It is a good idea to plant this variety towards the back of a large border, although the blooms are so fragrant that they should be easily accessed for frequent sniffing. It makes a very good cut flower because it lasts well in a vase and the fragrance will fill a room. 'Felicia' looks particularly effective in a mixed border with other plants such as *Delphinium*, *Veronicastrum* and *Campanula*, although care should be taken that they are not allowed to grow right around the base of the rose.

Another similar Pemberton rose introduced a little earlier, in 1925, is *Rosa* 'Cornelia', which has smaller flowers of copper-apricot fading to copper-pink on a shrub that grows to 1.5 metres (5 ft) tall. Two modern examples are David Austin's English roses: Scepter'd Isle (1996) and Gentle Hermione (2005). These are both smaller shrubs, measuring 120 by 90 centimetres (4 x 3 ft), and both offer soft-pink flowers with the shape and powerful fragrance of the old-rose hybrids. **MM**

Alternatives

Rosa Gentle Hermione = 'Ausrumba', *Rosa* 'Cornelia',
Rosa Scepter'd Isle = 'Ausland'

Rosa

Golden Beauty

Main feature Fragrant amber-yellow flowers in summer
Height 90 cm (3 ft) **Spread** 60 cm (24 in.)
Position ○
Hardiness RHS H6

Golden Beauty is a floribunda rose in that the flowers are produced in clusters. They attract bees into the garden and are produced from early summer to late autumn. Unlike many other yellow-flowering roses, it is vigorous and will produce masses of scented flowers.

Golden Beauty is a hungry rose, so it is best to add rose fertiliser during the growing season and plenty of garden compost at planting time. Plant in a sunny, open position in moist, well-drained soil. When planting in autumn, winter or spring, sprinkle the roots with a powder of mycorrhizal fungi. This ensures fast establishment of the plants and subsequent strong growth. Always keep newly planted specimens well watered in periods of dry weather. In order to get the best out of Golden Beauty, prune the plant in early spring, removing any crossed or diseased branches. Cut back the remaining shoots to around 30 centimetres (12 in.) from the soil level. Once the rose is actively growing and flowering, remove flower heads as they fade to encourage more bud production. Golden Beauty has good disease resistance and will not be troubled by the usual fungal and rust attacks experienced by many other roses.

Bred in Germany by W. Kordes' Söhne, the variety was a winner at the Gold Standard Trials in 2009. These are UK trials commissioned by rose growers, but run and judged independently. Only roses with exceptional performance across two years are given the award, confirming Golden Beauty as a tried and tested beautiful variety. **PM**

Alternatives

= 'Korberbeni'. *Rosa* 'South Africa'

Rosa
Westerland

Main features Clusters of apricot-coloured flowers; good disease resistance
Height 1.5–3.6 m (5–12 ft) **Spread** 1.5 m (5 ft)
Position ○ **Hardiness** RHS H6

Since their first appearance in 1969, the sensational, rich, apricot-coloured blooms of *R*. Westerland have been winning the hearts of gardeners throughout the world. Gorgeous flowers with a strong fragrance are matched by good, disease-resistant, dark-green foliage. A fantastic rose, it can be grown as a shrub but more likely as a climber. Westerland is not shy about blooming, producing flowers in the first year, and it repeat flowers well. Many other varieties in this colour class are susceptible to extreme cold, but Westerland is not bothered if the temperature drops. It is a rose for all seasons, with winter hardiness, attractive, bronze-tinted shoots in spring, followed by masses of blooms into the autumn.

This variety grows best in a sunny position, and flower colour is at its strongest in cooler conditions. If Westerland is grown in a shady spot, the shoots will grow quickly but will look stretched, will be lighter green, and will not produce the display that the plant is noted for. As with all cluster-flowered varieties, make it a daily routine during the flowering season to pick off flower heads that are going over and beginning to fade. This keeps plants looking good, reduces the chance of grey mould attacking the blooms, and encourages the plant to produce more flower buds. If hard pruned every winter or early spring, Westerland will grow as a shrub rose. If left to its own devices, it will behave as a climbing rose, covering any structure, such as a strong metal obelisk or wall, with a blanket of blooms. **PM**

Alternatives

= 'Korwest'. *Rosa* 'Autumn Sunset'

Rosa
R. *virginiana*

Main features Small, single, bright-pink flowers; very good autumn colour; lightly fragrant
Height 1.2 m (4 ft) **Spread** 90 cm (3 ft)
Position ○ ◑ **Hardiness** RHS H7

Most wild roses are very vigorous and as shrubs will easily reach 1.8 metres (6 ft) in height and spread, making them difficult to accommodate in smaller gardens. *R. virginiana* is more modestly sized and offers three good seasons of interest. The small, single flowers are bright pink and produced very prolifically over a long season. They are followed by small, brightly coloured hips that turn from orange to red. This coincides with the leaves changing colour to a superb mix of oranges, reds, coppers and bronzes. The leaves will stay attached to the plant for some weeks, while the hips will last until late winter, thereby providing a good source of food for wildlife (as will the flowers for insects).

A remarkably tough, reliable and healthy plant, *R. virginiana* stays free of the usual diseases. It is happiest in full sun, but would cope with only half a day's worth of sunshine, and will grow well in just about any soil except extremes of acid and alkaline. In order to encourage its natural habit, it is best not to prune *R. virginiana* at all, although some of the older stems could be cut out after several years on a mature plant.

The wilder, more informal parts of the garden will be where this plant will look the best, although it would also be excellent in a mixed border. A hedge of *R. virginiana* would be most effective, especially because it will then sucker and develop into an impenetrable barrier. There is also a white form, *R. virginiana* 'Alba', and a pretty double variety, *R. virginiana* 'Plena', which is a very old hybrid that was once used for buttonholes. *R. spinosissima* is equally tough and of a similar size to *R. virginiana*. Its leaves will turn a rich mixture of colours during the autumn, although the flowers are white and the hips black. Many of its hybrids will make a very worthwhile additions to the garden. **MM**

Alternatives

Rosa spinosissima 'Andrewsii', *Rosa spinosissima* 'Glory of Edzell', *Rosa spinosissima* 'Single Cherry', *Rosa stellata*

Rosa
'Octoberfest'

Main feature Orange blooms produced in clusters
Height 2 m (7 ft) **Spread** 1.2 m (4 ft)
Position ○
Hardiness RHS H5

The words 'exuberant', 'flamboyant' and 'zestful' only begin to describe this rose variety, which guarantees to light up your garden. Its blooms are an ever-changing mix of orange, red and yellow – produced at the peak of summer – and provide a taster of the autumn colours to come. Subtlety? Not a chance of it.

'Octoberfest' was introduced in 1996 by the McGredy family: rose breeders who settled in New Zealand in the 1970s and introduced a great many successful, brightly coloured, hybrid tea roses, including one of 'Octoberfest's' parents, *Rosa* 'New Zealand', in 1989. 'Octoberfest' is classed as a grandiflora type, which combines the shape of a hybrid tea with the cluster-flowering nature of floribundas. The flower buds are stylish and pointed, opening to high-centred, medium to large blooms that can reach 13 centimetres (5 in.) in diameter. As the flowers are produced in clusters, yet have the shape of old-fashioned Valentine's Day roses, stems can be cut to make attractive bouquets. The fragrance is moderately fruity.

In spring the new shoot growth of 'Octoberfest' is deep red, with leaves developing into a healthy, glossy, deep green. Plants can grow fairly tall and they are superb if used on their own in beds or as specimens near the back of a mixed border, adding plenty of drama to a hot-colour scheme. However, this variety needs a fertile soil in full sun to produce its best flowers. Prune in winter to maintain the shape and integrity of the plant and to ensure a wonderful garden display the following summer. The colour of the flowers will fade slightly in strong sun, but with so many blooms being produced by each plant, this is not too much of an issue. As the weather cools, the vibrancy returns. It is hard to keep 'Octoberfest' down. **PM**

Alternatives

Rosa 'Maclanter', *Rosa* 'Lantern', *Rosa* 'New Zealand'

Gardeners have always had the urge to collect plants that are exotic for their region, and have been prepared to build special structures to provide them with the conditions they need. Perhaps the most extravagant such edifices are the orangeries built at Versailles to house citrus plants. You don't need a palace, however: even an indoor windowsill could be home to any number of interesting little gems from afar.

Within this chapter is an eclectic mix of plants that perhaps have little in common apart from their preference for a bit of cosseting in colder weather. There are houseplants, both foliage and flowering kinds such as orchids and some curious talking points, such as cacti, carnivorous plants and bromeliads. A few are succulents that make drought-tolerant features on a sunny patio; others were originally jungle understory plants, so they like moist and shady conditions.

INDOOR AND PATIO

◐ *Dudleya brittonii* is an architectural succulent that tolerates a hot, dry patio.

Abutilon
'Kentish Belle'

Main features Long-flowering shrub from spring to autumn; vividly coloured, pendent flowers
Height 2.4 m (8 ft) **Spread** 2.4 m (8 ft)
Position ○ **Hardiness** RHS H3

There is something distinctly exotic-looking about this *Abutilon* – an indication perhaps of its Brazilian roots. Despite its South American origins, the hybrid 'Kentish Belle' is surprisingly resilient to winter cold, making it a brilliant choice for adding impact to walls in areas where the mercury does not dive too far and for too long below freezing.

The outstanding highlight of 'Kentish Belle' is its long-lived and vivid, but never brash, flowers. Dangling, tubular bells are held along long stalks, and its crimson buds unfurl to reveal orange-yellow skirts beneath. Below the petals a cluster of conspicuous stamen hang like the clappers of a bell. The plant's arching growth shows off the profuse, bell-shaped flowers to perfection. The palmate leaves are shallowly lobed and dark green and, in milder areas, they can persist through winter. In warmer regions, the flowers can also still be seen after Christmas, however, sunlight is essential for it to keep flowering. *Abutilon* is a member of the mallow family, which includes hollyhocks, lavatera and hibiscus, all of which seem to flower for months on end. 'Kentish Belle' is no exception, coming into bloom in late spring and putting on a nonstop, cheerful display well into autumn, even in colder places.

Despite its obvious charms, 'Kentish Belle' seems to be underused, certainly in the United Kingdom, which is not exactly overrun with long flowering, climbing plants, especially those that put on such a spectacular show. With its neat growing habit, 'Kentish Belle' is perfect against a sunny, sheltered house wall, or try combining it with more short-lived, flowering wall shrubs, such as *Ceanothus*. Do not be put off if where you live suffers from frost; if *Abutilon* succumbs, there is a good chance it will regenerate from new shoots at ground level. **ER**

Alternative

Abutilon 'Canary Bird'

Abutilon
A. megapotamicum 'Orange Hot Lava'

Main features Compact shrub; bright, bell-like flowers
from early summer to autumn; attracts hummingbirds
Height 1.2 m (4 ft) **Spread** 90 cm (3 ft)
Position ○ **Hardiness** RHS H3

This particularly free-flowering form of *Abutilon* has
vibrant, clear-orange bells veined in red and held in
conspicuous brick-red calyxes. The volcanic colours
and fascinating flower shape demand attention, and
it is a plant that calls for a prominent position in the
garden. The leaves are a typical maple shape, and in
mild conditions the plant will keep some leaves through
winter. Introduced in 2005 by Luen Miller of the Monterey
Bay Nursery in California, it is a multi-stemmed shrub
that forms a more compact plant than many abutilon,
including its parent *A. megapotamicum*.

Plant it in a sturdy tub in moisture-retentive compost.
In warm, temperate or subtropical regions, it will flourish
in a sheltered spot outside. Protect from strong wind,
which may break the branches. Pinch out new sideshoots
to promote bushiness. Prune in late winter as new growth
starts to shoot, and water regularly to keep the compost
moist. Pot-grown specimens will need feeding monthly
with a high-potash feed to encourage flowering. Plants
will survive short periods down to -5°C (23°F) if the soil
is dry, but they can be short-lived, so it is advisable to
root a few cuttings each year. Softwood cuttings taken
in late spring should root in four to six weeks; there will
be no shortage of people willing to home any spare
plants. Under glass, they are, like many plants, prone to
whiteflies, red spider mite and mealy bugs.

Although abutilon is known as the flowering maple,
it is not a maple at all, but a hibiscus relative in the
Malvaceae family. The family likeness can be seen in the
long staminal column with masses of fluffy pollen in the
middle of the flower. The alternative name of Chinese
lantern is also inaccurate as the wild species is native not
to China, but to Argentina, Brazil and Uruguay, where it
is pollinated by hummingbirds. **GHa**

Alternatives

Abutilon 'Fool's Gold', *Abutilon* 'Voodoo'

Aeonium

'Zwartkop'

Main features Good patio and container plant; drought tolerant; good for xeriscaping
Height 90–120 cm (3–4 ft) **Spread** 60–90 cm (2–3 ft)
Position ○ **Hardiness** RHS H1c

The genus *Aeonium* takes its name from the Greek word *aionos*, meaning 'timeless', 'everlasting', 'eternal'. Native to the Canary Islands, northern Africa and the Mediterranean, there are many versatile species, but the cultivars are most commonly found. Distinctive 'Zwartkop' has glossy, dark-purple, almost black leaves that form elegant rosettes at the end of its fleshy, central stem and side branches. Take out the central eye with a sharp knife to encourage a bushy habit. Although not frost hardy, 'Zwartkop' makes a beautiful container plant in cooler regions, grown in winter in frost-free garden rooms, conservatories or greenhouses. Placed outside in summer, it adds architectural interest and colour to seasonal patio displays. Other notable varieties include *A. haworthii*, an evergreen subshrub with a fleshy rosette of grey-green leaves at the end of each branch. It produces white or yellow flowers that are sometimes tinged pink. **RC**

Alternatives

Aeonium 'Blushing Beauty', *Aeonium haworthii* 'Variegatum', *Aeonium* 'Sunburst', *Aeonium tabuliforme*

Agave

A. americana

Main feature Exotic-looking, architectural evergreen
Height 1.8 m (6 ft) **Spread** 2.7 m (9 ft)
Position ○
Hardiness RHS H2

This spiny succulent is native to Mexico, where it is a key feature of the arid landscape. The spiky, often curved, glaucous leaves are arranged in striking rosettes. Up to 1.8 metres (6 ft) long, *A. americana* spines and tips are covered in sharp needles. Mexicans have long collected the sap to make a drink called *pulque*, and juice from the core of the plant is used to produce agave nectar, a sugar substitute. The fibres of the plant can be used to make rope, matting and cloth. *A. americana* is also known as the 'century plant', because it takes a very long time to flower. It is monocarpic, which means that after producing many yellow flowers on a very tall stem, followed by black seedpods, the plant dies. By then, however, it will have produced plenty of rhizomatous offshoots, which become new plants. *A. americana* grows anywhere with a sunny, dry climate and looks especially good in modern, 'dry', or gravel gardens, making a striking focal point. In cooler climates it needs very well-drained soil. **VP**

Alternatives

Agave americana 'Marginata', *Agave americana* 'Mediopicta Alba'

Agave americana 'Marginata' in gravel at Beth Chatto Gardens, Essex, UK. ●

Aloe
A. vera

Main features Useful succulent; architectural qualities
Height 45 cm (18 in.) **Spread** 60 cm (24 in.)
Position ○
Hardiness RHS H1c

Originally from West Africa but now naturalised in many warm countries, *A. vera* has been referred to as a 'wonder plant'. This is because it is used in food and food supplements, cosmetics, and herbal remedies. Familiar as an indoor plant, it is widely cultivated throughout the world – in countries such as Mexico, Australia and the United States – to supply the cosmetics industry with aloe vera gel, which is extracted from the fleshy leaves. A striking, clump-forming, suckering succulent, *A. vera* has rosettes of narrow, lance-shaped leaves with teeth along the margins. The upper surface of the leaves is sometimes marked with white flecks or spots, which add to their appeal. Large plants produce exotic panicles that bear tubular, orange or orange-red flowers. *A. vera* needs frost-free conditions over winter, but can be stood out in the garden in a sunny spot during the summer. The most impressive and free-flowering specimens will be ones grown in roomy pots, hot climates or planted out in a greenhouse or conservatory. **GS**

Alternatives

Syn. *Aloe barbadensis. Aloe arborescens, Aloe ferox*

Arctotis
A. × *hybrida*

Main features Tender perennial; daisy-like flowers from midsummer to early autumn
Height 45 cm (18 in.) **Spread** 30 cm (12 in.)
Position ○ **Hardiness** RHS H2

These large, daisy-like flowers adore the sun and put on a display that dazzles, although in dull weather and in late afternoon the flowers close up. Natives of South Africa, *A.* × *hybrida* need well-drained soil and plenty of sun to thrive. The blooms are around 8 centimetres (3 in.) in diameter and are available in carrot orange, fiery red, rich mahogany, pretty pink and cooling white. In addition many varieties have a silver sheen to the undersides of the leaves that flashes when the foliage is blown by summer breezes. *A.* × *hybrida* is perfect for container cultivation, where the addition of horticultural grit to the compost will ensure good drainage. Grown as single subjects in pots, their roots have evolved to seek out moisture, and easily suffer from competition. An alternative is to plant them in drifts or blocks. Orange-flowered *A.* × *hybrida* 'Flame' and the darker orange *A.* × *hybrida* 'Mahogany' are part of the hot-coloured beds at Sissinghurst in Kent. Other named varieties have pink flowers, whereas 'Holly' (pictured) produces deep-red flowers. **PM**

Alternative

Arctotis × *hybrida* 'China Rose'

⊖ *Aloe vera* grown in a container can easily be moved to a frost-free place in the autumn.

Argyranthemum
'Jamaica Primrose'

Main features Tender perennial; nonstop flowers from early summer to late autumn
Height 90 cm (3 ft) **Spread** 1.2 m (4 ft)
Position ○ **Hardiness** RHS H3

A tender perennial that hails from the Canary Islands and Madeira, *Argyranthemum* is a well-established treasure for summer displays in containers and the open garden. Recent introductions have included spectacular, crested and fully double flowers on increasingly compact plants, but 'Jamaica Primrose' is an old favourite that has stood the test of time and still gives other species a run for their money. This plant is one of the most prolific flowering plants in the world, and it is not unusual to see the single, yellow daisy heads still out on Christmas day in a mild winter. Combine this feat with an ease of cultivation – 'Jamaica Primrose' is very easy to propagate from stem cuttings taken in late summer – and it is no surprise that it has been awarded the Royal Horticultural Society Award of Garden Merit.

If you are able to overwinter mature plants in a frost-free environment or garden in a hot climate, it is well worth training 'Jamaica Primrose' into half or full standards. A matching pair – with tall stalks and rich-green leaves – can look very sophisticated in deep terra-cotta pots framing a front door. As you would with standard fuchsias, you simply train a strong shoot from a pot-grown plant up a cane, removing all other side shoots (but not the leaves on the main stem), and pinch out the tip at the required height. Further pinching will be required to form a bushy head. In fact, 'Jamaica Primrose' will benefit from some pinching at any size, because the side branches tend to be brittle and break away, especially when grown in rich, damp soils. Weekly deadheading will keep the plants looking tidy, and a light trim after each major flower flush will encourage new growth and more blooms. Suitable companion plants include *Lobelia erinus compacta* and *Petunia × hybrida* 'Storm Lavender'. **GS**

Alternatives

Argyranthemum gracile 'Chelsea Girl', *Argyranthemum* 'Vancouver', *Argyranthemum* Madeira Cherry Red = 'Bonmadcher'

Aspidistra
A. elatior

Main feature Resilient, evergreen, perennial grown for
its dark-green, lance-shaped leaves
Height 60 cm (24 in.) **Spread** 45 cm (18 in.)
Position ◐ ● **Hardiness** RHS H2

This plant earned the nicknames cast-iron plant and
bar room plant from its ability to survive under adverse
conditions, including being used as an ashtray in a smoky
bar. The species *A. elatior* originates from China and Japan
and was a popular feature of nineteenth-century homes
because it could cope with poor light conditions and the
fumes from gas lighting. Some plants from the Victorian
era are known to have survived and been passed down
the generations. The cast-iron plant was immortalised in
George Orwell's novel of 1938, *Keep the Aspidistra Flying*.

A. elatior is a low-maintenance houseplant with
glossy, dark-green leaves that will enhance any dull
corner of the house. It is a slow grower that does not
require repotting too often, and its leaves can grow
up to 90 centimetres (3 ft) in length and 13 centimetres
(5 in.) in width. It is often found as a pot plant in office
interiors and the indoor gardens of department stores.
Aspidistras can also be grown outside in containers or in
the ground, where they can withstand temperatures as
low as -5°C (23°F). They thrive in sheltered, shady, moist
conditions, where they associate well with ferns. Out of
direct sunlight the leaves are an attractive deep green.
In the ground, *A. elatior* produces rather insignificant,
star-shaped, crimson-purple flowers with a cream back
at soil level in the spring or early summer.

There are several variegated cultivars, including
A. elatior 'Variegata', which has irregular cream stripes,
adding a splash of colour to the dark foliage, and 'Milky
Way' (pictured), which is green with white spots. Note
that the variegated cultivars need slightly more light
than the common species. Generally, however, if there
is one plant you can put down in the ground or put in a
pot for indoors and pretty well leave to its own devices,
it has to be *A. elatior*. **NM**

Alternatives

Aspidistra elatior 'Milky Way', *Aspidistra elatior* 'Variegata',
Aspidistra lurida, *Aspidistra attenuata*, *Aspidistra elator*
'Asahi', *Aspidistra elator* 'Okame'

Astelia
A. chathamica 'Silver Spear'

Main features Evergreen, silver, grey-green leaves; good in containers
Height 90–150 cm (3–5 ft) **Spread** 1.2–1.5 m (4–5 ft)
Position ◑ ● **Hardiness** RHS H3

Evergreen and architectural, *A. chathamica* stands out as one of the few silver-leaved plants that thrives in shade. It originates from the Chatham Islands of New Zealand, and in its native habitat it is a woodland understorey that grows in damp soil with leaf mould. The low-maintenance cultivar 'Silver Spear' has become synonymous with the plant. Highly reflective foliage is combined with a bold architectural shape or habit. Leaves are ridged in texture, with silver on the topside and white underneath, which adds to its metallic glow. 'Silver Spear' is startlingly bright and makes an excellent night-time plant – add an outdoor spotlight to maximise this quality. Although its looks go well with sparse, spare, gravel gardens, where

pebble mulch aids moisture retention around plant roots, it prefers a soil that does not dry out. In mid to late spring, long stems of yellowish-green flowers emerge from female plants, and these are followed by orange berries in autumn.

'Silver Spear' underscores the white trunks and branches of silver birch to create pools of light in a garden. Alternatively, for added drama, contrast its silver shimmer with pitch-black mondo grass *Ophiopogon planiscapus* 'Nigrescens', the darkly glossy, purple rosettes of *Aeonium* 'Zwartkop', or the similarly sword-shaped leaves of *Phormium tenax* 'All Black'. Other cultivars to try include *Astelia nervosa* 'Westland', which has spiky clumps of red-flushed foliage, and 'Red Devil', a shorter cultivar with red-silver leaves. **RC**

Alternatives

Astelia banksii, Astelia nervosa 'Westland', *Astelia* 'Red Devil'

Brugmansia
B. suaveolens

Main features Flowers summer and autumn; year-round foliage; fragrant flowers; architectural plant
Height 1.8 m (6 ft) **Spread** 90 cm (3 ft)
Position ○ ◑ **Hardiness** RHS H1c

This is a plant of considerable stature, with the ability to put on a spectacular display. Its evergreen leaves are 20 centimetres (8 in.) long, but it is the flowers of *B. suaveolens* that steal the show: large, pendulous, widely flared, trumpets up to 30 centimetres (12 in.) long. They are sweetly scented, especially at night, when they attract pollinating moths. The flowers can be white, pale pink or yellow, and a double-flowered variety ('Flore Pleno') is also available. There are cultivars with variegated leaves, but it is arguable that the white-edged foliage detracts from the pureness of colour and dramatic effect of the flower.

A native to tropical South America, it can reach 5 metres (16 ft) in height in the wild, but in cultivation it can be kept much smaller by hard pruning and pinching out. It is much loved by ornamental gardeners with a taste for the exotic, but it must be protected from frost in winter. It makes a showy specimen in a pot when used as a focal point in the garden or when planted out as a summer addition to an otherwise hardy border in cooler climates.

For all its glorious beauty, *B. suaveolens* has a sinister history. It belongs to the family *Solanaceae*, which includes deadly nightshade (*Atropa belladonna*), potato and tobacco – all plants with potentially toxic properties. Historically, the psychotropic properties of *B. suaveolens* have been used in rituals by shamans to induce a trance-like state. All parts of the plant are toxic, especially the leaves and seeds, but that should not put you off growing this glorious plant. **PWi**

Alternative

Syn. *Datura suaveolens. Brugmansia suaveolens* 'Snow White'

Brunfelsia
B. pauciflora

Main feature Shrub with scented flowers in summer
and autumn
Height 90–240 cm (3–8 ft) **Spread** 1.2–1.8 m (4–6 ft)
Position ○ ◑ **Hardiness** RHS H3

Native to the woodlands of Brazil, this tropical shrub
features dark-green, leathery leaves and is a profuse
bloomer, with flowers that open deep violet, turn to light
violet, then become white as they age over the course of
three days. Flowering continuously from spring through
to the end of summer, *B. pauciflora* can display blooms of
all three colours at any one time, thus giving the plant a
charming, spangled effect. The long, tubular flowers have
flat, pansy-like faces with white centres and throats, and
their nectar attracts butterflies by day and moths at dusk.
In addition the flowers are intoxicatingly fragrant with a
sweet, candy-like scent that carries for quite a distance
and will delightfully perfume a summer patio or outdoor
seating area. *B. pauciflora* is perfect as a container plant, as
it flowers best when allowed to become potbound and
periodically dry out. It is also easily kept to a manageable
height with judicious pruning. Although there are several
cultivars available, they are actually all relatively similar
and have the same telltale, multi-coloured effect. **KK**

Alternatives

Brunfelsia nitida, Brunfelsia jamaicensis, Brunfelsia americana

Caesalpinia
C. pulcherrima

Main features Delicate leaves; brightly coloured flowers
Height 1.8 m (6 ft) **Spread** 2.4 m (8 ft)
Position ○ ◑
Hardiness RHS H1c

These large shrubs, or small trees, are valued for their finely
divided leaves and architectural flowers with long stamen,
which sit like candles above the branches.
C. pulcherrima has wide-spreading branches and fern-like
leaves. The flowers, on an open airy spike with filamentous
stems, are 5 to 8 centimetres (2–3 in.) in diameter. Each
flower has five crinkled, red-and-orange petals, and
prominent bright-red stamen that extend way beyond
the flower. There is also a yellow-flowered form, and both
are visited by insects, hummingbirds and monarch
butterflies. *C. pulcherrima* can be grown by a warm,
sheltered, sunny wall in cool, temperate climates. In the
tropics it is evergreen, but in cool climates it becomes
deciduous or even herbaceous, growing annually from
ground level. Fabulous as a specimen plant or in shrub
borders, *C. pulcherrima* is also used as informal hedging.
Plant it in a moderately fertile, well-drained soil in full sun
or light shade. *C. gilliesii* is a similar plant but bigger, with
pale-yellow trumpet flowers and long, red stamen. **MB**

Alternative

Caesalpinia gilliesii

Calathea
C. zebrina

Main features Perennial with striking, year-round foliage; architectural plant
Height 90 cm (3 ft) **Spread** 90 cm (3 ft)
Position ◑ ● **Hardiness** RHS H1b

This striking, Brazilian plant has paddle-like, evergreen leaves up to 45 centimetres (18 in.) long that are held on wiry stems. The leaf midrib is a conspicuous white, and the leaf is banded dark and light green, with a velvet sheen. Like other *Calathea*, the undersides of the leaves are purple, but as they grow horizontally, the colour cannot be appreciated. The leaves are useful as short-lived, cut foliage. The bold foliage can be made even more effective by growing it alongside the lacy foliage of the maidenhair fern (*Adiantum*) or the more fluffy-looking asparagus fern (*Asparagus setaceus*). If the leaves start to roll up along their edges, it is telling you it needs more water. The small, white or purple flowers are not regularly produced and are of little significance. *C. zebrina* is often seen as a houseplant in cooler climates, but in tropical regions it is a useful container plant for a shaded area or as ground cover under taller shrubs and trees. Indoors it needs a warm, humid site out of direct sunlight, such as a well-lit bathroom, but keep it away from heat sources. **PWi**

Alternatives

Calathea majestica, Calathea rufibarba

Calliandra
C. haematocephala

Main features Interesting, colourful buds and flowers; blooms midsummer to autumn; attracts pollinators
Height 1.8 m (6 ft) **Spread** 1.2 m (4 ft)
Position ○ ◑ **Hardiness** RHS H3

Also known as pink powderpuff, the flowers of *C. haematocephala* are this plant's talking point. From buds that form in midsummer, they open out into a fluffy ball of stamen, usually in autumn and winter. In its native South America, *C. haematocephala* (a relative of the mimosa) grows into a large, evergreen tree, but in cooler climates it is grown as a long-term container plant for the home or conservatory. In mild regions it is sometimes found as an outdoor shrub, where it can be long-lived and grow large, or it can be trained against a wall or grown as a hedge or screen. Container plants need regular watering, but if the roots sit in waterlogged conditions, they will rot. In warmer months container-grown specimens can be placed on a sunny patio. As summer fades and plants are brought back indoors, which is usually when flowering commences, they are slightly fragrant. *C. haematocephala* has oblong-shaped leaves that fold up at night. When first produced, they are often flushed a prawn-pink colour, but mature to a dark green. **PM**

Alternatives

Calliandra 'Dixie Pink', *Calliandra portoricensis*

Callistemon
C. citrinus 'Splendens'

Main features Evergreen shrub with flowers in summer; scented foliage; colourful conservatory plant
Height 4 m (13 ft) **Spread** 4 m (13 ft)
Position ○ **Hardiness** RHS H3

'Splendens' is certainly an instantly recognisable, impressive, eye-catching shrub with a most appropriate common name: bottlebrush. Its parent comes from Australia and Tasmania, home to so many extraordinary plants, but this excellent variety was raised at Kew Gardens, England, from Australian seed.

It forms a lax, evergreen bush, some 4 metres (13 ft) high by the same across. The leaves are stiff, narrow and dark green, and they give off a lemon scent when crushed, hence its specific name. The new growth is pleasantly soft and silky with a pinkish flush. From midspring into summer, the clusters of buds erupt into a dense cylindrical 'bottlebrush' shape, 10 to 13 centimetres (4–5 in.) long. The bright crimson stamen of 'Splendens' obscure the inconspicuous petals. After flowering, woody bobbly seed capsules develop, which persist for many years, and the next season's flowers develop beyond the previous seasons.

Grow this plant in a sheltered position and in full sun for the best effect, in a moist but well-drained, acidic to neutral soil. The bush tends to be a rather lax shape, but this can be improved by light pruning immediately after flowering, cutting just behind the occasional old flower head.

The striking appearance of 'Splendens' makes this plant ideal for a tropical or contemporary style of planting, in company with other Australasian plants, or in a Mediterranean-style garden. (In truth, it looks rather alien in a cottage-style garden.) 'Splendens' is marginally hardy and perfect for warmer climates. In less favourable climates 'Splendens' can be grown successfully in a container in a cool greenhouse or conservatory and then stood outside in a sunny position throughout the summer months. **MP**

Alternative

Callistemon subulatus

Camellia
'Quintessence'

Main feature Small, spreading, evergreen shrub; scented flowers in early spring
Height 1 m (3.5 ft) **Spread** 1.2 m (4 ft)
Position ◑ ● **Hardiness** RHS H4

This is not like a typical camellia. 'Quintessence' is a small, spreading, low-growing, evergreen bush with gorgeously scented flowers. Its growth habit means that it can be planted in a large hanging basket or tall pot and allowed to cascade down. Therefore, not only can you enjoy growing this camellia whatever your soil type, but even those with small urban spaces can grow it in a sheltered corner, porch or conservatory, where the early spring fragrance brings such joy.

The plant is not totally hardy, although being fairly compact in growth, that is not a major handicap. In mild regions it can be grown outside, perhaps at the front of a shrub border where other camellias already thrive, or in a rockery. It also makes good ground cover. Camellias require well-drained, acidic soil, so if planting in containers use an ericaceous (lime-free) compost, and in hard water areas use rainwater for watering. Feed with a camellia and azalea plant food in spring and remember to keep watered in summer, as that is when the buds form for the next year's display. The flowers are pretty and fairly plentiful: from neat pink buds they open to small, delicate white blooms tinged with pink and showing their yellow stamen. The foliage is glossy and dark green but new leaves often have bronze tints.

'Quintessence' is a fairly recent hybrid (*japonica* × *lutchuensis*), which was introduced in 1985. There are other camellia cultivars, for example *C. sasanqua*, that are prized for their scented flowers and which are also worth exploring if you have the right situation and winter climate for them, although they usually make bigger plants than 'Quintessence'. For example, an excellent contrast to 'Quintessence' is *C. sasanqua* 'Crimson King', with its crimson-red single flowers and golden-yellow stamen, which appear in late autumn to early winter. **NM**

Alternative

Camellia sasanqua 'Crimson King'

Catharanthus
C. roseus

Main feature Flowering annual; weather tolerant;
attracts wildlife but deer resistant
Height 30–60 cm (12–24 in.) **Spread** 25–30 cm (10–12 in.)
Position ○ ◑ ● **Hardiness** RHS H1c

Also known as the Madagascan periwinkle and originally
from Madagascar, today *C. roseus* is a pan-global bedding
plant. It has been used medicinally for centuries to treat
problems from wasp stings to diabetes. More recently, the
alkaloids present in the plant are being used in anticancer
drugs. Vincristine, its main abstract, has been credited
with raising the survival rate for childhood leukaemia.

C. roseus can grow virtually anywhere, but it excels in
high temperatures and high humidity. It is drought
tolerant, although it can cope with rain too. Grown as an
annual, but in some regions as a perennial, it can reseed,
which can be a bonus, but this can also make it invasive
in subtropical areas. In shades of white, through pink, rose,
red and purple, *C. roseus* can be found with and without
contrasting 'eyes'. American seed companies have led
the charge in breeding new varieties, with bigger flowers,
newer colours and greater resilience. Seed germinate fast
at a minimum temperature of 24°C (75°F), but the resulting
seedlings require high (95 per cent) humidity. As these
versatile plants grow stronger, humidity can be reduced,
but you should maintain minimum temperatures of
21°C (70°F). Young plants can then be watered and the
compost allowed to dry out before repeating, which
acclimatises them to outdoor garden conditions.

Grow *Catharanthus* in pots, containers or flower beds.
Plant en masse to maximise effect, but note that as their
roots have alkaloidal, allelopathic effects, they do not
always associate well with other plants. **IT**

Alternative

Syn. *Vinca rosea. Catharanthus roseus* 'Mediterranean Lilac'

Cestrum

C. nocturnum

Main features Shrub that flowers in summer to the first frost; blooms in flushes
Height 75–100 cm (2.5 3.5 ft) **Spread** 90 cm (3 ft)
Position ○ **Hardiness** RHS H4

This shrub has sprawling stems that give rise to sprays of small, tubular, greenish-white flowers. These blooms are not particularly showy, and the foliage is a basic green colour. During the day the plant's appearance is somewhat unremarkable; however, *C. nocturnum* is a night-blooming jasmine and possibly the most fragrant and sweetest- smelling plant you can grow. The scent is pungent and sugary, strong and sensual – there is nothing quite like it. Some say it is reminiscent of sweets or bubble gum; others detect a combination of traditional jasmine and a citrus overtone. The small flowers start pumping out fragrance as dusk descends, and the scent grows stronger as night progresses.

C. nocturnum is a delight by a patio or open window as the romantic and intoxicating fragrance wafts about. As a background plant by day, it can act as a foil for more florally exuberant neighbours before taking its nightly turn as star. In New Orleans, legend has it that *C. nocturnum* was traditionally planted near outhouses to mask unsavoury odours. In warm climates it becomes a large shrub, but elsewhere it makes an admirable container subject, and pruning can keep it a manageable size for a houseplant. If not deadheaded, *C. nocturnum* will produce white berries that are ornamental in their own right, beloved by birds, and useful in indoor arrangements. Blooming in flushes throughout warm weather, this West Indian native is a must-have plant for anyone who gardens for fragrance. **KK**

Alternatives

Cestrum diurnum, Cestrum aurantiacum

Chlorophytum
C. comosum 'Vittatum'

Everyone at some time in their lives has come into contact with the spider plant *C. comosum*. Perhaps it was the first plant grown at home, or in the workplace, where it was ever present, sitting neglected on top of a filing cabinet. This undoubtedly is an irradicable plant of our times.

The linear, strappy, green leaves of 'Vittatum' (pictured) have a central cream-white stripe, whereas 'Variegatum' has a cream-white leaf margin. The species *C. comosum* is plain green, but the variegated forms are more commonly found. The spider plant also produces long flowering stems, often up to 1.8 metres (6 ft) long, carrying starry, white flowers and tiny, young plants, identical to the parent, along their length. There is nothing more engaging than breaking the plantlets off the stem and rooting in them pots of compost or even in glasses of water. It is the simplest plant to propagate.

Spider plants grow best in a sunny or semi-shaded position in the home; they survive when neglected and do not suffer at all if a watering or two is missed. Ideally, the compost should be kept moist but not waterlogged. In warmer months plants can be moved outside and can be displayed to great effect when grown in hanging baskets. This allows the leaves and fecund flowering stems to cascade down completely unimpeded. Many are shoved on top of a kitchen cupboard, where they thrive without fuss. Even there, 'Vittatum' and 'Variegatum' thoroughly deserve their Royal Horticultural Society Awards of Garden Merit. The species is a native of South Africa and has adapted to periods of dry weather. Thick, white fleshy roots store water and food for times of hardship. If the leaves do start to turn brown, it can be assumed that watering, or a lack of it, has gone too far. Treated well, nothing harms or is even slightly detrimental to this stalwart. **PM**

Alternatives

Chlorophytum comosum, Chlorophytum comosum 'Aureomarginata'

Clivia
C. miniata var. citrina

Main feature Shade-loving evergreen with showy,
lemon-coloured, long-lasting blooms
Height 30–60 cm (12–24 in.) **Spread** 30–60 cm (12–24 in.)
Position ◑ ● **Hardiness** RHS H1c

Few plants will grow in shady areas, but for the Natal lily
C. miniata, which likes its roots in rich, moist soil, this is
home. Its natural habitat is on the forest floor, under trees
or between boulders on slopes. *C. miniata* is a fantastic
plant for shady containers or garden corners that do not
fall below 15°C (60°F); where temperatures fall below this,
grow it as a conservatory or houseplant.

The orange-flowered *C. miniata* was a popular
indoor plant with the Victorians. The first recorded
yellow form of the species was found in the forests of
Zululand, KwaZulu-Natal, by Captain Mansell in 1888. The
yellow-blooming Natal lily remained a rarity until today.
History occasionally relates the story of dedicated, even
fanatical, plant collectors. One such was Gordon McNeil
of Ofcolaco, who for fifty years collected all manner of
Clivia species and cultivars from within South Africa.
Thought to have introduced this yellow form across the
world, he was relentless in his experimental breeding.
The name *citrina* is derived from the word 'citrine', a
semiprecious yellow quartz; these plants were used to
introduce the colour yellow into other *Clivia*. Longwood
Gardens in the United States has since bred improved
yellow-flowered cultivars and hybrids.

Plants benefit from feeding as the flower spikes
develop. They grow continuously in tropical climates,
but plants have a winter rest elsewhere. Grow in clay pots
and use indoors or outside. Although botanically a bulb,
Clivia forms thick, branching roots and rhizomes and is
best purchased as a potted plant in flower to confirm the
correct colour. Allow plants to become overcrowded in
the pot, as this promotes flowering. *Clivia* can be grown
from seed too, but they only flower when they have
produced thirteen leaves, which takes four to six years.
Note that the leaves are toxic when nibbled by pets. **IT**

Alternatives

Clivia miniata var. *citrina* 'Butterball', *Clivia miniata*
'Longwood Debutante'

Conophytum
C. flavum

Main features Fascinating, dwarf succulent; blue-green leaves; gold-yellow flowers
Height 10 cm (4 in.) **Spread** 10 cm (4 in.)
Position ○ **Hardiness** RHS H2

This is a fascinating little plant guaranteed to keep all gardeners intrigued, particularly children. Perfect for the home and even outdoors during warmer, summer weather, *C. flavum* – also known as the yellow cone plant – is a beautiful curiosity. It is a dwarf succulent that forms low clumps of plant 'bodies' in dense mats or cushions. Each body is made up of a pair of swollen, extremely fleshy leaves fused at the lower part. They are blue-green in colour and frequently exhibit small spots of dark-brown tannin on the upper surface. If that isn't enough to get the botanic taste buds tingling, then this enigmatic succulent goes one step further. Single, gold-yellow, daisy-like blooms emerge from the central cleft between the two leaves in late summer and autumn. The blooms open in strong sunshine, but by around midafternoon they close up again. The leaves usually shrivel after flowering.

Originating in South Africa, where it grows wild on quartz, shale or granite outcrops, *C. flavum* needs a warm, sunny environment. Plants are therefore ideal for an indoor windowsill, a well-ventilated greenhouse or a conservatory. Grow in pots filled with well-drained compost; add sharp sand or fine grit to standard compost mixes. Water sparingly when the plants are in full growth and keep completely dry when they become dormant. The plant is usually dormant in summer and active in the autumn and winter, although they can grow all year round. A good rule of thumb is that when the plant shrivels, you need to give it a watering. Plants need sunlight, but protection from scorching sun in summer. A plant can stay in the same pot for many years, and if over potted, may not produce flowers for a few years. However, get the growing conditions right and *C. flavum* will transfix and delight the botanically minded. **PM**

Alternatives

Conophytum pearsonii, Conophytum meyeri, Conophytum verrucosum

Cordyline
C. australis 'Torbay Dazzler'

Main features Architectural plant; evergreen, sword-like leaves
Height 2.4–5 m (8–16 ft) **Spread** 2 m (7 ft)
Position ○ ◑ **Hardiness** RHS H3

These striking evergreen shrubs are grown for their architectural shape. The leathery, sword-like leaves – in shades of green, bronze and purple – can grow up to 90 centimetres (3 ft) long. The lower leaves are shed as the plant grows, which gives the plant a palm-like appearance, as well as its common name, the cabbage palm. In the summer *C. australis* has mid-green leaves and panicles of white flowers, followed by small, green-white berries. 'Torbay Dazzler' is variegated, with cream stripes and margins.

This cultivar makes a good specimen plant, especially in seaside, contemporary or urban gardens, where it can eventually reach 5 metres (16 ft) in height. It can also provide useful evergreen structure in a mixed border. Young plants are often grown in bedding displays or in containers. They do best in fertile, well-drained soil in a sheltered, sunny spot. Like all varieties with variegated or coloured leaves, 'Torbay Dazzler' thrives in partial shade because bright sun makes the colours fade. It is not fully hardy, but mature plants should survive the winter outside in temperate climates. Younger plants, and other varieties of *C. australis* with coloured leaves, are more tender, so their leaves should be tied together and wrapped in fleece for winter protection.

Cordylines are low maintenance: simply remove any browned leaves at the base of the plant, along with faded flower heads. Most plants are bought as mature specimens, but they can be grown from seeds, cuttings or suckers. Other good varieties to try include *C. australis* 'Albertii', which has matt-green, variegated leaves with cream edges and a pinkish midrib; *C. australis* 'Sundance', which is a popular compact cultivar with a red midrib on the leaves; and *C. australis* Purpurea Group, which has flushed purple leaves. **VP**

Alternatives

Cordyline australis 'Albertii', *Cordyline australis* Purpurea Group, *Cordyline australis* 'Sundance'

Cosmos
C. atrosanguineus
Chocamocha

Main features Tuberous perennial that flowers from
midsummer to autumn; chocolate-scented
Height 30 cm (12 in.) **Spread** 45 cm (18 in.)
Position ○ **Hardiness** RHS H3

The daisy-like flowers of *Cosmos* are stalwarts of summer
borders and containers. There are annual and perennial
types, and *C. astrosanguineus* Chocamocha is a tuberous
perennial that hails from Mexico. It derives its Latin name
from the dark, dried-blood colour of its sumptuous,
velvety flowers, but its common name is chocolate
cosmos thanks to its strong chocolate scent. A compact
plant flowering from mid- to early autumn, it looks good
planted with other hot-coloured plants, such as *Rudbeckia*,
Helenium and *Dahlia*, as well as with grasses. Flowers are
black velvet when they first open then they lighten to
crimson. Chocamocha is not frost hardy, so in temperate
climates it is best treated like *Dahlia*. After the first frost
has blackened the leaves, lift the tubers, remove all the
soil from the roots, and store in a cool, dry, frost-free
place. In early spring pot them up individually and put
them in a warm, bright spot to stimulate growth. Harden
them off before planting them out after the last frost. **VP**

Alternative

= 'Thomocha'. *Cosmos atrosanguineus*

Crassula
C. ovata

Main features Fleshy leaves; long-lived houseplant;
architectural shape
Height 90 cm (3 ft) **Spread** 60 cm (24 in.)
Position ○ ◑ **Hardiness** RHS H2

Known as jade plants, these long-lived succulents have
rounded, fleshy leaves with thick stems. As well as
the plain green species, there are several outstanding
cultivars, including the variegated 'Hummel's Sunset' and
'Gollum' (pictured, above top), which has tubular-shaped
leaves. 'Hummel's Sunset' is a bushy succulent reaching
around 90 centimetres (3 ft) high and has glossy leaves
edged with yellow and red. The beauty is in the leaves
and overall tree-like structure, but occasionally white or
pink flowers appear in autumn. A native of South Africa, it
needs a sunny place and free-draining compost. A potting
mix for cacti and succulents is ideal, but sharp sand or
fine grit can be added to other composts. Wait until
the compost is dry between waterings; water weekly in
spring and summer, reducing watering in winter. *C. ovata*
is best grown as a houseplant in most regions, but it can
be placed outside in a semi-shaded spot during summer
provided temperatures do not fall below 10°C (50°F). **PM**

Alternative

Crassula ovata 'Variegata'

Crassula ovata growing in a mixed container with dark-leaved
Aeonium 'Zwartkop' makes a long-lived houseplant. ➲

Ctenanthe

C. oppenheimiana 'Tricolor'

Main feature Dramatically variegated, leafy houseplant
Height 2 m (7 ft) **Spread** 60 cm (24 in.)
Position ◐
Hardiness RHS H1b

Also known as the never-never plant, *C. oppenheimiana* 'Tricolor' is one for experienced gardeners and those wanting a challenge, and seeing the superb foliage is rewarding. A bushy, evergreen perennial, it has lance-shaped leaves that are heavily variegated with cream and silvery green, with plum-purple undersides. An additional feature is that the leaves tend to fold up as it gets dark. It is a native of Brazil and likes warmth, humidity and plenty of water, so grow as a greenhouse plant or indoors. Pot up in free-draining compost and never let it dry out between watering. Give it a bright position, but not in direct, scorching sunlight. Draughts are fatal; try a hot, steamy bathroom as the temperature should always be above 10°C (50°F). Keep the foliage in peak condition with a fortnightly feed, and repot annually in late spring, when the plant begins to grow actively. Get all the growing conditions right and 'Tricolor' will grow quickly and last for years. **PM**

Alternatives

Ctenanthe lubbersiana 'Gold Splash', *Ctenanthe pilosa*

Cyclamen

C. persicum

Main feature Tuberous plant with colourful flowers from late winter to early spring
Height 15 cm (6 in.) **Spread** 15 cm (6 in.)
Position ○ ◐ **Hardiness** RHS H1b

In the dead of winter, when skies are grey and trees skeletal, the florist's cyclamen brings good cheer and brightens up any home. These pot plants are sold as temporary splashes of colour and are invariably not labelled, but they are cultivars of *C. persicum*. Amongst them you may find scented forms, or those with interesting leaf markings. *C. persicum* grows wild in the rocky hillsides of Turkey, the Middle East and eastern Mediterranean. It is less tolerant of cold and frost than the outdoor cyclamen, such as *C. coum* and *C. hederifolia*. Like these cyclamen, *C. persicum* is a tuberous plant. Plant hunters have collected seeds high up in mountains that produces hardier plants, but it has been found that plants are more resilient when kept under cover. Florist's cyclamen are sold as houseplants, but they like a cool environment between 13 to 21°C (55–70°F) and bright but indirect or filtered light. In a centrally heated home, a cool porch or conservatory often suits them better. **NM**

Alternative

Syn. *Cyclamen latifolium*. *Cyclamen persicum* Halios Series

Cyclamen persicum in a container scheme with winter-flowering heather and ornamental cabbage. ➲

Cymbidium
Showgirl

Main feature Orchid suitable as a houseplant;
long-lasting, waxy flowers from late winter onwards
Height 45 cm (18 in.) **Spread** 45 cm (18 in.)
Position ◑ **Hardiness** RHS H1c

These popular orchids are grown for their beautiful, waxy flowers. They are found growing naturally in China, Japan, the Himalayas, South East Asia and Australia, and there are around fifty species, from which thousands of hybrids have been bred, mostly flowering in winter and spring. Cymbidiums are amongst the easiest orchids to grow. In hot climates they can be grown in the garden; in temperate climates they are grown as houseplants. However, they prefer cooler temperatures than other types of orchid. In winter they need a temperature of around 10 to 14°C (50–57°F), and in summer, make sure that temperatures do not exceed 30°C (86°F). The plants require a distinct temperature drop between day and night during mid- to late summer, as this is when flower-spike initiation takes place. In a temperate climate this is best achieved by putting the plants outside for the summer.

For the best results ensure good light levels all year round – orchids need ten to fifteen hours of light each day – especially in winter, but shield them from strong sunlight. If the plants are growing outside, they do best in dappled shade. Water moderately in spring and summer and make sure that excess water can drain away. Let the compost in pots dry out before watering again. Cymbidium orchids generally flower for six to eight weeks, and the stems will need to be supported by a bamboo cane. Once flowering has finished, cut down the flowered stem to the base. Repot the plants in spring if they have become too big for their containers or have been in the same compost for two years. Use a specially formulated orchid bark compost.

Most orchids are sold unnamed, and only specialist orchid nurseries offer named plants. Showgirl is a hybrid between Sweetheart and Alexanderi. As a miniature type it is easier to accommodate as a houseplant. **VP**

Alternatives

Cymbidium 'Lisa Rose', *Cymbidium tigrinum*,
Cymbidium Showgirl 'Malibu'

Darlingtonia
D. californica

Main features Carnivorous plant; flowers in summer; insectivorous pitchers
Height 60 cm (24 in.) **Spread** 60 cm (24 in.)
Position ○ ◑ **Hardiness** RHS H3

No one can fail to be captivated by the sinister-looking but fascinating, carnivorous, or insect-eating, plants. They are often very popular with children, especially young boys. The cobra lily, *D. californica*, is native to northern California and southwest Oregon in the United States, where it lives in nutrient-poor, acidic bogs, and supplements its diet with nitrogen from unsuspecting passing insects that fall into its clutches.

The trap itself consists of a modified leaf that is rolled and sealed to create a watertight tube or pitcher, which is green or green red in colour. The top is curved, swollen and translucent, and ends with two leaf-like 'wings', which are reminiscent of the forked tongue of a cobra. The smell of nectar entices the insects into this trap, and once they have been caught, they cannot escape because the inside of the tube is slippery and the hole by which they could exit is very small. They then fall into a soup-like liquid at the base of the tube, where they will be 'digested' by fluid and enzymes. The plant then extracts the nutrients of the insects. The nodding flowers of *D. californica* are also interesting. Dark-purple petals are surrounded by green-yellow sepals that are held on slender stalks. The flowers hang downwards to prevent the pollen from getting wet; if the pollen is wet, it cannot pollinate the flowers. It is not yet known which insects pollinate *D. californica*; both beetles and spiders have been suggested.

These plants need quite specific conditions to grow well. They need either the moss sphagnum or a mixture of pure moss peat and perlite. The roots need to be watered daily with distilled or rainwater, to mimic the cool, flowing streams in their native habitat. The top of the plant prefers bright light but not direct sun. They are only moderately hardy, but they can be grown in a cool glasshouse. **MP**

Alternatives

Sarracenia purpurea, Sarracenia leucophylla, Dionaea muscipula

Dasylirion
D. wheeleri

Main features Unusual, sword-shaped leaves edged with hooked spines; architectural plant
Height 1.2–1.8 m (4–6 ft) **Spread** 90–120 cm (3–4 ft)
Position ○ **Hardiness** RHS H2

A plant for brave gardeners, this is the hardiest *Dasylirion*, hailing from high altitudes in its native range in the mountains of Mexico and southern parts of the United States. *D. wheeleri* makes a beautiful, but potentially dangerous, ball of glaucous, green-grey leaves, which are viciously armed with hooked spines along the leaves edges. The evergreen leaves are narrow and have a spoon-like base, giving rise to the plant's common names of spoon flower and spoon yucca.

Growing up to 6 metres (20 ft) high in the wild, *D. wheeleri* slowly forms a woody trunk. Typically, these plants grow fairly slowly in gardens, remaining shrub-like (1.2–1.8 m/4–6 ft) for years. However, the flower spikes, when they appear, can add a remarkable 2.4 to 3.6 metres (8–12 ft) to the height. Flowering occurs in summer, with each rosette producing an incredible, ramrod-straight, inflorescence covered in bell-shaped, white flowers. Fortunately for gardeners, unlike many rosette-forming plants, it does not die after flowering. The silvery leaves and beautiful, spurting firework-like shape of this and other *Dasylirion* work well in pots. By lifting them off the ground you can appreciate the nearly perfect spherical growth of the young plants. However, be warned that they will grab clothing and skin with their hooked leaf spines, so place them away from pathways.

D. wheeleri thrives in warm, sunny conditions in rocky or sandy soil. Always mulch plants with gravel; not only does this cut down on the potentially dangerous job of weeding, but it also echoes their natural rocky habitat and makes them look at home. They make wonderful focal points, either as potted specimens on a lawn or grown amongst other arid-climate plants in gravel gardens. For an unusual talking point, *Dasylirion* is hard to beat. **GAR**

Alternatives

Dasylirion acrotrichum, Yucca rostrata

Delosperma
D. cooperi

Main features Fleshy succulents with daisy-like flowers;
low-growing ground cover
Height 10 cm (4 in.) **Spread** 38 cm (15 in.)
Position ○ **Hardiness** RHS H5

Known as the hardy ice plant because the calcium deposits
on its leaves look like ice, *Delosperma* is surprisingly hardy,
but only in dry winters; therefore, in most regions they
are grown as container plants and overwintered as
houseplants. *D. cooperi* and *D. nubigenum* were originally
found in the Drakensberg Mountains of South Africa
by Panayoti Kelaidis of the Denver Botanic Gardens;
D. floribundum and *D. herbeum* were later discovered. In
1998, the hybrid 'Kelaidis' arose at Denver Botanic Gardens
in Colorado and is sold as 'Mesa Verde'.

The leaves of *Delosperma* species are succulent and
rounded in shape – two great attributes when growing
in dry conditions – and flower colour varies. Plants form
low mats, where drying winds have less deleterious
effects. Even if you do not have poor growing conditions
to really test the plants, they are quite happy performing
in containers on a hot, sunny patio or in rockeries and
scree gardens. In a xeric garden, plant en masse in the soil
for an impressive display. When growing in containers,
plant them on their own, not in mixed pots. Hardiness
varies from species to species, but given free-draining
soil, many will survive cold conditions. It is the wet that
can be a challenge.

D. cooperi produces shocking-pink blooms all
summer. *D. herbeum* features white or pale-lavender
blooms from midsummer to early autumn, although
many gardeners enjoy the peach-orange flowers of
D. dyeri. If cool white is in your garden colour scheme,
look out for *D. basuticum* 'White Nugget'. The choice is
wide with some varieties, such as *D. daveyi* producing
bronze-tinged foliage as an additional feature. Plant
collector Josef Halda from the Czech Republic has
introduced other hardy *Delosperma* species, including
D. deleeuwiae. **PM**

Alternatives

Delosperma floribundum, Delosperma herbeum

Dendrobium
D. nobile

Dichorisandra
D. thyrsiflora

Main feature Orchid that can be grown as a houseplant; flowers along the stems; long flowering
Height 90 cm (3 ft) **Spread** 30 cm (12 in.)
Position ◑ **Hardiness** RHS H3

Main features Evergreen perennial; large, jungle-like leaves; showy flowers in late summer
Height 1.8–2.4 m (6–8 ft) **Spread** 90 cm (3 ft)
Position ◑ **Hardiness** RHS H2

This is one of the easiest orchids to grow, and there is a long-lasting display of showy blooms along the stem. Flowers of the species range from pure white through to pink purple, and recent hybridising has resulted in many more colours becoming available. Markings on the flowers add to their exotic charm and fascination. They are perfect houseplants, but can be grown outdoors in summer. In the wild they are found in deciduous forests in the foothills of the Himalayas as epiphytes (lodging on host plants). Cultivated *D. nobile* is often attached to bark to mimic this; it shows off the plant's natural beauty, but it can be grown as a conventional pot plant. It flowers best if kept slightly potbound. All flowers are formed on erect bracts with individual blooms forming on the sides along the whole length. Grow *D. nobile* in small pots of bark or special orchid compost. Use rainwater to drench the plants when they require watering. Shade from direct sun, but give them as much light as possible in winter. There are many varieties in popular cultivation. **PM**

Known as blue ginger, *D. thyrsiflora* is a native of Brazil and has large, glossy leaves up to 30 centimetres (12 in.) long that spiral around the tall, cane-like stems. The leaves are deep green on the upper surfaces and purple beneath. Flowers appear from late summer to autumn at the top of the canes. Dense flower heads produce numerous electric-blue buds, which open to short-stalked, intense, violet-blue flowers with white stripes. The inflorescence can be slow to develop, and in colder climates the flowers may not open fully, but they can still be enjoyed at the bud stage. *Dichorisandra* grows best in warm, humid places, preferring well-drained but humus-rich soil, with a minimum winter temperature of 12°C (54°F). In many regions that means growing it as a houseplant in a large container with the compost kept evenly moist. In mild climes it can be grown outside, but needs shelter from hot sun. It also needs to be sheltered from strong winds or the leaves can become tattered. *Dichorisandra* associates well with ferns, orchids and prayer plants (*Maranta*). **GHa**

Alternative

Dendrobium nobile var. *virginale*

Alternative

Hedychium greenii

Dionaea
D. muscipula

Dioon
D. edule

Main feature Curious carnivorous plant with moving traps to catch flies
Height 20 cm (8 in.) **Spread** 20 cm (8 in.)
Position ○ ◑ **Hardiness** RHS H5

Main features Stiff, blue-green leaves; corky trunk
Height 3m (10 ft) **Spread** 90 cm (3 ft)
Position ○
Hardiness RHS H3

The Venus flytrap lives up to Charles Darwin's description of being one of the most wonderful plants in the world. Look closely and you can see hairs on the surface of the traps; when more than one of these is moved by a fly or insect, the trigger hairs initiate a sequence of chemical reactions resulting in the snapping shut of the traps. Enzymes are then released to digest the prey. *D. muscipula* grows wild in the bogs of North and South Carolina in the United States. When grown indoors it needs a specialist compost mix of moss, peat and sand. Full sun or dappled light is best as the plant will turn sickly yellow in dark conditions. In the growing season it is best to stand the pot on a saucer of water. Use rainwater if possible, and in winter reduce watering, so that the compost is barely moist. If flower spikes appear, nip them off. This will help the plant to use its energy to produce more traps. Plants can be fed tiny pieces of raw meat if there are no flies; if you keep teasing the plant to shut without providing any food, it will die. **PM**

Chestnut dioon is an ancient plant that is still endemic to the eastern coast of Mexico. It is a beautiful plant, classified as a cycad, with blue-green leaves, a corky trunk and great surviving power. The stiff, upright leaves give the plant a fern or palm-like appearance. Growing in tropical, deciduous forests, this plant can take the usually poor soil and harsh conditions. The storage trunk can contract into the surface of the soil, resulting in less surface area being exposed to the conditions and predators. *D. edule* is long lived, but slow growing. A plant with 30 centimetres (12 in.) of trunk on view is around twenty years old. Unlike many other cycads, *D. edule* does not have spines, but the leaflets do taper to a point, so it is best to grow them away from the edges of paths or steps. *D. edule* grows best if there is good air movement around the leaves. In summer, plants are happy outdoors on a sunny patio and can withstand cooler temperatures as autumn draws in. In cooler areas play safe and cultivate it indoors or in a greenhouse. **PM**

Alternative

Dionaea muscipula 'Akai Ryu'

Alternative

Dioon edule var. *angustifolium*

Disocactus
D. flagelliformis

Main features Trailing spiny cactus; magenta flowers
Height 30 cm (12 in.) **Spread** 90 cm (3 ft)
Position ○
Hardiness RHS H1b–H2

Rattail cactus is not the most evocative common name for a plant, especially one that has been honoured with a Royal Horticultural Society Award of Garden Merit, but this trailing cactus produces amazing magenta flowers over long periods in the summer months. *D. flagelliformis* is best grown in a conservatory or greenhouse, where the temperature does not drop below 6°C (43°F). In these ideal conditions the long stems can trail up to 90 centimetres (3 ft) in length, and the fuzzy groups of needles are yellow brown in colour. The slightly curved blooms are a gorgeous shade of magenta, and they can be up to 8 centimetres (3 in.) long. Although they are mainly produced in summer, they can pop out at any time throughout the year.

This easy-to-grow cactus needs a well-drained compost and a bright position. In addition, it is best to keep *D. flagelliformis* out of harsh, direct sunlight as it can scorch and burn. In order to pump up the tails, ensure that the plant gets plenty of water, but always allow the water to drain freely because waterlogged compost will encourage root rot. Reduce watering in late autumn and winter, but increase it again as the light levels improve in spring.

D. flagelliformis is the most cultivated species in the genus. It is a fast-growing plant and will need repotting every other spring. Wear gloves to protect yourself against the spines, and either pot up into the next size of container or – to control the growth yet retain a healthy plant – merely repot using fresh compost into the old pot. Any stems that have become discoloured or shrivelled can be cut back to their base in order to encourage new growth. Cuttings from healthy tails root easily and will be producing their own spectacular blooms within a couple of years. **PM**

Alternatives

Disocactus macranthus, Disocactus nelsonii, Disocactus phyllanthoides

Dracaena
D. marginata 'Tricolor'

Main feature Evergreen tree with lance-shaped leaves with coloured stripes or margins
Height 2 m (7 ft) **Spread** 1.5 m (5 ft)
Position ○ **Hardiness** RHS H1b

Plants in the genus *Dracaena* can be imposing trees, diminutive houseplants or anything in between. The linear, lance-shaped leaves can be green or red, mottled, or variegated, but all species have the capability of producing small, greenish-white flowers. However, it is the foliage that makes the plant worth growing.

D. marginata 'Tricolor' is a well-known houseplant in many regions, producing narrow, stripy, cream-coloured leaves. After a couple of years, the margins of the leaves can turn red. This plant can also get quite big, growing to 3 metres (10 ft) in a decade, and it is a popular choice for offices and many homes. 'Tricolor' is a consistent performer, and therefore has been awarded the Royal Horticultural Society Award of Garden Merit. Another award winning species is *D. draco*. This plant is at the top end of the height chart, potentially reaching 8 metres (26 ft), albeit over a period of thirty years or so. This beauty produces rosettes of sword-shaped leaves at the end of its branches, and if the ceiling of your greenhouse is not high enough – and not many are – it might be easier to view the plant growing naturally in the Canary Islands. A more practical houseplant specimen would be *D. fragrans* 'Massangeana'. Although it can reach 4 metres (13 ft) in height, this plant can be grown successfully in a root-restricting container, which will control its growth. 'Massangeana' is superb plant that has deep-green leaves with a central, greenish-yellow stripe.

All species of *Dracaena* need a sunny spot. Plenty of water is best, and the compost should always be free draining. A monthly treat of balanced fertiliser will maintain strong growth, but if for any reason a plant looks weak, it can be cut hard back in spring to within 15 centimetres (6 in.) of the base. It will soon reshoot and produce stronger, more vigorous growth. **PM**

Alternatives

Dracaena marginata, Dracaena draco, Dracaena fragrans 'Massangeana'

Drosera
D. capensis

Main features Carnivorous plant with sticky, hairy leaves; grown as a small curiosity plant
Height 30 cm (12 in.) **Spread** 20 cm (8 in.)
Position ○ **Hardiness** RHS H3

Sundews (*Drosera*) are carnivorous plants that can be found on every continent. All sundews have modified leaves covered with red hairs that secrete a sticky substance, via mucilaginous glands, to ensnare and tangle their prey. As the insect struggles, the leaves of the sundew slowly wrap around the victim, eventually suffocating it and absorbing nutrients from the corpse. This technique means that sundews can grow in areas where other nonspecialised plants are unable to.

The species *D. capensis* is the most popular. It originates from the subtropical regions of South Africa. It is considered a weed amongst some collections of carnivorous plants, due to the amount of viable seeds that is produced in the tall flower spikes. *D. prolifera* is endemic to the Queensland tropical rain forests, and *D. graomogolensis* is native to South America. *D. rotundifolia* and *D. filiformis* var. *filiformis* can be grown outside in areas with minimum night temperatures of -7°C (20°F) if they are given a well-lit position without direct sunlight. Peaty bogs are the perfect conditions for these plants to thrive. To grow *Drosera* at home, plant them in containers of wet, peaty or peat-substitute compost and stand them in saucers of rainwater. Alternatively, you could grow a bog garden with an area dedicated to carnivorous plants, but *Drosera* will not be able to compete with more vigorous bog plants. They like a light position but dislike strong direct sun.

Whenever you purchase *Drosera* to grow at home, always check the provenance of the plant. Certain species, such as *D. madagascariensis*, are now considered endangered because plants have been removed from the wild on a large scale for commercial use. Other species are similarly threatened due to removal of their habitats. **PM**

Alternatives

Drosera capensis 'Albino', *Drosera binata* subsp. *dichotomoa*, *Drosera slackii*

Drosera capensis and other carnivorous plants can be grown and cared for in planted-up displays. ➲

Dudleya
D. brittonii

Main features Succulent with evergreen rosette; drought tolerant; suits some coastal conditions
Height 30 cm (12 in.) **Spread** 30–60 cm (12–24 in.)
Position ○ **Hardiness** RHS H1b

With showstopper looks, *D. brittonii* has a perfectly formed, architectural, basal rosette of leaves that draws the eye and demands closer inspection. The leaves are coated with a chalky, blue-white 'wax', a substance that reflects the sun's rays efficiently, giving it amongst the highest ultraviolet reflectivity measured in any plant. Native to Baja California, Mexico, the genus is named after William R. Dudley, a botanist at Stanford University, and the species derives from Dr Nathaniel Lord Britton, botanist and first director of the New York Botanical Garden.

This slow-growing dudleya has a rosette of leaves, from which stems of yellow flowers appear from spring to summer. These flower stems elongate and turn red as flowers open. Despite its impressive looks, this is a plant that positively thrives on neglect. Summer dormancy means that it must be kept dry during this season. Plant it in a well-drained rock garden in warmer regions or as a container-grown succulent in cooler areas.

The chalk dudleya, *D. pulverulenta* is a California native and appears similar to *D. brittonii*. It is great for dry, sunny slopes and seems able to defy gravity with its ability to grow in rocky cracks. This cultivar is more frost tolerant than Britton's dudleya. *D. candelabrum* is a smaller, green succulent that can also survive frost. *D. cymosa* is found in the rocky areas of the lower elevations of California and southern Oregon. It puts on a colourful, orange-scarlet floral display that enlivens stony terrain. **RC**

Alternatives

Dudleya pulverulenta, Dudleya candelabrum, Dudleya cymosa

Echeveria
E. elegans

Main features Evergreen succulent; interest from both foliage and flowers
Height 5 cm (2 in.) **Spread** 50 cm (20 in.)
Position ○ **Hardiness** RHS H2

It is not surprising that this native to Mexico is one of the most widely grown succulents today, both indoors and out, for it has many desirable qualities. The evergreen rosettes of *E. elegans* (pictured, front) spread by forming side shoots and can quickly form a carpet of silvery blue. This is the perfect backdrop for the yellow-tipped, pink flowers that nod from the top of long stalks.

Also known as Mexican snowball, it looks well set on its side growing out of chinks in a wall, amongst rocks and boulders, in shallow terra-cotta pans and stone troughs; even in drought-busting hanging baskets mixed in with other succulents, like agave and aloe. It also makes a superb underplanting to contrast with black-leaved *Aeonium* 'Zwartkop'. Another novel idea is to grow your own house name or number by planting echeveria to form the letters or numbers in a container dressed with dark-coloured chippings, or contrasted with another succulent, like houseleeks (*Sempervivum*). A single plant can be multiplied by detaching the side shoots that often have a few roots attached or pulling off single leaves and pushing the thin end into a tray of gritty compost. Echeverias hate to have wet soil around the neck of the rosettes. Sharp grit can be worked into soil, and fine gravel or chippings used to dress the surface. On wet, clay soils, raised beds filled with friable soil will allow the cultivation of many alpine and succulent-leaved species that would otherwise perish. **GS**

Alternatives

Echeveria 'Duchess of Nuremberg', *Echeveria* 'Black Knight', *Echeveria secunda* var. *glauca*

Echeveria
'Perle von Nürnberg'

Main features Evergreen; year-round, colourful foliage; flowers in spring; drought tolerant
Height 15–30 cm (6–12 in.) **Spread** 20–30 cm (8–12 in.)
Position ○ **Hardiness** RHS H2

Named for a renowned Mexican botanical artist, *Echeveria* is an outstanding genus that is filled with desirable forms. 'Perle von Nürnberg' stands out as a real masterpiece in the genus and is worthy of exhibition in any garden or plant collection. This hybrid succulent (its parents are *E. gibbiflora* var. *metallica* and *E. potosina*) has beautiful, neat rosettes formed by slightly concave, overlapping grey leaves, which are tinged purplish pink. It has a definite pearlescent sheen, which gives the plant a glowing, luminescent quality. From this base, flowers appear in summer on 30- to 45-centimetre-long (12–18 in.), arching, reddish-stemmed inflorescences. Up to half a dozen or more flower spikes can be produced from one rosette. The small but showy flowers are a delicate coral pink on the outside with a yellow interior. Fortunately, the leaves of succulents do not fade, so their good looks remain year-round.

Although adapted to conditions of full sun and little water, in warmer climates it is best to protect 'Perle von Nürnberg' from the full glare of afternoon sun. Although a native of Mexico, it is a slightly hardier hybrid and can tolerate a moderate frost. In cooler locations grow it as a conservatory plant or on a bright windowsill, and put it outside for summer displays. 'Perle von Nürnberg' is easy to care for, wherever it is grown. As the plant ages, single rosettes slowly grow up into a short slender stem. Most attractive as a younger plant, it benefits from being re-rooted every three to four years. Offsets of small plants naturally occur and can be potted up into gritty cactus compost in spring. In cooler areas for a hardier, outdoor plant consider one of the saxifrages or houseleeks with similar colour qualities. For example, *Saxifraga frederici–augusti*, *Sempervivum montanum* and *Sempervivum* 'Pacific Red Rose'. **RC**

Alternatives

Echeveria agavoides, Echeveria elegans, Echeveria × gilva, Echeveria pulvinata, Echeveria rosea

Echinocactus
E. grusonii

Main features A characterful cactus decorated with
yellow spines; flowers when mature
Height 60 cm (24 in.) **Spread** 90 cm (3 ft)
Position ○ **Hardiness** RHS H1c

This popular cactus, known as the golden barrel cactus,
is often the first plant children grow on the windowsill. It
is endemic to eastern and central Mexico and is currently
listed as endangered by the International Union for the
Conservation of Nature, due to the destruction of its
habitat and illegal collecting. Millions of *Echinocactus* are
grown in nurseries each year as demand for them is high.

Their tubby shape gives them their character. Twenty
to forty angled ribs are armed with pale-yellow, incurved
spines, crossbanded with raised lines, surrounding the
barrel. The botanical name comes from the Greek word
echino, which means 'hedgehog'. The impressive flowers
are yellow, and star-shaped, and they appear in a ring
around the top of the barrel, though plants may be
twenty years old before they flower. *E. grusonii* is slow
growing, so it is often only a few inches tall if bought at
a young age. In the wild, old specimens can reach more
than 90 centimetres (3 ft) high. Keen gardeners who have
visited the volcanic island of Lanzarote will be familiar
with the Jardin de Cactus, where *E. grusonii* that are large
enough to flower have been planted en masse into the
black volcanic ash. They reach impressive proportions.

The golden barrel cactus can add contemporary
style to a modern, light indoor setting when it is grown
in matching, tall, steel containers or lined up along a
window in shallow bowls. These plants are quite capable
of surviving throughout the winter without water if they
are kept cool. If they are stood on saucers, make sure
they are not standing in water. Overwatering is the most
common cause for their downfall.

New plants can be generated by cutting off the
'pups' that form around the base with a sharp knife and
rooting them. This will produce a good-sized specimen
far more quickly than raising the plants from seeds. **GS**

Alternatives

Echinocactus grusonii var. *inermis*, *Echinocactus
horizonthalonius*

Echinopsis
E. multiplex

Main features Cactus with globular shape; flowers from a young age; good beginner cactus
Height 45 cm (18 in.) **Spread** 45 cm (18 in.)
Position ○ ◑ **Hardiness** RHS H2

The cactus *E. multiplex* is easy to grow and often produces massive flowers in vast numbers over a long period of time. Furthermore, it starts blooming from an early age and is simple to propagate. Originating in South America, species of *Echinopsis* produce blooms in a vast array of colours, and sometimes the flowers have a couple of different hues on the same bloom. Individual blooms can grow to more than 15 centimetres (6 in.) in diameter, often completely dwarfing the plant. Although they last in peak condition for little more than twenty-four hours, you can be sure that there is another one lining up to burst into colour.

Echinopsis plants need bright conditions, but they prefer not to be sunburned in the full, scorching, all-day sun. Once temperatures rise to above 27°C (80°F), the plants will want to flower. All species need a free-draining compost, so add a handful of horticultural grit even when using premixed cactus compost to ensure the drainage is sharp. Although cacti can survive periods of drought, they perform better if regular waterings are made throughout the warmer, growing months. Reduce watering in winter as the temperatures drop, and ensure that the plants are kept away from areas where the temperature might dip below freezing.

Of the numerous *Echinopsis* species available, *E. eyriesii* is a beauty, producing white blooms on stubby, cylindrical plants. *E. backebergii* subsp. *backebergii* produces carmine-red flowers, each with a pale centre. All *Echinopsis* readily produce new plants on the main plant. Often referred to as pups, these young versions of the parents need to be broken off. Any scars at the base of the cutting should be allowed to dry and heal for a couple of days before planting in a gritty, cactus compost. **PM**

Alternatives

Syn. *Echinopsis oxygona*. *Echinopsis backebergii* subsp. *backebergii*, *Echinopsis eyriesii*

Echium
E. candicans

Main features Shrub-like biennial; attracts bees, birds and butterflies; drought tolerant; spring and summer flowers
Height 1.5–2.4 m (5–8 ft) **Spread** 1.5–2.4 m (5–8 ft)
Position ○ **Hardiness** RHS H1c

Big, bold, fast-growing Pride of Madeira is an awesome plant that commands centre stage. *E. candicans* is a bushy, biennial, subshrub native to the island of Madeira in the Atlantic Ocean, where it grows on rocky cliffs and terraces. Its looks and qualities make an irresistible combination for gardeners in many other parts of the world.

This plant has grey-green, hairy, lance-shaped leaves in an architectural clump below dense terminal panicles of white or deep blue-purple flowers borne on red-tinged stamen in spring and summer. It manages to appear both spiky yet soft at the same time, with its architectural habit and fuzzy appearance of foliage and flowering stems. It is not frost hardy and is often short-lived, but reseeds quite freely. In colder climates it can either be container grown under glass through winter and placed on a sunny patio for summer, or grown outside with protection from frost and excess rain. Pride of Madeira looks at home in borders or beds in city courtyards – it likes the shelter of a sunny wall – and also in cottage-style and informal gardens. It is excellent on slopes, where there is space for it to spread out to its full potential.

Other interesting *Echium* cultivars include *E. pininana*, the tree echium, or giant viper's bugloss. Native to the Canary Islands, it is hardier despite its exotic looks, with silvery leaves and single flower spikes that can reach up to 4 metres (13 ft) tall. Also biennial, after flowering in the second year it dies, but reseeds itself. In colder regions sow seeds to ensure new plants. The same holds true for *E. wildpretii*, also known as tower of jewels. This bears a 1.8- to 3-metre-tall (6–10 ft) spike of dark-pink to rose-red flowers in late spring. Echium can be invasive, so show caution when planting near wild habitats. It can also be a skin irritant, so handle with care. **RC**

Alternatives

Echium pininana, *Echium pininana* 'Snow Tower',
Echium 'Pink Fountain', *Echium vulgare* 'Blue Bedder'

Ensete
E. ventricosum

Main features Evergreen in warm conditions; exotic, showy specimen; architectural plant
Height 4–6 m (13–20 ft) **Spread** 1.8 m (6 ft)
Position ○ ◑ **Hardiness** RHS H1b

If you like your plants on the large, exotic side, then this one is for you. *E. ventricosum* is a close relative of the banana plant and is very like it in appearance. Huge, upright, paddle-shaped leaves sprout from a trunk-like pseudostem that is made from the bases of old leaves. Growth can be rapid in a warm climate, and plants can reach a height of 6 metres (20 ft) or more – possibly twice that size in ideal conditions. The leaves can grow to between 5 and 6 metres (16–20 ft) in length, although in cultivation they are usually much shorter. The leaves are a fresh green colour with a strong, red midrib. The cultivar 'Maurelii' (pictured) has red-tinged leaves and makes a striking plant for an urban, jungle-style planting. It works well with the larger *Salvia*, such as *S. confertiflora*, and the dramatic leaves of *Tetrapanax papyrifer*.

E. ventricosum does produce flowers, but they are insignificant, as are the fruits. In temperate climates this plant works well in tropical-style plantings, along with other tender plants, or as a specimen plant in a pot. In areas prone to frost it will need protection during the winter, so it will need to be lifted and brought indoors. In areas where winters are less harsh, it is possible to remove the leaves and wrap the stem with hessian or another insulating material that will allow the plant to breathe over the winter. A waterproof 'hat' placed on the wrapping will help prevent any rotting.

These large leaves have evolved to cope with high winds and hurricanes, which they do by shredding along the side veins to reduce their sail effect. However, if they are allowed to this, it can leave the plants looking untidy, so a sheltered position will lead to much better looking plants. Rich, moist soil will give the best results, and the plant should avoid environments that are excessively hot and dry. **PWi**

Alternatives

Ensete ventricosum 'Maurelii' (syn. *Ensete ventricosum* 'Rubrum')

Eranthemum
E. pulchellum

Main feature Subshrub with winter flowers that emerge from white-green bracts
Height 90 cm (3 ft) **Spread** 90 cm (3 ft)
Position ◑ **Hardiness** RHS H2

E. pulchellum, also known as blue sage, is a tropical evergreen plant native to the Himalayas, west China and India. In cooler parts of the world it is a perfect plant for the conservatory or heated greenhouse, but it can also be cultivated outdoors in beds and borders in warmer regions. The main feature is the gorgeous gentian blue flowers that appear in winter and early spring, although flowering can continue on and off throughout the year.

E. pulchellum needs rich, fertile soil, and plenty of moisture. Soil, or compost, if growing in a large container in a conservatory, should be free draining to prevent waterlogging and subsequent root rot. The intricately veined white-green bracts develop just before the plant flowers, serving to heighten your anticipation before the plant bursts into a blue sensation. Even when it is not in flower *E. pulchellum* is a terrific plant, as the foliage is also attractive; the large, dark-green leaves can grow up to 20 centimetres (8 in.) long. They are oval-shaped, and heavily veined.

The plant prefers to be in an area of dappled shade, but it can also cope with both sun and shade. After several years some of the shoots will die down, but new growth will form, which will result in a more vigorous, bushier specimen than the previous plant. If *E. pulchellum* becomes straggly, it can be cut back hard to soil or compost level in order to encourage new growth and improved flowering. Plants can be propagated by taking softwood cuttings.

Plants that have been grown in conservatories can be placed in the garden during the warmer summer months. However, do keep an eye out for whitefly, aphid or mealy bug infesting the plant. If you do spot this, prompt removal will usually prevent any major problems from developing, and they are largely disease-free. **PM**

Alternatives

Brunfelsia pauciflora (syn. *Brunfelsia calycina*),
Plumbago auriculata

Erythrina
E. crista-galli

Main feature Spiny shrub or small tree bearing coral-red flowers in late summer and autumn
Height 2.4 m (8 ft) **Spread** 90 cm (3 ft)
Position ○ **Hardiness** RHS H3

Native to Brazil, Argentina and eastern Bolivia, *E. crista-galli* is one of the hardiest coral trees in the genus *Erythrina* and was introduced into cultivation in 1771. The spiny branches are adorned with leathery leaves with racemes of scarlet-red blooms that appear in late summer and autumn. The blooms are prodigious producers of sweet nectar that can end up dripping, tear-like from the blooms, hence the common names Christ's tears, cockspur tree, and crybaby tree. The plant is grown for its ornamental blooms and was awarded a Royal Horticultural Society Award of Garden Merit in 2012. Remove the flowers when they fade, as not only does it tidy up the plant, but it encourages fresh blooms.

In the right climate, such as the Mediterranean, *E. crista-galli* could be grown as a small free-standing tree. In a favourable spot in a temperate climate – such as the shelter of a sunny wall and an insulating mulch in winter – it could grow as a semi-woody shrub. The top growth can be cut to the ground in cold winters as it often comes back in spring. It can be planted in a large container of gritty, well-drained compost, which allows it to overwinter in a frost-free greenhouse or conservatory.

Specimens grown under glass are prone to red spider mites and mealy bugs. *E. crista-galli* can survive light frost, but only once it is established. An annual prune will enable the plant to keep its shape and its best flowers. It has naturalised in the southeastern United States and the coast of eastern Australia, so it could be considered a weed in these places. Santa Barbara, a coastal city in southern California, has the ideal climate for growing *Erythina* outside, and many species were introduced by Dr Francesco Franceschi between 1893 and 1939. San Marcos Growers introduced many species in the 1980s, but some did not survive the unseasonal years. **PM**

Alternatives

Erythrina × bidwillii, Erythrina flabbelliformis, Erythrina humeana (syn. *Erythrina princeps*)

Espostoa
E. melanostele

Main feature Columnar cactus with golden spines and white wool
Height 1.2 m (4 ft) **Spread** 60 cm (24 in.)
Position ○ **Hardiness** RHS H3

Old man of Peru is a distinctive cactus found growing high up in the Andes in Peru. It is a thick-stemmed, columnar cactus with a shock of white, woolly hair and sunlight-gold spines. If you get the growing conditions just right, beautiful, almost translucent, white blooms appear, but you will need patience together with gardening expertise as it can take fifteen years for plants to mature to a flowering age.

With time the plant will branch from its base, but younger plants are generally single bodies. More and more hair appears as it ages, which is a clever method of protecting the plant from scorching sun, drying winds and predatory animals. The Royal Horticultural Society awarded *E. melanostele* an Award of Garden Merit for its considerable virtues.

E. melanostele requires a sunny position and should never be exposed to frost. In most regions that means cultivating it in a greenhouse, where humidity should be maintained at a low level; it needs plenty of water in summer but requires a resting period in winter when watering should be reduced. In summer, water when the well-drained compost is dry to the touch, but in winter it can be bone dry for a few weeks before small amounts of water are needed. Overwatering of *E. melanostele* will induce root and stem rot. It is perhaps the perfect cactus for forgetful gardeners.

When growing the plant in compost, choose one formulated and mixed specifically for cacti. Before potting, add 10 per cent more grit by volume to be sure the drainage is as effective as possible. Even though plants are slow growing, they will need repotting every three years. Only move the plant up into the next size of pot to avoid the chance of wet, stagnant compost in an overlarge pot. **PM**

Alternatives

Espostoa lanata, Espostoa blossfeldiorum, Espostoa baumannii

Exacum
E. affine

Main features Annual pot plant with flowers in summer, autumn and winter; fragrant flowers
Height 30 cm (12 in.) **Spread** 30 cm (12 in.)
Position ○ ◐ **Hardiness** RHS H1b

A small plant with great charm and cheer, *E. affine* produces masses of tiny, fragrant, violet-blue, white or pink flowers, each with bright yellow stamen in the centre, over a long period of several months. The leaves are small and densely arranged, giving the plant a compact but bushy look. *E. affine* is from south Yemen, where it is now critically endangered in the wild due to habitat loss.

E. affine makes a neat, little houseplant and is suited to a well-lit position, although it should be kept out of direct, midday sun. Too little light, and it will lose its compact habit and become open and drawn. Beware of overwatering and keep it just moist rather than wet. It will not harm it to let it dry out between waterings.

Although it is a biennial or short-lived perennial, *E. affine* is usually treated as an annual, and while it is not difficult to raise from seed each year, the fuss and effort probably does not balance out against the convenience of simply throwing away the old plant and buying a new one. It can be propagated by cuttings taken in the autumn and overwintered, ready for potting in spring.

E. affine can only be grown outdoors year-round in tropical or subtropical conditions. It can also be used as an outdoor ornamental bedding plant, planted out for summer display when all risk of frost has passed. In a temperate climate grow it as a houseplant with a minimum winter temperature of 10°C (50°F), but keep it away from hot, drying radiators. **PWi**

Alternatives

Exacum affine 'Jupiter White', *Exacum affine* 'Rex24', *Exacum affine* 'Rococo'

Fenestraria

F. rhopalophylla

Main feature Small, club-shaped leaves with translucent, flattened tops
Height 10 cm (4 in.) **Spread** 20 cm (8 in.)
Position ○ **Hardiness** RHS H3

It must be difficult being a plant growing in southeastern Namibia, tussling with extreme high temperatures in summer, combined with little or no rainfall, and then light rain in winter. However, *F. rhopalophylla* (also known as baby's toes) manages it. Thriving in such conditions, this curious and compelling plant is equipped with enough survival techniques to make grown botanists weep with joy.

F. rhopalophylla forms low-growing mats or clumps in sandy soil. The glaucous green, club-shaped leaves are mostly hidden below the soil surface, but the tops have adapted to form flattened windows. This ensures that the ravages of the weather pass the plant by, yet light is still efficiently harvested and redirected within the adapted leaves. In severe heat the roots can actually pull the plant further into the soil to enhance the chance of survival. All available water is sucked into the root hairs, and then the surplus is stored in the thick, fleshy roots. In the wild the plant can survive merely on dew and water from mist and fog.

Grow in containers of well-drained, gritty, or sandy compost formulated for cacti, but add the same volume of horticultural sand before repotting. Get the conditions right and you will be rewarded with beautiful, white-and-yellow flowers. Overwatering can destroy a specimen, resulting in root rot and split leaves. Water sparingly at all times and keep dry in summer. **PM**

Alternative

Fenestraria rhopalophylla subsp. *aurantica*
(syn. *Fenestraria aurantica*)

Ferocactus
F. acanthodes

Main features Hooked spines; range of bright flower colours; easy to grow
Height 50 cm (20 in.) **Spread** 50 cm (20 in.)
Position ○ **Hardiness** RHS H3

Barrel cacti are fearsome-looking plants with fish-hook spines and a variety of brightly coloured flowers. *Ferocactus* species are easy to grow from seed, carefree when it comes to cultivation needs and have a compelling charm that turns ordinary gardeners into avid collectors. Once they have their spines into you, there is no turning back.

The magnificently hooked spines perform a number of tasks. First, and perhaps most importantly to the gardener, they look intriguing. The spines also protect the plant body from predators and heat, and they act as condensation points for any available moisture in the air. Interestingly, they also help move the plant around. *Ferocactus* species are shallow rooting and can be easily uprooted by flash floods or strong winds. The spines therefore enable the plant to roll to new positions or hook into the skin and fur of passing animals and hitch a ride. Even if the whole plant does not get on the move, the portion of plant attached to the spine can be ripped from the main body and dragged along. Flowers are readily produced, and depending on species, can be red, pink, purple or yellow. Not only are these flowers beautiful, but they also have to be tough. Developing and growing through a mat of spines would be terrifying for many blooms. *F. acanthodes* (right) is an easy but slow-growing species with yellow flowers.

There are plenty of species to choose from in the *Ferocactus* group, with *F. wislizenii* (candy barrel cactus) being a favourite with gardeners. It exhibits all the characteristic *Ferocactus* spines and produces yellow to red flowers. *F. glaucescens* (glaucous barrel cactus) has a grey-green body, yellow spines and pure-yellow blooms whereas *F. fordii* (Ford barrel cactus) features purplish-pink flowers. *F. viridescens* (coast barrel cactus) has curious-looking blooms in green tinged with red. **PM**

Alternatives

Syn. *Ferocactus cylindraceus* subsp. *cylindraceus*, *Ferocactus wislizenii*, *Ferocactus glaucescens*, *Ferocactus fordii*, *Ferocactus viridescens*

◒ *Ferocactus* species including the red-spined *F. pilous* growing in a heated greenhouse at Holly Gate Cactus Nursery, Sussex, UK.

Fittonia
F. albivenis Verschaffeltii Group

Main features Herbaceous perennial; distinctively marked or veined foliage; often grown as houseplant
Height 10–15 cm (4–6 in.) **Spread** 15–45 cm (6–18 in.)
Position ◑ **Hardiness** RHS H1b

The snakeskin plant or mosaic plant *F. albivenis* (Verschaffeltii Group) certainly lives up to its common names because its deep olive-green leaves have distinctive, net-like, pink markings. The plant occurs naturally in the warm, humid rainforests of Colombia and Peru, and when growing outdoors, will readily root wherever the stem touches the soil surface. The white flowers are insignificant and are rarely produced in cultivation.

F. albivenis is a low, mat-forming plant grown best as a houseplant in cooler areas or as a ground cover plant in hotter climates, as it needs a minimum temperature of 13°C (55°F). When grown as a houseplant, it is best to put containers away from direct sunlight, but still keep it in bright conditions. Regular misting with a hand spray is needed; if plants are allowed to dry out, they will wilt, and leaves may turn brown and crispy at the edges. For this reason they are a good candidate for terrariums and bottle gardens. In a heated conservatory with border soil, they can be grown as creeping ground cover.

F. albivenis grows best in loam-based composts and responds to a fortnightly feed with a balanced fertiliser when plants are in their active growth period from late spring through to midsummer. In winter, watering needs to be reduced to keeping the compost just moist. This may mean watering as little as once a month. Overwatering will cause the roots to rot and the first indication of this will be a few leaves turning yellow before dying. Maintain the shape of plants by pinching out the growing tips. These can be rooted in gritty compost to create new plants if desired. Plants do occasionally produce spikes of flowers, but these are best pinched off promptly to encourage plants to produce more of their striking leaves. **PM**

Alternatives

Fittonia albivenis Argyroneura Group (syn. *Fittonia argyroneura*, *Fittonia verschaffeltii* var. *argyroneura*)

Fuchsia
'Gartenmeister Bonstedt'

Main features Shrub with red-orange blooms; flowers
summer to autumn; dark-green, purple-veined foliage
Height 30–90 cm (12–36 in.) **Spread** 30–90 cm (12–36 in.)
Position ○ ◑ **Hardiness** RHS H2

This showy fuschia is native to the mountains of
Hispaniola. Due to its mountainous origin, it is able
to withstand surprisingly cold (although not freezing)
temperatures while also being adapted to the torrid
summers of the West Indies. This heirloom is an old
hybrid of *F. triphylla,* which was introduced in 1905 and
has recently been rediscovered.

As anyone can easily see from looking at the plant,
'Gartenmeister Bonstedt' is a fuchsia that does not look
the part. It has a bushy, upright habit that would never
work in a hanging basket, and where it is winter hardy, it
actually makes a woody shrub. Used as a summer annual
in temperate climates, it is a free-flowering, workhorse
grown for its multitude of tubular flowers. It is notable
as one of the only fuchsias that will stand up to the
summer heat and humidity of eastern North America
and will, in fact, bloom until the first frost. 'Gartenmeister
Bonstedt' is a hummingbird favourite. It is difficult to
describe the colour of its flowers. Some call it bright
or brick red; others, coral or orange. Suffice to say that
the flowers are spectacular and elegant, and positively
glow in a shaded setting. They stand out beautifully
against the foliage, which is a satiny, dark green with
striking reddish-purple veins. Plants produce numerous,
pendent clusters of flowers, making them a mainstay for
summertime container gardens or wherever a colourful
shade-tolerant annual is needed.

Like most fuchsias, 'Gartenmeister Bonstedt' needs
to be kept evenly moist at all times to look its best. Also,
because it is a flowering machine, regular feeding is
advised. It performs best with a full morning's sun and
then shade for the rest of the day. In cooler areas plants
should be overwintered indoors, where they should be
kept just moist. **KK**

Alternatives

Fuchsia 'Billy Green', *Fuchsia* 'Boy Marc', *Fuchsia* 'Coralle',
Fuchsia 'Elfriede Ott', *Fuchsia* 'Fuchsiarama '91'

Gardenia
G. jasminoides

Main features Shrub with richly scented, white flowers; glossy, evergreen leaves
Height 90–120 cm (3–4 ft) **Spread** 90–120 cm (3–4 ft)
Position ◐ **Hardiness** RHS H1c

In the world of scented plants, *G. jasminoides* packs a punch like no other. Its fragrance is not only floral; it is also deliciously complex, revealing layer upon layer of different notes. It is not surprising, therefore, that gardenia is a staple scent for many of the world's perfume houses. It is said that in the early twentieth century, no respectable gentleman's evening dress was complete without a gardenia in his buttonhole. The American jazz singer Billie Holiday memorably wore gardenias in her hair as her signature style from the 1930s to 1950s.

The flowers of certain cultivars of *G. jasminoides* have an almost virginal quality, and they feature some of the purest white of any blooms. They are native to the open woodlands of the Far East – Japan, Taiwan and China. Imagine their native forest home, and you will get a good idea of the ideal growing conditions for gardenias. They like bright, indirect light – dappled shade is perfect – and reasonable levels of humidity. Ericaceous (lime-free) compost is essential: do not pot plants into standard, multipurpose compost, because it contains lime that will kill gardenias pretty quickly. Keep them well watered in summer and reduce watering during winter.

Gardenias grow well outdoors in climates that have mild winters and ample summer heat (and humidity), such as those encountered in southeastern areas of the United States. Otherwise, they can be grown as houseplants, but care must be taken to meet their particular requirements. There are some cultivars that are hardier than the species; they include 'Kleim's Hardy', 'Crown Jewel' and 'Ice Diamond'. All these cultivars are well worth trying in sheltered gardens outside of traditional gardenia-growing areas. Even when not flowering, they make attractive, bushy, glossy-leaved, evergreen shrubs. **GAR**

Alternative

Syn. *Gardenia augusta, Gardenia florida, Gardenia grandiflora, Gardenia jasminoides* 'Kleim's Hardy'

Gasteria
G. batesiana

Main features Green-leaved succulent with white spots; beautiful racemes of red or pink flowers
Height 20 cm (8 in.) **Spread** 20 cm (8 in.)
Position ○ ◑ **Hardiness** RHS H2

All *Gasteria*, also commonly known as oxtongue, are native to South Africa and are best grown as houseplants in cooler areas. They are wonderful succulent plants; their leaves are waxy, sometimes smooth, while others are pointed and often exhibit beautiful, white spots and striations. Diversity and beauty abound within the genus.

G. batesiana shows the typical rosette of fleshy leaves. It has a popular hybrid, 'Little Warty' (pictured), which produces long, green, lightly spotted leaves. It produces many offsets, resulting in spectacular clumps of plants forming even when young. Soft red or pink flowers are produced in spring. *G. pillansii* var. *ernesti-ruschii* is a sensational plant with glossy, green leaves, pointy at the ends, and spotted in white. The plant turns a delicate apricot colour in summer. *G. maculata* has densely packed, deep-green leaves and produces lovely coral-pink blooms. Tolerating more shade than many succulents, they produce long racemes of red or pink flowers in spring, often continuing throughout summer.

Gasteria is undemanding and can survive on a neglected windowsill, but it will thrive given a little care and attention. Plants will be more compact if given some sun. They can ignore the occasional period of drought, but are at their best when watered frequently during the growing season. Well-drained compost is essential and must be allowed to dry out between watering. Leaves can develop black, sunken spots due to a fungal infection; the plant isolates the spread by shutting down that part of the leaf. The best practice is to reduce humidity and increase air circulation to prevent the fungal infection from first developing. Repot plants in spring using shallow or halfpots; *Gasteria* have shallow root systems, and using deep pots may produce stagnant conditions that could encourage root rot. **PM**

Alternatives

Gasteria pillansi var. *ernesti-ruschii*, *Gasteria maculata*

Glottiphyllum
G. oligocarpum

Graptopetalum
G. bellum

Main features Succulent with soft, tongue- or club-shaped leaves; vivid-yellow, fragrant blooms
Height 13 cm (5 in.) **Spread** 30 cm (12 in.)
Position ○ **Hardiness** RHS H2

Main features Succulent with eye-catching, pink-red flowers in spring and early summer; year-round foliage
Height 2.5 cm (1 in.) **Spread** 10 cm (4 in.)
Position ○ **Hardiness** RHS H1c

Tongue leaf plant (*G. oligocarpum*) is an ideal succulent for hot, sunny positions in the greenhouse or indoors on a bright windowsill. Soft, delicately fragrant flowers are produced in late summer and autumn. Native to the Cape Province of South Africa, it grows in cracks in rocks and in rocky soil. Plants have thick, fleshy leaves around 5 centimetres (2 in.) long that are capable of storing water for dry periods. Tongue leaf plant thrives in full sun and needs little water. When growing, irrigate every week, allowing the well-drained compost to fully dry out between waterings. The tongue-shaped leaves are blue green in colour with a white sheen and are tightly packed, forming a mat against the surface of the compost. *G. oligocarpum* can be easily raised from seeds, but seed-raised plants may not exhibit true characteristics of the parent. Alternatively, take cuttings at the end of summer. Mature plants can tolerate short spells of frost and will thrive in the protected environs of a greenhouse. **PM**

A neat rosette of oval, pointed, grey-green, fleshy leaves, each rimmed with a lighter grey edge, carries sprays of surprisingly large, eye-catching, pink-red flowers that last for weeks. As with most succulents, *Graptopetalum* needs lots of light to flower successfully, but it also needs a cold spell of below 15°C (60°F) for at least a month to initiate flowering. It grows wild in Mexico on cliffs and crevices in places out of direct sunlight, so in regions that experience intense sunshine, give the plant some shade. In cooler climates where the power of the midday sun is less severe, it will tolerate full sun. Most succulents are used to dry conditions in the wild, and overwatering can cause roots or stems to rot. Using a free-draining compost will help avoid waterlogging, and a mulch of grit will help prevent stem rot. Keep dry during winter, and water sparingly in spring and summer. Small succulents can look a little lost when not in flower, so plant two or three varieties in a pot together for better effect. **PWi**

Alternative

Glottiphyllum depressum

Alternatives

Graptopetalum filiferum, Graptopetalum paraguayense

Guzmania

G. *lingulata* var. *minor*

Gymnocalycium

G. *andreae*

Main features Bromeliad with long, strappy leaves; striking scarlet-orange bracts; long-lasting white flowers
Height 30 cm (12 in.) **Spread** 40 cm (16 in.)
Position ● **Hardiness** RHS H2

Main features Cactus with solitary spiny plants; beautifully coloured blooms
Height 15 cm (6 in.) **Spread** 20 cm (8 in.)
Position ○ **Hardiness** RHS H2

This bromeliad comes from the rainforests of Central America, Mexico and the West Indies. The tongue-shaped, shiny, green foliage of *G. lingulata* var. *minor* forms a watertight, star-shaped rosette from which scarlet-orange bracts are formed. Although classed as an epiphyte, it will grow in pots and soil. In hot areas it can be planted in rockeries and scree gardens, but elsewhere it makes a good houseplant. When plants are mature the inner leaves turn scarlet orange and white flowers appear. The flower spike can last up to three months, but another will not be produced in the plant's life span. The mother plant then produces smaller plants around the base. These can be left to grow and eventually flower themselves. Alternatively, they can be cut off, rooted and grown on. To water the plant, use rainwater and pour directly into the central rosette. This area (the 'tank') should be filled with water at all times. Use a hand sprayer to encourage the foliage to thrive. **PM**

There is no better starting point to a collection of cacti than a chin cactus. *Gymnocalycium* are easy to look after, slow growing, and guaranteed to produce colourful blooms. Most are solitary plants and rather globose in stature. Along the deep-green bodies, slightly tuberculated ribs give the plant a chin-like appearance. All chin cacti produce naked flowers in that they do not have spines, wool or bristles. The majority of species produce white or pink blooms, but some have deep-red or yellow flowers. Plants bloom when they are young; they need high temperatures for flowers to fully open, so a sunny position in a greenhouse is ideal. Shield from scorching sun, as this can turn the plant body a sunburned red. In spring and summer, water the well-drained compost when it is dry, but reduce watering in winter. Plants also require a winter rest, usually from autumn to midspring. *G. baldianum* produces stunning wine-red blooms and *G. andreae* (pictured) has large, soft-yellow blooms. **PM**

Alternatives

Guzmania lingulata, Guzmania musaica

Alternatives

Gymnocalycium rosanthemum, Gymnocalycium marquezii

Haemanthus
H. albiflos

Main features Evergreen plant with a long flowering season; white flowers with yellow pollen; strap-like leaves
Height 30 cm (12 in.) **Spread** 30 cm (12 in.)
Position ◑ ● **Hardiness** RHS H2

H. albiflos is an evergreen, bulbous plant with thick, leathery, strap-like leaves. The edges of the leaves may be fringed with fine hairs. It has a long flowering season, usually during autumn and winter and then sporadically throughout the rest of the year. White bracts enclose numerous small, white flowers with prominent, erect stamen bearing yellow pollen, giving it a brush-like appearance, and hence the common name of paintbrush plant. The flowers produce copious amounts of nectar and are attractive to both bees and butterflies. Orange or red, fleshy berries follow the flowers and some forms produce white berries.

H. albiflos is native to southern Africa, where it grows in a range of habitats from shady forest floors to rocky cliffs. The upper half of the bulb is often exposed and will remain green and photosynthesise. In cultivation it is very tolerant of varying conditions, although it prefers dappled shade. In full sun the leaves can go yellow, but it will still flower well. Grow *H. albiflos* in well-aerated, gritty compost, with added leaf mould if available. Water year-round; it will tolerate drought for several weeks. Leave undisturbed for two or three years before repotting, as plants flower well when potbound. *Haemanthus* are members of the *Amaryllidaceae* family and are related to bulbs such as amaryllis and hippeastrum. *Haemanthus* are not frost hardy, but in temperate climates they can be left on the patio during the summer months. Pests are rarely a problem, but watch out for mealy bugs if grown in glasshouse conditions.

Haemanthus bulbs were among the first plants gathered at the Cape of Good Hope by European explorers, and they have been cultivated in Europe since the early seventeenth century. The plant was used in its native land as a charm to ward off lightning. **GHa**

Alternatives

Haemanthus coccineus, Haemanthus sanguineus

Hatiora
H. gaertneri

Main features Cactus with flattened leaves; spectacular pink or red flowers
Height 15 cm (6 in.) **Spread** 30 cm (12 in.)
Position ◑ **Hardiness** RHS H2

A relatively new botanical name, *Hatiora* encompasses the various names that gardeners have had in the past for the Easter, or Whitsun, cactus. This genus grows naturally in trees in the tropical rain forests of southeastern Brazil. These plants are succulent, usually without spines, and they make lovely houseplants in certain cooler climates, or specimens for a hot and humid greenhouse.

The most popular species is *H. gaertneri*, also known as the Easter cactus. It is grown worldwide for its starburst blooms in red or pink, which are borne on flattened stems. It has a Royal Horticultural Society Award of Garden Merit and looks superb when it is displayed in bloom with the branches hanging downwards. *H. gaertneri* has been crossed with *H. rosea* to form hybrids that produce flowers in many different colours.

Once the last of *H. gaertneri*'s flowers fade, it is good practice to rest the plant. Reduce watering for around a month before beginning to water more frequently again. When it is growing, the plant needs to be in consistently moist soil, but it must never sit in water or become waterlogged, as the stems will turn yellow and rot. Apply a liquid feed when the cactus is in bud, but stop feeding it after flowering has finished. Pale or reddening stems are a sign the plant needs feeding. Be aware that once buds have formed, they can drop off if the plant is moved or if it experiences a sudden temperature drop.

Once you have experienced some success with Easter cactus, try experimenting with other *Hatiora* species. *H. salicornioides* (also known as *Rhipsalis salicornioides*) has abundant, bottle-shaped stems, but with smaller, and yellow flowers from spring to early summer. It is also known as drunkard's dream, spice cactus and dancing bones cactus. **PM**

Alternative

Hatiora salicornioides (syn. *Rhipsalis salicornioides*)

Haworthia
H. reinwardtii

Main features Succulent grown for its intricately marked foliage; small flowers
Height 15 cm (6 in.) **Spread** 30 cm (12 in.)
Position ◑ ● **Hardiness** RHS H2

The succulent leaves, often intricately marked with grey, variegated lines, make *Haworthia* an interesting plant for either indoors or the greenhouse. Various species are endemic to parts of South Africa and form low rosettes of stemless leaves. Most species produce firm, fleshy leaves covered in white, pearly beads or bands. Flower spikes can reach up to 40 centimetres (16 in.) long and are generally either white or pink white. *H. fasciata* (the zebra plant) is a readily available plant popular for its horizontal white stripes and ease of cultivation. The following species all have Royal Horticultural Society Awards of Garden Merit: *H. venosa* subsp. *tesselata* (veined haworthia) has a dense mat of rosettes of triangular, grey-green leaves, netted on the upper surface with pale-white lines. It produces greenish-white flowers. *H. retusa* has translucent, green leaves and produces white flowers in late autumn whereas *H. reinwardtii* (pictured) has white, spotted leaves and small, tubular, pink-white flowers.

Plant care is straightforward; the biggest threat is too much water. If the plants sit in waterlogged soil, the roots will rot, so allow compost to dry out between waterings. A cactus compost with added grit or sand will provide good drainage. Reduce the frequency and amount of water in winter, to allow plants to rest before the spring growth. *Haworthia* needs a bright situation, but it can tolerate some shade. If placed in scorching sun, the leaves can turn white. **PM**

Alternatives

Haworthia retusa, Haworthia fasciata, Haworthia venosa subsp. tesselata, Haworthia pimila

Hedychium
H. coronarium

Main features White flowers in summer; spring, summer, and autumn foliage; fragrant flowers, architectural plant
Height 3 m (10 ft) **Spread** 90 cm (3 ft)
Position ○ ◑ **Hardiness** RHS H1c

The name *Hedychium* comes from the Greek *hedys*, meaning 'sweet', and *chion*, meaning 'snow', and is particularly apt for this species, which has white, fragrant flowers. *Hedychium* are generally upright, leafy plants, and this species is no exception. The lance-like leaves are up to 60 centimetres (24 in.) long, and the plant, in ideal conditions, can reach up to 3 metres (10 ft) in height. *H. coronarium* is ideal for tropical-style plantings, where the effectiveness of the foliage is as important as the flowers. The sweetly scented flowers are shaped like butterflies. They are held on upright shoots at the top of the plant in mid- to late summer. Individually, they are not long-lived, but new flowers are produced regularly over three or four weeks. This is an easily grown plant given warmth, moisture and a fertile soil. In fact, so easy is it to grow that its robust, spreading rhizomes have made it a significant pest plant in several countries. Beware of its vigour if you are growing it in ideal conditions outdoors and perhaps keep it in a pot. Otherwise, it is a very good addition to the tropical style of garden, along with *Ensete*, *Musa*, *Tetrapanax* and *Canna*.

As this plant comes from tropical parts of India and southern Asia, it is not suitable for outdoor growing in colder zones. That said, it is easily overwintered in a dry, frost-proof place by lifting the plant, putting it into a pot or box, and leaving it to gradually dry out. Then, keep only just moist until new growth appears in spring. **PWi**

Alternatives

Hedychium coronarium 'Gold Spot', *Hedychium coccineum*, *Hedychium densiflorum*

Heliamphora
H. heterodoxa × nutans

Main feature Carnivorous, green pitchers with spoon-shaped endings
Height 30 cm (12 in.) **Spread** 30 cm (12 in.)
Position ○ ◑ **Hardiness** RHS H1a

The various species of *Heliamphora* are carnivorous plants that are quite a challenge to grow, requiring expertise, good facilities and patience – but they are rewarding. When growing naturally on the tabletop mountains of Venezuela, Brazil and Guyana, *Heliamphora* receives plenty of tropical light and revels in the high altitude and cool temperatures. *H. heterodoxa × nutans* is a slow-growing plant, often taking five years to be established enough to produce its first adult pitcher, and another five years before there are any signs of flowers.

Large fluctuations in temperature will slow down growth, so aim for 16 to 27°C (60–80°F). A windowsill can be sufficient, but when night-time temperatures start to drop, especially in winter, stabilise the conditions by putting the pot in an open-topped terrarium or large glass vase. Sunlight will cause the temperature in such a vase to rocket. It is therefore best to use fluorescent lighting to provide additional brightness.

Ideally the pot should always be standing in a saucer containing 0.6 centimetre (0.25 in.) of water. This keeps the compost, made up of live *Sphagnum* moss, permanently wet and adds a touch of humidity around the pitchers. Feeding a healthy pitcher plant does not involve any artificial fertilisers because the whole idea of the plant is that it can catch its own food; all *H. heterodoxa × nutans* needs is one or two flies a month. However, if you are really worried about your plant, it is quite acceptable to drop a recently killed fly into the pitcher. As the plants slow down in winter, reduce the feeding to nil by mouth. Although it is an effort to grow this plant well, to see a maturing *H. heterodoxa × nutans* specimen in prime condition is one of the great joys of gardening, and its worth has been recognised by a Royal Horticultural Society Award of Garden Merit. **PM**

Alternatives

Heliamphora heterodoxa x ionasi, Heliamphora heterodoxa, Heliamphora nutans

Helichrysum
H. petiolare 'Limelight'

Main features Tender perennial grown for its foliage;
year-round foliage
Height 10–50 cm (4–20 in.) **Spread** 50–100 cm (20–40 in.)
Position ◑ **Hardiness** RHS H3

The cultivar 'Limelight' is a lime-green variety of the
usually grey *H. petiolare*. It is a wiry, sprawling, perennial
plant that is perfectly suited to hanging baskets and
ornamental containers. The small leaves are neatly spaced
along the stem, and it will weave up, and through, other
nearby plants.

The fresh-looking, yellow-lime-coloured leaves are
neat, almost circular, and textured like soft felt. However,
to get the best from 'Limelight', it is important to grow
it well. It needs to be out of direct sunlight because if
it becomes dry, or scorched by the sun, it will lose its
vibrancy and may begin to look washed out and even
slightly shabby.

When arranged in a container, the lime-green leaves
provide a good background for plants of other colours,
including purple and vibrant red for jazziness, yellow
for harmony and white for coolness. 'Limelight' looks
impressive when grown with *Begonia sutherlandii*, which
features a lot of small, pale-orange flowers. The effect of
these plants together is stylish, soft and subtle.

As well as being used in mixed containers and
baskets, consider growing 'Limelight' as a single subject
plant in a hanging basket. It can also be encouraged
up a wall or through a trellis as a permanent sprawling
climber, in climates unaffected by frost. Another way to
use this plant is as a foliage filling in an annual summer
bedding scheme, as it will grow decoratively through the
other plants. At the end of the growing season, in regions
subject to frost, the whole bed should then be cleared.

First-year cuttings will not normally flower, but plants
aged two years and older show somewhat flattened
heads of small, cream-coloured, uninspiring flowers on
long stalks. 'Limelight' is vigorous, so may need trimming
during the growing season. **PWi**

Alternatives

Syn. *Helichrysum petiolare* 'Aureum'. *Helichrysum petiolare*
'Goring Silver', *Helichrysum petiolare* 'Variegatum'

Heliocereus
H. speciosus

Heliotropium
H. arborescens 'Chatsworth'

Main features Cactus with impressive trumpet flowers; long, spiny stems
Height 10 cm (4 in.) **Spread** 45 cm (18 in.)
Position ○ **Hardiness** RHS H1b

Main features Shrubby perennial; richly scented, violet or white flowers; attracts butterflies and bees
Height 60 cm (24 in.) **Spread** 60 cm (24 in.)
Position ○ **Hardiness** RHS H1c

The appearance of bright-red, trumpet-shaped flowers, up to 15 centimetres (6 in.) in diameter, make this easy-to-grow cactus a firm favourite. A devout sun worshipper, it is ideal on a warm, sunny windowsill where it can soak up the rays and reward the gardener with its blooms. *H. speciosus* originates in central Mexico. It has slender, heavily ribbed, spiny stems and extravagant blooms in summer. The stems start off life growing upwards, but with time and added plant weight, they tend to descend to form 45-centimetre-long (18 in.) trails. In addition to high levels of sunlight, *H. speciosus* likes humid conditions. In the main growing season of spring and summer, plants should be well watered, but the compost should be left to almost dry out between waterings. Plants also benefit from a balanced half-strength feed every fortnight. The growing regime changes in winter when watering should be reduced and no feed applied. New plants are easily raised from freshly sown seed. **PM**

A native of Peru, *Heliotropium* is often grown as a half-hardy annual with seed sown under cover in early spring. It was introduced to Europe in 1757 and became especially popular in Victorian times, when pots of heliotrope were brought into flower throughout the year to perfume the house. It was used extensively for bedding. A profusion of cultivars were raised, although sadly these are mostly now extinct. Most heliotrope flowers are in shades of mauve or purple; those with paler flowers tend to be more fragrant. *H. arborescens* 'Chatsworth' is an erect, bushy, evergreen shrub with dark-green, deeply veined leaves and clusters of small, very fragrant, purple flowers in summer. The nectar-rich flowers are attractive to bees, butterflies and moths, and their amazing cherry-pie fragrance makes them irresistible to people too. The cultivar is named after Chatsworth Estate in Derbyshire, England, where it was raised. 'Princess Marina' is a similar shade to 'Chatsworth' but not as well scented. **GHa**

Alternative

Syn. *Disocactus speciosus*. *Heliocereus serratus* (syn. *Disocactus serratus*)

Alternatives

Heliotropium arborescens 'White Lady', *Heliotropium arborescens* 'Dame Alice de Hales'

Heliotropium arborescens produces billowing clouds of colour and scent, here used as summer bedding. ➡

Hibiscus

H. moscheutos

Main features Woody perennial; flowers from summer to autumn; attracts butterflies and hummingbirds
Height 1.8 m (6 ft) **Spread** 1.2 m (4 ft)
Position ○ **Hardiness** RHS H3

This hibiscus, also known as swamp rose mallow, will bring a touch of tropical paradise to your garden. It is a woody, herbaceous perennial native to the United States. Like all perennial hibiscus, it comes into its own as a flowering plant in late summer with blossoms 15 to 25 centimetres (6–10 in.) wide. Each flower only lasts a day, but plenty of blooms are produced, so keep deadheading and plants will remain attractive. The flowers come in various colours depending on the cultivar: red, pink or white, but all with the unmistakable, crimson eye. The flowers are formed of five petals with a yellow stamen.

Keep *H. moscheutos* in a sunny, sheltered spot in moist, but well-drained, humus-rich, neutral to alkaline soil and it will reward you with beautiful blooms. The flowers also attract butterflies and hummingbirds, if nearby. *H. moscheutos* needs long, hot summers to flower well and it copes well with high humidity. Water container-grown plants before the compost dries out and use a high-potash fertiliser every six to eight weeks.

The dimensions of *H. moscheutos* make it ideal for the back of a perennial border. There are more compact cultivars, some of which are raised as half-hardy annuals. For example, the Disco Belle Series and Luna Series (pictured) are 60 to 90 centimetres (2–3 ft) high and can be raised from seed for gap filling or containers. Other perennials, such as the Southern Belle Group, can be pruned in autumn to form a bushy plant the next year. **NM**

Alternatives

Hibiscus moscheutos 'Cranberry Crush', *Hibiscus moscheutos* Disco Belle Series

Hibiscus
H. rosa-sinensis 'Cooperi'

Main features Flowers from spring to autumn; attracts bees, butterflies and birds; colourful, variegated foliage
Height 1.5 m (5 ft) **Spread** 90 cm (3 ft)
Position ○ **Hardiness** RHS H1b

Known also as the rose mallow or China rose, *H. rosa-sinensis* is a perennial found in the tropics, particularly South East Asia. However, it is also widely grown in temperate countries and, under the right conditions, can thrive there. The cultivar 'Cooperi' has crimson, 10-centimetre-wide (4 in.) blossoms, consisting of five single petals and a long, red stamen and stigma. It is more compact growing than most rose mallows, and its foliage is beautifully variegated with red, pink and white. Numerous cultivars of *H.rosa-sinensis* are available, with flowers ranging from yellow and orange to pink, with single and double petals. The dark-green, glossy leaves are coarsely serrated, and the flowers usually only last a day. 'Snow Queen' is an alternative variegated hibiscus, which bears similar flowers to 'Cooperi' but its leaves are green and speckled with white or pink.

As a tropical plant, it needs a minimum temperature of 10°C (50°F) in the winter, so in temperate countries it is best grown in a warm and humid glasshouse or conservatory, with minimum night temperatures of 7 to 10°C (45–50°F). Alternatively, a sunny windowsill is fine. If pot-grown, 'Cooperi' can be placed outside in summer, although it must be brought in for winter. Plants need to be repotted with loam-based compost in late winter to early spring, with weekly feeding with a liquid fertiliser six to eight weeks after repotting. In temperate glasshouses it flowers in summer and autumn. **NM**

Alternatives

Hibiscus rosa-sinensis 'Snow Queen', *Hibiscus schizopetalus*

Hibiscus

H. schizopetalus

Hildewintera

H. aureispina

Main features Perennial with lantern-like flowers in late spring and early summer; attracts butterflies and birds
Height 2 m (7 ft) **Spread** 1.5–1.8 m (5–6 ft)
Position ○ **Hardiness** RHS H1b

Main features Spiny cactus with long snake-like stems; tubular flowers
Height 15 cm (6 in.) **Spread** 1.5 m (5 ft)
Position ○ **Hardiness** RHS H1b

A perennial hibiscus originating from tropical East Africa, *H. schizopetalus* has crinkly, red, single flower petals that curl backwards on themselves to form a lantern with the impressive, long stamen. Against a backdrop of dark-green foliage, it is a sight to behold. Also known as the Japanese lantern, this evergreen shrub requires minimum winter temperatures of 10 to 16°C (50–61°F), so in colder regions it needs to be grown indoors, where it should be given as much light as possible. As a container plant it can be left outside in warmer months. *H. schizopetalus* will grow large, even in a container. The stems are lax and need some support, although it can be trained like a climber or carefully pruned to keep its shape. However, plants bloom better if left unpruned, as the flowers are produced on short spurs from the previous year's wood, so only prune every three or four years. The Japanese lantern blooms year-round in the tropics, but only in the summer months in temperate countries. **NM**

If spiny, yellow-bodied snakes up to 1.5 metres (5 ft) long give you nightmares then maybe *H. aureispina* is not for you. However, this is a great specimen with impressive, thick stems, golden-yellow spines, and masses of tubular flowers. Native to Argentina and Uruguay, this plant produces small, tubular, salmon-orange flowers with purple anthers from midspring through to the end of summer. Often many blooms are produced at the same time, making it a breathtaking sight. Young plants start off growing upright, but their stems soon begin to grow downwards as they age. *H. aureispina* is a robust and beautiful plant. It is one of the easiest cacti to grow at home, so try it in a hanging basket in a tall greenhouse. In the warmer summer months *H. aureispina* can go outside, but return it under cover when the temperatures start to fall. With no special treatment required, it will thrive in a bright position in well-drained soil and bring years of delight. **PM**

Alternative

Hibiscus rosa-sinensis 'Cooperi'

Alternative

Syn. *Cleistocactus aureispina*. *Cleistocactus winteri*

Huernia
H. zebrina

Main features Succulent with leafless stems; blooms smell of rotting meat
Height 20 cm (8 in.) **Spread** 20 cm (8 in.)
Position ◐ **Hardiness** RHS H1b

Many plants can be described as producing scented flowers, and *Huernia* species are no exception. The intricately constructed, coloured, and patterned flowers of this group of fascinating succulents are indeed scented. However, in this instance the fragrance is not lily of the valley, garden pink or mock orange, but that of rotting flesh. The putrid, fetid and downright disgusting smell attracts flies as pollinators. This makes *Huernia* a great plant for a glasshouse away from the home, and a perfect companion for an insect-eating plant. The leafless stems of *Huernia* species are heavily toothed, grey green in colour, and fleshy. The flowers appear from midsummer to autumn on short stalks from the base or middle of stems. Depending on the species, the blooms can be red, brown, purple, yellow, spotted or plain, and 'scented'. Species to try include *H. zebrina*, which has yellow-brown blooms with maroon stripes, and *H. pillansii*, with starfish-shaped blooms in deep maroon with white speckles. **PM**

Alternatives

Huernia guttata, Huernia hystrix, Huernia pillansii

Iochroma
I. australe

Main feature Shrub grown for its violet-purple trumpet flowers in spring and summer
Height 3 m (10 ft) **Spread** 2 m (7 ft)
Position ○ ◐ **Hardiness** RHS H2

This is an evergreen shrub that carries a mass of pendulous, violet-purple flowers in late spring and summer. In the wild it develops into a sprawling shrub some 3 metres (10 ft) high. The flowers are small versions of its close relation, the much larger angel's trumpet (*Brugmansia*), although this plant is much tougher than its larger cousin. It comes from the southern, cooler parts of Argentina and is able to stand a few degrees of frost over short periods. The branches are lax and arch gracefully under the weight of flowers when in full bloom. The leaves are simple with no particular merit. It is a versatile and vigorous shrub that can be grown as a freestanding plant in frost-free climates or, where the temperature is likely to go below freezing by a few degrees, benefits from being grown against a sheltered wall that faces the midday sun. It also makes an impressive specimen plant in a large container. In very cold climates container plants can be cut back hard in the autumn and brought indoors. **PWi**

Alternative

Iochroma australe 'Andean Snow'

Iresine
I. herbstii 'Brilliantissima'

Jatropha
J. podagrica

Main feature Houseplant or annual bedding with dramatic crimson leaves
Height 30–60 cm (12–24 in.) **Spread** 30–60 cm (12–24 in.)
Position ○ **Hardiness** RHS H1c

Main features Fascinating sculptural plant; attracts butterflies and hummingbirds
Height 45–60 cm (18–24 in.) **Spread** 45–60 cm (18–24 in.)
Position ○ ◑ **Hardiness** RHS H1a

With common names that include blood leaf, chicken gizzard and beefsteak plant, nobody will be unduly surprised to learn that *I. herbstii* is a foliage plant with leaves in vivid shades of red and pink. 'Brilliantissima' has particularly bright, crimson leaves with lighter veins and looks almost unnatural in its intensity. This is a dramatic plant to grow as annual bedding, or as a colourful houseplant on a sunny windowsill. Native to Brazil, the species likes warm temperatures and bright light. The best leaf colours are obtained in full sun. Plants are easily grown from seed, but cuttings root readily too, if taken in late summer and then overwintered on a bright windowsill. Pot into a loam-based potting compost. Feed regularly through the growing season with a balanced fertiliser. Ensure that the soil does not dry out excessively. Young plants will need the tips pinching out at regular intervals to keep plants neat and bushy. Plants are frost tender and require a minimum temperature of 10°C (50°F). **GHa**

This plant, which has a plethora of common names – including Buddha belly plant, bottleplant shrub, and gout plant – is perhaps not beautiful but it certainly has character. The most distinctive trait is the swollen, belly-like stem. This is green grey and shows the bristled scars of old leaf bases. The leaves that emerge on the top of the stem are initially red-edged with hairy centres, but they rapidly expand to waxy, five-lobed leaves. The leaves will drop in the cooler months, but throughout the year *Jatropha* will send up stalks of coral-red or yellow flowers held above the leaves. There are separate male and female flowers, which look similar, but the female flowers start to open first to reduce self-pollination. If fertilised, the plant will bear green, olive-like, seedpods that ripen and explode with an audible pop, expelling seed over a wide area. The seed, like the rest of the plant, is toxic. *Jatropha* is a member of the *Euphorbia* family and is very easy to grow. Treat it as you would cacti and succulents. **GHa**

Alternatives

Iresine herbstii 'Wallisii', *Iresine herbstii* 'Purple Lady'

Alternative

Jatropha podagrica 'Cintho Sunshine'

 Iresine herbstii 'Brilliantissima' as a foliage bedding plant in Fellow's Garden, Cambridge, UK.

Jovellana
J. violacea

Main features Shrub with aromatic foliage; profuse flowers in late spring and summer; attracts bees
Height 1.5–2.4 m (5–8 ft) **Spread** 60–90 cm (2–3 ft)
Position ○ ◑ **Hardiness** RHS H2

This spreading shrub, sometimes known as the violet slipper flower, is grown for its generous sprays of small, violet blooms. These reward close inspection as the nodding bells have interiors that are blotched with yellow and spotted with purple. They are reminiscent of foxglove flowers and are similarly attractive to bees. The small, green, toothed leaves, carried on red stems, are aromatic with a spicy, minty fragrance if rubbed.

Jovellana are deciduous in cold conditions, but in mild winters, or if grown in a conservatory, they will be evergreen. They prefer a warm, sunny position, but with protection from the midday sun. Provide a free-draining loam compost. Avoid excessive winter wet. Mild frost should not be a problem if the roots are well-mulched before the onset of winter. Propagate from seeds, which are very fine and should be watered into the surface of the compost. Do not cover as light will aid germination, but ensure the surface of the compost does not dry out by regularly misting, or covering with polythene. Semi-ripe cuttings taken in summer root readily.

The genus was named for Gaspar Melchor de Jovellanos, a Spanish statesman, philosopher, and student of Peruvian flora. *J. violacea* grows wild in Chile. The genus is of interest to plant geographers, as of the four species currently recognised, two occur in New Zealand and two in Chile. This distribution, broken by the Pacific Ocean, is believed to be the result of the break up of the landmass Gondwana. **GHa**

Alternatives

Jovellana punctata, Jovellana sinclairii

Justicia
J. brandegeeana

Main features Evergreen perennial; distinctive pink or red bracts; often grown as a houseplant
Height 90 cm (3 ft) **Spread** 90 cm (3 ft)
Position ◗ **Hardiness** RHS H1b

Native to Mexico, the false hop or Mexican shrimp plant, is an evergreen, shrubby perennial with rather weak spindly stems. They are popular plants in cultivation and can be trained as standard specimens with support for the main stem. The soft, green leaves are oval and lightly downy on the undersides. The plant produces overlapping, dusky-pink or brick-red bracts from which extend the tubular white flowers. These bracts have a prawn-like appearance. The flowers appear in late spring and continue into early autumn. Cultivated forms may have bright-yellow or lime-green bracts.

Justicia was named for the Scottish horticulturist Sir James Justice, whose profligate spending on greenhouses and soil mixtures was said to have led to his divorce and expulsion from Fellowship in the Royal Society. The species name commemorates the US botanist Townshend Stith Brandegee of Connecticut.

Grow in partial shade in a sheltered position, although some sun is important to encourage strong growth and stimulate flowering. Plants must be protected from frost, and they do well as houseplants. Pinch out shoots at the tips to promote more compact, bushy plants. Young plants can be cut back hard to encourage vigorous growth, but old, leggy specimens rarely respond well to being cut back, so it's best if they are replaced. Propagate from seeds sown in spring or by taking softwood or semi-ripe cuttings. Insert cuttings in a small pot of moist, free-draining compost. **GHa**

Alternatives

Justicia adhatoda, Justica carnea

Kalanchoe
K. beharensis

Main features Evergreen shrub; attractive, touchable, hairy leaves
Height 90–150 cm (3–5 ft) **Spread** 90–150 cm (3–5 ft)
Position ○ ◑ **Hardiness** RHS H1b

Soft and invitingly touchable, the leaves of this evergreen shrub have earned it the common names of elephant's ear, felt bush and velvet leaf. In cultivation, grown in a large tub, it can reach 1.5 metres (5 ft) tall, but in the hot, humid forests of Madagascar, it can reach as high as 6 metres (20 ft). The leaves are triangular and olive green, but are covered with dense woolly hairs that are rust brown on the upper surface of the leaves and silvery below. The plant produces small, yellow flowers with violet markings from winter through to summer. The plant was discovered in Behara in southern Madagascar and was once widely distributed across the entire island, but now only grows in the south, in dry, arid forests on a variety of soils.

Grow in full sun to partial shade in a gritty, loam-based mix. Allow the growing medium to dry between watering, and water sparingly during the winter. Apply a balanced liquid fertiliser a couple of times during the growing season. The plant is tolerant of neglect, but it will rot in cold, damp conditions. *Kalanchoe* are not particularly prone to pests and diseases, but mealy bugs can be troublesome in glasshouse cultivation or indoors. Severe infestations will reduce plant vigour and stunt growth and may result in an accumulation of honeydew, leading to the growth of unsightly, sooty mould.

Propagate from seeds or by stem or leaf cuttings. Leaf cuttings are a useful way to produce a larger number of new plants. Remove a leaf and cut across the midrib with a clean, sharp knife in several places. Secure the leaf to the surface of a sandy propagating mix with hairpins. New plants should form along the cut lines within a month and can be potted up separately once the old leaf has withered away. Many *Kalanchoe* species contain cardiac glycosides and are toxic to animals, so keep away from pets. **GHa**

Alternatives

Kalanchoe beharensis 'Fang', *Kalanchoe tomentosa*

Kohleria
'Sunshine'

Main features Houseplant; attractive, velvety foliage; showy, tubular flowers over a long season
Height 30 cm (12 in.) **Spread** 15–30 cm (6–12 in.)
Position ◑ **Hardiness** RHS H1c

The beautiful, velvety leaves of silver green with darker, sage-green veining would make this an appealing houseplant if grown for its foliage alone. However, there is added value to this robust, upright plant once it starts to flower. This popular plant is ideal for indoor hanging baskets to allow a view up inside the showy, tubular flowers. The tube itself is bright red and expands into five spreading lobes that are intricately marked with a network of red patterns. The flowers are softly hairy. They bloom profusely in late spring and early summer, but flowers may also be produced at other times of the year.

Kohleria grows from scaly rhizomes, which are adapted for periods of dormancy during the dry season. The rhizomes typically grow up to 5 centimetres (2 in.) long, but in the wild they can reach up to 15 centimetres (6 in.) in length. They are easy to grow in pots of fibre-based compost. Keep in light shade in a humid environment with protection from drafts. They need a minimum temperature of 15°C (60°F). Allow the compost to partially dry out between waterings and feed regularly with a high-potash liquid feed, such as those formulated for tomato plants. Plants should be virtually dry during the winter dormancy period. Extra plants are easily propagated by stem cuttings or division of the rhizomes.

Kohleria are members of the *Gesneriaceae* family, which includes popular houseplants such as *Gloxinia* and *Saintpaulia*. There are nineteen species of *Kohleria* distributed in Central America and South America, particularly in the highlands of Colombia, where they grow at the edges of forests. Many hybrids were developed in the nineteenth century – when the genus was named for a Swiss natural history teacher from Zurich – and there has been renewed interest in *Kohleria* from plant breeders in recent years. **GHa**

Alternatives

Kohleria 'Peridots Mango Martini', *Kohleria* 'Ryssiten'

Lavandula
L. pedunculata subsp. *pedunculata*

Main features Scented leaves and flowers; long flowering season
Height 60 cm (24 in.) **Spread** 60 cm (24 in.)
Position ○ **Hardiness** RHS H3

Hailing from the sunny shores of the Mediterranean, this is a species of *Lavandula* with a difference. Instead of the usual blue-mauve flowers seen on traditional English lavender (*L. angustifolia*), this beautiful small shrub bears short spikes of tubular flowers topped off with delightful top knots of purple-coloured bracts, which are often likened to rabbit ears.

It is much better behaved than many other lavenders, remaining small and easily managed in a container. It is also useful because it blooms over an extended period: usually for several months between late winter and midsummer, depending on where it is being grown. Bees appreciate the flowers even more than gardeners do, making a high-quality honey that is much loved in Crete. *L. pedunculata* subsp. *pedunculata* is one of the more tender lavenders, although fortunately for those in colder climates, it is easily grown from cuttings, which can be overwintered somewhere frost free. It is surprisingly tolerant of high humidity and is a great choice in areas where other lavenders are prone to wilting in high summer.

The scent of *L. pedunculata* subsp. *pedunculata* is somewhat different to that of *L. angustifolia*, having a more camphor-like note, which could perhaps be likened to a cross between lavender and rosemary. It is difficult to resist the temptation to gently squeeze the flower heads as you walk past the plant and then sniff your fingers. If hardy in your region, this plant will make a wonderful, fragrant, low hedge, but be sure to trim it at least once, if not, twice a year, straight after a flush of flowers has faded. Look out for seedlings around the bases of plants; they are a sure sign that the plant is happy. In addition, these seedlings are well worth potting up because they soon make usable plants. **GAR**

Alternatives

Syn. *Lavandula stoechas* 'Butterfly', *Lavandula stoechas* 'Papillon'. *Lavandula pinnata, Lavandula dentata*

Leptospermum
L. scoparium 'Red Damask'

Main features Shrub grown for its double, aromatic, evergreen leaves; good for poor soils
Height 1.8–2.4 m (6–8 ft) **Spread** 1.2–1.5 m (4–5 ft)
Position ○ **Hardiness** RHS H3

The New Zealand tea tree, *L. scoparium*, is known as manuka in its native land. Bees adore it, and manuka honey produced from the flowers is held in high esteem for its healing properties. The species is a plain-looking shrub with aromatic, silky leaves and small flowers and will grow in low-fertility soils. 'Red Damask' was bred by University of California (UCLA) professor Dr Walter Lammerts, an expert in avocado breeding who pioneered controlled hybridisation of *Leptospermum*. Using *L. scoparium* 'Nichollsii' and a double, pink form, Lammerts introduced the colour red for the first time in a double, tea tree flower. 'Red Damask' was the result, and this led the way for the multiple forms available today including the similar 'Crimson Glory' (pictured).

These miniature, frilly and tissue-like, carmine-red flowers with black 'kohl' centres are, in fact, quite tough and smother the branches completely, gently weighing them down in early summer. Yet, the flowers are not the only outstanding feature. It is known as the tea tree plant since the oil glands on the undersides of the dark, slender foliage of this cultivar contain a delightful scent, slightly reminiscent of honeyed turpentine. Persistent, black-berried fruits add further interest.

A quick-growing plant, drought tolerant, but of borderline hardiness, pot up in well-drained neutral to acidic soil. Position plant pots in full sun and where you can walk past to breathe in the distinctive, but delightful, perfume on warm days. Although tender in colder climates, 'Red Damask' can be grown as a shrub directly in the ground with the protection of a warm wall. Prune to the size wanted after flowering. 'Red Damask' can also be used as a cut flower. The species can self-seed in certain regions, however, the double flowers produce very little seed. **IT**

Alternative

Leptospermum scoparium 'Ruby Glow', *Leptospermum scoparium* 'Burgundy Queen'

Leucadendron
'Inca Gold'

Main features Brightly coloured foliage and bracts; unusual flower heads; great cut flower
Height 1.8 m (6 ft)   **Spread** 1.8 m (6 ft)
Position ○   **Hardiness** RHS H3

The *Leucadendron* originates from the exotic, sun-baked fynbos of South Africa, a place like no other on Earth. Here, in part of what has become known as the smallest of Earth's six 'botanical kingdoms', an area comprising 0.5 per cent of Africa's landmass contains an astonishing 20 per cent of the continent's plant species. 'Inca Gold' is a veritable artist's palette of a plant: an upright evergreen shrub, with handsome green leaves infused with burgundy. The yellow-green flower heads are surrounded by reddish bracts, which fade to golden yellow and pink as they mature. It makes quite a spectacle, especially when grown against a wall or other plain backdrop where it can be admired.

The plant's long-lasting flowers are much sought after by flower arrangers for their unusual looks and durability. Cut foliage and flowers will last for many weeks in water, and they can be dried for use in decorations, too. 'Inca Gold' thrives in a poor, neutral to acidic, well-drained soil, but in cold areas it is more likely that you will grow it in a pot. This wonderful plant brings colour to the garden or patio for months on end: the bracts surrounding the flowers remain bright for a particularly long time. One of the least fussy (and hardiest) of the South African *Protea* relatives, *Leucadendron* grows well in areas with Mediterranean or mild maritime climates. If you are successful with it, pruning will probably be unnecessary because all the flower arrangers in your neighbourhood will be lining up to do it for you! **GAR**

Alternative

Leucadendron 'Safari Sunset'

Lithops
L. julii

Main features Fascinating stone mimic; attractive multi-petalled flowers
Height 10 cm (4 in.) **Spread** 10 cm (4 in.)
Position ○ **Hardiness** RHS H2

The common name living stones aptly describes these intriguing plants that mimic small pebbles in order to avoid being eaten by herbivores in their native southern Africa. They are great for stimulating an interest in plants in children, who will be fascinated to see the daisy-like flowers seeming to emerge from a stone. *Lithops* will also appeal to collectors, who have a choice of more than 130 species and many hybrids from which to assemble their selection.

These plants are often sold as unnamed species in mixed collections of succulent plants, and they are fine for growing together in a pan. All species grow as pairs of flat-topped, fleshy leaves, but some will form spreading clumps of the paired leaves. The leaf colour and markings can be very variable. Most species will produce white or yellow flowers, which emerge from the fissure between the pair of leaves in the autumn. Flowers usually open in afternoon sun and close at night. Named species include *L. julii*, which has white flowers from midsummer to autumn that are large enough to cover the fleshy leaves. The golden-flowered *L. aucampiae* has red-brown leaves marked with darker dots. *L. marmorata* has grey-green leaves marbled with grey lines. The white flowers open in early autumn and are large enough to cover the leaves.

Lithops needs a bright, sunny position at all times and prefers good ventilation at night to allow the stomata to open for the absorption of carbon dioxide. Some species tolerate frost in their natural environment. **GHa**

Alternatives

Lithops bella, Lithops olivacea, Lithops otzeniana

Livistona
L. chinensis

Main features Elegant, single-trunk palm; distinctive fan-like foliage with long tips
Height 5 m (16 ft) **Spread** 1.8 m (6 ft)
Position ○ ◐ **Hardiness** RHS H3

The genus *Livistona* was named for Patrick Murray, Baron of Livingston, a keen horticulturalist whose plant collection became the basis of the Royal Botanic Garden Edinburgh. *L. chinensis* is native to the coastlines of Japan, Taiwan and the Guangdong region of southern China. In China the wood has been used for umbrella handles and walking sticks, the leaves are made into hats, and rope is produced from the fibres of the fronds. The broad-green leaves of *L. chinensis* can grow to 1.8 metres (6 ft) in diameter, and the long, ribbon extensions at the leaf tips move in the slightest breeze, giving a shimmering effect. *L. chinensis* is a medium-sized palm tree, and the robust grey trunk has evolved to withstand hurricane winds. Don't be put off by the height measurement – immature and dwarf cultivars are used widely in landscaping under trees. The flowers are pollinated by the wind and insects, and by early winter they have developed into large numbers of glossy, blue-green fruits. **GHa**

Alternatives

Livistona australis, Livistona nitida, Washingtonia robusta, Livistona chinensis

Lotus
L. berthelotii × maculatus

Main features Delicate foliage ideal for tall pots and hanging baskets; exotic blooms
Height 20 cm (8 in.) **Spread** 1.2 m (4 ft)
Position ○ **Hardiness** RHS H1c

The alternative name for this plant, fire vine, aptly describes its crowning glory – beak-like clusters of blooms that are yellow, flushed with red, and a dark line down the centre of the arching throat. A good hybrid combines the best qualities of each parent, both of which in this case grow wild in the Canary Islands. The hybrid's flowers are brighter than those of *L. berthelotii*, which are an orange-red, while it inherits the desirable, silvery-coloured, needle-like leaves from *L. berthelotii*. This parrot's beak looks superb getting baked on the sides of a tall, Mediterranean terra-cotta oil jar like the ones made in Crete. In fact, tall containers look better in the landscape with low, trailing plants, like lotus. To ensure plants flower profusely, give them the hottest, most sheltered spot, either in containers or the open ground. Planted near brickwork or paving: they will appreciate the absorbed heat given off at night. They associate well with other sun worshippers, like gazanias and osteospermums. **GS**

Alternatives

Lotus maculatus 'Gold Flash', *Lotus maculatus* 'Amazon Sunset', *Lotus berthelotii*

◒ *Livistona chinensis* in amongst ferns in Rupe Dell, Isola Madre, Lake Maggiore, Italy.

Luculia
L. gratissima

Main features Large shrub; richly fragrant pink flowers from autumn into winter
Height 3 m (10 ft) **Spread** 1.5 m (5 ft)
Position ○ ◑ **Hardiness** RHS H1c

Grown for the wonderful perfume of the flowers, *Luculia* is a semi-evergreen shrub with long, deeply veined leaves that turn red and are shed at intervals throughout the year. It is a member of the *Rubiaceae* family, which includes the coffee plant (*Coffea arabica*) and scented pot plants, such as *Gardenia*. In cultivation *L. gratissima* may reach 3 metres (10 ft) high, but wild plants may grow taller. Large, rounded clusters of baby-pink flowers, up to 20 centimetres (8 in.) in diameter, appear on the ends of the stems from autumn through winter. The beautiful perfume of these flowers is retained even in dried specimens. An inhabitant of forests in the foothills of the Himalayas, from northern India to western China, *L. gratissima* prefers a rich organic soil, but plants are prone to fungal disease if soil gets waterlogged. Mulch well with organic matter to retain moisture around the roots. In the Himalayas, plants will experience cool summers and frost-free winters. In temperate climates grow this plant in a tub in a cool glasshouse and put outdoors for the summer. **GHa**

Alternatives

Luculia intermedia, Luculia grandifolia

Ludisia
L. discolor

Main features Beautiful, velvety leaves; spikes of small, white-and-yellow flowers in winter
Height 30 cm (12 in.) **Spread** 30 cm (12 in.)
Position ◑ **Hardiness** RHS H1a

Ludisia is a terrestrial orchid that grows on the forest floors of South East Asia, from southern China to Sumatra and the Philippines. Its only species is *L. discolor*, which is unusual amongst orchids in that it is grown more for its foliage than for its flowers. The leaves have a wonderful velvety texture. In the usual form they are a deep chocolate-brown colour, highlighted with shimmering, pink or coppery-red veins. The undersides of the leaves are a uniform bronze. Clusters of small, white flowers with a yellow heart grow on upright stems, giving the impression of a flock of small birds with their wings outstretched. The flowers can last for six to eight weeks and usually emerge in winter; however, plants may repeat the display at other times of the year. Wild plants vary considerably in the colour and markings on the leaves, and a few of these variations can be seen in cultivated plants. *L. discolor* 'Alba' lacks the typical red pigmentation and has attractive fresh-green foliage with silver veining. A variant with white veins is sold as 'Silver Velvet'. **GHa**

Alternatives

Dossinia marmorata, Macodes petola

Lycianthes
L. rantonnetii

Main features Shrub with showy cascades of purple flowers in summer and early autumn; grows well in a pot
Height 2–4 m (7–13 ft) **Spread** 1.2–1.8 m (4–6 ft)
Position ○ **Hardiness** RHS H1c

Also known as *Solanum rantonnetii*, the blue potato bush is an incredibly generous plant. Beautiful and easy to grow, this lax evergreen shrub from South America brings a flood of purplish flowers to summer gardens. Borne over a long period, the blooms are generally a rich, velvety purple, but the colours can vary from mauve, blushed with pink, to pure white in *L. rantonnetii* 'Alba'. All have a central yellow 'eye' – betraying their botanical closeness to potatoes and aubergines. Despite its name, the blue potato bush is not edible, but it more than makes up for a lack of culinary usefulness with impressive flower power. Although *L. rantonnetii* is tender in many places, it makes a great plant for greenhouses, conservatories or patio pots. If you are lucky enough to live in an area with mild winters, it can be grown as an outdoor shrub, or trained as a small tree. This technique works well for pot plants too – the best way to grow them in containers is trained as a 'standard' (lollipop shape). Simply give them a light 'haircut' every few months to keep them in shape. **GAR**

Alternatives

Solanum crispum 'Glasnevin', *Solanum wendlandii*

Mackaya
M. bella

Main features Shrub with glossy, green leaves; tubular, pale-violet flowers throughout the year
Height 1.5 m (5 ft) **Spread** 90 cm (3 ft)
Position ○ ◑ **Hardiness** RHS H2

With its slender branches, *M. bella* can be grown as a shrub or small tree. It has glossy, green leaves that are 8 centimetres (3 in.) long and have wavy-toothed edges. Loose spikes of flowers sit at the ends of branches for much of the year. The flowers are tubular bells, 6 centimetres (2.5 in.) long, with five flared lobes at the mouth. They are white or a pale-violet colour, usually marked with fine purple veins. The profusion of flower was the inspiration for the specific name *bella*, which means 'beautiful'. After flowering, fruits are set. They are green, club-shaped capsules that change to brown as they mature and then explode into two parts to eject the seed. *M. bella* is the only species in the genus *Mackaya*, and it is native to the Eastern Cape, KwaZulu-Natal, Swaziland and Northern Province of South Africa, where it grows in forests as an understorey shrub, often at stream edges. The plant will grow in any well-drained soil in sun or part shade, but too much sun can scorch the leaves. It is a food plant for the larvae of *Junonia oenone*, the blue pansy butterfly. **GHa**

Alternative

Ruellia macrantha

Mammillaria
M. compressa

Main features Spiny cacti with clusters of spherical or columnar stems; rings of attractive flowers
Height 10–50 cm (4–20 in.) **Spread** 10–50 cm (4–20 in.)
Position ○ **Hardiness** RHS H2

Here is a large genus of low-growing cacti with stems covered in tubercles, with areoles on the ends from which emerge the spines. This contrasts with the areoles arranged in ribs as seen on many other cacti. *Mammillaria* are popular plants with hobbyists as they are easily grown and varied, with small colourful flowers in shades of bright pink or cream. The flowers often form a wreath around the crown of the plant. The flowers are followed by red, club-shaped fruits that are berry-like and edible. These are sometimes known as chilitos because they look like tiny, red chilli peppers. In species such as *M. theresae*, the fruits remains hidden within the plant body. Most species have a neat growth habit and are freely offsetting. The genus name is derived from the Latin word *mammilla* meaning 'little nipple', referring to the tubercles.

Mammillaria has a wide distribution in nature, from the southern states of America, through Central America to Colombia. The largest number of species is found in Mexico. Popular species include *M. compressa*, a globular solitary species that grows to form big clumps and has white "wool" and bristles; *M. bombycina*, known as the silken pincushion cactus, which has thick, white hairs between the tubercles; and *M. plumosa*, which has a mound of globose stems totally covered by dense, white spines. *M. bocasana*, known as the powder puff cactus, is a very attractive species with fine hair that hides the hooked spines. Several cultivars exist with varying quantity of wool, and flower colour.

Grow in full sun in a gritty, sandy mix. Plants require low humidity and should be watered moderately through spring and summer and kept dry from midautumn. Feed with a high-potash fertiliser while in flower. Many *Mammillaria* tolerate low temperatures if they are kept dry in winter. **GHa**

Alternatives

Mammillaria bombycina, Mammillaria elongata, Mammillaria gracilis

Maranta
M. leuconeura var. *erythroneura*

Main features Colourful foliage plants; beautifully patterned leaves
Height 30 cm (12 in.) **Spread** 45 cm (18 in.)
Position ◑ **Hardiness** RHS H1b

This is one of the most widely grown foliage houseplants. The velvety black-green leaves are oval and about 13 centimetres (5 in.) long with reddish undersides. The beautiful leaves lie flat during the day and fold together in an erect position at night, which gave rise to the common name of the prayer plant. *M. leuconeura* var. *erythroneura* is also known as the herringbone plant, and this name relates to the pattern of prominent carmine veins on the leaves, which look as though they have been hand-painted. Fairly insignificant small, white or pink-purple flowers are borne on slender stems just above the leaves.

The genus *Maranta* was named for the sixteenth-century Venetian botanist Bartolomeo Maranta. It is found in tropical Central and South America, as well as in the West Indies and Brazil. There are some forty to fifty species, including *M. arundinacea,* which is grown to produce the edible starch arrowroot. *M. leuconeura* var. *kerchoveana* has dark blotches between the leaf veins and whitish undersides to the leaves. *M. leuconeura* var. *leuconeura* has a light, blue-green central zone and radiating lateral veins that extend through a green-black background. These latter forms are worth seeking out if you do not like the carmine markings of the more widely sold *M. leuconeura* var. *erythroneura.*

In cultivation *Maranta* requires light shade and high humidity. Grow it in a humus-rich potting mixture and keep the plant evenly moist. In dry conditions mist the leaves regularly with soft water, and in order to increase humidity, stand the pot on a tray of wet pebbles. For the best results keep *Maranta* in warm conditions, out of drafts, and check for red spider mites regularly. The easiest way to propagate the plant is to divide the clumps in spring or take stem cuttings from spring to early summer. **GHa**

Alternatives

Maranta leuconeura var. *kerchoveana, Maranta leuconeura* var. *leuconeura*

Massonia
M. depressa

Main features Curiosity value; interesting leaves; flower and seed heads
Height 5 cm (2 in.) **Spread** 50 cm (20 in.)
Position ○ **Hardiness** RHS H2

This is a fascinating plant grown perhaps more for its curiosity value than for any beauty of flower or leaf. In the autumn bulbs produce pairs of oblong leaves that lie pressed flat against the ground. The leaves are smooth and dull green, sometimes with purplish markings or an attractive beetroot-red edge. They are followed in winter and spring by a brush-like flower head with upwards-pointing stamen. The white or pink flowers have a distinct yeasty odour, and in South Africa they are pollinated by small rodents, including gerbils. In early evening the flowers secrete nectar, which has a low sugar concentration but is particularly thick and jelly-like. This is thought to make it easier for the rodents to lap it up. The fruits of *M. depressa* consist of three-winged capsules, producing seed that germinate readily. Young plants will flower within two to three years of sowing. The seedlings need to be spaced well apart in pots; otherwise, their large leaves may overwhelm those of their neighbours. Grow the plants in pots of free-draining, sandy compost. **GHa**

Alternatives

Massonia echinata, Massonia pustulata

Melianthus
M. major

Main features Perennial; blue-grey leaves; brick-red flowers in autumn; year-round foliage in frost-free climates
Height 2–3 m (7–10 ft) **Spread** 1–3 m (3–10 ft)
Position ○ **Hardiness** RHS H3

This plant has majestic, jagged, blue-grey leaves up to 40 centimetres (16 in.) long, each deeply cut to the midrib into rows of up to eighteen leaflets that are carried on upright, hollow stems up to 2 metres (7 ft) high. In warm climates it produces spikes of flowers 60 centimetres (24 in.) long. In its native South Africa, the flowering season is spring to early summer, but in temperate climates the small, deep, brick-red flowers are produced later in the season. Winter frost can destroy or badly damage the foliage. It is worth cutting the plant to the ground in spring to encourage a set of fresh shoots whether or not the foliage has been damaged by the winter. Covering the crown with a deep layer of protective mulch before the onset of winter helps prevent frost from penetrating the ground. It is a useful plant for creating an exotic-looking border. Try it alongside species of *Hedychium* and *Canna*. In colder zones use it with varieties of *Miscanthus*. It also makes a bold container plant. Leaves smell of peanut butter, peapods or rubber: you decide. **PWi**

Alternatives

Melianthus comosus, Melianthus villosus

Melianthus major in a container in Washington, US (planting design by Dan Hinkley). ➔

Mimosa
M. pudica

Main features Subshrub grown as an annual; pompom flowers; year-round foliage; leaves sensitive to touch
Height 30–75 cm (12–30 in.) **Spread** 40–90 cm (16–36 in.)
Position ○ **Hardiness** RHS H1b

One of the fastest-moving plants that is sensitive to touch, *M. pudica* is a great selection to excite both children and adults alike. At first glance it is a fairly nondescript little plant, between 30 and 75 centimetres (12–30 in.) tall with pinnate leaves split into four, long, narrow leaflets, each of which is split into between ten and twenty-five segments. It looks rather like an acacia. It grows as a spreading, mat-forming annual or short-lived perennial. Its famous party piece is the speed at which the leaves will collapse when touched. The segments almost instantly fold along their rib, and apart from startling or dislodging a hungry herbivore, the whole plant looks wilted and, helped by its sharp prickles, unappetising. The collapse is due to a sudden change in the water pressure in certain cells. After a few minutes, pressure is restored and the leaves will stiffen once more. While there are other plant species that move their leaves – for example, common clover folds up at night to conserve moisture – they generally do so much more slowly. Small, pretty, pale-pink or pale-purple pompom flowers – 1 to 2 centimetres (0.5–0.75 in.) across – are produced during the summer. The specific name *pudica* comes from Latin, meaning 'bashful', for obvious reasons.

M. pudica is native to the tropical zones of South America, but it is naturalised in many places throughout the world. It is difficult to recommend it as an ornamental plant for use in the garden; however, it undoubtedly makes an interesting talking point when grown as a pot plant. If it is grown indoors, give it as much light as possible.

Despite reports of it being toxic to animals in large doses, in parts of the world it is used as a forage plant for cattle where regular grazing prevents older, thorn-carrying stems from developing. **PWi**

Alternatives

Mimosa pudica var. *hispida*, *Mimosa pudica* var. *pastoris*

Monstera
M. deliciosa 'Variegata'

Main feature Vigorous, evergreen, climbing shrub with
aerial roots
Height 3 m (10 ft) **Spread** 90 cm (3 ft)
Position ○ ◑ **Hardiness** RHS H1b

In the tropics, *M. deliciosa* is rather like the plant from the
fairy tale of Jack and the beanstalk: spreading its aerial
roots as it sprouts, leaf after leaf, and climbing up a wall
the way it would a tree trunk in the rainforest to reach for
the light. Its common name, Swiss cheese plant, comes
from the holes its mature leaves develop.

'Variegata' has similar leaves, but they are splashed
with cream; each leaf has a different pattern – some
leaves will be all cream on one half, whereas others will
be evenly splashed with cream, as if splattered with paint.
Occasionally, a leaf will be entirely cream. Fortunately,
this is a stable variety in that it does not revert to all
green or all cream, so it can be recommended as a highly
decorative and dramatic foliage specimen.

The leaves of *M. deliciosa* can grow up to 38 to
50 centimetres (15–20 inches) long, and the plant can
reach 3 metres (10 ft) high, but as a houseplant its growth
will be confined by the size of pot it is grown in and
the lower light levels. Coming from the tropics, a Swiss
cheese plant is happiest at temperatures of 18 to 29°C
(65–85°F) and can cope with a humidity of 40 per cent,
making it easy to accommodate its needs in a centrally
heated house. Once the plant is in its final pot, liquid feed
with a foliage houseplant feed as directed.

These large plants look good in a corner of the living
room or conservatory in a large pot. The thick, aerial
roots should be trained onto a moss pole, or they will
cling to the walls and damage the paintwork. When fully
mature, Swiss cheese plants flower and fruit, but the
main reason to grow them is their foliage. Often plants
eventually become ungainly and leggy. They can then
be discarded, but if you feel up to it, you can attempt to
propagate a new plant by cutting off the top with some
aerial roots and starting again. **NM**

Alternatives

Monstera deliciosa, Monstera adansonii

Musa
M. basjoo

Main features Architectural perennial; huge, paddle-shaped leaves
Height 4 m (15 ft) **Spread** 3.6 m (12 ft)
Position ○ **Hardiness** RHS H3

No other plant produces such large, architectural leaves as bananas. Their huge, green, paddle-shaped foliage makes them a striking feature in the garden. In warm climates they also produce flowers and fruits, but these are often not tasty enough to eat. Bananas look good in tropical or jungle-style planting schemes, where they combine well with cannas, ginger lilies and hot-coloured plants, such as dahlias. They can also be used as a focal point in a large pot. *M. basjoo* is known as the Japanese banana because it hails from Japan. Each arching leaf can grow up to 3 metres (10 ft) in length, and it can be a statuesque plant, reaching 4 metres (15 ft) in height. The stems are green at first, before turning brown and becoming papery. In summer hanging spikes of pale, cream-yellow, tubular flowers with colourful bracts are followed by greenish-yellow fruits that are not particularly tasty.

M. basjoo is a suckering, evergreen perennial. It is not fully hardy, but plants growing in the ground can be overwintered successfully in temperate climates. Apply a thick layer of mulch to protect the crown in autumn, and protect the foliage by gathering the leaves together and wrapping them in a blanket of fleece or straw. In cold areas, or in gardens with heavy soil, grow these plants in pots, so that they can be overwintered under glass. Japanese bananas are best grown in a sheltered location, as their leaves can be shredded by strong winds. They like a well-drained soil that has been enriched with organic matter, such as garden compost. To get the best foliage, water and feed generously throughout the growing season.

M. sikkimensis has bronze markings on the young leaves and trunk, and the foliage is more wind resistant. *M. acuminata* 'Dwarf Cavendish' is more compact, reaching 2 metres (7 ft). **VP**

Alternatives

Musa sikkimensis, Musa acuminata 'Dwarf Cavendish'

Musa basjoo is best grown in a sheltered spot for the best foliage. ➔

Nematanthus
N. gregarius

Main features Perennial; trailing stems of glossy leaves; orange, pouched flowers over many months; houseplant
Height 60 cm (24 in.) **Spread** 90 cm (3 ft)
Position ◑ **Hardiness** RHS H1c

It does not take much imagination to see, in a mature plant of this species, a school of golden fish feeding amongst glossy, green weed. The orange, pouched flowers with their small, mouth-like openings give this easy-to-grow specimen its common name of goldfish plant. A member of the *Gesneriaceae* family – that includes such popular plants as *Streptocarpus* (Cape primrose) and *Saintpaulia* (African violet) – the goldfish plant is naturally an epiphyte, growing in the coastal rainforests of southeastern Brazil.

Stems initially grow upright but then trail, which makes it an ideal plant for hanging baskets. The stems form roots readily at the nodes. The small, oval leaves are succulent and glossy green. A profusion of flowers are formed for up to nine months of the year. Wild plants are pollinated by hummingbirds.

Grow in a free-draining, organic compost. Keep evenly moist, allowing plants to become drier in winter when they will usually have a rest period. In dry conditions they may be prone to red spider mites. Plants respond well to a monthly feed with a high-potash or seaweed-based fertiliser. The species requires plenty of light to initiate flowering, but it needs protection from the midday sun. Cut back regularly to keep bushy and compact. Prunings can be treated as cuttings and will root easily in pots of moist compost.

N. gregarius was first described in 1974 by the US botanist Dale Lee Denham who, with his wife, Dr Miriam Denham, did much work with the Gesneriad family. It is one of over thirty species with flowers mainly in shades of red, yellow and orange. Some species in the genus, such as *N. corticola* and *N. crassifolius,* hold their flowers on long, dangling pedicels to make them easier for hummingbirds or large bees to reach them. **GHa**

Alternatives

Nematanthus gregarius 'Dibley's Gold', *Nematanthus* 'Tropicana'

Nepenthes
'Bill Bailey'

Main features Carnivorous plant; houseplant
Height 30 cm (12 in.) **Spread** 30 cm (12 in.)
Position ○ ◑
Hardiness RHS H1b

When tropical pitcher plants, or monkey cups, are on display – whether it be at a garden show, in a living room, or in a greenhouse – they attract attention. Their bright, green foliage sets off the curious and colourful pitchers that hang from the tendrils. The pitchers are modified leaves with honey glands that attract insects, which then slide down inside the pitcher. The insects are then digested in the liquid at the base of the pitcher, and so feed the plant with nutrients. This enables pitcher plants to grow in wet soils that are low in nutrients.

These carnivorous plants come from the highlands of South East Asia. The species are mostly endangered because of the destruction of their rainforest habitat, but there are plant nurseries who cultivate hybrids and crosses, and carnivorous plant specialists who can guide you to what is available. Sizes are difficult to give guidance on because of the shape of the plants. One example is the hybrid 'Bill Bailey', available from Borneo Exotics in Sri Lanka, who named the plant after the British comedian for his conservation work. This plant has pitchers that are a good size and a deep plum red colour. It is a hybrid cross (*N. ventricosa* × *singalana*), and it has the size of *N. ventricosa* from the mountains of the Philippines and the vigour of *N. singalana* from the highlands of Sumatra. Its mature pitchers are 15 centimetres (6 in.) long.

Pitcher plants will eat the flies and insects in the house, but if there are none available, you might need to feed them tiny strands of raw meat, such as minced beef. Coming from the tropics, *Nepenthes* need to be grown indoors in light or partial shade and require a humidity of 70 per cent, so regular misting is important. A greenhouse or indoors within a terrarium provides a good environment. **NM**

Alternatives

Nepenthes × *hookeriana*, *Nepenthes* 'Lady Pauline', *Nepenthes* 'Rebecca Soper'

Nephrolepis
N. exaltata

Nerium
N. oleander 'Variegatum'

Main features Fern with elegant, arching, sword-shaped fronds; grows well indoors or under glass
Height 60 cm (24 in.) **Spread** 60 cm (24 in.)
Position ● **Hardiness** RHS H1c

Main features Evergreen shrub with colourful foliage; pink, white or red flowers from spring to summer
Height 2 m (7 ft) **Spread** 2 m (7 ft)
Position ○ **Hardiness** RHS H2

Native to tropical and subtropical areas – such as Florida, Central America, Polynesia and Africa – this stately fern makes a wonderful houseplant in shady rooms, conservatories or porches. Grow in a hanging basket or in a container on a stand, which will allow the long, arching fronds to hang gracefully. Fronds can grow up to 2 metres (7 ft) long when conditions suit, but they tend to be much smaller in the relatively dry conditions found in most homes. However, *N. exaltata* tolerates low humidity better than many other ferns. For best results, keep compost slightly moist, and mist the leaves occasionally. If old plants look ragged, they can be cut back to the base and they will regrow fresh leaves. There are hundreds of cultivars with very varied leaf size, texture, colour and growth habit. Whichever variety you grow, these ferns will bring a lush, verdant feel to shady rooms – and can even be used as outdoor ground cover in warm areas, provided conditions are sufficiently shady. **GAR**

Oleanders are flowering, evergreen shrubs that combine great beauty with a very tough constitution. This makes them desirable plants in many parts of the world, but their weakness is frost, so how they are used depends on where you live. In frost-free regions they are widely used as landscape plants along roads. In the garden, choosing a variegated cultivar, such as 'Variegatum', adds extra colour when the plants are not flowering. Other variegated cultivars include 'Twist of Pink' and 'Mrs Runge', which is pink with double flowers. The ability of oleanders to cope with draughts, heat and salt makes them good candidates for hedging, screening or covering sunny, dry banks. They also make excellent garden shrubs in a Mediterranean-style planting. In colder regions oleanders can still be enjoyed by growing them in big containers on a sunny terrace or patio over summer and then moving them inside over winter. Note that plants are toxic if eaten, and the sap can cause blistering. **IT**

Alternative

Nephrolepis exaltata 'Bostoniensis'

Alternatives

Nerium oleander 'Twist of Pink', *Nerium oleander* 'Mrs Runge'

Nopalxochia
N. phyllanthoides

Main features Long, strap-shaped stems; showy pink or red flowers
Height 45 cm (18 in.) **Spread** 60 cm (24 in.)
Position ◑ **Hardiness** RHS H1c

The pond lily cactus is epiphytic and forms a bushy plant with branching, jointed stems made up of flattened, strap-shaped segments with wavy edges. The genus name *Nopalxochia* comes from an ancient Mexican word meaning 'cactus with scarlet flowers', and all members of this genus have large pink or red flowers that resemble those of water lilies. Flowers are usually 8 to 10 centimetres (3–4 in.) across. Unlike the *Epiphyllum* cacti, the flowers open during the day. Plants may repeat flower up to three times a year, and flowers are followed by fleshy, red fruits. Grow in a slightly acidic, epiphytic compost or a mix of bark and leaf mould. Water freely when growing and give a half-strength, balanced fertiliser monthly. Keep just moist in winter. Protect from direct sunlight to avoid scorching. Flower formation is dependent on temperature and plants should be kept dry and cool over winter (above 5°C/41°F). 'Deutsche Kaiserin' is an old cultivar, which can produce a great profusion of pink flowers. **GHa**

Alternative

Syn. *Disocactus phyllanthoides*

Olearia
O. × scilloniensis
'Master Michael'

Main features Abundant purple, daisy-like flowers; good for wildlife; attracts bees; evergreen
Height 1.8 m (6 ft) **Spread** 1.8 m (6 ft)
Position ○ **Hardiness** RHS H3

This is a hybrid between two daisybushes (*O. lirata* × *O. phlogopappa*), which arose in the gardens of Tresco Abbey on the Scilly Isles, a magical archipelago of islands in the Atlantic Ocean, off the southwestern tip of the United Kingdom. This is almost exactly on the other side of the world to the native range of its parents, in southeastern Australia and Tasmania. *O.* × *scilloniensis* 'Master Michael' looks good all year round, with handsome, greyish, wavy-edged, evergreen leaves, but its real glory comes in late spring, when the entire bush is smothered with purple, daisy-like flowers. Other cultivars produce white flowers. The quantity of flowers is truly phenomenal, and pollinating insects, such as bees and butterflies, love these open-centred, lightly fragrant blooms. Daisybushes tolerate salt spray and drought, but they need protection from frost and make a useful hedge in coastal areas. In cold areas grow plants in pots and overwinter them somewhere bright and frost free. **GAR**

Alternative

Olearia stellulata

Oreocereus
O. celsianus

Main features Tall, sculptural cactus; covered in long
coarse hairs
Height 90–180 cm (3–6 ft) **Spread** 60 cm (24 in.)
Position ○ **Hardiness** RHS H2

Known as old man of the Andes, this is a striking, columnar
cactus with ribbed and spiny stems that may grow as
tall as 1.8 metres (6 ft). The yellow or brown-coloured
spines are hidden amongst a dense layer of shaggy blond
hairs. The hairs protect and shade the green stem from
the intense, high-altitude sunlight and cold night-time
temperatures that the plant experiences on the rocky
cliffs of the Andes in Argentina, Bolivia, Chile and Peru.
The species name honours the French cacti and orchid
enthusiast Jean-François Cels, who first collected the
plant in the wild.

O. celsianus normally blooms in spring, producing a
crown of tubular, rose-pink flowers at the top of the plant.
These face upwards to attract hummingbirds and insect
pollinators. Plants do not always flower regularly in
cultivation, but specimens should flower as they mature.
Small, round fruits may follow the flowers, becoming
reddish and bursting open at the base when ripe.

The species can be difficult to grow as a houseplant,
since it requires a big difference between the day and
night-time temperatures. In its natural environment the
winter night temperatures may drop to freezing. Grow
in full sun using a free-draining, gritty potting mix. Water
regularly in spring and summer, but keep dry in winter.
As plants mature they will need a big, heavy pot to
ensure that they do not topple over with the weight of
the plant. Propagate from seeds, as plants in cultivation
do not readily form offsets. **GHa**

Alternatives

Oreocereus doelzianus, Oreocereus trolli

Oxalis
O. triangularis subsp. papilionacea

Main features Bulbous plant with purple foliage;
starry white or pink flowers in summer
Height 15 cm (6 in.) **Spread** 30 cm (12 in.)
Position ◑ **Hardiness** RHS H2

The purple-leaf false shamrock is a bulbous plant that produces purple foliage from spring to autumn. The leaves are divided into three leaflets, which are triangular in shape. They are a rich, purple-bronze colour, often highlighted with a bright, violet mark in the centre. During the summer a long succession of white to pale-pink, starry flowers crown the plant. The leaves of this species move in response to light levels, opening in the day and closing in low light levels. This movement occurs due to changes in turgor pressure in the cells at the base of the leaf. The flowers generally close in dull weather and at night.

This species is usually grown as a houseplant, but it also works well in summer hanging baskets. Plants benefit from a moisture-retentive, but well-drained soil mix of equal parts loam, leaf mould and horticultural grit. Water moderately when in growth and apply a balanced liquid fertiliser monthly. When dormant in the winter keep the compost just moist. Growth is best in bright, filtered light and at temperatures of around 15°C (60°F), but plants will tolerate dry shade. Propagate by division of the bulbs when they are dormant. Some success may be had from leaf cuttings taken in high summer.

O. triangularis comes from Brazil, where it grows amongst rocks and along streams. It grows from a swollen rootstock, which is adapted to survive droughts. A range of cultivars have been introduced with different colours or markings. *Oxalis* 'Irish Mist' is popular for its fresh-green leaves irregularly marked with cream. **GHa**

Alternatives

Syn. *Oxalis regnellii. Oxalis hirta, Oxalis smithiana*

Pachyphytum
P. oviferum

Main features Succulent with flowers in winter and spring; year-round attractive foliage; architectural plant
Height 13 cm (5 in.) **Spread** 30 cm (12 in.)
Position ○ **Hardiness** RHS H1c

The succulent *P. oviferum* is one of those plants with an irresistible, slightly unreal, shape and texture. It does not get very big – a maximum of 13 centimetres (5 in.) tall and 30 centimetres (12 in.) across – and even if the climate allows you to grow it outdoors, grow it in a pot so that you can enjoy it close-up. One advantage of growing it indoors in a heated greenhouse or conservatory or, in warmer climates, simply under cover is that it is less at the mercy of the weather, which can damage the bloom coating the fleshy, oval-shaped leaves and break the flower stalks. The flowers, which open in sequence, have large, pale blue-green calyxes and red petals and are held up on a long, pink-red, upright stalk bent over at the top. The bent tip straightens as the flowers open. *P. oviferum* is a Mexican plant that enjoys as much light as possible. Like most succulents, it needs good drainage and very little water in winter. Water moderately in summer. Display in a terra-cotta pot either as a single specimen or combine it with its close relative, *Echeveria*. **PWi**

Alternatives

Pachyphytum compactum, Pachyphytum hookeri

Pachystachys
P. lutea

Main feature Evergreen shrub with long-lasting, showy spikes of bright-yellow or amber, overlapping bracts
Height 60–90 cm (2–3 ft) **Spread** 60–90 cm (2–3 ft)
Position ○ ◑ **Hardiness** RHS H1b

The lollipop plant has dark-green, lance-shaped leaves that grow to 10 centimetres (4 in.) or more in length. They have conspicuous, deeply set veins giving a corrugated appearance. The chief attraction, though, is the profusion of dense, erect spikes of showy, bright-yellow or amber bracts, which earn the plant its alternative name of golden shrimp plant. Produced from spring to autumn, the individual bracts can last for three months or more, but the actual white flowers, which protrude from the bracts, last only a few days. They are two-lipped and tubular and form an effective contrast to the gold of the bracts. Originating in Peru, the lollipop plant is widely planted in tropical areas as a landscape shrub, but in temperate climates it is usually grown as a houseplant or as temporary summer bedding. Plants turn woody at the base as they mature. Prune them hard each year to give compact, bushy plants and avoid legginess. Repot plants annually in a loam-based potting mixture. Avoid dry conditions, which will cause leaves to drop. **GHa**

Alternatives

Pachystachys coccinea, Aphelandra squarrosa

Pachystachys lutea is grown for its yellow bracts that last longer than its white flowers. ➔

Parodia
P. magnifica

Pelargonium
Caliente Series

Main feature Slow-growing, globe-shaped cactus houseplant with sulphur-yellow flowers in summer
Height 8–20 cm (3–8 in.) **Spread** 15 cm (6 in.)
Position ○ ◐ **Hardiness** RHS H1c

Main features Summer-flowering, patio container plant; drought tolerant; low maintenance
Height 30–45 cm (12–18 in.) **Spread** 45–60 cm (18–24 in.)
Position ○ ◐ **Hardiness** RHS H1c

Even sitting in a pot, the *P. magnifica* cactus evokes visions of old Westerns. Its barrel shape, bluish-grey, ribbed, symmetrical segments and contrasting rusty-yellow furry spines make it a classic desert cactus. It blooms in summer, with sulphur-yellow flowers topping the compact ball. This architectural species, known also as *Eriocactus magnificus* or *Notocactus magnificus*, is found in one area of Brazil, where it is endangered, and in Uruguay, in hilly grasslands. The bristly, flexible spines are not formidable, unlike the sharper golden barrel cactus, which it somewhat resembles. *P. magnifica* grows easily from seed, is drought tolerant, lives a long time and starts flowering while young. The 5-centimetre-wide (2 in.) blooms appear intermittently, and several may flower together. Use small but deep pots, filled with a well-drained cactus mix; keep dry in winter. Outdoors, it can take temperatures as low as -4°C (25°F). **JW**

Pelargoniums are classified into 'zonal' and 'ivy-leaf' types; the former has an upright habit and hairy, sometimes bicoloured, leaves; and the latter has bright-green, shiny leaves and a lax, trailing habit. Plant breeders have crossed these two groups, creating a hybrid that combines these habits into a trailing, cascading mound. This breakthrough, the Caliente Series, comes in hot, vivid colours: 'Fire', 'Orange', 'Coral', 'Hot Coral', 'Rose', 'Dark Rose', 'Lavender' and 'Deep Red' (pictured). The green to mid-green foliage provides the perfect foil to cool these colours. The hybrid has more vigour than the parents, so these flower from spring to autumn, making them high-performance patio plants, yet they require little daily care. They are ideal for hanging baskets, window boxes, pots or raised beds. In warmer climates plants can be used as ground cover. When a flower fades, the petals drop to the ground, so there is no need to deadhead. **IT**

Alternatives

Parodia mammulosa subsp. *mammulosa*, *Parodia warasii*, *Mammillaria zeilmanniana*

Alternatives

Pelargonium Calliope Series, *Pelargonium* 'Glitterati Ice Queen'

Pelargonium
'Polka'

Main features Tall-growing; attractive sage-green leaves; salmon-orange flowers with deep-red markings
Height 50 cm (20 in.) **Spread** 50 cm (20 in.)
Position ○ ◑ **Hardiness** RHS H1c

The pelargonium 'Polka' produces flowers in an unusual shade of salmon orange. Plants are tall growing and are ideal for large patio tubs. They produce a profusion of flowers from late spring and through summer. 'Polka' belongs to a group of large shrubby plants with brightly coloured flowers known as Unique Pelargoniums. Uniques will flower profusely in small pots on a windowsill, but if planted in a large tub or bed in a conservatory, they can grow up to 3 metres (10 ft) tall, making imposing specimens. In frost-free regions they can be planted out to create a spectacular low hedge. 'Polka' was one of six Uniques raised by Frances Hartsook while she was living in a desert area of Mexico. She wanted to create plants with the splendid flowers of the regal pelargoniums, but with greater tolerance of the intense heat and dry conditions in which she gardened. She crossed the cultivar 'Old Scarlet Unique' with various regal plants. **GHa**

Alternatives

Pelargonium 'Bolero', *Pelargonium* 'Carefree',
Pelargonium 'Mystery'

Pelargonium
'Lady Plymouth'

Main features Container plant; aromatic foliage; prolific flowers from summer to autumn
Height 45–60 cm (18–24 in.) **Spread** 20–60 cm (8–24 in.)
Position ○ **Hardiness** RHS H1c

Just a single plant of 'Lady Plymouth' fills the space around it with its classic perfume. Even out of sight and within touching distance, essential oils are released from its variegated, aromatic leaves, perfuming the air with its distinctive rose-lemon fragrance. The combination of fragrance, fine foliage and abundant flower production make this a quality plant that packs a punch above its size. Upright in habit, its attractive leaves are deeply lobed, cut like lace, grey-green with cream-white margins. It produces many clusters of small, pale mauve-pink flowers with attractive darker flecks at their centre over a long period. Dead flowers should be removed regularly to keep their production flowing. The plant is tender, so must be kept frost free through winter, but in good light. In cooler climates, grow in a pot on a brightly lit windowsill, garden room, conservatory or greenhouse through winter, then place outside on a warm patio. **RC**

Alternatives

Pelargonium 'Grey Lady Plymouth', *Pelargonium* 'Graveolens', *Pelargonium* 'Mabel Grey'

Pelargonium

P. × *hortorum* 'Pinto Premium White to Rose'

Main features Early flowering; blooms change colour from white to rose pink; no need to deadhead
Height 25–60 cm (10–24 in.) **Spread** 30–45 cm (12–18 in.)
Position ○ ◑ **Hardiness** RHS H1c

This pelargonium won an All-America Selections bedding plant award in 2013. Pelargoniums are grown for their reliable production of colourful flowers, and this one does not disappoint. It produces large flower heads up to 13 centimetres (5 in.) across, each with twenty or more individual flowers that open white and then turn soft pink, and finally a deep, rose pink. Each flower head will contain a mix of the colours, giving an interesting display. 'Pinto Premium White to Rose' is a vigorous plant that will grow to 60 centimetres (24 in.) tall, depending on conditions. The heart-shaped leaves have a near-black zone, and scalloped margins. Flowering continues throughout summer, irrespective of deadheading. This cultivar is usually offered as seed, which is best sown in small individual pots or cells. Germination is generally within two weeks, but may take longer. Plants bloom earlier than many other seed-raised cultivars.

Grow in full sun, in patio containers, window boxes or in flower beds with other tender perennials. Ensure that soil or compost is free-draining and add grit if necessary. A good feed with a high-potash fertiliser on alternate weeks through the summer will ensure container-grown plants continue to thrive. Although usually grown as an annual, plants will continue to grow in frost-free conditions; in areas with cold winters they can be lifted and kept dry over winter before watering again when growth restarts in the spring. **GHa**

Alternatives

Pelargonium × *hortorum* 'Pinto Blush', *Pelargonium* Maverick Series 'Maverick Appleblossom'

Pelargonium
P. peltatum

Main features Flowers in summer; glossy, green, ivy-leaved foliage
Height 45 cm (18 in.) **Spread** 90 cm (3 ft)
Position ○ ◑ **Hardiness** RHS H1c

Ivy-leaved pelargoniums make an impressive display in full flower and are often seen in hanging baskets, window boxes or patio containers. Their common name comes from their trailing habit and ivy-like leaves. The leaves are usually glossy and plain green, but they can be bicoloured. Most of the cultivars have single flowers, although double forms are also popular. Colours range from vivid scarlet through pink and white to soft lilac.

Derived mainly from the wild species *P. peltatum*, which was introduced to the Netherlands in 1700 from the Cape of Good Hope, ivy-leaved pelargoniums became hugely popular as balcony plants in Switzerland and other countries in Europe. Plants are recognised as

P. 'Roi des Balcons Impérial', but are sold under colours prefixed by Balcon or Cascade. Cascade plants are generally smaller and less inclined to creep. They are thought to be crosses involving *P. acetosum*.

Plants are usually bought in spring as plug plants, however, sowing from seeds in early spring is an option. Once planted up after the last frost, they are easy to grow over summer and do not require deadheading. Grow in full sun to encourage flowering. Water and feed regularly with high-potash fertiliser to promote flowering, but plants are reasonably drought tolerant. High summer temperatures do not worry them, but they are frost sensitive, so either discard them at the end of the growing season or bring under cover. **GHa**

Alternatives

Pelargonium 'Decora Rose', *Pelargonium* 'Rouletta', *Pelargonium* 'Fringed Rouletta'

Pelargonium
P. sidoides

Main features Dark-magenta flowers in spring, summer, and autumn; attractive grey-green, velvety foliage
Height 30 cm (12 in.) **Spread** 30 cm (12 in.)
Position ○ **Hardiness** RHS H1c

This pelargonium looks delicate, but it packs a punch. It is a native of South Africa, and extracts of its root are used medicinally in cold and flu remedies. It has attractive, faintly aromatic, grey-green foliage; its leaves are covered in very fine down and feel velvety to the touch. Small, pretty flowers are carried in sprays at the end of delicate, arching stems. In certain lights the flowers look almost black, but they are, in fact, dark magenta. They look rather like exotic, jewel-coloured insects floating high above the plant's velvety, heart-shaped leaves for weeks on end. Beautiful foliage alone makes this an outstanding plant. However, it is the flowers, which are produced from late spring through to the first frost, that take this pelargonium to an even higher level. Although it is not hardy, there are few months without any flowers, whether it is grown outside or inside. It likes to be kept quite dry through winter and does not need much moisture during the summer months.

P. sidoides is an excellent specimen on its own when viewed close-up. It is also a delightful combination plant in greenhouse displays, patio container planting or in garden borders in warmer climates. Group it together with silver-leaved plants, such as *Astelia chathamica*, or against the similarly dark foliage of *Aeonium* 'Zwartkop'. Or try planting it to scramble through other patio plants with contrasting foliage texture and flower shapes; for example, *Arctotis* 'Holly'.

'Ardens' is another similar and popular species type, with blood-red flowers marked with a darker red. 'Grey Lady Plymouth' is grown for its strong minty-scented foliage, as much as its small, lavender-veined, pale-rose flowers. *P. tomentosum* has larger, velvety leaves with a good peppermint scent and is low growing with a spreading habit. **RC**

Alternatives

Pelargonium 'Ardens', *Pelargonium* 'Grey Lady Plymouth', *Pelargonium tomentosum*

Peperomia
P. obtusifolia Magnoliifolia Group

Main features Perennial grown for its evergreen foliage;
usually grown as a houseplant
Height 25 cm (10 in.) **Spread** 30 cm (12 in.)
Position ○ **Hardiness** RHS H2

There are more than 1,500 species of *Peperomia*, which
is related to the black pepper plant. Many are epiphytes
(plants that grow harmlessly on another plant) from hot,
humid tropical forests, but many are so pretty and robust
that they make very popular houseplants. One of these,
a South Florida and Caribbean native, is *P. obtusifolia*. It
is also known as baby rubber plant, although it has no
connection to the actual rubber plant, other than it also
boasts smooth, rounded or oval, glossy, leathery leaves.
Other common names include spoonleaf peperomia
and red margin peperomia.

In tropical habitats baby rubber plant makes good
ground cover. Stiffly upright and spreading, its small,
dark-green leaves are held on short, brittle, red-purple
stems. Mostly, however, it is found as a generally
uncomplicated houseplant. It is good in average
household temperatures, does fine with limited space
and looks great in a hanging basket. The 5- to
10-centimetre-long (2–4 in.) leaves are accompanied by
upright, slender, white flowers in summer. Variegated
types of *P. obtusifolia* are the prettiest, the most common
having shades of dark green, olive and cream white in
some irregular combinations, or marbled swirl. The more
exotic forms feature pink or gold. The leaves of the
Magnoliifolia Group of *P. obtusifolia* are more spoon
shaped than round. The variegated cultivar 'Greengold'
(pictured) is cream and bright green.

Grow the plant in bright, indirect sun in a warm humid
spot; keep above 15°C (60°F). If your plant gets leggy,
pinch it back and raise light levels, especially for
variegated forms. Plant in highly organic soil, such as bark
chips and peat, or small, shallow pots of fast-draining
houseplant mix with perlite. Overwatering is deadly;
allow the compost mix to dry between waterings. **JW**

Alternatives

Peperomia obtusifolia (Magnoliifolia Group) 'Golden Gate',
Peperomia obtusifolia 'Tricolor'

Peperomia

P. caperata 'Luna Red'

Main features Perennial with bold, year-round foliage;
tiny, green-white flowers in summer
Height 20 cm (8 in.) **Spread** 20 cm (8 in.)
Position ◐ ● **Hardiness** RHS H1b

All the *P. caperata* varieties have heart-shaped, deeply
corrugated leaves. 'Luna Red' is a particularly good purple
to dark crimson selection. The colour is strongest in
the furrows of the corrugation and paler on the ridges,
giving the leaf a very strong pattern. It is a useful plant for
indoor displays in temperate climates, and in subtropical
regions it can be used outdoors as shade-tolerant ground
cover. It makes a neat houseplant either on its own or
in combination with other foliage plants, such as *Pilea*
(aluminium plant) and *Hypoestes* (polka-dot plant). It
enjoys shade, which makes the colour stronger; too
much sunlight tends to bleach out the purple and give
the plant a washed-out look.

One of the intriguing things about all *Peperomia* is
their flowers. They are minute and borne along what
could be described as 'rat's tails', although 'slender
wands' probably sounds more appealing. So small
are the greenish-white flowers that you would not
necessarily know they were flowers.

This evergreen perennial, also known as the radiator
plant, dislikes waterlogging, which causes its roots to
rot, so water carefully. It will not do any harm to let
Peperomia get almost to the point of wilting before
watering. Remove dead leaves and flower stalks right
to the base of the plant to avoid the accumulation of
fleshy stalks, which, if kept wet, will cause rot in the heart
of the plant. **PWi**

Alternatives

Peperomia caperata 'Emerald Ripple', *Peperomia caperata*
'Little Fantasy'

Phalaenopsis
P. × hybridus

Main features Beautiful, robust houseplant;
long-lasting flowers
Height 45 cm (18 in.) **Spread** 25 cm (10 in.)
Position ◖ **Hardiness** RHS H1a

Nothing speaks of the glorious tropics quite as much as
the orchid, and *Phalaenopsis*, commonly known as the
moth orchid, is the bestselling orchid in the world. It is
robust enough to be grown as a houseplant without the
need for special conditions, such as an orchid house. The
flowers last for three months or more, and with attention
the plant will reproduce flowers within a year. Orchids
signify luxury and glamour, but thanks to commercial
micro-propagation by tissue culture, they are now
inexpensive and available year-round.

In the wild, moth orchids are epiphytes, which attach
themselves to other plants, such as trees, but they can
equally survive in a pot of compost. Use epiphytic orchid
mix, or equal parts medium- and fine-grade bark chips
with pumice chips. They flourish in a temperature of 20°C
(68°F) in a light area but away from direct sun. Orchids
naturally grow in high, humid areas, and therefore
appreciate regular misting, but this isn't essential. Use
an orchid feed during the growing season but do so
sparingly during the winter. Repotting in spring is
necessary every other year if the plant is not in flower.

Moth orchids are often bought when in flower and
are chosen based on their colours and markings, so
their labels contain little information about the names
of the plants. It is worth visiting an orchid nursery if you
would like something special. A few species exist, such as
P. amabilis, but most orchids are man-made hybrids. **NM**

Alternatives

Phalaenopsis Brother Little Amaglad gx 'Xavera',
Phalaenopsis amabilis

Philodendron
P. bipinnatifidum

Main feature Large, dramatically dissected, evergreen
leaves on an imposing, spreading plant
Height 4.5 m (15 ft) **Spread** 4.5 m (15 ft)
Position ◗ **Hardiness** RHS H3

There are hundreds of species of the dramatic tropical
foliage plant *Philodendron*, and all are evergreen vines
or shrubs, often with large, leathery, glossy leaves.
P. bipinnatifidum, the tree philodendron, is an arborescent
(tree-like) type that grows wild in southeast Brazil. A
strong, stout, upright stem is topped with unusually
long-stemmed, oval leaves that are up to 90 centimetres
(3 ft) in length, and split into many pairs of narrow, wavy-
edged segments. As the plant matures, it develops into
an impressive architectural feature, but the trunk may
start to lean under the weight of the heavy foliage, and
sturdy support may be necessary. The tree philodendron
makes a fine outdoor specimen in partial shade; leaves
develop pale-brown patches in too much sun. Plant
in well-drained, fertile soil or in a very large container.
This variety appreciates high humidity and a night
temperature of at least 15°C (60°F). In areas with cooler
nights it needs protection, and it usually becomes too large
to be grown indoors in anywhere except an atrium. **GR**

Alternative

Syn. *Philodendron selloum*

Phoenix
P. roebelenii

Main feature Neat date palm with attractive and
dramatic foliage
Height 2.4 m (8 ft) **Spread** 2.4 m (8 ft)
Position ◗ **Hardiness** RHS H1c

Date palms grow in a wide variety of habitats, from
swamps to deserts and coasts. They are found in north
and central Africa, the Canary Islands and Crete, and from
Turkey through southern China to Malaysia. Some date
palms develop a single trunk, some develop clustered
groups of trunks, but all are unusual amongst palms in
that they have large leaves, up to 6 metres (20 ft) long,
divided into opposite pairs of long, narrow leaflets that
are V-shaped in cross section. Only female trees produce
edible dates, but they need a nearby male for pollination.
The pigmy date palm, *P. roebelenii*, carries curved, deep-
green leaves up to 1.2 metres (4 ft) long, while the yellow
summer flowers are gathered into 45 centimetre (18 in.)
clusters and followed by small, edible fruits. Happy outside
where night temperatures do not drop below 10°C (50°F),
P. roebelenii enjoys moist, acidic, fertile soil. In cooler
conditions grow it in a conservatory. In a large container
of ericaceous (lime-free) compost, it can be kept outside
for most of the year, but moved inside in winter. **GR**

Alternatives

Phoenix canariensis, Phoenix dactylifera

Phormium
'Yellow Wave'

Main feature Architectural plant with evergreen,
strap-shaped leaves
Height 3 m (10 ft) **Spread** 90 cm (3 ft)
Position ○ ◑ **Hardiness** RHS H3

Phormium, like cordyline, is grown for its strong architectural shape, having clumps of sword- or strap-shaped, evergreen leaves. It is a native of New Zealand, and the fibre from the leaves was traditionally used in the same way as hemp or sisal, hence its alternative name New Zealand flax or flax lily. Phormiums thrive in coastal gardens as they are salt tolerant, but they are equally at home in contemporary gardens and courtyards, mixed borders or as a single, focal point. 'Yellow Wave' has arching, leathery, strap-like leaves that are green with yellow stripes, and grow up to 90 centimetres (3 ft) long. In summer it bears dark-red, 5-centimetre-long (2 in.) flowers on tall panicles; however, it is mostly grown for its foliage. Phormiums do best in fertile, moist, but well-drained soil in full sun or partial shade. In areas that are prone to frost, plants may need some winter protection; the coloured varieties are less hardy. Feeding plants in winter will encourage soft growth that may suffer in cold areas. In late spring, remove any dead or damaged leaves. **VP**

Alternatives

Phormium 'Bronze Baby', *Phormium* 'Sundowner'

Phygelius
P. × rectus 'African Queen'

Main features Magnificent, fuchsia-like flowers that
bloom from summer to autumn; attracts hummingbirds
Height 90–150 cm (3–5 ft) **Spread** 90–150 cm (3–5 ft)
Position ○ **Hardiness** RHS H5

'African Queen' in full flower is a truly splendid sight. A single plant produces hundreds of flowers all summer long. A native of South Africa, where it thrives on moist slopes and banks, it is surprisingly hardy. An evergreen shrub in warmer regions, in cooler locations it is treated as a herbaceous plant. With a suckering habit, it is fast growing, with dark-green, oval leaves on upright stems. From summer to autumn, stems also bear large panicles of tubular-shaped flowers; lobes appear pale orange, red on the outside, and yellow inside. Strikingly colourful, they resemble fuchsia blooms in style, although the plants are not related. Flowers are also pendent, giving the whole plant a gently nodding appearance. This quality makes it perfect for planting on sunny banks and slopes, as in its native homeland. It is also good planted at the base of a sunny garden wall and in containers. Blue-flowering agapanthus and salvia make jewel-bright plant combinations. It is easy to care for: simply cut back top growth to around 15 centimetres (6 in.) in spring. **RC**

Alternatives

Phygelius × *rectus* 'Devil's Tears', *Phygelius* × *rectus* 'Moonraker'

Pilea

P. involucrata

Main feature An easily propagated houseplant with rugged-textured foliage
Height 30 cm (12 in.) **Spread** 30 cm (12 in.)
Position ◑ **Hardiness** RHS H1c

The friendship plant *P. involucrata* is a highly attractive foliage plant suitable for small hanging baskets or terrariums or growing as ground cover in greenhouses. A small creeping or trailing plant, it has square, hairy stems and oval leaves with toothed edges. There are around 600 species in the genus *Pilea,* which are widely distributed in the warmer regions of the world. They are members of the *Urticaceae* or nettle family. *P.* 'Moon Valley' (pictured), collected from the mountains of Costa Rica, is more upright, with leaves that are strongly puckered and are said to resemble the craters on the surface of the moon, hence the cultivar name; the leaves are washed with burgundy. The sprays of flowers that sometimes occur are white, tinged with a soft baby-pink, but they are not particularly showy. 'Norfolk' has distinct silver-veined leaves, whereas 'Silver Tree' has a broad silver band along the centre of the leaf, and the sides are dotted with silver.

Native to Central and South America, the friendship plant needs warm conditions and high humidity out of direct sunlight. Use a well-aerated potting mix that is high in organic matter and sharp sand. Feed monthly with a balanced fertiliser in spring and summer. Plants may become straggly after a couple of years, but are easily replaced by new cuttings. The ease with which stem-tip cuttings root gives the plant its common name, meaning that the plant can be freely distributed amongst friends. Cuttings can be ready to pot on in four to six weeks. **GHa**

Alternatives

Pilea cadieri 'Nana', *Pilea grandifolia*

Platycerium

P. bifurcatum

Main feature Fern with dramatic, antler-shaped,
evergreen fronds all year round
Height 1.2 m (4 ft) **Spread** 1.2 m (4 ft)
Position ◑ ● **Hardiness** RHS H1b

Ferns come in many shapes and sizes, but none are
quite like the staghorn ferns, *Platycerium*. In fact, they
hardly resemble ferns at all. This group is also one of a
small number that, instead of rooting in the soil as most
ferns do, grows on tree trunks and in the crotches of
branches. Most of the fifteen species of *Platycerium* grow
in the subtropical and tropical rainforests of Asia, Africa
and Australia, but because of their size and growing
requirements, few are grown in gardens. They develop
two kinds of fronds. At the base of the plants, clasping
the tree trunk, are thick and spongy fronds that resemble
a series of overlapping bowls held convex side out; green
at first, they become crisp and brown as they age. The

main display comes from the green fronds that carry
the spores and that resemble a mass of green antlers
hanging down or held upright.

The common staghorn fern, *P. bifurcatum*, grows wild
on the trunks of trees in Indonesia and Australia. The basal
fronds are up to 45 centimetres (18 in.) across and mature
from green to brown. The 90-centimetre-long (3 ft) fertile
fronds stand upright, spread out or sometimes hang
down, and are divided into long, narrow, slightly grey-
green segments. The overall effect is very dramatic, but
it may vary depending on the age of the plant and
growing conditions. In gardens the staghorn fern can be
grown outside, where the night temperature remains
above 5°C (41°F), and is best tied to a tree trunk. It can also
be grown in a large greenhouse or conservatory. **GR**

Alternative

Platycerium superbum

Pleione
P. formosana

Main feature Bulbous orchid with intricate, colourful spring flowers
Height 15 cm (6 in.) **Spread** 30 cm (12 in.)
Position ◑ **Hardiness** RHS H3

This exotic jewel of a plant makes other spring bulbs look positively humdrum by comparison. Flamboyantly coloured, intricate blooms in shades of pink, white, purple and yellow erupt from the swollen pseudobulbs in midspring, drawing admiring glances from all who encounter them.

Hailing from the Far East – its Latin epithet *formosana* refers to Formosa, the old name for Taiwan – these beautiful, small orchids are listed as 'terrestrial' or 'lithophytic', which means that they grow in the soil or on rocks in their native habitat of sheltered woodlands at high altitudes. They are also referred to as 'pseudobulbs'. *P. formosana* is one of the hardiest pleiones and can be grown outdoors in rock gardens in mild areas. Otherwise, it makes an excellent candidate for pot culture in a greenhouse or porch, provided that it can be kept cool during the summer and given a winter resting period just above freezing point at 1 to 5°C (34–41°F). They are deciduous, so will naturally die back at the end of summer. In areas with warm winters the bulbs can be stored throughout winter in paper bags in the refrigerator, and will race into growth when potted up again in spring.

Pleiones are also known as Indian crocuses, Nepalese crocuses and windowsill orchids, and when in flower, they make wonderful houseplants for a cool, shady windowsill. Use a specially formulated orchid compost containing bark, moss and perlite. Treated well, the pseudobulbs will increase in number year after year to make a showstopping display of these most delightful of all spring flowers. Grow them in shallow containers and place them in an area where they can be seen close-up, as their colourful flowers are so complex that they demand closer inspection. **GAR**

Alternatives

Bletilla striata, Pleione Britannia 'Doreen'

Plumbago
P. auriculata

Main features Shrubby climber with attractive, long
flowering, abundant blooms; versatile and rapid climber
Height 4.5 m (15 ft) **Spread** 1.5 m (5 ft)
Position ○ **Hardiness** RHS H2

Clouds of sky-blue, phlox-like flowers make this versatile
drought-tolerant climbing plant indispensable to frost-
free gardeners. But fear not, those who experience winters
where temperatures regularly fall below 0°C (32°F) can
also enjoy its spectacular display by growing it indoors
in a cool or temperate greenhouse or conservatory.
Alternatively, it can be planted in a container and moved
inside over winter. Either way, the rewards justify the
effort involved.

    P. auriculata comes from South Africa, where it grows
as a shrub in its native habitat. It thrives in the heat and
will flower for most of the year in southernmost parts of
Texas and Florida. Elsewhere, it will certainly produce a
display from early summer to late autumn, its baby-blue
trusses contrasting against the apple green of its semi-
evergreen foliage. It may cope outside all year round in
less frosty sites further north in the United States and
also in more temperate parts of the United Kingdom,
as long as the site is properly free-draining. As an extra
precaution, cut it down in winter, protecting the crown
if necessary. In warmer environments cutting back hard
in early spring will boost the amount of flowers.

    The rapid, sprawling, scrambling habit of *P. auriculata*
makes it useful for covering a wall or training over a
pergola. It can also be trained to grow up the side of a
building. Trimming off unruly shoots will not only neaten
its appearance, but it will also stimulate an additional
flush of blooms. This plant also makes a tremendous
informal hedge, planted around a fence in a line and
clipped as required. *Plumbago* will also happily clamber
across a bank in a mounding, tumbling fashion, forming
an effective ground cover. An additional bonus for some
gardeners is that deer do not seem to like it, however,
butterflies do! **ER**

Alternative

Plumbago auriculata f. *alba*

Primula
P. malacoides

Main features Fragrant flowers from winter to spring; attracts butterflies; great for dappled shade
Height 30–45 cm (12–18 in.) **Spread** 15–20 cm (6–8 in.)
Position ◑ **Hardiness** RHS H1c

Known as the fairy primrose, this is a showy perennial, grown as an annual pot plant with fragrant winter or spring flowers in shades of white, pink, carmine, red and lilac. The dainty flowers encircle 20- to 30-centimetre-long (8–12 in.) stems held above whorls of mid-green, slightly frilly, downy leaves. Their delicate and dainty appearance is deceptive, and they are tougher than they first appear. Plants can be purchased ready for outdoor bedding in warmer climates. They are fabulous planted en masse as a winter display, and attract butterflies. In colder regions, they make colourful indoor plants. *P. malacoides* can also be grown from seeds; varieties are available in mixtures or separate colours. This primula is particularly popular in Japan, where breeders have produced other cultivars, including 'Momokomachi', 'Hiotome', 'Kurenai', 'Uguisu' and the Prima F1 Series. In England breeders have given us 'Ballerina', 'Brilliancy', 'Bright Eyes' and the Beauty Series.

The fairy primrose is best treated as a half-hardy annual and resown each year, although it is an evergreen perennial in mild climates. Treat as a cool houseplant, with no really high temperatures (maximum 18°C/64°F), sufficient indirect light and a constantly moist compost. Mirror their natural habitat, which is meadows, damp fields or edges of rice paddies in southwest China and across the border in Burma.

Correct compost is fundamental when growing this primrose, as this will have a marked effect on its development and growth. Loam-based compost will hold structure best and allow for a greater margin of error in watering. Sow seed uncovered in midsummer; prick out seedlings into pots, when they are strong enough; and plant out before the flowering stage. Buds form during winter and flower in spring. Note, for some people, handling the leaves can cause dermatitis. **IT**

Alternatives

Primula forbesii subsp. *delicata*, *Primula obconica*

Pteris

P. cretica var. albolineata

Main feature Fern with long, slender frond segments
with bold, cream-white stripes
Height 75 cm (30 in.) **Spread** 75 cm (30 in.)
Position ◑ ● **Hardiness** RHS H1b

Most ferns have green fronds. Very few varieties have
other colours in their foliage, and those that do are
prized for this feature. The young fronds of some can be
encrusted with gold- or rust-coloured hairs; some young
fronds emerge bronze tinted; whereas in other ferns, the
fronds turn a yellow colour in the autumn. One of the
most popular varieties that feature foliage of different
colours is *P. cretica* var. *albolineata*. The botanical name
cretica would indicate that it grows on the Greek island
of Crete, and this is indeed the case. But this widespread
species can also be found around the world in warm,
temperate, and tropical areas. It is naturalised in a few
American states.

   This is a fern that develops a mass of fronds from
compact, slowly spreading roots; the fronds come in two
forms. All are 30 to 45 centimetres (12–18 in.) in length –
oval or triangular in outline – and split into up to five
opposite pairs of long, slender, toothed segments; the
segments at the base are each split into two. Mostly, they
are rather spreading in the way they are held, but the
fronds that carry the spores are upright in growth and
have narrower segments and longer stems than others.

   The fronds of *P. cretica* var. *albolineata* are distinct
in having a broad, cream-white stripe along the centre of
each segment, sometimes leaving only a slender, green
margin. This attractive feature has made it a popular fern
around the world, and it has escaped into the wild in
Florida. In favourable conditions it can be grown outside
in fertile soil that is moist and limey; although happy in
the shade, it takes more light than many ferns. However,
note that plants can spread too freely from spores when
they are in favoured areas. In colder locations this fern is
often grown as a houseplant or in the shady corners of
a conservatory. **GR**

Alternative

Pteris cretica 'Mayi'

Radermachera
R. sinica

Main features Evergreen tree with glossy, dark-green leaves; architectural shape; best as a houseplant
Height 1.5 m (5 ft) Spread 90 cm (3 ft)
Position ○ ◑ Hardiness RHS H2–3

The *R. sinica* is a beautiful foliage plant that is capable of lasting for many years. It will quickly become a focal point to any room in the home. The main feature is the glossy, dark-green leaves, and the plant eventually forms a small tree. It has been awarded a Royal Horticultural Society Award of Garden Merit as a houseplant, and it is trouble free and tolerant.

Native to south-east China, *R. sinica* is an evergreen shrub that grows to a height of around 4.5 metres (15 ft) in the wild. It can produce cream-white, fragrant, trumpet-shaped flowers, which has led to the common name of Asian bell tree. However, *R. sinica* rarely flowers when it is grown as a houseplant. This is a shame, because seed collected from dry pods is the best way to propagate these plants, and they can be tricky to grow from cuttings. In the confines of a large pot indoors, it will reach a height of 1.5 metres (5 ft): an impressive size for a foliage houseplant without being too overwhelming.

A sunny position is ideal, but keep *R. sinica* away from direct sunlight. Settle for a bright room and a position away from a window. The plant is naturally branched, but if a branch begins to grow in a different direction, it can be cut back to encourage sideshoots. Feed *R. sinica* with a weak houseplant feed every fortnight to get the best from it. Watering and fertilising should be reduced in winter. The plant should never stand in water, as this will encourage the roots to rot. It is best to water it when the compost has just become dry to the touch. *R. sinica* will not tolerate draughts from windows or doors. If the leaves start to turn crispy and brown, particularly on one side of the plant, it is likely due to a draughty window or icy blast from an outside door. To recover the plant, reposition it, cut off the offending branches, and wait for new shoots to appear. **PM**

Alternative

Syn. *Stereospermum sinicum*

Rebutia
R. fiebrigii 'Muscula'

Main feature Small clustering cactus with white spines
and orange flowers
Height 6 cm (2.5 in.) **Spread** 6 cm (2.5 in.)
Position ○ **Hardiness** RHS H2

There are plenty of varieties of *Rebutia* cacti, ever since
botanists lumped some other popular cacti into this
broader group. Synonyms abound, including *Aylostera*,
Mediolobivia, *Sulcorebutia* and *Weingartia*. They are all
small, clustering, ball-shaped plants that evolved in
extreme landscapes, making them robust and tough to
kill. The orange crown cactus, *R. fiebrigii* 'Muscula' (also
known as *R. muscula*, amongst other names) comes
from the high Andes in rocky grasslands and exposed
slopes of Bolivia and Argentina, where many nooks and
crannies have produced localised varieties. This is why
R. fiebrigii in cultivation can differ greatly, with confusing
names for the same species. They are notable for their
variable white, silky spines on a dark-green stem; some
types look like an old, bearded, wild man, whereas others
seem almost manicured.

A great plant for beginners, orange crown cactus
thrives on neglect. Grow in a gritty cactus mix that drains
well, and then water and fertilise sparingly from spring
to summer and hardly at all the rest of the year. Do not
water in winter and do not overwater at any time. Keep
cool (15°C/60°F) in winter. This is a small plant for a small
space, slowly increasing by forming offsets around the
base to fill a 15-centimetre-wide (6 in.) pot. Bright light
not only helps it bloom, but it keeps stems compact and
dense. It also brings out intense colours in the stems,
with hues of purple and bronze sometimes evident under
the fuzzy spines. A flush of orange flowers can cover the
barrel for about a week in late spring or summer. Flowers
can also be yellow, red or pink; blooms, which can reach
5 centimetres (2 in.) wide, generally appear from the stem
sides. Distinct types include 'Donaldiana', which has
brown spines that set off the dark orange-red flowers,
and 'Narvaecensis' with soft-pink blooms. **JW**

Alternatives

Rebutia albipilosa, Rebutia buiningiana

Rhapis
R. excelsa

Main feature Glossy, green palm-like leaves on a slow-growing bamboo palm
Height 5 m (16 ft) **Spread** 4 m (13 ft)
Position ◐ **Hardiness** RHS H1b

The slender, adaptable bamboo palm is perfect for the home and is often seen in offices around the world. The evergreen leaves are made up of twenty or more glossy-green lobes, and given time, the plant will begin to form a clump. It is slow growing, so it will never become a nuisance and is easy to care for. Panicles of small, yellow flowers form on older plants followed by small fruits. Originating in South China, North Vietnam and Japan, this species requires heat, humidity and ideally, dappled light to thrive. All can be found in a hot glasshouse, a hardworking office or a bathroom setting. Additional humidity can be supplied by a weekly misting with water. *R. excelsa* can put on 30 centimetres (12 in.) of growth in a year if it is doing well. If left to bake in full sun, the leaves will turn brown. In the growing season the plant should be watered to ensure the compost stays moist. This should be reduced in winter as growth slows down. As well as its stunning foliage, the upright stems of *R. excelsa* are attractively clothed in woolly fibre. **PM**

Alternative
Rhapis humilis

Rumohra
R. adiantiformis

Main features Glossy, dark-green fronds on an evergreen fern; ideal for containers and hanging baskets
Height 90 cm (3 ft) **Spread** 90 cm (3 ft)
Position ◐ ● **Hardiness** RHS H3

Leather fern is a handsome specimen that is ideal for hanging baskets, containers and living in the home. It is highly valued by florists as the cut fronds are durable and can last in peak condition for weeks. *R. adiantiformis* is an evergreen with bold, heavy fronds that are made up of glossy-green, triangular leaflets. It is suitable for planting in soil borders beneath glasshouse benching or in summer hanging baskets, but it will need protection in colder areas during winter. In the wild it is often found growing on decaying logs or in branches of trees. It likes to nuzzle itself into the warmth and protection of soft tree ferns. Shade is the key to success, as direct sunlight will scorch the plant. It can tolerate periods of drought and is not fussy about the type of compost it grows in. A quick and easy way to produce new plants is to pull away a small section of the clump in late spring, ensuring some roots and shoots are attached. Pot up in well-drained compost, leave in semi-shade in a cool greenhouse for six months, and plant out the following spring. **PM**

Alternative
Nephrolepis exaltata

Russelia
R. equisetiformis

Main feature Constant, spring-to-autumn, shrubby
bloomer beloved by hummingbirds
Height 90–240 cm (3–8 ft) **Spread** 90–150 cm (3–5 ft)
Position ○ ◑ **Hardiness** RHS H3

The weeping, airy, feathery style of *R. equisetiformis* is
like an asparagus fern gone wild and then bursting with
scarlet firework-shaped flowers. An almost constant
bloomer from spring to autumn – all year in mildest
climates – the nectar-rich, firecracker plant, or coral plant,
is a hummingbird magnet. Butterflies love it too. Native
to Mexico and Guatemala, where it can spread in soft
masses, this shrubby showstopper has long, bright-green,
slender stems that start out erect and then tumble over in
a natural cascading habit, giving rise to another common
name, fountain plant. In mild climates it can be grown
outdoors year-round, often rooting where it has contact
with soil. A humus-rich, well-drained garden soil or good
potting mix with a little sand is ideal. Once established,
the plant is drought tolerant, though regular watering
and fertilising (and at least a half day of sun) create the
best blooms. In temperate areas *R. equisetiformis* is reliably
useful in the garden as an ornamental accent plant. Tie it
to a trellis or let it ramble over a raised bed or rock wall. **JW**

Alternatives

Cuphea ignea, Penstemon eatonii

Salvia
S. leucantha 'Purple Velvet'

Main features Tender shrub with flowers summer to
autumn; aromatic foliage
Height 90–150 cm (3–5 ft) **Spread** 45–90 cm (18–36 in.)
Position ○ **Hardiness** RHS H2

An upright shrub with narrow, pointed, grey-tinted, green
leaves that are 10 centimetres (4 in.) long and hairy. In
fact, the whole plant is hairy, particularly the flowers. The
species name means 'white flowered', but when you first
glance at the plant, it seems to have purple flowers. A
closer look, however, will show that the part that wraps
around the flower, the calyx, is very prominent and purple.
The calyx partly hides the flower, which is white but
not conspicuous. The combination of white flower and
purple calyx, both covered in soft down, makes for a
very pleasing effect. 'Purple Velvet' has purple flower
and calyx. The flower spikes can be up to 30 centimetres
(12 in.) long. It is a good plant for a large container display,
where you can get up close to enjoy the flowers and
smell the blackcurrant-scented foliage. Alternatively, use
it in a border display of tender perennials. In temperate
regions take cuttings in autumn for next year or lift the
plant, cut back and store in a frost-free place. *Salvia* roots
readily from semi-ripe cuttings taken in late summer. **PWi**

Alternatives

Salvia leucantha, Salvia leucantha 'Sanra Barbara'

Sansevieria
S. trifasciata var. laurentii

Main features Evergreen perennial; variegated leaves; scented flowers (in warm regions); architectural plant
Height 75 cm (2.5 ft) **Spread** 30 cm (12 in.)
Position ◑ **Hardiness** RHS H2

This member of the asparagus family belongs to a group of plants that all yield bow string hemp, a strong plant fibre used for making bow strings. The plant is native to southern Africa, and in temperate climates it is most frequently seen as a houseplant, while in warmer areas it can be used as a landscape plant with strong architectural qualities. Its succulent, stiff, strap-shaped leaves grow without a stem, emerging straight from a gently creeping rhizomatous rootstock. The leaves are dark green with irregular grey-green, mottled, horizontal stripes. *S. trifasciata* var. *laurentii* also has a narrow cream-yellow margin to the leaves. Cream-white, scented flowers appear on short spikes. This variety has two points of interest. Firstly, it is a periclinal chimera, which means that the normal method of propagating it from leaf cuttings fails to produce the yellow edge. It must be propagated by division. Secondly, it has the remarkable ability to absorb toxins, such as nitrogen oxide and formaldehyde, from the atmosphere, making it an ideal air-purifying plant. **MP**

Alternative

Sansevieria trifasciata 'Moonshine'

Sarracenia
S. leucophylla

Main feature Decorative, insect-eating pitchers
Height 45–100 cm (18–40 in.) **Spread** 90 cm (3 ft)
Position ◑
Hardiness RHS H5

Haunting wet places in the south-eastern United States, this bug-eating plant is beautiful yet deadly. As an adaptation to living in nutrient-poor environments, its leaves have evolved to become far more than a platform for photosynthesis. Over the course of millions of years, its leaves have curled over, sealed up, and become tall, elegant, vase-like pitchers – filled with a gruesome cocktail of digestive juices. Any hapless insect unlucky enough to land on the leaves' slippery rims will soon become the pitcher's next meal. Luckily for the gardener, *S. leucophylla* is one of the easiest carnivorous plants to grow. Give it acidic compost and rainwater, and it makes a rewarding houseplant for a sunny windowsill or greenhouse. Plants are surprisingly hardy, given their native range, and adapt well to cultivation. *S. leucophylla* makes a striking pot plant; its pitchers are patterned with white 'windows' set in a purple-red background that fades to green at the base. They often bear wine-purple flowers in spring, looking like a single hellebore bloom on a long stem. **GAR**

Alternatives

Sarracenia purpurea, Pinguicula vulgaris

Schefflera
S. taiwaniana

Main feature Tree or shrub with tropical-looking, evergreen foliage
Height 2.4 m (8 ft) **Spread** 1.5 m (5 ft)
Position ○ ◑ **Hardiness** RHS H3

The *Schefflera* has long been grown as a houseplant, but since the mid 1980s, plant hunters have been returning from South East Asia and China with some spectacular plants that are proving to be hardy in temperate climates. They are now much sought after by gardeners who are looking for something different. *S. taiwaniana* is an elegant, unusual evergreen that is native to the high mountain forests of central Taiwan. Left to its own devices, it naturally forms a tree with a broad canopy. If pinched out regularly, however, it will create an eye-catching, bushy shrub. The palmate leaves on long stalks have a tropical air, but the plant is fully hardy when established. It produces sprays of yellow-green flowers in late summer, followed by tiny black fruits, but it is primarily grown for its foliage. *S. taiwaniana* needs to be planted in a sheltered spot, as cold winds can scorch the growing tips of the leaves. In colder areas it should not be planted out until it has some toughened wood on its stem. It likes soil to be on the moist side, enriched with plenty of leaf mould. **VP**

Alternatives

Schefflera rhododendrifolia, Schefflera macrophylla

Schlumbergera
S. truncata

Main feature Succulent with tubular flowers in autumn and winter
Height 30 cm (12 in.). **Spread** 30–45 cm (12–18 in.)
Position ◑ **Hardiness** RHS H1a

The small *Schlumbergera* genus comprises only six species, all of which grow wild in the Brazilian rainforests. They make small, rather shrubby, plants and have no leaves. Most are epiphytic species in the wild: that is, they grow on trees and sometimes rocks. The plants are woody at the base and, instead of leaves, the stems develop flattened, succulent, leaf-like structures with notched edges along either side. The branches tend to grow upright at first and then arch as they age. Towards the tips of the shoots, the flamboyant 8-centimetre-long (3 in.) flowers develop; each is trumpet-shaped with additional recurved petals behind. One of these easy-to-grow succulents is *S. truncata*, also known as the Thanksgiving cactus. It is an early-flowering variety, starting in late autumn and its 'leaves' have points along the edges. The flowers may be red, orange, pink or white, and it is important not to move the plant when it is in bud because the developing flowers may drop off. It can be grown outside in suitable climates; in cooler areas, grow it as a houseplant. **GRw**

Alternatives

Hatiora rosea, Schlumbergera × buckleyi

Senecio
S. haworthii

Main feature Greenhouse succulent with white, felty leaves
Height 25 cm (10 in.) **Spread** 25 cm (10 in.)
Position ○ **Hardiness** RHS H2

Also known as ashweed or cocoon plant, *S. haworthii* is a tough little succulent plant with silver-white, densely felted leaves and the ability to produce roots from cuttings without any questions. It is a born survivor and adapted to its native South Africa, but it is also grown elsewhere as a greenhouse pot plant. When grown outdoors, the felt covering on the succulent, cylindrical leaves is a wonderful way not only to prevent damage to the plant from scorching sun, but also to maintain sufficient moisture within the plant. *S. haworthii* will rot in wet soils, so keep composts dry and ensure that the plant gets plenty of sun.

This plant grows best in a real terra-cotta pot, because this helps to keep the roots cool and dry. In good growing conditions, a pot plant will reach around 25 centimetres (10 in.) in height and will produce a multitude of butter-yellow blooms. Unfortunately, it is rare for viable seeds to be produced by the flowers, but genetically identical plants can be produced by simply pulling off a leaf, allowing the cut end to dry for two days, and then pushing it into well-drained compost. Given a little drop of moisture and warm conditions, roots will form within a few weeks. The new plants can then be potted up as they grow. Hundreds of ready-made cuttings are produced by cutting the plant hard back in early spring.

If *S. haworthii* is grown 'soft' by excess watering and the addition of fertiliser, the plant will grow tall and leggy and can be cut back in early spring. However, the perfect plant is smaller and squat, and looks solid. Only water it when the compost is bone-dry and reduce any irrigation to a few drops in winter. In the correct conditions *S. haworthii* is easy to grow. It was named after botanist Adrian Haworth, who first described it in 1803. **PM**

Alternatives

Senecio jacobsenii, Senecio crassissimus, Senecio citriformis

Senna
S. artemisioides

Main features Shrub with downy, grey-green leaves; subtle, yellow, fragrant blooms
Height 2.4 m (8 ft) **Spread** 2.4 m (8 ft)
Position ○ **Hardiness** RHS H1c

Also known as wormwood senna or silver cassia, *S. artemisioides* is a lovely shrub that has adapted superbly to hot, dry conditions and will tolerate any amount of neglect provided that the temperature stays above freezing. It is perfect for a greenhouse or a container placed in a position where the plant can revel in the summer sunshine, but come back under cover in autumn.

The leaves of *S. artemisioides* are downy and grey green in colour, divided into delicate-looking leaflets. Yellow, bowl-shaped flowers can appear at any time of the year, but they are more abundant in autumn and winter. Consequently, this is a great plant for brightening up an otherwise desolate greenhouse in the depths of a grey winter's day. Once the flowers have faded, they are followed by long pods containing seed. They turn from fresh green to a crisp brown within a month. The seeds can then be harvested and sown into well-drained compost in a heated propagator.

When planting *S. artemisioides* in a container, use a loam-based compost. The plant needs full sun and above-average humidity. If the plant is under glass in summer, splash water onto any hard surfaces early in the morning; the water quickly evaporates as the sun strengthens, and it increases humidity around the plant. *S. artemisioides* is a relatively slow-growing plant, but eventually it will reach 2.4 metres (8 ft) in height after fifteen years. Occasionally, a shoot may grow away quickly, thereby ruining the overall compact shape to the plant. Luckily, this plant responds to hard pruning, and if the pruning is done in spring, it will produce new growth. A severe haircut will rejuvenate an older, out-of-shape specimen. Cut the plant back to within 15 centimetres (6 in.) of the compost level, water it and wait until it springs into life again. **PM**

Alternative

Syn. *Cassia artemisoides. Senna corymbosa*

Solenostemon
'Winsome'

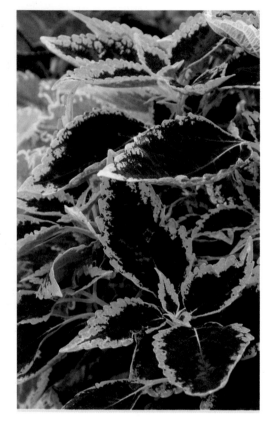

Main features Tender perennial with long-lasting foliage colour in summer; year-round display in warm climates
Height 75 cm (2.5 ft) **Spread** 75 cm (2.5 ft)
Position ○ ◑ ● **Hardiness** RHS H2

Normally, we think of variegated plants as having yellow or white edges on green leaves. The colourful *Solenostemon* – commonly known as coleus or painted nettles – make a mockery of such preconceptions. In fact, these tropical beauties provide some of the best foliage colour of any plant. There are hundreds of cultivars, with vividly coloured leaves ranging from purple and pink to yellow, with plenty of vivid, zesty green and red thrown in for good measure. These last two colours feature in the cultivar 'Winsome'. Its handsome red leaves are edged in a fresh lime green, making a colour combination rarely seen in other plants. The description 'red' hardly does the plant justice: the leaf veins are a deep, brazen scarlet that veers into purple and maroon, depending on the light and growing conditions.

The small, mauve flowers of *Solenostemon* are borne on spikes that some gardeners find attractive; however, it is generally recommended that flower spikes be pinched out to encourage bushy growth and the plentiful production of attractive leaves. Plants positively relish shady conditions and are wonderful for brightening up dull spots in the garden. In fact, shade tolerance is a useful attribute for any plant, especially one so amenable to being used as a bedding plant. The leaves may scorch in sunny conditions in warm areas, although plants are happy in most types of soil, as long as they are not allowed to get waterlogged or too dry. They are easily propagated from softwood cuttings in the growing season or by seeds in early spring.

Solenostemon combines well with many other plants, especially those with contrasting forms, for example, finely textured, small-leaved cultivars of *Helichrysum* or *Chlorophytum* (spider plants). **GAR**

Alternatives

Solenostemon 'Combat', *Solenostemon* 'Crimson Ruffles', *Solenostemon* 'Durham Gala'

Solenostemon with red leaves in flower at Centre de la Nature public garden, Laval, Quebec, Canada. ➔

Spathiphyllum
'Mauna Loa'

Main features Tolerant perennial; glossy foliage; long-lasting flowers
Height 1 m (3.5 ft) **Spread** 1 m (3.5 ft)
Position ◐ ● **Hardiness** RHS H1b

One of the most widely grown of houseplants, *Spathiphyllum* – commonly known as the peace lily or white sails – is popular for good reasons. It would be outstanding if grown simply as a foliage plant, with its large, glossy, green leaves that emerge from rhizomatous roots. However, *Spathiphyllum* has the added attraction of flowers produced on a club-like spadix surrounded by a sail-like, white spathe. Peace lilies are often sold unlabelled, but it is worth seeking out 'Mauna Loa'. It is a large cultivar with flowers that are scented when they first open, although the fragrance fades after a few days. The spathe itself can last for around six weeks. A well-grown peace lily can bloom twice a year, providing several months of flowers.

These are tolerant houseplants that flower well in the low light levels of a typical home because they grow in shade in their native habitats. Curled, pale leaves can indicate that the plant is getting too much light. They thrive in high humidity, so will benefit from being placed on trays of damp gravel if kept in a centrally heated house. During the summer water and mist frequently. In winter reduce watering, but never allow the soil to completely dry out.

The peace lily is not actually a lily, but, along with *Arisaema* and *Zantedeschia,* is a member of the *Arum* family. There are around forty species of *Spathiphyllum* in Central and South America, and they tend to look fairly similar to one another. They have been very popular in Hawaii for many years. The cultivar 'Mauna Loa' is named for one of five volcanoes that make up the island of Hawaii. It will bring a tropical ambience to any home. As well as its ornamental qualities, the peace lily is also known for its capacity to remove indoor air pollutants, such as trichloroethylene and formaldehyde. **GHa**

Alternatives

Spathiphyllum 'White Lightning', *Spathiphyllum* 'Golden Delicious'

Stephanotis
S. floribunda

Main features Evergreen climber; scented, long-lasting flowers from midsummer to autumn
Height 1.8–3 m (6–10 ft) **Spread** 30–60 cm (12–24 in.)
Position ○ ◑ **Hardiness** RHS H1b

The Madagascan jasmine, *S. floribunda*, has a strong, intense, sweet perfume that will unconsciously draw you towards it. The flower is said to signify 'happiness in marriage', and for centuries it has had an association with brides, bouquets and weddings. The meaning of the Greek genus name *Stephanotis* is 'crown' and 'ear', which refers to the arrangement of ear-shaped stamen within the flower. You will not regret finding a place for this well-behaved climber, either indoors or out.

In regions where temperatures are below 15°C (60°F), grow evergreen *Stephanotis* in tubs with some support to train the vines. Plants can therefore be moved away from freezing temperatures in autumn and winter. In warmer climes grow it against a warm, sheltered wall, training the slow-growing vines by tying them along horizontal wires. In tropical areas provide a strong structure to hold its weight, so the white, waxy flowers can release their fragrance as you sit under an arbour, gazebo or pergola. Madagascan jasmine prefers its roots cool, with its 'head in the sun', but it does not like changes in temperature, so gardeners should site plants where temperatures tend to remain constant, and acclimatise the plants when moving them between outdoors and indoors. Height varies greatly depending on where and how it is grown; both height and spread will be much greater in tropical regions than when grown as a houseplant.

An alternative is to grow a small plant in a pot as a permanent houseplant in a draught-free spot. Water Madagascan jasmine evenly during the growing season, reducing the frequency of watering in winter to give plants a rest. In hard water (limey) areas use rain water. If mealy bugs or scales appear, then act immediately to remove, as serious infestations can later become difficult to control. **IT**

Alternatives

Stephanotis floribunda 'Variegata', *Trachelospermum jasminoides*

Strelitzia
S. reginae

Main features Year-round foliage; striking, orange-and-blue blooms; good cut flower
Height 1.5–1.8 m (5–6 ft) **Spread** 90 cm (3 ft)
Position ◑ ● **Hardiness** RHS H1c

This evergreen perennial from South Africa is commonly known as bird of paradise. Its striking looks and colourful flowers that resemble a tiny bird make it a showstopper of a plant, wherever it is grown. Its long-stalked, green leaves are bold in shape and have year-round presence. Out of this central clump grow stems that end with beak-like spathes. From these emerge its striking orange-and-blue flowers, which appear in succession during late winter and spring, if given the right conditions. Flowers are the size of a small bird with an aerodynamic appearance – they appear to hover above the plant and look as though they could launch into flight. In fact, its strong stems can take the weight of a hummingbird, which enjoys the nectar produced by the showy blooms. After planting it can take a few years before flowers are produced again, but once they reappear, the plant will provide years of beauty. It needs little more than good light and water to produce its distinctive, signature blooms. Needless to say, it makes a striking cut flower.

'Mandela's Gold' is a yellow-flowering form. In 1996 its name was changed from 'Kirstenbosch Gold' in honour of Nelson Mandela, then president of South Africa. *Strelitzia juncea* is another species of the same scale with similar flowers, but it has very different, glaucous blue-grey, rush-like leaves. Flowers are held below the leaf tops in contrast to *S. reginae*.

Bird of paradise needs frost-free conditions; in cooler climates it is best treated as a houseplant or grown in a conservatory. Placing it outside in the warm summer months is optional, depending on the size and weight of the plant in its container. Plants grown outdoors year-round will tolerate a little frost. Remove any damaged leaves to maintain the plant's looks, but they may take some time to be replaced. **RC**

Alternatives

Strelitzia reginae 'Mandela's Gold', *Strelitzia juncea*

Streptocarpus
'Crystal Ice'

Main features Perennial pot plant; attractive foliage;
white flowers with violet-blue veining
Height 30 cm (12 in.) **Spread** 30 cm (12 in.)
Position ◑ **Hardiness** RHS H1c

This is a particularly long flowering form of the well-known and popular Cape primrose. It is a rosette-forming perennial plant with narrow, dark-green leaves, and sprays of white flowers with heavy, violet-blue veining on the lower lobes. Each flower stem carries between seven and thirteen flowers, so a plant in full flower will be smothered in blooms. 'Crystal Ice' was the first of a series of *Streptocarpus* bred to flower continuously. 'Crystal Snow' in the same series has pure-white flowers, and 'Crystal Wonder' is a rich, purple form. The Crystal Series was bred by Dibleys' nursery in Wales

Streptocarpus is native to the mountains of central, eastern and southern Africa, where it grows on shady hillsides and in rocky crevices. The species *S. rexii* was introduced to the gardens at Kew in 1824, and the first hybrid was created there in the mid-nineteenth century. *Streptocarpus* became popular in the Victorian period due to the range of colours and profuseness of flowers.

Grow *Streptocarpus* under glass in fibrous compost in bright, but filtered, light. Water regularly, but allow compost to dry between waterings. In dry, centrally heated rooms, stand pots on a saucer of grit or expanded clay granules, which are kept moist to increase humidity. Crystal Series plants may continue flowering through the year, so keep them in a very well-lit spot in winter. Remove the faded flower stalks to encourage further flower formation. Feed regularly with a high-potash liquid feed formulated for tomatoes or a feed for flowering houseplants. Plants are usually propagated by leaf cuttings. A whole leaf can be used or the leaf cut into sections with each section being inserted into compost. Place in a propagator or a clear plastic bag in a light place out of direct sunlight. When plantlets form, remove the cover and allow plants to grow on. **GHa**

Alternatives

Streptocarpus 'Ella', *Streptocarpus* 'Falling Stars'

Streptosolen
S. jamesonii

Main features Scrambling shrub with flowers in spring, summer, and autumn; evergreen foliage
Height 1.8–3 m (6–10 ft) **Spread** 90–240 cm (3–8 ft)
Position ○ **Hardiness** RHS H1c

This is a tall, lax, scrambling, evergreen shrub – with small, shiny, deep-green leaves – that looks nothing special until its orange and yellow flowers burst open in a blaze of cheer. The flowers are small but packed with vibrant colour: each starts off rich yellow and then turns orange as it matures, giving a 'marmalade' effect. Each cluster of flowers can be up to 15 centimetres (6 in.) in diameter. *S. jamesonii* is tender but easy enough to manage, requiring only moderate warmth during the winter. In temperate climates it makes an exciting conservatory plant because it flowers from late spring to autumn. Outdoors in milder regions its scandent branches are perfectly suited to being trained against a wall or through and over a pergola. The genus name *Streptosolen* means 'twisted tube', from the Greek *streptos* (twisted) and *solen* (tube), in reference to the flower tube, which is, of course, twisted. It is in the family *Solanaceae*, which rather surprisingly means it is a close relative of the potato, tobacco, *Brugmansia* and *Petunia*. **PWi**

Alternative

Syn. *Browallia jamesonii*

Strobilanthes
S. dyeriana

Main features Evergreen subshrub with purple and silver foliage; flowers in late autumn or winter
Height 60–120 cm (2–4 ft) **Spread** 60–120 cm (2–4 ft)
Position ◑ ● **Hardiness** RHS H1b

The Persian shield plant is an evergreen subshrub, although the term 'evergreen' does not do justice to the leaves, which when young are beautifully marked in silver with a rich purple overlay. The leaves are thick and deeply veined, so they look as though they are quilted. In tropical countries a plant may reach 1.2 metres (4 ft) in height and makes a striking individual specimen. However, in temperate climates *S. dyeriana* is usually grown as an annual bedding plant, and it will achieve around 20 to 30 centimetres (8–12 in.) in a border. The flowers are lavender-blue funnels held in short spikes. The related *S. kunthiana* from India has plain leathery leaves, but gives a better floral display with dense heads of bell-shaped, lilac flowers with green overlapping bracts in late summer. Persian shield is unusual amongst summer bedding plants in that it puts on a more captivating performance in shady situations. It will grow in sunny locations but the deep purple of the leaves, for which the plant is known, is more intense in shade-grown plants. **GHa**

Alternatives

Strobilanthes kunthiana, Strobilanthes wallichii

Stromanthe
S. sanguinea 'Triostar'

Main features Evergreen perennial with colourful foliage; good for the patio, greenhouse or home
Height 1.5 m (5 ft) **Spread** 1.5 m (5 ft)
Position ◑ ● **Hardiness** RHS H1b

Only nature can get away with splashing shades of olive green, red wine, white and orange together. *S. sanguinea* carries all these colours and is a dazzling houseplant that anyone can grow. Native to the Brazilian rainforests, this evergreen perennial is grown indoors in most regions. The upper surface of the lance-shaped leaves of 'Triostar' is white and green, whereas the under side is a burgundy-red colour. When in flower the blooms open to display white petals with orange sepals. Flowers can appear at any time of the year when plants are growing in the home or glasshouse. Humidity is the watchword when thinking about how to get the best from *S. sanguinea*. A warm, humid greenhouse is perfect, but in the home you will need to spray the plant by hand or keep it in a humid bathroom. The plant needs moist soil and a position out of direct sun otherwise the white areas of the leaves can scorch. It also responds well to a fortnightly application of a tomato feed when it is growing. In the height of summer *S. sanguinea* can spend some time outside. **PM**

Alternative

Stromanthe amabilis

Tecoma
T. stans 'Gold Star'

Main features Evergreen shrub with glossy, green leaves; succession of showy, trumpet-like flowers
Height 90–150 cm (3–5 ft) **Spread** 60–120 cm (2–4 ft)
Position ○ **Hardiness** RHS H3

Commonly known as yellow bells, the yellow elder or esperanza (the Spanish word for 'hope') is a shrub or small tree native to the southern United States, Mexico and South America. It has showy, yellow, trumpet-shaped flowers, which resemble those of other members of the trumpet vine family. The flowers are rich in nectar, and native plants are much visited by hummingbirds. The cultivar 'Gold Star' is particularly floriferous with dense clusters of flowers in constant succession from spring until autumn. It was selected by Greg Grant of the Stephen F. Austin State University in Texas, from a private garden in San Antonio, for its early flowering in a container. The glossy, compound leaves are very attractive too. Provide a rich, fertile growing medium and plenty of water and fertiliser throughout the growing season. Plants love the sun and show great tolerance of heat. Grown in a pot for the patio or conservatory, they will produce a mound of stems. In Mediterranean climates plants can survive in the ground if the roots are thickly mulched in autumn. **GHa**

Alternatives

Tecoma 'Orange Jubilee', *Tecoma capensis* 'Aurea'

Tibouchina
T. urvilleana

Main features Evergreen shrub with flowers in summer
and autumn; attracts butterflies
Height 2.4–4 m (8–13 ft) **Spread** 1.5–2.4 m (5–8 ft)
Position ○ **Hardiness** RHS H1c

The *T. urvilleana* is a showstopper when in full flower,
casting a spell over all who see it and demanding a
closer look. It is native to Brazil, and in the tropical to
subtropical conditions of its home, it often grows into a
small tree, but it is most usually seen as a shrub in cooler
climates. In colder regions it makes an excellent container
plant for a frost-free room in winter and a focal point of
summer patio displays. Alluring wherever it is planted,
T. urvilleana is an evergreen, bushy shrub with oval, grey-
green leaves. Each has a prominent central vein, and new
growth is covered with fine bronze-red hairs or down
that give the plant an attractive fuzzy look. However, it
is the flowers that are the standout feature: rich, regal,
violet purple, and large, measuring up to 10 centimetres
(4 in.) in diameter. The whole plant seems to glow with
the intensity of flower colour. *T. urvilleana* flowers from
summer to autumn and is fast growing. Its open habit
can sometimes appear lax, so pinch out growing tips
or prune lightly to keep the plant in good shape. **RC**

Alternative

Tibouchina urvilleana 'Edwardsii'

Tillandsia
T. argentea

Main features Epiphyte with salmon-red, tubular flowers
in spring; architectural, silver-grey foliage
Height 10 cm (4 in.) **Spread** 15 cm (6 in.)
Position ○ ◐ **Hardiness** RHS H2

Planted in little globes or on a piece of driftwood,
the air plant makes a lovely feature in a living room
or conservatory. *T. argentea* is an epiphyte that grows
on trees in the forest canopy of Mexico. It absorbs air
from the atmosphere through scales on its leaves, so
frequent misting with soft water several times a week
is important, especially in dry environments. It needs
bright, indirect light. It can only be grown outside
with daytime temperatures of 26 to 32°C (80–90°F)
and night-time temperatures of 10 to 15°C (50–60°F). It
needs to be taken indoors during winter. As an epiphyte
T. argentea does not need any soil, giving you freedom
to use mediums such as cork, bark and wood. It can be
hung on the base of a split bamboo or planted on bark.
Although *T. argentea* produces beautiful purple flowers
from salmon-pink flower bracts, its twisting, silver-grey
leaves are also attractive. *T. usneoides,* or Spanish moss, is
another indoor favourite, which hangs down in bunches
like roots. **NM**

Alternative

Tillandsia usneoides

Titanopsis
T. calcarea

Main features Succulent with curious, warty or pebbly growths; grey-green leaves; yellow flowers
Height 10 cm (4 in.) **Spread** 10 cm (4 in.)
Position ○ **Hardiness** RHS H2

The genus *Titanopsis* is both curious and cryptic. It is devilishly difficult to discover in the wild. Some say it is beautiful while others consider it beastly. It grows on rocks and scree in South Africa and has adapted to live in a hostile environment by producing warty growths on its succulent leaves that mimic the limestone it is growing on. It is a fascinating adaptation and one that works wonders, except when the plant needs to reproduce. In order to attract insects, *Titanopsis* has to put on a bit of a show. It flowers in late autumn and produces spectacular yellow blooms that are easily spotted. *T. calcarea* produces pebbly or warty growths on grey-green leaves. The plant forms low mats and is best grown in a sunny position. In shade the pebbly growths disappear and the leaves turn green. Yellow flowers appear in the autumn and winter. *T. calcarea* is a superb succulent, perfect for a greenhouse or sunny windowsill. It is low growing and requires a well-drained compost low in nutrients. Even when actively growing, this plant requires little water. **PM**

Alternative

Titanopsis fulleri

Tradescantia
T. zebrina 'Quadricolor'

Main feature Perennial; year-round, colourful foliage
Height 15 cm (6 in.) **Spread** 20 cm (8 in.)
Position ◐ ●
Hardiness RHS H1b

The species *T. zebrina* has striped foliage, hence the zebra reference, but the leaves also have a crystalline sparkle to them when they catch the light, which the cultivar 'Quadricolor' has inherited. 'Quadricolor' means four colours, and these are all in the foliage: silver, white, pink and green. It is a very easy plant to grow, as are most of the plants in the genus *Tradescantia,* requiring sufficient light, a bit of warmth, and a moist but not wet compost or soil. It is a popular houseplant, and it is very easy to root new plants from cuttings. Even pieces stood in a glass of water on a windowsill will root. The trailing or scrambling habit of 'Quadricolor' can look untidy if the plant loses leaves along its trailing stems, so occasionally cut back the long shoots so that they sprout new leaves and fill out the base of the plants. The flowers are insignificant but grow 'Quadricolor' alongside the spider plant *Chlorophytum* for a bright foliage combination. In warmer climates it can be used as a light ground cover plant for under larger shrubs. **PWi**

Alternative

Tradescantia fluminensis 'Quicksilver'

Verbena
'Sissinghurst'

Main features Semi-evergreen perennial with spreading or trailing plant; heads of vivid magenta-pink flowers
Height 30 cm (12 in.) **Spread** 60 cm (24 in.)
Position ○ **Hardiness** RHS H5

The Verbena family includes thirty-five genera of which the most important is the one after which the family is named. The genus *Verbena* includes annuals, perennials and some partially woody species, but those grown as seasonal summer flowers are the most widely seen. They vary in their habit, and therefore their use in the garden, and also in their hardiness and in how they are propagated. Their colour range has been expanding for many years, and it continues to do so.

Compact, bushy, rather upright types, reaching 20 to 30 centimetres (8–12 in.) in height and spread are used in containers and in seasonal summer plantings; they are usually raised from seeds. Also available, and generally more popular and raised from cuttings, are spreading types. These are intended for ground cover and, more importantly, for hanging baskets and other containers. They come in broad-leaved types, as well as those with dissected leaves; their range of colours, bicolours and patterns is extensive.

'Sissinghurst' is a spreading and trailing type with dissected leaves, and it is also one of the hardiest varieties. Its 1.2-centimetre-long (0.5 in.) flowers are carried in clusters about 2.5 to 5 centimetres (1–2 in.) in diameter. They open in vivid, magenta pink and then mature to paler tones, thereby making a splendid specimen for urns and as a matted ground cover. This cultivar is said to have been given to head gardeners Pamela Schwerdt and Sibylle Kreutzberger at the United Kingdom's legendary Sissinghurst Castle garden in Kent around the late 1970s, and the donor reported that she had collected it in the wild. However, in North America this plant has been grown as 'St Paul' and 'Texas Tuff Pink', which tends to indicate that it has arisen independently at different times or has originated in gardens. **GR**

Alternatives

Syn. *Verbena tenera* 'St Paul', *Verbena tenera* 'Texas Tuff Pink', *Verbena* 'Hot Lips', *Verbena* Lanai Deep Pink = 'Lan Depink'

Xanthosoma
X. mafaffa 'Lime Zinger'

Main feature Perennial houseplant grown for its
dramatic foliage in different colours
Height 1.2 m (4 ft) **Spread** 1.2 m (4 ft)
Position ◐ **Hardiness** RHS H1b

Also known as elephant ear, *Xanthosoma* is extravagant,
dramatic and luscious. Its vibrant leaves make it a
wonderful houseplant, and it is fairly easy to grow in a
home environment if humidity is maintained at a high
level. In the wild these plants can be found growing on
the floors of tropical rainforests, so *Xanthosoma* performs
well in a humid greenhouse or a warm room inside the
house, such as a hot bathroom. In some parts of the
world they are valued for their edible roots. They require
bright light, but their impressive leaves can be scorched
in patches by direct sunlight.

The cultivar 'Lime Zinger' cannot be missed: its
60-centimetre-long (2 ft), arrow-shaped leaves are lime
green in colour, and they certainly zing. Large specimens
are breathtaking. Container-grown plants can be placed
outside on a patio in summer, but they must be brought
inside as the temperature falls. Water this plant well in
the growing season and keep the compost moist, but
never let it get waterlogged.

Maintain *Xanthosoma* throughout the winter by
reducing the watering levels. As light levels drop, the
leaves tend to pale in colour, and one way of overcoming
this is to dry off the plants and allow them a dormancy
period. Cover the dormant corms with dry compost and
keep them in a dark, frost-free place over the winter.
Bring them back into growth the following spring.

All *Xanthosoma* varieties are bold houseplants, and the
effort it takes to grow them is rewarded with magnificent
foliage. *X. lindenii* 'Magnificum' has yellow-green leaves
with broad white veins, and healthy specimens have
a slight, white line around the margin of each leaf.
X. albo marginata produces swirly, variegated leaves, and
the leaves of *X. violaceum* have a red tinge, particularly
in the thick veins. **PM**

Alternatives

Xanthosoma lindenii 'Magnificum' (syn. *Caladium lindendii*
'Magnificum'), *Xanthosoma albo marginata*

Yucca
Y. elephantipes

Main features Dramatic, drought-tolerant, soft-tipped leaves; evergreen; cream-coloured flowers in summer
Height 6 m (20 ft) **Spread** 60–90 cm (2–3 ft)
Position ○ **Hardiness** RHS H2

There are about fifty species of these impressive drought-tolerant plants growing mainly in North and Central America. Reaching from 0.75 to 9 metres (3–30 ft) in height, all *Yucca* species have dramatic rosettes of long, pointed, evergreen leaves gathered at the top of a woody trunk, which can be so short as to be hardly noticeable or so tall as to create a tree-like plant. The spikes of large, bell-shaped, white flowers are even more arresting.

Many *Yucca* have foliage with dangerously sharp points, but this species is different. Reaching as much as 6 metres (20 ft) tall, *Y. elephantipes* may develop a single trunk, or the swollen base may generate a number of stems. The heavy, narrow, evergreen leaves are 50 to 100 centimetres (20–40 in.) in length and toothed all the way along their length. They are not sharply pointed but have soft tips, making this variety a more acceptable garden plant than many other species. The flowers develop from the centre of the rosettes in summer and tend to be held fairly close to the foliage. Stout stems carry tall, branched clusters of cream, bell-shaped flowers that are 5 centimetres (2 in.) in diameter.

Where should you grow *Y. elephantipes*? In areas where it is too cold for the plant to survive outside, it is often grown as a houseplant. Its size can be controlled by the size of the pot in which it is grown; plants in small pots stay small. Larger plants in large containers make striking specimens on the patio, where the lack of spines is a big advantage, and they tolerate irregular watering; in fact, overwatering will cause the roots to rot. In milder areas spineless *Yucca* make fine specimens in any reasonably well-drained soil in full sun, and once established they will tolerate long, dry spells. A number of forms with variegated leaves have been selected, but they are not always available with individual names. **GR**

Alternatives

Yucca elephantipes 'Jewel', *Yucca elephantipes* 'Puck', *Yucca flaccida*, *Yucca recurvifolia*

Zygopetalum
James Strauss gx 'Scentsation'

Main features Flowers in winter and early spring; fragrant houseplant
Height 55 cm (21 in.) **Spread** 30 cm (12 in.)
Position ◗ **Hardiness** RHS H1a

Whenever there are fragrance contests at orchid shows, the genus *Zygopetalum* is always on the list of top winners. Legendary for incredible perfumes, these exotic-coloured orchids are generally easy to grow and very free-flowering, making them rewarding winter-blooming houseplants. The daytime scent can fill the room, evoking hyacinth, freesia and baby powder, and the waxy flowers can last up to three months.

Species of *Zygopetalum* come from humid areas of tropical Central and South America, and they are epiphytes that grow on the sides of trees. The flower inflorescence boasts multiple blooms and can grow longer than the foliage, which sits atop a rounded bulb. Nowadays, hybrids are readily available, imparting the jungle-patterned flowers and great fragrances with hybrid vigour. The strength of fragrance can vary between *Zygopetalum* cultivars, from faint to spectacular.

James Strauss gx 'Scentsation' was created in 1984 from two stellar hybrid parents (*Zygopetalum* 'Artur Elle' and *Zygopetalum* 'B. G. White'). The blooms have the classic chocolate-mottled green petals and sepals, enlivened by contrasting purple lips. The cultivar 'Scentsation' (also known as 'Scent-sation') is a relatively new arrival, chosen for its spicy perfume in combination with a vigorous, tolerant nature. Fragrance is generally best in the mornings and will be gone by late afternoon.

Pot your 'Scentsation' in a medium-sized orchid mix and grow it in bright, indirect light. Leaf colour is a great clue as to whether the plant is getting enough light. Lush, dark green means not enough light; a light, grassy green is just right. The bright light of a windowsill with morning sun often works best, with a summer outdoors, hanging in a high shade tree. In ideal conditions 'Scentsation' may surprise you with two blooms a year. **JW**

Alternatives

Zygopetalum 'Artur Elle', *Zygopetalum* 'B. G. White', *Zygopetalum* 'John Banks', *Zygopetalum* 'Warringa Wonder'

For people who want to take the first step towards growing their own edibles, herbs are a good place to start. Herbs will fit into an available space, however small: there is no need to build a dedicated herb garden, although a sunny spot best brings out their flavour. The perennial herbs, such as sage, thyme and rosemary, are attractive enough to be incorporated into any ornamental bed that gets some sun. Other annual herbs, such as coriander, dill and basil, can be raised from seeds sown directly into little pots, kept on a sunny windowsill.

Our focus in this chapter is on the lesser-known versions of common culinary herbs, to provide you with something special to flavour your salads and sauces. But there is a whole world of other medicinal and historical herbs to explore if your interest is piqued by this taster.

⬤ *Angelica archangelica* is used to flavour Chartreuse, Vermouth and other liqueurs.

Agastache
'Blue Fortune'

Main features Aniseed-scented leaves with culinary uses; flowers summer to autumn; highly attractive to bees
Height 60–90 cm (24–36 in.) **Spread** 60–90 cm (24–36 in.)
Position ○ ◑ **Hardiness** RHS H6

Magnets for bees and butterflies, the spires of lavender-blue flowers of the giant hyssop also attract hummingbirds in the United States. The whole plant is attractive to gardeners, with sturdy stems that do not need staking and foliage that releases an agreeable, mild aniseed aroma when crushed. The leaves can be used fresh in salads and the stems can be harvested as the flowers fade and hung up to dry. Once dry and brittle, strip the leaves and flowers from the stems and use for herbal tea.

Selected by Gert Fortgens, the director of the Trompenburg Gardens in Rotterdam, the Netherlands, this is a hybrid between the North American anise hyssop, *Agastache foeniculum* and the Korean mint, *A. rugosa*. The flowers are sterile, so no seed is set, and plants will bloom for many weeks. The long, erect spikes are made up of many whorls of small tubular flowers. The North American parent is found in open woodland and prairies from Arctic Canada to Colorado and Kentucky. 'Blue Fortune' enjoys similar situations with well-drained soil and a reasonably sunny position. It is drought tolerant once established, but it does not like winter wet and can be short-lived.

Ideal for long-lasting flowers in the herb garden, plants can also be used in Mediterranean-style plantings in gravel or in a border with other late-flowering perennials, such as heleniums and crocosmias. The stems can be left to provide winter interest. Plants can be propagated by basal cuttings taken as the new growth appears, or by division, which is best carried out in spring. The plants are usually free of pests and diseases, but they may become infected by mildew in hot, dry summers, so try to ensure good air flow around them. They will not cope with too much competition. **GHa**

Alternatives

Agastache 'Blackadder', *Agastache* 'Firebird', *Agastache aurantiaca* 'Apricot Sprite'

Allium
A. schoenoprasum

Main features Mild, onion-scented leaves; edible pink flowers; attracts bees and butterflies
Height 30 cm (12 in.) **Spread** 20–30 cm (8–12 in.)
Position ○ ◑ **Hardiness** RHS H7

Loved for imparting an onion flavour without tears, chives are essential to any chef's repertoire and a traditional ingredient of the classic French *fines herbes*. Chives are tolerant plants, amongst the most easily grown of herbs, but they will be more productive given a sunny site and any fertile soil apart from waterlogged soils. They have a neat growing habit and are useful edging plants for borders or the herb garden. They make good companion plants to tomatoes grown in large tubs. The hollow, upright leaves can be used fresh all year or may be frozen or dried in a cool oven. The pompom-like flowers are popular with butterflies and will attract bees. Deadhead fading flowers to encourage greater leaf production. Plants can be susceptible to onion white rot and downy mildew.

Plants die down for the winter. In the autumn bulbs can be potted up for the winter windowsill, where they will produce fresh green leaves. Split congested clumps in spring or autumn. Seeds can be sown in late winter in a cold frame or outdoors in spring. There will be some variation in the colour of the flowers of resulting plants.

Chopped chives eaten with bread and butter were once advocated as a cure for whooping cough. Fortunately, modern immunisation programmes have rendered such folk remedies unnecessary. Today, chives are more often used stirred into soured cream or mayonnaise as a filling for baked potatoes or added to omelettes and as a garnish for fish and other dishes.

Pink flowers are choice colour selections, for example the Pink Perfection Group or 'Forescate'. The former originated at Poyntzfield Herb Nursery in Scotland and was grown and distributed by the proprietor Duncan Ross. Both need to be deadheaded promptly or the mauve-flowered species will return. **GHa**

Alternatives

Allium schoenoprasum 'Black Isle Blush', *Allium schoenoprasum* 'Silver Chimes'

Allium
A. tuberosum

Main features Flat, garlic-flavoured leaves; edible starry white flowers; attracts bees and butterflies
Height 30 cm (12 in.) **Spread** 30 cm (12 in.)
Position ○ ◑ **Hardiness** RHS H7

Chinese, or garlic, chives can be distinguished from common chives by the solid; flat, rather than hollow, leaves; and subtle garlic flavour. They are perennial plants with cylindrical bulbs that produce open heads of white flowers, held on long stalks, clear above the bluish-green leaves. The small starry flowers of *A. tuberosum* are long blooming from late summer through the autumn and are surprisingly sweetly scented, attracting a profusion of bees and butterflies to the garden.

The species is native to the Himalayas and Shanxi province of northern China. In mild growing conditions plants will remain green all year. Grow in full sun to encourage maximum flower production and to benefit butterflies, although they will tolerate partial shade. Plants look good and function well in tubs or at the front of borders with other late flowerers, such as sedums, asters, and *Geranium* 'Rozanne'. They make good cut flowers and can also be dried. They are easily grown from seeds or by division of the bulbs in spring or autumn. In some gardens plants will remain as a neat clump, but in favourable conditions they can self-sow profusely and become invasive. If they become overly proliferate, deadhead the flowers as they fade and keep cutting the leaves to reduce the vigour of the plant. Throw the cut leaves into a homemade soup.

As well as an ingredient in soups, garlic chives can be used in stirfries and in egg or cheese dishes. They are not as pungent as true garlic, and the flavour is further reduced by cooking. The white flowers are also edible and make an attractive addition to salads. Plants can be blanched with an upturned flower pot to produce tender yellow leaves with a milder taste, which is popular in Chinese cuisine. The sprouted seeds give an extra crunch and a peppery taste to salads. **GHa**

Alternative

Allium ursinum

Aloysia
A. citrodora

Main features Half-hardy deciduous shrub; aromatic, lemon-scented leaves; tiny purplish-white flowers
Height 1.5 m (5 ft) **Spread** 1.2 m (4 ft)
Position ○ **Hardiness** RHS H3

This half-hardy, deciduous shrub, or subshrub, has rough-textured, yellowish-green, lance-shaped leaves with pointed margins that are slightly toothed or toothless and fringed with hairs. These are arranged in groups of three or four whorls around ridged stems and release an uplifting lemon scent when crushed. A haze of tiny, delicate, lilac-tinged white tubular flowers appear in summer. The flowers too, have a fresh lemony perfume and flavour when eaten.

Commonly known as lemon verbena, this plant needs plenty of sunshine and free-draining soil and is best planted in a border against a sunny south- or west-facing wall in northern areas. In tropical areas it can easily reach 3 metres (10 ft) high; outdoors in warm areas, 1.5 metres (5 ft). In cold areas it is best grown in containers, which will confine its growth to 60 centimetres (24 in.) or so, depending on the pot size, but there will still be plenty of leaves to harvest. The pot can spend the summer on a warm patio and be housed indoors during the winter.

The leaves and flowers, both fresh and dried, are mostly used in cosmetics, drinks, puddings and to flavour savoury dishes, as well as oils, vinegars and marinades. It is also a key ingredient of potpourri and often used to make sachets. Lemon verbena has therapeutic properties, and drinking lemon verbena tea, especially at bedtime, has a calming influence and aids sleep. Its medicinal qualities have been prized for centuries, and it has been used to help digestion and ease fevers. Brought to Europe by the Spanish from South America in the seventeenth century, it was first used to make perfumes, love potions and aromatic oils, which during Victorian times, were used to sweeten the water in finger bowls at large banquets. Lemon verbena has also been put to good use as an air freshener and insect repellent. **AW**

Alternative

Syn. *Aloysia triphylla*

Anethum
A. graveolens 'Fernleaf'

Main feature A short cultivar of dill with highly aromatic, lacy foliage
Height 45 cm (18 in.) **Spread** 45 cm (18 in.)
Position ○ ◑ **Hardiness** RHS H6

The *A. graveolens* 'Fernleaf' is a dwarf cultivar of dill that is particularly suited to container cultivation. It is also useful in borders and should not need staking. It is slow to bolt and is grown more for its dark-green leaves than its seed. The feathery foliage looks attractive growing amongst roses, as well as in the herb bed. Yellow-green flowers appear late in the season and attract beneficial insects, such as hoverflies, which prey on aphids. Plants will do best in full sun in a fertile, well-drained soil. Seeds should be sown where the plants are required, as the long tap roots do not transplant readily. Keep them well watered to prevent bolting. Do not plant near fennel, as they will cross-pollinate, and the individual flavours will be lost.

Dill has a delicate taste that is valued in cream sauces with fish or chicken and is classically combined with cucumber in salads. The leaves can be added generously to soups and herb butters. Dill is much used in Scandinavian cuisine and is an essential ingredient of gravadlax. If seeds are set, they can be used as a tasty addition to potato salads or an ingredient when pickling vegetables. They can also add interest to risottos or even apple pies.

The common name dill comes from the Norse word *dilla*, which means 'to lull or soothe' as the herb was used to induce sleep. Nicholas Culpeper, the English herbalist, recommended dill as a cure for hiccups. Gripe water, which is still used to treat colic in babies, contains dill, amongst other ingredients. **GHA**

Alternative

Anethum graveolens 'Bouquet'

Angelica
A. archangelica

Main features Architectural stems; striking flowers in summer
Height 2.4 m (8 ft) **Spread** 1.5 m (5 ft)
Position ○ ◑ **Hardiness** RHS H7

In seventeenth-century England, *A. archangelica* was so widely grown that apothecary Nicholas Culpeper almost could not bring himself to expend energy describing it, explaining in his *Complete Herbal* (1653): 'To write a description of that which is so well known to be growing in almost every garden, I suppose is altogether needless; yet for its virtue it is of admirable use.' These days it is a relatively rare sight, although *A. archangelica* still deserves a place in the garden for so obligingly combining a charming, flat, 'cottagey' flower head with the tall, edgy architectural shape required by modern planting design. Indeed, 'architectural' truly is the right word to describe this plant, because its long, firm stems were apparently

the inspiration for the fluted Doric columns of ancient Greece. For all its beauty *A. archangelica* is also a herb, and its candied stems are an old favourite in cakes and puddings. For a healthier alternative, skip the sugar and eat the stems as a vegetable instead.

In earlier times, *A. archangelica* was used medicinally. Culpeper wrote: 'It resists poison, by defending and comforting the heart, blood, and spirits; it doth the like against the plague and all epidemical disease, if the root be taken in powder to the weight of half a dram at a time, with some good treacle in Carduus water, and the party thereupon laid to sweat in his bed; if treacle be not to be had take it alone in Carduus or Angelica-water.' It was also rumoured to help with bites from mad dogs or venomous creatures **LG**

Alternatives

Angelica atropurpurea, Angelica sylvestris

Anthriscus
A. cerefolium

Main features Fern-like, aromatic green leaves; attractive heads of small, white flowers
Height 30–60 cm (12–24 in.) **Spread** 30 cm (12 in.)
Position ◑ ● **Hardiness** RHS H6

One of the few herbs that grow best in shady conditions, chervil is a biennial usually grown as an annual. It is related to parsley and has a hollow, furrowed stem and fern-like divided leaves with fine downy hairs. Umbels of tiny, white flowers in early summer are followed by oval seeds. The plants are pretty enough to be grown amongst more robust flowers in informal, cottage-garden–style borders.

A succession of seeds should be sown where plants are required, as they produce a long tap root and do not transplant easily. Native from Europe to Western Asia, chervil can be grown in any well-drained soil, but it should be watered regularly in dry spells, or it will run to seed. Harvest leaves regularly to keep plants productive.

Chervil is one of the constituents of the classic French *fines herbes*. It has a delicate aniseed flavour, which is good with mild-flavoured foods, such as fish, chicken and egg. The eighteenth-century philosopher and writer Rousseau described in his autobiography how in passing through a hamlet, he caught scent of a good chervil omelette and was tempted to stop. Chervil leaves are best used fresh, as the flavour does not withstand long cooking or drying. Extracts from the leaves have been shown to have antioxidant properties. Sometimes equated with the plant *Scandix*, which was said by Pliny the Elder to reinvigorate the body when exhausted by sexual excesses, chervil may not have aphrodisiac qualities, but its leaves often blush pink and then red when the plant is fertilised and sets seeds. **GHa**

Alternative

Anthriscus sylvestris 'Ravenswing'

Apium

A. *graveolens* var. *secalinum* 'Par–cel'

Main features Attractive celery-flavoured leaves; useful container plant
Height 30 cm (12 in.) **Spread** 30 cm (12 in.)
Position ○ ◑ **Hardiness** RHS H5

Much easier to grow than common, stalked celery, the leaf celery 'Par-cel' is a compact plant that is ideal for growing in containers. The rich green leaves look much like those of a flat-leaved parsley. The scent is said to repel cabbage white butterflies, so plants are worth trialing amongst brassicas in the vegetable garden. The leaves are quite ornamental and make attractive border edging.

Although biennial, 'Par-cel' is usually grown as an annual. Germinate the seeds on a windowsill in late winter or early spring, transplanting into tubs, the potager or the herb border as the weather warms up in spring. Plants prefer full sun so long as the soil is moist, but they will tolerate shade for part of the day. Cut the leaves regularly to keep plants productive.

Celery has been used since ancient times. Howard Carter, who discovered the tomb of Tutankhamen, reported that sprigs of wild celery were woven with olive leaves and cornflowers into the band of a garland found there. Leaf celery is used today as a garnish and in soups, stews and stirfries. The taste is more intense than that of stalked celery. Leaf celery does also produce stalks that can be boiled as a vegetable. However, they are thin and deep green, unlike the pale succulent stems of common celery, which was developed in the seventeenth century from wild plants. The seeds are aromatic with a bitter tang and are excellent in risottos and fish or crab dishes. **GHa**

Alternative

Petroselinum crispum

Artemisia
A. dracunculus

Main features Shrubby herb with pungent, anise-flavoured leaves; tiny, yellow flowers in summer
Height 60–90 cm (24–36 in.) **Spread** 30–45 cm (12–15 in.)
Position ○ ◑ **Hardiness** RHS H3

A versatile perennial herb, French tarragon has an intense mint-anise flavour that complements chicken or egg dishes. The lance-shaped leaves, which are smooth and glossy, are traditionally used in French cuisine and should not be confused with the bitter-tasting and coarser Russian form (*A. dracunculoides*). French tarragon is best bought as a plant from a reputable herb nursery; unlike the Russian tarragon it is not raised from seeds. Alternatively, if you have a mature clump of tarragon, lift and divide a piece of root in spring. Tarragon thrives in a light, free-draining soil. While it is essential to keep it well watered during the growing season, when planted in damp soil, the roots are prone to decay. Cut back plants almost to ground level at the end of the season and cover with deep mulch. Tarragon can be grown in a deep container and brought indoors if the temperature drops to freezing. Tarragon has been used as a remedy for poor digestion, rheumatism and arthritis. It is also a key ingredient in perfumes, soaps and cosmetics. **AW**

Alternative

No alternative with that particular flavour.

Borago
B. officinalis

Main features Vivid blue flowers; hairy leaves with the flavour of cucumbers; attracts bees
Height 60 cm (24 in.) **Spread** 30 cm (12 in.)
Position ○ **Hardiness** Annual

The main attraction of *B. officinalis*, commonly known as borage, is the loose racemes of blue star-shaped flowers with distinctive black stamen that are produced throughout summer. The leaves, stems and sepals are covered with fine, silvery hairs that give the plant a soft sheen. It is thought that the word 'borage' may be derived from the Latin for a hairy garment, *burra*. The edible flowers can be used as garnish, candied in puddings and frozen in ice cubes to decorate and cool summer drinks. The young leaves will give soups and salads a light, salty, cucumber flavour. The nectar-rich flowers attract bees and other beneficial insects. Advocates of companion planting recommend planting borage near tomatoes, to improve their growth and disease resistance, and next to strawberries to improve yield and give a tastier crop. As borage matures, the leaves become prickly and unappealing. Handling leaves may cause contact dermatitis, so always wear gloves. It is used medicinally to balance female hormones and to treat eczema. **AW**

Alternative

Borago officinalis 'Alba'

Borago officinalis is often used as a companion plant in a kitchen garden. ➲

Calendula
C. officinalis

Main feature Bright, yellow-orange flowers with edible petals
Height 45 cm (18 in.) **Spread** 45 cm (18 in.)
Position ○ **Hardiness** RHS H2

More popularly known as the marigold, *C. officinalis* suffers the indignity of having to share its common name with another marigold, *Tagetes patula*, which similarly boasts bright-yellow flowers of a merry gold. This is a shame because *C. officinalis*, also known as the English marigold or pot marigold, most definitely deserves to have its own identity.

This little flower does not grow particularly tall, but its fresh green leaves cushion its happy, yellow-orange flowers, each with a keen quantity of petals in several layers. As befits its cheery appearance, *C. officinalis* has a charmingly easygoing disposition, managing to grow on most soils and flowering all through the summer and even into winter if it is mild. Moreover, in case the profusion of flowers is not enough, the plant can easily be encouraged to produce more blooms with a simple hard prune, as described by seventeenth-century garden writer John Evelyn: 'When Mary-Golds are tender, collect as many as you can, well compasse within your hand & fingers, and sinke them into the Earth-bed by thrusting them down strongly into it as they grow, having before a little stirred the mould. Then cutt off their topps so as but very little appeare, and they will produce goodly flowers.'

However, the truly good news is that *C. officinalis* can also bring colour to the dining table because the petals are edible and can be sprinkled into soups and rice dishes to offer a yellow tint when saffron is not available. They can also make a delicious addition to a salad. Consequently, it is no wonder that marigolds have been popular with so many generations of gardeners. Cultivars to try include *C. officinalis* 'Chrysantha' (double yellow flowers), 'Sun Glow' (bright-yellow flowers) and 'Variegata' (yellow variegated leaves). **LG**

Alternatives

Calendula officinalis 'Indian Prince', *Calendula officinalis* Fiesta Gitana Group, *Calendula officinalis* 'Art Shades'

◉ *Calendula officinalis* (pot marigold) as part of a mixed annual summer bed.

Coriandrum
C. sativum 'Calypso'

Cymbopogon
C. citratus

Main features Spicy leafy herb; can be harvested many times from one spring sowing
Height 15–20 cm (6–8 in.) **Spread** 15–20 cm (6–8 in.)
Position ○ ◑ **Hardiness** Annual

Main feature A tall grassy clump, with leaves that when crushed, release a strong lemon scent
Height 1.5 m (5 ft) **Spread** 90 cm (3 ft)
Position ○ ◑ **Hardiness** RHS H1c

Varieties of *Coriandrum* selected for producing lots of spicy leaves are the most useful to the home gardener, and of these, *C. sativum* 'Calypso' is the best one to grow. Not only is it slow to seed, but also its growing points are very close to the ground. This means that a single sowing can be cut down and will regrow three to five times – if the potting mix is kept moist – making it brilliant for small spaces. Cut the leaves with scissors when the plants reach around 10 centimetres (4 in.) high, trimming back to 2.5 to 5 centimetres (1–2 in.) above the base of the plants. As 'Calypso' is a cut-and-come-again variety, repeat the cut every month or so. It grows quickly and soon goes over, so freeze batches in ice-cube trays in early summer. 'Calypso' is difficult to grow outside in autumn and winter, but if you really want fresh leaves in winter, you can sow leafy varieties of *C. sativum* year-round in pots on the kitchen windowsill. Another slow-to-bolt variety is 'Confetti'. This has a mild flavour and very fine feathery leaves that make a pretty garnish. **LD**

This half-hardy perennial, known as lemongrass, makes a dense clump of leaves that are sharp and rough to the touch, with robust, cane-like stems that have an intense lemon flavour. In its native tropical climate, it produces clusters of greenish flowers with a reddish tinge in summer. In the garden it can fulfil the same role as any ornamental grass, providing it is given moist soil and full sun with some shade. In regions where temperatures at night fall below 8°C (48°F), grow it in a sturdy pot so it can be moved into a greenhouse. When light levels drop, the plant goes dormant, so it is important to reduce watering to the minimum. Lemongrass is one of the most versatile of herbs. It is central to Asian cuisine, especially Thai, and is used in soups and curries. The best flavour comes from the enlarged white area found at the base of the stems. The leaves make a delicious herbal tea, which will settle an upset stomach, reduce a fever and ease a cough. It can also be used as a relaxant in baths and is added to soaps and perfumes as well as candles for aromatherapy. **AW**

Alternatives

Coriandrum sativum 'Santo', *Coriandrum sativum* 'Lemon'

Alternative

Cymbopogon flexuosus

Foeniculum
F. vulgare 'Purpureum'

Main features Attractive foliage; flowers in summer; medicinal and herbal attributes
Height 2.4 m (8 ft) **Spread** 90 cm (3 ft)
Position ○ ◑ **Hardiness** RHS H4

Bronze fennel has a strong aniseed taste and smell, and the leaves and seeds are used widely to flavour dishes. However, in recent times, it has elevated itself from the herb garden to occupy a position as one of the most valued elements in contemporary perennial planting schemes. In summer it bears sunny-yellow umbels composed of tiny flowers, a mecca for all manner of insects. The purple-bronze feathery leaves that grow in clumps make *F. vulgare* 'Purpureum' easy to use in a mixed scheme, where it provides the perfect foil for large, bold-leaved plants, such as *Cynara cardunculus* or *Macleaya microcarpa* 'Kelway's Coral Plume'. Interplanted with different varieties from the daisy family and spiky flowers, such as *Veronicastrum*, 'Purpureum' forms soft, airy mounds that connect the whole scheme. In low light the transparent, fluffy foliage glows like a hazy cloud above the other plants. This effect will last through the winter months because 'Purpureum' is semi-evergreen and will retain its structure as other perennials die back. **ER**

Alternative

Foeniculum vulgare

Laurus
L. nobilis

Main feature Scented leaves with culinary use
Height 8 m (26 ft) **Spread** 10 m (33 ft)
Position ○ ◑
Hardiness RHS H4

For some, *L. nobilis* (bay) is a clipped piece of topiary outside a front door; for others it is an invaluable culinary herb that provides leaves to infuse food with flavouur throughout the year. Indeed, these varied but invaluable uses are at the heart of its long cultural history. The ancient Greeks celebrated bay, with Apollo decreeing that poets should be decorated with a crown of its glossy leaves; they also hung it over the doorways of the sick to keep away evil and death. Bay was important to the Romans too, and thus to the gardeners of the Italian Renaissance, who appreciated its tight evergreen forms. However, the reason for the enduring success of *L. nobilis* is most probably that it is simply a hardworking garden staple. You will not get much better than this vigorous but compliant evergreen with brittle, lozenge-shaped leaves that release a stunning, strong, sweet odour when snapped. When content, as the bay is most of the time, this splendid plant even produces elegant, cream-coloured flowers too. **LG**

Alternatives

Laurus nobilis 'Aurea', *Laurus nobilis* f. *angustifolia*

Lavandula
L. angustifolia 'Folgate'

Main features Aromatic, grey-green evergreen foliage; dense spikes of fragrant purple-blue flowers
Height 70 cm (28 in.) **Spread** 70 cm (28 in.)
Position ○ ◑ **Hardiness** RHS H5

For the sweetest scent and best flavour, it is best to grow named cultivars of English lavender (*L. angustifolia*). The reliable and very hardy variety 'Folgate' has spiky purple-blue flowers and makes a strong upright plant. It is also versatile and will adapt to some semi-shade as long as the soil is light and well drained. A stalwart of the traditional herb garden and for making folk medicines, such as antiseptic and sedatives, lavender is truly a 'modern' garden plant. It is useful for making mini-hedges or edging, as a container plant, or grown as a specimen plant in sunbaked gravel beds. The plant is valued for its fragrance, long flowering period and silvery foliage. Lavender's nectar-rich flowers are also a magnet to bees and butterflies, making it a very desirable perennial.

Lavender has many culinary uses in both sweet and savoury dishes, however, it is very powerful so use sparingly. A good way to introduce a subtle flavour is to steep a few buds into a carrying ingredient, such as sugar or milk, then discard the buds and use the ingredients as you would normally to make cakes, biscuits or ice cream. Oils and vinegars can also carry the flavour in savoury recipes.

The history of lavender has biblical roots and it has over 2500 years of recorded use, especially as a cure-all, for everything from insomnia and aching backs to insanity. The Romans in particular prized its flowers and used them to fragrance bathwater. According to legend, Cleopatra employed its romantic perfume to seduce Julius Caesar and Mark Antony.

There are plenty of named garden-worthy varieties including 'Hidcote', named for plantsman Laurence Johnston's famous garden in Gloucestershire, and the compact variety 'Munstead' are especially prized for the quality of the essential oil they produce. **AW**

Alternative

Lavandula angustifolia 'Imperial Gem'

Lavandula
L. viridis

Main feature Scented flowers and foliage
Height 75 cm (2.5 ft) **Spread** 75 cm (2.5 ft)
Position ○
Hardiness RHS H3

If you like your lavender purple and to smell of lavender, then this variety is probably not for you. If, however, you hanker after something unusual, then *L. viridis* is a particularly choice lavender that will prove to be a talking point with any visitors to your garden. Firstly, the flowers are not lavender but a pale yellow, almost cream green. Each flower spike is topped with tufty bracts, which resemble those of French lavender (*L. stoechas*). The foliage is similar in form and habit to common lavender, but is much lighter green; not the glaucous shade that we normally associate with most lavenders. It is taller than many other lavenders, reaching up to 75 centimetres (2.5 ft). The scent of both the flowers and the foliage is highly aromatic and has been described as lemony.

We are all aware of lavender's herbal properties, and yellow lavender, *L. viridis*, is no exception. Although this species is not cultivated commercially for its oil, the flowers may still be harvested for scented bags to freshen laundry and wardrobes. Furthermore, the leaves are particularly good added to desserts – they will bring an extra zing without a soapy lavender flavour.

Enjoy the heady fragrance by making sure it is planted somewhere you will brush against it. The yellow and green creates a striking visual contrast when grown alongside the purple and grey of a traditional lavender variety, such as 'Hidcote', 'Folgate' or 'Munstead'. And why stop at yellow? Lavender also comes in pink; for example, *L. angustifolia* 'Loddon Pink', and white, of which *L. × intermedia* 'Alba' is a lovely variety.

Originating from Spain and Portugal, yellow lavender is not as hardy as some other varieties – the tufty bracts are often a clue to lavenders' hardiness. However, this plant will tolerate a short spell of frost to -5°C (23°F) in a free-draining spot. **ER**

Alternative

Lavandula × intermedia 'Alba'

Levisticum
L. officinale

Main features Spicy, fragrant, shiny, green leaves; summer umbels of bee-attracting, tiny, yellowish flowers
Height 90–200 cm (3–7 ft) **Spread** 30–90 cm (1–3 ft)
Position ◐ **Hardiness** RHS H5

Once considered a love potion, lovage is a fresh-faced architectural perennial sweet herb, similar to angelica in dimensions and similarly grown for its fetching foliage and form. For centuries its sweet aromatic leaves were used to flavour food and make herbal tea; the young stems candied or blanched as a vegetable; seeds and roots used to make sweat-inducing cordials. It has since fallen out of favour but deserves to be more widely grown, either in your herb garden or as a foil for flowers in the border.

Lovage prefers a fertile and moist but well-drained soil, though it tolerates other soil conditions if kept well watered. Easy and effortless to grow, simply sow seeds directly where they are to develop, in late autumn or spring. Alternatively divide existing roots in early spring and transplant immediately. Ensure the surrounding area is kept watered and weed free.

Leaves of young plants resemble a flat-leaved parsley whereas the French call it *céleri bâtard*, or false celery, due to its resemblance to celery. Indeed, the taste is not dissimilar to a combination of parsley and celery. The dark, glabrous, green leaves are strongly and spicily perfumed, some say of citrus lime, and impart a hearty flavour to both cold and hot dishes. Harvest leaves fresh before flowering occurs or cut leaves in autumn to dry for winter use. Chopped lovage leaves can replace celery or 'Par-cel' to flavour soups and stews, except in winter when it dies down. Boost flavours further by adding to salads, potatoes, white meats and fish. **IT**

Alternative

Apium graveolens var. *secalinum* 'Par-cel'

Melissa
M. officinalis 'Aurea'

Main features Gold-splashed, lemon-scented leaves; tiny nectar-filled flowers in summer; attracts bees
Height 75 cm (2.5 ft) **Spread** 40 cm (16 in.)
Position ○ ◑ **Hardiness** RHS H5

The leaves of this fragrant, deciduous perennial are variegated green and gold, reverting to pure green in hot weather. They are typically oval shaped, with strong veins and scalloped edges. Minute short hairs dot the surface of the leaves, which when crushed give off a sweet, citrus scent. Tiny, nectar-filled, pale-cream flowers appear in whorls on spikes from midsummer to early autumn. Removing the spent flowers will prevent the plant from self-seeding and becoming invasive, but the ever-expanding clump of roots and shoots will still spread into other plants if not controlled.

Lemon balm grows well in all soils except waterlogged. It is tolerant of drought and unaffected by most pests and diseases. It is a good choice for herb beds and ideal for planting at the front of mixed borders, or close to paths where the decorative foliage, if allowed to billow out, will release its lemony scent when brushed against. Plant it close to sitting areas too, as it is said to repel flies and ants.

The leaves are traditionally used in potpourri and to flavour tea, which has a calming effect. It has long been used to make a tonic that lifts the spirits and also in skin care as an anti-inflammatory. Extract of lemon balm is used in alcoholic beverages and medicinal remedies for insect bites and sores. The ancient Greeks first appreciated its value with keeping honeybees happy. Greeks placed sprigs of lemon balm inside and around their hives to encourage honeybee swarms to stay. **AW**

Alternative

Melissa officinalis 'All Gold'

Mentha
M. × piperita

Main features Distinctive peppermint aroma; red-purplish overtones on foliage; lavender-violet flowers
Height 60–120 cm (2–4 ft) **Spread** 60–90 cm (2–3 ft)
Position ◑ ● **Hardiness** RHS H7

Of the many mints available, peppermint – with its cooling taste and calming aroma – is the most well known and commercially grown. Peppermint has been used medicinally and in cooking for many centuries. It is widely used in chewing gum, confectioneries, shampoos and shower gels, teas, tinctures and toothpastes. Peppermint's soothing and antiseptic properties come from the high level of menthol in its leaves.

Easy to grow, this exuberant plant is the result of a natural cross between water mint (*M. aquatic*) and spearmint (*M. spicata*) and will 'run' given the opportunity. A hardy herbaceous perennial, it survives where few other plants will grow in partial to deep shade. It prefers a deep, fertile, mostly moist soil, but it will grow in a wide range of conditions; soil can become exhausted so replant when vigour is reduced. It is wise to grow it in pots, window boxes or sunken bottomless buckets to contain its spread; regularly dig up runners to pot up and give away. Pinch out growing tips frequently to provide sweet-tasting shoots. Use prudently in the kitchen for cold or hot potato dishes, vinaigrettes, sauces, salads, soft cheeses and dips. Mint jelly made from peppermint melts in your mouth when teamed with lamb. Add sprigs to cold drinks and iced tea for summer refreshment.

Mints are perennials but the flavour of the leaves changes through the year. The leaves are at their peak for harvesting from early summer to early autumn. First, pinch out 2.5 centimetres (1 in.) of the growing tips; this will help the plant bush out. Later, when you want to dry a large quantity or make a batch of mint sauce, cut the plants down to the base. For fresh mint in winter, dig up runners in the autumn and lay them flat in a pot half full of potting mix, add a thin layer of potting mix then keep on an indoor windowsill. **IT**

Alternatives

Mentha × piperata f. *citrata*, *Mentha × piperata* f. *citrata* 'Bergamot'

Mentha
M. spicata 'Kentucky Colonel'

Main features Aromatic, spearmint-scented leaves with culinary uses; flowers in summer; attracts bees
Height 12–24 in. (30–60 cm) **Spread** 12–24 in. (30–60 cm)
Position ○ ◑ **Hardiness** USDA 5

This is an improved variety that can be used in any recipe calling for spearmint, including mint sauce and jelly. It is actually the official herb in the Kentucky Derby's bourbon-based cocktail mint julep, which gave rise to the common name of the cultivar. Most gardeners have no trouble at all growing mint, but they do have trouble containing it. Like all varieties of mint, *M. spicata* 'Kentucky Colonel' spreads vigorously and is best kept in check by continuous harvesting for beverages, jellies, or potpourri. The more it is cut, the more productive it becomes; frequent harvesting maintains the best flavor in the leaves and also suppresses flowering. Growing 'Kentucky Colonel' as a container plant is another recommended strategy for keeping it within bounds.

'Kentucky Colonel' will grow in sun or shade and flourishes where it is damp, yet it will also grow well in dry shade as a ground cover although with less flavorful foliage. However, it is not tolerant of drought. Wherever it is grown, it produces fresh, green, crinkled leaves. If permitted, later in the summer, flower spikes rise sporting white, pink, mauve, or purple flowers that bloom until the fall. All mint flowers are a delight to bees, but remember that the taste of the leaves will suffer if the plant is allowed to flower.

According to Greek mythology Minthe, a nymph adored by Hades, was transformed into a plant by Hades's jealous wife. To ease her banishment Hades gave her an enticing fragrance that would enrapture anyone who might tread upon her. It is also reported that if mint is planted or placed in a pot under a picnic table and then trimmed prior to a picnic, it will repel all manner of annoying insects from the area. Others have suggested that mint planted around the foundation of a house deters rodents. **KK**

Alternatives

Mentha spicata var. *crispa* 'Moroccan', *Mentha spicata* 'Mojito'

Mentha

M. spicata 'Tashkent'

Myrtus

M. communis

Main features Spearmint-scented and flavoured leaves; small, purple-mauve flowers on cylindrical spikes in summer
Height 60 cm (24 in.) **Spread** 45–60 cm (18–24 in.)
Position ◗ **Hardiness** RHS H7

Main features Shrub with glossy, aromatic leaves; fragrant, stamen-packed, white flowers; blue-black berries
Height 1.5–2.4 m (5–8 ft) **Spread** 1.5–2.4 m (5–8 ft)
Position ○ ◗ ● **Hardiness** RHS H4

Mints for tea drinking are often named after a country where mint tea is popular. *M. spicata* 'Tashkent' is a recognised form sold by nurseries. If you find spearmint described as Moroccan mint, it does not mean that it is the best to re-create a drink you might have enjoyed on holiday; a specialist herb nursery and plenty of tastings is the key. *M. spicata* is a perennial with erect stems that bear slightly curled and rounded leaves, with a distinct serrated edge. In summer, light purple-mauve, tubular flowers are produced in interrupted spikes. Like all mints, its creeping rhizomes will spread to make an extensive colony unless the roots are confined. Plant in a sunken, bottomless container in moist soil in partial shade. Never plant two types of mints together, as they readily cross-pollinate to produce plants with inferior flavours. Mint is an excellent remedy for digestion ailments. Use it to make a mint sauce to accompany lamb or add a small amount to chocolate desserts. Today, mint is also a component of deodorants, skin tonics and toothpastes. **AW**

This bushy, evergreen shrub has pointed leaves that when crushed, release a soft aroma of eucalyptus. In summer the plant is cloaked with fragrant white flowers with long gold-tipped stamen that are followed by blue-black berries. A classic shrub for Mediterranean gardens, and found growing wild in dry, warm areas of southern Europe, myrtle is heat, drought and salt tolerant, making it a useful shrub for coastal gardens and as a glossy, evergreen foil for flowering plants in sunny borders with well-draining soil. In a cooler climate, plant it against a sheltered, sunny wall, where it can be clipped to shape. Alternatively, grow it in a sizable container that can be moved indoors in winter. In the kitchen the leaves and berries can be used to flavour stews, soups and pork and game dishes. Adding dried leaves to the barbecue gives food a distinct bay-like flavour. An essential oil from the plant is used in perfumes, soaps and skincare products. In the Mediterranean, myrtle is a symbol of love and is used in wedding bouquets. **AW**

Alternatives

Mentha spicata 'Brundall', *Mentha spicata* var. *crispa*

Alternative

Myrtus communis subsp. *tarentina*

Myrtus communis is an evergreen with fragrant flowers and flavorsome leaves. ➔

Nepeta

N. *cataria* 'Citriodora'

Main features Lemon-scented leaves used in tea;
summer blooms; attracts bees
Height 45 cm (18 in.) **Spread** 45 cm (18 in.)
Position ○ ◑ **Hardiness** RHS H7

Standard *N. cataria* is, of course, common catnip, which is
irresistible to cats. Felines aside, catnip actually has a long
history of human medicinal use and is a delightful sleep
aid when taken as an infusion in tea before bed. Alas, it
has a somewhat foxy flavour that is not always palatable
to humans. Lemon catnip, or *N. cataria* 'Citriodora', on
the other hand, has a citrus fragrance that humans find
much more agreeable.

A herbaceous perennial, lemon catnip is great
grown in containers as it withstands a bit of drought. It
is an excellent companion plant in the kitchen garden
because it is a natural insect repellent. It is known to
deter a number of pests and will protect neighbouring
plants. Interestingly, it is said that rodents are also
repelled by catnip. Plants spread indefinitely by rhizomes
if not controlled and will reseed easily.

Lemon catnip is a slightly smaller plant than common
catnip. The foliage is an apple green rather than glaucous
green. The lemon scent is particularly noticeable on hot
days – one need only brush up against it. 'Citriodora'
is a lovely addition to any tea, even when not used
specifically to induce sleep. Its flowers are rather more
attractive to humans than standard catnip, having more
of a pink or pink-spotted hue. The bees love it, although
they equally adore standard catnip. Grow lemon catnip
for your own enjoyment; however, if you are growing
catnip for feline friends, standard catnip may, in fact, be
the better choice. **KK**

Alternative

Nepeta cataria

Ocimum
O. basilicum 'Genovese'

Main feature Pungent, cup-shaped foliage for use in
salads and for making pesto
Height 20 cm (8 in.) **Spread** 20 cm (8 in.)
Position ○ **Hardiness** RHS H3

Basil is a popular summer herb, and there are now several
ornamental varieties and different flavours. However,
for generous handfuls of this pungent leaf, you want to
grow the classic bush basil *O. basilicum* 'Genovese'. Basil
is very sensitive to frost and cold, damp conditions, and
the best way to get around this is by buying pot plants
in early summer or by sowing a bit later than usual and
placing the containers in warm spots – a deck, patio or
raised up on tabletops, shelves and window boxes –
rather than in soil borders.

Sow seed in pots from midspring onwards and place
them somewhere light and warm, such as a heated
propagator in a greenhouse or on the kitchen windowsill.

Sow three to four seeds in an 8-centimetre-deep (3 in.)
pot to keep root disturbance to a minimum. Pinch out
growing tips when the plants are 15 centimetres (6 in.) tall,
and plant out once the risk of frost has passed. Pinching
out the flower buds will encourage the plant to remain
bushy. Keep the potting mix on the dry side to avoid root
rots and diseases; it is also worth remembering to resow
little and often. Avoid taking too many leaves at one time
from a single plant when they are young. Later, harvest
larger quantities to make pesto, as the plants will die
anyway, when the first frost comes. Small-leaved basil,
such as *O. basilicum* 'Aristotle' can be trimmed to shape,
a bit like a temporary topiary: a pleasant task because
the aroma is lovely. Although the flavour is mild, you can
cut sprigs of whole leaves with scissors for garnish. **LD**

Alternatives

Ocimum basilicum 'Puck', *Ocimum basilicum* 'Green Ruffles'

Ocimum
O. basilicum 'Siam Queen'

Main features Exceptionally decorative large leaves with purple veins; fine flavour
Height 60 cm (24 in.) **Spread** 60 cm (24 in.)
Position ○ **Hardiness** RHS H3

A real head turner, *O. basilicum* 'Siam Queen' has lime-green leaves that contrast with vivid purple stems. If left to flower, the blooms are a bold shade of magenta. It has a fresh citrus aroma with a hint of cloves. The complex basil flavour is tinged with sweet liquorice or aniseed. Each plant develops into a neat bushy clump, making it ideal for container growing or making a statement in a mixed herb garden.

Regarded as far superior to other Thai basils, this award-winning variety has leaves at least twice the size of its rivals. It is ideal for Asian cooking and can be used in curries and stirfries, or as a decorative garnish. The heady fragrance and flavour are stable even at high temperatures, where many other herbs would become bland. Thai basil is distinct from traditional Italian basil (also known as sweet basil) in that it has a less peppery taste. Another advantage is that the leaves are still tasty even when the plant is allowed to flower, although it is best to prevent plants from flowering throughout most of the growing season in order to prolong each plant's life. Simply nip off any buds that appear at the top of the stalks. 'Siam Queen' sets seeds readily and so each spring the volunteer seedlings can be potted up or grown on for a continual supply.

This tender perennial is often grown as an annual. Hailing from tropical climes, 'Siam Queen' needs a sunny spot to really thrive, with a minimum of six to eight hours of sunshine each day. Regularly harvesting the leaves for cooking will help to encourage the plants to form a bushy shape. However, it is important not to remove more than a third of the growing stem at any one time. In Thailand there are three different basils used in national cuisine: holy basil (kaphrao, sometimes also known as Thai basil), Thai basil (horapha) and lemon basil. **PWa/JM**

Alternative

Ocimum basilicum 'Christmas Basil'

Ocimum
'African Blue'

Main features Exceptionally decorative large leaves with purple veins; abundant edible flowers
Height 75 cm (2.5 ft) **Spread** 35 cm (14 in.)
Position ○ **Hardiness** RHS H3

The name of this incredibly decorative basil is slightly misleading. Although it does hail from Africa, the young leaves are, in fact, a rich shade of purple. As they mature they become bright green, but they retain an attractive purple vein. Each leaf can be up to 5 centimetres (2 in.) long, therefore, they are extremely easy to prepare for the kitchen. The abundant flowers can also be a glorious pink-purple, placing them in great demand by chefs as an unusual garnish. They are also delicious scattered over salads or added to cold summer drinks.

Unlike other basils, *Ocimum* 'African Blue' can flower without setting seeds. This is due to the fact that it is a sterile hybrid of two other breeds ('Dark Opal' and 'Camphor'). Although this hybrid has the definite camphor scent of its parent, it also benefits from a very earthy basil flavour, with a spicy tang of rosemary and clove. It combines well with tomatoes, if used in small quantities in Italian dishes such as pasta and pizza.

The nectar-rich flowers are extremely popular with bees and butterflies. The fragrant flower spikes can grow up to 25 centimetres (10 in.) long. Very long lasting when cut, these are ideal for use in flower arrangements. Taller than most other basils, 'African Blue' is an ideal choice for the back of a herb border, as it is a vigorous grower and makes a great backdrop for other plants. Its highly decorative nature means that it can also be planted in pots on a patio. Caution must be taken when selecting pots, however. What looks like a tiny cutting can soon blossom into a verdant bush, so it is important to select large pots at least 35 centimetres (14 in.) in diameter. Some gardeners report that the strong camphor scent deters pests, therefore where space permits, it can be grown as a good companion plant for green beans and tomatoes. **PWa/JM**

Alternative

Ocimum × africanum

Origanum
O. majorana

Main feature Attracts bees
Height 60 cm (24 in.) **Spread** 60 cm (24 in.)
Position ○ ◑
Hardiness RHS H3

Although it holds its leaves throughout the year, there is something delightfully summery about *O. majorana*, or sweet marjoram, as it is also known. It is so warm and pleasant as to induce thoughts of bare feet on sun-baked hillsides, even if the plant is being picked from a small inner-city back garden. Its flavour is delightful in pasta sauces, but also adds a cheerful surprise to salads. However, this little plant is not only for gastronomic enjoyment. The ancient Greeks, for example, used it to cure narcotic poisoning, rheumatism and depression, whereas in eighteenth-century England it played its part in ornamental plantings alongside *Dianthus* and *Lavandula*. Today, *O. majorana* is a frequent player in horticultural endeavours. It has justified its place in the kitchen, but behaves nicely in the garden, too, where it not only enjoys soaking up the sun nestled into a patio, but also lends its bright leaves to liven up any gaps in a flower border, complementing pinks and purples in particular. **LG**

Alternatives

Origanum vulgare 'Aureum', *Origanum vulgare*

Petroselinum
P. crispum var. *crispum*

Main features Feathery, pepper-tasting, dark-green foliage; attracts bees, birds and butterflies
Height 45–60 cm (18–24 in.) **Spread** 30–45 cm (12–18 in.)
Position ◑ ●   **Hardiness** RHS H4

There is more to moss parsley (also known as curled parsley) than its curly good looks. Once used only to garnish dishes, it is seen as one of the best sources of iron and multiple vitamins. Its role as a garnish originated from the belief that chewing parsley leaves at the end of a meal both refreshed a diner and freshened their breath. The thickly curled leaves are so named for their resemblance to a mass of moss, and many cultivars exist today. 'Moss Curled' was one of the first to receive a Royal Horticultural Society Award of Garden Merit; other cultivars include 'Astra' with a tall uniform upright habit; 'Bravour' (pictured), a reliable cropper with curled leaves; 'Curlina', tightly curled, compact, and uniform; 'Frison' has tightly curled, almost double, deep-green leaves; and 'Marunka' forms a neat dome of tightly curled leaves. In practice, there is little difference in flavour, although the taste of moss parsley is not as dominant as flat-leaved parsley and is used in a variety of cuisines and dishes. **IT**

Alternative

Syn. *Petroselinum hortense*

Petroselinum

P. crispum var. neapolitanum

Main feature Flat-leaved leafy, flavourful herb
Height 45 cm (18 in.) **Spread** 20 cm (8 in.)
Position ○ ◐
Hardiness RHS H3

Flat-leaved parsley is viewed by many chefs as the finest culinary parsley: the mature leaves are an excellent flavouring for stocks, and the younger ones can be used chopped in salads. Leaves can stay fresh for two or more weeks if stored in an air-tight container in the refrigerator, although home gardeners can simply go out and pick more. Parsley freezes well too, so washed leaves can be chopped finely and frozen in ice-cube trays with a little water or olive oil. Alternatively, the large flat leaves dry very easily if bunches are hung up in a well-ventilated space. Once the leaves are completely dehydrated, they can be crumbled into glass jars to store for future use. Flat-leaved parsley is usually grown as an annual. It works well in a container, which keeps mud off the foliage, and even a small pot will yield useful leaves. For the largest plants, for preserving, grow *P. crispum* var. *neapolitanum* in a bed or border in a moist compost with some shade. Once the plant flowers, the leaves become bitter. **PWa/JM**

Alternative

Petroselinum crispum var. *crispum* 'Italian Giant'

Rosmarinus

R. officinalis 'Green Ginger'

Main features Distinct ginger-flavoured leaves; small pale-blue summer flowers; attracts bees; upright habit
Height 60–90 cm (2–3 ft) **Spread** 30–60 cm (12–24 in.)
Position ○ **Hardiness** RHS H4

If you love the smell of fresh ginger, plant *R. officinalis* 'Green Ginger' rosemary close to where you can brush it to release its delicious scent. It is an exotic variation on traditional rosemary. This cultivar is variably winter hardy; plant it in a sheltered spot, in full sun, and well-drained but moist soil; or in a pot that can be brought under cover for winter. Although it is reasonably drought tolerant, over winter ensure it never dries out or stands in water. Flowers, formed on the previous season's wood, are pale blue with darker stripes and central white markings arising from the throat. It forms a compact, upright shrub that is at home in a herb garden or at the base of a warm, sunny wall. Pinch plant shoots regularly during the growing season to promote steady new growth for culinary use. Steep 'Green Ginger' rosemary sprigs in olive oil and use to make an unusual salad dressing; otherwise, use in cooking as with other rosemaries, with meats, potatoes and in breads and herb butters. **IT**

Alternative

Rosmarinus officinalis 'Roseus'

Rosmarinus
R. officinalis 'Arp'

Main features Intense, sweetly fragrant leaves; attracts bees; companion plant for a range of vegetables
Height 90–180 cm (3–6 ft) **Spread** 60–120 cm (2–4 ft)
Position ○ **Hardiness** RHS H4

Bill Arp was the pen-name of nineteenth-century humourist Charles Henry Smith, an American writer from Georgia. Named for him is the tiny Texas town of Arp, where this cold-tolerant rosemary was discovered by respected herb pioneer and 'Grand Dame of Herbs', Madalene Hill, one snowy day in January 1972. Past president of the Herb Society of America and coauthor of *Southern Herb Growing*, her quest was to educate people on the use of herbs. Considered radical at the time, she used herbs in her cooking – a practice we take for granted today. As gardeners growing 'Arp' rosemary we honour the memory of the woman who facilitated the introduction of herbs for both culinary and landscape purposes to the US public at large. The cultivar *R. officinalis* 'Arp' allowed rosemary finally to be overwintered in northern gardens.

'Arp' rosemary is a very hardy, dense shrub with an upright form, fine needle-like leaves, and pale blue-violet flowers. It thrives in full sun in well-drained soil that is neutral to alkaline; try to manage a balance so that rosemary plants never dry out completely and never stand in water. Grow in pots, the landscape or use for informal hedging, lightly clipping after flowering. Originating from a Mediterranean coastal habitat, this plant enjoys the sea air. Historically, rosemary has both romantic and remembrance associations. It is the symbol of fidelity for lovers and was used at weddings and worn entwined in the bride's wreath; sprigs were also given out at funerals.

The leaves of rosemary contain pungent, volatile oils that are released with heat, making this a great herb for barbecues, roasted meats and vegetables. Vinaigrettes, rosemary jellies, herb butters and rosemary ciabattas are just a few of the recipes suited to this herb, which can be used either fresh or dried. **IT**

Alternatives

Rosmarinus officinalis 'Hill Hardy'

Salvia
S. elegans 'Golden Delicious'

Main features Pineapple-flavoured, bright-golden
foliage; vivid, red flowers in late summer and early autumn
Height 30–120 cm (12–48 in.) **Spread** 30–90 cm (12–36 in.)
Position ○ **Hardiness** RHS H3

This golden-leaved pineapple sage lights up the
landscape wherever it is planted – preferably in full sun.
Illuminate your garden with this triple treat – fabulous
foliage, flaming flowers and a flavoursome food. *S. elegans*
'Golden Delicious' (or golden pineapple sage) is a star
herb and a must-have plant that should find a place in
every garden. Autumn-flowering scarlet flowers float
above silky-haired, limey-yellow foliage and attract the
attention of visiting birds, bees and butterflies. This
cultivar's high visibility and nectar levels will especially
appeal to hummingbirds, and red is their favourite colour.
If you live in a region where hummingbirds visit, plant
a perch nearby for the males to guard this important
source of food in your garden.

Native to Mexico, this sage is not winter hardy;
grow it in a pot to be taken indoors if frost is likely, or
use annually in borders and overwinter plants for the
following year. Choose a warm site with neutral, well-
drained but moist soil, and, unusually for a sage, keep
well-watered throughout summer. Plant in full sun unless
in your region the sun is so strong that the leaves are
scorched, in which case half a day of sun is preferable.
As a tender perennial, overwinter in colder climes or
try it in sharply drained soil in warm regions to see if it
regenerates herbaceously the following year.

'Golden Delicious' pineapple sage is so named for
its colourful and tasty, tropical-smelling fruity leaves,
specifically the scent of pineapple. It is not a herb that
you can purchase at a store, so to enjoy it grow it yourself.
. Impress your dinner guests with grilled goat's cheese
on a bed of salad leaves garnished in the edible crimson
flowers interspersed with leaves of warm golden sage.
Pineapple sage is also useful in smoothies and iced tea.
The leaves and flowers can be dried for potpourri too. **IT**

Alternatives

Salvia rutilans, *Salvia elegans* 'Frieda Dixon'

Salvia

S. *officinalis* 'Berggarten'

Main features Pungent grey-green leaves; early to midsummer fragrant flowers; attracts bees and butterflies
Height 30–90 cm (12–36 in.) **Spread** 30–90 cm (12–36 in.)
Position ○ **Hardiness** RHS H4

The cultivar name 'Berggarten' means 'mountain garden' and refers to an historic German royal vegetable garden created in 1666. The garden was one of Europe's early breeding stations, and this superior, large-leaved, compact cultivar of common sage was one of its lasting legacies. 'Berggarten' is particularly useful for culinary purposes, having broader leaves than more common types, but it is also excellent for medicinal uses. *Salvia* means 'to be saved', referring to its therapeutic traits.

Sage is highly variable from seed, but this cultivar yields the most practical form to grow in a kitchen garden. A well-behaved herb, 'Berggarten' forms a uniquely compact, evergreen subshrub, bearing dark violet-blue flowers in summer that attract an array of beneficial insects. It enjoys a sunny, dry position in neutral to alkaline soil; it is drought tolerant, so avoid overly wet conditions. On hot sunny days its distinct aroma fills the air while crushed leaves emit a pleasantly antiseptic scent. 'Berggarten' is low maintenance; merely cut back stems every spring until the flower stems form, to induce fresh new leaves for cutting. Take cuttings when the plant becomes too woody, which happens less frequently than with the common form.

Use fresh leaves to make infusions of tea, sage butter or add to a stuffing for poultry and pork. For beekeepers, sage honey is considered a delicacy. It is said not to crystallise, and sweetens dishes without imparting a honey flavour. **IT**

Alternatives

Salvia officinalis 'Purpurascens', *Salvia officinalis* 'Tricolor'

Salvia
S. officinalis 'Purpurascens'

Main feature Purple-tinted fragrant leaves
Height 60 cm (24 in.) **Spread** 60 cm (24 in.)
Position ○
Hardiness RHS H5

Few plants tick as many boxes as *S. officinalis* 'Purpurascens', or purple sage, as it is also known. This modest plant requires almost no looking after, apart from making sure that it does not get waterlogged feet, and giving it a good haircut once a year to keep it fresh. In return it will furnish the garden with year-round foliage with a gorgeous purple tint that turns grey-green as it gets older. Moreover, 'Purpurascens' will scent the garden beautifully if you brush past its soft and slightly furry leaves. When in a good mood in midsummer, it produces long, simple, purple flowers as a bonus.

These visual attributes make it an extremely worthy garden plant in itself, but as a medicinal herb, purple sage has a phenomenal number of applications, from suppressing perspiration to relieving depression and use as an antiseptic. Historically, the ancient Egyptians used purple sage to promote fertility, and seventeenth-century English apothecary Nicholas Culpeper wrote of it helping to fight off the plague: 'The juice of Sage drank with vinegar, hath been of good use in time of plague at all times.' In the kitchen it is one of our culinary stalwarts and makes a lovely complement to pork and goose in particular.

In addition, an untrumpeted skill of 'Purpurascens' is that the strong flavour and smell of its leaves are amongst the few things that put off slugs and snails, so planting a purple sage next to your courgettes will do wonders for pest control – quite the trooper. **LG**

Alternatives

Salvia officinalis, Salvia fulgens

Satureja
S. hortensis

Main features Fragrant hairy leaves with culinary and medicinal uses; pale-lilac flowers; attracts bees
Height 20–30 cm (8–12 in.) **Spread** 30–45 cm (12–18 in.)
Position ○ **Hardiness** RHS H4

Published in 1672, John Josselyn wrote in his book *New-England's Rarities*, 'I shall now ... give you to understand what English herbs we have growing in our gardens that prosper there as well', and he listed summer savoury (*S. hortensis*) as one of these. He insightfully described the effect of the first English settlers on local Native American society, as well as the local flora and fauna.

Summer savoury is thought to have been brought to America by these English settlers, to whom it was officially recorded as introduced via Italy in 1562. However, it was probably used as early as the first century by Roman occupiers who cooked it with meat. Savoury has been in use for many centuries; especially if we consider Jacob served Isaac his father 'savoury food' from Esau's game (Genesis 27:4). The word 'savoury' comes from 'savour' and is used to describe a plant of the genus *Satureja*. *S. hortensis* and *S. montana* in particular are used in cookery.

Summer savoury is an annual sweet herb, best grown from fresh seed each year in spring, with further sowings to increase availability. Direct ground sow or use in containers, but keep both regularly watered. It thrives in a well-drained, light but rich, fertile soil in full sun; keep watered throughout the season.

As with other aromatic sweet herbs, summer savoury can be used fresh to flavour white meat and fish dishes or it can be used dried for stuffing and as part of a bouquet garni in soups and stews. As a tea it is said to be beneficial for sore throats. Using scissors, snip the top growth regularly. Summer savoury will enhance the flavour of freshly steamed beans, particularly broad beans. Summer savoury rubbed on bee or wasp stings is thought to give prompt relief, as it contains an essential oil known to have antiseptic properties. **IT**

Alternatives

Satureja montana, Satureja montana citriodora, Satureja montana subsp. *illyrica, Satureja spicigera*

Thymus
Coccineus Group

Main features Spicy, fragrant leaves; summer flowers; attracts bees and butterflies; can be used as a 'lawn'
Height 2.5–5 cm (1–2 in.) **Spread** 30–45 cm (12–18 in.)
Position ○ **Hardiness** RHS H5

Shakespeare wrote in *A Midsummer Night's Dream*: 'I know a bank where the wild thyme grows', referring to where Titania, queen of the fairies, slept. Pillows stuffed with thyme were once considered therapeutic to sleep on and gardeners used to plant a bed of creeping thyme as a home for fairies, legend declaring the fairies would come and eat tiny cakes if left there on Midsummer Night.

Indeed, creeping thyme, with flowers of the prettiest pink purple, not only creates the best incentive for our fairy friends to visit but can form a fragrant alternative to a grass lawn or scented path. An ornamental carpet of evergreen creeping thyme is lower maintenance and more drought tolerant than grass, particularly in drier, hotter conditions reminiscent of its Mediterranean origins. This procumbent thyme is suited to cascading over walls; you can also plant it in a rock garden, in clay pots top-dressed with gravel, or use it as underplanting to roses. Vegetable growers sometimes dot plants around the allotment to discourage detrimental bugs. Gardeners will find this creeping thyme easy to grow from seed, cuttings or young plants; the deep pink-purple flowers smother the foliage so that the dark-green leaves can remain hidden for several months. It thrives in a well-drained, light to sandy soil in full sun; it likes alkaline soils but dislikes excess moisture. Weed around plants until thyme is established and trim lightly after flowering. Pelleted chicken manure in spring will keep plants fed.

One of the French *fines herbes*, creeping thyme can be cut with scissors to include in a bouquet garni for use in French and other dishes, such as clam chowder, salads and meats in general. Thyme tea has antioxidant properties and is easily made by steeping fresh leaves in boiling water for ten minutes. **IT**

Alternative

Syn. *Thymus serpyllum coccineus* 'Minor'. *Thymus serpyllum* 'Pink Chintz'

Thymus

T. *vulgaris*

Main feature Edible leaves with strong scent
Height 30 cm (12 in.) **Spread** 30 cm (12 in.)
Position ○
Hardiness RHS H5

According to seventeenth-century apothecary Nicholas Culpeper, *T. vulgaris* is a fearsome, multipurpose beast: 'It is a noble strengthener of the lungs, as notable a one as grows; neither is there scarce a better remedy growing for that disease in children which they commonly call the Chin-cough, than it is. It purges the body of phlegm, and is an excellent remedy for shortness of breath. It kills worms in the belly, and being a notable herb of Venus, provokes the terms, gives sage and speedy delivery to women in travail, and brings away the after birth.' In the garden, *T. vulgaris* is a humble soul, growing low to the ground with tiny, oval, grey-green leaves and clusters of even tinier purple, pink, or white flowers that arrive in the early-summer heat. It shouts even less about its requirements, growing in most well-drained soils as long as there is sun, without taking up too much space or demanding attention. However, this plant really does require full sun and will not be fobbed off with a partially shaded position.

Truthfully, *T. vulgaris* is not simply a low-maintenance, evergreen perennial that gardeners should grow at some point in their lifetime. Rather, it is such a trouble-free and unfussy plant that it seems ridiculous not to grow it all the time. Which other plant fills garden gaps as obligingly, and with such a lovely scent, while also flavouring soups and stews so delightfully? Fortunately, it would seem that gardeners from across the world and through many generations have reached the same conclusion, because thyme has been grown by them all: from scholar Al-Biruni in the eleventh-century Persian desert, to botanist and garden writer Girolamo Fiorenzuola in sixteenth-century Italy, to Charles, Prince of Wales, in his well-known Thyme Walk at Highgrove in Gloucestershire. **LG**

Alternatives

Thymus 'Highdown', *Thymus citriodorus* 'Aureus', *Thymus vulgaris* 'Compactus'

Thymus vulgaris has low-growing leaves that can be kept clean with a gritty mulch over soil. ➔

Thymus
'Silver Queen'

Main features Lemon-scented leaves with culinary uses; flowers in summer; attracts bees and butterflies
Height 20–30 cm (8–12 in.) **Spread** 30–45 cm (12–18 in.)
Position ○ ◑ **Hardiness** RHS H5

This evergreen hardy perennial is lemon scented and one of the most useful herbs for cooking, cleaning and medicines. Its small, ovate grey-green leaves are edged with silvery white, and clusters of lilac-pink summer flowers also make it a great garden plant for a container or planting out. For the cook it is easiest to grow thyme in a pot so that it is near to hand, but this cultivar makes a good garden plant, too. For example, the low-spreading habit, and the delicious citrus scent that the leaves release when they are crushed, make it an ideal ground cover and alternative to a lawn for a sunny, well-drained site. Or plant in gravel and between slabs and stones. Other options include a rock garden or the front of a border and in a formal herb bed it lends itself to clipping and shaping.

Thyme flowers are attractive to honeybees and butterflies, yet the plant's strong aroma is also said to repel many insects, including greenfly, making it worth trying as a companion plant for vegetables and ornamentals, such as roses. Thyme thrives in sun and even drought conditions, although it will tolerate partial shade. A well-drained, chalky, even slightly deprived soil is ideal. Too rich a soil, and plants will become leggy.

In the ancient world, thyme was used by the Greeks in massage oil to give them courage, and by the Romans to give them vigour. Ancient Egyptians employed it in embalming. Generally, thyme is steeped in folklore and superstition. During the Middle Ages, for example, it was thought that having thyme in your garden would attract fairies. Burning sprigs of thyme indoors was believed to cleanse and provide protection against the plague. Even today, thyme is still used as a therapeutic herb, and it features in many disinfectants and antiseptics used to treat infections. Thyme is a versatile culinary herb, popular in Mediterranean, Italian and French cuisines. **AW**

Alternatives

Thymus vulgaris 'Silver Posie', *Thymus vulgaris* 'Silver Needle'

Tropaeolum
T. majus 'Blue Pepe'

Main features Peppery flavour; highly decorative; easy to grow from seeds
Height 30 cm (12 in.) **Spread** 30 cm (12 in.)
Position ○ ◑ **Hardiness** Annual

Given that nasturtium leaves are very tasty and contain around ten times as much vitamin C as lettuce, it is surprising that these plants are not grown more often for use in salads and sandwiches. However, *T. majus* 'Blue Pepe' has been bred specifically as a culinary variety. The glaucous (blue-green) foliage is a delightful contrast to the deep-orange blooms, and the flowers, buds, leaves and seed are all edible and nutritious.

The strong peppery leaves are perfect for adding a welcome kick to drab dishes and will have a spicier flavour when grown in hot, sunny conditions. Very young leaves taste a little like raw onion with a hint of garlic, and for garnishes it is best to pick the leaves when they are small and unblemished. The flowers make an excellent addition to a garnish too, and with a core that has a distinctly honeyed flavour, they are sweet enough for children to enjoy. The buds and seeds can be sprinkled over salads or pickled to make a tangy jam.

Unlike some salad leaves, 'Blue Pepe' is incredibly easy to grow and will be happy in sun or partial shade. It even copes well with hot, dry weather when many other leafy vegetables would bolt. Perhaps best of all, it is decorative enough to be grown in patio pots, on windowsills, or even in hanging baskets. It can be trained to climb up trellis at the back of a border if space is tight. It is so easy to grow that new plants are likely to emerge every spring from seeds set the previous fall. The seedlings can be eaten as baby leaves, potted up to give to friends or grown in any suitable site. If preferred, plants can be prevented from setting seeds by deadheading the flowers before they get a chance to develop the big round seed. For a continuous crop of baby leaves, keep sowing a few plants every two to three weeks during spring and summer. **PWa/JM**

Alternative

This is the only blue-green nasturtium bred as a salad leaf.

Valeriana
V. officinalis

Main features White to lavender-pink flowers in late spring to early summer; fragrant flowers
Height 90 cm (3 ft) **Spread** 90 cm (3 ft)
Position ○ ◑ **Hardiness** RHS H7

Valerian is an old-fashioned, cottage and herb garden plant that has a storied past – it is said that the Pied Piper used valerian root to lure rats out of Hamelin. Its name comes from the Latin for strength and health, and its pulverised roots have a long history of medicinal and herbal use as a mild relaxant going back to the Romans, and are said to bring the same joy to cats as catnip.

As an ornamental, however, valerian is attractive for its umbels of exceptionally fragrant white to light lavender-pink flowers, which appear in early to midsummer and are a lovely addition to mixed bouquets. The fragrance has been alternately described as vanilla or almond; it has the benefit of carrying for a long distance and can scent an entire garden. Many gardeners refuse to be without this heritage plant because its lovely fragrance scents the air in time to make late-spring or early-summer chores more pleasurable.

Plants grow about 90 centimetres (3 ft) tall from a basal rosette of deeply incised, ferny leaves. It is best to deadhead to avoid unwanted seeding. After flowering, the ferny foliage maintains a neat appearance in the border if the flowering stalk is cut down to the basal rosette. Valerian is easy to grow, thrives in almost any soil, and needs no support when given plenty of sun. It is also useful for the organic gardener, for the flowers attract pollinators and beneficial insects whereas the roots have the ability to fix phosphorus levels in the soil to the benefit of neighbouring plants. **KK**

Alternative

Valeriana officinalis subsp. *sambucifolia*

Wasabia
W. japonica

Main features Complex hot mustard flavour from stems; best eaten fresh
Height 15 cm (6 in.) **Spread** 35 cm (14 in.)
Position ● **Hardiness** RHS H4

Wasabi needs regular attention and highly specific conditions to grow well. What is more, plants take two years to mature from seed. The fact it is so tricky to cultivate means that it is very expensive to buy. However, to experience the best possible wasabi flavour, it must be eaten fresh. Thus, green-fingered devotees of Japanese food make the effort to grow this delicious herb-vegetable. The thick, fragrant stems are typically grated to form a paste. If left uncovered, this paste starts to lose its pungent tanginess around fifteen minutes after preparation. For this reason, many of the more exclusive restaurants only prepare the paste after the customer has ordered it.

Much of the paste that is labelled as 'wasabi-flavoured' is, in fact, made with horseradish, as this plant is easier to cultivate commercially and considerably cheaper. Although horseradish has a similar taste, wasabi has a more complex hot flavour caused by volatile compounds. This heat quickly dissipates, leaving a sweet tang. Fresh wasabi is a delicate shade of pale green. The vivid-green paste often seen in shops is usually created with dyes.

Although it is the stems that are usually grated fresh or dried to be ground into powder, the leaves are also spicy and can be enjoyed in salads or stirfries. They are traditionally pickled in sake brine or soy sauce, to be eaten with rice. Leaves can be harvested within a year of growing the plant, but the stems take at least eighteen months to mature. **PWa/JM**

Alternatives

Wasabia japonica 'Daruma', *Wasabia japonica* 'Mazuma'

The satisfaction of growing your own food is immense; the benefits of fresh, healthy produce are even greater. There are lots of possible crops a gardener could grow, but we have concentrated here on a few nuggets to give you a taste of the range out there, which is far greater than that available in any supermarket. We have quick-growers, tasty treats and a mix of the latest varieties with some heritage varieties to which those who buy their vegetables do not have access.

You do not need a large area to grow your own food: food plants can be grown in containers on the patio, fitted in amongst ornamental plants, or grown intensively in raised beds measuring as little as 1.2 by 1.2 metres (4 x 4 ft). It is amazing how productive a small space can be. Most vegetable crops are annuals, so you can keep replanting them after they have been harvested.

VEGETABLES

⊙ *Cucurbita pepo* 'Romanesco' is a reliable Italian heritage variety that is productive and attractive.

Allium

A. ampeloprasum var. *porrum* 'Lincoln'

Main features Very hardy baby leek; can also be grown to full size
Height 20–45 cm (8–18 in.) **Spread** 15 cm (6 in.)
Position ○ ◑ **Hardiness** RHS H6

A breakthrough in Dutch breeding has led to this gourmet baby leek, which is delicious enough to eat raw. If picked when pencil thin, it is mild and crisp, making it perfect as a crudité or in salads. Lightly cooked, it adds a subtle flavour and crunch to stirfries or barbecues, and it is also popular in soups, vegetable dishes and sauces. Additionally, it can be used as a decorative garnish for savoury dishes. This variety has an attractive appearance, with a long, white shank and pale-green foliage.

Baby leeks are ready to eat at around fifty days. Since the baby leeks mature so quickly, they can be sown in succession in order to produce a constant supply of tender young crops. Ideally, sow a new row of leeks every two weeks or so for months of fresh pickings. Seeds are sown close together, and one option is to harvest three out of every four baby leeks per row at regular intervals. This will give the remaining leeks in each row the space to grow on to reach adult size. 'Lincoln' is a disease-resistant variety that is open pollinated and fast growing. It is a dual-purpose leek and can be grown on to maturity. After around twelve weeks, plants reach the girth of a typical leek. They are hardy enough to stand in the ground for many weeks – withstanding frost and snow – and therefore offer gardeners an extremely long harvesting period. While still milder than many other leeks, 'Lincoln' has a more intense flavour upon reaching maturity, making it ideal for traditional favourites, such as Vichyssoise. **PWa/JM**

Alternative

Allium ampeloprasum var. *porrum* 'King Richard'

Allium

A. cepa 'Jermor'

Main features Long bulbs; easier to peel than round
varieties; exceptional flavour
Height 30 cm (12 in.) **Spread** 15 cm (6 in.)
Position ○ **Hardiness** RHS H6

Shallots are prized by cooks for their superior flavour.
Despite being more expensive than onions to buy in the
shops, they are easy to grow yourself and store better
than onions. Shallots tend to be smaller and milder than
traditional onions and have twice the vitamin C; they
also contain more flavonoids and phenols. 'Jermor' is
thought by many chefs to have the finest taste of all. It
is a 'longue' shallot, meaning that it is more banana-
shaped than typical round varieties. Although it was bred
in the southern Rhône Valley of France, it is hardy enough
to grow in northern areas of the United Kingdom.

'Jermor' has good-sized bulbs that are less fiddly to
prepare than many other shallots. They have an attractive,
almost shiny, coppery-coloured skin that contrasts with
the pink-tinged, white flesh. These good looks and their
uniform shape and size make them a favourite with
exhibitors. 'Jermor' is an ideal cultivar for autumn
planting and will yield much heavier crops if overwintered
in the ground. Each bulb that is planted soon bulks up
and starts to form several offsets. A fully grown plant will
yield a neat clump of around eight bulbs. Plants are
shallow rooted and must be watered regularly, but take
care not to overwater them, due to rot.

This variety is an excellent keeper. Harvest the bulbs
when 75 per cent of the plant top dries and begins to
droop. The bulbs should then be stored in an airy and
dry spot until the tops are completely dry. They can then
be stored in a cool place for several months. **PWa/JM**

Alternative

Allium cepa 'Simiane'

Allium

A. fistulosum
'White Lisbon'

Main features Quick-growing onion flavour; good for a small space
Height 15–25 cm (6–10 in.) **Spread** 2.5 cm (1 in.)
Position ○ **Hardiness** RHS H4

You may be forgiven for thinking onions are crude everyday vegetables, but when grown less for their fully grown bulbs and more as spring onions, these familiar stalwarts become little gems of delight. They can be planted successionally from early summer to autumn, from tiny black seeds directly in the bed where they are to grow. After only a fortnight tiny green needles will pierce their way through the soil. Wait a few more weeks and you will reliably have handfuls of crisp, sweet onion stalks that can be used in stirfries or salads. Unlike many vegetables, the ones you harvest at home will look as pristine as those you can buy. Growing salad onions is ideal for those with the desire to grow food but not much space, as even in a patch of earth no bigger than a footprint, a dozen salad onions can be squeezed quite happily. 'White Lisbon' is one of the oldest cultivars and is still the most popular. Red-purple-tinted cultivars are also available. **LG**

Alternative

Allium fistulosum 'Deep Purple'

Allium

A. sativum
'Solent Wight'

Main features A garlic yielding medium-sized bulbs; exceptional flavour; stores well
Height 12–18 in. (30–45 cm) **Spread** 6–10 in. (15–25 cm)
Position ○ **Hardiness** RHS H6

This is a classic cultivar with large, pure-white bulbs. The individual cloves are cream coloured with a slight hint of pink at their bases. They have hard, dense flesh, which is ideal for slicing and chopping. Best of all, 'Solent Wight' offers a delicious flavour and an elegant aroma that is retained even after cooking, making it the chef's choice for slow-cooked dishes, such as stews and casseroles. A softneck garlic, 'Solent Wight' has long stems that are easy to plait into ropes. Hung up in a well-ventilated place, these garlic plaits are decorative and convenient for storage. Originating from the Isle of Wight, 'Solent Wight' is an exceptional all-rounder, offering heavy yields of up to eighteen cloves per bulb. It is hardy and well suited to areas that have cold, wet winters. 'Solent Wight' can even be grown in large containers. Although all garlic varieties need regular watering and rich, freely draining soil, this cultivar requires less maintenance than other types, making it a good choice for beginners. **PWa/JM**

Alternative

Allium sativum 'Germidour'

● *Allium fistulosum* (salad onions) are also available with red-purple skins.

Allium

A. sativum var. *ophioscorodon* 'Lautrec Wight'

Main features Exceptional flavour; decorative bulbs; ideal for exhibition
Height 60 cm (24 in.) **Spread** 15 cm (6 in.)
Position ○ **Hardiness** RHS H6

France is world renowned for the quality of its garlic and *A. sativum* var. *ophioscorodon* 'Lautrec Wight' – originally from near Toulouse in the southwest region – is widely regarded as the finest-tasting cultivar of all. Although not as large as some other bulbs, it has a strong, creamy flavour with no hint of bitterness, making it ideal for culinary dishes in which cloves are baked in their skins and eaten whole. The richly aromatic cloves are also extremely popular and flavoursome when sliced or crushed and can be added to an extensive range of savoury dishes, breads, soups and salads.

The bulbs have smooth, white skin, with subtle, vertical, pink stripes, and each clove has a deep-pink, papery coating. It is suitable for both autumn and spring planting, and although it is an undemanding hardy bulb, it does not perform well when planted in heavy soil. If this is the case, plant the bulbs in a raised bed. 'Lautrec Wight' is often referred to as a hardneck garlic. The 'hardneck' is actually a flowering stalk that should be snapped off as soon as it appears. This edible stalk is delicious in soups or stirfries. Removing it encourages the plant to put all its energy into the bulbs and can therefore double the size of the yield. Hardneck garlics often have stronger flavours and larger cloves than softneck cultivars, but they cannot be stored for as long.

The plants should be harvested as soon as the leaves start to turn yellow, because the bulbs start to open up if harvesting is delayed. This is the reason that 'Lautrec Wight' does not last very well in storage. However, if allowed to dry off thoroughly in a bright, airy location, the bulbs can be stored in a dry place at room temperature for many weeks. Avoid storing garlic in a very cold place because this replicates winter conditions and actually encourages it to try and sprout. **PWa/JM**

Alternatives

Allium sativum var. *ophioscorodon* 'Red Sicilian',
Allium sativum var. *ophioscorodon* 'Chesnok Wight'

Asparagus
A. officinalis

Main features Delicately flavoured edible spears; attractive airy foliage; herbaceous perennial
Height 1.8 m (6 ft) **Spread** 1.2 m (4 ft)
Position ○ ◑ **Hardiness** RHS H3

This attractive herbaceous perennial has never dipped in popularity since it was enjoyed by the ancient Romans, having originated on the steppes of Eastern Europe and the Mediterranean coast. In the wild it grows in temperate grassland, dunes and heaths. However, it can be a tricky vegetable to cultivate. Essentially, this is an issue of time, patience and deference to the plant. Asparagus crowns can be easily purchased from any number of nurseries, but before they can be planted, the gardener must spend an inordinate amount of time painstakingly preparing a bed for this horticultural treasure, as it must not be obliged to compete with troublesome perennial weeds.

Then once the crowns are in their suitably luxurious bed, you must wait. You must wait for not one season, but two or even three. During the springs of this time, if you are on track, tempting spears will push themselves through the ground and wave their delicious heads at you, but you must not harvest them. Asparagus spears must be allowed two or three interminable rounds of taunting before you may take a knife and slice them down and then take them triumphantly to the kitchen to be steamed and eaten with butter. Even mature plants need to have some spears left to grow to full size (pictured) to sustain these perennial plants.

For many gardeners there are few pleasures greater than growing your own food, and it stands to reason that the more delicious the food, the greater the pleasure in growing it. This is undoubtedly part of the reason why we remain so determined to grow asparagus, despite the obstacles in our way, but perhaps the other is that the harder it is to grow, the more determined we are to succeed. Give it a go, and emerge triumphant. Protect asparagus beds with fleece during hard frost. **LG**

Alternatives

Asparagus officinalis 'Connover's Colossal', *Asparagus officinalis* 'Gijnlim', *Asparagus officinalis* 'Lucullus'

Beta

B. vulgaris
'Burpee's Golden'

Main features Distinctive root colours; heritage varieties; good for salad use or cooking; crops in as few as ten weeks
Height 30 cm (12 in.) **Spread** 15 cm (6 in.)
Position ○ ◐ **Hardiness** Annual

The origins of the tasty culinary beetroot belong with the wild sea beet, *B. vulgaris*, which can be found growing on the coastlines of Europe and Western Asia. The colourful beetroot 'Burpee's Gold' hails from breeding work in North America and qualifies as a heritage variety because its lasting quality and uniqueness has stood the test of time. 'Burpee's Golden' was bred by Burpee Seeds in the 1940s and is enjoying a new lease of life having been rediscovered by modern-day chefs. The globe-shaped roots are bright orange in colour, and the internal flesh turns a bright golden-yellow while cooking. Many people prefer the taste of these golden beetroot to their red cousins. The foliage of 'Burpee's Golden' can be used for baby-leaf growing or cooked and used in a similar way to spinach. Another great variety is 'Chioggia', first recorded in the 1840s as being grown in the market gardens of Vienna. It is somewhat milder than other beet and brings a candy-stripe effect to the salad bowl. **TS**

Alternatives

Beta vulgaris 'Yellow Detroit', *Beta vulgaris* 'Albina Vereduna'

Beta

B. vulgaris
'Alto'

Main features High-quality, long, cylindrical roots; ideal for slicing; efficient use of space
Height 30 cm (12 in.) **Spread** 15 cm (6 in.)
Position ○ ◐ **Hardiness** Annual

Unlike heritage varieties such as *B. vulgaris* 'Chioggia' and 'Burpee's Golden', which have survived as distinct varieties through many years of selection and roguing, 'Alto' – an F1 hybrid, with long cylindrical roots – represents the more modern way to achieve a breeding objective by working with two pure-breeding parent lines. The result is a top-quality, uniform variety of excellent taste. It does mean, though, that the cross has to be remade each year, and the seeds are more expensive. The development of the cylindrical types is proving very popular with modern chefs, as it is the ideal shape for slicing quickly. An added benefit is that 'Alto' has much better holding ability, meaning that the roots stay in better condition for longer. Like other beetroot, the foliage tops of 'Alto' can be used when the roots are harvested at a young stage, but the leaves should be twisted off rather than cut, because this will discourage 'bleeding' of juice from the top of the root. **TS**

Alternatives

Beta vulgaris 'Cylindra', *Beta vulgaris* 'Forono'

Beta

B. vulgaris
'Bright Lights'

Main features Attractive, colourful stems; harvest through the winter
Height 60 cm (24 in.) **Spread** 30 cm (12 in.)
Position ○ ◐ **Hardiness** RHS H4

Budding vegetable gardeners take note: it is impossible to fail with 'Bright Lights'. All cultivars of Swiss chard or silverbeet are brilliant for their willingness to provide us with a green, leafy vegetable even in the most unpromising circumstances. 'Bright Lights' has the ability to do all this and be particularly attractive at the same time. Its large green-and-purple leaves are held by stems in a multitude of exuberant colours from red to yellow to orange. 'Bright Lights' brings a bit of French potager glamour to any garden by being easily attractive enough to hold its own in the flower border while being tough enough to hold its head high in the allotment too. This fabulous vegetable grows so enthusiastically that you can simply pop its seeds into even the most unprepossessing ground and the result will be a plant. Swiss chard is one of the few vegetables that will survive through the winter and provide a supply of fresh leaves during the coldest months. **LG**

Alternative

Beta vulgaris subsp. *cicla* var. *flavescens* 'Lucullus'

Brassica

B. oleracea
'Savoy King'

Main features Fast growing; long harvest; high-quality crop
Height 30 cm (12 in.) **Spread** 45 cm (18 in.)
Position ○ ◐ **Hardiness** RHS H6

Winter cabbage varieties are worthy of a place in the vegetable garden, but the Savoy Group deserves special attention. The leaves are dark green with pale veins and have a wonderfully rumpled appearance. This latter feature gives rise to a lovely, crunchy bite. Their flavour tends to be robust while the texture of the leaves makes them an ideal ingredient in stirfries. They also make an inviting change when they are steamed or boiled and served as a side dish. There are several varieties, some cropping earlier or later in the season, but *B. oleracea* 'Savoy King' is particularly good because it grows faster than other winter cabbages. Speed of harvest does not mean that you compromise when it comes to the size of the crop. This is a heavy-yielding cabbage that rewards the gardener with dense, heavy, slightly flattened heads that measure roughly 20 centimetres (8 in.) in diameter. When they are cut and in the kitchen, they make you feel like you've grown something significant. **PWa/JM**

Alternatives

Brassica oleracea 'Resolution', *Brassica oleracea* 'Mila'

Brassica
B. rapa var. *chinensis* 'Joi Choi'

Main features Fast growing; strong flavour; slow to bolt
Height 15–60 cm (6–24 in.) **Spread** 15–30 cm (6–12 in.)
Position ○ ◑
Hardiness Annual

One of the most versatile cultivars of pak choi, 'Joi Choi' is very fast-growing and can be harvested to use raw as a delicious baby-leaf salad vegetable just thirty days after planting. It can also be grown on for longer periods, for use as a semi-mature or fully grown plant, which tastes excellent in stirfries, soups and Asian dishes. The mature leaves have a strong flavour, and the thick stems are crisp and succulent.

As pak choi is shallow rooted and leafs up very quickly, it can be prone to 'bolting'. This is when the plant stops growing roots and leaves and instead concentrates all its energy on sending up flower heads so that it can set seeds. The leaves of plants that have bolted can have a noticeably bitter flavour. One of the reasons 'Joi Choi' is so popular is that it is less likely to bolt than other varieties of pak choi, although it still requires regular watering. In contrast to deeper-rooted plants, pak choi benefits from being watered often, but only a little each time, and it responds better to a daily splash rather than a weekly drench. It is also hardy enough to sow from early spring into autumn, and even into winter. In cooler weather it will need light protection with a cloche or a layer of horticultural fleece.

Due to its bolt-resistant nature and shallow roots, 'Joi Choi' is the perfect variety for growing in containers on a patio or balcony. Young plants can even be enjoyed as a 'cut-and-come-again' leaf crop: you can simply snip a few leaves from each plant whenever you want to cook with them. It can be harvested up to late autumn, a time when few other fresh leaves will be available. 'Joi Choi' is also a handy crop to fill the space that has been left after early crops, such as peas, have been harvested. Remember to keep the soil moist, to guard against slugs and to use a crop cover of fine mesh to keep insects away. **PWa/JM**

Alternatives

Brassica chinensis 'Canton Dwarf', *Brassica chinensis* 'Mei Qing Choi'

Brassica
B. oleracea 'Cavolo Nero'

Main features Hardy brassica; fresh winter greens; rich, intense flavour; ornamental foliage
Height 45 cm (18 in.) **Spread** 45 cm (18 in.)
Position ○ ◑ **Hardiness** RHS H4

The hardiest of the winter greens, kale is a highly nutritious vegetable and a versatile brassica to grow. Both modern and heritage varieties liven up potagers, ornamental borders and containers with their curly or puckered foliage in a range of colours from red purple, almost black, and blue green to mossy green. Kale will also keep you healthy since it is full of vitamins, as well as iron and fibre. The chef's favourite for flavour is the black kale 'Cavolo Nero' (also known as 'Nero di Toscana'), a heritage, open-pollinated kale that has been grown in Tuscany for hundreds of years. It has strap-shaped, blue-grey to black leaves with a puckered appearance. 'Black Magic' is a modern version that produces more uniform plants and leaves. It is tasty and easy to cut up into strips with scissors, but do clean kale carefully first, as the leaf texture and darker colour hides dirt and pests.

Kale, or borecole, is a type of collard (a general term for cabbage plants). Kale and collards are very primitive plants that have been around for at least 2,000 years. They are native to the eastern Mediterranean and Asia Minor and were grown by the ancient Greeks and Romans. Whereas some cabbage-type plants went on to form heads, the more primitive kales and collards remained the same.

Sow seeds in spring and then plant out in its final position during the summer. The seed is large so it's easy to handle. Kale will tolerate a lower fertility than most brassicas, but the usual additions of well-rotted organic matter and liming for acidic soils still apply. A sunny site will be the most productive, although kale will still produce leaves in partial shade. Kale for use as cooked greens can be harvested from late autumn and onwards. Pick a few outer or middle leaves from each plant, leaving the youngest ones to grow on. **LD**

Alternatives

Syn. = *Brassica* 'Nero di Toscana', *Brassica oleracea* 'Black Magic'

Brassica
B. *oleracea* 'Petit Posy'

Main features New hybrid; winter vegetable; frilly, colourful foliage; sweet, nutty flavor
Height 75 cm (30 in.) **Spread** 60 cm (24 in.)
Position ○ ◑ **Hardiness** RHS H5

'Petit Posy' is an entirely new vegetable, also known as Kalettes, which is a cross between kale and Brussels sprouts. It tastes sweeter and milder than a Brussels sprout. The actual plants are tall and look like traditional Brussels sprout plants, but instead, where you expect to find the little 'button' sprouts, there are little tufts of mini-kale leaves. These little tufts are easier to detach from the parent than Brussels sprouts, which can be tricky when your fingers are numb with cold in winter.

Once picked, Kalettes look very pretty with their touches of pink, and little preparation is required beyond washing and cooking. They can be steamed, stirfried, grilled, roasted or microwaved as a side vegetable, and they also work well in pasta dishes or added to robust soups. They are a winter to early spring vegetable rather than a year-round crop. 'Petit Posy' was developed by the UK-based vegetable breeder Tozer Seeds and was launched in 2010 as Flower Sprout, but it did not take off until it was rebranded as Kalettes in the United States.

Grow them as you would a Brussels sprout crop. Kalettes are extremely hardy and produce large crops, even through a cold winter. The plants do take up a fair amount of space for a long period; maturity dates range from 110 to 138 days. As with most brassicas, you need to prepare the soil ahead of time with well-rotted organic matter, such as garden compost. After planting and staking the plants, be on hand to feed and water so there is no check to their growth. They suffer from the same pests as most brassicas, so in order to avoid spraying with chemicals, use barriers such as crop covers and bird netting over a tall, sturdy fame. If you already have brassicas in your annual vegetable plan, they are no extra bother, and they do offer something unusual for the kitchen. **LD**

Alternative

Syn. *Brassica oleracea* Kalettes, *Brassica oleracea* Flower Sprout

Brassica
B. oleracea 'Dynamo'

Main features Very fast-growing cabbage; matures early
Height 30 cm (12 in.) **Spread** 45 cm (18 in.)
Position ○ ◑
Hardiness Annual

With any vegetable plant, part of the skill involved in cultivation revolves around prolonging the harvest for as long as possible. Few gardeners want a huge glut of produce for two or three months followed by a lean period in which there is nothing to do but wait for vegetables to grow. That is why plant breeders work hard to introduce new varieties, either with a very long and progressive cropping period or that are productive early or late in the season. For a cabbage that produces a head quickly, look for those described in seed catalogues as 'summer cabbages' or 'early cultivars'.

'Dynamo' is an early growing cabbage, ready to harvest within sixty-five days. It forms a compact round head, and growers will need to check early varieties daily once the cabbage head has formed. As they are fast growing, they are prone to splitting open, but an advantage of 'Dynamo' is that it 'stands well', so it is less likely to split than other varieties.

One of the earliest of all cabbage varieties to mature is *B. oleracea* 'Earliana', which can be sown indoors and grown on for six to eight weeks before being transplanted outside. It will then be ready to harvest just sixty days after planting. The heads are small – around 10 to 13 centimetres (4–5 in.) in diameter and weighing around 1 kilogram (2 lb) – but this is still plenty of cabbage for most family kitchens. They have a very good flavour, perfect for the first cabbage of the season.

They are troublefree and low-maintenance additions to the vegetable garden, and therefore a good choice for less experienced gardeners. A major benefit of being so early to mature is that they are sown, planted, grown and cut before most cabbage pests are ready to do damage. Pigeons do attack young brassica leaves, but these birds are easily deterred with netting. **PWa/JM**

Alternatives

Brassica oleracea 'Earliana', *Brassica oleracea* 'Hispi', *Brassica oleracea* 'Hotspur'

Brassica
B. oleracea 'Artwork'

Main features Sweet-tasting, tender stems; abundant sideshoots
Height 60 cm (24 in.) **Spread** 20 cm (8 in.)
Position ○ ◑ **Hardiness** Annual

Until recently, the stem, or baby, broccoli was only available in gourmet markets and high-end restaurants. That all changed with 'Artwork', a new dark-green stem broccoli now available to home gardeners. It was a national winner in the All-America Selections trials. 'Artwork' starts out similarly to regular broccoli, but after harvesting that first crown, or head, easy-to-harvest, tender, tasty side shoots continue to appear long into the growing season, resisting warm temperature bolting better than other broccoli. A few 'Artwork' plants will provide stems for several meals. Harvest will be maximised if you remove the head about fifty-five days after moving plants to their final growing site. The optimal stage to remove the main head is when it is 2.5 to 4 centimetres (1–1.5 in.) across; simply snap or cut the stem below the head. The first harvest usually occurs ten days after the head removal. Harvest stems when they are 15 to 20 centimetres (6–8 in.) long and 2.5 centimetres (1 in.) in diameter. **DB**

Alternatives

Brassica oleracea 'Apollo' F1, *Brassica oleracea* 'Aspabroc' F1

Brassica
B. oleracea 'Redhead'

Main features Reliable, late-cropping cultivar; rich purple colour
Height 90 cm (3 ft) **Spread** 60 cm (24 in.)
Position ○ ◑ **Hardiness** RHS H5

This purple-sprouting broccoli is a frost-hardy, biennial crop typically planted in autumn and harvested in spring. A member of the *Brassicaceae* family, it differs from cauliflower in having more divided leaves and less dense flower heads. Like the other close relatives of cabbage, broccoli is native to the Mediterranean area and Asia Minor. It has been cultivated in Italy since the days of the Roman Empire and is thought to be the same plant described as '*Bruttium broccoli*' by the naturalist Pliny. It was referred to as sprout cauliflower and Italian asparagus in Miller's *Gardeners Dictionary* of 1724. Sprouting broccoli is popular in the United Kingdom since it can be harvested in that time of year when overwintered crops are finished and new season ones are not ready. 'Redhead' is a strong-growing form of purple-sprouting broccoli, which forms large primary heads and good-size secondary shoots. It crops over an eight-week period. It is a good, rich-purple colour due to high levels of anthocyanin pigments. **GHa**

Alternatives

Brassica oleracea 'Red Arrow', *Brassica oleracea* 'Red Spear', *Brassica oleracea* 'Cardinal' Italica Group

Brassica oleracea Italica Group **'Purple Sprouting'** produces a second crop of tasty, edible flowering shoots on tall plants. ➲

Capsicum
C. annuum 'Basket of Fire'

Main features Compact plant; self-supporting; produces hundreds of pods
Height 30 cm (12 in.) **Spread** 60 cm (24 in.)
Position ○ **Hardiness** Annual

Chillis are often called ornamental varieties, but do not let this put you off *C. annuum* 'Basket of Fire'. It is referred to as ornamental because it grows into a beautiful compact plant covered in yellow, orange and red chilli pods that point outwards through the small, green foliage. This is an ideal plant for growing on a kitchen windowsill, and its semi-trailing quality means that it looks great grown in a hanging basket too. The small but fleshy pods can be used chopped or whole in most dishes that need chillis. If you pick some of each colour, they are great sliced up in a salsa, bringing a bit of colour to what can otherwise be a red concoction.

'Basket of Fire' can grow up to 30 centimetres (12 in.) high and twice that wide. It is described as having a compact branching habit, and in order to further enhance its bushy behaviour, you can pinch out the growing tips once they have reached 15 centimetres (6 in.) long. The plant will take about eighty days to reach maturity from transplanting. Each of the 5- to 8-centimetre-long (2–3 in.) pods will start off pale yellow and then turn orange and finally red. They can be picked and used in culinary dishes at any point, and they will be hotter when they are red. With possibly more than 200 pods, in different colours/stages of maturity on the plant at the same time, it is easy to see why this *C. annuum* was given the cultivar name 'Basket of Fire'.

The heat of chillis is rated in Scoville heat units (SHUs), and the higher the number, the hotter the chilli. A typical jalapeño rates at about 5,000 SHUs, whereas a sweet pepper will rate 0 SHU. The active ingredient is capsaicin, which in its pure form would rate 16,000,000 SHUs. The 'Basket of Fire' is a hot chilli at around 80,000 SHUs, which is hot enough so that you will know when you have eaten one. **DF**

Alternative

Capsicum annuum 'Chenzo'

Capsicum
C. annuum 'NuMex Twilight'

Main features Compact plant; very colourful display; needs no support; productive
Height 60 cm (24 in.) **Spread** 45 cm (18 in.)
Position ○ **Hardiness** Annual

This is one of the most beautiful ornamental chillis that gardeners can grow. It was released in 1992 after being developed by Paul Bosland at New Mexico State University. It was not hybridised, but plants were selected from a larger population for their positive traits. Seed were then collected for three generations before a single plant was selected from which to breed. *C. annuum* 'NuMex Twilight' was developed as a commercial plant that could be sold as seed or as a pot plant in garden centres. It is small and compact, at 45 to 60 centimetres (18–24 in.) high, and does not need support for the hundreds of small 2-centimetre-long (0.75 in.) erect pods that it produces. These pods mature from purple, through yellow to orange and red, with pods at all stages of maturity at the same time. This plant has been a great commercial success because it offers dramatic colour and something edible, grown in the smallest of spaces.

In fact, 'NuMex Twilight' can be grown on a windowsill and should overwinter well, so it is possible for each plant to last a few years. Although this plant is called ornamental, the pods are hot in terms of chilli heat, at between 30,000 and 50,000 Scoville heat units (SHU). They can be used in cooking for added heat, but are probably not best suited to all culinary uses because of their slightly bitter aftertaste.

Where the local climate is warm enough, these plants can be grown outside in flower beds as long as the soil is moist and well-drained. They like sunny, warm conditions and will make a unique talking point. If the plants are grown in a greenhouse, expect a much heavier yield. An up-and-coming alternative, and a development from the 'NuMex Twilight' is 'Fairy Lights', which is very similar but has purple-tinged leaves, bright-purple flowers, and hotter fruits. **DF**

Alternative

Capsicum annuum 'Fairy Lights'

Capsicum
C. annuum
'Mama Mia Giallo'

Main features Compact plant; beautiful, tapered, yellow pods
Height 30–60 cm (12–24 in.) **Spread** 38 cm (15 in.)
Position ○ **Hardiness** Annual

Here is an early-ripening Italian sweet pepper that takes eighty-five days from transplanting to produce golden-yellow pods. A compact plant, *C. annuum* 'Mama Mia Giallo' likes a sunny position but has lots of dark-green foliage that will protect the pods from sunburn as they ripen. In the right conditions, you can expect more than twenty-four 18- to 22-centimetre-long (7–9 in.) pods from each plant. Pick when the pods are fully mature and golden yellow in colour. They have a smooth skin and a thick flesh, but they are not the best for stuffing due to their shape. However, they are excellent roasted over an open flame, until the skin has charred, then placed in a plastic bag to cool before carefully peeling away the skin. Do not wash away any flecks of the skin that remain; just let the peppers cool and then slice them up. Added to a salad or used to flavour a soup, 'Mama Mia Giallo' works well with tomato or butternut squash. Alternatives to try include 'Marconi Golden' and 'Corno di Toro Giallo'. **DF**

Alternative

Capiscum annuum 'Marconi Golden'

Capsicum
C. annuum
'Orange Blaze'

Main features Ideal for containers; matures quickly; beautiful, blocky, orange pods
Height 60–90 cm (24–36 in.) **Spread** 60 cm (24 in.)
Position ○ **Hardiness** Annual

Orange sweet peppers are not always the easiest to grow and can take their time to ripen. However, *C. annuum* 'Orange Blaze' is simple to grow; it is an early variety and changes colour very quickly from its immature deep green to a most impressive orange colour. The thick, firm flesh is very crunchy, which makes it a nice addition to a salad. The pods are also ideal for stuffing, due to their shape and volume. Try stuffing them with chilli: place a small amount of cooked rice in the bottom of each pod, topping this with already-cooked chilli and adding a layer of grated cheese before placing the peppers in a hot oven. 'Orange Blaze' likes full sun and a well-drained but moist bed; as a disease-resistant and very low-maintenance plant, it is ideal for the occasional gardener. Developed by Monsanto, this is an F1 hybrid, so seed saving will not produce the same variety. However, a very good, open-pollinated variety called 'Orange Sun' is well worth looking out for too. **DF**

Alternative

Capiscum annuum 'Golden Sun'

Capsicum

C. annuum
'Cayennetta'

Main features Compact plant; pods ripen to a bright red
Height 60–75 cm (24–30 in.) **Spread** 60 cm (24 in.)
Position ○
Hardiness Annual

This is one of the best patio chilli plants, and it produces an abundance of fairly hot (10,000 to 20,000 Scoville heat units), cayenne-style pods. Developed specifically by Floranova for growing in containers, *C. annuum* 'Cayennetta' was an All-America Selections winner in 2012. Cayenne-style peppers are very popular and have been purported to have many medicinal benefits. Numerous commercial hot sauces are based on this style of pepper, but you can easily make a quick hot sauce at home with only twenty fully ripe 'Cayennetta' chillis and these basic ingredients: white wine vinegar or cider vinegar, cloves of garlic and salt. A compact plant with a bushy habit, 'Cayennetta' produces lots of dense foliage that protects the pods from sunburn, making this plant ideally suited to hot and sunny positions. Even with a full crop of chillis, it should not need support. It will take sixty-five to seventy days from transplantation for the pods to turn from bright green to a glossy red. **DF**

Alternatives

Capiscum annuum 'Apache', *Capiscum annuum* 'Loco'

Capsicum

C. annuum
'Hungarian Hot Wax'

Main features Compact plant; ideal for cooler climates
Height 60 cm (24 in.) **Spread** 30 cm (12 in.)
Position ○
Hardiness Annual

A one-time winner of a Royal Horticultural Society Award of Garden Merit, this is one of the most reliable and easiest chillis to grow. It produces copious amounts of conical pods that ripen from green via yellow to crimson red. If picked when yellow, the pods are slightly sweeter with less heat. When fully ripe *C. annuum* 'Hungarian Hot Wax' can reach up to 10,000 to 12,000 Scoville heat units; more typically it is in the 5,000 to 8,000 range. The cultivar takes its name from the shiny, waxy-looking skin and its origins in Hungary. Its popularity is due to its suitability for cooler climates and that it is one of the earliest chilli plants to start producing pods. Although the chillis are tasty when yellow, if you pick the pods in the immature yellow state, it will promote the production of even more pods. However, as the season comes to an end, let the pods ripen fully and then use a dehydrator to dry them. This way, you can make a fine chilli powder that will keep you going until the next crop is available. **DF**

Alternative

Capsicum annuum 'Santa Fe Grande'

Capsicum
C. annuum 'Pimiento de Padron'

Main features Delicious, mild-to-hot chilli pepper; low-maintenance plant
Height 60–90 cm (2–3 ft) **Spread** 30–35 cm (12–14 in.)
Position ○ **Hardiness** Annual

This chilli from Padron, a town in the Galicia region of north-western Spain, has become a sensation after the explosion in popularity of Spanish tapas. You will find *C. annuum* 'Pimiento de Padron' (or Padron peppers) sold fresh in supermarkets and grocery stores, and they are excellent when fried whole in a little, very hot olive oil – until the skin starts to char – and then served sprinkled with sea salt. The best way to eat the fried peppers is by holding on to the stalk and biting through the thick-fleshed pod, or by eating them whole if they are small enough. Eating this dish has become known as a form of Spanish roulette, because when young, the green pods are not always hot, with only about one in ten having matured enough to have any significant heat, so eating them can be a variable experience in terms of heat.

Timing is a slight problem when harvesting these chilli peppers; leave them too long on the plant and they will all become hot and eventually turn red. If you grow them at home, remember to pick them as soon as you feel they are large enough, but of course, you could just fry up a few to make sure. Although they have become well known as a tapas, Padron peppers are also delicious used in a stirfry or stuffed and grilled. In fact, you could use them in place of regular green chillis.

'Pimiento de Padron' is generally considered to be a heritage variety. Although its history is not well documented, it has been around for hundreds of years and survived being passed down by growers due to its ease of growing and its much-prized flavour.

Good soil, sun and water will usually result in strong, vibrant plants. In cooler areas these chillis need to be grown in a greenhouse or polytunnel if you are going to get a significant harvest. They can grow into large plants, around 60 to 90 centimetres (24–36 in.) high. **DF**

Alternative

Capsicum annuum 'Telicia'

Cichorium
C. endivia 'Natacha'

Main features Tasty, slightly bitter leaves; quick to mature; slow to bolt
Height 20 cm (8 in.) **Spread** 40 cm (16 in.)
Position ○ ◐ **Hardiness** Annual

Known predominantly as endive in the United States and sometimes chicory or escarole, 'Natacha' is an exceptional example of *C. endivia*, a tasty salad vegetable with a slightly bitter flavour. It is the leading *scarole* (or broad-leaved salad endive) in France, where the crispy leaves are usually eaten raw. They combine well with other strong flavours, such as garlic, blue cheese or chilli. Since 'Natacha' contains less milky sap than lettuce, the leaves retain their crispness longer after being cut, and they are much slower to turn brown at the edges.

'Natacha' is popular with gardeners because it is fast to mature yet slow to bolt (run to seed), provided that the soil is moist but not waterlogged. This means baby leaves can be ready to harvest in as little as ten weeks from sowing, but can then be picked over a long season. It is a relatively hardy chicory, so is therefore a good option for planting in early spring or winter.

Although many people enjoy the bitter tang of this vegetable it is something of an acquired taste, and there are various ways to reduce the level of natural chemicals that cause this sharpness. Cooking the leaves reduces their natural bitterness and brings out a more mellow, buttery flavour. The hearts are popular when served lightly baked, braised or grilled.

Blanching the leaves of mature plants by excluding light for ten to twenty days will also give them a milder flavour than leaves grown in the sunshine. One option is to cover each plant with a pot or bucket to keep it entirely in the dark. Alternatively, the outer leaves can be bunched up around the heart and tied with string. After two weeks or so, the pale, blanched leaves can be harvested. Keep plants dry while covered to avoid rotting. Chicory grows similarly to lettuce, but is tolerant of higher temperatures. **PWa/JM**

Alternative

Cichorium endivia 'Wallonne'

Cichorium

C. *intybus* 'Witloof'

Main features Heads of crisp leaves; tangy, bitter flavour; can be forced for sweeter, pale yellow leaves
Height 8 in. (20 cm) **Spread** 10 cm (4 in.)
Position ◐ ● **Hardiness** Annual

Sometimes called Belgian endive or forcing chicory, this is a densely packed heart of crisp, young leaves known as a chicon. The tender, pale leaves have a unique tang due to a naturally occurring substance called intybin. If the chicons are exposed to sunlight, they start to turn green and the flavour becomes too bitter. These plants are therefore not only grown under cover, they are also often wrapped in dark paper after harvesting to preserve their mild taste. The curled shape of the individual leaves makes them ideal for serving whole with fillings, or with dipping sauces. The heads are also delicious when cooked, and they can be baked, roasted, fried or stewed. Heating the chicons reduces the level of intybin.

'Witloof' was discovered by accident in Belgium (the name is Flemish for 'white leaf'), when the head gardener at the botanical gardens in Brussels left some roots covered in soil in a cellar. On tasting the resulting chicons, he found them to be delicious. Once the commercial growing method had been perfected, 'Witloof' became a national favourite.

In winter the large, thick roots are planted in a frost-free area, such as a shed or garage, to be forced in complete darkness. Single plants can be covered with a bucket to exclude light, or grown completely underground. A white chicon will form on each root every three to six weeks. Once they reach 20 centimetres (8 in.), they can be cut off at the base and eaten. **PWa/JM**

Alternatives

Cichorium intybus 'Witloof Zoom', *Cichorium intybus* 'Palla Rossa', *Cichorium intybus* 'Rossa di Treviso'

Citrullus

C. lanatus 'Faerie'

Main features Cream-yellow rind with thin stripes; sweet, pink-red flesh with high sugar content; crisp texture
Height 60 cm (24 in.) **Spread** 3.4–3.6 m (11–12 ft)
Position ○ **Hardiness** Annual

Watermelon, or *C. lanatus*, is a member of the *Cucurbitaceae* family. Like the pepper, tomato and pumpkin, watermelon is a fruit, botanically, but because it is planted as seed (or young plants) and cleared from the field each year, it is considered a vegetable by home gardeners. It is the fruit of a plant originally from a vine in southern Africa, so it can only be grown in warmer regions.

'Faerie' is different from a traditional watermelon in that it has a cream-yellow rind with thin stripes, yet it still yields sweet, pink-red flesh with a high sugar content and crisp texture. If you live in a region where watermelons can be grown to fruiting size, this new variety is worth trying.

Growers will appreciate the disease and insect tolerance of 'Faerie', as well as its prolific fruit set that starts with an early appearance of female flowers and continues through the season. The skin colour turns from green (pictured) to cream yellow, indicating maturity and the time to harvest; a great indicator for less-experienced watermelon growers. The All-America Selections judges held taste trials, and all over North America, 'Faerie' was voted the best-tasting, yellow-skinned watermelon.

Start off seeds indoors four weeks prior to the last frost, keeping them at 24°C (75°F). Harden off and transplant into the final growing space after soil and air temperature have warmed. In areas with long growing seasons, seed may be sown directly into prepared ground. **DB**

Alternatives

Citrullus lanatus 'Golden Crown', *Citrullus lanatus* 'Vanguard', *Citrullus lanatus* 'New Queen'

Citrullus
C. lanatus 'Harvest Moon'

Main features Seedless, tasty fruits; early ripening; easy-to-grow variety
Height 25–60 cm (10–24 in.) **Spread** 90–150 cm (3–5 ft)
Position ○ **Hardiness** Annual

Not every region is suitable for growing watermelons, but for those that are, this cultivar is a new take on the old heritage variety C. lanatus 'Moon and Stars'. Both have dark-green rinds speckled with yellow dots, and sweet, crisp, pink-red flesh. However, 'Harvest Moon' is earlier ripening and higher yielding, with seedless fruits. The earlier cropping makes it easier for gardeners to get fruits before the end of the growing season, plus, it has shorter, more compact vines. Potentially, each plant can yield four or five watermelons, around 30 to 38 centimetres (12–15 in.) long. 'Harvest Moon' has been recognised as a national winner of an All-America Selections Award. Triploid (seedless) watermelons can be tricky to germinate, so start seed indoors and keep the soil temperature at 30 to 32°C (85–90°F) until germination occurs. Sow seeds four weeks prior to the last frost, directly into pots filled with well-watered compost that has been allowed to drain. Wrap in plastic and keep in a protected environment before planting out in warmer weather. **DB**

Alternative

Citrullus lanatus 'Moon and Stars'

Cucumis
C. melo 'Melemon'

Main feature Piel-de-sapo- or honeydew-type melon with a unique sweet-tart taste
Height 60–90 cm (24–36 in.) **Spread** 30–60 cm (12–24 in.)
Position ○ **Hardiness** Annual

Early maturing, piel-de-sapo-type melons on strong, healthy plants that produced a large number of melons with superior taste were all factors that contributed to 'Melemon' becoming an All-America Selections winner. Judges linked the taste of this hybrid melon to a honeydew, but with a surprising citrusy tanginess. A uniform fruit shape (15 cm/6 in. in height and 17 cm/6.5 in. in diameter) also makes it perfect for market growers and home gardeners. Each fruit has a beautiful, lime-green rind that, when cut open, reveals refreshingly crisp flesh with a unique, sweet-and-sour taste. Compact plants produce a large number of melons per plant. Judges noted that this melon was more disease resistant compared with similar melons. For cooks, this melon lends itself perfectly to fresh, summery fruit salads and is wonderful puréed in smoothies. Although piel de sapo literally translates as 'skin of toad', it is recommended that you give 'Melemon' a try as you never know what treasures lie under an unattractive exterior. **DB**

Alternatives

Cucumis melo 'Lambkin', Cucumis melo 'Kermit'

Cucumis melo plants trained up wire frame supports in a garden in Oxfordshire, UK. ➔

Cucumis
C. sativus 'Pick a Bushel'

Main features Compact, bush-type cucumber; high yields; excellent heat tolerance; firm texture
Height 60–90 cm (24–36 in.) **Spread** 60 cm (24 in.)
Position ○ **Hardiness** Annual

Typically, when choosing a cucumber variety, you have to decide whether you want one that produces lots of small, 8-centimetre-long (3 in.) fruits for pickling, or a variety with fewer but bigger (15 cm/6 in.) fruits for using fresh, usually in salads. However, with 'Pick a Bushel' you can do both. It offers the best of both worlds and is a handy cultivar for gardeners who might only have room for a couple of plants. The name of this All-America Selections winner (Heartland and Great Lakes regions) certainly explains the productivity of this compact plant that can be grown using a trellis or cage either in the ground or in patio containers. The flesh has a good, firm texture with a sweet flavour.

Cucumbers need a site in full sun. Plant seed in light, fertile, and well-drained soil, with plenty of compost added to ensure good yields. Seeds should be sown when the soil has warmed up to 21°C (70°F). Sow one seed every 15 centimetres (6 in.), pushing it into the soil to a depth of 2.5 centimetres (1 in.). Cover and keep moist. When the plants are 5 centimetres (2 in.) high, thin them to 25 centimetres (10 in.) apart. Alternatively, plant seed in a series of hills or mounds 1.2 to 1.5 metres (4–5 ft) apart; a hill or mound of soil is typically 30 centimetres (12 in.) in diameter. Start by sowing four or five seeds and then thin to three per hill. In short-summer areas, gardeners may wish to start cucumbers indoors. Plant seeds in individual pots or a similar container two or three weeks before the last frost. Harden off the seedlings for several days before planting in the garden.

The vines of 'Pick a Bushel' will spread 60 to 90 centimetres (24–36 in.) so plant them accordingly, using a trellis or cage, which will save space and make the cucumbers easier to harvest. You can expect fifteen to twenty fruits per plant if you harvest regularly. **DB**

Alternatives

Cucumis sativus 'County Fair', *Cucumis sativus* 'Regal', *Cucumis sativus* 'Calypso'

Cucumis
C. sativus 'Saladmore Bush'

Main features Prolific, compact, dual-purpose bush;
ideal for growing in containers
Height 60 cm (24 in.) **Spread** 60 cm (24 in.)
Position ○ **Hardiness** Annual

Perfect for growing where space is limited, this dual-purpose cucumber can either be picked small to be processed for pickling, or allowed to grow into long, straight cucumbers, which are best harvested when about 20 centimetres (8 in.) in length. C. sativus 'Saladmore Bush' has a compact, bushy habit and grows to around 60 centimetres (24 in.) in both height and spread, making it ideal for growing in containers. Offering a series of bright-yellow flowers, these neat bushes are decorative enough to be featured on a patio.

'Saladmore Bush' is surprisingly fast to mature and, if grown in the right conditions, it is not unusual to be able to pick the first mature fruits only fifty-five days after sowing the seeds. Although each plant is relatively compact, it is also prolific, offering an average of twelve fruits per bush. Regular harvesting encourages the plants to keep flowering. Ideally, cut the fruits in the morning when temperatures remain cool. Like all cucumbers, 'Saladmore Bush' is especially crisp and firm in the morning and keeps better than if it is harvested in the afternoon. Each tapered, cylindrical fruit has a dark-green, slightly spiky outer skin and pale-green flesh, as well as a strong fragrance and crisp, sweet flavour. This cucumber is ideal for slicing in salads or cutting into batons to use with dips.

Another advantage of this award-winning variety is that it has good resistance to disease and mildew. It is ideal for growing in warmer areas where other plants succumb to late-season diseases. However, these are thirsty plants, so for the best results keep the soil constantly moist by watering around the base of each plant instead of over the leaves. This means that not only is more moisture taken up by the plant, but the risk of powdery mildew is reduced. **PWa/JM**

Alternatives

Cucumis sativus 'Bush Champion',
Cucumis sativus 'Salad Bush', *Cucumis sativus* 'Fanfare'

Cucurbita

C. *pepo* 'Romanesco'

Main features Attractive, ribbed fruits; firm texture;
nutty flavour; edible yellow flowers
Height 90 cm (3 ft) **Spread** 90–120 cm (3–4 ft)
Position ○ **Hardiness** Annual

This species is native to northeastern Mexico and the
southern United States. Cultivated for centuries, *C. pepo*
has resulted in many different fruiting forms, including
squashes, pumpkins, marrows and ornamental gourds.
It was in northern Italy that the cylindrical fruit known as
summer squash, courgette, or zucchini was developed.
They are eaten when immature, before seeds have
developed. The Italian name *zucchini* means 'little
squash'; the word 'courgette', which is used in the United
Kingdom, comes from French.

'Romanesco' is a reliable Italian heritage variety that
produces a long succession of attractive, glossy fruits
on a bushy, sprawling plant. The plants, which have

large, lobed leaves covered in scratchy hairs, are usually
grown as half-hardy annuals. Large yellow flowers in
summer are followed by the light-green fruits, which
have characteristic raised ribs running along their length.
The courgettes have a firm, creamy texture even when
allowed to grow quite large. They have more flavour
than many other cultivars, with an almost nutty taste.
The flowers are also edible and are useful for stuffing or
can be dipped in tempura batter and fried.

Sow seeds 2.5 centimetres (1 in.) deep in individual
pots in spring. Transplant plants outdoors four to five
weeks later when all danger of frost has passed. Space
plants around 90 centimetres (3 ft) apart in ground
prepared with plenty of organic matter. **GHa**

Alternatives

Cucurbita pepo 'Lungo di Firenze', *Cucurbita pepo*
'Striato d'Italia'

Cucurbita
C. moschata 'Waltham Butternut'

Main features Long-season keeper; sweet, orange flesh; good source of winter vitamins; edible seed
Height 25–30 cm (10–12 in.) **Spread** 60–90 cm (24–36 in.)
Position ○ **Hardiness** Annual

The word 'squash' comes from an Algonquin word *askutasquash,* meaning 'food to eat raw'. Squash are divided into winter and summer varieties, with butternut squash being a winter squash, because you can eat it during winter. It is one of the best 'keepers' – you can keep it up to a year – thanks to the protective tan skin that encloses the orange, dry-textured, sweet flesh.

'Waltham Butternut' is named for Waltham Suburban Experiment Station in Massachusetts, where it is said to have been developed from crosses between a wild African squash and the New Hampshire butternut. However, a hobby farmer and amateur breeder Charles A. Leggett is also said to have developed the butternut

squash pre–World War Two. He reputedly named it for its attributes of being 'smooth as butter and sweet as a nut' and presented it to the Waltham field station, who subsequently introduced it. 'Waltham Butternut' became the most popular butternut squash available. Specifically developed to be superior to other varieties, it had an improved shape and size, a thickened neck, a smoother skin, a smaller seed cavity, higher yields, and better storage. A winner of an All-America Selections Award in 1970, it can be grown in a variety of conditions.

Butternut squash is an adaptable vegetable that lends itself to be mashed or puréed for soups. It also holds its shape well if cubed and cooked in stews, barbecued on the grill and roasted in the oven. **IT**

Alternatives

Cucurbita moschata 'Early Butternut', *Cucurbita moschata* 'Butterscotch', *Cucurbita moschata* 'Harrier'

Cucurbita

C. moschata 'Sweet Dumpling'

Main features Small, tasty, attractive fruits; versatile vegetable; stores well
Height 90 cm (3 ft) **Spread** 90 cm (3 ft)
Position ○ **Hardiness** Annual

The cucurbit to grow for the best-tasting flesh – and sound fruits that will store for months – is the winter squash. There are many tasty varieties to choose from; the best have a dense texture that is creamy smooth when cooked and a taste that is not merely sweet, but has a nuttiness to it. Many of the commercial varieties are bred to be large for processing, but for home gardeners they are simply too big to manage or to enjoy. Therefore, opt for a small-fruited variety, such as 'Sweet Dumpling'. Simply cut one ripe squash in half, scoop out the seed, add butter and seasoning and microwave in minutes. 'Sweet Dumpling' produces plenty of small fruits, with attractive striped skins that are excellent when shown whole in autumn displays.

Of course, the main reason to grow them is the particularly good flavour of the light-yellow flesh.

Like all cucurbits, winter squash are very sensitive to frost, so there is no point sowing seed or planting out starter plants too early. However, you have to be sure of fruits before the first frost; this one matures eighty-two days from sowing. In warm regions the seeds can be pushed into the ground a couple of weeks after the last frost. In colder areas it pays to start the seed off in pots at 21°C (70°F), then gradually harden off plants to outside conditions. Plant into a rich, well-drained soil that has been mounded into a small hill; an alternative is to plant on the flat on ground laid with mulch. Protect from winds while they are establishing, but for most of the summer they can be left while the weather is fine. **LD**

Alternative

Cucurbita moschata 'Harlequin'

Cucurbita
C. maxima 'Cinderella's Carriage'

Main features Heritage-type pumpkin; bright, reddish-orange skin
Height 1.5–1.8 m (5–6 ft) **Spread** 45 cm (18 in.)
Position ○ **Hardiness** Annual

The challenge of growing a large pumpkin is a fun family project: start by sowing a seed in spring, watch the plant grow like a triffid, peep under the leaves to witness the fruits swell. Then bring home the bounty in the autumn. Big pumpkins impress, of course, but rather than the huge ones that exhibitors grow – which are often too big to manage, unsymmetrical and deformed – home gardeners should get a variety that has vertical ridges, so the fruits will hold their shape and look attractive.

There are various French heritage pumpkins that fit the bill – 'Cinderella', 'Fairytale' and for foodies, the flavoursome 'Musquee de Provence' or red 'Rouge Vif d'Etampes', but the latter pair are more flat than round

and all these are open-pollinated varieties, so results are variable. Growing pumpkins takes up a lot of space, so for more guarantees, turn to modern breeding in the form of 'Cinderella's Carriage'. This bright, red-orange pumpkin is the first F1 hybrid, Cinderella-type pumpkin. The improved yield should mean five to seven fruits per vine (depending on growing conditions) – more than the one or two fruits one would get with open-pollinated varieties. The typical fruit size is 11 to 16 kilograms (25–35 lb) – impressive but manageable for lifting. This variety also has a good resistance to the dreaded powdery mildew. 'Cinderella's Carriage' is an All-America Selections winner and is well-suited for autumn decoration, as well as baking and cooking. **DB/LD**

Alternative

Cucurbita maxima 'Rouge Vif d'Etampes'

Cucurbita
C. pepo 'Sunburst'

Main features Fast-growing, vigorous, attractive fruits; delicious, tender, buttery flesh
Height 90 cm (3 ft) **Spread** 90 cm (3 ft)
Position ○ **Hardiness** Annual

Also known as yellow pattypan or custard squash, this bright-gold summer squash tastes as wonderful as it looks. Each fruit resembles an old-fashioned spinning top in shape, with delicate, scalloped edges around the central ridge. 'Sunburst' can be harvested as a melt-in-the-mouth baby squash when very tiny, with the yellow flower still attached. The edible flowers can be stuffed and baked or fried. However, this squash is most commonly grown to around the size of a teacup. This cultivar is unusual in that it retains its fine texture and flavour even if grown into larger squash of up to 20 centimetres (8 in.) across, when many other varieties would be tough and tasteless.

The tender, delicious flesh of 'Sunburst' has a buttery quality and can simply be either steamed or boiled. However, it is often sliced and fried or grilled. It retains its attractive, pleasing shape when baked, so it is therefore popularly served as a stuffed vegetable. Pattypans are also excellent pickled whole in sweet vinegar, and the golden fruits of 'Sunburst' are especially attractive when preserved in this way.

'Sunburst' has been recognised by All-America Selections for its vigorous growth, productivity and fruit quality. Pattypan plants grow into a relatively tidy, bushy shape, with large, yellow flowers that attract bees and other pollinators. They are decorative enough to be featured in a kitchen garden or in the beds of a cottage garden. Another advantage of this cultivar's vivid yellow colouring is that the fruits are always highly visible, which makes harvesting them while still very young easier than with green squash. Picking the fruits on a daily basis ensures that they can be enjoyed at their freshest, and it also encourages the plant to keep producing new flowers. **PWa/JM**

Alternatives

Cucurbita pepo 'Peter Pan', *Cucurbita pepo* 'Atena', *Curcurbita pepo* 'Summer Ball'

Cucurbita

C. *pepo* 'Hijinks'

Main features Small-sized pumpkin for carving; smooth, deep-orange skin; strong, durable stem
Height 4.5 m (15 ft) **Spread** 90 cm (3 ft)
Position ○ **Hardiness** Annual

Making the most of autumn with festivals, fun and celebration is a good opportunity to get the children outside before the weather turns colder. At one time, the bigger the pumpkin the better, but there is now a trend to have smaller ones so that each child can carve their own small jack-o'-lantern. 'Hijinks' is a large vine, but it produces a number of smallish fruits of an even, easy-to-manage size for children and is a variety well worth growing. Typically, fruits will be 18 to 20 centimetres (7–8 in.) long and weigh 3 to 4 kilograms (7–9 lb); they should also be very uniform in size and shape. Smooth, deep-orange skin with distinctive grooves gives a very classy appearance to autumn decorations and is ideal for painting or carving. The long, dark, durable stem makes a great handle for small hands. Gardeners can expect high yields, notable resistance to powdery mildew, easy fruit removal from the vines and strong stems that stay attached to the pumpkin. This is a perfect pumpkin to get children interested in gardening and producing a specimen they can use for Halloween. It was an All-America Selections Award winner in 2011.

To grow, sow seed directly in mounded hills of garden soil with plenty of space for the long vines. Space plants 90 centimetres (3 ft) apart with 1.5 metres (5 ft) between rows. Pumpkins produce both female and male flowers, so they will therefore need pollination. Early to mature, this *C. pepo* is ready for harvest in about one hundred days from sowing or eight-five days from planting a transplant. Most pumpkins need plenty of moisture and nutrients, so testing the garden soil fairly frequently will help ensure successful growing. Drip irrigation or a soaker hose is recommended for pumpkins to direct water to the base of the vines, avoiding wet foliage, which can lead to disease. **DB**

Alternatives

Cucurbita pepo 'Orange Smoothie', *Cucurbita pepo* 'Hybrid Pam'

Cynara
C. cardunculus 'Gros Vert de Lâon'

Main features Edible flower buds; spring to summer foliage; architectural plant
Height 1.5 m (5 ft) **Spread** 60 cm (24 in.)
Position ○ **Hardiness** RHS H6

Best reserved for larger gardens, globe artichokes take up a lot of space, considering that they offer only a small number of edible buds each year. That said, C. cardunculus 'Gros Vert de Lâon' is not only a heavy cropper (for an artichoke), but it is also utterly delicious. It is a traditional French variety that used to be quite hard to find, but thankfully, the Internet has made tracking down plants much easier. It is worth taking the time to find this one for the simple reason that this heritage favourite produces the largest hearts of any artichoke variety.

In terms of dinner-party prestige, serving home-grown artichokes is a hard act to follow, but they are good to grow even if you never cut a single bud. Tall, stately, and highly architectural, the plants add instant class to flower beds and borders. If left on their stems, the edible heads will open into spectacular firework blooms beloved not only of bees, but also of flower arrangers. The globe-shaped, green buds of 'Gros Vert de Lâon' are a real focal point and look particularly good paired with its purple-headed cousin 'Violetta di Chioggia'. The latter is equally popular with gourmands and certainly very decorative.

Artichokes can be grown from seeds, but the resulting plants do not always come completely true to their variety; instead, you may find slight variations in size, shape and colour if you grow them this way. If you want to be sure you are growing 'Gros Vert de Lâon', buy young plants. As they grow, these will produce rooted side shoots called offsets, and by lifting the plants and dividing them, you can expand your stock or pass on plants to friends. In the first year the plants may not produce particularly big artichokes, but subsequent harvests will be at their best in midsummer and should be picked when the scales are still closed. **PWa/JM**

Alternatives

Cynara cardunculus 'Green Globe', *Cynara cardunculus* 'Violetta di Chioggia'

❦ *Cynara cardunculus* needs plenty of room but the reward is lots of globe artichokes.

Daucus
D. carota 'Nantes'

Main features High-quality, uniform roots; heavy yields and reliable cropping
Height 30 cm (12 in.) **Spread** 5–8 cm (2–3 in.)
Position ○ ◐ **Hardiness** Annual

There are many different kinds and colours of carrot but it is not always straightforward to know which variety to grow. However, *D. carota* 'Nantes', named after the city in France, is a good choice if you are new to growing carrots. Very much a heritage type, 'Nantes' was bred in the 1850s by Henry de Vilmorin of the French seed company Vilmorin & Cie, which is still around and thriving today. It represented a quantum leap in the history of carrot breeding. So successful has the 'Nantes' type been that there are now well over forty cultivars in commerce today, derived from the original.

The well-known Vilmorin seed catalogue from 1885 makes interesting reading, describing 'Nantes' as 'having a near-perfect cylindrical root with smooth skin and entirely edible near-red flesh, both sweet and mild in flavour'. The 'Nantes' carrot is further characterised by having a rounded top and bottom to its roots, and in the world of carrots it is classified as medium sized, growing up to 20 centimetres (8 in.) in length. The variety is revered for its high sugar content and crisp texture as well as for having a small central core. Another reason for its success has been its reliable performance in a range of different soil types.

Although perhaps not the best choice for storing, all the 'Nantes' types may be harvested as young or mature roots and are extremely versatile as an ingredient for fresh use or cooking. When young they are particularly tender and sweet and do not require peeling. There is now a number of F1 hybrid 'Nantes' carrots on the market, which offer even greater uniformity and better pest and disease resistance. The mere fact, however, that this type has survived more than 150 years is a great tribute to Henry de Vilmorin and his team of vegetable breeders. **TS**

Alternatives

Daucus carota 'Early Nantes 5', *Daucus carota* 'Nantes 2 Mars', *Daucus carota* 'Maestro', *Daucus carota* 'Artemis'

Daucus
D. *carota* subsp. *sativus* 'Purple Haze'

Main feature A tasty carrot with different-coloured skin to add interest on the plate
Height 30 cm (12 in.) **Spread** 5–8 cm (2–3 in.)
Position ○ ◐ **Hardiness** Annual

Carrots have not always been orange, so the new varieties in purple, red, white and yellow forms actually exemplify carrot breeders simply taking this vegetable back to its roots. Purple carrots have more anthocyanin, thanks to the purple pigment in them. However, the main reason to grow them is not for their health benefit, but because they taste great and add interest on the plate.

The cultivar 'Purple Haze' as a dark-purple skin in contrast with the orange interior. This carrot looks impressive when served in slanted slices so that both colours are visible. It is sweet and tasty and has a national All-America Selections Award. 'Deep Purple' is a much darker purple and the pigment continues through the whole carrot. It looks appealing when served mixed with orange or red carrots.

The effect of the colour variation is best displayed on full-size, 18-centimetre-long (7 in.) carrots. To produce a crop of carrots to store over winter, make one sowing in early summer. Thin out the carrots to 5 to 8 centimetres (2–3 in.) between plants. Protect with fine mesh if carrot root fly is a problem. In the autumn lift the roots and store them in moist sand in sturdy wooden or metal boxes and keep them in a cool, dark place, such as a garage or shed.

There are references to carrots being grown in gardening books from 1599, by American colonists in 1600s, and before that, the Romans spread them throughout Europe. Purple carrots were grown in the Middle East and spread by the Moors in the eighth century; some of these are still in seed libraries today. Long Orange Dutch carrots – developed with a denser carotene pigment – first appeared in 1720, and were cultivated by the Dutch. These were the progenitors of the modern carrot, and from this time on, orange became the most popular colour for carrots. **LD**

Alternatives

Daucus carota 'Purple Sun', *Daucus carota* 'Rainbow Mixed'

Hibiscus
H. esculentus 'Clemson Spineless'

Main features Spineless, edible pods; flowers attract bees; extreme heat and drought tolerance
Height 1.2–1.5 m (4–5 ft) **Spread** 60–90 cm (2–3 ft)
Position ○ **Hardiness** Annual

Okra came to America via the slave trade from Africa, where it grows wild. A stew known as gumbo in the southern United States (*ki ngombo* is the original West African name) is an okra-based stew subsequently claimed by Creole cuisine. Related to *Hibiscus*, *A. esculentus* has huge, pale-yellow flowers with a contrasting maroon base, making it an interesting plant for your vegetable or flower garden. The curious, edible, ridged seed pods, which are eaten as a vegetable, tend to be pale green, but they can also be red, red-orange and burgundy. 'Clemson Spineless' is the most practical and popular variety to grow, the reason being in its name. Named for the Agricultural Experiment Station in South Carolina, its pods have no spines. A slightly taller, more open form, 'Clemson Spineless 80' was released in 1980.

A pan-global annual plant popular in warmer climes, okra dislikes soil temperatures below 18°C (65°F) and requires a long growing season of sixty days. Improve germination by soaking seeds overnight and sowing at a minimum temperature of 21°C (70°F). Plant 30 to 45 centimetres (12–18 in.) apart, as plants can be large, and pinch out to encourage bushiness. Following flowering, pick pods at 8 centimetres (3 in.) long. Do not allow to ripen, or plants will cease to produce.

Sauté or simmer okra in sauces, soups, stews and curries, or deep-fry. The mucilaginous pods are mainly used to thicken dishes, but interestingly, the leaves, flowers, and seed pods are also edible. The petals can be used in salads; the toasted, ground seed are a coffee substitute; and the nutritious leaves, steamed or raw, have high levels of protein. Recent research has been centred around the plant's potential to manage diabetes. Be warned, hairs on the seed pods can be a skin irritant to some people. **IT**

Alternative

Syn. *Abelmoschus esculentus. Abelmoschus manihot*

Ipomoea
I. batatas 'Beauregard'

Main features Attractive, tasty, nutritious roots; good for warm and temperate areas
Height 2.7 m (9 ft) **Spread** 15–30 cm (6–12 in.)
Position ○ **Hardiness** Annual

Native to the United States, the sweet potato is an important crop not only in that country, but also in many parts of Asia. Although it is often referred to as 'yam', this is a misnomer because yam is a completely different species in the genus *Dioscorea*.

Ipomoea is a short-lived perennial, but it is usually grown as an annual. The relatively new variety known as *I. batatas* 'Beauregard' produces large, long tubers with a red skin and attractive salmon-orange flesh. These tubers are a nutritious, healthy part of a diet, because they are low in fat and calories yet high in vitamins A and C and also contain high levels of potassium, calcium and iron. In addition to the nutritious tubers, the leaves and young shoots may be harvested and used as cooked greens. The plant leaves are heart-shaped and the stems can trail to around 2.7 metres (9 ft). Attractive, white, trumpet-shaped flowers, each of which comes and goes within a day, are carried above the foliage and attract butterflies, moths and the occasional hummingbird.

'Beauregard' has the bonus of being reasonably hardy for a sweet potato, which means that it is a good all-rounder for both warm and temperate climes. Plants are produced traditionally from 'slips' (long shoots created by encouraging selected tubers into growth), but increasingly they are grown from rooted cuttings. 'Beauregard' tubers mature some ninety days from planting. As the shorter days arrive, the foliage turns yellow and blackens, and at this point the tubers may be carefully lifted. They can be used fresh or prepared for storage by curing. Lifted tubers should be left in the sun for a few hours and then placed in a warm, humid place, such as a glasshouse, for around ten days. Once the skin has cured, tubers should be kept cool and dry and will store well for a few months. **TS**

Alternatives

Ipomoea batatas 'O'Henry', *Ipomoea batatas* 'Nugget'

Lactuca
L. sativa 'Buttercrunch'

Main features Loosely packed heads of large, pale-green leaves; good flavour
Height 15–30 cm (6–12 in.) **Spread** 30 cm (12 in.)
Position ○ ◐ **Hardiness** Annual

Butterhead lettuce, such as 'Buttercrunch', have round, compact heads of loosely packed, smooth, soft leaves. In the United States they are commonly called loose heads. They have more flavour than the crisphead type and are excellent in green salads, but they can also be made into a surprisingly tasty soup. In Korean cuisine they are sometimes used as an alternative to Chinese cabbage and pak choi as wraps for slices of grilled meats flavoured with sesame oil or soy sauce.

An annual plant in the daisy family (*Asteraceae*), *L. sativa* is native to North Africa, Asia and Europe and has been cultivated since ancient times. In Egypt it was associated with the fertility god, Min.

Lettuce grows best in cool seasons. Seed germination is poor at temperatures above 25ºC (77ºF). The seed can be sown from midwinter onwards under cover, ready for planting outside in early spring with a fleece covering to protect against frost. Starting seedlings off in modules allows them to be planted out without root disturbance. Plant out when they have five or six leaves. They prefer fertile, moisture-retentive soil in an open site or light shade. Space plants 25 centimetres (10 in.) apart in rows 30 centimetres (12 in.) apart. Summer sowings are best made outdoors to prevent seedlings wilting on transplanting. In hot weather, water the drills before sowing to reduce soil temperatures. Cold-hardy cultivars, such as 'Valdor' can be sown outdoors in late summer and overwintered under fleece for an early spring crop. **GHa**

Alternatives

Lactuca sativa 'Clarion', *Lactuca sativa* 'Diana'

Lactuca
L. sativa 'Red Salad Bowl'

Main features Long cropping period; crisp, succulent leaves; easy to grow
Height 10–30 cm (4–12 in.) **Spread** 10–30 cm (4–12 in.)
Position ○ ◑ **Hardiness** Annual

There are a number of different sorts of lettuce, and *L. sativa* 'Red Salad Bowl' belongs to a group known as loose-leaved lettuce. The variety qualifies for heritage status, having been introduced in 1955, and it is still so good that it has acquired the Royal Horticultural Society Award of Garden Merit.

'Red Salad Bowl' is aptly named because the mature heads – with a diameter of 30 centimetres (12 in.) – nicely fill an average-sized salad bowl. The deeply cut, crimped leaves are green at the base, turning into a rich bronze-red colour, which is accentuated in cool weather. In fact, 'Red Salad Bowl' is a truly versatile variety since it has three distinct uses.

Firstly, it is often used in salad mixes as baby leaves, when the young bronze-red leaves are harvested when they are only three to four weeks old and the plants 8 to 10 centimetres (3–4 in.) high. This is the simplest way to produce salad leaves, and it can be done easily on a well-lit windowsill, in a patio pot or in the garden soil. Secondly, 'Red Salad Bowl' can be used as a true 'picking' lettuce, and you can walk through the rows picking off leaves as required. Pick the young leaves from the outside and be selective. Too many from one plant will severely affect the subsequent yield. Thirdly, you can allow this nonhearting lettuce to grow to maturity and harvest it as one head, as you would conventional lettuce. The all-green variety, *L. sativa* 'Salad Bowl', is equally versatile (both pictured). **TS**

Alternatives

Lactuca sativa 'Delicato', *Lactuca sativa* 'Granada'

Lactuca
L. *sativa* 'Little Gem'

Main features Great-tasting lettuce; compact habit
for small spaces; crisp, succulent leaves; easy to grow
Height 20 cm (8 in.) **Spread** 20 cm (8 in.)
Position ○ ◑ **Hardiness** Annual

Lettuce has been cultivated since early Egyptian times,
when it was grown not only for its salad leaves but also
for its seeds, which were used for the production of
cooking oil. It was also used as a medicinal herb and was
considered to be something of an aphrodisiac!

L. *sativa* 'Little Gem' is a small, upright lettuce that
is recognised as a heritage variety. It is thought to have
originated in France from a cross between 'Romaine
Cos' and 'Butterhead'. The 'Romaine Cos' heritage
provides the distinctive crisp leaves of 'Little Gem',
and the 'Butterhead' linkage provides the sweetness
in the leaves. Unlike many 'Cos' lettuce varieties, 'Little
Gem' has a thinner internal stalk, which results in more

edible content. It is a winner of the prestigious Royal
Horticultural Society Award of Garden Merit.

The compact nature of 'Little Gem' – 20 centimetres
(8 in.) high with a similar ground spread – is ideal where
space is limited in small gardens or for growing in a
container on the patio. It is one of the fastest-growing
lettuce varieties, producing leaves that can be used as
baby leaf in salads in only twenty-one to twenty-eight
days, or a mature lettuce in forty-eight days. The variety
has also been shown to have good resistance to attack
from the lettuce root aphid. Primarily, 'Little Gem' is used
in salads, sandwiches and wraps and is favoured for use
in the well-known Caesar salad. In addition, it can be
used in lettuce soup. Normally, grown in summer, there
is also a winter selection. **TS**

Alternatives

Lactuca sativa 'Vailan', *Lactuca sativa* 'Amaze'

Lactuca
L. sativa 'Mottistone'

Main features Decorative; fine flavour; good disease and mildew resistance
Height 45 cm (18 in.) **Spread** 45 cm (18 in.)
Position ○ ◑ **Hardiness** Annual

One of the pleasures of growing your own vegetables is that you can seek out tasty cultivars that offer something a bit different from those sold in the supermarket. *L. sativa* 'Mottistone' is a great example because the unusual foliage puts off commercial growers and retailers. However, for the home gardener wanting to incorporate edibles into their flower borders, the crinkly leaves of this lime-green lettuce, dotted with red freckles, are a pretty tasty addition. The flavour is excellent, with none of the bitterness that some red-leaved varieties possess.

Crunchy hearts can be harvested in as few as fifty-five days after planting. Alternatively, for a cut-and-come-again crop of baby leaves, seeds can be sown closely together and the new leaves harvested in as few as thirty to forty days after sowing. If plants are watered regularly and left to grow on, it can be possible to get three or sometimes four harvests from a single sowing from this dual-purpose lettuce.

'Mottistone' is usually eaten raw, and the red-and-green leaves make a striking addition to a mixed salad. However, a surplus can be stirfried, grilled, braised or baked. The pretty leaves can also be made into a stylish entrée or canapé when stuffed and folded into tiny parcels. If any heads of 'Mottistone' are accidentally left growing for so long that they become old and tired, they can be harvested, lightly drizzled with oil, and warmed in a hot oven until they melt like baked spinach. The cooking process enhances the sweet flavour. **PWa/JM**

Alternative

Lactuca sativa 'Forellenschluss' (syn. 'Speckled Trout Back')

Nasturtium
N. officinale 'Aqua'

Main features Edible, glossy, green leaves with a strong peppery flavour; small, white flowers; attracts bees
Height 50 cm (20 in.) **Spread** 50 cm (20 in.)
Position ○ ◑ **Hardiness** Annual

Watercress is grown for its edible, glossy, green leaves, which have a strong peppery flavour. As the common name implies, it is a water plant that grows wild along the edges of streams. The stems are hollow, allowing the plant to float. Like other members of the *Brassicaceae* family, it is the food plant of several butterflies. The small, white flowers bloom from summer through to autumn and attract bees and other insects. Once plants start to flower, the leaves can become unpleasantly bitter to taste.

Contrary to popular belief, watercress does not need a stream or even waterlogged soil in which to grow. It can be grown successfully in troughs, a bog garden or in the garden pond. It will even grow happily in pots of any reasonably moist compost in partial shade. It prefers a constant temperature of around 10°C (50°F). In warm weather, stand the pots in a saucer of water. Cuttings from a bunch bought from the supermarket can be rooted in a glass of water on the windowsill, or grow cultivars, such as 'Aqua', from seeds. Watercress makes a useful cut-and-come-again crop, best sown in spring or fall, as it may run to seed in high summer temperatures.

Native throughout Europe, particularly in limestone areas, watercress has been consumed for centuries. The Greek physician Hippocrates grew watercress as a medicinal plant on the island of Kos around 400 BCE. It was spread around the world by European explorers, who used it to prevent scurvy, the disease caused by a vitamin C deficiency. Watercress is a useful source of vitamins and minerals, particularly vitamins A and C. It is sometimes used as a water-purifying plant in ponds that are full of algae since it will outcompete the algae for nutrients, such as nitrates and phosphates, in the water. Remember that watercress spreads indefinitely in suitable conditions. **GHa**

Alternative

Eruca sativa

Phaseolus
P. coccineus 'Saint George'

Main features Climbing runner bean with colourful flowers; high yields
Height 3 m (10 ft) **Spread** 30 cm (12 in.)
Position ○ **Hardiness** Annual

Climbing beans originated in Central and South America and there is evidence that they were cultivated from around 2,000 BCE onwards. They were brought to Europe in the sixteenth century; the British favoured the runner bean (*P. coccineus*) whereas in the rest of Europe, *P. vulgaris* was preferred (hence the term French beans). Both species were grown only as ornamental vines up until the 1800s, when their tasty pods were discovered. We have now come full circle, since there is a renewed interest in having edibles that also earn their place as ornamentals as more people with small urban gardens and tiny patios want to grow their own food. Even in larger plots the cottage-garden–style puts the accent, as well as the productivity, on a flower. In any situation where flower colour is a consideration, runner beans have the edge over French beans. One of the most colourful runner beans is 'Saint George', with red and white flowers. The variety won a Royal Horticultural Society Award of Garden Merit in 2006 and scores highly on both counts with plenty of 25- to 30-centimetre-long (10–12 in.) pods.

Runner beans have colourful flowers to attract bees to pollinate their flowers, whereas French beans are self-pollinating and have less showy, white or pale-lavender flowers. When pollinators such as bees are in short supply, or night temperatures are over 15°C (59°F), pods either abort or deform, or the yield is reduced on runner beans. That is when French beans have the advantage.

Is it possible to have a self-fertile runner bean? Breeders Tozer launched 'Moonlight', a runner bean crossed with a French bean, in 2010, but despite good yields, it has not taken off, perhaps because of its white flower. Newer, self-fertile varieties 'Firestorm' (red) and 'Tenderstar' (red and pink) are recommended both for their appearance and versatility in the kitchen. **LD**

Alternatives

Phaseolus 'Firestorm', *Phaseolus* 'Tenderstar'

Phaseolus

P. vulgaris

Main features Climbing, annual bean; very productive yields for the space
Height 1.8–2.7 m (6–9 ft) **Spread** 45 cm (18 in.)
Position ○ **Hardiness** Annual

Climbing beans are incredibly productive crops that most home gardeners find worth growing. There are different types, and depending on where you live, the preference might be for pole bean, a French climbing bean, or a runner bean. Within each type there are many varieties, including heritage and new hybrids. All climbing beans require a degree of forward planning; you need to decide early on what supports to have and where to put them. A tepee arrangement of poles laid out in a circle at least 90 centimetres (3 ft) across will fit into most potager or ornamental beds and make an attractive and productive summer feature in a sheltered garden. Alternatively, as many climbing beans are attractive in flower, use them

alongside ornamental, annual climbers over an arch or trained up a pergola. For the serious veg grower, or if your site is windy, a double row of poles 60 to 90 centimetres (24–36 in.) apart and braced with horizontal struts at the top will give you firm support for a line of beans. This system will produce a large crop, so it suits those who are able to freeze or preserve produce.

There are many varieties of pole bean, usually grouped by the type or colour of pod: flat pod, round pod, purple pod, yellow pod, and shelling beans. A good one to start with is 'Kentucky Blue' as it is the latest version of two reliable classics – flat pod 'Kentucky Wonder' and round pod 'Blue Lake'. 'Kentucky Blue' should give you large crops of straight, stringless pods that will be ready for picking when they are 18 centimetres (7 in.) long. **LD**

Alternatives

Phaseolus vulgaris 'Romano', *Phaseolus vulgaris* 'Blauhilde'

Phaseolus
P. *vulgaris* 'Mascotte'

Main features Prolific crops on self-supporting plants;
disease resistant
Height 45 cm (18 in.) **Spread** 30 cm (12 in.)
Position ○ **Hardiness** Annual

Also known as a French bean or green bean, the dwarf
cultivar 'Mascotte' is one of the best options for home
growers. It has a compact root system and a neat, bushy
growing habit, so it is perfect for planting in pots, raised
beds, window boxes and troughs. It is ideal for providing
a worthwhile crop in a tiny space, such as a balcony or
patio garden. The plants are decorative when the little
white flowers are in bloom, and they will attract a variety
of bees and other pollinating insects. 'Mascotte' plants
do not need stakes or supports, as neighbouring plants
will support them.

The delicious beans are extra fine and completely
stringless, so they are very easy to prepare in the kitchen.

They are also very simple to harvest because 'Mascotte'
produces all the flowers and pods right at the top of
the plant, held well outside the foliage. The fact it is so
easy to spot them means that the plant is unlikely to go
to seed, which in turn means that the cropping period
is extended for as long as possible. If the beans are
harvested regularly, it is not unusual to be picking tasty
pods of 'Mascotte' for up to sixteen weeks. However, to
guarantee a continuous harvest all summer long, it is
worth sowing more seeds every few weeks.

Another advantage of this variety is that it is resistant
to common mosaic virus and halo blight, making it ideal
for gardeners who prefer to grow crops without using
artificial chemicals. Heavy cropping, it is ideal for freezing
in batches. **PWa/JM**

Alternative

Phaseolus vulgaris 'Green Arrow', *Phaseolus vulgaris* 'Stanley'

Phaseolus

P. vulgaris 'Berggold'

Main feature Reliable producer of colourful, yellow-podded beans
Height 50 cm (20 in.) **Spread** 30 cm (12 in.)
Position ○ **Hardiness** Annual

This is a stringless French bean with straight, pencil-thin, yellow pods of around 13 centimetres (5 in.) in length. The pods contrast well with the dark-green, heart-shaped leaves. They look particularly attractive cascading out of a large hanging basket or window box, especially if grown together with a purple-podded cultivar, such as 'Amethyst'. 'Berggold' is a dwarf variety that is early to crop, very vigorous and productive. The seed are white and can be dried for winter use.

P. vulgaris is native to the Americas and was an essential crop for the indigenous North American people, along with squash and maize, together known as the 'three sisters'. The beans were first introduced into Europe by the Spanish conquistadors. In Italy they were an established crop in vegetable gardens as early as 1569.

French beans will not tolerate frost, but early sowings can be made in pots under cover, planting out after the risk of frost has passed. Outdoor sowings can be made from late spring, if plants are protected with cloches or fleece against late frost. Space plants 15 centimetres (6 in.) apart. They are best grown in small blocks so that neighbouring plants provide support. Water well during periods of prolonged dry weather. Feed with a high-potash feed, such as a liquid tomato fertiliser. As with other members of the legume family, French beans acquire the nitrogen they need through an association with rhizobia, a species of nitrogen-fixing bacteria. Start to harvest the pods when they are about 10 centimetres (4 in.) long. Pods are ready when they snap easily and before the beans can be seen through the pod. When picked regularly, the plants will continue to produce for several weeks. Once all the pods have been harvested, water the plants well and feed with a liquid fertiliser. This will encourage a further crop of smaller pods. **GHa**

Alternatives

Phaseolus vulgaris 'Concador', *Phaseolus vulgaris* 'Creso', *Phaseolus vulgaris* 'Sonesta'

Physalis
P. philadelphica 'Purple De Milpa'

Main features Prolific, low-calorie vegetable with antioxidants and multivitamins; unique, tart flavour
Height 45–80 cm (18–32 in.) **Spread** 2.4–3 m (8–10 ft)
Position ○ **Hardiness** Annual

Affectionately called little tomato in Spanish, tomatillo – a relative of the tomato – originates from Mexico, where it grows wild in cornfields. This spherical-shaped berry, enclosed in its own papery husk, was grown by the Aztecs and has been used as a vegetable for centuries. Archaeological evidence dates its cultivation to about 5090 BCE, making it one of the oldest-known cultivated foods. The tomatillo is a stalwart of Mexican cuisine and adds a sharp piquancy, particularly to salsas. Use the fruits raw or cooked; roasting or grilling will intensify the flavour.

Also known as green tomatoes, most tomatillos are fresh green in colour, but they also come in yellow or dark purple. 'Purple De Milpa' is a heritage variety with a particularly deep-purple skin that is occasionally coloured throughout, pointing to the levels of antioxidants contained within it. The fruit is slightly smaller than other cultivars and has a more tart, more distinct flavour, which is preferred by some cooks.

Tomatillos like a rich, well-drained soil that is neutral to slightly alkaline, full sun and moderate watering. Grow tomatillos from fresh seeds annually and they will be ready to harvest within seventy to ninety days of sowing. Sow four weeks before the first frost; plant at least two of them to cross-pollinate and set fruit. Plants tend to sprawl, but gardeners can 'cage' or trellis them, providing greater air circulation while the fruits stay off the ground. Alternatively, grow them in large pots, 'ridges' or raised beds, where they benefit from improved drainage and faster-warming soil. Pick when the papery husk splits to reveal the firm flesh and remove the husks before eating. (All parts of the plant are poisonous except for the fruit.) Tomatillos tend to be sticky when handled. 'Purple De Milpa' fruits are smaller but more prolific than other cultivars. **IT**

Alternatives

Syn. *Physalis ixocarpa* 'Purple De Milpa'. *Physalis ixocarpa* 'Purple', *Physalis* 'Mexican Green Husk'

Pisum

P. sativum
'Sugar Ann'

Main features Compact plants; early to mature; sweet, crisp pods; can grow without support
Height 45 cm (18 in.) **Spread** 5–13 cm (2–5 in.)
Position ○ **Hardiness** Annual

Snap peas, or sugar snap peas, are a fairly modern development, produced when snow peas were crossed with shell peas, creating an edible pea pod. These peas do not have a membrane and do not open when mature. The short, compact-growth habit of 'Sugar Ann' makes it ideal for urban gardens with limited space. Another useful feature of 'Sugar Ann' is its earliness, up to two weeks earlier than comparable varieties. Its plump, crisp, edible pods are very sweet and grow to 6 centimetres (2.5 in.) long. The pods grow on compact, 45-centimetre-high (18 in.), bushy plants and can be grown with or without support. Peas can be planted when the soil is still cool, so you do not have to worry about frost. The main challenges are pests, such as mice, and mildew. Later sowings do not produce as prolific a harvest. Plant the first crop in early spring, as soon as the soil can be worked. 'Sugar Ann' pods are delicious eaten raw, as crudités or sliced into a salad, as well as sautéed, stirfried, roasted and steamed. **DB**

Alternatives

Pisum sativum 'Mr Big', *Pisum sativum* 'Sugar Snap'

Pisum

P. sativum
'Oregon Giant'

Main feature High yields of edible, sweet-tasting, pea pods
Height 90 cm (3 ft) **Spread** 5–13 cm (2–5 in.)
Position ○ **Hardiness** Annual

'Oregon Giant' is a form of the snow pea that produces vigorous annual vines that will scramble up trellis to a height of around 90 centimetres (3 ft). Sometimes called snowman, this popular cultivar is high yielding with long, straight, and very sweet pods. They tend to curl somewhat as they mature. The pods are usually cooked, but they can be eaten raw. The young tips, known as pea shoots, may also be harvested and cooked. They are particularly popular in Chinese cuisine. The pea is thought to have originated in central or south-eastern Asia, but is no longer known in the wild. The name snow pea comes from the Chinese and is thought to have arisen because they can emerge early in the spring and get caught in late snowfalls. The name *mangetout* (French for 'eat all') can apply both to snow peas and to sugar snap peas (*P. sativum* var. *macrocarpon*), which have thicker, but still edible, pods. Snow peas are high in vitamin C and contain useful minerals, such as iron and manganese. **GHa**

Alternatives

Pisum sativum 'Kennedy', *Pisum sativum* 'Snowbird'

Pisum

P. savitum
'Kelvedon Wonder'

Main features High yields of delicious peas; relatively trouble-free plants
Height 45 cm (18 in.) **Spread** 5–13 cm (2–5 in.)
Position ○ **Hardiness** Annual

In the 1900s, peas were considered to be the most delicious of all vegetables, rated higher than any other gourmet vegetable. Many of these heritage varieties are still available today, and they include numerous, reliable cultivars. One such example is *P. savitum* 'Kelvedon Wonder', a shelling pea with pods that open to reveal sweet, succulent peas. Producing two well-filled pods per node, this cultivar is an 'early', which means that it matures quickly. The individual pods are not very long, but they are densely packed, which makes shelling efficient. Masses of peas can be harvested around twelve weeks after sowing, so to enjoy fresh crops of 'Kelvedon Wonder' from late spring to early winter, it is worth sowing a short row or two every month from early spring until midsummer. The young shoots are delicious when eaten in salads and sandwiches. 'Kelvedon Wonder' has pretty little cream-coloured flowers, which make it suitable for growing in large pots on the patio. **PWa/JM**

Alternative

Pisum sativum 'American Wonder'

Raphanus

R. sativus
'French Breakfast'

Main features Sweet-tasting radish; decorative, cylindrical shape
Height 15 cm (6 in.) **Spread** 10 cm (4 in.)
Position ○ ◑ **Hardiness** Annual

Few vegetables are as quick and easy to grow as summer radishes. They are currently enjoying a revival as a gourmet salad ingredient. The heritage variety 'French Breakfast' has been popular since around 1885 and is still winning awards today. Rather than the typical round shape, it is elongated and has a rich, dark-pink colour with a white base. It gets its name from the European habit of eating this mild, sweet, crisp vegetable with a little salt, and bread and butter in the morning. Although they are usually served raw, 'French Breakfast' radishes can be sautéed in butter and served warm. The leaves are also edible, and when young, the tangy leaves are ideal in salads or in sandwiches with mayonnaise. Radishes have a delicious peppery flavour and add depth when cooked with sweeter vegetables, such as peppers and squash. 'French Breakfast' is ideal for growing in containers, window boxes or greenhouse borders, where it will offer a generous return for the small space given to it. **PWa/JM**

Alternative

Raphanus sativus 'Ping Pong'

Rheum
R. rhabarbarum
'Victoria'

Main feature A perennial vegetable grown for its edible leaf stalks, which can be cooked early in the year
Height 90 cm (3 ft) **Spread** 90 cm (3 ft)
Position ○ ◑ **Hardiness** RHS H4

Rhubarb is a rewarding crop that requires very little effort. In fact, all this perennial needs is space to be left alone. Ideally, rhubarb plants should be in a sunny position, but they are worth trying if the only option is partial shade. The harvest comes early in the year, when there is little on the vegetable plot and no other fruits to pick for months. Simply pull some colourful red stems for cooking; quick poaching or dry roasting is the way to keep the flavour. The best stems are those that are blanched; that is, deprived of light. These will be a pretty pink, and tender with no stringiness. For a crop of blanched rhubarb in early spring, cover a dormant clump with a terra-cotta forcing pot, a large flower pot or an upturned dustbin in early winter. Rhubarb is grown around the world but is particularly associated with England. 'Victoria' is a variety that was selected in the 1820s and 1830s by Joseph Myatt, a market gardener from London, for its yield, stem colour and early cropping. **LD**

Alternative

Rheum rhabarbarum 'Timperley Early'

Solanum
S. lycopersicum
'Terenzo'

Main features Ideal home-garden variety; easy to grow; cherry-sized fruits
Height 10–24 in. (25–60 cm) **Spread** 20 in. (50 cm)
Position ○ **Hardiness** Annual

Bred in England, *S. lycopersicum* 'Terenzo' is a bush type (determinate) tomato, which is ideal both for container growing and garden planting. It is an All-America Selections winner and produces cherry-type fruits about 2.5 centimetres (1 in.) in diameter and around 20 grams (0.75 oz) in weight. The fruit is sweet with a slight acidity and is produced in abundance. 'Terenzo' is a true bush variety and lacks the vigour of a very similar but semi-determinate variety, 'Lizzano', bred by the same breeder. 'Terenzo' is best suited to hanging baskets or growing in small spaces. It has good resistance to fruit splitting, which is a big advantage in some weather conditions. Determinate varieties tend to crop over a shorter period, so in addition to salad use, 'Terenzo' is well suited to canning, freezing, drying and juicing. The advantage of a more vigorous variety such as 'Lizzano' is that it produces larger crops over a longer period. This long season of cropping makes 'Lizzano' ideal for fresh salad use. **TS**

Alternative

Solanum lycopersicum 'Tumbler'

Solanum lycopersicum 'Lizzano' is rather vigorous for a hanging basket but it crops over a long period. ➲

Solanum

S. *lycopersicum* 'Fantastico'

Main features Early to crop; high yields of small, sweet fruits
Height 90 cm (3 ft) **Spread** 45–50 cm (18–20 in.)
Position ○ **Hardiness** Annual

This speedy selection, cropping early in only fifty days after planting, can produce 5.5 kilograms (12 lb) of fruit per plant. The plants are bushy and compact, and so they are ideal for tubs or large hanging baskets. 'Fantastico' is a determinate variety, which means that all the fruits set at once, thereby resulting in a really attractive display of glossy, red, grape-sized fruits that are easy to harvest. They look particularly ornamental cascading out of raised beds. The fruits have firm skins and an excellent, tangy taste.

This tomato is raised from seeds in the usual way. Fill pots and baskets with a good-quality loamy compost for best results. There is no need to remove the sideshoots, although if you want to, you can root them in water for fun. Water the plants frequently, aiming to keep the compost evenly moist. Feed regularly with a high-potash plant food once the first truss of fruits has formed.

Tomatoes originated in the coastal highlands of western South America, where they were grown by the Aztec and Maya peoples. New varieties arose by natural cross-pollination and selection to suit different climates and tastes, and now there are more than 5000 varieties, which can make choosing which one to grow something of a challenge. Bush forms such as 'Fantastico' are easy plants for inexperienced gardeners to trial, and children will love the profusion of small, sweet fruits that beg to be eaten straight off the bush. **GHa**

Alternatives

Solanum lycopersicum 'Rosada', *Solanum lycopersicum* 'Tumbling Tom Red'

Solanum
S. lycopersicum 'Chef's Choice Orange'

Main features Large, bright-orange fruits; vigorous plant
Height 1.5 m (5 ft) **Spread** 60 cm (24 in.)
Position ○
Hardiness Annual

A new selection from the heritage cultivar *Solanum lycopersicum* 'Amana Orange', which was raised by Gary Staley of Florida, *S. lycopersicum* 'Chef's Choice Orange' retains the brilliant tangerine colouring and mild taste of its parent but has a shorter time before it is harvested: it is ready to pick seventy-five days after planting out. It is a beefsteak cultivar, producing fruits 15 centimetres (6 in.) in diameter that weigh from 250 to 450 grams (9–16 oz). The tomatoes have a solid flesh with few seed.

Plants will usually be grown in a glasshouse but may be happy outdoors in sunny, sheltered conditions. For outdoor culture, sow the seeds indoors five to six weeks before the date of the expected last frost. It is important to wait until all risk of frost has passed before transplanting. A fertile, well-drained soil is required, and plants should be gradually acclimatised to outdoor conditions. Water evenly to avoid blossom end rot on the fruit, and feed regularly with a high-potash plant food. An F1 hybrid and an All-America Selections winner, 'Chef's Choice Orange' is a vigorous plant and will need sturdy stakes for support.

The meaty flesh of this tomato makes it a good choice for slicing and eating in sandwiches but it is more easily admired if sliced thinly on a plate and sprinkled with torn basil leaves. It is also delicious grilled with a drizzle of olive oil or used in soups and sauces. The intense orange colour is retained during cooking. **GHa**

Alternatives

Solanum lycopersicum 'Dr Wyche's Yellow', *Solanum lycopersicum* 'Gold Medal'

Solanum
S. lycopersicum 'San Marzano Lungo'

Main feature Elongated, plum-shaped fruits
Height 1.8 m (6 ft) **Spread** 60 cm (24 in.)
Position ○
Hardiness Annual

A high-yielding tomato that crops consistently over a long period, *S. lycopersicum* 'San Marzano Lungo' is one of the best cultivars for cooking. The long, plum-shaped fruits are an even rich-red colour and have a dry, mealy texture. They weigh up to 110 grams (4 oz) each. They are also easy to peel and excellent for drying, either outdoors in sunny climates or in a low oven. Best of all, perhaps, the fruits remain in good condition on the vine for longer than many other cultivars.

The 'San Marzano' is the tomato of choice in kitchens throughout Italy for sauces, pastes and passata. It is thought to have originated in the nineteenth century in southern Italy and was named for the town of San Marzano sul Sarno, near Naples, where it was grown on the rich volcanic soil of Mount Vesuvius. It was introduced commercially in 1926 and remains very important for the canning industry. 'San Marzano Lungo' is one of several recent selections with improved characteristics and earlier cropping.

For the best results sow seeds in individual pots indoors in spring. Harden off plants over about a week, so that they are used to outdoor conditions before they are planted out in early summer. The vines are indeterminate and need their sideshoots removed in order to keep the plants under control. In good conditions 'San Marzano' starts to crop around seventy-five days from planting. When growing in a heated glasshouse, plants may be transplanted as soon as the first flowers are showing. Water plants frequently, to keep the compost evenly moist and prevent blossom end rot, and feed regularly with a tomato feed (high in potash) once the first truss of fruits has formed. The plants show good resistance to diseases, but outdoor plants may succumb to late blight in wet humid seasons. **GHa**

Alternatives

Solanum lycopersicum 'Jersey Giant', *Solanum lycopersicum* 'Rio Grande', *Solanum lycopersicum* 'Speckled Roman'

Solanum
S. *lycopersicum* 'Chocolate Cherry'

Main features High yields of bite-size fruits; unusual colour and rich, fruity flavour
Height 1.5 m (5 ft) **Spread** 60 cm (24 in.)
Position ○ **Hardiness** Annual

Lower in calories than real chocolate and high in vitamin C, this cherry tomato makes an ideal sweet snack for children, and they will find it hard to resist eating the fruits of *S. lycopersicum* 'Chocolate Cherry' straight from the vine. The vines produce masses of small tomatoes, usually with eight per truss. They are a deep maroon-black colour and have an excellent flavour. The thick skins are resistant to splitting, so fruits keep well after picking if they manage to make it to the kitchen and are not eaten en route.

Raised in the United States, the cultivar is suitable for glasshouse cultivation or outdoors in a sunny frost-free position. Sow seeds indoors some five to six weeks before the expected last frost date for your area. When established, plant 'Chocolate Cherry' into a large patio pot or growing bag and leave in a cool, frost-free greenhouse or move outdoors when the risk of frost has passed. The growth habit is indeterminate, otherwise known as a cordon, and plants will benefit from the sideshoots being removed. Staking is important, too, to prevent the stems from breaking under the weight of the fruits. Cropping starts some seventy days after planting and will continue until the first frost. Whitefly can be a problem if tomatoes are grown under glass.

Like those of other black- and plum-coloured tomatoes, the fruits of 'Chocolate Cherry' contain high levels of anthocyanins. These are naturally occurring chemicals that act as antioxidants and may have health benefits. The unusual colour makes for an interesting salad when it is combined with red and yellow cultivars. Slow roasting with a drizzle of oil really brings out the flavour of this tomato and it is excellent in omelettes and quiches. If the plants have been particularly productive, use the fruits in chutneys and jams. **GHa**

Alternatives

Solanum lycopersicum 'Black Cherry', *Solanum lycopersicum* 'Black Opal', *Solanum lycopersicum* 'Indigo Rose'

Solanum
S. *lycopersicum* 'Sungold'

Main features Tasty, large, cherry-sized fruit; gold-orange colour; ideal for the home garden; early to fruit
Height 2 m (7 ft) **Spread** 50 cm (20 in.)
Position ○ **Hardiness** Annual

'Sungold' is a relatively recent variety that has made a big impact since its introduction from Japan in 1992. It's a large cherry tomato, and the fruits are a bright, shiny, gold-orange colour due to the presence of carotene and a flavonoid pigment, resulting in a health-promoting fruit. Tomatoes are divided into those with a sweet-acidic flavour or those with a sweeter, mellow taste. 'Sungold' is the ideal tomato for those with the latter preference. The fruit is firm and thin skinned, which tends to improve the eating quality but makes it prone to fruit splitting in adverse conditions. It does, however, have good disease resistance. When it was first introduced in Europe and North America, 'Sungold' was by far the best of its type in its colour range, and it remains a great favourite today. An early variety, it fruits about sixty days after sowing. Fruit is borne on long clusters on robust plants. Grow 'Sungold' in a glasshouse or conservatory, or outside in sheltered areas. **TS**

Alternatives

Solanum lycopersicum 'Golden Gem', *Solanum lycopersicum* 'Sunsugar'

Solanum
S. *lycopersicum* 'Shirley'

Main features High-quality, dual-purpose variety; good yield potential
Height 2 m (7 ft) **Spread** 50 cm (20 in.)
Position ○ **Hardiness** Annual

'Shirley' was one of the first high-quality tomato hybrids introduced by the Netherlands in the early 1980s, and subsequently its use spread around the world. It was one of the first to illustrate the benefits of hybrid seeds to the home gardener. This manifested itself in higher, better-quality yields while maintaining tasty fruits. Other benefits came in the form of improved plant vigour and disease resistance. Initially, 'Shirley' was intended for commercial growers, but it was not long before seed companies saw the benefits for the amateur grower and began to sell seeds and plants. The fruit is best described as on the large side of medium – with uniform, glossy, red skin – and the rounded shape now seen in supermarkets. Unlike some modern hybrids, however, this shape is not at the expense of taste. The actual flesh is meaty and juicy, which makes it a good variety both for eating raw and for cooking. Watch out for new, leaf-blight resistant varieties, like 'Cloudy Day' and 'Crimson Crush'. **TS**

Alternatives

Solanum lycopersicum 'Cloudy Day', *Solanum lycopersicum* 'Crimson Crush', *Solanum lycopersicum* 'Mountain Magic'

Solanum
S. tuberosum 'Yukon Gold'

Main features An early to midseason variety; great for container growing; tasty, pale-yellow flesh
Height 45–60 cm (18–24 in.) **Spread** 45–60 cm (18–24 in.)
Position ○ **Hardiness** Annual

The pale-yellow flesh of 'Yukon Gold' makes you think the butter has already been added. This potato variety has a tasty flavour and is good baked, fried or boiled. 'Yukon Gold' was introduced in 1981 as part of a breeding programme at the University of Guelph in Canada. It is a cross between the North American, white-fleshed variety 'Norgleam' and a wild, yellow-fleshed South American variety. Breeder Gary Johnston recalled in a letter in 1998 that Dutch and Belgian settlers to Canada, who became commercial vegetable growers, had petitioned for a yellow-fleshed potato such as they had in their homeland. The Wisconsin Potato Introduction Station supplied Johnston with hybrids between 'Yema de huevo' and 'Katahdin', the former being from the species *S. phureja*. He succeeded in breeding a tasty variety with normal-sized tubers and yellow flesh. If you want to grow potatoes in containers, look for certified seed varieties that are described as early, second early or early-mid. **LD**

Alternatives

Solanum tuberosum 'Yellow Finn', *Solanum tuberosum* 'Kennebec', *Solanum tuberosum* 'Michigold'

Solanum
S. tuberosum 'King Edward'

Main features Historic variety valued for its taste and fluffy texture; requires good growing conditions
Height 45–60 cm (18–24 in.) **Spread** 45–60 cm (18–24 in.)
Position ○ **Hardiness** Annual

'King Edward' is one of the most famous potato varieties. It has been around for over 200 years for the simple reason that it is tasty. This hybrid variety was first called 'Fellside Hero', before being released as 'King Edward' at the time of the coronation in 1902. One of its parents is 'Beauty of Hebron', a heritage US variety with a floury texture and good cooking qualities. 'King Edward' is not easy to grow at home, however, as it is prone to late blight and needs good soil conditions and plenty of fertiliser. It does not respond well to drought or too little or overwatering, so yields are often low compared to modern varieties. This is a main crop, which takes ninety days from planting to harvest. Grow in well-prepared ground, planting out sprouted, certified seed potatoes in late spring. 'King Edward' is perfect for roasting, frying or baking. The oval tubers are cream-coloured with red splashes; there is also a red-skinned version ('Red King Edward') and a purple-splashed type ('Yetholm Gypsy'). **LD**

Alternatives

Solanum tuberosum 'Red King Edward', *Solanum tuberosum* 'Yetholm Gyspy', *Solanum tuberosum* 'Cara'

Solanum

S. tuberosum 'Vitelotte'

Main features French, gourmet, heritage variety grown
for its taste; quick-maturing potato; purple skin and flesh
Height 45–60 cm (18–24 in.) **Spread** 45–60 cm (18–24 in.)
Position ○ **Hardiness** Annual

This French heritage potato dates to pre-1850 and is still
grown and served in restaurants in France by its name.
'Vitelotte' is more than a purple-fleshed novelty. The
flesh is smooth and its taste is described as nutty or
chestnut flavoured. 'Vitelotte' was served at a meal for
garden writers in a Loire restaurant in autumn, 2012, when
it caused much positive comment; so much so that the
chef came out and handed round samples of the tubers.
As a quick-maturing variety, 'Vitelotte' (or one of its kin)
is worth growing if you can obtain seed potatoes from a
specialist. Grow in pots or potato sacks, since yields will
be low compared to modern varieties.

There is a theory that the variety originated in the
early 1800s in Peru or Bolivia and found its way to France.
There are other Peruvian purple potatoes; legend has
it that they were special and kept for the Incan kings.
Potatoes have been cultivated in South America since
5000 BCE, and they have a far wider range of types and
species than are generally available. In the sixteenth
century, Spanish colonists described them as 'truffles',
and purple-fleshed ones are still sometimes called this.

'Vitelotte' has a purple skin and purple flesh, but
there are other variations. Note that often a variety
with 'purple' in its name only has a purple skin. The
heritage variety 'Congo' is said to be similar genetically
to 'Vitelotte', but 'Congo' gets few plaudits for its taste.
'Negresse' is another you may come across. There are
other varieties with coloured flesh, including blue and
red-pink. Usually, they are heritage potatoes and are
worth trying just for the experience of growing them
and to encourage potato specialists to keep listing them.
The worst thing you can do with coloured-flesh potatoes
is to boil them, as the colour dilutes to a wishy-washy
hue. Steaming, baking or frying invariably works best. **LD**

Alternatives

Solanum tuberosum 'Negresse', _Solanum tuberosum_ 'Salad
Blue', _Solanum tuberosum_ 'Highland Burgundy Red'

◑ _Solanum tuberosum_ 'Vitelotte' grown by guerrilla gardeners in France.

Solanum
S. *tuberosum* 'Rose Finn Apple'

Main features Unusual, finger-shaped tubers; excellent for storage; nutty taste; holds shape in cooking
Height 30–60 cm (12–24 in.) **Spread** 1.2 m (4 ft)
Position ○ **Hardiness** Annual

Fingerling potatoes, so named for their narrow finger-shaped tubers, are considered gourmet food in the Western world. Originating from the Andean mountains, they have been grown since 1836 in North America. Today, Andean Peruvians grow and eat multiple forms and colours of fingerling potatoes that are considered the progenitors of cultivars such as 'Rose Finn Apple'.

The tubers are medium-sized, finger shaped, and knobbly. As the name suggests, the skin is rose pink (it is often called the pinkie potato) and encloses a deep-yellow–fleshed potato with a waxy texture. The English 'Pink Fir Apple' is a similar variety. Like most potatoes, 'Rose Finn Apple' thrives in a fertile to sandy loam in full sun. This variety can be grown in rows in the traditional way, or in smaller quantities in raised beds under a black sheet mulch or in potato bags. A mid- to late-maturing potato (sometimes listed in catalogues as a 'late main crop') it takes 90 to 110 days from planting to harvest.

'Rose Finn Apple' potatoes are delicious hot or cold. As they can be tricky to peel, it is best to steam them in their cleaned skins and eat with a knob of melted butter; or they can be roasted or even fried. As a waxy potato, it holds its shape well in cold dishes, particularly potato salad, where cutting the tubers into cubes is simplified by their long, slim shape. Their flavour is described as nutty. For a more winter warming dish, parboil and sauté them with onions and crushed garlic. IT

Alternatives

Solanum tuberosum 'Pink Fir Apple', *Solanum tuberosum* 'Belle de Fontenay'

Solanum

S. tuberosum 'Sárpo Mira'

Main feature Blight-resistant variety; good for organic gardeners; yields well, even in poor conditions
Height 45–60 cm (18–24 in.) **Spread** 45–60 cm (18–24 in.)
Position ○ **Hardiness** Annual

Late blight is a serious potato disease that thrives in warm, humid summers. The results can be devastating with the whole crop lost. Infection starts with the foliage and then goes down to the tubers, which soon become inedible, rotten and foul smelling. There are no sprays available to home gardeners to control blight, and although some old varieties claim to be resistant, these days they are not resistant to new, mutated strains of the disease.

Dr Sárvári Sr, the director of a potato research centre in Hungary, was asked to produce a hardy strain of potatoes for growing across the Soviet Union that would survive the ravages of climate and disease. Using wild potato material, resistance to viruses and late blight were bred into his stocks. Further research at the Sárvári Research Trust in Wales produced 'Sárpo Mira', which is now the benchmark variety for blight resistance. However, it is much more than this, as it has been bred to produce high yields in poor growing conditions, such as drought or lack of fertiliser. It is an excellent variety for organic growers or those in developing countries. Foodies have been critical of its taste, but the flavour is fine if you grow it well. The secret to this vigorous plant is not to leave the top growth growing for too long. Cut the tops off by late summer; otherwise they stay green and the tubers carry on growing until they are huge, and their texture deteriorates. Tubers can be left for two to four weeks after cutting the foliage before harvesting. **LD**

Alternatives

Solanum tuberosum 'Sárpo Axona', _Solanum tuberosum_ 'Sárpo Shona'

Solanum
S. melongena 'Fairy Tale'

Main features Mild flavour; decorative flowers and fruit; ideal for container growing
Height 45 cm (18 in.) **Spread** 30 cm (12 in.)
Position ○ **Hardiness** Annual

Aubergines are tricky to grow in some regions since they need a longer growing period to form the fruit than their relative, the tomato. However, if you can provide them with warmth – by growing under glass or in a very warm, sheltered terrace – they are rewarding vegetables.

'Fairy Tale' (pictured centre) has particularly attractive fruit; vivid purple with pure-white splashes along its length. The densely textured fruits can be harvested when egg sized, at 5 centimetres (2 in.) long. At this size they can simply be sliced in half, drizzled with oil, and grilled. Alternatively, fruits can be grown on to 15 centimetres (6 in.) in length. Even when larger they retain their juicy flavour and soft skin. The adult-sized fruits are ideal for stuffing and roasting or baking with tomato, basil and Parmesan cheese to make traditional Italian parmigiana. 'Fairy Tale' is considerably less bitter than other aubergine, and each fruit has far fewer seed, making them ideal for eating lightly sautéed with herbs or for using in a classic ratatouille. If any fruits are accidentally left to get old and past their prime, they are still delicious when curried. They will soak up lots of oil in cooking to achieve a wonderful silky texture.

The plants have attractive purple flowers with bright, yellow centres. These are followed by the developing fruits. The compact plants are prolifically branching, and fruits grow in clusters of six. As each plant only grows to around 45 centimetres (18 in.) tall and 30 centimetres (12 in.) wide, they make ideal subjects for growing in containers on a patio or balcony. 'Fairy Tale' is fast to mature and resistant to many of the pests and diseases that can affect other varieties. It has been given a Royal Horticultural Society Award of Garden Merit in the United Kingdom and an All-America Selections Award in the United States. **PWa/JM**

Alternative

Solanum melongena 'Rosa Bianca'

Spinacia
S. oleracea 'Tyee'

Main features Dark-green, leafy vegetable; good
disease resistance
Height 15–20 cm (6–8 in.) **Spread** 15 cm (6 in.)
Position ○ ◑ **Hardiness** Annual

Spinach is a fast-growing, annual crop with rich, green
leaves that can be harvested as baby leaves for salads or
left to mature before cutting as a vegetable. 'Tyee' – like
the similar cultivar 'Space' – is a semi-savoy variety with
vigorous, upright growth that is less likely to suffer mud
splatter than the standard savoy cultivars. Its dark-green
leaves are slightly rumpled. Plants are resistant to downy
mildew, and they show improved bolt resistance. The
cultivar can be grown year-round in areas with mild
winters, where it will provide an excellent source of winter
greens. It is a useful cut-and-come-again vegetable.

Spinach is a cool-season plant, and seedlings may
survive temperatures of -9°C (15°F). Sow seed directly
where you want it to grow in spring, late summer, or
autumn. It does not usually germinate well in the heat
of summer. Grow in rows 30 centimetres (12 in.) apart.
Thin the seedlings to 8 centimetres (3 in.) apart if they are
being grown for baby leaves, but allow a wider spacing
for mature plants. Make successional sowings as the
seedlings emerge. They tolerate light shade, but they
tend to bolt if allowed to dry. The leaves can be harvested
from five to ten weeks after sowing. Individual leaves can
be cut, or the whole heads cut to 2.5 centimetres (1 in.)
above the ground, with the roots left to resprout.

The species *S. oleracea* is only known today as a
cultivated plant, but it is thought to have originated in
south-west Asia. It was cultivated in China by the seventh
century and in Ethiopia before the fourteenth century.
Charred remains of the plant have been found in the
Pyrenean village of Montaillou in France, in a house
dated from the late-twelfth to mid-thirteenth century.
Spinach is now widely cultivated and has naturalised in
temperate and subtropical regions. It is a highly regarded
vegetable for its nutritional qualities. **GHa**

Alternatives

Spinacia oleracea 'Galaxy', *Spinacia oleracea* 'Jovita'

Tetragonia
T. tetragonoides

Main features Tasty leaves and shoots; long, trailing stems
Height 60 cm (24 in.) **Spread** 1.2 m (4 ft)
Position ○ **Hardiness** Annual

True spinach is an annual, and while everyone loves its flavour, for the gardener it is tricky to grow a regular supply as it soon runs to seed. That is where plants with a more perennial nature, but that can be grown as annuals, are so useful, because the crop is less likely to run to seed. There are many types throughout the world, each with their own regional names, and *T. tetragonoides* is an example with a maritime history.

Captain Cook had the right idea when he ordered his crew aboard the *Endeavour* to eat *T. tetragonoides* to prevent scurvy. As a result it is known as Cook's cabbage, as well as New Zealand spinach or Botany Bay spinach. It is a good ground cover plant with trailing stems that can reach 1.2 metres (4 ft) in spread. The leaves and young shoots are prepared in the kitchen as you would spinach, and are packed with vitamins. It is easy to grow from seeds, trouble free and looks great either grown as ground cover, in containers and hanging baskets or as an edible ornamental in any vegetable patch.

T. tetragonoides is a vegetable that asks for little but gives a lot. Seeds sown in spring will produce harvestable crops within two months, and the more that is cut will encourage more to be produced. If plants ever become straggly, they will respond to being cut back to ground level, always reshooting and quickly producing more edible leaves within weeks.

It is best grown as an annual, although it is classified as a half-hardy perennial, so it is slower to run to seed. Newly sown plants always seem to have more vigour and, most importantly, tastier new shoots and leaves. Plants can be overwintered with a little protection using horticultural fleece or a cloche. *T. tetragonoides* grown in containers can easily be brought under cover in periods of harsh weather. **PM**

Alternatives

Atriplex hortensis, Chenopodium bonus-henricus

Valerianella
V. locusta

Main features Soft and succulent, mild-tasting salad leaves; long, spoon-shaped leaves
Height 15–25 cm (6–10 in.) **Spread** 25 cm (10 in.)
Position ○ ◑ **Hardiness** Annual

Also known as lamb's lettuce (due to its leaf's resemblance to the size and shape of a lamb's tongue), or in France *mâche*, corn salad is a low-growing plant, forming rosettes of long, spoon-shaped leaves. The leaves are soft and succulent and tend to stay in good condition throughout the winter. In harsh winters they will continue to grow with the protection of a cloche. They have a mild, delicate, tangy taste that is sometimes described as nutty. The small-leaved cultivar 'Verte de Cambrai' from northern France has the best flavour. 'Large Dutch' unsurprisingly forms a rosette of larger, dark-green leaves 20 centimetres (8 in.) high. The small-leaved forms tend to be hardier. Corn salad is usually treated as a salad leaf, but it can also be cooked in soups and omelettes or used as a substitute for spinach.

Corn salad is very hardy and is usually grown as a winter leaf crop, from seed sown in late summer or early autumn. Protect the emerging seedlings from birds and slugs. They require fertile, well-drained soil high in organic matter. Keep the soil moist, and mulch the plants to help retain water in dry spells. In warm climates it tends to run to seed very quickly. Harvest by pulling the leaves as required. Corn salad is often used for inter- or undercropping vegetables, such as winter brassicas.

Corn salad grows wild across Europe, Asia and northern Africa. It was often foraged as a wild salad plant when found growing in cornfields, from which the usual common name is derived. It was grown commercially in London in the late-eighteenth and early-nineteenth centuries, but then fell out of favour. The US president Thomas Jefferson grew it at Monticello in Virginia in the early 1800s. Today, it is becoming popular once more and is often found in mixed, prepared bags of salad leaves in shops and supermarkets. **GHa**

Alternative

Montia perfoliata

Vicia
V. faba 'Crimson Flowered'

Main features A hardy broad bean; often self-supporting; impressive crimson flowers followed by pods
Height 90 cm (3 ft) **Spread** 40 cm (16 in.)
Position ○ ◑ **Hardiness** Annual

These broad beans, also known as fava beans, are hardier than other beans, and in cold regions they help fill a gap in early summer before other beans start cropping. There are many heritage broad bean varieties with much to offer the home gardener, but this is an example with gorgeous, red flowers, blue-green foliage, and green beans that was rescued from extinction and reintroduced to catalogues by a seed library.

'Crimson Flowered' seed was originally donated to the Garden Organic Heritage Seed Library in 1978 by Rhoda Cutbush of Kent. The exact age of the variety is not known, but crimson-flowered broad beans were mentioned as long ago as 1778. The crimson flowers bring early colour to a potager bed or border (most broad beans have smaller, white flowers) and do not usually need staking in a sheltered garden. Broad bean varieties do cross-pollinate, so if you want to save the seeds, it is best to grow one type of broad bean. To save your broad bean seed from year to year, wait until the pods are ready to clean, when they are black and crispy; if wet weather is forecast, bring the pods into a warm place with good air circulation. Bean weevils can eat the seed (small holes in the seed are a sign they are present), and once they attack the embryo, the seed will not germinate. Seed collectors suggest keeping saved seed in a fridge for seven days (or five days in a freezer) to kill the beetles. Some people have an adverse reaction to uncooked beans, so make sure they are properly cooked. **LD**

Alternatives

Vicia faba 'Lunga delle Cascine', *Vicia faba* 'Green Windsor'

Vicia
V. faba 'The Sutton'

Main features Small, sweet bean seed; self-supporting; plants may be overwintered
Height 38–45 cm (15–18 in.)   **Spread** 20–30 cm (8–12 in.)
Position ○   **Hardiness** Annual

'The Sutton' qualifies for heritage status in that it was bred by British seed firm Suttons back in 1923 and is still the prominent dwarf broad bean variety today. Originally found in North Africa, it is grown in various continental countries with a temperate climate, but it is still thought of as a very British crop. *Vicia* is, of course, grown for its succulent, edible seed, and 'The Sutton' produces upwards-facing, deep-green pods 15 centimetres (6 in.) long. Normally, these pods will contain up to five small, white-seeded beans that are rich in protein and vitamins A, C and E. These beans have a nutty taste and must be picked young before they become hard and full of starch. The young tips of the broad bean plants can be removed and boiled for the table in a similar way you would for spinach. 'Setting' of the pods is preceded by the production of attractive, white flowers with black markings. These flowers are a good early source of nectar for garden bees and butterflies.

There is no need to provide growing supports for 'The Sutton', and where space is a problem, it can be grown in large containers. It is extremely hardy, meaning that it has a long sowing and harvesting period and can be overwintered in temperate climates. Protection by garden cloches or polyethylene tunnels may be needed in the coldest weather. This variety is a good reliable cropper and can crop in as few as fourteen weeks from sowing, dependent on the time of cropping. It is often sown in succession to produce a long season. **TS**

Alternatives

Vicia faba 'Express', *Vicia faba* 'De Monica'

Zea
Z. mays 'Mirai'

Main features Fast-growing variety; very sweet flavour
Height 2 m (7 ft) Spread 30–35 cm (12–14 in.)
Position ○
Hardiness Annual

The Japanese word *mirai* means 'taste of the future', which accurately describes this very modern sweet corn. It was first popularised in Japan as a fruit, where raw cobs are frozen and served as healthy ice pops. The cultivar 'Mirai' is now sold all over the world, including in the United States. This is ironic as 'Mirai' was initially bred by Twin Gardens Farm in Harvard, Illinois, but the delicate cell walls meant it could only be harvested by hand, so it was not viable for farms that harvest it mechanically.

If you are in a region where you can grow sweet corn, it is a real treat to pick a cob, strip the leaves and bite into it. It is so juicy and sweet. In fact, that is the benefit of growing any sweet corn, to get it fresh and sweet before the sugars turn to starch. To grow sweet corn you need enough space for a block of six plants, minimum, and somewhere warm, sunny, and sheltered. Also, as with any supersweet, you need to keep it well away from other sweet corn or they will cross-pollinate, and the benefits will be lost. The roots go deep down into the soil, so the area needs to be dug over with plenty of well-rotted, organic matter added. Plants occupy the space for a long time, but since the roots go deep, you can also use the space to sow quick crops, such as lettuce.

In mild regions seed can be sown directly into the ground in midspring, but in most areas it will be sown in pots under cover. It is fast cropping, with a maturity date of seventy-five days. Use tall, 7-centimetre-wide (2–3 in.) pots (or the cardboard centres of toilet rolls), so that the main root is not damaged or its growth checked. Plants need to be acclimatised before planting after there is no more risk of frost. Sweet corn is a member of the grass family and is pollinated by wind, hence, it is often grown in a block of three plants by three plants to aid pollination. **LD**

Alternative

Zea mays 'Xtra Tender and Sweet'

Zea
Z. mays 'Painted Mountain'

Main features Psychedelic-coloured kernels; plants capable of growing in harsh conditions
Height 1.5m (5 ft) **Spread** 30–35 cm (12–14 in.)
Position ○ **Hardiness** Annual

The yellow sweet corn that was bred for the kitchen has been further developed to produce even sweeter cobs, but other types of heritage sweet corn are also available. Early civilisations, from the Aztecs in South America to the Native Americans in North America, grew corn with multi-coloured seeds. 'Painted Mountain' is no ordinary variety of corn. More than forty years of breeding has accumulated a diverse range of ancient genes into one variety that can grow in most conditions and has the capability of feeding some of the hungriest populations in the world.

The success of 'Painted Mountain' is due to the dedication of corn breeder Dave Christensen. This variety has been developed using corns grown by Native Americans and homesteaders who lived in the harshest parts of the United States and Canada. It is a genetic resource full of essential information, and it has the potential for further breeding.

As well as being tasty raw, the fantastic multi-coloured kernels are delicious when cooked or processed into flour. 'Painted Mountain' grows fast, even in cool regions, and produces great yields in adverse weather. The plants grow to around 1.5 metres (5 ft) high, and the ears of the corn are usually around 18 centimetres (7 in.) long. At maturity the individual kernels can be a mix of yellow, orange, gold, red, black and blue. The ears will mature around one hundred days from sowing.

'Painted Mountain' can grow in a range of soils and can survive in most conditions, but it will grow best in fertile soil with plenty of water. Once it has germinated it is difficult to stop, but seeds will not grow in cold soil. It is best to wait for a few weeks after the last frost. Alternatively, seed can be started off indoors, ready to be planted outside in the spring. **PM**

Alternative

Zea mays 'Indian Summer'

Fruits are perhaps the most challenging plants to grow successfully. The reward is to pick fruit from your own garden that has ripened naturally, and can be eaten at its peak. No cold storage, transportation or packaging involved! The quickest fruit to grow is the strawberry, and one of the most rewarding too: imagine the aroma and complex flavour of a ripe berry still warm from the sun.

Fruiting bushes that produce berries and currants are no more difficult to grow than shrubs, so they are also worthwhile. Cane fruits, such as blackberries and raspberries, need more training, but, if you have the space, they are very productive. As this book does not cover trees, we haven't covered tree fruits, but apples sneak in because they can be grown neatly as cordons and other trained forms.

● *Malus domestica* 'Bramley's Seedling' is the world's favourite cooking apple.

Actinidia
A. deliciosa 'Jenny'

Main features Self-fertile fruits; fast-growing climber; small white flowers in summer
Height 6 m (20 ft) **Spread** 4 m (13 ft)
Position ○ **Hardiness** RHS H4

The kiwi fruit is a native of southern China and it certainly brings an air of the exotic to the garden, with lush-leaved vines that twine languidly through neighbouring plants or along wire or timber supports. The fact that 'Jenny' is the only self-fertile, hardy kiwi fruit vine makes it far and away the most popular of the cultivated varieties. All-female alternatives, such as *A. deliciosa* 'Hayward', need a male partner in order to bear fruit, and few gardeners have the space to spare for such a requirement.

A strong climbing habit, attractive stems, and lush foliage make 'Jenny' a wonderful choice for growing over a trellis or arbour, where the attractive red-tipped, heart-shaped leaves will offer privacy and shade. 'Jenny'

carries small white flowers through the summer, and the fruits, which are ready to harvest in late summer or early autumn, hang from the vines in pleasing clusters. The kiwis are roughly the size and shape of hens' eggs, with furry brown skin and wonderfully bright-green flesh that has a sweet, fresh taste and an appealing texture.

It is a very vigorous grower that will need pruning to control its size in all but the most spacious gardens. This makes it an ideal option for covering large and unsightly expanses of fencing or masonry. It fruits best in warm and sunny conditions, but 'Jenny' is not a good greenhouse resident as it will quickly crowd all its neighbours. Instead, plant outdoors and train a few of the vines into the greenhouse, perhaps using them to shade other plants in high summer. **PWa/JM**

Alternative

Actinidia arguta 'Issai'

Amelanchier
A. alnifolia

Main features Beautiful spring blossom; sweet red-black fruits in midsummer
Height 3–4 m (10–13 ft) **Spread** 3–4 m (10–13 ft)
Position ○ ◑ **Hardiness** RHS H7

Variously known as June berries, service berries or saskatoons, the fruits of this suckering shrub or small tree look similar to blueberries but have a slightly tangier flavour. The showy, white flowers appear in early spring. The red berries ripen in midsummer, changing first to an attractive purple and then to blue-black with a waxy bloom. They have a mealy texture and can be eaten fresh or used in pies and jams. As a finale the plant puts on an excellent show of red and yellow leaf colour in autumn.

Native to North America, the plant is very hardy and less fussy about soil conditions than blueberries. Plant in fertile, well-drained soil; blossoms come early, so avoid planting in frost pockets. These shrubs are self-fertile, so only one plant is necessary. The fruits ripen best in full sun, but plants tolerate partial shade. Cultivars grown for their fruits include *A. alnifolia* 'Smoky', which is the most widely available one raised in Canada. It has large, sweet, mild-flavoured fruits and is very productive. 'Martin' is used in commercial orchards due to the uniformity in ripening of the berries. 'Northline' crops heavily from an early age but suckers profusely. 'Obelisk' is a dense, upright cultivar, useful for restricted spaces.

The saskatoon was widely used by North American native people and later by European settlers. The wood is hard but flexible and was used for arrows. The berries were added to the dried meat pemmican, which was an important winter staple. The fruit has given its name to a city in central Saskatchewan, Canada. **GHa**

Alternatives

Amelanchier canadensis, Amelanchier × grandiflora

Citrus
C. × *latifolia*

Main features Seedless fruits; dark, glossy foliage in spring and summer; architectural plant
Height 2.4 m (8 ft) **Spread** 4 m (13 ft)
Position ○ **Hardiness** RHS H2

A popular and widely grown lime tree, *C.* × *latifolia*, known also as Persian or Tahiti lime, is an excellent choice for temperate conditions. It can make a very appealing focal point in a sheltered, Mediterranean-style garden, where the dark, glossy leaves and clusters of delicate, white blooms offer interest throughout the summer. The flowers are exotically scented, and on a warm day their perfume can fill the air around the tree. The fruits that follow can take as long as a year to ripen, but they are definitely worth waiting for. Large, round, dark green, and seedless, they are also fragrant and juicy; this lime is perfect for use in the kitchen or in cocktails. A popular ingredient in Asian, Mexican and North African cooking, limes are an excellent source of vitamin C. In fact, during the nineteenth century, the British navy issued limes to its sailors in order to prevent scurvy, and this is the origin of the nickname used by Americans for a British person – 'limey'.

Lime trees are hungry feeders and appreciate a well-drained soil with plenty of organic matter dug in. To keep the ground below the tree clear of weeds and grass, that would otherwise compete for water and nutrients, use an organic mulch, such as compost or shredded bark. Do not let the mulch touch the trunk of the tree, however, or you risk harming the plant. A specialised citrus feed should be given in spring and autumn, and the plant should be watered regularly in hot weather to allow the flowers and fruits to develop.

C. × *latifolia* is capable of surviving only brief cold snaps below freezing point. In cooler climates a lime tree is best grown in a large container, in which it can be moved indoors to a bright, frost-free position from autumn to spring. As it is self-fertilising, the Tahiti lime does not need a companion for pollination. **PWa/JM**

Alternatives

Citrus × *latifolia* 'Bearss', *Citrus* × *aurantiifolia*, *Citrus limettioides*

Citrus
C. × *limon* 'Meyer'

Main feature Versatile fruits with a sweet flavour; spring
and summer foliage; an architectural plant
Height 3 m (10 ft) **Spread** 1.5 m (5 ft)
Position ○ **Hardiness** RHS H2

While its fruits may be smaller than those of the true
lemon, *C. × limon* 'Meyer' has become popular in cold
countries because it can grow to half the usual size in
containers. The fruits have a fresh flavour and a lack of
bitterness. They are sweet enough to be eaten raw or
pressed for drinking, and the flesh and juice both have
a delicate pink colour that intensifies to pink red in some
climates and soils. This colour makes it a wonderful choice
for homemade lemonade, as does the low acidity, since
less sugar is needed to balance the flavour. It is ideal for
use in puddings, poultry or rice dishes and even salads.

A close relative of the true lemon, 'Meyer' was
discovered by chance in 1908 when American plant-
hunter Frank Meyer spotted it growing in a front garden
in suburban Beijing. It is thought to be a natural orange-
lemon, or mandarin-lemon hybrid, hence the sweet,
slightly floral, taste. The ends of the fruits are rounded;
more like the ends of an orange or mandarin than the
pointed ends of a true lemon. Despite its appealing
flavour, 'Meyer' has not been commercially successful
because its delicate skin makes it hard to transport. This
means homegrown fruits are even more valuable and
make a great talking point when served at events.

A few degrees of frost will not harm the tree, but
sustained temperatures below -3°C (26°F) can be fatal.
Fruiting is also impaired by low temperatures, but 'Meyer'
grows well in containers, which will allow you to bring
plants indoors through the colder months to reduce this
risk. Depending on the severity of the winter, carefully
insulating the tree with horticultural fleece may be
enough in some sheltered locations. As temperatures
climb, water the plant well to ensure the fruits can form.
In some countries you may find 'Improved Meyer', which
was developed in California in the 1970s. **PWa/JM**

Alternatives

Citrus × limon 'Eureka', *Citrus × limon* 'Lisbon',
Citrus × limon 'Variegata'

Ficus
F. carica 'Rouge de Bordeaux'

Main features Spring and summer foliage; an architectural plant
Height 3 m (10 ft) **Spread** 4 m (13 ft)
Position ○ ◑ **Hardiness** RHS H4

'Rouge de Bordeaux' is a classic French variety of fig that offers fruits with succulent, ruby-red flesh and sumptuous, deep-red skin, verging on purple, or even black if they are left to ripen fully on the tree. The fruits are medium in size, somewhat flat in shape and dusted with a luxurious, almost luminescent, bloom.

This fig tree would make a worthy addition to any garden based on looks alone, but the superb flavour of the fruit is an even better reason to choose this plant if growing conditions allow. A ripe 'Rouge de Bordeaux', still warm from the sun, is very hard to beat. It is a deservedly popular variety for jam making, and the fruits also dry very well, so they can be enjoyed year-round rather than for just a few short weeks in late summer.

Not as reliably hardy as some other cultivars, 'Rouge de Bordeaux' will withstand some cold, but it is best grown under glass or against a sheltered wall. In particularly harsh winters, a protective layer of horticultural fleece would be a wise investment, to reduce the damage that might be caused by frost. The warmer and sunnier the conditions in the growing season, the better the yield and the quality of the fruits will be.

An advantage of fig trees is that they are self-fertilising, meaning they will produce fruits even if no other trees are nearby to pollinate them. This is a real advantage for smaller gardens, but if you have the space, then growing two or more trees of different, well-selected cultivars can spread the harvest to late in the season. A good way to grow a fig tree is to train it into a fan shape against a warm wall. The roots are best restricted, which often happens when the plant is at the base of a wall. An old gardener's trick is to line the sides of a small hole with paving slabs. The plants like well-drained soil that could include rubble or chalk. **PWa/JM**

Alternatives

Ficus carica 'Brown Turkey', *Ficus carica* 'Brunswick', *Ficus carica* 'White Marseille'

Ficus carica trained against a warm wall saves space and encourages fruits to ripen. ➲

Ficus

F. carica 'Panachée'

Main features Prolific cropper; variegated skin of fruits; architectural plant
Height 3 m (10 ft) **Spread** 4 m (13 ft)
Position ○ ◑ **Hardiness** RHS H4

In cultivation since the mid-seventeenth century, this cultivar of fig tree is, surprising, not particularly widely grown today. *F. carica* 'Panachée' is a prolific cropper and produces high-quality fruits that are deliciously sweet; their flavour is especially intense after a hot and sunny summer. The most striking feature, however, is the delightful variegation of the skin of the fruit. This characteristic has resulted in its common name of tiger fig. A tree well-laden with ripening fruits is sure to become a central feature in any late-summer garden. When it is ready for harvesting, the flesh of the fruit becomes a glorious red, and some growers have likened it to that of ripe strawberries.

As with the flavour, the striped skin can be more pronounced in warmer years, while cooler weather may result in a violet tint to the fruit. Therefore 'Panachée' is a good choice if you have a sheltered garden in a mild region, or you can grow it in a container in a greenhouse or conservatory. Varieties such as 'Brown Turkey' and 'Brunswick' will be more reliable in cooler conditions.

Fig trees are statement plants even without their fruit, as their lush, broad leaves add a touch of the exotic to the garden. They are vigorous growers that will quickly crowd neighbouring plants if left unchecked, but their final size can be controlled by judicious pruning in spring. Alternatively, a large container makes an ideal home for a fig, as the tree's size will be determined by the limits of the pot. **PWa/JM**

Alternatives

Syn. *Ficus carica* 'Panache', *Ficus carica* 'Madeleine'

Fragaria

F. vesca 'Mara des Bois'

Main features Fantastic flavour to fruits; the aroma of wild alpine strawberries
Height 50 cm (20 in.) **Spread** 60 cm (24 in.)
Position ○ ◑ **Hardiness** RHS H6

Any dedicated fan of strawberries knows that the wild alpine varieties have a sweet, aromatic taste all their own, but also that the fruit is usually impossible to buy and is often so small as to be almost not worth the picking. What a joy it is then that modern breeding has given us this wonderful variety, which has all the incredible flavour of its alpine heritage, but delivered in much more satisfyingly sized fruits. No other strawberry manages such a feat, and as a result the variety is highly sought after by in-the-know gardeners and foodies alike. The produce can sometimes be found in French markets. However, it is not widely sold elsewhere, so growing your own is a rewarding option.

The berries are a lovely deep-red colour when ripe and are simply irresistible, not only to humans, but also to garden birds! For this reason they do need to be protected with netting as the harvest approaches. The fruits are deliciously fragrant, with an aroma that transports you to a vibrant, summer woodland. The best way to eat them is straight from the plant, when they are still warm from the summer sun.

Another advantage of this cultivar is its long cropping season. There are earlier- and later-fruiting strawberries, but 'Mara des Bois', produces flavoursome fruits from late spring through to early autumn, and it is hard to match for its staying power. Although generally easy to grow, strawberry plants can be prone to various diseases depending on your region and climate. **PWa/JM**

Alternatives

Fragaria × ananassa 'Symphony', *Fragaria vesca* 'Alexandra'

Fragaria

F. × ananassa 'Malwina'

Main features Late-fruiting variety; dark red fruits and flesh; exceptionally sweet flavour
Height 15–25 cm (6–10 in.) **Spread** 30–45 cm (12–18 in.)
Position ○ ◑ **Hardiness** RHS H5

Nothing compares to eating fresh fruit straight off the plant, but it is the nature of such things that we can only enjoy them for a few fleeting weeks as the harvest ripens. Strawberries in summer are a fine example of this. Happily, modern breeding techniques have allowed gardeners to grow several different varieties, from early-fruiting types to late developers, and so spread the enjoyment through a longer season. Therein lies the appeal of strawberry 'Malwina', which is a particularly late variety that ripens just as other crops are finishing.

'Malwina' is a relatively new introduction from a breeding programme in Switzerland, and its development has focused on general health. It is resistant to several problems common to strawberries, including verticillium wilt, crown rot, red core and mildew. It even withstands heavy rain, which can sometimes damage plants so badly that they do not fruit at all.

The practicalities of an extended growing season and healthier crop do not come at the expense of this strawberry's other qualities. This variety has such deep-red fruits that they are considered too dark for the supermarket shelves – all the more reason to grow them at home. The fruits are large and rounded, with an exceptionally sweet flavour and a delightful scent. The plants themselves are vigorous, but compact rather than straggling, and they grow well in open ground or containers. They have large, glossy, green leaves and a generally perky, healthy appearance. **PWa/JM**

Alternatives

Fragaria × *ananassa* 'Florence', *Fragaria* × *ananassa* 'Fenella'

Fragaria

F. × *ananassa* 'Sallybright'

Main feature Superb-tasting, early-season fruits
Height 15–25 cm (6–10 in.) **Spread** 30–45 cm (12–18 in.)
Position ○ ◑
Hardiness RHS H6

While heritage varieties of fruits and vegetables are worth growing for many reasons, modern cultivars can often have the edge when it comes to all-round garden performance. Strawberries have been the subject of intense research in recent years and several new varieties have been introduced as a result. 'Sallybright' is a 2007 introduction from a British breeding programme and has quickly gathered praise. It is a vigorous and robust variety, with a pleasing growing habit, with 'Alice' and 'Eros' in its parentage.

It offers that much-anticipated early-season crop, which is ready to harvest slightly before that of the popular *F.* × *ananassa* 'Elsanta'. The flowers are borne on upright stems, above the leaf canopy of the plant, and, of course, this is also where the fruits form, so they are held well clear of the ground and suffer less from slug damage and rain splash. This factor also makes them easier to spot, and therefore to harvest. The fruits are large and very uniform in shape with shiny, bright-red skin. The yield is good if not exceptional.

The media is full of studies and surveys advising what product to buy, but one such investigation by UK consumer rights organisation *Which?* is worth taking note of. Researchers spent two years investigating strawberry varieties and had over a thousand people involved in the taste testing. The results proclaimed 'Sallybright' the joint tastiest of the early-fruiting varieties, sharing the top spot with *F.* × *ananassa* 'Darlisette'. **PWa/JM**

Alternatives

Fragaria × *ananassa* 'Darlisette', *Fragaria* × *ananassa* 'Mae'

Fragaria
F. × ananassa 'Ogallala'

Main features Ever-bearing; extremely hardy
Height 15–25 cm (6–10 in.) **Spread** 30–45 cm (12–18 in.)
Position ○ ◑
Hardiness RHS H7

Developed over twenty-five years by the US Department of Agriculture and the University of Nebraska, 'Ogallala' counts not only popular garden varieties, but also wild Rocky Mountain strawberries amongst its ancestors. The enticing aroma and flavour of the wild plants are still present in this descendent, as is a remarkably hardy constitution. Indeed, many people have suggested that this is the hardiest variety available today, because it tolerates cold, wet, winter weather, extended periods of drought and less-than-perfect soil conditions. From the more cultivated side of its breeding, 'Ogallala' receives an ever-bearing habit, which means it offers a steady supply of berries from early summer right through to autumn, provided the weather allows. It also inherits larger-sized fruits and an ability to crop more prolifically than any wild plant. The fruits are full of flavour and have attractive red flesh. They are good eaten fresh but are also noted as an excellent variety for freezing. **PWa/JM**

Alternatives

Fragaria × ananassa 'Quinault', *Fragaria × ananassa* 'Tribute', *Fragaria × ananassa* 'Tristar'

Fragaria
F. × ananassa 'Fort Laramie'

Main features Ever-bearing; withstands cold weather
Height 15–25 cm (6–10 in.) **Spread** 30–45 cm (12–18 in.)
Position ○ ◑
Hardiness RHS H7

While there are many good varieties of strawberry to choose from, getting a successful crop is sometimes a question of selecting the right plant for your local conditions. It can be frustrating to prepare the ground, plant, and care for the plants, only for them to fruit poorly. Growers in cooler climates would do well to consider 'Fort Laramie', which is particularly resistant to cold weather and will produce a healthy quantity of fruits when other more sensitive varieties would struggle. It is a vigorous grower and generally trouble free, which means it is also a good choice for novice gardeners. This variety has good all-round disease resistance but, as with any strawberry plant, only purchase certified disease-free stock. In fact, 'Fort Laramie' crops heavily, producing huge piles of fruits that have a bright-red colour, firm flesh and a honey-sweet flavour and scent. They are wonderful eaten fresh and are also ideal for processing into jams and a range of puddings. **PWa/JM**

Alternatives

Fragaria × ananassa 'Albion', *Fragaria × ananassa* 'Seascape', *Fragaria × ananassa* 'Ozark Beauty'

Malus
M. domestica

Main features High yields of large fruits; strong, sharp apple flavour so good for cooking; stores well
Height 9 m (30 ft) **Spread** 9 m (30 ft)
Position ○ **Hardiness** RHS H6

There are few activities more fulfilling than harvesting your own apples and carrying the haul straight to the fruit bowl, where it will spill over resplendently, heavy with a crisp, warm scent that supermarkets cannot provide. According to the fruit historian Joan Morgan, apples have their origins in the Tien Shan Mountains between China and Kazakhstan and travelled along the Silk Road to the Balkans before moving across Europe with the Romans. Today, they are popular across the world but are grown with particular pride in the British Isles. 'Bramley's Seedling' is now grown worldwide, which is unusual, as different regions will often have their own thriving apple varieties. This one copes in most places but it does need other apples to pollinate it. 'Bramley's Seedling' was raised from a pip sown by a girl in a cottage garden in Nottinghamshire, United Kingdom, between 1809 and 1813. The original tree is still alive and the trees grown today are clones of the original. **LG**

Alternatives

Malus domestica 'Rhode Island Greening', *Malus domestica* 'Arthur Turner'

Malus
M. domestica Redlove Era

Main features Red-skinned apples with pink flesh; dark pink blossom in spring
Height 3 m (10 ft) **Spread** 3 m (10 ft)
Position ○ ◑ **Hardiness** RHS H6

With its spectacular crimson flesh, *M. domestica* Redlove Era is an incredibly decorative, versatile apple to use in any recipe. It will brighten up fruit salads, tarts, pies and jams. The red colouring extends right through the flesh, and when sliced, there is also an attractive marbled white ring surrounding the core. It is the result of many years of careful selection and pollination by a Swiss plant breeder named Markus Kobelt. Redlove Era tastes as good as it looks, and boasts a good balance of tartness and sweetness, as well as a satisfying crunch. While some apples are best eaten raw and others are only suitable for culinary use, Redlove Era is fully dual purpose, and the flesh stays firm and vividly coloured when cooked. The cut flesh is slow to turn brown. While many apples have decorative blooms, few can rival the vivid-pink blossom of 'Redlove', which is fragrant and long-lasting, making this a good all-round garden tree. It is also very popular with bees and pollinating insects. **PWa/JM**

Alternatives

Malus domestica Redlove Calypso, *Malus domestica* Redlove Odysso, *Malus domestica* Redlove Circe

---

Physalis
P. peruviana

Main features Decorative sweet fruits; exceptional shelf life
Height 60–90 cm (2–3 ft) **Spread** 90 cm (3 ft)
Position ○ **Hardiness** RHS H2

A sweet berry with a complex flavour and a hint of tartness, *P. peruviana* has a pleasantly crisp texture and is usually eaten raw. It is popular in fruit salads or salsas, but it can also be cooked for use in pies or jams. Alternatively, the berries can be dried and used rather like raisins. The marble-sized fruits have a papery calyx around each bright-orange berry. These husks can be peeled back to form a decorative frame for the fruit within, which has made *P. peruviana* berries a popular garnish for puddings. The husks also protect the fruits inside from spoiling. If left intact in their husks, fruits can have a shelf life of up to forty-five days at room temperature. Originating from Peru, *P. peruviana* needs a very sunny, sheltered spot to thrive, but in the right conditions, it romps away. It can also be grown as an annual under cover. Taller cultivars, such as 'Giant', can reach 1.8 metres (6 ft) high and may need support. In summer it has pretty pale-yellow flowers with darker centres. Although each flower is small, they are plentiful and are popular with bees. **PWa/JM**

Alternative

Syn. *Physalis edulis*

Ribes
R. nigrum 'Ebony'

Main features Large, exceptionally sweet fruits; good mildew resistance
Height 1.5 m (5 ft) **Spread** 1.5 m (5 ft)
Position ○ **Hardiness** RHS H6–7

While all blackcurrants are popular as a culinary fruit, *R. nigrum* 'Ebony' is perhaps the only variety that can be eaten fresh from the bush without the need for sugar. The large, firm fruits are so sweet, they have a Brix value of up to 17 per cent. Ideal for jams, jellies, pies and puddings, the sweet flavour of 'Ebony' is also particularly suited for making juices, smoothies, syrups and cordials. Like all blackcurrants, this plant has aromatic leaves that are edible and these can be used to flavour tea, jam or alcoholic drinks. Although 'Ebony' is a self-fertile plant that is quite vigorous, it has a fairly open habit, so harvesting is simple. Once the fruits are glossy and fragrant, the easiest option is to cut off whole fruiting branches and place them in a pile on a table. Then, taking each branch in turn, hold it at the top end and run a large table fork down its length to pull each of the berries from their strigs into a large bowl. 'Ebony' bushes reach maturity at around five years old, when each bush can be expected to offer yields of up to 4 kilograms (9 lb). **PWa/JM**

Alternative

Ribes nigrum 'Ben Connan'

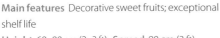
◑ *Physalis peruviana* at an early stage of growth. These protective husks will later dry and split, revealing the berries, which are best eaten ripe.

Ribes

R. *rubrum* 'Gloire de Sablons'

Main features Unusual pink fruits; trouble-free plants; good disease resistance
Height 1.2 m (4 ft) **Spread** 1.2 m (4 ft)
Position ○ **Hardiness** RHS H7

One of the first fruits of the season to ripen, this red currant is an unusual and attractive shade of pale pink. It can be eaten fresh or cooked in sweet or savoury dishes. Furthermore, as red currants contain a high level of pectin, they are excellent for turning into jams and jellies, and the long strigs of delicate, translucent berries are also highly valued as a decorative addition to cakes, pastries, and puddings. *R. sativum* 'Gloire de Sablons' is a particularly fragrant, juicy currant. It has a sweet flavour with an interesting hint of tartness.

This plant produces a heavy crop in midsummer and often fruits well in the first year after planting. However, the best yields come from mature plants from around sixteen to twenty months old. Bushes can be surprisingly long-lived, and if well tended, they will still produce fruit up to twenty years after planting. 'Gloire de Sablons' is a robust and problem-free variety, which is resistant to white pine blister, rust and mildew. It is self-fertile, so will still produce good yields, even if it is the only red currant grown in the garden. The tiny yellow-green flowers in spring are laden with nectar and attract bees and other pollinating insects.

Like all red currants, 'Gloire de Sablons' is shallow-rooted, so it is important to keep the plants well watered during any dry spells, especially when the fruits are forming. In spring feed the plants with a top dressing of general-purpose organic fertiliser, then apply a generous mulch of well-rotted manure. As 'Gloire de Sablons' gives such an early crop, the red currants are a favourite with birds, so it can be helpful to protect the bush with netting during the summer. Remember that red currants fruit on old wood, so prune your plants with care. Remove any diseased branches in winter, as well as any wood that is older than three years. **PWa/JM**

Alternatives

Ribes rubrum 'Rovada', *Ribes rubrum* 'Pink Champagne'

Ribes
R. uva-crispa 'Pax'

Main features Largish red fruits; vigorous, spine-free plants; good mildew resistance
Height 90–120 cm (3–4 ft) **Spread** 90–120 cm (3–4 ft)
Position ○ **Hardiness** RHS H7

The *R. uva-crispa* 'Pax' is an excellent culinary gooseberry that is sweet enough to be enjoyed as a dessert fruit picked straight from the plant. Fruits mature in midsummer and turn a pleasing shade of red, which makes them a popular addition to summer puddings. The soft, tangy berries are also ideal for pies, crumbles, jams and jellies. Although some minor spines can appear on new growth, the mature, upright bushes are virtually spineless, which makes this cultivar particularly easy to harvest. The fact that it has such good mildew and leaf-spot resistance also makes this an ideal choice for inexperienced or busy gardeners. In order to get the biggest, juiciest fruits in midsummer, it is well worth thinning the berries in late spring or early summer. Working from the centre of the bush outwards, remove every other berry along each branch. The immature fruits are too sharp to eat raw, but they are delicious cooked with added sugar in pies or other puddings.

'Pax' is extremely vigorous, and each plant soon offers a good yield. However, this means that plants will usually need to be shaped by annual pruning. They can be grown as espaliers (trained to grow flat against a support), although they are typically grown as a largish open bushes, spaced 1.5 metres (5 ft) apart. In winter cut away any dead, diseased or damaged wood, and trim any low-lying shoots. Spur prune side shoots by trimming them to three buds from the base. Then branch tips can be trimmed by around a quarter, cutting to an outwards-facing bud. In summer it is possible to shape the bushes by shortening the current season's growth. Importantly, this should not affect fruiting, as the berries grow on older wood. Once the plant is established, watering is seldom required, but it may be necessary during very dry spells. **PWa/JM**

Alternatives

Ribes uva-crispa 'Invicta', *Ribes uva-crispa* 'Pixwell'

Rubus
R. fruticosus 'Reuben'

Main features Blooms in summer; attracts bees; huge fruits of exceptional sweetness; easy to grow
Height 1.8 m (6 ft) **Spread** 1.2 m (4 ft)
Position ○ ◑ **Hardiness** RHS H7

This unusual blackberry is a 'primocane', which means that it fruits on the first year's growth (like an autumn raspberry), so gardeners do not have to wait too long before enjoying a harvest. What is more, each berry is exceptionally large, often up to 5 centimetres (2 in.) in length. These fruits are deliciously sweet, with a Brix value of 11.5 per cent. (For comparison, a sweet strawberry typically measures between 8.5 and 9.5 per cent.) *R. fruticosus* 'Reuben' gives a very heavy yield of berries, which can be enjoyed on their own or made into delicious pies, jellies and jams. Plants reach maturity in just two years, each offering around 4 kilograms (9 lb) of fruit. The canes are spineless, which makes harvesting easy.

'Reuben' has relatively large white flowers and a long flowering period, from midspring to midsummer, thereby ensuring that a succession of bees and butterflies can enjoy the nectar. The plant can also be trained over walls and fences, planted as part of a mixed edible hedge, or used as a great backdrop to a wildlife garden. In addition, the dark-green pinnate foliage is quite attractive and turns a pale-yellow shade in the autumn.

This plant has an upright growth habit, which makes training and pruning it very straightforward. 'Reuben' is therefore a great option for beginner gardeners. Simply cut all the canes to just above ground level in winter or early spring. When the new growth emerges, apply a liquid feed. As the canes reach around 90 centimetres (3 ft) high, remove the top 5 centimetres (2 in.) because this will encourage branching and increase the yield too. If you would prefer two crops a year, cut the canes that have fruited in autumn by half, and these will produce an extra crop in early summer. An annual mulch of well-rotted compost will also help to keep the soil moist and encourage heavy harvests. **PWa/JM**

Alternatives

Rubus fruticosus 'Chester', *Rubus fruticosus* 'Loch Ness'

Rubus
R. idaeus 'Joan J'

Main features A generous crop of sweet berries from summer to autumn; attracts pollinating insects
Height 1.5 m (5 ft) **Spread** 60 cm (24 in.)
Position ○ **Hardiness** RHS H7

Offering a long cropping period from summer to autumn, this outstanding variety has large berries of a superior flavour to many of its older rivals. The deep-red fruits are delicious when eaten fresh, but yields are so generous that there will be plenty available for freezing or preserving. Trials have shown that this raspberry freezes exceptionally well and the fruits retain their sweet flavour, unlike many other raspberries that sadly taste more acidic once they have been frozen and defrosted.

    R. idaeus 'Joan J' is resistant to most problem insects, and the canes are sturdy and virtually spine free, which makes harvesting easy. Known as an 'autumn-fruiting' or 'primocane' variety, it can bear berries for at least seven weeks from late summer until the first frost. This cultivar has large, firm, juicy fruits that are around 30 per cent bigger than those of *R. idaeas* 'Autumn Bliss', which was previously considered to be one of the best primocane varieties.

    As with all raspberries it is important to ensure that the plants have their roots just below the surface of the soil. Planting raspberries too deeply will kill the canes. Primocane varieties are exceptionally easy to cultivate because they bear fruit on new growth each year. In late winter simply cut down all the canes to ground level using sharp secateurs. In spring mulch around each plant with a generous layer of organic matter. If necessary, tie the new canes in as they appear. 'Joan J' has such sturdy canes that it can usually be grown without support, although it will need to be tied onto horizontal wires if grown in a windy position. In addition, 'Joan J' is self-fertile and does not need to be grown with other raspberries in order to produce heavy yields. The plants can be kept in the same beds and will produce crops for many years. **PWa/JM**

Alternatives

Rubus idaeus 'Tulameen', *Rubus idaeus* 'Heritage'

Rubus

R. idaeus 'Valentina'

Main features Unusual apricot-coloured berries with fine flavour and texture; early flowers; attracts bees
Height 1.5 m (5 ft) **Spread** 60 cm (24 in.)
Position ○ **Hardiness** RHS H7

In a tempting shade of apricot pink, this unusual raspberry has a particularly fine flavour and soft, delicate skin. Ideal eaten freshly picked and with cream, the medium-sized berries are a delightful addition to a fruit salad and can be used to make exotic-looking juices, jellies and jams. Perfect for busy gardeners, *R. idaeus* 'Valentina' is a low-maintenance, summer-fruiting raspberry with good resistance to disease and aphids. The strong, upright canes have very few spines, which makes the fruits much easier to harvest than those of traditional varieties. Best of all, this cultivar offers consistently high yields of fruit. Although it flowers early, it is resistant to frost damage. The spring flowers are a boon to hungry bees and other pollinating insects.

Like all raspberries, 'Valentina' needs to be grown in a sunny position on moist, free-draining soil. A thick mulch of organic matter, such as bark chippings, will help to keep the soil moist and weed free. In dry spells, and for the best results, it is worth watering the canes during the period when the fruits are developing. Although 'Valentina' is low maintenance, all raspberries need support as they grow. A popular cultivation method is to prepare a raspberry bed by removing all the weeds, enriching the soil with organic matter, and then hammering a row of posts in the ground at 2.7-metre (9 ft) intervals with heavy-gauge wires in between. Summer-fruiting raspberries grow on older wood, so it is important to cut the fruited canes back to ground level after they have finished fruiting. The unfruited canes (which will be a brighter shade of green) will provide the following year's berries. Select around seven canes per plant and tie them onto wire supports. Cut any remaining stems at ground level. Check plants in spring and trim any unruly growth. **PWa/JM**

Alternative

Rubus idaeus 'Anne Yellow'

Vaccinium
V. corymbosum 'Northland'

Main features White or pink spring flowers; tasty summer berries; vivid autumn foliage; very hardy cultivar
Height 1.2 m (4 ft) **Spread** 1.5 m (5 ft)
Position ○ ◐ **Hardiness** RHS H7

This early-fruiting blueberry is ideal for wildlife gardeners. It has a spreading habit and dense foliage, so the mature shrubs provide ideal cover and nesting sites for wild birds. The nectar-rich blooms in late spring attract bees, and the leaves are a larval food source for several butterflies. The clusters of medium-sized berries have an exceptionally sweet flavour, and the low-growing nature of this cultivar means that it is easy for children to help themselves to a healthy treat straight from the bush. Rich in vitamins and antioxidants, the berries can be eaten fresh or used in a variety of puddings.

V. corymbosum 'Northland' often grows to be wider than it is tall, so it is perhaps more suited to growing in the ground than in a container. The foliage turns a fabulous vivid-orange colour in autumn, thereby providing a perfect backdrop to late-flowering plants such as dahlias and chrysanthemums. This cultivar even offers interest in winter as the stems range from a shade of yellow green to bright red. Relatively low maintenance,'Northland' requires minimal pruning, although a trim in winter will help to keep it in shape. It is not a self-fertile plant and needs to be grown alongside another blueberry in order to set fruit. Choosing a cultivar that crops slightly later in the summer will extend the harvesting season and visual appeal.

All blueberries need acidic soil that is moist but well draining, so incorporate plenty of organic matter into the planting hole. For the best results, water the plants regularly and position them in full sun or only partial shade. Adding a thick mulch of organic matter around (but not touching) the stem will help to conserve moisture and suppress the weeds. It is possible to increase yields by feeding 'Northland' with an ericaceous (lime-free) fertiliser in early summer. **PWa/JM**

Alternative

Vaccinium corymbosum 'Patriot'

Vaccinium

V. corymbosum 'Liberty'

Main features Delicious large berries for pudding or culinary use; spring blooms; attractive autumn foliage
Height 1.2 m (4 ft) **Spread** 90 cm (3 ft)
Position ○ ◐ **Hardiness** RHS H7

Also known as highbush blueberry, this plant has a vigorous, upright habit and soon grows into a tall, shapely shrub that offers interest for most of the year. Best of all, the fruits are large, firm and juicy. While they are delicious eaten straight from the bush, they also have a good shelf life and can be cooked or used in preserves. In addition, the powder-blue fruits are held away from the bush, which makes this one of the easiest blueberries to harvest.

Offering good resistance to cold weather, *V. corymbosum* 'Liberty' fruits in late summer, and the berries ripen over a long period, meaning that freshly picked fruits can be enjoyed every day for weeks on end. Like all blueberries, 'Liberty' is decorative enough to grow in containers on a patio. The pretty bell-shaped blooms in spring are followed by the berries, but perhaps the bush is most striking in autumn when the foliage turns red and orange. The height of this particular variety makes it ideal for growing as a statement plant in a container.

Blueberries are most productive in full sun but will tolerate partial shade. They must be watered regularly if grown in pots or until their roots are established if grown in the ground. These plants need acidic soil, so in gardens with alkaline soil, it is best to grow them in pots of ericaceous (lime-free) compost. In midsummer long canes appear from the centre of the bush; these can be pinched out to provide a bushy framework. Remove any damaged or crossing branches and shorten any very long canes to encourage branching. **PWa/JM**

Alternative

Vaccinium corymbosum 'Bluecrop'

Vitis

V. vinifera 'Boskoop Glory'

Main features Black grapes; attractive foliage in spring and summer; very decorative
Height 11 m (36 ft) **Spread** 5 m (16 ft)
Position ○ **Hardiness** RHS H5

This black grape is reliable and easy to grow outdoors, making it a sensible choice for busy gardeners or anyone new to growing grapes. The fruit has very few seed and is tasty enough to eat as a dessert grape straight from the vine. Since it crops heavily, *V. vinifera* 'Boskoop Glory' is also ideal for juicing or making wine, jellies or conserves.

Hailing from the Netherlands, this cold-tolerant grape is widely grown in England, Germany and northern Europe, where other varieties would need to be grown in a greenhouse or conservatory. It is a vigorous grower and can be put to good use as a decorative addition to sunny walls and fences, or even for covering pergolas or outbuildings. Like all grapes, 'Boskoop Glory' has edible leaves that can be harvested in late spring. After picking some of the largest leaves and briefly steaming them, traditional recipes suggest adding a spoonful of cooked rice and herbs to the centre of each leaf and rolling them up into a cylinder shape to make stuffed vine leaves.

Most outdoor grape varieties need to be trained along wires and pruned regularly. The Guyot system is often used for training grapes in open ground, whilst the rod-and-spur system is ideal for growing fruits against walls and fences. Generally, the main pruning is carried out in early winter, while new shoots are trained and pinched out in spring and summer. As the bunches of fruits start to appear, it is also worth removing any leaves that are shading the grapes. Not only does this improve the airflow, but sunlight improves the flavour. **PWa/JM**

Alternatives

Vitis vinifera 'Perlette', *Vitis vinifera* 'Schiava Grossa'

Index by hardiness zone

UK hardiness zones are based on the ratings introduced by the Royal Horticultural Society (RHS) in 2013. Plants are listed from least to most hardy.

Annual

Ageratum houstonianum 'Blue Horizon' **22**
Alcea rosea Halo Series **23**
Amaranthus cruentus × powellii 'Hopi Red Dye' **24**
Amberboa moschata **25**
Ammi majus 'Graceland' **27**
Beta vulgaris 'Alto' **860**
Beta vulgaris 'Burpee's Golden' **860**
Borago officinalis **820**
Brassica rapa var. *chinensis* 'Joi Choi' **862**
Brassica oleracea 'Dynamo' **865**
Brassica oleracea 'Artwork' **866**
Calendula officinalis 'Indian Prince' **35**
Callistephus chinensis 'Milady Mixed' **37**
Capsicum annuum 'Basket of Fire' **868**
Capsicum annuum 'NuMex Twilight' **869**
Capsicum annuum 'Mama Mia Giallo' **870**
Capsicum annuum 'Orange Blaze' **870**
Capsicum annuum 'Hungarian Hot Wax' **871**
Capsicum annuum 'Cayennetta' **871**
Capsicum annuum 'Pimiento de Padron' **872**
Celosia argentea Plumosa Group **39**
Centaurea cyanus 'Black Ball' **39**
Cichorium endivia 'Natacha' **873**
Cichorium intybus 'Witloof' **874**
Citrullus lanatus 'Faerie' **875**
Citrullus lanatus 'Harvest Moon' **876**
Clarkia unguiculata 'Apple Blossom' **41**
Cleome Senorita Rosalita **42**
Cleome serrulata 'Solo' **43**
Consolida regalis **44**
Coriandrum sativum 'Calypso' **824**
Cosmos sulphureus 'Polidor' **46**
Cosmos bipinnatus Sonata Series **46**
Cucumis melo 'Melemon' **876**
Cucumis sativus 'Pick a Bushel' **878**
Cucumis sativus 'Saladmore Bush' **879**
Cucurbita pepo 'Romanesco' **880**
Cucurbita pepo **49**
Cucurbita moschata 'Waltham Butternut' **881**
Cucurbita moschata 'Sweet Dumpling' **882**
Cucurbita maxima 'Cinderella's Carriage' **883**
Cucurbita pepo 'Sunburst' **884**
Cucurbita pepo 'Hijinks' **885**
Daucus carota subsp. *sativus* 'Purple Haze' **889**
Daucus carota 'Nantes' **888**
Eschscholzia californica Thai Silk Series **59**
Gomphrena globosa **64**

Helianthus annuus 'Italian White' **65**
Helianthus annuus 'Solar Flash' **65**
Helianthus annuus 'Suntastic Yellow' **66**
Helianthus annuus 'Valentine' **67**
Helianthus annuus 'American Giant' **68**
Hibiscus esculentus 'Clemson Spineless' **890**
Impatiens hawkeri 'Florific Sweet Orange' **72**
Ipomoea batatas 'Beauregard' **891**
Lactuca sativa 'Buttercrunch' **892**
Lactuca sativa 'Red Salad Bowl' **893**
Lactuca sativa 'Little Gem' **894**
Lactuca sativa 'Mottistone' **895**
Leonotis leonurus **75**
Limnanthes douglasii **75**
Lobelia erinus Super Star **76**
Molucella laevis **80**
Nasturtium officinale 'Aqua' **896**
Nemesia 'Sweet Lady' **83**
Nemophila menziesii **84**
Nierembergia scoparia 'Mont Blanc' **87**
Nigella hispanica 'Midnight' **88**
Orlaya grandiflora **91**
Panicum elegans 'Frosted Explosion' **93**
Papaver commutatum 'Ladybird' **95**
Phaseolus coccineus 'Saint George' **897**
Phaseolus vulgaris **898**
Phaseolus vulgaris 'Mascotte' **899**
Phaseolus vulgaris 'Berggold' **900**
Phlox drummondii 'Moody Blues' **98**
Physalis philadelphica 'Purple de Milpa' **901**
Pisum sativum 'Sugar Ann' **902**
Pisum sativum 'Oregon Giant' **902**
Pisum sativum 'Kelvedon Wonder' **903**
Portulaca oleracea Rio Series **101**
Raphanus sativus 'French Breakfast' **903**
Ricinus communis 'Impala' **102**
Salvia coccinea 'Summer Jewel Pink' **106**
Salvia viridis var. *comata* 'Claryssa Mixed' **107**
Solanum lycopersicum 'Terenzo' **904**
Solanum lycopersicum 'Fantastico' **906**
Solanum lycopersicum 'Chef's Choice Orange' **907**
Solanum lycopersicum 'San Marzano Lungo' **908**
Solanum lycopersicum 'Chocolate Cherry' **909**
Solanum lycopersicum 'Sungold' **910**
Solanum lycopersicum 'Shirley' **910**
Solanum tuberosum 'Yukon Gold' **911**
Solanum tuberosum 'King Edward' **911**
Solanum tuberosum 'Vitelotte' **913**
Solanum tuberosum 'Rose Finn Apple' **914**
Solanum tuberosum 'Sárpo Mira' **915**

Solanum melongena 'Fairy Tale' **916**
Spinacia oleracea 'Tyee' **917**
Tagetes tenuifolia 'Lemon Gem' **111**
Tagetes patula 'Cinnabar' **113**
Tagetes patula 'Tiger Eyes' **114**
Tagetes patula 'Harlequin' **115**
Tetragonia tetragonoides **918**
Tithonia rotundifolia 'Torch' **117**
Trachymene coerulea 'Blue Lace' **120**
Tropaeolum majus 'Blue Pepe' **849**
Tropaeolum majus Alaska Series **120**
Vicia faba 'Crimson Flowered' **920**
Vicia faba 'The Sutton' **921**
Viola Sorbet Series **124**
Zea mays 'Mirai' **922**
Zea mays 'Painted Mountain' **923**

H1a warmer than 15°C (59°F)

Heliamphora heterodoxa × nutans **734**
Ipomea lobata **617**
Jatropha podagrica **743**
Ludisia discolor **754**
Phalaenopsis × hybridus **779**
Polianthes tuberosa **204**
Schlumbergera truncata **793**
Zygopetalum James Strauss gx 'Scentsation' **809**

H1b 10 to 15°C (50–59°F)

Browallia speciosa **34**
Calathea zebrina **687**
Ctenanthe oppenheimiana 'Tricolor' **698**
Cyclamen persicum **698**
Dracaena marginata 'Tricolor' **707**
Dudleya brittonii **710**
Ensete ventricosum **716**
Eucharis amazonica **162**
Exacum affine **720**
Fittonia albivenis Verschaffeltii Group **724**
Heliocereus speciosus **736**
Hibiscus schizopetalus **740**
Hibiscus rosa-sinensis 'Cooperi' **739**
Hildewintera aureispina **740**
Huernia zebrina **741**
Justicia brandegeeana **745**
Kalanchoe beharensis **746**
Maranta leuconeura var. *erythroneura* **757**
Mimosa pudica **760**
Monstera deliciosa 'Variegata' **761**
Nepenthes 'Bill Bailey' **765**

Glossary

Botanical plant names
Each plant in the book is referred to by its botanical name.
Family A group of genera that share defined features, such as flower shape or fruit type.
Genus A group of closely-related species.
Species Members of a species share characteristics and can interbreed.

Subspecies A subdivision of a species that has features different from the parent species.
Variety A variation within a species that occurs naturally in the wild.
Cultivar A 'cultivated variety'. A man-made plant maintained in cultivation and often bred to enhance characteristics.
Hybrid Offspring of genetically different

parents, often different species of the same genus. 'F1 hybrid' refers to the first generation cross between two distinct pure-bred lines.
Group A group of cultivars within a species with similar characteristics.
Series A group of different coloured versions of the same cultivar selected by breeders of bedding plants to sell together.

Balanced fertilizer
A plant feed that contains the major nutrients (nitrogen, phosphorus and potassium) in equal proportions to encourage leafy growth.
Bedding plant
A plant that gives just one season's interest.
Bract
A small leaf-type structure below the true flower, often coloured and ornamental.
Brix value
A unit of measurement for the sugar concentration of a liquid that is used to compare the sweetness of fruits.
Cloche
A temporary or movable plant cover put over bare earth or young plants for protection.
Cold frame
A structure with a transparent lid that retains a temperature that is about halfway between a greenhouse and the open air.
Conifer
An evergreen tree or shrub that belongs to the group of plants that produce cones.
Corm
An underground swollen stem often surrounded by a papery covering.
Cut-and-come-again
A way to grow young salad crop. Plants are sown together closely and the stems of young plants are cut. They regrow and can be recut.
Deadheading
Removing faded or dead flowers to encourage more flowers to grow.
Determinate
When the main stem does not continue growing beyond a certain height.
Early
Relating to potatoes that are ready for harvesting ten weeks or so from planting.
Ericaceous
Plants that do not tolerate lime in their soil or compost and grow at a pH of 6.5 or less. Ericaceous compost is lime-free.
Everbearing
Fruiting little and often through the season.

Fleece
A lightweight sheet draped over plants to protect them from light frosts.
Floribunda rose
A modern-bred rose that is cross between a hybrid tea and a polyantha rose. It produces many clusters of flowers on one stem.
Hermaphrodite
Flowers with both female and male parts. This means, for example, that berries can grow on a single plant.
High-potash fertilizer
A plant feed that contains a higher proportion of potassium than nitrogen and phosphorus. This encourages flower and fruit production.
Humus
A residue of decayed vegetation that coats soil particles and improves soil conditions.
Hybrid musk rose
Shrub roses developed by Reverend Joseph Pemberton. The flowers are medium-sized and come in large clusters, often scented.
Hybrid tea rose
A cross between a perpetual rose and a tea rose that produces the classic, beautifully shaped blooms, usually one per stem.
Leaf mold
Decomposed leaves used as a soil improver or, if sieved, as an ingredient in potting mixes.
Maincrop
Relating to potatoes that are ready fifteen to twenty weeks from planting.
Modular tray
A tray that has been divided so that each plant develops in its own cell. This protects roots from damage. Also known as starter trays.
Mulch
A material applied to the soil surface to suppress weeds and conserve moisture. It could be a loose material, such as bark chips, or a sheet, such as woven polypropylene.
Mycorrhizae
Soil fungi associated with plant roots that benefit plant growth. Often sold as a root dip, it is used when planting out woody plants.

Open-pollinated
The natural transfer of pollen from anthers to the stigma, achieved by insects or the wind.
pH levels
A measure of how acid or alkaline a substance is, such as soil. The pH scale is 1 to 14 and pH7 is neutral. Figures below 7 are acidic and figures greater than 7 are alkaline.
Plug plant
A very young plant, akin to a rooted cutting or rooted seedling. Often sold in packs in spring.
Rhizome
An underground stem that acts as a storage organ and can be divided for propagation.
Rosette
A cluster of leaves coming out from the same point at ground level.
Second early
Relating to potatoes that are ready thirteen weeks or so from planting.
Self-fertile
A plant that produces viable seed when fertilized with its own pollen. This is a useful attribute of fruits growing in small spaces.
Self-seed
A plant that produces fertile seeds that fall to the ground and grow. This causes many annuals to reappear each year.
Semideterminate
Used to describe tomato plants that grow to 4 feet (1.2 m) tall. Also known as cordon tomato plants.
Spathe
A large modified bract that encloses a flower.
Strig
The stalk of a flowering or fruiting plant; often applied to the stalk that bears currant crops.
Tissue culture
The growing and propagation of parts of a plant in sterile conditions in a laboratory. This has made propagation easier, and has been used to remove viruses from plant stock.
Tuber
A swollen underground organ, often used to store food. Potatoes are an example.

Contributors

Zia Allaway (ZA) is an author and editor-in-chief of a range of gardening books, including the RHS *How to Grow Practically Everything* and the RHS *What Plant Where*. Zia is also a regular contributor to the magazines *Homes & Gardens* and *Garden Design Journal* in the UK, and the lifestyle blog Achica Living.

Matthew Biggs (MB) is a gardening writer and broadcaster who travels the world in search of great plants. He has presented gardening TV programmes in the UK and is a panel member of BBC Radio 4's 'Gardeners' Question Time' and has written several book on plants and gardening.

Diane Blazek (DB) is executive director of All-America Selections® and National Garden Bureau. Diane has been immersed in gardening both personally and professionally for more than twenty years. Growing up on a small family farm in northern Missouri, Diane spent years helping her parents plant, tend and harvest a large home vegetable garden.

Val Bourne (VB) is a lifelong, hands-on, organic gardener with a passion for plants. She writes for many publications, judges RHS floral and dahlia trials, lectures widely and produces books with an organic theme – always enthusiastically. Most of all, Val gardens at Spring Cottage, wrestling with windswept conditions in both her garden and allotment in the cold, UK Cotswolds.

Ruth Chivers (RC) is a writer, designer and a Fellow of the Society of Garden Designers. She has designed gardens in both the UK and in California, US. She has also contributed to *The Gardener's Garden* and *1001 Gardens You Must See Before You Die* and lectures on garden design.

Everard Daniel (ED) is a botany and geology graduate with a keen interest in all wildlife and horticulture, especially birds and woody plants. He has spent around forty years diversifying his late grandfather's rose garden in Surrey, UK. After nineteen years teaching science he currently works for a specialist rhododendron nursery.

Liz Dobbs (LD) studied biology and plant physiology to degree level before organising trials of plants, gardens and products for gardening magazines. A former editor of *Gardens Monthly* in the UK, she is now a freelance writer, consultant and author of ten international books on plants and gardening.

David Floyd (DF) has been involved in chillis for many years. He has grown chillis, developed chilli recipes and also edits and writes the blog www.chilefoundry.com, which has grown to be one of the largest specialist chilli blogs in the world.

Linden Groves (LG) is a qualified landscape historian working to achieve conservation through engagement, and co-author of the award-winning book *The Gardens of English Heritage*. She specialises in engaging children with historic parks and gardens though her website: www.outdoorchildren.co.uk

Gail Harland (GHa) combines her work as a paediatric dietitian with writing on horticultural and poultry subjects. She is author of five gardening books including works on cottage gardens and tomatoes. She has her own large cottage garden in the east of England.

Jenny Hendy (JH) is a lifelong gardener who trained in botany before joining the staff of a national gardening magazine in the UK. Her design practice, workshops and broadcasts for local BBC Radio continue to inspire her writing. She has authored more than twenty books, published worldwide.

Geoff Hodge (GH) writes for various UK gardening magazines and websites and has written eight books. He appears on BBC local radio gardening programmes, Q&A panels at flower shows and gives demonstrations and talks to garden centres and gardening clubs.

Klaus Kirschbaum (KK) has gardened in both New York and California. He currently works in international publishing at Rizzoli International Publications and was formerly director of the Garden Book Club.

Jacqueline van der Kloet (JK) is a garden and landscape designer with a passion for plants. Her speciality is impressionistic planting schemes involving annuals, biennials, bulbs and perennials. Jacqueline lives in Weesp, the Netherlands, and has a garden open to the public, which can be seen online at www.theetuin.nl

Michael Marriott (MM) has been a passionate plants person and gardener all of his life. For the last thirty years, since joining David Austin Roses, he has developed a love of roses. He now designs rose garden plans and is a font of information on all matters relating to roses.

Jeannine McAndrew (JM) is an editor and author with more than twenty years of experience in garden writing. She has launched and edited several leading magazines. Now working freelance, she grows her own produce and cut flowers and keeps rescued rare-breed chickens.

Phil McCann (PM) started gardening at an early age and says he has been lucky enough to study plant science and work in horticulture all of his life. When he is not writing about plants he is busy growing them in his garden in the East Midlands, UK.

Andy McIndoe (AMcI) is managing director of Hillier Nurseries, Hampshire, UK where he has masterminded their Gold Medal winning exhibit at the Royal Horticultural Society's Chelsea Flower Show for more than two decades. Andy is a seasoned author and broadcaster and lectures widely. He blogs to an enthusiastic following and is a tutor at my-garden-school.com

Nooraini Mydin (NM) is a freelance writer based in the UK covering lifestyle and travel for publications in Malaysia and Singapore. She has previously worked as a writer for Weber Shandwick Malaysia and as a feature writer for *The Sun* and the *New Straits Times* in Kuala Lumpur. She has also worked in public relations in the UK and for several international hotels in Malaysia.

Mary J Payne (MP) is a lecturer, broadcaster for TV and radio, writer and horticultural consultant for both private and public gardens. As a garden designer she specialises in planting schemes and her own tiny garden opens for the National Gardens Scheme. Mary has a M. Hort (RHS) qualification and was awarded a MBE for services to horticulture in south west England.

Veronica Peerless (VP) is a writer and editor specialising in gardening. She writes for gardening magazines in the UK and is the author of *The Gardener's Year*, which was published by Dorling Kindersley. Her blog, www.throughthegardengate.co.uk/blog celebrates other people's gardens, both large and small.

Gil Pidduck (GP) works in one of the largest garden centres in the UK, advising customers on garden-related issues including the best plants to suit their needs. Prior to this, for twenty-three years, she was a researcher for *Which? Gardening* magazine, which was published by the UK Consumers' Association.

Fi Reddaway (FRe) has an extensive herb garden in Devon, UK, having first started growing herbs in the late 1980s. Since 2014, she has held two Plant Heritage National Collections of *Nepeta* (catmint) and *Monarda* (bee balm, horsemint, bergamot).

Emma Reuss (ER) trained in garden design and garden history at Capel Manor College, UK. She has written for *Country Life*, *The Guardian* and the *Garden Design Journal*, and her highly acclaimed first book, *Garden Design Close Up*, was published in 2014. She has created many lovely outdoor spaces for clients, as well as cultivating plants and vegetables in her compact London garden.

Graham Rice (GR) is an award-winning writer on plants who trained at London's Royal Botanic Gardens and has grown and written about a vast variety of plants from his Pennsylvania garden. He is particularly interested in new plants, plant names and the stories behind the plants.

Gareth Richards (GAR) is the online features editor for the RHS. A keen gardener and allotment holder, he gardened in France, Italy and New Zealand before settling in the UK. His passions include tender plants and unusual edibles, as well as keeping chickens.

Frans Roozen (FR) worked for the International Flowerbulb Centre in the Netherlands for over thirty-five years. He is also a co-founder of www.allabouttulips.nl

Tom Sharples (TS) has a BSc in Horticulture from Bath University and has spent over forty years with the Suttons Group, most recently as senior horticultural manager for Suttons Seeds. His responsibilities have included running trial grounds, product development, seed catalogue production and marketing.

Janice Shipp (JS) manages the ornamental plant trials and is a writer for *Which? Gardening* magazine. Initially a student at Capel Manor College, she studied to the level of Royal Horticultural Society Master of Horticulture, and used to run a garden maintenance and design business.

Rae Spencer-Jones (RSJ) studied horticulture before joining the editorial team of *Gardens Illustrated* magazine. After a career as a freelance horticultural journalist and author, she currently works at the Royal Horticultural Society as publisher of RHS Books. Rae is the author of *Wild Flowers of Britain and Ireland* and general editor of *1001 Gardens You Must See Before You Die*.

Miek Stap (MS) is a freelance writer with fifteen years of experience in horticulture, including at the International Flowerbulb Centre in the Netherlands. Since 2012 Miek has been involved with www.allabouttulips.nl

Graham Strong (GS) has been a keen gardener since his early teens. He developed his love of plants and landscaping from working at the Savill Garden, Chelsea Physic Garden and the Royal Botanic Garden, Edinburgh, UK. He is an award-winning author, designer and photographer.

Irene Tibbenham (IT) trained as a horticulturist, then worked in the seed industry in the UK and the Netherlands and has lived and gardened in California and Texas. She now lives in an English barn surrounded by a relaxed but botanically diverse garden nestled in the Suffolk countryside. She is assisted in her gardening duties by a menagerie of Rex cats, chickens, ducks and her long-suffering husband.

Paul Wagland (PWa) is a former editor of several leading gardening magazines and a writer specialising in allotments, sustainable living and the cultivation of fruits and vegetables. Himself a keen grower of edible plants, he is always keen to share his enthusiasm for self-reliance.

Rosemary Ward (RKW) is a UK-based gardening writer and adviser with more than thirty years of experience under her belt. Her particular garden interests are trees, scented plants, wildlife gardening and growing things to eat.

judywhite (JW) was editor-in-chief of Time Inc's *Virtual Garden*, has authored three books about orchids and houseplants and wrote the 2015 feature film, *Lies I Told My Little Sister*. Judy trained as a research biologist and is also a well-known photographer at GardenPhotos.com

Adrienne Wild (AW) trained in horticulture at the Royal Botanic Gardens, Edinburgh, UK. She is an award-winning writer and editor of gardening magazines and has for more than forty years written gardening columns for a variety of newspapers and magazines.

Paul Williams (PWi) is an author, writer, garden designer, lecturer and broadcaster on all horticulture matters. He is currently the head gardener at Whichford Pottery in Warwickshire, UK.

Janine Wookey (JWo) is a well-travelled and experienced gardening writer, and is the former editor of *The English Garden*, which is published in the UK and USA.

Picture credits

2 © inga spence/Alamy 20 GAP/Jenny Lilly 22 GAP/Carole Drake 23 GAP/Julia Boulton 24 GAP/Jonathan Buckley 25 © Floramedia 26 © Carol Sharp/Flowerphotos/ardea.com 27l © Trevor Sims 27r GAP/Clive Nichols 28l All-America Selections 28r GAP/Dave Bevan 29l GAP/Jonathan Buckley 29r GAP/Annie Green-Armytage 30 GAP/Graham Strong 31l LDI 31r Graham Rice/GardenPhotos.com 32 Graham Rice/GardenPhotos.com 33 All-America Selections 34 © GWI 35 GAP/Jonathan Buckley 36 GAP/Jonathan Buckley 37 Ellen McKnight/Alamy 38 LDI 39l Haydn Hansell/Alamy 39r Graham Rice/GardenPhotos.com 40 © Dave Zubraski/Flowerphotos/ardea.com 41 GAP/Julie and Vic Pigula 42 © GWI 43 LDI 44 GAP/Jonathan Burkley 45 GAP/Tim Gainey 46l GAP/Paul Debois – Heather Osborne 46r GAP 47 GAP/Christa Brand – Weihenstephan Gardens 48 Graham Strong 49l GAP/Mark Bolton 49r Graham Rice/GardenPhotos.com 50l © Thomas Marent/ardea.com 50r LDI 51l GAP/Paul Debois 51r GAP/Thomas Alamy 52 LDI 53 GAP/J S Sira – Design: Hilliers. Sponsors: Hilliers 54l GAP/Chris Burrows 54r © Liz Cole 55 GAP/Abigail Rex 56 GAP/Rob Whitworth – Design: Piet Oudolf 57l © Carol Sharp/Flowerphotos/ardea.com 57r © Carol Sharp/Flowerphotos/ardea.com 58 LDI 59 GAP/Gary Smith 60 GAP/Gary Smith 61 Horticultureimages.com 62 GAP/Jonathan Buckley – Design: Derry Watkins, Special Plants 63 Graham Strong 64l GAP/Jonathan Buckley – Design: Derry Watkins, Special Plants 64r © GWI 65l GAP/Elke Borkowski – Design: Christian Meyer 65r GAP/Graham Strong 66 © Oscar D'arcy 67 LDI 68l GAP/Christina Bollen 68r Val Duncan/Kenebec Images/Alamy 69 Tim Gainey/Alamy 70 GAP/J S Sira 71 © Botanic Images Inc 72 All-America Selections 73 GAP 74l GAP/Jerry Pavia 74r GAP/Pernilla Bergdahl 75l GAP/Dave Bevan 75r GAP/FhF Greenmedia 76 GAP/Visions 77 © Botanic Images Inc. 78 © Carol Sharp/Flowerphotos/ardea.com 79l © Carol Sharp/Flowerphotos/ardea.com 79r LDI 80 GAP/John Glover 81 GAP/Jonathan Buckley – Design: Sarah Raven 82 GAP/J S Sira 83l GAP/Jo Whitworth 83r Graham Strong 84 GAP/Tommy Tonsberg 85 GAP/Fiona McLeod 86 GAP/Elke Borkowski 87 All-America Selections 88 GAP/Sabina Ruber 89 GAP/John Glover 90 GAP/Nicola Stocken 91 GAP/Carole Drake 92 GAP/Jonathan Buckley 93 GAP/Graham Strong 94 GAP/Clive Nichols – Painswick Rococo Garden, Gloucestershire 95l GAP/Jenny Lilly 95r GAP/Howard Rice 96l © Richard Shiell 96r Select Seeds 97l GAP/Friedrich Strauss 97r GAP/Geoff du Feu 98 LDI 99 GAP/Sue Heath 100 GAP/Thomas Alamy 101 © GWI 102l © Adrian James 102r © Susan Edwards/Flowerphotos/ardea.com 103 GAP/Tim Gainey 104 GAP/Jonathan Buckley 105 GAP/Tim Gainey 106l All-America Selections 106r GAP/J S Sira 107l GAP/Jan Smith 107r GAP/Paul Debois 108 © Jonathan Buckley/Flowerphotos/ardea.com 109 GAP/Pernilla Bergdahl 110 GAP/Jenny Lilly 111 GAP/Dave Bevan 112 GAP/Jonathan Buckley 113 GAP/Jonathan Buckley 114 GAP/Tommy Tonsberg 115 © MAP/Nathalie Pasquel 116 GAP/Howard Rice 117 GAP/Jenny Lilly 118 GAP/Visions 119 © MAP/Nicole and Patrick Mioulane 120l Steffen Hause/botanikfoto/Alamy 120r GAP/Tommy Tonsberg 121 GAP/Graham Strong 122 GAP/Joanna Kossak 123l GAP/Annette Lepple – Maison de l'Arbre – owners: Elaine and David Morgan 123r All-America Selections 124l GAP/Marg Cousens 124r GAP/Friedrich Strauss 125 ©judywhite/GardenPhotos.com 126l GAP/FhF Greenmedia 126r Graham Strong 127l GAP/Manuela Goehner 127r Graham Rice/GardenPhotos.com 128 GAP/Richard Wareham 130 GAP/Juliette Wade 131 © Carol Sharp/Flowerphotos/ardea.com 132 GAP/Jonathan Buckley 133l © Duncan Smith/Flowerphotos/ardea.com 133r LDI 134l LDI 134r GAP/Frederic Didillon 135 © Sue Kennedy/Flowerphotos/ardea.com 136 GAP/Geoff du Feu 137 GAP/Visions 138 Graham Strong 139 GAP/Visions 140 GAP/Jonathan Buckley 141l GAP/Jonathan Buckley – Design: Christopher Lloyd, Great Dixter 141r GAP/Lynn Keddie 142 GAP/John Glover 143l Graham Strong 143r GAP/Juliette Wade 144l GAP/Jonathan Buckley 144r GAP/BIOS – Gilles Le Scanff and Joëlle-Caroline Mayer 145 LDI 146l LDI 146r GAP/Bjorn Hansson 147l © Edith Ulrich/Flowerphotos/ardea.com 147r GAP/Marg Cousens 148 Graham Strong 149 GAP/Richard Bloom 150 GAP/Carol Casselden 151 GAP/Dave Zubraski 152 GAP/Dianna Jazwinski 153l © David C Dixon/ardea.com 153r GAP/Jonathan Buckley 154l GAP/Dave Zubraski 154r GAP/Carol Casselden 155l LDI 155r GAP/Jonathan Need 156 GAP/Clive Nichols 157 GAP/Charles Hawes 158 © David Dixon/ardea.com 159l GAP/Graham Strong 159r LDI 160 GAP/John Glover 162 GAP/Jenny Lilly 163 GAP/Jonathan Buckley – Design: John Massey 164l GAP/Richard Bloom 164r © Carol Sharp/Flowerphotos/ardea.com 165 Graham Strong 166 GAP/Clive Nichols 167 GAP/J S Sira 168 GAP/John Glover 169 Graham Strong 170 GAP/Jenny Lilly 171l GAP/Nicola Stocken 171r GAP/FhF Greenmedia 172 GAP/Elke Borkowski 173 GAP/Tommy Tonsberg 174 GAP/Jonathan Buckley 175 The Garden Collection/Flora Press/Andrew Lawson 176l GAP/Jonathan Buckley 176r The Garden Collection/Flora Press/Martin Hughes-Jones 177 GAP/Clive Nichols 178 GAP/Bjorn Hansson 179 GAP/Heather Edwards – Pennings Bulbs 180 GAP/Elke Borkowski 181l Graham Strong 181r GAP/Jonathan Buckley 182 GAP/Jonathan Buckley 183 LDI 184l GAP/Dave Bevan 184r GAP/Heather Edwards 185l © John Swithinbank 185r Graham Strong 186 GAP/Visions 187 GAP/Howard Rice 188 GAP/Janet Johnson 189l GAP/Janet Johnson 189r GAP/Jonathan Buckley 190l GAP/Ron Evans 190r © Carol Sharp/Flowerphotos/ardea.com 191 GAP/Jonathan Buckley – Design: John Massey, Ashwood Nurseries 192 GAP/Virginia Grey 193l GAP/Jonathan Buckley – Design: Sue and Wol Staines 193r GAP/Elke Borkowski 194 GAP/John Glover 195 GAP/Lynne Brotchie 196 Graham Strong 197l GAP/Juliette Wade 197r GAP/Sharon Pearson 198l © Edith Ulrich/Flowerphotos/ardea.com 198r © Paul Tomlins/Flowerphotos/ardea.com 199l The Garden Collection/Flora Press/Christine Ann Föll 199r Graham Strong 200 LDI 201 The Garden Collection/Flora Press/Martin Hughes-Jones 202 GAP/Dave Bevan 203 © Emma Townsend/Flowerphotos/ardea.com 204 GAP/Visions 205 Graham Strong 206l GAP/S & O 206r GAP/David Dixon 207l GAP/Fiona Lea 207r GAP/Mark Bolton 208 GAP/Rob Whitworth 209 GAP/Visions 210 GAP/Fiona Lea 211l GAP/Jonathan Buckley 211r GAP/Jonathan Buckley 212 GAP/Bjorn Hansson 213 GAP/Richard Bloom 214 GAP/Mark Bolton 215 © John Swithinbank 216 GAP/Clive Nichols – Oxford Botanic Garden 217 GAP/Juliette Wade – Woodpeckers, Essex 218 GAP/Jenny Lilly 219l GAP/Lynn Keddie 219r GAP/Rob Whitworth 220 GAP/Visions 221 GAP/Dave Zubraski 222l GAP/Pernilla Bergdahl 222r The Garden Collection/Flora Press/Bildagentur Beck 223 © Bob Gibbons/ardea.com 224 GAP/Jerry Harpur 225l GAP/Howard Rice 225r GAP/Juliette Wade 226l GAP/Sabina Ruber 227l GAP/Richard Wareham 227r LDI 228l LDI 228r GAP/J S Sira 229l GAP/David Dixon 229r GAP/Visions 230 GAP/John Glover 231 GAP/John Glover 232 © Julian Nieman/Flowerphotos/ardea.com 234 GAP/Neil Holmes 235l GAP/J S Sira 235r GAP/John Glover 236 GAP/Jo Whitworth 237 GAP/Christa Brand 238 GAP/Jo Whitworth – Design: Tom Stuart-Smith 239l GAP/Jo Whitworth – Design: Tom Stuart-Smith 239r GAP/Richard Bloom 240 © Rex May/Alamy 241 GAP/Richard Bloom 242l GAP/Amy Vonheim 274l GAP/Frederic Didillon 274r GAP/Chris Burrows 275l GAP/Amy Vonheim 274l GAP/Frederic Didillon 274r GAP/Chris Burrows 275l GAP 275r GAP/Neil Holmes 276 GAP/Tommy Tonsberg 277 GAP/Jo Whitworth 278 GAP/Dave Zubraski 279l GAP/Jonathan Need 279r GAP/Marg Cousens 280 GAP/Martin Staffler 281 GAP/Howard Rice 282 GAP/Jonathan Buckley 283 GAP/Maddie Thornhill 284 GAP/Marcus Harpur 285 GAP/Matt Anker 286 GAP/Adrian Bloom 287 GAP/John Glover 288l GAP/Jonathan Buckley – Design: Carol Klein 288r GAP/FhF Greenmedia 289 GAP/Graham Strong 290 GAP/John Glover – RHS Wisley, Surrey 291l GAP/John Glover 291r © Mark Bolton 292 GAP/Visions 293 GAP/Kit Young 294 GAP/Carole Drake 295l GAP/Richard Bloom 295r GAP/Martin Staffler 296l GAP/J S Sira 296r GAP/Richard Bloom 297 GAP/Graham Strong 298 GAP/Dave Zubraski 299 GAP/Graham Strong 300l GAP 300r GAP/Sharon Pearson 301l GAP/Matt Anker – Design: Peter Reader. Sponsor: Provender Nurseries 301r GAP/Andrea Jones 302l GAP/J S Sira 302r © Steffen Hauser 303l GAP/S & O 303r GAP/Amanda Darcy 304 GAP/Howard Rice – Design: Sally and Don Edwards 305 GAP/Juliette Wade 306 GAP/Sue Heath 307 GAP/Carol Casselden 308l GAP/Fiona Lea – Design: Oxford College of Garden Design. 308r GAP/Martin Staffler 309 GAP/Martin Staffler 310 GAP/Howard Rice 311l GAP/Howard Rice 311r GAP/Elke Borkowski 312 GAP/Matt Anker 313 GAP/Howard Rice 314 GAP/Nicola Stocken 315 GAP/Elke Borkowski 316 GAP/Neil Holmes 317 GAP/Sharon Pearson 318 © GWI 319 GAP/Jonathan Buckley 320 GAP/Lee Avison 321 GAP/Lynn Keddie 322 GAP/Richard Bloom 323 ©judywhite/GardenPhotos.com 324l ©Graham Rice/GardenPhotos.com 324r GAP/Marg Cousens 325 GAP/Visions 326 GAP/Maddie Thornhill 327 GAP/Carole Drake 328 GAP/Fiona McLeod – Design: Leeds City Council 329 GAP/Jenny Lilly 330 GAP/Mark Bolton 331 GAP/Mark Bolton 332 GAP/Heather Edwards – Design: Roger Platts 333l GAP/Marcus Harpur 333r GAP/S & O 334 GAP/J S Sira 335 GAP/Dave Bevan 336 GAP/Visions 337 GAP/Richard Bloom 338l www.PerennialResource.com 338r GAP/Jonathan Buckley – Design: John Massey, Ashwood Nurseries 339 GAP/Neil Holmes 340 GAP/Tommy Tonsberg 341 GAP/Richard Bloom 342l GAP/Howard Rice 342r GAP/Joanna Kossak 343 GAP/Sue Heath 344 © Anne Gilbert/Alamy 345l GAP/Richard Bloom 345r GAP/Jan Smith 346l GAP/Carole Drake 346r GAP/Jonathan Buckley – Design: John Massey, Ashwood Nurseries 347l GAP/Fiona Lea 347r GAP/Jo Whitworth 348 GAP/Graham Strong 349 GAP/Carole Drake – Helmsley Walled Garden Trust 350 GAP/Dave Zubraski 351 GAP/Julie Dansereau 352 © William S. Kuta/Alamy 353 GAP/Frederic Didillon 354 GAP/Tommy Tonsberg 355 GAP/

Frederic Didillon 356 GAP/Richard Bloom 357 GAP/Mark Bolton 358 GAP/Howard Rice 359 GAP/John Glover 360l ©judywhite/GardenPhotos.com 360r GAP/Clive Nichols 361 GAP/Elke Borkowski 362 GAP/Howard Rice 363 GAP/Neil Holmes 364l GAP/Heather Edwards – Design: Lindsay Withycombe 364r GAP/Tim Gainey 365 GAP/Howard Rice 366 © Steffen Hauser/botanikfoto/Alamy 367 GAP/Jenny Lilly 368 GAP/Visions 369l GAP/Jerry Harpur 369r GAP/Geoff Kidd 370l GAP/Pernilla Bergdahl 370r GAP/Clive Nichols 371l GAP/Matt Anker 371r GAP/Pernilla Bergdahl 372 GAP/Howard Rice 373l GAP/Visions 373r GAP/J S Sira 374 GAP/Howard Rice 375 GAP/Visions 376 GAP/Marg Cousens 377 GAP/Carole Drake – Owner: Ms Christine Wood 378l GAP/Fiona Lea 378r GAP/Friedrich Strauss 379 GAP/Martin Staffler 380 GAP/Mark Bolton 381 GAP/Christa Brand 382 GAP/FhF Greenmedia 383 GAP/Rob Whitworth 384l GAP/Joanna Kossak 384r GAP/Fiona McLeod 385l GAP/Abigail Rex 385r GAP/David Dixon 386 The Garden Collection/Flora Press/Nova Photo Graphik/ 387 © Liz Every 388 GAP/Marg Cousens 389 GAP/Tim Gainey 390 The Garden Collection/Flora Press/Biosphoto/Hervé Lenain 391 GAP/J S Sira 392l The Garden Collection/Flora Press/Torie Chugg 392r © Tim Gainey/Alamy 393l GAP/J S Sira 393r GAP/Lynn Keddie 394 GAP/Heather Edwards 395 GAP/Pernilla Bergdahl 396 GAP/Christina Bollen 397 GAP/Jonathan Buckley 398l © Oscar D'arcy 398r GAP/Neil Holmes 399l GAP/Richard Bloom 399r GAP/Manuela Goehner 400 GAP/Andrea Jones – Design: Oehme, van Sweden Associates 401l GAP/Dave Zubraski 401r GAP/Annette Lepple 402l GAP/Dave Zubraski 402r GAP/John Glover 403 GAP/Howard Rice 404 GAP/Howard Rice 405 GAP/Julie Dansereau – RHS Wisley 406 GAP/Elke Borkowski 407 The Garden Collection/Flora Press/Derek Harris 408 GAP/Dave Bevan 409 GAP/Jacqui Hurst 410 © Sue Kennedy/Flowerphotos/ardea.com 411 GAP/Fiona McLeod 412 The Garden Collection/Flora Press/Bildagentur Beck 413 GAP/Friedrich Strauss 414 GAP/Carole Drake 415 GAP/Richard Bloom 416 GAP/John Glover 417 GAP/Chris Burrows 418l GAP/Fiona McLeod 418r GAP/Dave Bevan 419l GAP/S & O 419r GAP/Sharon Pearson 420 GAP/Frederic Didillon 421 GAP 422 GAP/Howard Rice 423 GAP/Christa Brand 424 GAP/Neil Holmes 425 GAP/Elke Borkowski 426 © blickwinkel/Alamy 427 GAP/Fiona Lea 428 GAP/Juliette Wade 429l GAP/Richard Bloom 429r GAP/Richard Bloom 430 GAP/Rob Whitworth 431 GAP/Matt Anker 432l GAP/Visions 432r GAP/Virginia Grey 433l © Trevor Sims 433r © Julian Nieman/Flowerphotos/ardea.com 434 GAP/Jo Whitworth 436 Photos Horticultural/Photoshot 437 GAP/Richard Bloom – Winter Garden, Bressingham Gardens 438 GAP/Graham Strong 439l GAP/Dave Zubraski 439r GAP/Jo Whitworth 440l GAP/Marcus Harpur 440r © John Richmond/Alamy 441l Nova Photo Graphik 441r The Garden Collection/Flora Press/Richard Bloom 442l © REDA &CO srl/Alamy 442r GAP/Charles Hawes – Garden created by Anne Wareham and Charles Hawes 443 GAP/Suzie Gibbons – Design: Sue Milward 444 GAP/Rob Whitworth 445 GAP/J S Sira 446 GAP/Richard Bloom 447 GAP/Adrian Bloom 448 GAP/Dianna Jazwinski 449 GAP/Rob Whitworth 450l The Garden Collection/Flora Press/Andrew Lawson 450r GAP/Joanna Kossak 451 GAP/Jacqui Hurst 452 GAP/Jerry Pavia 453l GAP/Jason Ingram 453r GAP/FhF Greenmedia 454l GAP/Carol Casselden 455l GAP/Thomas Alamy 455r © Rex May/Alamy 456 © Trevor Sims 457 GAP/Richard Bloom 458 GAP/Jenny Lilly 459 GAP/John Swithinbank 460 GAP/Matt Anker 461 GAP/Jenny Lilly 462 GAP/Carole Drake 463l GAP/Joanna Kossak 463r GAP/Richard Bloom 464 © Zoonar GmbH/Alamy 465 GAP/Carole Drake – Design: Dave and Tina Primmer 466l GAP/Charles Hawes 466r © flowerphotos/Alamy 467l The Garden Collection/Flora Press/Nova Photo Graphik/ 467r GAP/Ray Cox 468l © Jonathan Ward/Alamy 468r GAP/Dave Zubraski 469 GAP/Howard Rice 470 © Photoshot Holdings Ltd/Alamy 471l GAP/Graham Strong 471r GAP/Chris Burrows 472 GAP/Nicola Stocken 473 GAP/Trevor Nicholson Christie 474 GAP/Martin Staffler 475 GAP/Geoff Kidd 476 GAP/Carole Drake 477 GAP/Richard Bloom – The Winter Garden at The Bressingham Gardens, Norfolk 478 © Steffen Hauser/botanikfoto/Alamy 479l © John Glover/Alamy 479r GAP/Neil Overy 480l GAP/Jonathan Buckley – Design: Christopher Lloyd, Great Dixter 480r GAP/Jonathan Buckley 481l GAP/Jenny Lilly 481r GAP/FhF Greenmedia 482 © John Glover/Alamy 483l GAP/Lee Avison – Design: Maureen Sawyer 483r The Garden Collection/Flora Press/Martin Hughes-Jones 484 GAP/Howard Rice 485 © John Martin/Alamy 486 GAP/Julie Dansereau 487 GAP/Jonathan Buckley 488l GAP/Charles Hawes 488r GAP/Dave Bevan 489l © Rex May/Alamy 489r © Rex May/Alamy 490l GAP/J S Sira 490r © Niall McDiarmid/Alamy 491 Photos Horticultural/Photoshot 492l GAP/Carole Drake 492r GAP/Dave Zubraski 493 GAP/Jerry Harpur 494 GAP/Howard Rice 495l © Natural Garden Images/Alamy 495r GAP/Fiona Lea 496 © Rex May/Alamy 497 GAP/Rob Whitworth 498 GAP/Richard Bloom 499 GAP/Elke Borkowski 500 © Kevin Richardson/Alamy 501 © Trevor Chriss/Alamy 502 © Doug Houghton/Alamy 503 © Rex May/Alamy 504 GAP/Juliette Wade 505 © Organica/Alamy 506l © John Richmond/Alamy 506r GAP/Marg Cousens 507l Dave Zubraski/Alamy 507r GAP/Jerry Pavia 508 GAP/Dave Bevan 509 GAP/Matt Anker 510 © Photos Horticultural 511 GAP/John Glover 512 GAP/Dianna Jazwinski 513 The Garden Collection/FP/Derek St. Romaine 514l GAP/Howard Rice 514r Sue Milliken, Far Reaches Farm 515l GAP/Lee Avison 515r GAP/Carole Drake 516 GAP/Elke Borkowski 517 GAP/Richard Bloom 518 GAP/Marcus Harpur 519 GAP/Neil Holmes 520 © Rob Whitworth Garden Photography/Alamy 520 GAP/Marg Cousens 522 GAP/Neil Holmes 523 GAP/Marcus Harpur – RHS Wisley, Surrey 524 The Garden Collection/FP/Martin Hughes-Jones 525 GAP/Neil Holmes 526 GAP/S & O 526 GAP/Elke Borkowski 527 GAP/Richard Bloom 528 The Garden Collection/FP/Bildagentur Beck 529 Willoway Nurseres 530 GAP/Jenny Lilly 531 GAP/Lee Avison 532l GAP/Tomek Ciesielski 532r GAP/Richard Bloom 533l GAP/Lee Avison 533r GAP/Adrian Bloom 534 © Holmes Garden/Alamy 535 © Adrian James 536 GAP/Geoff Kidd 537 GAP/Clive Nichols 538 © Niall McDiarmid/Alamy 539l GAP/Paul Debois 539r GAP/Fiona Lea 540l GAP/Christina Bollen – The Himalayan Garden, North Yorkshire 540r GAP/Tommy Tonsberg 541l GAP/Jerry Pavia 541r GAP/Jerry Pavia 542l GAP/Tommy Tonsberg 542r GAP/Clairc Takacs 543 GAP/Adrian Bloom 544 © Picture Alliance/Photoshot 545l GAP/Christina Bollen 545r GAP/Heather Edwards 546 © gardeningpix/Alamy 547 © Mark Summerfield/Alamy 548 GAP/Howard Rice – NCCPG National Collection. Barry Clarke 549 GAP/FhF Greenmedia 550 GAP/Howard Rice 551 GAP/Adrian Bloom 552 GAP/Jo Whitworth 553 GAP/Manuela Goehner 554 © DPA/Photoshot 555l GAP/Marcus Harpur – Design: Rodney and Pam Burn 555r GAP/Jonathan Buckley 556 GAP/Carole Drake 557 © Andrea Jones Images/Alamy 558l GAP/Jenny Lilly 558r © Photos Horticultural 559l GAP/Fiona McLeod 559r LDI 560 GAP/Neil Holmes 561 © Christopher Lavis-Jones 562 GAP/Thomas Alamy 563l ©judywhite/GardenPhotos.com 563r GAP/J S Sira 564 © Rita Coates 565 GAP/Clive Nichols – Moors meadow garden, Herefordshire 566 GAP/Thomas Alamy 567 GAP/Fiona Lea 568 © Tim Wright/Alamy 569 GAP/Heather Edwards – Design: Ruth Gwynn 570 GAP/Clive Nichols 571 GAP/Carole Drake – courtesy The Sir Harold Hillier Gardens/Hampshire County Council 572 GAP/Nicola Stocken 573 GAP/Howard Rice 574 GAP/Charles Hawes 575 GAP/Richard Bloom 576 GAP/Marcus Harpur 577 GAP/Clive Nichols 578 GAP/S & O 579 GAP/Jan Smith 580l © John Martin/Alamy 580r © Terry Jennings 581l © MAP/Alain Guerrier 581r GAP/Joanna Kossak 582 © blickwinkel/Alamy 584 © blickwinkel/Alamy 585 Christer Johansson 586 GAP/Neil Holmes 587 Wayside Gardens 588 GAP/Christa Brand 589 GAP/Neil Holmes 590 GAP/Carole Drake – courtesy Nicholas Wray, Curator, University of Bristol Botanic Garden 591 GAP/Howard Rice 592 GAP/Paul Debois 593l The Garden Collection/Flora Press/Gary Rogers 593r GAP/Neil Holmes 594 © Allan Munsie/Alamy 595 © Anne Gilbert/Alamy 596l The Garden Collection/Flora Press/Nova Photo Graphik/ 596r The Garden Collection/Flora Press/Bildagentur Beck 597 GAP/Robert Mabic 598 GAP/John Glover 599 GAP/J S Sira 600 GAP/J S Sira 601 GAP/Matt Anker 602 GAP/Jenny Lilly 603 GAP/Jonathan Buckley 604 GAP/Dave Zubraski 605 GAP/Gary Smith 606l GAP/Jo Whitworth 606r Ron Rabideau 607l GAP/Geoff Kidd 607r GAP/Jonathan Need 608 GAP/Geoff Kidd 609 Lewis Jackson/Alamy 610 GAP/Carole Drake – courtesy Nicholas Wray, Curator, Bristol University Botanic Garden 611 GAP/Clive Nichols 612 GAP/Graham Strong 613l GAP/Clive Nichols 613r John Glover/Alamy 614 © Geraldine Buckley/Alamy 615 GAP/Geoff Kidd 616l GAP/Neil Holmes 616r GAP/Frederic Didillon 617l © Florapix/Alamy 617r GAP/FhF Greenmedia 618l © Roberto Nistri/Alamy 618r GAP/Neil Holmes 619 GAP/Friedrich Strauss 620 GAP/J S Sira 621 GAP/Paul Debois 622 GAP/Christina Bollen 623 GAP/Tommy Tonsberg 624 GAP/Neil Holmes 625 GAP/Neil Holmes 626l GAP/Marcus Harpur 626r GAP/Neil Holmes 627l GAP/Jonathan Buckley 627r © Florapix/Alamy 628 GAP/Howard Rice 629 GAP/Howard Rice 630l GAP/Rob Whitworth 630r GAP/Matt Anker 631 GAP/Richard Bloom 632 © Jack Glisson/Alamy 633 GAP/David Dixon 634 GAP/Jerry Harpur 635 © Andrea Jones Images/Alamy 636 © Rex May/Alamy 637l GAP/Carole Drake 637r GAP/Nicola Stocken 638l GAP/Marg Cousens 638r GAP/David Dixon 639l GAP/Elke Borkowski 639r GAP/Friedrich Strauss 640 GAP/Fiona Lea 641 GAP/J S Sira 642 GAP/S & O 643 GAP/Dave Bevan 644l Photos Horticultural/Photoshot 644r The Garden Collection/Flora Press/Tim Gainey 645 GAP/Friedrich Strauss 646 GAP/Howard Rice – David Austin Roses Ltd. 648 GAP/Elke Borkowski 649 GAP/Elke Borkowski 650 GAP/Howard Rice 651l GAP/FhF Greenmedia 651r Flora Press/Biosphoto/Jean-Yves Grospas 652 GAP/Juliette Wade 653 GAP 654 GAP/Jonathan Buckley 655 © Garden Photo World/Alamy 656 GAP/Michael King 657l GAP/Joanna Kossak 657r © Donaldl Fackler Jr/Alamy 658l GAP/Tommy Tonsberg 658r © GWI 659l GAP/Charles Hawes 659r GAP/Charles Hawes 660 GAP/Howard Rice 661 The Garden Collection/Flora Press/Christine Ann Föll 662 GAP/Elke Borkowski 663 GAP/Lynn Keddie 664 GAP/FhF Greenmedia 665 GAP/Mark Bolton 666 GAP/Howard Rice – Hengrave Hall, Suffolk 667 GAP/Howard Rice – David Austin Roses Ltd. 668 GAP/Christina Bollen 669 GAP/Richard Bloom 670 GAP/Carole Drake 671 GAP/Heather Edwards 672 GAP/Howard Rice 673 © Georgianna Lane/Garden Photo World/Corbis 674 GAP/S & O 676 GAP/Howard Rice 677 GAP/Nicola Stocken 678l GAP/Pernilla Bergdahl 678r GAP/Clive Nichols – Design: Amir Schlezinger/My Landscapes 679 GAP/Howard Rice 680 © Floramedia/GWI 681l GAP/John

Picture credits

Glover 681r GAP/Chris Burrows 682 GAP/Jo Whitworth 683 GAP/Carole Drake 684 GAP/Jonathan Buckley 685 GAP/Neil Holmes 686l GAP/Dave Bevan 686r GAP/Tim Gainey 687l © Nigel Cattlin/Alamy 687 GAP/S & O 688 GAP/Michael King 689 © Photos Horticultural/Photoshot 690 GAP/Friedrich Strauss 691 GAP/Friedrich Strauss 692 GAP/Graham Strong 693 GAP/Sue Heath 694 GAP/J S Sira 695 GAP/Joanna Kossak – Design; stylist: Danuta Mlozniak 696l GAP/Michael Howes 696r GAP/Brian North 697 GAP/Jerry Pavia 698l GAP/Howard Rice 698r GAP/Visions 699 GAP/Elke Borkowski 700 GAP/John Glover 701 GAP/Lynne Brotchie 702 GAP/Lee Avison – Design: Gordon Cooke 703 GAP/Thomas Alamy 704l LDI 704r Mike Comb/Science Photo Library 705l GAP/J S Sira 705r © REDA &CO srl/Alamy 706 © Photoshot Holdings Ltd/ Alamy 707 © GWI 708 GAP/Clive Nichols 709 GAP/Visions 710 GAP/S & O 711 GAP/Juliette Wade 712 © Ernie Janes/Alamy 713 GAP/Heather Edwards – Design: Sarah Eberle 714 © REDA &CO srl/Alamy 715 GAP/Jerry Harpur – Design: Mary Effron, Pat Bauer 716 GAP/Manuela Goehner 717 © GWI 718 GAP/Gary Smith 719 GAP/Trevor Nicholson Christie 720 GAP/Howard Rice 721 © blickwinkel/Alamy 722 GAP/Maddie Thornhill – Holly Gate Cactus Nursery 723 GAP/Marcus Harpur 724 GAP/Matt Anker 725 © Dorling Kindersley ltd/Alamy 726 GAP/Jerry Harpur 727 The Garden Collection/Flora Press/Nova Photo Graphik/ 728l GAP/J S Sira 728r © Maximilian Weinzierl/ Alamy 729l © Organica/Alamy 729r GAP/J S Sira 730 GAP/Neil Overy 731 © dpa picture alliance/Alamy 732 GAP/Lynn Keddie 733 © Dennis Frates/Alamy 734 GAP/Matt Anker 735 GAP/Carole Drake 736l Royal Botanic Garden Edinburgh/Science Photo Library 736r GAP/Dave Bevan 737 GAP/Thomas Alamy 738 GAP/Visions Premium 739 © kpzfoto/Alamy 740l © Zena Elea/Alamy 740r © Tony Cooper 741l © REDA &CO srl/Alamy 741r GAP/Howard Rice 742 GAP/Howard Rice – Fellows' Garden, Clare College, Cambridge 743l GAP/Dave Zubraski 743r GAP/Visions 744 GAP/Dave Bevan 745 © Rex May/Alamy 746 GAP/Thomas Alamy 747 GAP/Sarah Cuttle 748 GAP/ Jonathan Buckley 749 GAP/Geoff Kidd 750 GAP/Jenny Lilly 751 © MARKA/Alamy 752 GAP/Charles Hawes 753l © dpa picture alliance/Alamy 753r © blickwinkel/Alamy 754l © Florapix/Alamy 754r GAP/Chris Burrows 755l GAP/Thomas Alamy 755r GAP/Jenny Lilly 756 GAP/Lynn Keddie 757 GAP/Jo Whitworth 758l © Martin Hughes-Jones/Alamy 758r GAP/Marcus Harpur 759 GAP/Jerry Harpur – Design: Dan Hinkley 760 GAP/Heather Edwards 761 GAP/John Glover 762 GAP/John Glover 763 GAP/ Howard Rice – St Barnabas Road, Cambridge 764 © Trevor Sims 765 GAP/Sarah Cuttle 766l GAP/Leigh Clapp 766r © REDA &CO srl/Alamy 767l © Jenny Lilly 767r GAP/ John Glover 768 © REDA &CO srl/Alamy 769 GAP/Richard Bloom 770l © ArtesiaWells/Alamy 770r GAP/Jenny Lilly 771 GAP/Friedrich Strauss 772l GAP/Amy Vonheim 772r GAP/Friedrich Strauss 773l GAP/Paul Debois 773r GAP/Geoff Kidd 774 All-America Selections 775 © Hervé Lenain/Alamy 776 GAP/Lynn Keddie 777 GAP/Lee Avison 778 GAP/Jo Whitworth 779 Reto Puppetti 780l © John Richmond/Alamy 780r © Photos Horticultural/Photoshot 781l GAP/Jonathan Need 781r GAP/Richard Bloom 782 GAP/J S Sira 783 © Rafael Ben-Ari/Alamy 784 GAP/John Glover 785 GAP/Zara Napier 786 GAP/John Glover 787 GAP/Maddie Thornhill 788 GAP/Jenny Lilly 789 GAP/Jenny Lilly 790l © songsak aromyim/Alamy 790r GAP/Amy Vonheim 791l GAP/David Dixon 791r GAP/Thomas Alamy 792l GAP/Jerry Pavia 792r GAP 793l © Rex May/Alamy 793r GAP/Neil Holmes 794 GAP/Carole Drake 795 GAP/Carole Drake 796 GAP/Carole Drake 797 GAP/Perry Mastrovito – Centre de la Nature public garden, Saint-Vincent-de-Paul, Laval, Quebec, Canada 798 GAP/Jerry Harpur 799 GAP/FhF Greenmedia 800 GAP/Jerry Harpur 801 GAP/Matt Anker 802l GAP/ Friedrich Strauss 802r GAP/Pernilla Bergdahl 803l © John Richmond/Alamy 803r Eric Peterson 804l GAP/Jonathan Buckley 804r Tropic Flore 805l © shapencolour/Alamy 805r GAP/Visions 806 GAP/Howard Rice 807 © flowerphotos/Alamy 808 GAP/Jo Whitworth 809 GAP/John Glover 810 GAP/Dianna Jazwinski 812 © blickwinkel/Alamy 813 GAP/Sue Heath 814 GAP/Jonathan Buckley – Design: Sarah Raven 815 GAP/Friedrich Strauss 816 GAP/Gary Smith 817 GAP/Dianna Jazwinski 818 GAP/Martin Staffler 819 GAP/Geoff Kidd 820 LDI 820l © Bob Gibbons/ardea.com 821r GAP/Elke Borkowski 822 GAP/Fiona Lea 823 GAP/Gary Smith 824l GAP © dpa picture alliance/Alamy 825l GAP/Fiona McLeod 825r GAP/Charles Hawes – Garden created by Anne Wareham and Charles Hawes 826 GAP/Maddie Thornhill 827 © Steffen Hauser/botanikfoto/Alamy 828 © Floramedia 829 GAP/Graham Strong 830 GAP/John Glover 831 GAP/Geoff Kidd 832l LDI 832r GAP/Geoff Kidd 833 GAP/Janet Johnson 834 The Garden Collection/FP/Martin Hughes-Jones 835 GAP/Friedrich Strauss 836 GAP/Graham Strong 837 GAP/Jonathan Buckley 838l GAP/Friedrich Strauss 838r GAP/Jonathan Buckley – Design: Christopher Lloyd 839l The Garden Collection/FP/Biosphoto/Jean-Louis Le Moigne 839r © Rex May/Alamy 840 GAP/John Glover 841 The Garden Collection/Flora Press/Nova Photo Graphik 842 © Steffen Hauser/botanikfoto/Alamy 843 GAP/Jo Whitworth 844 GAP/Thomas Alamy 845 GAP/Thomas Alamy 846 © Carol Sharp/Flowerphotos/ardea.com 847 GAP/Thomas Alamy 848 GAP/Lee Avison 849 GAP 850 GAP/John Glover 851 © CTK/Alamy 852 GAP/FhF Greenmedia 854 GAP/Leigh Clapp 855 GAP/Jo Whitworth 856 GAP/Chris Burrows 857l GAP/Heather Edwards – Design: Charles Dowding 857r © Martin Hughes-Jones/ Alamy 858 GAP/Elke Borkowski 859 GAP/Heather Edwards 860l GAP/Chris Burrows 860r © Christopher Burrows/Alamy 861l GAP/Juliette Wade 861r © Trevor Sims 862 © Anne Gilbert/Alamy 863 GAP/Tommy Tonsberg 864 © Tim Hill/Alamy 865 © GWI 866l All-America Selections 866r GAP/Christina Bollen 867 GAP/Heather Edwards 868 GAP/Jan Smith 869 GAP/Elke Borkowski 870l All-America Selections 870r www.millettegardenpictures.com 871l www.millettegardenpictures.com 871r © Dave Bevan 872 Jonathan Buckley – Design: Sarah Raven 873 © Anne Gilbert/Alamy 874 © Martin Hughes-Jones 875 © Nigel Cattlin/Alamy 876l All-America Selections 876r All-America Selections 877 GAP/Tim Gainey 878 All-America Selections 879 GAP/Clive Nichols – Design: Clare Matthews 880 GAP/FhF Greenmedia 881 © Lena Ason/Alamy 882 GAP 883 © Zoonar GmbH/Alamy 884 GAP/Juliette Wade 885 All-America Selections 886 GAP/Jonathan Buckley 887 GAP/Jonathan Buckley – Design: Sarah Raven 888 GAP/Chris Burrows 889 GAP/John Glover 890 © blickwinkel/Alamy 891 GAP/Jonathan Need 892 © Diarmuid/Alamy 893 GAP/J S Sira 894 GAP/Claire Davies 895 GAP/Jenny Lilly 896 GAP/Sarah Cuttle 897 Suttons Seeds 898 GAP 899 Suttons Seeds 900 GAP/Graham Strong 901 © Wildlife GmbH/Alamy 902l GAP/John Glover 902r GAP/FhF Greenmedia 903l GAP/Fiona Lea 903r GAP 904l GAP/Tim Gainey 904r GAP/Howard Rice – Pro Veg Seeds Ltd. 905 GAP/Howard Rice – Pro Veg Seeds Ltd. 906 GAP/Howard Rice – Pro Veg Seeds Ltd. 907 Seeds By Design, Inc 908 GAP/Maxine Adcock 909 GAP/Clive Nichols 910l GAP/Chris Burrows 910r GAP/Geoff Kidd 911l © Brian Yarvin/Alamy 911r © Simon Hadley/Alamy 912 The Garden Collection/Flora Press/Christine Ann Föll 913 © Bon Appetit/Alamy 914 David Q. Cavagnaro 915 GAP/Pat Tuson 916 GAP/Graham Strong 917 GAP/Jerry Pavia 918 GAP/Thomas Alamy 919 GAP/Christa Brand 920 © Alec Scaresbrook/ Alamy 921 GAP/FhF Greenmedia 922 GAP/Howard Rice 923 The Garden Collection/FP/Martin Hughes-Jones 924 GAP/Neil Holmes 926 GAP/Claire Higgins 927 © All Canada/Alamy 928 © William Clevitt 929 © Andrea Jones 930 GAP/Howard Rice 931 GAP/Andrea Jones 932 © Andrea Jones Images/Alamy 933 GAP/Claire Higgins 934 Harriet Rycroft at Whichford Pottery 935 GAP/Elke Borkowski 936l GAP/Jonathan Buckley – Design: Sarah Mead, Yeo Valley Garden 936r GAP/Dave Bevan 937l GAP/Neil Holmes 937r GAP/Sarah Cuttle 938 GAP/Pernilla Bergdahl 939l The Garden Collection/FP/Nova Photo Graphik/ 939r Claire Higgins 940 GAP/Claire Higgins 941 GAP/Claire Higgins 942 GAP/Claire Higgins 943 Trevor Sims 944 GAP/Paul Debois 945 GAP/Claire Higgins 946 GAP/Tim Gainey 947 GAP/Elke Borkowski

Acknowledgements

This book would have been far harder without the resources of The Royal Horticulture Society (RHS) who publish up-to-date lists of AGM awards and the annual RHS *Plant Finder*. Thanks also to the All-America Selections organisation for their state wide trials of new varieties. Thank you to the following for allowing me to view their trials over very many years: Thompson & Morgan, Mr. Fothergill's, Suttons Seeds, Tozer Seeds, Ball Colegrave and the British Association of Rose Breeders. Members of the International Clematis Society advised on clematis varieties. For US roses: Harry A. Landers of the International Rose Test Garden, Portland, Oregon.

A heartfelt thank you to all the staff at Quintessence who have worked so hard on this book but particularly Sophie Blackman for her efficiency and support. To the many contributors, garden owners and photographers whose work has made this book possible. Finally, thank you to my husband Stephen Mercer for keeping our garden going while I was otherwise occupied.